The Life and Work of Our Lord

C. H. Spurgeon

Volume 2

Jesus the Messiah

A Division of Baker Book House Co
Grand Rapids, Michigan 49516

Reprinted 1996 by Baker Books
a division of Baker Book House Company
P.O. Box 6287, Grand Rapids, MI 49516-6287

Previously published in 1979 as part of
A Treasury of Spurgeon on the Life and Work of Our Lord

Originally published in London by Passmore and Alabaster
Vol. 1: *Christ in the Old Testament: Sermons on the Foreshadowing of Our Lord in Old Testament History, Ceremony and Prophecy,* 1899
Vol. 2: *The Messiah: Sermons on Our Lord's Names, Titles and Attributes,* 1898
Vol. 3: *Our Lord's Passion and Death,* 1904

Printed in the United States of America

ISBN 0-8010-1115-9

Contents

A Root Out of a Dry Ground 1
    Isaiah 53:2

Rivers of Water in a Dry Place 13
    Isaiah 32:2

The Messenger of the Covenant 25
    Malachi 3:1

The Sitting of the Refiner 35
    Malachi 3:3

Christ, the End of the Law 47
    Romans 10:4

Christ, the Conqueror of Satan 59
    Genesis 3:15

Christ, the Overcomer of the World 71
    John 16:33

"God With Us" 83
    Matthew 1:23

Immanuel—The Light of Life 95
    Isaiah 9:1, 2

His Name—Wonderful 107
    Isaiah 9:6

His Name—The Counsellor 115
    Isaiah 9:6

His Name—The Mighty God 123
    Isaiah 9:6

His Name—The Everlasting Father 131
                Isaiah 9:6

Shiloh 143
                Genesis 49:10

The Prince of Life 155
                Acts 3:15

A Prince and a Saviour 167
                Acts 5:31

The Mediator—Judge and Saviour 179
                Acts 10:42, 43

Who Is This? 191
                Jeremiah 30:21

The Great Arbitration Case 203
                Job 9:33

Jehovah Tsidkenu, The Lord Our Righteousness 215
                Jeremiah 23:6

Ecce Rex 223
                John 19:14

Jesus, the King of Truth 235
                John 18:37

The Breaker and the Flock 247
                Micah 2:12, 13

Jesus—The Shepherd 259
                Isaiah 40:11

Our Own Dear Shepherd 271
                John 10:14, 15

Behold the Lamb 283
                John 1:36

The Lamb—The Light 295
                Revelation 21:23

The Lamb in Glory 307
                Revelation 5:6, 7

The Man of Sorrows 319
                Isaiah 53:3

The Shame and Spitting	331
Isaiah 50:6	
The Nazarene and the Sect of the Nazarenes.	343
Matthew 2:3; Acts 24:5	
The Great Itinerant................................	355
Acts 10:38	
Our Compassionate High Priest.......................	367
Hebrews 5:2	
The Ever-living Priest	379
Hebrews 7:23-25	
The Sinner's Advocate	391
I John 2:1	
The Way..	403
John 14:6	
"Eyes Right"	415
Proverbs 4:25	
The One Foundation................................	427
I Corinthians 3:11	
The Head Stone of the Corner	439
Psalm 118:22-25	
The Head of the Church	451
Colossians 1:18	
Victor Emmanuel, Emancipator	463
Isaiah 42:7	
The Great Physician and His Patients	475
Matthew 9:12	
"Supposing Him to Be the Gardener"	487
John 20:15	
"The Sun of Righteousness".........................	499
Psalm 19:4-6; Malachi 4:2	
The Way to Honour	511
Proverbs 27:18	
The Unrivalled Friend...............................	523
Proverbs 17:17	

The Meat and Drink of the New Nature 535
  John 6:55

The Best Bread 547
  John 6:48

Spiritual Appetite 559
  Proverbs 27:7

The Fourfold Treasure 571
  I Corinthians 1:30, 31

The Lord's Famous Titles 583
  Psalm 146:7-9

Christ Our Life—Soon to Appear 593
  Colossians 3:4

A Portrait No Artist Can Paint........................... 605
  Revelation 1:16

Christ with the Keys of Death and Hell.................. 615
  Revelation 1:18

Jesus Christ Himself 627
  Ephesians 2:20

Jesus Only.. 639
  Matthew 17:8

The Rule of the Race..................................... 651
  Hebrews 12:1, 2

Alpha and Omega 663
  Revelation 22:13

The Amen... 675
  Revelation 3:14

All and All in All 687
  Colossians 3:11; I Corinthians 15:28

A Root Out of a Dry Ground

"A root out of a dry ground"—Isaiah liii. 2.

THE prophet is speaking of the Messiah. He declares of him, "He shall grow up before him as a tender plant, and as a root out of a dry ground: he hath no form nor comeliness; and when we shall see him, there is no beauty that we should desire him." It is marvellous that with such plain prophecies concerning the Messiah, the Jews should have made such a fatal mistake in reference to him. They looked for a temporal prince, who would come in splendour, notwithstanding that this and other Scriptures speak of his humiliation in express terms. Every unprejudiced person might have seen from this passage that the Messiah, when he came, was not to be surrounded with pomp, but would come as "a man of sorrows, and acquainted with grief," to be "despised and rejected of men." Yet, though the truth was written as with a sunbeam, and the Jewish people were pretty generally acquainted with their own Scriptures, so that they had the opportunity of knowing it, yet when the Messiah came unto his own, his own received him not, and though favoured with the clearest prophecies concerning him they rejected his claims, and cried, "Let him be crucified!" Does not this teach us that the plainest instruction, earnestly and forcibly delivered, will not be understood by the unregenerate mind? The carnal mind discerns not spiritual things, its eye is darkened, its ear is heavy. Inspiration itself cannot put a spiritual truth so clearly that men will see it, unless their eyes be opened by the Holy Spirit. Vain is the best light to blind men. Beloved, remember that what was true of the Jews is equally true of the Gentiles. The gospel of Jesus Christ is the simplest thing in the world, but yet no man truly understands it until he is taught of God. There are preachers who labour after simple words, and seek out instructive similitudes, by which to make the gospel clear to every apprehension; but yet of the unregenerate it may be said, "Their foolish heart is darkened." Sin has brought upon the human race a mental incapacity with regard to spiritual subjects. They rush on in darkness, though the gospel creates a noonday around them; they grope for the wall like the blind, though the Sun of Righteousness shines with infinite brightness. Alas! to what has our nature fallen! How is the image of God marred within us! How ardently should we adore the Holy Spirit, that he stoops to us even in this our blindness, and is pleased to remove the scales and pour light into our souls. Whatever we have rightly discerned has been revealed to us by his teaching, for apart from his illumination we should have been as obstinately unbelieving as the Jews, who knew not their King. Dear hearers, how is it with you? Are ye blind also? Though living in the gospel day, it may be you have never seen the Saviour with the eye of faith. Are ye blind also? Oh, if ye be, may he who alone can teach you to profit, instruct you in the faith of Jesus, and in his light may you see light!

Now, turning to the text itself, you will observe that Isaiah describes our Lord Jesus as growing up like " a tender plant," a weak branch, a suckling, a sapling, a plant that very readily might be destroyed. We cannot pass over that comparison without a note or two, though we intend to dwell mainly upon the next clause. Our Lord Jesus Christ in his humiliation appeared in great feebleness; born a helpless babe, he was in his infancy in great danger from the hand of Herod, and though preserved, it was not by a powerful army, but by flight into another land. His early days were not spent amid the martial music of camps, or in the grandeur of courts, but in the retirement of a carpenter's shop,—fit place for " a tender plant." His life was gentleness, he was harmless as a lamb. At any time it seemed easy to destroy both him and his system. When he was nailed to the cross to die, did it not appear as if his whole work had utterly collapsed and his religion would be for ever stamped out? The cross threatened to be the death of Christianity as well as of Christ; but it was not so, for in a few days the power of the divine Spirit came upon the church. At its first setting up, how feeble was the kingdom of our Lord! When Herod stretched out his hand to vex certain of the church, unbelief might have said, " there will be an utter end ere long." When, in after years, the Roman Emperors turned the whole imperial power against the gospel, stretching forth an arm long enough to encompass the entire globe, and uplifting a hand more heavy than an iron hammer, how could it be supposed that the Christian church would still live on? It bowed before the storm like a tender shoot, but it was not uprooted by the tempest; it survives to this day; and although we do not rejoice at this moment in all the success which we could desire, yet still that tender shoot is full of vitality, we perceive the blossoms of hope upon it, and expect soon to gather goodly clusters of success.

Christianity in our own hearts,—the Christ within us,—is also a " tender plant." In its upspringing it is as the green blade of corn, which any beast that goeth by may tread upon or devour. Oftentimes to our apprehension, it has seemed that our spiritual life would soon die: it was no better than a lily, with a stalk bruised and all but snapped in twain. The mower's scythe of temptation has cut down the outgrowth of our spiritual life, but, blessed be God, he who cometh down like rain upon the mown grass has restored our verdure and maintained our vigour to this day. Tender as our religion is, it is beyond the power of Satan to destroy it. Weak as we are, we have not utterly fallen, nor shall we; for the feeble shall be victorious and the "lame shall take the prey." Though grace is often like to the hyssop for its weakness, it is ever as the oak for endurance. Man threatens to crush the church, or hopes to uproot true grace from the heart of the timid believers, but it shall not be done: the "tender plant" shall become a goodly cedar, and the weakness of God shall baffle the power of man.

Now let us turn to the similitude which we have selected for our text, —"A root out of a dry ground."

First, we will *explain the meaning of the metaphor* ; then, secondly, speak of *our experimental knowledge of its truth;* thirdly, dwell for a while upon *the encouragements which it affords;* and, fourthly, upon *the glory which it displays.*

I. First, then, this morning, our Lord Jesus is said to be "a root out of a dry ground." What is THE HISTORICAL MEANING OF THIS METAPHOR ? We believe that it applies to the person of the Lord, and also to his cause and kingdom :—to himself personally and to himself mystically. He is "a root out out of a dry ground."

A root which springs up in a fat and fertile field, owes very much to the soil in which it grows. We do not wonder that some plants thrive abundantly, for the earth in which they are planted is peculiarly congenial to their growth ; but if we see a root or a tree luxuriating upon a flinty rock, or in the midst of arid sand, we are astonished and admire the handiwork of God. Our Saviour is a root that derives nothing from the soil in which it grows, but puts everything into the soil. Christ does not live because of his surroundings, but he makes those to live who are around him ; and Christianity in this world derives nothing from the world except that which alloys and injures it ; but it imparts every blessing to the place where it comes. Note, then, this truth, —that Christ is always "a root out of a dry ground ;" he derives nothing from without, but is self-contained and self-sustained in all the strength and excellence which he displays. Let us dwell on that truth.

It is quite certain that our Lord derived nothing whatever from *his natural descent.* He was the Son of David, and lawful heir to the royal dignities of the tribe of Judah ; but his family had fallen into obscurity, had lost position, wealth, and repute. Joseph, his nominal father, was only a carpenter ; Mary, his mother, but a humble village maiden. The glory had altogether departed from Judah when Shiloh came. No crown was treasured amid the heirlooms of Joseph, and no sceptre was comprehended in the scanty portion of Mary. He who was born king of the Jews inherited nothing from his parents by way of honour and dignity,—his only portion was the danger of being sought out by the cunning and cruelty of Herod. Now, had our Lord been descended from the Pharaohs, had he come into the world as the scion of a long line of Cæsars, or as the heir to a wide-spread monarchy, it would have been said, "Every man respects pedigree and descent, and hence the triumphs of his teaching."

But who shall do otherwise than magnify the Lord alone, when the blessed and only Potentate is born in lowliest poverty.

> "Lo God bedews old Jesse's root
> With blessings from the skies;
> He makes the Branch of promise shoot,
> The promised Prince arise."

Nor did our Lord derive assistance from *his nationality;* it was no general recommendation to his teaching. that he was of the seed of Abraham. Why, to this day, to many minds, it is almost shameful to mention that our Saviour was a Jew. Though certainly the Jew is of an honourable race, ancient and venerable, as having been chosen of God of old, yet among the sons of men the name of Jew has not yet lost the opprobrium which long ages of cruel oppression and superstitious hate have cast upon it. It is said that there was no nation, immediately after the time of our Saviour, that the Romans ardently hated except the Jews. The Romans were peculiarly tolerant of all religions and customs; by conquest their empire had absorbed men of all languages and creeds, and they usually left them undisturbed: but the Jewish faith was too peculiar and intolerant to escape derision and hatred. After the siege of Jerusalem by Titus, the Jews were hunted down, and the connection of Christianity with Judaism so far from being an advantage to it became a serious hindrance to its growth. Christianity was confounded with Judaism, and made to share the political obloquy of the Jewish nation as well as its own reproach. Had our Saviour been born in Greece, there is no doubt that as a religious teacher he would have commanded far more attention than as coming forward from Jerusalem or Nazareth. He owed nothing to his Jewish birth, for if anything good could have come out of Israel in former days, behold into what a state it had fallen,—it was dead politically, religiously, and mentally. Look at Phariseeism, what shall I say of it, but that it had perverted the noblest into the basest? Look at Sadduceeism, with its profession of superior wisdom, its intense unbelief, and I may add its consequent folly. Whatever power the Jewish Monotheism may have had in the world, had perished beneath the destructive influences of a ritualistic Phariseeism and a broad church Sadduceeism. Our Saviour, could he have disowned all connection with Israel, might have been rather strengthened than weakened by so doing. He was in this respect "a root out of a dry ground." Mentally, among the Jews nothing was left; no harp resounded with psalms like those of David; no prophet mourned in plaintive tones like Jeremy, or sang in the rich organ tones of Isaiah; there remained not even a Jonah to startle, or a Haggai to rebuke. No wise man gave forth his proverbs, nor preacher took up his parable. The nation had mentally reached its dregs, its scribes were dreaming over the letters of Scripture, insensible to its inner sense, and its elders were drivelling forth traditions of the fathers, and so sinking lower and lower in an inane superstition. It was a "dry ground" out of which Jesus sprang.

Nor did the Saviour owe anything to *his followers.* He might have selected, had he pleased, certain eminent persons as his first converts.

Casting his eye upon the reigning Cæsar and his royal subordinates, he might have turned their hearts to serve him, and so have surrounded himself with a discipleship culled from men of renown; but he did not so, else would men have said, "His religion might well spread with such powerful men at its head." The man chosen out of the people passed by the noble and elected the base. He might have journeyed at once to Athens, and have collected from the remnant of the old philosophic schools the choice thinkers of the age. There still survived the sects of the Stoics and the Epicureans, and the old learning of Socrates and Plato was not quite forgotten; he might have called to his feet the leaders in the more potent schools of thought; but he did not so, else they would have said that Christianity might well triumph with such master minds to propagate it. He might have gone to the Forum at Rome, and there have selected men of mighty eloquence; he might have converted the orators of the tribune, or the persuasive speakers of the senate, and have set such men to lead the van of the new faith; but he did not so, else they would have said that rhetoric achieved the victory, and eloquence with her charms had spell-bound the world. See ye not how he hastens to the fisher boats on the Lake of Gennesaret, and calls men of the roughest exterior and the least cultured intellect. Shall a world-subduing religion be disseminated by peasants and mariners? So did he ordain it. He selected men commonly known to be unlearned and ignorant, and made them apostles of the faith. Whatever they became in after life, he made them that. Peter did not make Christianity, but Christianity made Peter what he was. Paul brought nothing to Christ, but Christ gave everything to Paul. I admit that the apostles became great men; they were eloquent and learned in the truest sense of the term, being taught of God, but Jesus, as "the root," bore them, not they the root. This wondrous root fertilised the soil in which it grew; it derived nothing from the men, but gave the men all they possessed. But we will pass on.

Our Saviour is "a root out of a dry ground" as to *the means which he chose for the propagation of his faith.* Nobody wonders that Mahometanism spread. After the Arab prophet had for a little while himself personally borne the brunt of persecution, he gathered to his side certain brave spirits who were ready to fight for him at all odds. You marvel not that the sharp arguments of scimitars made many converts. Any religion will win assent when the alternative is conversion or instant death. Give a man a strong right hand and a sharp sabre, and he is a fit missionary of Mahomet's doctrine. Our Saviour gave to his soldiers neither spears nor swords, but said, "Put up again thy sword into his place: for all they that take the sword shall perish with the sword." He asked no aid from governments, he disowned the temporal arm altogether as his ally. Had our Saviour been a State-churchman, and not, as he was, the grandest of nonconformists, it would have been said that under the wings of the State his church was fostered into power. If Cæsar had said, "I will gather thy children together as a hen gathereth her chickens under her wings," it would not have been surprising if the brood of Christians had multiplied indefinitely. But our Saviour sought no succour from potentates, and rested not upon an arm of flesh.

The people would have made him a king, but he hid himself, for his kingdom was not of this world, therefore did not his servants fight.

Our Saviour as he used no force, so neither did he use any means which might enlist man's lower nature on his side. When I have heard of large congregations gathered together by the music of a fine choir, I have remembered that the same thing is done at the opera-house and the music-hall, and I have felt no joy. When we have heard of crowds enchanted by the sublime music of the pealing organ, I have seen in the fact rather a glorification of St. Cecilia than of Jesus Christ. Our Lord trusted in no measure or degree to the charms of music for the establishing his throne. He has not given to his disciples the slightest intimation that they are to employ the attractions of the concert room to promote the kingdom of heaven. I find no rubric in Scripture commanding Paul to clothe himself in robes of blue, scarlet, or violet; neither do I find Peter commanded to wear a surplice, an alb, or a chasuble. The Holy Spirit has not cared even to hint at a surpliced choir, or at banners, processions, and processional hymns. Now, if our Lord had arranged a religion of fine shows, and pompous ceremonies, and gorgeous architecture, and enchanting music, and bewitching incense, and the like, we could have comprehended its growth; but he is "a root out of a dry ground," for he owes nothing to any of these. Christianity has been infinitely hindered by the musical, the æsthetic, and the ceremonial devices of men, but it has never been advantaged by them, no, not a jot. The sensuous delights of sound and sight have always been enlisted on the side of error, but Christ has employed nobler and more spiritual agencies. Things which fascinate the senses are left to be the chosen instruments of Antichrist, but the gospel, disdaining Saul's armour, goes forth in the natural simplicity of its own might, like David, with sling and stone. Our holy religion owes nothing whatever to any carnal means; so far as they are concerned, it is " a root out of a dry ground."

Neither did the Saviour owe anything to *the times in which he lived.* Christianity, it is said by some, came upon the field at a time when it was likely to succeed. I utterly deny it: it was born at a period of history when the world by wisdom knew not God, and men were most effectually alienated from him. The more thinking part of the world's inhabitants at the time of Christ's coming were atheistic, and made ridicule of the gods, while the masses blindly worshipped whatever was set before them. The whole set and current of thought at the advent of our Lord was in direct opposition to such a religion as he came to inculcate. It was an age of luxury—Rome was full of wealth and the desire for self-indulgence. Wherever Romans settled, they built magnificent villas, and used all the arts for the gratification of the flesh: was this a preparation for the doctrines of the cross? It was an age of universal vice. It is a great mercy that most of the ancient cities have been destroyed, and their works of art dashed to shivers, for many of them were unutterably vicious, and such as remain are doing not a little to degrade humanity. Vices which now we dare not speak of were then perpetrated in public; things that are now detested were performed as a part of sacred worship. The world was rotten through and through. If darkness be a preparation for light, I grant you the world did prepare itself for Christ. If an Augean stable, pestilential with a putridity which supersedes all common rottenness, be in readiness for the coming of him who shall cleanse it, the world was prepared for Jesus, but not else. I deny that he owed anything to his times. He came when the times could not help him in any degree whatever, and his religion was "a root out of a dry ground."

Neither, again, let me say, did the religion of Jesus owe anything to *human nature?* It is sometimes said that it commends itself to human nature. It is false: the religion of Jesus opposes unrenewed human nature. In Christ's day revenge was one of the most glorious things known; it was sung of, it was preached upon, it was the joy of men; and what religion but Christianity ever taught men never to retaliate? Christ said, "Love your enemies, and pray for them that despitefully use you." Is this in human nature? Is there anything in the commands of Christ that at all flatters pride or conciliates lust? He judges our thoughts as well as our actions. "He that looketh upon a woman to lust after her hath committed adultery with her already in his heart." Is that agreeable to human nature? Does that run in the same vein as our passions, think you? Mahomet prospered because his religion pandered to human weakness; but there is in the religion of Christ no yielding to what are called the natural passions, no providing for sensual desires. "Take up," saith he, "not thy scimitar but thy cross." He says not, "Increase thine harem." No, but "Crucify the flesh." Is there any glorification of human intellect in the religion of Jesus? Is not its invariable command, "Believe, and live." If Christianity spreads, it spreads in opposition to human nature, by changing human nature, by making it what it never was and never could have been, had not the incorruptible truth of God been planted in it like "a root in a dry ground."

Thus much, and perhaps too much, upon the historical meaning of the metaphor.

II. Now, briefly, but earnestly, OUR KNOWLEDGE OF ITS TRUTH EXPERIMENTALLY. Beloved, you remember your own conversion. When Jesus Christ came to you to save you, did he find any fertile soil in your heart for the growth of his grace? I must bear witness that to convince me of sin and humble me, he had need of all the mighty hammers of his power to break my rocky heart. Conviction of sin was no natural product of my mind. Repentance was a plant of the Lord's right hand planting, and not a native of the soil. Remorse we might have had by nature, but repentance never. And brethren, if now we have believed in Christ Jesus, and are resting in him, I am sure we must own that faith never sprang up naturally in the garden of our hearts: the Holy Spirit taught us how to believe in Jesus, and led us to look unto him that we might be saved. So far from helping Christ, my whole soul was opposed to him. If now I bow before his feet, and delight to call him my Master and my Lord, it is because I am subdued by his power, not because I have educated myself to it, or was at all inclined thereto. Religion, true religion, in the heart at conversion is "a root out of a dry ground."

Let me ask you who look into your own hearts, how have you found them since? Has there been anything in your natural humanity congenial with the new life which grace has begotten within you? You have the higher life in your souls, has it found sustenance in your flesh? Ah, it is sadly the reverse. Christ's life has come into us like Israel into the wilderness, and it finds in us no food; if manna do not drop from heaven, and water leap from the smitten rock, it must die in the desert of our soul. "In me, that is, in my flesh," said the apostle, "there dwelleth no good thing." Our carnal nature is still as evil as ever it was: "The carnal mind is enmity against God, it is not reconciled to God, neither indeed can it be." If you have grace in your hearts to-day, beloved, you have been made to feel that it is "a root out of a dry ground."

I bless the Lord that we have felt this at peculiar seasons. When you have had great joy in God, great exhilaration and delight, has it not usually been at times when you might least have expected it? When the body is gradually pining away with sickness, we have seen the spirit more triumphant than it was in health, deriving none of its joy from the strength of nature, but flourishing upon a secret provender of which the world knows nothing: it has been "a root out of a dry ground." Sometimes we have been desponding in spirit, our animal spirits as they are called, have been quite dried up, and yet or ever we were aware, our souls have been made like the chariots of Amminadib, and we have flashed and glowed with sacred delight. "A root out of a dry ground" again. Children have died, and perhaps a beloved wife has been taken away; possibly business has been against us, trials have multiplied, and yet at that very season we have walked nearer to God than ever we did before, and had more delight in his company, and have known more of the power of the Holy Spirit in our souls, than ever we did in days of prosperity;—all to show us that the grace within us lives by its own inward vigour and by supernatural help, and owes nothing to bodily health, nothing to outward circumstances, but is still a root flourishing best in a dry ground. There is much that is painful about this experience of the dryness of the ground, but there is something delightful in the experience of the growing of the root under such circumstances; for then all the glory is given to the Lord alone, and we dare not touch it, nay, not so much as with one of our fingers.

III. But I will pass on. This whole subject appears to me to afford much ENCOURAGEMENT to many.

And first, let me speak as earnestly as I can a word to those of you who are seeking after the Saviour, but are very conscious of your own sinfulness. You are depressed under a sense of being unworthy to be saved, and what is perhaps worse, you feel that though the gospel be preached to you you are unable to receive it of yourself. Deadness and powerlessness are the main thoughts upon your mind. Now, beloved, let this console you. Christ Jesus, when he saves a sinner, borrows no help whatever from the sinner himself. "It pleased the Father that in *him* should all fulness dwell." If there be all fulness in him, he does not need any contribution from us, and, blessed be his name, he never waits for any. We can give none, and he will receive none. Christ is all—does not that cheer you? Do you say, "I want power"? In him is strength. "I want wisdom" say you :—he is "made of God unto us wisdom." "I want a tender heart" ;—who can give it you but Christ? "But, ah, I want to repent":—is he not "exalted on high to give repentance"? "But I long for faith." Well, and have you never read, "it is not of yourselves, it is the gift of God"? He is "a root out of a dry ground," and your ground is very, very dry, but he will come and put fertility into it; he does not first want fertility in you. Poor, helpless, hopeless, stripped, and emptied one, thou needst not look for nor desire anything in thyself to prepare thee for Jesus; he delights to come into empty hearts to fill them with his love, into cold hearts to warm them with his sacred flame, and into dead hearts to give them life.

Now, the same thought which may thus comfort the seeker, and I pray it may, ought also to encourage any Christian who has been making discoveries of his own barrenness. It is not every child of God that knows himself thoroughly. We may go on a long time after our first conversion without any very deep understanding of what poor things we are. Have you begun to see yourself in the looking-glass of the word, and does the sight alarm and distress you? Are you crying, "My barrenness! my barrenness!" Beloved brother, Christ "is a root out of a dry ground," and though thou be thus barren now, thou art not one whit more barren than thou always hast been: thy sin alarms thee, but it was always there; thy natural death disgusts thee, but it is no new thing. "Oh, but I seem to be less than I was!" You never were anything, and if you had begun by understanding you were nothing, you would have begun in a wiser and happier way than you have done. Whenever the child of God says, "I find my total of natural strength is getting smaller," he is only approximating to the truth, for his strength is "perfect weakness." Beloved, when we get to realise the lesson taught us in our baptism, we are drawing near to truth. What is that? say you. Why, it is the burial of the creature in Christ's tomb. Circumcision signifies the putting away of the filth of the flesh, but baptism teaches us the burial of it altogether, as an incorrigible and utterly corrupt thing, not to be reformed and mended, but to be reckoned as dead and buried. "Mortify therefore your members which are upon the earth." Be nothing at all, and let Jesus be all in all. When at any time you are cast down by a sense of your nothingness, remember that your Lord is "a root out of a dry ground."

The same comfort avails for every Christian worker. You who work for Jesus in the pulpit, or in the Sunday school, or elsewhere, I am quite sure if God blesses you you do not always feel alike. Those machines that preach regularly in the same way accomplish very little. God means to use *men*, and while men are men they will be sensitive and changeable. Flesh and blood are not like marble,—they change, and God means to use the feelings of his ministers and his servants for divine ends and purposes. If God ever honours a man in public, he will whip him every now and then behind the door, and make him cry out, "Who is sufficient for these things?" Now, brother, when you feel you are barren, do not fret or despair about it, but rather say, "Lord, here is a dry tree, come and make it bear fruit, and then I shall joyfully confess "from thee is my fruit found." Lord, I am a withered branch by nature, come and put sap into me, and make me bud and blossom like Aaron's rod; so shall men see a miracle of grace and thou shalt have all the praise of it. Do not think that your unfitness to be used is really a disqualification with God. The last thing a man might choose to fight with would be the jaw bone of an ass, and yet Samson found it handy enough, and it made his victory the more famous. The last instrument God might choose to use might be yourself, and yet if he pleases there is a fitness in your unfitness, and a qualification in your disqualification. A man's conceit that he is well prepared for God to use him, will prove fatal to him. If a man be possessed of polished diction, very learned, a man of high family, a man of great repute, and so on, the likelihood is that he will be esteemed by his fellows so much that the Lord will say, "I cannot use this man lest men glorify him." Therefore God often uses young men, because people know they are fools; he honours illiterate men, that people may know that it is not by their learning. He chooses home-spun people, who speak without the polish which others have gained, and he uses them because the world says, " He is an unlearned man, and a rough vulgar fellow." Do you not see that thus all the glory goes to God. The man's disqualifications are his fitness. " The rather, therefore," saith the Apostle, "will I glory in infirmities, that the power of Christ may rest upon me." Go on, dear worker, for Jesus is "a root out of a dry ground," and in your dryness he will flourish.

Do you not think that this also ought to comfort all of us with regard to the times in which we live? They are said to be very horrible times,—they always were ever since I have known anything of the world, and I suppose they always were in our fathers' time. We are always at a crisis according to some people. I am not about to defend the times, they are, no doubt, very bad, for the innumerable spirits of evil are bold and active, while good men seem to have lost their courage. We find amalgamations and compromises *ad infinitum*, and the precious truth of God is trodden as the mire of the streets. What about all this ? Are we discouraged ? Far from it. Bad times are famous times for Christ. When Wycliffe came, the times were dark enough in England, and therefore the morning star was the more welcome. When Luther came into the world, the times were almost as black as they could be and therefore good times for reformation ! The times were dead enough when Wesley and Whitfield came : but they proved glorious days for the Lord to work in ! And if you discern now that there is not much prayerfulness, nor much spirituality, nor much truthful doctrine, nor much zeal, do not fret; it is thoroughly dry soil, and now the root of grace will grow. John Bunyan once said that when he heard the young fellows swear so profanely in his parish, he used to think what men God would make of them when he converted them! Let us think of that. Suppose he saves those wretched priests who are trying to swallow down England, suppose he converts these profane rationalists, who almost deny God's existence,— what penitent sinners they will make when he once breaks their hearts, and what preachers of the word they will be when he renews them.

Let us have good hope. Our faith does not rise when people say the times are improving, nor do we despond when men denounce the times as bad. Eternity is the life time of God, and he will work out his purposes. Time may ebb and flow, God is in no hurry; but if the world goes on for a million of years God, will triumph in the end, and the poem of human history will not wind up with a dirge, but will end with a triumphant hymn after all. Let us be of good courage about that.

And thus we may be encouraged concerning any particularly wicked place. Do not say, "It is useless to preach down there, or to send missionaries to that uncivilized country." How do you know? Is it very dry ground? Ah, well, that is hopeful soil; Christ is a "root out of a dry ground," and the more there is to discourage the more you should be encouraged. Read it the other way. Is it dark? Then all is fair for a grand show of light; the light will never seem so bright as when the night is very very dark. Come with the salt of Christ where there is most putridity. Where is the scene for the triumph of the physician but where disease has reigned supreme? Go with Christ's gospel in your hands where it is most required.

The same is true of individual men, you should never say, "Well, such a man as that will never be converted." You parents do not say, "Now, there is Mary, she has a sweet temper, I expect to see her brought to Christ, and there is John, an open-hearted lad, seems very attentive in the house of God, I expect to see him saved; but, as for Tom, he is such a wild dare-devil fellow, I shall never see him saved." I should not wonder that he is just the very one whom God will bring to himself, and make him to be the joy and gladness of your old age. Who are you that you should set up to elect God's people? He has done that years ago, and he has often elected the very ones whom you would have cast out. Seek the conversion of all persons, and all classes, all men, and all your relatives, and all your children, and you do not know whether any shall be saved, this or that. He is "a root out of a dry ground." Look for the dry ground, and rather rejoice when you see it is dry ground, with the comfortable hope that the root will spring up there.

IV. I must close with a few words upon THE GLORY WHICH ALL THIS DISPLAYS. Christ's laurels, beloved, at this day are none of them borrowed. When he shall come in his glory there will be none among his friends who will say, "O King, thou owest that jewel in thy crown to me." None will whisper among themselves, that if the honour be given to the Captain yet it was a soldiers' battle after all. No, but everyone will own that he was the author and the finisher of the whole work, and therefore he must have all the glory of it, since we who were with him were dry ground, and he gave life to us but borrowed nothing from us. In the end of the world it will be seen how Christ has sedulously shaken off from him everything that could have marred his victory. This is most prominent in history. The church of God went on gloriously and subdued the nations, till that unbaptised heathen Constantine thought, as a piece of state policy, that he would get the Christians on his side to secure for him a throne which else he would have lost; and that old sinner made Christianity a national religion, and from that day it was pure Christianity no more. You could not find pure religion then, except you went to the valleys of Piedmont, amongst the persecuted Waldenses, where it was maintained. Religion, as far as real, true, pure holiness was concerned, almost ceased to exist from the day when the royal hand inflicted a spiritual scrofula upon the church by its touch. The dark ages were a chastisement to the church for leaning upon an arm of flesh. Then came the Reformation, and as long as men preached the gospel, and depended upon spiritual power only, even persecution made it spread; but those sinners, Henry the Eighth and Elizabeth, must needs extend the royal wing over it, and it sickened almost to death. The despised Puritans became the representatives of the crucified Lord. And then there came a time when these Puritans were multiplied, and they erred, and they took the sword (and if Puritans take the sword they can fight, mark you), and they got the upper hand by the arm of flesh, and then down went the spirituality of Puritanism, because whoever it is that thinks to bring glory to God in that way, God will have nothing to do with him. And now, at this day the Lord may bless his dissenting people in this country: but if they seek political power, and lean upon the education of their ministers, or any other earthly thing, God will cast them off as he has all the others. History shows that Christ blesses a humble, believing, trustful, spiritually minded people; but when they cringe before the king, or use sword or bayonet, from that moment the Master puts them down, and begins again at the first foundation, for it is "not by might, nor by power, but by my Spirit, saith the Lord of hosts." And so it shall be. When at the last the entire church shall rise in all its splendour, not a single stone shall bear the mark of the carver's tool of human workmanship: from basement to pinnacle there shall be no token of human masonry; no king shall be able to say, "I gave that glorious window of chrysolite," no prince shall say, "I contributed that pinnacle of sapphire or chrysoprasus"; no minister shall be able to say, "My eloquence made yonder gate of agate, and opened those windows of carbuncle." No angel even shall be able to say, " I spread the sacred pavement of transparent gold like unto pure glass," but it shall be to God, to God, to God alone;—the foundations laid in the divine decree, the stones cemented with the fair vermillion of the Saviour's atoning blood, each gem fashioned and placed by the mysterious Spirit of the living God, and the whole temple fitly framed together;—glowing with the glory of God, bright with the presence of God, from foundation to pinnacle, it shall speak of God, God, God alone. When that palace shall be complete, then from the ends of the earth shall be heard the shout, "Hallelujah, Hallelujah, Hallelujah, the Lord God omnipotent reigneth!" Hushed be every other acclamation! this anthem drowns them all. Let it in our hearts drown them all. The Lord, the Lord alone, shall be exalted in that day, for he is God, and beside him there is none else!" Amen and Amen.

Rivers of Water in a Dry Place

"As rivers of water in a dry place"—Isaiah xxxii. 2.

I SUPPOSE it must be conceded that the surface sense of this passage refers to Hezekiah and to other good kings who were the means of great blessing to the declining kingdom of Judah. We can scarcely be thankful enough for a righteous government. If for a few years we could feel the yoke of despotism we should better appreciate the joys of freedom. In the prophecy before us very much is said in praise of a king who shall reign in righteousness, and princes who shall rule in judgment; such men are the protectors of the State, enriching it by commerce and blessing it with peace; they deserve honour and the word of God renders it to them. But I cannot bring my mind to believe that these expressions were intended by the Holy Spirit to have no other and higher reference. They appear to me to be far too full of meaning to be primarily or solely intended for Hezekiah or any other mere man. When the Holy Spirit declared by the mouth of the prophet, "A man shall be as a hiding place from the wind and a covert from the tempest, as rivers of water in a dry place, as the shadow of a great rock in a weary land," it can scarcely be conceived that he referred only to Hezekiah and his princes. It cannot be that the church of God has erred these many years in applying such a passage as this to the Lord Jesus Christ. Surely the words are not only applicable to him, but can never be fully understood until they are applied to his ever blessed and adorable person. At any rate, this much is sure, that if a king who rules in righteousness brings so much blessing on his people, then Jesus, who is peculiarly the King of righteousness, "the blessed and only Potentate, the King of kings and Lord of lords," must bring these blessings in the highest conceivable degree, and therefore these expressions are, beyond all possibility of exaggeration, applicable in their widest sense to him whom we this day delight to hail as Lord of all.

Applying the language of the whole verse to the Lord Jesus Christ, the King in Zion, we are struck with the number of the metaphors. He is not merely a hiding place and a covert, and a river, but he is a shadow of a great rock. Yes, my brethren, if we attempt to set forth our Lord's glories by earthly analogies we shall need a host of them, for no one can set him forth to perfection, each one has some deficiency, and even altogether they are insufficient to display all his loveliness. We need a thousand types and images to depict the varied beauties of his character, the manifold excellencies of his offices, the merit of his sufferings, the glory of his triumphs, and the innumerable blessings which he bestows on the sons of men. Should you focus all the rays of nature's sun you could not equal a solitary beam of his splendour—

> "Nor earth, nor sea, nor sun, nor stars,
> Nor heaven his full resemblance bears;
> His beauties you can never trace
> Till you behold him face to face."

It is very pleasant to see that our Beloved is such a many-sided Christ, that from all points of view he is so admirable, and that he is supremely precious in so many different ways, for we have so many and so varied needs, and our circumstances are so continually changing, and the incessant cravings of our spirit are so constantly taking fresh turns. Blessed be his name, these changes of ours, and wants of ours, and cravings of ours, shall only put us in fresh positions in which to see yet more fully his surpassing excellencies, his superabounding fulness, and how completely he is adapted to meet the wants of our nature in every conceivable condition. Blessed be the name of the Lord Jesus that while he is one he is many, while he is altogether lovely he is also many lovelinesses combined, while he is perfect under one aspect he is equally complete under every other.

The point to note in the text, applying it to Christ is this, that it is *a man* who is to be as rivers of water in a dry place. Note that—*a man!* We glory in the Godhead of Jesus Christ; about that we entertain no question. This is not the place wherein to attempt to prove it, for we are all persuaded of it, and we know him to be divine by personal dealings with him; we have found him to be the Son of the Highest, and he ever must be so to us,—" very God of very God." Yet none the less, but all the more, do we tenaciously hold to the truth of the true and proper manhood of the Lord Jesus Christ, and it is as God in human flesh that he is to us as rivers of water in a dry place. Think of it for a minute. If God loves us so much as to become man, then the blessings which he intends to bestow must be incalculable. The Incarnation is in itself a promise big with untold blessing. Gaze upon the Son of God in Bethlehem's manger, and you feel sure that if the Infinite has assumed the form of an infant, his incarnation betokens infinite love, foreshadows intimate intercourse, and foretells unbounded blessedness for the sons of Adam. If Jehovah himself in human flesh walks toilsomely over the acres of Judea, if he bears human sicknesses and sorrows, if he in human form gives his hands to the nails and his heart to the spear, there must be boundless affection in his heart towards the seed chosen from among men. What rivers of blessings must come to us if God himself comes to us, and comes in such a fashion and in such a spirit. What meaneth the union of Godhead with humanity but this, that though he was rich yet for our sakes he became poor? And what can his purpose be but "that we through his poverty might be made rich"? rich with riches as vast as those which he renounced in order to espouse our nature in all its poverty and degradation? Let us at this time joy and rejoice in the Son of Mary, the Son of Man, who is also the Son of God; let us exult to-day as we believe that Jesus is as truly man as he is truly God.

> "Oh joy! There sitteth in our flesh,
> Upon a throne of light,
> One of a human mother born,
> In perfect Godhead bright!"

This is the source, the channel, and the stream, bringing to us and containing within itself all the blessings with which God has enriched us. This is that river of God which is full of water.

Come we, then, with this as our guide, to *study the metaphor of our text.* When we have done so for a little, we shall *remark upon a special excellence which is indicated;* and, having so done, we shall *close by gathering up the practical lessons of the whole.*

I. As setting forth the benedictions which come to us through the incarnate God, LET US STUDY THE METAPHOR of rivers of water in a dry place. This means, first, *great excellence* of blessing. A river is the fit emblem of very great benefits, for it is of the utmost value to the land through which it flows. A river in its own way creates life wherever it flows; grass and reeds and rushes are sure to spring up, and willows fringe the water-courses. The water of the river fosters and nourishes the vegetation along its banks, and sustains an infinite number of fishes and creeping things. The silver stream lights up the landscape with its brightness; "the joyous and abounding river" is the theme of song, and a song in itself. It is a glad sight to trace the winding line of silver light amongst green fields. Who can refuse to render thanks to the God who thus visits the earth, and waters it? Now, what the river is to the land that the Lord Jesus Christ is to us. He is the spring and source of spiritual life, and where he comes divine life springs up and flourishes like a tree by the rivers of water, whose leaf never withers. The life which he bestows he also nourishes, watering it every moment; nourishing it, he makes it fruitful; making it fruitful, he causes it to be fair to look upon, and brings it to perfection. Vegetation owes much to the river which waters it. What were the meads without the streams? That were the saints without the Saviour. What were the villages without their springs and waterbrooks? That were believers without the covenant blessings which are given us in Christ Jesus.

The analogy is so very obvious that I need not pursue it. The place of broad rivers and streams is the place where plentiful good things are looked for, and not in vain shall we look for good things in our Lord Jesus. He is that river the streams whereof make glad the city of God. Of him it may be truly said that "everything that liveth which moveth, whithersoever the rivers shall come, shall live." Because the Word was made flesh and dwelt among us, therefore do rivers of mercy flow to many, and we who believe shall be made to drink of the river of his pleasures. Here, O my heart, is reason for adoration. I need not see any difficulty in it. Having believed the testimony of the Lord, all difficulty has vanished. "The Word was God," and the Word was also "made flesh and dwelt among us," and through being made flesh and dwelling among us, he has opened rivers in high places and fountains in the midst of the valleys. God has come down to man that man may go up to God. God has veiled himself in an infant's form that babes may learn his love; the Christ has grown in stature from childhood to manhood that we also may grow up into him in all things; he has been perfect man that we also may come unto the fulness of the stature of men in Christ Jesus. Christ the man, the God, connects man with God; the river flows direct from the throne of God to the hearts of mortals, and brings God himself to us to fill us with all fulness. Observe the excellence of the Lord Jesus, and meditate upon it.

The metaphor chiefly implies, in the second place, *abundance.* Jesus is as rivers of water, because he is full of grace and truth. It would be a very difficult thing to calculate the body of water to be found in the Thames, but in rivers such as our American friends are favoured with it must be almost beyond the power of mind to conceive the mass of water that must come rolling down into the sea. Gallons and hogsheads seem quite ridiculous by the side of the Mississippi and the St. Lawrence. I always feel very fidgety when theologians begin making calculations about the Lord Jesus. There used to be a very strong contention about particular redemption and general redemption, and though I confess myself to be to the very backbone a believer in Calvinistic doctrine, I never felt at home in such discussions. It is one thing to believe in the doctrines of grace, but quite another thing to accept all the encrustations which have formed upon those doctrines, and also a very different matter to agree with the spirit which is apparent in some who profess to propagate the pure truth. I can have nothing to do with calculating the value of the atonement of Christ. I see clearly the speciality of the purpose and intent of Christ in presenting his expiatory sacrifice, but I cannot see a limit to its preciousness, and I dare not enter into computations as to its value or possible efficacy. Appraisers and valuers are out of place here. Sirs, I would like to see you with your slates and pencils calculating the cubical contents of the Amazon: I would be pleased to see you sitting down and estimating the quantity of fluid in the Ganges, the Indus, and the Orinoco; but when you have done so, and summed up all the rivers of this earth, I will tell you that your task was only fit for school-boys, and that you are not at the beginning of that arithmetic which can sum up the fulness of Christ, for in him dwelleth all the fulness of the Godhead bodily. His merit, his power, his love, his grace surpass all knowledge, and consequently all estimate. Limits are not to be found, neither shore nor bottom are discoverable. Instead of coldly calculating with a view to systematize our doctrines, let us joyfully sing with the poet of the sanctuary—

> "Rivers of love and mercy here
> In a rich ocean join;
> Salvation in abundance flows,
> Like floods of milk and wine."

All idea of stint or insufficiency is out of place in reference to the Lord Jesus. When any man enquires, "Is there enough merit in the Saviour's death to make atonement for my sin?" The answer is, "The blood of Jesus Christ his Son cleanseth us from all sin." When any say, "Perhaps I may not taste his love and believe on his name," the reply is, "Whosoever will, let him take of the water of life freely." O, sirs, would you measure the air? Could you calculate the contents of the atmosphere which surrounds the globe? Yes, that might be done. Would you measure space? I suppose that also might be accomplished. Will you measure eternity? Will you calculate infinity? You must begin by problems like these before you can discover a bound to that abundant grace which comes to sinners through God in human flesh, who bore human sin, and gave up his life, the just for the unjust, to bring us to God.

Anything approaching to a narrow spirit is unseemly in connection with the merits of our Redeemer. Niggardliness at an imperial banquet is not more out of place than an ungenerous spirit in a Christian. Our Lord does things upon such a royal scale that we ought to be of a kingly spirit also. Saint and bigot are a strange mixture: saint and miser cannot agree. I remember hearing of a man who used to go out preaching, and happened to have a well upon his premises, to which his neighbours came more frequently than he liked, and he therefore put up a notice that trespassers would be prosecuted. It was not at all surprising that a witty friend soon adorned the preacher's residence with a bill in prominent capitals, bearing these words, "*Come to Jesus, but you must not take water out of my well.*" In a great many other ways the same remark might be applied. Come to Jesus, but do not crowd me up in my pew! Come to Jesus, but do not ask me for a shilling. Certain people are very free with the gospel, for it costs them nothing: very free indeed with the tracts which are given them to distribute, but they hang back when the hungry want feeding or the naked need clothing. Are such churls any credit to the gospel, think you? Yea, and are there not preachers who appear to be half afraid that some poor non-elect sinner may get into heaven by accident. Hear how they define, and distinguish, and denounce. I confess I have no sympathy with those who would drive men back; far rather would I draw them forward. When one once gets to know that Jesus is as rivers of water, a large-hearted loving spirit seems to spring up in the soul as a matter of course. The Holy Ghost enlarges the heart by revealing to us the glorious fulness of our Lord. I pray, my brethren, ye may be all enlarged, and that none of you may ever slander the Lord Jesus Christ by bearing a narrow, contracted testimony concerning him. Never may you help to straiten other people's apprehensions of what the gospel is by depicting your

Lord as if he were some cramped up straightlined canal, with locks, and
pumps, and measured wharfs, for he is as rivers of water. There is in
Christ Jesus such an abundance that if you come, O great sinner, there
is enough of mercy in Christ for you ; yea, if the teeming myriads of
the human race should all come rushing to this river to drink, they
could not drain it dry—nay, it should seem all the fuller, and the lands
should be made all the gladder as the undiminished stream flowed on.

In a river we see not only excellence and abundance, but *freshness*.
A pool is the same thing over again, and gradually it becomes a stag-
nant pond, breeding corrupt life and pestilential gases. A river is
always the same, yet never the same ; it is ever in its place, yet
always moving on. Filled to the brim with living water, even as in
ages long gone by, and yet flowing fresh from the spring, it is an
ancient novelty. We call our own beautiful river, " Father Thames,"
yet he wears no furrows on his brows, but leaps in all the freshness of youth. You shall live by the banks of a river for years, and
yet each morning its stream shall be as fresh as though its fountain had been unsealed but an hour ago when the birds began to
awake the morning and the sun to sip the dews. Is it not so with
our Lord Jesus Christ ? Is he not evermore as bright and fresh as
when first you met with him ? I remember when first I knew him,
and my soul was married to him. I had a blessed honeymoon in
dearest fellowship. That sweet communion is not over yet, nay, it is
deeper, nearer, more constant than ever. He is as good a Christ to
me now as at first : I may not say that he is better, but I must confess
that I know him better, I love him more fervently, and prize him more
highly. If you serve a master twenty years I should not wonder but
what you find him out by that time. Some of you have served the Lord
Jesus these forty years, and what think you of him ? You have
found him out by this time, and you may without fear tell all that you
have discovered. Do not words fail you to express his excellence ?
All others become stale, but Jesus has the dew of his youth. These
fine ribbons and bits of colour, which are attracting the people to certain Episcopal churches for a time, will soon fade. They tell us that
such and such a church is quite full, because they have a surpliced
choir, and pretty processions and tasteful banners, and many other
childish toys, which turn their churches into dolls' houses ; but let
them not dream that these prettinesses will long draw the people.
Go into the Popish churches on the continent, and you will see in
some cases fine marbles and gems, and in others twopenny-halfpenny
artificial flowers and daubs of paint, but where are the people?
Rarely enough do you see a crowd. In general you only spy out
a few women, dupes of the priests; the manhood of the nation is
not to be entrapped by such transparent tomfooleries. These things
grow old and effete, but the gospel does not. Centuries ago
Wickliffe preached the gospel of Christ beneath an oak in Surrey,
and crowds assembled ; not long ago I preached beneath the same old
tree the self-same gospel, and its attractive power was none the less.
Even so, in the ages yet to come, others will arise with the same
message on their tongues, and the people will gather to hear them, and
own the gospel's power. Some will come to find fault, and will gnash

their teeth with rage, but they *must* come and hear it: it is impossible for them to do otherwise, for the novelty of the gospel will always attract. Is it not always news? And is not news a thing ever sought after? Does a man want something new? Tell him "the old, old story." Our naked fathers crossed the Thames in their coracles, and we sail upon it in our steam-vessels, but it is the same glad river, and yet when it first flowed it was not more fresh and sparkling than it is to-day. It is ever changing, ever fresh, ever new, yet ever the same; and so is Jesus Christ, the same yesterday, to-day, and for ever.

Again, Jesus Christ may well be compared to a river, from his *freeness*. We cannt say this of all the rivers on earth, for men generally manage to claim the banks and shores, and the fisheries and water-powers. I sometimes wonder our great men do not map out the stars. Will no duke claim the Pole star, and no earl monopolise Castor and Pollux? Could we not have an Enclosure Act for the Zodiac, or at least for some of the brighter constellations? Well is it written, "The heaven, even the heavens, are the Lord's: but the earth hath he given to the children of men." Yet rivers can scarcely be parcelled out, they refuse to become private property. See how freely the creatures approach the banks. I took pleasure the other day in seeing the cattle come to the river to drink. The cows sought out a sloping place, and then stood knee deep in the stream and drank and drank again! I thought of Behemoth, who trusted he could snuff up Jordan at a draught, they drank so heartily, and no one said them nay, or measured out the draught. The dog as he ran along lapped eagerly, and no tax was demanded of him. The swan was free to plunge her long neck into the flood, and the swallow to touch the surface with its wing. To ox and fly, and bird, and fish, and man, the river was alike free. So thou ox of a sinner with thy great thirst, come and drink; and thou dog of a sinner, who thinkest thyself unworthy even of a drop of grace, yet come and drink. I read near one of our public ponds a notice, "Nobody is allowed to wash dogs here." That is right enough, for a pond, but it would be quite needless for a river. In a river the foulest may bathe to his heart's content. The fact of its fulness creates a freeness which none may restrict. How I delight to talk about this, for I remember when I thought that the Lord Jesus was not free to me; I dreamed that I wanted him and he would not have me, whereas it was all the other way: he was willing enough, but I was unwilling. O, poor sinner, there is nothing so free in all the world as Christ is. To all who pant after him, desire him, and need him, he is free as the air you breathe.

Christ is like a river for *constancy*, too. Pools and cisterns dry up, but the river's song is—

> "Men may come and men may go,
> But I go on for ever."

So is it with Jesus. The grace to pardon and the power to heal are not a spasmodic force in him; they abide in him evermore. He saved a thousand years ago, he saveth still; he saveth all day long, and all night long. Whether we sleep or wake, the river still flows on, sounding no trumpet, but steadily pursuing its course, and so the pardoning grace of God is flowing all day and all night long, all the year round, quietly blessing thousands. Blessed be God for this! To-day is the Sabbath, and to me it seems as if the river widened out and poured its bounty over a greater area. Oh that you would drink of it, poor sinner, to-day. It flows still, whether you refuse it or accept it. Oh suffer it not to flow in vain for you.

The text speaks of rivers, which implies both *variety and unity*— upon this we cannot enlarge, but must dwell upon the idea of *force*. Nothing is stronger than a river ; it cuts its own way, and will not be hindered in its course. Who shall dam up the Mississippi ? Who shall enchain the Amazon ? They roll whither they will, following the course which infinite sovereignty marked out for them. If the rock be in the river's way it will wear it down. If the cliff intrude, it must fall, being undermined by the current, and falling it must disappear. The river waiteth not for man, neither tarrieth for the sons of men, but follows its predestined course. Glory be to God, Christ Jesus will accomplish the divine purposes, the pleasure of the Lord shall prosper in his hand. None can stay his course: winding this way and that, he must needs go to this sinner and the other ; he cleanses a dying thief and waters some of " Cæsar's household." Between the high hills of proud opposition he speeds his way, and makes glad the lowly valleys of the contrite in heart. Neither death nor hell can stay his course ; he sweeps away all opponents even as that mighty river, the river Kishon, swept away the armies of Jabin ; and when it seems as if there were no longer a channel for the gospel the truth leaps adown the precipice in some great reformation or revival like a glorious Niagara, and the wonders of divine power are still more clearly seen, the Lord making bare his arm in the eyes of all the people. Flow on, O river of God, for evermore.

II. Secondly, WE WILL CONSIDER A SPECIAL EXCELLENCE which the text mentions. "Rivers of water *in a dry place*."

I cannot tell you how I leaped at that word on my own account. In this country we do not value rivers so much because we have springs and wells in all our villages and hamlets ; but in the country where Isaiah lived the land is parched and burnt up without rivers. You can trace the Jordan and the other streams by the fringe of vegetation skirting their banks, and consequently a river is greatly prized in a dry place. Ah, my brethren, when the Man Jesus Christ came hither with blessings from God, he brought rivers into the dry place of our humanity ; when he came down among Abraham's race, he brought rivers of water into the dry old stock of Jesse ; when Judah had lost her king, he came to renew the royalty of the house of David ; and to-day, we Gentiles, who had been cut off from all covenant blessings and left like the desert while Israel was like a garden,—we have Jesus Christ coming among us as rivers of water in a dry place. Jesus has come to you, my brother, and what a dry place your heart was by nature. Ah, think how dry it was before Christ came and caused springs of life to water your soul. As I think of my own state by nature, I can only compare it to a waste howling wilderness, " a salt land, and not inhabited," in which there was great drought,—a dry and thirsty land where no water is. The Sahara is not more destitute of waterbrooks than is human nature of aught that is good, and yet Jesus Christ has come into your human nature and into mine and made the dry land springs of water. O brethren, what a dry place our nature would still be at this very moment if it were not for the presence of Jesus as the river of the water of life. We have grown older, but our nature has not improved; years have gone over us, but not even a cloud the size of a man's hand has come to us by nature's energy, our only watering has been through our interceding Saviour.

So far as the flesh is concerned, I see myself more prone to sin than ever, weaker than ever for all good things, more consciously dead and withered apart from Christ. If you have found springs in the waste places of your nature, I confess I have not: my nature is, indeed, still a dry place. Emptiness!—Oh, that is hardly the word for it: one feels worse than empty. Dead, oh how dead! Even those of us who try to live near to God have cold seasons. I suppose the perfect people have no such confessions to make, but I am not one of them. I mourn over seasons in which I cannot pray as I would, and rise groaning from my knees; I suffer from temptations without and fightings within, and I cannot always alike rejoice in God, although I know he is always worthy of all my joy. I lament that it is so, but so it is with me. There may be persons who can always glide along like a tram-car on the rails without a solitary jerk, but I find that I have a vile nature to contend with, and spiritual life is a struggle with me; I have to fight from day to day with inbred corruption, coldness, deadness, barrenness, and if it were not for my Lord Jesus Christ my heart would be as dry as the heart of the damned, and have no more life, or light, or goodness in it than hell itself. This, however, I can say, I value his fulness all the more because I am so empty; and I prize his power the more because I am so weak. I find I cannot speak or think well-enough of my Lord, nor ill-enough of myself. Nothingness and emptiness, vanity and sin are my sole and only heritage by nature, and all my fulness lies in Christ, and every excellence I can ever claim must come from him and him alone.

Do not many of you find your outward circumstances very dry places? Are you rich? Ah, my brethren, wealthy society is generally as dry a place as the granite hills. "Gold and the gospel seldom do agree." Are you poor? Poverty is a dry place to those who are not rich in faith. Are you engaged in business from day to day? How often do its cares parch the soul, like the hot simoon of the desert! To rise up early and to toil late amid losses and crosses is to dwell in a dry place. Oh, to feel the love of Christ flowing then! This is to have rivers of water. To have Christ near when you are losing your money, when bills are being dishonoured, and commercial houses falling, this is true religion. To rejoice in Christ when you are out of work, poor man, to have Christ when the wife is sick, Christ when the darling child has to be buried, Christ when the head is aching, Christ when the poor body is half starved; this is sweetness. Ah, you will never know the sweetness of Christ till you know the bitterness of trial. You cannot know his fulness till you see your emptiness, I pray that it may be our experience always to feel ourselves going down and Christ going up, ourselves getting poorer and poorer apart from him, while we know more and more of the priceless riches which are ours in Christ Jesus our Lord.

The point then, of the whole, seems to me to be this—that Christ is a river of abounding grace, but he is most so to those who are most dry. Alms are only sought by the poor, the physician is only esteemed by the sick, the lifeboat is only valued by the man that is drowning; so, my brethren, Christ will be dearer and dearer to you just in proportion as you have less and less esteem of yourself. " Rivers of water in a dry place."

III. Now, WE CLOSE WITH THE PRACTICAL LESSON from it all.

First, *see the goings out of God's heart to man, and man's way of communing with God.* Other rivers rise in small springs, and many tributaries combine to swell them, but the river I have been preaching about rises in full force from the throne of God. It is as great a river at its source as in its after course. Oh, my brother, whenever you stoop down to drink of the mercy which comes to you by Jesus Christ you are having fellowship with God, for what you drink comes direct from God himself. Do think of this, now. You desire to have a communication established between you and God, and the Lord says, " Here am I coming to you, coming in a great river of blessedness; take of me; accept of what comes to you through Jesus Christ. Every drop of it has come from my throne, and is full of the love which is my essence." Oh, poor sinner, do you see this? What a simple, what a safe, what a suitable way God has prepared to bring you into communion with himself! You are to be the receiver, and he the giver; he the everlasting source of all your supplies, and you simply the partaker of his benefits. Ask what God is, and the answer is, God is a river of goodness streaming down to men through the person of Jesus Christ.

Secondly, *see what a misery it is that men should be perishing and dying of soul-thirst when there is this river so near.* That men should die of thirst would be horrible, but that such deaths should happen all along the banks of a river is shocking indeed. What ails them? Have they never heard of it? Dear brethren, let the thought press heavily on you, that millions of our race have never heard of Jesus. In China, in parts of India, in Africa, in large tracts of country myriads live and die without having heard the sweet name of Jesus. Are we doing all we can for missions, do you think? Are we all sure that we give as much as we should, and pray as we should, and work as we should for missions? It is a sad thing that Christ has come into the world and yet men perish by millions.

Ah, yet there is a sadder thought still, for millions of men know all about this river and yet do not drink. Many of our own fellow-citizens know the plan of salvation by Jesus Christ, but they are struck with a strange insanity; they would sooner die of thirst than drink of God's own river. O God, we sometimes say, "Have pity," but thou hast had pity, and therefore we had better pray, "Teach men to have pity upon themselves."

Another lesson is, *let us learn if we have any straitness, where it must lie.* It cannot be in Christ, because he is as rivers of water; so the next time we feel that we are straitened, that we have little grace, little power, little joy, let us know where the fault lies. Our cup is small, but the river is not. If you have not, brethren, it is not because God does not give, it is because you are not open to receive. "Ye have not because ye ask not, or because ye ask amiss." O church of God, if thou art weak it is not because God is weak; if thou canst not get at sinners it is not because God cannot reach them. Ye are not straitened in him, ye are straitened in your own bowels.

Is Christ a river, then, last of all, *drink of him,* all of you. To be carried along on the surface of Christianity, like a man in a boat, is not enough, you must drink or die. Many are influenced by the externals of religion, but Christ is not *in* them; they are on the water, but the water is not in them; and if they continue as they are they will be lost. A man may be in a boat on a river and yet die of thirst if he refuses to drink; and so you may be carried along and excited by a revival, but unless you receive the Lord Jesus into your soul by faith, you will perish after all. Faith is as simple a thing as drinking, but you must have it; you must believe or die. If a man were set up to his neck in water like Tantalus, and if all the rivers in the world flowed by him, he would expire in the pangs of thirst if he did not drink. Some of you have been up to your neck in the river for years. As I look at those pews I cannot but remember that rivers of love and mercy have been flowing right up to your lips, and yet you have not drunk. He who dies so deserves to die; he who perishes of thirst in such a condition must perish with a sevenfold emphasis. God help you. I know not what more I can ask him to do for you. Has he not done enough in giving rivers of mercy to you in Christ?

And if you have drunk of this stream, the next thing I say is, *live near it.* We read of Isaac that he dwelt by the well. It is good to live hard by an inexhaustible spring. Commune with Christ, and get nearer to him each day. Wade into this river, as you have done, till the water is up to your ankles; go on till it is up to your knees; go on till it washes your heart and loins, yea, go on till you find it a river to swim in.

I should like to say, last of all, if Christ be like a river, let us be like the fishes that *live in it.* The fish is an ancient Christian emblem for Jesus and his people. I sat under a beech tree some months ago in the New Forest; I gazed up into it, measured it, and marked the architecture of its branches, but suddenly I saw a little squirrel leap from bough to bough, and I thought, " After all, this beech tree is far more to you than to me, for you live in it. It delights me, it instructs me, and it affords me shade, but you live in it and upon it." So we know something about rivers, and they are very useful to us, but to the fish the river is its element, its life, its all. So, my brethren, let us not merely read about Christ, and think of him, and speak of him, but let us live on him, and in him, as the squirrel in the tree and the fish in the river. Live *by* him, and live *for* him : you will do both if you live *in* him.

> Roll over me, thou heavenly stream,
>   I find my element in thee.
> This my true life and bliss I deem,
>   In Christ, my Lord, absorb'd to be.

The Messenger of the Covenant

"The messenger of the covenant, whom ye delight in"—Malachi iii. 1.

THE Lord's people delight in the covenant itself. It is an unfailing source of consolation to them so often as the Holy Spirit leads them to its green pastures, and makes them to lie down beside its still waters. They can sweetly sing of it from youth even to hoar hairs, from childhood even to the tomb, for this theme is inexhaustible:

> "Thy covenant the last accent claims
> Of this poor faltering tongue;
> And that shall the first notes employ
> Of my celestial song."

They delight to contemplate *the antiquity* of that covenant, remembering that before the day-star knew its place, or planets ran their round, the interests of the saints were made secure in Christ Jesus. It is peculiarly pleasing to them to remember *the sureness* of the covenant. They love to meditate upon "the sure mercies of David." They delight to celebrate the covenant in their songs of praise, as "signed and sealed, and ratified, in all things ordered well." It often makes their hearts dilate with joy to think of its *immutability*, as a covenant which neither time nor eternity, life nor death, things present, nor things to come, nor angels, nor principalities, nor powers, shall ever be able to violate;—a covenant as old as eternity and as everlasting as the Rock of ages. They rejoice also to feast upon *the fulness* of this covenant, for they see in it all things provided for them.—God is their portion, Christ their companion, the Spirit their comforter, earth their lodge and heaven their home. They see in it not only some things, but all things; not only a help to obtain some desirable possessions, but an inheritance reserved and entailed to every soul that has an interest in this ancient and eternal deed of gift. Their eyes sparkled when they saw it as a treasure-trove in the Bible; but O how their souls were gladdened when they saw in the last will and testament of their divine kinsman that it was bequeathed to them! More especially it is the pleasure of God's people to contemplate *the graciousness* of this covenant. They see that the law was made void because it was a covenant of works and depended upon merit, but this they perceive to be enduring because grace is the basis, grace the condition, grace the strain, grace the bulwark, grace the foundation, grace the topstone. From the beginning even to the end, it is all of grace. They see that the covenant runneth on this wise, not "I will if you will," but "I will and you shall ;" not "I will reward if you deserve," but "I will forgive even if you sin ;" not "I will cleanse if you are clean," but "I will cleanse if you are filthy;" not "I will keep if you assist," but "I will bring you back even if you be lost, I will surely save you and preserve you even to the end." I know some Christians—bleared-eyed, like Leah—who cannot see afar off, and hence the councils of eternity they cannot behold. I know some believers of weak knees and feeble joints who are afraid of that strong word "Covenant." But they that are men in Christ Jesus, who by reason of years have had their senses exercised, know that the covenant is a treasury of wealth, a granary of food, a fountain of life, a store-house of salvation, a charter of peace, and a haven of joy. The covenant! let my soul but anchor here, then howl ye winds, and roar ye hurricanes! I will not fear. The covenant! let my soul but cast its anchor here, and come life with all its tribulations, and death with all its pains and terrors, my soul laughs them all to scorn.

> "The gospel bears my spirit up;
> A faithful and unchanging God
> Lays the foundation for my hope,
> In oaths, and promises, and blood.

We advance a step further towards our text, and remark that the "Messenger of the covenant" is a welcome ambassador to those who are interested in those exceeding great and precious promises which pertain to life and godliness. But, waiving further preface, let us notice, first, *that we delight in the office of Christ as the messenger of the covenant;* next, *that we delight in the way in which he fulfils that office;* and then, we shall conclude by noticing *some ways in which we show our delight.*

I. First, then, WE DELIGHT IN CHRIST IN HIS OFFICE OF MESSENGER OF THE COVENANT.

What is that office? I shall need two or three words to explain it. When we read of Christ as messenger of the covenant, I think we may understand him to be a *covenanted messenger.* Now, God has sent many messengers, whose words, when they have spoken in His name, he has not suffered to fall to the ground. So far they were covenanted messengers; but these persons sometimes spoke of themselves, and then God had not bound himself by promise to keep their words. Sometimes, even like the apostle Paul, they would have to pause and say, "I think I have the Spirit of God," but they might not be certain. But Christ is a covenanted messenger. God hath sworn to him to do for us whatever he may promise to us, so that if we believe in God we may believe also in him, since he speaks for God, and his every word is settled in heaven—

> "Array'd in mortal flesh,
> He like an angel stands,
> And holds the promises
> And pardons in his hands:
> Commission'd from his Father's throne
> To make his grace to mortals known."

Again, he is the covenanted messenger; on our behalf Christ swore to God to carry out that part of the covenant which was left for man, and so he stood as a covenanted messenger between God and man. The word "plenipotentiary" just hits my thought. You know sometimes kings send out ambassadors to try and negotiate peace, but they have limited powers. On other occasions ambassadors are sent with unlimited, unrestricted power, to make peace or not, and to make it just as they will. Now Christ comes as the covenanted ambassador of God, as the plenipotentiary of heaven. Let him do what he will, God is with him; let him promise what he may, God ratifies it; let him speak what he will to our souls, his word shall certainly be fulfilled. Now do you not rejoice in Christ in this office. He has said to us, "Come unto me all ye that labour and are heavy laden and I will give you rest." "Rest," saith the eternal Father, as he confirms Jesus' word. "Go in peace, thy sins which are many are forgiven thee." "They *are* forgiven thee," saith the court of heaven, "go in peace." "He that believeth on me is not condemned," saith Christ; and the Father saith himself "He is not condemned." There is not a word of the gospel which the Father has left unsanctioned. You need not therefore, when you venture upon Christ's word and Christ's merit, think you are resting on a something which God will not accept. He is God's covenanted messenger. He is sworn to accept whom Christ accepts, and since Christ saves all that trust in him, the Father accepts them likewise. He will save certainly all whom Christ hath declared shall be saved.

This, however, does not exhaust the meaning. Christ is the messenger of the covenant, in the next place, as *the messenger of the Father to us*. Moses was messenger of the covenant of works, and his face shone, for the ministration of death was glorious; but Christ is the messenger of the covenant of grace. O let his face shine in your esteem, ye saints of the Lord, for the ministration of life must be more glorious, far! Christ comes to us to tell us all that God will tell. The revelation of God is Christ. If you would know God, he that hath seen Christ hath seen the Father. God's *word* is Jesus, he speaketh fully by him. Would you know the father's decree? "I will declare the decree," saith Christ. Would you know his character? See every attribute of God in the man, Christ. Would you know his designs? See the designs of God effected in the works of Jesus. Would you know in fact all that is knowable of God? Understand that you can see it, not in nature, nor in providence, but in Jesus,

"God in the person of his Son,
Hath all his mightiest works outdone."

And will you not delight in him as such—as God's messenger to you? —If the very ministers of Christ are delightful to you, if their feet are beautiful upon the tops of the mountains when they bring glad tidings, how much more beautiful is he who comes from God to man, with messages of peace, declaring to us that God is reconciled to us, and accepteth us in the beloved. Sing his praises, O ye that have heard his voice. Glory ye in his holy name, O ye that have received his report, unto whom the arm of the Lord has been revealed, for as God's messenger to you, ye should delight in him.

But then, he is, as the messenger of the covenant, *our messenger and mediator with the Father.* You want to tell your Father something; Jesus stands to carry the message for you. George Herbert, in one of his poems, pictures Christ as using the hole in his side as a bag to carry our letters to glory—

> " If ye have anything to send or write,
> (I have no bag, but here is room)
> Unto my father's hands and sight
> (Believe me) it shall safely come.
> That I shall mind, what you impart;
> Look, you may put it very near my heart."

In the wounds of Christ we put our messages to God, and they go up to heaven with something more added to them. The blots and blurs of our petition Christ wipeth out, and then he savoureth our prayers, and incenseth them by putting with them the costly mixture of his own precious righteousness. See! In his golden censer yonder smokes the incense of your prayer, accepted for the incense sake, and for the sake of him who swings it to and fro as it smokes before the Most High. "The messenger of the covenant;" this name is peculiar to our Lord. Let not any man arrogate this office to himself, for it is Christ's alone. God never did hear a message from man that he accepted, except through this messenger. I cannot get to God directly, I must have a mediator. Well said Luther, "I will have nothing to do with an absolute God; for our God is a consuming fire." No sigh ever reached the Most High, except through Christ—I mean so as to move his heart to pour out his grace. Prayers, groans, tears, all these are like arrows without a bow, till Christ comes and fits them to the string, and shoots them home for you and me. All our prayers are like a victim, with the wood and altar; Christ must bring the fire, and then the sacrifice smokes to heaven. He is the messenger. Oh Christian, do you not rejoice in him then as the messenger of the covenant? He is doing thy errands before the throne to-night, pleading for me, pleading for you. "I have prayed for thee, that thy faith fail not." You came to this house to-night, you offered prayer, Christ is offering it now, as an offering most divinely sweet. As you are sitting here, you are breathing a vow, or a desire to heaven; Christ presents it, for he stands at the golden altar, having a censer full of the prayer and vows of saints. Give him an errand now. Try him at this moment, entreat him to plead on your behalf. Thus view him; thus exercise your faith upon him as the plenipotentiary from God to man, as the revealer of God to man, and as spokesman from man to God.

" Look up, my soul, with cheerful eye,	He sweetens every humble groan,
See where the great Redeemer stands,—	He recommends each broken prayer;
The glorious Advocate on high,	Recline thy hope on him alone,
With precious incense in his hands!	Whose power and love forbid despair."

II. But briefly on the second point. WE DELIGHT IN THE WAY IN WHICH CHRIST HAS CARRIED OUT THIS OFFICE AS MESSENGER OF THE COVENANT.

And here let us dwell on that part of the office which relates to *the revelation of God to man.* Oh, what a full messenger has he been! He has not dropped half the message; he has not told us a part of God, but all that his heavenly Father bade him declare, he has revealed unto us as we could bear it; and he has given us this day the Holy Spirit, who shall lead us into all truth, who shall take of the things of Christ, which the Father gave him, and reveal them unto us. What a full messenger, and how faithful! Surely the Master could say, "I have kept back nothing that is profitable for you." With greater emphasis than ever Paul could say it, he might have declared, "I am clear from the blood of all men. For I have not shunned to declare unto you all the counsel of God." We poor messengers mar the Master's message in the telling of it, but "Never man spake like this man." So full and faithful is he who speaketh with Jehovah's bidding to his chosen people, that he can say, "All things that I have heard of my Father I have made known unto you."

Then, *how willingly he does it!* "I delight to do thy will, O God." How sweet it seemed to him to show God out to us! Even his tears, though bitterly they flowed, were cheerfully bestowed; and his very death, though it was an awful baptism, yet was one for which he longed. How was he straitened until it was accomplished! I hate a man to be a messenger who goes unwillingly, and who mumbles out the message as if he had no interest in it; but oh! our sweet Lord Jesus tells God's message to us as though he were more interested in it than we are; tells it so lovingly, so affectionately, so tenderly, with all his heart, turning his soul out that we may see it, writing his very nature out in streams of blood, that we might see in crimson lines what otherwise we might not have been able to perceive. Oh, how well—better than ministers, better than prophets, better than apostles, better than angels, Christ hath performed the office of messenger from God. Solomon's proverb is all outdone in our Redeemer's case. "As the cold of snow in the time of harvest, so is a faithful messenger to them that send him: for he refresheth the soul of his masters."

Beloved, let us delight equally as much in *the way in which he has performed our message from ourselves to God.* Ah, I have been to my advocate a thousand times, but I never found him a weary messenger. You have a servant, and you give him many things to do; but towards nightfall it may be that you give him one thing too many, and the poor man's weary feet and languid looks chide you when you give him the errand. But I have been to my Master, and so have you, in the dead of night, and I never found him asleep. I have been to him in the heat of summer, but I never found him point to his bloody sweat, and say he could not go. I have been to him a thousand times, and yet I have never, never heard him say, "I have served thee enough, I will not be thy messenger again." But cheerfully, willingly hath he taken our request to God, again, and again, and again, and presented it there. And how full of sweet powers of memory and generous recollections he has been! We have often failed to tell him the message aright, and sometimes there was a part of it that we could not tell him—groanings that could not be uttered—but he read the message, and then told it perfectly out in the other place, within the veil, never forgetting one desire nor one faint wish; sometimes erasing one that was evil and putting in another that was right, but he hath never forgotten us. The blessed Master hath a thousand souls to plead for; nay, what if I say millions!

but never hath he forgotten one. The meanest lamb in his flock he has tended; the poorest subject in his dominions has been the object of his advocacy. And then, brethren, with what passionate love hath he pleaded for us in heaven! Oh, you cannot conceive him, for he is high above us; but if we could see him to-night, standing before the throne, we should say, " I never thought I had such an advocate as this;"—not with sighs and tears, for they are over now, but with authority he pleads, points to his wounded hands and to his side, and urges the case of his people as though it were his own case, and so indeed, it is, for he may well say—
"I feel at my heart all thy sighs and thy groans,
For thou art most near me—my flesh and my bones."
Never such an advocate as this. Fathers might plead for sons, and a wife might throw herself on the ground to plead with a judge for her husband, but never such a pleader as this. Thou messenger of the covenant, none can plead as thou dost.

And then, dear friends, I think we ought to delight in him, when we think how unflaggingly *he perseveres in his intercession*, though we are continually forgetful and ungrateful for his kindness. I am sure if we had a friend's cause to plead, and he were as unworthy and forgetful as we are, we should tell him to suit himself, and find some other advocate. But he, for Zion's sake, doth not hold his peace, for Jerusalem's sake he doth not rest. Going to and fro from heaven to earth, from earth to heaven, he speaketh messages of love from God to our souls, bearing messages of pleading and of intercession from our souls to God. Take thou, beloved, a sweet delight in Jesus, for he doth his errand well. He is a choice messenger, one among a thousand, yea the chief among ten thousand.

III. But time flies, and therefore we hasten onward to carry out our third proposal. HOW ARE WE TO SHOW THAT WE DO REALLY DELIGHT IN CHRIST? Well, there is one way of doing it, and that is by again *employing him to-night.* Thou hast been upon my errands so many times, my sweet Lord, that thou shalt even go again. I ask thee, brother Christian, to let me speak to thee a moment. I know thou hast some very heavy matter on thy mind to-night, some very heavy trial awaiteth thee to-morrow, and thou hast been troubled about it all the week. Dost thou delight in the messenger of the covenant? Ah, then send thy Jesus with it as a message to the throne to-night. Say thou unto Jesus, " I pray thee tell the Father that one of his adopted who can say, 'Abba,' is in trouble deep and sore. Send thou from heaven and deliver me, and pluck me out of the deep waters." Thou wilt show thy delight in him by trusting him in thy great matters. Oh, but you mean to do it yourself; you have all your wits about you and mean to get through it yourself do you? You shall flounder in the mire. But give the matter up to *Him* and let him take it to thy God and see whether prayer does not more often prevail in trial than all the energies and wits of man. And sister over yonder, thou hast a secret, one thou wouldst not tell to me, no, nor to thy dearest friend, but it rankles and it makes thy heart bleed in secret till sometimes thou art weary of thy life. Dost thou love the messenger of the covenant?

Whisper into his ear what thou canst tell to none beside, and ask him to speak for thee to the king, to the captain of the host. Say unto him, "Jesus, lover of my soul, I'll trust thee with this most secret grief. That which no creature can intermeddle with, thou shalt know; behold I bare the wound before thy tender eye; go tell the Father that a child of his is weeping in secret, walking in darkness and seeing no light." Thou wilt show thy delight in him by trusting him now. Minister, send a messenger by him to-night for thy flock! Sunday school teacher, give him a missive from thy heart for thy class! Mother, the messenger waits for thee, ask him to plead for thy sons and daughters! Father, the messenger is ready to bear thy wish to heaven! Tell him thou wouldst have no greater joy than this, to see thy children walk in the truth! Jesus, say thou to thy Father that *my* prayer to-night is that I would have this congregation saved. Oh speak thou; bear the ponderous message; ask that not one within these walls may perish. Lift up thy hands, and plead for every man, and woman, and child, beneath this tabernacle's dome to-night, and ask that every one may be a partaker of the grace that saves. I know that thou wilt prevail if thou wilt ask, for if thou shouldest ask anything of thy Father he will do it for thee. Thou hast but to will it and 'tis done. Behold, by faith I would lay hold upon the skirt of thy garment thou great High Priest, the sweetly sounding bells of thy ephod I hear to-night; upon thy glittering breast-plate the eyes of my faith are fixed. Take that request, and plead it solemnly before the awful throne of heaven, and let the answer come to all this multitude—an answer of grace and peace! Thus, my beloved, we must show our delight in him—by bidding him plead for us.

Leaving for a moment the thought of messenger, I want to add some other things, not quite, perhaps, in keeping with our text, but quite in harmony with our delight in Jesus. You are coming round the table, brothers and sisters, and you delight in Christ. Shall I tell you how it is that we show that we delight in him?

One way is by *waiting for him*. There is the wife at evening. It is past the proper hour for her husband to return. She goes to the window and looks out into the cold dark night, and then she goes back to the chair, and to the little one, and takes her needle and whiles away the time, but soon she is up again looking out of the window once more, and listening to every foot-fall in the street, or looking out from the open door. Why is not her spouse at home? How is it that he is away? She sits down again, she tries to ease her mind with household business, but every ticking of the clock, and every striking of the hour suggests to her, "Why is he so long in coming?" See she is again drawing back the curtains and looking out into the black night for the hundredth time, longing for her husband, and why? because she takes delight in him, and wants to see his face. So when Christians look out into the dark world and say, "When will he come?" and when they go to their labour, and say, "Why are his chariot-wheels so long in coming?" and when they can cry with John, "Come quickly, even so, come quickly, Lord Jesus," and are waiting for and hasting unto the coming of the Son of man, then they prove that they have intense delight in him. Do you show this, Christian? Are you waiting for him? Are you getting ready for the time when the Lord himself shall descend from heaven with a shout, with the trump of the archangel and the voice of God?

"Come, my beloved, haste away,
Cut short the hours of thy delay:
Fly like a youthful hart or roe,
Over the hills where spices grow."

We prove our delight in him in another way, by *working for him.* There is a woman there; she is working hard at her embroidery needle; she is making a little coat; it is a linen ephod. I wonder why that woman smiles so, while she works with her needle? There, she must put it away, for there is other work to do. I wonder why next day she goes to the drawer, so pleased to get that work out and continue it? I will tell you her name; her name is Hannah, the wife of Elkanah, and she is making a little coat for her son Samuel, whom she has left with Eli at the Tabernacle; now you perceive wherefore is she so pleased in making this ephod? Because she delighteth in Samuel. So I see the Sunday school teacher pleased to meet his children; I see the minister go to the pulpit with beaming eye, and I see the missionary leaving house and home, kindred and cherished associations, joyfully giving up everything for Christ, and I ask why? Because he delights in Christ, and therefore he can work for him. Is it so with you, friends, are you working for Christ? Yes, methinks you are, or else I fear me you are not delighting in him.

And then another thing. I have seen the boy at school—I knew such a boy myself—and one day that child was at play, and merry was he at his games, and well intent thereat, but some lad ran across the ground, and said, "Your father's come to see you," and he laid aside his playthings and his games, and ran at once into his father's arms because he delighted in his parent. And I have seen the Christian when he is delighting in his God, when lecture or prayer-meeting night came, say, "Well, I will gladly lose a little of my business, that I may run into my Father's arms in the hour of worship." There has been a saint to be visited, or a sinner to be warned, and I have seen the lovers of Jesus leave their nets that they may follow Christ, and forsake the world, that they might serve him. Beloved, if he were to come to-night and bid us choose whether we would be in heaven or here, I think we would not long delay, but say to him, "Thou leavest me no choice." To be with thee is so much better than aught beside, that I embrace thee now. Oh take me up to thee!

Further, we may show our delight in Christ by *searching after him when we lose his presence.* There is the spouse in the Canticles; she is going about in the city in the dark night—"Saw ye him whom my soul loveth?" The watchmen meet her and pluck away her veil rudely, and they smite her. Why is not that delicate woman at home at rest? See, she wanders on, cold and weary, with tears rolling down her cheeks, and hanging like pearls from her eyes. Wherefore is this woman weeping and searching thus? The answer is—"Tell me O thou whom my soul lovest, where thou feedest?" She hath such a delight in him, that she will search a thousand nights; yea, a believing soul would search hell through to find Christ, if he were to be found nowhere else; and I know what Rutherford said was no great exaggeration, when he said, "If there were fifty hells between my soul and Christ, and he bade me wade through them and he would come and meet me, I fain would dash through them all to reach his fond embrace." Jesu, our thirst for thee is insatiable; we must have thee, and thus we prove our delight in thee.

Lastly, we may prove our delight in Christ by *being very happy ourselves and trying to make others partakers of our joy.* Do not go to the Lord's table to-night if you can help it burdened with your groans and moans. If you cannot come without bringing them, then come; come anyhow. But I would have you to-night, if you could, delight yourselves in the Lord. You are very poor.—Ah! but you are very rich in him. You are sick, you say.—Ay! but remember what he suffered for you. Oh! but you are a sinner. Ay! but remember his precious blood! Fix your eye on *him* to-night and on nothing else, and oh be glad! Come to his table with delight. I often say I know the people that come here—our regular people that come here—because they have a way of walking, and a look on the Sabbath that is different from most people that go to other places of worship. Other folks are so solemn, as if they were going to an execution. They look so grave, as if it were an awful work to serve God, as bad as going to prison, to attend a service, and as disagreeable as the pillory o stand up and praise the Lord. But I notice that you come here with joy, looking upon the Sabbath as a joyous day, not a time to pull the blinds down and shut out the light, but a day to feast yourselves in God. Now I think ordinance days are especially times of rejoicing. You and I have been all the week up to our elbows in work. By-and-bye we shall have to go back to that dingy workroom among those persecuting worldlings. Never mind; Lord make this as a sanctuary to us to-night. Shut us in and shut the world out, and let us rejoice ourselves in our God.

"As myrrh new bleeding from the tree,
Such is a dying Christ to me;
And while he makes my soul his guest,
Thy bosom, Lord, shall be my rest.

No beams of cedar, or of fir,
Can with thy courts on earth compare;
And here we wait, until thy love
Raise us to nobler seats above."

Beloved brethren, if you have this delight *tell it to others.* Do not be tongue-tied and dumb any of you. Speak out what God has done for you. Tell! tell!—

"Tell to sinners round,
What a dear Saviour you have found."

If you should have any enjoyment to-night, let others partake of the honey which you have discovered. God help you thus to live to his praise.

I am about to retire a few moments, while our friends get to their seats for the communion. Before I retire, I have a message to tell from the Messenger of the Covenant. He is willing to take a message from any poor, troubled, sin-burdened, conscience-stricken sinner in this Tabernacle. Has any one of you a message for him? The Lord Jesus Christ is willing to receive and stamp with his own blood-marked hand any earnest, heart-written message you are willing to send to God to-night. Is there any one who has this to send—"God be merciful to me a sinner?" What! Not one of you? Is there not a heart here that would say, "Lord save or I perish?" Surely there are some! Breathe thy desire out now silently; Jesus hears it; trust him to carry it to God. Believe that his blood can cleanse thee. Trust him, trust his merits to clothe thee. Trust especially his intercession to prevail for thee as the messenger of the covenant. Do it soul. "Oh but," you say, "my hand is black." Never mind, he will touch it and make it white. "Oh but I cannot pray." He can pray for you. "Oh but I cannot plead." He can plead in your stead. Tell him your wants. As Rowland Hill once did, so would I do with you. It is said that Rowland once had to put up in a village where there was no other house to put up at but a tavern; and having a pair of horses to bait, and going into the best room of the inn, he was considered to be a valuable guest for the night. So the host came in, and he said, "Glad to see you Mr. Hill." "I am going," was the reply, "to stay with you to-night; will you let me have family prayer to-night in this house?" "I never had such a thing as family prayer here," said the landlord, "and I don't want to have it now." "Very well, then just fetch my horses out; I can't stop in a house where they won't pray to God. Take the horses out." Now being too good a guest to lose, the man thinks better of it, and promises to have family prayer. "Ah but," said Hill, "I'm not in the habit of conducting prayer in other people's houses. You must conduct it yourself." The man said he could not pray. "But you must," said Rowland Hill. "Oh but I never did pray." "Then my dear man you will begin to-night," was the answer. So when the time came, and the family were on their knees, "Now," said Rowland Hill, "every man prays in his own house; you must offer prayer to-night." "I can't pray, *I can't*," said the landlord. "What, man, you have had all these mercies to-day, and are you so ungrateful that you cannot thank God for them? Besides, what a wicked sinner you have been. Can't you tell God what a sinner you've been and ask for pardon?" The man began to cry, "I can't pray, Mr. Hill, I can't, indeed I can't." "Then tell the Lord, man, you can't; tell him you can't pray," said Mr. Hill, "and ask him to help you." Down went the poor landlord on his knees. "O Lord I can't pray; I wish I could." "Ah! you have begun to pray," said Rowland Hill, "you have begun to pray, and you will never leave off. As soon as God has once set you to pray, faint though it be, you will never leave off. Now I'll pray for you." And so he did, and it was not long before the Lord was pleased, through that strange instrumentality, to break the landlord's hard heart and to bring him to Christ. Now I say, if any of you can't pray, tell the Lord you can't. Ask him to help you to pray; ask him to show you your need to be saved; and if you can't pray, ask him to give you everything that you need. Christ will make as well as take the message. He will put his own blood upon your prayer; and the Father will send down the Holy Ghost to you to give you more faith and more trust in Christ.

May the Lord send you away with his blessing to-night. **Amen.**

The Sitting of the Refiner

"And he shall sit as a refiner and purifier of silver: and he shall purify the sons of Levi, and purge them as gold and silver, that they may offer unto the Lord an offering in righteousness"—Malachi iii. 3.

THIS is spoken of as one of the results of the coming of the Lord: he would test and try all things, destroy the false and the evil, and make those pure whom he permitted to remain. Behold, the Promised One has come! He whom Israel sought suddenly appeared in his temple as the messenger of the covenant. Glad were the eyes of Simeon, and Anna, and all those who waited for him, and glad this day are our voices as we proclaim that the Messiah has appeared. The glorious Son of God, the anointed of the Most High, has been among men, and faithful witnesses have testified concerning him, "We beheld his glory, the glory as of the only begotten of the Father, full of grace and truth." That coming, heralded by songs of angels, and prophetic of countless blessings, should have been a day of unmingled light to men; but because of hypocrisy, pride, and self, it was not so; on the contrary, it was to many a day of darkness and not of light. We have abundant historical evidence that our Lord's first advent was a day of great trial to the Jewish people; and when we remember the siege of Jerusalem, and kindred events, we do not marvel that the prophet asked, "But who may abide the day of his coming? and who shall stand when he appeareth? for he is like a refiner's fire, and like fuller's sope." His ministry tried the religion, the orthodoxy, and the saintship of the period, and because it revealed the hollowness of the whole of the profession of the day, it aroused all the enmity of the religious classes. Those who were the leaders of the so-called religious thought of the age were aroused to hate the Lord Jesus, and to take a delight in nailing him to the tree; for his teaching was so true and good that their word-chopping and ceremony-making could not endure it.

Our Lord, when he came, sat as a refiner, and assayed the age then present; and ever since then his gospel in the world, his Spirit, his teaching, yea, the very fact of his life,—these all together have been a test, a trial, a sort of standard of weights and measures among men. All things are on their trial. You are constantly hearing of this time and that time as being "crises"; and the saying is true. There is always a crisis to something or other during these days of the Lord's sitting as a refiner. All things are being thrust into the furnace, and the fire is kept burning at a white heat, and nothing evil can abide the flame. Everything that is good shall be conserved, purified, made brilliant; but all that is evil, be it what it may, the whole world over, since Christ has come, shall be tried and dissolved as by fire. When our Lord comes the second time, the trial will be still more intense. "Who shall abide the day of his coming" when he shall still further be revealed, and when his purpose shall be rather that of judgment than of mercy?

It is well for us to know that, whenever Jesus Christ draws near to a soul, he comes in utmost mercy to make it clean. Because he is in himself the incarnation of ineffable love, his coming always means that he is about to purify the soul, for the highest mercy is to rid us of sin. The grandest thing that God himself can do in the purpose of his love is to purify us into his own glorious holiness. Christ loved his church, and this is how he showed it; "He gave himself for it, that he might present it to himself a glorious church, not having spot, or wrinkle, or any such thing." The Well Beloved seeks to purify his chosen by the washing of water through the word. It is the way his love takes: for true love doth ever choose the way of holiness. That love which would lead its beloved into sin is lust; it deserves not the name of love; but true love will ever seek the highest health and wholeness (which is holiness) of its object. Pure affection will grieve to see a fault, mourn over a folly, and seek to remove a blot. Perfect love seeks the perfection of the thing it loves. Such is the perfect love of Christ: whenever he comes to a soul in love he comes as a refiner. He comes with this object,—to take away the dross from the silver, and to make the fine gold purer still. In his sharpest dispensations he means no ill to us, but the divinest good; seeking not to grieve, but to lead up to the eternal blessedness, of which the root and flower are both found in absolute perfection.

If any of you, my hearers, are seeking the Lord at this time, I want you to understand what it means: you are seeking a fire which will test you, and consume much which has been dear to you. We are not to expect Christ to come and save us in our sins, he will come and save us from our sins; therefore, if you are enabled by faith to take Christ as a Saviour, remember that you take him as the purger and the purifier, for it is from sin that he saves us. "They shall call his name Jesus, for he shall save his people from their sins." This is the particular salvation which he aims at. Though he does deliver men from hell, it is by delivering them from the sin which is the fuel of Tophet's flame. Though he does give us heaven, yet his way of bringing us to heaven is by giving us a heavenly mind, a heart obedient to the holy and loving Father. The refinement of our nature and character is the way in which his infinite love most wisely displays itself.

We are going to talk of this purifying process. "He shall sit as a refiner." *How is the refining carried on?*

It is carried on in part *by the word of God.* "Is not my word like a fire?" Wherever the gospel is preached thoroughly, out and out, it is a wonderful consumer of dross. I have known certain congregations that have been dead in worldliness, the haunts of wealthy professors, whose love to Christ is a mere pretence. Close to them I have seen another church which has been lively in spirit, and full of zeal for the Lord. Whence the difference? The reason has usually been this —that in the one case there was man's ministry, and in the other there was the word of the Lord. Ministries of the Spirit worldly people cannot bear. They are displeased with a plain testimony. It rasps their conscience. There is no need to turn them out of the church; they drop away of themselves: it is not the place for them; it is too hot for them, I mean too holy, too spiritual, too devout. By-and-by they are offended, and murmuringly they prepare to emigrate. There are so many things that they do not approve of, they see so much that is dreadfully orthodox, narrow-minded, and bigoted; and so they trot off among their own cattle. Yes, and so they should. That is God's way of keeping his flock to itself. Those that are rooted up by the word of God are best rooted up. We may always be practising this kind of separating the tares from the wheat, for it leaves the testing with God and a man's own conscience, and hence no injustice will be done. It would be ill by excommunications to seek to root up the tares from among the wheat, lest we root up the wheat with them; but by the word, if it be preached in the power of the Holy Ghost, the process will be always going on. God's furnace stands in Zion. If any of you are ever displeased by the word, I pray you be displeased: we shall certainly never alter the word for you. If the truth comes too closely home to your consciences and angers you, be angry, not alone with him that speaks it, but with him from whom it comes; and then you will see the folly of such anger, and humble yourselves before God, and accept his truth, which will live, and your sin shall die. God grant it may be so.

Another purging operation is by causing his chosen to have *more fellowship* with his own blessed and glorious self. Of all the means of purging the heart none surpasses this, for when the Lord in great mercy draws his child near to him, and makes him feel his love, and know it beyond a doubt, then the favoured heart longs to be holy in all things. When the Lord fills his servant full of his love, and makes him to be joyed and overjoyed with the sweet consciousness that he is the Beloved's, and that the Beloved is his, then a holy jealousy burns within the soul, and the heart cries, "Is there anything that can grieve the Beloved? Let it be slain! Is there aught that I think, or wish, or say, or do, that might break the sacred spell of communion, and cause him to be gone? Let it be driven out at once!" The heart institutes a diligent search that, if possible, it may put away the accursed thing, that Christ may not be grieved. Of all fires that ever burned this is one of the fiercest. Jealousy is cruel as the grave, and a holy jealousy does stern work in our hearts with sin. It hangs up the darling sin before the face of the sun, and calls upon the fowls of heaven to come and feast upon the slain. Oh, that we knew Christ better, and lived more in the light of his countenance, for then should we be purged as with the spirit of burning.

After all, *the Holy Spirit* is the great fire that burns in Zion to purge believers from the love of sin. It is he that makes use of the Word, and makes use of fellowship, and makes use of everything else, to sever sin from the saint, and take away the dross from the silver. He is the immediate agent of our sanctification, all else we must regard as only the means in his skilful hand. To him be our love and our praise evermore.

As a subsidiary means the Lord uses *providence*. I have no doubt that he uses very frequently gracious providences, as we call them; that is, providences which please us by gratifying our natural wishes. Some people have been sanctified by prosperity; but I do not think very many have been. Few good medicines are pleasant to the palate. If we were as we ought to be, every joy that comes to us would tend to make us grateful, and so it would make us love God; and what is that but to be more like God and more holy? But, alas, in that we are weak through the flesh, the gentler modes of love far oftener fail than her rougher processes. It remains then that, if we cannot be preserved in honey, we must be salted with fire, lest corruption should take hold upon us. Such is the stubbornness of our flesh, that the Lord uses for fuel in his furnace sharp and heavy trials of different kinds. Adversity assumes many forms, and in each and all of its shapes the Lord knows how to use it for his people's benefit. Christ sits as a refiner when he takes away prosperity, and brings the wealthy down to poverty. He often refines men by the losses which they sustain of beloved friends. Bereavement burns like a blast-furnace; and, oh, how much of carnal love has been consumed by it!

We have known persons greatly purified by the Holy Spirit by passing through depression of spirit, inward grief, and soul sorrow. Spiritual pain has been blessed to some, and physical pain to more. In itself pain will sanctify no man: it may even tend to wrap him up within himself, and make him morose, peevish, selfish; but when God blesses it then it will have a most salutary effect—a suppling, softening influence. Sorrow is made to act as a kind of flux upon the hard metal to make the dross separate from the precious ore.

Yes, *affliction* is what most believers think of when they read such a passage as this; but I warn them not to think too much of it, for that is not the refiner's only fire, nor is it even his best fire. Affliction is but one part of the machinery of the Royal Refinery,—one of the fluxes by which the great Lord separates the precious from the vile.

I desire to call your attention to the text by leading you to mark three things. First, I want you to watch *the attitude of the refiner.* —" And he shall sit as a refiner and purifier of silver." Secondly, *the object of his refining,* —" He shall purify the sons of Levi, and purge them as gold and silver." And, thirdly, *the result of the refinement,*— " That they may offer unto the Lord an offering in righteousness."

I. Notice carefully THE ATTITUDE OF THE REFINER,—" He shall sit." The posture would not have been mentioned had it not been instructive.

Sitting *looks like the attitude of indifference.* There is the metal vexed with a white heat: here is the refiner sitting down. There is the child of God upon the bed of pain, and he cries, "My Lord, come and help me"; and there the refiner sits, looks on, but does not stir a hand. The child of God is sinking in trouble; he fears, like Peter, that the next step may drown him; and there is his Lord, calm and unmoved. When the apostolic ship was out at sea, and tossed with tempest, Christ was asleep in the hinder part of the vessel Unbelief dares challenge his love because of this apparent apathy: How can he sit still and see us suffer? She mutters—" He is indifferent: he does not care." " Carest thou not that we perish?" is the cry of unbelief; and before the heart actually utters it, it begins to think, " Where is the tenderness of Christ? Where is the gentleness of God? Am I thus to be tortured? Am I thus to be tried? Am I thus to be tossed from billow to billow without a helper?" Yet after all our crying and tears the refiner sits still! Yes, he to all appearance disregards our prayers and entreaties, and fulfils the description of the text—" He sits."

It is wonderful how often God seems utterly indifferent to his people, and how a Christ filled with compassion, because he has been tried in all points like as we are, yet seems to look down upon our sorrows with undisturbed serenity. I once heard a Welshman preach in his own native tongue. It was a sermon in which he got into the spirit of his subject, and spake as one inspired. He used a very simple illustration when he said, "The mother has her dear babe upon her knee. It is time for washing; she washes its face. The little one cries; it loves not the soap; it loves not the water; and therefore it cries. Here is a great sorrow! Listen to its lamentations! It is ready to break its heart! What does the mother do? Is she sorrowful? Does she weep? No; she is singing all the while, because she understands how good it is that the child should suffer a little temporary inconvenience in order that its face, all smeared and foul, should become bright and beautiful again. Thus does the great Father rest in his love, and rejoice over us with singing while we are sighing and crying." Ours is but a child's sorrow, sharp and shallow, of which the greatest source is our own ignorance of the great designs of the Perfecter of men. The Lord pities our childish sorrow, but he does not so regard it as to stay his hand from his cleansing work. " Let not thy soul spare for his crying," said Solomon; and our wise Father when he is chastening us does not spare us for our crying. What if the metal that is put into the furnace should be sentient when the crucible is hot, and should cry out, " Oh, take me out; the fire is too hot; I cannot bear it. I am dissolving; I am melting; take me out." Would the assayer regard the entreaties of the metal? Ah, no! The refiner sits still. Why should he be flurried? He knows what he is at, and he knows that his divine methods are wise and infallible. He is not hurting the silver, but doing it lasting service. He is not even putting it through a needless process. He is taking the shortest way of working when he seems to be longest in his assays. There is a haste that is not good speed, and God uses not such haste as that; he moves at the pace of perfection, and that may seem slow to petulance. He shall sit as a refiner till thou shalt say, " Does he care at all for me?"

Carnal reason may judge as it pleases as to the indifference of him who seems to sit at ease while his people are melted in the flames, but faith is full well assured that in the attitude of the divine Refiner there is *real attention*. Why does the refiner sit, but because he is resolved steadily to watch the crucible? He will not go away and leave it, even for a moment, lest the heat should grow too great or a certain point should be passed over when his presence would be essential to the success of the process. I have often heard that a refiner sits and looks at the silver till he can see his own portrait in it; but, though I have heard that venerable story many times, and can see the evident moral of it, I have my suspicions as to its being a matter of fact. I certainly should not like to be the refiner who had such a task to do, for when a crucible is in the white heat of the furnace, it is almost enough to burn out your eyes to look at it even for an instant; and I do not believe that any human being could watch a mass of molten silver glowing in the furnace till he saw his own image there. Christ's eye can bear the blaze, and he can watch us in the fires. But I use not the illustration, because I have my doubts about the truth of it. Our Lord sits as the refiner at the furnace mouth, because he is all attention. He has, as it were, given up all other cares just to sit there, and watch his treasure. He is determined that his servants shall be purified—that the sons of Levi shall be purged; and so there he is, everything else laid aside, giving his whole heart and soul to those whom he is refining. "Oh," say you, "but you exaggerate if you talk about the Lord's giving all his heart and soul to one of his people." No, I do not. The Lord Jesus watches each one of his people as intensely as if he had not another. Finite minds must have a centre somewhere, and as that centre changes so our circumference of thought and action shifts; but God's centre is everywhere, and his circumference is nowhere. Each one of us may be in the centre of the divine mind, and yet none of the redeemed may be any the less near because of it. Jesus watches each one—you, me, fifty thousand others —all of them his chosen ones that are undergoing the purifying process. He watches each one as if there were never another for his blessed eye to rest upon. He is all attention, watching not as children gaze on soldiers in the fire, but as practical refiners watch their precious metal. Poor, bowed heart, Jesus is all attention. His sitting down is not because he forgets, but because he remembers.

"God's furnace doth in Zion stand,
But Zion's God sits by,
As the refiner views his gold,
With an observant eye."

Always observing, always watching. Jesus shall sit,—" He shall sit as a refiner."

But we may notice more than this. I think I see in the sitting down of the refiner a *settled patience*, as if he seemed to say, "This is stern work, and I will sit down to it, for it will need care, and time, and constant watchfulness. This metal may need to be purified in a furnace of earth seven times, but I am set upon the perfecting of the work, and, therefore, here I place myself. I shall bear with this man till I have delivered him from his faults. I shall bear with this woman till I have made something of her—till I have got away that which weakens and injures her character. I mean to bear with this poor, petulant, unbelieving, complaining, selfish, groaning mortal; he has some love to me, and some life in me; and, therefore, I will bear with him till his life and love shall have conquered all earthly grossness, and he shall be a lump of pure metal fit **for my Father's treasury.**"

THE SITTING OF THE REFINER

The Lord has had boundless patience with some of us already, for we required a world of purifying, and we have been very slow to receive it. How many sermons have we heard, and yet how little have we been purified by the word? How often has the Spirit striven with us, and yet every thought is not yet brought into captivity. How often have we had near and true fellowship with Christ, and yet have again forsaken him! How frequently have we had to endure the furnace of affliction and yet our dross and tin are not removed. The Refiner still perseveres with settled resolve of ceaseless love. He will not give up his gracious task. He did not come hastily to the furnace door and shut us in, and then leave us while he minded other matters; but he has been sitting near his work ever since he began it, even as the refiner sits close to his work; and he means to stay as long as the work remains unfinished; he will not be gone till all is over. Here then faith sees divine attention and settled patience where unbelief dared to suspect unfeeling indifference.

I find in looking at the original that the word for "sit" is one which is used many times in Scripture for the posture of a king upon a throne: it is a sort of regal sitting down. So that we have here *the posture of power.* "He shall sit as a refiner," signifies, then, I take it, that he who seems indifferent, but who is constantly observant and patient, is seated on his throne possessing infinite power over all things, so that the process which he is watching can be checked or quickened according to his own will and wish. He reigns as a refiner, he has power over every coal, over every single jet of gassy flame, power over every breath of air that fans the fire, power over the furnace to its inmost centre and its utmost vehemence, power over the metal itself and its dross, and all that is excellent about it as well as all that is vile. Oh, this is a grand consolation! He that has undertaken to purify us can do it, for he sits on the throne of boundless might. Nothing short of an omnipotent Saviour could have saved *me.* It were ill news for me if men could show that Christ were not divine; for short of a divine Redeemer I shall never be perfected, I know. No strength but that which made me can new-make me. Only he that says, "I kill and I make alive," can ever kill my sin and make me alive unto God. Oh, Christian, this ought to be a delight to you, that he who sits as a refiner sits on the throne while he is refining you, and exercises sovereign grace and infinite power while dealing with your soul. Jesus reigns in the work of sanctification, having all things at his disposal, and he can and will perform that which he has begun.

> "Grace will complete what grace begins,
> To save from sorrows or from sins;
> The work that wisdom undertakes
> Eternal mercy ne'er forsakes."

Eternal power performs what everlasting love designs. So I conceive that the text may also teach us *the perfect perseverance of Christ* in the work of the purifying of his people. "He shall sit as a refiner." Might not your backsliding after you had once reached a great height of sanctity have disappointed Christ, and made him leave you? Yes, if it were not true of him, "I am God: I change not," he would have left you to be consumed. But therefore ye are not consumed, because from his blessed purpose he will not swerve. Oh, how many times you and I have seemed to make advances towards purity, but have gone back again to folly, thus manifesting the abundance of our alloy. It did seem as if, at last, the blessed flame of grace had begun to make us bright; and yet we have dulled again back to the old state. But where is the Refiner? Has he gone? By no means. There he is! He has been sitting as a refiner, and he is sitting still. That is a blessed text: "He shall not fail nor be discouraged." There is much to discourage him, but he is not discouraged; there is much to make him relinquish the work, but he determines not to fail in it. His mind is made up, and well it may be, for he has paid in bloody sweat and in his heart's blood the ransom price to purchase us, and he will never leave half effected what he has spent his life to achieve. What he has redeemed he will refine. Gethsemane and Calvary have bound the refiner to his task. He undertook a stupendous labour, and he went through with it till he shouted from the tree, "It is finished," and therefore we may rest assured that he will go on with the further portions of his great enterprise till, from his throne above, he will say, "It is finished," as he surveys every one of us, "without spot, or wrinkle, or any such thing,"—pure lumps of gold and silver, brought home by himself, without a speck of dross about us. Oh, blessed hope! where should we dare to indulge it but in the presence of an almighty Saviour, whose immutable oath has bound him to carry out the work of our perfection.

II. Now, dear brethren, suffer a few words upon THE GREAT OBJECT OF OUR LORD'S REFINING WORK. This point has come up all along. May the Spirit of God instruct us concerning it.

The great object of his refining is that he may deliver us from all evil, and make us perfect. Recollect, *the subjects of purifying are his own chosen ones,*—" He shall purify the sons of Levi." Levi was the tribe taken out of the rest for God's service. The Lord has a people whom he has set apart unto himself, and these he will purify. Do others think that he does them an injustice by this act of choice? Would they like to be purified? Then, depend upon it, he will not refuse it to them. Nay, the quibble lies in words, and has no truth in it. Men pretend to be angry with electing love, though they have no desire for it themselves. God's election is an election to holiness, and this is a thing which men in their heart of hearts do not desire. Sirs, if you do not wish for purification and holiness, wherefore should you quarrel with God that he gives it not to you? Yet unholy men rave at election to holiness, and call it partiality, and I know not what besides. Ye dogs in the manger, will ye always howl at God because he gives to his own sheep that which you will not care to have? If you wish for it, you may have it. Free is the gospel to every soul under heaven that desires it. The Lord proclaims, "Whosoever will, let him come and take the water of life freely;" but if men turn their backs on heaven's ever-flowing fountain, shall they afterwards quarrel with the election of God because he causes some to come whom he makes willing in the day of his power. They may quarrel if they will; but high overhead rolls the dread thunder of that awful word, "He will have mercy on whom he will have mercy, and he will have compassion on whom he will have compassion." God is sovereign in his gifts of grace, and does after his own mind. He refuses grace to none, but yet he will have a people of his own on whom his sanctifying work shall be wrought. "He shall purify the sons of Levi."

The refiner begins his work by discovering to his people their need of purity. What! purify the sons of Levi? Do they want it? Surely, Reuben, Manasseh, Gad—these might want purifying; but Levi opens and shuts the door of the house of God. It is a Levite that sacrifices, that enters within the veil. Does *he* require purifying? Ay, that he does. "He shall purify the sons of Levi,"—the best, the very best, the holiest—those that come near to God—the true silver and the real gold. He shall purify these. Brother, sister, have you a notion that you do not need purifying? Discard it, for if we walk in the light as God is in the light, and have closest fellowship with God, yet still we need the cleansing blood. "The blood of Jesus Christ, his Son," still "cleanseth us from all sin." Still we need the purging Spirit, or else there remains enough of evil about the man that is nearest heaven's gates to make a Judas Iscariot of him, if grace do not prevent. "He shall purify the sons of Levi": the pure shall be purified, the clean shall be yet further cleansed. Did you ever notice that the branch which feels most of the knife, and gets most of the pruning, is not the dead branch? Not that withered, crooked branch does the husbandman wound with the knife. No, the best branch, that bears most fruit, is most worthy of the gardener's visits and shall be most favoured with them. That ore which has the most gold in it, in proportion to the quartz, is the likeliest to get into the fire. He that has most of refinement is he on whom Christ will carry out his refining work. "He shall purify the sons of Levi."

Further, observe that he not only discovers to them their need of this purity, but he remedies their impurity. He shall actually purify them as gold and silver. The point is the thoroughness of it. This piece of wood which makes my pulpit, if it is defiled, it is dusted, and it is at once sufficiently cleansed. Your platters are washed: that is all. Your furniture may need beating, dusting, and many processes; but there is nothing thorough in them compared with the metaphor of the text,—"He shall purify them as gold and silver." They must go into the fire. The purging that God gives his people is not the washing of the outside of the cup and platter, it is the cleansing of the soul, the heart—the purging of the inward parts of the man—a fiery purging. Fire does not merely go about the metal, but it penetrates, and passes right into it. The metal is hot; it is melted; it flows; the fire has dissolved the mass. We say in the hymn, "Refining fire, go through my heart;" and that is the nearest approximation of language: but fire does something more than go through the metal. It seems to get into the very essence and nature and character of the metal, and fuse it all, making it all feel its supreme force. The Lord's purification of his people in order to make them fit to be with him in heaven is a fire process, mysterious, inward, penetrating, consuming, transforming. His Spirit burns like fire. His word like fire goes through and through the soul. His holy fellowship causes us to say, "My heart melted while my beloved spoke"; and his fiery trials, too, when blest by the Spirit, seem to melt the very being of the man.

This fire-process is intended to be thorough, that it may be abiding. If you get a piece of gold or silver, though it has been through the fire, it may grow dull again, but it cannot again become impure and alloyed. Silver will soon oxidize upon the surface, but for all that the bulk of the silver vessel is not injured at all: it remains pure silver after it has been through the fire. The work is done, and done thoroughly. The purifications of God will last throughout eternity. Have you ever reflected upon the fact that when Christ's refining work is done upon us there will never be any need for it again? Blessed be God, there is no purgatorial fire. We need not dread that we have yet to pass through purging flames in another world, for Jesus has well refined the sons of Levi and they are clean every whit. Believers are taken up to heaven at once as soon as they quit this world. If we were not thoroughly purified before we entered there, we should be under a strong temptation to pride. Only think of yourself with a palm branch, my brother! You fought very badly, too. You with a harp in your hand! Is there not a temptation to strike just one gentle string in praise of what you did or suffered? Say not that you could not be thus tempted. Why, an angel fell from heaven; the son of the morning, a greater being than you, could not stand amidst the glories of Paradise. Pride dragged Lucifer from heaven, and hurled him down to the darkest deeps. Oh, joy, joy, joy, the like shall never happen to you. You will never be proud in Paradise: you will never be discontented in heaven. Say you, "I should think not"? I do not know. If you could go to heaven as you are you would be. You would be sorry to think that there is no temple there, and no more sea; and a great many things might make you dissatisfied, but you will not be discontented, for you will be purified. You will not speak sharply to your neighbour in heaven; you will not think he sings too loudly, or is too demonstrative in his worship. You will not quarrel with anybody up in heaven, for you will have nothing in you which can lead to sin. See how splendidly the refiner will do his work, then, so that throughout eternity, when this poor world shall all dissolve in smoke, and the sun shall have burnt out like an expiring coal, and the moon shall be black as sackcloth of hair, and all earth-born things shall have grown hoary and given way to corruption's finger, you shall still be young and fresh and pure and perfect as the God that loved you, and that made you so. Oh, well may we be content to let the fire burn and let the coals glow as much as ever they will, since it can be only for a very little while, and then come the ages, the eternities, the God, the Christ, the heaven which he has prepared for us when we are prepared for them. This, then, is the object of his refining.

III. Thirdly, and to conclude, WHAT WILL BE THE IMMEDIATE RESULT OF THIS REFINING AS CHRIST CARRIES IT ON? It will be this —"That they may offer to the Lord an offering of righteousness."

First, these Levites shall attend to their business. They ought to have been working at the temple, but they had forgotten their high calling. The sons of Levi had taken up their portion in the world, though their God had never given them any, for he gave no portion to

Levi when the land was divided among the tribes. "The Lord's portion is his people," and the Lord is the portion of their inheritance. The Levites had got away from their spiritual calling, and had given themselves up to mind this and that; but it is pleasant to observe that when God purifies them, then they begin to do their own business,—" That they may offer to the Lord." Oh, beloved, if you have been refined by the Word, if you have been refined by the Spirit, if you have been refined by heavenly joys, if you have been refined by sanctified sorrows, you wish to serve God much more than ever you did before. You now pray that if you have lived to self in any degree, you may be forgiven, for you wish to live to Christ, and to him alone. Now, as a Levite, you say, "What can I do for God? There is nothing here worth living for, but to love and serve him. Here, Lord, tell me what thou wouldest have me to do. I desire to do it at once." Brother, thank God for every trial you have suffered, if it leads you to offer your sacrifice. I will bless God for all I have endured myself, if I am enabled to fulfil my priesthood; for are we not a nation of priests, a peculiar people, set apart to offer sacrifice to God? And this is to be the result of refinement: that we do good work and service unto God. Some of you want a little pushing on in this direction, for I know a great many Christians who live as if the main point in religion was to enjoy yourself. "I enjoyed that sermon. I enjoyed that prayer-meeting." Yes, that is quite right. But have you done anything? Have you served the Master? Have you offered anything to Jesus? Have you brought forth fruit to his glory? Oh, it is a good thing to be watered; it is a blessed thing to stand in the warm sunlight and grow; but after the watering and the sunshine must come the fruit-bearing, or we shall be barren fig trees after all. And so it is in the text, you see—" That they may offer unto the Lord an offering."

But then, next, they are not only to do their work, but they are to do it well. "They must offer unto the Lord an offering in righteousness," for, oh, we may do much for God that looks very pretty, but when we get into trial and look back upon our service by the furnace light we do not think much of it. Have you ever taken a little time to look back upon your service of God, and have you not wondered at yourself that you have done it so badly? Have you not said, "Please God I may address that class again, I will be more passionately in earnest"? Have you not said, "Please God I may get out to that village to preach again, I will speak with all my soul, and nothing else but Christ shall be my theme"? Have we not often wished we could do our lifework over again, that we might do it better? I do not think that there is any use in that wish. Let us improve what is to be done in the future, rather than wish to undo the past. Let us buckle on our harness, and ask God to give us more spiritual intensity, that what is done may be a sacrifice offered in righteousness unto the Lord.

And then another result of this purification is that they were accepted, for the next verse says, "Then shall the offering of Judah and Jerusalem be pleasant unto the Lord as in the days of old." When God accepts our persons, he accepts our offerings, but if we are not ourselves accepted, then that which we do is rejected. When the Lord Jesus Christ enables us to live by faith in him, and to see that we are "accepted in the Beloved," and when that faith helps us to work in a right spirit and serve God from a pure motive, then we ourselves and our work are pleasant unto God as in former days.

God grant that the blessed processes of his providence and of his grace which are being carried on in his people may be carried on in you and me, that we may serve God with perfect hearts all our days.

I think I heard somebody say, "I do not want putting through that process. I do not wish for such purifying." You have seen the great masses of slag that they throw out from the furnace. They lie in great heaps at the pit's mouth. Will these be a picture of you and your eternal condition? Reprobate silver shall men call them, because God has rejected them. Will you be the slag cast away? the dross left for ever? Oh, eternity, eternity, what must it be to be shipwrecked on thy shoreless sea, and drifted for ever as a waif and stray from God and hope? Eternity, eternity, what must it be to be rejected and cast away from the presence of God and from the glory of his power, thrown out upon the waste-heap of the universe, for ever given up? God save any man from that! Oh, it were worth wading through a thousand hells to obtain that which makes existence worth the having—namely, rightness with God. But, oh, if there were nothing else to lose but God's love, nothing else to earn by neglect of things divine but to be rejected of God, I would plead with you with my whole soul that you should seek the Lord now. Cry mightily to the divine Saviour that he may now purge you with his precious blood from all the guilt of sin, that he may then go on with the second process by which he shall purge you from the power and habit and defilement of sin, and make you, like himself, immaculate before the Omniscient. God grant it, for Jesus's sake. Amen.

Christ, the End of the Law

"For Christ is the end of the law for righteousness to every one that believeth"—Romans x. 4.

You remember we spoke last Sabbath morning of "the days of the Son of man." Oh that every Sabbath now might be a day of that kind in the most spiritual sense. I hope that we shall endeavour to make each Lord's Day as it comes round a day of the Lord, by thinking much of Jesus, by rejoicing much in him, by labouring for him, and by our growingly importunate prayer, that to him may the gathering of the people be. We may not have very many Sabbaths together, death may soon part us; but while we are able to meet as a Christian assembly, let us never forget that Christ's presence is our main necessity, and let us pray for it and entreat the Lord to vouchsafe that presence always in displays of light, life and love! I become increasingly earnest that every preaching time should be a soul-saving time. I can deeply sympathize with Paul when he said, "My heart's desire and prayer to God for Israel is that they might be saved." We have had so much preaching, but, comparatively speaking, so little believing in Jesus; and if there be no believing in him, neither the law nor the gospel has answered its end, and our labour has been utterly in vain. Some of you have heard, and heard, and heard again, but you have not believed in Jesus. If the gospel had not come to your hearing you could not have been guilty of refusing it. "Have they not heard?" says the apostle. "Yes, verily:" but still "they have not all obeyed the gospel." Up to this very moment there has been no hearing with the inner ear, and no work of faith in the heart, in the case of many whom we love. Dear friends, is it always to be so? How long is it to be so? Shall there not soon come an end of this reception of the outward means and rejection of the inward grace? Will not your soul soon close in with Christ for present salvation? Break! Break, O heavenly day, upon the benighted ones, for our hearts are breaking over them.

The reason why many do not come to Christ is not because they are not earnest, after a fashion, and thoughtful and desirous to be saved, but because they cannot brook God's way of salvation. "They have a zeal for God, but not according to knowledge." We do get them by our exhortation so far on the way that they become desirous to obtain eternal life, but "they have not submitted themselves to the righteousness of God." Mark, "submitted themselves," for it needs submission. Proud man wants to save himself, he believes he can do it, and he will not give over the task till he finds out his own helplessness by unhappy failures. Salvation by grace, to be sued for *in forma pauperis*, to be asked for as an undeserved boon from free, unmerited grace, this it is which the carnal mind will not come to as long as it can help it: I beseech the Lord so to work that some of you may not be able to help it. And oh, I have been praying that, while this morning I am trying to set forth Christ as the end of the law, God may bless it to some hearts, that they may see what Christ did, and may perceive it to be a great deal better than anything they can do; may see what Christ finished, and may become weary of what they themselves have laboured at so long, and have not even well commenced at this day. Perhaps it may please the Lord to enchant them with the perfection of the salvation that is in Christ Jesus. As Bunyan would say, " It may, perhaps, set their mouths a watering after it," and when a sacred appetite begins it will not be long before the feast is enjoyed. It may be that when they see the raiment of wrought gold, which Jesus so freely bestows on naked souls, they will throw away their own filthy rags which now they hug so closely.

I am going to speak about two things, this morning, as the Spirit of God shall help me: and the first is, *Christ in connection with the law*—he is "the end of the law for righteousness"; and secondly, *ourselves in connection with Christ*—" to everyone that believeth Christ is the end of the law for righteousness."

I. First, then, CHRIST IN CONNECTION WITH THE LAW. The law is that which, as sinners, we have above all things cause to dread; for the sting of death is sin, and the strength of sin is the law. Towards us the law darts forth devouring flames, for it condemns us, and in solemn terms appoints us a place among the accursed, as it is written, " Cursed is every one that continueth not in all things that are written in the book of the law to do them." Yet, strange infatuation! like the fascination which attracts the gnat to the candle which burns its wings, men by nature fly to the law for salvation, and cannot be driven from it. The law can do nothing else but reveal sin and pronounce condemnation upon the sinner, and yet we cannot get men away from it, even though we show them how sweetly Jesus stands between them and it. They are so enamoured of legal hope that they cling to it when there is nothing to cling to; they prefer Sinai to Calvary, though Sinai has nothing for them but thunders and trumpet warnings of coming judgment. O that for awhile you would listen anxiously while I set forth Jesus my Lord, that you may see the law in him.

Now, what has our Lord to do with the law? He has everything to do with it, for he is its end for the noblest object, namely, for righteousness. He is the "end of the law." What does this mean? I think it signifies three things: first, that Christ is *the purpose and object* of the law; secondly, that he is *the fulfilment* of it; and thirdly, that he is *the termination* of it.

First, then, *our Lord Jesus Christ is the purpose and object of the law.* It was given to lead us to him. The law is our schoolmaster to bring us to Christ, or rather our attendant to conduct us to the school of Jesus. The law is the great net in which the fish are enclosed that they may be drawn out of the element of sin. The law is the stormy wind which drives souls into the harbour of refuge. The law is the sheriff's officer to shut men up in prison for their sin, concluding them all under condemnation in order that they may look to the free grace of God alone for deliverance. This is the object of the law: it empties that grace may fill, and wounds that mercy may heal. It has never been God's intention towards us, as fallen men, that the law should be regarded as a way to salvation to us, for a way of salvation it can never be. Had man never fallen, had his nature remained as God made it, the law would have been most helpful to him to show him the way in which he should walk: and by keeping it he would have lived, for "he that doeth these things shall live in them." But ever since man has fallen the Lord has not proposed to him a way of salvation by works, for he knows it to be impossible to a sinful creature. The law is already broken; and whatever man can do he cannot repair the damage he has already done; therefore he is out of court as to the hope of merit. The law demands perfection, but man has already fallen short of it; and therefore let him do his best he cannot accomplish what is absolutely essential. The law is meant to lead the sinner to faith in Christ, by showing the impossibility of any other way. It is the black dog to fetch the sheep to the shepherd, the burning heat which drives the traveller to the shadow of the great rock in a weary land.

Look how the law is adapted to this; for, first of all, *it shows man his sin.* Read the ten commandments and tremble as you read them. Who can lay his own character down side by side with the two tablets of divine precept without at once being convinced that he has fallen far short of the standard? When the law comes home to the soul it is like light in a dark room revealing the dust and the dirt which else had been unperceived. It is the test which detects the presence of the poison of sin in the soul. "I was alive without the law once," said the apostle, "but when the commandment came sin revived and I died." Our comeliness utterly fades away when the law blows upon it. Look at the commandments, I say, and remember how sweeping they are, how spiritual, how far-reaching. They do not merely touch the outward act, but dive into the inner motive and deal with the heart, the mind, the soul. There is a deeper meaning in the commands than appears upon their surface. Gaze into their depths and see how terrible is the holiness which they require. As you understand what the law demands you will perceive how far you are from fulfilling it, and how sin abounds where you thought there was little or none of it. You thought yourself rich and increased in goods and in no need of anything, but when the broken law visits you your spiritual bankruptcy and utter penury stare you in the face. A true balance discovers short weight, and such is the first effect of the law upon the conscience of man.

The law also shows *the result and mischief of sin*. Look at the types of the old Mosaic dispensation, and see how they were intended to lead men to Christ by making them see their unclean condition and their need of such cleansing as only he can give. Every type pointed to our Lord Jesus Christ. If men were put apart because of disease or uncleanness, they were made to see how sin separated them from God and from his people; and when they were brought back and purified with mystic rites in which were scarlet wool and hyssop and the like, they were made to see how they can only be restored by Jesus Christ, the great High Priest. When the bird was killed that the leper might be clean, the need of purification by the sacrifice of a life was set forth. Every morning and evening a lamb died to tell of daily need of pardon, if God is to dwell with us. We sometimes have fault found with us for speaking too much about *blood;* yet under the old testament the blood seemed to be everything, and was not only spoken of but actually presented to the eye. What does the apostle tell us in the Hebrews? "Whereupon neither the first testament was dedicated without blood. For when Moses had spoken every precept to all the people according to the law, he took the blood of calves and of goats, with water, and scarlet wool, and hyssop, and sprinkled both the book, and all the people, saying, this is the blood of the testament which God hath enjoined unto you. Moreover he sprinkled with blood both the tabernacle, and all the vessels of the ministry. And almost all things are by the law purged with blood; and without shedding of blood is no remission." The blood was on the veil, and on the altar, on the hangings, and on the floor of the tabernacle: no one could avoid seeing it. I resolve to make my ministry of the same character, and more and more sprinkle it with the blood of atonement. Now the abundance of the blood of old was meant to show clearly that sin has so polluted us that without an atonement God is not to be approached: we must come by the way of sacrifice or not at all. We are so unacceptable in ourselves that unless the Lord sees us with the blood of Jesus upon us he must away with us. The old law, with its emblems and figures, set forth many truths as to men's selves and the coming Saviour, intending by every one of them to preach Christ. If any stopped short of him, they missed the intent and design of the law. Moses leads up to Joshua, and the law ends at Jesus.

Turning our thoughts back again to the moral rather than the ceremonial law, it was intended to teach men *their utter helplessness*. It shows them how short they fall of what they ought to be, and it also shows them, when they look at it carefully, how utterly impossible it is for them to come up to the standard. Such holiness as the law demands no man can reach of himself. "Thy commandment is exceeding broad." If a man says that he can keep the law, it is because he does not know what the law is. If he fancies that he can ever climb to heaven up the quivering sides of Sinai, surely he can never have seen that burning mount at all. Keep the law! Ah, my brethren, while we are yet talking about it we are breaking it; while we are pretending that we can fulfil its letter, we are violating its spirit, for pride as much breaks the law as lust or murder. "Who can bring a clean thing out of an unclean? Not one." "How can he be clean that is born of a woman?"

No, soul, thou canst not help thyself in this thing, for since only by perfection thou canst live by the law, and since that perfection is impossible, thou canst not find help in the covenant of works. In grace there is hope, but as a matter of debt there is none, for we do not merit anything but wrath. The law tells us this, and the sooner we know it to be so the better, for the sooner we shall fly to Christ.

The law also shows us *our great need*—our need of cleansing, cleansing with the water and with the blood. It discovers to us our filthiness, and this naturally leads us to feel that we must be washed from it if we are ever to draw near to God. So the law drives us to accept of Christ as the one only person who can cleanse us, and make us fit to stand within the veil in the presence of the Most High. The law is the surgeon's knife which cuts out the proud flesh that the wound may heal. The law by itself only sweeps and raises the dust, but the gospel sprinkles clean water upon the dust, and all is well in the chamber of the soul. The law kills, the gospel makes alive; the law strips, and then Jesus Christ comes in and robes the soul in beauty and glory. All the commandments, and all the types direct us to Christ, if we will but heed their evident intent. They wean us from self, they put us off from the false basis of self-righteousness, and bring us to know that only in Christ can our help be found. So, first of all, Christ is the end of the law, in that he is its great purpose.

And now, secondly, he is *the law's fulfilment*. It is impossible for any of us to be saved without righteousness. The God of heaven and earth by immutable necessity demands righteousness of all his creatures. Now, Christ has come to give to us the righteousness which the law demands, but which it never bestows. In the chapter before us we read of "the righteousness which is of faith," which is also called "God's righteousness"; and we read of those who "shall not be ashamed" because they are righteous by believing, "for with the heart man believeth unto righteousness." What the law could not do Jesus has done. He provides the righteousness which the law asks for but cannot produce. What an amazing righteousness it must be which is as broad and deep and long and high as the law itself. The commandment is exceeding broad, but the righteousness of Christ is as broad as the commandment, and goes to the end of it. Christ did not come to make the law milder, or to render it possible for our cracked and battered obedience to be accepted as a sort of compromise. The law is not compelled to lower its terms, as though it had originally asked too much; it is holy and just and good, and ought not to be altered in one jot or tittle, nor can it be. Our Lord gives the law all it requires, not a part, for that would be an admission that it might justly have been content with less at first. The law claims complete obedience without one spot or speck, failure, or flaw, and Christ has brought in such a righteousness as that, and gives it to his people. The law demands that the righteousness should be without omission of duty and without commission of sin, and the righteousness which Christ has brought in is just such an one that for its sake the great God accepts his people and counts them to be without spot or wrinkle or any such thing. The law will not be content without spiritual obedience, mere outward compliances will not satisfy. But our Lord's obedience was as deep as it was broad, for his zeal to do the will of him that sent him consumed him. He says himself, " I delight to do thy will, O my God, yea thy law is within my heart." Such righteousness he puts upon all believers. " By the obedience of one shall many be made righteous "; righteous to the full, perfect in Christ. We rejoice to wear the costly robe of fair white linen which Jesus has prepared, and we feel that we may stand arrayed in it before the majesty of heaven without a trembling thought. This is something to dwell upon, dear friends. Only as righteous ones can we be saved, but Jesus Christ makes us righteous, and therefore we are saved. He is righteous who believeth on him, even as Abraham believed God and it was counted unto him for righteousness. " There is, therefore, now no condemnation to them that are in Christ Jesus," because they are made righteous in Christ. Yea, the Holy Spirit by the mouth of Paul challengeth all men, angels, and devils, to lay anything to the charge of God's elect, since Christ hath died. O law, when thou demandest of me a perfect righteousness, I, being a believer, present it to thee; for through Christ Jesus faith is accounted unto me for righteousness. The righteousness of Christ is mine, for I am one with him by faith, and this is the name wherewith he shall be called—" The Lord our righteousness."

Jesus has thus fulfilled the original demands of the law, but you know, brethren, that since we have broken the law there are other demands. For the remission of past sins something more is asked now than present and future obedience. Upon us, on account of our sins, the curse has been pronounced, and a penalty has been incurred. It is written that he "will by no means clear the guilty," but every transgression and iniquity shall have its just punishment and reward. Here, then, let us admire that the Lord Jesus Christ is the end of the law as to penalty. That curse and penalty are awful things to think upon, but Christ has ended all their evil, and thus discharged us from all the consequences of sin. As far as every believer is concerned the law demands no penalty and utters no curse. The believer can point to the Great Surety on the tree of Calvary, and say, " See there, oh law, there is the vindication of divine justice which I offer to thee. Jesus pouring out his heart's blood from his wounds and dying on my behalf is my answer to thy claims, and I know that I shall be delivered from wrath through him." The claims of the law both as broken and unbroken Christ has met: both the positive and the penal demands are satisfied in him. This was a labour worthy of a God, and lo, the incarnate God has achieved it. He has finished the transgression, made an end of sins, made reconciliation for iniquity, and brought in everlasting righteousness. All glory be to his name.

Moreover, not only has the penalty been paid, but Christ has put great and special honour upon the law in so doing. I venture to say that if the whole human race had kept the law of God and not one of them had violated it, the law would not stand in so splendid a position of honour as it does to-day when the man Christ Jesus, who is also the Son of God, has paid obeisance to it. God himself, incarnate, has in his life, and yet more in his death, revealed the supremacy of law; he has shown that not even love nor sovereignty can set aside justice. Who shall say a word against the law to which the Lawgiver himself submits? Who shall now say that it is too severe when he who made it submits himself to its penalties. Because he was found in fashion as a man, and was our representative, the Lord demanded from his own Son perfect obedience to the law, and the Son voluntarily bowed himself to it without a single word, taking no exception to his task. " Yea, thy law is my delight," saith he, and he proved it to be so by paying homage to it even to the full. Oh wondrous law under which even Emmanuel serves! Oh matchless law whose yoke even the Son of God does not disdain to bear, but being resolved to save his chosen was made under the law, lived under it and died under it, "obedient to death, even the death of the cross."

The law's stability also has been secured by Christ. That alone can remain which is proved to be just, and Jesus has proved the law to be so, magnifying it and making it honourable. He says, "Think not that I am come to destroy the law, or the prophets: I am not come to destroy, but to fulfil. For verily I say unto you, till heaven and earth pass, one jot or one tittle shall in no wise pass from the law, till all be fulfilled." I shall have to show you how he has made an end of the law in another sense, but as to the settlement of the eternal principles of right and wrong, Christ's life and death have achieved this for ever. " Yea, we establish the law," said Paul, " we do not make void the law through faith." The law is proved to be holy and just by the very gospel of faith, for the gospel which faith believes in does not alter or lower the law, but teaches us how it was to the uttermost fulfilled. Now shall the law stand fast for ever and ever, since even to save elect man God will not alter it. He had a people, chosen, beloved, and ordained to life, yet he would not save them at the expense of one principle of right. They were sinful, and how could they be justified unless the law was suspended or changed? Was, then, the law changed? It seemed as if it must be so, if man was to be saved, but Jesus Christ came and showed us how the law could stand firm as a rock, and yet the redeemed could be justly saved by infinite mercy. In Christ we see both mercy and justice shining full orbed, and yet neither of them in any degree eclipsing the other. The law has all it ever asked, as it ought to have, and yet the Father of all mercies sees all his chosen saved as he determined they should be through the death of his Son. Thus I have tried to show you how Christ is the fulfilment of the law to its utmost end. May the Holy Ghost bless the teaching.

And now, thirdly, he is the end of the law in the sense that he is *the termination of it.* He has terminated it in two senses. First of all, his people are not under it as a covenant of life. "We are not under the law, but under grace." The old covenant as it stood with father Adam was "This do and thou shalt live": its command he did not keep, and consequently he did not live, nor do we live in him, since in Adam all died. The old covenant was broken, and we became condemned thereby, but now, having suffered death in Christ, we are no more under it, but are dead to it. Brethren, at this present moment, although we rejoice to do good works, we are not seeking life through them, we are not hoping to obtain divine favour by our own goodness, nor even to keep ourselves in the love of God by any merit of our own. Chosen, not for our works, but according to the eternal will and good pleasure of God ;

called, not of works, but by the Spirit of God, we desire to continue in this grace and return no more to the bondage of the old covenant. Since we have put our trust in an atonement provided and applied by grace through Christ Jesus, we are no longer slaves but children, not working to be saved, but saved already, and working because we are saved. Neither that which we do, nor even that which the Spirit of God worketh in us is to us the ground and basis of the love of God toward us, since he loved us from the first, because he would love us, unworthy though we were; and he loves us still in Christ, and looks upon us not as we are in ourselves, but as we are in him; washed in his blood and covered in his righteousness. Ye are not under the law, Christ has taken you from the servile bondage of a condemning covenant and made you to receive the adoption of children, so that now ye cry, Abba, Father.

Again, Christ is the terminator of the law, for we are no longer under its curse. The law cannot curse a believer, it does not know how to do it; it blesses him, yea, and he shall be blessed; for as the law demands righteousness and looks at the believer in Christ, and sees that Jesus has given him all the righteousness it demands, the law is bound to pronounce him blessed. "Blessed is he whose transgression is forgiven, whose sin is covered. Blessed is the man unto whom the Lord imputeth not iniquity, and in whose spirit there is no guile." Oh, the joy of being redeemed from the curse of the law by Christ, who was "made a curse for us," as it is written, "Cursed is every one that hangeth on a tree." Do ye, my brethren, understand the sweet mystery of salvation? Have you ever seen Jesus standing in your place that you may stand in his place? Christ accused and Christ condemned, and Christ led out to die, and Christ smitten of the Father, even to the death, and then you cleared, justified, delivered from the curse, because the curse has spent itself on your Redeemer. You are admitted to enjoy the blessing because the righteousness which was his is now transferred to you that you may be blessed of the Lord world without end. Do let us triumph and rejoice in this evermore. Why should we not? And yet some of God's people get under the law as to their feelings, and begin to fear that because they are conscious of sin they are not saved, whereas it is written, "he justifieth the ungodly." For myself, I love to live near a sinner's Saviour. If my standing before the Lord depended upon what I am in myself and what good works and righteousness I could bring, surely I should have to condemn myself a thousand times a day. But to get away from that and to say, "I have believed in Jesus Christ and therefore righteousness is mine," this is peace, rest, joy, and the beginning of heaven! When one attains to this experience, his love to Jesus Christ begins to flame up, and he feels that if the Redeemer has delivered him from the curse of the law he will not continue in sin, but he will endeavour to live in newness of life. We are not our own, we are bought with a price, and we would therefore glorify God in our bodies and in our spirits, which are the Lord's. Thus much upon Christ in connection with the law.

II. Now, secondly, OURSELVES IN CONNECTION WITH CHRIST—for "Christ is the end of the law *to every one that believeth*." Now see the point "to every one that believeth," there the stress lies. Come, man, woman, dost thou believe? No weightier question can be asked under heaven. "Dost thou believe on the Son of God?" And what is it to believe? It is not merely to accept a set of doctrines and to say that such and such a creed is yours, and there and then to put it on the shelf and forget it. To believe is, to trust, to confide, to depend upon, to to rely upon, to rest in. Dost thou believe that Jesus Christ rose from the dead? Dost thou believe that he stood in the sinner's stead and suffered the just for the unjust? Dost thou believe that he is able to save to the uttermost them that come unto God by him? And dost thou therefore lay the whole weight and stress of thy soul's salvation upon him, yea, upon him alone? Ah then, Christ is the end of the law for righteousness to thee, and thou art righteous. In the righteousness of God thou art clothed if thou believest. It is of no use to bring forward anything else if you are not believing, for nothing will avail. If faith be absent the essential thing is wanting: sacraments, prayers, Bible reading, hearings of the gospel, you may heap them together, high as the stars, into a mountain, huge as high Olympus, but they are all mere chaff if faith be not there. It is thy believing or not believing which must settle the matter. Dost thou look away from thyself to Jesus for righteousness? If thou dost he is the end of the law to thee.

Now observe that there is no question raised about the previous character, for it is written, "Christ is the end of the law for righteousness to *every one that believeth.*" But, Lord, this man before he believed was a persecutor and injurious, he raged and raved against the saints and haled them to prison and sought their blood. Yes, beloved friend, and that is the very man who wrote these words by the Holy Ghost, "Christ is the end of the law for righteousness to every one that believeth." So if I address one here this morning whose life has been defiled with every sin, and stained with every transgression we can conceive of, yet I say unto such, remember "all manner of sin and of blasphemy shall be forgiven unto men." If thou believest in the Lord Jesus Christ thine iniquities are blotted out, for the blood of Jesus Christ, God's dear Son, cleanseth us from all sin. This is the glory of the gospel that it is a sinner's gospel; good news of blessing not for those without sin, but for those who confess and forsake it. Jesus came into the world, not to reward the sinless, but to seek and to save that which was lost; and he, being lost and being far from God, who cometh nigh to God by Christ, and believeth in him, will find that he is able to bestow righteousness upon the guilty. He is the end of the law for righteousness to everyone that believeth, and therefore to the poor harlot that believeth, to the drunkard of many years standing that believeth, to the thief, the liar, and the scoffer who believeth, to those who have aforetime rioted in sin, but now turn from it to trust in him. But I do not know that I need mention such cases as these; to me the most wonderful fact is that Christ is the end of the law for righteousness *to me*, for I believe in him. I know whom I have believed, and I am persuaded that he is able to keep that which I have committed to him until that day.

Another thought arises from the text, and that is, that there is nothing said by way of qualification as to the strength of the faith. He is the end of the law for righteousness to everyone that believeth, whether he is Little Faith or Greatheart. Jesus protects the rear rank as well as the vanguard. There is no difference between one believer and another as to justification. So long as there is a connection between you and Christ the righteousness of God is yours. The link may be very like a film, a spider's line of trembling faith, but, if it runs all the way from the heart to Christ, divine grace can and will flow along the most slender thread. It is marvellous how fine the wire may be that will carry the electric flash. We may want a cable to carry a message across the sea, but that is for the protection of the wire, the wire which actually carries the message is a slender thing. If thy faith be of the mustard-seed kind, if it be only such as tremblingly touches the Saviour's garment's hem, if thou canst only say "Lord, I believe, help thou mine unbelief," if it be but the faith of sinking Peter, or weeping Mary, yet if it be faith in Christ, he will be the end of the law for righteousness to thee as well as to the chief of the apostles.

If this be so then, beloved friends, all of us who believe are righteous. Believing in the Lord Jesus Christ we have obtained the righteousness which those who follow the works of the law know nothing of. We are not completely sanctified, would God we were; we are not quit of sin in our members, though we hate it; but still for all that, in the sight of God, we are truly righteous, and being qualified by faith we have peace with God. Come, look up, ye believers that are burdened with a sense of sin. While you chasten yourselves and mourn your sin, do not doubt your Saviour, nor question his righteousness. You are black, but do not stop there, go on to say as the spouse did, "I am black, but comely."

> "Though in ourselves deform'd we are,
> And black as Kedar's tents appear,
> Yet, when we put Thy beauties on,
> Fair as the courts of Solomon."

Now, mark that the connection of our text assures us that being righteous we are saved; for what does it say here, "If thou shalt confess with thy mouth the Lord Jesus, and shalt believe in thine heart that God hath raised him from the dead, thou shalt be *saved.*" He who is justified is saved, or what were the benefit of justification? Over thee, O believer, God hath pronounced the verdict "*saved,*" and none shall reverse it. You are saved from sin and death and hell; you are saved even now, with a present salvation; "He hath saved us and called us with a holy calling." Feel the transports of it at this hour. "Beloved, now are we the sons of God."

And now I have done when I have said just this. If any one here thinks he can save himself, and that his own righteousness will suffice before God, I would affectionately beg him not to insult his Saviour. If your righteousness sufficeth, why did Christ come here to work one out? Will you for a moment compare your righteousness with the righteousness of Jesus Christ? What likeness is there between you and him? As much as between an emmet and an archangel. Nay, not so much as that: as much as between night and day, hell and heaven. Oh, if I had a righteousness of my own that no one could find fault with, I would voluntarily fling it away to have the righteousness of Christ, but as I have none of my own I do rejoice the more to have my Lord's. When Mr. Whitefield first preached at Kingswood, near Bristol, to the colliers, he could see when their hearts began to be touched by the gutters of white made by the tears as they ran down their black cheeks. He saw they were receiving the gospel, and he writes in his diary " as these poor colliers had no righteousness of their own they therefore gloried in Him who came to save publicans and sinners." Well, Mr. Whitefield, that is true of the colliers, but it is equally true of many of us here, who may not have had black faces, but we had black hearts. We can truly say that we also rejoice to cast away our own righteousness and count it dross and dung that we may win Christ, and be found in him. In him is our sole hope and only trust.

Last of all, for any of you to reject the righteousness of Christ must be to perish everlastingly, because it cannot be that God will accept you or your pretended righteousness when you have refused the real and divine righteousness which he sets before you in his Son. If you could go up to the gates of heaven, and the angel were to say to you, "What title have you to entrance here?" and you were to reply, "I have a righteousness of my own," then for you to be admitted would be to decide that your righteousness was on a par with that of Immanuel himself. Can that ever be? Do you think that God will ever allow such a lie to be sanctioned? Will he let a poor wretched sinner's counterfeit righteousness pass current side by side with the fine gold of Christ's perfection. Why was the fountain filled with blood if you need no washing? Is Christ a superfluity? Oh, it cannot be. You must have Christ's righteousness or be unrighteous, and being unrighteous you will be unsaved, and being unsaved you must remain lost for ever and ever.

What! has it all come to this, then, that I am to believe in the Lord Jesus Christ for righteousness, and to be made just through faith? Yes, that is it: that is the whole of it. What! trust Christ alone and then live as I like! You cannot live in sin after you have trusted Jesus, for the act of faith brings with it a change of nature and a renewal of your soul. The Spirit of God who leads you to believe will also change your heart. You spoke of "living as you like," you will like to live very differently from what you do now. The things you loved before your conversion you will hate when you believe, and the things you hated you will love. Now, you are trying to be good, and you make great failures, because your heart is alienated from God; but when once you have received salvation through the blood of Christ, your heart will love God, and then you will keep his commandments, and they will be no longer grievous to you. A change of heart is what you want, and you will never get it except through the covenant of grace. There is not a word about conversion in the old covenant, we must look to the new covenant for that, and here it is—" Then will I sprinkle clean water upon you, and ye shall be clean: from all your filthiness, and from all your idols, will I cleanse you. A new heart also will I give you, and a new spirit will I put within you: and I will take away the stony heart out of your flesh, and I will give you an heart of flesh. And I will put my spirit within you, and cause you to walk in my statutes, and ye shall keep my judgments, and do them." This is one of the greatest covenant promises, and the Holy Ghost performs it in the chosen. Oh that the Lord would sweetly persuade you to believe in the Lord Jesus Christ, and that promise and all the other covenant engagements shall be fulfilled to your soul. The Lord bless you! Spirit of God, send thy blessing on these poor words of mine for Jesus' sake. Amen.

Christ, the Conqueror of Satan

"And I will put enmity between thee and the woman, and between thy seed and her seed; it shall bruise thy head, and thou shalt bruise his heel"—Genesis iii. 15.

THIS is the first gospel sermon that was ever delivered upon the surface of this earth. It was a memorable discourse indeed, with Jehovah himself for the preacher, and the whole human race and the prince of darkness for the audience. It must be worthy of our heartiest attention.

Is it not remarkable that this great gospel promise should have been delivered so soon after the transgression? As yet no sentence had been pronounced upon either of the two human offenders, but the promise was given under the form of a sentence pronounced upon the serpent. Not yet had the woman been condemned to painful travail, or the man to exhausting labour, or even the soil to the curse of thorn and thistle. Truly "mercy rejoiceth against judgment." Before the Lord had said "Dust thou art and unto dust thou shalt return," he was pleased to say that the seed of the woman should bruise the serpent's head. Let us rejoice, then, in the swift mercy of God, which in the early watches of the night of sin came with comfortable words unto us.

These words were not directly spoken to Adam and Eve, but they were directed distinctly to the serpent himself, and that by way of punishment to him for what he had done. It was a day of cruel triumph to him: such joy as his dark mind is capable of had filled him, for he had indulged his malice, and gratified his spite. He had in the worst sense destroyed a part of God's works, he had introduced sin into the new world, he had stamped the human race with his own image, and gained new forces to promote rebellion and to multiply transgression, and therefore he felt that sort of gladness which a fiend can know who bears a hell within him. But now God comes in, takes up the quarrel personally, and causes him to be disgraced on the very battle-field upon which he had gained a temporary success. He tells the dragon that he will undertake to deal with him; this quarrel shall not be between the serpent and man, but between God and the serpent. God saith, in solemn words, "I will put enmity between thee and the woman, between thy seed and her seed," and he promises that there shall rise in fulness of time a champion, who, though he suffer, shall smite in a vital part the power of evil, and bruise the serpent's head. This was the more, it seems to me, a comfortable message of mercy to Adam and Eve, because they would feel sure that the tempter would be punished, and as that punishment would involve blessing for them, the vengeance due to the serpent would be the guarantee of mercy to themselves. Perhaps, however, by thus obliquely giving the promise, the Lord meant to say, "Not for your sakes do I this, O fallen man and woman, nor for the sake of your descendants; but for my own name and honour's sake, that it be not profaned and blasphemed amongst the fallen spirits. I undertake to repair the mischief which has been caused by the tempter, that my name and my glory may not be diminished among the immortal spirits who look down upon the scene." All this would be very humbling but yet consolatory to our parents if they thought of it, seeing that mercy given for God's sake is always to our troubled apprehension more sure than any favour which could be promised to us for our own sake. The divine sovereignty and glory afford us a stronger foundation of hope than merit, even if merit can be supposed to exist.

Now we must note concerning this first gospel sermon that on it the earliest believers stayed themselves. This was all that Adam had by way of revelation, and all that Abel had received. This one lone star shone in Abel's sky; he looked up to it and he believed. By its light he spelt out "sacrifice," and therefore he brought of the firstlings of his flock and laid them upon the altar, and proved in his own person how the seed of the serpent hated the seed of the woman, for his brother slew him for his testimony. Although Enoch the seventh from Adam prophesied concerning the second advent, yet he does not appear to have uttered anything new concerning the first coming, so that still this one promise remained as man's sole word of hope. The torch which flamed within the gates of Eden just before man was driven forth lit up the world to all believers until the Lord was pleased to give more light, and to renew and enlarge the revelation of his covenant, when he spake to his servant Noah. Those hoary fathers who lived before the flood rejoiced in the mysterious language of our text, and resting on it, they died in faith. Nor, brethren, must you think it a slender revelation, for, if you attentively consider, it is wonderfully full of meaning. If it had been on my heart to handle it doctrinally this morning, I think I could have shown you that it contains all the gospel. There lie within it, as an oak lies within an acorn, all the great truths which make up the gospel of Christ. Observe that here is the grand mystery of the incarnation. Christ is that seed of the woman who is here spoken of; and there is a hint not darkly given as to how that Incarnation would be effected. Jesus was not born after the ordinary manner of the sons of men. Mary was overshadowed of the Holy Ghost, and "the holy thing" which was born of her was as to his humanity the seed of the woman only; as it is written, "Behold a virgin shall conceive and bear a son, and they shall call his name Immanuel." The promise plainly teaches that the deliverer would be born of a woman, and, carefully viewed, it also foreshadows the divine method of the Redeemer's conception and birth. So also is the doctrine of the two seeds plainly taught here—" I will put enmity between thee and the woman, between thy seed and her seed." There was evidently to be in the world a seed of the woman on God's side against the serpent, and a seed of the serpent that should always be upon the evil side even as it is unto this day. The church of God and the synagogue of Satan both exist. We see an Abel and a Cain, an Isaac and an Ishmael, a Jacob and an Esau; those that are born after the flesh, being the children of their father the devil, for his works they do, but those that are born again—being born after the Spirit, after the power of the life of Christ, are thus in Christ Jesus the seed of the woman, and contend earnestly against the dragon and his seed. Here, too, the great fact of the sufferings of Christ is clearly foretold—" Thou shalt bruise his heel." Within the compass of those words we find the whole story of our Lord's sorrows from Bethlehem to Calvary. " It shall bruise thy head ": there is the breaking of Satan's regal power, there is the clearing away of sin, there is the destruction of death by resurrection, there is the leading of captivity captive in the ascension, there is the victory of truth in the world through the descent of the Spirit, and there is the latter-day glory in which Satan shall be bound, and there is, lastly, the casting of the evil one and all his followers into the lake of fire. The conflict and the conquest are both in the compass of these few fruitful words. They may not have been fully understood by those who first heard them, but to us they are now full of light. The text at first looks like a flint, hard and cold; but sparks fly from it plentifully, for hidden fires of infinite love and grace lie concealed within. Over this promise of a gracious God we ought to rejoice exceedingly.

We do not know what our first parents understood by it, but we may be certain that they gathered a great amount of comfort from it. They must have understood that they were not then and there to be destroyed, because the Lord had spoken of a " seed." They would argue that it must be needful that Eve should live if there should be a seed from her. They understood, too, that if that seed was to overcome the serpent and bruise his head, it must augur good to themselves: they could not fail to see that there was some great, some mysterious benefit to be conferred upon them by the victory which their seed would achieve over the instigator of their ruin. They went on in faith upon this, and were comforted in travail and in toil, and I doubt not both Adam and his wife in the faith thereof entered into everlasting rest.

This morning I intend to handle this text in three ways. First, we shall notice *its facts;* secondly, we shall consider *the experience within the heart of each believer which tallies to those facts;* and then, thirdly, *the encouragement* which the text and its connection as a whole afford to us.

I. THE FACTS. The facts are four, and I call your earnest attention to them. The first is *Enmity was excited.* The text begins, " I will put enmity between thee and the woman." They had been very friendly; the woman and the serpent had conversed together. She thought at the time that the serpent was her friend; and she was so much his friend that she took his advice in the teeth of God's precept, and was willing to believe bad things of the great Creator, because this wicked, crafty serpent insinuated the same. Now, at the moment when God spake, that friendship between the woman and the serpent had already in a measure come to an end, for she had accused the serpent to God, and said, "The serpent beguiled me, and I did eat." So far, so good. The friendship of sinners does not last long; they have already begun to quarrel, and now the Lord comes in and graciously takes advantage of the quarrel which had commenced, and says, "I will carry this disagreement a great deal further, I will put enmity between thee and the woman." Satan counted on man's descendants being his confederates, but God would break up this covenant with hell, and raise up a seed which should war against the Satanic power. Thus we have here God's first declaration that he will set up a rival kingdom to oppose the tyranny of sin and Satan, that he will create in the hearts of a chosen seed an enmity against evil, so that they shall fight against it, and with many a struggle and pain shall overcome the prince of darkness. The divine Spirit has abundantly achieved this plan and purpose of the Lord, combating the fallen angel by a glorious man: making man to be Satan's foe and conqueror. Henceforth the woman was to hate the evil one, and I do not doubt but what she did so. She had abundant cause for so doing, and as often as she thought of him it would be with infinite regret that she could have listened to his malicious and deceitful talk. The woman's seed has also evermore had enmity against the evil one. I mean not the carnal seed, for Paul tells us, "They which are the children of the flesh, these are not the children of God: but the children of the promise are counted for the seed." The carnal seed of the man and the woman are not meant, but the spiritual seed, even Christ Jesus and those who are in him. Wherever you meet these, they hate the serpent with a perfect hatred. We would if we could destroy from our souls every work of Satan, and out of this poor afflicted world of ours we would root up every evil which he has planted. That seed of the woman, that glorious *One*,—for he speaks not of seeds as of many but of seed that is one,—you know how he abhorred the devil and all his devices. There was enmity between Christ and Satan, for he came to destroy the works of the devil and to deliver those who are under bondage to him. For that purpose was he born; for that purpose did he live; for that purpose did he die; for that purpose he has gone into the glory, and for that purpose he will come again, that everywhere he may find out his adversary and utterly destroy him and his works from amongst the sons of men. This putting of the enmity between the two seeds was the commencement of the plan of mercy, the first act in the programme of grace. Of the woman's seed it was henceforth said, "Thou lovest righteousness, and hatest wickedness: therefore God, thy God, hath anointed thee with the oil of gladness above thy fellows."

Then comes the second prophecy, which has also turned into a fact, namely *the coming of the champion.* The seed of the woman by promise is to champion the cause, and oppose the dragon. That seed is the Lord Jesus Christ. The prophet Micah saith, "But thou, Bethlehem Ephratah; though thou be little among the thousands of Judah, yet out of thee shall he come forth unto me that is to be ruler in Israel;

whose goings forth have been from of old, from everlasting. Therefore will he give them up, until the time that she which travaileth hath brought forth." To none other than the babe which was born in Bethlehem of the blessed Virgin can the words of prophecy refer. She it was who did conceive and bear a son, and it is concerning her son that we sing, " Unto us a child is born, unto us a Son is given: and his name shall be called Wonderful, Counsellor, the Mighty God, the Everlasting Father, the Prince of Peace." On the memorable night at Bethlehem, when angels sang in heaven, the seed of the woman appeared, and as soon as ever he saw the light the old serpent, the devil, entered into the heart of Herod if possible to slay him, but the Father preserved him, and suffered none to lay hands on him. As soon as he publicly came forward upon the stage of action, thirty years after, Satan met him foot to foot. You know the story of the temptation in the wilderness, and how there the woman's seed fought with him who was a liar from the beginning. The devil assailed him thrice with all the artillery of flattery, malice, craft and falsehood, but the peerless champion stood unwounded, and chased his foeman from the field. Then our Lord set up his kingdom, and called one and another unto him, and carried the war into the enemy's country. In divers places he cast out devils. He spake to the wicked and unclean spirit and said, " I charge thee come out of him," and the demon was expelled. Legions of devils flew before him : they sought to hide themselves in swine to escape from the terror of his presence. " Art thou come to torment us before our time ?" was their cry when the wonder-working Christ dislodged them from the bodies which they tormented. Yea, and he made his own disciples mighty against the evil one, for in his name they cast out devils, till Jesus said, " I beheld Satan as lightning fall from heaven." Then there came a second personal conflict, for I take it that Gethsemane's sorrows were to a great degree caused by a personal assault of Satan, for our Master said, " This is your hour, and the power of darkness." He said also, " The Prince of this world cometh." What a struggle it was. Though Satan had nothing in Christ, yet did he seek if possible to lead him away from completing his great sacrifice, and there did our Master sweat as it were great drops of blood, falling to the ground, in the agony which it cost him to contend with the fiend. Then it was that our Champion began the last fight of all and won it to the bruising of the serpent's head. Nor did he end till he had spoiled principalities and powers and made a show of them openly.

"Now is the hour of darkness past,
Christ has assumed his reigning power;
Behold the great accuser cast
Down from his seat to reign no more."

The conflict our glorious Lord continues in his seed. We preach Christ crucified, and every sermon shakes the gates of hell. We bring sinners to Jesus by the Spirit's power, and every convert is a stone torn down from the wall of Satan's mighty castle. Yea, and the day shall come when everywhere the evil one shall be overcome, and the words of John in the Revelation shall be fulfilled. " And the great dragon was cast out, that old serpent, called the Devil, and Satan, which deceiveth the whole world : he was cast out into the earth, and his angels were cast out with him. And I heard a loud voice saying in heaven, Now is come salvation, and strength, and the kingdom of our God, and the power of his Christ: for the accuser of our brethren is cast down, which accused them before our God day and night." Thus did the Lord God in the words of our text promise a champion who should be the seed of the woman, between whom and Satan there should be war for ever and ever: that champion has come, the man-child has been born, and though the dragon is wroth with the woman, and makes war with the remnant of her seed which keep the testimony of Jesus Christ, yet the battle is the Lord's, and the victory falleth unto him whose name is Faithful and True, who in righteousness doth judge and make war.

The third fact which comes out in the text, though not quite in that order, is that *our Champion's heel should be bruised.* Do you need that I explain this? You know how all his life long his heel, that is, his lower part, his human nature, was perpetually being made to suffer. He carried our sicknesses and sorrows. But the bruising came mainly when both in body and in mind his whole human nature was made to agonize; when his soul was exceeding sorrowful even unto death, and his enemies pierced his hands and his feet, and he endured the shame and pain of death by crucifixion. Look at your Master and your King upon the cross, all distained with blood and dust! There was his heel most cruelly bruised. When they take down that precious body and wrap it in fair white linen and in spices, and lay it in Joseph's tomb, they weep as they handle that casket in which the Deity had dwelt, for there again Satan had bruised his heel. It was not merely that God had bruised him, "though it pleased the Father to bruise him," but the devil had let loose Herod, and Pilate, and Caiaphas, and the Jews, and the Romans, all of them his tools, upon him whom he knew to be the Christ, so that he was bruised of the old serpent. That is all, however! It is only his heel, not his head, which is bruised! For lo, the Champion rises again; the bruise was not mortal nor continual. Though he dies, yet still so brief is the interval in which he slumbers in the tomb that his holy body hath not seen corruption, and he comes forth perfect and lovely in his manhood, rising from his grave as from a refreshing sleep after so long a day of unresting toil! Oh the triumph of that hour! As Jacob only halted on his thigh when he overcame the angel, so did Jesus only retain a scar in his heel, and that he bears to the skies as his glory and beauty. Before the throne he looks like a lamb that has been slain, but in the power of an endless life he liveth unto God.

Then comes the fourth fact, namely, that while his heel was being bruised, *he was to bruise the serpent's head.* The figure represents the dragon as inflicting an injury upon the champion's heel, but at the same moment the champion himself with that heel crushes in the head of the serpent with fatal effect. By his sufferings Christ has overthrown Satan, by the heel that was bruised he has trodden upon the head which devised the bruising.

> "Lo, by the sons of hell he dies;
> But as he hangs 'twixt earth and skies,
> He gives their prince a fatal blow,
> And triumphs o'er the powers below."

Though Satan is not dead, my brethren, I was about to say, would God he were, and though he is not converted, and never will be, nor will the malice of his heart ever be driven from him, yet Christ has so far broken his head that he has missed his mark altogether. He intended to make the human race the captives of his power, but they are redeemed from his iron yoke. God has delivered many of them, and the day shall come when he will cleanse the whole earth from the serpent's slimy trail, so that the entire world shall be full of the praises of God. He thought that this world would be the arena of his victory over God and good, instead of which it is already the grandest theatre of divine wisdom, love, grace, and power. Even heaven itself is not so resplendent with mercy as the earth is, for here it is the Saviour poured out his blood, which cannot be said even of the courts of paradise above. Moreover he thought, no doubt, that when he had led our race astray and brought death upon them, he had effectually marred the Lord's work. He rejoiced that they would all pass under the cold seal of death, and that their bodies would rot in the sepulchre. Had he not spoiled the handiwork of his great Lord? God may make man as a curious creature with intertwisted veins and blood nerves, and sinews and muscles, and he may put into his nostrils the breath of life; but, "Ah," saith Satan, "I have infused a poison into him which will make him return to the dust from which he was taken." But now, behold, our Champion whose heel was bruised has risen from the dead, and given us a pledge that all his followers shall rise from the dead also. Thus is Satan foiled, for death shall not retain a bone, nor a piece of a bone, of one of those who belonged to the woman's seed. At the trump of the archangel from the earth and from the sea they shall arise, and this shall be their shout, "O death, where is thy sting? O grave, where is thy victory?" Satan, knowing this, feels already that by the resurrection his head is broken. Glory be to the Christ of God for this!

In multitudes of other ways the devil has been vanquished by our Lord Jesus, and so shall he ever be till he shall be cast into the lake of fire.

II. Let us now view OUR EXPERIENCE AS IT TALLIES WITH THESE FACTS. Now, brothers and sisters, we were by nature, as many of us as have been saved, the heirs of wrath even as others. It does not matter how godly our parents were, the first birth brought us no spiritual life, for the promise is not to them which are born of blood, or of the will of the flesh, or of the will of man, but only to those who are born of God. "That which is born of the flesh is flesh"; you cannot make it anything else and there it abides, and the flesh, or carnal mind, abideth in death; "it is not reconciled to God, neither indeed can be." He who is born into this world but once, and knows nothing of the new birth, must place himself among the seed of the serpent, for only by regeneration can we know ourselves to be the true seed. How does God deal with us who are his called and chosen ones? He means to save us, and how does he work to that end?

The first thing he does is, he comes to us in mercy, and *puts enmity between us and the serpent.* That is the very first work of grace. There was peace between us and Satan once; when he tempted we yielded; whatever he taught us we believed; we were his willing slaves. But perhaps you, my brethren, can recollect when first of all you began to feel uneasy and dissatisfied; the world's pleasures no longer pleased you; all the juice seemed to have been taken out of the apple, and you had nothing left but the hard core, which you could not feed upon at all. Then you suddenly perceived that you were living in sin, and you were miserable about it, and though you could not get rid of sin yet you hated it, and sighed over it, and cried, and groaned. In your heart of hearts you remained no longer on the side of evil, for you began to cry, "O wretched man that I am, who shall deliver me from the body of this death?" You were already from of old in the covenant of grace ordained to be the woman's seed, and now the decree began to discover itself in life bestowed upon you and working in you. The Lord in infinite mercy dropped the divine life into your soul. You did not know it, but there it was, a spark of the celestial fire, the living and incorruptible seed which abideth for ever. You began to hate sin, and you groaned under it as under a galling yoke; more and more it burdened you, you could not bear it, you hated the very thought of it. So it was with you: is it so now? Is there still enmity between you and the serpent? Indeed you are more and more the sworn enemies of evil, and you willingly acknowledge it.

Then came the champion: that is to say, "Christ was formed in you the hope of glory." You heard of him and you understood the truth about him, and it seemed a wonderful thing that he should be your substitute and stand in your room and place and stead, and bear your sin and all its curse and punishment, and that he should give his righteousness, yea, and his very self, to you that you might be saved. Ah, then you saw how sin could be overthrown, did you not? As soon as your heart understood Christ then you saw that what the law could not do, in that it was weak through the flesh, Christ was able to accomplish, and that the power of sin and Satan under which you had been in bondage, and which you now loathed, could and would be broken and destroyed because Christ had come into the world to overcome it.

Next, do you recollect how you were led to see *the bruising of Christ's heel* and to stand in wonder and observe what the enmity of the serpent had wrought in him? Did you not begin to feel the bruised heel yourself? Did not sin torment you? Did not the very thought of it vex you? Did not your own heart become a plague to you? Did not Satan begin to tempt you? Did he not inject blasphemous thoughts, and urge you on to desperate measures; did he not teach you to doubt the existence of God, and the mercy of God, and the possibility of your salvation, and so on? This was his nibbling at your heel. He is at his old tricks still. He worries whom he can't devour with a malicious joy. Did not your worldly friends begin to annoy you? Did they not give you the cold shoulder because they saw something about you so strange and foreign to their tastes? Did they not impute your conduct to fanaticism, pride, obstinacy, bigotry, and the like? Ah, this persecution is the serpent's seed beginning to discover the woman's seed, and to carry on the old war. What does Paul say? "But as then he that was born after the flesh persecuted him that was born after the Spirit, even so it is now." True godliness is an unnatural and strange thing to them, and they cannot away with it. Though there are no stakes in Smithfield, nor racks in the Tower, yet the enmity of the human heart towards Christ and his seed is just the same, and very often shows itself in "trials of cruel mockings" which to tender hearts are very hard to bear. Well, this is your heel being bruised in sympathy with the bruising of the heel of the glorious seed of the woman.

But, brethren, do you know something of the other fact, namely, that *we conquer, for the serpent's head is broken in us?* How say you? Is not the power and dominion of sin broken in you? Do you not feel that you cannot sin because you are born of God? Some sins which were masters of you once, do not trouble you now. I have known a man guilty of profane swearing, and from the moment of his conversion he has never had any difficulty in the matter. We have known a man snatched from drunkenness, and the cure by divine grace has been very wonderful and complete. We have known persons delivered from unclean living, and they have at once become chaste and pure, because Christ has smitten the old dragon such blows that he could not have power over them in that respect. The chosen seed sin and mourn it, but they are not slaves to sin; their heart goeth not after it: they have to say sometimes "the thing I would not that I do," but they are wretched when it is so. They consent with their heart to the law of God that it is good, and they sigh and cry that they may be helped to obey it, for they are no longer under the slavery of sin; the serpent's reigning power and dominion is broken in them.

It is broken next in this way, that the guilt of sin is gone. The great power of the serpent lies in unpardoned sin. He cries "I have made you guilty: I brought you under the curse." "No," say we, "we are delivered from the curse and are now blessed, for it is written, 'Blessed is the man whose transgression is forgiven, and whose sin is covered.' We are no longer guilty, for who shall lay anything to the charge of God's elect? Since Christ hath justified, who is he that condemneth?" Here is a swinging blow for the old dragon's head, such as he never will recover.

Oftentimes the Lord also grants us to know what it is to overcome temptation, and so to break the head of the fiend. Satan allures us with many baits; he has studied our points well, he knows the weakness of the flesh: but many and many a time, blessed be God, we have foiled him completely to his eternal shame! The devil must have felt himself mean that day when he tried to overthrow Job, dragged him down to a dunghill, robbed him of everything, covered him with sores, and yet could not make him yield. Job conquered when he cried, "Though he slay me yet will I trust in him." A feeble man had vanquished a devil who could raise the wind and blow down a house, and destroy the family who were feasting in it. Devil as he is, and crowned prince of the power of the air, yet the poor bereaved patriarch sitting on the dunghill covered with sores, being one of the woman's seed, through the strength of the inner life won the victory over him.

> "Ye sons of God oppose his rage,
> Resist, and he'll be gone:
> Thus did our dearest Lord engage
> And vanquish him alone."

Moreover, dear brethren, we have this hope that the very being of sin in us will be destroyed. The day will come when we shall be without spot or wrinkle, or any such thing; and we shall stand before the throne of God, having suffered no injury whatever from the fall and from all the machinations of Satan, for "they are without fault before the throne of God." What triumph that will be! "The Lord will tread Satan under your feet shortly." When he has made you perfect and free from all sin, as he will do, you will have bruised the serpent's head indeed.

And your resurrection, too, when Satan shall see you come up from the grave like one that has been perfumed in a bath of spices, when he shall see you arise in the image of Christ, with the same body which was sown in corruption and weakness raised in incorruption and power, then will he feel an infinite chagrin, and know that his head is bruised by the woman's seed.

I ought to add that every time any one of us is made useful in saving souls we do as it were repeat the bruising of the serpent's head. When you go, dear sister, among those poor children, and pick them up from the gutters, where they are Satan's prey, where he finds the raw material for thieves and criminals, and when through your means, by the grace of God, the little wanderers become children of the living God, then you in your measure bruise the old serpent's head. I pray you do not spare him. When we by preaching the gospel turn sinners from the error of their ways, so that they escape from the power of darkness, again we bruise the serpent's head. Whenever in any shape or way you are blessed to the aiding of the cause of truth and righteousness in the world, you, too, who were once beneath his power, and even now have sometimes to suffer from his nibbling at your heel, you tread upon his head. In all deliverances and victories you overcome, and prove the promise true,—"Thou shalt tread upon the lion and adder: the young lion and the dragon shalt thou trample under feet. Because he hath set his love upon me, therefore will I deliver him: I will set him on high, because he hath known my name."

III. Let us speak awhile upon THE ENCOURAGEMENT which our text and the context yields to us; for it seems to me to abound.

I want you, brethren, to exercise faith in the promise and be comforted. The text evidently encouraged Adam very much. I do not think we have attached enough importance to the conduct of Adam after the Lord had spoken to him. Notice the simple but conclusive proof which he gave of his faith. Sometimes an action may be very small and unimportant, and yet, as a straw shows which way the wind blows, it may display at once, if it be thought over, the whole state of the man's mind. Adam acted in faith upon what God said, for we read, "And Adam called his wife's name Eve (or Life); because she was the mother of all living" (verse 20). She was not a mother at all, but as the life was to come through her by virtue of the promised seed, Adam marks his full conviction of the truth of the promise though at the time the woman had borne no children. There stood Adam, fresh from the awful presence of God, what more could he say? He might have said with the prophet, "My flesh trembleth for the fear of thee," but even then he turns round to his fellow-culprit as she stands there trembling too, and he calls her Eve, mother of the life that is yet to be. It was grandly spoken by Father Adam : it makes him rise in our esteem. Had he been left to himself he would have murmured or at least despaired, but no, his faith in the new promise gave him hope. He uttered no word of repining against the condemnation to till with toil the unthankful ground, nor on Eve's part was there a word of repining over the appointed sorrows of motherhood ; they each accept the well-deserved sentence with the silence which denotes the perfection of their resignation ; their only word is full of simple faith. There was no child on whom to set their hopes, nor would the true seed be born for many an age, still Eve is to be the mother of all living, and he calls her so. Exercise like faith, my brother, on the far wider revelation which God has given to you, and always extract the utmost comfort from it. Make a point, whenever you receive a promise from God, to get all you can out of it : if you carry out that rule, it is wonderful what comfort you will gain. Some go on the principle of getting as little as possible out of God's word. I believe that such a plan is the proper way with a man's word ; always understand it at the minimum, because that is what he means ; but God's word is to be understood at the maximum, for he will do exceeding abundantly above what you ask or even think.

Notice by way of further encouragement that we may regard our reception of Christ's righteousness as an instalment of the final overthrow of the devil. The twenty-first verse says, " Unto Adam also and to his wife did the Lord God make coats of skins, and clothed them." A very condescending, thoughtful, and instructive deed of divine love ! God heard what Adam said to his wife, and saw that he was a believer, and so he comes and gives him the type of the perfect righteousness, which is the believer's portion—he covered him with lasting raiment. No more fig leaves, which were a mere mockery, but a close fitting garment which had been procured through the death of a victim ; the Lord brings that and puts it on him, and Adam could no more say, " I am naked." How could he, for God had clothed him. Now, beloved, let us take out of the promise that is given us concerning our Lord's conquest over the devil this one item and rejoice in it, for Christ has delivered us from the power of the serpent who opened our eyes and told us we were naked, by covering us from head to foot with a righteousness which adorns and protects us, so that we are comfortable in heart, and beautiful in the sight of God, and are no more ashamed.

Next, by way of encouragement in pursuing the Christian life, I would say to young people, expect to be assailed. If you have fallen into trouble through being a Christian, be encouraged by it ; do not at all regret or fear it, but rejoice ye in that day, and leap for joy, for this is the constant token of the covenant. There is enmity between the seed of the woman and the seed of the serpent still, and if you did not experience any of it you might begin to fear that you were on the wrong side. Now that you smart under the sneer of sarcasm and oppression rejoice and triumph, for now are ye partakers with the glorious seed of the woman in the bruising of his heel.

Still further encouragement comes from this. Your suffering as a Christian is not brought upon you for your own sake ; ye are partners with the great seed of the woman, ye are confederates with Christ.

You must not think the devil cares much about you: the battle is against Christ in you. Why, if you were not in Christ, the devil would never trouble you. When you were without Christ in the world you might have sinned as you like, your relatives and work-mates would not have been at all grieved with you, they would rather have joined you in it; but now the serpent's seed hates Christ in you. This exalts the sufferings of persecution to a position far above all common afflictions. I have heard of a woman who was condemned to death in the Marian days, and before her time came to be burned a child was born to her, and she cried out in her sorrow. A wicked adversary, who stood by said, "How will you bear to die for your religion if you make such ado?" "Ah," she said, "Now I suffer in my own person as a woman, but then *I* shall not suffer, but Christ in me." Nor were these idle words, for she bore her martyrdom with exemplary patience, and rose in her chariot of fire in holy triumph to heaven. If Christ be in you, nothing will dismay you, but you will overcome the world, the flesh, and the devil by faith.

Last of all, let us resist the devil always with this belief, that he has received a broken head. I am inclined to think that Luther's way of laughing at the devil was a very good one, for he is worthy of shame and everlasting contempt. Luther once threw an inkstand at his head when he was tempting him very sorely, and though the act itself appears absurd enough, yet it was a true type of what that greater Reformer was all his life long, for the books he wrote were truly a flinging of the inkstand at the head of the fiend. That is what we have to do: we are to resist him by all means. Let us do this bravely, and tell him to his teeth that we are not afraid of him. Tell him to recollect his bruised head, which he tries to cover with a crown of pride, or with a popish cowl, or with an infidel doctor's hood. We know him, and see the deadly wound he bears. His power is gone; he is fighting a lost battle; he is contending against omnipotence. He has set himself against the oath of the Father; against the blood of the incarnate Son; against the eternal power and Godhead of the blessed Spirit, all of which are engaged in the defence of the seed of the woman in the day of battle. Therefore, brethren, be ye steadfast in resisting the evil one, being strong in faith, giving glory to God.

> " 'Tis by thy blood, immortal Lamb,
> Thine armies tread the tempter down;
> 'Tis by thy word and powerful name
> They gain the battle and renown.
>
> " Rejoice ye heavens; let every star
> Shine with new glories round the sky:
> Saints, while ye sing the heavenly war,
> Raise your Deliverer's name on high."

Christ, the Overcomer of the World

"Be of good cheer; I have overcome the world"—John xvi. 33.

WHEN these words were spoken our Saviour was about to leave his disciples to go to his death for their sakes. His great anxiety was that they might not be too much cast down by the trials which would come upon them. He desired to prepare their minds for the heavy sorrows which awaited them, while the powers of darkness and the men of the world wrought their will upon him. Now observe, beloved, that our Lord Jesus, in whom dwells infinite wisdom, knew all the secret springs of comfort, and all the hallowed sources of consolation in heaven and under heaven, and yet in order to console his disciples he spoke, not of heavenly mysteries nor of secrets hidden in the breast of God, but he spake concerning himself. Doth he not herein teach us that there is no balm for the heart like himself, no consolation of Israel comparable to his person and his work. If even such a divine Barnabas, such a first-born son of consolation as the Lord himself must point to what he himself has done, for only so can he make his followers to be of good cheer, then how wise it must be in ministers to preach much of Jesus by way of encouragement to the Lord's afflicted, and how prudent it is for mourners to look to him for the comfort they need. "Be of good cheer," he saith, "*I*"—something about himself—"*I have* overcome the world." So then, beloved, in all times of depression of spirit hasten away to the Lord Jesus Christ; whenever the cares of this life burden you, and your way seems hard for your weary feet, fly to your Lord. There may be, and there are, other sources of consolation, but they will not at all times serve your turn; but in Him there dwelleth such a fulness of comfort, that whether it be in summer or in winter the streams of comfort are always flowing. In your high estate or in your low estate, and from whatever quarter your trouble may arise, you can resort at once to him and you shall find that he strengthens the hands that hang down and confirms the feeble knees.

A further remark suggests itself that the Lord Jesus must be more than man from the tone which he assumed. There are certain persons who deny the godhead of our Lord and yet think well of Jesus as a man; indeed, they have uttered many highly complimentary things with regard to his character: but I wonder it should not strike them that there is a great deal of assumption, presumption, pride, egotism, and all that style of folly in this man if he be nothing more than a man. For what good man whom you would wish to imitate would say to others "Be of good cheer; I have overcome the world." This is altogether too much for a mere man to say. The Lord Jesus Christ frequently spoke about himself and about what he has done, and commended himself to his disciples as one who was only a man and of a lowly mind could never have done. The Lord was certainly meek and lowly in heart, but no man of that character would have told others so. There is an inconsistency here which none can account for but those who believe him to be the Son of God. Understand him to be divine, put him in his true position as speaking down out of the excellency of his deity to his disciples, and then you can comprehend his so speaking, yea, it becomes infinitely seemly and beautiful. Deny his godhead, and I for one am quite unable to understand how the words before us, and others like them, could ever have fallen from his lips, for none will dare to say that he was boastful. Blessed be thou, O, Son of man, thou art also Son of God, and therefore thou dost not only speak to us with the sympathizing tenderness of a brother man, but with the majestic authority of the Only Begotten of the Father. Divinely condescending are thy words, "I have overcome the world."

If you look at this claim of Jesus without the eye of faith, does it not wear an extraordinary appearance? How could the betrayed man of Nazareth say, "I have overcome the world"? We can imagine Napoleon speaking thus when he had crushed the nations beneath his feet, and shaped the map of Europe to his will. We can imagine Alexander speaking thus when he had rifled the palaces of Persia and led her ancient monarchs captive. But who is this that speaketh on this wise? It is a Galilean, who wears a peasant's garment, and consorts with the poor and the fallen! He has neither wealth nor worldly rank nor honour among men, and yet speaks of having overcome the world. He is about to be betrayed by his own base follower into the hands of his enemies, and then he will be led out to judgment and to death, and yet he says, "I have overcome the world." He is casting an eye to his cross with all its shame, and to the death which ensued from it, and yet he saith, "I have overcome the world." He had not where to lay his head, he had not a disciple that would stand up for him, for he had just said, "Ye shall be scattered, every man to his own, and shall leave me alone"; he was to be charged with blasphemy and sedition, and brought before the judge, and find no man to declare his generation; he was to be given up to a brutal soldiery to be mocked and despitefully used and spat upon; his hands and feet were to be nailed to a cross, that he might die a felon's death, and yet he saith, "I have overcome the world." How marvellous, and yet how true! He spoke not after the manner of the flesh nor after the sight of the eye. We must use faith's optics here and look within the veil, and then we shall see not alone the despised bodily person of the Son of man, but the indwelling, noble, all-conquering soul which transformed shame into honour, and death into glory. May God the Holy Spirit enable us to look through the external to the internal, and see how marvellously the ignominious death was the rough garment which concealed the matchless victory from the purblind eyes of carnal man.

During the last two Sabbath mornings I have spoken of our Lord Jesus Christ: first, as the end of the law; and secondly, as the conqueror over the old serpent; now we come to speak of him as *the overcomer of the world*. Addressing his disciples he said, "Be of good cheer; I have overcome the world."

Now, *what is this world that he speaks about?* and *how has he overcome it?* and *what good cheer is there in the fact for us?*

I. WHAT IS THIS WORLD WHICH HE IS REFERRING TO? I scarcely know a word which is used with so many senses as this word "world." If you will turn to your Bibles you will find the word "world" used in significations widely different, for there is a world which Christ made, " He was in the world and the world was made by him "—that is, the physical world. There is a world which God so loved that he gave his only begotten Son that whosoever believeth in him might not perish. There are several forms of this favourable signification. Then there is a world, the world here meant, which " lieth in the wicked one," a world which knows not Christ, but which is evermore opposed to him: a world for which he says that he does not pray, and a world which he would not have us love—" Love not the world, neither the things which are in the world." Without going into these various meanings, and shades of meaning, which are very abundant, let us just say that we scarcely know how to define what is meant here in so many words, though we know well enough what is meant. Scripture does not give us definitions, but uses language in a popular manner, since it speaks to common people. "The world" is very much the equivalent of the " seed of the serpent," of which we spoke last Sabbath-day. The world here means the visible embodiment of that spirit of evil which was in the serpent, and which now worketh in the children of disobedience; it is the human form of the same evil force with which our Lord contended when he overcame the devil; it means the power of evil in the unregenerate mass of mankind, the energy and power of sin as it dwells in that portion of the world which abideth in death and lieth in the wicked one. The devil is the god of this world, and the prince of this world, and therefore he who is the friend of this world is the enemy of God. The world is the opposite of the church. There is a church which Christ has redeemed and chosen out of the world and separated unto himself, from among men, and of these as renewed by the power of divine grace, he says, " Ye are not of the world, even as I am not of the world," and again " Because ye are not of the world, but I have chosen you out of the world, therefore the world hateth you." Now, the rest of mankind not comprehended amongst the chosen, the redeemed, the called, the saved, are called the world. Of these our Lord said, " O, righteous Father, the world hath not known thee ; " and John said, " The world knoweth us not because it knew him not." This is the power which displays a deadly enmity against Christ and against his chosen; hence it is called "this present evil world," while the kingdom of grace is spoken of as "the world to come." This is the world of which it is said, "He that is born of God overcometh the world."

You will see that "the world" includes the ungodly themselves, as well as the force of evil in them, but it marks them out, not as creatures nor even as men who have sinned, but as unregenerate, carnal and rebellious, and therefore as the living embodiments of an evil power which works against God; and so we read of "the world of the ungodly."

Perhaps I ought to add that there has grown up out of the existence of unconverted men and the prevalence of sin in them certain customs, fashions, maxims, rules, modes, manners, forces, all of which go to make up what is called "the world," and there are also certain principles, desires, lusts, governments and powers which also make up a part of the evil thing called "the world." Jesus says "My kingdom is not of this world." James speaks of keeping ourselves "unspotted from the world." John says, "the world passeth away and the lust thereof;" and Paul says, "Be not conformed to this world, but be ye transformed."

Moreover, I may say that the present constitution and arrangement of all things in this fallen state may be comprehended in the term "world," for everything has come under vanity by reason of sin, and things are not to day according to the original plan of the Most High, as designed for man in his innocence. Behold there are trials and troubles springing out of our very existence in this life of which it is said, "in the world ye shall have tribulation." To many a child of God there have befallen hunger and disease and suffering, and unkindness, and various forms of evil which belong not to the world to come, nor to the kingdom which Christ has set up, but which come to them because they are in this present evil world, which has so become because the race of men have fallen under the curse and consequence of sin.

Now the world is all these matters put together, this great conglomeration of mischief among men, this evil which dwelleth here and there and everywhere wherever men are scattered,—this is the thing which we call the world. Every one of us know better what it is than we can tell to anybody else, and perhaps while I am explaining I am rather confounding than expounding. You know just what the world is to some of you—it is not more than your own little family, as to outward form, but much more as to influence. Your actual world may be confined to your own house, but the same principles enter into the domestic circle which pervade kingdoms and states. To others the world takes a wide sweep as they necessarily meet with ungodly men in business, and this we must do unless we are to go altogether out of the world, which is no part of our Lord's plan, for he says, "I pray not that thou shouldest take them out of the world." To some who look at the whole mass of mankind, and are called thoughtfully to consider them all because they have to be God's messengers to them, the tendencies and outgoings of the human mind towards that which is evil, and the spirit of men's actions as done against God in all nations and ages,—all these go to make up to them "the world." But be it what it may, it is a thing out of which tribulation will be sure to come to us, Christ tells us so. It may come in the form of temporal trial of some shape or other ; it may come in the form of temptation which will alight upon us from our fellow-men ; it may come in the form of persecution to a greater or less extent according to our position : but it will come. "In the world ye shall have tribulation." We are sojourners in an enemy's country, and the people of the land wherein we tarry are not our friends, and will not help us on our pilgrimage to heaven. All spiritual men in the world are our friends, but then, like ourselves, they are in the world but they are not of it. From the kingdom of this world whereof Satan is lord we must expect fierce opposition against which we must contend even unto victory if we are to enter into everlasting rest.

II. Now this brings me to the more interesting topic in the second place of HOW HAS CHRIST OVERCOME THE WORLD ? And we answer. first he did so *in his life:* then *in his death:* and then *in his rising and his reigning.*

First, Christ *overcame the world in his life.* This is a wonderful study, the overcoming of the world in the life of Christ. I reckon that those first thirty years of which we know so little were a wonderful preparation for his conflict with the world, and that though only in the carpenter's shop, and obscure, and unknown to the great outside world, yet in fact he was not merely preparing for the battle, but he was then beginning to overcome it. In the patience which made him bide his time we see the dawn of the victory. When we are intent upon doing good, and we see mischief and sin triumphant everywhere, we are eager to begin : but suppose it were not the great Father's will that we should be immediately engaged in the fray, how strongly would the world then tempt us to go forward before our time. A transgression of discipline may be caused by over zeal, and this as much breaks through the law of obedience as dulness or sloth would do. The Roman soldier was accounted guilty who, when the army was left with the orders that no man should strike a blow in the leader's absence, nevertheless stepped forward and slew a Gaul ; the act was one of valour, but it was contrary to military discipline, and might have had most baleful results, and so it was condemned. Thus is it sometimes with us ; before we are ready, before we have received our commission, we are in haste to step forward and smite the foe. That temptation must have come to Christ from the world : many a time as he heard of what was going on in the reign of error and hypocrisy his benevolent impulses might have suggested to him to be up and doing, had it not been that he was incapable of wrong desires. Doubtless he was willing to be healing the sick. Was not the land full of sufferers ? He would fain be saving souls—were they not going down to the pit by thousands ? He would gladly have confuted error, for falsehood was doing deadly work, but his hour was not yet come. Yet our Lord and Master had nothing to say till his Father bade him speak. Strongly under an impulse to be at work we know he was, for when he went up to the temple he said, "Wist ye not that I must be about my Father's business?" That utterance revealed the fire that burned within his soul, and yet he was not preaching nor healing, nor disputing, but still remained in obscurity all those thirty years, because God would have it so. When the Lord would have us quiet we are doing his will best by being quiet, but yet to be still and calm for so long a time was a wonderful instance of how all his surroundings could not master him, not even when they seemed to work with his philanthropy; he still remained obedient to God, and thus proved himself the overcomer of the world.

When he appears upon the scene of public action you know how he overcomes the world in many ways. First, *by remaining always faithful to his testimony.* He never modified it, not even by so much as a solitary word to please the sons of men. From the first day in which he began to preach even to the closing sentence which he uttered it was all truth and nothing but truth, truth uncoloured by prevailing sentiment, untainted by popular error. He did not, after the manner of the Jesuit, disguise his doctrine by so shaping it that men would hardly know but what it was the very error in which they had been brought up, but he came out with plain speaking, and set himself in opposition to all the powers which ruled the thought and creed of the age. He was no guarder of truth. He allowed truth to fight her own battles in her own way, and you know how she bares her breast to her antagonist's darts, and finds in her own immutable, immortal, and invulnerable life her shield and her spear. His speech was confident, for he knew that truth would conquer in the long run, and therefore he gave forth his doctrine without respect to the age or its prejudices. I do not think that you can say that of anybody else's ministry, not even of the best and bravest of his servants. We can see, in looking at Luther, great and glorious Luther, how Romanism tinged all that he did more or less; and the darkness of the age cast some gloom even over the serene and steadfast soul of Calvin; of each one of the reformers we must say the same: bright stars as all of these were, yet they kept not themselves untarnished by the sphere in which they shone. Every man is more or less affected by his age, and we are obliged, as we read history, to make continual allowances, for we all admit that it would not be fair to judge the men of former times by the standard of the nineteenth century. But, sirs, you may test Christ Jesus if you will by the nineteenth century light, if light it be; you may judge him by any century, ay, you may try him by the bright light of the throne of God: his teaching is pure truth without any admixture, it will stand the test of time and of eternity. His teaching was not affected by the fact of his being born a Jew, nor by the prevalence of the Rabbinical traditions, nor by the growth of the Greek philosophy, nor by any other of the peculiar influences which were then abroad. His teaching was in the world, but it was not of it, nor tinged by it. It was the truth as he had received it from the Father, and the world could not make him add to it, or take from it, or change it in the least degree, and therefore in this respect he overcame the world.

Observe him next in *the deep calm which pervaded his spirit at times when he received the approbation of men.* Our Lord was popular to a very high degree at certain times. How the people thronged around him as his benevolent hands scattered healing on all sides. How they approved of him when he fed them; but how clearly he saw through that selfish approbation, and said, "Ye seek me because of the loaves and fishes." He never lost his self-possession: you never find him elated by the multitudes following him. There is not an expression that he ever used which even contains a suspicion of self-glorification. Amid their hosannahs his mind is quietly reposing in God. He leaves their acclamations and applause to refresh himself by prayer upon the cold mountains, in the midnight air. He communed with God, and so lived above the praises of men. He walked among them, holy, harmless, undefiled and separate from sinners, even when they would have taken him by force and made him a king. Once he rides in triumph, as he might often have done if he had pleased, but then it was in such humble style that his pomp was far other than that of kings, a manifestation of lowliness rather than a display of majesty. Amid the willing hosannas of little children, and of those whom he had blessed, he rides along, but you can see that he indulges none of the thoughts of a worldly conqueror, none of the proud ideas of the warrior who returns from the battle stained with blood. No, he is still as meek and as gentle and as kindly as ever he was, and his triumph has not a grain of self-exaltation in it. He had overcome the world. What could the world give him, brethren? An imperial nature like to his, in which the manhood held such close communion with Deity as is not readily to be imagined, what was there here below to cause pride in him? If the trump of fame had sounded out its loudest note, what could it have been compared with the songs of cherubim and seraphim to which his ear had been accustomed throughout all ages? No, allied with his deity, his manhood was superior to all the arts of flattery, and to all the honours which mankind could offer him. He overcame the world.

He was the same when the world tried the other plan upon him. *It frowned at him, but he was calm still.* He had scarcely commenced to preach before they would have cast him from the brow of the hill headlong. Do you not expect, as they are hurrying him to the precipice, to see him turn round upon them and denounce them at least with burning words, such as Elias used? But no, he speaks not an angry word; he passes away and is gone out of their midst. In the synagogue they often gnashed their teeth upon him in their malice, but if ever he was moved to indignation it was not because of anything directed against himself; he always bore all, and scarcely ever spoke a word by way of reply to merely personal attacks. If calumnies were heaped upon him he went on as calmly as if they had not abused him, nor desired to slay him. When he is brought before his judges what a difference there is between the Master and his servant Paul. He is smitten, but he does not say like Paul, "God shall smite thee, thou whited wall;" no, but like a lamb before her shearers he is dumb and openeth not his mouth. If they could have made him angry they would have overcome him; but he was loving still; he was gentle, quiet, patient, however much they provoked him. Point me to an impatient word—there is not even a tradition of an angry look that he gave on account of any offence rendered to himself. They could not drive him from his purposes of love, nor could they make him say anything or do anything that was contrary to perfect love. He calls down no fire from heaven: no she bears come out of the wood to devour those who have mocked him. No, he can say, "I have overcome the world," for whether it smile or whether it frown, in the perfect peace and quiet of his spirit, in the delicious calm of communion with God, the Man of Sorrows holds on his conquering way.

His victory will be seen in another form. He overcame the world as to *the unselfishness of his aims.* When men find themselves in a world like this they generally say, "What is our market? what can we make out of it?" This is how they are trained from childhood. " Boy, you have to fight your own way, mind you look to your own interests and rise in the world." The book which is commended to the young man shows him how to make the best use of all things for himself, he must take care of "number one," and mind the main chance. The boy is told by his wise instructors "you must look to yourself or nobody else will look to you : and whatever you may do for others, be doubly sure to guard your own interests." That is the world's prudence, the essence of all her politics, the basis of her political economy,—every man, and every nation must take care of themselves: if you wish for any other politics or economics you will be considered to be foolish theorists and probably a little touched in the head. Self is the man, the world's law of self-preservation is the sovereign rule, and nothing can go on rightly if you interfere with the gospel of selfishness; so the commercial and political Solomons assure us. Now, look at the Lord Jesus Christ when he was in the world and you will learn nothing of such principles, except their condemnation: the world could not overcome him by leading him into a selfish mode of action. Did it ever enter into his soul, even for a moment, what he could do for himself? There were riches, but he had not where to lay his head. The little store he had he committed to the trust of Judas, and as long as there were any poor in the land they were sure to share in what was in the bag. He set so little account by estate, and stock, and funds that no mention is made of such things by either of his four biographers. He had wholly and altogether risen above the world in that respect; for with whatever evil the most spiteful infidels have ever charged our Lord they have never, to my knowledge, accused him of avarice, greed, or selfishness in any form. He had overcome the world.

Then again the Master overcame the world in that *he did not stoop to use its power.* He did not use that form of power which is peculiar to the world even for unselfish purposes. I can conceive a man even apart from the Spirit of God rising superior to riches, and desiring only the promotion of some great principle which has possessed his heart; but you will usually notice that when men have done so, they have been ready to promote good by evil, or at least they have judged that great principles might be pushed on by force of arms, or bribes, or policy. Mahomet had grasped a grand truth when he said, "There is no God but God." The unity of the godhead is a truth of the utmost value; but then here comes the means to be used for the propagation of this grand truth,—the scimitar. "Off with the infidels' heads ! If they have false gods, or will not own the unity of the godhead, they are not fit to live." Can you imagine our Lord Jesus Christ doing this? Why then the world would have conquered him. But he conquered the world in that he would not employ in the slightest degree this form of power. He might have gathered a troop about him, and his heroic example, together with his miraculous power, must soon have swept away the Roman empire, and converted the Jew; and then across Europe and Asia and Africa his victorious legions might have gone trampling down all manner of evil, and with the cross for his banner and the sword for his weapon, the idols would have fallen, and the whole world must have been made to bow at his feet. But no, when Peter takes out the sword, he says, "Put up thy sword into its sheath, they that take the sword shall perish with the sword." Well did he say, "My kingdom is not of this world, else would my servants fight."

And he might if he had pleased have allied his church with the state, as his mistaken friends have done in these degenerate times, and then there might have been penal laws against those who dared dissent, and there might have been forced contributions for the support of his church and such like things. You have read, I dare say, of such things being done, but not in the Gospels, nor in the Acts of the Apostles. These things are done by those who forget the Christ of God, for he uses no instrument but love, no sword but the truth, no power but the Eternal Spirit, and, in the very fact that he put all the worldly forces aside, he overcame the world.

So, brethren, he overcame the world by *his fearlessness of the world's elite*, for many a man who has braved the frowns of the multitude cannot bear the criticism of the few who think they have monopolized all wisdom. But Christ meets the Pharisee, and pays no honour to his phylactery; he confronts the Sadducee and yields not to his cold philosophy, neither does he conceal the difficulties of the faith to escape his sneer; and he braves also the Herodian, who is the worldly politician, and he gives him an unanswerable reply. He is the same before them all, master in all positions, overcoming the world's wisdom and supposed intelligence by his own simple testimony to the truth.

And he overcame the world in his life best of all *by the constancy of his love*. He loved the most unlovely men, he loved those who hated him, he loved those who despised him. You and I are readily turned aside from loving when we receive ungrateful treatment, and thus we are conquered by the world, but he kept to his great object—" he saved others, himself he could not save"; and he died with this prayer on his lips, "Father, forgive them, for they know not what they do." Not soured in the least, thou blessed Saviour, thou art at the last just as tender as at the first. We have seen fine spirits, full of generosity, who have had to deal with a crooked and perverse generation, until they have at last grown hard and cold. Nero, who weeps when he signs the first death warrant of a criminal, at last comes to gloat in the blood of his subjects. Thus do sweet flowers wither into noxious corruption. As for thee, thou precious Saviour, thou art ever fragrant with love. No spot comes upon thy lovely character, though thou dost traverse a miry road. Thou art as kind to men at thy departure as thou wast at thy coming, for thou hast overcome the world.

I can only say on the next point that *Christ by his death overcame the world* because, by a wondrous act of self-sacrifice, the Son of God smote to the heart the principle of selfishness, which is the very soul and life-blood of the world. There, too, by redeeming fallen man he lifted man up from the power which the world exercises over him, for he taught men that they are redeemed, that they are no longer their own but bought with a price, and thus redemption became the note of liberty from the bondage of self-love, and the hammer which breaks the fetters of the world and the lusts thereof.

By reconciling men unto God through his great atonement, also he has removed them from the despair which else had kept them down in sin, and made them the willing slaves of the world. Now are they pardoned, and, being justified, they are made to be the friends of God, and being the friends of God they become enemies to God's enemies, and are separated from the world, and so the world by Christ's death is overcome.

But chiefly has he overcome *by his rising and his reigning,* for when he rose he bruised the serpent's head, and that serpent is the prince of this world, and hath dominion over it. Christ has conquered the world's prince and led him in chains, and now hath Christ assumed the sovereignty over all things here below. God hath put all things under his feet. At his girdle are the keys of providence; he ruleth amongst the multitude and in the council chambers of kings. As Joseph governed Egypt for the good of Israel, so doth Jehovah Jesus govern all things for the good of his people. Now the world can go no further in persecuting his people than he permits it. Not a martyr can burn, nor a confessor be imprisoned without the permit of Jesus Christ who is the Lord of all; for the government is upon his shoulders and his kingdom ruleth over all. Brethren, this is a great joy to us to think of the reigning power of Christ as having overcome the world.

There is yet this other thought that he has overcome the world *by the gift of the Holy Spirit.* That gift was practically the world's conquest. Jesus has set up a rival kingdom now: a kingdom of love and righteousness; already the world feels its power by the Spirit. I do not believe that there is a dark place in the centre of Africa which is not to some extent improved by the influence of Christianity; even the wilderness rejoices and is glad for him. No barbarous power dares to do what once it did, or if it does there is such a clamour raised against its cruelty that very soon it has to say *peccavi,* and confess its faults. This moment the stone cut out of the mountain without hands has begun to smite old Dagon, it is breaking his head and breaking his hands and the very stump of him shall be dashed in pieces yet. There is no power in this world so vital, so potent as the power of Christ at this day. I say naught just now of heavenly or spiritual things; but I speak only of temporal and moral influences,—even in these the cross is to the front. He of whom Voltaire said that he lived in the twilight of his day, is going from strength to strength. It was true it was the twilight, but it was the twilight of the morning and the full noon is coming. Every year the name of Jesus brings more light to this poor world; every year hastens on the time when the cross which is the Pharos of humanity, the world's lighthouse amid the storm, shall shine forth more and more brightly over the troubled waters till the great calm shall come. The word shall become more and more universally true, "I, if I be lifted up, will draw all men unto me." Thus hath he overcome the world.

III. Now, lastly, WHAT CHEER IS THERE HERE FOR US? Why, this first, that if the man Christ Jesus has overcome the world at its worst, we who are in him shall overcome the world too through the same power which dwelt in him. He has put his life into his people, he has given his Spirit to dwell in them, and they shall be more than conquerors. He overcame the world when it attacked him in the worst possible shape, for he was poorer than any of you, he was more sick and sad than any of you, he was more despised and persecuted than any of you, and he was deprived of certain divine consolations which God has promised never to take away from his saints, and yet with all possible disadvantages Christ overcame the world: therefore be assured we shall conquer also by his strength.

Besides, he overcame the world when nobody else had overcome it. It was as it were a young lion which had never been defeated in fight: it roared upon him out of the thicket and leaped upon him in the fulness of its strength. Now if our greater Samson did tear this young lion as though it were a kid and fling it down as a vanquished thing, you may depend upon it that now it is an old lion, and grey and covered with the wounds which he gave it of old, we, having the Lord's life and power in us, will overcome it too. Blessed be his name! What good cheer there is in his victory. He does as good as say to us, "I have overcome the world, and you in whom I dwell, who are clothed with my spirit, must overcome it too."

But then, next, remember he overcame the world as our Head and representative, and it may truly be said that if the members do not overcome, then the head has not perfectly gained the victory. If it were possible for the members to be defeated, why then, the head itself could not claim a complete victory, since it is one with the members So Jesus Christ, our covenant Head and representative, in whose loins lay all the spiritual seed, conquered the world for us and we conquered the world in him. He is our Adam, and what was done by him was actually done for us and virtually done by us. Have courage then, for you must conquer; it must happen to you as unto your head: where the head is shall the members be, and as the head is so must the members be: wherefore be assured of the palm branch and the crown.

And now, brethren, I ask you whether you have not found it so? Is it not true at this moment that the world is overcome in you? Does self govern you? Are you working to acquire wealth for your own aggrandisement? Are you living to win honour and fame among men? Are you afraid of men's frowns? Are you the slave of popular opinion? Do you do things because it is the custom to do them? Are you the slaves of fashion? If you are, you know nothing about this victory. But if you are true Christians I know what you can say: "Lord, I am thy servant, thou hast loosed my bonds; henceforth the world hath no dominion over me; and though it tempt me, and frighten me, and flatter me, yet still I rise superior to it by the power of thy Spirit, for the love of Christ constraineth me, and I live not unto myself and unto things that are seen, but unto Christ and to things invisible." If it be so, who has done this for you? Who but Christ the Overcomer, who is formed in you the hope of glory: wherefore be of good cheer, for you have overcome the world by virtue of his dwelling in you.

So, brethren, let us go back to the world and its tribulations without fear. Its trials cannot hurt us. In the process we shall get good, as the wheat doth out of the threshing. Let us go forth to combat the world, for it cannot overcome us. There was never a man yet with the life of God in his soul whom the whole world could subdue; nay, all the world and hell together cannot conquer the veriest babe in the family of the Lord Jesus Christ. Lo, ye are harnessed with salvation, ye are panoplied with omnipotence, your heads are covered with the ægis of the atonement, and Christ himself, the Son of God, is your captain. Take up your battle cry with courage, and fear not; for more is he that is for you than all they that be against you. It is said of the glorified saints, "They overcame through the blood of the Lamb"; "and this is the victory which overcometh the world, even our faith," wherefore be ye steadfast, even to the end, for ye shall be more than conquerors through him that hath loved you. Amen.

"God with Us"

"They shall call his name Emmanuel, which being interpreted is, God with us"
—Matthew i. 23.

THOSE words, "being interpreted," salute my ear with much sweetness. Why should the word "Emmanuel" in the Hebrew, be interpreted at all? Was it not to show that it has reference to us Gentiles, and therefore it must needs be interpreted into one of the chief languages of the then existing Gentile world, namely, the Greek. This "being interpreted" at Christ's birth, and the three languages employed in the inscription upon the cross at his death, show that he is not the Saviour of the Jews only, but also of the Gentiles. As I walked along the quay at Marseilles, and marked the ships of all nations gathered in the port, I was very much interested by the inscriptions upon the shops and stores. The announcements of refreshments or of goods to be had within were not only printed in the French language, but in English, in Italian, in German, in Greek, sometimes in Russian and Swedish. Upon the shops of the sail-makers, the boat-builders, the ironmongers, or the dealers in ship stores, you read a polyglot announcement, setting forth the information to men of many lands. This was a clear indication that persons of all nations were invited to come and purchase, that they were expected to come, and that provision was made for their peculiar wants. "Being interpreted" must mean that different nations are addressed. We have the text put first in the Hebrew "Emmanuel," and afterwards it is translated into the Gentile tongue, "God with us;" "being interpreted," that we may know that we are invited, that we are welcome, that God has seen our necessities and has provided for us, and that now we may freely come, even we who were sinners of the Gentiles, and far off from God. Let us preserve with reverent love both forms of the precious name and wait the happy day when our Hebrew brethren shall unite their "Emmanuel" with our "God with us."

Our text speaks of a *name* of our Lord Jesus. It is said, "They shall call his name Emmanuel." In these days we call children by names which have no particular meaning. They are the names, perhaps, of father or mother or some respected relative, but there is no special meaning as a general rule in our children's names. It was not so in the olden times. Then names meant something. Scriptural names, as a general rule, contain teaching, and especially is this the case in every name ascribed to the Lord Jesus. With him names indicate things. "His name shall be called Wonderful, Counsellor, the Mighty God, the everlasting Father, the Prince of Peace," because he really is all these. His name is called Jesus, but not without a reason. By any other name Jesus would not be so sweet, because no other name could fairly describe his great work of saving his people from their sins. When he is said to be called this or that, it means that he really is so. I am not aware that anywhere in the New Testament our Lord is afterwards called Emmanuel. I do not find his apostles, or any of his disciples, calling him by that name literally; but we find them all doing so in effect, for they speak of him as "God manifest in the flesh", and they say, "The word was made flesh and dwelt among us, and we beheld his glory, the glory as of the only-begotten of the Father, full of grace and truth." They do not use the actual word, but they again interpret and give us free and instructive renderings, while they proclaim the sense of the august title and inform us in divers ways what is meant by God being with us in the person of the Lord Jesus Christ. It is a glorious fact, of the highest importance, that since Christ was born into the world God is with us.

You may divide the text, if you please, into two portions :—" GOD," and then " God WITH US." We must dwell with equal emphasis upon each word. Never let us for a moment hesitate as to the Godhead of our Lord Jesus Christ, for his Deity is a fundamental doctrine of the Christian faith. It may be we shall never understand fully how God and man could unite in one person, for who can by searching find out God. These great mysteries of godliness, these " deep things of God," are beyond our measurement : our little skiff might be lost if we ventured so far out upon this vast, this infinite ocean, as to lose sight of the shore of plainly revealed truth. But let it remain as a matter of faith that Jesus Christ, even he who lay in Bethlehem's manger, and was carried in a woman's arms, and lived a suffering life and died on a malefactor's cross, was, nevertheless, " God over all, blessed for ever," " upholding all things by the word of his power." He was not an angel—that the apostle has abundantly disproved in the first and second chapters of the epistle to the Hebrews : he could not have been an angel, for honours are ascribed to him which were never bestowed on angels. He was no subordinate deity or being elevated to the Godhead, as some have absurdly said—all these things are dreams and falsehoods; he was as surely God as God can be, one with the Father and the ever-blessed Spirit. If it were not so, not only would the great strength of our hope be gone, but as to this text the sweetness had evaporated altogether. The very essence and glory of the incarnation is that he was God who was veiled in human flesh: if it was any other being who thus came to us in human flesh, I see nothing very remarkable in it, nothing comforting, certainly. That an angel should become a man is a matter of no great consequence to me : that some other superior being should assume the nature of man brings no joy to my heart, and opens no well of consolation to me. But "God with us" is exquisite delight. "GOD with us": all that "God" means, the Deity, the infinite Jehovah with us ; this, this is worthy of the burst of midnight song, when angels startled the shepherds with their carols, singing "Glory to God in the highest, and on earth peace, good will to men." This was worthy of the foresight of seers and prophets, worthy of a new star in the heavens, worthy of the care which inspiration has manifested to preserve the record. This, too, was worthy of the martyr deaths of apostles and confessors who counted not their lives dear unto them for the sake of the incarnate God ; and this, my brethren, is worthy at this day of your most earnest endeavours to spread the glad tidings, worthy of a holy life to illustrate its blessed influences, and worthy of a joyful death to prove its consoling power. Here is the first truth of our holy faith—"Without controversy great is the mystery of godliness, God was manifest in the flesh." He who was born at Bethlehem is God, and "God with us." God—there lies the majesty ; "God with us," there lies the mercy. *God*—therein is glory; "God *with us*," therein is grace. God alone might well strike us with terror ; but "God with us" inspires us with hope and confidence. Take my text as a whole, and carry it in your bosoms as a bundle of sweet spices to perfume your hearts with peace and joy. May the Holy Spirit open to you the truth, and the truth to you. I would joyfully say to you in the words of one of our poets—

"Veil'd in flesh the Godhead see ;
Hail the incarnate Deity !
Pleased as man with men to appear,
Jesus our Immanuel here."

First, *let us admire this truth;* then *let us consider it more at length;* and after that *let us endeavour personally to appropriate it.*

I. LET US ADMIRE THIS TRUTH. "God with us." Let us stand at a reverent distance from it as Moses when he saw God in the bush stood a little back, and put his shoes from off his feet, feeling that the place whereon he stood was holy ground. This is a wonderful fact, God the Infinite once dwelt in the frail body of a child, and tabernacled in the suffering form of a lowly man. "God was in Christ." "He made himself of no reputation, and took upon him the form of a servant, and was made in the likeness of men."

Observe first, the wonder *of condescension* contained in this fact, that God who made all things should assume the nature of one of his own creatures, that the self-existent should be united with the dependent and derived, and the Almighty linked with the feeble and mortal. In the case before us the Lord descended to the very depth of humiliation, and entered into alliance with a nature which did not occupy the chief place in the scale of existence. It would have been great condescension for the infinite and incomprehensible Jehovah to have taken upon himself the nature of some noble spiritual being, such as a seraph or a cherub ; the union of the divine with a created spirit would have been an unmeasurable stoop, but for God to be one with man is far more. Remember that in the person of Christ manhood was not merely quickening spirit, but also suffering, hungering, dying, flesh and blood. There was taken to himself by our Lord all that materialism which makes up a body, and a body is after all but the dust of the earth, a structure fashioned from the materials around us. There is nothing in our bodily frame but what is to be found in the substance of the earth on which we live. We feed upon that which groweth out of the earth, and when we die we go back to the dust from whence we were taken. Is not this a strange thing that this grosser part of creation, this meaner part, this dust of it, should nevertheless be taken into union, with that pure, marvellous, incomprehensible, divine being of whom we know so little, and can comprehend nothing at all? Oh, the condescension of it! I leave it to the meditations of your quiet moments. Dwell on it with awe. I am persuaded that no man has any idea how wonderful a stoop it was for God thus to dwell in human flesh, and to be "God with us."

Yet, to make it appear still more remarkable, remember that the creature whose nature Christ took was a being that had sinned. I can more readily conceive the Lord's taking upon himself the nature of a race which had never fallen; but, lo, the race of man stood in rebellion against God, and yet a man did Christ become, that he might deliver us from the consequences of our rebellion, and lift us up to something higher than our pristine purity. "God sending his own Son in the likeness of sinful flesh, has condemned sin in the flesh." "Oh, the depths," is all that we can say, as we look on and marvel at this stoop of divine love.

Note, next, as you view this marvel at a distance, what *a miracle of power* is before us. Have you ever thought of the power displayed in the Lord's fashioning a body capable of union with Godhead? Our Lord was incarnate in a body, which was truly a human body, but yet in some wondrous way was prepared to sustain the indwelling of Deity. Contact with God is terrible; "He looketh on the earth and it trembleth; he toucheth the hills and they smoke." He puts his feet on Paran, and it melts, and Sinai dissolves in flames of fire. So strongly was this truth inwrought into the minds of the early saints, that they said, "No man can see God's face and live;" and yet here was a manhood which did not merely see the face of God, but which was inhabited by Deity. What a human frame was this which could abide the presence of Jehovah! "A body hast thou prepared me." This was indeed a body curiously wrought, a holy thing, a special product of the Holy Spirit's power. It was a body like our own, with nerves as sensitive, and muscles as readily strained, with every organization as delicately fashioned as our own, and yet God was in it. It was a frail barque to bear such a freight. Oh, man Christ, how couldst thou bear the Deity within thee! We know not how it was, but God knoweth. Let us adore this hiding of the Almighty in human weakness, this comprehending of the Incomprehensible, this revealing of the Invisible, this localization of the Omnipresent. Alas, I do but babble! What are words when we deal with such an unutterable truth? Suffice it to say, that the divine power was wonderfully seen in the continued existence of the materialism of Christ's body, which else had been consumed by such a wondrous contact with divinity. Admire the power which dwelt in "God with us."

Again, as you gaze upon the mystery, consider what *an ensign of good will* this must be to the sons of men. When the Lord takes manhood into union with himself in this matchless way it must mean good to man. God cannot mean to destroy that race which he thus weds unto himself. Such a marriage as this, between man and God, must mean peace; war and destruction are never thus predicted. God incarnate in Bethlehem, to be adored by shepherds, augurs nothing but "peace on earth and mercy mild." O ye sinners who tremble at the thought of the divine wrath, as well you may, lift up your heads with joyful hope of mercy and favour, for God must be full of grace and mercy to that race which he so distinguishes above all others by taking it into union with himself. Be of good cheer, O men of women born, and expect untold blessings for "unto us a child is born, unto us a Son is given." If you look at rivers you can often tell whence they come, and the soil over which they have flowed by their colour: those which flow from melting glaciers are known at once. There is a text concerning a heavenly river which you will understand if you look at it in this light: "He showed me a pure river of the water of life, clear as crystal, proceeding out of the throne of God, and *of the Lamb*." Where the throne is occupied by Godhead, and the appointed Mediator, the incarnate God, the once bleeding Lamb, then the river must be pure as crystal, and be a river, not of molten lava of devouring wrath, but a river of the water of life. Look you to "God with us" and you will see that the consequences of incarnation must be pleasant, profitable, saving, and ennobling to the sons of men.

I pray you to continue your admiring glance, and look upon God with us once more *as a pledge of our deliverance*. We are a fallen race, we are sunken in the mire, we are sold under sin, in bondage and in slavery to Satan; but if God comes to our race, and espouses its nature, why then we must retrieve our fall, it cannot be possible for the gates of hell to keep those down who have God with them. Slaves under sin and bondsmen beneath the law, hearken to the trump of jubilee, for one has come among you, born of a woman, made under the law, who is also mighty God, pledged to set you free. He is a Saviour, and a great one: able to save, for he is Almighty, and pledged to do it, for he has entered the lists and put on the harness for the battle. The champion of his people is one who will not fail nor be discouraged till the battle is fully fought and won. Jesus coming down from heaven is the pledge that he will take his people up to heaven, his taking our nature is the seal of our being lifted up to his throne. Were it an angel that had interposed, we might have some fears; were it a mere man, we might go beyond fear, and sit down in despair; but if it be "God with us," and God has actually taken manhood into union with himself, then let us "ring the bells of heaven" and be glad; there must be brighter and happier days, there must be salvation to man, there must be glory to God. Let us bask in the beams of the Sun of Righteousness, who now has risen upon us, a light to lighten the Gentiles, and to be the glory of his people Israel.

Thus we have admired at a distance.

II. And, now, in the second place, let us come nearer and CONSIDER THE SUBJECT MORE CLOSELY. What is this? What means this, "God with us"? I do not expect this morning to be able to set forth all the meaning of this short text, "God with us," for indeed, it seems to me to contain the whole history of redemption. It hints at man's being without God, and God's having removed from man on account of sin. It seems to tell me of man's spiritual life, by Christ's coming to him, and being formed in him the hope of glory. God communes with man, and man returns to God, and receives again the divine image as at the first. Yea, heaven itself is "God with us." This text might serve for a hundred sermons without any wire drawing; yea, one might continue to expatiate upon its manifold meanings for ever. I can only at this time give mere hints of lines of thought which you can pursue at your leisure, the Holy Spirit enabling you.

This glorious word Emmanuel means, first, that God in Christ is *with us in very near association*. The Greek particle here used is very forcible, and expresses the strongest form of "*with*." It is not merely "in company with us" as another Greek word would signify, but "with," "together with," and "sharing with." This preposition is a close rivet, a firm bond, implying, if not declaring, close fellowship. God is peculiarly and closely "with us." Now, think for a while, and you will see that God has in very deed come near to us in very close association. He must have done so, for *he has taken upon himself our nature*, literally our nature,—flesh, blood, bone, everything that made a body; mind, heart, soul, memory, imagination, judgment, everything that makes a rational man. Christ Jesus was the man of men, the second Adam, the model representative man. Think not of him as a deified man any more than you would dare to regard him as a humanized God, or demigod. Do not confound the natures nor divide the person: he is but one person, yet very man as he is also very God. Think of this truth then, and say, "He who sits on the throne is such as I am, sin alone excepted." No, 'tis too much for speech, I will not speak of it; it is a theme which masters me, and I fear to utter rash expressions. Turn the truth over and over, and see if it be not sweeter than honey and the honey-comb.

"Oh joy! there sitteth in our flesh,
Upon a throne of light,
One of a human mother born,
In perfect Godhead bright!"

Being with us in our nature, God was with us in *all our life's pilgrimage*. Scarcely can you find a halting-place in the march of life at which Jesus has not paused, or a weary league which he has not traversed. From the gate of entrance even to the door which closes life's way the footprints of Jesus may be traced. Were you in the cradle? He was there. Were you a child under parental authority? Christ was also a boy in the home at Nazareth. Have you entered upon life's battle? Your Lord and Master did the same; and though he lived not to old age, yet through incessant toil and suffering he bore the marred visage which attends a battered old age. Are you alone? So was he, in the wilderness, and on the mountain's side, and in the garden's gloom. Do you mix in public society? So did he labour in the thickest press. Where can you find yourself, on the hill top, or in the valley, on the land or on the sea, in the daylight or in darkness,— where, I say, can you be without discovering that Jesus has been there before you? What the world has said of her great poet we might with far more truth say of our Redeemer—

"A man so various that he seemed to be
Not one, but all mankind's epitome."

One harmonious man he was, and yet all saintly lives seem to be condensed in his. Two believers may be very unlike each other, and yet both will find that Christ's life has in it points of likeness to their own. One shall be rich and another shall be poor, one actively laborious and another patiently suffering, and yet each man in studying the history of the Saviour shall be able to say—his pathway ran hard by my own. He was made in all points like unto his brethren. How charming is the fact that our Lord is " God with us," not here and there, and now and then, but evermore.

Especially does this come out with sweetness in his being "God with us" *in our sorrows*. There is no pang that rends the heart, I might almost say not one which disturbs the body, but what Jesus Christ has been with us in it all. Feel you the sorrows of poverty? He "had not where to lay his head." Do you endure the griefs of bereavement? Jesus "wept" at the tomb of Lazarus. Have you been slandered for righteousness' sake, and has it vexed your spirit? He said "Reproach hath broken mine heart." Have you been betrayed? Do not forget that he too had his familiar friend, who sold him for the price of a slave. On what stormy seas have you been tossed which have not also roared around his boat? Never glen of adversity so dark, so deep, apparently so pathless, but what in stooping down you may discover the footprints of the Crucified One. In the fires and in the rivers, in the cold night and under the burning sun, he cries, " I am with thee. Be not dismayed, for I am both thy companion and thy God."

Mysteriously true is it that when you and I shall come to *the last, the closing scene,* we shall find that Emmanuel has been there. He felt the pangs and throes of death, he endured the bloody sweat of agony and the parching thirst of fever. He knew the separation of the tortured spirit from the poor fainting flesh, and cried, as we shall, " Father, into thy hands I commend my spirit." Ay, and the grave he knew, for there he slept, and left the sepulchre perfumed and furnished to be a couch of rest, and not a charnel-house of corruption. That new tomb in the garden makes him God with us till the resurrection shall call us from our beds of clay to find him God with us in newness of life. We shall be raised up in his likeness, and the first sight our opening eyes shall see shall be the incarnate God. "I know that my Redeemer liveth, and though after my skin worms devour this body, yet in my flesh shall I see God." " God with us." I in my flesh shall see him as the man, the God. And so *to all eternity* he will maintain the most intimate association with us. As long as ages roll he shall be " God with us." Has he not said, " Because I live ye shall live also"? Both his human and divine life will last on for ever, and so shall our life endure. He shall dwell among us and lead us to living fountains of waters, and so shall we be for ever with the Lord.

Now, my brethren, if you will review these thoughts, you shall find good store of food; in fact, a feast even under that one head. God in Christ is with us in the nearest possible association.

But, secondly, *God in Christ is with us in the fullest reconciliation.* This, of course, is true, if the former be true. There was a time when we were parted from God; we were without God, being alienated from him by wicked works, and God also was removed from us by reason of the natural rectitude of character which thrusts iniquity far from him. He is of purer eyes than to behold iniquity, neither can evil dwell with him. That strict justice with which he rules the world requires that he should hide his face from a sinful generation. A God who looks with complacency upon guilty men is not the God of the Bible, who is in multitudes of places set forth as burning with indignation against the wicked. "The wicked and him that loveth violence his soul hateth." But, now the sin which separated us from God has been put away by the blessed sacrifice of Christ upon the tree, and the righteousness, the absence of which must have caused a gulf between unrighteous man and righteous God, that righteousness, I say, has been found, for Jesus has brought in everlasting righteousness. So that now in Jesus God is with us, reconciled to us, the sin which caused his wrath being for ever put away from his people. There are some who object to this view of the case, and I, for one, will not yield one jot to their objections. I do not wonder that they cavil at certain unwise statements, which I like no better than they do; but, nevertheless, if they oppose the atonement as making a recompense to injured justice, their objections shall have no force with me. It is most true that God is always love, but his stern justice is not opposed thereto. It is also most certainly true that towards his people he always was, in the highest sense, love, and the atonement is the result and not the cause of divine love; yet, still viewed in his rectoral character, as a judge and lawgiver, God is "angry with the wicked every day," and apart from the reconciling sacrifice of Christ, his own people were "heirs of wrath even as others." There was anger in the heart of God, as a righteous judge, against those who have broken his holy law, and the reconciliation has a bearing upon the position of the judge of all the earth as well as upon man. I for one shall never cease to say, "O Lord, I will praise thee, for though thou wast angry with me, thine anger is turned away, and thou comfortest me." God can now be with man, and embrace sinners as his children, as he could not have righteously done had not Jesus died. In this sense, and in this sense only, did Dr. Watts write some of his hymns which have been so fiercely condemned. I take leave to quote two verses, and to commend them as setting forth a great truth if the Lord be viewed as a judge, and represented as the awakened conscience of man rightly perceives him. Our poet says of the throne of God:

> "Once 'twas the seat of dreadful wrath,
> And shot devouring flame;
> Our God appeared, consuming fire,
> And vengeance was his name.

> "Rich were the drops of Jesus' blood,
> Which calmed his frowning face,
> Which sprinkled o'er the burning throne,
> And turn'd the wrath to grace."

So that now Jehovah is not God against us, but "God with us," he has "reconciled us to himself by the death of his Son."

A third meaning of the text "God with us" is this, *God in Christ is with us in blessed communication.* That is to say, now he has come so near to us as to enter into commerce with us, and this he does in part by hallowed conversation. Now he speaks to us and in us. He has in these last days spoken to us by his Son and by the Divine Spirit with the still small voice of warning, consolation, instruction, and direction. Are you not conscious of this? Since your souls have come to know Christ, have you not also enjoyed intercourse with the Most High? Now, like Enoch, you "walk with God," and, like Abraham, you talk with him as a man talketh with his friend. What are those prayers and praises of yours but the speech which you are permitted to have with the Most High; and he replies to you when his Spirit seals home the promise or applies the precept, when with fresh light he leads you into the doctrine or bestows brighter confidence as to good things to come. Oh yes, God is with us now, so that when he cries, "Seek ye my face" our heart says to him, "Thy face, Lord, will I seek." These Sabbath gatherings, what mean they to many of us but "God with us." That communion table, what means it but "God with us"? Oh, how often in the breaking of bread and the pouring forth of the wine in the memory of his atoning death have we enjoyed his real presence, not in a superstitious, but in a spiritual sense, and found the Lord Jesus to be "God with us." Yes, in every holy ordinance, in every sacred act of worship, we now find that there is a door opened in heaven and a new and living way by which we may come to the throne of grace. Is not this a joy better than all the riches of earth could buy?

And it is not merely in speech that the Lord is with us, but God is with us now by powerful *acts* as well as words. "God with us," why it is the inscription upon our royal standard which strikes terror to the heart of the foe, and cheers the sacramental host of God's elect. Is not this our war cry, "The Lord of hosts is with us, the God of Jacob is our refuge." As to our foes within, God is with us to overcome our corruptions and frailties; and as to the adversaries of truth without, God is with his church, and Christ has promised that he ever will be with her "even to the end of the world." We have not merely God's word and promises, but we have seen his acts of grace on our behalf, both in providence and in the working of his blessed Spirit. "The Lord hath made bare his holy arm in the eyes of all the people." "In Judah is God known: his name is great in Israel. In Salem also is his tabernacle, and his dwelling place in Zion. There brake he the arrows of the bow, the shield, and the sword, and the battle." "God with us"—oh, my brethren, it makes our hearts leap for joy, it fills us with dauntless courage. How can we be dismayed when the Lord of hosts is on our side?

Nor is it merely that God is with us in acts of power on our behalf, but in emanations of his own life into our nature by which we are at first new born, and afterwards sustained in spiritual life. This is more wonderful still. By the Holy Spirit the divine seed which "liveth and abideth for ever" is sown in our souls, and from day to day we are strengthened with might by his Spirit in the inner man.

Nor is this all, for as the masterpiece of grace, the Lord, by his Spirit, even dwells in his people. God is not incarnate in us as in Christ Jesus, but only second in wonder to the incarnation is the indwelling of the Holy Spirit in believers. Now is it "God with us" indeed, for God dwelleth in us. "Know ye not," says the apostle, "that your bodies are the temples of the Holy Ghost." "As it is written, I will dwell in them, and I will walk in them." Oh, the heights and depths then comprehended in those few words, "God with us."

I had many more things to say unto you, but time compels me to sum them up in brief. The Lord becomes "God with us" *by the restoration of his image in us.* "God with us" was seen in Adam when he was perfectly pure, but Adam died when he sinned, and God is not the God of the dead but of the living. Now we, in receiving back the new life and being reconciled to God in Christ Jesus, receive also the restored image of God, and are renewed in knowledge and true holiness. "God with us" means sanctification, the image of Jesus Christ imprinted upon all his brethren.

God is with us, too, let us remember, and leave the point, *in deepest sympathy.* Brethren, are you in sorrow? God is in Christ sympathetic to your grief. Brethren, have you a grand object? I know what it is, it is God's glory: therein also you are sympathetic with God, and God with you. What, let me inquire, is your greatest joy? Have you not learned to rejoice in the Lord? Do you not joy in God by Jesus Christ? Then God also joyeth in you. He rests in his love, and rejoices over you with singing, so that there is God with us in a very wonderful respect, inasmuch as through Christ our aims and desires are like those of God. We desire the same thing, press forward with the same aim, and rejoice in the same objects of delight. When the Lord says, "This is my beloved Son, in whom I am well pleased," our heart answers, "Ay, and in him we are well pleased too." The pleasure of the Father is the pleasure of his own chosen children, for we also joy in Christ; our very soul exults at the sound of his name.

III. I must leave this delightful theme when I have said two or three things about OUR PERSONAL APPROPRIATION of the truth before us.

"God with us." Then, if Jesus Christ be "God with us," let us come to God without any question or hesitancy. Whoever you may be you need no priest or intercessor to introduce you to God, for God has introduced himself to you. Are you children? Then come to God in the child Jesus, who slept in Bethlehem's manger. Oh, ye grey-heads, ye need not keep back, but like Simeon come and take him in your arms, and say, "Lord, now lettest thou thy servant depart in peace according to thy word, for mine eyes have seen thy salvation." God sends an ambassador who inspires no fear: not with helmet and coat of mail, bearing lance, does heaven's herald approach us, but the white flag is held in the hand of a child, in the hand of one chosen out of the people, in the hand of one who died, in the hand of one who though he sits in glory wears the nail-print still. O man, God comes to you as one like yourself. Do not be afraid to come to the gentle Jesus. Do not imagine that you need to be prepared for an audience with him, or that you want the intercession of a saint, or the intervention of priest or minister. Anyone could have come to the babe in Bethlehem. The horned oxen, methinks, ate of the hay on which he slept and feared not. Jesus is the friend of each one of us, sinful and unworthy though we be. You, poor ones, you need not fear to come, for, see, in a stable he is born, and in a manger he is cradled. You have not worse accommodation than his, you are not poorer than he. Come and welcome to the poor man's Prince, to the peasants' Saviour. Stay not back through fear of your unfitness; the shepherds came to him in all their deshabille. I read not that they tarried to put on their best garments, but in the clothes in which they wrapped themselves that cold midnight they hastened just as they were to the young child's presence. God looks not at garments, but at hearts, and accepts men when they come to him with willing spirits, whether they be rich or poor. Come, then; come, and welcome, for God indeed is "God with us."

But, oh, let there be no delay about it. It did seem to me, as I turned this subject over, yesterday, that for any man to say, "I will not come to God," after God has come to man in such a form as this, were an unpardonable act of treason. Peradventure, you knew not God's love when you sinned, as you did; peradventure, though you persecuted his saints, you did it ignorantly in unbelief; but, behold your God extends the olive branch of peace to you, extends it in a wondrous way, for he himself comes here to be born of a woman, that he may meet with you who were born of women too, and save you from your sin. Will you not hearken now that he speaks by his Son? I can understand that you ask to hear no more of his words when he speaks with the sound of a trumpet, waxing exceeding loud and long, from amidst the flaming crags of Sinai; I do not wonder that you are afraid to draw near when the earth rocks and reels before his awful presence; but now he restrains himself and veils the splendour of his face, and comes to you as a child of humble mien, a carpenter's son. Oh, if he comes so, will you turn your backs upon him? Can ye spurn him? What better ambassador could you desire? This embassage of peace is so tenderly, so gently, so kindly, so touchingly put, that surely you cannot have the heart to resist it. Nay, do not turn away, let not your ears refuse the language of his grace, but say, "If God is with us, we will be with him." Say it, sinner, say, "I will arise and go to my Father and will say unto him, Father, I have sinned."

And as for you who have given up all hope, you that think yourselves so degraded and fallen that there can be no future for you,— there is hope for you yet, for you are a man, and the next being to God is a man. He that is God is also man, and there is something about that fact which ought to make you say, "Yes, I may yet discover, mayhap, brotherhood to the Son of man who is the Son of God, I, even I, may yet be lifted up to be set among princes, even the princes of his people, by virtue of my regenerated manhood which brings me into relation with the manhood of Christ, and so into relation with the Godhead." Fling not yourself away, oh man, you are something too hopeful after all to be meat for the worm that never dies, and fuel for the fire that never can be quenched. Turn you to your God with full purpose of heart, and you shall find a grand destiny in store for you.

And now, my brethren, to you the last word is, let us be with God since God is with us. I give you for a watchword through the year to come, " Emmanuel, God with us." You, the saints redeemed by blood, have a right to all this in its fullest sense, drink into it and be filled with courage. Do not say, " We can do nothing." Who are ye that can do nothing? God is with you. Do not say " The church is feeble and fallen upon evil times,"—nay, " God is with us." We need the courage of those ancient soldiers who were wont to regard difficulties only as whetstones upon which to sharpen their swords. I like Alexander's talk—when they said there were so many thousands, so many millions perhaps of Persians. " Very well," says he, " it is good reaping where the corn is thick. One butcher is not afraid of a thousand sheep." I like even the talk of the old Gascon, who said when they asked him, " Can you and your troops get into that fortress ? it is impregnable." " Can the sun enter it ?" said he. " Yes." " Well, where the sun can go we can enter." Whatever is possible or whatever is impossible, Christians can do at God's command, for God is with us. Do you not see that the word, " God with us," puts impossibility out of all existence ? Hearts that never could else be broken will be broken if God be with us. Errors which never else could be confuted can be overthrown by " God with us." Things impossible with men are possible with God. John Wesley died with that upon his tongue, and let us live with it upon our hearts.—" The best of all is God with us." Blessed Son of God, we thank thee that thou hast brought us that word. Amen.

Immanuel—The Light of Life

"Nevertheless the dimness shall not be such as was in her vexation, when at the first he lightly afflicted the land of Zebulun and the land of Naphtali, and afterward did more grievously afflict her by the way of the sea, beyond Jordan, in Galilee of the nations. The people that walked in darkness have seen a great light: they that dwell in the land of the shadow of death, upon them hath the light shined "—Isaiah ix. 1, 2.

As in this case the Revised Version is much to be preferred, we will now read it:—

"But there shall be no gloom to her that was in anguish. In the former time he brought into contempt the land of Zebulun and the land of Naphtali, but in the latter time hath he made it glorious, by the way of the sea, beyond Jordan, Galilee of the nations. The people that walked in darkness have seen a great light: they that dwelt in the land of the shadow of death, upon them hath the light shined "—Isaiah ix. 1, 2.

When Judah was in sore distress, the sign that she should be delivered was Immanuel. "Behold, a virgin shall conceive, and bear a son, and shall call his name Immanuel" (Isaiah vii. 14). When no other ray of comfort could be found, light came from the promise of the wondrous birth of him whose name is "God with us." God alone would be the deliverer of Judah when over-matched by her two enemies. God would be with them, and he gave them as a pledge a vision of that time when, in very deed, God would dwell among men, and wear their nature in the person of The Virgin-born.

It is noteworthy that the clearest promises of the Messiah have been given in the darkest hours of history. If the prophets had been silent upon the Coming One before, they always speak out in the cloudy and dark day; for well the Spirit made them know that the coming of God in human flesh is the lone star of the world's night. It was so in the beginning, when our first parents had sinned, and were doomed to quit the Paradise of delights. It was not meet that rebels should be dwellers in the garden of the Lord, they must go forth to till the ground from whence they were taken; but ere they went, there fell upon their ear the prophecy of the Deliverer who would be born: "The seed of the woman shall bruise the serpent's head." How bright shone that one promise amid the surrounding gloom! The earliest believers found in this hope of the coming Conqueror of the serpent a solace amid their labour and sorrow. When Israel was in

Egypt, when they were in the sorest bondage, and when many plagues had been wrought on Pharaoh, apparently without success; for he knew not the Lord, neither would he let his people go; then Israel saw the Messiah set before her as the Paschal lamb, whose blood sprinkled on the lintel and the two side posts secured the chosen from the avenger of blood. The type is marvellously clear, and the times were marvellously dark. It seemed as if the Lord would make the consolation to abound even as the tribulation abounded.

I will not multiply instances; but I will quote three cases from the prophetical books which now lie open before us. In Isaiah, turn to his twenty-eighth chapter, and the sixteenth verse, and you read that glorious prophecy: "Behold, I lay in Zion for a foundation a stone, a tried stone, a precious corner stone, a sure foundation: he that believeth shall not make haste." When was that given? It was pronounced when the foundation of society in Israel was rotten with iniquity, and when its corner stone was oppression. Read from verse fourteen: "Wherefore hear the word of the Lord, ye scornful men, that rule this people which is in Jerusalem. Because ye have said, We have made a covenant with death, and with hell are we at agreement; when the overflowing scourge shall pass through, it shall not come unto us: for we have made lies our refuge, and under falsehood have we hid ourselves." Thus, when lies and falsehoods ruled the hour, the Lord proclaims the blessed truth that the Messiah would come and would be a sure foundation for believers. Next, look into Jeremiah, and pause at the twenty-third chapter and the fifth verse: "Behold, the days come, saith the Lord, that I will raise unto David a righteous Branch, and a King shall reign and prosper, and shall execute judgment and justice in the earth. In his days Judah shall be saved, and Israel shall dwell safely: and this is his name whereby he shall be called, THE LORD OUR RIGHTEOUSNESS." When was this clear testimony given? Read the former verses of the chapter, and see that the pastors were destroying and scattering the sheep of Jehovah's pasture. When the people of the Lord thus found their worst enemies where they ought to have met with friendly care, then they were promised happier days through the coming of the divine Son of David. I will only further detain you while we glance at Ezekiel xxxiv. 23, where the Lord says, "And I will set up one shepherd over them, and he shall feed them, even my servant David; he shall feed them, and he shall be their shepherd." When came this cheering promise concerning that great Shepherd of the sheep? It came when Israel is thus described: "And they were scattered, because there is no shepherd: and they became meat to all the beasts of the field, when they were scattered. My sheep wandered through all the mountains, and upon every high hill: yea, my flock was scattered upon all the face of the earth, and none did search or seek after them." Thus you see that, in each case, when things were at their worst, the Lord Jesus was the one well of consolation in a desert of sorrows.

> "Midst darkest shades, if he appear,
> Our dawning has begun;
> He is our soul's bright morning star,
> And he our rising sun."

In the worst times we are to preach Christ, and to look to Christ. In Jesus there is a remedy for the direst of diseases, and a rescue from the darkest of despairs. Ahaz, as the chapter tells us, was in great danger, for he was attacked by two kings, each one stronger than himself; but the Lord promised him deliverance, and commanded him to choose a sign either in the heights, or in the depths. This, under a hypocritical pretence, he refused to do; and therefore the Lord chose as his own token the appearance of the heavenly Deliverer, who would be God, and yet born of a woman. "Behold, a virgin shall conceive, and bear a son, and shall call his name Immanuel." He was to eat butter and honey, like other children in that land of milk and honey, and yet he was to be the Mighty God, the Everlasting Father, the Prince of Peace. We see here Godhead in union with manhood. We behold Jesus man "of the substance of his mother," and yet "God over all, blessed for ever." Surely this God-appointed sign was both in the depth and in the height above: the Man of sorrows, the Son of the Highest. This vision was the light of the age of Ahaz. It is God's comfort to troubled hearts in all the ages; it is God's sign of grace to us this morning. The sure hope of sinners and the great joy of saints is the incarnate Lord, Immanuel, God with us. May he be your joy and mine even this day. He it is who is the great light of the people who dwell in the land of the shadow of death: if any among you are in that dreary land, may he be light and life to you! He alone could make the darkness of Zebulun and Naphtali to disappear in a blaze of glory: he can do the same for those who sorrow at this hour.

Now, if I may have your patient attention, I shall, as I am enabled, *illustrate this fact by the context.* Scripture best explains Scripture, as diamond cuts diamond. The Word of God carries its own keys for all its locks. It is profitable to study Scripture, not in fragments, but in connected paragraphs. It is well to see the glory of a star, but better to behold the whole constellation in which it shines. When I have dwelt upon the context, I shall, in the second place, *press home certain joyful truths connected with the subject.*

I. There is to be a light breaking in upon the sons of men who sit in darkness, and this light is to be found only in the incarnate God. Let me ILLUSTRATE THIS FACT BY THE CONTEXT.

I must carry you back to the fourteenth verse of the seventh chapter. *The sign of coming light is Jesus.* "Therefore the Lord himself shall give you a sign; Behold, a virgin shall conceive, and bear a son, and shall call his name Immanuel." In Judah's trouble, the Virgin-born was God's token that he would deliver, and that speedily; for in less time than it would take such a child to reach years of knowledge, both Judah's royal adversaries would be gone. The sign was good for Ahaz; but it is better far for us. Behold the incarnate Son of God born of Mary at Bethlehem; what can this intend for us but grace? If the Lord had meant to destroy us, he would not have assumed our nature. If he had not been moved with mighty love to a guilty race, he would never have taken upon himself their flesh and blood. It is a miracle of miracles that the Infinite should become an infant; that he who is pure spirit, and filleth all things, should be wrapped in swaddling bands, and cradled in a manger. He took not on him the nature of angels, though that would have been a tremendous stoop from Deity, but he descended lower still; for he took on him the seed of Abraham. "He was made in all things like unto his brethren"; though "he counted it not robbery to be equal with God." It is not in the power of human lips to speak out all the comfort which this one sign contains. If any troubled soul will look believingly at God in human flesh, he must take heart of hope. If he looks believingly, his comfort will come right speedily. The birth of Jesus is the proof of the good will of God to men: I am unable to conceive of proof more sure. He would not have come here to be born among men, to live among them, suffer and to die for them, if he had been slow to pardon, or unwilling to save. O despairing soul, does not Immanuel, God with us, make it hard to doubt the mercy of the Lord?

We have comfort in the fact that our Lord was truly man. He whom we worship became one with us in nature. He was born as other children are born, save that his mother was a virgin. He was fed as other children were fed, upon curds and honey, the food of a pastoral country. He had to be developed, as to his natural powers, even as other little ones. He grew up from childhood to youth, and from youth to manhood, passing through all the gradations of human weakness, even as we have done; and he was obedient to his parents, even as other children should be. He is, therefore, really and truly a man; and this fact is a bright particular star for sinners' eyes. Come to Jesus, all ye who languish under terror and dread because of the majesty of Deity; for here you see how compassionate he is, how sympathetic he can be, yea, how near of kin he has become. He is God; but he is God *with us*. He is bone of our bone, and flesh of our flesh, a brother born for adversity; and here the most trembling may be at rest. God in our nature is a grand prophecy of salvation and bliss for us. Why has he come down to us but that we may come up to him? Why has he taken our nature in its sorrow, but that we may be made partakers of the divine nature in righteousness and holiness? He comes down, not to thrust us lower, but to lift us to heights of perfectness and glory. That Jesus is man and yet God, is full of hope and joy for us who believe in him. I do not feel as if I wanted to enlarge upon this glorious truth with words alone. Oh, that the Holy Spirit would convey to each one of my hearers the light which shines from the star of incarnation! Oh, that at this moment the people who walk in darkness may see in the incarnate God a great light, and perceive in him the prophecy and assurance of all good things! Not long shall evil oppress the believer; for in Christ Jesus God is with us; and if God be for us, who can be against us?

> "O joy! there sitteth in our flesh,
> Upon a throne of light,
> One of a human mother born,
> In perfect Godhead bright!
>
> "For ever God, for ever man,
> My Jesus shall endure;
> And fix'd on him, my hope remains
> Eternally secure."

Further on we see our Lord Jesus as *the hold-fast of the soul in time of darkness.* See in the eighth verse of the eighth chapter the whole country overwhelmed by the fierce armies of the Assyrians, as when a land is submerged beneath a flood. Then you read—"And he shall pass through Judah; he shall overflow and go over, he shall reach even to the neck; and the stretching out of his wings shall fill the breadth of thy land, O Immanuel." The one hope that remained for Judah was that her country was Immanuel's land. There would Immanuel be born, there would he labour, and there would he die. He was by eternal covenant the King of that land, and no Assyrian could keep him from his throne. Whatever the enemy might do, the land was still "thy land, O Immanuel!" If, my dear friend, you are a believer in Christ, you belong to him, and you always were his by sovereign right, even when the enemy held you in possession. The devil had set his mark upon you, so that you might be for ever his branded slave; but he had no legal right to you, for Immanuel had redeemed you, and he claimed you as his own. Had we known, we might exultingly have gloried over you, "Thy soul, O Immanuel!" The Father gave you to Jesus, and Jesus himself bought you with his blood; and, though you knew it not, he had the title-deeds of you, and would not lose his inheritance. Herein lay your hope when all other hope was gone. Herein is your hope now. If you belong to Jesus, he will have you. If he bought you with his blood, he will not shed that blood in vain. If on the cross he bore your sin, he will not suffer you to bear it, and so to make void his sacrifice. If you belong to him he will deliver you, even as David snatched the lamb of his flock from the jaw of the lion and the paw of the bear. O sinner, this is the great hope we have for you : if you were given of old to Jesus he will rescue you from the hand of the enemy. This, also, is your own hope: if you believe in Jesus you belong to Jesus ; if you trust him, he has redeemed you with a price, and will also redeem you with power. If you cast your guilty soul at his dear feet, and take him to be your own Saviour, you are not your own, but bought with a price; and sooner shall heaven and earth pass away than one whom Jesus calls his own shall be left to perish. "Having loved his own, he loved them unto the end." Immanuel, God with us, is strong to rescue his own out of the enemy's hand.

Further on in the chapter we learn that Jesus is *our star of hope as to the destruction of the enemy.* The foes of God's people shall be surely vanquished and destroyed because of Immanuel. Note well, in verses 9 and 10, how it is put twice over, like an exultant taunt : " Gird yourselves, and ye shall be broken in pieces; gird yourselves, and ye shall be broken in pieces. Take counsel together, and it shall come to nought; speak the word, and it shall not stand: for Immanuel." Our version translates the word into " God with us," but it is "Immanuel." In him, even in our Lord Jesus Christ, dwelleth all the fulness of the Godhead bodily, and he has brought all that Godhead to bear upon the overthrow of the foes of his people. Let the powers of darkness consult and plot as they may, they can never destroy the Lord's redeemed. Lo ! I see councils of evil spirits : they sit down in Pandemonium, and conspire to ruin a soul redeemed by blood. They lay their heads together, they use a cunning deep as hell: they are eager to destroy the soul that rests in Jesus. In vain their devices, for the incarnate God is embodied wisdom. Now see them: they rise from the council table, they put on their harness; their arrows are dipped in malice, and their bows are strong to shoot afar. Each foul spirit takes his sword, his sharp sword, that will cut a soul to the centre, and kill it with despair; but their weapons shall all fail. If we fly to Jesus, who is God with us, no weapon that is formed against us shall prosper. His name Immanuel is the terror of the hosts of hell. God with us means confusion to our foes. As the death of death, and hell's destruction, our Immanuel cries to the legions of the pit, "Gird yourselves, and ye shall be broken in pieces. Gird yourselves, and ye shall be broken in pieces"! Let us take courage and defy the legions of darkness. Let us charge them with this war-cry, "God is with us." Immanuel, who has espoused our cause, is God himself, almighty to save: the enemies of our souls shall be trodden under his feet, and he shall bruise Satan even under our feet shortly. Satan from the first hated God in our nature, for thus man was exalted beyond the angel; and this his pride could not endure. The Lord Jesus is as the star Wormwood to our spiritual adversaries, rousing their fiercest hate, and foreboding their sure overthrow.

Further on we find *the Lord Jesus as the morning light after a night of darkness*. The last verses of the eighth chapter picture a horrible state of wretchedness and despair: "And they shall pass through it, hardly bestead and hungry: and it shall come to pass, that when they shall be hungry, they shall fret themselves, and curse their king and their God, and look upward. And they shall look unto the earth; and behold trouble and darkness, dimness of anguish; and they shall be driven to darkness." But see what a change awaits them! Read the fine translation of the Revised Version: "But there shall be no gloom to her that was in anguish." What a marvellous light from the midst of a dreadful darkness! It is an astounding change, such as only God with us could work. Many of you know nothing about the miseries described in those verses; but there are some here who have traversed that terrible wilderness; and I am going to speak to them. I know where you are this morning: you are being driven as captives into the land of despair, and for the last few months you have been tramping along a painful road, "hardly bestead and hungry." You are sorely put to it, and your soul finds no food of comfort, but is ready to faint and die. You fret yourself: your heart is wearing away with care, and grief, and hopelessness. In the bitterness of your soul you are ready to curse the day of your birth. The captive Israelites cursed their king who had led them into their defeat and bondage; in the fury of their agony, they even cursed God and longed to die. It may be that your heart is in such a ferment of grief that you know not what you think, but are like a man at his wits' end. Those who led you into sin are bitterly remembered; and as you think upon God you are troubled. This is a dreadful case for a soul to be in, and it involves a world of sin and misery. You look up, but the heavens are as brass above your head;

your prayers appear to be shut out from God's ear; you look around you upon the earth, and behold "trouble and darkness, and dimness of anguish"; your every hope is slain, and your heart is torn asunder with remorse and dread. Every hour you seem to be hurried by an irresistible power into greater darkness, yea, even into the eternal midnight. In such a case none can give you comfort save Immanuel, God with us. Only God, espousing your cause, and bearing your sin, can possibly save you. See, he comes for your salvation! Behold, he has come to seek and to save that which was lost. God has come down from heaven, and veiled himself in our flesh, that he might be able to save to the uttermost. He can save the chief of sinners: he can save *you*. Come to Jesus, you that have gone furthest into transgression, you that sit down in despondency, you that shut yourselves up in the iron cage of despair. For such as you there shines this star of the first magnitude. Jesus has appeared to save, and he is God and man in one person: man that he may feel our woes, God that he may help us out of them. No minister can save you, no priest can save you—you know this right well; but here is one who is able to save to the uttermost, for he is God as well as man. The great God is good at a dead lift; when everything else has failed, the lever of omnipotence can lift a world of sin. Jesus is almighty to save! That which in itself is impossibility is possible with God. Sin which nothing else can remove is blotted out by the blood of Immanuel. Immanuel, our Saviour, is God with us; and God with us means difficulty removed, and a perfect work accomplished. But I fail to tell you in words. Oh, that the light itself would shine into your souls, that those of you who have as yet no hope may see a great light, and may from henceforth be of good courage!

Once more, dear friends, we learn from that which follows our text, that *the reign of Jesus is the star of the golden future*. He came to Galilee of the Gentiles, and made that country glorious, which had been brought into contempt. That corner of Palestine had very often borne the brunt of invasion, and had felt more than any other region the edge of the keen Assyrian sword. They were at first troubled when the Assyrian was bought off with a thousand talents of silver; but they were more heavily afflicted when Tiglath-pileser carried them all away to Assyria, for which see the fifteenth chapter of the second book of the Kings. It was a wretched land, with a mixed population, despised by the purer race of Jews; but that very country became glorious with the presence of the incarnate God. It was there that all manner of diseases were healed; there the seas were stilled, and the multitudes were fed; it was there that the Lord Jesus found his apostles, and there he met the whole company of his followers when he had risen from the dead. That first land to be invaded by the enemy was made the head-quarters of the army of salvation: this very Zebulun and Naphtali, which had been so downtrodden and despised, was made the scene of the mighty works of the Son of God. Even so, at this day his gracious presence is the day-dawn of our joy.

If Christ comes to you, my dear hearer, as God with us, then shall your joy be great; for you shall joy as with the joy of harvest, and as those rejoice that divide the spoil. Is it not so? Many of us can bear our witness that there is no joy like that which Jesus brings. Here read and interpret the third verse of the ninth chapter.

Then shall your enemy be defeated, as in the day of Midian. Gideon was, in his dream, likened to a barley-cake, which struck the tent of Midian, so that it lay along. He and his few heroes, with their pitchers and their trumpets, stood and shouted, "The sword of the Lord and of Gideon!" and Midian melted away before them. So shall it be with our sins, and doubts, and fears, if we believe in Jesus, the incarnate God; they shall vanish like the mists of the morning. The Lord Jesus will break the yoke of our burden, and the rod of our oppressor, as in the day of Midian. Be of good courage, ye that are in bondage to fierce and cruel adversaries; for in the name of Jesus, who is God with us, you shall destroy them. This you see in the fourth verse. Please follow me as I dwell on each verse.

When Jesus comes, you shall have eternal peace; for his battle is the end of battles. "All the armour of the armed man in the tumult, and the garments rolled in blood, shall even be for burning, for fuel of fire." This is the rendering of the Revision; and it is good. The Prince of peace wars against war, and destroys it. What a glorious day is that in which the Lord breaketh the bow and cutteth the spear in sunder, and burneth the chariot in the fire! I think I see it now. My sins, which were the weapons of my foes, the Lord piles in heaps. What mountains of prey! But see! he brings the fire-brand of his love from the altar of his sacrifice, and he sets fire to the gigantic pile. See how they blaze! They are utterly consumed for ever. The enemy has now no weapon that he can use against my soul. The incarnate God has broken the power of the adversary, for the sting of death is sin, and that he has made an end of. He has thus destroyed the war which raged in our souls, and now he reigns as Prince of peace, and we have peace in him.

Now is it that the Lord Jesus becomes glorious in our eyes; and he whose name is Immanuel is now crowned in our heart with many crowns, and honoured with many titles. What a list of glories we have here! What a burst of song it makes when we sing of the Messiah: "His name shall be called Wonderful, Counsellor, The mighty God, The everlasting Father, The Prince of Peace"! Each word sounds like a salvo of artillery. It is all very well to hear players on instruments and sweet singers rehearse these words; but to believe them, and realize them in your own soul, is better far. When every fear and every hope, and every power and every passion of our nature fill the orchestra of our heart, and all unite in one inward song unto the glorious Immanuel, what music it is! He is to us the Wonderful, the Counsellor, the Mighty God, the Everlasting Father, the Prince of Peace, and much more than words can tell. Do but get Christ Jesus in your soul, as the incarnate God, and he will set up a government within your nature which shall bring you peace, and righteousness, and joy, and eternal glory. He will so reign over you that your happiness shall know no bound; but you shall climb from grace to grace, from joy to joy, from peace to peace, yea, from heaven to the highest heaven. This all along shall be your divinest comfort, that Jesus is both God and man, even God with us.

Thus have I very briefly skimmed over the connection. Had we time and grace, what a wealth of thought might be drawn from these inexhaustible mines!

II. But now, secondly, I want to PRESS HOME CERTAIN TRUTHS CONNECTED WITH MY THEME. Come, Holy Spirit, to help the preacher! Come, divine Comforter, to troubled hearts, and give them rest in Immanuel!

Immanuel is a grand word. "God with us" means more than tongue can tell. It means enmity removed on our part, and justice vindicated on God's part. It means the whole Godhead engaged on our side, resolved to bless us.

But you say to me, "Who is this? Are you sure that Immanuel is Jesus of Nazareth?" Yes, *Jesus is Immanuel*. Will you turn to Matthew i. 21, and read onward, "And she shall bring forth a son, and thou shalt call his name Jesus: for he shall save his people from their sins. Now all this was done, that it might be fulfilled which was spoken of the Lord by the prophet, saying: Behold, a virgin shall be with child, and shall bring forth a son, and they shall call his name Emmanuel, which being interpreted is, God with us." Do you see this? They call his name Jesus to fulfil the prophecy that they should call his name Immanuel! It is a singular fulfilment surely. It can only be accounted for by the fact that the Holy Spirit regards the name "Jesus" as being tantamount to the name "Immanuel." The Saviour is God with us. Jesus, a Saviour, is, in the Hebrew, Joshua, or Jehoshua, that is, Jehovah saving. The sense is the same as that of Immanuel, or "God with us," or for us; since God for us is sure to save us. The two names are the same in essential meaning. If God has come to save, then God is with us; if God himself is our salvation, then God is on our side; and if the child born of the virgin be indeed the Lord of glory, then is God our friend. Strong Son of God! Immortal Love! We have not seen thy face; but we can trust thy power, and rest upon thy love. Thy very birth brings hope; but as for thy death, when thou didst bear our sins in thine own body on the tree, this is the fulfilment of all our desires, in the cancelling of sin, the removal of wrath, and the securing of eternal life. Yes, Jesus is God with us.

Perhaps you wish to know a little more of the incident in the text which exhibits *Jesus as the great light*. We have spoken of Zebulun and Naphtali: were those regions really benefited by the coming of the Lord Jesus? Just look a little further on, to Matthew iv. 12: "Now when Jesus had heard that John was cast into prison, he departed into Galilee; and leaving Nazareth, he came and dwelt in Capernaum, which is upon the sea coast, in the borders of Zabulon and Nephthalim: that it might be fulfilled which was spoken by Esaias the prophet, saying, The land of Zabulon, and the land of Nephthalim, by the way of the sea, beyond Jordan, Galilee of the Gentiles; the people which sat in darkness saw great light; and to them which sat in the region and shadow of death light is sprung up. From that time Jesus began to preach, and to say, Repent: for the kingdom of heaven is at hand." Yes, beloved, our Lord made his home in the darkest parts. He looked about and saw no country so ignorant, no country so sorrowful, as Galilee of the Gentiles, and therefore he went there, and lifted it up to heaven by priceless privileges! His ministry of repentance and faith was in itself a glorious light; but he did many mighty works to confirm it. Why, the whole country round was full of sick folk whom he had restored. You could not go half a mile but what you met a blind man who told of how Jesus had restored his sight, or a sick woman who had been raised up from the fever, or some paralytic who had been made whole. That country must have been glad indeed. Multitudes would never forget how they heard him by the sea. They said, "What sermons he preached! He made our hearts dance for joy; and then he fed us, and we ate of barley loaves and little fish till we were filled. He is a wonderful prophet, and this is a wonderful country; once dark enough, but now enlightened by his presence." Beloved, I pray that Jesus may come to you if you are in the dark to-day, and work miracles for you, feed you, and teach you, and make you glad, so that, though you were the most unhappy of beings, you may become the happiest of mortal men. Galilee, plundered, despoiled, despised, became, by-and-by, glorious, because of him who is Immanuel. This is a happy omen for you, dear friends: if you have been the most sorrowful of beings, the Lord Jesus may come at once to you and make you rejoice with great joy. Jesus rescues from contempt, from ignorance, from misery, from despair, and therein reveals himself as "God with us."

We will turn back to where we opened our Bibles at the first, and there we learn that, to be God with us, *Jesus must be accepted by us*. He cannot be with us if we will not have him. Hear how the prophet words it: "Unto us a child is born, unto us a son is given." As a child he was born, as a son he was given. He comes to us in two ways—in his human nature, born; in his divine nature, given. But I want you to see that all the sweetness and light that can come to you through him, must come by your putting both your hands upon him, and taking him to be your own. Here is one hand, "*Unto us* a child is born"; here is the other, "*Unto us* a son is given." Do you ask, "What are these two hands?" I received a note from one of my hearers, who pleads, "Tell me, sir, what faith is; tell me what you mean by believing and trusting." My dear friend, I am always telling you *that*, and I mean to keep on always telling you it so long as I have a tongue to move. By a daring act of appropriation take Jesus to be yours, and say with me—oh, that we could all say it in one great shout!—"UNTO US A CHILD IS BORN, UNTO US A SON IS GIVEN." God gives him, we take him. He is born, we take him up in our arms, and feel ready to cry, "Lord, now lettest thou thy servant depart in peace; for mine eyes have seen thy salvation." He is a Son given. Shall we not accept this gift of gifts, and love him because he has first loved us? To believe is to take freely what God gives freely. It is the simplest thing that can be. I could not explain to you what to drink is; but I will put this glass to my lips, and actually perform the action. Now you see what it is. The water is put to the lip, it is allowed to flow into the mouth and down the throat, and so it is drunk. Take Christ just so. Up to the very lip of your reception he flows; open the mouth of your soul, and take him into yourself. "May I?" say you. May you? You are threatened with damnation if you do not; for this is one side of the gospel message, "He that believeth and is baptized shall be saved; he that believeth not shall be damned." A man may certainly do that which involves him in condemnation if he does not do it. That awful threatening is one of the most powerful bits of gospel that I know of: it drives while the promise draws. If you want Christ, you may have him. If you desire to have God with you, he waits to be gracious unto you. If you wish for Immanuel, behold him in Jesus, your Lord.

"Oh, but I wish I had some sign that I might be sure!" What sign do you want beyond the gift of God, the birth of Jesus? Away with demands which are wild and ungenerous. The Word of God bids you believe and live. The moment you believe in Jesus he is yours. Say, then, this morning, "Unto us a child is born, unto us a son is given," and say it with fulness of delight.

Be sure that you go on with the verse to the end—"and the government shall be upon his shoulder." If Christ is your Saviour he must be your King.

> "But know, nor of the terms complain,
> Where Jesus comes he comes to reign:
> To reign, and with no partial sway;
> Lusts must be slain that disobey."

The moment we really believe in Jesus as our salvation we fall before him, and call him Master and Lord. We serve when he saves. He has redeemed us unto himself, and we own that we are his. A generous man once bought a slave-girl. She was put upon the block for auction, and he pitied her and purchased her; but when he had bought her he said to her, "I have bought you to set you free. There are your papers, you are a free woman." The grateful creature fell at his feet and cried, "I will never leave you; if you have made me free I will be your servant as long as you live, and serve you better than any slave could do." This is how we feel towards Jesus. He sets us free from the dominion of Satan, and then, as we need a ruler, we say, "And the government shall be upon his shoulder." We are glad to be ruled by "Immanuel, God with us." This also is a door of hope to us. That Jesus shall be the monarch of our hearts is our exceeding joy. To us he shall be always "Wonderful." When we think of him, or speak about him, it shall be with reverent awe. When we need advice and comfort, we will fly to him, for he shall be our Counsellor. When we need strength, we will look to him as our Mighty God. Born again by his Spirit, we will be his children, and he shall be the Everlasting Father. Full of joy and rest, we will call him Prince of Peace.

Are you willing to have Christ to govern you? Will you spend your lives in praising him? You are willing to have Christ to pardon you, but we cannot divide him, and therefore you must also have him to sanctify you. You must not take the crown from his head; but accept him as the monarch of your soul. If you would have his hand to help you, you must obey the sceptre which it grasps. Blessed Immanuel, we are right glad to obey thee! In thee our darkness ends, and from the shadow of death we rise to the light of life. It is salvation to be obedient to thee. It is the end of gloom to her that was in anguish to bow herself before thee. May God the Holy Spirit take of the things of Christ and show them unto us, and then we shall all cry—

> "Go worship at Immanuel's feet!
> See in his face what wonders meet!
> Earth is too narrow to express
> His worth, his grace, his righteousness."

His Name—Wonderful!

" His name shall be called Wonderful'?—Isaiah ix. 6.

ONE evening last week I stood by the sea-shore when the storm was raging. The voice of the Lord was upon the waters; and who was I that I should tarry within doors, when my Master's voice was heard sounding along the water? I rose and stood to behold the flash of his lightnings, and listen to the glory of his thunders. The sea and the thunders were contesting with one another; the sea with infinite clamour striving to hush the deep-throated thunder, so that his voice should not be heard; yet over and above the roar of the billows might be heard that voice of God, as he spake with flames of fire, and divided the way for the waters. It was a dark night, and the sky was covered with thick clouds, and scarce a star could be seen through the rifts of the tempest; but at one particular time, I noticed far away on the horizon, as if miles across the water, a bright shining, like gold. It was the moon hidden behind the clouds, so that she could not shine upon us; but she was able to send her rays down upon the waters, far away, where no cloud happened to intervene. I thought as I read this chapter last evening, that the prophet seemed to have stood in a like position, when he wrote the words of my text. All round about him were clouds of darkness; he heard prophetic thunders roaring, and he saw flashes of the lightnings of divine vengeance; clouds and darkness, for many a league, were scattered through history; but he saw far away a bright spot—one place where the clear shining came down from heaven. And he sat down, and he penned these words: "The people that walked in darkness have seen a great light: they that dwell in the land of the shadow of death, upon them hath the light shined;" and though he looked through whole leagues of space, where he saw the battle of the warrior "with confused noise and garments rolled in blood," yet he fixed his eye upon one bright spot in futurity, and he declared, that there he saw hope of peace, prosperity and blessedness; for said he, "Unto us a child is born, unto us a son is given: and the government shall be upon his shoulder: and his name shall be called Wonderful."

My dear friends, we live to-day upon the verge of that bright spot. The world has been passing through these clouds of darkness, and the light is gleaming on us now, like the glintings of the first rays of morning. We are coming to a brighter day, and "at evening time it shall be light." The clouds and darkness shall be rolled up as a mantle that God needs no longer, and he shall appear in his glory, and his people shall rejoice with him. But you must mark, that all the brightness was the result of this child born, this son given, whose name is called Wonderful; and if we can discern any brightness in our own hearts, or in the world's history, it can come from nowhere else, than from the one who is called "Wonderful, Counsellor, the mighty God."

The person spoken of in our text, is undoubtedly the Lord Jesus Christ. He is a child born, with reference to his human nature; he is born of the virgin, a child. But he is a son given, with reference to his divine nature, being given as well as born. Of course, the Godhead could not be born of woman. That was from everlasting, and is to everlasting. As a child he was born, as a son he was given. "The government is upon his shoulder, and his name shall be called Wonderful." Beloved, there are a thousand things in this world, that are called by names that do not belong to them; but in entering upon my text, I must announce at the very opening, that Christ is called Wonderful, because he is so. God the Father never gave his Son a name which he did not deserve. There is no panegyric here, no flattery. It is just the simple name that he deserves, they that know him best will say that the word doth not overstrain his merits, but rather falleth infinitely short of his glorious deserving. His name is called Wonderful. And mark, it does not merely say, that God has given him the name of Wonderful—though that is implied; but "his name shall be *called*" so. It *shall* be; it is at this time called Wonderful by all his believing people, and it shall be. As long as the moon endureth, there shall be found men, and angels, and glorified spirits, who shall always call him by his right name. "His name shall be called Wonderful."

I find that this name may bear two or three interpretations. The word is sometimes in Scripture translated "marvellous." Jesus Christ may be called marvellous; and a learned German interpreter says, that without doubt, the meaning of miraculous is also wrapt up in it. Christ is the marvel of marvels, the miracle of miracles. "His name shall be called *Miraculous*," for he is more than a man, he is God's highest miracle. "Great is the mystery of godliness; God was manifest in the flesh." It may also mean separated, or distinguished. And Jesus Christ may well be called this; for as Saul was distinguished from all men, being head and shoulders taller than they, so is Christ distinguished above all men; he is anointed with the oil of gladness above his fellows, and in his character, and in his acts, he is infinitely separated from all comparison with any of the sons of men. "Thou art fairer than the children of men; grace is poured into thy lips." He is "the chief among ten thousand and altogether lovely." "His name shall be called the *Separated One*," the distinguished one, the noble one, set apart from the common race of mankind.

We shall, however, this morning, keep to the old version, and simply read it thus, "His name shall be called Wonderful." And first I shall notice that Jesus Christ deserveth to be called Wonderful for *what he was in the past;* secondly, that he is called Wonderful by all his people for *what he is in the present;* and in the third place, that he *shall* be called Wonderful, *for what he shall be in the future.*

I. First, Christ shall be called Wonderful for WHAT HE WAS IN THE PAST. Gather up your thoughts, my brethren, for a moment, and centre them all on Christ, and you will soon see how wonderful he is. Consider his eternal existence, "begotten of his Father from before all worlds," being of the same substance with his Father: begotten, not made, co-equal, co-eternal, in every attribute, "very God of very God." For a moment remember that he who became an infant of a span long, was no less than the King of ages, the everlasting Father, who was from eternity, and is to be to all eternity. The divine nature of Christ is indeed wonderful. Just think for a moment, how much interest clusters round the life of an old man. Those of us who are but as children in years, look up to him with wonder and astonishment, as he tells us the varied stories of the experience through which he has passed; but what is the life of an aged man—how brief it appears when compared with the life of the tree that shelters him. It existed long before that old man's father crept a helpless infant into the world. How many storms have swept over its brow! how many kings have come and gone! how many empires have risen and fallen since that old oak was slumbering in its acorn cradle! But what is the life of the tree compared with the soil on which it grows? What a wonderful story that soil might tell! What changes it has passed through in all the eras of time that have elapsed since "in the beginning God created the heavens and the earth." There is a wonderful story connected with every atom of black mould which furnishes the nourishment of the oak. But what is the history of that soil compared with the marvellous history of the rock on which it rests—the cliff on which it lifts its head. Oh! what stories might it tell, what records lie hidden in its bowels. Perhaps it could tell the story of the time when "the earth was without form and void, and darkness was upon the face of the earth." Perhaps it might speak and tell us of those days when the morning and the evening were the first day, and the morning and the evening were the second day, and could explain to us the mysteries of how God made this marvellous piece of miracle,—the world. But what is the history of the cliff, compared with that of the sea that rolls at its base—that deep blue ocean, over which a thousand navies have swept, without leaving a furrow upon its brow! But what is the history of the sea, compared with the history of the heavens that are stretched like a curtain over that vast basin! What a history is that of the hosts of heaven—of the everlasting marches of the sun, moon, and stars! Who can tell their generation, or who can write their biography? But what is the history of the heavens, compared with the history of the angels? They could tell you of the day when they saw this world wrapped in swaddling bands of mist—when, like a new-born infant, the last of God's offspring, it came forth from him, and the morning stars sang together, and the sons of God shouted for joy. But what is the history of the angels that excel in strength, compared with the history of the Lord Jesus Christ? The angel is but of yesterday, and he knoweth nothing; Christ, the Eternal One, chargeth even his angels with folly, and looks upon them as his ministering spirits, that come and go at his good pleasure. Oh, Christians, gather with reverence and mysterious awe around the throne of him who is your great Redeemer; for "his name is called Wonderful," since he has existed before all things, and "by him all things were made; and without him was not anything made that was made."

Consider, again, the incarnation of Christ, and you will rightly say, that his name deserveth to be called "Wonderful." Oh! what is that I see? Oh! world of wonders, what is that I see? The Eternal of ages, whose hair is white like wool, as white as snow, becomes an infant. Can it be? Ye angels, are ye not astonished? He becomes an infant, hangs at a virgin's breast, draws his nourishment from the breast of woman. Oh wonder of wonders! Manger of Bethlehem, thou hast miracles poured into thee. This is a sight that surpasses all others. Talk ye of the sun, moon, and stars; consider ye the heavens, the work of God's fingers, the moon and the stars that he hath ordained; but all the wonders of the universe shrink into nothing, when we come to the mystery of the incarnation of the Lord Jesus Christ. It was a marvellous thing when Joshua bade the sun to stand still, but more marvellous when God seemed to stand still, and no longer to move forward, but rather, like the sun upon the dial of Ahaz, did go back ten degrees, and veil his splendour in a cloud. There have been sights matchless and wonderful, at which we might look for years, and yet turn away and say, "I cannot understand this; here is a deep into which I dare not dive; my thoughts are drowned; this is a steep without a summit; I cannot climb it; it is high, I cannot attain it!" But all these things are as nothing, compared with the incarnation of the Son of God. I do believe that the very angels have never wondered but once and that has been incessantly ever since they first beheld it. They never cease to tell the astonishing story, and to tell it with increasing astonishment too, that Jesus Christ, the Son of God, was born of the Virgin Mary, and became a man. Is he not rightly called Wonderful? Infinite, and an infant—eternal, and yet born of a woman—Almighty, and yet hanging on a woman's breast—supporting the universe, and yet needing to be carried in a mother's arms—king of angels, and yet the reputed son of Joseph—heir of all things, and yet the carpenter's despised son. Wonderful art thou, O Jesus, and that shall be thy name for ever.

But trace the Saviour's course, and all the way he is wonderful. Is it not marvellous that he submitted to the taunts and jeers of his enemies—that for a long life he should allow the bulls of Bashan to gird him round, and the dogs to encompass him? Is it not surprising that he should have bridled in his anger, when blasphemy was uttered against his sacred person? Had you or I been possessed of his matchless might, we should have dashed our enemies down the brow of the hill, if they had sought to cast us there; we should never have submitted to shame and spitting; no, we would have looked upon them, and with one fierce look of wrath, have dashed their spirits into eternal torment. But he hears it all—keeps in his noble spirit—the lion of the tribe of Judah, but bearing still the lamb-like character of

"The humble man before his foes,
A weary man, and full of woes."

I do believe that Jesus of Nazareth was the king of heaven, and yet he was a poor, despised, persecuted, slandered man; but while I believe it I never can understand it. I bless him for it; I love him for it; I desire to praise his name while immortality endures for his infinite condescension in thus suffering for me; but to understand it, I can never pretend. His name must all his life long be called Wonderful.

But see him die. Come O my brothers, ye children of God, and gather round the cross. See your Master. There he hangs. Can you understand this riddle: God was manifest in the flesh, and crucified of men? My Master, I cannot understand how thou couldst stoop thine awful head to such a death as this—how thou couldst take from thy brow the coronet of stars which from old eternity had shone resplendent there; but how thou shouldst permit the thorn-crown to gird thy temples astonishes me far more. That thou shouldst cast away the mantle of thy glory, the azure of thine everlasting empire, I cannot comprehend; but how thou shouldst have become veiled in the ignominious purple for awhile, and then be bowed to by impious men, who mocked thee as a pretended king, and how thou shouldst be stripped naked to thy shame, without a single covering, this is still more incomprehensible. Truly thy name is Wonderful. Oh thy love to me is wonderful, passing the love of woman. Was ever grief like thine? Was ever love like thine, that could open the flood gates of such grief. Thy grief is like a river; but was there ever spring that poured out such a torrent? Was ever love so mighty as to become the fount from which such an ocean of grief could come rolling down? Here is matchless love—matchless love to make him suffer, matchless power to enable him to endure all the weight of his Father's wrath. Here is matchless justice, that he himself should acquiesce in his Father's will, and not allow men to be saved without his own sufferings; and here is matchless mercy to the chief of sinners, that Christ should suffer even for them. "His name shall be called Wonderful."

But he died. He died! See Salem's daughters weep around. Joseph of Arimathea takes up the lifeless body after it has been taken down from the cross. They bear it away to the sepulchre. It is put in a garden. Do you call him Wonderful now?

"Is this the Saviour long foretold
To usher in the age of gold?"

And is he dead? Lift his hands! They drop motionless by his side. His foot exhibits still the nail-print; but there is no mark of life. "Aha," cries the Jew, "is this the Messiah? He is dead; he shall see corruption in a little space of time. Oh! watchman, keep good ward lest his disciples steal his body. His body can never come forth, unless they do steal it; for he is dead. Is this the Wonderful the Counsellor?" But God did not leave his soul in Hades, nor did he suffer his body—" his holy one"—to see corruption? Yes, he *is* wonderful, even in his death. That clay-cold corpse is wonderful. Perhaps this is the greatest wonder of all, that he who is "Death of death and hell's destruction" should for awhile endure the bonds of death. But here is the wonder. He could not be holden of those bonds. Those chains, which have held ten thousand of the sons and daughters of Adam, and which have never been broken yet by any man of human mould, save by a miracle, were but to him as green withes. Death bound our Samson fast, and said, "I have him now; I have taken away the locks of his strength; his glory is departed, and now he is mine; but the hands that kept the human race in chains were nothing to the Saviour; the third day he burst them, and he rose again from the dead, from henceforth to die no more. Oh! thou risen Saviour—thou who couldst not see corruption—thou art wonderful in thy resurrection. And thou art wonderful too in thine ascension—as I see thee leading captivity captive and receiving gifts for men. "His name shall be called Wonderful."

Pause here one moment, and let us think—Christ is surpassingly wonderful. The little story I have told you just now—not little in itself, but little as I have told it—has in it something surpassingly wonderful. All the wonders that you ever saw are nothing compared with this. As we have passed through various countries we have seen a wonder, and some older traveller than ourselves has said, "Yes, this is wonderful to you, but I could show you something that utterly eclipses that." Though we have seen some splendid landscapes, with glorious hills, and we have climbed up where the eagle seemed to knit the mountain and the sky together in his flight, and we have stood and looked down, and said, "How wonderful!" Saith he, "I have seen fairer lands than these, and wider and richer prospects far." But when we speak of Christ, none can say they ever saw a greater wonder than he is. You have come now to the very summit of everything that may be wondered at. There are no mysteries equal to this mystery; there is no surprise equal to this surprise; there is no astonishment, no admiration that should equal the astonishment and admiration that we feel when we behold Christ in the glories of the past. He surpasses everything.

And yet again. Wonder is a short-lived emotion; you know, it is proverbial that a wonder grows grey-headed in nine days. The longest period that a wonder is found to last is about that time. It is such a short-lived thing. But Christ is, and ever shall be wonderful. You may think of him through three-score years and ten, but you shall wonder at him more at the end than at the beginning. Abraham might wonder at him, when he saw his day in the distant future; but I do not think that even Abraham himself could wonder at Christ so much as the very least in the kingdom of heaven of to-day wonders at him, seeing that we know more than Abraham, and therefore wonder more. Think again for one moment, and you will say of Christ that he deserves to be called Wonderful, not only because he is always wonderful, and because he is surpassingly wonderful, but also because he is altogether wonderful. There have been some great feats of skill in the arts and sciences; for instance, if we take a common wonder of the day, the telegraph—how much there is about that which is wonderful! But there are a great many things in the telegraph that we can understand. Though there are many mysteries in it, still there are parts of it that are like keys to the mysteries, so that if we cannot solve the riddle wholly, yet it is disrobed of some of the low garments of its mystery. But now if you look at Christ anyhow, anywhere, anyway, he is all mystery; he is altogether wonderful, always to be looked at and always to be admired.

And again, he is universally wondered at. They tell us that the religion of Christ is very good for old women. I was once complimented by a person, who told me he believed my preaching would be extremely suitable for blacks—for negroes. He did not intend it as a compliment, but I replied, "Well sir, if it is suitable for blacks I should think it would be very suitable for whites; for there is only a little difference of skin, and I do not preach to people's skins, but to their hearts." Now, of Christ we can say that he is universally a wonder, the strongest intellects have wondered at him. Our Lockes and our Newtons have felt themselves to be as little children when they have come to the foot of the cross. The wonder has not been confined to ladies, to children, to old women and dying men; the highest intellects, and the loftiest minds have all wondered at Christ. I am sure it is a difficult task to make some people wonder. Hard thinkers and close mathematicians are not easily.

brought to wonder; but such men have covered their faces with their hands and cast themselves in the dust, and confessed that they have been lost in wonder and amazement. Well then may Christ be called Wonderful.

II. "His name shall be called Wonderful." He is wonderful for WHAT HE IS IN THE PRESENT. And here I will not diverge, but will just appeal to you personally Is he wonderful to *you?* Let me tell the story of my own wonderment at Christ, and in telling it, I shall be telling the experience of all God's children. There was a time when I wondered not at Christ. I heard of his beauties, but I had never seen them; I heard of his power, but it was nought to me; it was but news of something done in a far country—I had no connection with it, and therefore I observed it not. But once upon a time, there came one to my house of a black and terrible aspect. He smote the door; I tried to bolt it—to hold it fast. He smote again and again, till at last he entered, and with a rough voice he summoned me before him; and he said, "I have a message from God for thee; thou art condemned on account of thy sins." I looked at him with astonishment; I asked him his name. He said, "My name is the Law;" and I fell at his feet as one that was dead. " I was alive without the law once: but when the commandment came, sin revived, and I died." As I lay there, he smote me. He smote me till every rib seemed as if it must break, and the bowels be poured forth. My heart was melted like wax within me; I seemed to be stretched upon a rack—to be pinched with hot irons—to be beaten with whips of burning wire. A misery extreme dwelt and reigned in my heart. I dared not lift up mine eyes, but I thought within myself, "There may be hope, there may be mercy for me. Perhaps the God whom I have offended may accept my tears and my promises of amendment, and I may live." But when that thought crossed me, heavier were the blows and more poignant my sufferings than before, till hope entirely failed me, and I had nought wherein to trust. Darkness black and dense gathered round me; I heard a voice as it were, of rushing to and fro, and of wailing and gnashing of teeth. I said within my soul, "I am cast out from his sight, I am utterly abhorred of God, he hath trampled me in the mire of the streets in his anger." And there came one by, of sorrowful but of loving aspect, and he stooped over me, and he said, "Awake thou that sleepest, and arise from the dead, and Christ shall give thee light." I arose in astonishment, and he took me, and he led me to a place where stood a cross, and he seemed to vanish from my sight. But he appeared again hanging there. I looked upon him as he bled upon that tree. His eyes darted a glance of love unutterable into my spirit, and in a moment, looking at him, the bruises that my soul had suffered were healed; the gaping wounds were cured; the broken bones rejoiced; the rags that had covered me were all removed; my spirit was white as the spotless snows of the far-off north; I had melody within my spirit, for I was saved, washed, cleansed, forgiven, through him that did hang upon the tree. Oh, how I wondered that I should be pardoned! It was not the pardon that I wondered at so much; the wonder was that it should come to me. I wondered that he should be able to pardon such sins as mine, such crimes, so numerous and so black, and that after such an accusing conscience he should have power to still every wave within my spirit, and make my soul like the surface of a river, undisturbed, quiet, and at ease. His name then to my spirit was Wonderful But, brethren and sisters, if you have felt this, you can say you thought him wonderful then—if you are feeling it, a sense of adoring wonder enraptures your heart even now.

And has he not been wonderful to you since that auspicious hour, when first you heard Mercy's voice spoken to you? How often have you been in sadness, sickness, and sorrow! But your pain has been light, for Jesus Christ has been with you on your sick-beds; your care has been no care at all, for you have been able to cast your burden upon him. The trial which threatened to crush you, rather lifted you up to heaven, and you have said "How wonderful that Jesus Christ's name should give me such comfort, such joy, such peace, such confidence." Various things bring to my recollection a period now removed by the space of nearly two years. Never shall we forget, beloved, the judgments of the Lord, when by terrible things in righteousness he answered our prayer that he would give us success in this house. We cannot forget how the people were scattered—how some of the sheep were slain, and the shepherd himself was smitten. I may not have told in your hearing the story of my own woe. Perhaps never soul went so near the burning furnace of insanity, and yet came away unharmed. I have walked by that fire until these locks seemed to be crisp with the heat thereof. My brain was racked.

I dared not look up to God, and prayer that was once my solace, was the cause of my affright and terror, if I attempted it. I shall never forget the time when I first became restored to myself. It was in the garden of a friend. I was walking solitary and alone, musing upon my misery, much cheered as that was by the kindness of my loving friend, yet far too heavy for my soul to bear, when on a sudden the name of Jesus flashed through my mind. The person of Christ seemed visible to me. I stood still. The burning lava of my soul was cooled. My agonies were hushed. I bowed myself there, and the garden that had seemed a Gethsemane became to me a Paradise. And then it seemed so strange to me, that nought should have brought me back but that name of Jesus. I thought indeed at that time that I should love him better all the days of my life. But there were two things I wondered at. I wondered that he should be so good to me, and I wondered more that I should have been so ungrateful to him. But his name has been from that time "Wonderful" to me, and I must record what he has done for my soul.

And now, brothers and sisters, you shall all find, every day of your life, whatever your trials and troubles, that he shall always be made the more wonderful by them. He sends your troubles to be like a black foil, to make the diamond of his name shine the brighter. You would never know the wonders of God if it were not that you find them out in the furnace. "They that go down to the sea in ships, that do business in great waters, these see the works of the Lord, and his wonders in the deep;" and we shall never see the wonders of God except in that deep; we must go into the deeps before we know how wonderful his power and his might to save.

I must not leave this point without one more remark. There have been times when you and I have said of Christ, "His name is wonderful indeed, for we have been by it transported entirely above the world, and carried upward to the very gates of heaven itself." I pity you, beloved, if you do not understand the rhapsody I am about to use. There are moments when the Christian feels the charms of earth all broken, and his wings are loosed, and he begins to fly; and up he soars, till he forgets earth's sorrows and leaves them far behind; and up he goes, till he forgets earth's joys, and leaves them like the mountain tops far below, as when the eagle flies to meet the sun; and up, up, up he goes, with his Saviour full before him almost in vision beatific. His heart is full of Christ; his soul beholds his Saviour, and the cloud that darkened his view of the Saviour's face seems to be dispersed. At such a time the Christian can sympathise with Paul. He says, "Whether in the body or out of the body I cannot tell—God knoweth!" but I am, as it were, "caught up to the third heaven." And how is this rapture produced? By the music of flute, harp, sackbut, psaltery, and all kinds of instruments? No. How then? By riches? By fame? By wealth? Ah, no. By a strong mind? By a lively disposition? No. By the name of Jesus. That one name is all sufficient to lead the Christian into heights of transport that verge upon the region where the angels fly in cloudless day.

III. I have no more time to stay upon this point, although the text is infinite, and one might preach upon it for ever. I have only to notice that his name shall be called Wonderful IN THE FUTURE.

The day is come, the day of wrath, the day of fire. The ages are ended; the last century, like the last pillar of a dilapidated temple, has crumbled to its fall. The clock of time is verging to its last hour. It is on the stroke. The time is come when the things that are made must disappear. Lo, I see earth's bowels moving. A thousand hillocks give up the slumbering dead. The battle fields are clothed no more with the rich harvests that have been manured with blood; but a new harvest has sprung up. The fields are thick with men. The sea itself becomes a prolific mother, and though she hath swallowed men alive, she gives them up again, and they stand before God, an exceeding great army. Sinners! ye have risen from your tombs; the pillars of heaven are reeling; the sky is moving to and fro; the sun, the eye of this great world, is rolling like a maniac's, and glaring with dismay. The moon that long has cheered the night now makes the darkness terrible, for she is turned into a clot of blood. Portents, and signs, and wonders past imagination, make the heavens shake, and make men's hearts quail within them. Suddenly upon a cloud there comes one like unto the Son of Man. Sinners! picture your astonishment and your wonder when you see him. Where art thou, Voltaire? Thou saidst, "I will crush the wretch." Come and crush him now! "Nay," saith Voltaire, "he is not the man I thought he was." Oh how will he wonder when he finds out what Christ is! Now, Judas, come and give him a traitor's kiss! "Ah! nay," says he, "I knew not what I kissed: I thought I kissed only the son of Mary, but lo! he is the everlasting God." Now, ye kings and princes, that stood up and took counsel together against the Lord and against his anointed, saying, "Let us break his bands asunder, and cast his cords from us!" Come now, take counsel once more; rebel against him now! Oh! can ye picture the astonishment, the wonder, the dismay, when careless, godless infidels and Socinians find out what Christ is? "Oh!" they will say, "this is wonderful; I thought not he was such as this;" while Christ shall say to them, "Thou thoughtest that I was altogether such as yourselves; but I am no such thing; I am come in all my Father's glory to judge the quick and dead."

Pharaoh led his hosts into the midst of the Red Sea. The path was dry and shingly, and on either shore stood like a wall of alabaster the clear white water, stiff as with the breath of frost, consolidated into marble. There it stood. Can ye guess the astonishment and dismay of the hosts of Pharaoh, when they saw those walls of water about to close upon them? "Behold, ye despisers, and wonder, and perish!" Such will be your astonishment, when Christ, whom ye have despised to-day—Christ, whom ye would not have to be your Saviour—Christ, whose Bible ye left unread, whose Sabbath ye despised—Christ, whose gospel ye rejected, shall come in the glory of his Father, and all his holy angels with him. Ay, then indeed will ye "behold, and wonder, and perish," and you shall say, "His name is Wonderful."

But perhaps, the most wonderful part of the day of judgment is this, do you see all the horrors yonder—the black darkness, the horrid night, the clashing comets, the pale stars, sickly and wan, falling like figs from the fig tree? Do you hear the cry, "Rocks, hide us, mountains, on us fall?" "Every battle of the warrior is with confused noise;" but there never was a battle like this. This is with fire and smoke indeed. But do ye see yonder? All is peaceful, all serene and quiet. The myriads of the redeemed, are they shrieking, crying, wailing? No; see them! They are gathering—gathering round the throne. That very throne that seems to scatter, as with a hundred hands, death and destruction on the wicked, becomes the sun of light and happiness to all believers. Do you see them coming, robed in white, with their bright wings? while gathering round him they veil their faces. Do ye hear them cry, "Holy, holy, holy, Lord God of hosts, for thou wast slain, and thou hast risen from the dead; worthy art thou to live and reign, when death itself is dead?" Do ye hear them? It is all song, and no shriek. Do ye see them? It is all joy, and no terror. His name to them is Wonderful; but it is the wonder of admiration, the wonder of ecstacy, the wonder of affection, and not the wonder of horror and dismay. Saints of the Lord! ye *shall* know the wonders of his name, when ye shall see him as he is, and shall be like him in the day of his appearing. Oh! my enraptured spirit, thou shalt bear thy part in thy Redeemer's triumph, unworthy though thou art, the chief of sinners, and less than the least of saints. Thine eye shall see him and not another; "I know that my Redeemer liveth, and when he shall stand in the latter day upon the earth, though worms devour this body, yet in my flesh shall I see God." Oh! make yourselves ready, ye virgins! Behold the bridegroom cometh. Arise and trim your lamps, and go ye out to meet him. He comes—he comes—he comes; and when he comes, you shall well say of him as you meet him with joy, "Thy name is called Wonderful. All hail! all hail! all hail!"

His Name—The Counsellor

"For unto us a child is born, unto us a son is given: and the government shall be upon his shoulder: and his name shall be called Wonderful, Counsellor "—Isaiah ix. 6.

LAST Sabbath morning we considered the first title, "His name shall be called Wonderful:" this morning we take the second word, "Counsellor." I need not repeat the remark, that of course these titles belong only to the Lord Jesus Christ, and that we cannot understand the passage except by referring it to Messiah—the Prince. It was by a Counsellor that this world was ruined. Did not Satan mask himself in the serpent, and counsel the woman with exceeding craftiness, that she should take unto herself of the fruit of the tree of knowledge of good and evil, in the hope that thereby she should be as God? Was it not that evil counsel which provoked our mother to rebel against her Maker, and did it not as the effect of sin, bring death into this world with all its train of woe? Ah! beloved, it was meet that the world should have a Counsellor to restore it, if it had a Counsellor to destroy it. It was by counsel that it fell, and certainly, without counsel it never could have arisen. But mark the difficulties that surrounded such a Counsellor. 'Tis easy to counsel mischief; but how hard to counsel wisely! To cast down is easy, but to build up how hard! To confuse this world, and bring upon it all its train of ills was an easy thing. A woman plucked the fruit and it was done; but to restore order to this confusion, to sweep away the evils which brooded over this fair earth, this was work indeed, and "Wonderful" was that Christ who came forward to attempt the work, and who in the plentitude of his wisdom hath certainly accomplished it, to his own honour and glory, and to our comfort and safety.

We shall now enter upon the discussion of this title which is given to Christ, a title peculiar to our Redeemer; and you will see why it should be given to him, and why there was a necessity for such a Counsellor.

Now, our Lord Jesus Christ is a Counsellor in a three-fold sense. First, he is *God's Counsellor;* he sits in the cabinet council of the King of heaven; he has admittance into the privy chamber, and is the Counsellor with God. In the second place, Christ is a Counsellor in the sense which the Septuagint translation appends to this term. Christ is said to be *the angel of the great council.* He is a Counsellor in that he communicates to us in God's behalf, what has been done in the great council before the foundation of the world. And thirdly, Christ is *a Counsellor to us and with us,* because we can consult with him, and he doth counsel and advise us as to the right way and the path of peace.

I. Beginning then, with the first point, Christ may well be called Counsellor, for he is a COUNSELLOR WITH GOD. And here let us speak with reverence, for we are about to enter upon a very solemn subject. It hath been revealed to us that before the world was, when as yet God had not made the stars, long ere space sprang into being, the Almighty God did hold a solemn conclave with himself; Father, Son and Spirit held a mystic council with each other, as to what they were about to do. That council, although we read but little of it in Scripture, was nevertheless most certainly held; we have abundant traces of it, for though it is a doctrine obscure through the effulgence of that light to which no man can approach, and not simply and didactically explained, as some other doctrines are, yet we have continual tracings and incidental mentionings of that great, eternal and wonderful council, which was held between the three glorious persons of

Trinity before the world began. Our first question with ourselves is, why did God hold a council at all? And here, we must answer, that God did not hold a council because of any deficiency in his knowledge, for God understandeth all things from the beginning; his knowledge is the sum total of everything that is noble, and infinite is that sum total, infinitely above everything that is counted noble by us. Thou, O God, hast thoughts that are unsearchable, and thou knowest what no mortal ken can ever attain unto. Nor, again, did God hold any consultation for the increase of his satisfaction. Sometimes men, when they have determined what to do, will nevertheless seek counsel of their friends, because they say, " If their advice agrees with mine it adds to my satisfaction, and confirms me in my resolution." But God is everlastingly satisfied with himself, and knoweth not the shadow of a doubt to cloud his purpose; therefore, the council was not held with any motive or intent of that sort. Nor, again, was it held with a view of deliberation. Men take weeks and months and sometimes years, to think out a thing that is surrounded with difficulties; they have to find the clue with much research; enveloped in folds of mystery, they have to take off first one garment and then another, before they find out the naked, glorious truth. Not so God. God's deliberations are as flashes of lightning; they are as wise as if he had been eternally considering, but the thoughts of his heart, though swift as lightning, are as perfect as the whole system of the universe. The reason why God is represented as holding a council, if I think rightly, is this: that we might understand how wise God is. " In the multitude of counsellors there is wisdom." It is for us to think that in the council of the Eternal Three, each Person in the undivided Trinity being omniscient and full of wisdom, there must have been the sum total of all wisdom. And again, it was to show the unanimity and co-operation of the sacred persons: God the Father hath done nothing alone in creation or salvation. Jesus Christ hath done nothing alone; for even the work of his redemption, albeit that he suffered in some sense alone, needed the sustaining hand of the Spirit, and the accepting smile of the Father, before it could be completed. God said not, " *I* will make man," but " Let *us* make man in our own image." God saith not merely, " I will save," but the inference from the declarations of Scripture is, that the design of the three persons of the blessed Trinity was to save a people to themselves, who should show forth their praise. It was, then, for our sakes, not for God's sake, the council was held—that we might know the unanimity of the glorious persons, and the deep wisdom of their devices.

Yet another remark concerning the council. It may be asked, " What were the topics deliberated upon at that first council, which was held before the day-star knew its place, and planets ran their round?" We reply, " The first topic was creation." We are told in the passage we have read, (Proverbs viii,) that the Lord Jesus Christ, who represents himself as Wisdom, was with God before the world was created, and we have every reason to believe that we are to understand this as meaning, that he was not only with God in company, but with God in co-operation. Besides, we have other Scriptures to prove that " all things were made by him, and without him was not any thing made that was made." And to quote yet another passage that clinches this truth. God said, " Let *us* make *man;*" so that a part of the consultation was with reference to the making of worlds, and the creatures that should inhabit them. I believe that in the sovereign council of eternity, the mountains were weighed in scales, and the hills in balances; then was it fixed in sovereign council how far the sea should go, and where should be its bounds —when the sun should arise and come forth, like a giant from the chambers of his darkness, and when he should return again to his couch of rest. Then did God decree the moment when he should say, " Let there be light," and the moment when the sun should be turned into darkness, and the moon into a clot of blood. Then did he ordain the form and size of every angel, and the destinies of every creature; then did he sketch in his infinite thought, the eagle as he soared to heaven, and the worm as he burrowed into the earth. Then the little as well as the great, the minute as well as the immense, came under the sovereign decree of God. There was that book written, of which Dr. Watts sings—

> " Chained to his throne a volume lies,
> With all the fates of men,
> With every angel's form and size,
> Drawn by th' eternal pen."

Christ was a Counsellor in the matter of creation; with none else took he counsel; none else instructed him. Christ was the Counsellor for all the wondrous works of God.

The second topic that was discussed in this council was the *work of Providence.* God does not act towards this world like a man who makes a watch, and lets it have its own way till it runs down; he is the controller of every wheel in the machine of providence. He has left nothing to itself. We talk of general laws, and philosophers tell us that the world is governed by laws, and then they put the Almighty out of the question. Now, how can a nation be governed by laws apart from a sovereign, or apart from magistrates and rulers to carry out the laws? All the laws may be in the statute book, but put all the police away, take away every magistrate, remove the high court of parliament, what is the use of laws? Laws cannot govern without active agency to carry them out; nor could nature proceed in its everlasting cycles, by the mere force of law. God is the great motive-power of all things; he is in everything. Not only did he make all things, but by him all things consist. From all eternity, Christ was the Counsellor of his Father with regard to providence—when the first man should be born, when he should wander, and when he should be restored—when the first monarchy should rise, and when its sun should set—where his people should be placed, how long they should be placed, and where they should be moved. Was it not the Most High who divided to the nations their inheritance? Hath he not appointed the bounds of our habitation? Oh! heir of heaven, in the day of the great council, Christ counselled his Father as to the weight of thy trials, as to the number of thy mercies, if they be numerable, and as to the time, the way, and the means whereby thou shouldst be brought to himself. Remember, there is nothing that happens in your daily life, but what was first of all devised in eternity, and counselled by Jesus Christ for your good and in your behalf, that all things might work together for your lasting benefit and profit. But, my friends, what unfathomable depths of wisdom must have been involved, when God consulted with himself with regard to the great book of providence! Oh, how strange providence seems to you and to me! Does it not look like a zig-zag line, this way and that way, backward and forward, like the journeyings of the children of Israel in the wilderness? Ah! my brethren, but to God it is a straight line. Directly, God always goes to his object; and yet to us, he often seems to go round about. Ah! Jacob, the Lord is about to provide for thee in Egypt, when there is a famine in Canaan, and he is about to make thy son Joseph great and mighty. Joseph must be sold for a slave; he must be accused wrongfully; he must be put into the pit, and in the round-house prison he must suffer. But God was going straight to his purpose all the while: he was sending Joseph before them into Egypt that they might be provided for, and when the good old patriarch said, "All these things are against me," he did not perceive the providence of God, for there was not a solitary thing in the whole list that was against him, but everything was ruled for his weal. Let us learn to leave providence in the hand of the Counsellor; let us rest assured that he is too wise to err in his predestination, and too good to be unkind, and that in the council of eternity, the best was ordained that could have been ordained—that if you and I had been there, we could not have ordained half so well, but that we should have made ourselves eternal fools by meddling therewith. Rest certain, that in the end we shall see that all was well, and must be well for ever. He is "Wonderful, the Counsellor," for he counselled in matters of providence.

And now with regard to *matters of grace.* These were also discussed in the everlasting council. When the Three Divine Persons in the solemn seclusion of their own loneliness consulted together with reference to the works of grace, one of the first things they had to consider was, how God should be just and yet the justifier of the ungodly—how the world should be reconciled unto God. Hence you read in the book of Zechariah, if you turn to the sixth chapter and the thirteenth verse, this passage—"The council of peace shall be between them both." The Son of God with his Father and the Spirit, ordained the council of peace. Thus was it arranged. The Son must suffer; he must be the substitute, must bear his people's sins and be punished in their stead; the Father must accept the Son's substitution and allow his people to go free, because Christ had paid their debts. The Spirit of the living God must then cleanse the people whom the blood had pardoned, and so they must be accepted before the presence of God, even the Father. That was the result of the great council. But O my brethren, if it had not been for that council, what a question would have been left unsolved? Neither you nor I could ever have thought how the two should meet together—how mercy and justice should kiss each other over the mountain of our sins. I have always thought that one of the greatest proofs that the gospel is of God, is its revelation that Christ died to save sinners. That is a thought so original, so new, so wonderful; you have not got it in any other religion in the world; so that it must have come from God. As I remember to have heard an un-schooled and illiterate man say, when I first told him the simple story of how Christ was punished in the stead of his people: he burst out with an air of surprise, "Faith! that's the gospel, I know; no man could have made that up; that must be of God." That wonderful thought, that a God himself should die, that he himself should bear our sins, that so God the Father might be able to forgive and yet exact the utmost penalty, is super-human, super-angelic; not even the cherubim and seraphim could have been the inventors of it: but that thought was first struck out from the mind of God in the councils of eternity, when the "Wonderful, the Counsellor," was present with his Father.

Again, another part of the great council was this—*who should be saved?* Now, my friends, you that like not old Calvinistic doctrine will perhaps be horrified, but that I cannot help; I will never modify a doctrine I believe to please any man that walks upon earth; but I will prove from Scripture that I have the warrant of God in this matter, and that it is not my own invention. I say that one part of the council of eternity was the predestination of those whom God had determined to save, and I will read you the passage that proves it. "In whom also we have obtained an inheritance, being predestinated according to the purpose of him that worketh all things after the counsel of his own will." The predestination of everyone of God's people was arranged at the eternal council, where God's will sat as the sovereign umpire and undisputed president. There was it said of each redeemed one, "At such an hour I will call him by my grace, for I have loved him with an everlasting love, and by my lovingkindness will I draw him." There was it originated when the peace-speaking blood shall be laid to that elect one's conscience, when the Spirit of the living God shall breathe joy and consolation into his heart. There was it settled how that chosen one should be "kept by the power of God through faith unto salvation;" and there was it determined and settled by two immutable things, wherein it is impossible for God to lie, that everyone of these should be eternally saved, beyond the shadow of a risk of perishing. The apostle Paul was not like some preachers, who are afraid to say a word about the everlasting council; for he says in his epistle to the Hebrews—"God willing more abundantly to show unto the heirs of promise the immutability of his council, confirmed it by an oath." Now, you hear some talk about the immutability of the promise: that is good. But the immutability of God's counsel,—that is to fathom to the very uttermost the doctrines of grace. The council of God from all eternity is immutable; not one purpose has he ever altered, not one decree has he ever changed; he has nailed his decrees against the pillars of eternity, and though the devils have sought to rend them down from the posts of his magnificent palace, yet, saith he, "have I set my king upon my holy hill of Zion;" the decree shall stand; I will do all my pleasure. Thy counsels of old are faithfulness and truth; thou, Lord, in the beginning hast made the heavens and laid the foundations of the earth; thou hast determined thy plans and purposes, and they stand fast for ever and ever.

I think I have sufficiently declared how Christ was the Counsellor, in the transcendent affairs of nature, providence, and grace, in the everlasting council-chamber of eternity. But now I would have you notice what a mercy it was that there was such a counsellor with God, and how fit Christ was to be the Counsellor. Christ himself is wisdom. He chargeth his angels with folly; but he is God only wise himself. If a fool undertake to be a counsellor, his counsel is folly; but when Christ counselled, his counsel was full of wisdom. But there is another qualification necessary for a counsellor. However wise a man be, he has no right to be a counsellor with a king, unless he has some dignity and standing. There may happen to be in my congregation some person of great talent; but if my friend should present himself at the cabinet council and give his advice, he would most probably be unceremoniously dismissed, for they would say, "Art thou of the king's council; if not, what right hast thou to stand here?" Now Christ was glorious; he was equal with his Father, therefore he had a right to counsel God—to counsel with God. Had an angel offered his advice to God it would have been an insufferable impertinence; had the cherubim or seraphim volunteered to give so much as one word of counsel it would have been blasphemy. He would take no counsel from his creatures. Why should wisdom stoop from its throne, to counsel with created folly? But because Christ was far above all principalities and powers and every name that is named, therefore he had a right, not only from his wisdom, but from his rank, to be a Counsellor with God.

But there is one thing that is always necessary in a man, before we can rejoice in his being a counsellor. There are some counsellors concerning the legislation of our country in whom you or I could not rejoice much, because we feel that in their counsels the most of us would be forgotten. Our farming friends would probably rejoice in them; they will consult their interests, there is not much doubt; but whoever heard of a counsellor yet who counselled for the poor? or who has these many years heard so much as an inkling of the name of a man who really counselled for economy and for the good of his nation. We have plenty of men who promise us that they will counsel for us—abundance of men who, if we would but return them to parliament, would most assuredly pour forth such wisdom in our behalf that without doubt we should be the most happy and enlightened people in the world according to their promise; but alas! when they get into office they have no hearty sympathy with us; they belong to a different rank from the most of us, they do not sympathize with the wants and the desires of the middle class and of the poor. But, with regard to Christ, we can put every confidence in him, for we know that in that council from eternity he symphathized with man. He says, "My delights were with the sons of men." Happy men to have a counsellor who delights in them! Moreover, he then, though he was not man, yet foresaw that he was to be "bone of our bone and flesh of our flesh," and therefore in the counsels of eternity he pleaded his own cause when he pleaded our cause, for he well knew that he was to be tempted in all points like as we are, and was to suffer our sufferings and to be our covenant head in union with ourselves. Sweet Counsellor! I love to think thou wast in the everlasting council, my friend, my brother born for adversity!

II. Having thus discussed the first point, I shall proceed to consider briefly the second, according to the translation of the Septuagint. Christ is THE ANGEL OF THE GREAT COUNCIL. Do you and I want to know what was said and done in the great council of eternity? Yes, we do. I will defy any man, whoever he may be, not to want to know something about destiny. What means the ignorance of the common people, when they appeal to the witch, the pretender? when they enquire of the astrologer, and read the book of the pretended soothsayer? Why, it means that man wants to know something about the everlasting council. And what mean all the perplexing researches of certain persons into the prophecies? I consider very often that the inferences drawn from prophecy are very little better, after all, than the guesses of the Norwood gipsey, and that some people who have been so busy in foretelling the end of the world, would have been better employed if they had foretold the end of their own books, and had not imposed on the public by predictions, assaying to interpret the prophecies, without the shadow of a foundation. But, from their credulity we may learn, that among the higher class as well as among the more ignorant, there is a strong desire to know the councils of eternity. Beloved, there is only one glass through which you and I can look back to the dim darkness of the shrouded past, and read the counsels of God, and that glass is the person of Jesus Christ. Do I want to know what God ordained with regard to the salvation of man from before the foundation of the world? I look to Christ; I find that it was ordained in Christ that he should be the first elect, and that a people should be chosen in him. Do you ask the way in which God ordained to save? I answer, he ordained to save by the cross. Do you ask how God ordained to pardon? The answer comes, he ordained to pardon through the sufferings of Christ, and to justify through his resurrection from the dead. Everything that you want to know with regard to what God ordained, everything that you ought to know, you can find out in the person of Jesus Christ. And again, do I long to know the great secret of destiny? I must look to Christ. What mean these wars, this confusion, these garments rolled in blood? I see Christ born of a virgin, and then I read the world's history backwards, and I see that all this led to Christ's coming. I see that all these leaned one upon another, as I have sometimes seen clusters of rocks leaning on each other, and Christ the great leading rock bearing up the superincumbent mass of all past history. And if I want to read the future I look at Christ, and I learn that he who has gone up to heaven, is to come again from heaven in like manner as he went up to heaven. So all the future is clear enough to me. I do not know whether the Pope of Rome is to obtain universal empire or not; I do not mind whether the Russian empire is to swallow up all the nations of the continent; there is one thing I know; God will overturn, overturn, overturn, till he shall come whose right it is to reign; and I know that though the worms devour my body, yet when he shall stand in the latter day upon the earth, in my flesh shall I see God, and there is enough in that for me. All the rest of history is unimportant compared with its end, its issues, its purpose. The end of the first Testament is the first advent of Christ; the end of this second Testament of modern history is the second advent of the Saviour; and then shall the book of time be closed. But none could open the Old Testament history and make it out, except through Christ. Abraham could understand it, for he knew that Christ was to come; Christ opened the book for him. And so modern history is never to be understood except through Christ. None but the Lamb can take the book and open every seal; but he who believeth in Christ and looks for his glorious advent, he may open the book and read therein, and have understanding, for in Christ there is a revelation of the eternal councils.

"Now," says one, "Sir, I want to know one thing, and if I knew that, I would not care what happened. I want to know whether God from all eternity ordained me to be saved." Well, friend, I will tell you how to find that out, and you may find it out to a certainty. "Nay," says one, "but how can I know that? You cannot read the book of fate; that is impossible." I have heard of some divine, of a very hyper school indeed, who said, "Ah! blessed be the Lord, there are some of God's dear people here; I can tell them by the very look of their faces; I know that they are among God's elect." He was not half so discreet as Rowland Hill, who, when he was advised to preach to none but the elect, said, "He would certainly do so if some one would chalk them all on the back first." That was never attempted by anybody; so Rowland Hill went on preaching the gospel to every creature, as I desire to do. But you may find out whether you are among his chosen ones. "How?" says one. Why, Christ is the angel of the covenant, and you can find it out by looking to him. Many people want to know their election before they look to Christ. Beloved, you cannot know your election, except as you see it in Christ. If you want to know your election, thus shall you assure your hearts before God.—Do you feel yourself this morning to be a lost, guilty sinner? go straightway to the cross of Christ, and tell Christ that, and tell him that you have read in the Bible, "That him that cometh unto him he will in no wise cast out." Tell him that he has said, "This is a faithful saying and worthy of all acceptation, that Jesus Christ came into the world to save sinners, of whom you are chief." Look to Christ and believe on him, and you shall make proof of your election directly, for so surely as thou believest thou art elect. If thou wilt give thyself wholly up to Christ and trust him, then thou art one of God's chosen ones; but if you stop and say, "I want to know first whether I am elect," that is impossible. If there be something covered up, and I say, "Now, before you can see this you must lift the veil;" and you say, "Nay, but I want to see right through that veil," you cannot. Lift the veil first, and you shall see. Go to Christ, guilty, just as you are. Leave all curious inquiry about thy election alone. Go straight away to Christ, just as you are, black, naked, penniless and poor, and say,

"Nothing in my hands I bring,
Simply to thy cross I cling,"

and you shall know your election. The assurance of the Holy Spirit shall be given to you, so that you shall be able to say, "I know whom I have believed, and I am persuaded that he is able to keep that which I have committed to him." Now, do notice this. Christ was at the everlasting council: he can tell you whether you were chosen or not; but you cannot find that out anyhow else. You go and put your trust in him, and I know what the answer will be. His answer will be—"I have loved thee with an everlasting love, therefore in lovingkindness have I drawn thee." There will be no doubt about his having chosen *you*, when you shall feel no doubt about having chosen *him*.

So much for the second point. Christ is the Counsellor. He is the angel of the council, because he tells out God's secrets to us. "The secret of the Lord is with them that fear him, and he will show them his covenant."

III. The last point was, Christ is A COUNSELLOR TO US. And here I shall want to give some practical hints to God's people. Some how or other, brethren, it is not good for man to be alone. A lonely man must be, I think, a miserable man; and a man without a Counsellor, I think, must of necessity go wrong. "Where there is no counsellor," says Solomon, "the people fall." I think most persons will find it so. A man says, "Well, I'll have my own way, and I will ask nobody." Have it, sir,—have it—and you will find that in having your own way you have probably had the worst way you could. We all feel our need at times of a counsellor. David was a man after God's own heart and dealt much with his God; but he had his Ahithophel, with whom he took sweet counsel, and they walked to the house of God in company. Kings must have some advisers. Woe unto the man that hath got a bad counsellor. Rehoboam took counsel of the young men, and not of the old men, and they counselled him so that he lost ten-twelfths of his empire. Some take counsel of stocks and stones. We know many who counsel at the hands of foolish charms, instead of going to Christ. They shall have to learn that there is but one Christ, who is to be trusted; and that however necessary a counsellor may be, yet none other shall be found to fulfil the necessity, but Jesus Christ the Counsellor. Let me make a remark or two with regard to this Counsellor, Jesus Christ.

And, first, Christ is a *necessary Counsellor*. So sure as we do anything without asking counsel of God we fall into trouble. Israel made a league with Gibeon, and it is said, they took of their victuals, and they asked not counsel at the mouth of the Lord, and they found out that the Gibeonites had deceived them. If they had asked counsel first, no cunning deception could have imposed on them in the matter. Saul, the son of Kish, died before the Lord upon the mountains of Gilboa, and in the book of Chronicles it is written, he died because he asked not counsel of God, but sought unto the wizards. Joshua, the great commander, when he was appointed to succeed Moses, was not left to go alone, but it is written, "And Eliezer the priest shall be his counsellor, and he shall ask counsel of the Lord for him." And all the great men of olden times, when they were about to do an action, paused, and they said to the priest, "Bring hither the ephod," and he put on the Urim and the Thummim, and appealed to God, and the answer came, and sound advice was vouchsafed. You and I will have to learn how necessary it is always to take advice of God. Did you ever seek God's advice on your knees about a difficulty and then go amiss? Brethren, I can testify for my God that when I have submitted my will to his directing Spirit, I have always had reason to thank him for his wise counsel. But when I have asked at his hands, having already made up my own mind, I have had my own way; but like as he fed the Israelites with the quails of heaven, while the meat was yet in their mouth, the wrath of God came upon them. Let us take heed always that we never go before the cloud. He that goes before the cloud goes a fool's errand, and will be glad to get back again. An old puritan used to say, "He that carves for himself will cut his fingers. Leave God to carve for you in providence, and all shall be well. Seek God's guidance and nothing can go amiss." It is necessary counsel.

In the next place, Christ's counsel is *faithful counsel*. When Ahithophel left David, it proved that he was not faithful, and when Hushai went to Absalom and counselled him, he counselled him craftily, so that the good counsel of Ahithophel was brought to nought. Ah! how often do our friends counsel us craftily! We have known them do so. They have looked first to their own advantage, and then they have said, "If I can get him to do so-and-so it will be the best for me." That was not the question we asked them. It was what would be best for ourselves. But we may trust Christ, that in his advice to us there never can be any self-interest. He will be quite certain to advise us with the most disinterested motives, so that the good shall be to us, and the profit to ourselves.

Again, Christ's counsel is *hearty counsel*. I hate to go to a lawyer above all people, to talk with him upon matters of business. The worst kind of conversation is, I think, conversation with a lawyer. There is your case! Dear me, what an interest *you* feel in it! You spread it out before him, and he says, "There is a word upon the second page not quite correct." You look at it, and you say, "Ah! that is totally unimportant; that does not signify." He turns to another clause and he says, "Ah! there is a good deal here!" "My dear fellow," you say, "I do not care about those petty clauses, whether it says lands, properties, or hereditaments: what I want you to do is to set this difficulty right in point of law." "Be patient," he says; you must go through a great many consultations before he will come to the point, and all the while your poor heart is boiling over because you feel such an interest in the main point. But he is as cool as possible; you think you are asking counsel of a block of marble. No doubt his advice will come out all right at last, and it is pretty certain it will be good for you; but it is not hearty. He does not enter into the sympathies of the matter with you. What is it to him whether you succeed or not—whether the object of your heart shall be accomplished or not. It is but a professional interest he takes. Now, Solomon says, "As ointment for perfume, so is hearty counsel." When a man throws his own soul into your case, and says, "My dear friend, I'll do anything I can to help you; let me look at it," and he takes as deep an interest in it as you do yourself. "If I were in your position," he says, "I should do so-and-so; by-the-bye, there is a word wrong there." Perhaps he tells you so, but he only tells you because he is anxious to have it all right; and you can see that his drift is always towards the same end you are seeking, and that he is only anxious for your good. Oh! for a Counsellor that could tie your heart into unison with his own! Now Christ is such a Counsellor as that. He is a hearty Counsellor. His interests and your interests are bound up together, and he is hearty with you.

But there is another kind of counsel still. David says of one, who afterwards became his enemy, "We took sweet counsel together." Christian, do you know what sweet counsel is? You have gone to your Master in the day of trouble, and in the secret of your chamber you have poured out your heart before him. You have laid your case before him, with all its difficulties, as Hezekiah did Rabshakeh's letter, and you have felt, that though Christ was not there in flesh and blood, yet he was there in spirit, and he counselled you. You felt that his was counsel that came from the very heart. But he was something better than that. There was such a sweetness coming with his counsel, such a radiance of love, such a fulness of fellowship, that you said, "Oh that I were in trouble every day, if I might have such sweet counsel as this!" Christ is the Counsellor whom I desire to consult every hour, and I would that I could sit in his secret chamber all day and all night long, because to counsel with him is to have sweet counsel, hearty counsel, and wise counsel, all at the same time. Why, you may have a friend that talks very sweetly with you, and you will say, "Well, he is a kind, good soul, but I really cannot trust his judgment." You have another friend, who has a good deal of judgment, and yet you say of him, "Certainly, he is a man of prudence above a great many, but I cannot find out his sympathy; I never get at his heart; if he were ever so rough and untutored, I would sooner have his heart without his prudence, than his prudence without his heart." But we go to Christ, and we get wisdom; we get love, we get sympathy, we get everything that can possibly be wanted in a Counsellor.

And now we must close by noticing that Christ has special counsels for each of us this morning, and what are they? Tried child of God, your daughter is sick; your gold has melted in the fire; you are sick yourself, and your heart is sad. Christ counsels you, and he says, "Cast thy burden upon the Lord, he will sustain thee; he will never suffer the righteous to be moved." Young man, you that are seeking to be great in this world, Christ counsels you this morning. "Seekest thou great things for thyself? seek them not." I shall never forget Midsummer Common. I was ambitious; I was seeking to go to college, to leave my poor people in the wilderness that I might become something great; and as I was walking there that text came with power to my heart—"Seekest thou great things for thyself? seek them not." I suppose about forty pounds a year was the sum total of my income, and I was thinking how I should make both ends meet, and whether it would not be a great deal better for me to resign my charge and seek something for the bettering of myself, and so forth. But this text ran in my ears, "Seekest thou great things for thyself? seek them not." "Lord," said I, "I will follow thy counsel and not my own devices;" and I have never had cause to regret it. Always take the Lord for thy guide, and thou shalt never go amiss. Backslider! thou that hast a name to live, and art dead, or nearly dead, Christ gives thee counsel. "I counsel thee to buy of me, gold tried in the fire and white raiment, that thou mayest be clothed." And sinner! thou that art far from God, Christ gives thee counsel. "Come unto me, all ye that are weary and heavy laden, and I will give you rest," Depend on it, it is loving counsel. Take it. Go home and cast yourself upon your knees. Seek Christ; obey his counsel, and you shall have to rejoice that you ever listened to his voice, and heard it, and lived.

His Name—The Mighty God

"The mighty God"—Isaiah ix. 6.

OTHER translations of this divine title have been proposed by several very eminent and able scholars. Not that they have any of them been prepared to deny that this translation is after all most accurate; but rather that whilst there are various words in the original, which we render by the common appellation of "GOD," it might be possible so to interpret *this* as to show more exactly its definite meaning. One writer, for example, thinks the term might be translated "The Irradiator,"—he who gives light to men. Some think it bears the meaning of "The Illustrious,"—the bright and the shining one. Still there are very few, if any, who are prepared to dispute the fact that our translation is the most faithful that could possibly be given—"the mighty God."

The term here used for God, *El*, is taken from a Hebrew root, which, as I take it, signifies strength; and perhaps a literal translation even of that title might be, "The Strong one," the strong God. But there is added to this an adjective in the Hebrew, expressive of mightiness, and the two taken together express the omnipotence of Christ, his real deity and his omnipotence, as standing first and foremost among the attributes which the prophet beheld. "The mighty God." I do not propose this morning to enter into any argument in proof of the divinity of Christ, because my text does not seem to demand it of me. It does not say that Christ *shall be* "the mighty God,"—that is affirmed in many other places of Sacred writ; but here it says, "He shall be *called* Wonderful," *called* "Counsellor," *called*, "The mighty God;" and I think that therefore I may be excused from entering into any proof of the fact, if I am at least able to establish the truth of that which is here foretold, inasmuch as Christ is indeed called at this day, and shall be called to the end of the world, "the mighty God."

First, this morning, I shall speak for a moment on *the folly of those who profess to be his followers, but who do not call him "the mighty God."* In the second place I shall try to show *how the true believer practically calls Christ "the mighty God," in many of the acts which concern his salvation;* and then I shall close by noticing *how Jesus Christ has proved himself to be indeed "the mighty God" to us, and in the experience of his church.*

I. First let me point out THE FOLLY OF THOSE WHO PROFESS TO BE THE DISCIPLES OF CHRIST, YET DO NOT, AND WILL NOT, CALL HIM GOD. The question has sometimes been proposed to me, how it is that those of us who hold the divinity of Christ manifest what is called uncharitableness towards those who deny him. We do continually affirm that an error, with regard to the divinity of Christ, is absolutely fatal, and that a man cannot be right in his judgment upon any part of the gospel unless he think rightly of him who is *personally* the very centre of all the purposes of heaven, and the foundation of all the hopes of earth. Nor can we admit of any latitudinarianism here. We extend the right hand of fellowship to all those who love the Lord Jesus Christ in sincerity and truth; but we cannot exchange our Christian greetings with those who deny him to be "very God of very God." And the reason is sometimes asked; for say our opponents, "We are ready to give the right hand of fellowship to you, why don't you do so to us?" Our reply shall be given thus briefly: "You have no right to complain of us, seeing that in this matter we stand on the defensive. When you declare yourselves to believe that Christ is not the Son of God, you may not be conscious of it, but you have charged us with one of the blackest sins in the entire catalogue of crime." The Unitarians must, to be consistent, charge the whole of us, who worship Christ, with being idolators. Now idolatry is a sin of the most heinous character; it is not an offence against men it is true, but it is an intolerable offence against the majesty of God. We are ranked by Unitarians, if they be consistent, with the Hottentots. "No," say they, "we believe that you are sincere in your worship." So is the Hottentot; he bows down before his Fetich, his block of wood or stone, and he is an idolator; and although you charge us with bowing before a man, yet we do hold that you have laid at our door a sin insufferably gross, and we are obliged to repel your accusation with some severity. You have so insulted us by denying the Godhead of Christ, you have charged us with so great a crime, that you cannot expect us to sit coolly down and blandly smile at the imputation. It matters not what a man worships, if it be not God, he is an idolator. There is no distinction in principle between worship to a god of mud and a god of gold, nay further, there is no distinction between the worship of an onion and the worship of the sun, moon, and stars. These are alike idolatries. And though Christ be confessed by the Socinian to be the best of men, perfection's own self; yet if he be nothing more, the vast mass of the Christian world is deliberately assailed with the impudent accusation of being idolators. Yet those who charge us with idolatry, expect us to receive them with cordial kindness. It is not in flesh and blood for us to do so, if we take the low ground of reason; it is not in grace or truth to do so, if we take the high ground of revelation. As men, we are willing to shew them respect, we regard them, we pray for them, we have no anger or enmity against them. But when we come to the point of theology, we cannot as we profess to be followers of Christ, tamely see ourselves charged with an offence so dreadful and so heinous as that of idol worship.

I confess I would almost rather be charged with a religion that extenuated murder, than with one that justified idolatry. Murder, great as the offence is, is but the slaying of man; but idolatry is in its essence the killing of God; it is the attempt to thrust the Eternal Jehovah out of his seat, and to foist into his place the work of his own hand, or the creature of my own conceit. Shall a man charge me with being so besotted as to worship a mere man? Shall he tell me I am so low and grovelling in my intellect, that I should stoop down to worship my own fellow-creature? and yet does he expect me after that to receive him as a brother professing the same faith? I cannot understand his presumption. The charge against our sanctity of heart is so tremendous, the accusation is so frightful, that if there have been some severity and bitterness of temper in the controversy, the sin lies upon our opponent, and not on us. For he has charged us with a crime so dreadful, that an upright man must repel it as an insult. But to go further; if Jesus Christ be not a Divine person; if I could once imagine that he was no more than a mere man, I should prefer Mahomet to Christ; and if you ask me why, I think I could clearly prove to demonstration, that Mahomet was a greater prophet than Christ. If Jesus Christ be not the Son of God, co-equal, co-eternal with the Father, he so spake as to induce that belief in the minds of his own disciples, and of his adversaries likewise. Mahomet, with regard to the unity of the Godhead, is so clear and so distinct, that there is no Mahometan to this day, that has ever fallen into idolatry. You will find that throughout the whole of the Mahometan world the cry is still sternly uttered and faithfully believed, " There is but one God, and Mahomet is his prophet." Now, if Christ were but a good man and a prophet, why did he not speak more decisively? Why has he not left on record a war cry for the Christian, which would be as explicit and decisive as that of Mahomet? If Christ did not mean to teach that he himself is God, at least he was not very clear and definite in his denial and he has left his disciples extremely in the dark, the proof whereof is to be found in the fact, that at the present day, nine hundred and ninety-nine out of every thousand of the whole of the professed followers of Christ, do receive him, and bow down before him, as being the very God. And if he is not God, I deny his right to be esteemed as a prophet. If he is not God, he was an imposter, the grandest, the greatest of deceivers that ever existed. This, of course, is no argument to the man who denies the faith, and does not avow himself to be a follower of Christ. But to the man that is Christ's follower, I do hold that the argument is irresistible, that Christ could not have been a good and great prophet, if he were not what he certainly led us to believe himself to be, the Son of God, who thought it not robbery to be equal with God,—the very God, by whom all things were made, and without whom was not anything made that is made.

I will say yet another thing, which may startle the believer, but which is intended rather to reduce the heterodox doctrine of Christ not being God, to an absurdity. If Christ were not the Son of God, his death, so far from being a satisfaction for sin, was a death most richly and righteously deserved. The Sanhedrim before which He was tried was the recognised and authorised legislature of the country. He was brought before that Sanhedrim, charged with blasphemy, and it was upon that charge that they condemned him to die, because he made himself the Son of God. Now, I do not hesitate honestly to aver, that if I had been called on to plead in that case, I should have pleaded an avowal, and that moreover, I should have stood up, and said and felt, that I had a clear case before me, which nothing but lying and perjury could ever have put on one side, if Jesus of Nazareth had been charged with having declared himself to be the Son of God. Why, his whole preaching seemed to derive from thence it's unrivalled authority. There was continually in his actions and in his words, a claim to be something more than man ever could lay claim to. And when he was brought before the Sanhedrim, witnesses enough might have been found, to prove that he had made himself the Son of God; if he were not so, his condemnation for blasphemy was the justest sentence that ever was pronounced, and his crucifixion on Calvary, was absolutely the most righteous execution that ever was performed by the hand of the government. It is his being verily God, that frees him from the charge of blasphemy. It is the fact that he is God. and that his Godhead is not to be denied, that makes his death an unrighteous deicide at the hand of apostate man, and renders it, as before God, an acceptable sacrifice for the sins of all the people whom he redeemed with his most precious blood. But if he be not God, I do repeat, that there is no reason whatever, why we should have had a New Testament written; for there would be then nothing in the sublime central-fact of that New Testament but the righteous execution of one, who certainly deserved to die.

Do you remember, my dear friends, when the apostle Paul was preaching on the resurrection of the dead, in his letter to the Corinthians, how he uses an *ex post facto* argument, to show the natural consequences, if it were possible to overturn the truth? He says, "If Christ be not risen, then is our preaching vain, and your faith is also vain, and ye are yet in your sins." Now, I may fairly use the apostle's line of argument in reference to the Godhead and Sonship of Christ, of which his resurrection gave such a palpable demonstration: "If Christ be not the Son of God, then is our preaching vain, and your faith is also vain, and ye are yet in your sins:" all our visions of heaven are blasted and withered; the brightness of our hope is quenched for ever; that rock on which our trust is built, turns out to be nothing better than mere sand if the divinity of Christ be not proved. All the joy and consolation we ever had in this world, in our belief that his blood was sufficient to atone for sin, has been but a dream of fancy and a "figment of idle brains;" all the communion we have ever had with him has been but an illusion and a trance, and all the hopes we have of beholding his face in glory, and of being satisfied when we awake in his likeness, are but the foulest delusions that ever cheated the hopes of man. Oh, my brethren, and can any of you believe that the blood of all the martyrs has been shed as a witness to a lie? Have all those who have rotted in Roman dungeons, or have been burned at the stake because they witnessed that Christ was God, died in vain? Verily, if Christ be not God, we are of all men the most miserable. To what purpose is the calumny and abuse that we have had to endure day after day; to what purpose are our repentance, our sighs, our tears; to what purpose is our faith; to what purpose have our fears and bodings been supplanted by our hope and confidence; to what purpose our joy and our rejoicing, if Christ be not the Son of God? Will you put yourselves all down for fools; can you imagine that God's Word has misguided you; that prophets and apostles, and martyrs and saints, have all leagued together to lead you into a trap and to delude your souls? God forbid that we should think such a thing. There is no folly in the world that has in it so much as a doit of madness, compared with the folly of denying the divinity of Christ, and then professing to be his followers. No, beloved:

> "Let all the forms that men devise,
> Assault our faith with treacherous art;
> We'll call them vanity and lies,
> And bind the gospel to our heart!"—

We will write *this* on the forefront of our banner,—"Christ is God; co-equal and co-eternal with his Father: very God of very God, who counted it not robbery to be equal with God."

II. This brings me to the second part of the subject: How do we call Christ "the mighty God?" Here there is no dispute whatever; I am now about to speak of matters of pure fact. Whether Christ be mighty God or not, it is quite certain that we are in the constant habit of calling him so. Not, I mean, by the mere utterance of the term, but we do so in a stronger way—in fact;—and actions speak louder than words.

Now, beloved, I will soon prove that you and I are in the habit of calling Christ God. And I will prove it first, because it is our delight, and our joy and our privilege to attribute to him the attributes of Deity.

In hours of devout contemplation, how often do we look up to him as being *the Eternal Son*. You and I sit down in our chambers, and in our house of prayer, and as we muse upon the great covenant of grace, we are in the habit of speaking of our Lord Jesus Christ's everlasting love to his people. This is one of the jewels of our life, one of the ornaments with which we array ourselves as a bride doth. This is a part of the manna that tasteth like wafers made with honey, upon which our souls are wont to feed. We speak of God's eternal love, of our names having been inscribed in his eternal book, and of Christ's having borne them from before the foundation of the world upon his breast, as our great high-priest, our remembrancer before the throne of heaven. In so doing, we have virtually called him the mighty God; because none but God could have been from everlasting to everlasting. As often as we profess the doctrine of election, we call Christ the mighty God; as often as we talk of the eternal covenant, ordered in all things and sure, so often do we proclaim him to be God: because we speak of him as an everlasting one, and none could be from everlasting but one who is self-existent, who is God.

Again: how frequently do we repeat over to ourselves that precious verse, "Jesus Christ the same yesterday, and to-day, and for ever." We are always in the habit of ascribing to him *immutability*. Some of our choicest hymns are founded on that circumstance, and our richest hopes flow from that attribute. We know that all things will change. We are convinced that we ourselves are mutable as the winds, and as easily moved as the sand by the waves of the sea; but we know that our Redeemer liveth, and we cannot entertain a suspicion of any change in his love, his purpose, or his power. How often do we sing:—

> "Immutable his will,
> Though dark may be my frame,
> His loving heart is still
> Unchangeably the same.
> My soul through many changes goes:
> His love no variation knows!"

Do you not see that you have in fact called him God, because none but God is immutable? The creature changes. This is written on the forefront of creation— "Change!" The mighty ocean, that knows no furrows on its brow, changeth at times, and at times shifteth its level. It moveth hither and thither, and we know that it is to be licked up with forked tongues of flame, and yet we ascribe to Christ immutability. We do, then, in fact, ascribe to him, divinity; for, none but the divine can be immutable.

Is it not also our joy to believe that wherever two or three are gathered together in Christ's name, there is he in the midst of them? Do we not repeat it in all our prayer-meetings? Perhaps some minister in Australia began the solemnities of public worship this day with the reflection that Jesus Christ was with him, according to his promise, and I know that as I came here the same reflection comforted me, "Yea, I am with you alway even to the end of the world,"—that wherever a Christian is found, there God is. And though there be but two or three met in a barn, or on the greensward under the canopy of God's blue sky, yet there Christ vouchsafes his presence. Now I ask you, have we not ascribed to Christ, omnipresence; and who can be omnipotent but God? Have we not thus in fact then, though not in words, called Christ "God?" How is it possible for us to dream of Him as being here, and there, and everywhere; in the bosom of his Father, with the angels, and in the hearts of the contrite all at the same time, if he be not God? Grant me that he is omnipresent, and you have said that he is God, for none but God can be present everywhere. Again, are we not also wont to ascribe to Christ omniscience? You believe when your heart is aching that Christ knows your pains, and that he reckons every groan; or at least if *you* do not believe it, it is always *my* satisfaction to know that—

> "He feels at his heart,
> All my sighs and my groans."

And so he does yours. Wherever you are, you believe that he hears your prayers that he sees your tears, that he knows your wants, that he is ready to pardon your sins; that you are better known to him, than you are to yourself. You believe that he searches your hearts, and tries your reins, and that you never can come to him without finding him full of sympathy, and full of love. Now do you not see that you have ascribed omniscience to him; and therefore, though not in words, you have, in accents louder than words, called him the mighty God; for you have assumed that he is omniscient; and who can be omniscient but the very God of very God?

I shall not stop to descant upon the other attributes, but I think we might prove that we have each of us ascribed to Christ all the attributes of the Godhead in our daily life and in our constant trust and intercession. I am sure that it is true of many loving hearts of God's own children here. We have called him the mighty God, and if others have not called him so, nevertheless the text is verified by our faith. "He shall be called wonderful, counsellor, the mighty God." So he is, and so he shall be, world without end.

And now I have another proof to offer, that Christ is called "the mighty God." We call him so in many of his offices. We believe this morning that Christ is the mediator between God and man. If we would understand the term mediator or daysman, we must interpret it as Job did; one "that might lay his hand upon us both." We are accustomed to say that Jesus Christ is the mediator of the new covenant, and we offer our prayers to God through him, because we believe that he mediates between us and the Father. Let it once be granted then that Christ is the mediator, and you have asserted his divinity. You have virtually called him the Son of God; and you have granted his humanity, for he must put his hand upon both; therefore he must put his hand upon man in our nature; he must be touched with a feeling of our infirmities, and be in all points like as we are. But he is not a mediator unless he can put his hand upon God, unless as fellow of the Eternal One he shall be able without blasphemy to place his hand upon the divine Being. There is no mediatorship unless the hand is put on both, and who could put his hand on God but God? Can cherubim or seraphim talk of laying their hands on the Divine? Shall they touch the Infinite? "Dark with insufferable light his skirts appear"—then what is He Himself in the glorious Essence of Deity?—an all-devouring and consuming fire. Only God can put his hand on God, and yet Christ hath this high prerogative, for mark, there is no mediatorship established, there cannot be, unless the two are linked. If you wished to build a bridge you might commence on this side of the river, but if you have not connected it with the other side, you have not built the bridge. There can be no mediatorship unless the parties are fully linked. The ladder must have its feet on earth but it must reach to heaven, for if there were a single breach we should fall from its summit and perish. There must be entire communication between the two. Do you not see therefore that in calling Christ mediator we have in fact called him the mighty God.

But again, we call Christ our Saviour. Now, have any of you that foolish credulity which would lead you to trust in a man for the everlasting salvation of your soul? If you have, I pity you: your proper place is not in a Protestant assembly, but among the deluded votaries of Rome. If you can commit the keeping of your soul to one like yourself, I must indeed mourn over you, and pray that you may be taught better. But you do trust your salvation to him whom God hath set forth for a propitiation, do you not, O follower of Jesus? Can you not say all your hope is fixed on him, for he is all your salvation and all your desire? Does not your spirit rest on that unbuttressed pillar of his entire satisfaction, his precious death and burial, his glorious resurrection and ascension? Now, observe, you are either resting on man, or else you have declared Christ to be "the mighty God." When I say I put my faith in him, I do most honestly declare that I dare not trust even to him, if I did not believe him to be God. I could not put my trust in any being that was merely created. God forbid that my folly should ever go to such an extent as that. I would sooner trust myself than trust any other man, and yet I dare not trust myself, for I should be accursed. "Cursed is he that trusteth in man, and maketh flesh his arm." And would the Socinian have me to believe that I am to preach faith in Christ, and that yet, if my hearers trust Christ, they will be accursed, as they assuredly must be, if he is nothing but man, for, again I repeat it, "cursed is he that trusteth in man, and maketh flesh his arm." You get a blessing by faith in Jesus, but how? Is it not because—"Blessed is he that trusteth in the Lord, and whose hope the Lord is?" Christ is very Jehovah, and therefore the blessing comes to those who trust in him. So, then, as often as ye put your trust in Jesus, for time and eternity, ye have called him "the mighty God."

This subject is capable of the greatest expansion, and I do believe there is sufficient interest attaching to it to warrant me in keeping you to a late hour this day, but I shall not do so. There has been enough said, I think, to prove at least, that we are in the habit continually of calling Christ "the mighty God."

III. My third proposition is to explain to you HOW CHRIST HAS PROVED HIMSELF TO US TO BE "THE MIGHTY GOD." And here beloved, without controversy, great is the mystery of Godliness, for the passage from which the text is taken says, "Unto us a child is born." A child! what can that do? A child! it totters in its walk, it trembles in its steps—and it is a child newly born. Born! what an infant hanging on its mother's breast, an infant deriving its nourishment from a woman? That! can that work wonders? Yea, saith the prophet, "Unto us a child is born." But then it is added, "Unto us a Son is given." Christ was not only born, but given. As man he is a child born, as God he is the Son given. He comes down from on high; he is given by God to become our Redeemer. But here behold the wonder! "His name," this child's name, "shall be called Wonderful, Counsellor, the mighty God." Is this child, then, to us the mighty God? If so, O brethren, without controversy, great is the mystery of Godliness indeed! And yet, just let us look look through the history of the church, and discover whether we have not ample evidence to substantiate it. This child born, this Son given, came into the world to enter into the lists against sin. For thirty years and upwards he had to struggle and wrestle against temptations more numerous and more terrible than man had ever known before. Adam fell when but a woman tempted him; Eve fell when but a serpent offered fruit to her, but Christ, the second Adam, stood invulnerable against all the shafts of Satan though tempted he was in all points, like as we are. Not one arrow out of the quiver of hell was spared; the whole were shot against him. Every arrow was aimed against him with all the might of Satan's archers, and that is no little! And yet, without sin or taint of sin, more than conqueror he stood. Foot to foot with Satan, in the solitude of the wilderness; hand to hand with him on the top of the pinnacle of the temple; side by side with him in the midst of a busy crowd—yet ever more than conqueror. He gave him battle wherever the adversary willed to meet him, and at last, when Satan gathered up all his might, and seized the Saviour in the garden of Gethsemane, and crushed him till he sweat as it were great drops of blood, then when the Saviour said, "Nevertheless, not as I will but as thou wilt," the tempter was repulsed. "Hence! hence!" Christ seemed to say; and away the tempter fled, nor dare return again. Christ, in all his conquests over sin, does seem to me to have established his Godhead. I never heard of any other creature that could endure such temptation as this. Look at the angels in heaven; how temptation entered there I know not; but this I know, that Satan, the great archangel, sinned, and I know that he became the tempter to the rest of his companions, and drew with him a third part of the stars of heaven. Angels were but little tempted, some of them not tempted at all, and yet they fell. And then look at man; slight was his temptation, yet he fell. It is not in a creature to stand against temptation; he will yield, if the temptation be strong enough. But Christ stood, and it seems to me, that in his standing he proved Himself to have the omni-radiant purity, the immaculate holiness of Him before whom angels veil their faces, and cry, "Holy holy, holy, Lord God of Sabaoth."

But these proofs might appear insufficient, if he did not accomplish more than this. We know also that Christ proved himself to be the "mighty God" from the fact that at last all the sins of all his people were gathered upon his shoulders, and "he bare them in his own body on the tree." The heart of Christ became like a reservoir in the midst of mountains. All the tributary streams of iniquity, and every drop of the sins of his people, ran down and gathered into one vast lake, deep as hell, and shoreless as eternity. All these met, as it were, in Christ's heart, and yet he endured them all. With many a sign of human weakness, but with convincing signs of divine omnipotence, he took all our griefs and carried all our sorrows. The divinity within strengthened his manhood, and though wave after wave rolled over his head, till he sank in deep mire where there was no standing, and all God's waves and his billows had gone over him, yet did he lift up his head, and more than a conqueror, at length, he put the sins of his people to a public execution. They are dead. They have ceased to be; and, if they be sought for, they shall not be found any more for ever. Certainly if this be true, he is "the mighty God" indeed.

But he did more than this, he descended into the grave, and there he slept, fast fettered with the cold chains of death. But the appointed hour arrives—the sunlight of the third day gave the warning, and he snapped the bands of death as if they were but tow, and came forth to life as "the Lord of life and glory." His flesh did not see corruption, for he was not able to be holden by the bands of death. And who shall be the death of death, the plague of the grave, the destroyer of destruction, but God? Who but immortal life, who but the Self-existent, shall trample out the fires of hell; who, but he whose Being is eternal, without beginning, and without end, shall burst the shackles of the grave? He proved himself then, when he led captivity captive, and crushed death and ground his iron limbs to powder—he proved himself then to be the mighty God.

Oh, my soul, thou canst say, that he has proved himself in thy heart to be a mighty God. Sins, many hath he forgiven thee and relieved thy conscience of the keen sense of guilt, griefs inumerable hath he assuaged, temptations insurmountable hath he overcome; virtues once impossible hath he implanted, grace in its fulness hath he promised, and in its measure hath he given. My soul bears record that what has been done for me could never have been done by a mere man; and you would rise from your seats, I am sure, if it were needful, and say, "Yes, he that hath loved me, washed me from my sins, and made me what I am, must be God; none but God could do what he has done, could bear so patiently, could bless so lavishly, forgive so freely, enrich so infinitely. He is, he must be, we will crown him such—'The mighty God.'"

And, in conclusion, lest I weary you, permit me now to say, I beg and beseech of you all present, as God the Spirit shall help you, come and put your trust in Jesus Christ; he is "the mighty God." Oh, Christians, believe him more than ever; cast your troubles constantly on him; he is "the mighty God;" go to him in all your dilemmas, when the enemy cometh in like a flood, this mighty God shall make a way for your deliverance; take to him your griefs, this mighty God can alleviate them all; tell him your backslidings and sins, this mighty God shall blot them out. And, O sinners, ye that feel your need of a Saviour, come to Christ and trust him for he is "the mighty God." Go to your houses, and fall on your knees and confess your sins, and then cast your poor, guilty, helpless, naked, defenceless souls before his omnipotence, for he is able to save unto the uttermost them that come unto God by him, because when he died he was not manhood, without divinity, but he was "the mighty God." This, I say, we will write on our banners, from this day forth and for ever; this shall be our joy and our song—the child born and the son given is to us "the mighty God."

His Name—The Everlasting Father

"The everlasting Father"—Isaiah ix. 6.

How complex is the person of our Lord Jesus Christ! Almost in the same breath the prophet calls him a "child," and a "counsellor," a "son," and "the everlasting Father." This is no contradiction, and to us scarcely a paradox, but it is a mighty marvel that he who was an infant should at the same time be infinite, he who was the Man of Sorrows should also be God over all, blessed for ever; and that he who is in the Divine Trinity always called the Son, should nevertheless be correctly called "the everlasting Father." How forcibly this should remind us of the necessity of carefully studying and rightly understanding the person of our Lord Jesus Christ! We must not suppose that we shall understand him at a glance. A look will save the soul, but patient meditation alone can fill the mind with the knowledge of the Saviour. Glorious mysteries are hidden in his person. He speaks to us in plainest language, and he manifests himself openly in our midst, but yet in his person itself there is a height and depth which human intellect fails to measure. When he has looked long and steadily the devout observer perceives in his Well-beloved beauties so rare and ravishing that he is lost in wonder; continued contemplation conducts the soul, by the power of the Holy Spirit, into an elevation of delighted admiration which the less thoughtful know nothing of. So deep is the mystery of the person of our Lord that he must reveal himself to us or we shall never know him. He is not discovered by research nor discerned by reason. "Blessed art thou, Simon Barjonas," said Christ to Peter, "for flesh and blood hath not revealed this unto thee." "When it pleased God," says the apostle, "to reveal his Son in me." Another apostle asked the question, "How is it that *thou* dost manifest thyself unto us?" There is no seeing Jesus except by his own light. He is the door, but no man openeth that door but Jesus himself; for "*he* openeth, and no man shutteth; he shutteth, and no man openeth." He is the lesson, but he is also the schoolmaster. He is both key and lock, answer and riddle, way and guide. He is that which is to be seen, for we are to look unto him; but it is by him that we are enabled to see, for he giveth sight to the blind. Let us then, dear friends, if we really desire to understand that most excellent of all sciences, the science of Christ crucified, entreat the Lord himself to be our Rabbi, and beg to be allowed to sit with Mary at the Master's feet. Be this our prayer, that "we may know him;" and be this our desire, that "we may grow in grace and in the knowledge of our Lord and Saviour Jesus Christ;" for "to know him is life eternal," and to be taught of him is to be "wise unto salvation."

The title before us is a somewhat difficult one. Some years ago I preached to you from "His Name—Wonderful." I felt I could expatiate upon that with ease. We advanced as far as "Counsellor," and then we halted a while. After a time we were led to preach upon "The Mighty God;" but we have been somewhat diffident of our ability to open up this particular title, for there is a depth in it which we are not able to fathom. This morning I cannot pretend to dive into the profound depths of the word, but can only skim the surface as the swallow skims the sea. Silver of deep learning and gold of profound thought have I none; but such as I have, give I you. If my basket contains nothing more than a barley loaf and a few small fishes, may the Master of the feast multiply the food in the breaking, that there may be food convenient for his people.

It is necessary at the outset to observe that the Messiah is not here called "Father," by way of any confusion with him who is pre-eminently called "THE FATHER." Our Lord's proper name, so far as Godhead is concerned, is not the Father, but the Son. Let us beware of confusion. The Son is not the Father, neither is the Father the Son; and though they be one God, essentially and eternally, being for evermore one and indivisible, yet still the distinction of persons is to be carefully believed and observed. For the mere word "Persons" we do not contend; it is but a make-shift word, although we know not what better term to use; but the fact is all-important that the Father is not the Son, and the Son is not the Father. Our text has no bearing upon the position and titles of the three Persons with regard to each other; it does not indicate the relation of Deity to itself, but the relation of Jesus Christ to us. He is *to us* "the everlasting Father."

The light of the text divides itself into three rays:—Jesus is "*Everlasting;*" he is a "*Father;*" he is the "*Everlasting Father.*"

I. First, Jesus Christ is EVERLASTING. Of him we may sing with David, "Thy throne, O God, is for ever and ever." A theme for great rejoicing on our part. Rejoice, believer, in Jesus Christ, the same yesterday, to-day, and for ever.

Jesus always *was*. The Babe born in Bethlehem was united to the Word, which was in the beginning, by whom all things were made. The title by which Jesus Christ revealed himself to John in Patmos was, "Him which is, and which was, and which is to come." "His head and his hairs were white like wool, as white as snow," to betoken that he is the Ancient of Days.

> "Ere sin was born, or Satan fell,
> He led the host of morning stars;
> (Thy generation who can tell,
> Or count the number of thy years?)"

In his priesthood, Jesus, like unto Melchisedec, "has neither beginning of days nor end of life." His pedigree is thus declared by Solomon:— "When there were no depths, I was brought forth; when there were no fountains abounding with water. Before the mountains were settled, before the hills was I brought forth; while as yet he had not made the earth, nor the fields, nor the highest part of the dust of the world. When he prepared the heavens, I was there: when he set a compass upon the face of the depth: when he established the clouds above: when he strengthened the fountains of the deep: when he gave to the sea his decree, that the waters should not pass his commandment: when he appointed the foundations of the earth: then I was by him, as one brought up with him: and I was daily his delight, rejoicing always before him; rejoicing in the habitable part of his earth; and my delights were with the sons of men." Think not that the Son of God ever commenced to be.

> "Ere the blue heavens were stretch'd abroad,
> From everlasting was the Word;
> With God he was; the Word was God,
> And must divinely be adored."

If he were not God from everlasting, we could not so devoutly love him; we could not feel that he had any share in the eternal love which is the fountain of all covenant blessings. He must be eternal who has a part in the eternal purpose. Since our Redeemer was from all eternity with the Father, we trace the stream of divine love to himself equally with his Father and the blessed Spirit. We were chosen in him from before the foundation of the world, and thus in our eternal election he shines forth gloriously. We bless and praise, and magnify him that the name "Son" does not at all import any time of birth or generation, or of beginning, but we know that he is as eternally the Son as the Father is eternally the Father, and must be looked upon as God from everlasting. For he is "the image of the invisible God, the firstborn of every creature : for by him were all things created, that are in heaven, and that are in earth, visible and invisible, whether they be thrones, or dominions, or principalities, or powers : all things were created by him and for him : and he is before all things, and by him all things consist."

As our Lord always *was*, so also he *is* for evermore the same. Jesus is not dead; he ever liveth to make intercession for us. He has not ceased to be; he hath gone out of sight; but he sits at the right hand of the Father. Of him we read, "And, Thou, Lord, in the beginning hast laid the foundation of the earth; and the heavens are the works of thine hands : they shall perish; but thou remainest; and they all shall wax old as doth a garment; and as a vesture shalt thou fold them up, and they shall be changed: but thou art the same, and thy years shall not fail." Jesus is as truly the I AM, as that Jehovah who spoke out of the burning bush to Moses, at Horeb. *He lives! He lives!* This is the foundation of your comfort, "Because he lives you shall live also." "Seeing then that we have a great high priest, that is passed into the heavens, Jesus the Son of God, let us hold fast our profession. For we have not an high priest which cannot be touched with the feeling of our infirmities; but was in all points tempted like as we are, yet without sin. Let us therefore come boldly unto the throne of grace, that we may obtain mercy, and find grace to help in time of need." Resort to him in all your times of need, for he is waiting to bless you still. He is made higher than the heavens, but he still receiveth sinners, and effectually puts away their sins; and since "he ever liveth to make intercession for them, he is able to save unto the uttermost them that come unto God by him."

Jesus, our Lord, ever *shall be*. He could not be called everlasting if it were supposable that he must one day cease to exist. No, believer; if God shall spare your life to fulfil your full day of threescore years and ten, you shall find that his cleansing fountain is still opened and his precious blood has not lost its power; you shall find that the Priest who filled the healing fount with his own blood still lives to purge you from all iniquity. When only your last battle remains to be fought, you shall find that the hand of your conquering Captain has not grown feeble, nor his arm waxed short; the living Saviour shall cheer the living saint. Nor is this all, for when death has taken you away as with a flood, and all the men of your generation have fallen like grass beneath the mower's scythe, Jesus shall live, and you, caught up to heaven, shall find him there bearing the dew of his youth; and when the sun's burning eye shall be dim with age, and the lamps of heaven shall be paled into eternal midnight, when all this world shall melt as melts the winter's ice at the approach of spring; then shall you find the Lord Jesus still remain the perennial spring of joy, and life, and glory to his people. Living waters may you draw from this sacred well! Jesus always was, he always is, he always shall be. He is eternal in all his attributes, and in all his offices, and in all his might, and power, and wilingness to bless, comfort, guard, and crown his chosen people.

The connection of the word "Father" with the word "everlasting" allows us very fairly to remark that our Lord is as everlasting as the Father, since he himself is called "the everlasting Father;" for whatever antiquity paternity may imply is here ascribed to Christ. According to our common notions, of course, the Father must be before the Son, but we must understand that the terms used in Scripture to represent Deity to us are not intended to be literally understood, and rendered in their exact terrestrial sense; they are only so far descriptive as they may be but do not compass the whole truth, for human language utterly fails to convey the very essence and fulness of celestial things. When God condescends to speak to men, who are but as infants before him, he adopts their childish speech, and brings down his loftiness of thought to the littleness of their capacities. Babes have no words for the thoughts of senators and philosophers, and such matters must be stated in childish language if babes are to know them, and then the statement must inevitably fall far short of the great fact. The relation between the Father and the Son is a case in point; it is not precisely the same as the relation between a father and a son on earth, but that happens to be the nearest approach to it among men. We must beware of stretching and straining the word in its letter, especially in points where it would make us err from the spirit of the truth. Christ Jesus is as eternal as the Father, or he would never have been called "the everlasting Father."

It is the manner of the Easterns to call a man the father of a quality for which he is remarkable. To this day, among the Arabs, a wise man is called "the father of wisdom;" a very foolish man "the father of folly." The predominant quality in the man is ascribed to him as though it were his child, and he the father of it. Now, the Messiah is here called in the Hebrew "the Father of eternity," by which is meant that he is pre-eminently the possessor of eternity as an attribute. Just as the idiom, "the father of wisdom," implies that a man is pre-eminently wise, so the term, "Father of eternity," implies that Jesus is pre-eminently eternal; that to him, beyond and above all others, eternity may be ascribed. No language can more forcibly convey to our minds the eternity of our Lord Jesus. Nay, without straining the language, I may say that not only is eternity ascribed to Christ, but he is here declared to be the parent of it. Imagination cannot grasp this, for eternity is a thing beyond us; yet if eternity should seem to be a thing which can have no parent, be it remembered that Jesus is so surely and essentially eternal, that he is here pictured as the source and Father of eternity. Jesus is not the child of eternity, but the Father of it. Eternity did not bring him forth from its mighty bowels, but he brought forth eternity. Independent, self-sustained, uncreated, eternal existence is with Jesus our Lord and God.

In the highest possible sense, then, Jesus Christ is "the everlasting Father." I will only pause one minute to draw a practical inference from this doctrine. If our Immanuel be indeed then eternal and ever living, let us never think of him as of one dead, whom we have lost, who has ceased to be. What could be a greater sorrow than the thought of a dead Christ? He *lives*, and lives to care for us. He lives in all the attributes which adorned him upon earth, as gentle and kind and gracious now as he was then. Come to him, Christian, rest upon him now, just as if he were visible in this place, and you could tell into his ear your troubles, and confess your sins at his feet. He is here spiritually; your eyes cannot see him, but faith will be better evidence to you than eyesight. Trust him now with your cares! Rest upon him in your present difficulties! And thou, poor sinner, if Christ were on this platform wouldst thou not come and touch the hem of his garment, and cry, "Jesus, let thy pitying eye look on me and change my heart"? Well, dear friend, Jesus lives; he is the same to-day as he was in the streets of Jerusalem; and though your feet cannot bear you to him, yet your desires shall serve you instead of feet; and though your finger cannot touch him, your confidence shall be instead of a hand to you. Trust him now! He whose love made him die lives on. His precious blood can never lose its power. Come ye now, humbly come, and confide in "the everlasting Father."

II. We come, in the second place, to the difficult part of the subject; namely, Christ being called FATHER.

In what sense is Jesus a Father? Answer, first. He is *federally* a Father representing those who are in him, as the head of a tribe represents his descendants. The apostle Paul comes to our help here, for in the memorable chapter in the Corinthians, he speaks of those who are in Adam, and then he talks of a second Adam. Adam is the father of all living; he federally stood for us in the garden, and federally fell and ruined us all. He was the representative man by whose obedience we should have been blessed, through whose disobedience we have been made sinners. The curse of the fall comes upon us because Adam stood in a relation towards us in which none of us stand towards our fellows. He was the representative head for us; and what a fall was there when he fell! for every one of us in his loins fell in him. "In Adam all die." Since his day there has been but one other father to the human race federally. It is true, Noah was the father of the present race of men, for we have all sprung of him; but there was no covenant with Noah in which he represented his posterity, no condition of obedience by which he might have obtained a reward for us, and no condition of disobedience for the breach of which we are called to smart. The only other man who is a representative man before God is the second Adam, the man Christ Jesus, the Lord from heaven. Brothers and sisters, we call Adam father mournfully, for we are cast out of Eden by him, and we till the ground with the sweat of our face; in sorrow did our mothers bring us forth, and to the grave in sorrow must we go; but we who have believed in Jesus call another man father, namely, the Lord Jesus; and we speak this not sorrowfully but joyfully, for he has opened the gates of a better Paradise; he has taken away the sweat of toil from our faces spiritually, for we who have believed do " enter into rest;" he has borne himself the pangs which were brought upon us by sin, he took our sicknesses and bore our sorrows; while death itself, the heaviest affliction, he has overcome, so that he that liveth and believeth in him shall never die, but pass out of this world into the life celestial.

The grand question for us is this, Are we still under the old covenant of works? If so, we have Adam to our father, and under that Adam we died. But are we under the covenant of grace? If so, we have Christ to our Father, and in Christ shall we be made alive. Generation makes us the sons of Adam; regeneration acknowledges us as the sons of Christ. In our first birth we come under the fatherhood of the fallen one; in our second birth we enter into the fatherhood of the innocent and perfect One. In our first fatherhood we wear the image of the earthy; in the second we receive the image of the heavenly. Through our relation to Adam we become corrupt and weak, and the body is put into the grave in dishonour, in corruption, in weakness, in shame; but when we come under the dominion of the second Adam we receive strength, and quickening, and inward spiritual life, and therefore our body rises again like seed sown which rises to a glorious harvest in the image of the heavenly, with honour, and power, and happiness, and eternal life.

In this sense, then, Christ is called Father; and inasmuch as the covenant of grace is older than the covenant of works, Christ is, while Adam is not, " the everlasting Father;" and inasmuch as the covenant of works as far as we are concerned passes away, being fulfilled in him, and the covenant of grace never passes but abideth for ever, Christ, as the head of the new covenant, the federal representative of the great economy of grace, is " the everlasting Father." Secondly, Christ is a Father in the sense of a *Founder*. You know, perhaps, or at least you readily remember when I remind you, that the Hebrews are in the habit of calling a man a father of a thing which he invents. For instance, in the fourth chapter of Genesis, Jubal is called the father of such as handle the harp and organ; Jabal was the father of such as dwell in tents, and have cattle; not that these were literally the fathers of such persons, but the inventors of their occupations. Jabal first took upon himself a nomadic tent life, and set the example of wandering about with flocks and herds; and Jubal first put his fingers to musical strings, and his lips to pipes from which the wind is breathed melodiously. The Lord Jesus Christ is in this sense the Father of a wonderful system. Now, our Lord Jesus Christ, who brought life and immortality to light, and introduced a new phase of worship to this world is, in that respect, a Father; he is the Father of all Christians, the Father of Christianity, the Father of the entire system under which grace reigns through righteousness. Jesus is the Father of a great *doctrinal* system. All the great truths which we are in the habit of delivering in your hearing as the precious truths of God sent down from heaven fell first, clearly and powerfully, from the lips of Jesus. These things were dimly hinted at in the ceremonies of the law, but Christ first of all put them into plain letter so that he who runs may read. Practically it is Jesus who teaches us the doctrine of electing love; it is Christ who reveals to us redemption by blood; it is Christ that reveals regeneration by the work of the Spirit, saying plainly, "Ye must be born again." It is Christ that reveals the perseverance of the saints. In fact, there is no doctrine of the Christian system which is not so clearly set in the light of his own glorious Spirit by his teaching that we may not fairly call him the Father of it.

Our great Master is also the Father of a great *practical* system. If there be any in the world who "love their neighbours as themselves," the Man of Nazareth is their Father; for, albeit that the law signified all that, yet men had not discovered it, but had misread the law. "Eye for eye and tooth for tooth" was their version of law; but Christ comes and says, "I say unto you, Resist not evil; if any man smite you on the one cheek, turn to him the other also." If any man can suffer with patience and can return good for evil, heaping coals of fire upon the head of his foes, this man is a child of Christ. If men worship God in the spirit and have no confidence in the flesh, if they know no holy place, but recognize every place as holy where a holy man is found, such are the true children of Christ, for he said, "They that worship God must worship him in spirit and in truth." He is the Father of spiritual worship. It has been common to call Socrates the "father of philosophy;" Jesus is Father of the philosophy of salvation; Galen, the "father of medicine," Jesus is Father of the medicine of souls; Herodotus, "father of history;" but Jesus is the Father of heaven on earth. He is the Father of disinterested living, of true love to men; he is the Father of forgiving one's enemies; the Father, in fact, of the divine system of Christian life.

The system of salvation claims Christ to be its Father. Who ever said, "By grace are ye saved through faith, and that not of yourselves, it is the gift of God"? Who but the apostle of this man, Christ Jesus? Who told men that it was not by works of righteousness which they had done, but by the merit of his passion and his life that they were saved? Who revealed the way of faith to men but Christ, the great doctrine of "Believe and live"? and those who receive it may claim Christ as Father. He is the Father of the Christian faith—a faith, my brethren, which, albeit that it has done much already for the world, for in old Rome it put down the fights in the Coliseum, threw down the bestial gods of heathendom, and albeit that it is doing much for the world even now, and helping to purge the vast Augean stable of humanity, is to do more still; it is to cast out war, it is to destroy error, it is to regenerate the human race. The Father of this purifying system which is doctrinal and practical, and which has already worked the best results to men, is the Lord Jesus, and since it was devised of old, and will be prolonged as long as the world standeth, he is called "the everlasting Father."

Now, there is a third meaning. The prophet may not so have understood it, but we so receive it, that Jesus is, in the third place, a Father in the great sense of a *Life Giver*. That is the main sense of "father" to the common mind. Through our fathers we are called into this world. Now it is by Christ that there is a communication of divine energy to the soul, it is through him, through his teaching, through the Spirit that he hath given, through the blood that he hath shed, that life is given to those who were dead in trespasses and sins. He that sitteth upon the throne saith, "Behold, I make all things new." "If any man be in Christ, he is a new creature; old things have passed away; behold, all things have become new." "This is the record, that God hath given to us eternal life, and this life is in his Son." "For as the Father raiseth up the dead, and quickeneth them; even so the Son quickeneth whom he will. Verily, verily, I say unto you, The hour is coming, and now is, when the dead shall hear the voice of the Son of God; and they that hear shall live. For as the Father hath life in himself; so hath he given to the Son to have life in himself." We know that through Jesus Christ the divine life is given to us. "In him was life, and the life was the light of men." He gives the living water, and then it is in us "a well of water springing up into everlasting life." He is that living grain of wheat which was cast into the ground to die, that it might not abide alone, but become a root that bringeth forth fruit, which fruit we now are, receiving life from him as the stem receives life from the seed from which it sprang. Jesus is our Father in that sense. It is the Spirit of God who operatively quickens the soul and makes us live, but Jesus Christ's gospel is the channel through which the Spirit works, and Jesus Christ is the true life to us. Receiving Christ we receive life, and without him we cannot have life. "He that hath the Son hath life; he that hath not the Son shall not see life, but the wrath of God abideth on him." As through the energy of Adam this vast world is peopled till hill and dale are covered with a teeming population, so through the life-energy of our Lord Jesus Christ the plains of heaven and the celestial hills shall be peopled with a throng that no man can number. Out of every realm, and people, speaking every language, having been bronzed by the heats of the torrid zone, or frozen amidst the frosts of the frigid north, Christ shall find a people into whom his quickening shall come, and they shall live through the energy of his Spirit, and he shall be their everlasting Father. It is in this sense, because that life is everlasting and can never die out, that Jesus Christ is called "the everlasting Father."

Everything in us calls Christ "Father." He is the author and finisher of our faith. If we love him, it is because he first loved us. If we patiently endure, it is by considering "him who endured such contradiction of sinners against himself." He it is who waters and sustains all our graces. We may say of him, "All my fresh springs are in thee." The Spirit brings us the water from this well of Bethlehem, but Jesus is the well itself. Spring up, O Well! Spring up, O Well! Divine Father, blessed Jesus, prove thy Fatherhood by re-quickening our souls this morning according to thy word!

4. Fourthly, I do not think that we have yet come to the bottom of this title of "Everlasting Father." The term implies that Jesus Christ is to be in the future, *the Patriarch of an age.* Many translators render the

passage, "the Father of the future age." So Pope in his famous Poem of the Messiah understands it, and calls him, "The promised Father of the future age." It has been the custom with men to speak of ages as "the age of brass or iron," and "the age of gold." This age of gold we are always looking for; the world's face is constantly turned to it; so much so that quacks play upon the simplicity of men and tell them when this golden age is coming, and fleece them of their pence, and sometimes of their pounds, under the notion that they can tell them somewhat about the good times which are coming. They know nothing about it whatever; they are blind leaders of the blind: but this one thing is clear to every one who cares to see it, namely, that such an age of gold *shall* come, that a period brighter far than fancy paints will dawn upon this poor, darkened, enslaved world. I am always jealous with a godly jealousy lest you should forget this doctrine, or throw it up in disgust, because of the shameful way in which it is made merchandize of by others. Brethren, calculate no dates, sit down to devise no charts, but in your heart be satisfied with this, that *there will be* a kingdom and a reign, and that in that kingdom there shall be no strife to vex the nations, there shall be no affliction to grieve the people; in that kingdom Jesus, the King, shall be conspicuous, and his refulgent glory shall be the light of all the inhabitants; it shall be a New Jerusalem coming down from heaven, prepared by God, as a bride is prepared for her husband, worthy of her Lord, and a meet recompense for the crown of thorns, for the flagellation of his shoulders, for the shame, the spitting, and the cross. High lift the cross, my brethren, for it *shall* be lifted high. Speak not of Christ with bated breath, for he comes to be a King. Ye Christians, think not yourselves, though despised and rejected of men, to be men of a mean birth, for "it doth not yet appear what you shall be; but we know that when he shall appear ye shall be like him, for ye shall see him as he is." Joyfully drink the cup of bitterness, for you shall soon drink the wines on the lees well refined; cheerfully pass through the darkness, for the morning breaketh, and the day dawneth, and the shadows flee away. Be content to be the offscouring of all things, for one day, when kings shall bow down before *him*, and all nations shall call him blessed, you shall partake in his honour, and shall be as princes upon the throne with him. Yes, he is to be the Father of a future age. Men have called certain great patriots the fathers of their country. To-day let us call Christ the Father of our world. O Jesus, thou hast given to earth far better than a creation. Thou hast not only formed it from chaos into order, and then brought it from darkness into light, and then from death into warm life and beauty, but thou hast recovered it from worse than pristine chaos, and saved it from a darkness worse than the primeval gloom, and a death more horrible than the primeval shades. Thou hast descended into the depths into which this pearl, the world, was cast, and like a mighty diver all the waves and billows have gone over thee, but thou hast come up again bringing this pearl with thee, and it shall glisten in thy crown for ever when thou shalt be admired of angels and adored of all created spirits. This shall be the sweetest part of their admiration and their adoration, thou wast slain and hast redeemed *us* unto God by thy blood, and therefore unto thee be glory for ever and ever. He shall be in this sense, then, the Father of an everlasting age.

5. Once more—for the text is very prolific—Christ may be called a Father *in the loving and tender sense of a Father's office.* Here is a text to show what I mean. God is called the Father of the fatherless, and Job, I think, says of himself, that he became a father to the poor. You know what it means, of course, at once; it means that he exercised a father's part. Now, albeit that the Spirit of adoption teaches us to call God our Father, yet it is not straining truth to say that our Lord Jesus Christ exercises to all his people a Father's part. According to the old Jewish custom the elder brother was the father of the family in the absence of the father; the firstborn took precedence of all, and took upon him the father's position; so the Lord Jesus, the firstborn among many brethren, exercises to us a Father's office. Is it not so? Has he not succoured us in all time of our need as a father succours his child? Has he not supplied us with more than heavenly bread as a father gives bread unto his children? Does he not daily protect us, nay, did he not yield up his life that we his little ones might be preserved? Will he not say at the last, " Here am I, and the children that thou hast given me; I have lost none"? Does he not chastise us by hiding himself from us, as a father chasteneth his children? Do we not find him instructing us by his Spirit and leading us into all truth? Has he not told us to call no man father upon earth in the sense that he is to be our true guide and instructor, and we are to sit at his feet and make him our Rabbi and our authoritative Teacher? Is he not the head in the household to us on earth, abiding with us, and has he not said, "I will not leave you orphans (that is the Greek word); I will come unto you"? As if his coming was the coming of a Father. If he be a Father, will we not give him honour? If he be the head of the household, will we not give him obedience, and say in our hearts, "Other lords have had dominion over us, but henceforth, thou everlasting Father, we will give thee reverence." If he be in all these senses " the everlasting Father,"

" Then let us adore, and give him his right,
 All glory and power, and wisdom and might,
All honour and blessing, with angels above,
 And thanks never-ceasing, for infinite love."

III. Lastly, we weigh the words, "EVERLASTING FATHER." I have already explained what this means. Christ is called " the everlasting Father " because he does not himself, as a Father, die or vacate his office. He is still the Federal Head and Father of his people; still the Founder of gospel truth and of the Christian system; not allowing archbishops and popes to be his vicars and to take his place. He is still the true Life-giver, from whose wounds and by whose death we are quickened; he reigns even now as the patriarchal King; he is still the loving family Head; and so, in every sense, *he lives as a Father.* But here is a sweet thought. He neither himself dies, nor becomes childless. *He does not lose his children.* If his church could perish, he would not be the Father. How a Father without a son? And this is the best of all, that he is " an everlasting Father " to all those to whom he is a Father at all. If thou hast entered into this relationship so as to be in union with Christ, and to be covered with the skirts of his garment, thou art his child, and thou shalt for ever be. There is no unfathering Christ, and there is no unchilding us. He is everlastingly a Father to those who trust in him, and he never does at any one moment cease to be a

Father to any one of these. This morning you may have come here in trouble, but Christ is still your Father. This day you may be much depressed in spirit and full of doubts and fears; but a true father never ceases, if he be a father, to exercise his kindness to a child; nor does Jesus cease to love and pity you. He will help you. Go to him, and you shall find that loving Friend to be as tender as in the days of his flesh.

He is *the author of an eternal system.* As I glanced at the words "everlasting Father," and thought of him as the Founder of an everliving system, I said to myself, "Ah then, the Christian religion will never die out!" It is not possible that the truth as it is in Jesus should ever be put away if he is "the everlasting Father." I feel as if I could quote again Master Hugh Latimer, when, standing back to back with Ridley, "Courage, Master Ridley," said he, "we shall this day light such a candle in England as shall never be put out." Look yonder at Christ on the cross! He did that day light such a candle as never can be put out. He is "the everlasting Father." He set rolling that day as it were a snow-flake of truth as he died upon the cross; and you know what the snow-flake does upon the high Alps; a bird's wing perhaps sets it rolling, and it gathers another and another and another, till, as it descends, it becomes a mass of snow; and by-and-bye as it leaps from crag to crag, it grows greater and greater and greater, until ponderous masses of ice and snow cohere together, and at the last, with an awful thundering crash the avalanche rolls down, fills the valley, and sweeps all before it; even so this Everlasting Father on the cross set in motion a mighty force which has gone on swelling and increasing, gathering to be a ponderous mass of mighty teaching, and the day shall come when, like an irresistible avalanche it shall fall upon the palaces of the Vatican and upon the towers of Rome, when the mosques of Mahomet and the temples of the gods shall be crushed beneath its stupendous weight, and the Everlasting Father shall have done the deed.

"The everlasting Father," last of all, because he is the Father, in all his people, of eternal life. Adam, thou art a father, but where are thy sons? If thou couldst return to earth, O Mother Eve! where wouldst thou find thy children? Methinks I see her as she paces round the earth and finds nothing but little grassy mounds, heaps of turf, and sometimes a valley sodden blood red where her children have been slain in battle. I hear her weeping for her children; she will not be comforted because they are not! But hush, Mother Eve, what life didst thou give them? What life was that which Father Adam conferred upon thy sons and daughters? Why, only life terrestrial, a bubble life, that melted and disappeared. But Jesus as he comes again will find none of his children dead, none of his sons and daughters lost; because he lives they live also, for he is the everlasting Father, and makes those to have everlasting life who live and breathe through him. Thrice happy they who have an interest in the truth of our text!

Now, dear hearers, may I ask you whether Christ is an everlasting Father to you? There are other fathers. The Jew said, "We have *Abraham* to our father," and to this day certain divines teach that we have covenant rights because of our earthly fathers. They believe in the Abrahamic covenant much after the manner of the Jews. "We have Abraham to our father;" therefore we have a right to baptism, therefore we are church members; "born into the church." Yes, I have heard it said, "born into the church." Let no man deceive you; this is not Christ's teaching. "Ye must be born again." If not, though your mother were a saint in heaven, and your father an undoubted apostle of God, you should derive no advantage, but a world of solemn responsibility from the fact, except you be yourself born again. Do not then say unto yourself, "we have Abraham to our father," for God is able of the very stones to raise up children unto Abraham. We had a very remarkable instance not very long ago in this Tabernacle, of how God does sometimes bless the outcasts and leaves some of you, the children of godly parents, in the hardness of your heart to perish. There was a man known in the village where he lives by the name of Satan, because of his being so thoroughly depraved. He was a sailor, and as another sailor in that town had been the means of the conversion of all the sailors in a vessel that left the town, this man desired to sail with him to try and beat his religion out of him. He did his best, but he signally failed; and as they happened to be coming to London, his friend asked him whether he would come to the Tabernacle. He did not mind coming to hear me, for as it happened, I was brought up near the place where he lived. This Satan came here on the Lord's day morning, when the text was upon soul murder, and he sat (some of you noticed him that day), and sobbed and cried under the sermon at such a broken-hearted rate that he could only say, "People are noticing me, I had better go out;" but his companion would not let him go out, and that man from that day forth was begotten by the Everlasting Father, and is living and walking in the truth, an earnest believer, doing all that he can for the spread of the kingdom, and singularly clear in his doctrinal knowledge. Here is a man who had been everything that was possible in the way of badness, yet God met with him; and some of you who have Abraham to your father, and are related to godly people, are just all the more hardened for all the preaching you have heard. May God have pity upon you and save you yet! Do not be content with fleshly fatherhood; get the spiritual fatherhood which comes from Christ.

Others of you are this day perhaps saying, "Well, we can trust in our good works." Well, then, *Adam* is your father, and you know what will come of you. Adam was driven out of Paradise, and you will never be admitted there. Adam lost all his hopes, and you will lose yours. On the ground of the law shall no flesh living be justified. Alas! I fear that many here have another father. How does Christ put it? "Ye are of your father, *the devil*," says he, "for his works ye do." Not works merely of open sin in the form of adultery, uncleanness, theft, and such like, but opposition to Christ is peculiarly a work of the devil, and unbelief in Christ is the devil's masterpiece. If you do not then trust the Lord Jesus, do not say to-night when you kneel at the bedside, "Our Father, which art in heaven," for your father is not in heaven, your father is in hell. Go to the blood of Jesus and ask that you may be cleansed from all iniquity, and then may you say through the everlasting Father, "O God, thou hast made me thy child, and I love and bless thy name." May God be pleased to give you all his blessing for Jesus' sake. Amen.

Shiloh

"Until Shiloh come; and unto him shall the gathering of the people be "—Genesis xlix. 10.

THE dying patriarch was speaking of his own son Judah; but while speaking of Judah he had a special eye to our Lord, who sprang from the tribe of Judah. Everything therefore which he says of Judah, the type, he means with regard to our greater Judah, the antitype, our Lord Jesus Christ. You will remember how Jacob gathered his twelve sons around his bed, and, addressing them individually as representatives of the twelve tribes that bear their names, uttered divers predictions, and gave to each a special blessing. After first apostrophising Reuben and Simeon and Levi, he proceeds to salute Judah in words full of majesty:—"*Judah, thou art he whom thy brethren shall praise.*" A happy expression; for the word "Judah" signifies "praise." The name was given to him by his mother as expressing her gratitude to God at his birth. It is now confirmed to him by his father, who discerns in it a presage of his character and his destiny. And verily this is true of Jesus. If the virgin mother hailed his advent, how much more do his grateful brethren laud his career! Do not his brethren recognise in him a leader and commander, a Saviour and a friend? Is it not here, on earth, our sweetest employment, and will it not be in heaven our highest delight to praise his name? The praise we bestow on men is mere flattery: the praise we receive from men is fulsome. But Jesus hath a peerless name, and his brethren derive from him priceless benefits. In Jesus are fulfilled the dreams of Joseph. The sun and the moon and the eleven stars all bow before him; all the sheaves make obeisance unto his sheaf. Let him be crowned with majesty who bowed his head to death is the common verdict of all the brotherhood of the house of God. "*Thy hand shall be in the neck of thine enemies.*" As one that gets his hand upon the neck of his prey, stops its breath and destroys it; or as one who seizes his enemy by the throat and flings him down to death. How true has this been of Jesus. He has laid his hand upon the neck of his enemies. When he came to the cross, fought foot to foot with the old Serpent, and there vanquished sin and death and hell for us, it was a terrible battle, but it ended in a splendid victory, of which we shall never cease to sing. Nor do we doubt but the hand of Jesus Christ is at this moment in the neck of his enemies. They may be very rebellious, and, for a time, they may seem to get the ascendancy; but he has got the upper hand of them, and as surely as truth and righteousness must flourish and prevail, as surely as Jehovah is the living God, the kingdom of Christ will yet break in pieces all the powers that resist it. "He shall break them as with a rod of iron : he shall dash them in pieces like potters' vessels." *" Thy father's children shall bow down before thee."* To the descendants of Judah in the persons of David and Solomon the whole nation did fealty. But worship of a higher order, homage of deeper significance, and adoration from a wider circle pertain to him, for whom our Father in heaven demands of all his faithful children love, honour, and obedience. *"Judah is a lion's whelp: from the prey, my son, thou art gone up."* And how does this describe the Saviour—that "Lion of the tribe of Judah"—that strong and mighty Lion who entered into conflict with the lion of the pit and overcame him. From the prey he has gone up again, up into his glory, gone up beyond the stars, up to the right hand of the infinite majesty, there to sit in perpetual peaceful triumph. *" He stooped down, he couched as a lion, and as an old lion."* The lion may have been an emblem that befitted the son of Jesse. The *lion couchant* might have been fitly chosen for his heraldic device, when the Lord had delivered him out of the hand of all his enemies and of Saul. Yet with how much more propriety may this emblem be emblazoned on the arms of Prince Emmanuel! Did he not stoop down? Was ever such a stoop as his? Let him be crowned with majesty who bowed his head to death. It is for this that he deserves to conquer, because he was willing to submit to shame and death itself for the sake of his people. How glorious is it to think that he has gone up, seeing that he once came down! Who should deserve such honours but he who laid such honours aside for a while? *" Who shall rouse him up?"* A grand question. Who shall rouse up the Lion of the tribe of Judah? Who dare do it? Who can stand against him? He is a lamb, gentle and tender; "A bruised reed he will not break, and the smoking flax he will not quench;" but let him be provoked, then fiercer than a lion that roareth from the forest will he be upon his foes. So shall it come to pass on that tremendous day when he will ease him of his adversaries and shake himself clear of all his enemies. Remember ye not these terrible words of his :—" Beware, ye that forget God, lest I tear you in pieces, and there be none to deliver"? *" The sceptre shall not depart from Judah, nor a lawgiver from between his feet, until Shiloh come."* The sovereignty remained with Judah. It did continue to be the royal tribe till the prophetic epoch. When other tribes lost their peculiar position and their positive distinctiveness, Judah still remained, and it survives in the common appellation of the Hebrew people to this day. The Israelites are more commonly called

Jews than by any other name. Jesus, of the tribe of Judah, is the King of the Jews, even though they reject him. Over his head upon the cross was written the indelible truth in letters of Hebrew, and Greek, and Latin, " This is Jesus, the King of the Jews." Yea, he is King of all faithful Jews and of all believing Gentiles at this hour, with a sovereignty wider than that of emperors—yea, as wide as the dwelling places of all mankind. He is " King of kings, and Lord of lords." Of Shiloh it is the patriarch speaks when with the vision of a seer he describes the grand climax. Before the dim organs of his sight he saw all his twelve sons gathered to take leave of their dying sire. Before the beaming eyes of his faith he beheld the gathering of all their distant posterity, or peradventure of all the kindreds of the earth to greet with glad acclaim the everlasting King, of whose kingdom there shall be no end. " *Unto him shall the gathering of the people be.*" Thus simply and thus pointedly does Jacob refer to the Lord Jesus Christ by the name of Shiloh. Of that name and of that prophecy I shall try to speak.

First, let the title, "SHILOH," and secondly the TESTIMONY, " To him shall the gathering of the people be," engage our attention.

The title, "SHILOH." What an old word it is! What an old world word! I should not wonder if it was one of Jacob's own coining. A pet name is often the product of peculiar love. Tender affection takes this kindly turn. Those whom we fondly regard we familiarly call by some other name than chance has bequeathed or choice bestowed. Not content with the names that others understand or use, there is often a new mode of recognition between two who love each other, as much as to say, " You are to me what you are to none upon earth beside me." Even God gives to his people new names ; and I do not wonder if they give to him new names. Well may believers have each a favourite name for Jesus. Which name of your Lord do you love the best ? If the question were passed round, perhaps some would say—and the majority might—" Jesus : the name divinely sweet." Another would say,

" Sweeter sounds than music knows
Charm me in *Emmanuel's* name."

"That is the choice name." Others it may be might put in a claim for pre-eminence to the title of "The Well-beloved," which always seems to me to have a great charm about it; and if George Herbert were here, you know he would say, " How sweetly doth 'My Master' sound ! " " My Master." That was the name he loved to call his Lord by. Well, Jacob's name for Jesus was " Shiloh ; " and it is so long ago since he called him Shiloh that I do not wonder that we have almost forgotten the meaning of it. He knew it had a wealth of meaning as it came from his lips, and the meaning is there still ; but the well is deep; and those that have studied the learned languages have found this to be a word of such rare and singular occurrence, that it is difficult, with any positive certainty, to define it. Not that they cannot find a meaning, but that it is possible to find so many meanings of it. Not that it is not rich enough, but that there is an embarrassment of riches. It may be interpreted in so many different ways. I will give you, one by one, some of the meanings that have been proposed. There is something to be said for each one. Though I shall not trouble you with the names of the learned authors who stand up for each particular translation, as that would be useless, I will take care to put last the one which I conceive to be the best, has the most authority, and will probably commend itself to you as the most acceptable.

Some maintain that the word "Shiloh" signifies "sent." Like that word you have in the New Testament, "He said to him, go to the pool of Siloam, which is, by interpretation, *Sent.*" You observe the likeness between the words *Siloam* and *Shiloh*. They think that the words have the same meaning; in which case *Shiloh* here would mean the same as *Messiah*—the *sent* one—and would indicate that Jesus Christ was the messenger, the sent one of God, and came to us, not at his own instance, and at his own will, but commissioned by the Most High, authorised and anointed to that end. Here let us stop a minute. We rejoice to know that, whatever this title means, it is quite certain that Jesus Christ was sent. It is a very precious thing to know that we have a Saviour; but often and often it has cheered my heart to think that this dear Saviour who came to save me did not come as an amateur, unauthorised from the courts of heaven, but he came with the credentials of the Eternal Father, so that, whatever he has done, we may be sure he has done it in the name of God. Jehovah will never repudiate that which Jesus has accomplished. Him hath God set forth to be a propitiation; he is a mediator of God's own sending. He is our Substitute; but he is a Substitute of God's own finding. "I have laid help upon one that is mighty." So saith the oracle, and who shall gainsay it? "The Lord hath laid upon him the iniquity of us all." It is the Lord that has done it. An ambassador who had no credentials from the court he represented would be but a dubious boon to the people; but when as a plenipotentiary, with full authority from his sovereign, he comes with terms of peace, he might well be received without hesitation or demur. Sinner, have you received the Saviour Jesus? You profess to acknowledge the God who sent him, but know that in turning from the Emissary you are spurning the Sovereign. If you deny Jesus you defy God himself; yea, you make God a liar, because you have not believed his testimony concerning his Son. Beloved, do you welcome Jesus Christ as being sent to you *personally?* When you have laboured under a sense of sin, burdened to the very ground with trouble of conscience, was Jesus ever sent to you to say, "Look unto me and be ye saved, all ye ends of the earth"? Was he ever sent to lead you to look? Did you look unto him, and were you lightened? Oh, then, you will for ever bless his name, the name of the Most High, who sent such an one that he might lift you up out of your miseries, bring the bondaged one out of the dungeon, and set the captive free. Dwell, sweetly dwell, upon this meaning of the word Shiloh. If it means "sent," there is great sweetness in it.

Others have referred it to a word, the root of which signifies *the Son*. Upon such a hypothesis the name would be strictly appropriate to our Lord. He is the "Son of God;" he is the "Son of Man;"

he was the "Son of Judah;" he was the "Son of David:" "Unto us a child is born, unto us a Son is given." Let us linger for a while upon this gloss—"Until Shiloh," "Until the Son shall come." Be the annotation right or wrong, Jesus is the Son of God. He that hath come to save us is divine. No angel could bear the stupendous burden of redemption. Sooner might angels create than redeem, but they can do neither the one nor the other; they can only sing the high praises of him who is able to do both. Who but God himself could snatch a sinner from hell? God has done it. He that died upon the cross was none other than he that made the world. Trust the divine Saviour? O sinner! if thou hast had any doubts about the sufficiency of Jesus Christ to save, cast them all aside; for, if he be the Son of the Highest, and "God over all, blessed for ever," they that rest in him shall never be confounded. The Son of God is he, but he is also the *Son of Man*, and this is an equal joy to us. Jesus Christ is "bone of our bone, and flesh of our flesh," a man like ourselves. Though he is now in heaven, think not that he is transformed into a spirit there, or that he hath discarded our nature, or disowned our flesh and blood. Oh, no. After he was risen from the dead he appeared to his disciples, and eat with them; he partook of a fish and of honeycomb, to show that he was not spirit but flesh, and he said, "Handle me, and see, a spirit hath not flesh and bone: as ye see me have." In that very body of his he has gone up into his glory, and to-day, at the right hand, there sits he—a man clothed in a body like our own. Oh, beloved! let not terror affright us, or misgivings keep us back from a high priest that can be touched with a feeling of our infirmities, a dear Saviour who is not ashamed to call us brethren. "This man receiveth sinners." Oh, sinners! may ye be willing to be received by him. Let us bless him as the Son—the Son of God, the Son of Man.

A third meaning has been given to the word "Shiloh" which rather paraphrases than translates it. The passage, according to certain critics, would run something like this:—" Until he come *to whom it belongs, to whom it is, for whom it is reserved;*" or, as Ezekiel puts it, "Overturn, until he shall come *whose right it is*, and thou wilt give it him." It may mean, then, "The sceptre shall not depart from Judah until he shall come whose that sceptre is." This meaning is supported by many learned authorities, and has its intrinsic value. The sceptre belongs to Christ. All sceptres belong to him. He will come by-and-by and verify his title to them. Have you not seen the picture that represents Nelson on board a French man-of-war, receiving the swords of the various captains he has conquered, while there stands an old tar at his side putting all these swords underneath his arm as they are brought up. I have often pictured to myself our great Commander, the only King by divine right, coming back to this our earth, and gathering up the sceptres of the kings in sheaves, and putting them on one side, and collecting their crowns; for he alone shall reign King of kings and Lord of lords. When the last and greatest of all monarchs shall come a second time, "without a sin-offering unto salvation"—oh, the glory of his triumph! He has a right to reign. If ever there was a king by nature, and by birth, it is the Son of David; if ever there was one who would be elected to the monarchy by the suffrages of all his subjects, it is Jesus Christ. How often do we sing—

> "Bring forth the royal diadem,
> And crown him Lord of all;"

and we cannot repeat it too often. Our hearts and lips ought to be always saying, "Crown him; crown him; crowns become the victor's brow." His is the right to reign. Dear souls, acknowledge that right. If you never have acknowledged it, acknowledge it now. "Kiss the Son, lest he be angry and ye perish from the way, while his wrath is kindled but a little." You that do love him, and have made him your King, oh, kiss his feet again! Let him have your highest homage, your purest love, your perpetual service. Was ever such a King as thou art, O Jesus! "the chief among ten thousand, and the altogether lovely"? Let him be crowned with majesty for ever and ever. To him the royalty belongs, for him it is reserved.

The interpretation, however, which has the most support, and which I think has the fairest claim to be accorded correct, is that which derives the word "Shiloh" from the same root as the word "Salem." This makes it signify *peace*. "Until the *peace*, or the *peace-bearer*, or the *peace-giver*," or, if you like it better, "the *rest*, or the *rest-maker*—shall come." Select the word you prefer, it will sufficiently represent the sense. "Until the *peace-bringer* come, until *the rest-maker* come." His advent bounds the patriarch's expectation and his desire. Oh, beloved, what a vein of soul-charming reflection this opens! Do you know what rest means? Such "peace, peace," such perfect peace as he hath whose soul is stayed; because he trusteth, as the prophet Isaiah hath it. Have you ever said to yourself, "There is nothing I desire—nothing that I wish for; I am satisfied—perfectly content; I am without a fear, without a dread"? "No," say you, "I never reached that elysium. You may be worth millions of money without ever coming to that pass. All the gold in the world will never fill a man's heart; and you may have broad acres across which a swift horse could hardly rush in a day, but you will not have enough. All the land in the world cannot fill a heart. You may have all the beauty, rank, honour, and fame that ever can come to a human being, and yet say, "Ah me! I am wretched still." But full many who have found Jesus have been able to say, "It is enough: I need no more." Believing in Jesus, and learning to yield up everything to his will, living to his glory, and loving him supremely, we do enjoy peace with God—a "peace that passeth all understanding," which "keeps our heart and mind" by Jesus Christ. Are we adopted into the family of God?—we are sure that he never did cast a child out of the family that was once received into it. Are we made members of the body of Christ? There is no fear of dismemberment; that which is perfected and compacted together cannot be mangled or torn asunder. Our good hope through grace is not precarious. Well may we sing with the seraphic Toplady—

> "Yes, I to the end shall endure,
> As sure as the earnest is given;
> More happy, but not more secure,
> Are the glorified spirits in heaven."

Here is rest! Man may well take his rest when he has nothing to do, when it is all done for him. And that is the gospel. The world's way of salvation is "*Do,*" God's way of salvation is, "It is all done for you; accept and believe." The world, that says "*Do,*" never does anything, while the gospel which tells us "It is all done," imparts such joy and peace within that we spring to our feet ready and willing to do and dare ought for him who gave himself up for us. While active and passive obedience spring out of the doctrine of grace, nothing but pride and self-righteousness can come out of the religion which prates of merit and prescribes duties to be done in order that you may be saved. All that ever will be saved were saved on Calvary's bloody tree. Jesus said, "It is finished." Here his humiliation reached its climax; he humbled himself even unto death. It *was* finished. Those for whom he died were there and then redeemed. The ransom price paid for them exempted them from the penalty of their transgressions, exonerated them from legal responsibilities, and extinguished for them the fiery threat of perdition. He had suffered in their stead, and they could not be called upon to suffer for themselves. He had offered a righteousness to God on their behalf, and they were accepted because of that righteousness. Do you say, " I wish I were one of those people "? Dost thou believe in Jesus? Then thou art one of them. Dost thou trust Jesus? Then thou art saved. The moment a sinner believes and trusts in his crucified Lord, he is pardoned at once; he receives salvation in full through Christ's blood. Do but rest thy soul on Jesus, and it is *done,* and peace will enter thy soul—oh, such a deep and blessed peace, the like of which is not to be found out of heaven! for Jesus is the great peace-giver and peacemaker: he is our peace. God grant us to know him and to understand this aspect of his mediatorial character. Believe me, my hearers, I feel in my soul, as I look round upon you, the utmost longing for you all. Oh, that you did know my Lord and the peace he gives. It is years ago—three and twenty years or more—since I went to him. I could not believe it possible that he would receive me. I felt myself too great a sinner. How should there be mercy for me? But I heard a sermon from the text, " Look unto me and be ye saved, all ye ends of the earth!" I never understood it before, but when I came to understand that all I had to do was *to look,* oh, what a revelation it was to me! No feelings, no workings, no doings, no purchase-money demanded as a qualification. Christ on the cross was evidently set forth crucified before my eyes. I did but *look,* and I was saved; saved the moment I looked. When I turned to the Scriptures I found that was just what the Scriptures said, " He that believeth in him is not condemned." I did believe it, I did trust it, I did simply rest there. Neither shall I ever forget the rush of joyous feeling that went through my spirit, the cessation of long years of melancholy, bordering on despair, and the coming out into a clear light, which I thank God I have never lost, for, with all the troubles of this material life, I would not change places with any man that breathes, no, nor with the angels before God's throne. The station and the privilege of angels will not bear comparison with the eternal dignities reserved for the saints. For an angel no redeemer ever died, and no angel will be able to sing, "Worthy is he that hath washed me in his blood!" Oh, to be superlatively indebted to the infinite love of Jesus, to be a cleansed sinner, and to be put among the children, is so enchanting that it is enough to make one say, "Ah! not even an angel would I envy, nor with one of those celestial ministers would I change my happy lot." I wish you could all sympathise in this. Would that you all had fellowship with us in this grace wherein we stand. Many of you have, thank God. Some of you have not. What do you poor people do without a Saviour? I cannot make out why you who have got so little in this life do not look out for the promise of a better inheritance. And what do you poor rich people do without a Saviour? I pity you most of all, for your lives are generally passed in a very senseless and insipid fashion. With nothing but a round of visits to pay, and a few elegant trifles to attend to, like butterflies you flit from flower to flower. A poor man's time is taken up with hard labour; but you often ask yourselves, and consult one another how best you can spend the hours and kill the time that hangs heavily on your hands. If you cannot think upon Christ, if you cannot fall back upon the covenant of grace, if you cannot look up to the eternal God, and say, "My Father, thou art mine, and with thee shall I dwell for ever," I pity you, whether you be rich or poor. God grant you to have and to enjoy the fulness of treasure that is in Jesus Christ; then you can say :—

> "I would not change my blest estate
> With all that earth calls good or great;
> And while my faith can keep her hold,
> I envy not the sinner's gold."

Trusting, then, dear friends, that your faith has identified the Shiloh of Jacob's vision, let us occupy the few minutes that remain to us in considering the TESTIMONY which the patriarch here bears. "Unto him shall the gathering of the people be."

"UNTO HIM," as the Hebrew runs, "shall the *gatherings* of the *peoples* be." So wide the circumference that converges in this glorious centre. It comprehends all the peoples of the Gentiles as well as Jews. Of course it includes the favoured nation, but it also takes in the isles afar off; yea, all of us, my brethren. "Unto him shall the gatherings of the peoples be." What joy this announcement should give us! Do you realise it, that around Jesus Christ, around his cross, which is the great uplifted standard, the people shall gather? Just open your eyes and look. If you can see, and your eyes have been touched with eyesalve, you may perceive the power of attraction by which this magnificent issue is already in progress. Over yonder in America a poor sinner is seeking eternal life. If he is seeking aright, he is being gathered to Christ. Or, look at home in your own country. Perhaps, to-night, in many thousands of places that are open for divine worship, the like magnetic influence is at work. I only wish I could hope that there was some one in every assembly that was looking for eternal life. If it be so, they are all looking to Jesus Christ. Cast your eye now to India, or France, or Prussia, or over to Australia, in whatever direction you will; every soul that is in earnest seeking life is seeking it through Jesus Christ. I see them coming; he is the centre, and they are all drawing near to him. Every soul that is saved is drawn to Jesus; none are saved without him. The people gather to him as their only hope, and all succour else has failed. They do not fly to him until they have tried every other hope. Nobody ever comes to Christ until he cannot go anywhere else. The sinner comes to him by stress of weather—driven in sometimes, as ships are into harbours of refuge, because they cannot keep pace with it outside the bar. It is when the sinner is in difficulties that he is driven to Jesus Christ; and every soul that really is looking for eternal life in the right place is looking to Jesus and gathering to Jesus; and I see little silver threads going out from Christ, the centre, from all over the world, drawing men to himself. I hope there is one of these threads drawing you. Oh! yield to the gentle pressure! Follow it; for there is your only hope.

Look again, and you will see that all over the world those that are saved are gathering to Jesus, rallying round him, and accepting him as their leader, instructor, and king. The Jews said, "We have no king but Cæsar;" the Christians say, "We have no king but Jesus." I mean no spiritual lord, no teacher, no leader, except Jesus Christ himself. "Unto him shall the gathering of the people be." His people out of all nations shall come and take his easy yoke and wear it, and find rest unto their souls. And now, at this moment, my eyes can see myriads all over the world who are coming nearer and nearer to Jesus, with instant eager cry, saying, "Draw us, Lord, draw us nearer to thyself; make us more like thyself; help us to live more to thy glory." Is there one of these golden threads drawing you? Then run if you are drawn, and seek to love your Lord and serve him better than ever you have done, for "unto him shall the gathering of the people be."

Be assured of this; Christ is the only centre of true unity to his people. There is a society, I believe, for the promotion of the unity of Christendom. I am afraid it does not do much good, or cement much fellowship. The unity of Christendom! That will all depend upon what is the key-stone of the arch you are going to build. If you expect there will be a unity of the Greek Church, and the Latin Church, and the Anglican Church, I can only say that were all three united the union of Christians would be as far off as ever. In the midst of that *professed* Christendom, but distinct from it, there is an inner Christendom, a secret, sacred brotherhood of real Christians that knows little about these great secular churches. The true Christendom consists of all that worship God in the spirit, not having confidence in the flesh. The true church consists of all that believe in the Lord Jesus Christ and are quickened by the Holy Ghost, the only unity that society could ever get would be a confederation ecclesiastical, to be dominated over by some lordly priest or other. No desirable thing certainly. Christ is the centre of the church, and true unity will be found in him. "Unto him shall the gathering of the people be." Were I to give you a book to read about Jesus Christ, full of love to him, and when you had read it were I to ask you who wrote it, I warrant you would not guess rightly what denomination the man belonged to. Perhaps you will say, "Well, there is a flavour in it of Roman Catholicism now and then; but really it is so good a book I cannot think a Roman Catholic could have written it." "Or," you will say, "it has a little of the Plymouth Brother here and there, and that is not a sweet flavour; but still, it is so good I hardly think he could have written it." By-and-by you will say, "I do not know at all; I am at a loss." Often and often after reading books which have a savour of Christ in them, I have felt a love to the author, though I may have found out, perhaps, that he was an ecclesiastical opponent of mine. I do not care; I love him if he loves my Master, be he who he may, wherever he comes from. When we are down on our knees praying for the kingdom of Christ, or standing up to sing Messiah's praise, it is wonderful how like we are to each other. Mr. Wesley did not like Toplady, and Mr. Toplady did not like Wesley, called him "an old fox," and said that he would pluck him, and have him "tarred and feathered;" but take up any hymn book you like, and you will find, side by side, Charles Wesley's "Jesus, Lover of my Soul," and Toplady's "Rock of Ages, cleft for me;" and which is the better hymn of the two I am sure I do not know, they are so much alike. So were these men, after all, two blessed souls, for all their mistakes and all their misunderstandings of one another. When you get to the cross you get together. "Unto him shall the gathering of the people be." When you come to talk of him and what he did—his life and death, his atoning sacrifice, his glorious conquest of all our foes—then are you agreed.

Oh, brethren, we must therefore strive vigorously, and try incessantly, to lift Christ up. We want to see, during this year, a great gathering of souls. Well, we shall see it if we lift Christ up. Here is a lot of steel filings among a heap of ashes. How can I separate them? There are a great many ways of trying to do it. Bring a magnet in; put a magnet into the heap; see how it draws the steel filings away. In this congregation there is a great number of individuals, but who among them are God's elect I do not nor can I know; but let me preach Jesus Christ, and Jesus Christ will draw his own. "My sheep hear my voice; I know them and they follow me; and I give unto them eternal life." Preach Christ; that is the magnet; he will draw his own to himself. And, dear friends, if we want to see conversions in this beyond all past years there must be more preaching, more constant preaching of Christ; Christ must be in every sermon, and he must be top and bottom too of all the theology that is preached—"Jesus Christ and him crucified," and nothing else. I am bound to preach Jesus Christ and him crucified, for I do not know anything else to preach. My simplicity is my safeguard. I have often felt to be of Paul's mind: "I determined to know nothing among you save Jesus Christ and him crucified." Some are wise to interpret prophecies; I am not: enough for me to know about the cross. Some are able to split a hair, they can a hair divide betwixt the north and the north-west side. I am no logician. If, knowing the terrors of the Lord, I can persuade men to fly to Christ, and escape from the wrath to come, I shall fulfil my mission to my heart's delight. Consider this, all of you. Let each of us go back to the first principles of the gospel, and bring out, again and again, the old, old story of sinners lost and a Saviour come to redeem, of guilt sinking a man to hell like a millstone, and the Saviour taking all that guilt away. If you preach the blood, the precious blood of Jesus, you set forth the great soul-saving gospel, and you do honour to him unto whom "shall the gathering of the people be."

And, brethren, by the climax of destiny that is opened up, let the conduct of our daily life be disciplined. Let us aim to gather more and more to Jesus ourselves. We cannot get too near to him. Be it ours to strive to get closer than ever we have been. Even if a cross should be necessary to raise us, let us not be afraid of the cross, so long as it brings us nearer to Jesus. You are happiest, healthiest, and holiest when you are nearest to Christ. To him shall the continual "gathering of the people be."

And oh! let us pray, also, that this gathering may go on both among saints and sinners—that saints may gather nearer to Jesus, and that sinners may gather savingly to him. The text says, "To him shall the gathering of the people be." It is a faithful saying, and we do believe it. Not death nor hell can keep back the Lord's elect from coming to Christ. Come they must and shall; for the divine decree shall be accomplished, and each one for whom Jesus specially shed his blood shall be saved infallibly, saved beyond all risk; but it is ours to pray for it. Oh, Lord Jesus, it is said, "Unto thee shall the gathering of the people be." Make it so. The gathering shall be wrought by thyself. "He shall gather the lambs in his arms;" it is his to gather the strayed sheep; he gathereth together the outcasts. Surely he is the great gatherer. Well may they be gathered to him when he himself gathers them. Ask him to gather your children. Ask him to gather your dear beloved ones under your house-roof, your servants, your neighbours. Ask him to gather them. Ask him to gather this great city. Oh, what a city it has grown to be! Would God that Jesus had it! It would be a glorious koh-i-noor in the state jewels of Christ if he could call London his own. The biggest of cities— would God it were the holiest. Oh, that it were wholly Christ's from one end to the other. They used to say, in Cromwell's day, that if you walked down Cheapside at a certain hour, you would have heard the voice of family prayer and praise at every house in the whole street, both morning and evening. I trow it is not so in any street in London now. We have gone back since the grand old Puritanic times. But we will repair to the throne again by God's good grace, and yet shall there be a salt in this city, for the city shall be seasoned through and through with the power of the gospel of Jesus. Only to your knees! to your knees! to your knees! if you would have it so. You should get this fulfilled among your fellow citizens, if you would get it first vouchsafed to you as a boon of your God. Tell him he has said, "Unto him shall the gathering of the people be." Hold him to his word, plead with him that he cannot break it, and we shall live to see the day yet. "To him shall the gathering of the people be."

Oh, my dear hearers! as I draw these reflections to a close one thought passes over my mind to which I must give expression. You will all of you either be gathered to Christ to be saved, or else you will have to be gathered by-and-by for another purpose. There shall ring out upon the midnight air a trumpet call that shall be loud enough to be heard east and west, and south and north; it shall startle all the sleepers, and more than that, it shall arouse the dead; at its sound the sepulchre shall vomit forth its prey, and they that are rocked in slumber beneath the waves of ocean shall hear that trumpet call and rise, the whole mass of Adam's family, the myriads of all our race. Oh, what an assembly will that be! The motley throng within these walls is but as a grain of sand, compared with the sea-shore, to the multitudes that will then be congregated. Gather ye! gather ye! ye that have been dead these six thousand years. Gather ye! gather ye! ye that were drowned in Noah's flood. Gather ye! gather ye! all ye hosts of Egypt, and ye myriads of Chaldea, and of Babylon, of Persia, and of Greece. Gather ye! ye legions of Rome! ye myriads of the middle ages! ye countless millions of China and of swarthy Hindostan, and you of the world across the sea! Gather ye! gather ye! men of every skin and every tongue! For ye must gather, and there in the midst of you all shall be the cloud sailing through the air, and on it the great white throne of him whose spotless justice is mirrored in it. There will you stand, and if you have not looked at Christ on the cross, you will have to look at the Christ upon the throne; and if ye have never trusted him, ye will then have to tremble at him. Hark, how the trumpet sounds! How that clarion rings out again and again and again! And lo! all are there. And now he comes, whose pomp is beyond conception, and the books are opened. As they are opened, page after page, he reads the story of each man's life, and he has come to yours, and he reads the page that chronicles this fleeting hour. On such a night, gathered with this great congregation, you were bidden to believe in Jesus, and bow down before the great Peace-giver; you refused, and sealed your doom for ever. Shall it be so? Oh! shall it be so? God grant it may not be so. May there be another book opened, which is the Book of Life, and in that book may your name stand recorded as one who humbly trusted in the finished work of Jesus, and therefore was accepted in the Beloved, and found mercy on that day. The Lord grant it to every one of you. I may not ever again speak to some of you as long as I live. This then I *do* say to you while your ears are open and attentive to my voice, Lay hold on eternal life; put your trust in Jesus. And if, beloved, any of you to whom I am so familiar, to whom I speak so often, if you should depart from the world while I am absent, or if I should never return, but find a grave in some distant land, I charge you, meet me on the other side of Jordan; I charge you, meet me at my Master's right hand; I charge you, cling to the atoning sacrifice by faith; and we will meet together where he sits and reigns—our best beloved—the Judah, the Jesus, whom all his brethren shall praise—the Shiloh, the Prince of peace, for whose glorious advent all his saints look, and to whom they shall be gathered in fulness of joy for ever and for ever. Amen and amen.

The Prince of Life

"And killed the Prince of life, whom God hath raised from the dead; whereof we are witnesses "—Acts iii. 15.

PETER does not conceal the death of Christ: he is not ashamed of the fact that his Lord was crucified. God forbid that any of us should be ashamed of the cross: may we speak of it without a blush! Peter does not flatter his hearers; but he declares that they "killed the Prince of life." This was literally true, and it was needful that they should know and feel it. There is no gospel without the cross, and no useful preaching which does not appeal to the conscience; yes, there must be the cross for doctrine, and honest rebuke as the trumpet to awaken men's hearts. Ye ministers, take note of this!

Mark well that, in the same sentence in which he testified to the Lord's death, Peter bears witness to his resurrection. The verse is very short, and yet contains the two greatest events of human history: "Ye killed the Prince of life, whom God raised from the dead." The crucifixion and the resurrection come close together. There are no intervening words in Peter's speech, as there was scarcely an interval as a matter of fact. On the Friday evening our Redeemer is laid in the grave, and he quits it on the Sunday morning early. It is called "three days" by Oriental custom; but, as a matter of fact, the interval only consisted of parts of two days, and one whole day. God has a way of handling time which makes a day as a thousand years, and a thousand years as one day; and in this case he compressed into the smallest space the three days during which the Great Hostage remained in durance vile in the grave. Beloved, I wish you would learn a lesson here: never draw out sorrow and dread beyond the shortest necessary period. You that have been made to feel your death, and are at this time, as it were, wrapped in your grave-clothes; I pray that you may know no long interval between the time when you are slain by the law and made alive again by grace! Why should we tarry longer than may be under the bondage of the law? Dark is that night in which Jesus has not yet come, and yet the storm is raging. When the soul has only life enough to mourn its death it is a painful condition. Let that period be made as short as possible. Is it not written, "After two days will he revive us: in the third day he will raise us up, and we shall live in his sight"? Why should we make months and years of that which need be scarcely three days? If God contracts three days into one, may we not by holy faith make short work of our time of conviction and fear? When we know our death, we have in measure begun to live, and we should be eager that our life should quit the sepulchre of doubt and enjoy the light of joy.

I am about to speak of our Lord for that very purpose. I hope that the music of his charming name may bring rejoicing to sad hearts. Here is your power to quit your spiritual death; here is your sole hope of spiritual life: Jesus who rose from the dead is "the Prince of life." We will begin with that. *Consider a title*—" Prince of life." When we have done with that, we will look further into our text, and *unfold a roll of wonder*—" Ye killed the Prince of life, whom God hath raised from the dead; whereof we are witnesses." There are many riddles in that paradoxical statement—" Ye killed the Prince of life." When we have done with these points, we will come to a speedy close, as we *suggest an inquiry* which may be practically profitable to you.

I. First, then, let us CONSIDER A TITLE—"The Prince of life." This is not a literal translation, though it is a valuable interpretation. The word here is that which is translated " author " in that place wherein our Lord is said to be " the author and finisher of our faith " (Heb. xii. 2); and yet again it is rendered " captain " (in Hebrews ii. 10), where he is called " the captain of our salvation," made perfect through suffering. The word " Prince " is not inaccurate, for the idea of princedom lies on the surface of the Greek word, and therefore I shall keep to our own thrice precious version, which, take it for all in all, remains the Queen of all the versions. Still, you will not forget that it does include the sense of "*author of life*." Here it may be well to say that we think that Christ is indeed the Creator of all things, and especially of life: " All things were made by him; and without him was not anything made that was made. In him was life." Our Lord Jesus is peculiarly the Creator in connection with life; and I take pleasure in thinking of all life as proceeding from him by whom all things consist. But this is assuredly true of all spiritual life, which is a higher and a nobler thing than life vegetable, animal, or mental. From him, the Sun of Righteousness, every vital spark of heavenly flame has been sent forth: he is the quickening Spirit, and by union with him we live unto God, if, indeed, we so live. There is no spiritual life of which he is not the author, and there never will be. When you and I come to deal with men for their salvation, we discover our inability; for we perceive that the creation of life is out of our power, since it remains the sole prerogative of the Son of God. To him is given power over all flesh, that he may give eternal life to as many as the Father has given him. "As the Father raiseth up the dead, and quickeneth them; even so the Son quickeneth whom he will." All our preaching is in vain unless Jesus send forth life. " He that hath the Son hath life; and he that hath not the Son of God hath not life" (1 John v. 12); and what can we do among the dead? Come, thou Lord and Giver of life; for without thee we are but as the dead burying the dead.

But now we will handle our text as it stands in our version. It is a beautiful name this—"the Prince of life." Though seldom preached upon, it is one of our Lord's famous titles. He will be gloriously known by this name in the day of his appearing, when he shall raise the dead; but it is a title which belonged to him before he was nailed to the tree; for they "killed the Prince of life." The title belonged to him even when he was dead; for when killed he was still "the Prince of life." The title is his to the full now that he is risen, and ever lives to make intercession for us. None can share it with him, much less can any take it away from him. He alone is "the Prince of life."

Upon this famous title we would remark that it is justified by the fact that *he possesses life supremely.* In him is life emphatically, to its deepest and highest degree. In him is life superlatively, and beyond all others. Of him John well said, "The life was manifested, and we have seen it, and bear witness, and shew unto you that eternal life, which was with the Father, and was manifested unto us." He bears the name of "The Life" in that famous passage, "I am the way, the truth, and the life." He says of himself, "I am he that liveth." As surely as we have a living God we have a living Saviour. He is life self-existent, sustained by nothing from without. He is life essential, life eternal. He is the Prince of life, because in him life dwells in all its fulness, force, and independence. "As the Father hath life in himself; so hath he given to the Son to have life in himself" (John v. 26). Jesus lives: he must live : he cannot cease to live. All things else may pass away, and like the bubbles on the wave dissolve into their native nothingness; but the Christ of God must live, and live in full energy, and hence he is "the Prince of life."

Life is his natural patrimony. Life is his royal heritage. We hear of ladies who are peeresses in their own right; so is Christ the Prince of life in his own right; not only by purchase, or attainment, or reward, but by his nature and relationship to the Highest; for he is in himself God that liveth for ever. Moreover, he has power over his own life, in a way in which none of us can imitate him : as the God-man his life is absolutely at his own disposal. In the realm of life he is Prince, but we are only subjects. He says of his own life, "I have power to lay it down, and I have power to take it again;" this is not our case. We pay the debt of nature, and die; but our Lord owed no debt to nature, seeing he is the Maker of all. He died voluntarily, and of his own accord; you and I may not do this except under the compulsion of obedience to God. He resumed possession of life at his own will, which you and I could not do. He had the right, the authority, the power thus to deal with his own life. If this had not been so, he could not have offered himself to die in our place and stead; but, having a power and princedom over his own life, such as we have not, he could lay down his life for us, and he could take it again. O man! thou hast not life in thine own right : it is lent to thee by him who is still owner of it. Thou canst not lay down thy life at will; for it is not thine, but God's. Live thine appointed time, else wilt thou commit a crime against the majesty of the Life-giver! Our Lord Jesus assumed the life of men, and when he chose he could lay it down; for he was still the ever-living God. When he chose he could raise his human body from among the dead, and walk again among the sons of men: this he hath done, and many witnesses have attested the fact. Let us rejoice that we worship the living God through a living Mediator! How glad are we that we are comforted by the same assurance which sustained the heart of Job, "I know that my Redeemer liveth"! In an hour of great depression of spirit Luther was seen to write on the table before him these two words—*Vivit! Vivit!* and when he had so written, he arose, and went about his business calmly and quietly, as well he might, since his Almighty Helper lived. "The Lord is risen indeed." Is not this enough to make us all Luthers if we could but drink it in? For if Jehovah Jesus lives, his cause can never die; and our acceptance before God can never fail. The great Redeemer lives emphatically and eternally, and therefore let our faith in him rise to full assurance, and let that full assurance lift us to the summit of delight.

> "He lives, he lives, and sits above,
> For ever interceding there;
> Who shall divide us from his love?
> Or what shall tempt us to despair?"

In the next place, consider that our Lord is "the Prince of life" because *he won it for us right gloriously.* We had forfeited life, and had come under the sentence, "Thou shalt surely die." We fell under bondage to the power of death, and became dead to God, and righteousness, and hope. Our Lord Jesus entered into the lists against our great adversary, who had the power of death, that is, the devil. He had skirmishes with him in the wilderness, and he struggled with him in the garden, even to a bloody sweat. Our enemy was strong through our sin and the curse of the law which follows it; but our Lord was strong in love to bear our sin in his own body, and to endure the chastisement of our peace upon the cross. He fought the foes of our souls, and returned with dyed garments from Edom, having trampled under his lone foot all the powers of darkness, as the grapes are trodden in the winepress. He himself bowed his head to death, and by death he overcame the prince of darkness. By his patient suffering and painful death he won for us the right to live for ever. His endurance of the death-penalty blotted out the writ of judgment which had been issued against us: he himself putting it out of the way, nailing it to his cross.

> "Bruisèd is the serpent's head,
> Hell is vanquish'd, death is dead,
> And to Christ gone up on high,
> Captive is captivity."

By dying, the just for the unjust, our Lord, who was both Victim and Victor became our "Prince of life," handing us the pardon and justification, by which our eternal life is secured. As by the first Adam came death, so by the second Adam life has been bestowed. "There is therefore now no condemnation to them which are in Christ Jesus," for the condemnation has been passed upon him; and by this grand transference, while death has passed upon him, life has come to us. Our life is the glorious spoil which "the Prince of life" has snatched from the Destroyer, and granted freely to us. Well may we crown him Prince of life "who hath abolished death, and hath brought life and immortality to light through the gospel"!

Thirdly, our Lord may well be called "the Prince of life," because *he gives it so plentifully.* With both hands he scatters it where else all had been death. As he hath life most abundantly, and has won for us the right to it, so he actually imparts it to his chosen by the Spirit of life. Where the Tartar's horse trod, the grass never grew; but where Christ's feet tread, life springs up in the midst of the arid wilderness. He cannot live without scattering life all around him, even as the sun cannot exist without giving out his light on all sides. None but he can give life to men; but he can give it without measure. To those furthest sunken in death, even to the corrupt in heart, who stink in the nostrils of their fellow-men, he can give life. His voice can be heard in the innermost prison of spiritual death. As he called Lazarus, and made him live by his own supreme power, so can he quicken the corrupt sinner to sweetness and heavenliness of life. None have yet been met with so far gone in corruption as to be beyond his quickening energy. None have ever trusted him without receiving life, though their case seemed desperate. Yea, the feeblest trust in him is life. They live that believe

"There is life in a look at the Crucified One."

On all sides he dispenses that everlasting life which he compares to water springing up within a well. They that come under his benign influence live for ever, because of their contact with him; for this is life eternal, to know the Lord Jesus, as sent of God. Beloved, the day will come when our Lord will prove his life-giving power on a grand scale by causing the resurrection of the dead. When he shall come in the glory of the Father, they that are in the grave shall hear the voice of the Son of God, and they that hear shall live. What an Exodus will it be! The slaves of death shall quit the Egypt of the sepulchre, and march forth from the house of bondage. Land and sea shall teem with the uncountable multitude, and he that called them forth shall be seen to be "the Prince of life." Who but he could have released this vast multitude from their long prison? The Roman Emperor Theodosius, in a fit of great good humour, set at liberty all persons in prison, or in captivity; and then he sighed, and wished that he could release the dead from their graves. Theodosius could not reach the keys of the grave; these hang at the girdle of "the Prince of life." He shall open the iron gate, and bid the myriads pour forth, as bees from the hive. They sleep together in the dust, but when he calls they shall answer him. Hear this, O mourner: "Thy brother shall rise again!" Every man's brother shall rise again; an exceeding great army shall be seen where now we mourn a valley of dry bones. Until that glorious morning, nothing pleases our Lord better than to be working spiritual resurrections. He saith,

"He that believeth in me, though he were dead, yet shall he live; and whosoever liveth and believeth in me shall never die. Believest thou this?" Do you know anything about being quickened from the death wherein you lay dead in trespasses and in sins? Remember that marvellous sentence—"I am the resurrection and the life." Your Lord himself is the resurrection; do you know this? Those who have him have life eternal. Have you proved this truth? God grant that we may have many exemplifications of that fact in this house at this moment! May many of you look to Jesus, and begin the life which never ends!

Next, I think we may fitly style our Lord "Prince of life," because *he so wondrously sustains it.* If thou hast life, yet dost thou need food. Thou knowest where to find food for thy body; the fields and the floods yield it to thee; but where wilt thou find food for thy soul? There is but one place to which thou canst resort. Apart from Christ Jesus, not even heaven itself can yield it to thee, though it drop with manna; "for your fathers did eat manna in the wilderness, and are dead." Heaven itself can only give us the nutriment of spiritual life in that one form, namely, Christ Jesus. He says, "I am the living bread which came down from heaven: if any man eat of this bread, he shall live for ever: and the bread that I will give is my flesh, which I will give for the life of the world." He says again, "Whoso eateth my flesh, and drinketh my blood, hath eternal life; and I will raise him up at the last day. For my flesh is meat indeed, and my blood is drink indeed. As the living Father hath sent me, and I live by the Father: so he that eateth me, even he shall live by me." Brother, do you know this bread from heaven by handling and tasting it? If so, renew your acquaintance with it by receiving it anew. O soul, there is supreme virtue in this food which Jesus gives thee! Art thou faint this morning? Resort again to him who first gave thee life. Dost thou hunger? Come thou to him who is that Word of God by whom men live. He shall satisfy thy mouth with good things, and renew thy youth like the eagle's. He doth not bid thee take life from him, and then go elsewhere for bread wherewith to nourish it; no, he causes thee to live by thy constant and never-ending union with him, even as the branch lives in the vine. Pray, "Lord, evermore give us this bread." If thou feedest upon him whom God hath set forth to be the bread that never perishes, thou also shalt never perish, but live for ever. Oh, for a banquet upon this heavenly bread this morning! "Eat ye that which is good, and let your soul delight itself in fatness." Then, rising from the table well satisfied, you shall each one say, "Verily, he is the Prince of life, for we live by him."

Brethren, this name may be illustrated yet further by the fact that *he rules life most lovingly.* "The Prince of life" is not a mere title. I suppose the Prince of Wales does not govern Wales, as a matter of fact; and other princes who derive their names from different places do not necessarily rule over those places, but merely wear a title which means little or nothing. Our Lord Jesus wears no empty title, he is really Prince and Lord wherever he is Quickener. There is no spiritual life in the world which does not yield obedience to Jesus.

Other life may be rebellious, struggling against his sway; for "the kings of the earth set themselves, and the rulers take counsel together, saying, Let us break his bands asunder, and cast away his cords from us"; but the spiritually living, quickened by faith in him, cry each one to him, at the very first moment of their life, "Lord, what wouldst thou have me to do?" The spirit of life in Christ Jesus is the spirit of obedience. The life that Jesus gives does not go off at a tangent from him: it remains circulating about him as the planet around the sun. The life that Jesus gives is like the life of a body which is obedient to the head. My head says, "Lift your hand." Up goes the hand. "Close the fingers": they close. "Open the hand": it opens at once, without so much as a wish to rebel. The rule is where the life is, namely, in the head. Such is Christ to all truly living men and women: their life, their rule is in Christ Jesus. Where Jesus lives he reigns. I know there is in us another law working against the law of our mind, and sometimes bringing us into captivity to the law of sin and death; but this appertains not to our new-born life, it is a relic of our death. Sin comes of that "body of this death" over which we groan so deeply, crying, "Who shall deliver me?" As for the life which comes to us through our Lord Jesus, it is pure and heavenly. That which is born of God sinneth not; it followeth after righteousness, and keeps the way of holiness, and must do so eternally. The Prince of life is a real ruler, and the life he has created is subservient to his sway. He is head over all things *in* his church as well as *to* his church. Ruling with a mysterious, omnipotent, and effective power he worketh in the spiritual, so that they gladly pay their heart's homage to him.

I must give you observation the sixth, for I cannot else bring out all my thoughts on this marvellous name, "the Prince of life." Our Lord is *he who is the crown and glory of our life.* The prince, as the representative of the country, stands for it in the place of dignity and honour. At great ceremonials a country is represented and honoured by the presence of its crown prince. Among men it is but nominally that the prince is the glory of the nation; but in the divine life, Christ is indeed the flower, and crown, and glory of the people who are in him, even all the living in Zion. If you want to see the spiritual life, you may see it in any one of the members of the mystical body; but not to perfection. There is life in the hand, there is life in the foot, there is life even in our uncomely parts; but if you want to see the life of a man, you naturally look in his face. If you would see eternal life, behold it in the face of Jesus; for in him dwelleth eternal life to the full. He is the embodied, incarnate life of God for men, and in him is that life made perfect. Beloved, the glory of our manhood, as it is spiritually renewed and quickened, is Christ! He it is that hath raised our nature to the right hand of God. It is something to be a man, now that the Son of God is also man. It is much to be alive unto God, now that our life is hid with Christ in God. What a noble second Adam we have! How glorious he makes our nature! He is the flower of our manhood. All else is the branch, and leaf, and bud; but the supreme beauty, the image of God in man, finds full expression in the Firstborn from the dead, the altogether-lovely One.

He is the glory of our life, and hence he is well called "the Prince of life."

And, seventhly, which must bring this discussion of the title to a close—*it is he who himself is glorified by spiritual life.* Princes and kings reckon that the prosperity of their country reflects honour upon *them.* That monarch is great because he rules a great country: this king is famous because his armies have made him so. The people make the king. In our Lord's case, his living ones are his joy and crown. From him, and through him, and therefore *to* him, are all things in the realm of spiritual life. All spiritual life glorifies the living Christ. There is not a beat of the spiritual heart, there is not a breath of the spiritual lung, but what means love and loyalty to the Christ of God. That we should repent, that we should believe, that we should do good works—all this is to make Jesus a glorious prince, glorified by such holy and heavenly life. Your highest ambition, ye quickened ones, is that you may crown him Lord of all. If you had a wish and could now obtain your highest desire, your wish would be that he might be extolled, and be very high. I am sure it is so with you. You would forego at once ten thousand desires that lurk within your spirit, and that might, in themselves, be lawful enough; you would, I say, forego them all without regret, if *he* might have a glorious high throne, and be great unto the ends of the earth. I am sure it is so among the glorified in the New Jerusalem. In heaven they rejoice, but they joy before their Lord; in heaven they worship, but they worship the Lamb; in heaven they sing, but the song is, "Unto him that loved us, and washed us from our sins in his own blood." As in the aloe, all those long years of green leafage are tending to the production of one glorious flower in the end; as at last a flower-stalk shoots upward like a tree, and then is hung about with abundant flowering, so that the whole plant spends itself upon its blossoms, living only till they are displayed, so is it with the life of the saints of God. The aloe has no other reason for its growing than to bear that towering glory in the end; so is it with the entire mass of spiritual life which God has made—it is growing and gathering up all its strength throughout these ages, that Christ may be glorified. In the ages to come, Christ is to be manifested to principalities and powers in the heavenlies, in and through his church. We who live spiritually, make up his body; and as all the body ministers to the head, so do we all strive to bring honour and dominion to our Lord Jesus. It pleases the Holy Ghost in us to reveal Christ and magnify his name. Are we not, all of us, if children of God, yet all of us so many younger sons increasing the honour of the "Firstborn among many brethren?" All spiritual life is for him who is our life. "He shall live, and daily shall he be praised": we live alone for this. Bring forth your trophies to him, ye conquerors of sin! Pour out your treasures at his feet, ye who are rich toward God! Crown him King of kings, and Lord of lords. Hallelujah! Hallelujah! All spiritual life that was, and is, and ever shall be, is to the glory of him who saith, "I am he that liveth, and was dead, and am alive for evermore; and have the keys of hell and of death."

It is clear that he is well named "the Prince of life." I have been doing my work very badly because it is beyond me. My subject masters me. I am reminded of a story about Mr. Moody. Mr. Moody finished his sermon, and as he walked away dissatisfied with himself, he said to a good Scotchman with whom he was staying, "I cannot get to the end of it." "Man," said the other, "did you think you ever could?" Who can compass the infinite? I did not imagine that I could reach the height of this great argument; but still, I hoped to do better than this. The Lord forgive my feebleness, and yet use it to his glory. I am not astonished at my failure, but I am weary of the ignorance which makes me fail. I wish I could glorify my Lord more. Help to make up for my deficiencies. Let this precious name lie like a sweet wafer on your tongue. Go to sleep to-night with it in your mouth, and may it flavour your very dreams, and may you wake up in the morning and find yourselves still with him who is "the Prince of life"!

II. Now, secondly, I have to UNFOLD A ROLL OF WONDERS, which I see in my text: "Ye killed the Prince of life."

See here, beloved, in the murder of Christ, *the height and infamy of human sin*. They chose a murderer, but they killed "the Prince of life." He lived for their sakes, but they slew him: he would die that men might live, but they killed him. You blame the Jews: nay, rather blame yourselves. Those who did this deed were representatives of the whole race. We, also, put the Lord to death. Our hands were crimsoned in his blood.

> "'Twas you my sins, my cruel sins,
> His chief tormentors were;
> Each of my crimes became a nail,
> And unbelief the spear."

Sin is Christicide. I have in my reading, in old books, found holy men speaking of sins as "accursed kill-Christs." The name was well deserved. When sin was full-blown, it brought forth Christ-murder as its chief product. Hear how the wicked husbandmen cry: "This is the heir; come, let us kill him, and the inheritance shall be ours." He had nothing to do with our death but to bear the penalty of it, and he came hither only to make us live; but we with wicked hands have crucified him. What an evil and a bitter thing is sin! What a malicious and bloodthirsty monster! Oh, for grace to escape from it! A sevenfold depth of cursing lies within the heart of man; for he would kill his God, his Saviour. You, my hearer, will either be guilty of the death of Christ, or you will live by it. Which shall it be? You either kill *him*, or you live by him.

Another wonder is *our Lord's condescension*. How could he stoop to die? To die by the hands of wicked men? Behold the condescension of Christ, that being the Prince of life he should deign to die. A look of his would have made his murderers melt away, as it shall one day make heaven and earth to flee from his face. One word from him, and where would Caiaphas, and Annas, and Pilate, and the Roman soldiery have been? They would have become as the fat of rams, which speedily is consumed in smoke, had he but willed it; for by his will the old creation shall be dissolved. When he hung on the cross the nails could not have kept him there of themselves. He could have stepped from the tree among his adversaries, and made them scatter like sheep when a wolf leaps into the flock. He died; but that loud cry of, "It is finished"! proved that his strength was in him, and that he died not of necessity. He could have lived; but for our sakes he submitted to death. How was it that there was a possibility for the Prince of life to die? I cannot enter into that mystery; but it was so. Though he was Lord of life, he could die, and he could yet continue to have such power that soon his spirit would return to his body, which remained dead in the tomb, but could not see corruption.

As I unroll my text I see another wonder, and that is, *the folly of rebellion against Christ*. They killed the Prince of life! What was the effect of this vain malice? Could they really kill the Prince of life? Go and extinguish the sun; go stop the heart of this great earth, so that there shall be no more pulsings in her tides; but you can never in very deed destroy "him who only hath immortality." Yet, they thought they had killed the Prince of life; and, in a sense, they had done so. And this is the idle dream of men to this day: they hope to quench the gospel, to silence the doctrines of grace, to exterminate the ancient orthodoxy, and to put modern heresies in its place. Vanity of vanities! Even as the resurrection mocked the guards, the watch, the stone, so shall the revival of true godliness and the restoration of true doctrine baffle the devices of men. They that count the towers, to pull them down, and go about Zion in the hope of destroying her bulwarks, shall yet know that the virgin daughter of Zion hath shaken her head at them, and laughed them to scorn. As the Lord Jesus liveth, "the Way, the Truth, and the Life" shall remain eternally the same. Ye fools, when will ye be wise, and quit your vain rebellions?

The text also exhibits *the triumph of his life*. "The Prince of life, whom God hath raised from the dead." His Godhead raised him, his Father raised him, his Spirit raised him. He resumed his life, and thus was declared to be the Son of God with power. This glorious resurrection of Christ should cause the universe to sing. Rejoice; for Jesus hath left the dead, no more to die. A dead Christ? Then, there would have been a dead gospel! What had we to preach to you if Jesus had not risen? Now that he hath risen again we have justification to proclaim. Go, tell it all the world over: "The Lord hath risen indeed; the Lord hath risen indeed." His resurrection is the cornerstone of the good news which the Lord hath sent to believing men. Wherefore, with such a truth to publish, we faint not. This moved the apostles to preach with such boldness, because they knew that he whom they preached lived again.

Notice here in the text *the assurance of that fact*—" Whereof we are witnesses." There stood Peter and John, two evidently honest men; everything about them was straightforward; they had nothing to conceal, and nothing to gain by their testimony. They could have called upon all the twelve, and even upon above four hundred brethren, who at once had seen the risen Lord. The witness is perfect and unquestionable. Jesus assuredly overcame the pains of death, his soul was not left among the dead. His victory is proven. "Oh," say you, "those witnesses died nearly nineteen hundred years ago." Yes, yes; but a testimony does not lose certainty by the lapse of years. If what they witnessed was true when they witnessed it, it is true now. They saw the Lord Jesus alive after his resurrection, and that settles the question. If hundreds of persons saw the Lord Jesus after he was risen, then he did certainly rise. Hallelujah! Here is a stone to build upon which the Goths and Vandals of modern doubt cannot tear from its place. The resurrection is as certain as any fact recorded in history. Jesus of Nazareth, though he was killed, did rise from the dead, and we rejoice therein.

Let us put the resurrection of Christ to its proper uses. Let us believe in him as "able to save them to the uttermost that come unto God by him, seeing he ever liveth to make intercession for them." Let us feel that our justification is certified by his resurrection, and our own resurrection is guaranteed by the self-same fact. We are safe in the hands of his living wisdom, his living power, his living love. Above all, let us look for our Lord's second coming; for he lives, and cannot for ever stay away from his people. He that brought again from the dead that great Shepherd of the sheep by the blood of the everlasting covenant will also cause him to appear as the chief Shepherd in the latter days. The heavens have received him for a while, but he must come to gather in his people and cause them to reign with him. "Wherefore comfort one another with these words."

III. I have done when I have taken time to SUGGEST AN ENQUIRY. Let each hearer say, "What has the Prince of life to do with me?" Beloved, do you know the Lord Jesus Christ? Is he alive to you, and do you live by him; or are you dead in sin? Which is it? A man must be either dead or alive. There is no space between death and life. You are either dead in sin or alive unto righteousness; which are you? Everyone may tell, if he will make searching enquiry into his own state. A brother said to me this morning, "When you preach I generally find I have enough to do to mind my own business." May you all find it so! Mind your own business, and enquire, "Have I received divine life from Christ?" I will suppose the answer comes from one, "No, I am afraid I have not received it." Well, then, do you wish for it? Is there in your heart a desire to possess this new life? "The Prince of life" is to be found if you seek him. Scripture gives us this as one of the rules of the kingdom, "He that seeketh findeth." But mind that you make a thorough and sincere search. A farmer, by some means, lost a five-pound-note in his barn. It was of great importance to him that he should find it, for it was the most of what he possessed. So he said to himself, "I am certain that I lost this note in the barn; and as I must find it, I will turn over every straw in the barn rather than lose it. I will never leave off looking for it till I find it." After some days' search, as "for a needle in a bottle of hay," he spied out his precious bank-note among the straw, and came home greatly rejoicing. Sometime afterward, it pleased God to visit him with a deep sense of sin, and he said to his wife, "I wish I could believe in the Saviour; but, alas! I cannot find him." She wisely replied, "If you will look for him as you looked for that bank-note in the barn, you will find him." "Well," said he, "that is what I will do"; and by grace his seeking of Jesus led to finding, and he was saved, and knew it. O brothers, turn over those trusses of memories of the Word which you heard long ago, and among them you may find the Saviour. O sisters, stir up the dust of what you learned in the Sunday-school, and you shall come upon your Lord before long. It is written, "Ye shall seek me, and find me, when ye shall search for me with all your heart."

If Christ were dead and motionless, he would be hard to discover; but life cannot long be hidden. On the hillside yonder soldiers are waiting to come down upon our army, but our watchers cannot see them, because the men lie quiet behind rocks and trees. The moment the soldiers begin to move we shall discern them: a living and moving object our glasses will soon detect. O souls, the Lord Jesus is living and moving, and therefore he is visible to the naked eye of faith! Look *for* him, and then look *to* him. Because he is life, he cannot be hid. Oh, that you may behold him soon! "Oh," says one, "I do long to find eternal life!" Then, seek it in the right way. Follow only one track: Jesus is the one and only way to life. In the old times of slavery in the States, when men escaped from their masters, they did so by knowing that the north star would lead them to freedom, and by following that heavenly guide. They had to travel by night, for fear of being captured and taken back; and therefore they learned little of the geography of the country: they cared for nothing but the star. As they hastened through the woods, they did not study botany; as they flitted through towns and villages along the road, they learned nothing of politics or social reform: they knew one thing, and minded that one thing only: they kept on following the pole-star. Brother, there are hosts of things that you do not know at present, and many things that you will never know; but see that you know Jesus, who is the pole-star of salvation. Keep Christ in your eye. Follow the crucified and risen One. Trust him, rely upon him, follow him, receive the life of which he is the Prince, and it shall be well with your soul. May you live in Christ Jesus, and glorify him as "the Prince of life" for ever and ever! Amen.

A Prince and a Saviour

"Him hath God exalted with his right hand to be a Prince and a Saviour, for to give repentance to Israel, and forgiveness of sins"—Acts v. 31.

THE same fact appears very differently to different people. Our Lord Jesus, having risen from the dead, was exalted with the right hand of God. To the Jewish priests and rulers this was a dreadful announcement. They could not endure to hear that Jesus, whom they slew and hanged on a tree, was yet alive. As the murderer is startled at the apparition of the ghost of the man he has slain, so were these rulers altogether dismayed at the idea that Jesus of Nazareth, whom they had nailed to the cross, was risen from the grave; and they were astounded at the very thought that he whom they had put to death with all the shame that they could devise was with the full might and majesty of God exalted to the highest heavens. They were cut to the heart by the announcement as though a sword had cut them in twain, dividing their very bones. Full of indignation, they consulted how they could compass the death of those who had brought such evil tidings to their ears.

The fact had a very different effect upon the apostles. They were the friends of Jesus, and witnesses to his majesty; and when they were certified that, though they had seen him laid in the grave, he had risen and had ascended, and was now sitting at the right hand of God, even the Father, filled them with the greatest boldness and consolation. They might well speak in such a name, for it was assuredly divine. He who had conquered death, and opened the gates of heaven, must be able to take care of his own followers, and therefore with delight and courage they bearded his enemies in their dens. There was no need of trembling; who could harm them? They blushed not; there was nothing to blush at, for it was a triumphant cause. They feared not; there was nothing to fear, for the name high over all in heaven, and earth, and hell, would surely protect them from all peril. What was to the rulers a source of dismay was to the apostles a cause of courage.

Let me now enquire of you all how this fact of the exaltation of Christ impresses you? What think ye of Christ? As time would fail me to press this enquiry upon all classes in this assembly, I shall confine myself to those who have not yet found peace with God, and shall set the Ascended One before them, that in him they may find salvation. That is to be my subject: I want this morning to find out seekers, and by the help of God's Holy Spirit to encourage them, to direct them, so that if possible this may be the last morning in which they shall be called seekers, and the first day in which they shall be finders, and know how sweet Christ is to those who find him, and how inestimably precious his salvation is to those who receive it by faith in him.

I should be very glad this morning if we could get to business; for a great deal of hearing is not earnest hearing, but mere playing at hearing. Too many of you have ears to hear and yet do not truly hear. The word reaches the outward ear and goes no further, because you do not hear heartily and with earnest heed. Thousands of hearers are like spectators at a banquet who come into the gallery and look down upon the guests who are feasting below, but never taste a morsel themselves. For them there are no dainties for actual tasting: they look at the oxen and the fatlings, they see the enjoyment of the feasters, sometimes they feel their own mouths watering for the good things, and they almost envy those who are banqueting; but they do not seek a place at the loaded tables for themselves, they remain lookers-on. I pray this morning, and may God hear the desire of my soul, that you may all become partakers of the exceeding grace of God in Christ Jesus at this moment. May you who have fed feed again as you see the feast prepared in Christ, and may you who have never ventured to "taste and see that the Lord is good" approach the provisions of love this morning, and be fed with bread to the full. I want to see an end of mere wishes and desires, and to rejoice over the commencement of actual faith, and realized salvation. Come to business, and let us have no more talk or delay. I long to see you saved and saved at once, or perhaps you may never be saved at all.

Seeker, you know right well that if you are ever to be saved your salvation lies in Jesus Christ. "There is none other name given under heaven whereby we must be saved," and you know that it is so. The point is to obtain the salvation which is in that name, and so to lay hold of Christ, that what is stored in him may become your own. May the Spirit of God bless you now, so that while we speak to our text you may be led by it to actual salvation in Christ Jesus.

I. First, then, let me invite you to NOTE HIS TITLES and learn their meaning. He is called "*a Prince and a Saviour.*" You must know the Saviour, or you cannot be saved. It is important to you to understand the nature and character of him whom the Lord has set forth to be the only salvation of guilty men. The Lord Jesus is here described to you under two instructive names which comprehend within themselves the most of his offices and relationships; consider him now with deep attention.

He is called *a Prince* first. This tells you that he is receiving *honour* at this time as the reward of his sufferings on earth. While he was here below he was treated by his rebellious subjects as if he had been a felon.

What a mass of presents the Prince of Wales has brought home from his foreign travel; but when the Prince of Glory visited his dominions here below what did he take home with him except his wounds? "He came unto his own, and his own received him not." The shame and the rejection are now ended, and in the glory yonder our Lord Jesus is manifestly a Prince, reverenced, obeyed, and honoured. Every angel in heaven delights to sing, "Thou art the King of glory, O Christ!" The highest powers and potentates of the spiritual kingdom bow before him, and hail him, joyfully hail him, as Lord over all, blessed for ever. His dominion extends over all creation; all things are put under his feet; he is the Prince of the kings of the earth, yea, he is Lord of all. Think of him, then, O seeking sinner, in this honourable estate. Let your mind conceive of Christ as worthy of all the homage and reverence that you can ever pay to him. Do not approach him without serious thought and careful reverence, for though he be condescending and gentle, yet is he a Prince to whom honour and obeisance must be paid.

The title of "prince" in our Lord's case signifies not only honour, but actual *power*. His is no nominal princedom—he has both glory and strength. Unto him is given the mediatorial kingdom, which includes all power in heaven and in earth, so that he is well styled "the blessed and only Potentate."

> "His hands the wheels of nature guide
> With an unerring skill,
> And countless worlds, extended wide,
> Obey his sovereign will."

Was it not said of old, "The government shall be upon his shoulder, and his name shall be called Wonderful, Counsellor, the Mighty God, the Everlasting Father, the Prince of Peace." He is the Prince of the house of David, he openeth and no man shutteth; he shutteth and no man openeth. There is no bound to the power of Christ. If you seek his salvation think of him as Almighty, and remember that his power is now employed for the salvation of those who trust in him. He is exalted on high to be a Prince that he may give repentance and forgiveness of sins, so that the power which you see in him is all available for your salvation. Is not this encouraging? Does not this remove those fears which are suggested by your own feebleness? I desire that you may be led by the power of the Holy Spirit to conceive of our glorified Lord with the reverence which his honour deserves, and with the confidence which his power should command.

Remember, too, that a Prince signifies one who has *dominion*, and if Christ is to be yours to-day you must let him have dominion over you. "He must reign." He claims to be Master and Lord to those who ask salvation at his hands; and is not the claim a just one? Whom should we serve but the Lord who became a servant for our sakes? It must be so, or salvation is impossible; those who serve sin are not saved, nor can they be except by being brought to serve the Christ of God.

> "This know, nor of the terms complain,
> Where Jesus comes he comes to reign;
> To reign, and with no partial sway;
> Lusts must be slain that disobey."

You must accept Jesus to be a leader and a commander to you, or you cannot win the battle of life. You must yield him loving obedience, or he will not be married to your souls. His dominion is sweetly tempered by love; so that, as the prophet writes, " Thou shalt call me no more Baali," that is, " My Lord," with a hardness of rulership, but *Ishi,* " My Lord," because thou art my man, my husband; even so Jesus is our head and Lord, but his rule is that of supreme affection. There must be obedience to Jesus if there be faith in him, for true faith worketh by love. Will you render it?

Thus, then, Christ Jesus our Prince is crowned with honour and clothed with power, and he rightly claims and exercises dominion. I pray, dear hearer, that you may pay homage before him at once as your Prince.

The other title of the text is " *A Saviour,*" and this name, it seems to me, should be very delightful to every seeking soul. Struggling into light, and prizing every ray of hope, it must be sweet to you to know that the Son of God is still a Saviour, though manifestly a Prince. Observe here *the perseverance of the Lord's love.* He was a Saviour here below ; he is a Saviour now that he has reached his throne. We read of him while on earth, "The Son of Man has come to seek and to save that which was lost," and now that he has gone we still hear concerning him, " He is able, therefore, to save them to the uttermost that come unto God by him, seeing he ever liveth to make intercession for them." He has not paused in his blessed work of love. " He is the Saviour of the body." Saviour he was when he wore the garment without seam, and traversed the weary leagues of Palestine ; Saviour he is now that he is girt about the paps with a golden girdle, and sits upon the throne; and Saviour he shall be in his second advent, for which we look, even the glorious appearing of our God and Saviour. Saviour he was when he wept over Jerusalem, Saviour he is still, though his eyes are like a flame of fire, and Saviour shall he be to his own redeemed when before his glance this earth shall flee away. Look up to him under that aspect.

O ye who seek him, remember that our exalted Lord is a Saviour in virtue of *the prevalence of the work which he achieved while here below.* When he dwelt here among men he was able to save, but his salvation was not complete, for he had not yet said, " It is finished." Now his redeeming work is done, and saving is a simple matter to him. Never did he so well deserve the name of Saviour as when he climbed to his throne. The ransom price has all been paid, and now, O Jesus, thou art Saviour indeed. The head of the serpent has been broken beneath thy heel : Saviour indeed thou art. The gates of the grave have been burst, the sepulchre is bereaven of its prey, and the resurrection is brought to light ; thou art henceforth a Saviour to the uttermost, O Jesus. " By thine agony and bloody sweat, by thy cross and passion, by thy precious death and burial," thou hast finished salvation, and now our spirits shall rejoice in God our Saviour. I pray that you who seek him may have grace this morning to see him in the light of a Saviour, as pursuing still the work of saving souls, but yet pursuing it only to apply the atonement which his death completed. Look at him, O ye ends of the earth, as the Saviour, for such he is, and there is none else.

If he be a Saviour too, remember, this shows to trembling hearts *how approachable he is.* You might be abashed at coming to a prince, but you may be encouraged in coming to a Saviour. O thou that wouldst be rid of thy sin, dost thou fear the Prince? Well mayest thou, for he can punish thee. But fear not, for the Saviour will forgive thee. Diseased with sin, dost thou think thyself unworthy of his princely presence? Yet he is Physician as well as Prince: therefore come thou where the glance of his eye, or the touch of his hand, will make thee perfectly whole. I wish I knew how to put my Lord before you in the best of words, and describe him so sweetly that you would all fall in love with him: but, indeed, I believe him to be so beautiful that if I can only convey to you the faintest idea of him you must be enamoured of him, if you love that which is good and fair. While I am describing him I feel I do but put a mist about him; but, then, he is the sun, and he can break through my cloudy language, and cause your hearts to see him in all his glory.

"A Prince and a Saviour." Suppose I put the words together and say, a Prince-saviour: one who is lordly and kingly in the salvation which he brings, and deals out no stinted grace, but makes us to receive of his fulness grace for grace. Turn the titles the other way, and reverse the order, and truly he is a Saviour-prince whose glory it is to save, whose kingdom and power and dominion are all turned in full force to achieve the work of rescuing his people from destruction. "A Prince and a Saviour." This is the Christ to whom you must come, O ye who would be delivered from your sins. Look to him and live.

II. APPROACH HIM, THEN, UNDER THESE TWO CHARACTERS. I would come to very close quarters with you who are seeking the Lord, while I urge you to approach Jesus Christ as a *Prince.* "And how shall we do that?" say you. I answer, come to him at once, with the *sorrowful confession* of your past rebellion. You have lived I do not know how many years, you unconverted ones, without paying due homage to Jesus; you have known about him, but you have not obeyed him. Up to this moment you have resisted his love, and said, " Let us break his bands asunder and cast his cords from us." Confess this, and be ashamed, for it is a great disgrace not to be swayed by such love as that of Christ; it is a great sin not to be in love with such an inimitable character as that which shines in the person of the Son of God; it shows great moral hardness of heart, and bluntness of perception, and prejudice of soul, and ignorance of mind not to be at once the willing subject of Christ. These many years you have said, " I will not have this man to reign over me." Oh, may the gentle Spirit cause you now to see the folly and the sin of this conduct, and may you confess it with tearful eyes while you obey the bidding of the old Psalm, and "Kiss the Son, lest he be angry."

When you have confessed the past before this Prince, then I charge you *accept his great purpose, and submit to his rule.* He is a Prince, therefore yield yourself to be his subject. Do you know what the object of his rule is? It is to make you love God, and to be like God. You are created, and therefore launched upon the sea of existence; you cannot help this fact or alter it; your existence has been given you and you cannot lose it. How can this creation of yours be an eternal blessing, and the danger be removed of its becoming a never-ending curse? The answer is simple; if you are right with your Creator you are right with everything; if you are reconciled to him you will be happy in time and in eternity. But you cannot be right with your Creator until past guilt is forgiven and sin is given up, and the love of wrongdoing, the love of everything that is contrary to his pure and holy mind is destroyed in you. Now, Jesus comes in order that he may kill in you everything that is contrary to the mind of God; he comes to make you holy, ay, to make you perfect. Will you yield yourself to his gentle purpose? Are you ready to obey his precepts by means of which his Spirit will sanctify you wholly—spirit, soul, and body? He is able to save from sin; his name is Jesus, " for he shall save his people from their sins." Do you really wish to be saved from sin? Jesus once asked a sick man, " Wilt thou be made whole?" It is the question which he asks of you to-day, dear friend. You would be glad to be saved from going to hell; ay, that is not it; do you desire to be saved from that which created hell, from that which is the fuel of the unquenchable fire and the tooth of the undying worm—namely, the love of iniquity, the love of sin? Christ can save from sin as a Saviour, and lead you into the kingdom of righteousness, of which he is the Prince. Are you willing that he should do so?

If it be taken for granted that you have approached the Lord Jesus in this way, I would next say, as he is a Prince, *surrender everything to him.* Christ claims of you that if you are saved, since it is through his redemption, you should henceforth be his. If he has redeemed you then you belong to him; henceforth you are not your own, you are bought with a price. It is an inevitable consequence of being redeemed from death and hell by Jesus' blood that you should be Christ's for ever. Oh, can you lift your eye to heaven and say, " If he will have me, I will cheerfully be his "? Can you make over now, this morning, by the help of God's Spirit, your body and your soul as a living sacrifice? Can you give to him now all that you owe, and all that you have? Could you stand at the foot of the cross and say—

> " And if I might make some reverse,
> And duty did not call,
> I love my God with zeal so great,
> That I would give him all"?

He asks it of you: will you do it, O seeking soul, will you do it? For if that be done surely then Christ is to you a Prince and a Saviour?

And if this be accomplished, and he be Lord, then *pay your loving, loyal homage to your Prince.* Behold him in his glory, where all the angels cast their crowns before him, while the elders adore him with vials full of sweet odours. If Christ is to be your Saviour he must be your prince, and you must have a loyal attachment to him, deep and true. Is this a hard thing to ask of you? Methinks it is the joy of my life to be the subject and the servant of King Jesus. The name of the Queen stirs the British soldier's heart, and oftentimes in the hour of battle he has thought of his sovereign and his country, and has been willing to lay down his life; but the love of Jesus is a more intense passion by far, and the loyalty of a good soldier to Jesus Christ is a stronger force than any loyalty to earthly princes. You must have this. Do you see how right it is that you should have it? Towards such an one as Jesus we are proud to cherish a love which many waters cannot quench, a love stronger than death. Approach him, then, with loving hearts, or at least bring your hearts, and ask to have them made loving.

You must also approach the Lord Jesus as *Saviour*. Do not proudly murmur at this. I have known some who have been willing to take Christ for their example, and as their teacher; and so far they have owned him as a Prince, but they cannot brook it that they should confess their need of a Saviour: but you must have Jesus as a Saviour as well as a Prince, or you will be lost for ever. I do now affectionately urge the sinner who is seeking mercy to come to Christ Jesus, *confessing that he needs a Saviour*. Look at your sin, and consider your past life with all its transgressions. Are you not ashamed of it? Are you not afraid to stand before that judgment-seat where you must give an account for every idle word that you have spoken? Does not conscience fill you with trembling? Well, come and tell the Saviour; tell him all. Pour out your heart before him; acknowledge that you are undone, and condemned, unless he can in his pity obtain a pardon for you. Are you actually doing so now? Come to business, as I have said before; make the confession now from your heart while we are yet speaking.

That done, since Christ is a Saviour, *believe that he is able to save you*. Seeing he died the bitter death of the cross, suffering from divine justice in a most terrible manner upon Calvary, there must be in those five wounds power enough to be the death of every sin. O crimson blood, thou must have merit enough in thee to wash out crimson sin. It must be so. He who died upon the cross is God as well as perfect man, and a sacrifice offered by him must have infinite power and efficacy to remove sin. Believe thou this also, and when thou hast believed it then understand that thou must *submit thyself entirely to his processes of salvation*. He is able to save thee, but he has a way of his own, and he will not save thee in thy way but in his way; and his way of saving thee is to make thee feel the smart and bitterness of sin, to make thee hate that sin and loathe it, and so to turn thee from it for ever. Thus he saves thee: art thou willing to have it so? Canst thou say " Farewell " this morning to the sins thou hast so long loved? Is there any attraction to thee yet in the harlots and the riotous livers with whom thou hast spent thy Father's substance? Hast thou still a lingering love to the far country, or canst thou bid its citizens a long farewell? Do the swine attract thee? Hast thou a hankering after the husks which they do eat, so that thou canst refuse to go to Christ when he would take thee away from these filthy pleasures and degrading delights? Canst thou say, "I cannot linger longer here; it is Sodom, and the fire will soon descend from heaven; I must flee for my life, and look not behind me; I must and will do so, for Jesus takes me by the hand and leads me on"? If thou hast sincerely done this and thou art willing to have a divorce from thy sins, *mensa et thoro*, from table and bed, and hearth, and in all ways, so that sin and thee shall no more be on loving terms, then, I say, if thou art willing for this, all thou hast now to do is to *trust thy Saviour*. Lean all thy weight on him; repose thy whole self on him. Thou seest thy need of him, thou seest his power to save thee, and thou knowest what is meant by being saved, namely, delivered from the power of sin: wilt thou now trust him to make thee pure? If thou dost, thou hast come to him as a Prince and a Saviour, and he has said, "Him that cometh to me I will in no wise cast out," and he will not, cannot cast thee out.

This approach to the Lord Jesus should be made at this moment, where you now are. There is no need to go elsewhere, or tarry for an hour. While yet you are here God's Holy Spirit can enable you to come to Christ as your Prince and your Saviour.

I am putting the truth very plainly. I have scarcely used one figure of speech or a single ornament of language, but I have tried to tell you the way of salvation very plainly, and having told you it I can do no more but earnestly ask you, will you have this Prince and Saviour or not? May the Spirit of God persuade you to give the right reply.

III. In the third place, NOTE THE GIFTS OF THE LORD JESUS. He is "exalted with God's right hand to give repentance and forgiveness of sins." Now if, dear hearer, thou art distressed this morning beneath the burden of sin, I pray thee to catch at this blessed sentence, for there is honey here which shall take away the bitterness of thy soul. I think I heard thee say, "Fain would I have Christ as Prince and Saviour; I am willing enough; but this hard heart, this rebellious will, what can I do with them?" Listen: "He is exalted to give *repentance*." This does not mean, as some have said, to give space for repentance. We must not add words to Scripture. Nor does it mean to make repentance acceptable. Look at the text, and no trace of such a meaning is there. But "to give repentance," and repentance itself is intended, which is as much the gift of the ascended Saviour as the forgiveness which follows upon it. What is repentance? If we keep to its literal meaning it is a change of mind, but then it is a very wonderful change of mind. He can give thee to change thy mind about all the past, so that the things which pleased thee shall grieve thee, that which charmed thee shall disgust thee, that which thou dost love thou shalt hate, and that which thou dost desire thou shalt abhor. This is his gift to his chosen: "I will take away the stony heart out of their flesh, and I will give them a heart of flesh; a new heart also will I give them, and a right spirit will I put within them." What a marvellous thing this change of mind as to the past is. He can also change thy mind as to the present and the future, so that instead of looking for present pleasure thou wilt find thy delight in future glory realized by faith. Dost thou understand me? It shall be pleasure enough to thee to think of the pleasures at God's right hand for evermore. Jesus can save thee from living like the beast which looks not an hour ahead, but is content with the pasturage around it, and will even walk into the slaughter-house to be slain, so little does it know what is reserved for it. Jesus can save thee from being so brutish, and make thee look into the eternal future with the eye of a wise man. He can give thee a good hope, and inspire thee with a good object worthy of the eternity which lies before thee. Christ can give such a change of mind as shall make the whole world seem new, and thyself most changed of all.

Repentance includes a most needful sense of sin, and the Saviour can give thee this by his Spirit. He can fill thy soul with the barbed arrows of conviction till thy heart bleeds with inward grief on account of sin, or he can work more gently and make thee repent by melting thee beneath the smiles of love. He can make thee sing—

> "Thy mercy is more than a match for my heart,
> Which wonders to feel its own hardness depart;
> Dissolved by thy goodness, I fall to the ground,
> And weep to the praise of the mercy I've found."

He can work in thee desires after holiness and hatred of every false way; he can take the guile out of thy soul as well as the guilt out of thy life; he can give thee to be true and upright before him, and cleansed in the inward parts.

Everything that is included in "repentance" Jesus Christ is exalted to give. Now, if no one obtains repentance, then Christ is exalted in vain; but somebody must have it, for Christ is not exalted in vain; why then shouldst not thou have it? Thou needest it: thy heart seems hard as granite and cold as a block of ice. Well, if thou needest it, why shouldst thou not have it? To whom does a man give his alms but to the needy? Do not the wise distribute their gifts to those who want them? If thou wantest them come and freely take of them. Repentance will not spring out of thy unrenewed heart, but the Prince and Saviour can create it in thee; come thou to him for it.

> "True belief and true repentance,
> Every grace that brings you nigh,
> Without money,
> Come to Jesus Christ and buy."

Here I preach Christ not merely to penitent sinners, but to impenitent sinners. O rock, be smitten with this rod! The cross can fetch the waters of repentance out of stony hearts! O hard heart be melted with this sacred fire! The fire of Jesus' love can dissolve the northern iron and steel of obdurate impenitence. He is exalted on high to give repentance, therefore, O sinners, look to him for repentance.

It is added as his second gift, "to give *forgiveness*;" and the forgiveness which Jesus gives is very blessed. I pray thee, seeking soul, catch at each word I now say on this point. He can pass an act of amnesty and oblivion for all thy sin. If he forgive thee, all thy transgressions shall be as though they had never been. He will make clean work of it, blotting out every record of thy sin, so that in God's book there shall be no grieving memory of thy having been a sinner at all. So powerful is the atoning blood that all manner of sin and transgression shall be forgiven unto men for its sake. Sins against a holy God, sins against Christ's love and blood, sins against conscience, sins against the law, sins against the gospel, sins which have lain in your bones from your youth up, sins of your middle age, sins of your old age, aggravated sins, black sins, damnable sins, all are gone when he saith, "I have blotted out thy sins like a cloud, and as a thick cloud thy transgressions." Jesus has gone to heaven on purpose to give this complete forgiveness.

Now mark, when full forgiveness comes it brings with it the eternal removal of the penalty. The forgiven man cannot be punished; for him there is no hell, no worm that dieth not, nor fire that never can be quenched. God cannot forgive and then punish. If he remove thy transgressions from thee as far as the east is from the west, then who is he that shall lay anything to thy charge? Who is he that can condemn? And who is he that can punish thee?

With the pardon of sin there shall come also a restoration of every privilege. All that Adam had in the garden you shall have to be yours—not all of it to enjoy just now, but all and more than all shall really be restored to you, for the man who wears the righteousness of Christ and is accepted in the Beloved may not have a paradise on earth, but he has a paradise above; for him there may be no golden apples of Eden, but there shall be the fruit of the tree of life, of which he shall eat for ever and ever.

"What Adam had, and forfeited for all,
Christ hath who cannot fail nor fall."

He that believeth on Christ Jesus shall dwell in bliss and be satisfied with the goodness of the Lord.

And mark thee once again, thou shalt, when forgiven, have *quiet in thy soul,* for when thou art pardoned all the hurly-burly of thy spirit shall turn into a deep calm; thou shalt have the "peace of God which passeth all understanding" to "keep thy heart and mind by Christ Jesus." "Oh," saith one, "I would give my eyes for it." You shall have it without giving your eyes. Give your heart: nay, and not even give your heart as a price for it, but take the blessing freely, for freely it is given. Jesus is exalted on high that he may grant free pardons to great offenders. I come back to that statement: if Jesus is exalted on purpose to give pardon, then if he does not give forgiveness to some one he is exalted in vain. He must therefore give it to some: why should he not bestow it upon you?

The text says, "to give repentance to Israel." Who and what was Israel? The people of Israel in our Lord's time were surely the very worst of sinners, for it was by them that the Lord was nailed to the cross. It was the Jews who cried "Crucify him, crucify him." It means, then, that Jesus is exalted to give repentance and pardon to the chief of sinners, and if I be one, if instead of blaming Jews or the Romans I blame myself, if I take the death of Christ on my own shoulders and say,

"'Twas you my sins, my cruel sins,
His chief tormentors were;
Each of my crimes became a nail,
And unbelief the spear."

Then is he exalted to give me repentance and remission for my great sins.

Do I need to ask you, will you have these two gifts? Ah, friends, it shows how deep is the depravity of the human heart that we should have need to press our Master's mercies on you. If sin were not a madness, it would only need the preacher to come and tell out this blessed gospel, and you would begin to sing, "How beautiful upon the mountains are the feet of him that bringeth good tidings, that publisheth salvation, that saith unto Zion, Thy God reigneth as a Prince and a

Saviour in heaven." Instead, however, of offering my Lord a joyful reception, some of you will count it a weariness to be entreated and pleaded with. I feel in my own soul that though my Master enables me to put these things before you, you will not receive them unless his love constrains you. We can bring the horse to the water, but we cannot make it drink; and we can bring Christ before you, but we cannot make you accept him. I pray that there may be some soft relentings, some gentle meltings of your spirit this very morning, for "unto you is the word of this salvation sent."

My dear hearer, I may never have addressed you before; happy shall I be if at the very first assault I win your soul for my Master. Or perhaps I have spoken with you many, many times, and my voice is getting rather stale and flat to you. Well, I am sorry if I mar the message, but still it is so good that, though I stammered it, you ought still to catch at it and say, "Yes, if he is exalted to give repentance and pardon, here is my bosom, Lord, pour them both into my soul at this good hour."

IV. As I said to you about the titles, approach the Lord Jesus as such, so now I say about his gifts—ASK HIM FOR THEM. Ask now, at this moment. Again I say, I want you to come to business, and be doing as well as listening; while I am speaking may the Holy Ghost incline your hearts to practical obedience. At this moment ask the Lord Jesus *humbly* for repentance and pardon. You do not deserve these gifts; if he leaves you to perish he will be just. He will have mercy on whom he will have mercy, and he will have compassion on whom he will have compassion. You have no claim to his love, and must not set up any. Your heart is hard, and he can leave you in your unbelief: you are guilty, and he can justly leave you to bear your punishment. Ask humbly, therefore, not daring to claim anything, but appealing to his sovereign grace. Sing—

> "O save a guilty sinner, Lord,
> Whose hope still hovering round thy word;
> Would light on some sweet promise there,
> Some sure support against despair."

Ask *importunately*. Do not come to mercy's gate this morning with a cold heart and a trifling spirit. Come with this resolve, "I will not leave the cross till my sins have left me. I will plead for the grace of God until I obtain it. With importunity will I wrestle saying—

> 'Lord, I cannot let thee go
> Till a blessing thou bestow.'"

The angel is near this morning; seize him; grasp him; and if he seem to fling thee off yet hold him still, and say, "I will not let thee go except thou bless me, and bless me now?" You will get the blessing if you can pray like that: with deep humility because you are unworthy, but with violent importunity because you are in such fearful peril, and you cannot endure to be lost.

But I ask you to pray *believingly*, and this is indeed the pith of the matter. Ask for remission and repentance this morning, believing that Christ can give it, and believing that he is as willing as he is able. If you can look up and see those dear eyes which wept over sinners;

if you can see those wounds, still open for sinners, like so many
gates of heaven, you will perceive that Jesus still calls to you, and
bids you trust him. Do not think him unwilling to forgive. That
would be too cruel a suspicion after he has died. Trust him wholly,
only, sincerely, solely. Have done with those works, and prayers, and
tears which you have been wont to rely upon. All that you ever did to
save yourself must be undone. Nature's spinning must all be unravelled,
her figleaves will wither; sin's nakedness requires a better covering.
Your only hope lies in him who is Prince and Saviour. Cry at once to
him—

"A guilty, weak, and helpless worm,
  On thy kind arms I fall ;
Thou art my strength and righteousness,
  My Jesus, and my all."

And—and this is the last word—*ask now*. Do not put me off this
morning. I am in earnest if you are not. But oh, it is *your* soul, not
mine, that is now at stake. I pray thee be in earnest, O man, and be
so now. Perhaps thou wilt never hear another pleading; it may be
this is the last Sabbath thou wilt spend on earth; and where wilt
thou be if thou reject the Saviour? Where the Sabbath bell shall never
ring out its happy summons, where the silver voice of mercy shall
never again salute thee. There is another world; you will not die like
a dog; there is a judgment to come, and you will have to stand before
your Maker to give an account of all your life. There is an everlasting
punishment as surely as there is an eternal reward. Now I ask thee,
and I charge thee, to go not further till thou hast answered this
question—is it worth while to lose thy soul whatever thou canst gain
by it? The Romans when they meant to bring things to an issue with
an Oriental tyrant, sent their ambassador, and the ambassador was to
bring his answer back—yes or no, war or peace. What think you the
messenger did? When he saw the king he stooped down, and with his
wand he drew a ring upon the ground round the monarch; and then
said, "Step outside that ring, and it means war with Rome; before you
leave that circle you must accept our terms of peace, or know that
Rome will use her utmost force to fight with you." I draw a ring
round you while you are sitting in that pew, or standing in that aisle,
and I demand an answer. Sinner, wilt thou now be saved or not?
To-day is the accepted time, to-day is the day of salvation. O Holy
Spirit, lead the sinner now to ask and he shall receive, to believe, and
he shall be saved. Amen and Amen.

The Mediator—Judge and Saviour

"*And he commanded us to preach unto the people, and to testify that it is he which was ordained of God to be the judge of quick and dead. To him give all the prophets witness, that through his name whosoever believeth in him shall receive remission of sins*"—Acts x. 42, 43.

THESE two verses are an extract from a very remarkable sermon, a sermon preached by Peter in the house of Cornelius upon the occasion of the Gentile Pentecost. I think we are entitled to call the event by that name, for then upon the Gentiles was poured out the gift of the Holy Ghost. Peter preached at the first Pentecost, when the Holy Ghost fell upon the company of Jewish believers; and it is remarkable that he should be the preacher at the second Pentecost, when the Holy Ghost descended upon those of the uncircumcision while they were listening to the gospel. Philip was at Cæsarea, and might have been called in, but God had determined that the strict Peter, the minister of the circumcision, should himself open the door of faith to the Gentiles. Paul was at that time converted, and it might have seemed to be more appropriate to have used him in enlightening this Italian officer, but the Lord thought not so: he would send the Spirit upon the Gentiles in connection with the same person who preached when this visitation blessed the converts of Israel. Peter preached as it were upon the ruins of the middle wall of partition which once divided the sons of men.

The occasion was very special, and hence the sermon is the more worthy of our earnest consideration. What kind of discourse is that which is likely to be sealed by the Holy Spirit? We may learn something upon that point from the instance before us.

Notice that it was a sermon "preached by request." I have seen those words printed upon the title page of very poor sermons, as a sort of apology for their being printed. I have wondered who it was that did request them, and whether the requesters were pleased with what they got by their petition. I should think that they would hardly have asked that the same words should be spoken unto them again. But this request was a very honest and hearty one, for Cornelius sent many miles to fetch the preacher, and the preacher came a long day's journey in order to deliver his discourse. It were devoutly to be wished that many such sermons would both be preached and published by request. When men are anxious to hear such discourses, and count the preacher to be their benefactor, there is every hope that the truth will work their salvation.

This discourse was delivered to a model congregation. One might be satisfied to preach in the middle of the night to such an assembly, for a devout family had come together at the earnest request of a leading kinsman to have the gospel preached to them. To that assembly not a single person came in late: every one was there before the speaker arrived. Late attendance frequently means heartless worship, disturbance, and distraction. "Now, therefore," said Cornelius before Peter began, "are we all here present before God?" This was well: O that all hearers were punctual, that all worship might be undisturbed. Better still would it be if all our audiences felt that they were "before God:" this would create a solemn feeling and ensure devout attention. The hearers were all in a waiting and expectant mood, and all in a receptive condition, desiring, as Cornelius said, "to hear all things that are commanded thee of God." Never was the ground better ploughed, nor in a finer condition for receiving the living seed.

Peter gave them a very plain and simple sermon: you cannot find a flourish in it, nor a metaphor, nor even the least attempt at oratory, as indeed you do not find in the sermons of inspired men. Those gentlemen who preach grandiloquently are uninspired, you may depend upon that, or else they would not attempt the high and mighty style. The inspiration which the Holy Ghost gives leads men to use great plainness of speech. Not in words only was Peter plain, but the truths which he taught were the first principles of the faith, and it is generally by these that men are saved: points of difficult theology are not often the means of conversion. What have we to do with the fireworks of rhetoric, or the playthings of controversy, when men are anxious to know the way of salvation? Simple as the discourse was it was a very powerful one; so powerful, indeed, that all that heard it were converted. I do not see any intimation that one of them remained unconvinced; for the forty-fourth verse says, "The Holy Ghost fell on all them which heard the word." What a very remarkable occasion was this, when all who heard the truth felt the power of the Holy Spirit. What would I not give to be enabled to preach after that fashion, and to see such a result?

This sermon, however, was never finished: it remains for ever a homiletical fragment, a broken column of the temple of wisdom, a discourse of which we shall never know the conclusion intended by its author. I am sure that Peter felt full of matter that day, for so a minister usually feels when he knows that he is sent by the Lord himself with a special commission, and sees a people with open heart receiving all that he utters. He then feels like a vessel wanting vent, his heart is inditing a good matter, his tongue is the pen of a ready writer. Yet the sermon was never finished, but closed abruptly. Oh that our sermons were incomplete for the same cause that Peter's was; for the Holy Spirit, who speaketh better by himself than by the most earnest voice, caused a divinely joyful interruption:—"The Holy Ghost fell on all them which heard the word." The sermon was stopped while they heard the converts speak with tongues, and magnify God, and the preacher did not return to his sermon, but together with his converts attended to baptism and then enjoyed holy fellowship. Oh that the Spirit of God would in the same manner interrupt us! We have too much talk, and too little of those blessed silences which he is sure to cause. It were better for our lips to be sealed by the hour than for us to speak except as he opens our mouth to show forth the praises of the Lord. A sacred irregularity would be far better in our public services than the prim monotony of death. For all these reasons I think I have a claim upon your very earnest attention while we look at Peter's sermon more intently: surely a sermon produced under such circumstances, leading up to such results, and interrupted so divinely, deserves to be reverently studied.

What was the subject? What was Peter preaching upon? He was preaching Christ and him crucified. No other subject ever does produce such effects as this. The Spirit of God bears no witness to Christless sermons. Leave Jesus out of your preaching, and the Holy Spirit will never come upon you. Why should he? Has he not come on purpose that he may testify of Christ? Did not Jesus say, "He shall glorify me: for he shall receive of mine, and shall shew it unto you"? Yes, the subject was Christ, and nothing but Christ, and such is the teaching which the Spirit of God will own. Be it ours never to wander from this central point: may we determine to know nothing among men but Christ and his cross.

I think there were six heads in the sermon, though he spoke only of one subject, that is, Christ. The apostle spake of the Lord's *person*. I will not enlarge, but simply give you his words. He said, "Preaching peace by Jesus Christ: he is Lord of all." He did not teach the Socinian gospel, which sets forth a Christ who is not God. We love "the man Christ Jesus," but we cannot endure the doctrine that he is no more than man. How could he save us? Could a mere man redeem us? "He is Lord of all," and because he is thus supreme we feel we can trust him with the salvation of our souls. Peter is very clear upon the sovereign Godhead of Jesus. His words are few, but they are exceedingly explicit. Having spoken of his person, he then spoke of his *life*, and what a pithy summary it is: "How God anointed Jesus of Nazareth with the Holy Ghost and with power." There was the spring of his life's power, his anointing from the Holy Ghost, who bare witness of him in Jordan and at other times. He saith, "The Spirit of the Lord is upon me, for the Lord hath anointed me." The tenor of his life is set out in the next sentence, "Who went about doing good." That one stroke gives a full portrait of Christ. You have summed up in that sentence the biography of Jesus as he lived among men: he was an itinerant missionary, a travelling preacher, a general benefactor, and "he went about doing good." Then Peter passed on to his third point, which was the Saviour's *death*, of which he says, "Whom they slew and hanged on a tree." He does not take away the offence of the cross, nor put it in smooth language, as some would have done; but he confesses that they hanged him on a tree. Hanging or crucifixion was an accursed and shameful death in the judgment of all mankind, and Peter confesses that his Lord thus died: there is no concealing, or even veiling of the matter; he acknowledges that he died by hanging upon a tree. I rejoice in this bold telling out of the doctrine of the cross in what some may call its baldness, but in what we will regard as its sublime simplicity. In Christ's death the shame is honour, and the disgrace renown: to deck the cross with flowers and make crucifixion honourable is to rob the august transaction of its leading element, namely, the endurance of shame because of man's shameful sin. Then Peter passed on to our Lord's *resurrection*, for that is an essential part of the gospel, and the gospel is not preached where a risen Christ is forgotten. "Him God raised up the third day, and showed him openly." It was no fiction; he was openly shown on many occasions to those best able to recognize him. The risen Christ was seen, and seen clearly, yea, and spoken with, and touched with finger and hand by his disciples. He was not shown to all the people, for he was not to be exhibited to gratify curiosity, but to secure faith. The evidence of five hundred persons is quite sufficient to the establishment of an historical fact, and perhaps better for the purpose than the witness of unnumbered crowds. If you suppose those five hundred to have been deceived, you would just as readily believe that a whole nation was mistaken. Had the nation of the Jews received the truth of Christ's resurrection they could not have given us better evidence than we have already that Christ is risen: rather it would have been said,—This is all an Israelitish fable: the Jewish nation, prejudiced in their own favour, have banded together to maintain the fiction of a risen Messiah in order to add to their own national repute. There is something far more convincing in the testimony of men who themselves were persecuted and put to death for bearing such witness, and died adhering unaminously to the truth of their common testimony. God gave to the whole world sufficient evidence to establish the resurrection of Christ, for many did eat and drink with him after he rose from the dead. Then Peter came to the last two points of his sermon, which were, *the judgment*, which he felt it necessary to preach—declaring that Jesus Christ who died and rose again is now designated the Judge of all mankind: and lastly, as the gem of all, Peter preached *salvation* by the Lord Jesus most fully and graciously when he said, "Through his name whosoever believeth in him shall receive remission of sins." This was what he was driving at; and when he had reached this point enough truth had been taught to save a soul, and God, the Holy Spirit, at once used it.

I purpose this morning to confine your attention to those last two points of Peter's sermon, for I am sure that there is much profitable matter in them. Not that I intend to bring out the meaning of each of these verses separately so much as the connection of the two, to show how Christ's being made Judge of all mankind has a connection with his being the Saviour of all those who believe in him, to whom he forgives their sins. May God bless the meditation to our souls' profit.

I. OUR DIVINE MEDIATOR'S POSITION INVOLVES TWO OFFICES. We are not now living under the immediate government of God, but under the reign of Jesus Christ the Mediator; for God hath committed all judgment unto the Son. Jesus now reigns, according to the word of the psalmist, "Thou hast put all things in subjection under his feet." We are living under a mediatorial dispensation, in which all power is delivered unto Jesus in heaven and in earth. God shineth upon us now through the person of his dear Son, not therefore with those fierce and strong beams which in justice must have consumed us, but through the medium of the accepted person of Jesus; with mild, soft, genial radiance for our comfort and our salvation. Inasmuch as Christ has thus received mediatorial power in its fulness, there are two offices in it.

The first is that of Judge, and the second is that of Saviour. First, Jesus Christ as mediator has become our *Judge*. "The Father judgeth no man, but hath committed all judgment unto the Son." "To this end Christ both died, and rose, and revived, that he might be Lord both of the dead and living, for we shall all stand before the judgment seat of Christ;" mark that—"*of Christ.*" Jesus of Nazareth has become "Judge of quick and dead." In this capacity he has judicial authority over all mankind. Offences now are offences against him, transgressions against the royal Son of God. He has authority over men, and he will try all of us at the last, as he is even now sitting in judgment upon all our acts and thoughts and intents. We shall all have to stand before him, "that every one may receive the things done in the body, according to that he hath done, whether it be good or bad." He will sum up the evidence and decide the doom of all. We shall each one appear before his great white throne, and he shall divide the nations as a shepherd divideth the sheep from the goats. If any are condemned, his lips shall say, "Depart, ye cursed": if any are glorified, from his lips shall proceed the sentence, "Come, ye blessed of my Father, inherit the kingdom prepared for you from the foundation of the world." Yes, he that hung upon the cross sitteth now as King upon the holy hill of Zion, and he must reign till all his enemies are made his footstool, and he must come a second time without a sin-offering unto the judgment of mankind. That judgment of our Saviour's will be authoritative and final, and it will concern all the race of Adam. It is of divine appointing and can never be questioned, for God "hath appointed a day, in the which he will judge the world in righteousness by that man whom he hath ordained; whereof he hath given assurance unto all men, in that he hath raised him from the dead." The Lord Jesus is Judge of the quick, that is, of the living, and of the dead. All that will be alive at his coming, kings and peasants, professing saints and avowed sinners, must alike stand before his bar; and all the myriads whose mouldering bodies have turned the world into one huge graveyard must live again, and all answer to his trumpet summons. The Jews that accused him, the Romans that executed him, the ancient Gentiles that persecuted his apostles, the scoffers of modern times who ridicule his claims, all kings and patriarchs before the flood, with all the numerous host destroyed by the deluge, and the myriads upon myriads of all the nations that have come and gone since then, and all that shall come and shall yet go, must all without exception put in a personal appearance before the bar of the Nazarene, who is also the Son of God. This is part of his work as Mediator between God and man, and well will he discharge the solemn trust.

The second part of his office is to be a *Saviour*, "that through his name whosoever believeth in him should receive remission of sins." He is a Prince and a Saviour; power in him attends his grace. He has the sovereign right of condemnation or justification: the final judgment is with him: he saith, "Behold I come quickly, and my reward is with me to give every man according as his work shall be." The powers of life and death are entrusted to Jehovah Jesus, the Son of God. He has authority to pass by transgression, iniquity, and sin in his own name, as in the name of the Eternal God. His atonement has made it possible for him to do this in perfect consistency with his character as Judge: he pardons, and when he pardons it is as just an act as when he condemns. If this seem a paradox to you, read the New Testament, and see how he can be just and yet the justifier of him that believeth: see how it is that in the atoning sacrifice "righteousness and peace have kissed each other," and how God is severely just in all that he does, and yet aboundeth towards believers in richness of grace in passing by their sin.

It seems to me to be a very blessed thought that the same universality which pervades the Mediator's dignified proceedings as judge, is to be seen in his condescending operations as Saviour; for it is not to the Jews alone that he has come, though to them he is preached; would God they did receive him: but he is come to the Gentiles also, that "whosoever believeth in him shall receive remission of sins." Now, there is neither black nor white, nor male nor female, nor rich nor poor with him: humanity is one great family fallen, and out of it shall arise a great family restored, who come and trust the Saviour. Jesus Christ is able to save to the uttermost all them that come unto God by him. As well of the ages past was he the Saviour of believers as of this age and of ages yet to come: he is mighty always to save; the anointed Saviour, yesterday, to-day, and for ever the same. See ye then, because Christ is the Interposer, and has intervened between God and man, and has royal authority so to do, he therefore takes upon himself the double work of judging and of pardoning. Let the two works dwell together in your minds: "He is a just God and a Saviour."

II. Kindly follow me in the next consideration: BOTH THESE OFFICES REGARD MEN AS SINNERS. I am sick to the death of hearing men talk about the goodness which is latent in human nature. I read the other day an instruction to missionaries, that when they go to a foreign land they should always believe that men are good, that there is a natural religiousness in them, which, like sparks in the embers, only needs blowing up a little, and it will certainly flame up into a wonderful fire of true devotion, and so on. Pooh! There not a word of truth in all this flattery. No doctrine could be more untrue to the very existence of Christ. If natural religion would have sufficed, why need a divine Saviour to have descended among us? The best that the light of nature can do falls short of righteousness. The case of Cornelius in the chapter we have been reading makes it evident that the best natural religion needs to be illuminated by revelation and instructed by the doctrine of the cross; for there is Cornelius, a man worshipping the true God devoutly, and living correctly, and yet what must be done for him? Is he to be saved without Christ? Is he to find his own way to life by the development of his good qualities? No, but he must be told to fetch Peter, to tell him about Jesus the Saviour, and if no other means will answer an angel must descend to guide him to the appointed teacher. When he had gone as far as he could go, it became essential that he should hear the gospel of Jesus Christ. Now, it is clear as noonday that if for this best of cases the gospel was absolutely needful, it must assuredly be required by the myriads who are not so excellent.

Brethren, Jesus Christ comes to judge mankind because there are sinners to be judged. If you find me a nation which has no tribunals, no punishments, no courts of justice, no judges, it must either be the scene of utter anarchy or else a nation where all obey the law, and such a thing as a criminal is unknown. The setting up of the last great assize, and the making of that assize to have reference to all men, the quick and the dead, and the appointment of the supremest person in existence, even the Son of God, to conduct that assize,—all these facts imply guilt somewhere, and abundance of it. If it is not thereby proved that every one of the quick and the dead have offended, it at least implies that they are all under suspicion: that they are all actually guilty we learn from other portions of God's word. The judgment held by the Mediator is proof that the mediatorial office has reference to sin, and deals with men as transgressors of the law.

The second part of our Lord's mediatorial office implies this most certainly; for he comes as Saviour, and such an office would be needless if there were no sin and ruin; it is idle to talk of saving those who have never fallen. He comes to remit sin, but there can be no remission of sins to those who have never transgressed. The largeness of the promise here used that "whosoever believeth in him shall receive remission of sins," goes to prove that there is sin in everybody. However wide the "whosoever" is, so wide, depend upon it, is the guilt: the remedy measures the disease. Remission is promised upon belief in Jesus Christ, because fallen man needs to be pardoned.

Putting the two things together, the very fact that there is a Mediator at all regards man as fallen. God could have dealt with us immediately, without an Intercessor had we been as the first Adam was before his fall. It is by reason of sin's influence upon the race, the fall and corruption of the progeny of Adam, that it became necessary there should be a "daysman that might lay his hand upon both," and deal with God in his divine person, and yet deal with fallen man in his humanity. Yes, Christ as Mediator deals with sinners on God's behalf, and the point I want you practically to note is this—do not let us get away from the consciousness of being sinners, because we must then move away from Christ the Mediator. In proportion as you set up any righteousness of your own, in that proportion you become independent of the Saviour, and are divided from him. If you deny that you are liable to be judged and condemned you will deny also the necessity of your being forgiven, and while denying your guilt you never can be forgiven, for confession of guilt is a necessary preliminary to pardon. "If we confess our sins, he is faithful and just to forgive us our sins." Put yourselves, then, with broken hearts beneath the covert of the Saviour's wing. Come and stand before his majestic judgment-seat and plead guilty; there and then cry, "Remit my sin through thy great sacrifice and precious blood." Do not try to disprove the accusation or to extenuate the guilt, but plead guilty, and, as guilty, sue for a free pardon. Do not labour against your conscience to deny your sin, but take the publican's place and cry, "God be merciful to me a sinner." That is the second point of the text, and it is clear enough. May we be wise enough to put it into practice. May the Holy Spirit work in us a tender, humble, and contrite spirit.

III. Notice a third consideration: THE QUALIFICATIONS REQUIRED BY OUR LORD AS MEDIATOR TO FULFIL HIS FIRST OFFICE OF JUDGE MATERIALLY COMFORT US IN LOOKING AT HIM UNDER HIS SECOND OFFICE AS SAVIOUR.

Note, then, first, that as Judge the Lord Jesus *has full authority*: he is fully commissioned of God to acquit or to condemn. Oh, then, if he gives me pardon through his blood it is an authorised pardon, it is a free pardon under the King's own hand and seal. I rejoice to think of this. If Jesus the Judge had said, "Depart, ye cursed," I should be certain that it was true and sure, though I sank into unutterable despair for ever; and even so when he saith, "I have blotted out, as a thick cloud, thy transgressions, and, as a cloud, thy sins," I am equally certain that his sentence is sure and fixed. Therefore, being justified by such a justifier, we have peace with God through Jesus Christ our Lord. The pardon is as authorized as the condemnation would have been. Is not this sweet to think on? Is not this a solid pillar for hope to rest upon?

In order that our Lord might be a competent Judge, he *possesses the amplest knowledge*. A judge should be the most instructed among men, or otherwise he is not fit to decide in matters of great difficulty and importance. Jesus Christ as Judge is incomparably fit to judge men, for he knows men thoroughly. He is himself a man, and therefore he knows our temptations, and our weaknesses, in fact, he knows all about us by experience as well as by observation. He carries a man's heart within him to the judgment-seat, and in man's nature he sits there, to weigh us in the balances of truth. This fits him to judge the world with equity. Next, he knows the law. Hath he not said, "Yea, thy law is within my heart"? No one knows the law of God as Jesus did, for he kept it in every point: he has not merely read it and learned it, but obeyed it to the full. The law is written out in living characters in his holy life and obedient death. How qualified he is to judge, since he is Master of every line in the royal statute book! Moreover, he knows what sin is—not that he ever sinned, but he has lived among sinners as a Physician, and studied their complaints, making a specialty of the disease of sin. Though he had no sin of his own, yet all sin was laid on him. "He was made sin for us, that we might be made the righteousness of God in him." The Lord Jesus also knows the punishment of sin. A judge must know what penalties to award. Jesus knows this well enough, for he himself also hath once suffered for sin, the Just for the unjust, to bring us to God. He knows the deserved penalty of human guilt, for on his shoulders the ploughers made deep furrows, and his very soul was crushed within him in the winepress of divine wrath.

Pause here and think awhile. Inasmuch as this knowledge qualifies Christ to be thy Judge, O my soul, it equally qualifies him to pardon thee, for he knows thee thoroughly, and can cleanse thee thoroughly. He knows sin, dear brethren, your sin and mine, so that when he gives pardon it will be of all sin, of all manner of transgressions, iniquities, and crimes, of which all are open before him. He knows the law, and therefore he knows how legally to acquit, so that no further question can be raised. He will make no mistake about the matter, for he knows the ways of the courts of heaven. Since he knows the penalty, because he has borne it all, he will take care that none of it shall ever fall on us. The pardon of believers is not given by a blind God, nor granted in error: there are no flaws in the divine judgment, no schemes and quibbles by which to evade the meaning of the statute in that case made and provided, but all is done in justice and equity. The Lord doth not keep to the ear that which is avoided in fact, but all his judgments are done in truth. The Judge of all the earth must do right. If thou hast pardoned me, my Lord, thou hast known what thou hast done, and thou hast done it thoroughly and well, and wisely, and it will stand in the highest court against all gainsayers. I shall not be condemned when I am judged, but shall be cleared and justified even before the bar of God, for Jesus Christ the Judge himself has put away my sin: see here the full remission granted to my faith. Who shall lay anything to the charge of God's elect since God hath justified? Do you see this?

Do you not also see, dear friends, that all the personal qualifications of our Lord to act as Judge remarkably tend to make the pardon of his people the more blessedly clear; for, first of all, as a Judge he is very just. "Thou lovest righteousness and hatest wickedness, therefore God, thy God, hath anointed thee with the oil of gladness above thy fellows." "He is called Faithful and True, and in righteousness he doth judge and make war." He is impartial and unchanging, and sitting on the judgment-seat the highest and noblest qualities of humanity and deity are conspicuous in him. Well, then, when he forgives it must be just to forgive: when he pardons us it must be consistent with the holiness of God for us to be pardoned. Such an One as he whom God accounteth worthy to judge the sons of men at the last great day, when he saith "thy sins are forgiven thee," has not perverted judgment, nor turned aside from right. Our pardon is affirmed and established by the wisdom and truth of the divine Judge, and its authenticity and correctness are proven by the same attributes. Who can dispute our acquittal since it comes from the Judge himself? If you have caught my thought, and seen the truth, it must tend to your comfort and delight: all the pomp of judgment, all the authority of the throne, all the justice of the statute-book, all the power of the mediatorial government, and all the holiness of the Judge himself are engaged to maintain the verdict of his grace, and make it as firm as the sentence of his wrath. Herein is ground for quiet assurance.

IV. Let us next notice the fact, that OUR KNOWLEDGE OF THE FIRST OFFICE OF THE MEDIATOR IS EXCEEDINGLY NECESSARY TO OUR ACCEPTANCE OF HIM IN HIS SECOND CAPACITY. This was why Peter preached it: this was why Paul before Felix reasoned concerning righteousness, temperance, and judgment to come. This is why the Holy Spirit himself convinces the world of sin, of righteousness, and of judgment. Dear hearer, if you do not believe in Christ as your Judge you never will accept him as your Saviour. Unless you set yourself before that awful throne, that great white throne, as John calls it, and realise yourself as standing there to give in your account, you will not fly to the Saviour for mercy. I would have every unconverted person set before his mind the hour of his death, the moment of the appearance of his naked spirit before the tribunal of Christ, and then the resurrection and the solemnities of that great day for which all other days are made, when heaven and earth shall pass away and all things melt like dreams, and the only real thing shall be the man, his deeds, his Judge, his future. Oh, think of this! Some of you are unpardoned this morning, and as sure as you live, unless you repent, you will stand before God to receive nothing but condemnation, condemnation irreversible and eternal. Let those who would bewitch you say what they will, you will receive a condemnation which will thunder after you throughout ages without end, to wither all your hopes and dry up the springs of comfort within your nature, and leave you an eternal desolation. I cannot speak upon this topic at any length, the theme is too dreadful. May none of you ever incur the doom of the last day. May it never happen that one who sat in the Tabernacle while we tried to preach the gospel shall be driven by the whirlwind of divine justice away from the presence of God and the glory of his power. And yet it will be so with some of you, I am afraid, for you do not turn to God; you do not seek the Saviour, and you are as likely as not to die in your sins, and, if you do, "there remaineth no more sacrifice for sin, but a fearful looking for of judgment and of fiery indignation" which must devour you.

Oh that you would feel this, and now under a sense of it come and trust in Jesus Christ the Saviour. He is never dear to any but to sinners. Christ is never valued by any but the guilty. He came into the world to save sinners; it is well he did, for no one else will have him but those who feel their sin and condemnation. Oh, come and take him as your Saviour, and let that blessed word " *Whosoever* believeth in him" be like a wide door to let you in. " Whosoever believeth in him shall receive remission of sins"; why should you not at this moment obtain that full remission? Here are some lines which I would have you think upon when you are in your own chambers at home; may their concluding prayer be yours :—

"That day of wrath, that dreadful day,
When heaven and earth shall pass away,
What power shall be the sinner's stay!
How shall he meet that dreadful day,
When, shrivelling like a parched scroll,
The flaming heavens together roll ;
When louder yet, and yet more dread,
Swells the high trump that wakes the dead.

"O ! on that day, that wrathful day,
When man to judgment wakes from clay,
Be Thou the trembling sinner's stay,
Though heaven and earth shall pass away! "

V. The last observation is that THE SAVING WORK OF CHRIST'S MEDIATORIAL OFFICE IS THAT WHICH CONCERNS US MOST AT THIS PRESENT TIME. What does Jesus do as Mediator? He judges, but he also forgives. Note the words, " Shall receive remission of sins." What is remission of sin? Hear it and be astonished that it is possible: it is the causing of sin to cease to be. Granted that you have sinned; lamented that you have sinned; granted also that your sin deserves the utmost punishment; yet God in wondrous mercy is prepared to forget your sin, to blot it out, to cast it behind his back, to cast it into the depths of the sea; all which Scriptural expressions go to set forth that he will put it quite away, so that he will regard you as if you had never offended at all. Guilty man, dost thou hear this? You that are not guilty, you self-righteous people, I do not care whether you hear it or not, for Christ did not come to call you, since the whole have no need of a physician, but O, ye guilty ones, who know that you are guilty, listen to this. There is remission, and it is preached to you in Jesus Christ's name. God is a God of mercy, and he passeth by iniquity, transgression, and sin, and the guilty can be justly treated by him as if they were perfectly innocent.

Note this grand fact, and then observe that this is to be done in Christ's name. There is no other name in which pardon can be bestowed, but it can come in the name of Jesus. Without shedding of blood there is no remission, and this blood is the blood of Jesus Christ, God's dear Son, which cleanseth us from all sin. It is in the name of Jesus the Nazarene, despised and rejected of men, who is also Lord of all,—it is in his name that pardon is freely presented to the most guilty of the human race. Be they where they may, God is ready to kiss away their sins, and to accept them through Jesus Christ.

According to the text this is to be had through faith, for the text saith, "he that believeth on him." The plan is very simple. Every great discovery is very simple when it is complete. Did you ever notice that when a machine is complicated you feel sure that it is only in its infancy? The more perfect it becomes the more simple it becomes, till at last, when there is no improvement to be made, you can see it is so because all complications have been removed. Such is the gospel. It is not a science which needs to be learned at universities: it is not a mysterious doctrine which needs the intellect of a doctor of divinity to grasp it; it is just an A B C gospel which babes often receive when wise men miss it. It is, trust Jesus Christ: trust God in Jesus Christ, and you are reconciled to him, and your sins are blotted out for Christ's sake.

Lastly, this blessed news has reference to every one in the whole world that will believe in Jesus. That great, comprehensive word, "whosoever," is worthy of your devout notice. "Whosoever believeth in him." This excludes no race of men, neither the most degraded Hottentot, nor the most intellectual Hindoo: this shuts out no king, and no beggar, no moralist, and no whoremonger, no adulterer, no swearer, no thief, no murderer. Blessed be the God of all grace, it does not shut out me. I greatly rejoice in this. I am one of the "whosoevers," for I do believe in Jesus with all my heart. I have no hope but in him, and therefore I know that I have remission of my sins. I long for you all to have it too: not because of any merits of yours, not because of any feelings of yours, not because of any doings of yours, but for his dear sake who was hanged on a tree you shall have remission if you believe in him. Oh, trust ye him; trust ye him, and ye shall have pardon. My heart longs that you should at this moment accept Jesus and live. Why not? Often when we have spoken like this the Holy Spirit has cheered the hearts of men and brought them to Christ, and why should he not do it this morning? Pray for it, believers! This moment offer your intense prayers to heaven in silent ejaculations. The Spirit of God is here in this assembly, and he will work in answer to our warm desires. I have preached the gospel: I know it is the very gospel of the blessed God. Will he not bear witness to his own truth? Has he not pledged himself to do it? I have preached his truth as well as I can, relying only upon his help, and I have earnestly avoided all tawdry speech of human wisdom, telling you in all simplicity the old, old story of my blessed Lord, and therefore I confidently expect to see the word prosper. The Holy Spirit must bless the preaching of the cross: it is his office, his nature, his usual way to do so. He has not changed, nor ceased to be what he used to be, and therefore he will bless his people and make his gospel the power of God unto salvation. O my dear hearer, seize the blessing by an instant faith. God help you to do it, for Jesus Christ's sake. Amen.

Who Is This?

"For who is this that engaged his heart to approach unto me? saith the Lord"—Jeremiah xxx. 21.

I MENTIONED in the reading that there is a very remarkable change of tone in the Book of Jeremiah, at the thirtieth chapter. You read on through the twenty-nine chapters, and you hear nothing but "a weeping and wailing," while the prophet stands before you, girt with sackcloth, bidding Israel "lament and howl: for the fierce anger of the Lord is not turned back from us." When you come to the middle of the thirtieth chapter all is changed: you have left the dungeon for the pleasant meads, and you hear "thanksgiving, and the voice of them that make merry." Here flowers of promise glorify the fields, and birds of praise sweeten the air with music. The people are first made to tremble and fear on account of sin, and all faces are turned into paleness; and then the Lord declares his immeasurable grace, saying, "I am with thee to save thee: though I make a full end of all nations whither I have scattered thee, yet will I not make a full end of thee." The condition of the sinful people is brought home to them, and the nation is solemnly told—"Thy bruise is incurable, and thy wound is grievous. There is none to plead thy cause, that thou mayest be bound up: thou hast no healing medicines. Why criest thou for thine affliction? thy sorrow is incurable for the multitude of thine iniquity: because thy sins were increased, I have done these things unto thee." And then man's extremity of misery becomes God's opportunity of mercy. When and where sin aboundeth grace doth much more abound, and the Lord displays his wonders of love. He graciously declares—"I will restore health unto thee, and I will heal thee of thy wounds." The reason of the change is not difficult to find. The prophet is led to speak of covenant promises, such as that in the twenty-second verse, "Ye shall be my people, and I will be your God." No wonder that his strain grew more cheerful and jubilant. Was there ever such a box of perfume as the covenant? Was there ever such a harp of golden strings, all tuned to the music of consolation, as the covenant? Inspired by this subject, he exclaims in the next chapter,—" For thus saith the Lord; Sing with gladness for Jacob, and shout among the chief of the nations: publish ye, praise ye, and say, O Lord, save thy people, the remnant of Israel."

Moreover, he introduces to us that glorious Messenger of the covenant whom we delight in. He speaks of the Messiah, who is the glorious One who has engaged his heart to approach unto God; and, as when the sun ariseth darkness flees, so when the Saviour appeareth his sorrows vanish, and Jeremiah becomes as eloquent with joy as Isaiah himself. Think no more of Jeremiah as exclusively the weeping prophet; for the flashes of his delight make the night of his sorrow brilliant with an aurora of heavenly brilliance.

The answer to the question of our text is the reason why Jeremiah put away his dust and ashes and girt himself with beauteous array. God had for awhile, on account of their great sin, put away his people, and wounded them with the chastisement of a cruel one for the multitude of their iniquities. They could not walk with him, for they were not agreed with him. He could not accept their sacrifices, for they were polluted; he could not listen to their prayers, for they were hypocritical; he could not dwell with them, for they were proud-hearted and rebellious. So Zion came to be called an outcast whom no man seeketh after. God himself seemed to have given her a bill of divorce, and to have put her away; but it was in seeming only. In Jehovah's heart of hearts he was still bound to his people, whom he loved with an everlasting love. He could not cast away the seed of Abraham, his friend; and his bowels yearned towards the people whom he had loved of old, and borne with in great longsuffering. He had put them under a cloud necessarily, because of their sin, yet he did earnestly remember them still, for he bears witness, saying, "I am a father to Israel, and Ephraim is my firstborn." The Lord loved the distance which sundered his people from him, but he longed to see them approach to him that he might comfort them and satiate their souls with his goodness.

How was this to be done? This was the problem of that age, as it is the problem of all ages. How can guilty man return unto the Holy God? How can there be peace and amity, love and concord between the Judge of all the earth and his revolting and polluted creature man? It was necessary that one should arise who would approach to God on the behalf of the people, so that God might be well pleased with them for his righteousness' sake. But where was he to be found? Some one must come to God, and by his own coming make a way through which those whom he represented might have access. But where was this representative to be found? Paradise was lost; who was he by whom it could be regained? The question was asked, and in man's ear it seemed to be asked in vain, for it is written, "There is none to plead thy cause; all thy lovers have forsaken thee."

"Who is this that engaged his heart to approach unto me? saith the Lord." One was needed to bridge the chasm which divided man from God. Who could do it? God himself asked the question because he had himself found the person, and would have us see him and understand his glorious character. My text comes from Jehovah's own lip: "Who is this that engaged his heart to approach unto me? saith the Lord." He sets the Mediator before us and asks, " Who is this ? " We are sure that the Lord does not need to ask questions of us that he may gain information from us. " Known unto God are all his works," and much more must he be known by whom his grandest work is accomplished. Speaking in the name of wisdom our glorious Mediator saith of the Lord, "I was by him, as one brought up with him: and I was daily his delight, rejoicing always before him." So that the Lord only asks the question for our good, to set us thinking. This enquiry is fitly the sinner's question, when, trembling and convinced of sin, and led to seek his God, he needs an interposer, one of a thousand, who can put his hand upon the offender and the offended, and reconcile the rebel to his Lord. Therefore, in love the Lord takes up the sinner's question and answers it by another. Behold a Daysman of Jehovah's own providing, who can lay his hand upon both : look at him and answer, " Who is he ? "

The enquiry is made, I think, with three great designs, upon which I shall speak as I am enabled of the Spirit of God.—First, *to direct attention to this glorious person*—" Who is this ? " Secondly, *to excite admiration of his wondrous work* " that engaged his heart to approach unto me, saith the Lord " ; and then, thirdly, *to arouse our interest in the result of this marvellous approach unto God;* for by it we are permitted and enabled to approach unto the Lord ourselves, and we become his people, and he confesses himself to be our God. O for the Holy Spirit's own teaching, that I may speak aright to you upon this transcendant subject !

I. The question of our text is asked TO DIRECT ATTENTION TO THIS GLORIOUS PERSON. "Who is this that engaged his heart to approach unto me? saith the Lord." We read the chapter, and if you have read it attentively, or will do so, you will learn that the person who must draw near to God *must be one of ourselves.* " Their nobles," or their glorious one, "shall be of themselves, and their governor shall proceed from the midst of them ; and I will cause him to draw near, and he shall approach unto me." It is clear that a fit representative for men must be himself a man. It would not have been seemly that Adam, the representative of our race, should have been an angel; it was natural that he should be a man. In the same way, as man blocked up the road of communion with God, it was fitting that a man should make a new road, and re-establish divine intercourse. In Adam we transgressed and died to God : in another Adam must we be restored. If an angel were capable in all other respects of drawing near to God, yet it is clear that he could not do it on man's behalf ; for an angel can only represent angels. Each order of beings must be represented by its own kind. Our Lord, as man, took not up angels, for he was not made in their nature; but he took up the seed of Abraham because he had assumed their nature. It needed a man perfect in his manhood to head us up, and stand as our federal head and representative, or otherwise we could not be restored by him.

Now, then, brethren, where is this man to be found ? " Who is this?" If he is to come of ourselves, where is he ? Not among this assemblage ; nor if all the myriads that dwell on the face of the earth could be gathered together would there be found one who could undertake this enterprise,—" For all have sinned, and come short of the glory of God." We have none of us that perfection which is required for such a work. How shall a sinner atone for sinners ? He cannot make atonement for his own sin, he cannot render unto God for himself and on his own sole account the righteousness which justice demands of him ; and how, then, can he have anything to spare for his fellow men ? The best of men are each one in the condition of the wise virgins who, when the foolish virgins said, " Give us of your oil, for our lamps have gone out," replied, " Not so, lest there be not enough for us and you ; but go ye rather to them that sell, and buy for yourselves." If the whole roll of history be searched, from Adam's fall to this moment, there is not one mere man to be found who could represent the race and make an approach for them to God on the ground of personal perfection ; for this is God's own verdict,—" All have sinned, and come short of the glory of God." The Lord looked from heaven to see if there were any among the children of men that had not transgressed, but he found none, for " they are all gone out of the way, they are together become unprofitable ; there is none that doeth good, no, not one."

Nor is it merit alone that is needed, for he that would approach unto the Lord as mediator must be prepared with strength to suffer. Who can sustain the load of human sin ? Who can endure the indignation of the Lord against iniquity ? Assuredly none of us could do it : the fire would consume him as stubble. O for an interposer; but where can he be found ? Who is this who can as man appear for men, and by his personal righteousness and sacrifice render man acceptable with God ? There was a Man of matchless birth, at whose coming angels sang, for they were told that he would bring glory to God in the highest, and on earth peace. Find him in Bethlehem's manger : there he lies, the son of Mary, truly man, one of ourselves, partaker of our flesh and blood, subject to human wants, weaknesses, and woes, and able therefore to sympathize with us and have compassion upon us ; that Man grew up in this world without taint or spot, free from sin whether natural or acquired, and yet he was in the truest sense one of ourselves, so that he is not ashamed to call us brethren. When the malicious eyes of Satan searched him through and through, he found nothing of evil in him. He was without spot or wrinkle, or any such thing, and he it is—glory be to his name—he it is that hath engaged his heart to approach unto God on our behalf. He is the Son of man, most truly, anointed with the oil of gladness above his fellows, but still truly fellow with men. Though he counted it no robbery to be equal with God, yet he took upon himself the form of a servant, and was made in the likeness of men that he might redeem us from our sin.

Now look at the context, and you will see that the person who must approach to God for us *must be a prince-priest;* for he is called " their glorious One " and "their governor," and yet it is said of him, "I will cause him to draw near," which work of drawing near is in other places ascribed to priests, for these God had set apart for the service of his sanctuary. The Hebrew word "to draw near" signifies that peculiar action of a priest when he stands dealing with God on the behalf of men. The person, then, must be a priest and yet a prince. Who is he and where is he ? It is not David, for if David would approach unto God in the office of a priest he must not ; he must resort to the priest who hath the Urim and the Thummim, and the priest of the house of Aaron must inquire of God for David. This was one distinction between David and Saul, that David knew the limits of his office and never thought to overstep it. David and Solomon never attempted to intrude into the holy office: they knew that they were not priests, but only kings ; and when Uzzah stood to sacrifice like a priest you know how the leprosy fell upon him, and they drove him out of the house of God which he was desecrating by intruding himself into the priestly office, and he had to be shut up in a separate house all the rest of his life. Where shall we find one that even as a priest can really draw near to God for mankind? For remember, brethren, that the priests of old only drew near to God in figure and in metaphor; they could not actually and in very deed do so; for God is a consuming fire. Even when Moses went up unto the mount with God, and did draw near in a certain sense, yet he never saw the face of God; for the Lord said, " Thou canst not see my face and live." The brightest vision that ever Moses had was that he saw the skirts of Jehovah's robe, or what Scripture styles his backparts, for the face of God could not be seen. Mercy draws us near to God in Christ Jesus, but apart from the Mediator an approach to absolute Deity means destruction. Neither among kings nor priests could the one man be found who could open the way to the Father, and certainly no king-priest could be found, —the combination of the two offices falls not to the house of Aaron. A reverend personage had passed before the camera of history, and left a shadowy trace of himself. But where now is he who was named Melchisedec, king of Salem, priest of the Most High God, to whom Abraham gave tithes of all. He was raised up for a special purpose, and no one has inherited his peculiar call. That vision taught us what to look for, but it did not supply the object of our search. It has prophesied the coming of the true Melchisedec, the man without beginning of days or end of years, the man without predecessor or successor, who is greater than Abraham, and abideth both priest and king for ever, having once for all drawn near to God on our behalf. You know him, —the true priest of God, not of the order of Aaron, and the king eternal, immortal, invisible, King of kings, and Lord of lords. It is he that engaged his heart to draw near to God on our behalf.

The question, however, may be answered in another way, so as to bring out more clearly the matchless Person whom our hearts adore at this moment. It was necessary that *he who should draw near to God should be chosen to that office by God himself, and should be qualified for it by divine power.* " I will cause him to draw near, and he shall approach to me." Now, is there anyone among us all that God has ever chosen to represent our fellow men as their mediator, acting as the head of the race, and as such entering into the immediate presence of God on his own merits? We have not, I hope, the presumption to imagine such a thing. " There is one Mediator between God and man, the man Christ Jesus." He it is that takes upon himself our nature and our sin, and then goes in unto God and stands there amidst the blaze of the ineffable light to represent manhood; but there is none else. On him rested the Spirit of God without measure. The Dove descended on him in the waters of his baptism, and the Father said, " This is my beloved Son, in whom I am well pleased." This was the great One elect of heaven, ordained of the Father before the foundation of the world, and the Spirit of glory and of might did rest upon him, that he might be equipped for his mighty service, and might engage his heart to approach unto God. This is he who said, "I looked, and there was none to help; and I wondered that there was none to uphold: therefore mine own arm brought salvation unto me."

Moreover, to close this description, he was not only appointed of God and qualified, but he was *one who was willing to undertake the task and ready to pledge himself to it.* He voluntarily covenanted to do it, as it is written, "Lo, I come: in the volume of the book it is written of me, to do thy will, O God: yea, thy law is my delight." He engaged his heart to this gracious office, resolving to carry out to a happy issue the work of reconciliation. Moved by inconceivable, immeasurable love, and counting all the cost, he devoted himself to the supreme effort. "Christ loved the church, and gave himself for it." Of his own free will he placed himself before offended justice to meet its claims, and so he removed every barrier which stood between us and the throne of God. He is that Breaker who has gone up before us, that King who is at the head of all his chosen ones.

Now, where is such an One to be found unless it be the Lord Jesus? I trust many of us have given ourselves up to God and to his fear, drawn by almighty love; but it was never in our hearts to imagine that by giving up ourselves to holy service we could stand before God, and open a way to him for our fellow-men: we are well aware of our incompetence for so grand a task. None of us have struck hands and covenanted with God to mediate, for we could not do it. I dread the thought of seeming to intrude into so divine a work. We are priests unto God, but not mediators for men. When I hear of men pretending to hear the confessions of their fellow-men and absolving them of their sins, I wonder that they sleep of nights after professing so tremendous an act. I wonder what the power of Satan over them must be that they can rest after having assumed to act as vicars of Jehovah, he having given them no warrant and no authority for such a mediatorial position. Brethren, this hugest of blasphemies may well become the Mother of Harlots, but the Bride of Christ abhors it. But oh, when my eyes rest upon Jesus, the only-begotten Son of God, in human flesh, then I cry, "This is he! Glory be to his name!" Anon, lost in wonder, my soul exclaims, "Who is this? Who is this? What manner of man is this? Who is a God like unto thee?" All this in wonder, but not in doubt, for the Lord Jesus can do this great work, and he wills to do it; he resolves, and he will not fail nor be discouraged. Glory be to his name, *he has done it.* He has approached with engaged heart unto God on our behalf, and by his sacrifice has made a way by which each one of us who is willing to do so may now approach unto God, even the Father, without fear. "Who is this?" Our soul is filled with amazement, but not with ignorance, for we answer this question in a word,—He is God himself, light of lights, very God of very God, veiled in human flesh, who has opened the kingdom of heaven to all believers. "Who is this?" I answer, it is the Lawgiver himself who has put himself under the law, and who has borne the penalties of the law that the law may be glorified, while sin is pardoned and law-breakers are justified. "Who is this?" It is infinite holiness which has burdened itself with human sin. "For he hath made him to be sin for us, who knew no sin; that we might be made the righteousness of God in him." Oh, had I words to speak with I would try to extol him who, being infinitely pure, nevertheless was numbered with the transgressors; who, being incapable of spot, yet did bear upon himself the enormous and horrible load of human guilt. In his own body on the tree, in flesh and soul, he suffered, the just for the unjust, to bring us to God. Mark that word, for it shows his end and object, "to bring us to God." This is the way by which he brought us nigh, even by his own most precious blood. Ay, it is the heavenly One who is blessed for evermore who was made a curse for us; on whom, being everlastingly the object of Jehovah's love, there fell Jehovah's wrath on our account. Mystery of mystery! Miracle of miracles! This has astonished heaven and earth and hell. Jesus of Nazareth, King of the Jews and Son of the Highest, engaged his heart that he might wait upon the Judge of all the earth, and answer for rebellious man with his own life, and so complete a way of access by which we may rise from our abyss of woes to the bosom of the Eternal.

Though I have thus spoken to the best of my knowledge, I know that I cannot set out before you the full glory of the person of our covenant head. I shall go home saying to myself, "Who is this? Who is this?" and I shall have succeeded in my endeavour if you will each one say, "He could not tell us who he was: he could not reach the height of that great argument, but we shall all through time and in eternity go on wondering and saying, Who is this?" The more we wonder the more shall we love and praise the Lord Jesus with our heart of hearts and say, "He hath done all things well. We are made nigh by him, never more to be separated from the love of God which is in Christ Jesus our Lord."

Thus much upon the Person. How freely could I weep because I speak in words so poor and ill chosen. I do but hold a candle to show the sun!

II. I come now TO EXCITE ADMIRATION OF HIS MATCHLESS WORK. If Jesus Christ is to approach to God for us it is clear that he must come down into our condition, for he must first descend or he cannot ascend. Naturally there is such a oneness between the blessed Persons of the Trinity that there can be no approaching in their case to one another; but Jesus, though he was for ever in the highest sense with God, left his place of glory and took the position of our shame. "Himself took our infirmities and bare our sicknesses." There he stands, even where we stood by nature. Where we lay in our blood, there he came and engaged his heart to deliver us. He stood at the judgment bar because we had brought ourselves there; he was rejected of the people because we were rejected as reprobate silver; he was condemned because we were condemned; and he was put to death because such was the sentence upon us. He descended into our depths to engineer a way from the lowest to the highest, to come back from Bashan, and from the depths of the sea, leading the van of the armies of his chosen as they return unto God with songs and everlasting joy upon their heads.

This lowly place being taken, behold our Lord actually approaching unto the offended Majesty on high. Though found in fashion as a man, and by reason of his becoming a curse for us, denied the presence of the Father, so that he cried in anguish, "My God, my God, why hast thou forsaken me?" yet he did approach unto God: he did come near; nay, he remaineth near, able to save them to the uttermost that come unto God by him. He hath passed under the cloud, and the darkness, and through the consuming fire, and now he is the Lamb in the midst of the throne. He has gone into the Holy of Holies and revealed the mercy-seat. He has bridged the great gulf which sin had made. "It is finished," said he, ere he bowed his head and gave up the ghost. The pathway is open; every gulf is filled; every valley is exalted, and every mountain and hill laid low. It is finished,—the way from man to God has been already trodden by myriads of cleansed feet; for our glorious One has cast up the king's highway and made straight paths for our feet. Come, let us tread the road. With holy confidence let us draw nigh unto God.

Our Lord with all his heart desired to do this: he "engaged his heart" to perform it. Before all worlds his master purpose was to approach unto God as man's representative. He is styled "the Lamb slain from before the foundations of the world," because this was the firm resolve and bent of his entire being, or ever the earth was. He had vowed in his soul that he would restore the banishment of the fall, and bridge the distance between man and God. When God would not have sacrifice and offering at man's hand, then Jesus said, "Lo, I come." He says of himself, "The Lord God will help me; therefore shall I not be confounded: therefore have I set my face like a flint, and I know that I shall not be ashamed." His heart was determined and resolved, for so the expression means, when the text saith, "he engaged his heart."

But why this readiness, this eagerness? Love is the one reply. His heart was occupied with love to God and love to man, and he could not rest till he had restored the broken concord between these divided ones. With all the forcefulness of his divine nature, and with all the energy of his perfect humanity, he was resolved to bring men back to God. While he was yet a boy he felt bound to be about his Father's business. When he first appeared among the multitude it was by submission to the Father's ordinance to fulfil all righteousness. He could not hold his peace or take rest, because his mission was urgent and his heart was in it. Many a time he set aside a crown to bear a cross. All the kingdoms of this world could not bribe him from his sacred purpose, though displayed before him by the arch-tempter in a sudden blaze of brightness. If any endeavoured to dissuade him from his purpose, even though they did it out of love, he saw the evil spirit who was using them as his instruments, and with indignation he broke the snare. Even though it were the beloved Peter, he looked on him as the devil's advocate, and said, "Get thee behind me, Satan." How full of meaning is that sigh, "I have a baptism to be baptized with; and how am I straitened till it be accomplished!" He was shut up like a man in a narrow prison, and his only enlargement was to be by anguish and death. He was straitened till he could give himself up a sacrifice, and so open a door for us to our God. The insatiable desire of our Lord's vehement spirit was the finishing of the work which the Father had given him to do. It was his meat and his drink to accomplish the purpose of love. "Who is this?" "Who is this?" The more I turn it over and think of it the more I am astonished that so condescending, gracious, and glorious a work should engage the heart of the Lord of all. We had not loved him, but he loved us. We were his enemies, but what a friend was he! Our hearts were set on wandering, but his heart was engaged to bring us nigh to God. Let us each pause here and admire as we say, " He loved me, and gave himself for me." Who is this that thus has spent his love upon so poor a being!

Having thus determined that he would approach unto God on our behalf he took all the consequences. A correct reading of the passage would be, "Who is this that hath pledged his heart or his life to approach unto me, saith the Lord?" If you take the meaning of the word "heart" to be life, since the heart is the source of life, then we read that our Lord pledged his life, put his life in surety that he would approach unto God, the Judge of all, and bring us near to him. When he came as the representative of sinful men—then vengeance with its sword must smite him, and he was willing to be smitten. Voluntarily he gave his back to the smiters, and his cheeks to them that plucked off the hair; he did not hide his face from shame and spitting. He must die, if he draws near to God, for sinful men, for such is the penalty due; but he willingly laid down his life of himself, and bowing his head he gave up the ghost. He must be deserted of God, and he even submits to that, till he cries "My God, my God, why hast thou forsaken me?" He might have drawn back from his undertaking if he would; but he never thought of drawing back. With desire he desired to eat that passover. In order to die he broke off in the middle of a discourse, saying, "Arise, let us go hence." His motto was "The cup which my Father hath given me, shall I not drink it?" He saved others, but himself he could not save, because love held him bound in her chains. How intensely ought we to love Jesus, since he thus reckoned nothing too hard or heavy, that he might appear in the presence of God for us and make a way to God for poor sinners such as we are. He even delighted in suffering and dishonour for this end. " For the joy that was set before him he endured the cross, despising the shame." He made pledge, not merely of hand or eye, but of his heart and life; he came with his life in his hand before Jehovah's face, and gave up that life that he might remove from us the death penalty due to justice, and so reconcile us to the Lord of all. Tune your harps, ye angels! make this Sabbath on which we think of this sublime mystery a special festival of song. Oh, sing unto the Lord, ye redeemed ones who see his face! You are before the throne of glory because he stood before the throne of vengeance, and made it possible for your robes to be washed white as snow. As for you, ye redeemed with blood who are still below, bring forth your loudest notes, and praise him who has once for all cleared the way and opened an avenue of grace to you. Who is this wonderful Saviour? Who shall declare the generation of him who pledged his life that he might draw near to God for us, and endured all the consequences to the bitter end?

And now to-day, beloved, Jesus Christ rejoices to think that he has approached unto God on our behalf, and made eternal amity between God and man. Let us rejoice with him. Let us become happy in fellowship with our God.

> " 'Tis finish'd all; the veil is rent,
> The welcome sure, the access free;
> Now then, we leave our banishment,
> O Father, to return to thee!"

This is the joy of Christ's heart for ever. He welcomes our return to God; he is glad when our communion is hearty and continuous. By his Holy Spirit he draws us near. Blessed be his name.

III. Let me try, and may the Spirit of God help me, TO AROUSE YOUR INTEREST IN THE SWEET RESULTS OF JESUS CHRIST'S HAVING APPROACHED TO GOD FOR US.

The first result is found in the chapter. Read that twenty-second verse. Read it with your own eyes, and wonder that it should be put there. "Who is this that engaged his heart to approach unto me? saith the Lord. And ye shall be my people, and I will be your God." That is, because our royal High Priest approached unto God for us, therefore we who were called outcasts, we whose wound was incurable and grievous, we that were utterly ruined and undone; we, believing in this Jesus, shall in him become the people of God. Let me speak plainly with you, beloved brethren: how many of you have realized this? It is all idle for me to talk about Christ making the way unless you run in the way. Are you the Lord's people? Many of you humbly rejoice in this high honour; but there may be a few here who are of another mind; you care nothing for having the Lord to be your God. Possibly you sneer, and call it *cant*. Yes, but if you knew the truth you would not do so. When we hear you speaking contemptuously of being God's people, all we can say is, "Father, forgive them, for they know not what they do." Will you mind thinking just for half a minute? Will you try to think justly and rightly? Must it not be good and right that the creature should love the Creator? Must it not be a wise thing that the children whom God has formed should love their heavenly Father and be on good terms with him? Is it not likely that it would be a happy thing for you if you were one of God's people? You can never rest till you are. But you say, "How can I be?" Why, it all follows upon what I have been talking of. Jesus Christ went in unto the Father for us, that we might approach unto the Father in him and through him, that we might become the Lord's own people, and that the Lord might become our God. I tell you I would sooner say, "This God is my God," than anything else that I can imagine. To say, "This kingdom is my kingdom," or "This whole world is mine," were a miserable business compared with saying, "My Beloved is mine, and I am his." You would not think I exaggerated if you tried it. I invite you to an honest, practical test. See if there be not joy in the salvation of God. Religion is with some people a sort of dreamy thing on Sundays : you sit in your pews and bear with us long-winded talkers about things which you do not care for. Oh, but if you did value and enjoy them! If you could but taste and handle them you would say, "Go on, preacher; go on! You are a poor hand at it, for your themes are so great and wondrous that you cannot reach to them; but, still, go on. Ring that bell again: open more doors, and let us peep in upon the secret treasures. Bring us more clusters of the grapes of Eshcol, and let us at least pluck a berry here and there if we cannot carry away a whole cluster, and so fill our mouths with the inexpressible delight of being God's people, and having Jehovah to be our God." This bliss comes to those of us who rejoice in Christ Jesus and have no confidence in the flesh, because Jesus said, "I will wait upon the Lord that hideth his face from the house of Jacob." The face of the Lord is no longer hidden from us, but we have access with confidence into this grace wherein we stand, and rejoice in hope of the glory of God.

I seem to see in my spirit that old legend of Rome worked out in very deed. So saith the story: in the Roman Forum there gaped a vast chasm which threatened the destruction of the Forum, if not of Rome. The wise men declared that the gulf would never close unless the most precious thing in Rome was cast into it. See how it yawns and cracks every moment more horribly. Hasten to bring this noblest thing! For love of Rome sacrifice your best! But what, or who is this? Where is a treasure meet for sacrifice? Then Curtius, a belted knight, mounted his charger, and rightly judging that valour and love of country were the noblest treasures of Rome, he leaped into the gulf. The yawning earth closed upon a great-hearted Roman, for her hunger was appeased. Perchance it is but an idle tale: but what I have declared is truth. There gaped between God and man a dread abyss, deep as hell, wide as eternity, and only the best thing that heaven contained could fill it. That best thing was He, the peerless Son of God, the matchless, perfect man, and he came, laying aside his glory, making himself of no reputation, and he sprang into the gulf, which there and then closed, once for all.

> "Down from the shining seats above
> With joyful haste he fled,
> Enter'd the grave in mortal flesh,
> And dwelt among the dead.
>
> Oh, for this love let rocks and hills
> Their lasting silence break,
> And all harmonious human tongues
> The Saviour's praises speak."

One great result of Christ's having died is to leave us a way of access, which is freely opened to every poor, penitent sinner. Come. Are you using that way of access? Do you use it every day? Having used it, and thus having drawn near to God, do you dwell near to God? Do you abide in God? Is God the main thought of your life, the chief delight and object of your being? If it be not so, I earnestly invite you by the Spirit's help to make it so. You must engage your heart to come to God in Christ. There is no coming to God without sincere resolve and eager desire. Are you engaged to such an end? Alas! it may be you are drawn elsewhere. Are you engaged? Alas! some are engaged to Madame Bubble; some are engaged to Belial; some are engaged to self; some are engaged to Mammon; some seem engaged to the very devil of the pit. Be wise, and break these unlawful engagements. Let your covenant with death be broken, and your league with hell be disannulled. Though you be weary of my words, yet would I stir you up to interest in this all-important matter. Break these deadly bands asunder. God help you, by a sudden energy which he shall give you, to snap your fetters once for all, and then at once firmly engage your hearts to Christ. Never such loveliness, never such love will you find elsewhere. Come, say now,—Whatever else I do or do not do, I will do this : I will approach to God by the way that Christ has opened for me : I will arise and go to my Father : I will throw myself at my Father's feet : I must be reconciled : I cannot live an enemy to him : I must be made a friend:

"I will approach thee—I will force
My way through obstacles to thee,"

Jesus goes before me, and I gladly follow. I will not leave the throne till thou, O Lord, hast said, "I have loved thee with an everlasting love, therefore with lovingkindness have I drawn thee." I shall be greatly happy, I shall be exceeding glad, if I may induce one spirit to come to God by Jesus Christ; but if the whole of you will come at once, if God's spirit shall now prompt all believers to come, and all unbelievers to become believers, and so to come, what a splendid company of us will enter into the golden gates, and what joy there will be in heaven over all of us as we approach unto the Most High.

I think I note a seraph, as he takes down his harp, stand in the centre of the heavenly choir and suggest to his fellow choristers that their theme should be, "Who is this that hath engaged his heart to approach unto the living God?" Hark how ten thousand voices say—"Who is this?" Let us in humble notes lift up our praises. Here is a verse which may serve our turn—

"Who is this that enters glory,
Clearing for his saints a way?
Who shall tell the wondrous story !
Who his glorious work display?
Jesus makes our access clear,
To the Father brings us near."

Thus the question "Who is this?" admits of a second answer, for now in Christ Jesus all believers with engaged hearts are approaching unto God. Who is this? At first it is Jesus, Son of man and Son of God; and next it is his church with all her heart engaged approaching unto God by Jesus Christ. My hearers, can you join in the song of praise which is now rising from heaven and earth? Angels are waiting till you approach their God. Come, hurry up : hasten to be blest. At once approach your God by Christ Jesus, and as angels see you coming their song shall grow yet louder, till it shall excel the noise of many waters, and out-voice the last great thunderings. They come ! They come ! Sinners are coming to God! Hallelujah ! Hallelujah ! Hallelujah ! Amen.

The Great Arbitration Case

"Neither is there any daysman betwixt us, that might lay his hand upon us both"
Job ix. 33.

THE patriarch Job, when reasoning with the Lord concerning his great affliction, felt himself to be at a disadvantage and declined the controversy, saying, "He is not a man, as I am, that I should answer him, and we should come together in judgment." Yet feeling that his friends were cruelly mis-stating his case, he still desired to spread it before the Lord, but wished for a mediator, a middleman, to act as umpire and decide the case. In his mournful plight he sighed for an arbitrator who, while dealing justly for God, would at the same time deal kindly with poor flesh and blood, being able to lay his hand upon both. But, dear friends, what Job desired to have, the Lord has provided for us in the person of his own dear Son, Jesus Christ. We cannot say with Job that there is no daysman who can lay his hand upon both, because there is now "one Mediator between God and man, the man Christ Jesus." In him let us rejoice, if indeed we have an interest in him; and if we have not yet received him, may almighty grace bring us even now to accept him as our advocate and friend.

There is an old quarrel between the thrice holy God and his sinful subjects, the sons of Adam. Man has sinned; he has broken God's law in every part of it, and has wantonly cast off from him the allegiance which was due to his Maker and his King. There is a suit against man, which was formally instituted at Sinai and must be pleaded in the Court of King's Bench, before the Judge of quick and dead. God is the great plaintiff against his sinful creatures who are the defendants. If that suit be carried into court, it must go against the sinner. There is no hope whatever that at the last tremendous day any sinner will be able to stand in judgment if he shall leave the matter of his debts and obligations towards his God unsettled until that dreadful hour. Sinner, it would be well for thee to "agree with thine adversary quickly, whiles thou art in the way," for if thou be once delivered up to the great Judge of all the earth, there is not the slightest hope that thy suit can be decided otherwise than to thine eternal ruin. "Weeping, and wailing, and gnashing of teeth," will be the doom adjudged thee for ever, if thy case as before the living God shall ever come to be tried at the fiery throne of absolute justice. But the infinite grace of God proposes an arbitration, and I trust there are many here who are not anxious to have their suit carried into court, but are willing that the appointed daysman should stand betwixt them and God, and lay his hand upon both, and propose and carry out a plan of reconciliation. There is hope for thee, thou bankrupt sinner, that thou mayest yet be at peace with God. There is a way by which thy debts may yet be paid; that way is a blessed arbitration in which Jesus Christ shall stand as the daysman.

Let me begin *by describing the essentials of an arbitrator, or daysman;* then let me *take you into the arbitrator's court and show you his proceedings;* and then for a little time, if there be space enough, let us dwell upon *the happy success of our great Daysman.*

I. First of all, let me describe what are THE ESSENTIALS OF AN UMPIRE, AN ARBITRATOR, OR A DAYSMAN.

The first essential is, that *both parties should be agreed to accept him.* Let me come to thee, thou sinner, against whom God has laid his suit, and put the matter to thee. God has accepted Christ Jesus to be his umpire in his dispute. He appointed him to the office, and chose him for it before he laid the foundations of the world. He is God's fellow, equal with the Most High, and can put his hand upon the Eternal Father without fear, because he is dearly beloved of that Father's heart. He is "very God of very God," and is in no respect inferior to "God over all, blessed for ever." But he is also a man like thyself, sinner. He once suffered, hungered, thirsted, and knew the meaning of poverty and pain. Nay, he went farther, he was tempted as thou hast been, and farther still, he suffered the pangs of death, as thou poor mortal man wilt one day have to do. Now, what thinkest thou? God has accepted him; canst thou agree with God in this matter, and agree to take Christ to be thy daysman too? Does foolish enmity possess thee, or does grace reign and lead thee to accept Emmanuel, God with us, as umpire in this great dispute? Let me say to thee that thou wilt never find another so near akin to thee, so tender, so sympathetic, with such bowels of compassion towards thee. Love streamed from his eyes in life, and poured from his wounds in death. He is "the express image" of Jehovah's person, and you know that Jehovah's name is "Love." "God is love," and Christ is love. Sinner, has divine grace brought thee to thy senses? Wilt thou accept Christ now? Art thou willing that he should take this case into his hands and arbitrate between thee and God? for if God accepteth him, and thou accept him too, then he has one of the first qualifications for being a daysman.

But, in the next place, *both parties must be fully agreed to leave the case entirely in the arbitrator's hands.* If the arbitrator does not possess the power of settling the case, then pleading before him is only making an opportunity for wrangling, without any chance of coming to a peaceful settlement. Now God has committed "all power" into the hands of his Son. Jesus Christ is the plenipotentiary of God, and has been invested with full ambassadorial powers. He comes commissioned by his Father, and he can say in all that he does towards sinners, that his Father's heart is with him. If the case be settled by him, the Father is agreed. Now, sinner, does grace move thy heart to do the same?

Wilt thou agree to put thy case into the hands of Jesus Christ, the Son of God and the Son of Man? Wilt thou abide by his decision? Wilt thou have it settled according to his judgment, and shall the verdict which he gives stand absolute and fast with thee? If so, then Christ has another essential of an arbitrator; but if not, remember, though he may make peace for others, he will never make peace for thee; for this know, that until the grace of God has made thee willing to trust the case in Jesu's hands, there can be no peace for thee, and thou art wilfully remaining God's enemy by refusing to accept his dear Son.

Further, let us say, that to make a good arbitrator or umpire, *it is essential that he be a fit person*. If the case were between a king and a beggar, it would not seem exactly right that another king should be the arbitrator, nor another beggar; but if there could be found a person who combined the two, who was both prince and beggar, then such a man could be selected by both. Our Lord Jesus Christ precisely meets the case. There is a very great disparity between the plaintiff and the defendant, for how great is the gulf which exists between the eternal God and poor fallen man! How is this to be bridged? Why by none except by one who is God and who at the same time can become man. Now the only being who can do this is Jesus Christ. He can put his hand on thee, stooping down to all thine infirmity and thy sorrow, and he can put his other hand upon the Eternal Majesty, and claim to be co-equal with God and co-eternal with the Father. Dost thou not see, then, his fitness? Surely it were the path of wisdom, sinner, to accept him at once as the arbitrator in the case. See how well he understands it! I should not do to be an arbitrator in legal cases, because, though I should be anxious to do justice, yet I should know nothing of the law of the case. But Christ knows your case, and the law concerning it, because he has lived among men, and has passed through and suffered the penalties of justice. There cannot surely be a better skilled or more judicious daysman than our blessed Redeemer.

Yet there is one more essential of an umpire, and that is, that *he should be a person desirous to bring the case to a happy settlement.* If you appoint a quarrelsome arbitrator, he may delight to "set dogs by the ears;" but if you elect one who is anxious for the good of both, and wishes to make both friends, then he is just the very man, though, to be sure, he would be a man of a thousand, very precious when found, but very hard to discover. Oh that all law-suits could be decided by such men. In the great case which is pending between God and the sinner, the Lord Jesus Christ has a sincere anxiety both for his Father's glory and for the sinner's welfare, and that there should be peace between the two contending parties. It is the life and aim of Jesus Christ to make peace. He delighteth not in the death of sinners, and he knows no joy greater than that of receiving prodigals to his bosom, and of bringing lost sheep back again to the fold. You cannot tell how high the Saviour's bosom swells with an intense desire to make to himself a great name as a peace-maker. Never had warrior such ambition to make war and to win victories therein, as Christ has to end war, and to win thereby the bloodless triumphs of peace. From the heights of heaven he came leaping like a young roe down to the plains of earth. From earth he leaped into the depths of the grave;

then up again at a bound he sprang to earth, and up again to heaven; and still he resteth not, but presseth on in his mighty work to ingather sinners, and to reconcile them unto God; making himself a propitiation for their sins.

Thou seest then, sinner, how the case is. God has evidently chosen the most fitting arbitrator. That arbitrator is willing to undertake the case, and thou mayest well repose all confidence in him; but and if thou shalt live and die without accepting him as thine arbitrator, then, the case going against thee, thou wilt have none to blame but thyself. When the everlasting damages shall be assessed against thee in thy soul and body for ever, thou shalt have to curse only thine own folly for having been the cause of thy ruin. May I ask you to speak candidly? Has the Holy Ghost so turned the natural bent and current of your will, that you have chosen him because he has first chosen you? Do you feel that Christ this day is standing before God for you? He is God's anointed; is he your elected? God's choice pitches upon him, does your choice agree therewith? Remember, where there is no will towards Christ, Christ as yet exercises no saving power. Christ saves no sinner who lives and dies unwilling. He makes unwilling sinners willing before he speaks a word of comfort to them. It is the mark of our election as his people, that we are made willing in the day of God's power. Lay your hope where God has laid your help, namely, on Christ, mighty to save. You cannot have an arbitrator except both sides be agreed. Dost thou say ay, ay, with all my soul I choose him? Then let us proceed.

II. And now I shall want, by your leave, to TAKE YOU INTO THE COURT WHERE THE TRIAL IS GOING ON, AND SHOW YOU THE LEGAL PROCEEDINGS BEFORE THE GREAT DAYSMAN.

"The man, Christ Jesus," who is "God over all, blessed for ever," opens his court *by laying down the principles upon which he intends to deliver judgment*, and those principles I will now try to explain and expound. They are two-fold—first, *strict justice;* and secondly, *fervent love*.

The arbitrator has determined that let the case go as it may *there shall be full justice done*, justice to the very extreme, whether it be for or against the defendant. He intends to take the law in its sternest and severest aspect, and to judge according to its strictest letter. He will not be guilty of partiality on either side. If the law says that the sinner shall die, the arbitrator declares that he will judge that the sinner shall die; and if, on the other hand, the defendant can plead and prove that he is innocent, he intends to adjudge to him the award of innocence, namely ETERNAL LIFE. If the sinner can prove that he has fairly won it, he shall have his due. Either way, whether it be in favour of the plaintiff or of the defendant, the condition of judgment is to be strict justice.

But the arbitrator also says that he will judge according to the second rule, that of *fervent love*. He loves his Father, and therefore he will decide on nothing that may attaint his honour or disgrace his crown. He so loves God, the Eternal One, that he will suffer heaven and earth to pass away sooner than there shall be one blot upon the character of the Most High. On the other hand, he so loves the poor defendant, man, that he will be willing to do anything rather than inflict penalty upon him unless justice shall absolutely require it. He loves man with so large a love that nothing will delight him more than to decide in his favour, and he will be but too glad if he can be the means of happily establishing peace between the two. How these principles are to meet, will be seen by and by. At present he lays them down very positively. "He that ruleth among men must be just." An arbitraton must be just; or else he is not fit to hold the scales in any suit. Or the other hand, he must be tender; for his name, as God, is love; and his nature as man is gentleness and mercy. Both parties should distinctly consent to these principles. How can they do otherwise? Do they not commend themselves to all of you? Let justice and love unite if they can.

Having thus laid down the principles of judgment, the arbitrator *next calls upon the plaintiff to state his case.* Let us listen while the great Creator speaks: may God give me grace now reverently to state it in his name, as one poor sinner stating God's case against us all. " Hear, O heavens, and give ear, O earth: for the Lord hath spoken, I have nourished and brought up children, and they have rebelled against me. The ox knoweth his owner, and the ass his master's crib: but Israel doth not know, my people doth not consider. Ah sinful nation, a people laden with iniquity, a seed of evildoers, children that are corrupters: they have forsaken the Lord, they have provoked the Holy One of Israel unto anger, they are gone away backward." The Eternal God charges us, and let me confess at once most justly and most truly charges us, with having broken all his commandments—some of them in act, some of them in word, all of them in heart, and thought, and imagination. He charges upon us, that against light and knowledge we have chosen the evil and forsaken the good; that knowing what we were doing we have turned aside from his most righteous law and have gone astray like lost sheep, following the imaginations and devices of our own hearts. The great Plaintiff claims that inasmuch as we are his creatures we ought to have obeyed him, that inasmuch as we owe our very lives to his daily care we ought to have rendered him service instead of disobedience, and to have been his loyal subjects instead of turning traitors to his throne. All this, calmly and dispassionately, according to the great Book of the law, is laid to our charge before the Daysman. No exaggeration of sin is brought against us. It is simply declared of us that the whole head is sick and the whole heart is faint; that there is none that doeth good, no, not one; that we have all gone out of the way, and altogether become unprofitable. This is God's case. He says, "I made this man; curiously was he wrought in the lowest parts of the earth; and all his members bear traces of my singular handiwork. I made him for my honour, and he has not honoured me. I created him for my service, and he has not served me. Twenty, thirty, forty, fifty years I have kept the breath in his nostrils; the bread he has eaten has been the daily portion of my bounty; his garments are the livery of my charity; and all this while he has neither thought of me, his Creator and Preserver, nor done anything in my service. He has served his family, his wife and children, but his Maker he has despised. He has served his country, his neighbours, the borough in which he dwells; but I who made him, I have

had nothing from him. He has been an unprofitable servant unto me."
I think I may put the plaintiff's case into your hands. Which of you
would keep a horse, and that horse should yield you no obedience?
What excuse is it that though I might not use him he would carry
another? Nay, the case is worse than this. Not only has man done
nothing, but worse than nothing. Which of you would keep a dog,
which, instead of fawning upon you, would bark at you—fly at you, and
tear you in his rage? Some of us have done this to God; we have
perhaps cursed him to his face; we have broken his sabbaths, laughed
at his gospel, and persecuted his saints. You would have said of
such a dog, let it die. Wherefore should I harbour in my house a dog
that treats me thus? Yet, hear, O heavens; and give ear, O earth;
God has borne with your ill manners, and he still cries "forbear."
He puts the lifted thunder back into the arsenal of his dread artillery.
I wish I could state the case as I ought. My lips are but clay; and
these words should be like fire in the sinner's soul. When I meditated
upon this subject alone, I felt much sympathy with God, that he should
have been so ill treated; and whereas some men speak of the flames of
hell as too great a punishment for sin, it seems ten thousand marvels
that we should not have been thrust down there long ago.

The plaintiff's case having thus been stated *the defendant is called upon
by the Daysman for his*; and I think I hear him as he begins. First of
all the trembling defendant sinner pleads—"*I confess to the indictment,
but I say I could not help it. I have sinned, it is true, but my nature
was such that I could not well do otherwise; I must lay all the blame of
it to my own heart; my heart was deceitful and my nature was evil.*"
The Daysman at once rules that this is no excuse whatever, but an
aggravation, for inasmuch as it is conceded that the man's heart itself
is enmity against God, this in an admission of yet greater malice and
blacker rebellion. It was only alleged against the offender in the first
place that he had outwardly offended; but he acknowledges that he
does it inwardly, and confesses that his very heart is traitorous against
God, and is fully set upon working the King's damage and dishonour.
It is determined, therefore, by the Daysman that this excuse will not
stand, and he gives a case in point:—a thief is brought up for stealing,
and he pleads that his heart was thievish, that he felt a constant inclin-
ation to steal, and that therefore he could not help running off with
any goods within his reach. The judge very properly answers, "Then
I shall give you twice as much penalty as any other man who only fell
into the fault by surprise, for according to your own confession, you are
a thief through and through; what you have said is not an excuse, but
an aggravation."

Then the defendant pleads in the next place that albeit he acknowledges
the facts alleged against him, yet *he is no worse than other offenders*,
and that there are many in the world who have sinned more grievously
than he has done. He says he has been envious, and angry, and worldly,
and covetous, and has forgotten God; but then he never was an
adulterer, or a thief, or a drunkard, or a blasphemer, and he pleads that
his lesser crimes may well be winked at. But the great Daysman at
once turns to the Statute Book, and says that as he is about to give his
decision by law that plea is not at all tenable, for the law book has it—

"Cursed is every man that continueth not in all things that are written in the book of the law to do them." The offence of one sinner doth not excuse the offence of another; and the arbitrator declares that he cannot mix up other cases with the case now in hand; that the present offender has on his own confession broken the law, and that as the law book stands that is the only question to be decided, for "the soul that sinneth it shall die," and if the defendent has no better plea to offer, judgment must go against him.

The sinner urges further, that though he has offended, and offended very greatly and grievously, yet *he has done a great many good things.* It is true he did not love God, but he always went to chapel. It is true he did not pray, but still he belonged to a singing-class. It is quite correct that he did not love his neighbour as himself, but he always liked to relieve the poor. But the Daysman, looking the sinner full in the face, tells him that this plea also is bad, for the alleged commission of some acts of loyalty will not make compensation for avowed acts of treason. "Those things," saith he, "ye ought to have done, but not to have left the others undone;" and he tells the sinner, with all kindness and gentleness, that straining at a gnat does not exonerate him for having swallowed a camel; and that having tithed mint, and anise, and cummin, is no justification for having devoured a widow's house. To have forgotten God is in itself a great enormity; to have lived without serving him is a crime of omission so great, that whatever the sinner may have done on the *contra*, stands for nothing at all, since he has even then in that case done only what he ought to have done. You see at once the justice of this decision. If any of you were to say to your grocer, or tailor, when they send in their bills, "Well, now, you ought not to ask for payment of that account, because I did pay you another bill—you ought not to ask me to pay for that suit of clothes, because I did pay you for another suit;" I think the answer would be, "But in paying for what you had before, you only did what you ought to do; but I still have a demand upon you for this." So all the good deeds you have ever done are only debts discharged which were most fully due, (supposing them to be good deeds, which is very questionable) and they leave the great debt still untouched.

The defendant has no end of pleas, for the sinner has a thousand excuses; and finding that nothing else will do, he begins to appeal to the mercy of the plaintiff, and says *that for the future he will do better.* He confesses that he is in debt, but he will run up no more bills at that shop. He acknowledges that he has offended, but he vows he will not do so again. He is quite sure that the future shall be as free from fault as angels are from sin. Though it is true that he just now said his heart was bad, still he feels inclined to think that it is not so very bad after all; he is conceited enough to think that he can in the future keep himself from committing sin; thereby, you see, admitting the worthlessness of his former plea on which he relied so much "Now," he says, "if for life I become a teetotaller, then surely I may be excused for having been a drunkard; suppose now that I am always honest and steady, and never again say one ill word, will not that exonerate me from all my wrong-doings, and for having blasphemed God?" But the Daysman rules, still with kindness and gentleness, that the greatest imaginable virtue in the future will be no recompense for the sin of the past; for he finds in the lawbook no promise whatever made to that effect: but the statute runs in these words, "He will by no means spare the guilty;" "Cursed is every one that continueth not in all things which are written in the book of the law to do them."

You would think that the defendant would now be fairly beaten, but he is not: he asks leave to step across the way *to bring in a friend of his.* He is allowed to do so, and comes back with a gentleman dressed in such a queer style, that, if you had not sometimes seen the like in certain Puseyite Churches, you would suppose him to have arrayed himself for the mere purpose of amusing children at a show, where a merry-andrew is the presiding genius. The defendant seems to imagine that if the case be left to this gentleman in the white shirt and ribbons, he will settle it with ease. He has with him a little bottle of water, by which he can turn hearts of stone into flesh, making heirs of wrath into "members of Christ, children of God, and inheritors of the kingdom of heaven." He has a certain portion of mystical bread, and magical wine, the reception with which he can work wonderful transformation, producing flesh and blood therefrom at his reverence's will and pleasure. In fact, this gentleman trades and gets his living by the prosecution of magic. He has occult influences streaming from his fingers, which influences he derived originally from a gentleman in lawn; and he now pretends to have ability derived from the apostles, most probably from Judas, by marvellous manipulations—how I cannot tell you, but by a kind of sleight of hand—to settle the case. But the Daysman, with a frown, hurls a thunderbolt from his hand against the impudent impostor, and bids him take himself away, and not again deceive poor sinners with his vain pretensions. He warns the defendant that the priest is an arrant knave, that whatever professions he may make of being a "successor of the apostles," he knows nothing about apostolical doctrine, or else he would not have intruded his sinful, silly self, between men's souls and God. He bids him advise the man to dress himself like a person in his right mind, who was about honest work, and not as a necromancer or priest of Baal, and give himself to preaching the gospel, instead of propagating the superstitious inventions of Rome.

What is the poor defendant to do now? He is fairly beaten this time. He falls down on his knees, and with many tears and lamentations he cries, "I see how the case stands; *I have nothing to plead, but I appeal to the mercy of the plaintiff;* I confess that I have broken his commandments; I acknowledge that I deserve his wrath; but I have heard that he is merciful, and I plead for free and full forgiveness."

And now comes another scene. The plaintiff seeing the sinner on his knees, with his eyes full of tears, makes this reply, "I am willing at all times to deal kindly and according to lovingkindness with all my creatures; but will the arbitrator for a moment suggest that I should damage and ruin my own perfections of truth and holiness; that I should belie my own word; that I should imperil my own throne; that I should make the purity of immaculate justice to be suspected, and should bring down the glory of my unsullied holiness, because this creature has offended me, and now craves for mercy? I cannot, I will not spare the guilty; *he has offended, and he must die!* 'As I live, I have no pleasure in the death of the wicked, but would rather that he should turn from his wickedness and live.' Still, this 'would rather' must not be supreme. I am gracious and would spare the sinner, but I am just, and must not unsay my own words. I swore with an oath, 'The soul that sinneth shall die.' I have laid it down as a matter of firm decree, ' Cursed is every one that continueth not in all things which are written in the book of the law to do them.' This sinner is righteously cursed, and he must inevitably die; and yet I love him. How can I give thee up, Ephraim? how can I make thee as Admah? How can I set thee as Zeboim? And yet, how can I put thee among the children? Would it not be a worse calamity that I should be unjust than that earth should lose its inhabitants? Better all men perish, than that the universe should lose the justice of God as its stay and shield." The arbitrator bows and says, "Even so; justice demands that the offender should die, and I would not have thee unjust."

What more does the arbitrator say? He sits still, and the case is in suspense. There stands the just and holy God, willing to forgive if it can be done without injury to the immutable principles of right. There sits the arbitrator, looking with eyes of love upon the poor, weeping, trembling sinner, and anxious to devise a plan to save him, but conscious that that plan must not infringe upon divine justice; for it were a worse cruelty to injure divine perfections than it were to destroy the whole human race. The arbitrator, therefore, after pausing awhile, puts it thus: " I am anxious that these two should be brought together; I love them both: I cannot, on the one hand, recommend that my Father should stain his honour; I cannot, on the other hand, endure that this sinner should be cast eternally into hell; I will decide the case, and it shall be thus: *I* will pay my Father's justice all it craves; I pledge myself that in the fulness of time *I will suffer in my own proper person all that the weeping, trembling sinner ought to have suffered.* My Father, wilt thou stand to this?" The eternal God accepts the awful sacrifice! What say you, sinner, what say you? Why, methinks you cannot have two opinions. If you are sane—and may God make you sane—you will melt with wonder. You will say, " I could not have thought this! I never called in a daysman with an expectation of this! *I* have sinned, and *he* declares that *he* will suffer; *I* am guilty, and *he* says that *he* will be punished for me!"

Yes, sinner, and he did more than say it, for when the fulness of time came—you know the story. The officers of justice served him with the writ, and he was taken from his knees in the garden of Gethsemane away to the court, and there he was tried and condemned; and you know how his back was scourged till the white bones stood like islands of ivory in the midst of a crimson sea of gore; you know how his head was crowned with thorns, and his cheeks were given to those who plucked off the hair! Can you not see him hounded through the streets of Jerusalem, with the spittle of the brutal soldiery still upon his unwashed face, and his wounds all unstanched and bleeding? Can you not see him as they hurl him down and fasten him to the accursed tree?—then they lift the cross and dash it down into its socket in the earth, dislocating every bone, tearing every nerve and sinew, filling his soul as full of agony as this earth is full of sin, or the depths of the ocean filled with its floods? You do not know, however, what he suffered within. Hell held carnival within his heart. Every arrow of the infernal pit was discharged at him, and heaven itself forsook him. The thunderbolts of vengeance fell upon him, and his Father hid his face from him till he cried in his agony, "My God, my God, why hast thou forsaken me?" And so he suffered on, and on, and on, till "It is finished" closed the scene.

Here, then, is the arbitration. Christ himself suffers; and now I have to put the query, "Hast thou accepted Christ?" O dear friend, if thou hast, I know that God the Holy Ghost has made thee accept him; but if thou hast not, what shall I call thee? I will not upbraid thee, but my heart would weep over thee. How canst thou be so mad as to forego a compromise so blessed, an arbitration so divine! Oh! kiss the feet of the Daysman; love him all thy life, that he has decided the case so blessedly.

III. Let us now look at THE DAYSMAN'S SUCCESS.

For every soul who has received Christ, Christ has made a full atonement which God the Father has accepted; and his success in this matter is to be rejoiced in, first of all, because *the suit has been settled conclusively*. We have known cases go to arbitration, and yet the parties have quarrelled afterwards; they have said that the arbitrator did not rule justly, or something of the kind, and so the whole point has been raised again. But O beloved, the case between a saved soul and God is settled once and for ever. There is no more conscience of sin left in the believer; and as for God's Book, there is not a sin recorded there against any soul that has received Christ. I know some of our Arminian brethren rather think that the case is not settled; or they suppose that the case is settled for a time, but that it will one day come up again. Beloved, I thank God that they are mistaken. Christ has not cast his people's sins into the shallows, where they may be washed up again, but he has cast them into the depths of the sea, where they are drowned for ever. Our scape-goat has not carried our sins to the borders of the land, where they may be found again, but he has taken them away into the wilderness where, if they be searched for, they shall not be found. The case is so settled that in eternity you shall never hear of it again except as a case which was gloriously decided.

Again, the case has been settled *on the best principles*, because, you see, neither party can possibly quarrel with the decision. The sinner cannot, for it is all mercy to him: even eternal justice cannot, for it has had its due. If there had been any mitigation of the penalty, we might yet fear that perhaps the suit might come up again; but now that everything has been paid, that cannot be. If my creditor takes from me, by a settlement in the Court of Insolvency, ten shillings in the pound, I know he will not disturb me yet; but I cannot feel quite at ease about the other ten shillings; and if I am ever able, I should like to pay him. But, you see, Christ has not paid ten shillings in the pound, but he has paid every farthing.

"Justice now demands no more,
He has paid the dreadful score."

For all the sins of all his people he has made such a full and satisfactory atonement, that divine justice were not divine justice at all if it should ask to be paid twice for the same offence. Christ has suffered the law's fullest and severest penalty, and there is now no fear whatever that the case can ever be revived, by writ of error, or removal into another court, because it has been settled on the eternal and immutable principles of justice.

Again, the case has been so settled, *that both parties are well content.* You never hear a saved soul murmur at the substitution of the Lord Jesus. If ever I get to see his face, I'll fall down before him and kiss the dust beneath his feet. Oh! if ever I see the Saviour who has thus delivered me from ruin; if I have a crown I will cast it at his feet, and never, never wear it; it must, it shall be his. I feel like the good woman who said, that if Christ ever saved her, he should never hear the last of it; and I am sure he never shall, for I will praise him as long as immortality endures, for what he has done for me. I am sure that every saved sinner feels the same. And Jehovah, on the other side, is perfectly content. He is satisfied with his dear Son. "Well done!" he saith to him. He has received him to the throne of glory, and made him to sit at his right hand, because he is perfectly content with the great work which he has accomplished.

But, what is more and more wonderful still, *both parties have gained in the suit.* Did you ever hear of such a law-suit as this before? No, never in the courts of man. The old story of the two oyster-shells, you know, awarded to the plaintiff and defendant, while the oyster is eaten in court, is generally the result; but it is not so in this case, for both the plaintiff and the defendant have won by the arbitration. What has God gained? Why, glory to himself, and such glory as all creation could not give him, such glory as the ruin of sinners, though so well-deserved, could not give him. Hark how

"Heaven's eternal arches ring
With shouts of sovereign grace!"

Angels, too, as well as those who have been redeemed, strike their harps, which they have turned afresh to a nobler strain, as they sing, "Worthy is the Lamb, and blessed is the eternal God!" And, as for us, the poor defendants, why, what have we not gained? We were men before; now we are something more than Adam was. We were "a little lower than the angels" before, but now we are "lifted up far above all principalities and powers." We were God's subjects once, but this arbitration has made us his sons. We were at our very best only the possessors of a paradise on earth, but now we are joint-heirs with Christ of a paradise above the skies. Both sides have won, and both sides must therefore be blessedly content with their glorious Daysman.

And, to conclude, through this Daysman *both parties have come to be united in the strongest, closest, dearest, and fondest bond of union.* This law-suit has ended in such a way that the plaintiff and the defendant are friends for life, nay, friends through death, and friends in eternity. How near God is to a pardoned sinner,

"So near, so very near to God,
Nearer we cannot be;
For in the person of his Son,
We are as near as he."

What a wonderful thing is that union between God and the sinner! We have all been thinking a great deal lately about the Atlantic Cable. It is a very interesting attempt to join two worlds together. That poor cable, you know, has had to be sunk into the depths of the sea, in the hope of establishing a union between the two worlds, and now we are disappointed again. But oh! what an infinitely greater wonder *has been* accomplished. Christ Jesus saw the two worlds divided, and the great Atlantic of human guilt rolled between. He sank down deep into the woes of man till all God's waves and billows had gone over him, that he might be, as it were, the great telegraphic communication between God and the apostate race, between the Most Holy One and poor sinners. Let me say to you, sinner, there was no failure in the laying down of that blessed cable. It went down deep; the end was well secured, and it went down deep into the depths of our sin, and shame, and woe; and on the other side it has gone right up to the eternal throne, and is fastened there eternally fast, by God himself. You may work that telegraph to-day, and you may easily understand the art of working it too. A sigh will work it; a tear will work it. Say, "God be merciful to me a sinner," and along the wire the message will flash, and will reach God before it comes from you. It is swifter far than earthly telegraphs; ay, and there will come an answer back much sooner than you ever dream of, for it is promised—"Before they call I will answer, and while they are yet speaking I will hear." Who ever heard of such a communication as this between man and man; but it really does exist between sinners and God, since Christ has opened up a way from the depths of our sin to the heights of his glory.

This is for you who are at a distance from him, but he has done more for us who are saved, for he has taken us right across the Atlantic of our sin and set us down on the other side; he has taken us out of our sinful state, and put us into the Father's bosom, and there we shall dwell for ever in the heart of God as his own dear children.

I would to God that some might now be led to look to the Saviour, that some would come with weeping and with tears to him, and say,

"'Jesus lover of my soul,
Let me to thy bosom fly.'

Take my case, and arbitrate for me; I accept thine atonement; I trust in thy precious blood; only receive me and I will rejoice in thee for ever with joy unspeakable and full of glory."

May the Lord bless you evermore. Amen.

Jehovah Tsidkenu
The Lord Our Righteousness

"This is his name whereby he shall be called, The Lord our Righteousness"—Jeremiah xxiii. 6.

MAN by the fall sustained an infinite loss in the matter of righteousness. He suffered the loss of a righteous nature, and then a two-fold loss of legal righteousness in the sight of God. Man sinned; he was therefore no longer innocent of transgression. Man did not keep the command; he therefore was guilty of the sin of omission. In that which he *committed*, and in that which he *omitted*, his original character for uprightness was completely wrecked. Jesus Christ came to undo the mischief of the fall for his people. So far as their sin concerned their breach of the command, that he has removed by his precious blood. His agony and bloody sweat have for ever taken away the consequences of sin from believers, seeing Christ did by his one sacrifice bear the penalty of that sin in his flesh. He, his own self, bare our sins in his own body on the tree. Still it is not enough for a man to be pardoned. He of course is then in the eye of God without sin. But it was required of man that he should actually keep the command. It was not enough that he did not break it, or that he is regarded through the blood as though he did not break it. He must keep it, he must continue in all things that are written in the book of the law to do them. How is this necessity supplied? Man must have a righteousness, or God cannot accept him. Man must have a perfect obedience, or else God cannot reward him. Should He give heaven to a soul that has not perfectly kept the law; that were to give the reward where the service is not done, and that before God would be an act which might impeach his justice. Where, then, is the righteousness with which the pardoned man shall be completely covered, so that God can regard him as having kept the law, and reward him for so doing? Surely, my brethren, none of you are so besotted as to think that this righteousness can be wrought out by yourselves. You must despair of ever being able to keep the law perfectly. Each day you sin. Since you have passed from death unto life, the old Adam still struggles for dominion within you. And by the force of the lusts of the flesh you are brought into captivity to the law of sin which is in your members. The good you would do, you do not, and the evil you would not, that you too often do. Some have thought the works of the Holy Spirit in us would give us a righteousness in which we might stand. I am sure, my brethren, we would not say a word derogatory to the work of the Holy Spirit.

It is divine. But we hold it to be a great cardinal point in divinity that the work of the Spirit was never meant to supplant the merits of the Son. We could not depreciate the Lord Jesus Christ in order to exalt the office of the Holy Spirit of God. We know that each particular branch of the divine salvation which was espoused by the persons of the Trinity has been carried out by each one to perfection. Now as we are accepted in the Beloved, it must be by a something that the Beloved did ; as we are justified in Christ it must be by a something not that the Spirit has done, but which Christ has done. We must believe, then,—for there is no other alternative—that the righteousness in which we must be clothed, and through which we must be accepted, and by which we are made meet to inherit eternal life, can be no other than the work of Jesus Christ. We, therefore, assert, believing that Scripture fully warrants us. that the life of Christ constitutes the righteousness in which his people are to be clothed. His death washed away their sins, his life covered them from head to foot ; his death was the sacrifice to God, his life was the gift to man, by which man satisfies the demands of the law. Herein the law is honoured and the soul is accepted. I find that many young Christians who are very clear about being saved by the merits of Christ's death, do not seem to understand the merits of his life. Remember, young believers, that from the first moment when Christ did lie in the cradle until the time when he ascended up on high. he was at work for his people ; and from the moment when he was seen in Mary's arms, till the instant when in the arms of death he "bowed his head and gave up the ghost," he was at work for your salvation and mine. He completed the work of obedience in his life, and said to his Father, "I have finished the work which thou gavest me to do." Then he completed the work of atonement in his death, and knowing that all things were accomplished, he cried, "It is finished." He was through his life spinning the web for making the royal garment, and in his death he dipped that garment in his blood In his life he was gathering together the precious gold, in his death he hammered it out to make for us a garment which is of wrought gold. You have as much to thank Christ for living as for dying, and you should be as reverently and devoutly grateful for his spotless life as for his terrible and fearful death. The text speaking of Christ, the son of David, the branch out of the root of Jesse, styles him, THE LORD OUR RIGHTEOUSNESS.

Having introduced the doctrine of imputed righteousness, I proceed to map out my subject. First, by way of *affirmation ;* we say of the text—it is so—Christ is the Lord our righteousness ; secondly, I shall exhort you to do him *homage ;* let us call him so : for this is the name whereby he shall be called ; and thirdly, I shall appeal to your *gratitude ;* let us wonder at the reigning grace, which has caused us to fulfil the promise, for we have been sweetly compelled to call him the Lord our righteousness.

First, then, *He is so.* Jesus Christ is the Lord *our* righteousness. There are but three words, "JEHOVAH,"—for so it is in the original,—" OUR RIGHTEOUSNESS." He is Jehovah. Read that verse, and you will clearly perceive that the Messiah of the Jews, Jesus of Nazareth the Saviour of the Gentiles, is certainly Jehovah. He hath the incommunicable title of the Most High God. "Behold, the days come, saith the Lord, that I will raise unto David a righteous branch, and a king shall reign and prosper, and shall execute judgment and justice in the earth. In his days Judah shall be saved, and Israel shall dwell safely : and this is his name whereby he shall be called, THE LORD OUR RIGHTEOUSNESS." Oh, ye Arians and Socinians, who monstrously deny the Lord who bought you and put him to open shame by denying his divinity, read you that verse and let your blasphemous tongues be silent, and let your obdurate hearts melt in penitence because ye have so foully sinned against him. He *is* Jehovah, or, mark you, the whole of God's word is false, and there is no ground whatever for a sinner's hope. We know, and this day we testify in his name, that the very Christ who did lie in the manger as an infant was infinite even then ; that he who cried, cried for very pain as a child, was nevertheless saluted at that very moment as God by the songs of the creatures that his hands had made. He who walked in pain over the flinty acres of Palestine, was at the same time possessor of heaven and earth. He who had not where to lay his head, and was despised and rejected of men, was at the same instant God over all, blessed for evermore. He that sweat great drops of blood did bear the earth upon his shoulders. He who was flagellated in Pilate's hall was adored by spirits of the just made perfect. He who did hang upon the tree had the creation hanging upon him. He who died on the cross was the ever living, the everlasting One. As a man he died, as God he lives. As Mary's son he bled, as the son of the Eternal God he had the sway and the dominion over all the world. In nature Christ proves himself to be universal God. Without him was not anything made that was made. By him all things consist. Who less than God could make the heavens and the earth? Bow before him, bow before him, for he made you, and should not the creatures acknowledge their Creator?

Providence attests his Godhead. He upholdeth all things by the word of his power. Creatures that are animate have their breath from his nostrils; inanimate creatures that are strong and mighty stand only by his strength. He can say concerning the earth, " I bear the pillars thereof." In the deep foundations of the sea his power is felt, and in the towering arches of the starry heavens his might is recognised to the full. And as for Grace, we claim for Christ that he is Jehovah in the great kingdom of his grace. Who less than God could have carried your sins and mine and cast them all away? Who less than God could have interposed to deliver us from the jaws of hell's lions, and bring us up from the pit, having found a ransom? On whom less than God could we rely to keep us from the innumerable temptations that beset us? How can he be less than God, when he says, " Lo I am with you always, unto the end of the world?" How could he be omnipresent if he were not God! How could he hear our prayers, the prayers of millions, scattered through the leagues of earth, and attend to them all, and give acceptance to all, if he were not infinite in understanding and infinite in merit? How were this if he were less than God? Let Atheists scoff, let Deists sneer, let the vain Socinian boast, let the Arian lift up his puny voice, but we will glory in this fact, that he that bought us with his blood is Jehovah—very God of very God. At his footstool we bow and pay him the very homage that we pay to his Father and to the Spirit.

" Blessings more than we can give,
Be Lord for ever thine."

But the text speaks about righteousness too—"Jehovah our righteousness." And he is so. Christ in his life was so righteous, that we may say of the life, taken as a whole, that it is righteousness itself. Christ is the law incarnate. Understand me. He lived out the law of God to the very full, and while you see God's precepts written in fire on Sinai's brow, you see them written in flesh in the person of Christ.

" My dear Redeemer and my Lord,
I read my duty in thy word,
But in thy life the law appears
Drawn out in living characters."

He never offended against the commands of the Just One. From his eye there never flashed the fire of unhallowed anger. On his lip there did never hang the unjust or licentious word. His heart was never stirred by the breath of sin or the taint of iniquity. In the secret of his reins no fault was hidden. In his understanding was no defect; in his judgment no error. In his miracles there was no ostentation. In him there was indeed no guile. His powers being ruled by his understanding, all of them acted and co-acted to perfection's very self, so that never was there any flaw of omission or stain of commission. The law consists in this first, "Thou shalt love the Lord thy God with all thy heart." He did so. It was his meat and his drink to do the will of him that sent him. Never man spent himself as he did. Hunger and thirst and nakedness were nothing to him, nor death itself, if he might so be baptised with the baptism wherewith he must be baptised, and drink the cup which his Father had set before him. The law consists also in this, "Thou shalt love thy neighbour as thyself." In all he did, and in all he suffered, he more than fulfilled the precept, for "he saved others, himself he could not save." He exhausted the utmost resources of love in the deep devotion and self-sacrifice of loving. He loved man better than his own life. He would sooner be spit upon than that man should be cast into the flames of hell, and sooner yield up the ghost in agonies that cannot be described than that the souls his Father gave him should be cast away. He carried out the law, then, I say to the very letter; he spelt out its mystic syllables; and verily he magnified it, and made it honourable. He loved the Lord his God, with all his heart, and soul, and mind, and he loved his neighbours as himself. Jesus Christ was righteousness impersonated. "Which of you convinceth me of sin?" he might well say. One thousand eight hundred years have passed since then, and blasphemy itself has not been able to charge him with a fault. Strange as it may appear, the most perverted judges have nevertheless acknowledged the awful dignity of his character. They have railed at his miracles; they have denied his Godhead; but his righteous character I know not that they have dared to impugn. They have hatched jokes about his generation; they have made his poverty a jest, and his death has been the theme of ribald song; but his life has staggered even the most unbelieving, and made the careless wonder how such a character could have been conceived even if it be a fiction, and much more, how it could have been executed if it be a fact. No one that I know of has dared to charge Christ with unrighteousness to man, or with a want of devotedness to God. See then, it is so. We do not stay to prove his righteousness any more than we did to prove his Godhead. The day is coming when men shall acknowledge him to be Jehovah, and when looking upon all his life while he was incarnate here, they shall be compelled to say that his life was righteousness itself. The pith, however, of the title, lies in the little word "our,"—"Jehovah *our* righteousness." This is the grappling iron with which we get a hold on him—this is the anchor which dives into the bottom of this great deep of his immaculate righteousness. This is the sacred rivet by which our souls are joined to him. This is the blessed hand with which our soul toucheth him, and he becometh to us all in all, "Jehovah *our* Righteousness."

You will now observe that there is a most precious *doctrine* unfolded in this title of our Lord and Saviour. I think we may take it thus: When we believe in Christ, by faith we receive our justification. As the merit of his blood takes away our sin, so the merit of his obedience is imputed to us for righteousness. We are considered, as soon as we believe, as though the works of Christ were our works. God looks upon us as though that perfect obedience, of which I have just now spoken, had been performed by ourselves,—as though our hands had been busy at the loom, as though the fabric and the stuff which have been worked up into the fine linen, which is the righteousness of the saints, had been grown in our own fields. God considers us as though we were Christ—looks upon us as though *his* life had been *our* life—and accepts, blesses, and rewards us as though all that he did had been done by us, his believing people. Accordingly, if you will turn to the thirty-third chapter of this same prophet Jeremiah, and look at the sixteenth verse, you will see it written, "This is the name wherewith *she* shall be called, the Lord our righteousness." I know that Socinus in his day used to call this an execrable, detestable, and licentious doctrine: probably it was, because he was an execrable, detestable, and licentious man. Many men use their own names when they are applying names to other persons; they are so well acquainted with their own characters, and so suspicious of themselves, that they think it best, before another can express the suspicion, to attach the very same accusation to someone else. Now we hold, you know, that this doctrine is not execrable, but most delightful; that it is not abominable, but Godlike; that it is not licentious, but holy: and let others say what they will of it, we will repeat the praise which we have been singing,—

"Jesus, thy perfect righteousness
My beauty is, my glorious dress;"

and we will wait the day when all things shall be tried by fire, for we feel confident that—

"Bold shall we stand in that great day,
For who aught to our charge shall lay,"

when we are clothed with the righteousness divine?

Imputation, so far from being an exceptional case with regard to the righteousness of Christ, lies at the very bottom of the entire teaching of Scripture. How did we fall, my brethren? We fell by the imputation of Adam's sin to us. Adam was our federal head; he represented us; and when he sinned, we sinned representatively in him, and what he did was imputed to us. You say that you never agreed to the imputation. Nay, but I would not have you say thus, for as by representation we fell, it is by the representative system that we rise. The angels fell personally and individually, and they never rise; but we fell in another, and we have therefore the power given by divine grace to rise in another. The root of the fall is found in the federal relationship of Adam to his seed; thus we fell by imputation. Is it any wonder that we should rise by imputation? Deny this doctrine, and I ask you—How are men pardoned at all? Are they not pardoned because satisfaction has been offered for sin by Christ? Very well, then, but that satisfaction must be imputed to them, or else how is God just in giving to them the results of the death of another, unless that death of the other be first of all imputed to them? When we say that the righteousness of Christ is imputed to all believing souls, we do not hold forth an exceptional theory, but we expound a grand truth, which is so consistent with the theory of the fall and the plan of pardon, that it must be maintained in order to make the gospel clear. I think it was this doctrine which Martin Luther called the article of standing or falling of the Church. I find a passage in his works which seems to me to refer to this doctrine rather than to justification by faith. He ought certainly to have said, "Justification by faith is *the* doctrine of standing or falling of the Church." But in Luther's mind, imputed righteousness was so interwoven with justification by faith, that he could not see any distinction between the two. And I must confess, in trying to observe a difference, I do not see much. I must give up justification by faith if I give up imputed righteousness. True justification by faith is the surface soil, but then imputed righteousness is the granite rock which lies underneath it; and if you dig down through the great truth of a sinner's being justified by faith in Christ, you must, as I believe, inevitably come to the doctrine of the imputed righteousness of Christ as the basis and foundation on which that simple doctrine rests.

And now let us stop a moment and think over this whole title—"The Lord our righteousness." Brethren, the Law-giver has himself obeyed the law. Do you not think that his obedience will be sufficient? Jehovah has himself become man that so he may do man's work: think you that he has done it imperfectly? Jehovah—he who girds the angels that excel in strength—has taken upon him the form of a servant that he may become obedient: think you that his service will be incomplete? Let the fact that the Saviour is Jehovah strengthen your confidence. Be ye bold. Be ye very courageous. Face heaven, and earth, and hell with the challenge of the apostle, "Who shall lay anything to the charge of God's elect?" Look back upon your past sins, look upon your present infirmities, and all your future errors, and while you weep the tears of repentance, let no fear of damnation blanch your cheek. You stand before God to-day robed in your Saviour's garments, "with his spotless vestments on, holy as the Holy One." Not Adam when he walked in Eden's bowers was more accepted than you are,—not more pleasing to the eye of the all-judging, the sin-hating God, than you are if clothed in Jesus' righteousness and sprinkled with his blood. You have a better righteousness than Adam had. He had a human righteousness; your garments are divine. He had a robe complete, it is true, but the earth had woven it. You have a garment as complete, but *heaven* has made it for you to wear. Go up and down in the strength of this great truth and boast exceedingly, and glory in your God; and let this be on the top and summit of your heart and soul: "Jehovah, the Lord our righteousness."

You will remember that in Scripture, Christ's righteousness is compared to fair white linen; then I am, if I wear it, without spot. It is compared to wrought gold; then I am, if I wear it, dignified and beautiful, and worthy to sit at the wedding feast of the King of kings. It is compared, in the parable of the prodigal son, to the best robe; then I wear a better robe than angels have, for they have not the best; but I, poor prodigal, once clothed in rags, companion to the nobility of the stye,—I, fresh from the husks that swine do eat, am nevertheless clothed in the best robe, and am so accepted in the Beloved.

Moreover, it is also everlasting righteousness. Oh! this is, perhaps, the fairest point of it—that the robe shall never be worn out; no thread of it shall ever give way. It shall never hang in tatters upon the sinner's back. He shall live, and even though it were a Methusaleh's life, the robe shall be as if it were woven yesterday. He shall pass through the stream of death, and the black stream shall not foul it. He shall climb the hills of heaven, and the angels shall wonder what this whiteness is which the sinner wears, and think that some new star is coming up from earth to shine in heaven. He shall wear it among principalities and powers, and find himself no whit inferior to them all. Cherubic garments and seraphic mantles shall not be so lordly, so priestly, so divine, as this robe of righteousness, this everlasting perfection which Christ has wrought out, and brought in and given to all his people. Glory unto thee, O Jesus, glory unto thee! Unto thee be hallels for ever; Hallelu—Jah! Thou art Jah —"Jehovah, the Lord our righteousness."

II. Having thus expounded and vindicated this title of our Saviour, I would now APPEAL TO YOUR FAITH.

Let us call him so. "This is the name whereby he shall be *called*, the Lord our righteousness." Let us call him by this great name, which the mouth of the Lord of Hosts hath named. Let *us* call him—poor sinners!—even we, who are to-day smitten down with grief on account of sin. I want this text to be fulfilled in your ears and in your case to-day. You are guilty. Your own conscience acknowledges that the law condemns you, and you dread the penalty. Soul! he that trusteth Christ Jesus is saved, and he that believeth on him is not condemned. To every trustful spirit. Christ is "the Lord our righteousness." Call him so, I pray thee. "I have no good thing of my own," sayest thou? Here is every good thing in him. "I have broken the law," sayest thou? There is his blood for thee. Believe in him; he will wash thee. "But then I have not kept the law." There is his keeping of the law for thee. Take it, sinner, take it. Believe on him. "Oh, but I dare not," saith one. Do him the honour to dare it. "Oh, but it seems impossible." Honour him by believing the impossibility then. "Oh, but how can he save such a wretch as I am?" Soul! Christ is glorified in saving wretches. As I told you the other day, Christ cures incurable sinners; so I say now he accepts unacceptable sinners. He receives sinners that think they are not fit to be received. Only do thou trust him, and say, "He shall be *my* righteousness to-day." "But suppose I should do it and be presumptuous?" It is impossible. He bids you; he commands you. Let that be your warrant. "This is *the* commandment, that ye believe on Jesus Christ whom he hath sent." If you cannot say it with a loud voice, yet with the trembling silence of your soul let heaven hear it. Yes, Jesus, "All unholy and unclean, I am nothing else but sin; yet I dare with fervent venture of these quivering lips to call thee, and to call upon thee now, as the Lord my righteousness."

And you who have passed from a state of trembling hope into that of lively faith, I beseech you call him so. Let your faith say, as you see him suffering, bleeding, dying, "Thus my sins were washed away." But let not your faith stay there. As you see him sweating, toiling, living a self-denying laborious life, say, "Thus the law was kept for me." Come up to the foot of Sinai now, and if you see its lightnings flash, and hear its thunders roar, be brave, and say like Moses, "I will ascend above those thunders; I will stand enwrapped within the storm-cloud, and I will talk with God, for *I* have no cause for fear; there are no thunderbolts for me; for me no lightning flash can spend its arrow; I am perfectly, completely justified in the sight of God, through the righteousness of Jesus Christ." Say that, child of God! Does yesterday's sin make thee stammer? In the teeth of all thy sins believe that he is thy righteousness still. Thy good works do not improve his righteousness; thy bad works do not sully it. This is a robe which thy best deeds cannot mend and thy worst deeds cannot mar. Thou standest in him, not in thyself. Whatever, then, thy doubts and fears may have been, do now, poor troubled, distressed, distracted believer, say again, "Yes, he *is* the Lord my righteousness."

And some of us can say it yet better than that; for we can say it not merely by faith, but by fruition. We remember well the day when we first called him "the Lord our righteousness." Oh, the peace it brought, the joy, the gladness, the transport! Since then we have proved it to be true; for we have had privileges we could not have had if he had not been our righteousness. We have had the privilege of reconciliation with God; and He could not be reconciled to one that had not a perfect righteousness; we have had access with boldness to God himself, and He would never have suffered us to have access if we had not worn our brother's garments. We have had adoption into the family, and the Spirit of adoption, and God could not have adopted into his family any but righteous ones. How should the righteous Father be God of an unrighteous family? Our prayers have been heard, and we have had gracious answers, and that could not have been—for he could not hear the prayer of the wicked; he could not have heard us—if it had not been that he seemed to hear Christ crying through us, and to have seen Christ's merits in us, and therefore granted the desire of our hearts. We have had in daily rich and sweet experience such manifestations of fellowship with the Father and with his Son Jesus Christ, that to us it is a matter of fact as well as a matter of faith, a matter of praise as well as a matter of profession, that Jesus Christ is "the Lord our righteousness."

Brethren, your divinity must be experimental or it will not profit you. I would not give a straw for your theology if you learned it merely out of a college, or out of a system of man's teaching. No, no, we must prove these things to be true in our lives. I can say it, and I must say it—the testimony is not egotistical—I *know* there is a comfort in the faith of Christ's imputed righteousness which no other doctrine can yield. There is something that a man can sleep on and wake on, can live on and die on, in the firm conviction that he is received by God as though the deeds of Christ were his deeds, and the righteousness of Christ his righteousness. Take away his filthy garments from him; set a fair mitre on his head; array him in fine linen. O Joshua, priest of the Most High, thou man greatly beloved, come thou forth now in thy garments and offer acceptable sacrifice, seeing thou wearest the garments of Jesus, our great High Priest." Let *us*, then, call upon his name and extol him in our worship as "the Lord *our* righteousness."

And now let the whole universal Church of Christ, in one glad song, call Jesus Christ the Lord their righteousness Wake up, ye isles of the sea; shout, thou wilderness that Kedar doth inhabit; ye people of God, scattered and peeled, banished among the heathen, vexed with the filthy conversation of the idolaters, from your huts, from the destitute places that ye inhabit, sing, "The Lord our righteousness!" Let no heir of heaven be silent at this hour; let every soul be stirred. Though tempest-tossed and half a wreck, yet, mariner in Christ, say, "Thou art the Lord my righteousness." Though cast down into the deep dungeon, thou despairing soul, yet say, "The Lord my righteousness." Let no one of the entire believing family keep back his song, but together let us sing, "The Lord our righteousness." And you, ye spirits that walk in white, ye glorious ones that "day without night circle his throne rejoicing," ye saints that ere his day beheld him, and died, not having received the promise, but having beheld it afar off,—Abraham, and Isaac, and Jacob, and Moses, and Samuel, and Jephthah, and David, and Solomon, and all the mighty host, sing ye, sing ye, sing ye unto him to-day; and let this be the summit of your song, "The Lord our righteousness." Our spirit bows before him now. Sweet fellowship beyond the stream! We clasp our hands with those that went before; and while the cherubim can only say, "Holy, holy, holy; he is righteous," we lift up a higher note, and say, "Yes, thrice holy, but the Lord our righteousness is he." Let none, then, of all his saints in heaven and in earth, refuse to call him "the Lord our righteousness."

III. I now conclude, in the third place, by appealing to your GRATITUDE. Let us admire that wonderful and reigning grace which has led you and me to call him, "The Lord our righteousness."

When I look back some ten or twelve years upon a foolish boy, who cared little for the things of God, who was burdened with an awful sense of sin, and thought that he never could be pardoned—a lad so often driven to the borders of despair that he was fain to make away with his own life, because he thought there was no happiness on earth for him— I can only say for my own self. O the riches of the grace of God in Christ, that ever *I* should stand not only conscious that he is the Lord my righteousness, but to preach him to you! O God, thou hast done wonderful things! Thou saidst by the mouth of Jeremy, "This is the name whereby he shall be called." I call him so this day from my inmost soul. Jesus of Nazareth! suffering man! glorious God! thou art the Lord my righteousness! If I were to pass this question round these galleries, and down below, oh, what hundreds of responses would there be from such as joyously obey the summons of gratitude! And among those about to be added to the Church (I am sure they would permit me to tell, for the honour of the glorious grace of God), there are very many who are special instances of that grace which has sweetly constrained them to call Christ their righteousness. Some of them, according to their own confession before us at the Church meeting, were not only revelling in drunkenness, one until he had well nigh drank away his reason by thirty years of habitual intoxication ; but others of them were unclean and unchaste, till they had rioted in debauchery, and gone to the utmost lengths of crime. There be many in this place to-day, who would not, though they would blush for the past, refuse to tell, to the honour of redeeming grace, that once they had committed every crime in the catalogue except murder ; and if they have not committed that, it was nothing but the sovereign grace of God that restrained them. Some members of this Church have sinned in every part of the world—have sinned in every quarter of the globe—have committed every form of lust and vice—and if you had asked them ten years ago whether they should ever be in a place of worship, they would have repelled with an oath what they would have thought an insult, and would have cursed you for supposing that they should so degrade themselves as to profess the faith of Christ. Brothers and sisters, I should not be surprised if you were to stand up now and say, " Yes, still Jehovah Jesus is the Lord our righteousness." Oh !—

> " Wonders of grace to God belong ;
> Repeat his mercies in your song."

Who would have thought that the lip of the blasphemer should fulfil that very prophecy—that the tongue that could scarce move without an oath should, nevertheless, glorify Christ,—that the heart that was black with accumulated lust,—the mouth which must have become a very sepulchre, breathing forth deadly miasma, has now become a place for song, and the heart a house for music, while heart and tongue say, " Yes, he is the Lord my righteousness this very day ?"

It would be a wonder if God should vow that the devils should yet sing his praise ; but I do not think it would be a greater wonder than when he makes some of us sing his glorious praise. Brethren, you and I know that there is nothing in free-will doctrine ; for in our case, at any rate, it was not true. Left to ourselves, where should we have been ? What could Arminianism have done for us ? Oh, no ! it was irresistible grace that brought us to call him " the Lord our righteousness." It was that divine *shall* that broke in pieces our *will*. It was that strong arm that broke the iron sinew of our proud neck, and made us bow, even us, who would not have this man to reign over us. It was his finger that opened the blind eye ; for once we could see no beauty in him. It was his breath that thawed our icy heart ; for once we felt no love to him ;—

> " But now, subdued by sovereign grace,
> Our spirit longs for his embrace ;
> Our beauty this our glorious dress,
> Jesus the Lord our righteousness."

And this shall be our glory here, and our song for ever—" The Lord our righteousness."

Ecce Rex

"He saith unto the Jews, Behold your King!"—John xix. 14.

PILATE said much more than he meant, and, therefore, we shall not restrict our consideration of his words to what *he* intended. John tells us considering Caiaphas, " and this spake he not of himself," and we may say the same of Pilate. Everything said or done in connection with the Saviour during the day of his crucifixion was full of meaning, far fuller of meaning than the speakers or actors were aware. Transformed by the cross, even the commonplace becomes solemn and weighty. When Caiaphas said that it was expedient that one man should die for the people, that the whole nation perish not, he little thought that he was enunciating the great gospel principle of substitution. When the Jewish people cried out before Pilate " His blood be on us and on our children," they little knew the judgment which they were bringing upon themselves, which would commence to be fulfilled at the siege of Jerusalem, and follow them, hanging like a heavy cloud over their race, for centuries. When the soldier with a spear pierced his side he had no idea that he was bringing forth before all eyes that blood and water which are to the whole church the emblems of the double cleansing which we find in Jesus, cleansing by atoning blood and sanctifying grace. The fulness of time had come, and all things were full. Each movement on that awful day was brimming with mystery, neither could the Master or those around him stir or speak without teaching some gospel, or enforcing some lesson. Whereas on certain days frivolity seems to rule the hour, and little is to be gathered from much that is spoken; on the day of the passion even the most careless spake as men inspired. Pilate, the undecided spirit, with no mind of his own, uttered language as weighty as if he too had been among the prophets. His acquittal of our Lord, his mention of Barabbas, his writing of the inscription to be fixed over the head of Jesus, and many other matters, were all fraught with instruction.

It was to the Jews that Pilate brought forth Jesus arrayed in garments of derision, and to them he said, " *Ecce rex* "—" Behold your King ! " It was by the seed of Abraham that he was rejected as their King ; but we shall not think of them in order to blame that unhappy nation, but to remind ourselves that we also may fall into the same sin. As a nation favoured with the gospel we stand in many respects in the same privileged condition as the Jews did. To us is the word of God made known, to our keeping the oracles of God are committed in these last days, and we, though by nature shoots of the wild olive, are engrafted into that favoured stock from which Israel have for a while been cut off. Shall we prove equally unworthy ? Shall any of us be found guilty of the blood of Jesus ? We hear of Jesus this day ; are we rejecting him ? The suffering Messiah will be brought forth again this morning, not by Pilate, but by one who longs to do him honour, and when he stands before you, and is proclaimed again in the words, " Behold your King ! " will you also cry, " Away with him, away with him " ? Let us hope that there will not be found here hearts so evil as to imitate the rebellious nation and cry, " We will not have this man to reign over us." Oh that each one of us may acknowledge the Lord Jesus to be his King, for beneath his sceptre there is rest and joy. He is worthy to be crowned by every heart, let us all unite in beholding him with reverence and receiving him with delight. Give me your ears and hearts while Jesus is evidently set forth as standing among you, and for the next few minutes let it be your only business to " Behold your King."

I. Come with me, then, to the place which is called the Pavement, but in the Hebrew Gabbatha, and there "behold your King." I shall first ask you to BEHOLD YOUR KING PREPARING HIS THRONE, yea, and making himself ready to sit thereon. When you look in answer to the summons, " Behold your King," what do you see ? You see the " Man of sorrows and acquainted with grief, " wearing a crown of thorns and covered with an old purple cloak, which had been thrown about him. In mockery ; you can see, if you look narrowly, the traces of his streaming blood, for he has just been scourged, and you may also discover that his face is blackened with bruises and stained with shameful spittle from the soldiers' mouths.

> " Thus trimmed forth they bring him to the rout,
> Who 'Crucify him' cry with one strong shout,
> God holds his peace at man, and man cries out."

It is a terrible spectacle, but I ask you to gaze upon it steadily and see the establishment of the Redeemer's throne. See how he becomes your mediatorial King. He was setting up a new throne on Gabbatha, whereon he would reign as the King of pardoned sinners and the Prince of Peace. He was King before all worlds as Lord of all by right of his eternal power and Godhead ; he had a throne when worlds were made, as King of all kings by creation ; he had also always filled the throne of providence, upholding all things by the word of his power. On his head were many crowns, and to Pilate's question, " Art thou a king then ?" he did fitly answer, " Thou sayest that I am a king." But here before Pilate and the Jews, in his condition of shame and misery, he was about to ascend, and first of all to prepare the throne of the heavenly grace, which now is set up among the sons of men, that they may flee to it and find eternal salvation. Mark how he is preparing this throne of grace, it is *by pain and shame endured in our room and stead.* Sin was in the way of man's happiness, and a broken law, and justice requiring a penalty: and all this must be arranged before a throne of grace could be erected among men. If you look at our suffering Lord you see at once the ensigns of his *pain*, for he wears a crown of thorns which pierce his brow. Pain was a great part of the penalty due for sin, and the great Substitute was therefore sorely pained. When Pilate brought forth our martyr Prince he was the very mirror of agony, he was majesty in misery, misery wrought up to its full height and stature. The cruel furrows of the scourge, and the trickling rivulets of his blood adown his face were but the tokens that he was about to die in cruel pangs upon the cross, and these together were incumbent upon him because there could be no throne of grace till first there had been a substitutionary sacrifice. It behoved him to suffer that he might be a prince and a Saviour. Behold your King in his pains, he is laying the deep foundations of his kingdom of mercy. Many a crown has been secured by blood, and so is this, but it is his own blood; many a throne has been established by suffering, and so is this, but he himself bears the pain. By his great sacrificial griefs our Lord has prepared a throne whereon he shall sit till all the chosen race have been made kings and priests to reign with him. It is by his agony that he obtains the royal power to pardon: by his stripes and bruises he wins the right to absolve poor sinners. We shall have no cause to wonder at the greatness of his mediatorial power if we consider the depth of his sacrificial sufferings: as his misery is the source of his majesty, so the greatness of his pains has secured to him the fulness of power to save. Had he not gone to the end of the law, and honoured justice to the highest degree, he had not now been so gloriously able to dispense mercy from his glorious high throne of mediatorial grace. Behold your King, then, as he lays deep in his own pain and death the basis of his throne of grace.

Nor is it only pain, for he wears also the tokens of *scorn.* That crown of thorns meant mainly mockery: the soldiers made him a mimic monarch, a carnival king, and that scarlet robe, too, was cast upon his shoulders in bitter scorn: thus did this world deride its God. The evangelists give you the description in brief sentences, as if they stopped between each line to cover their faces with their hands and weep. So there he stands before the crowd, helpless, friendless, with none to declare his generation or give him a good word. He is deserted by all who formerly called him Master, and he has become the centre of a scene of rioting and ridicule. The soldiers have done their worst, and now the chief men of the nation look at him with contempt, and are only kept back from the most ribald scorn by a hate too furiously eager for death to afford them leisure for their scoffs. His enemies had done everything in their power to clothe him with scorn, and they were asking for permission to do more, for they cried, "Let him be crucified." Behold ye, how he has left all the honour of his Father's house, and his own glory among the angels, and here he stands with a mock robe, a mimic sceptre, and a thorny crown, the butt of ridicule, scoffed at by all! Yet this must be, because sin is a shameful thing, and a part of the penalty of sin is shame, as they will know who shall wake up in the day of judgment to everlasting contempt. Shame fell on Adam when he sinned, and then and there he knew that he was naked ; and now shame has come down in a tremendous hail upon the head of the Second Adam, the substitute for shameful man, and he is covered with contempt. "All they that see me laugh me to scorn." It is hard to say whether cruelty or mockery had most to do with the person of our Lord at Gabbatha; but by enduring these two things together he laid on an immovable foundation the corner stone of his dominion of love and grace. How could he have been the king of a redeemed people if he had not thus redeemed them? He might have been lord over a people doomed to die, the stern ruler of a people who continued in sin, and would so continue till they perished for ever from his presence ; but no such a kingdom did he seek; he sought a kingdom over hearts that should eternally be under obligation to him, hearts that, being redeemed from the lowest hell by his atoning death, would for ever love him with the utmost fervency. His sorrow secured his power to save, his shame endowed him with the right to bless.

"Behold your King." Look at him with steady eye and see what a King he now is *by right of benefit conferred*. Behold, he hath put away sin for ever by the sacrifice of himself, and therefore all the ransomed ones agree that he should be king who smote the great dragon which devoured the nations. Behold by his stooping to shame he hath dethroned Satan, who was the prince of this world; and who should occupy the throne but he who has won it, and cast out the strong one who ruled aforetime. Christ has done more for men than the prince of darkness could or would, for he has died for them, and so he has earned a just supremacy over all grateful hearts. As for death, Jesus, by yielding to death, has conquered it. Let him be crowned with the victor's wreath who has destroyed the world's destroyer. In his shame you also see the Lord Jesus Christ fulfilling the law and making it honourable. He who could honour that law, which else would have cursed us, deserveth to have all honour and homage paid to him by the sons of men, whom he has rescued from the curse. You see, then, our Lord, when he put on the old red cloak, and submitted his brows to be environed with thorns, was really establishing for himself an empire the foundations of which shall never be shaken: he was performing that saving work which has made him king among sinners whom he saves, and Lord of the kingdom of grace, which through his death is bestowed upon men.

Note this, too, that men are kings among their fellows when they can show *deep sympathy, and give substantial succour*. He who can sympathise wins power of the best sort, not coarse force, but refined spiritual influence. For this cause our Lord was afflicted, as you see him afflicted, that he might have sympathy with you in your direst grief, and in your most grievous dishonour. As the children were partakers of flesh and blood, he himself also took part of the same, and as they must suffer, so the Captain of their salvation was made perfect by suffering. This gives him his glorious power over us. He is a faithful high priest, for he can be touched with the feeling of our infirmities, and this ability to enter into our infirmities and sorrows makes him supreme in our hearts. Look at your King in pain and mockery, and see how royal he is to your heart! How sovereignly he commands your heart to rejoice. With what regal power he commands your fears to lie still, and how obediently your despondency yields to his word. Now, as it is with you, so is it on a larger scale in the world. The suffering nations will yet see their true deliverer in their suffering Lord. That sceptre of a reed will secure him power far greater than a rod of iron. His love to man is proved by his suffering to the death on their behalf, and this, when the Holy Ghost hath made men wise, shall be to the myriads of our race the reason for proclaiming him Lord of all. The kings and princes who rule mankind by reason of their descent or by the force of arms have but the names of kings, the true kings are the great benefactors. The heroes are our kings after all. We look upon those as royal who can risk their lives for their fellow men, to win them liberty, or to teach them truth. The race forgets its masters, but it remembers its friends. Earth, but for Jesus, had been a vast prison, and men a race of condemned criminals, but he who stands before us in Gabbatha, in all his shame and grief, hath delivered us from our lost estate, and therefore he must be King. Who shall say him nay ? If love must ultimately triumph; if disinterested self-sacrifice must obtain homage, then Jesus is and shall be King. If eventually when the morning breaketh and man's heart is purged from the prejudice and injustice occasioned by sin, the might shall be with the right, and truth must prevail; then Jesus must reign. The eternal fitness of things demands that the best should be highest, that he who does men most service should be most honoured among them ; in a word, that he who was made nothing of for man's sake should become everything to him: See you, then, how the crown of thorns is mother to the crown which Jesus wears in his church ! The scarlet robe is the purchase price of the vesture of universal sovereignty, and the mock sceptre of reed is the precursor of the rod of nations wherewith the whole earth will yet be ruled. " Behold your King," and see the sources of his mediatorial power.

II. O you who see in your bleeding and rejected Lord " the King in his beauty," come ye hither yet again and BEHOLD HIM CLAIMING YOUR HOMAGE. See in what way he comes to win your hearts. What is his right to be King over you ? There are many rights, for on his head are many crowns, but the most commanding right which Jesus has over any of us is signified by that crown of thorns: it is *the right of supreme love* : he loved us as none other could have loved. If we put all the loves of parents and of wives and children all together, we can never rival even for a moment the love of Christ to us, and whenever that love touches us, so that we feel its power, we crown him King directly. Who can resist his charms ? One look of his eyes overpowers us. See with your heart those eyes when they are full of tears for perishing sinners, and you are a willing subject. One look at his blessed person subjected to scourging and spitting for our sakes will give us more idea of his crown rights than anything besides. Look into his pierced heart as it pours out its life-flood for us, and all disputes about his sovereignty are ended in our hearts. We own him Lord because we see how he loved. How could we do otherwise ? Love in action, or rather love suffering, carries an omnipotence about it. Behold what his love endured, and so " Behold your King."

Jesus in the garb of mockery, marred with traces of his pain, also reminds us of *his complete purchase* of us by his deeds and death. "Ye are not your own, ye are bought with a price." Behold your King, and see the price. It is the price of suffering immense, of shame most cruel. It is an incalculable price, for the Lord of all is set at nought. It is an awful price, for he who only hath immortality yields himself to die. It is the price of blood. It is the scourging and bleeding and woe of Jesus; nay, it is himself. If you would see the price of your redemption, " Behold your King." 'Tis he that hath redeemed us unto God by his blood, he that "made himself of no reputation, and took upon him the form of a servant; and being found in fashion as a man, humbled himself, and became obedient unto death, even the death of the cross." You own that claim, the love of Christ constraineth you; you feel that henceforth you live for him alone, and count it joy that in all respects he should reign over you with unlimited sway.

Jesus, because he suffered, hath acquired a power over us which is far superior to any which could be urged in courts of law, or enforced by mere power, for our hearts have voluntarily surrendered to him and given him *the right of our free submission*, charmed to own allegiance to such imperial love. Is it possible for a believer to look at the Lord Jesus Christ without feeling that he longs to be more and more his servant and disciple? Do you not thirst to serve him? Can you behold him in the depth of shame without pining to lift him up to the heights of glory? Can you see him stooping thus for you without pleading with God that a glorious high throne may be his, and that he may sit upon it and rule all the hearts of men? There is no need to argue out the right of King Jesus, for you feel it; his love has carried you by storm, and it holds fast its capture. You cannot have a Saviour without his being your King, and seeing such a Saviour in such a condition, you cannot even think of him without delighting to ascribe to him all power and dominion. Could we escape his sway it would be bondage to us, and when we at any time fail to own it, it is our worst affliction.

" Behold your King," then, for he himself is his own claim to your obedience. See what he suffered for you, my brethren, and henceforth never draw back from any labour, shame, or suffering for his dear sake. " Behold your King," and reckon to be treated like him. Do you expect to be crowned with gold where he was crowned with thorns? Shall lilies grow for you and briars for him? Never again be ashamed to own his glorious name, unless indeed you can be so vile as to prove a traitor to such a Lord. See to what shame he was put, and learn from him to despise all shame for his truth's sake. Shall the disciple be above his master, or the servant above his lord? If they have thus maltreated the master of the house, what shall they do to the household? Let us reckon upon our share of this treatment, and by accepting it prove to all men that the despised and rejected of men is really the King over us, and that the subjects blush not to be like their monarch. Even though the cost be all the shame the world can possibly pour upon us, or all the suffering that flesh and blood can in any condition endure, let us be faithful in our loyalty, and cry, "Who shall separate us? Shall persecution, or distress, or tribulation divide us from our King? Nay, in all these things we are more than conquerors. King of griefs, thou art King of my soul! O King of shame, thou art absolute monarch of my heart. Thou art King by right divine, and King by mine own voluntary choice. Other lords have had dominion over us, but now, since thou hast revealed thyself after this fashion, thy name only shall govern our spirit." Do you not see, then, that Jesus before Pilate reveals his claim in the appearance which he wears. "Behold your King."

III. "Behold your King," for a third time, that you may see him SUBDUING HIS DOMINIONS. Dressed in robes of scorn, and with a visage marred with pain, he comes forth conquering and to conquer. This is not very apparent at a superficial glance, for he is not arrayed like a man of war. You see no sword upon his thigh, nor bow in his hand. No fiery threatenings fall from his lips, nor does he speak with eloquent persuasion. He is unarmed, yet victorious ; is silent, but yet conquering. In this garb he goeth forth to war. His shame is his armour, and his sufferings are his battle axe. How say you? How can it be so? I speak no fiction, but sober fact, and it shall be proved.

Missionaries have gone forth to win *the heathen* for Christ, and they have commenced with the uncivilized sons of sin by telling them that there is a God, and that he is great and just : the people have listened unmoved, or have only answered, "Dost thou think we know not this?" Then they have spoken of sin and its punishment, and have foretold the coming of the Lord to judgment, but still the people stirred not, but coolly said, "'Tis true," and then went on their way to live in sin as before. At last these earnest men have let fall the blessed secret, and spoken of the love of God in giving his only begotten Son, and they have begun to tell the story of the matchless griefs of Immanuel. Then have the dry bones stirred, then have the deaf begun to hear. They tell us that they had not long told the story before they noticed that eyes were fastened on them, and that countenances were beaming with interest which had been listless before, and they have said to themselves, "Why did we not begin with this?" Ay, why indeed? for this it is that touches men's hearts. Christ crucified is the conqueror. Not in his robes of glory does he subdue the heart, but in his vestments of shame. Not as sitting upon the throne does he at first gain the faith and the affections of sinners, but as bleeding, suffering, and dying in their stead. "God forbid that I should glory," said the apostle, " save in the cross of our Lord Jesus Christ "; and though every theme that is connected with the Saviour ought to play its part in our ministry, yet this is the master theme. The atoning work of Jesus is the great gun of our battery. The cross is the mighty battering-ram wherewith to break in pieces the brazen gates of human prejudices and the iron bars of obstinacy. Christ coming to be our judge alarms, but Christ the man of sorrows subdues. The crown of thorns has a royal power in it to compel a willing allegiance, the sceptre of reed breaks hearts better than a rod of iron, and the robe of mockery commands more love than Cæsar's imperial purple. There is nothing like it under heaven. Victories ten thousand times ten thousand have been achieved by him whom Pilate led forth to the multitude,—victories distinctly to be ascribed to the thorny crown and vesture of mockery, are they not written in the book of the wars of the Lord? There will be more such as he is more frequently set forth in his own fashion, and men are bidden in the Man of sorrows to behold their King.

Has it not been so *at home* as well as among the far-off heathen? What winneth men's hearts to Christ to-day? What but Christ in shame and Christ in suffering? I appeal to you who have been newly converted; what has bound you as captives to Jesus' chariot? What has made you henceforth vow to be his followers, rejoicing in his name? What but this, that he bowed his head to the death for your sake and hath redeemed you unto God by his blood? You know it is so.

And oh, dear *children of God*, if ever you feel the power of Christ upon you to the full, till it utterly overcomes you, is it not the memory of redeeming grief which doeth it? When you become like harps, and Jesus is the minstrel and layeth his finger amongst your heart-strings and bringeth out nothing but praise for his dear name, what is it that charms you into the music of grateful love but the fact of his condescension on your behalf? Is not this your song, that he was slain and hath redeemed you unto God by his blood? I confess I could sit me down at his cross' foot and do nothing else but weep until I wept myself away, for his sufferings make my soul to melt within me. Then if the call of duty is heard I feel intensely eager to plead with others, ready to make any sacrifice to bring others under my Lord's dominion, and full of a holy passion that even death could not quench—all this, I say, if I have but just come from gazing on the Redeemer's passion, and drinking of his cup and being baptized with his baptism. The sceptre of reed rules as nothing else ever did, for it rouses enthusiasm. The thorn-crown commands homage as no other diadem ever did, for it braces men into heroes and martyrs. No royalty is so all-commanding as that which has for its insignia the chaplet of thorn, the reed, the red cloak, and the five wounds. Other sovereignties are forced, and feigned, and hollow compared with the sovereignty of "the despised of men": fear, or custom, or self-interest make men courtiers elsewhere, but fervent love crowds the courts of King Jesus. We do not merely say that the marred countenance is the most majestic ever seen, but we have felt it to be so on many an occasion, yea, and feel it to be so now. Do you want to make our hard hearts soft? Tell us of Jesus' grief. Would you make us, strong men, into children? Set the Man of sorrows in our midst; there is no resisting *him*.

Look ye also at *backsliders* if ye would see the power of the despised Nazarene. If they have gone away from Christ, if they have become lukewarm, if their hearts have become obdurate to him who once could charm them, what can bring them back? I know but one magnet which in the hands of the Holy Spirit will attract these sadly fallen ones: it is Jesus in his shame and pains. We tell them that they crucified the Son of God afresh, and put him to an open shame, and they look on him whom they have pierced, and mourn for him. O ye that after having sipped of the communion cup have gone to drink at the table of Bacchus, ye who after having talked of love to Christ have followed after the lusts of the flesh, ye who after singing his praises have blasphemed the sacred name with which ye are named—may his omnipotence of love be proved in you also. What can ever bring you back but this sad reflection, that ye also have twisted for him a crown of thorns and caused him to be blasphemed among his enemies? Still the merit of his death is available for you: the power and efficacy of his precious blood have not ceased even for you, and if you come back to him—and oh, may a sight of him draw you—he will receive you graciously as at the first. I say to you, "Behold your King," and may the sovereignty of his humiliation and suffering be proved this morning in some of you as you shall come bending at his feet, conquered by his great love and restored to repentance and faith by his marvellous compassion. A sight of his wounds and bruises heals us, so that we grieve at our rebellions and long to be brought home to God, never to wander more.

Ah, dear brethren, we shall always find, as long as the world standeth, that among saints, sinners, backsliders, and all classes of men Jesus Christ's power is most surely felt when his humiliation is most faithfully declared and most believingly known. It is by this that he will subdue all things to himself. If we will but preach Jesus Christ to the Hindoo it will not be necessary to answer all his metaphysical subtleties —the sorrows of Jesus are as a sharp sword to cut the Gordian knot. If we will go down amongst the degraded inhabitants of Africa we shall not need first to civilize them; the cross is the great lever which lifts up fallen men: it conquers evil and establishes truth and righteousness. The most depraved and hardened learn his great love, and hearts of stone begin to beat; they see Jesus suffering to the death out of nothing else but love to them, and they are touched by it, and eagerly enquire what they must do to be saved by such a Saviour. The Holy Spirit worketh in the minds of many by setting forth the great love and grief of Jesus. May we who are his ministers have great faith in his cross, and henceforth say, as we preach the suffering Jesus, "Behold your King."

IV. In the fourth place I beg you to "Behold your King" SETTING FORTH THE PATTERN OF HIS KINGDOM. When you look at him you are struck at once with the thought that if he be a king he is like no other monarch, for other kings are covered with rich apparel and surrounded with pomp, but he has none of these. Their glories usually consist in wars by which they have made others suffer, but his glory is his own suffering; no blood but his own has flowed to make him illustrious. He is a king, but he cannot be put in the list of sovereigns such as the nations of the earth are compelled to serve. When Antoninus Pius set up the statue of Jesus in the Pantheon as one of a circle of gods and heroes, it must have seemed strangely out of place to those who gazed upon its visage if the sculptor was at all true to life. It must have stood apart as one that could not be numbered with the rest. Neither can you set him among the masters of the human race who have crushed mankind beneath their iron heel. He was no Cæsar; you cannot make him appear like one: call him not autocrat, emperor, or czar,—he has an authority greater than all these, yet not after their kind. His purple is different from theirs, and his crown also, but his face differs more, and his heart most of all. "My kingdom," saith he, "is not of this world." For troops he has a host of sorrows, for pomp a surrounding of scorn, for lofty bearing humility, for adulation mockery, for homage spitting, for glory shame, for a throne a cross. Yet was there never truer king, indeed all kings are but a name, save this King, who is a real ruler in himself and of himself, and not by extraneous force. Right royal indeed is the Nazarene, but he cannot be likened unto the princes of earth, nor can his kingdom be reckoned with theirs. I pray that the day may soon come when none may dream of looking upon the church as a worldly organization capable of alliance with temporal sovereignties so as to be patronized, directed, or reformed by them. Christ's kingdom shines as a lone star with a brightness all its own. It standeth apart like a hill of light, sacred and sublime: the high hills may leap with envy because of it, but it is not of them nor like unto them. Is not this manifest even in the appearance of our Lord as Pilate brings him forth and cries, "Behold your King!"?

Now as he sets before us in his own person the pattern of his kingdom, we may expect that we shall see some likeness to him in his subjects; and if you will gaze upon the church, which is his kingdom from the first day of her history until now, you will see that it too is wearing its purple robe. The martyrs' blood is the purple vesture of the church of Christ; the trials and persecutions of believers are her crown of thorns. Think of the rage of persecution under Pagan Rome, and the equally inhuman proceedings of Papal Rome, and you will see how the ensign of Christ's kingdom is a crown of thorns; a crown and yet thorns, thorns but still a crown. The bush is burning, but it is not consumed. If you, beloved, are truly followers of Jesus, you must expect to take your measure of shame and dishonour, and you may reckon upon your allotment of griefs and sorrows. The "Man of sorrows" attracts a sorrowful following. The lamb of God's passover is still eaten with bitter herbs. The child of God cannot escape the rod, for the elder brother did not, and to him we are to be conformed. We must "fill up that which is behind of the afflictions of Christ for his body's sake, which is the church " (Colossians i. 24).

Recollect, however, that Christ's sufferings as a pattern were not for his own sins, nor brought upon him as a chastisement for his own faults, so that the sufferings which belong to his kingdom are those which are endured for his name and for his glory's sake, and for the good of others. If men lie in prison for their own crimes, that has nothing to do with his kingdom; if we suffer for our sins, that is no part of his kingdom; but when a man loseth of his substance for Christ's cause, layeth out himself to toil even unto death, beareth contempt and suffers hardness as a Christian—this is after the type of Christ's kingdom. When the missionary goeth forth with his life in his hand among the heathen, or when a believer in any way divesteth himself of comfort for the good of others, it is then that he truly copies the pattern set him in Pilate's hall by our great King. I say to you Christians who court ease, to you who are hoarding up your gold, to you who will do nothing that would bring you under the criticism of your fellow men, to you who live unto yourselves,—would it not be irony of the severest kind if I were to point to Jesus before

Pilate and say, " Behold your King." Living in undue luxury, amassing wealth, rolling in ease, living to enjoy yourselves! Is that your King? Poor subjects you, and very unlike your Lord; but if there be among us those who for his sake can make sacrifices, we may look upon our King without fear. You who are undaunted by contempt, and who would give all that you have, yea, and give yourselves to know Jesus, and are doing so, to such I say, "Behold your King," for you are of his kingdom and you shall reign with him. In your your conquest of yourselves you have already become kings. In reigning over your own desires and carnal inclinations, for the sake of his dear love, you are already kings and priests unto God, and you shall reign for ever and ever He who is ruled by his passions in any degree is still a slave, but he who lives for God and his fellow men hath a royal soul. The insignia of a prince unto God are still shame and suffering: which adornments are readily worn when the Lord calls him so to do. In Christ's kingdom those are peers of the highest rank who are most like their Lord and are the lowest and humblest in mind, and most truly the servants of all. The secondary princes of his kingdom approximate less closely to him, and the lower you descend in the scale the less you are like him in those respects. The Christian surrounded with every comfort, who never endured hardness for Christ, who never knew what it was to be sneered at for Jesus' sake, who never made a sacrifice which went so far as to pinch him in the least, he, if indeed he be a Christian, is least in the kingdom of heaven. Proud, rich men who give but trifles to Christ's cause are pariahs in his kingdom, but they are the chief who are willing to be least of all, they are princes who make themselves the offscouring of all things for his name's sake, such as were the apostles and first martyrs, and others whom his love has greatly constrained.

V. Our concluding remark shall be, "Behold your King"—PROVING THE CERTAINTY OF HIS EMPIRE,—for if, beloved, Christ was King when he was in Pilate's hands, after being scourged and spit upon, and while he was wearing the robe and crown of mockery, when will he not be King? If he was King at his worst, when is it that his throne can ever be shaken? They have brought him very low, they have brought him lower than the sons of men, for they have made him a worm and no man, despised of the people, *and yet he is King!* Marks of royalty were present on the day of his death. He dispensed crowns when he was on the cross,—he gave the dying thief a promise of an entrance into Paradise. In his death he shook the earth, he opened the graves, he rent the rocks, he darkened the sun, and he made men smite on their breasts in dismay. One voice after another, even from the ranks of his foes, proclaimed him to be King, even when dying like a malefactor. Was he a King then? When will he not be King? and who is there that can by any means shake his throne? In the days of his flesh " the Kings of the earth stood up, and the rulers took counsel together, saying, Let us break his bonds asunder, and cast his cords from us"; but he that sat in the heavens did laugh, the Lord did have them in derision, and Christ on the cross was acknowledged, in Hebrew, and Greek, and Latin, to be still the King of the Jews. When will he not be King? If he was King before he died and was laid in the grave, what is he now that he has risen from the dead, now that he has vanquished the destroyer of our race, and lives no more to die? **What is he now?** Ye angels, tell what glories surround him now! If he was King when he stood at Pilate's bar, what will he be when Pilate shall stand at his bar, when he shall come on the great white throne and summon all mankind before him to judgment? What will be his acknowledged sovereignty and his dreaded majesty in the day of the Lord? Come, let us adore him; let us pay our humble homage in the courts of the Lord's house this day; and then let us go forth to our daily service in his name, and make this our strong resolve, his Spirit helping us, that we will live to crown him in our hearts and in our lives, in every place where our lot may be cast, till the day break and the shadows flee away, and we behold the King in his beauty and the land that is very far off. None can overturn a kingdom which is founded on the death of its King; none can abolish a dominion whose deep foundations are laid in the tears and blood of the Prince himself. Napoleon said that he founded his empire by force, and therefore it had passed away; but, said he, " Jesus founded his kingdom upon love, and it will last for ever." So it must be, for whatever may or may not be, it is written—" *He must reign.*"

As for us, if we wish to extend the Redeemer's kingdom we must be prepared to deny ourselves for Christ, we must be prepared for weariness, slander, and self-denial. In this sign we conquer. The cross will have to be borne by us as well as by him if we are to reign with Jesus. We must both teach the cross and bear the cross. We must participate in the shame if we would participate in the glory. No thorn no throne. When again shall be heard the voice, " Behold your King," and Jew and Gentile shall see him enthroned, and surrounded with all his Father's angels, with the whole earth subdued to his power, happy shall he be who shall then in the exalted Saviour behold his King. The Lord grant us this day to be loyal subjects of the Crucified that we may be favoured to share his glory.

Jesus, the King of Truth

"Pilate therefore said unto him, Art thou a king then? Jesus answered, Thou sayest that I am a king. To this end was I born, and for this cause came I into the world, that I should bear witness unto the truth. Every one that is of the truth heareth my voice "—John xviii., 37.

THE season is almost arrived when by the custom of our fellow-citizens we are led to remember the birth of the holy child Jesus, who was born " king of the Jews." I shall not, however, conduct you to Bethlehem, but to the foot of Calvary ; there we shall learn, from the Lord's own lips, something concerning the kingdom over which he rules, and thus we shall be led to prize more highly the joyous event of his nativity.

We are told, by the apostle Paul, that our Lord Jesus Christ before Pontius Pilate witnessed a good confession. It was a good confession as to the manner of it, for our Lord was truthful, gentle, prudent, patient, meek, and yet, withal, uncompromising, and courageous. His spirit was not cowed by Pilate's power, nor exasperated by his sneers. In his patience he possessed his soul, and remained the model witness for the truth—both in his silence and in his speech. He witnessed a good confession also, as to the matter of it ; for, though he said but little, that little was all that was needful. He claimed his crown rights, and, at the same time, declared that his kingdom was not of this world, nor to be sustained by force. He vindicated both the spirituality and the essential truthfulness of his sovereignty. If ever we should be placed in like circumstances, may we be able to witness a good confession too! We may never, like Paul, be made to plead before Nero; but, if we should, may the Lord stand by us, and help us to play the man before the lion! In our families, or among our business acquaintances, we may have to meet some little Nero, and answer to some petty Pilate; may we then also be true witnesses. O that we may have grace to be prudently silent or meekly outspoken, as the matter may require, in either case being faithful to our conscience and our God! May the sorrowful visage of Jesus, the faithful and true witness, the Prince of the kings of the earth, be often before our eye, to check the first sign of flinching, and to inspire us with dauntless courage !

We have before us, in the words of the text, a part of our Saviour's good confession touching his kingdom.

I. Note, first of all, that OUR LORD CLAIMED TO BE A KING. Pilate said, " Art thou a king, then ? " asking the question with a sneering surprise that so poor a being should put forth a claim to royalty. Do you wonder that he should have marvelled greatly to find kingly claims associated with such a sorrowful condition ? The Saviour answered, in effect, " It is even as thou sayest, I am a king." The question was but half earnest; the answer was altogether solemn: "I am a king." Nothing was ever uttered by our Lord with greater certainty and earnestness.

Now, notice, that our Lord's claim to be a king was made without the slightest ostentation or desire to be advantaged thereby. There were other times when, if he had said "I am a king," he might have been carried upon the shoulders of the people, and crowned amid general acclamations. His fanatical fellow countrymen would gladly have made him their leader at one time; and we read that they would have "taken him by force and made him a king." At such times he said but little about his kingdom, and what he did say was uttered in parables, and explained only to his disciples when they were alone. Little enough did he say in his preaching concerning his birthright as the Son of David and a scion of the royal house of Judah ; for he shrank from worldly honours, and disdained the vain glories of a temporal diadem. He who came in love to redeem men, had no ambition for the gewgaws of human sovereignty. But now, when he is betrayed by his disciple, accused by his countrymen, and in the hands of an unjust ruler; when no good can come of it to himself; when it will bring him derision rather than honour ; he speaks out plainly and replies to his interrogator, " Thou sayest that I am a king."

Note well the clearness of our Lord's avowal ; there was no mistaking his words: "I am a king." When the time has come for the truth to be spoken, our Lord is not backward in declaring it. Truth has her times most meet for speech, and her seasons for silence. We are not to cast our pearls before swine, but when the hour has come for speech we must not hesitate, but speak as with the voice of a trumpet, giving forth a certain sound, that no man may mistake us. So, though a prisoner given up to die, the Lord boldly declares his royalty, though Pilate would pour derision upon him in consequence thereof. O, for the Master's prudence to speak the truth at the right time, and for the Master's courage to speak it when the right time has come. Soldiers of the cross, learn of your Captain.

Our Lord's claim to royalty must have sounded very singularly in Pilate's ear. Jesus was, doubtless, very much careworn, sad, and emaciated in appearance. He had spent the first part of the night in the garden in an agony; in the midnight hours he had been dragged from Annas to Caiaphas, and from Caiaphas to Herod ; neither at daybreak had he been permitted to rest, so that, from sheer weariness, he must have looked very unlike a king. If you had taken some poor ragged creature in the street, and said to him, " Art thou a king, then?" the question could scarcely have been more sarcastic. Pilate, in his heart, despised the Jews as such, but here was a poor Jew, persecuted by his own people, helpless and friendless; it sounded like mockery to talk of a kingdom in connection with him. Yet never earth saw truer king! None of the line of Pharaoh, the family of Nimrod, or the race of the Cæsars, was so intrinsically imperial in himself as he, or so deservedly reckoned a king among men by virtue of his descent, his achievements, or his superior character. The carnal eye could not see this, but to the spiritual eye it is clear as noonday. To this day, pure Christianity, in its outward appearance, is an equally unattractive object, and wears upon its surface few royal tokens. It is without form or comeliness, and when men see it, there is no beauty that they should desire it. True, there is a nominal Christtianity which is accepted and approved of men, but the pure gospel is still despised and rejected. The real Christ of to-day, among men, is unknown and unrecognised as much as he was among his own nation eighteen hundred years ago. Evangelical doctrine is at a discount, holy living is censured, and spiritual-mindedness is derided. "What," say they, "This evangelical doctrine, call you it the royal truth? Who believes it now-a-days? Science has exploded it. There is nothing great about it; it may afford comfort to old women, and to those who have not capacity enough for free thought, but its reign is over, never to return." As to living in separation from the world, it is called Puritanism, or worse. Christ in doctrine, Christ in spirit, Christ in life —the world cannot endure as king. Christ chanted in cathedrals, Christ personified in lordly prelates, Christ surrounded by such as are in king's houses, *he* is well enough; but Christ honestly obeyed, followed, and worshipped in simplicity, without pomp or form, they will not allow to reign over them. Few now-a-days will side with the truth their fathers bled for. The day for covenanting to follow Jesus through evil report and shame appears to have gone by. Yet, though men turn round upon us, and say, "Do you call your gospel divine? Are you so preposterous as to believe that your religion comes from God and is to subdue the world?"—we boldly answer; "Yes!" Even as beneath the peasant's garb and the wan visage of the Son of Mary we can discern the Wonderful, the Counsellor, the Mighty God, the Everlasting Father! so beneath the simple form of a despised gospel we perceive the royal lineaments of truth divine. We care nothing about the outward apparel or the external housing of truth; we love it for its own sake. To us, the marble halls and the alabaster columns are nothing, we see more in the manger and the cross. We are satisfied that Christ is the king still where he was wont to be king, and that is not among the great ones of the earth, nor among the mighty and the learned, but amongst the base things of the world and the things which are not, which shall bring to nought the things that are, for these hath God from the beginning chosen to be his own.

Let us add, that our Lord's claim to be a king shall be acknowledged one day by all mankind. When Christ said to Pilate, according to our version, "Thou sayest that I am a king," he virtually prophesied the future confession of all men. Some, taught by his grace, shall in this life rejoice in him as their altogether lovely King. Blessed be God, the Lord Jesus might look into the eyes of many of us, and say, "Thou sayest that I am a king," and we would reply, "We do say it joyfully." But the day shall come when he shall sit upon his great white throne, and then, when the multitudes shall tremble in the presence of his awful majesty, even such as Pontius Pilate, and Herod, and the chief priests, shall own that he is a king! Then to each of his astounded and overwhelmingly convinced enemies he might say, " Now, O despiser, thou sayest that I am a king," for to him every knee shall bow, and every tongue shall confess that he is Lord!

Let us remember, here, that when our Lord said to Pilate, "Thou sayest that I am king," he was not referring to his divine dominion. Pilate was not thinking of that at all, nor did our Lord, I think, refer to it: yet, forget not that, as divine, he is the King of kings and Lord of lords. We must never forget that, though he died in weakness as man, yet he ever lives and rules as God. Nor do I think he referred to his mediatorial sovereignty, which he possesses over the earth for his people's sake; for the Lord has all power committed unto him in heaven and in earth, and the Father has given him power over all flesh, that he may give eternal life to as many as are given him. Pilate was not alluding to that, nor our Lord either, in the first place ; but he was speaking of that rule which he personally exercises over the minds of the faithful, by means of the truth. You remember Napoleon's saying, " I have founded an empire by force, and it has melted away ; Jesus Christ established his kingdom by love, and it stands to this day, and will stand." That is the kingdom to which our Lord's word refers, the kingdom of spiritual truth in which Jesus reigns as Lord over those who are of the truth. He claimed to be a king, and the truth which he revealed, and of which he was the personification, is, therefore, the sceptre of his empire. He rules by the force of truth over those hearts which feel the power of right and truth, and therefore willingly yield themselves to his guidance, believe his word, and are governed by his will. It is as a spiritual Lord that Christ claims sovereignty among men; he is king over minds that love him, trust him, and obey him, because they see in him the truth which their souls ; pine for. Other kings rule our bodies, but Christ our souls, they govern by force, but he by the attractions of righteousness ; theirs is, to a great extent, a fictitious royalty, but his is true, and finds its force in truth.

So much, then, upon Christ's claims to be a king.

II. Now, observe, secondly, that OUR LORD DECLARED THIS KINGDOM TO BE HIS MAIN OBJECT IN LIFE. " To this end was I born, and for this cause came I into the world." To set up his kingdom was the reason why he was born of the virgin. To be King of men, it was necessary for him to be born. He was always the Lord of all ; he needed not to be born to be a king in that sense, but to be king through the power of truth, it was essential that he should be born in our nature. Why so ? I answer, first, because it seems unnatural that a ruler should be alien in nature to the people over whom he rules. An angelic king of men would be unsuitable ; there could not exist the sympathy which is the cement of a spiritual empire. Jesus, that he might govern by force of love and truth alone, became of one nature with mankind; he was a man among men, a real man—but a right noble and kingly man, and so a King of men.

But, again, the Lord was born that he might be able to save his people. Subjects are essential to a kingdom ; a king cannot be a king if there be none to govern. But all men must have perished through sin, had not Christ come into the world and been born to save. His birth was a necessary step to his redeeming death ; his incarnation was necessary to the atonement.

Moreover, truth never exerts such power as when it is embodied. Truth spoken may be defeated, but truth acted out in the life of a man is omnipotent, through the Spirit of God. Now, Christ did not merely speak the truth, but he *was* truth. Had he been truth embodied in an angelic form, he had possessed small power over our hearts and lives ; but perfect truth in a human form has royal power over renewed humanity. Truth embodied in flesh and blood has power over flesh and blood. Hence, for this purpose was he born. So when ye hear the bells ringing out at Christmas, think of the reason why Jesus was born ; dream not that he came to load your tables and fill your cups ; but in your mirth look higher than all earth-born things. When you hear that in certain churches there are pompous celebrations and ecclesiastical displays, think not for this purpose was Jesus born. No ; but look within your hearts, and say, for this purpose was he born : that he might be a King, that he might rule through the truth in the souls of a people who are by grace made to love the truth of God.

And then he added, "For this cause came I into the world ;" that is, he came out of the bosom of the Father that he might set up his kingdom, by unveiling the mysteries which were hid from the foundation of the world. No man can reveal the counsel of God, but one who has been with God; and the Son who has come forth of the ivory palaces of gladness, announces to us tidings of great joy ! For this cause also came he into the world, from the obscure retirement of Joseph's workshop, where, for many years he was hidden like a pearl in its shell. It was needful that he should be made known, and that the truth to which he witnessed should be sounded in the ears of the crowd. Since he was to be a King, he must leave seclusion, and come forth to do battle for his throne; he must address the multitudes on the hill-side; he must speak by the sea-shore; he must gather disciples, and send them forth by two and two to publish on the housetops the secrets of mighty truth ! He came not forth because he loved to be seen of men, or courted popularity; but for this purpose—that, the truth being published, he might set up his kingdom. It was needful that he should come out into the world and teach, or truth would not be known, and consequently could not operate. The sun must come forth, like a bridegroom out of his chamber, or the kingdom of light will never be established; the breath must come forth from the hiding-place of the winds, or life will never reign in the valley of dry bones. During three years, our Lord lived conspicuously, and emphatically " came into the world." He was seen of men so closely as to be beheld, looked upon, touched, and handled. He was intended to be a pattern, and therefore, it was needful that he should be seen. The life of a man who lives in absolute retirement may be admirable for himself and acceptable with God, but it cannot be exemplary to men : for this cause the Lord came forth into the world, that all he did might influence mankind. His enemies were permitted to watch his every action, and to endeavour to entrap him in his speech, by way of test ; his friends saw him in privacy, and knew what he did in solitude; thus his whole life was reported— he was observed on the cold mountain-side at midnight, as well as in the midst of the great congregation. This was permitted to make the truth known, for every action of his life was truth, and tended to set up the kingdom of truth in the world.

Let us pause here. Christ is a king, a king by force of truth in a spiritual kingdom ; for this purpose was he born ; for this cause came he into the world. My soul, ask thyself this question:—Has this purpose of Christ's birth and life been answered in thee ? If not, what avails Christmas to thee ? The choristers will sing, " Unto us a child is born ; unto us a Son is given." Is that true to thee ? How can it be unless Jesus reigns in thee, and is thy Saviour and thy Lord ? Those who can in truth rejoice in his birth are those who know him as their bosom's Lord, ruling their understanding by the truth of his doctrine ; their admiration by the truth of his life ; their affections by the truth of his person. To such he is not a personage to be pourtrayed with a crown of gold and a robe of purple, like the common theatrical kings of men; but one brighter and more heavenly, whose crown is real, whose dominion is unquestionable, who rules by truth and love ! Do we know this King ?

This question may well come home to us, for, beloved, there are many who say, " Christ is my King," who know not what they say, for they do not obey him. He is the servant of Christ who trusts in Christ, who walks according to Christ's mind, and loves the truth which Jesus has revealed : all others are mere pretenders.

III. But now I must pass on. Our Lord, in the third place, REVEALED THE NATURE OF HIS ROYAL POWER. I have already spoken on that, but I must do so again. We should have thought the text would have run thus : " Thou sayest that I am a king ; to this end was I born, and for this cause came I into the world, that I should establish my kingdom." It is not so in words, but so it must mean, for Jesus was not incoherent in his speech. We conclude that the words employed have the same meaning as that which the context suggests, only it is differently expressed. If our Lord had said, " That I might establish a kingdom," he might have misled Pilate ; but when he availed himself of the spiritual explanation, and said that his kingdom was truth, and that the establishment of his kingdom was by bearing witness to the truth, then, though Pilate did not understand him—for it was far above his comprehension—yet, at any rate, he was not misled.

Our Lord, in effect, tells us that truth is the pre-eminent characteristic of his kingdom, and that his royal power over men's hearts is through the truth. Now, the witness of our Lord among men was emphatically upon real and vital matters. He dealt not with fiction, but with facts; not with trifles, but with infinite realities. He speaks not of opinions, views, or speculations, but of infallible verities. How many preachers waste time over what may be or may not be ! Our Lord's testimony was pre-eminently practical and matter-of-fact, full of verities and certainties. I have sometimes, when hearing sermons, wished the preacher would come to the point, and would deal with something that really concerned our soul's welfare. What concern have dying men with the thousand trivial questions which are flitting around us? We have heaven or hell before us, and death within a stone's-throw; for God's sake do not trifle with us, but tell us the truth at once! Jesus is king in his people's souls, because his preaching has blessed us in the grandest and most real manner, and set us at rest upon points of boundless importance. He has not given us well-chiselled stones, but real bread. There are a thousand things which you may not know, and you shall be very little the worse for not knowing them; but O, if you do not know that which Jesus has taught, it shall go ill with you. If you are taught of the Lord Jesus, you shall have rest for your cares, balm for your sorrows, and satisfaction for your desires. Jesus gives sinners who believe in him the truth which they need to know; the assurance of sin forgiven through his blood, favour ensured by his righteousness, and heaven secured by his eternal life.

Moreover, Jesus has power over his people because he testifies not to symbols, but to the very substance of truth. The Scribes and Pharisees were very fluent upon sacrifices, offerings, oblations, tithes, fastings, and the like; but what influence could all that exert over aching hearts? Jesus has imperial power over contrite spirits, because he tells them of his one real sacrifice and of the perfection which he has secured to all believers. The priests lost their power over the people because they went no further than the shadow, and sooner or later all will do so who rest in the symbol. The Lord Jesus retains his power over his saints because he reveals the substance, for grace and truth are by Jesus Christ. What a loss of time it is to debate upon the fashion of a cope, or the manner of celebrating communion, or the colour suitable for the clergyman's robes in Advent, or the precise date of Easter. Vanity of vanities, all is vanity! Such trifles will never aid in setting up an everlasting kingdom in men's hearts. Let us take care lest we also set great store by externals, and miss the essential, spiritual life of our holy faith. Christ's kingdom is not meat and drink, but righteousness and peace, and joy in the Holy Ghost!

The power of King Jesus in the hearts of his people lies much in the fact that he brings forth unalloyed truth, without mixture of error. He has delivered to us pure light and no darkness; his teaching is no combination of God's word and man's inventions; no mixture of inspiration and philosophy; silver without dross is the wealth which he gives his servants. Men taught of his Holy Spirit to love the truth, recognise this fact and surrender their souls to the royal sway of the Lord's truth, and it makes them free, and sanctifies them; nor can anything make them disown such a sovereign, for as the truth lives and abides in their hearts, so Jesus, who is the truth, abides also. If you know what truth is, you will as naturally submit yourselves to the teachings of Christ as ever children yield to a father's rule.

The Lord Jesus taught that worship must be true, spiritual, and of the heart, or else it would be nothing worth. He would not take sides with the temple at Gerizim or that on Zion, but he declared that the time was come when those who worshipped God would worship him in spirit and in truth. Now, regenerate hearts feel the power of this, and rejoice that it emancipates them from the beggarly elements of carnal ritualism. They accept gladly the truth that pious words of prayer or praise are vanity, unless the heart has living worship within it. In the great truth of spiritual worship, believers possess a Magna Charta, dear as life itself. We refuse to be again subject to the yoke of bondage, and cleave to our emancipating king.

Our Lord taught, also, that all false living was base and loathsome. He poured contempt on the phylacteries of hypocrites and the broad borders of the garments of oppressors of the poor. With him, ostentatious alms, long prayers, frequent fasts, and the tithe of mint and cummin, were all nothing when practised by those who devoured widows' houses. He cared nothing for white-washed sepulchres and platters with outsides made clean, he judged the thoughts and intents of the heart. What woes were those which he denounced upon the formalists of his day! It must have been a grand sight to have seen the lowly Jesus roused to indignation, thundering forth peal on peal his denunciations of hypocrisy. Elias never called fire from heaven one half so grandly. "Woe unto you Scribes and Pharisees, hypocrites," is the loudest roll of heaven's artillery! See how, like another Samson, Jesus slays the shams of his age, and piles them heaps upon heaps to rot for ever. Shall not he who teaches us true living be king of all the sons of truth? Let us even now salute him as Lord and King.

Besides, beloved, our Lord came not only to teach us the truth, but a mysterious power goes forth from him, through that Spirit which rests on him without measure—which subdues chosen hearts to truthfulness, and then guides truthful hearts into fulness of peace and joy. Have you never felt when you have been with Jesus, that a sense of his purity has made you yearn to be purged of all hypocrisy and every false way? Have you not been ashamed of yourself when you have come forth from hearing his word, from watching his life, and, above all, from enjoying his fellowship—quite ashamed that you have not been more real, more sincere, more true, more upright, and so a more loyal subject of the truthful King? I know you have. Nothing about Jesus is false or even dubious; he is transparent—from head to foot he is truth in public, truth in private, truth in word, and truth in deed. Hence it is that he has a kingdom over the pure in heart, and is vehemently extolled by all those whose hearts are set upon righteousness.

IV. And now, in the fourth place, our Lord DISCLOSED THE METHOD OF HIS CONQUEST. "To this end was I born, and for this cause came I into the world, *that I should bear witness for the truth.*" Christ never yet set up his kingdom by force of arms. Mahomet drew the sword, and converted men by giving them the choice of death or conversion; but Christ said to Peter, "Put up thy sword into its sheath." No compulsion ought to be used with any man to lead him to receive any opinion, much less to induce him to espouse the truth. Falsehood requires the rack of the Inquisition, but truth needs not such unworthy aid; her own beauty, and the Spirit of God, are her strength. Moreover, Jesus used no arts of priestcraft, or tricks of superstition. The foolish are persuaded of a dogma, by the fact that it is promulgated by a learned doctor of high degree, but our Rabboni wears no sounding titles of honour; the vulgar imagine that a statement must be correct if it emanates from a person who wears lawn sleeves, or from a place where the banners are of costly workmanship, and the music of the sweetest kind : these things are arguments with those who are amenable to no other ; but Jesus owes nothing to his apparel, and influences none by artistic arrangements. None can say that he reigns over men by the glitter of pomp, or the fascination of sensuous ceremonies. His battle-axe is the truth; truth is both his arrow and his bow, his sword and his buckler. Believe me, no kingdom is worthy of the Lord Jesus but that which has its foundations laid in indisputable verities; Jesus would scorn to reign by the help of a lie.

True Christianity was never promoted by policy or guile, by doing a wrong thing, or saying a false thing. Even to exaggerate truth is to beget error, and so to pull down the truth we would set up. There are some who say, "Bring out one line of teaching, and nothing else, lest you should seem inconsistent." What have I to do with that ? If it be God's truth, I am bound to deliver it all, and to keep back none of it. Policy, like a sailing vessel, dependant on the wind, tacks about hither and thither; but the true man, like a vessel having its motive power within, goes straight onward in the very teeth of the hurricane. When God puts truth into men's souls, he teaches them never to tack or trim, but to hold to truth at all hazards. This is what Jesus always did. He bore witness to the truth, and there left the matter; being guileless as a lamb.

Here it will be fit to answer the question, "What truth did he witness to ?" Ah, my brethren what truth did he *not* witness to ? Did he not mirror all truth in his life ? See how clearly he set forth the truth that God is love. How melodious, how like a peal of Christmas bells, was his witness to the truth that "God so loved the world, that he gave his only begotten Son, that whosoever believeth in him might not perish but have everlasting life." He also bore witness that God is just. How solemnly he proclaimed that fact ! His flowing wounds, his dying agonies rang out that solemn truth, as with a knell which even the dead might hear. He bore witness to God's demand for truth in the inward parts ; for he often dissected men and laid them bare, and opened up their secret thoughts and discovered them to themselves, and made them see that only sincerity could bear the eye of God. Did he not bear witness to the truth that God had resolved to make for himself a new people and a true people ? Was he not always telling of his sheep who heard his voice, of the wheat which would be gathered into the garner, and of the precious things which would be treasured up when the bad would be thrown away ? Therein he was bearing witness that the false must die, that the unreal must be consumed, that the lie must rust and rot; but that the true, the sincere, the gracious, the vital, shall stand every test, and outlast the sun. In an age of shams, he was always sweeping away pretences and establishing truth and right by his witness. And now, beloved, this is the way in which Christ's kingdom is to be set up in the world. For this cause was the church born, and for this end came she into the world, that she might set up Christ's kingdom by bearing witness to the truth. I long, my beloved, to see you all witness-bearers. If you love the Lord, bear witness to the truth. You must do it personally; you must also do it collectively. Never join any church whose creed you do not entirely and unfeignedly believe, for if you do you act a lie, and are, moreover, a partaker in the error of other men's testimonies. I would not for a moment say anything to retard Christian unity, but there is something before unity, and that is, "truth in the inward parts" and honesty before God. I dare not be a member of a church whose teaching I knew to be false in vital points. I would sooner go to heaven alone than belie my conscience for the sake of company. You may say, "But I protest against the error of my church." Dear friends, how can you consistently protest against it when you profess to agree with it, by being a member of the church which avows it? If you are a minister of a church, you do in effect say before the world, " I believe and teach the doctrines of this church;" and if you go into the pulpit and say you do not believe them, what will people conclude? I leave you to judge that. I saw a church tower the other day, with a clock upon it, which startled me by pointing to half-past ten when I thought it was only nine; I was, however, quite relieved when I saw that another face of the clock indicated a quarter past eight. "Well," thought I, "whatever time it may be, that clock is wrong, for it contradicts itself." So if I hear a man say one thing by his church-membership and another by his private protest, why, whatever may be right, he certainly is not consistent with himself.

Let us bear witness to the truth, since there is great need of doing so just now, for witnessing is in ill repute. The age extols no virtue so much as "liberality," and condemns no vice so fiercely as bigotry, *alias* honesty. If you believe anything and hold it firmly, all the dogs will bark at you. Let them bark: they will have done when they are tired! You are responsible to God, and not to mortal men. Christ came into the world to bear witness to the truth, and he has sent you to do the same; take care that you do it, offend or please; for it is only by this process that the kingdom of Christ is to be set up in the world.

Now, the last thing is this. Our Saviour, having spoken of his kingdom and the way of establishing it, DESCRIBED HIS SUBJECTS: "Everyone that is of the truth heareth my voice." That is to say, wherever the Holy Spirit has made a man a lover of truth, he always recognises Christ's voice and yields himself to it. Where are the people who love the truth? Well, we need not enquire long. We need not Diogenes' lantern to find them, they will come to the light; and where is light but in Jesus? Where are those that would not seem to be what they are not? Where are the men who desire to be true in secret and before the Lord? They may be discovered where Christ's people are discovered ; they will be found listening to those who bear witness to the truth. Those who love pure truth, and know what Christ is, will be sure to fall in love with him and hear his voice. Judge ye, then, this day, brethren and sisters, whether ye are of the truth or not ; for if you love the truth, you know and obey the voice which calls you away from your old sins, from false refuges, from evil habits, from everthing which is not after the Lord's mind. You have heard him in your conscience rebuking you for that of the false which remains in you ; encouraging in you that of the true which is struggling there. I have done, when I have urged on you one or two reflections.

The first is, beloved, Dare we avow ourselves on the side of truth at this hour of its humiliation ? Do we own the royalty of Christ's truth when we see it every day dishonoured. If gospel truth were honoured everywhere, it would be an easy thing to say " I believe it ;" but now, in these days, when it has no honour among men, dare we cleave to it at all costs ? Are you willing to walk with the truth through the mire and through the slough ? Have you the courage to profess unfashionable truth ? Are you willing to believe the truth against which science, falsely so-called, has vented her spleen ? Are you willing to accept the truth although it is said that only the poor and uneducated will receive it ? Are you willing to be the disciple of the Galilean, whose apostles were fishermen ? Verily, verily, I say unto you, in that day in which the truth in the person of Christ shall come forth in all its glory, it shall go ill with those who were ashamed to own it and its Master.

In the next place, if we have heard Christ's voice, do we recognise our life-object ? Do we feel, " For this end were we born, and for this cause came we into the world, that we might bear witness to the truth ? " I do not believe that you, my dear brother, came into the world to be a linendraper, or an auctioneer, and nothing else. I do not believe that God created you, my sister, to be merely and only a sempstress, a nurse, or a housekeeper. Immortal souls were not created for merely mortal ends. For this purpose was I born, that, with my voice in this place, and everywhere else, I might bear witness to the truth. You acknowledge that : then I beg you, each one, to acknowledge that you have a similar mission. "I could not occupy the pulpit," says one. Never mind that : bear witness for the truth where you are, and in your own sphere. O waste no time or energy, but at once testify for Jesus.

And now, last of all, do you own Christ's superlative dignity, beloved ? Do you see what a King, Christ is ? Is he such a King to you as none other could be ? It was but yesterday a prince entered one of our great towns, and they crowded all their streets to welcome him—yet he was but a mortal man. And then at night they illuminated their city, and made the heavens glow as though the sun had risen before his appointed hour. Yet what had this prince done for them? Loyal subjects were they, and that was the reason of their joy. But O, beloved, we need not ask, "What has Christ done for us?"—we will ask, "What has he not done for us?" Emmanuel, we owe all to thee! Thou art our new creator, our Redeemer from the lowest pit of hell! In thyself resplendent and altogether lovely, thy beauties command our adoration! Thou hast lived for us, thou hast bled for us, thou hast died for us; and thou art preparing a kingdom for us, and thou art coming again to take us to be with thee where thou art! All this commands our love. All hail! all hail! Thou art our King, and we worship thee with all our soul!

Beloved, I beseech you love Christ, and live for him while you can. Work while opportunity serves. While I have been laid aside, and able to do nothing, the great sorrow of my heart has been my inability to do him service. I heard my brethren shouting in the battle-field, and I saw my comrades marching to the fight, and I lay like a wounded soldier in the ditch, and could not stir, save that I breathed a prayer that you might all be strong in the Lord and in the power of his might. This was my thought: "Oh, that I had preached better while I could preach, and lived more for the Master while I could serve him!" Don't incur such regrets in the future by present sluggishness, but live now for him who died for you!

If any present in this assembly have never obeyed our King, may they come to trust in him to-night; for he is a tender Saviour, and is willing to receive the biggest and blackest sinner who will come to him. Whosoever trusts in him, will never find him fail; for he will save to the uttermost them that come unto God by him. May he bring you to his feet, and reign over you in love. Amen.

The Breaker and the Flock

"I will surely assemble, O Jacob, all of thee; I will surely gather the remnant of Israel; I will put them together as the sheep of Bozrah, as the flock in the midst of their fold: they shall make great noise by reason of the multitude of men. The breaker is come up before them: they have broken up, and have passed through the gate, and are gone out by it: and their king shall pass before them, and the Lord on the head of them "—Micah ii. 12, 13.

You will remember, dear friends, from our reading last Sabbath morning, in the second chapter of the Book of Micah, that the prophet was delivering reproofs and rebukes against a sinful people, a people who tried to straiten the Spirit and silence the voice of prophecy, and refused to listen to the messengers of God. He threatened them with condign punishment from the Most High. To our surprise, in the very midst of the threatening he delivers a prediction brimming with mercy. Not only is not the Spirit of the Lord straitened, but even the people of the Lord are not to be straitened; for one has come forth who will be to them both liberator and leader. Judgment is God's strange work, and he rejoices even in the midst of threatening to turn aside and utter gracious words to obedient souls. Surely the brightest and most silvery drops of love that have ever distilled upon men have fallen in close connection with storms of divine justice. The acceptable year of the Lord is hard by the day of vengeance of our God. The blackness of the tempest of his wrath acts as a foil to set forth more brightly the glory of his grace. In this case the thunder-bolts stay their course in mid-volley : when the prophet is hurling destruction upon sin and sinners he pauses to interpose a passage of promise most rich and gracious—a passage which I wish to open up to you at this time, as the Spirit of God shall enable me.

Certain wilful persons were proudly confident that no enemy could reach them behind the walls of their cities, though the Lord declared that he would make Samaria a heap, and would strip Jerusalem. They coveted fields and took them by violence, and went on with their oppressions as if there had been no Judge of all the earth. The Lord warned them again and again, and assured them that they must not expect to be preserved from chastisement because they were the Lord's people. They boasted that God would protect them, yea, they leaned upon the Lord, and said, "Is not the Lord among us? none evil can come upon us." He told them that Zion should be ploughed as a field, and Jerusalem should become heaps. They were by no means to escape the rod; rather might they look for grace after they had been severely chastened. They would be carried away into captivity, but yet there would come a day in which they should be gathered out of the places wherein they had been scattered, and brought back to their own land. The prophet cried to the daughter of Zion, "Thou shalt go even to Babylon; there shalt thou be delivered; there the Lord shall redeem thee from the hand of thine enemies."

Truly, the Lord forgets not to devise means to bring again his banished ones. The words of Micah in the passage before us agree with many others which fell from the lips of prophets; for it is the way of the Lord to restore his chosen in the day of their repentance. Did he not say by his servant Amos, "Lo, I will command, and I will sift the house of Israel among all nations, like as corn is sifted in a sieve; yet shall not the least grain fall upon the earth." He will preserve the chosen race even in their scattering, and then in his own appointed time he will seek them out, according to his own word, "He that scattered Israel will gather him, and keep him, as a shepherd doth his flock." These gathered ones were to be led back to their land under the guidance of a great shepherd, whose business it should be to break down all obstacles and clear the road for them, so that they might safely reach their resting-place.

I have no doubt that the first fulfilment of this prophecy was given when Cyrus conquered Babylon and gave permission for Israel to return to their own land. Cyrus may be regarded as "the Breaker;" for the prophet Isaiah wrote concerning him: "Thus saith the Lord to his anointed, to Cyrus, whose right hand I have holden, to subdue nations before him; and I will loose the loins of kings, to open before him the two leaved gates; and the gates shall not be shut; I will go before thee, and make the crooked places straight: I will break in pieces the gates of brass, and cut in sunder the bars of iron." Then the willing-hearted of Israel gathered together to rebuild the house of the Lord, and to this centre multitudes hastened, the Lord being with them and sending them prosperity. It was of these favoured ones that we find a striking fulfilment of our text as to the noise made by the concourse of men. Ezra tells us that "the people shouted with a loud shout, and the noise was heard afar off." Then was this promise in a measure fulfilled.

But, brethren, the promises of the Lord are perennial springs for ever overflowing with new fulfilments. In the latter days, the God of Israel, in abundant grace, will remember his covenant with Abraham, Isaac, and Jacob, and will gather together his ancient nation, who are at this time a people scattered and peeled. These shall be converted to the Christ of God, and then shall be accomplished the word of the prophet: "I the Lord will be their God, and my servant David a prince among them." The Son of David, whom their fathers slew, not knowing what they did, shall be made known to them as the promised seed, and then they shall look on him whom they have pierced, and they shall mourn for him. May this day soon come! Then shall the veil be taken away from their hearts, and the cloud shall no longer hang over Israel's head, but the Lord shall restore them, and they shall rejoice in him. The day cometh when the Breaker shall go up before them, and the King at the head of them, and they shall be brought again unto the inheritance of their fathers.

Even this will not exhaust the prophecy. I regard this passage as setting forth a vision of spiritual things in which Micah dimly saw the gathering together, and the heavenward march of the true Israel, namely, the elect of God, whom he hath given to his Son Jesus, and whom the Lord Jesus has undertaken to save. "He is a Jew, which is one inwardly; and circumcision is that of the heart." (Rom. ii. 29.) As Paul, by the Spirit of God, interpreteth the whole story of the covenant made with Abraham, Isaac, and Jacob, it is clear that we, brethren, the children of the promise, are the true seed, even those who are born by divine power and as believers are the *spiritual* family of believing Abraham. If we have the faith of Abraham, we are the children of Abraham, and with us is the covenant made; for the seed of Abraham is not reckoned according to descent by the flesh, else would the covenant blessing have fallen to Ishmael and not to Isaac, to Esau and not to Jacob. The covenant is to a spiritual seed, born according to divine promise through divine power. The line in which the Lord has determined that the covenant blessing should run was ordered by divine sovereignty, "that the purpose of God according to election might stand." The Lord purposed that they which are born after the spirit should be the true heirs, and not those that are born after the flesh. We, therefore, believe that to us, even to us who rejoice in Christ Jesus and have no confidence in the flesh, appertain the promises and the covenant. It shall come to pass that all the elect of God shall yet be gathered together from the places whereto they have wandered in their sin, and for them a clear way shall be opened up to the land of their inheritance. The Breaker, who is also their King and God, shall lead them through all opposition, and bring them without fail to their quiet resting-place. Even as at the first all Israel was brought out of Egypt and safely led with a high hand and an outstretched arm through sea and desert, so shall the Lord Jesus lead the whole host of his redeemed to the place of his glory. Hath not the Lord God declared it— "The redeemed of the Lord shall return, and come with singing unto Zion; and everlasting joy shall be upon their head: they shall obtain gladness and joy; and sorrow and sighing shall flee away"?

An august spectacle is set before us in our text. May our eyes be anointed of the Holy Spirit, that we may behold its glories, so that our hearts shall leap for joy!

First, in the text I see *the flock gathered:* "I will surely assemble, O Jacob, all of thee; I will surely gather the remnant of Israel. I will put them together as the sheep of Bozrah, as the flock in the midst of their fold: they shall make great noise by reason of the multitude of men." Secondly, we behold *the champion Shepherd clearing the way of the flock:* "The breaker is come up before them." He, with the arm of his strength, breaks all opposers, and breaks up for them a way from their captivity. Thirdly, behold *the flock advancing,* with their great Shepherd at their head : "They have broken up, and have passed through the gate, and are gone out by it : and their king shall pass before them, and the Lord on the head of them." Jehovah leads the van, and the hosts of his redeemed march triumphantly after him.

I. To begin then, brethren ; here is THE FLOCK GATHERED : "I will surely assemble, O Jacob, all of thee."

Who knows where God's chosen are ? Babylon was far off from Jerusalem, but our places of wandering are farther off from God than that. "All we like sheep have gone astray ; we have turned every one to his own way." In the cloudy and dark day we have wandered to the uttermost ends of the earth. The Lord's chosen ones lie wide of one another, and they are far off from God himself. What a mercy it is that in the text we have a promise that they shall be gathered *divinely!* "*I* will surely assemble, O Jacob, all of thee; *I* will surely gather the remnant of Israel." Who else could gather them but the Lord ? What power less than divine could fetch such wanderers from their haunts and hidings ? One is aloft yonder on the hill side in his pride and self-conceit ; another is down below in the despondency of his disappointment. One wanders in the pastures of worldliness, sporting himself in the plenty thereof, and hard to be brought back for that reason ; another is entangled in the briars of poverty, half-starved and ready to die, and hopeless of ever seeing the face of God with joy. They are everywhere, my brethren,—these lost sheep : they seem to have chosen out, as if deliberately, the most dangerous places ; they stumble on the dark mountains, they are caught in the tangled thickets, they have fallen into pits. O sin, what hast thou done ? rather, what hast thou not done ? for men seem to have gone to the utmost extreme of rebellion against God, and to have done evil with both hands earnestly. Therefore doth God himself come to the rescue. He himself shall assemble Jacob, and gather the remnant of Israel. Driving with the terrors of his law, drawing with the sweetnesses of his gospel, he shall surely bring them in. By one instrumentality or by another, and in some cases, apparently, without instrumentality at all, he will bring them from all points of the compass to the place where he will meet with them.

> "There is a period known to God,
> When all his sheep, redeemed by blood,
> Shall leave the hateful ways of sin,
> Turn to the fold, and enter in."

This is the result of the divine working, and of that alone. Our hope of the salvation of God's elect lies in the fact that it is God himself who undertakes to gather them. Remember his word by the prophet Ezekiel, "For thus saith the Lord God; Behold, I, even I, will both search my sheep, and seek them out."

Following the text closely, we notice that this gathering is to be performed *surely*. I dwell with great pleasure upon that word "surely," because it is spoken twice, "I will *surely* assemble, O Jacob, all of thee; I will *surely* gather the remnant of Israel." There are no "ifs" where there is a God : there are no "peradventures" where divine predestination rules the day. Let Jehovah speak, and it is done; let him command, and it shall stand firm. Inasmuch as he saith "surely" twice, it reminds me of Joseph's word to the Egyptian king: "And for that the dream was doubled unto Pharaoh twice, it is because the thing is established by God." God will not change his purpose, nor turn from his promise, nor forget his covenant: he will surely gather together his chosen people wherever they may be. O thou that art buffeted by opposition, and driven to sore distress in thy holy service, be not thou dismayed, for the purpose of the Lord shall stand. *Thou* mayest fail, but the eternal God will not. Thy work may be washed away like the work of little children in the sand of the sea shore, but that which God doeth endureth for ever. God shaketh the earth out of its place, but who can move *him?* When God saith *surely,* who shall cast doubt in the way? The Lord will without fail call out his redeemed from among men. As a worker and a soul-winner I grasp at these words, "I will surely gather the remnant of Israel," and I feel that I shall not labour in vain, nor spend my strength for nought. When the end cometh, and the whole business of salvation shall be complete, it shall be seen that the Lord hath achieved his purpose. Jesus saith, "All that the Father giveth me shall come to me," and it shall surely be so. Wherefore let us be of good courage, and seek out the lost ones in full confidence that they must and shall be found.

This leads us to notice that they shall be gathered *completely.* "I will surely assemble, O Jacob, *all of thee.*" Not some of the chosen, but all of them, shall be brought out from the world which lieth in the wicked one. Not some of the redeemed, but each one of them, shall be made to walk at liberty under the leadership of their Shepherd-king. The Lord will leave none of his sheep in their wanderings, and surrender none to the lion or the bear. Dear friend, sighing and crying afar off and thinking that God will never gather you, have faith in him. Helpless as thou art, trust him to do his work as a Saviour. It is written, "I will surely gather, O Jacob, all of thee," and thou mayest not think that thou hast wandered beyond the reach of the infinite arm. Is the Spirit of the Lord straitened? Thou must not dream that thou hast sinned thyself beyond the power of grace, for his mercy endureth for ever! Only do thou look unto Christ, and let thy soul stay itself on him, and God will not overlook thee in the day when he gathers his own. Though thou be least in Israel, and most unworthy of his regard, yet he has expressly said, "I will seek that which was lost, and bring again that which was driven away, and will bind up that which was broken, and will strengthen that which was sick." He will not forget thee, thou weakest of all the flock. Thou art needful to the completeness of the company. If thou be not there, how shall the Lord keep his word, "I will surely assemble, O Jacob, all of thee"?

Further, our text declares that the people shall be gathered *unitedly.* There shall be a wonderful union among them: "I will put them together as the sheep of Bozrah." Oh that the Lord would in these days more fully and evidently carry out this promise in the happy unity of his visible church! Sinners hate each other while they wander in their different ways; but when the Lord brings them together by his grace, then love is born in their hearts. What enmities are cast out by the power of divine grace! When lusts are conquered, wars and fightings cease. God is not the author of confusion, but of peace. It is grace which causes that Ephraim shall not envy Judah, nor Judah vex Ephraim. I notice that sinners, when they are under conviction of sin, are not apt to quarrel with one another; and saints, when they behold the Saviour and rejoice in pardoning love, come together in holy love. In that visible community which stands for the Church of God—I mean the combined external organization of Christendom—there are many divisions and fierce heart-burnings; but in the real Church of God, that spiritual body which the Holy Spirit inhabits, these evils are buried. The truly spiritual are really one in heart. You may meet with a man from whom you differ in many respects, but if the life of God is in him, and in yourself also, you will feel a kinship with him of the nearest kind. Often have I read books which have awakened in my soul a sense of true brotherhood with their authors, although I have known them to be of a church opposed to many of my own views. If they praise my divine Lord, if they speak of the inner life, and touch upon communion with God, and if they do this with that unction and living power which are the tokens of the Holy Spirit, then my heart cleaves to them, be they who they may. Is it not so with you? When the Lord brings people to himself, he brings them to one another. Though depraved nature divides, and pride and self set men apart, yet the Lord overcomes these dividing elements by his renewing grace, and his divine word is accomplished—" I will put them together!" When the Lord puts us together, no man can put us asunder. What is wanted in the much-divided visible church of God is, that we should all come under the divine hand more fully, that we should all feel the touch of the divine life, and yield ourselves more completely to the teaching of the divine truth. Schemes of union are of small value; it is the spirit of union which is wanted. Our Lord Jesus prayed, " that they all may be one; that the world may believe that thou hast sent me"; and his prayer cannot fall to the ground. The church is one in Christ, and none can rend the seamless vesture. Yet more openly as the days pass on, the Lord will gather together in one the children of God that were scattered abroad (John xi. 52.)

This gathering together will be done *happily:* they are to be gathered " as the flock in the midst of their fold." God's gathering of his chosen is not to a place of barrenness and misery, but to a place of security and quietude, even to his appointed fold. The Lord Jesus Christ, that great Shepherd of the sheep, maketh us to lie down in green pastures; he leadeth us beside the still waters. He folds his flock, and makes it to lie down in peace. He saith, " Fear not, little flock; for it is your Father's good pleasure to give you the kingdom." He gives us all things richly to enjoy. O you that are wandering afar from God, there can be no rest for you until the Lord gathers you to the fold of which Jesus is the centre and the Shepherd. When you come to Jesus you shall find rest unto your souls, but not till then. "The peace of God that passeth all understanding shall keep your hearts and minds by Christ Jesus," but by Christ Jesus only. Christians are not a miserable company of restless spirits; they are not a pack of dogs howling at one another, and smarting under the keeper's lash; but they are a flock feeding in happy communion, while Jesus in their midst finds for them a place where they may rest at noon. He so loves his own, and so reveals himself to his own, that they are a happy people, highly favoured, and greatly honoured. God hath blessed them, and they shall be blessed, let the world say what it will concerning them.

One more note must be made on this head: they shall be gathered *numerously:* "They shall make great noise by reason of the multitude of men." The Lord's camp is very great. If you have taken into your head the idea that the Lord has chosen for himself a very small company, and that in the end there will be only a few saved, dismiss the notion. The redeemed are a number that no man can number. Now, a man can count to a very great extent; and if the chosen are beyond the numbering of men, they are a multitude indeed. The prophet represents them as making a great noise by reason of their multitude: he alludes to "the busy hum of men," the buzz of the crowd as when the bees are swarming. As in a city there is an indescribable sound by reason of the multitude who are making traffic in it, so shall there be a noise in the church of a great concourse of men. Conceive of the noise heard at Bozrah, in the sheep country of Edom, when all the flocks of the country were gathered together to be numbered for the purposes of tribute. Hearken to the indescribable noise of the bleating myriads. What a suggestion of the voices of the innumerable hosts of the redeemed when they shall finally be brought together, and shall all in fullest joy lift up their voices! If all the gathered-out company were to pray together, what a sound of supplication would go up by reason of the multitude of men! But when they all sing—what a sound shall that be! Do you wonder that John said, "I heard a voice from heaven, as the voice of many waters, and as the voice of a great thunder"? It makes my eyes water to think of the incomparable armies of the redeemed gathered together in one place. Well might the prophet turn poet when he began to picture that countless flock, and speak of the "great noise by reason of the multitude of men"! I believe we shall not any one of us restrain our voices in that day when we shall meet together with our Lord at our head. I saw one stand up at the opening of this service to look around the Tabernacle, to see the multitude; and well he might, for it is a thing to do one's eyes good to behold this vast assembly. But what shall be our joy when we shall stand up in the midst of the great company of the redeemed? We shall look far and wide, and see no end of the great gathering. When they begin to sing, how will our spirits bear the swell of that majestic psalmody? I know I shall find my best voice that day, when in the midst of the congregation of the faithful I shall sing praise unto the Lord my God. The "great noise by reason of the multitude of men" sets forth the enthusiasm of the praise, and the immense number of the perfected ones who shall pour out their hearts before the throne. Thus I have set before you in a feeble way the gathering of the flock.

II. Follow me while, next, I speak of THE CHAMPION SHEPHERD clearing the way. "The breaker is come up before them." In the tenth verse the Lord says to his people, "Arise ye, and depart; for this is not your rest: because it is polluted." But we say to ourselves— How are they to depart from the place where they now are, and press forward to the pastures on the hill-tops of heaven? They are as sheep.

How can they find their way? How can they face their foes? How can they break down barriers? A flock is but ill fitted to tramp over pathless deserts, infested by ferocious wolves. How shall the church attain to the abodes of the perfected? Long leagues of distance must be traversed, hills of guilt must be crossed, and nights of blackest darkness must be experienced. Ah, Lord God! how canst thou expect that this thy church, which is like a flock of sheep, should find its way through all difficulties and adversaries unto thyself? The answer to our fears is before us : " The breaker is come up before them." That great Shepherd of the sheep, whose name is " The Through-breaker" or "The Breaker-up," makes a way for his people, yea, creates it by force of arms.

Between us and heaven once lay the tremendous Alps of sin. Not one of all the flock of God could climb those hills ; all must perish who attempt to cross those awful barriers. The way to heaven was effectually blocked by these heaven-defying mountains, for no passes existed: even the eagle's eye could not discover a way. One sin might keep a man out of heaven ; but the multitudes of our iniquities, the blackness, the aggravation, the repetition of our offences made the case hopeless to all human power or wisdom. I see those awful hills, and wonder how the flock of God can hope to reach eternal bliss with those in the way. Behold he comes, "The Breaker," before whom the mountains sink. " He his own self bare our sins in his own body on the tree; and by that bearing he put them all away." He took upon himself the whole load of his people's iniquities ; he endured the entire weight of the crushing burden, and by his atoning death he cast their iniquities into the depths of the sea. The pass of the atonement is our clear way to glory. In the sepulchre of Jesus all our sins are buried. To as many as believe in Jesus Christ no sin remaineth.

> " This Breaker once made sin to be,
> Broke from the curse his people free.
> He broke the power of death and hell,
> And cleared the road for Israel."

" In those days, and in that time, saith the Lord, the iniquity of Israel shall be sought for, and there shall be none ; and the sins of Judah, and they shall not be found: for I will pardon them whom I reserve." The glorious Breaker, with his pierced hands, and nailed feet, and opened side, hath wrought a miracle of miracles by putting away sin through the sacrifice of himself. Jesus saith, "I am the way"; and the way he is: the way which neither past nor present sin can effectually close. But, my brethren, if our sins were all forgiven us, there are other difficulties in the way ; for we are without strength, and the depravity of our nature is not readily to be overcome. Think of the hardness of our hearts, the waywardness of our wills, the blindness of our judgments, the readiness of our minds to yield to temptation ! How can we force our way through such obstacles ? Why, if the Lord would forgive me all my sin, and give me heaven on condition that I should find my way to it, mine would still be a hopeless case. Even the regenerate find that they have a hard struggle with the flesh ; how can we win our way in the teeth of our fallen nature ? Beloved, the Breaker has gone up before us. The Lord Jesus Christ assumed our nature, and was "tempted in all points like as we are"; he overcame the adversary at every point of the conflict, that through his victory we might be more than conquerors. He sends forth the Holy Spirit to renew us in the spirit of our minds; he takes the stony heart out of our flesh; he rules the will, he governs the affections, he enlightens the understanding, he sanctifies the soul; and thus, though weak in ourselves, we are made strong in him; so strong that we shall not perish in the wilderness, but shall pursue our pilgrimage till we cross the Jordan, and stand in our lot at the end of the days. Because the Breaker has gone up before us, we shall break through the ramparts of sinfulness, and cut our way to holiness and perfection.

Yet, even though this be so, that sin is forgiven and our corrupt nature overcome, still there is another difficulty: the prince of darkness has set himself to obstruct the way: he defies us to advance, he stands across the road, and swears that he will spill our souls. By no means let us be afraid, for the Breaker is gone up before us, and the enemy knows the force of his strong right hand. In the wilderness and in the garden our Lord vanquished this great adversary, and therein gave us full assurance that he will bruise Satan under our feet shortly. We need not fear all the devils in hell: if by faith we have courage to resist them they will flee from us. We shall reach the haven of our rest, the heaven of our bliss. Our glorious Breaker with the mace of the cross has broken the head of leviathan, and made an open show of his adversaries. Thus was it spoken of our Lord at the gates of Eden concerning the old serpent—"Thou shalt bruise his heel": and now by his ascension to heaven he has done the deed, leading captivity captive.

> "Gone up as God's co-equal Son,
> With all his blood-stained garments on,
> While seraphs sing his deathless fame,
> And chant the Breaker's glorious name."

This brings us face to face with the last enemy. Death blocks the way to eternal life. Be of good courage, the Breaker has gone up before you in this matter also. Jesus died: the Ever-blessed bowed his head and yielded up the ghost. Hearken yet again: he has risen from the dead; he slept a while in the cold prison of the tomb, but he could not be holden with the bands of death, and therefore in due time he arose. He arose in newness of life, that all his own might also rise in him. Come, be not afraid to die, for you will travel a well-beaten track. Be not afraid to go down into the heart of the earth, for there your Emmanuel has slept. Nor will he suffer you to go by this dark road alone. "He hath said, I will never leave thee, nor forsake thee." He will go down into this Egypt with you, and he will surely bring you up again. The Breaker goeth up before you.

But can I hope I shall ever enter the gates of heaven? Those gates of pearl whose mild, pure radiance chides my perturbed and guilty heart —can I hope to pass their portal? Can I hope to stand where all is absolutely perfect? I shrink in the presence of such matchless purity. But, brethren, the Breaker has gone up before us. He hath opened the kingdom of heaven to all believers. It will be safe for us to enter where he has gone : yea, we must enter; for where he is, there also shall his servants be. He will welcome each one of us with, "Come in, thou blessed of the Lord; wherefore standest thou without?" Adown those streets of pure gold like unto transparent glass we shall walk without fear, and up to that blazing throne of purest light we shall pass without dismay; for Jesus has gone in before us. Behold him!

> "He is at the Father's side,
> The Man of Love, the Crucified."

The way into the holiest is now made manifest. The Breaker has rent the veil from the top to the bottom, and given us free access to heaven itself.

But I must pause. Certainly my matter is not exhausted : time alone restrains.

III. Lastly, I have to show you for a minute or two THE FLOCK ADVANCING, their royal Breaker leading the way. As the Lord Jesus, in his death, resurrection, and ascension, has gone up before us, so by his grace we are led to follow him from grace to glory. "They go from strength to strength." He saith to them, "Follow me": they know his voice, and as his sheep they follow him.

Along the way which the great Champion clears we find the whole of the flock proceeding. "The Breaker is come up before them," therefore they keep to his footprints. "They have broken up, and have passed through the gate, and are gone out by it." Behold, my brethren, the vision of visions : the whole company of God's elect following their triumphant Leader ! Do you see yonder the pillar of fire and cloud leading the way through the desert ? Do you see the host of Israel in glorious order marching to their predestined inheritance ? Such is the Church of God as it is seen by spiritual eyes. All down the centuries, in every land, they are marching along that appointed road which Jesus, the Breaker, has cleared for them. You and I, I hope, are in that goodly company : sometimes our following is lame and halting, but yet we are not turned out of the way. To whom else could we go if we were to leave our chosen Leader ? Faint we may be, but pursuing we will be. Oh, that we could keep closer to the Breaker ! Oh, that he would break our hearts with his love ! Oh, that all our evil habits might be broken by his grace. We would follow our King whithersoever he goeth. Yes, we are in that company, I trust; and God grant we may never stray from it ! No other road is prepared by a great Breaker as this road is prepared. This is the King's highway, and we will keep to it all our days.

Observe, that in the text the people of God are described as imitating their King ; for it is written, "They have broken up." He is the Breaker ; and are they breakers too ? Yes, they also have broken up. Christ is the great warrior for his people ; but not without conflict will any one of them be crowned. It is so arranged in the wisdom of God, that everything is so done for us as not to drive us into inaction, but to draw us into holy diligence. Christ's warfare is repeated in his saints in their measure. The crown is of grace ; but we must run for it. Christ has conquered sin, and we have to overcome through faith in him. He has subdued the adversary, but we also shall have to wrestle with spiritual wickednesses. "They have broken up." Herein is condescending love. Christ might have saved us, and there might have been nothing for us to do; but, to display his grace, he intends to conform us to himself, in conflict and in crown, in breaking up, and in going forth, and in entering in. He makes us know the fellowship of his sufferings. Come, brethren and sisters, let us ask God to fulfil in us the words of the text, "They have broken up." Let us be resolved to break down all sin. Let us be determined to overcome through the blood of the Lamb. This is the victory which overcometh the world, even our faith. If we have it, let us use it to good purpose this day.

Notice that as these people were led on by the Breaker: they persevered in following him. "They have broken up; they have passed through the gate, and are gone out by it." They did a little at a time; they advanced step by step; they stopped at nothing, but went onward and upward. So do saints go from grace to grace, from faith to greater faith. Note the sentences: "they have broken up, they have passed through the gate, and have gone out by it": this looks as if they did it slowly but surely, gradually but grandly. So, when the grace of God enters into the heart, and we, the sheep of God, are made to follow him, we are attentive to detail, and notice each part of our obedience. You cannot in grace, any more than in anything else, do a great deal at once, and do it effectually. I find that advance in grace, if it be suppositious, can be rapid; but if it be real, it requires patience. Our Lord gives us line upon line, precept upon precept; here a little, and there a little. Let us be sure even if we be slow.

But now I would have you dwell upon the fact that they are marching under royal leadership: "Their King shall pass before them." Christ is always at the head of his own church. Why? because he loves it so that he cannot be away from it. He is at the head of his own flock because he has purchased it with his own blood. He will not send an angel to lead his chosen, but he himself will watch over the objects of his everlasting love. He knows the necessities of his church to be such as he, and only he, can meet: therefore as the King he always remains at their head. Brethren, let us always reverence, honour, and obey him. Our active, present King must be loyally and earnestly served. As Breaker he did us service; as King we must render him service. Remember how the Psalmist put it to the chosen bride: "He is thy Lord, and worship thou him." As a church, we know no other head; as the people of his pasture, we know no other leader. Let us follow him boldly and gladly.

Let us give him praise this day; yea, let us worship and adore him, for he is Jehovah. He who is at our head is Lord: in him dwelleth all the fulness of the Godhead bodily. Is it not written, "The Lord shall go before thee"? Let us rejoice because the Lord is our King, and he will save us. Do you ever fear that the cause of truth and righteousness will fail? Shake this dust from off thee. Banish such a thought. If Jehovah leads the van, who shall stand against him? If Jesus Christ, once the man of sorrows, but now the King of kings, is to the fore, he will reckon with our adversaries, and make short work of their boastings. Wherefore, follow quietly and unquestioningly as sheep follow the shepherd, and your way shall be prosperous. The Lord of hosts is with us, the God of Jacob is our refuge : wherefore comfort one another with these words.

I cannot express the joy I feel in the belief that I am one of the company which is following the Breaker's lead ; but my sorrow is that some of you are not of his flock. Oh, that you may belong to those of whom he says, " Other sheep I have which are not of this fold : them also I must bring." Oh, that he may bring you in speedily! Do you feel a desire towards Christ this morning ? Have you any longings to be reconciled to God by him ? Then you may freely come, with the confident assurance that him that cometh to him he will in no wise cast out. He invites you to his cross, yea, to himself. Obey the gentle impulse which is now stirring your bosom. Jesus has come on purpose to seek and to save the lost : you are lost; therefore pray that he may save you.

Should the enemy of all good tell you that if you should believe, yet you would never hold out to the end, remind him that the Breaker has gone up before his people, and their King at the head of them, and therefore you are not afraid of meeting anything upon the road which can beat you back from hope and heaven. Join the army which marches under our victorious Joshua, and through sin, and hell, and death the Breaker will clear your way. To him be praise for ever and ever! Amen.

Jesus—The Shepherd

"He shall feed his flock like a shepherd"—Isaiah xl. 11.

Our Lord Jesus is very frequently described as the shepherd of his people. The figure is inexhaustible, but it has been so often handled that I suppose it would be difficult to say anything fresh upon it. We all know, and are very glad and comforted in the knowledge, that the Lord Jesus Christ, as our Shepherd, exercises towards us all the kind and necessary offices which a shepherd performs towards his sheep. With gentle sway he *rules* us for our good: "Let us worship and bow down; let us kneel before the Lord our Maker; for he is our God, and we are the people of his pasture and the sheep of his hand." He *guides* us: "And when he putteth forth his own sheep he goeth before them, and the sheep follow him, for they know his voice." He *provides* for us: "The Lord is my shepherd, I shall not want. He maketh me to lie down in green pastures: he leadeth me beside the still waters." He *protects* us from all forms of evil; therefore, "though we walk through the valley of the shadow of death, we will fear no evil, for he is with us: his rod and his staff, they comfort us." If we wander, he *seeks* us out and brings us back. "He restoreth my soul; he leadeth me in the paths of righteousness for his name's sake." If we be broken, he binds us up; if we be wounded, he heals according to his own word, "I will bind up that which was broken, and will strengthen that which was sick." The sheep is an animal of many diseases and many wants, and so the Christian is an individual of many sins and many infirmities; but as the shepherd endeavours to meet all the wants of his flock, so our Lord Jesus succours all the blood-bought company in all their needs.

We propose to illustrate the great doctrine of the text in a scriptural, and therefore we hope in an interesting, manner. First, we shall consider in connection with the text, *Old Testament illustrations;* in the second place, *New Testament descriptions;* and, in the third place, *Impressive applications.*

I. We commence with Old Testament Illustrations of the manner in which the Lord Jesus Christ discharges the office of feeding his flock like a shepherd.

Out of five great types we begin with *Abel, the shepherd slain.* The second man who was born into the world was a shepherd, and was in many respects typical of our good shepherd. "Abel was a keeper of sheep, but Cain was a tiller of the ground." Abel was a type of the Saviour in that, being a shepherd, *he sanctified his work to the glory of God, and he offered sacrifice of blood upon the altar of the Lord,* and the Lord had respect unto Abel and his offering. This early type of our Lord is not very full and comprehensive, but it is exceedingly clear and distinct. Like the first streak of light which tinges the east at the sunrise, it does not reveal everything, but it clearly manifests the great fact that the sun is coming. Abel is nothing like so complete and perfect a portrait of our own Lord Jesus, as other shepherds of whom we have to speak; but as we see him standing a shepherd and yet a sacrificing priest offering upon the altar a sacrifice of sweet smell unto God, we discern there at once the picture of our Lord, who brings before his Father a sacrifice of precious blood, to which Jehovah ever hath respect. Abel, the sacrificing shepherd, was hated by his brother—hated without a cause; and even so was the Saviour: the spirit of this world, the natural and carnal man, hated the better man, the accepted man in whom the Spirit of grace was found, and rested not until his blood had been shed. Abel fell, and sprinkled his own altar and his sacrifice with his own blood; and he must be blind indeed who cannot behold the Lord Jesus slain by the enmity of man while serving as a priest before the Lord. Abel is the type of Jesus the slain shepherd; let us attentively consider him. We have been reading in the tenth chapter of John, this morning, that the good Shepherd layeth down his life for the sheep—let us weep over him as we view him stretched upon the ground by the hatred of mankind at the foot of his own altar of sacrifice, pouring out his blood. We read of *Abel's blood,* in the New Testament, that it *speaketh.* "He being dead yet speaketh." "The Lord said unto Cain, The voice of thy brother's blood crieth unto me from the ground." Herein we have a blessed type of the Lord: his blood had a mighty tongue, and the import of its prevailing cry is not vengeance but mercy.

"the rich blood of Jesus slain
Speaks peace as loud from every vein."

It is precious beyond all preciousness to stand at Jesus Christ's altar, and to see him himself offered there as a whole burnt-offering acceptable unto God; to see him lying bleeding there as the slaughtered priest, and then to hear the voice of his blood speaking peace in our consciences, peace in the Church of God, peace between Jew and Gentile, peace between man and his offended Maker—speaking peace all down the ages of eternity for blood-washed man. Abel is first in order of time, and Jesus first in order of excellence. The earth opened her mouth to receive Abel's blood, and Jesus' sacrifice has blessed this poor, sin-ruined world. Abel received divine witness to his righteousness, and Jesus obtained the same in the day of his resurrection; but fulness of other matter forbids us to linger.

Further down the page of sacred history we find another shepherd. He is a more instructive type of the Saviour, perhaps, than the first, but in Abel we discover a truth which is absent in all others. Abel is the only one of the typical shepherds who dies at the foot of the altar, he is the only sacrificing shepherd; and herein you see Jesus Christ in the very earliest ages set forth to mankind as the slaughtered victim; that whatever else the early saints might not see, yet they might know that the seed of the woman would shed his precious blood. This most vital truth is not withheld even for a little season.

Now we turn to *Jacob, the toiling shepherd*. Here is a type of the good Shepherd not as dying, but as keeping sheep with a view to get unto himself a spouse and a flock. Jacob left his father's house. He departed from all the joy and comfort of the house in which he was the recognized heir, both by his own purchase and his Father's promise. Our Lord Jesus Christ, out of the love which he bore us, left his Father's house above, and came down to tabernacle among men. Jacob repaired to his mother's brethren; and even so our Lord, on the mother's side, counts men his brethren. "He came unto his own." That vision which Jacob saw the first night after he had left his father's house, seems to me to be a representation of the great object which our Lord had set before him as the intent of his mission here below. Jacob slept, and dreamed that he saw a ladder the foot whereof stood upon the earth, while the top reached to the heaven of heavens, whence a Covenant God spoke to his chosen servant; and so, before the Saviour's eye, as the great reward of all his life's travail, he saw a ladder set up by which earth should be connected with heaven. He saw fallen man at the foot of it, but he beheld a Covenant God at the top, while the angels of God ascending and descending upon his own person, as upon the divine road of communication by which prayer mounts, and mercy descends. As soon as Jacob arrived at the house of his mother's brethren, he began to work out of the love he bore to Rachel; and Jesus Christ no sooner descended upon this lower earth, than he began at once to labour to win his spouse. Now there were in the house of manhood two daughters to both of whom Jesus must be affianced. There was first of all the Jewish Church, which was in his eyes his Rachel, his dearly beloved, and he toiled for her; but in the days of his flesh his own received him not. Though while he was here below, he declared that he was not sent save to the lost sheep of the house of Israel, yet Israel was not gathered; yet Jesus lost not his reward, for the Gentile Church, the tender-eyed Leah, was his reward. "Though Israel be not gathered, yet shall I be glorious in the eyes of the Lord, and my God shall be my strength. And he said, It is a light thing that thou shouldest be my servant to raise up the tribes of Jacob, and to restore the preserved of Israel: I will also give thee for a light to the Gentiles, that thou mayest be my salvation unto the end of the earth." Leah, the Gentile Church, is far more fruitful unto Christ in spiritual children than the Rachel for whom he served in the days of his flesh; but the day cometh when Rachel shall be more fully increased, when the fulness of the Gentiles having been gathered in, the Jew shall recognise Messiah, and the Jewish people shall own their King. We understand from Jacob's own description of his toil, that his labour in order to get to himself his spouse was of the most arduous character; and it will be well for the intelligent Christian to see Jesus Christ in just such toil, seeking to redeem unto himself his own beloved, that they might for ever be one with himself in his own glory. In the thirty-first chapter of Genesis, at the thirty-eighth verse, Jacob, while expostulating with Laban, thus describes his own toil: "This twenty years have I been with thee; thy ewes and thy she-goats have not cast their young, and the rams of thy flock have I not eaten. That which was torn of beasts I brought not unto thee: I bare the loss of it; of my hand didst thou require it, whether stolen by day, or stolen by night. Thus I was; in the day the drought consumed me, and the frost by night; and my sleep departed from mine eyes. Thus have I been twenty years in thy house: I served thee fourteen years for thy two daughters, and six years for thy cattle; and thou hast changed my wages ten times." Even more toil some than this was the life of our Saviour here below. He watched over all his sheep till he could give in as his last account, "Of all those whom thou hast given me I have lost none, but the son of perdition, that the Scriptures might be fulfilled." His hair was wet with dew, and his locks with the drops of the night. Sleep departed from his eyes, for all night he was in prayer wrestling with God. One night it is Peter who must be pleaded for; another time, another claims his tearful intercession. No shepherd sitting beneath the cold skies, looking up to the stars, could ever utter such complaints because of the hardness of his toil as Jesus Christ might have brought, if he had chosen to do so, because of the sternness of his service in order to gather unto himself his people.

> "Cold mountains and the midnight air,
> Witnessed the fervour of his prayer;
> The desert his temptation knew,
> His conflict and his victory too."

It is sweet to dwell upon the spiritual parallel of Laban having required all the sheep at Jacob's hand. If they were torn of beasts he must make it good; if any of them died, he must stand as surety for the whole. And did not the Saviour stand just so while he was here below? Was not his toil for his Church just the toil of one who felt that he was under suretyship obligations to bring every one of them safe to the hand of him who had committed them to his charge? Look upon toiling Jacob and you see a representation of him of whom the text says, "He shall feed his flock like a shepherd." One other point of resemblance there is here, namely, that when Jacob had thus purchased to himself his spouse, and had received a reward for all his toil out of the flock which he himself tended, he then conducted both his family and his flock away from Laban. This is a point never to be forgotten. Shouldering his cross, Jesus went without the camp, and in so doing he speaks to each of us. "Let us therefore go forth without the camp, bearing his reproach." He went to his mother's brethren that he might fetch out his chosen from among men, and his voice to his spouse is, "Hearken, O daughter, and consider: forget also thine own people, and thy father's house. So shall the king greatly desire thy beauty: for he is thy Lord; and worship thou him." Jacob coming back from Laban to the Promised Land, is a true picture of Jesus Christ coming up from the world, followed by his Church, to enter upon that better Canaan which has been given to us by a covenant of salt for ever. The toiling shepherd has never ceased his work till he has bidden farewell to Laban once for all, and has come to dwell in tents where Abraham and Isaac had dwelt before him; and Christ's work is not accomplished in us till he has made us like himself, holy, harmless, undefiled, and separate from sinners. Although these types are very full, I choose rather to give them to you as suggestions to think out for yourselves, than to enlarge upon them myself.

Joseph is a type of Jesus, *reigning in the Egypt of this world for the good of his own people, while they are here below.* Remember Joseph's history. We find that he kept his father's flock with his brethren. So did our Saviour when he began to teach and to preach. In the midst of the envious Scribes and Pharisees he kept his father's flock. They could not, however, brook him in whom they discerned a royalty not in themselves. As Joseph wore a coat of many colours, indicative of princely rank and of his father's love, even so Jesus Christ in the perfections of his nature, being something more than ordinary man, was soon spied out by envious shepherds as anointed with the oil of gladness above his fellows. Then began they to find fault with his words. He had seen a dream, in which the sun, and moon, and the eleven stars made obeisance unto him. And as the envious Scribes and Pharisees listened to the word of the Saviour, and heard him claim that he was the Son of God, and that he came down from heaven, they thought that he dreamed; they charged him with blasphemy, and straightway their hearts were set against him, and they were determined upon his destruction. They sold him for thirty pieces of silver, the price of a slave. So our Joseph was sold into Egypt to the powers of evil. There he was falsely accused, though in him was no sin. Our Joseph, our blessed Shepherd, was cast into the prison of the grave, and there he abode for awhile, but by-and-by he came out of prison, and Joseph—Jesus—it matters not which word I use, Joseph was made ruler over all the land of Egypt. That same Shepherd of ours who was sold by his envious brethren, and who went down into the prison-tomb, is now exalted high above all principalities and powers, and every name that is named; and even here, in this Egypt, where his people now dwell, Jesus Christ is king. Not a dog dare move his tongue in all the land of Egypt without the permission of Joseph, and surely no enemy can forge a weapon against Christ's Church here on earth.

"He overrules all mortal things,
And manages our mean affairs."

The Father hath committed all power unto his Son. Jesus Christ is King over Egypt's realm. Now observe the likeness between Joseph and Jesus in this respect. Joseph was of very singular advantage to the Egyptians. They must have starved in the years of famine, if his prescient eye had not foreseen the famine, and stored up the plenty of the seven previous years. And Jesus Christ is of great service even to this wicked world. It is by him that it is preserved. The barren fig-tree was spared because the husbandman pleaded for it, and the intercession of Jesus Christ spares the lives of the unregenerate; and though they will be swept away with the besom of destruction when their iniquity is fully ripe, yet meanwhile they are spared because of the mediatorial sovereignty of the great Shepherd. Jesus Christ, like Joseph, rules over the land of Egypt; but Joseph ruled for a special purpose. God had sent Joseph to Egypt, but not mainly for the sake of the Egyptians. "God hath sent me hither to save your souls alive;" this was Joseph's own testimony. Jesus Christ now hath power over all flesh—why? "That he should give eternal life to as many as thou hast given him." The universal reign of Christ, in which respect his redemption comes to all the sons of men, has for its object that special redemption, in which respect it comes only to his own people, who are his sheep. Perhaps some of you may wonder how I venture to call Joseph a shepherd. You grant me that in his early days he kept his father's flock, but was he a shepherd while he was in Egypt? You will believe the dying words of his father Jacob, will you not? His father Jacob, when speaking of him said, "Joseph is a fruitful bough, even a fruitful bough by a well; whose branches run over the wall; the archers have sorely grieved him, and shot at him, and hated him: but his bow abode in strength, and the arms of his hands were made strong by the hands of the mighty God of Jacob;"—then there comes a sentence between brackets—"from thence is the shepherd, the stone of Israel." Joseph is here called the shepherd and the stone. I could not make out in meditation why he should be both a shepherd and a stone, but you remember that Jesus Christ was at once the shepherd and the stone which the builders refused, which afterwards became the headstone of the corner; and so Joseph in being a shepherd of his people, and in having been the corner stone of the Israelitish race while they were in Egypt, was both the shepherd and the stone of Israel. Beloved, it seems to me to be such a delightful thought to think that Jesus Christ is King to-day in the world. The Lord reigneth: let the earth rejoice. Jesus Christ wears the crown this day of universal monarchy. "The Lord said unto my lord, sit thou on my right hand until thine enemies are made thy footstool;" so that nothing happens now, but that which Jesus permits, ordains, and overrules. Let empires go to wreck, it is Christ who breaks them with a rod of iron, and shivers them like potters' vessels: let conflagrations burn down cities, and let diseases devastate nations, let war succeed to war, and pestilence to famine, yet still our Joseph rules all things well, and we know that all things work together for good to them that love God, that are called according to his purpose. The saints are in the world, but Christ reigns over the world for his Church, that it may be kept and preserved in the midst of an evil generation. You remember that remarkable saying, "Now every shepherd is an abomination unto the Egyptians"—a strange thing, and yet in Egypt the shepherds found their shelter. Now every Christian is an abomination to the world, and yet it is in this world that at the present time we dwell in so much temporal comfort, under such excellent government, with so little disturbance. To what can we attribute it but to this, that Jesus sits upon the throne and rules Egypt for the good of Israel, and the world is made subservient to the blessedness of the Church of God. I must not tarry any longer, though it is a very tempting theme, but I want to take you on to the next shepherd.

Jesus Christ will be represented to you in quite a different character under the next illustration. Moses was not a ruler in Egypt, but quite a distinct character. Moses, when he kept sheep, kept them in the wilderness, far away from all other flocks; and when he became a shepherd over God's people Israel, his business was not to preserve them in Egypt, but to conduct them out of it. Here, then, is a representation of Jesus Christ as *the Shepherd of a separated people*, called from among men, and made to be a distinguished nation, not numbered among the people. Jesus, like Moses, might have been a king. The devil said to him, "All these things will I give thee if thou wilt fall down and worship me." The people would have taken him, we read, and made him a king, for he was naturally of royal race, but he refused. As Moses refused to be called the son of Pharaoh's daughter, so Jesus Christ said, "Get thee behind me, Satan," to all the pomp and glory of this present world, and preferred to take part with his poor, despised people, who were crushed down by the reigning powers in the Egypt of his days. Now, Moses began his mission, you remember, by going to Pharaoh and saying, "Thus saith the Lord, Let my people go, that they may serve me." Jesus Christ begins as the Shepherd of the separate ones by demanding that they should be let go from the bondage of their natural estate. With a high hand and with an outstretched arm, he fetches out his people from among men: plagues and marvels does he work, but he brings them all out. "Not a hoof shall be left behind;" not one child of God, not one sheep of his pasture left in the Egypt of sin and death. They shall all be made to go without the camp—leaving even Goshen to go into a wilderness because they must be alone with God, and they cannot worship him in a land full of idols. I might dwell for a long time on all the transactions of Moses in Egypt, and especially upon the paschal supper, all of which was doubtless typical of him of whom the text says, "He shall feed his flock like a shepherd." Our main point is the great exodus of Moses, who at the head of all the tribes goes forth to Succoth. There they pitch their tents. By-and-by they advance to Pi-hahiroth with the Red Sea before them. With Moses' staff to lead the van they pass through the sea dry-shod, and come absolutely into the wilderness of separation, as, beloved, every heir of heaven is brought right out of Egypt, led through the Red Sea of Jesus Christ's blood, baptized into Jesus, and brought out into the separated position in the wilderness. Now, it is easy to see how Moses was a shepherd to the people while in the wilderness. He led them in all their wanderings. He was King in Jeshurun over the people whom God had given to him. When they wanted food his prayer brought down the manna or the quails; when they needed drink it was his voice that made the rock burst forth with floods, or his rod that smote, and lo, the flinty rock gushed with torrents. If there were Amalekites to fight, the uplifted arm of Moses did more than the sharp sword of Joshua. They sometimes received chastisement from him. He ground the golden calf to pieces, and strewed the powder on water and made them drink. They were equally dependent upon him for comfort too; his speech distilled as the dew and dropped as the rain, the small rain upon the tender herb. Moses, like a shepherd, had to carry all the people in his bosom as God's appointed messenger, and often did he find it a very weary load, so that he said, "I cannot bear the burden of this great people alone."

You have here a suggestive type of Jesus Christ, the leader of the separated Church. Brethren, I think we may all of us not only catch the idea but live it out, the Church is in the desert now. We have left the world, we have left its maxims, its customs, its religion. We hate the world's religion as much as we do its irreligion. We have forsaken it for good, never to go back again; and though the flesh sometimes falls a lusting and would fain go back to the old bondage, yet, under the guidance of our greater Shepherd, who leads his people far away from Mizraim's polluted shore, we march onward by devious ways to the promised rest.

The last type I mean to give you is *David*. This shepherd represents *Jesus Christ*, not at all as the others, but *as King in the midst of his Church*. David, like Jesus Christ, begins his life with trials. He is anointed and straightway he begins to suffer. The world's king recognizes him, fixes his eye upon him, hurls the javelin at him, hunts him like a partridge on the mountains, and rests not till he himself is slain. Poor David is the apt picture of Jesus Christ in the days of his flesh, hunted by the world's king who would fain put him down and crush out his spark. David at length mounts to his throne, quietly and in peace he sits in Jerusalem as king over Israel and Judah; and even at this day, though the kings of the earth set themselves against him, and their rulers take counsel together, yet this is the decree concerning our Lord, "Yet have I set my king upon my holy hill of Zion." That same Shepherd who of old snatched the lamb out of the jaw of the lion and delivered his sheep from the paw of the bear; that same Shepherd who, in pangs of death, took the lion of hell by the beard and slew him; that same shepherd sits as King in the Jerusalem above, and all his saints delight to do him homage. All hail, thou Son of David! Reign thou for ever! Hosanna unto thee! Thine enemies cannot dispossess thee; thou hast smitten them terribly, and they shall yet feel the terror of thine arm. The Shepherd reigns, Jesus Christ is King of God's Church, and one of these days the reign of David will blossom into the reign of Solomon. We shall see Jesus Christ under a yet more glorious type, for he shall reign from the river even unto the ends of the earth. There shall be no war with the Ammonites, no war anywhere; all enemies shall have been put beneath his feet, and the kings of the nations shall bow before him, and they that dwell in the wilderness shall lick the dust. May that millennial splendour soon dawn, when the Son of David shall be King for ever and ever as the great Shepherd, reigning over all lands. Think these five illustrations over, and there will be much instruction here concerning him who feeds his flock like a shepherd.

II. Now let the Christian who is not **weary** follow me in three NEW TESTAMENT DESCRIPTIONS.

Jesus Christ the Shepherd, is described in the New Testament, as I dare say you all remember, in three ways. He is first of all spoken of as the *good* Shepherd, next, as the *great* Shepherd, and thirdly, as the *chief* Shepherd. I do not know that any other adjective is appended to his name of Shepherd. First, turn to the tenth of John, there you find him described as the *good* Shepherd. "The good shepherd giveth his life for the sheep." Goodness is the special excellence which seems to gleam in the character of our Lord in his earthly life and in his passion for the sons of men. As I look upon my Lord and Master here, despised and rejected of men, I know he is the great Shepherd, but his greatness does not strike me; his flock is so few. We read in the Acts that "the number of the names together were about one hundred and twenty." "Foxes have holes, and the birds of the air have nests, but I, the Son of Man, have not where to lay my head." Herein is goodness, but the greatness is concealed. When he saw the multitude, he had compassion upon them, for they were as sheep having no shepherd. Here is the good Shepherd: he healed their sicknesses and wept over their sins—here is goodness indeed. When it was time for him to die, he crossed the brook Kedron, and suffered till he sweat great drops in the garden; he went to trial and condemnation, and then to the mount of doom, to suffer, bleed, and die. Here is the good Shepherd—the good Shepherd bleeding for the sheep. Can you tell me *how* good a Shepherd Jesus was? Can you measure the height and depth of the extraordinary goodness that dwelt in him?—so good that he saved others, himself he could not save—so good that when he rendered in his account, he could say, "I have lost none." He had kept them all safely, though he himself had bowed his head and given up the ghost.

You will find in Hebrews xiii. 20, that he is called the *great* Shepherd. Does that refer to his life on earth, and to his death? Not at all. Kindly observe the connexion. "Now the God of peace which brought again from the dead our Lord Jesus Christ, that *great* Shepherd of the sheep, through the blood of the everlasting covenant, make you perfect in every good work to do his will." Do you perceive? He is not the great Shepherd when he dies: he is the good Shepherd, but he is the great Shepherd when he is brought again from the dead. In resurrection you perceive his greatness. He lies in the grave slumbering; he is the good Shepherd then, having laid down his life for the sheep; life appears again in him, the stone is rolled away, the watchmen are seized with terror, and he stands out the risen one, no more the dying—now he is the great Shepherd. He manifests himself for forty days among his own disciples, and then at last taking them to the hill of Galilee a cloud receives him out of their sight, and up he mounts as the great Shepherd. When he has told them to go to Jerusalem, they sit waiting till the time of the fulness is come, and suddenly there is heard the sound of a rushing mighty wind, and fiery tongues sit upon all of them. Who has given this boon to each? Who is it? This is the great Shepherd. He has ascended on high, and has received gifts for men; the Shepherd still you see, but now he is the great Shepherd, the Shepherd riding in triumphal state through the midst of New Jerusalem, amidst the acclamations of angels, and sending to his sheep down below the precious gift of apostles and ministers of various orders, according to his own will. He was the good Shepherd before, he is the good Shepherd now; but he is also pre-eminently the great Shepherd. Let us delight to think of this greatness of our Lord Jesus Christ. Let us extol and bless him. Observe, carefully, that while the good Shepherd lays down his life, that you may have life, and have it more abundantly, he is the great Shepherd for another purpose. What does it say? "Make you perfect in every good work to do his will." Yes, he dies to wash away your sin, but he rises for your justification and your complete sanctification, that as the Lord left his graveclothes behind him, you may leave your sins behind you; and as he left the tomb behind him, never to enter it, you may leave the old dead world in which you once lived, and live in newness of life.

We have a third text remaining—the first Epistle of Peter, fifth chapter and fourth verse. Here you have the Saviour called the *chief* Shepherd. When is this? In Peter he is not the good Shepherd—he is not the great Shepherd—he is all that, but he is a great deal more—he is the chief Shepherd. When will he wear this title? Do you notice, beloved, this one thing; let me have your hearts here. While he is the good Shepherd he is all alone, no other mentioned; while he is the great Shepherd he is still alone, and only a bare hint of others, but when he is the chief Shepherd, it is implied that there are others among whom he is chief. Notice, then, that in the atonement Jesus is alone—there is no one with the good Shepherd: in resurrection for our justification he is alone—no one aids the great Shepherd: but at the second advent he will be with his people chief among many. Read the verse: "And when the chief Shepherd shall appear, ye shall receive a crown of glory that fadeth not away." So you see Christ is the *chief* Shepherd at the second advent; then shall the world be astonished to find that though alone in atonement, and alone in justification, he is not alone in service or in glory. Then every minister who has fed his sheep, every teacher who has fed his lambs—all of you, holy men and women, who have in any way whatever contributed under him towards the guidance, and the government, and the feeding, and the protection of his dear, blood-bought flock—you shall appear. He has no crown, you perceive, as the good Shepherd; we do not read of a crown for him as the great Shepherd, but when he comes with the crown wherewith his mother crowned him, then shall ye also appear with him in glory, having the crown of life that fadeth not away. I do not know whether this peculiar circumstance interests you, but it did me when I observed it: *Good* in his dying, *great* in his rising, *chief* in his coming. It seems to me to gather such force—*good* to me as a sinner, *great* to me as a saint, *chief* to me as one with him in his glorious reign. I pass, as it were, through three stages—a sinner, then I look to the good Shepherd laying down his life for the sheep; I reach higher ground, and I am a saint, I look to the great Shepherd to make me perfect in every good work to do his will; I mount higher still, I die, I rise again, I walk in resurrection life, and now I look to the chief Shepherd, and hope to receive at his hands the crown of life which he shall give to me, and not to me only, but unto all them that love his appearing, the good, great, chief Shepherd. May God give us grace, meditating upon these things, to know them and enter into them.

III. In conclusion I promised one or two IMPRESSIVE APPLICATIONS.

The first application is one of *comfort and satisfaction* to you who are poor, needy, weary, troubled lambs or sheep of the flock. Our own text runs thus, "He shall feed his flock like a shepherd." What next? "He shall gather the lambs with his arms, and carry them in his bosom, and shall gently lead those that are with young." The lambs have not the value of mature sheep, yet they are the most thought of under the great Shepherd. They might fetch the least price in the market, but they have the greatest portion of his heart. You needy, troubled ones, I want you to look here and note down in your memories that though there are promises for all saints, there are special promises for you. Jesus Christ will take care that the lambs and those who are with young, shall be specially housed. Notice this in Jacob, whom I introduced to you as the toiling shepherd; when he met with Esau, Esau wanted him to accept a guard to go with him, but he said, "My lord knoweth that the children are tender, and the flocks and herds with young are with me: and if men should overdrive them one day, all the flock will die." Jesus, the good Shepherd, will not travel at such a rate as to overdrive the lambs. He has tender consideration for the poor and needy. Kings usually look to the interests of the great, and the rich, but in the kingdom of our great Shepherd, he cares most for the poor. "He shall judge the poor of the people." The weaklings and the sickly of the flock are the special objects of the Saviour's care. A proof of this you find at the thirty-fourth chapter of Ezekiel, sixteenth verse, "I will seek that which was lost, and bring again that which was driven away, and I will bind up that which was broken, and I will strengthen that which was sick." Inexpressibly comforting words to the broken, sick, needy, Christian! Thou thinkest dear heart, that thou art forgotten, because of thy nothingness and weakness, and poverty. This is the very reason why thou art remembered. There is a mother here this morning: she has seven children; I know what child she has been thinking of while we have been preaching. She has not been thinking of John, who is married and away, nor of Mary who is in health, nor of Thomas who is sitting by her side, but she has been thinking of the poor little one at home in bed, and she has wondered whether it has had any sleep this morning, and whether it has been well taken care of. You know that my guess is correct. Now Jesus Christ, our loving Shepherd, if he should forget those of us who are strong and in sound health, will be sure to recollect the sickly ones. He shall feed his flock like a shepherd: he shall gather the lambs with his arms and carry them in his bosom. He shall gently lead those that are with young.

A second application containing *comfort* and *warning* too. Sinner, to you our Lord Jesus Christ now represents himself as being a Shepherd who is come to seek and to save that which was lost. Here are his own words: "What man of you having a hundred sheep, if he lose one of them, doth not leave the ninety and nine in the wilderness and go after that which is lost, until he find it? And when he hath found it, he layeth it on his shoulders, rejoicing; and calleth together his friends and his neighbours, saying, Rejoice with me for I have found the sheep which was lost." Such is Jesus now, looking after stray sheep. Where are you, where are you this morning? The great Shepherd comes after you, and oh, what joy will be in his heart, what joy there will be in heaven when the great Shepherd shall throw you on his shoulders and bring you home.

But hark you. Did you ever notice that the same Shepherd who saves the lost, will curse the finally impenitent? He shall separate them one from another as a shepherd divideth his sheep from the goats, and he shall set the sheep on his right hand, but the goats on the left. Then shall he say unto them on the left hand, "Depart ye cursed." What lips are those which pronounce those dreadful words? The

Shepherd's lips; the lips of that same Shepherd who flies over the mountains to the lost sheep, of whom I trust it will yet be said, "We were as sheep going astray, but we have now returned unto the Shepherd and Bishop of our souls." That same seeker of the lost and gatherer together of them that are scattered, will say, Depart ye cursed into everlasting fire in hell prepared for the devil and his angels. Oh, sinner, may you know the Shepherd as binding up your broken bones and healing your wounds, and rejoicing over your saved soul, for if you do not, you will have to know him in another and more terrible character, when he shall curse you, separating you from his own sheep as the Shepherd divideth the sheep from the goats.

So we shall conclude with these words, which may be for both *saint and sinner*. Let it never be forgotten, that in all we have said about Jesus Christ, still, as a Shepherd, he is pre-emiently to be preached as the suffering One. I began with Abel and I must conclude with Abel. Zechariah has recorded these remarkable words of Jehovah, "Awake, O sword, against my shepherd, and against the man that is my fellow, saith the Lord. Smite the shepherd, and the sheep shall be scattered." O sinner, you have most of all to do to-day with the Abel-shepherd—with the Shepherd dead at the altar; with the Shepherd with his blood crying up to heaven, with the sword of Jehovah in his bowels. You shall know about the toiling-shepherd by-and-by; the Shepherd reigning in Egypt, the Joseph you shall know soon; the Shepherd of the separated flock, you shall follow ere long; the Shepherd reigning in Jerusalem, the David you shall rejoice to serve; but now you have to do with the Shepherd bleeding and dying. Hark to these words, and I have done: "All we like sheep have gone astray, we have turned everyone to his own way, and the Lord hath laid on him the iniquity of us all." Herein is Jesus to be seen, suffering, bleeding, dying, on yonder accursed tree. He is there, the Shepherd to whom if we look we shall live, and live for ever. God enable you to turn those poor eyes of yours which have been red with weeping over sin, or red with the drunkenness of wickedness, and see in Jesus Christ your iniquity put away, Jehovah reconciled, and your souls eternally saved. Amen.

Our Own Dear Shepherd

"I am the good Shepherd, and know my *sheep*, and am known of mine. As the Father knoweth me, even so know I the Father: and I lay down my life for the sheep "—John x. 14, 15.

As the passage stands in the Authorized Version, it reads like a number of short sentences with scarcely any apparent connection. Even in that form it is precious; for our Lord's pearls are priceless even when they are not threaded together. But when I tell you that in the Greek the word "and" is several times repeated, and that the translators have had to leave out one of these "ands" to make sense of the passage on their line of translation, you will judge that they are none too accurate in this case. To use many "ands" is after the manner of John; but there is usually a true and natural connection between his sentences. The "and" with him is usually a real golden link, and not a mere sound; we need a translation which makes it so. Observe also that in our Version the word "sheep" is put in italics, to show that it is not in the original. There is no need for this alteration if the passage is more closely rendered. Hear, then, the text in its natural form—

"*I am the good Shepherd; and I know mine own, and mine own know me, even as the Father knoweth me, and I know the Father; and I lay down my life for the sheep.*"

This reading I have given you is that of the Revised Version. For that Revised Version I have but little care as a general rule, holding it to be by no means an improvement upon our common Authorized Version. It is a useful thing to have it for private reference, but I trust it will never be regarded as the standard English translation of the New Testament. The Revised Version of the Old Testament is so excellent, that I am half afraid it may carry the Revised New Testament upon its shoulders into general use. I sincerely hope that this may not be the case, for the result would be a decided loss. However, that is not my point. Returning to our subject, I believe that, on this occasion, the Revised Version is true to the original. We will therefore follow it in this instance, and we shall find that it makes most delightful and instructive sense. " I am the good Shepherd; and I know mine own, and mine own know me, even as the Father knoweth me, and I know the Father; and I lay down my life for the sheep."

He who speaks to us in these words is the Lord Jesus Christ. To our mind every word of Holy Scripture is precious. When God speaks to us by priest or prophet, or in any way, we are glad to hear. Though when, in the Old Testament, we meet with a passage which begins with "Thus saith the Lord" we feel specially charmed to have the message directly from God's own mouth, yet we make no distinction between this Scripture and that. We accept it all as inspired; and we are not given to dispute about different degrees and varying modes of inspiration, and all that. The matter is plain enough if learned unbelievers did not mystify it; "all Scripture is given by inspiration of God, and is profitable for doctrine, for reproof, for correction, for instruction in righteousness" (2 Tim. iii. 16). Still, there is to our mind a peculiar sweetness about words which were actually spoken by the Lord Jesus Christ himself: these are as honey in the comb. You have before you, in this text, not that which comes to you by prophet, priest, or king, but that which is spoken to you by one who is Prophet, Priest, and King in one, even your Lord Jesus Christ. He opens his mouth, and speaks to you. You will open your ear, and listen to him, if you be indeed his own.

Observe here, also, that we have not only Christ for the speaker, but we have Christ for the subject. He speaks, and speaks about himself. It were not seemly for you, or for me, to extol ourselves; but there is nothing more comely in the world than for Christ to commend himself. He is other than we are, something infinitely above us, and is not under rules which apply to us fallible mortals. When he speaketh forth his own glory, we feel that his speech is not vain-glory; nay, rather, when he praises himself, we thank him for so doing, and admire the lowly condescension which permits him to desire and accept honour from such poor hearts as ours. It were pride for us to seek honour of men; it is humility in him to do so, seeing he is so great an One that the esteem of beings so inferior as we are cannot be desired by him for his own sake, but for ours. Of all our Lord's words, those are the sweetest in which he speaks about himself. Even he cannot find another theme which can excel that of himself.

My brethren, who can speak of Jesus but himself? He masters all our eloquence. His perfection exceeds our understanding; the light of his excellence is too bright for us, it blinds our eyes. Our Beloved must be his own mirror. None but Jesus can reveal Jesus. Only he can see himself, and know himself, and understand himself; and therefore none but he can reveal himself. We are most glad that in his tenderness to us he sets himself forth by many choice metaphors, and instructive emblems, by which he would make us know some little of that love which passeth knowledge. With his own hand he fills a golden cup out of the river of his own infinity, and hands it to us that we may drink and be refreshed. Take, then, these words as being doubly refreshing, because they come directly from the Well-beloved's own mouth, and contain rich revelations of his own all-glorious self. I feel that I must read them again;—"I am the good Shepherd; and I know mine own, and mine own know me, even as the Father knoweth me, and I know the Father; and I lay down my life for the sheep."

In this text there are three matters about which I shall speak. First, I see here *complete character.* "I am the good Shepherd." He is not a half shepherd, but a shepherd in the fullest possible sense. Secondly, I see *complete knowledge,* "and I know mine own, and mine own know me, even as the Father knoweth me, and I know the Father." Thirdly, here is *complete sacrifice.* How preciously that sentence winds up the whole, "and I lay down my life for the sheep"! He goes the full length to which sacrifice can go. He lays down his soul in the stead of his sheep; so the words might be not incorrectly translated. He goes the full length of self-sacrifice for his own.

I. First, then, here is COMPLETE CHARACTER. Whenever the Saviour describes himself by any emblem, that emblem is exalted, and expanded; and yet it is not able to bear all his meaning. The Lord Jesus fills out every type, figure, and character; and when the vessel is filled there is an overflow. There is more in Jesus, the good Shepherd, than you can pack away in a shepherd. He is the good, the great, the chief Shepherd; but he is much more. Emblems to set him forth may be multiplied as the drops of the morning, but the whole multitude will fail to reflect all his brightness. Creation is too small a frame in which to hang his likeness. Human thought is too contracted, human speech too feeble, to set him forth to the full. When all the emblems in earth and heaven shall have described him to their utmost, there will remain a somewhat not yet described. You may square the circle ere you can set forth Christ in the language of mortal men. He is inconceivably above our conceptions, unutterably above our utterances.

But notice that he here sets himself forth as a shepherd. Dwell on this for a moment. A shepherd is hardly such a man as we employ in England to look after sheep for a few months, till they are large enough to be slaughtered; a shepherd after the Oriental sort, such as Abraham, Jacob, or David, is quite another person.

The Eastern shepherd is generally *the owner* of the flock, or at least the son of their owner, and so their proprietor in prospect. The sheep are his own. English shepherds seldom, or never, own the sheep: they are employed to take care of them, and they have no other interest in them. Our native shepherds are a very excellent set of men as a rule —those I have known have been admirable specimens of intelligent working-men—yet they are not at all like the Oriental shepherd, and cannot be; for he is usually the owner of the flock which he tends. He remembers how he came into possession of the flock, and when and where each of the present sheep was born, and where he has led them, and what trials he had in connection with them; and he remembers this with the emphasis that they are his own inheritance.

His wealth consists in them. He very seldom has much of a house, and he does not usually own much land. He takes his sheep over a good stretch of country, which is open common for all his tribe; but his possessions lie in his flocks. Ask him, "How much are you worth?"

He answers, "I own so many sheep." In the Latin tongue the word for money is akin to the word "sheep," because, to many of the first Romans, wool was their wealth, and their fortunes lay in their flocks. The Lord Jesus is our Shepherd: we are his wealth. If you ask what is his heritage, he tells you of "the riches of the glory of his inheritance in the saints." Ask him what are his jewels, and he replies, "*They* shall be mine in that day." If you ask him where his treasures are, he will tell you, "The Lord's portion is his people. Jacob is the lot of his inheritance." The Lord Jesus Christ has nothing that he values as he does his own people. For their sakes he gave up all that he had, and died naked on the cross. Not only can he say, "I gave Ethiopia and Seba for thee," but he "loved his church, and gave himself for it." He regards his church as being his own body, "the fulness of him that filleth all in all."

The shepherd, as he owns the flock, is also *the caretaker*. He takes care of them always. One of our brethren now present is a fireman; and, as he lives at the fire-station, he is always on duty. I asked him whether he was not off duty during certain hours of every day; but he said, "No; I am never off duty." He is on duty when he goes to bed, he is on duty while he is eating his breakfast, he is on duty if he walks down the street. Any time the bell may ring the alarm, and he must be in his place, and hasten to the fire. Our Lord Jesus Christ is never off duty. He has constant care of his people day and night. He has declared it,—"For Zion's sake will I not hold my peace, and for Jerusalem's sake I will not rest." He can truly say what Jacob did. "In the day the drought consumed me, and the frost by night." He says of his flock what he says of his garden, "I the Lord do keep it; I will water it every moment: lest any hurt it, I will keep it night and day." I cannot tell you all the care a shepherd has over his flock, because his anxieties are of such a various kind. Sheep have about as many complaints as men. You do not know much about them, and I am not going to enter into details, for the all-sufficient reason that I do not know much about them myself; but the shepherd knows, and the shepherd will tell you that he leads an anxious life. He seldom has all the flock well at one time. Some one or other is sure to be ailing, and he spies it out, and has eye and hand and heart ready for its succour and relief. There are many varieties of complaints and needs, and all these are laid upon the shepherd's heart. He is both possessor and caretaker of the flock.

Then he has to be *the provider* too, for there is not a woolly head among them that knows anything about the finding and selecting of pasturage. The season may be very dry, and where there once was grass there may be nothing but a brown powder. It may be that herbage is only to be found by the side of the rippling brooks, here and there a bit; but the sheep do not know anything about *that*; the shepherd must know everything for them. The shepherd is the sheep's providence. Both for time and for eternity, for body and for soul, our Lord Jesus supplies all our need out of his riches in glory. He is the great storehouse from which we derive everything. He has provided, he does provide, and he will provide; and each one of us may therefore sing, "The Lord is my Shepherd; I shall not want."

But, dear friends, we often dream that we are the shepherds, or that we, at any rate, have to find some of the pasture. I could not help saying just now to our friends at our little prayer-meeting, "There is a passage in the Psalms which makes the Lord do for us what one would have thought we could have done for ourselves—'He maketh me to lie down in green pastures.'" Surely, if a sheep can do nothing else it can lie down. Yet to lie down is the very hardest thing for God's sheep to do. It is here that the full power of the rest-giving Christ has to come in to make our fretful, worrying, doubtful natures lie down and rest. Our Lord is able to give us perfect peace, and he will do so if we will simply trust to his abounding care. It is the shepherd's business to be the provider; let us remember this, and be very happy.

Moreover, he has to be *the leader*. He leads the sheep wherever they have to go. I have often been astonished at the shepherds in the South of France, which is so much like Palestine, to see where they will take their sheep. Once every week I saw the shepherd come down to Mentone, and conduct all his flock to the sea-beach. I could see nothing for them but big stones. Folk say that perhaps this is what makes the mutton so hard; but I have no doubt the poor creatures get a little taste of salt, or something which does them good. At any rate, they follow the shepherd, and away he goes up the steep hillsides, taking long steps, till he reaches points where the grass is growing on the sides of the hills. He knows the way, and the sheep have nothing to do but to follow him wherever he goes. Theirs not to make the way; theirs not to choose the path; but theirs to keep close to his heel.

Do you not see our blessed Shepherd leading your own pilgrimage? Cannot you see him guiding your way? Do you not say, "Yes, he leadeth me, and it is my joy to follow"? Lead on, O blessed Lord; lead on, and we will follow the traces of thy feet!

The shepherd in the East has also to be *the defender* of the flock, for wolves yet prowl in those regions. All sorts of wild beasts attack the flock, and he must be to the front. Thus is it with our Shepherd. No wolf can attack us without finding our Lord in arms against him. No lion can roar upon the flock without arousing a greater than David. "He that keepeth Israel shall neither slumber nor sleep."

He is a shepherd, then, and he completely fills the character—much more completely than I can show you just now.

Notice that the text puts an adjective upon the shepherd, decorating him with a chain of gold. The Lord Jesus Christ himself says, "I am the *good* Shepherd." "The *good* Shepherd"—that is, he is not a thief that steals, and only deals with the sheep as he bears them from the fold to the slaughter. He is not a hireling: he does not do merely what he is paid to do, or commanded to do, but he does everything *con amore*, with a willing heart. He throws his soul into it. There is a goodness, a tenderness, a willingness, a powerfulness, a force, an energy in all that Jesus does that makes him to be the best possible Shepherd that can be. He is no hireling; neither is he an idler. Even shepherds that have had their own flocks have neglected them, as there are farmers who do not well cultivate their own farms; but it is never so with Christ. He is the good Shepherd: good up to the highest point of goodness, good in all that is tender, good in all that is kind, good in all the directions in which a shepherd can be needed; good at fight, and good at rule; good in watchful oversight, and good in prudent leadership; good every way most eminently.

And then notice he puts it, "I am *the* good Shepherd." That is the point I want to bring out. Of other shepherds we can say, he is *a* shepherd; but this is *the* Shepherd. All others in the world are shadows of the true Shepherd; and Jesus is the substance of them all. That which we see in the world with these eyes is after all not the substance, but the type, the shadow. That which we do not see with our eyes, that which only our faith perceives, is after all the real thing. I have seen shepherds; but they were only pictures to me. *The* Shepherd, the real, the truest, the best, the most sure example of shepherdry is the Christ himself; and you and I are the sheep. Those sheep we see on yonder mountain-side are just types of ourselves: but we are the true sheep, and Jesus is the true Shepherd. If an angel were to fly over the earth to find out the real sheep, and the real Shepherd, he would say, "The sheep of God's pasture are men; and Jehovah is their Shepherd. He is the true, the real Shepherd of the true and real sheep." All the possibilities that lie in a shepherd are found in Christ. Every good thing that you can imagine to be, or that should be, in a shepherd, you find in the Lord Jesus Christ.

Now, I want you to notice that, according to the text, the Lord Jesus Christ greatly rejoices in this. He says, "I am the good Shepherd." He does not confess that fact as if he were ashamed of it, but he repeats it in this chapter so many times that it almost reads like the refrain of a song. "I am the good Shepherd": he evidently rejoices in it. He rolls it under his tongue as a sweet morsel. Evidently it is to his heart's content. He does not say, "I am the Son of God, I am the Son of man, I am the Redeemer"; but this he does say, and he congratulates himself upon it: "I am the good Shepherd."

This should encourage you and me to get a full hold of the word. If Jesus is so pleased to be my Shepherd, let me be equally pleased to be his sheep; and let me avail myself of all the privileges that are wrapped up in his being my Shepherd, and in my being his sheep. I see that it will not worry him for me to be his sheep. I see that my needs will cause him no perplexity. I see that he will not be going out of his way to attend to my weakness and trouble. He delights to dwell on the fact, "I am the good Shepherd." He invites me, as it were, to come and bring my wants and woes to him, and then look up to him, and be fed by him. Therefore I will do it.

Does it not make you feel truly happy to hear your own Lord say himself, and say it to you out of this precious Book, "I am the good Shepherd"? Do you not reply, "Indeed thou art a good Shepherd. Thou art a good Shepherd to me. My heart lays emphasis upon the word 'good,' and says of thee, 'there is none good but One, but thou art that good One.' Thou art the good Shepherd of the sheep"?

So much, then, concerning the complete character.

II. May the Holy Spirit bless the word still more, while I speak in my broken way upon the next point: THE COMPLETE KNOWLEDGE

The knowledge of Christ towards his sheep, and of the sheep towards him, is wonderfully complete. I must read the text again—" I kno mine own, and mine own know me, even as the Father knoweth me, and I know the Father."

First, then, consider *Christ's knowledge of his own, and the comparison by which he sets it forth:* "As the Father knows me." I cannot conceive a stronger comparison. Dost thou know how much the Father knows the Son, who is his glory, his darling, his *alter ego*, his other self—yea, one God with him? Dost thou know how intimate the knowledge of the Father must be of his Son, who is his own wisdom, ay, who is his own self? The Father and the Son are one spirit. We cannot tell how intimate is that knowledge ; and yet so intimately, so perfectly, does the great Shepherd know his sheep.

He knows their *number*. He will never lose one. He will count them all again in that day when the sheep shall pass again under the hand of him that telleth them, and then he will make full tale of them. "Of all that thou hast given me," says he, "I have lost none." He knows the number of those for whom he paid the ransom-price.

He knows their *persons*. He knows the age and character of every one of his own. He assures us that the very hairs of our head are all numbered. Christ has not an unknown sheep. It is not possible that he should have overlooked or forgotten one of them. He has such an intimate knowledge of all who are redeemed with his most precious blood that he never mistakes one of them for another, nor misjudges one of them. He knows their constitutions,—those that are weak and feeble, those that are nervous and frightened, those that are strong, those that have a tendency to presumption, those that are sleepy, those that are brave, those that are sick, sorry, worried, or wounded. He knows those that are hunted by the devil, those that are caught up between the jaws of the lion, and shaken till the very life is almost driven out of them. He knows their feelings, fears, and frights. He knows the secret ins and outs of every one of us better than any one of us knows himself.

He knows our *trials*,—the particular trial under which you are now bowed down, my sister ; our difficulties,—that special difficulty which seems to block up your way, my brother, at this very time. All the ingredients of our life-cup are known to him. "I know mine own, as the Father knoweth me." It is impossible to conceive a completer knowledge than that which the Father has of his only-begotten Son ; and it is equally impossible to conceive a completer knowledge than that which Jesus Christ has of every one of his chosen.

He knows our *sins*. I often feel glad to think that he always did know our evil natures, and what would come of them. When he chose us, he knew what we were, and what we should be. He did not buy his sheep in the dark. He did not choose us without knowing all th devious ways of our past and future lives.

> "He saw us ruined in the fall,
> Yet loved us notwithstanding all."

Herein lieth the splendour of his grace. "Whom he did foreknow, he also did predestinate." His election implies foreknowledge of all our ill manners. They say of human love that it is blind ; but Christ's love has many eyes, and all its eyes are open, and yet he loves us still.

I need not enlarge upon this. It ought, however, to be very full of comfort to you that you are so known of your Lord, especially as he knows you not merely with the cold, clear knowledge of the intellect, but with the knowledge of love and of affection. He knows you in his heart. You are peculiarly dear to him. You are approved of him. You are accepted of him. He knows you by acquaintance with you ; not by hearsay. He knows you by communion with you ; he has been with you in sweet fellowship. He has read you as a man reads his book, and remembers what he reads. He knows you by sympathy with you : he is a man like yourself.

> "He knows what sore temptations mean,
> For he has felt the same."

He knows your weaknesses. He knows the points wherein you suffer most, for

> "In every pang that rends the heart
> The Man of sorrows had a part."

He gained this knowledge in the school of sympathetic suffering. "Though he were a Son, yet learned he obedience by the things which he suffered." "He was in all points made like unto his brethren ;" and by being made like to us he has come to know us, and he does know us in a very practical and tender way. You have a watch, and it will not go, or it goes very irregularly, and you give it into the hands of one who knows nothing about watches ; and he says, "I will clean it for you." He will do it more harm than good. But here is the very person who made the watch. He says, "I put every wheel into its place ; I made the whole of it, from beginning to end." You think to yourself, "I feel the utmost confidence in trusting that man with my watch ; he can surely put it right, for he made it." It often cheers my heart to think that since the Lord made me he can put me right, and keep me so to the end. My Maker is my Redeemer. He that first made me has made me again, and will make me perfect, to his own praise and glory. That is the first part of this complete knowledge.

The second part of the subject is *our knowledge of the Lord, and the fact by which it is illustrated.* "And mine own know me, even as I know the Father." I think I hear some of you say, "I do not see so much in that. I can see a great deal more in Christ's knowing us." Beloved, I see a great deal in our knowing Christ. That he should know me is great condescension, but it must be easy to him to know me. Being so divine, with such a piercing eye as his, it is amazingly condescending, as I say, but it is not difficult for him to know me. The marvel is that I should ever know him. That such a stupid, blind, deaf, dead soul as mine should ever know him, and should know him as he knows the Father, is ten thousand miracles in one. Oh, sirs, this is a wonder so great that I do not think you and I have come at it yet to the full, or else we should sit down in glad surprise, and say,—This proves him to be the good Shepherd indeed, not only that he knows his flock, but that he has taught them so well that they know him ! With such a flock as Christ has, that he should be able to train his sheep so that they should be able to know him, and to know him as he knows the Father, is miraculous.

O beloved, if this be true of us, that we know our Shepherd, we may clap our hands for very joy! And yet I think it is true even now. At any rate, I know so much of my Lord that nothing gives me so much joy as to hear of him. Brethren, there is no boasting in this personal assertion of mine. It is only the bare truth. You can say the same; can you not? If anybody were to preach to you the finest sermon that was ever delivered, would it charm you if there was no Christ in it? No. But you will come and hear me talk about Jesus Christ in words as simple as ever I can find, and you cry one to another, "It was good to be there."

> "Thou dear Redeemer, dying Lamb,
> We love to hear of thee :
> No music's like thy charming name,
> Nor half so sweet can be."

Now mark that this is the way in which Jesus knows the Father. Jesus delights in his Father, and you delight in Jesus. I know you do; and herein the comparison holds good.

Moreover, does not the dear name of Jesus stir your very soul? What is it that makes you feel as if you wish to hasten away, that you might be doing holy service for the Lord? What makes your very heart awake, and feel ready to leap out of your body? What but hearing of the glories of Jesus? Play on what string you please, and my ear is deaf to it; but when you once begin to tell of Calvary, and sing the song of free grace, and dying love, oh, then my soul opens all her ears, and drinks in the music, and then her blood begins to stir, and she is ready to shout for joy! Do you not even now sing—

> "Oh, for this love let rocks and hills
> Their lasting silence break,
> And all harmonious human tongues
> The Saviour's praises speak.

> "Yes, we will praise thee, dearest Lord,
> Our souls are all on flame,
> Hosanna round the spacious earth
> To thine adorèd name?"

Yes, we know Jesus. We feel the power of our union with him. We know him, brethren, so that we are not to be deceived by false shepherds. There is a way nowadays of preaching Christ against Christ. It is a new device of the devil to set up Jesus against Jesus, his kingdom against his atonement, his precepts against his doctrines. The half Christ in his example is put up, to frighten souls away from the whole Christ, who saves the souls of men from guilt as well as from sin, from hell as well as from folly. But they cannot deceive us in that way. No, beloved, we know our Shepherd from all others. We know him from a statue covered with his clothes. We know the living Christ, for we have come into living contact with him, and we cannot be deceived any more than Jesus Christ himself can be deceived about the Father. "Mine own know me, even as I know the Father." We know him by union with him, and by communion with him. "We have seen the Lord." "Truly our fellowship is with the Father, and with his Son Jesus Christ."

We know him by love: our soul cleaves to him, even as the heart of Christ cleaves to the Father. We know him by trusting him—" He is all my salvation, and all my desire." I remember once feeling many questions as to whether I was a child of God or not. I went into a little chapel, and I heard a good man preach. He was a simple working-man. I heard him preach, and I made my handkerchief sodden with my tears as I heard him talk about Christ, and the precious blood. When I was preaching the same things to others I was wondering whether this truth was mine, but while I was hearing for myself I knew it was mine, for my very soul lived upon it. I went to that good man, and thanked him for the sermon. He asked me who I was. When I told him, he turned all manner of colours. "Why," he said, " Sir, that was your own sermon." I said, "Yes, I knew it was, and it was good of the Lord to feed me with food that I had prepared for others." I perceived that I had a true taste for what I myself knew to be the gospel of Jesus Christ. Oh, yes, we do love our good Shepherd ! We cannot help it.

And we know him also by a deep sympathy with him ; for what Christ desires to do, we also long to do. He loves to save souls, and so do we. Would we not save all the people in a whole street if we could ? Ay, in a whole city, and in the whole world ! Nothing makes us so glad as that Jesus Christ is a Saviour. "There is news in the paper," says one. That news is often of small importance to our hearts. I happened to hear that a poor servant girl had heard me preach the truth, and found Christ; and I confess I felt more interest in that fact than in all the rise and fall of Whigs or Tories. What does it matter who is in Parliament, so long as souls are saved ? That is the main thing. If the kingdom of Christ grows, all the other kingdoms are of small account. That is the one kingdom for which we live, and for which we would gladly die. As there is a boundless sympathy between the Father and the Son, so is there between Jesus and ourselves.

We know Christ as he knows the Father, because we are one with him. The union between Christ and his people is as real and as mysterious as the union between the Son and the Father.

We have a beautiful picture before us. Can you realize it for a minute ? The Lord Jesus here among us—picture him ! He is the Shepherd. Then, around him are his own people, and wherever he goes they go. He leads them into green pastures, and beside the still waters. And there is this peculiarity about them : he knows them as he looks upon every one of them, and they every one of them know him. There is a deeply intimate and mutual knowledge between them. As surely as he knows them, they know him. The world knows neither the Shepherd nor the sheep, but they know each other. As surely as truly, and as deeply, as God the Father knows the Son, so does this Shepherd know his sheep ; and as God the Son knows his Father, so do these sheep know their Shepherd. Thus in one band, united by mutual intercourse, they travel through the world to heaven. "I know mine own, and mine own know me, even as the Father knoweth me, and I know the Father." Is not that a blessed picture ? God help us to figure in it !

III. The last subject is COMPLETE SACRIFICE. The complete sacrifice is thus described,—"*I lay down my life for the sheep.*"

These words are repeated in this chapter in different forms some four times. The Saviour keeps on saying, "I lay down my life for the sheep." Read the eleventh verse: "The good Shepherd giveth his life for the sheep." The fifteenth verse: "I lay down my life for the sheep." The seventeenth verse: "I lay down my life, that I may take it again." The eighteenth verse: "I have power to lay it down, and I have power to take it again." It looks as if this was another refrain of our Lord's personal hymn. I call this passage his pastoral song. The good Shepherd with his pipe sings to himself and to his flock, and this comes in at the end of each stanza, "I lay down my life for the sheep."

Did it not mean, first, that he was always doing so? All his life long he was, as it were, laying it down for them; he was divesting himself of the garments of life, till he came to be fully disrobed on the cross. All the life he had, all the power he had, he was always laying it out for his sheep. It means that, to begin with.

And then it means that the sacrifice was actively performed. It was ever in the doing as long as he lived; but he did it actively. He did not die for the sheep merely, but he laid down his life, which is another thing. Many a man has died for Christ: it was all that he could do. But we cannot lay down our lives, because they are due already as a debt of nature to God, and we are not permitted to die at our own wills. That were suicidal and improper. With the Lord Christ it was totally different. He was, as it were, actively passive. "I lay down my life for the sheep. I have power to lay it down, and I have power to take it again. This commandment have I received of my Father."

I like to think of our good Shepherd, not merely as dying for us, but as willingly dying—laying down his life: while he had that life, using it for us; and when the time came, putting off that life on our behalf. This has now been actually done. When he spoke these words, it had not been done. At this time it has been done. "I lay down my life for the sheep" may now be read, "I have laid down my life for the sheep." For you, beloved, he has given his hands to the nails, and his feet to the cruel iron. For you he has borne the fever and the bloody sweat; for you he has cried "Eloi, Eloi, lama sabachthani;" for you he has given up the ghost.

And the beauty of it is that he is not ashamed to avow the object of it. "I lay down my life *for the sheep.*" Whatever Christ did for the world—and I am not one of those who would limit the bearings of the death of Christ upon the world—yet his peculiar glory is, "I lay down my life *for the sheep.*"

Great Shepherd, do you mean to say that you have died for such as these? What! for these sheep? Died for them? What! die for sheep, Shepherd? Surely you have other objects for which to live beside sheep. Have you not other loves, other joys? We know that it would grieve you to see the sheep killed, torn by the wolf, or scattered; but you really have not gone so far in love for them that for the sake of those poor creatures you would lay down your life? "Ah, yes," he says, "I would, I have!" Carry your wondering thoughts to Christ Jesus. What! What! What! Son of God, infinitely great and inconceivably glorious Jehovah, wouldst thou lay thy life down for men and women? They are no more in comparison with thee than so many ants and wasps, pitiful and obnoxious creatures. Thou couldst make ten thousand millions of them with a word, or crush them out of existence at one blow of thy hand. They are poor things, make the most you can of them. They have hard hearts, and wandering wills; and the best of them are no better than they should be. Saviour, didst thou die for such? He looks round, and says, "Yes, I did. I did. I laid down my life for the sheep. I am not ashamed of them, and I am not ashamed to say that I died for them." No, beloved, he is not ashamed of his dying love. He has told it to his brethren up yonder, and made it known to all the servants in his Father's house, and this has become the song of that house, "Worthy is the Lamb that was slain!" Shall not we take it up, and say, "For thou wast slain, and hast redeemed us to God by thy blood"? Whatever men may talk about particular redemption, Christ is not ashamed of it. He glories that he laid down his life for the sheep. *For the sheep*, mark you. He says not for the world. There is a bearing of the death of Christ towards the world; but here he boasts, and glories in the specialty of his sacrifice. "I lay down my life *for the sheep*,"—"instead of the sheep," it might be read. He glories in substitution for his people. He makes it his boast, when he speaks of his chosen, that he suffered in their stead—that he bore, that they might never bear, the wrath of God on account of sin. What he glories in, we also glory in. "God forbid that I should glory save in the cross of our Lord Jesus Christ, by whom the world is crucified unto me, and I unto the world!"

O beloved, what a blessed Christ we have who loves us so, who knows us so—whom we also know and love! May others be taught to know him, and to love him! Yea, at this hour may they come and put their trust in him, as the sheep trust to the shepherd! **We ask it for Jesu's sake.** Amen.

Behold the Lamb

"Behold the Lamb of God!"—John i. 36.

It is the preacher's principal business, I think I might say, his only business, to cry, "Behold the Lamb of God!" For this reason was John born and sent into the world, and such were the prophecies which went before concerning him. If he had been the most eloquent preacher of repentance, if he had been the most earnest declaimer against the sins of the times, he would, nevertheless, have missed his life-work, if he had forgotten to say, "Behold the Lamb of God." He did well when he baptized the repenting crowd, he spake nobly when he faced the Pharisees, and was a true hero when he rebuked Herod, but after all his chief errand was to herald the Messiah, to bear witness to the Son of God. What we have said of John we may say of every God-sent minister: he is sent to bear witness to the Christ of God, and whatever else he may do, if he do not this continually, habitually, earnestly, he is not fulfilling the errand for which his Master sent him, but has turned aside to baser ends. When any one of us who are called ministers shall die, and come before the Lord to give in our account, it will be a sorry thing for us if we can only say, "Lord, I have preached the dogmas of the church to which I belonged," unless we can also add that we have directed men to the living Saviour. Vain will it be to have argued with accurate logic, and persuaded with lofty rhetoric, unless we have uplifted Christ among the people. It will be idle to say, "I have preached against the scepticism of the times, I have rebuked the sins which raged around me, and have proclaimed what I knew of the glory of God in nature and in providence," for our chief and distinguishing work is to declare the name of the Lord Jesus and the power of his precious blood. As the stars called "the Pointers" always point to the Pole star, so must we always point to the Redeemer. Methinks the minister who has failed to cry, "Behold the Lamb of God," may expect at the last to be cut in pieces, and to have his portion with the tormentors.

I can scarce conceive a doom too terrible for the man who dazzled his hearers with oratorical fire works, when he ought to have lifted up the cross, and mocked immortal souls with the carved stone of his elocution when they were starving for the bread of heaven. Sermons without Christ condemn the preacher and delude the hearer. Sermons which do not point to Christ in them will be as hard to answer for as blasphemy or murder when the Judge is on his great white throne. It is cruel to amuse with trifles those whose souls are in jeopardy of eternal fire. Playing with men's souls is murderous work, and truly if the Lamb of God be not preached, the ministry is playing with souls, if not worse. John, however, most thoroughly discharged his life-work, for he was ever saying, "Behold the Lamb of God."

Notice in the text the attitude of the preacher, for it is very instructive. "Looking upon Jesus as he walked, John said, "Behold the Lamb of God!" The preacher's eye should be *upon* his Master while he points *to* his Master. They preach Christ best who see him best. John had his own eyes fastened upon Jesus, and therefore did he by his own example as well as by his word say, "Behold the Lamb of God." If you will take your place in a crowded street, and stand for a few minutes looking at a certain object in the heavens, or gaze upward as if something were there to be seen, you will soon find that without asking others to do the same a company will gather round you and begin to look in the same direction. Indeed, a vast crowd might be collected, by no other action than by you yourself gazing intently into the air. So John, in addition to his saying, "Behold the Lamb of God," was doing the best thing to attract others to behold him—when he fixed his own eyes on Jesus, with fixed wondering, admiring, adoring gaze. John had no eye for any one but "the Lamb of God that taketh away the sin of the world," and therefore his words had point and power in them. And note that John's eye was upon Christ, not only when Christ was coming to him, but as he walked by him. Well may the preacher have his Master before him when his Master is cheering him with his fellowship and honouring him with his presence; but, on this occasion, Jesus was walking alone, as though in meditation, with his eyes probably bent upon the ground. It was not meet that he should always be coming to John; he had done that once, and so had put an honour upon his servant, but this time he came not to him lest men should think that he had any dependence upon John, but he walked in quiet musing as though his thoughts were otherwise occupied. Nevertheless, the Baptist had not forgotten his Lord, but again pointed him out. If the Lord deny to the preacher his comfortable presence, if no light of fellowship shine forth from the brow of the Crucified, it is still ours whenever and wherever we preach to let the eye of faith realise Christ as present, and still to cry to others with a heart that palpitates in union with our words, "Behold the Lamb of God, which taketh away the sin of the world." Even when I preach in chains I would labour to honour Jesus, looking to him as the end and object of every word I utter.

It is mine to preach a Saviour in whom I believe, whom having not seen I love. I am looking to him now for everything, even as I would have you do. I see in him superlative beauties which I wish you to see, and I worship a divinity in him which I desire you to worship. I preach not to you an unknown God, or an untried Saviour.

There is something notable in our text as to the hearers. This was a brief but weighty sermon, worthy to be preached a thousand times. Nobody needs a new sermon when " Behold the Lamb of God " is the old one. John had delivered this same discourse before an assembled crowd; but now he had only two hearers, and those two were not unconverted persons; they were disciples of his own, and they were at least very near to the kingdom if not already in it. Yet to the solitary two and those already discipled he had only the same message to deliver, " Behold the Lamb of God." He was a man of rich mind and ready utterance, yet he kept to his one point in all companies. It is thought that if we go into the theatre to preach to the mob, we must be sure to preach Christ : let me ask you what subject would be fitter for an assembly of saints ? I pray you tell me. It has been said that he who preaches in the street ought to confine himself to the simple gospel : my brethren, in what place would that subject be inappropriate or unprofitable ? Paul knew nothing among the Corinthians save Jesus Christ and him crucified, the resolve is a safe one for all companies. In this respect some preachers know too much, and the sooner they join the holy know-nothings the better. Christ is appropriate as a subject for two disciples as well as for a thousand scoffers, for while he is the resurrection to those who are dead, he is also the life of those who have been already quickened. No subject is more sweet, more refreshing, more inspiriting, more sanctifying to the saint than the Cross of our dying Lord : the sinner needs it if he would be saved, but the saint requires it that he may persevere, advance, conquer, and attain perfection. Give me that harp and let my fingers never leave its strings, the harp whose strings resound the love of Christ alone. To harp upon the name of Jesus is the blessed monotony of a true ministry, a monotony more full of variety than all other subjects besides. When Jesus is the first, the midst, and the last, yea, all in all, then do we make full proof of our ministry. We do well when we are able to say, " of the things which we have spoken this is the sum, we have such an high priest who is set on the right hand of the throne of the Majesty in the heavens." May Christ be "all in all" in all our ministries, for so shall we prove that God hath called us to testify concerning his son Jesus.

This may serve as an introduction to our subject. Now let us take the text itself : John saith, " Behold Lamb of God."

And first let us behold Jesus, and *know him to be the Lamb of God.* It will be well to be fully assured upon that point, and heartily to accept the witness of God concerning his Son. When we have so done let us secondly behold Him, that is *contemplate Him*, and humbly and attentively view Him as the great propitiation, the true sacrifice for sin ; then thirdly, beholding Him again, *let us gather instruction from* the Redeemer's appearance as the Lamb of God ; and fourthly, let us behold Him, that is, *reverently adore Him* in his blessed capacity as the Lamb slain.

I. First then, let us behold our Lord, and LEARN THAT HE IS THE LAMB OF GOD.

What means the term, "the Lamb of God?" The Hebrews are accustomed to use the expression that a thing is "of God" when they mean that it is the greatest, the noblest, the chief of the kind. For instance, they call the cedars "trees of God," and the thunder is the "voice of God." So that we may understand in the first place by the expression "the Lamb of God" that Jesus is *the chief of all sacrifices,* the first of all offerings by which atonement is made to God for sin. And truly he is so. He stands above all others because he contains all others. All other sacrifices of God's ordaining were but pictures, representations, symbols, and shadows of himself. There is only one sacrifice for sin, there never was another and there never can be. All those offerings under the Aaronic priesthood which were presented because of sin were only representations of the One Sacrifice; they were that and nothing more. Jesus far excels them all. Beloved, if you want to see the lamb that Abel offered on the altar, the lamb because of which God accepted his faith, and had respect unto him, you must see Jesus Christ, for we are accepted in the Beloved. God hath respect unto any man who brings this sacrifice; but unto any who bring a bloodless sacrifice, such as the Cainites of Rome foolishly do when they offer the unbloody sacrifice of the mass, unto them God hath no respect, and never can have. The blood of Jesus once presented has for ever put away sin, and no further sin-offering can be brought. Whoever resteth in Jesus as the true and only sacrifice is accepted in his faith. If you desire to see the lamb which Noah offered when he came out of the ark, together with other sacrifices of which it is said that "The Lord smelled a sweet savour of rest," you must look to Jesus Christ; for the bullocks, and rams, and lambs of Noah all pointed to the one sweet savour offering of Christ Jesus offered upon the cross, where God and the souls of all believers meet in blessed union and find sweetest rest. This, beloved, is the Lamb of which Abraham spake when he said to Isaac, "My son, God will provide himself a lamb." And to-day if you would understand the paschal supper first of all spread on that dread night when the destroying angel went through Egypt and smote the first born of all her land, if you would know who it is whose blood is the true passover when it is sprinkled upon the conscience, and whose flesh is meat indeed when it is fed upon by the children of God, you must look to Jesus, for he is the Lamb of God's passover. And if, pursuing your studies, your thoughts should turn into the tabernacle of old, or into Solomon's Temple, and you should see each morning a lamb slaughtered and its blood poured out, and each evening the same sacrifice repeated, if you desire to know what was intended by the morning and evening lambs you will find that they were but lambs of men, lambs presented by men, but they pointed to the Lamb of God, in whom their teaching is all summed up. He is the substance of that of which they were but the shadow. Jesus is the Lamb of the morning slain from before the foundation of the world, and the Lamb of the evening offered up in these last days for his people. Thus might we speak of all other sacrifices, and show that in Jesus they are all fulfilled. Atonement for sin is truly and in very deed to be found in the Son of God. In him alone is there remission, for in his blood alone is there efficacy to satisfy the law.

Stern as the truth is, we ought never to flinch from repeating it, that sin cannot be put away under the moral government of God without punishment. This is a rule from which there is no variation, and there should be none, for if justice be left unsatisfied the foundations of society are out of course. Infinite wisdom has found for us a door of escape by the way of vicarious sacrifice, but that way does not violate justice. Seeing that we originally fell by the sin of another, namely, our representative Adam, God has seen fit that we should rise through the righteousness and sufferings of another, namely, Jesus, the second Adam. Because Jesus was one with his people, and their federal head, it was just to allow him to suffer in their stead, and he has so done. Apart from this, every man must bear his own burden of sin and punishment. The only possible way by which a man can be forgiven his sin is by that sin being punished in his legal representative—the Lord Jesus. Jesus has borne what every believing sinner ought to have borne in his own person, or an equivalent for it, sufficient to recompense the injury done to eternal justice. No other person could be a substitute for our sin, for no other is our head and representative before God, and yet himself innocent. There is none other name given under heaven by which we may be saved. The Lord Jesus is of God appointed, and provided to be the one vicarious sufferer, the true bearer away of the sin of the world by enduring its penalty in is own person, so that whosoever believeth in him is redeemed from the punishment of sin. That is the gospel. I would sooner state it in the most simple language than have the power to deliver an impromptu poem, though it should excel the productions of Homer or Milton. There is more of precious truth and priceless learning in that faithful saying that " Jesus Christ came into the world to save sinners " than in the most profound discourse, or the most stately epic. Be thankful that you have heard it, that there is forgiveness with God because Jesus Christ has become the Saviour of men. O fellow sinner, you may approach your God without being plunged into suffering yourself, or needing to bring a victim with you, for Jesus Christ has been brought as a lamb to the slaughter, and his soul has been made an offering for sin. Tremble not, but receive the reconciliation effected by the Lamb of God. Come boldly, for the way is open, and man is invited to approach his God.

Moreover, our Saviour is called the Lamb of God, not only, *par excellence*, because he is, beyond all others such ; but, secondly, because he is *the Lamb of God's appointing*. God from all eternity appointed the Lord Jesus. He was chosen and ordained to be the great Sacrifice for Sin. So was it decreed and written of him in the volume of the Book, that oldest of books, " I delight to do thy will O, God." In the fulness of time Jesus came to do the Father's will, and therefore it is plain that there was such a will to do, such a decree to fulfil. Jesus is elect, precious. Peter tells us that the Lord Jesus is " a lamb without blemish and without spot, who verily was foreordained from before the foundation of the world." Jesus is the choice of the Father. Our hearts rejoice that it is so, for when we rely upon Jesus Christ to save us we trust in one whom God has appointed to save his people. If as a poor guilty sinner I leave my sin upon Christ the Lamb of God, I leave it where God has bidden me cast, namely, on the appointed scapegoat; I rest in a sacrifice which God himself ordained of old to be the sacrifice for sin. O soul, there can be no question that if thou comest to the Father in the way in which he himself appoints thou comest acceptably; for if thou wert not accepted thou mightest well say, "O God, thou hast set forth Christ as a Saviour, and yet thou dost not save men through him. Thou hast bidden him say, 'Him that cometh to me I will in no wise cast out,' yet I have come and thou hast cast me out. This be far from thee, Lord." Such an event shall never happen. No human lips shall utter such a complaint. God's appointment is the guarantee of the acceptance of everyone that believeth in Jesus.

Thirdly. Christ is called the "Lamb of God" because *he is of God's providing*. The Father not only appointed his Son to be the sacrifice for sin, but he gave him freely to be such. Out of the bosom of God came Jesus Christ as love's richest benison. He is the Father's only begotten, God's dear Son, and to us "his unspeakable gift." "He spared not his own Son, but freely delivered him up for us all." "Herein is love, not that we loved God, but that he loved us, and sent his Son to be the propitiation of our sins." Men were bidden to provide the sacrifice under the law, but the one sacrifice of the Gospel is the gift of God. "This is the record that God hath given to us, eternal life, and that life is in his Son." It endears Jesus to us know that he is the dearest pledge of Jehovah's love to his chosen.

And then, fourthly. He is not only of God's appointing and God's giving, but he is of *God's offering*. Let us never forget that Jesus Christ was not presented to God by a human priest; there might then have been some mistake in the sacrifice. It was not left to the sons of Aaron to offer up this true sacrifice to God; that we may be quite sure that the offering was presented in fit order and in an acceptable way, it is written, "It pleased the Father to bruise him, he hath put him to grief. The Lord hath laid on him the iniquity of us all." God himself had a hand in the sufferings of his Son. What means that cry, "My God, my God, why hast thou forsaken me?" But that God himself had turned away from him, and so had brought his soul into the extremity of woe. What saith the Scriptures? Is it not the Father's voice which saith "Awake, O sword, against my Shepherd, and against the man that is my fellow." Oh, beloved, when I think of this, that God chose his Son to be the atonement, that he gave his Son, and then himself did, as it were like another Abraham, offer up his own Isaac, I feel that the sacrifice must be acceptable and all sufficient, so that he who rests in it, need not have a shadow of a doubt but that his soul is saved.

One other reflection here; this sacrifice is also of *God's setting forth* to the sons of men. Remember the text, "Whom God hath set forth to be a propitiation through faith in his blood, to declare his righteousness for the remission of sins that are past, through the forbearance of God." When we, as God's ambassadors, tell you of Jesus Christ, we do not so in our name but we do our Lord's bidding, and God himself by us is setting Christ forth, showing him, revealing him, exhibiting him, and bidding you come to him. "Behold," saith God "I have given him for a covenant to the people, a leader and commander to the people." This is God's will, that Christ should be made known to the ends of the earth. Everywhere Jesus is to be preached, whether men will bow before him or no. We are quite sure we are doing God's will when we are setting forth Christ, for we are bidden to go into all the world and preach him to every creature. Assuredly, what the Lord thus sets forth he intends to give to those who seek it. There are no mockeries with God. He does not exhibit bread and refuse it to the hungry, or set rainment before the naked and refuse it to them. Happy are the men who see Jesus set forth manifestly crucified among them, for they have good ground to hope in him.

Now then, sinner, look at this. Thou wantest to be rid of thy sin; thou art conscious of it this morning, and thou dost confess it with shame. Well then, God's way of pardoning thee is that thy sin be laid on Jesus. As far as thou art concerned, thou canst obtain all the merit of the great atonement of Calvary by a simple act of faith. As of old the Jew laid his hand upon the victim, and then the victim was his substitute, so if thou dost but lay thy trembling hand upon Christ, he suffered for thee; he was an atonement for thee, and what a blessed atonement! Let us rehearse that point again, he is the chief of all sacrifices, the sacrifice of God's ordaining, of God's bestowing, of God's presenting, and now of God's setting forth to thee. What more wouldst thou have? In order that all things might be of God in this matter, from first to last Jesus is the Lamb of God; is not this well? Jesus is God's own chosen Saviour, what can be better? On what surer ground wouldst thou wish to rest? O that thou wert led to receive him now to be thine for ever. Jesus is my all, and I am a man as thou art; why should he not be thine also?

I feel as if I could tarry here just a minute and pass round among all this audience, this one solemn question for each one to answer—wilt thou accept Jesus of Nazareth, the Son of God, to be unto thy soul the Lamb of God which taketh away thy sin? Come, what sayest thou? It is ours to point to him and to bear our witness, wilt thou accept our testimony? Truly he is a great God and a Saviour. We have trusted in him and we are not confounded. Oh, if the Spirit of God sweetly leads thee now to say from thy heart—

"My faith doth lay her hand
On that dear head of Thine,
While like a penitent I stand,
And there confess my sin—"

it is indeed well with thee both for time and eternity. Be of good cheer, thy sins, which are many, are forgiven thee! Go thy way, thou art accepted in the beloved! Thine iniquities are blotted out like a cloud: not one of them shall be mentioned against thee any more for ever. O blessed Spirit of God out of thy great mercy grant that many and many a heart may lay hold upon the Lord Jesus to this at this hour.

II. But now we must pass on to a second point. "Behold the Lamb of God," that is, let us CONTEMPLATE JESUS UNDER THAT CHARACTER. Let us meditate upon him for a few minutes and then let us constantly fix our thoughts upon him.

Jesus Christ, as the atoning sacrifice, ought to be *the principal* object of every believer's thoughts. There are other subjects in the world which we must think of, for we are yet in the body; but this one subject ought to engross our souls, and, as the birds fly to their nests so ought we, whenever our minds are let loose, to fly back to Jesus Christ. He should be the main topic of each day's consideration and of each night's reflection. We might, with truthfulness, transfer the words of the first psalm, and say, " Blessed is the man whose delight is in the Christ of God and who meditates in him both day and night; for he shall be as a tree planted by the rivers of water, that bringeth forth his fruit in his season; his leaf also shall not wither, and whatsoever he doeth shall prosper."

To meditate much upon the Lamb of God, is to occupy your minds with *the grandest* subject of thought in the universe. All others are flat compared with it? What are the sciences but human ignorance set forth in order? What are the classics but the choicest of Babel's jargon when compared with his teachings? What are the poets but dreamers, and philosophers but fools in his presence? Jesus alone is wisdom, beauty, eloquence and power. No theme for contemplation can at all equal this noblest of all topics,—God allied to human nature, God the Infinite, incarnate among sons of men, God in union with humanity taking human sin, out of love stupendous condescending to be numbered with the transgressors, and to suffer for sin that was not his own? O wonder and romance, if men desire ye, they may find you here! O love, if men seek thee, here alone, they may behold thee! O wisdom, if men dig for thee, here shall they discover thy purest ore! O happiness, if men pine for thee, thou dwellest with the Christ of God, and they enjoy thee who live in him. O Lord Jesus, thou art all we need!

"Such as find thee find such sweetness
Deep, mysterious, and unknown;
Far above all worldly pleasures,
If they were to meet in one."

Ye may search the heavens above and the earth beneath; ye may penetrate the secret mysteries to find out the callow principles and the beginnings of things, but ye shall find more in the man of Nazareth, the equal with God, than in all else besides. He is the sum and substance of all truth, the essence of all creation, the soul of life, the light of light, the heaven of heavens, and yet he is greater far than all this, or all else that I could utter. There is no subject in the world so vast, so sublime, so pure, so elevating, so divine; give me to behold the Lord Jesus, and my eye seeth every precious thing.

Brethren, no subject so well *balances the soul* as Jesus, the Lamb of God. Other themes disturb the mental equilibrium, and overload one faculty at the expense of others. I have noticed in theology that certain brethren meditate almost exclusively upon doctrine, and I think it is not severely critical to say that they have a tendency to become hard, rigid, and far too militant. It is to be feared that some doctrinalists miss the spirit of Christ in fighting for the words of Christ. God forbid I should speak against earnestly contending for the true faith, but still without fellowship with the living Saviour we may through controversy become ill-developed and onesided. I think I have noticed that brethren who give all their thoughts to experience are also somewhat out of square. Some of them dwell upon the experience of human corruption until they acquire a melancholy temperament, and are at the same time apt to censure those why enjoy the liberty of the children of God. Other brethren turn all their attention to the brighter side of experience, and these are not always free from the spirit of carnal security which leads them to look down upon trembling and anxious hearts as though they could not possess true faith in God. I think also that I have noticed that those who pay all their homage at the shrine of practical theology have a tendency to become legal, and to exchange the privileges of believers for the bondage of servants. This also is a grievous fault. But when a man takes Christ Jesus crucified to be his mind's main thought he has all things in one; doctrine, experience, and practice combined. As Canaan contained Carmel, and Sharon, and Eschol, and Hermon, so Jesus comprehends all good things. If "the Lamb of God that taketh away the sin of the world" be the object of our thoughts we have wine and milk, butter and honey, the fat of the kidneys, of wheat and oil out of the rock, all in one. "A bundle of myrrh is my beloved unto me," "a cluster of camphire in the vineyards of En-gedi."

>All human beauties, all divine
>In my beloved meet and shine.

Beloved, this indeed is *the most needful subject* of contemplation that can be brought before you. You may forget many other things without serious damage, and even upon important matters you may somewhat err and yet be safe; but you must live upon Christ, your souls must meditate on him, else you have left the bread from the feast and missed the water from the well. The crucified Saviour is as needful for our meditation as the air is for our breathing. The blood of Jesus is the life-blood of true religion; a bloodless faith is a lifeless faith. I stood yesterday by the little open grave of one of our orphans, and it said far more to me than I could say to those who mourned around it, for it reminded me that there is nothing worth living for beneath the sky, since all things are as a dream. Then I thought within myself as I looked on the poor orphan lads around me—yes, there is something to live for, to help the poor and train the young, and to make men holier and happier; but then I recollected that they too, like myself, were dying creatures, and therefore even the benefit received by them would also pass away. To live, then, for men is, as far as eternity is concerned, an unsatisfactory thing, unless there be some higher light in which to view it. But when the heart lives for Jesus it is not less philanthropic, for it loves men for his sake, but its object melts into the divine, for we love God when we love Jesus, since he is very God of very God. Beloved, this leads me to the very marrow of the matter; to believe in Jesus as divine is essential to real Christianity, and one of the distinguishing subjects of faith which separate Christians from other men. Individuals are to be found who possess great admiration for the prophet of Nazareth, but they know him not as the Son of God, or as the Lamb of God; they deny his divinity, and reject his atonement. With fair words and oily speeches they compliment his character, and bedaub his name with their worthless praises.

Yet they are not Christians, and the name is dishonoured when they wear it. Of late we have heard deniers of our Lord's divinity spoken of as Christian brethren; now, my common sense does not enable me to see how a man can be called a Christian who rejects Christ. Charity by all manner of means, but not falsehood. Union certainly, but not union in deadly error. Confederacy with those who do not believe Jesus Christ to be God, and deny his atoning sacrifice, is treason to the Lord of glory. Such persons may be excellent Mahometans, or Jews, or pure Theists, but they are not Christians ; and if they wrongly assume that title we ought not to concede it to them. In this matter he that is not with our Lord is against him, and he that gathereth not with him scattereth abroad. Without a distinct and hearty recognition of our Lord's deity and atonement, how can a man be a partaker of Christ at all? True Christians about these truths have no question ; Jesus is to them the Lamb of God that taketh away the sin of the world, and the Son of God, whom the world shall yet adore.

III. Now, let us pass on to a third run of thought, but indulge in it very briefly. Let us behold the Lamb of God, that is, GATHER INSTRUCTION FROM JESUS UNDER THAT ASPECT.

I beg you to gather some *doctrinal* instruction. If the sacrifice provided by God for human sin must be none other than the Son of God himself, then sin is a gigantic evil, and then necessarily the punishment of sin is stupendous too. I observe with pain the attempt that is made to lower the meaning of Scripture upon the subject of the penalty due to sin. It has been usually believed to be everlasting, but this is now denied, denied in the teeth of express Scriptures. Now, the moment we begin to mitigate our thought of hell's terrors we also lower our idea of sin's evil, and with it we also decrease our estimate of the Saviour. All things in the temple of truth are to scale. If you take the inch scale which now seems to be getting popular you diminish the dimensions throughout! A little hell involves a little atonement. But, to be consistent, grant a divine Saviour, an infinite sacrifice, and you grant the infinite demerit of sin and then the eternity of future punishment is seen to be consistent. All these truths in Scripture lean the one upon the other, and your judgment upon every other will be affected by your opinion of any one. Do not err I pray you. Uplift the Christ of God and believe in the Lamb of God as none other than "very God of very God" and have him in high reverence whatever that reverence may involve. What though your inmost soul be awed with the deepest dread and made to tremble at the fate of those who reject the Saviour and perish in their sins, yet seek not to save your feelings at your Saviour's cost.

Moreover, what a conception of the love of God, the gift of the Lord Jesus for our salvation gives us. Despite the terrible wrath of God against sin he loved the sinner so much that he gave his only son to die for his redemption ! Herein is love. Let us infer from that gift his willingness to answer prayer. "He that spared not his own Son but freely delivered him up for us all, how shall he not with him also freely give us all things." Let us also see herein sure proof of the security of the saints, for if Christ be the Lamb of God and no less than divine, how shall they perish for whom such a sacrifice was offered ? If it be the blood of the Son of God which has bought us, we must be most effectually redeemed beyond all fear of perishing. So far you get doctrinal truth from beholding the Lamb of God.

Now, if you desire *experimental* aid look to the Lamb of God also. Is there a heart here troubled with sin ? Do not meditate upon your sin hoping to find comfort from any consideration connected with it : as well look for heaven in hell. Do not look to your own resources for consolation,—as well search the Arctic ocean for tropical heat. " Behold the Lamb of God ! " Sin vanishes when the Saviour appears. Are you tormented with the power of sin ? Beloved, if you long to conquer sin within you, behold the Lamb of God ! Crucified, your sin shall be upon that cross where Jesus died. Contemplations of the Saviour are the death of sin, but no other weapon will destroy them. If you suffer to-day from personal affliction and need fresh strength to bear it, " Behold the Lamb of God ! His way was much rougher and darker than yours,—pluck up courage, he will bear you through. He is familiar with all your griefs, his pitying eye beholds your sorrows; and oh, if you are getting weary in the battle of life and tired of serving God, " Behold the Lamb of God ! " wrestling unto blood, and your courage will return. Reaper in the summer's heat, see him as he grasps the sickle with that pierced hand ! What strides he makes, how untiringly he labours till his bloody sweat falls on the ground. Up and do thy reaping too, working at his side. Builder in the house of God, if thou seest not the temple rising as thou couldst desire, lay not down thy trowel or thy mallet, but see the master-builder standing there with indefatigable perseverance following out his glorious design. Let not self-denial or self-sacrifice be hard when the Lamb of God is before thee. Let not perseverance be difficult, or shame, or scorn be hard to endure, or defeat, or death itself, be impossible to triumph in, when the Lamb of God is before them. He conquered upon Golgotha, perhaps thou wilt only conquer there. Only keep thine eye upon the Lamb of God and this will make thee strong to do and to endure.

I might thus continue urging children of God to their profit to look to the Lamb of God, but I shall only add this, that if at any time we grow discouraged about God's work, and are afraid that it will not succeed and so on, the very best encouragement for us is to Behold the Lamb of God. You get afraid that sin will conquer in your soul,— how can it, when Jesus died for you ? Sin seemed to win the day when Christ was dead, but he rose again, and so shalt thou rise, and thou shalt be more than a conqueror. And in this world, is it not a very weary business to be a minister of Christ to-day ? If I might have my choice I would sooner follow any avocation, so far as the comfort of it is concerned, than this of ministering to the sons of men, for we beat the air, this deaf generation will not hear us. What is this perverse generation the better for years and years and years of preaching ? Here is this land going back to the foul doctrines which its fathers would not bear : while those who know better act in concert and continue in fellowship with the priests of Rome. The world is not worth the preaching to—we have piped unto it, and it has not danced ; we have mourned unto it, but it has not lamented. It wants an Elias, a man of fire and thunder, to deal with such an age as this. But for all that, there is no room for discouragement, for the truth will win the day ; it is in the hand of one who cannot fail or falter. He shall not fail or be discouraged till he hath set judgment in the earth, and the isles wait for his law. The fight may seem to hang in the scales to-day, but the conquest is sure to come unto him whose right it is. He shall gather all the sceptres of kings beneath his arm in one mighty sheaf, and take their diadems from off their brows, and be himself crowned with many crowns, for God hath said it, and heaven and earth shall pass away, but every promise of his must and shall be fulfilled. Push on, then, through hosts of enemies ye warriors of the Cross. Fight up the hill, ye soldiers of Christ, through the smoke and through the dust. Ye may not see your banner just now, neither do ye hear the trumpet that rings out the note of victory, but the mist shall clear away, and you shall gain the summit of the hill, and your foes shall fly before you, and the King himself shall come, and you shall be rewarded who have continued stedfast in his service.

IV. Now the last thought was to be this. Behold the Lamb of God WITH REVERENCE. I will not dwell upon it for I have not time. Lift up your eyes and worship him now. He exists, he is as truly there in heaven as he was here on earth. Behold him, worship him, trust him, love him, for be this remembered, he will come ere long, and that which we shall have to dread if we are unbelievers will be the wrath *of the Lamb.* Read through the book of Revelations and you shall find there, I think, more than twenty times, the Lord described as a Lamb. The song is the " song of Moses and of the Lamb." Worship is given " unto the Lamb, for he is worthy." He it is that takes the book and looses the seven seals thereof, and it is the Lamb that shall come "to judge the quick and the dead." "Wherefore kiss the Son lest he be angry, and ye perish from the way while his wrath is kindled but a little." Worship him at this hour for he cometh ere long. As the Lord liveth before whom I stand, he will summon every one of you to his bar. Take heed that he be not an object of terror to you as he will be if you continue in unbelief, but turn unto him that he may be your joy and gladness in the day of his appearing. Amen.

The Lamb—The Light

"And the city had no need of the sun, neither of the moon, to shine in it: for the glory of God did lighten it, and the Lamb is the light thereof"—Rev. xxi. 23.

To the lover of Jesus it is very pleasant to observe how the Lord Jesus Christ has always stood foremost in glory from before the foundation of the world, and will do so as long as eternity shall last. If we look back by faith to the time of the creation, we find our Lord with his Father as one brought up with him. "When there were no depths, I was brought forth; when there were no fountains abounding with water. While as yet he had not made the earth, nor the fields, nor the highest part of the dust of the world. When he prepared the heavens, I was there: when he set a compass upon the face of the depth: when he established the clouds above: when he strengthened the fountains of the deep." He was that wisdom who was never absent from the Father's counsels in the great work of creation, whether it be the birth of angels or the making of worlds of men. One of the first events ever recorded in Scripture history is, "When he bringeth in the first-begotten into the world, he saith, let all the angels of God worship him." Such words were never spoken of any creature, but only of him who is co-equal and co-eternal with the Father, glorious for ever: the firstborn of every creature, the head of the household of God, the express image of his person, and the fulness of his glory. In the earliest periods of which we possess any knowledge, Jesus Christ stood exalted far above all principalities and powers, and every name that is named. When human history dawns, and the history of God's Church commences, you still find Christ pre-eminent. All the types of the early Church are only to be opened up by him as the key. It would have been nothing to be of the seed of Israel, if it had not been for the promise of the Shiloh that was to come; it would have been in vain that the sacrifices were offered in the wilderness, that the ark abode between the curtains, or that the golden pot which had the manna was covered with the mercy-seat, if there had not been a real signification of Christ in all these. The religion of the Jew would have been very emptiness if it had not been for Christ, who is the substance of the former shadows. Run on to the period of the prophets, and in all their prophesyings do you not see additional glimpses of the glory of Christ? When they mount to the greatest heights of eloquence do they not speak of him? Whenever their soul is carried up, as in a chariot of fire, is not the mantle left behind them a word telling of the glory of Jesus? They could never glow with fervent heat, except concerning him. Even when they denounced the judgments of God, they paused between the crashes of God's thunder to let some drops of mercy fall on man in words of promise concerning him who was to come. It is always Christ from the opening leaf of Genesis to the closing note of Malachi—Christ, Christ, Christ, and nothing but Christ. It is very delightful, brethren, when we come to such a text as this, to observe that what was in the beginning, is now, and ever shall be, world without end, Amen. In that millennial state of which the text speaks, Jesus Christ is to be the light thereof, and all its glory is to proceed from him; and if the text speaketh concerning heaven and the blessedness hereafter, all its light, and blessings, and glory, stream from him: "The Lamb is the light thereof." If we read the text and think of its connection with us to-day, we must confess that all our joy and peace flow from the same fountain. Jesus Christ is the Sun of Righteousness to us, as well as to the saints above.

I shall try then—though I am conscious of my feebleness to handle so great a matter—I shall try, as best I can, to extol the Lord Jesus, first of all, in the excellence of his glory *in the millennial state;* next, *in heaven;* and then, thirdly, *in the condition of every heavenly-minded man who is on his way to paradise*—in all these cases " the Lamb is the light thereof."

I. First, then, a few words concerning THE MILLENNIAL PERIOD.

We are not given to prophesyings in this place. There are some of our brethren who delight much in them. Perhaps it is well that there should be some who should devote their time and thoughts to that portion of God's Word which abounds in mysteries; but for our part, we have been so engaged in seeking to win souls, and in endeavouring to contend with the common errors of the day, that we have scarcely ventured to land upon the rock of Patmos, or to peer into the dark recesses of Daniel and Ezekiel. Yet this much we have ever learned most clearly, that on this earth, where sin and Satan gained victory over God through the fall of man, Christ is to achieve a complete triumph over all his foes—not on another battle-field, but on this. The fight is not over. It commenced by Satan's attack upon our mother Eve; and Christ has never left the field from that day until now. The fight has lasted thousands of years; it grows sterner every day; it is not over; and it never shall be stayed until the serpent's head is effectually bruised, and Christ Jesus shall have gotten unto himself a perfect victory. Do not think the Lord will allow Satan to have even so much as one battle to call his own. In the great campaign, when the history shall be written, it shall be said, " The Lord reigneth;" all along the line he hath gotten the victory. There shall be victory in every place and spot; and the conquest of Jesus shall be complete and perfect. We believe, then, that in this very earth, where superstition has set up its idols, Jesus Christ shall be adored. Here, where blasphemy has defiled human lips, songs of praise shall rise from islands of the sea and from the dwellers among the rocks. In this very country, among those very men who became the tools of Satan, and whose dwelling-places were dens of mischief, there shall be found instruments of righteousness, lips to praise God, and occasions of eternal glory unto the Most High. O Satan, thou mayst boast of what thou hast done, and thou mayst think thy sceptre still secure, but he cometh, even he who rides upon the white horse of victory; and when he comes, thou shalt not stand against him, for the two-edged sword which goeth out of his mouth shall drive thee and thy hosts back to the place from whence thou camest. Let us rejoice that Scripture is so clear and so explicit upon this great doctrine of the future triumph of Christ over the whole world!

We are not bound to enter into any particulars concerning what form that triumph shall assume. We believe that the Jews will be converted, and that they will be restored to their own land. We believe that Jerusalem will be the central metropolis of Christ's kingdom; we also believe that all the nations shall walk in the light of the glorious city which shall be built at Jerusalem. We expect that the glory which shall have its centre there, shall spread over the whole world, covering it as with a sea of holiness, happiness, and delight. For this we look with joyful expectation. During that period the Lord himself by his glorious presence shall set aside the outward rites of his sanctuary. "The city hath no need of the sun, neither of the moon, to shine in it." Perhaps by sun and moon here, are intended those ordinary means of enlightenment which the Church now wants. We want the Lords' Supper to remind us of the body and blood of Christ; but when Christ comes there will be no Lord's Suppers, for it is written, "Do this until he come;" but when he comes, then will be the final period of the remembrance-token, because the person of Christ will be in our midst. Neither will you need ministers any longer, any more than men need candles when the sun ariseth. They shall not say one to another, "Know the Lord: for all shall know him, from the least to the greatest." There may be even in that period certain solemn assemblies and Sabbath-days, but they will not be of the same kind as we have now; for the whole earth will be a temple, every day will be a Sabbath, the avocations of men will all be priestly, they shall be a nation of priests—distinctly so, and they shall day without night serve God in his temple, so that everything to which they set their hand shall be a part of the song which shall go up to the Most High. Oh! blessed day. Would God it had dawned, when these temples should be left, because the whole world should be a temple for God. But whatever may be the splendours of that day—and truly here is a temptation to let our imagination revel—however bright may be the walls set with chalcedony and amethyst, however splendid the gates which are of one pearl, whatever may be the magnificence set forth by the "streets of gold," this we know, that the sum and substance, the light and glory of the whole will be the person of our Lord Jesus Christ, "for the glory of God did lighten it, and the Lamb is the light thereof." Now, I want the Christian to meditate over this. In the highest, holiest, and happiest era that shall ever dawn upon this poor earth, Christ is to be her light. When she puts on her wedding garments, and adorns herself as a bride is adorned with jewels, Christ is to be her glory and her beauty. There shall be no ear-rings in her ears made with other gold than that which cometh from his mine of love; there shall be no crown set upon her brow fashioned by any other hand than his hands of wisdom and of grace. She sits to reign, but it shall be upon *his* throne; she feeds, but it shall be upon *his* bread; she triumphs, but it shall be because of the might which ever belongs to him who is the Rock of Ages. Come then, Christian, contemplate for a moment thy beloved Lord. Jesus, in a millennial age, shall be the light and the glory of the city of the new Jerusalem. Observe then, that Jesus makes the light of the millennium, because *his presence will be that which distinguishes that age from the present.* That age is to be akin to paradise. Paradise God first made upon earth, and paradise God will last make. Satan destroyed it; and God will never have defeated his enemy until he has re-established paradise, until once again a new Eden shall bless the eyes of God's creatures. Now, the very glory and privilege of Eden I take to be not the river which flowed through it with its four branches, nor that it came from the land of Havilah which hath dust of gold—I do not think the glory of Eden lay in its grassy walks, or in the boughs bending with luscious fruit—but its glory lay in this, that the "Lord God walked in the garden in the cool of the day." Here was Adam's highest privilege, that he had companionship with the Most High. In those days angels sweetly sang that the tabernacle of God was with man, and that he did dwell amongst them. Brethren, the paradise which is to be regained for us will have this for its essential and distinguishing mark, that the Lord shall dwell amongst us. This is the name by which the city is to be called— Jehovah Shammah, the Lord is there. It is true we have the presence of Christ in the Church now—"Lo, I am with you alway, even unto the end of the world." We have the promise of his constant indwelling: "Where two or three are gathered together in my name, there am I in the midst of them." But still that is vicariously by his Spirit, but soon he is to be personally with us. That very man who once died upon Calvary is to live here. He—that same Jesus—who was taken up from us, shall come in like manner as he was taken up from the gazers of Galilee. Rejoice, rejoice, beloved, that he comes, actually and really comes; and this shall be the joy of that age, that he is among his saints, and dwelleth in them, with them, and talketh and walketh in their midst.

The presence of Christ it is which will be the means of the peace of the age. In that sense Christ will be the light of it, for *he* is our peace. It will be through his presence that the lion shall eat straw like an ox, that the leopard shall lie down with the kid. It will not be because men have had more enlightenment, and have learned better through advancing civilisation, that they shall beat their swords into ploughshares. It is notorious that the more civilised nations become the more terrible are their instruments of destruction; and when they do go to war, the more bloody and protracted their wars become. I venture to say, that if in a thousand years' time Christ shall not come, if war were to break out, where we now fight for ten or twenty years we shall have the venomous hatred of one another and the means of carrying on a war for a century. Instead of advancing in peacefulness, I do fear me the world has gone back. We certainly cannot boast now of living in halcyon days of peace. But Christ's presence shall change the hearts of men. Then spontaneously at sight of the great Prince of Peace, they shall cast away their armour and their weapons of war, and shall learn war no more. In that sense then, because his presence will be the cause of that happy period, he is the light of it.

Again, Christ's presence is to that period *its special instruction*. They shall need no candle, neither light of the sun, nor of the moon. Why? Because Christ's presence will be sufficiently instructive to the sons of men. When the Lord Jesus Christ comes, superstition will not need an earnest testimony to confute it—it will hide its head. Idolatry will not need the missionary to preach against it—the idols he shall utterly abolish, and shall cast them to the moles and to the bats. Men and women, at the sight of Christ, and at the knowledge that he is reigning gloriously upon earth, will give up their unbelief. The Jew will recognise the Son of David, and the Gentile will rejoice to worship him who was once slain as the King of the Jews. The presence of Christ shall do more for the enlightenment of his Church than the teaching of all her officers and ministers in all ages. She shall then in the sight of her Lord come to a fulness of knowledge, and have a perfect understanding of God's Word.

Once again, Christ will be the light of that period *in the sense of being its glory.* Oh! it is the glory of the Christian now to think that Christ reigns in heaven. In this we boast in every season of depression and of downcasting, that he is exalted and sits at the right hand of the Father. But the glory of that age shall be that Christ is come, that he sits upon the throne of David as well as upon the throne of God; that his enemies bow before him and lick the dust. Think, my brethren, of the splendour of that time, when from every nation and land they shall bring him tribute, when praises shall ascend from every land, when the streets of that city shall be thronged every day with adoring worshippers, when he shall ride forth conquering and to conquer, and his saints shall follow him upon white horses! We sometimes have high days and holidays, when kings and princes go abroad, and the streets are full, and people crowd even to the chimney-pots to see them as they ride along; but what shall it be to see King Jesus crowned with the crown wherewith his mother crowned him in the day of his espousals! What a contrast between the cavalcade winding its way along the streets of Jerusalem, along the *via dolorosa* up to the mount of execution— what a contrast, I say! Then women followed him and wept, but now men will follow him and shout for joy: then he carried his cross, but now he shall ride in state: then his enemies mocked him and gloated their eyes with his sufferings; but *then* his enemies shall be put to confusion and covered with shame, and upon himself shall his crown flourish: then it was the hour of darkness and the time of the prince of the pit, but now it shall be the day of light and the victory of Emmanuel, and the sounding of his praise both in earth and heaven. Contemplate this thought; and though I speak of it so feebly, yet it may ravish your hearts with transport that Christ is the Sun of that long-expected, that blessed day, that Christ shall be the highest mountain of all the hills of joy, the widest river of all the streams of delight, that whatever there may be of magnificence and of triumph, Christ shall be the centre and soul of it all. Oh! to be present and to see him in his own light, the King of kings, and Lord of lords!

II. And now we will turn our thoughts another way from the millennial period to THE STATE OF THE GLORIFIED IN HEAVEN ITSELF. "The city hath no need of the sun, neither of the moon, to shine in it."

The inhabitants of the better world are *independent of creature comforts.* Let us think that over for a minute. We have no reason to believe that they daily pray, "Give us this day our daily bread." Their bodies shall dwell in perpetual youth. They shall have no need of raiment; their white robes shall never wear out, neither shall they ever be defiled. Having food and raiment on earth therewith we are content, but in heaven "they toil not, neither do they spin: and yet I say unto you, That even Solomon in all his glory was not arrayed like one of these;" yet the fields yield them neither flax nor any other material for clothing, neither do the acres of heaven yield them bread. They are satisfied by leaning upon God, needing not the creature for support. They need no medicine to heal their disease, "for the inhabitant shall not say, I am sick." They need no sleep to recruit their fatigue, and although sleep is sweet and balmy—God's own medicine—yet they rest not day nor night, but unweariedly praise him in his temple.

They need no social ties in heaven. We need here the associations of friendship and of family love, but they are neither married nor are given in marriage there. Whatever comfort they may derive from association with their fellows is something extra and beyond, they do not need any: their God is enough. They shall need no teachers there; they shall doubtless commune with one another concerning the things of God, and tell to one another the strange things which the Lord hath wrought for them, but they shall not need this by way of instruction; they shall all be taught of the Lord, for in heaven "the glory of God doth lighten it, and the Lamb is the light thereof." There is an utter independence in heaven, then, of all the creatures. No sun and no moon are wanted—nay, no creatures whatever. Here we lean upon the friendly arm, but there they lean upon their beloved and upon him alone. Here we must have the help of our companions, but there they find all they want in Christ alone. Here we look to the meat which perisheth, and to the raiment which decays before the moth, but there they find everything in God. We have to use the bucket to get water from the well, but there they drink from the well-head, and put their lips down to the living water. Here the angels bring us blessings, but we shall want no messengers from heaven then. They shall need no Gabriels there to bring their love-notes from God, for there they shall see *him* face to face. Oh! what a blessed time shall that be, when we shall have mounted above every second cause and shall hang upon the bare arm of God! What a glorious hour when God, and not his creatures, God, and not his works, but God himself, Christ himself shall be our daily joy.

"Plunged in the Godhead's deepest sea,
And lost in His immensity."

Our souls shall then have attained the perfection of bliss.

While in heaven, it is clear that the glorified are quite independent of creature aid, do not forget that *they are entirely dependent for their joy upon Jesus Christ.* He is their sole spiritual light. They have nothing else in heaven to give them perfect satisfaction but himself. The language here used, "the Lamb is the light thereof," may be read in two or three ways. By your patience, let us so read it.

In heaven Jesus is the light in the sense of *joy*, for light is ever in Scripture the emblem of joy. Darkness betokens sorrow, but the rising of the sun indicates the return of holy joy. Christ is the joy of heaven. Do they rejoice in golden harps, in palm branches and white robes? They may do so, but they only rejoice in these things as love-gifts from *him*. Their joy is compounded of this—"Jesus chose us, Jesus loved us, Jesus brought us, Jesus washed us, Jesus robed us, Jesus kept us, Jesus glorified us; here we are, entirely through the Lord Jesus—through him alone." Each one of these thoughts shall be to them like a cluster from the vines of Eshcol. Why methinks there is an eternal source of joy in that one thought, "Jesus bought me with his blood." Oh! to sit on the mountains of heaven and look across to the lowly hill of Calvary, and see the Saviour bleed! What emotions of joy shall stir the depths of our soul, when we reflect that there upon the bloody tree he counted not his life dear unto him that he might redeem us unto God.

> "Calvary's summit shall I trace,
> View the heights and depths of grace,
> Count the purple drops, and say,
> 'Thus my sins were washed away.'"

In glory they think of the character and person of Jesus, and these are wells of delight to them. Thus they muse—Jesus is eternal God; his enemies reviled him, but still he is God. Jesus became the virgin's child; Jesus lived a life of holiness, and Jesus died; but see what triumph springs from his condescension and his shame: he rises, he ascends, and leads captivity captive; he scatters gifts amongst men; he reigns over earth, and hell, and heaven; King of kings, and Lord of lords. "The government shall be upon his shoulder: and his name shall be called Wonderful, the Counseller, The mighty God, The everlasting Father, The Prince of Peace." When I have listened to Handel's music in "The Messiah," where that great musician wakes every instrument to praise the name of Jesus, I have felt ready to die with excess of delight that such music should ever have been composed by mortal man to the honour of our great Messiah; but what will be the music of celestial choirs? How would such hearts as ours burst, and such souls as ours leap out of their bodies, if they could but know while here, such joys as celestials know above. But, beloved, our faculties shall be strengthened, our capacities shall be enlarged, our whole being shall be expanded, and thus we shall be able to bear the full swell of seraphic music, and join in it without fainting from delight, while they sing of the glory of the Son of Man—the Son of God. Christ is the light of heaven, then, because he is the substance of its joy.

Light may be viewed in another sense. Light is the cause of *beauty*. That is obvious to you all. Take the light away, and there is no beauty anywhere. The fairest woman charms the eye no more than a heap of ashes when the sun has departed. Your garden may be gay with many coloured flowers, but when the sun goeth down you cannot know them from the grass which borders them. You look upon the trees, all fair with the verdure of summer, but when the sun goes down they are all hung in black. Without light no radiance flashes from the sapphire, no peaceful ray proceedeth from the pearl. There is nought of beauty left when light is gone. Light is the mother of beauty. In such sense the Lord God Almighty and the Lamb are the light of heaven; that is to say, all the beauty of the saints above comes from God incarnate. Their excellence, their joy, their triumph, their glory, their ecstatic bliss, all spring from him. As planets, they reflect the light of the Sun of Righteousness; they live as beams proceeding from the central orb, as streams leaping from the eternal fountain. If he withdrew, they must die; if his glory were veiled, their glory must expire. Think of this, Christian, and I am sure you will be reminded how true this is beneath the sky, as well as above, that if light be the mother of beauty, Christ is the light; there is nothing good, nor comely, nor gracious about any one of us, except as we get it from Christ, and from Christ Jesus alone. "The Lamb is the light thereof."

Another meaning of light in Scripture is *knowledge*. Ignorance is darkness. Now, in heaven they need no candle, neither light of the sun, because they receive light enough from Christ, Christ being the fountain of all they know. I think it is Dr. Dick who speaks about the enjoyments of heaven, consisting very likely in going from star to star, and viewing the works of God in different portions of his universe, admiring the anatomy of living creatures, studying geology, ferrying across the waving of ether, and voyaging from world to world. I do not believe in such a heaven for a moment. I do not conceive it a worthy employment for immortal spirits, and, if there were nothing else to make me think so, the text would be enough. "And the city had no need of the sun, neither of the moon, to shine in it." There is no need of the works of God to give instruction to its inhabitants, "for the glory of God did lighten it." The glory, not of God's works, but of God's Son, is their glorious light.

> "The spacious earth and spreading flood
> Proclaim the wise and powerful God;
> And thy rich glories from afar
> Sparkle in every rolling star.
>
> But in his looks a glory stands,
> The noblest labour of thy hands;
> The pleasing lustre of his eyes
> Outshines the wonders of the skies."

They need no light of the sun and moon where Jesus is. However well the sun and moon may tell of God, we shall not want them from day to day to send forth their line throughout all the earth, and their word unto the end of the world, for the glory of Christ will teach us all we wish to learn; and beholding the unveiled glory of God will be better far than prying into the works of nature, even though we had an angel's power of discovery. We shall know more of Christ in five minutes, I ween, when we get to heaven, than we shall know in all our years on earth. Dr. Owen was a master of theology, but the smallest child who goes to heaven from a Sunday-school knows more of Christ after being in heaven five minutes, than Dr. Owen did. John Calvin searched very deep, and Augustine seemed to come to the very door of the great secret; but Augustine and Calvin would be but children on the first form there—I mean if they knew no more than on earth. Oh! what manifestations of God there will be! Dark dealings of providence which you never understood before will then be seen without the light of a candle or of the sun. Many doctrines puzzled you, and you could not find the clue to the labyrinth of mystery; but there all will be simple and plain, so that the wayfaring man may run and understand it. You have had many experiences and tossings to and fro, and you have felt your ignorance, your corruption and weakness; but there you shall see to the very bottom of human nature, you shall understand the virulence of man's depravity, and the heights of God's sovereignty, the marvels of his electing love, and the magnificence of his divine power, by which he has made us to be partakers of the divine nature.

> "There you shall see and hear and know
> All you desired or wished below,
> And every power find sweet employ
> In that eternal world of joy."

And this knowledge, I say, shall not come from any inferior agent, but from the Lord God who shall be your glory, and from Jesus Christ himself who shall teach you all truth.

I must not dwell longer on this point except to say this one thing, that light also means *manifestation*. "Every one that doeth evil hateth the light, neither cometh to the light, lest his deeds should be reproved. But he that doeth truth cometh to the light, that his deeds may be made manifest, that they are wrought in God." Light manifests. In this world it doth not yet appear how great we must be made. God's people are a hidden people—their life is hid with Christ in God. They possess God's secret, and that secret other men cannot discover. Christ in heaven is the great revealer of God's mind; and when he gets his people there, he will touch them with the wand of his own love, and change them into the image of his manifested glory. They were poor and wretched, but what a transformation! Their rags drop off and they are acknowledged as princes. They were stained with sin and infirmity, but one touch of his finger, and they are bright as the sun, and clear as crystal, transformed even as he was upon Mount Tabor, whiter than any fuller can make them. They were ignorant and weak on earth, but when he shall teach them, they shall know even as they are known. They were buried in dishonour, but they are raised in glory; they were sown in the grave in weakness, but they are raised in power; they were carried away by the hands of remorseless Death, but they arise to immortality and life. Oh! what a manifestation. Light is sown for the righteous, and Christ is the sacred rain that brings the harvest above ground. The righteous are always pearls, but they are hidden, as it were, in the oyster now, and Christ brings them forth. They were always diamonds, they were far away in the Golconda of sin; but Christ hath fetched them up from the deep mines. They were always stars, but they were hidden behind the clouds; Christ, like a swift wind, hath blown the clouds away, and now they shine like stars in the firmament for ever and ever. In this sense Christ is the light of heaven, because it is through him that the true and real character of all the saints has been manifested.

Come, my soul, take wing a moment—it is not far for thee to fly—mount thee and walk the golden streets, and as thou walkest thou shalt see nothing but Jesus glorified. Come up to the throne, and thou shalt see Christ on it. Sit down and listen to the song, Christ is the theme; go to the banquet, Christ is the meat; mingle with the dancers, Christ is their joy; make thou one in their great assemblies, and Christ is the God they worship:—

"'Worthy the Lamb that died,' they cry,
'To be exalted thus:'
'Worthy the Lamb,' our lips reply,
'For he was slain for us.'"

III. Let us turn to our last thought; and here I hope we can speak experimentally, whereas on the other two points we could only speak by faith in the promise of God. THE HEAVENLY MAN'S STATE MAY BE SET FORTH IN THESE WORDS.

First, then, even on earth *the heavenly man's joy does not depend upon the creature.* Brethren, in a certain sense we can say to-day that "the city hath no need of the sun, neither of the moon, to shine in it." We love and prize the happy brightness which the sun scatters upon us; as for the moon, who does not admire the fair moonlight when the waves are silvered, and silent nature wears the plumage of the dove; but we do not need the sun or the moon, we can do without them; for the Sun of Righteousness has risen with healing beneath his wings. There are brothers and sisters here this morning who are very happy, and yet it is long since they saw the sun. Shut up in perpetual night, through blindness, they need not the light of the sun, nor of the moon, for the Lord God is their glory—Christ is their light. If our eyes should be put out, we could say, "Farewell, sweet light, farewell, bright sun and moon—we prize ye well, but we can do without ye—Christ Jesus is to us as the light of seven days."

As we can do without these two most eminent creatures, so we can be happy without other earthly blessings. Our dear friends are very precious to us—we love our wife and children, our parents and our friends, but we do not need them. May God spare them to us! but if they were taken, it does not come to a matter of absolute need, for you know, beloved, there is many a Christian who has been bereft of all, and he thought, as the props were taken away one after another, that he should die of very grief; but he did not die, his faith surmounted every wave, and he still rejoices in his God. I know that at the thought of those dear ones who are taken from you, the sluices of your grief are drawn up, but still I hope you will not be so false to Christ as to deny what I now say, that his presence can make amends for all losses, that the smilings of his face will make a paradise so sweet, that no sorrow or sighing shall be heard in it.

"Thee, at all times, will I bless;
Having thee, I all possess;
How can I bereaved be,
Since I cannot part with thee?"

It is a very happy thing to be placed in circumstances where one knows no lack of bread—to have a house, a comfortable home, and sufficiency for our family is very pleasant: but O dear friends, if it comes to actual need, the Christian does not want this, he needs no sun nor moon even here. Look at the chosen sons of poverty—they toil from morning to night and never get a single inch beyond, just living from hand to mouth, but they are happy, ah! some of them infinitely happier than the rich man with all his sumptuous faring, and the fine linen with which he wraps himself. Why there have been men reduced all but to beggary who have rejoiced far more in their poverty than others in their wealth: we have seen some of God's saints in the workhouse, or lingering in a dark ill-furnished almsroom, and we have heard them speak as joyously about God and their state as if they were dwelling in mansions or palaces. Yes, many a poor child of God has learned to sing—

"I would not change my bless'd estate
For all the world calls good or great;
And while my faith can keep her hold,
I envy not the sinner's gold."

For "this city hath no need of the sun, nor of the moon, to shine in it, for the glory of God doth lighten it, and the Lamb is the light thereof." *Health* too—who can prize it enough? When stretched upon the bed of sickness, then we begin to know how priceless a boon was a sound body, but ah! the Christian, though he loves health, can do without it. I have heard of Christians who have been blind, and who have been bedridden and have not stirred from their bed for many years, who could scarcely lift their hands through paralysis, and who never had stood upon their feet for years, through some stroke of God's hand, yet have they delighted themselves in the Lord. They have laid there ill-nursed, ill-cared for—simply living to illustrate to what degree a mortal man may become a mass of suffering and a prodigy of grief, and yet as I have sometimes stood by such bed-sides, I have heard more rapturous expressions concerning present joy and future prospects, than from God's strongest saints in their healthiest hours. The dying girl, when consumption has paled her cheek and taken the flesh from off her poor aching bones, has nevertheless appeared in a sacred majesty of might which showed me that she needed no moon nor sun to lighten her, no health nor strength to give her spirits, for the presence of Christ made her conqueror in the extremity of weakness, and victorious in the grim presence of Death itself. The Christian then, dear friends, leans upon the arm of God—he has pressed through the crowd of creatures—he has bidden them all retire that he might live nearer to his all-sufficient Lord, and if when he has reached his Lord the creatures turn their backs and go away, he saith, " There, ye may all go; I have him now; I embrace him now; he hath kissed me with the kisses of his lips; ye may spit on me and ye will; now *he* has spoken softly to me ye may curse me if ye please; now that he has told me I am his and he is mine, even my father and mother may forsake me, for the Lord hath taken me up." Yes, the heavenly man, even before he gets to heaven hath no need of the sun nor of the moon, for the glory of God doth lighten him.

We finish by observing that such a man, however, has great need of

Christ—he cannot get on without Christ. O beloved, if the sun were struck from the spheres, what a poor, dark, dreary world this would be. We should go groping about it, longing for the grave; but that would be nothing compared with our misery if Christ were taken away. O Christian man, what would you do without a Saviour? We should be of all men the most miserable—we who have once known him. Ah! you who do not know Christ, you can get on pretty well without him, like a poor slave who has never known liberty, and rests content in bondage. The bird in its cage, which never did fly over the fields, which has been born in the cage, can be pretty easy; but after we have once stretched our wings, and once know what liberty means, we cannot be shut out from our Lord. As the dove mourns itself to death when its mate is taken away, so should we if Christ were gone. We can do without light, without friendship, without life, but we cannot live without our Saviour. Oh! to be without Christ! My soul, what wouldst thou do in the world without him, in the midst of its temptations and its cares? What wouldst thou do in the morning without him, when thou wakest up and lookest forward to the day's battle? What wouldst thou do if he did not put his hand upon thee, and say, "Fear not, I am with thee?" And what wouldst thou do at night, when thou comest home jaded and weary, if there were no prayer, no door of access between thee and Christ? What should we do without Christ in our trials, our sicknesses? What should we do when we come to die, with no one to make our dying bed feel soft as downy pillows are? Oh! if the infidel's laugh has truth in it, it may well ring bitterly in our ears, for it were a bitter truth to us. No Christ! Then to die indeed is dreadful. To have such high hopes, and to have them all blasted; such high, loud boastings, and to have our mouths stopped for ever! But, beloved, we need not suppose such a thing, for we know that our Redeemer liveth, and we know that he never forsakes the work of his own hand. Married as he is to our souls, he will never sue out a divorce against any one of his dear people, but he will hold, and keep, and bless us till we die; and we on our part will confess of our spiritual life that the Lamb is the light thereof. Of every day and every night, of every joy and every sorrow, the Lamb has been until now our light, and shall be till we die.

If this be so, how dark is the case of those who do not know the Lamb! In what misery and ignorance do you grope who do not know the Saviour! Would you know Christ, would you have the happiness of resting upon his bosom? Trust him, then, for whosoever trusteth him is saved. To trust Christ is that saving faith which brings the soul out of condemnation. "He that believeth on him is not condemned." Trust thou, guilty as thou art, trust thou to his atonement, and it shall wash thee; trust to his power, it shall prevail for thee; trust to his wisdom, it shall protect thee; trust to his heart, it shall love thee, world without end. Amen.

The Lamb in Glory

"And I beheld, and, lo, in the midst of the throne and of the four living creatures, and in the midst of the elders, stood a Lamb as it had been slain, having seven horns and seven eyes, which are the seven Spirits of God sent forth into all the earth. And he came and took the book out of the right hand of him that sat upon the throne "—Revelation v. 6, 7.

THE apostle John had long known the Lord Jesus as the Lamb. That was his first view of him, when the Baptist, pointing to Jesus, said, " Behold the Lamb of God, which taketh away the sin of the world." He had been very familiar with this blessed personage, having often laid his head upon his bosom, feeling that this tender goodness of the Saviour proved him to be in nature gentle as a lamb. He had beheld him when he was brought " as a lamb to the slaughter," so that the idea was indelibly fixed upon his mind that Jesus, the Christ, was the Lamb of God. He knew that he was the appointed sacrifice, set forth in the morning and evening Lamb, and in the Paschal Lamb, by whose blood Israel was redeemed from death. In his last days the beloved disciple was to see this same Christ, under the same figure of a lamb, as the great revealer of secrets, the expounder of the mind of God, the taker of the sealed book, and the looser of the seals which bound up the mysterious purposes of God towards the children of men. I pray that we may have on this earth a clear and constant sight of the sin-bearing Lamb, and then, in yonder world of glory, we shall behold him in the midst of the throne and the living creatures and the elders.

The appearance of this Lamb at the particular moment described by John was exceedingly suitable. Our Lord usually appears when all other hope disappears. Concerning the winepress of wrath, it is he who saith, " I have trodden the winepress alone, and of the people there was none with me." In the instance before us, the strong angel had proclaimed with a loud voice, " Who is worthy to open the book, and to loose the seals thereof ? " And there was no response from heaven, or earth, or hell. No man was able to open the book, neither to look therein. The divine decrees must remain for ever sealed in mystery unless the once slain Mediator shall take them from the hand of God, and open them to the sons of men. When no one could do this, John wept much. At that grave moment the Lamb appeared. Old Master Trapp says, "Christ is good at a dead lift"; and it is so. When there is utter failure everywhere else, then in him is our help found. If there could have been found another bearer of sin, would the Father have given his Only-Begotten to die? Had any other been able to unfold the secret designs of God, would he not have appeared at the angel's challenge? But he that came to take away the sin of the world now appears to take away the seals which bind up the eternal purposes. O Lamb of God, thou art able to do what none beside may venture to attempt! Thou comest forth when no one else is to be found. Remember, next time you are in trouble, that when no man can comfort and no man can save, you may expect the Lord, the ever-sympathetic Lamb of God, to appear on your behalf.

Before the Lamb appeared, while as yet no one was found worthy to look upon that book which was held in the hand of him that sitteth on the throne, John wept much. By weeping eyes the Lamb of God is best seen. Certain ministers of this age, who make so little of the doctrine of substitutionary sacrifice, would have been of another mind if they had known more contrition of heart and exercise of soul. Eyes washed by repentance are best able to see those blessed truths which shine forth from our incarnate God, the bearer of our sins. Free grace and dying love are most appreciated by the mourners in Zion. If tears are good for the eyes, the Lord send us to be weepers, and lead us round by Bochim to Bethel. I have heard the old proverb, "There is no going to heaven but by Weeping Cross"; and there seems no way of even seeing heaven, and the heavenly One, except by eyes that have wept. Weeping makes the eyes quick to see if there be any hope; and while it dims them to all false confidences, it makes them sensitive to the faintest beam of divine light. "They looked unto him, and were lightened: and their faces were not ashamed." Those who have laid eternal matters to heart so much as to weep over their own need, and that of their fellow-men, shall be the first to see in the Lamb of God the answer to their desires.

Yet observe, that even in this case human instrumentality was permitted; for it is written, "One of the elders saith unto me, Weep not." John the apostle was greater than an elder. Among them that are born of women, in the Church of God we put none before John, who leaned his head upon his Master's bosom; and yet a mere elder of the Church reproves and instructs the beloved apostle! He cheers him with the news that the Lion of the tribe of Juda had prevailed to open the book, and to loose the seven seals thereof. The greatest man in the Church may be under obligations to the least: a preacher may be taught by a convert; an elder may be instructed by a child. Oh that we might be always willing to learn!—to learn of anyone, however lowly. Assuredly, we shall be teachable if we have the tenderness of heart which shows itself in weeping. This will make our souls like waxen tablets, whereon the finger of truth may readily inscribe its teaching. God grant us this preparation of heart!

May we come in a teachable spirit to the text, and may the Lord open our eyes to see and learn with John! It is no small favour that we have the record of the vision. Does not the Lord intend us to be partakers in it? The vision is that of a Lamb, a Lamb that is to open the book of God's secret purposes, and loose the seals thereof. The teaching of the passage is that the Lord Jesus, in his sacrificial character, is the most prominent object in the heavenly world. So far from substitution being done with, and laid aside as a temporary expedient, it remains the object of universal wonder and adoration. He that became a Lamb that he might take away the sin of the world, is not ashamed of his humiliation, but still manifests it to adoring myriads, and is, for that very reason, the very object of their enthusiastic worship. They worship the Lamb even as they worship him that sits upon the throne; and they say, "Worthy is the Lamb," because he was slain and redeemed his people by his blood. His atoning sacrifice is the great reason for their deepest reverence and their highest adoration. Some dare to say that the life of Jesus should alone be preached, and that no prominence should be given to his death. We are not of their religion. I am not ashamed of preaching Christ Jesus in his death as the sacrifice for sin; but, on the contrary, I can boldly say, "God forbid that I should glory, save in the cross of our Lord Jesus Christ." We do not so believe the doctrine of Atonement as to leave it in the dark as a second-rate article of faith; but we hold it to be the first and foremost teaching of inspiration, the greatest well of the believer's comfort, the highest hill of God's glory. As our Lord's sacrificial character is in heaven most prominent, so would we make it most conspicuous among men. Jesus is to be declared as the sin-bearer, and then men will believe and live. May God the Holy Spirit help us in our attempt this morning!

I. Jesus in heaven appears in his sacrificial character; and I would have you note that THIS CHARACTER IS ENHANCED BY OTHER CONSPICUOUS POINTS. Its glory is not diminished, but enhanced, by all the rest of our Lord's character: the attributes, achievements, and offices of our Lord all concentrate their glory in his sacrificial character, and all unite in making it a theme for loving wonder.

We read that *he is the Lion of the tribe of Juda;* by which is signified the dignity of his office, as King, and the majesty of his person, as Lord. The lion is at home in fight, and "the Lord is a man of war: the Lord is his name." Like a lion, he is courageous. Though he be like a lamb for tenderness, yet not in timidity. He is terrible as a lion, "who shall rouse him up?" If any come into conflict with him, let them beware; for as he is courageous, so is he full of force, and altogether irresistible in might. He hath the lion's heart, and the lion's strength; and he cometh forth conquering and to conquer. This it is that makes it the more wonderful that he should become a lamb—

"A lowly man before his foes,
A weary man, and full of woes."

It is wonderful that he should yield himself up to the indignities of the cross, to be mocked with a thorn-crown by the soldiers, and to be spit upon by abjects. O wonder, wonder, wonder, that the Lion of Juda, the offshoot of David's royal house, should become as a lamb led forth to the slaughter!

Further, it is clear that *he is a champion:* "The Lion of the tribe of Juda hath prevailed." What was asked for was worthiness, not only in the sense of holiness, but in the sense of valour. One is reminded of a legend of the Crusades. A goodly castle and estate awaited the coming of the lawful heir: he and he only could sound the horn which hung at the castle gate; but he who could make it yield a blast would be one who had slain a heap of Paynim in the fight, and had come home victorious from many a bloody fray. So here, no man in earth or heaven had valour and renown enough to be worthy to take the mystic roll out of the hand of the Eternal. Our champion was worthy. What battles he had fought! What feats of prowess he had performed! He had overthrown sin; he had met face to face the Prince of darkness, and had overcome him in the wilderness; ay, he had conquered death, had bearded that lion in his den; had entered the dungeon of the sepulchre, and had torn its bars away. Thus he was worthy, in the sense of valour, on returning from the far country to be owned as the Father's glorious Son, heaven's hero, and so to take the book and loose the seals thereof. The brilliance of his victories does not diminish our delight in him as the Lamb. Far otherwise, for he won these triumphs as a Lamb, by gentleness, and suffering, and sacrifice. He won his battles by a meekness and patience before unknown. The more of a conqueror he is, the more astounding is it that he should win by humiliation and death. O beloved, never tolerate low thoughts of Christ! Think of him more and more, as did the blessed Virgin, when she sang, "My soul doth magnify the Lord." Make your thoughts of him great. Be-greaten your God and Saviour, and then add to your reverent thoughts the reflection that still he looks like a lamb that has been slain. His prowess and his lion-like qualities do but set forth more vividly the tender, lowly, condescending relationship in which he stands to us as the Lamb of our redemption.

In this wonderful vision we see Jesus as *the familiar of God.* He it was who, without hesitation, advanced to the burning throne and took the book out of the right hand of him that sat upon it. He was at home there: he counted it not robbery to be equal with God. He is "very God of very God"; to be extolled with equal honour with that which is given unto the Lord God Almighty. He advances to the throne, he takes the book, he communes with Jehovah, he accepts the divine challenge of love, and unseals the mysterious purposes of his glorious Father. To him there is no danger in a close approach to the infinite glory, for that glory is his own. Now, it is he who thus stood on familiar terms with God who also stood in our place, and bore for us the penalty of sin. He who is greater than the greatest, and higher than the highest, became lower than the lowest, that he might save to the uttermost them that come to God by him. He who is Lord of all stooped under all the load and burden of sin. Fall down on your faces and worship the Lamb; for though he became obedient unto death, he is God over all, blessed for ever, the Beloved of the Father.

We observe, in addition to all this, that *he is the prophet of God.*

He it was that had the seven eyes to see all things and discern all mysteries; he it is that opened the seven seals, and thus unfolded the parts of the Book one after another, not merely that they might be read, but might be actually fulfilled; and yet he had been our substitute. Jesus explains everything: the Lamb is the *open sesame* of every secret. Nothing was ever a secret to him. He foresaw his own sufferings; they came not upon him as a surprise.

> "This was compassion like a God,
> That when the Saviour knew
> The price of pardon was his blood,
> His pity ne'er withdrew."

Since then he has not been ignorant of our unworthiness, or of the treachery of our hearts. He knows all about us; he knows what we cost him, and he knows how ill we have repaid him. With all that knowledge of God and of man, he is not ashamed to call us brethren; nor does he reject that truth, so simple, yet so full of hope to us, that he is our sacrifice and our substitute. "He who unveils the eternal will of the Highest is the Lamb of God which taketh away the sin of the world."

Our Lord always was, and is now, *acknowledged to be Lord and God*. All the church doth worship him; all the myriads of angels cry aloud in praises unto him; and to him every creature bows, of things in heaven, and things on earth, and things that are under the earth. When you call him King of kings and Lord of lords, lofty as these titles are, they fall far below his glory and majesty. If we all stood up with all the millions of the human race, and with one voice lifted up a shout of praise to him, loud as the noise of many waters and as great thunders, yet would our highest honours scarcely reach the lowest step of his all-glorious throne. Yet, in the glory of his Deity, he disdains not to appear as the Lamb that has been slain. This still is his chosen character. I have heard of a great warrior, that on the anniversary of his most renowned victory he would always put on the coat in which he fought the fight, adorned, as it was, with marks of shot. I understand his choice. Our Lord to-day, and every day, wears still the human flesh in which he overthrew our enemies, and he appears as one that has but newly died, since by death he overcame the devil. Always, and for ever, he is the Lamb. Even as God's prophet and revealer he remains the Lamb. When you shall see him at the last, you shall say, as John did, "I beheld, and, lo, in the midst of the throne and of the four living creatures, and in the midst of the elders, stood a Lamb as it had been slain."

Write, then, the passion of your Lord upon the tablets of your hearts, and let none erase the treasured memory. Think of him mainly and chiefly as the sacrifice for sin. Set the atonement in the midst of your minds, and let it tinge and colour all your thoughts and beliefs. Jesus bleeding and dying in your room, and place, and stead, must be to you as the sun in your sky.

II. In the second place, let us note that, IN THIS CHARACTER, JESUS IS THE CENTRE OF ALL. "In the midst of the throne, and of the four living creatures, and in the midst of the elders, stood a Lamb as it had been slain." The Lamb is the centre of the wonderful circle which makes up the fellowship of heaven.

From him, as a standpoint, all things are seen in their places. Looking up at the planets from this earth, which is one of them, it is difficult to comprehend their motions—progressive, retrograde, or standing still; but the angel in the sun sees all the planets marching in due course, and circling about the centre of their system. Standing where you please upon this earth, and within human range of opinion, you cannot see all things aright, nor understand them till you come to Jesus, and then you see all things from the centre. The man who knows the incarnate God, slain for human sins, stands in the centre of truth. Now he sees God in his place, man in his place, angels in their place, lost souls in their place, and the saved ones in their place. Know him whom to know is life eternal, and you are in the position of vantage from which you may rightly judge of all things. The proper bearings and relationships of this to that, and that to the next, and so on, can only be ascertained by a firm and full belief in Jesus Christ as the atoning sacrifice.

> "Till God in human flesh I see,
> My thoughts no comfort find,
> The Holy, Just, and sacred Three,
> Are terrors to my mind.
>
> "But if Immanuel's face appears,
> My hope, my joy begins:
> His name forbids my slavish fears,
> His grace removes my sins."

In Christ you are in the right position to understand the past, the present, and the future. The deep mysteries of eternity, and even the secret of the Lord, are all with you when once you are with Jesus. Think of this, and make the Lamb your central thought—the soul of your soul, the heart of your heart's best life.

The Lamb's being in the midst, signifies, also, that *in him they all meet in one.* I would speak cautiously, but I venture to say that Christ is the summing up of all existence. Seek you Godhead? There it is. Seek you manhood? There it is. Wish you the spiritual? There it is in his human soul. Desire you the material? There it is in his human body. Our Lord hath, as it were, gathered up the ends of all things, and hath bound them into one. You cannot conceive what God is; but Christ is God. If you dive down with materialism, which by many is regarded as the drag and millstone of the soul, yet in Jesus you find materialism, refined and elevated, and brought into union with the divine nature. In Jesus all lines meet, and from him they radiate to all the points of being. Would you meet God? Go you to Christ. Would you be in fellowship with all believers? Go you to Christ. Would you feel tenderness towards all that God has made? Go you to Christ; for "of him, and through him, and to him are all things." What a Lord is ours! What a glorious being is the Lamb; for it is only as the Lamb that this is true of him! View him only as God, and there is no such meeting with man. View him as being only man, and then he is far from the centre: but behold him as God and man, and the Lamb of God, and then you see in him the place of rest for all things.

Being in the centre, *to him they all look.* Can you think for a moment how the Lord God looks upon his Only-Begotten? When Jehovah looks on Jesus, it is with an altogether indescribable delight. He saith, "This is my beloved Son, in whom I am well pleased." When he thinks of the passion through which he passed, and the death which he accomplished at Jerusalem, all the infinite heart of God flows high and strong towards his Best-beloved. He hath rest in his Son as he hath nowhere else. His delight is in Jesus; indeed, he hath so much delight in him, that for his sake he takes delight in his people. As the Father's eyes are always on Jesus, so are the eyes of the living creatures and the four-and-twenty elders which represent the church in its divine life and the church in its human life. All who have been washed in his blood perpetually contemplate his beauties. What is there in heaven which can compare with the adorable person of him by whom they were redeemed from among men? All angels look that way, also, waiting his august commands. Are they not all ministering spirits, whom he sends forth to minister to his people? All the forces of nature are waiting at the call of Jesus; all the powers of providence look to him for direction. He is the focus of all attention, the centre of all observation throughout the plains of heaven. This, remember, is as "the Lamb." Not as king or prophet chiefly, but pre-eminently as "the Lamb" is Jesus the centre of all reverence, and love, and thought, in the glory-land above.

Once more, let me say of the Lamb in the centre, that *all seem to rally round him as a guard around a king.* It is for the Lamb that the Father acts: he glorifies his Son. The Holy Spirit also glorifies Christ. All the divine purposes run that way. The chief work of God is to make Jesus the first-born among many brethren. This is the model to which the Creator works in fashioning the vessels of grace: he has made Jesus Alpha and Omega, the beginning and the end. All things ordained of the Father work towards Christ, as their centre; and so stand all the redeemed, and all the angels waiting about the Lord, as swelling his glory and manifesting his praise. If anything could enter the minds of heavenly beings that would contribute to lift Jesus higher, it would be their heaven to speed throughout space to carry it out. He dwelleth as a King in his central pavilion, and this is the joy of the host, that the King is in the midst of them.

Beloved, is it so? Is Jesus the centre of the whole heavenly family? Shall he not be the centre of our Church life? Will we not think most of him—much more of him than of Paul, or Apollos, or Cephas, or any party-leaders that would divide us? Christ is the centre; not this form of doctrine nor that mode of ordinance, but the Lamb alone. Shall we not always delight in him, and watch to see how we can magnify his glorious name? Shall he not be also the centre of our ministry? What shall we preach about but Christ! Take that subject away from me, and I have done. These many years I have preached nothing else but that dear name, and if that is to be dishonoured, all my spiritual wealth is gone: I have no bread for the hungry, nor water for the faint. After all these years my speech has become like the harp of Anacreon, which would resound love alone. He wished to sing of Atreus and of Cadmon, but his harp resounded love alone. It is so with my ministry: with Christ, and Christ alone am I at home. Progressive theology! No string of my soul will vibrate to its touch. New divinity! Evolution! Modern thought! My harp is silent to these strange fingers; but to Christ, and Christ alone, it answers with all the music of which it is capable. Beloved, is it so with you? In teaching your children, in your life at home, in your dealing with the world, is Jesus the centre of your aim and labour? Does his love fill your heart? In the old Napoleon's days, a soldier was wounded by a bullet, and the doctor probed deep to find it. The man cried out, "Doctor, mind what you are at! A little deeper, and you will touch the Emperor." The Emperor was on that soldier's heart. Truly, if they search deep into our life they will find Christ. Queen Mary said that when she died they would find the name of *Calais* cut upon her heart; for she grieved over the loss of the last British possession in France. We have not lost our Calais, but hold still our treasure; for Christ is ours. We have no other name engraven on our heart but that of Jesus. Truly can we say,

> "Happy if with my latest breath
> I may but gasp his name;
> Preach him to all, and cry in death,
> 'Behold, behold the Lamb!'"

III. Thirdly, our Lord is seen in heaven as the Lamb slain, and IN THIS CHARACTER HE EXHIBITS PECULIAR MARKS. None of those marks derogate from his glory as the sacrifice for sin; but they tend to instruct us therein.

Note well the words: "Stood a Lamb as it had been slain." "Stood," here is the posture of life; "as it had been slain," here is the memorial of *death*. Our view of Jesus should be twofold; we should see his death and his life: we shall never receive a whole Christ in any other way. If you only see him on the cross, you behold the power of his death; but he is not now upon the cross; he is risen, he for ever liveth to make intercession for us, and we need to know the power of his life. We see him as a lamb "as it had been slain"; but we worship him as one that "liveth for ever and ever." Carry these two things with you as one: a slain Christ, a living Christ. I notice that feeling and teaching in the church oscillates between these two, whereas it should comprehend them both. The Romish church continually gives us a babe Christ, carried by his mother; or a dead Christ, on the cross. Go where we may, these images are thrust upon us. Apart from the sin of image-worship, the thing set forth is not the whole of our Lord. On the other hand, we have a school around us who endeavour to put the cross out of sight, and they give us only a living Christ, such as he is. To them Jesus is only an example and teacher. As a true and proper expiatory substitute they will not have him; BUT WE WILL. We adore the Crucified One upon the throne of God. We believe in him as bleeding and pleading: we see him slain, and behold him reign. Both of these are our joy; neither one more than the other, but each in its own place. Thus, as you look at the Lamb, you begin to sing, "Thou art he that liveth, and wast dead, and art alive for evermore." The mark of our Saviour is life through death, and death slain by death.

Note, next, another singular combination in the Lamb. He is called "a little lamb"; for the diminutive is used in the Greek; but yet how great he is! In Jesus, as a Lamb, we see great tenderness and exceeding familiarity with his people. He is not the object of dread; there is about him nothing like "Stand off, for I am too holy to be approached." A lamb is the most approachable of beings. Yet there is about the little Lamb an exceeding majesty. The elders no sooner saw him than they fell down before him. They adored him, and cried with a loud voice, "Worthy is the Lamb." Every creature worshipped him, saying, "Blessing, and honour, and glory, and power, be unto the Lamb." He is so great that the heaven of heavens cannot contain him; yet he becomes so little that he dwells in humble hearts. He is so glorious that the seraphim veiled their faces in his presence: he is so condescending as to become bone of our bone, and flesh of our flesh. What a wonderful combination of *mercy and majesty,* grace and glory! Never divide what God has joined together: do not speak of our Lord Jesus Christ as some do, with an irreverent, unctuous familiarity; but, at the same time, do not think of him as of some great Lord for whom we must feel a slavish dread. Jesus is your next-of-kin, a brother born for adversity, and yet he is your God and Lord. Let love and awe keep the watches of your soul!

Further, let us look at the peculiar marks of him, and we see that he hath *seven horns and seven eyes.* His power is equal to his vigilance; and these are equal to all the emergencies brought about by the opening of the seven seals of the Book of Providence. When plagues break forth, who is to defend us? Behold the seven horns. If the unexpected occurs, who is to forewarn us? Behold the seven eyes.

Every now and then some foolish person or other brings out a pamphlet stuffed with horrors which are going to happen in a year or two. The whole of it is about as valuable as the Norwood Gipsy's Book of Fate, which you can buy for two-pence; but still, if it were all true that these prophecy-mongers tell us, we are not afraid; for the Lamb has seven horns, and will meet every difficulty by his own power, having already foreseen it by his own wisdom. The Lamb is the answer to the enigma of providence. Providence is a riddle, but Jesus explains it all. During the first centuries, the Church of God was given up to martyrdom: every possible torment and torture was exercised upon the followers of Christ: what could be God's meaning in all this? What but the glory of the Lamb? And now to-day the Lord seems to leave his Church to wander into all kinds of errors: false doctrines are, in some quarters, fearfully paramount. What does this mean? I do not know; but the Lamb knows, for he sees with seven eyes. As a Lamb, as our Saviour, God and man, he understands all, and has the clues of all labyrinths in his hands. He has power to meet every difficulty, and wisdom to see through every embarrassment. We should cast out fear, and give ourselves wholly up to worship.

The Lamb also works to perfection in nature and in providence; for with him are "the seven Spirits of God sent forth into all the earth." This refers not merely to the saving power of the Spirit which is sent forth unto the elect; but to those powers and forces which operate upon all the earth. The power of gravitation, the energy of life, the mystic force of electricity, and the like, are all forms of the power of God. A law of nature is nothing but our observation of the usual way in which God operates in the world. A law in itself has no power: law is but the usual course of God's action. All the Godhead's omnipotence dwells in the Lamb: he is the Lord God Almighty. We cannot put the atonement into a secondary place; for our atoning sacrifice hath all the seven Spirits of God. He is able to save to the uttermost them that come unto God by him. Let us come to God by him. He has power to cope with the future, whatever it may be. Let us secure our souls against all threatening dangers, committing ourselves to his keeping.

How I wish I had power to set the Lord before you this morning evidently glorified! But I fail utterly. My talk is like holding a candle to the sun. I am grateful that my Lord does not snuff me out; perhaps my candle may show some prisoner to the door, and when he has once passed it, he will behold the sun in its strength. Glory be to him who is so great, so glorious, and yet still the Lamb slain for sinners, whose wounds in effect continually bleed our life, whose finished work is the perpetual source of all our safety and our joy.

IV. I close with my fourth point, which is this: Jesus appears eternally as a Lamb, and IN THIS CHARACTER HE IS UNIVERSALLY ADORED.

Before he opened one of the seals this worship commenced. When he had taken the book, the four living creatures and the four-and-twenty elders fell down before the Lamb, and sung a new song, saying, "Thou art worthy to take the book." While yet the book is closed, we worship him. We trust him where we cannot trace him. Before he begins his work as the revealing Mediator, the church adores him for his work as a sacrifice. Jesus our Lord is worshipped not so much for what benefits he will confer as for himself. As the Lamb slain he is the object of heavenly reverence. Many will reverence him, I do not doubt, when he comes in his second Advent, in the glory of the Father. Every knee will bow before him, even of apostates and infidels, when they shall see him take to himself his great power and reign; but that is not the worship which he accepts, nor that which proves the offerer to be saved. You must worship him as a sacrifice, and adore him in his lowly character, as the "despised and rejected of men." You must reverence him while others ridicule him, trust his blood while others turn from it with disdain, and so be with him in his humiliation. Accept him as your substitute, trust in him as having made atonement for you; for in heaven they still worship him as the Lamb.

That adoration *begins with the church of God.* The church of God, in all its phases, adores the Lamb. If you view the church of God as a divine creation, the embodiment of the Spirit of God, then the living creatures fall down before the Lamb. No God-begotten life is too high to refuse obeisance to the Lamb of God. Look at the church on its human side, and you see the four-and-twenty elders falling down and worshipping, having every one harps and vials. Well may the whole company of redeemed men worship the Mediator, since in him our manhood is greatly exalted! Was ever our nature so exalted as it is now that Christ is made Head over all things to his church? Now are we nearest to God, for between man and God no creature intervenes: Immanuel—God with us—has joined us in one. Man is next to the Deity, with Jesus only in between, not to divide, but to unite. The Lord in Christ Jesus hath made us to have dominion over all the works of his hands; he hath put all things under our feet: all sheep and oxen, yea, the fowl of the air, and fish of the sea, and whatsoever passeth through the paths of the sea. O Lord our God, how excellent is thy name in all the earth!

The Lord is adored by the church in all forms of worship. They worship him in prayer; for the vials full of sweet odours are the prayers of saints. They worship him in praise with a new song, and with the postures of lowliest reverence.

But, beloved, the Lamb is not only worshipped by the church, *he is worshipped by angels.* What a wonderful gathering together of certain legions of the Lord's hosts we have before us in this chapter! " Ten thousand times ten thousand, and thousands of thousands." Their company cannot be enumerated in human arithmetic. With perfect unanimity they unite in the hallowed worship, shouting together, " Worthy is the Lamb that was slain."

Nay, it is not merely the church and angelhood; but *all creation,* east, west, north, south, highest, lowest, all adore him. All life, all space, all time, immensity, eternity: all these become one mouth for song, and all the song is, " Worthy is the Lamb."

Now, then, dear friends, if this be so, shall we ever allow anybody in our presence to lower the dignity of Christ, our sacrifice? ["No."] A friend says, emphatically, No; and we all say, No. As with a voice of thunder, we say, No, to all attempts to lower the supreme glories of the Lamb. We cannot have it: our loyalty to him will not permit. Besides, no man will willingly lose his all. Take the Lamb away you take all away. "Who steals my purse, steals trash": who steals my Christ, steals myself, and more than myself—my hopes that are to be my future joys. Life is gone, when his death is rejected, his blood despised. Our souls burn with indignation when this vital truth is assailed.

> " Stand up, stand up for Jesus,
> Ye soldiers of the cross!
> Lift high his royal banner,
> It must not suffer loss! "

Wherever you are, to whatever church you belong, do not associate with those who decry the atonement. Enter not into confederacy with those who, even by a breath, would disparage his precious blood. Do not bear that which assails the Lamb; grow indignant at the foul lie! The wrath of the Lamb may with safety be copied by yourself in this case: you will be angry, and sin not.

Once more, if this be so, if the glorious sacrifice of our Lord Jesus be so much thought of in heaven, cannot you trust it here below? O you that are burdened with sin, here is your deliverance: come to the sin-bearing Lamb. You that are perplexed with doubts, here is your guide: the Lamb can open the sealed books for you. You that have lost your comfort, come back to the Lamb, who is slain for you, and put your trust in him anew. You that are hungering for heavenly food, come to the Lamb, for he shall feed you. The Lamb, the Lamb, the bleeding Lamb: be this the sign upon the standard of the Church of God. Set that ensign to the front, and march boldly on to victory, and then, O Lamb of God, that taketh away the sin of the world, grant us thy peace! Amen.

The Man of Sorrows

"A man of sorrows, and acquainted with grief"—Isaiah liii. 3.

POSSIBLY a murmur will pass round the congregation, "This is a dreary subject and a mournful theme." But, O beloved, it is not so, for great as were the woes of our Redeemer, they are all over now, and are to be looked back upon with sacred triumph. However severe the struggle, the victory has been won ; the labouring vessel was severely tossed by the waves, but she has now entered into the desired haven. Our Saviour is no longer in Gethsemane agonising, or upon the cross expiring ; the crown of thorns has been replaced by many crowns of sovereignty ; the nails and the spear have given way to the sceptre. Nor is this all, for though the suffering is ended, the blessed results never end. We may remember the travail, for the Man Child is born into the world. The sowing in tears is followed by a reaping in joy. The bruising of the heel of the woman's seed is well recompensed by the breaking of the serpent's head. It is pleasant to hear of battles fought when a decisive victory has ended war and established peace. So that the double reflection that all the work of suffering is finished by the Redeemer, and that, henceforth, he beholds the success of all his labours, we shall rejoice even while we enter into fellowship with his sufferings.

Let it never be forgotten that the subject of the sorrows of the Saviour has proved to be more efficacious for comfort to mourners than any other theme in the compass of revelation, or out of it. Even the glories of Christ afford no such consolation to afflicted spirits as the sufferings of Christ. Christ is in all attitudes the consolation of Israel, but he is most so as a man of sorrows. Troubled spirits turn not so much to Bethlehem as to Calvary ; they prefer Gethsemane to Nazareth. The afflicted do not so much look for comfort to Christ as he will come a second time in splendour of state, as to Christ as he came the first time, a weary man and full of woes. The passion-flower yields us the best perfume, the tree of the cross bleeds the most healing balm. Like in this case cures like, for there is no remedy for sorrow beneath the sun like the sorrows of Immanuel. As Aaron's rod swallowed up all the other rods, so the griefs of Jesus make our griefs disappear. Thus you see that in the black soil of our subject light is sown for the righteous, light which springs up for those who sit in darkness and in the region of the shadow of death. Let us go, then, without reluctance to the house of mourning, and commune with "The Chief Mourner," who above all others could say, "I am the man that hath seen affliction."

We will not stray from our text this morning, but keep to it so closely as even to dwell upon each one of its words. The words shall give us our divisions :—" *A man;* " " *a man of sorrows;* " " *acquainted with grief.*"

I. "A MAN." There is no novelty to anyone here present in the doctrine of the real and actual manhood of the Lord Jesus Christ; but, although there be nothing novel in it, there is everything important in it, therefore, let us hear it again. This is one of those gospel church-bells which must be rung every Sabbath-day : this is one of those provisions of the Lord's household, which, like bread and salt, should be put upon the table at every spiritual meal. This is the manna which must fall every day round about the camp. We can never meditate too much upon Christ's blessed person as God and as man. Let us reflect that he who is here called a man was certainly "very God of very God;" "a man," and "a man of sorrows," and yet at the same time, "God over all, blessed for ever." He who was "despised and rejected of men" was beloved and adored by angels, and he from whom men hid their faces in contempt, was worshipped by cherubim and seraphim. This is the great mystery of godliness, God was "manifest in the flesh." He who was God, and was in the beginning with God, was made flesh, and dwelt among us. The Highest stooped to become the lowest, the Greatest took his place among the least. Strange, and needing all our faith to grasp it, yet is it true that he who sat upon the well of Sychar, and said "Give me to drink," was none other than he who digged the channels of the ocean, and poured into them the floods. Son of Mary, thou art also Son of Jehovah ! Man of the substance of thy mother, thou art also essential Deity ; we worship thee this day in spirit and in truth !

Remembering that Jesus Christ is God, it now behoves us to recollect that his manhood was none the less real and substantial. It differed from our own humanity in the absence of sin, but it differed in no other respect. It is idle to speculate upon a heavenly manhood, as some have done, who have, by their very attempt at accuracy, been borne down by whirlpools of error. It is enough for us to know that the Lord was born of a woman, wrapped in swaddling bands, laid in a manger, and needed to be nursed by his mother as any other little child ; he grew in stature like any other human being, and as a man we know that he ate and drank, that he hungered and thirsted, rejoiced and sorrowed. His body could be touched and handled, wounded and made to bleed. He was no phantasm, but a man of flesh and blood, even as ourselves; a man needing sleep, requiring food, and subject to pain, and a man who, in the end, yielded up his life to death. There may have been some distinction between his body and ours, for inasmuch as it was never defiled by sin, it was not capable of corruption; otherwise in body and in soul, the Lord Jesus was perfect man after the order of our manhood, "made in the likeness of sinful flesh," and we must think of him under that aspect. Our temptation is to regard the Lord's humanity as something quite different from our own; we are apt to spiritualise it away, and not to think of him as really bone of our bone and flesh of our flesh. All this is akin to grievous error; we may fancy that we are honouring Christ by such conceptions, but Christ is never honoured by that which is not true. He was a man, a real man, a man of our race, the Son of Man; indeed a representative man, the second Adam: "As the children are partakers of flesh and blood, he also himself took part of the same." "He made himself of no reputation, and took upon him the form of a servant, and was made in the likeness of men."

Now this condescending participation in our nature brings the Lord Jesus very near to us in relationship. Inasmuch as he was man, though also God, he was, according to Hebrew law, our *goel*—our kinsman, next of kin. Now it was according to the law that if an inheritance had been lost, it was the right of the next of kin to redeem it. Our Lord Jesus exercised his legal right, and seeing us sold into bondage and our inheritance taken from us, came forward to redeem both us and all our lost estate. A blessed thing it was for us that we had such a kinsman. When Ruth went to glean in the fields of Boaz, it was the most gracious circumstance in her life that Boaz turned out to be her next of kin; and we who have gleaned in the fields of mercy praise the Lord that his only begotten Son is the next of kin to us, our brother, born for adversity. It would not have been consistent with divine justice for any other substitution to have been accepted for us, except that of a man. Man sinned, and man must make reparation for the injury done to the divine honour. The breach of the law was caused by man, and by man must it be repaired; man had transgressed, man must be punished. It was not in the power of an angel to have said, "I will suffer for man"—for angelic sufferings would have made no amends for human sins. But the man, the matchless man, being the representative man, and of right by kinship allowed to redeem, stepped in, suffered what was due, made amends to injured justice, and thereby set us free! Glory be unto his blessed name!

And now, beloved, since the Lord thus saw in Christ's manhood a suitableness to become our Redeemer, I trust that many here who have been under bondage to Satan will see in that same human nature an attraction leading them to approach him. Sinner, thou hast not to come to an absolute God, thou art not bidden to draw nigh to the consuming fire. Thou mightest well tremble to approach him whom thou hast so grievously offended; but, there is a man ordained to mediate between thee and God, and if thou wouldst come to God, thou must come through him—the man Christ Jesus. God out of Christ is terrible out of his holy places, he will by no means spare the guilty :—but look at yonder Son of man!

> "His hand no thunder bears,
> No terror clothes his brow;
> No bolts to drive your guilty souls
> To fiercer flames below."

He is a man with hands full of blessing, eyes wet with tears of pity, lips overflowing with love, and a heart melting with tenderness. See ye not the gash in his side?—through that wound there is a high-way to his heart, and he who needs his compassion may soon excite it. O sinners! the way to the Saviour's heart is open, and penitent seekers shall never be denied. Why should the most despairing be afraid to approach the Saviour? He has deigned to assume the character of the Lamb of God,—I never knew even a little child that was afraid of a lamb; the most timorous will approach a lamb, and Jesus used this argument when he said to every labouring and heavy laden one, "Take my yoke upon you, and learn of me, for I am meek and lowly in heart." I know you feel yourselves sad and trembling, but need you tremble in *his* presence? If you are weak, your weakness will touch his sympathy, and your mournful inability will be an argument with his abounding mercy. If I were sick and might have my choice where I would lie, with a view to healing, I would say, place me where the best and kindest physician upon earth can see me, put me where a man with great skill, and equal tenderness, will have me always beneath his eye: I shall not long groan there in vain—if he can heal me he will. Sinner, place thyself by an act of faith this morning beneath the cross of Jesus; look up to him and say, "Blessed Physician, thou whose wounds for me can heal me, whose death for me can make me live, look down upon me! Thou art man, thou knowest what man suffers. Thou art man, wilt thou let a man sink down to hell who cries to thee for help? Thou art a man, and thou canst save, and wilt thou let a poor unworthy one who longs for mercy be driven into hopeless misery, while he cries to thee to let thy merits save him?" Oh, ye guilty ones, have faith that ye can reach the heart of Jesus. Sinner, fly to Jesus without fear; he waits to save, it is his office to receive sinners and reconcile them to God. Be thankful that you have not to go to God at the first, and as you are, but you are invited to come to Jesus Christ, and through him to the Father May the Holy Spirit lead you to devout meditation upon the humility of our Lord; and so may you find the door of life, the portal of peace, the gate of heaven!

Then let me add, before I leave this point, that every child of God ought also to be comforted by the fact that our Redeemer is one of our own race, seeing that he was made like unto his brethren, that he might be a merciful and faithful High Priest; and he was tempted in all points, like as we are, that he might be able to succour them that are tempted. The sympathy of Jesus is the next most precious thing to his sacrifice. I stood by the bedside of a Christian brother the other day, and he remarked, "I feel thankful to God that our Lord took our sicknesses." "Of course," said he, "the grand thing was, that he took our sins, but next to that, I, as a sufferer, feel grateful that he also took our sicknesses." Personally, I also bear witness that it has been to me, in seasons of great pain, superlatively comfortable to know that in every pang which racks his people the Lord Jesus has a fellow-feeling. We are not alone, for one like unto the Son of man walks the furnace with us. The clouds which float over our sky have aforetime darkened the heavens for him also—

"He knows what strong temptations mean,
For he has felt the same."

How completely it takes the bitterness out of grief to know that it once was suffered by him. The Macedonian soldiers, it is said, made long forced marches which seemed to be beyond the power of mortal endurance, but the reason for their untiring energy lay in Alexander's presence. He was accustomed to walk with them, and bear the like fatigue. If the king himself had been carried like a Persian monarch in a palanquin, in the midst of easy, luxurious state, the soldiers would soon have grown tired ; but, when they looked upon the king of men himself, hungering when they hungered, thirsting when they thirsted, often putting aside the cup of water offered to him, and passing it to a fellow-soldier who looked more faint than himself, they could not dream of repining. Why, every Macedonian felt that he could endure any fatigue if Alexander could. This day, assuredly, we can bear poverty, slander, contempt, or bodily pain, or death itself, because Jesus Christ our Lord has borne it. By his humiliation it shall become pleasure to be abased for his sake, by the spittle that distilled adown his cheeks it shall become a fair thing to be made a mockery for him, by the buffeting and the blind-folding it shall become an honour to be disgraced, and by the cross it shall become life itself to surrender life for the sake of such a cause and so precious a Master! May the man of sorrows now appear to us, and enable us to bear our sorrows cheerfully. If there be consolation anywhere, surely it is to be found in the delightful presence of the Crucified: "*A man* shall be a hiding-place from the wind, and a covert from the tempest."

II. We must pass on to dwell awhile upon the next words, "A MAN OF SORROWS." The expression is intended to be very emphatic, it is not "a sorrowful man," but "a man of sorrows," as if he were made up of sorrows, and they were constituent elements of his being. Some are men of pleasure, others men of wealth, but he was "a man of sorrows." He and sorrow might have changed names. He who saw him, saw sorrow, and he who would see sorrow, must look on him. "Behold, and see," saith he " if there was ever sorrow like unto my sorrow which was done unto me."

Our Lord is called the man of sorrows for *peculiarity,* for this was his peculiar token and special mark. We might well call him " a man of holiness ; " for there was no fault in him : or a man of labours, for he did his Father's business earnestly; or " a man of eloquence," for never man spake like this man. We might right fittingly call him in the language of our hymn, "The man of love," for never was there greater love than glowed in his heart. Still conspicuous as all these and many other excellencies were, yet had we gazed upon Christ and been asked afterwards what was the most striking peculiarity in him, we should have said his sorrows. The various parts of his character were so singularly harmonious that no one quality predominated, so as to become a leading feature. In his moral portrait, the eye is perfect, but so also is the mouth; the cheeks are as beds of spices, but the lips also are as lilies, dropping sweet-smelling myrrh. In Peter, you see enthusiasm exaggerated at times into presumption, and in John, love for his Lord would call fire from heaven on his foes. Deficiencies and exaggerations exist everywhere but in Jesus. He is the perfect man, a whole man, the holy one of Israel. But there was a peculiarity, and it lay in the fact that "his visage was so marred more than any man, and his form more than the sons of men," through the excessive griefs which continually passed over his spirit. Tears were his insignia, and the cross his escutcheon. He was the warrior in black armour, and not as now the rider upon the white horse. He was the lord of grief, the prince of pain, the emperor of anguish, a "man of sorrows, and acquainted with grief."

"Oh! king of grief! (a title strange, yet true,
To thee of all kings only due),
Oh! king of wounds! how shall I grieve for thee,
Who in all grief preventest me."

Is not the title of "man of sorrows" given to our Lord by way of eminence? He was not only sorrowful, but pre-eminent among the sorrowful. All men have a burden to bear, but his was heaviest of all. Who is there of our race that is quite free from sorrows? Search ye the whole earth through, and everywhere the thorn and thistle will be found, and these have wounded every one of woman born. High in the lofty places of the earth there is sorrow, for the royal widow weeps her lord: down in the cottage where we fancy that nothing but content can reign, a thousand bitter tears are shed over dire penury and cruel oppression. In the sunniest climes the serpent creeps among the flowers, in the most fertile regions poisons flourish as well as wholesome herbs. Everywhere "men must work and women must weep." There is sorrow on the sea, and sadness on the land. But in this common lot, the "firstborn among many brethren" has more than a double portion, his cup is more bitter, his baptism more deep than the rest of the family. Common sufferers must give place, for none can match with him in woe. Ordinary mourners may be content to rend their garments, but he himself is rent in his affliction; they sip at sorrow's bowl, but he drains it dry. He who was the most obedient Son smarted most under the rod when he was stricken of God and afflicted; no other of the smitten ones have sweat great drops of blood, or in the same bitterness of anguish, cried, "My God, my God, why hast thou forsaken me."

The reasons for this superior sorrow may be found in the fact that with his sorrow there was no admixture of sin. Sin deserves sorrow, but it also blunts the edge of grief by rendering the soul untender and unsympathetic. We do not start at sin as Jesus did, we do not tremble at the sinner's doom as Jesus would. His was a perfect nature, which, because it knew no sin, was not in its element amid sorrow, but was like a land bird driven out to sea by the gale. To the robber the jail is his home, and the prison fare is the meat to which he is accustomed, but to an innocent man a prison is misery, and everything about it is strange and foreign. Our Lord's pure nature was peculiarly sensitive of any contact with sin; we, alas, by the fall, have lost much of that feeling. In proportion as we are sanctified, sin becomes the source of wretchedness to us; Jesus being perfect, every sin pained him much more than it would any of us. I have no doubt there are many persons in the world who could live merrily in the haunts of vice—could hear blasphemy without horror, view lust without disgust, and look on robbery or murder without abhorrence; but to many of us, an hour's familiarity with such abominations would be the severest punishment. A sentence in which the name of Jesus is blasphemed is torture to us of the most exquisite kind. The very mention of the shameful deeds of vice seizes us with horror. To live with the wicked would be a sufficient hell to the righteous. David's prayer is full of agony wherein he cries, "Gather not my soul with sinners, nor my life with bloody men." But the perfect Jesus, what a grief the sight of sin must have caused him! Our hands grow horny with toiling, and our hearts with sinning; but our Lord was, as it were, like a man whose flesh was all one quivering wound, he was delicately sensitive of every touch of sin. We go through thorn brakes and briars of sin because we are clothed with indifference, but imagine a naked man, compelled to traverse a forest of briars—and such was the Saviour, as to his moral sensitiveness. He could see sin where we cannot see it, and feel its heinousness as we cannot feel it: there was therefore more to grieve him, and he was more capable of being grieved.

Side by side with his painful sensitiveness of the evil of sin, was his gracious tenderness towards the sorrows of others. If we could know and enter into all the griefs of this congregation, it is probable that we should be of all men most miserable. There are heart-breaks in this house this morning, which, could they find a tongue, would fill our heart with agony. We hear of poverty here, we see disease there, we observe bereavement, and we mark distress, we note the fact that men are passing into the grave and, (ah, far more bitter grief,) descending into hell; but, somehow or other, either these become such common things, that they do not stir us, or else we gradually harden to them: the Saviour was always moved to sympathy with another's griefs, for his love was ever at flood-tide. All men's sorrows were his sorrows. His heart was so large, that it was inevitable that he should become "a man of sorrows."

We recollect that besides this our Saviour had a peculiar relationship to sin. He was not merely afflicted with the sight of it, and saddened by perceiving its effects on others, but sin was actually laid upon him, and he was himself numbered with the transgressors; and therefore he was called to bear the terrible blows of divine justice, and suffered unknown, immeasurable agonies. His Godhead strengthened him to suffer, else mere manhood had failed. The wrath whose power no man knoweth, spent itself on him; "It pleased the Father to bruise him, he hath put him to grief." Behold the man, and mark how vain it would be to seek his equal sorrow.

The title of "man of sorrows," was also given to our Lord to indicate the *constancy* of his afflictions. He changed his place of abode, but he always lodged with sorrow. Sorrow wove his swaddling bands, and sorrow spun his winding sheet. Born in a stable, sorrow received him, and only on the cross at his last breath did sorrow part with him. His disciples might forsake him, but his sorrows would not leave him. He was often alone without a man, but never alone without a grief. From the hour of his baptism in Jordan, to the time of his baptism in the pains of death, he always wore the sable robe and was "a man of sorrows."

He was also "a man of sorrows," for the *variety* of his woes ; he was a man not of *sorrow* only, but of "*sorrows.*" All the sufferings of the body and of the soul were known to him ; the sorrows of the man who actively struggles to obey ; the sorrows of the man who sits still, and passively endures. The sorrows of the lofty he knew, for he was the King of Israel ; the sorrows of the poor he knew, for he "had not where to lay his head." Sorrows relative, and sorrows personal ; sorrows mental, and sorrows spiritual ; sorrows of all kinds and degrees assailed him. Affliction emptied his quiver upon him, making his heart the target for all conceivable woes. Let us think a minute or two of some of those sufferings.

Our Lord was a man of sorrows as to his poverty. Oh, you who are in want, your want is not so abject as his : he had not where to lay his head, but you have at least some humble roof to shelter you. No one denies you a cup of water, but he sat upon the well at Samaria, and said, " I thirst." We read more than once, that he hungered. His toil was so great that he was constantly weary, and we read of one occasion where they took him, " even as he was," into the ship—too faint was he to reach the boat himself, but they carried him as he was and laid him down near the helm to sleep ; but he had not much time for slumber, for they woke him, saying, " Master, carest thou not that we perish :" a hard life was his, with nothing of earthly comfort to make that life endurable.

Remember ye who lament around the open grave, or weep in memory of graves but newly filled, our Saviour knew the heart-rendings of bereavement. Jesus wept, as he stood at the tomb of Lazarus.

Perhaps the bitterest of his sorrows were those which were connected with his gracious work. He came as the Messiah sent of God, on an embassage of love, and men rejected his claims. When he went to his own city, where he had been brought up, and announced himself, they would have cast him headlong from the brow of the hill. It is a hard thing to come on an errand of disinterested love, and then to meet with such ingratitude as this. Nor did they stay at cold rejection, they then proceeded to derision and to ridicule. There was no name of contempt which they did not pour upon him ; nay, it was not merely contempt, but they proceded to falsehood, slander, and blasphemy. He was a drunken man, they said ; hear this, ye angels, and be astonished ! Yes, a wine-bibber did they call the blessed Prince of Life ! They said he was in league with Beelzebub, and had a devil, and was mad ; whereas he had come to destroy the works of the devil ! ! They charged him with every crime which their malice could suggest. There was not a word he spoke but they would wrest it ; not a doctrine but what they would misrepresent it : he could not speak but what they would find in his words some occasion against him. And all the while he was doing nothing but seeking their advantage in all ways. When he was earnest against their vices it was out of pity for their souls; if he condemned their sins it was because their sins would destroy them; but his zeal against sin was always tempered with love for the souls of men. Was there ever man so full of good-will to others who received such disgraceful treatment from those he longed to serve?

As he proceeded in his life his sorrows multiplied. He preached, and when men's hearts were hard, and they would not believe what he said, "he was grieved for the hardness of their hearts." He went about doing good, and for his good works they took up stones again to stone him; alas, they stoned his heart when they could not injure his body. He pleaded with them, and plaintively declared his love, and received instead thereof a hatred remorseless and fiendish: slighted love has griefs of peculiar poignancy: many have died of hearts broken by ingratitude. Such love as the love of Jesus could not for the sake of those it loved bear to be slighted; it pined within itself because men did not know their own mercies and rejected their own salvation. His sorrow was not that men injured him, but that they destroyed themselves; this it was that pulled up the sluices of his soul, and made his eyes o'erflow with tears: "O Jerusalem! Jerusalem! how often would I have gathered thy children together as a hen gathereth her chickens under her wings, and ye would not." The lament is not for his own humiliation, but for their suicidal rejection of his grace. These were among the sorrows that he bore.

But surely he found some solace with the few companions whom he had gathered around him. He did; but for all that he must have found as much sorrow as solace in their company. They were dull scholars, they learned slowly; what they did learn they forgot, what they remembered they did not practise, and what they practised at one time they belied at another. They were miserable comforters for the man of sorrows. His was a lonely life, I mean that even when he was with his followers, he was alone. He said to them once, "Could ye not watch with me one hour," but indeed he might have said the same to them all the hours of their lives, for even if they sympathised with him to the utmost of their capacity, they could not enter into such griefs as his. A father in a house with many little children about him, cannot tell his babes his griefs; if he did they would not comprehend him. What know they of his anxious business transactions, or his crushing losses? Poor little things, their father does not wish they should be able to sympathise with him, he looks down upon them and rejoices that their toys will comfort them, and that their little prattle will not be broken in upon by his great griefs. The Saviour, from the very dignity of his nature, must suffer alone. The mountain-side with Christ upon it seems to me to be a suggestive symbol of his earthly life. His great soul lived in vast solitudes, sublime and terrible, and there amid a midnight of trouble, his spirit communed with the Father, no one being able to accompany him into the dark glens and gloomy ravines of his unique experience. Of all his life's warfare he might have said in some senses "of the people there was none with me"; and at the last it became literally true, for they all forsook him—

one denied him and another betrayed him, so that he trod the winepress alone.

In the last, crowning sorrows of his life, there came upon him the penal inflictions from God, the chastisement of our peace which was upon him. He was arrested in the garden of Gethsemane by God's officers before the officers of the Jews had come near to him. There on the ground he knelt, and wrestled till the bloody sweat started from every pore, and his soul was "exceeding sorrowful, even unto death." You have read the story of your Master's woes, and know how he was hurried from bar to bar ; and treated with mingled scorn and cruelty before each judgment seat. When they had taken him to Herod and to Pilate, and almost murdered him with scourging, they brought him forth, and said, *Ecce homo*—" Behold the man." Their malice was not satisfied, they must go further yet, and nail him to his cross, and mock him while fever parched his mouth and made him feel as if his body were dissolved to dust. He cries out, "I thirst ; " and is mocked with vinegar. Ye know the rest, but I would have you best remember that the sharpest scourging and severest griefs were all within ; while the hand of God bruised him, and the iron rod of justice broke him, as it were, upon the wheel.

He was fitly named a "man of sorrows !" I feel as if I had no utterance, as if my tongue were tied, while trying to speak upon this subject. I cannot find goodly words worthy of my theme, yet I know that embellishments of language would degrade rather than adorn the agonies of my Lord. There let the cross stand sublime in its simplicity ! It needs no decoration. If I had wreaths of choicest flowers to hang about it, I would gladly place them there, and if instead of garlands of flowers, each flower could be a gem of priceless worth, I would consider that the cross deserved the whole. But as I have none of these I rejoice that the cross alone, in its naked simplicity, needs nought from mortal speech. Turn to your bleeding Saviour, O my hearers. Continue gazing upon him, and find in the "man of sorrows" your Lord and your God.

III. And now the last word is, he was "ACQUAINTED WITH GRIEF." With grief he had an *intimate* acquaintance. He did not know merely what it was in others, but it came home to himself. We have read of grief, we have sympathised with grief, we have sometimes felt grief : but the Lord felt it more intensely than other men in his innermost soul ; he, beyond us all, was conversant with this black letter lore. He knew the secret of the heart which refuseth to be comforted. He had sat at grief's table, eaten of grief's black bread, and dipped his morsel in her vinegar. By the waters of Marah he dwelt, and knew right well the bitter well. He and grief were bosom friends.

It was a *continuous* acquaintance. He did not call at grief's house sometimes to take a tonic by the way, neither did he sip now and then of the wormwood and the gall, but the quassia cup was always his hand, and ashes were always mingled with his bread. Not only forty days in the wilderness did Jesus fast ; the world was ever a wilderness to him, and his life was one long Lent. I do not say that he was not, after all, a happy man, for down, deep in his soul, benevolence always supplied a living spring of joy to him. There was a joy into which we are one day to enter—the "joy of our Lord"—the "joy set before him" for which "he endured the cross, despising the shame;" but that does not at all take away from the fact that his acquaintance with grief was continuous and intimate beyond that of any man who ever lived. It was indeed a *growing* acquaintance with grief, for each step took him deeper down into the grim shades of sorrow. As there is a progress in the teaching of Christ and in the life of Christ, so is there also in the griefs of Christ. The tempest lowered darker, and darker, and darker. His sun rose in a cloud, but it set in congregated horrors of heaped-up night, till, in a moment, the clouds were suddenly rent in sunder, and, as a loud voice proclaimed, "It is finished," a glorious morning dawned where all expected an eternal night.

Remember, once more, that this acquaintance of Christ with grief was a *voluntary* acquaintance for our sakes. He need never have known a grief at all, and at any moment he might have said to grief, farewell. He could have returned in an instant to the royalties of heaven and to the bliss of the upper world, or even tarrying here he might have lived sublimely indifferent to the woes of mankind. But he would not, he remained to the end, out of love to us, grief's acquaintance.

Now, then, what shall I say in conclusion, but just this: let us admire the superlative love of Jesus. O love, love, what hast thou done! What hast thou not done! Thou art omnipotent in suffering. Few of us can bear pain, perhaps, fewer still of us can bear misrepresentation, slander, and ingratitude. These are horrible hornets which sting as with fire: men have been driven to madness by cruel scandals which have distilled from venomous tongues. Christ, throughout life, bore these and other sufferings. Let us love him, as we think of how much he must have loved us. Will you try, this afternoon, before you come to the communion table, to get your souls saturated with the love of Christ? Lay them a-soak in his love all the afternoon, till like a sponge, ye drink into your own selves the love of Jesus; and then come up to-night, as it were, to let that love flow out to him again, while ye sit at his table and partake of the emblems of his death and of his love. Admire the power of his love, and then pray that you may have a love somewhat akin to it in power. We sometimes wonder why the church of God grows so slowly, but I do not wonder when I recollect what scant consecration to Christ there is in the church of God. Jesus was "a man of sorrows, and acquainted with grief;" but many of his disciples who profess to be altogether his are living for themselves. There are rich men who call themselves saints, and are thought to be so, whose treasures are hoarded for themselves and families. There are men of ability who believe that they are bought with Christ's blood, yet their ability is all spent on other things and none upon their Lord. And let us come nearer home; here are we, what are we doing? Teaching in the school are you,—are you doing it with all your heart for Jesus? Preaching in the street?—yes, but do you throw your soul into it for him? Mayhap, you have to confess you are doing nothing; do not let this day conclude till you have begun to do something for your Lord. We are always talking about the church doing this and that,—what is the church? I believe there is a great deal too much said, both of bad and good, about that abstraction ; the fact is, we are individuals. The church is only the aggregation of individuals, and if any good is to be done it must be performed by individuals, and if all individuals are idle there is no church work done ; there may be the semblance of it, but there is no real work done. Brother, sister, what art thou doing for Jesus ? I charge thee by the nail-prints of his hands, unless thou be a liar unto him, labour for him ! I charge thee by his wounded feet—run to his help ! I charge thee by the scar in his side—give him thy heart ! I charge thee by that sacred head, once pierced with thorns,—yield him thy thoughts ! I charge thee by the shoulders which bore the scourges,—bend thy whole strength to his service ! I charge thee by himself, give him thyself. I charge thee by that left hand which has been under thy head, and that right hand which has embraced thee, by the roes and by the hinds of the field, by the beds of spices, and the banquets of love, render thyself, thy heart, thy soul, and strength to him ! Live in his service, and die in service ! Lay not down thy harness, but work on as long as thou shalt live. Whilst thou livest let this be thy motto—" All for Jesus, all for Jesus ; all for the man of sorrows, all for the man of sorrows ! " O ye that love him, and fight for him, you are summoned to the front. Hasten to the conflict, I pray you, and charge home for the "man of sorrows ! " Make this the battle-cry to-day! Slink not back like cowards ! Hie not to your homes as lovers of ease ! but press to the front for the "man of sorrows," like good men and true. By the cross which bore him, and by the heavy cross he bore, by his deadly agony, and by the agony of his life, I cry, "forward, for the man of sorrows ! " Write this word, "for the man of sorrows," on your own bodies, wherein ye bear the marks of the Lord Jesus ; brand, if not in your flesh, yet in your souls, for henceforth ye are servants to the man of sorrows ! Write this on your wealth, bind this inscription on all your possessions—" This belongs to the man of sorrows." Give your children to the "man of sorrows," as men of old consecrated their sons to patriotism, and to battle with their country's foes. Give up each hour to the "man of sorrows ! " Learn even to eat and drink and sleep for the "man of sorrows," doing all in his name. Live for him and be ready to die for him, and the Lord accept you for the "man of sorrows' " sake. Amen.

The Shame and Spitting

"I gave my back to the smiters, and my cheeks to them that plucked off the hair: I hid not my face from shame and spitting"—Isaiah l. 6.

OF whom speaketh the prophet this? Of himself or of some other? We cannot doubt but what Isaiah here wrote concerning the Lord Jesus Christ. Is not this one of the prophecies to which our Lord himself referred in the incident recorded in the eighteenth chapter of Luke's gospel at the thirty-first verse? "Then he took unto him the twelve, and said unto them, Behold, we go up to Jerusalem, and all things that are written by the prophets concerning the Son of man shall be accomplished. For he shall be delivered unto the Gentiles, and shall be mocked, and spitefully entreated, and spitted on: and they shall scourge him, and put him to death." Such a remarkable prophecy of scourging and spitting as this which is now before us must surely refer to the Lord Jesus; its highest fulfilment is assuredly found in him alone.

Of whom else, let me ask, could you conceive the prophet to have spoken if you read the whole chapter? Of whom else could he say in the same breath, "I clothe the heavens with blackness, and I make sackcloth their covering. I gave my back to the smiters, and my cheeks to them that plucked off the hair." (Verses 3 and 6.) What a descent from the omnipotence which veils the heavens with clouds to the gracious condescension which does not veil its own face, but permits it to be spat upon! No other could thus have spoken of himself but he who is both God and man. He must be divine: how else could he say, "Behold, at my rebuke I dry up the sea, I make the rivers a wilderness"? (Verse 2.) And yet he must at the same time be a "Man of sorrows and acquainted with grief," for there is a strange depth of pathos in the words, "I gave my back to the smiters, and my cheeks to them that plucked off the hair: I hid not my face from shame and spitting." Whatever others may say, we believe that the speaker in this verse is Jesus of Nazareth, the King of the Jews, the Son of God and the Son of man, our Redeemer. It is the Judge of Israel whom they have smitten with a rod upon the cheek who here plaintively declares the griefs which he has undergone.

We have before us the language of prophecy, but it is as accurate as though it had been written at the moment of the event. Isaiah might have been one of the Evang͏͏ ͏ ͏'s, so exactly does he describe what our Saviour endured.

I have already laid before you in the reading of the Scriptures some of the passages of the New Testament wherein the scourging and the shame of our Lord Jesus are described. We saw him first at the tribunal of his own countrymen in Matthew xxvi., and we read, "Then did they spit in his face, and buffeted him ; and others smote him with the palms of their hands." It was in the hall of the high priest, among his own countrymen, that first of all the shameful deeds of scorn were wrought upon him. "He came unto his own, and his own received him not." His worst foes were they of his own household ; they despised and abhorred him, and would have none of him. His own Father's husbandmen said among themselves,—" This is the heir ; let us kill him, and let us seize on his inheritance." This was his treatment at the hand of the house of Israel.

The same treatment, or the like thereto, was accorded him in Herod's palace, where the lingering shade of a Jewish royalty still existed. There what I might venture to call a pattern mixture of Jew and Gentile power held court, but our Lord fared no better in the united company. By the two combined the Lord was treated with equal derision (Luke xxiii. 11). "Herod with his men of war set him at nought, and mocked him, and arrayed him in a gorgeous robe."

Speedily came his third trial, and he was delivered altogether to the Gentiles. Then Pilate, the governor, gave him up to the cruel process of scourging. Scourging as it has been practised in the English army is atrocious, a barbarism which ought to make us blush for the past, and resolve to end it for the future. How is it that such a horror has been tolerated so long in a country where we are not all savages? But the lash is nothing among us compared with what it was among the Romans. I have heard that it was made of the sinews of oxen, and that in it were twisted the hucklebones of sheep, with slivers of bone, in order that every stroke might more effectually tear its way into the poor quivering flesh, which was mangled by its awful strokes. Scourging was such a punishment that it was generally regarded as worse than death itself, and indeed, many perished while enduring it, or soon afterwards. Our blessed Redeemer gave his back to the smiters, and the ploughers made deep furrows there. O spectacle of misery! How can we bear to look thereon ? Nor was that all, for Pilate's soldiers, calling all the band together, as if there were not enough for mockery unless all were mustered, put him to derision by a mock enthronement and a mimic coronation ; and when they had thus done they again buffeted and smote him, and spat in his face. There was no kind of cruelty which their heartlessness could just then invent which they did not exercise upon his blessed person : their brutal sport had full indulgence, for their innocent victim offered neither resistance nor remonstrance. This is his own record of his patient endurance, "I gave my back to the smiters, and my cheeks to them that plucked off the hair : I hid not my face from shame and spitting."

Behold your King! I bring him forth to you this morning in spirit and cry, "Behold the Man!" Turn hither all your eyes and hearts and look upon the despised and rejected of men! Gaze reverently and lovingly, with awe for his sufferings and love for his person. The sight demands adoration. I would remind you of that which Moses did when he saw the bush that burned and was not consumed—fit emblem of our Lord on fire with griefs and yet not destroyed; I bid you turn aside and see this great sight, but first attend to the mandate—"put off thy shoes from off thy feet, for the place whereon thou standest is holy ground." All round the cross the soil is sacred. Our suffering Lord has consecrated every place whereon he stood, and therefore our hearts must be filled with reverence while we linger under the shadow of his passion.

May the Holy Spirit help you to see Jesus in four lights at this time. In each view he is worthy of devout attention. Let us view him first as *the representative of God*; secondly, as *the substitute of his people*; thirdly, as *the servant of Jehovah*; and fourthly, as *the Comforter of his redeemed*.

I. First, I invite you to gaze upon your despised and rejected Lord as THE REPRESENTATIVE OF GOD. In the person of Christ Jesus, God himself came into the world, making a special visitation to Jerusalem and the Jewish people, but at the same time coming very near to all mankind. The Lord called to the people whom he had favoured so long and whom he was intent to favour still. He says, in the second verse, "I came" and "I called." God did in very deed come down into the midst of mankind.

Be it noted, that when our Lord came into this world as the representative of God, he came with all his divine power about him. The chapter before us says, "Is my hand shortened at all, that it cannot redeem? or have I no power to deliver? behold, at my rebuke I dry up the sea, I make the rivers a wilderness." The Son of God, when he was here, did not perform those exact miracles, because he was bent upon marvels of beneficence rather than of judgment. He did not repeat the plagues of Egypt, for he did not come to smite, but to save; but he did greater wonders and wrought miracles which ought far more powerfully to have won men's confidence in him because they were full of goodness and mercy. He fed the hungry, he healed the sick, he raised the dead, and he cast out devils. He did equal marvels to those which were wrought in Egypt when the arm of the Lord was made bare in the eyes of all the people. It is true he did not change water into blood, but he turned water into wine. It is true he did not make their fish to stink, but by his word he caused the net to be filled even to bursting with great fishes. He did not break the whole staff of bread as he did in Egypt, but he multiplied loaves and fishes so that thousands of men and women and children were fed from his bounteous hand. He did not slay their firstborn, but he restored the dead. I grant you that the glory of the Godhead was somewhat hidden in the person of Jesus of Nazareth, but it was still there, even as the glory was upon the face of Moses when he covered it with a veil. No essential attribute of God was absent in Christ, and every one might have been seen in him if the people had not been wilfully blind. He did the works of his Father, and those works bare witness of him that he was come in his Father's name. Yes, God was personally in the world when Jesus walked the blessed fields of the Holy Land, now, alas, laid under the curse for rejecting him.

But when God thus came among men he was unacknowledged. What saith the prophet? "Wherefore when I came was there no man? when I called was there none to answer?" A few, taught by the Spirit of God, discerned him and rejoiced; but they were so very few that we may say of the whole generation that they knew him not. Those who had some dim idea of his excellence and majesty yet rejected him. Herod, because he feared that he was a king, sought to slay him. The kings of the earth set themselves, and the rulers took counsel together, against the Lord, and against his anointed. He was emphatically and beyond all others "despised and rejected of men." Though, as I have said, the Godhead in him was but scantily veiled, and gleams of its glory burst forth ever and anon, yet still the people would have none of it, and the cry, "Away with him, away with him, let him be crucified," was the verdict of the age upon which he descended. He called and there was none to answer; he spread out his hands all the day long unto a rebellious people who utterly rejected him.

Yet our Lord when he came into the world was admirably adapted to be the representative of God, not only because he was God himself, but because as man his whole human nature was consecrated to the work, and in him was neither flaw nor spot. He was untouched by any motive other than the one desire of manifesting the Father and blessing the sons of men. Oh, beloved, there was never one who had his ear so near the mouth of God as Jesus had. His Father had no need to speak to him in dreams and visions of the night, for when all his faculties were wide awake there was nothing in them to hinder his understanding the mind of God; and therefore every morning when his Father wakened him he spake into his ear. Jesus sat as a scholar at the Father's feet that he might learn first, and then teach. The things which he heard of the Father he made known unto men. He says that he spake not his own words but the words of Him that sent him, and he did not his own deeds, but "my Father," saith he, "that dwelleth in me, he doeth the work." Now, a man thus entirely agreeable to the mind and will of the great God was fitted to be the representative of God. Both the alliance of his manhood with the Godhead and its perfect character qualified it to be the fittest dwelling of God among men. Yes, dear friends, our Saviour came in a way which should at once have commanded the reverent homage of all men. Even his great Father said, "They will reverence my Son." Enough of the Godhead was manifested to impress and no more, lest it should alarm. With a soul of gentlest mould and a body like our own he was altogether adapted to be the representative of God. His errand, too, was all gentleness and love, for he came to speak words in season to the weary, and to comfort those that were cast down: surely such an errand should have secured him a welcome. His course and conduct were most conciliatory, for he went among the people, and ate with publicans and sinners; so gentle was he that he took little children in his arms, and blessed them; for this, if for nothing else, they ought to have welcomed him right heartily and rejoiced at the sight of him. Our text tells us how contrary was their conduct towards him to that which he deserved: instead of being welcomed he was scourged, and instead of being honoured he was scorned. Cruelty smote his back and plucked off the hair from his face, while derision jeered at him and cast its spittle upon him. Shame and contempt were poured upon him, though he was God himself. That spectacle of Christ spat upon, and scourged, represents what man virtually does to his God, what he would do to the Most High if he could. Hart well puts it:—

> "See how the patient Jesus stands,
> Insulted in his lowest case!
> Sinners have bound the Almighty hands,
> And spit in their Creator's face."

When our parents broke the command of their Maker, obeying the advice of the devil rather than the word of God, and preferring a poor apple to the divine favour, they did as it were spit into the face of God; and every sin committed since has been a repetition of the same contempt of the Eternal One. When a man will have his pleasure, even though it displeases God, he as good as declares that he despises God, prefers himself, and defies the wrath of the Most High. When a man acts contrary to the command of God he does as good as say to God, "This is better for me to do than what thou bidst me do. Either thou art mistaken, in thy prohibitions, or else thou dost wilfully deny me the highest pleasure, and I, being a better judge of my own interests than thou art, snatch at the pleasure which thou dost refuse me. I judge thee either to be unwise or unkind." Every act of sin does despite to the sovereignty of God: it denies him to be supreme, and refuses him obedience. Every act of sin does dishonour to the love and wisdom of God, for it seems to say that it would have been greater love to have permitted us to do evil than to have commanded us to abstain from it. All sin is in many ways an insult to the majesty of the thrice Holy God, and he regards it as such.

Dear friends, this is especially the sin of those who have heard the gospel and yet reject the Saviour, for in their case the Lord has come to them in the most gracious form, and yet they have refused him. The Lord might well say, "I have come to you to save you, and you will not regard me. I have come saying to you, 'Look unto me and be ye saved, all the ends of the earth,' and you close your eyes in unbelief. I have come saying, 'Let us reason together: though your sins be as crimson, they shall be as wool,' but you will not be cleansed from your iniquity. I have come with the promise, 'All manner of sin and iniquity shall be forgiven unto men.' What is your reply?" In the case of many the answer is, "We prefer our own righteousness to the righteousness of God." If that is not casting spittle into the face of God I know not what is, for our righteousnesses are well described as "filthy rags," and we have the impudence to say that these are better than the righteousness of God in Christ Jesus. Or if we do not say this when we reject the Saviour we tell him that we do not want him, for we do not need a Saviour: this is as good as to say that God has played the fool with the life and death of his own Son. What greater derision can be cast upon God than to consider the blood of atonement to be a superfluity? He who chooses sin sooner than repentance prefers to suffer the wrath of God rather than be holy and dwell in heaven for ever. For the sake of a few paltry pleasures men forego the love of God, and are ready to run the risk of an eternity of divine wrath. They think so little of God that he is of no account with them at all. All this is in reality a scorning and despising of the Lord God, and is well set forth by the insults which were poured upon the Lord Jesus.

Woe's me that it should ever be so. My God! my God! To what a sinful race do I belong. Alas, that it should treat thine infinite goodness so despitefully! That thou shouldst be rejected at all, but especially that thou shouldest be rejected when dressed in robes of love and arrayed in gentleness and pity is horrible to think upon. Do you mean it, O men? Can you really mean it? Can you deride the Lord Jesus who died for men? For which of his works do ye stone him, when he lived only to do good? For which of his griefs do you refuse him, when he died only that he might save? "He saved others, himself he cannot save," for he had so much love that he could not spare himself. I can understand your resisting the thunder of Jehovah's power, for I know your insanity; but can you resist the tenderness of Jehovah's love? If you do I must charge you with brutality, but therein I wrong the brutes, to whom such crimes are impossible. I may not even call this cruel scorning *diabolical*, for it is a sin which devils never did commit, perhaps would not have committed had it been possible to them. They have never trifled with a Redeemer, nor rejected the blood of atonement, for our Lord took not up the fallen angels, but he took up the seed of Abraham. Shall the favoured race spit upon its friend? God grant we may be brought to a better mind. But there is the picture before you. God himself set at nought, despised, rejected, put to shame, perpetually dishonoured in the person of his dear Son. The sight should breed repentance in us. We should look to him whom we have scourged, and mourn for him. O Holy Spirit, work this tender grace in all our hearts.

II. And now, secondly, I want to set the Lord Jesus before you in another light, or rather beseech him to shine in his own light before your eyes:—AS THE SUBSTITUTE FOR HIS PEOPLE. Recollect when our Lord Jesus Christ suffered thus it was not on his own account nor purely for the sake of his Father, but he "was wounded for our transgressions, he was bruised for our iniquities: the chastisement of our peace was upon him; and with his stripes we are healed." There has risen up a modern idea which I cannot too much reprobate, that Christ made no atonement for our sin except upon the cross: whereas in this passage of Isaiah we are taught as plainly as possible that by his bruising and his stripes, as well as by his death, we are healed. Never divide between the life and the death of Christ. How could he have died if he had not lived? How could he suffer except while he lived? Death is not suffering, but the end of it. Guard also against the evil notion that you have nothing to do with the righteousness of Christ, for he could not have made an atonement by his blood if he had not been perfect in his life. He could not have been acceptable if he had not first been proven to be holy, harmless, and undefiled. The victim must be spotless, or it cannot be presented for sacrifice. Draw no nice lines and raise no quibbling questions, but look at your Lord as he is and bow before him.

Understand, my dear brothers and sisters, that Jesus took upon himself our sin, and being found bearing that sin he had to be treated as sin should be treated. Now, of all the things that ever existed sin is the most shameful thing that can be. It deserves to be scourged, it deserves to be spit upon, it deserves to be crucified ; and because our Lord had taken upon himself our sin, therefore must he be put to shame, therefore must he be scourged. If you want to see what God thinks of sin, see his only Son spat upon by the soldiers when he was made sin for us. In God's sight sin is a shameful, horrible, loathsome, abominable thing, and when Jesus takes it he must be forsaken and given up to scorn. This sight will be the more wonderful to you when you recollect who it was that was spat upon, for if you and I, being sinners, were scourged, and smitten, and despised, there would be no wonder in it ; but he who took our sin was God, before whom angels bow with reverent awe, and yet, seeing the sin was upon him, he was made subject to the most intense degree of shame. Seeing that Jesus stood in our stead, it is written of the eternal Father that " He spared not his own Son." " It pleased the Father to bruise him : he hath put him to grief"; he made his soul an offering for sin. Yes, beloved, sin is condemned in the flesh and made to appear exceeding shameful when you recollect that, even though it was only laid on our blessed Lord by imputation, yet it threw him into the very depths of shame and woe ere it could be removed.

Reflect, also, upon the voluntariness of all this. He willingly submitted to the endurance of suffering and scorn. It is said in the text, "He *gave* his back to the smiters." They did not seize and compel him, or, if they did, yet they could not have done it without his consent. He gave his back to the smiters. He gave his cheek to those that plucked off the hair. He did not hide his face from shame and spitting : he did not seek in any way to escape from insults. It was the voluntariness of his grief which constituted in great measure the merit of it. That Christ should stand in our stead by force were a little thing, even had it been possible ; but that he should stand there of his own free will, and that being there he should willingly be treated with derision, this is grace indeed. The Son of God was willingly made a curse for us, and at his own desire was made subject to shame on our account. I do not know how you feel in listening to me, but while I am speaking I feel as if language ought scarcely to touch such a theme as this : it is too feeble for its task. I want you to get beyond my words if you can, and for yourselves meditate upon the fact that he who covers the heavens with blackness, yet did not cover his own face, and he who binds up the universe with the girdle which holds it in one, yet was bound and blindfolded by the men he had himself made ; he whose face is as the brightness of the sun that shineth in its strength was once spit upon. Surely we shall need faith in heaven to believe this wondrous fact. Can it have been true, that the glorious Son of God was jeered and jested at ? I have often heard that there is no faith wanted in heaven, but I rather judge that we shall want as much faith to believe that these things were ever done as the patriarchs had to believe that they would be done. How shall I sit down and gaze upon *him* and think that his dear face was once profaned with spittle ? When all heaven shall lie prostrate at his feet in awful silence of adoration will it seem possible that once he was mocked ? When angels, and principalities, and powers shall all be roused to rapture of harmonious music in his praise, will it seem possible that once the most abject of men plucked out the hair ? Will it not appear incredible that those sacred hands, which are "as gold rings set with the beryl," were once nailed to a gibbet, and that those cheeks which are "as a bed of spices, as sweet flowers," should have been battered and bruised? We shall be quite certain of the fact, and yet we shall never cease to wonder, that his side was gashed, and his face was spit upon? The sin of man in this instance will always amaze us. How could you commit this crime? Oh, ye sons of men, how could ye treat such an one with cruel scorn? O thou brazen thing called sin, thou hast, indeed, as the prophet saith, "a whore's forehead"; thou hast a demon's heart, hell burns within thee. Why couldst thou not spit upon earthly splendours? Why must heaven be thy scorn? Or if heaven, why not spit on angels! Was there no place for thy base deed but the Well-beloved's face? Was there no place for thy spittle but *his* face? *His* face! Woe is me! His face! Should such loveliness receive such shame as this? I could wish that man had never been created, or that, being created, he had been swept into nothingness rather than have lived to commit such horror.

Yet here is matter for our faith to rest upon. Beloved, trust yourselves in the hands of your great Substitute. Did he bear all this shame? then there must be more than enough merit and efficacy in this, which was the prelude of his precious death—and especially in his death itself —there must be merit sufficient to put away all transgression, iniquity, and sin. Our shame is ended, for he has borne it! Our punishment is removed: he has endured it all. Double for all our sins has our Redeemer paid. Return unto thy rest, O my soul, and let peace take full possession of thy weeping heart.

III. But time fails us, and therefore we will mention, next, the third light in which it is our desire to see the Saviour. Beloved, we desire to see the Lord Jesus Christ AS THE SERVANT OF GOD. He took upon himself the form of a servant when he was made in the likeness of man. Observe how he performed this service right thoroughly, and remember we are to look upon this third picture as our copy, which is to be the guide of our life. I know that many of you are glad to call yourselves the servants of God; take not the name in vain. As Jesus was, so are you also in this world, and you are to seek to be like him.

First, as a servant, Christ was personally prepared for service. He was thirty years and more here below, learning obedience in his father's house, and the after years were spent in learning obedience by the things which he suffered. What a servant he was, for he never went about his own errands nor went by his own will, but he waited always upon his Father. He was in constant communication with heaven, both by day and by night. He says, "He wakeneth morning by morning, he wakeneth mine ear to hear as the learned." The blessed Lord or ever the day broke heard that gentle voice which called him, and at its whisper he arose before the sunrise, and there the dawning found him, on the mountain side, waiting upon God in wrestling prayer, taking his message from the Father that he might go and deliver it to the children of men. He loved man much, but he loved his Father more, and he never came to tell out the love of God without having as man received it fresh from the divine heart. He knew that his Father heard him always, and he lived in the spirit of conscious acceptance. Have you ever noticed that sometimes a passage will begin, "At that time Jesus answered and said," and yet there is no notice that he had been speaking to anybody before, or that anybody had been speaking to him? What he said was an answer to a voice which no ear heard but his own, for he was always standing with opened ear, listening to the eternal voice. Such service did Jesus render, and you must render the same. You cannot do your Lord's will except you live near to him. It is of no use trying to preach with power unless we get our message from our heavenly Father's own self. I am sure you as hearers know the difference between a dead word which comes from a man's own brain and lip, and a living word which the preacher delivers fresh as the manna which fell from heaven. The word should come from the minister like bread hot from the oven, or better still, like a seed with life in it; not as a parched grain with the germ dead and killed, but as a living seed which roots itself in your souls, and springs up to a harvest. This made our Lord such a good servant that he listened to his Father's voice and yielded himself to the Father's will to perfection.

Our text assures us that this service knew no reserve in its consecration. *We* generally draw back somewhere. I am ashamed to say it, but I mourn that I have done so. Many of us could give to Christ all our health and strength, and all the money we have, very heartily and cheerfully; but when it comes to a point of reputation we feel the pinch. To be slandered, to have some filthy thing said of you; this is too much for flesh and blood. You seem to say, "I cannot be made a fool of, I cannot bear to be regarded as a mere impostor;" but a true servant of Christ must make himself of no reputation when he takes upon himself the work of his Lord. Our blessed Master was willing to be scoffed at by the lewdest and the lowest of men. The abjects jeered at him; the reproach of them that reproached God fell upon him. He became the song of the drunkard, and when the rough soldiery detained him in the guard-room they heaped up their ridicule, as though he were not worthy of the name of man.

> "They bow their knees to me, and cry, 'Hail, King':
> Whatever scoffs or scornfulness can bring,
> I am the floor, the sink, where they it fling:
>   *Was ever grief like mine?*
>
> "The soldiers also spit upon that face
> Which angels did desire to have the grace
> And prophets once to see, but found no place:
>   *Was ever grief like mine?*"

Herod and Pilate were the very dross of men, and yet he permitted them to judge him. Their servants were vile fellows, and yet he resigned himself to them. If he had breathed upon them with angry breath, he might have flashed devouring fire upon them, and burned them up as stubble; but his omnipotent patience restrained his indignation, and he remained as a sheep before her shearers. He allowed his own creatures to pluck his hair and spit in his face. Such patience should be yours as servants of God. We are to be willing to be made nothing of, and even to be counted as the offscouring of all things. It is pitiful for the Christian to refuse to suffer, and to become a fighting man, crying, "We must stand up for our rights." Did you ever see Jesus in that posture? There is a propensity in us to say, "I will have it out." Yes, but you cannot picture Jesus in that attitude. I defy a painter to depict him so: it is somebody else, and not Christ. No! he said, "I gave my back to the smiters, and my cheeks to them that plucked off the hair: I hid not my face from shame and spitting."

There is something more here than perfect consecration in the mere form of it, for its heart and essence are manifest in an obedient delight in the will of the Father. The words seem to me to express alacrity. It is not said that he reluctantly permitted his enemies to pluck his hair, or smite his back, but it is written, "I *gave* my back to the smiter, and my cheeks to them that plucked off the hair." He could not delight in it; how could he delight in suffering and shame? These things were even more repugnant to his sensitive nature than they can be to us; and yet, "For the joy that was set before him he endured the cross, despising the shame." He was ready for this dreadful treatment, for he said, "I have a baptism to be baptized with, and how am I straitened until it be accomplished!" He was ready for the cup of gall, and willing to drink it to its dregs, though it was bitterness itself to him. He gave his back to the smiters.

All this while—now follow me in this next point—there was no flinching in him. They spat in his face, but what says he in the seventh verse. "I have set my face like a flint." If they are about to defile his face he is resolved to bear it; he girds up his loins, and makes himself more determined. Oh, the bravery of our Master's silence! Cruelty and shame could not make him speak. Have not your lips sometimes longed to speak out a denial and a defence? Have you not felt it wise to be quiet, but then the charge has been so excessively cruel, and it has stung you so terribly that you hungered to resent it. Base falsehoods aroused your indignation, and you felt you must speak and probably you did speak, though you tried to keep your lips as with a bridle while the wicked were before you. But our own beloved Lord in the omnipotence of his patience and love would not utter a word, but like a lamb at the slaughter he opened not his mouth. He witnessed a good confession by his matchless silence. Oh, how mighty—how gloriously mighty was his patience! We must copy it if we are to be his disciples. We, too, must set our faces like flints, to move or to sit still, according to the Father's will, to be silent or to speak, as most shall honour him. "I have set my face like a flint," saith he, even though in another place he cries, "My heart is like wax, it is melted in the midst of my bowels."

And do you notice all the while the confidence and quiet of his spirit? He almost seems to say, "You may spit upon me, but you cannot find fault with me. You may pluck my hair, but you cannot impugn my integrity; you may lash my shoulders, but you cannot impute a fault to me. Your false witnesses dare not look me in the face: let me know who is mine adversary, let him come near to me. Behold, Adonai Jehovah will keep me, who is he that shall condemn me! Lo, they all shall wax old as a garment, the moth shall eat them up." Be calm then, O true servant of God! In patience possess your soul. Serve God steadily and steadfastly though all men should belie you. Go to the bottom of the service, dive even to the very depth, and be content even to lie in Christ's grave, for you shall share in Christ's resurrection. Do not dream that the path to heaven is up the hill of honour, it winds down into the valley of humiliation. Imagine not that you can grow great eternally by being great here. You must become less, and less, and less, even though you should be despised and rejected of men, for this is the path to everlasting glory.

I have not time to expound the last two verses of the chapter, but they read you a noble lesson. "He gave his back to the smiters;" if, then, any of you walk in darkness and have no light, this is no new thing for a servant of God. The chief of all servants persevered, though men despised him. Follow him, then. Stay yourselves upon God as he did, and look for a bright ending of your trials. He came out into the light ultimately, and there he sits in inconceivable splendour at his Father's right hand, and so shall all the faithful come out of the cloud and shine forth as the sun in the kingdom of their Father. Only bear on with resolute patience, and glory shall be *your* reward, even as it is his.

IV. Lastly, I am to set him forth in his fourth character, as THE COMFORTER OF HIS PEOPLE; but I must ask *you* to do this, while I just, as it were, make a charcoal sketch of the picture I would have painted.

Remember, first, our blessed Lord is well qualified to speak a word in season to him that is weary, because he himself is lowly, and meek, and so accessible to us. When men are in low spirits they feel as if they could not take comfort from persons who are harsh and proud. The comforter must come as a sufferer; he must come in a lowly, broken spirit, if he would cheer the afflicted. You must not put on your best dress to go and visit the daughter of poverty, or go with your jewels about you to show how much better off you are than she. Sit down by the side of the downcast man and let him know that you are meek and lowly of heart. Your Master "gave his back to the smiters, and his cheek to them that plucked off the hair," and therefore he is the Comforter you want.

Remark not only his lowliness, but his sympathy. Are you full of aches and pains this morning? Jesus knows all about them, for he "gave his back to the smiters." Do you suffer from what is worse than pain, from scandal and slander? "He hid not his face from shame and spitting." Have you been ridiculed of late? Have the graceless made fun of your godliness? Jesus can sympathise with you, for you know what unholy mirth they made out of him. In every pang that rends your heart your Lord has borne his share. Go and tell him. Many will not understand you. You are a speckled bird, differing from all the rest, and they will all peck at you; but Jesus Christ knows this, for he was a speckled bird too. He was "holy, harmless, undefiled, and separate from sinners," but not separate from such as you. Get you to him and he will sympathise with you.

In addition to his gentle spirit and his power to sympathise, there is this to help to comfort us—namely, his example, for he can argue thus with you, "I gave my back to the smiters. Cannot you do the like? Shall the disciple be above his master?" If I can but get on the doorstep of heaven and sit down in the meanest place there I shall feel I have an infinitely better position than I deserve, and shall I think of my dear, blessed Lord and Master giving his face to be spit upon, and then give myself airs, and say, " I cannot bear this scorn, I cannot bear this pain"! What, does the King pass over the brook Kedron, and must there be no brook Kedron for you? Does the Master bear the cross, and must your shoulders never be galled? Did they call the Master of the house "Beelzebub," and must they call you "Reverend Sir"? Did they laugh at him, and scoff at him, and must you be honoured? Are you to be "gentleman" and "lady" where Christ was " that fellow"? For his birth they loaned him a stable, and for his burial he borrowed a grave. O friends, let pride disappear, and let us count it our highest honour to be permitted to stoop as low as ever we can.

And, then, his example further comforts us by the fact that he was calm amid it all. Oh, the deep rest of the Saviour's heart! They set him up upon that mock throne, but he did not answer with an angry word; they put a reed into his hand, but he did not change it to an iron rod, and break them like potters' vessels, as he might have done. There was no wincing and no pleading for mercy. Sighs of pain were forced from him, and he said, "I thirst," for he was not a stoic; but there was no fear of man, or timorous shrinking of heart.

The King of Martyrs well deserves to wear the martyr's crown, for right royally did he endure: there was never a patience like to his. That is your copy, brother, that is your copy, sister—you must write very carefully to write as well as that. You had need your Master held your hand; in fact, whenever children in Christ's school do write according to his copy, it is always because he holds their hand by his Spirit.

Last of all, our Saviour's triumph is meant to be a stimulus and encouragement to us. He stands before us this morning as the Comforter of his people. Consider Him that endured such contradiction of sinners against himself lest ye be weary and faint in your minds; for though he was once abased and despised, yet now he sitteth at the right hand of God, and reigns over all things; and the day is coming when every knee shall bow before him, and every tongue confess that Jesus Christ is Lord, to the glory of God the Father. They that spat upon him will rue the day. Come hither, ye that derided him! He has raised you from the dead, come hither and spit upon him now! Ye that scourged him, bring your rods, see what ye can do in this day of his glory! See, they fly before him, they invoke the hills to shelter them, they ask the rocks to open and conceal them. Yet it is nothing but his face, that selfsame face they spat upon, which is making earth and heaven to flee away. Yea, all things flee before the majesty of his frown who once gave his back to the smiters, and his cheeks to them that plucked off the hair. Be like him, then, ye who bear his name; trust him, and live for him, and you shall reign with him in glory for ever and ever. Amen.

The Nazarene and the Sect of the Nazarenes

> "And he came and dwelt in a city called Nazareth: that it might be fulfilled which was spoken by the prophets, He shall be called a Nazarene"—Matt. ii. 23.

WE find the Jews speaking of Paul, and they say,

> "We have found this man a pestilent fellow, and a mover of sedition among all the Jews throughout the world, and a ringleader of the sect of the Nazarenes"—Acts xxiv. 5.

Thus it appears that our Lord and Master is called a Nazarene, and his disciples are styled "the sect of the Nazarenes," while Christian doctrine was called by the Jews the heresy of the Nazarenes.

Our Saviour, though actually born at Bethlehem, was commonly known as Jesus of Nazareth, because Nazareth was the place where he was brought up. There he remained with his reputed father in the carpenter's shop until the time of his showing unto the people. This Nazareth was a place very much despised. It was a small country town, and the people were rough and rustic. They were some three days' distance from Jerusalem, where I suppose the Jews thought that everything that was learned and polite could be found, as we are apt to think of our own city, or of Oxford, and Cambridge, and other seats of learning. The people of Nazareth were the boors of Galilee, the clowns of the country.

More than that, you will generally find in every nation—I was about to say in every county of our own country—some town made the butt of ridicule. I do not know that "silly Suffolk," is any sillier than any other part of the world; but I do know that I myself happen to have been born in the next parish to the town of Coggeshall, in Essex, concerning which all sorts of jokes are made; so that when any stupid thing is done they call it "a Coggeshall job." I merely mention this because it is an illustration of what used to be said concerning Nazareth. It was a primitive place. It was situated in Galilee, which was thought to be quite boorish enough, and Nazareth was the most rustic of all. The name signifies, in rough words, "sprouts," and the Jews, who were great at puns upon names, threw it as a jest at the people who came from that town. We Anglicize it in a more refined way by the word "branch;" for "Netzar," or "Nazareth," signifies a branch.

You will begin to understand why the Saviour is said to be called by the prophet a Netzar, or a Nazarene, and you will guess that Matthew refers to the passage in Isaiah, in the eleventh chapter at the first verse, where it is said that a rod shall come out of the stem of Jesse, and "a Netzar, a Nazarene, a Branch shall grow out of his roots." There is another passage in Jeremiah where we read of the man, the branch,—the Netzar,—the Nazarene; and again in Isaiah, "And his name shall be called a branch," or Nazarene. Those are the passages, I think, to which Matthew referred when he said, "That it might be fulfilled which was spoken by the prophets, He shall be called a Netzar, a branch, a Nazarene." The Hebrews made a great deal out of names, a great deal more than you and I generally do with names of places in England, and they had reason for so doing, for there was generally a meaning in the names of places. Perhaps Nazareth was called "branch" because trees flourished there, and not much else; or because they thought that the people were rather verdant, and they therefore called them "sprouts" and "greens," making the same use of language as the vulgar do at this day when they wish to express contempt. That may have been the origin of the term "Nazareth." Certain it is that the place was the subject of the jests of the Jews of our Lord's time; for even Nathanael, in whom was no guile, one who spoke in a simple-hearted, honest way, and had no prejudices, but wished well to everybody, said, "Can there any good thing come out of Nazareth?" As if he felt that prophets and saints were by no means likely to spring from a town so low down in the scale of progress and education. How could he of whom Moses spake be found away down there amongst the country folk of Nazareth?

As Nazarene was a term of contempt in the olden times, so it has continued to be. The apostate emperor Julian was wont always to call our Lord the Galilean; and when he died, in his agony of death, he cried, "O Galilean, thou hast vanquished me." He was obliged to confess our Lord's supremacy, though he still showed his contempt by calling him the Galilean. The Jews to this day, when they feel wroth against our Christ, are wont to call him the Nazarene.

Nazarene is not at all the same word as Nazarite. It is a different word in the Hebrew, and you must not confound the two. Never suppose that when you say, "He shall be called a Nazarene," that it signifies that he was called a Nazarite. Nazarite among the Jews would have been a title of honour, but Nazarene is simply a name of contempt. A late traveller tells us that he had a Mahometan guide through Palestine, and whenever they came to a village that was very dirty, very poor, and inhabited by professed Christians, he always said, "These are not Moslems; they are *netza*," or "Nazarenes," throwing all the spite he possibly could into the word, as if he could not have uttered a more contemptuous term. To this day, then, our Lord has the name of the Nazarene affixed to him by those who reject him, and to this day Christians are called among Mahometans, *Nazarenes*.

Our Lord Jesus Christ was never ashamed of this name: in fact, he called himself "Jesus of Nazareth" after he had risen from the dead.

He told Paul when he smote him to the earth, "I am Jesus of Nazareth whom thou persecutest." His disciples were not ashamed to call him by that name; for as they walked to Emmaus, and he joined them, and asked them what they were speaking of, they said they were talking of Jesus of Nazareth. This is a name at which devils tremble, for they besought him, even Jesus of Nazareth, that they should not be sent into the deep when he cast them out. It was the name which in contempt was nailed above his head upon the cross—"Jesus of Nazareth the king of the Jews." Oh, but it is a glorious name, as I shall have to show ere I have done. But still this is the meaning of it—the meaning of Matthew when he says that the prophets declared that he should be called a Nazarene. He meant that the prophets have described the Messiah as one that would be despised and rejected of men. They spoke of him as a great prince and conqueror when they described his second coming; but they set forth his first coming when they spoke of him as a root out of a dry ground without form or comeliness, who when he should be seen would have no beauty that men should desire him. The prophets said that he would be called by a despicable title, and it was so, for his countrymen called him a Nazarene.

I want you to notice our divine Redeemer's condescension, before I plunge further into this matter. It was a marvel that Jesus should live on this world at all. He who inhabits all things, whom space is not wide enough to contain, dwells on this poor, dusky planet. If he must dwell in this world, why is he born in Judæa? for though I am grieved it should be so, yet the Jews are a people greatly despised,—shame on Christians when they ever join in such despising. But still if Jesus must be a man in this world, why is he not born in Rome, in the capital of the nations? Why must it be in a little miserable country like Judæa? Yet if he shall be born in Judæa, why must he live in Galilee —that Bœotia of Israel, that most despicable part of Judæa? If he must live in Galilee, why not at Capernaum? Why does he choose Nazareth? Why must he go to the lowest of the low—that most despised place of a despised country? And if he must come to Nazareth, —follow him a step lower—why must he be a carpenter's son? Why, if he lives there, can he not be the son of the minister of the synagague, or some respectable scribe? No; but he must be reputed to be a poor man's son. And then if he must be a carpenter's son, why can he not so constrain men's hearts that they shall receive him? for the deepest depth of all is that even as a carpenter's son his fellow citizens will not endure him; but they take him to the brow of the hill to cast him down headlong from the cliff whereon the city stood. Was there ever such condescension as that of the Saviour? If in the lowest depth there be a lower deep, he plunges into it for our sakes. He emptied himself. Our old version says, "He made himself of no reputation," but the new one is in this case much better,—"He emptied himself." Nothing was left him of honour or respect. He gave up all. "Though he was rich, yet for your sakes he became poor"—poor to the last degree, poor in reputation. He was born a man, a Jew, a Galilean, a Nazarene.

You have gone down as far as language can descend; and I invite you now to think of *the way in which Jesus, the Nazarene, is still despised.* That shall be our first head. When we have thought upon that we will say a little upon *his disciples:* the sect of the Nazarenes must expect to be despised till brighter days shall dawn. When we have talked about that we shall have to say in conclusion that there is *nothing despicable either in the Master or in the servants,* though they are called Nazarenes by a contemptuous world.

I. First, then, OUR MASTER, THE NAZARENE, WAS DESPISED, AND IS DESPISED EVEN TO THIS DAY.

He was despised, first, because in *his person,* his parentage, his state, his apparel, his language, his habits, there was nothing of grandeur, nothing of parade, nothing but what was simple, gentle, lowly. He did ride once, but it was on a colt, the foal of an ass. It was said, "Behold thy king cometh"; but his coming was meek and lowly. He might have been a king: he was very near being taken by force to be pushed up into a throne; but he withdrew himself, for he did not strive, nor cry, nor cause his voice to be heard in the streets. He was no popularity-hunter, or flatterer of the great. He was no man of confusion and strife, who sought to push himself forward and tread down others. Those that opposed him were weak like bruised reeds; but he would not break them though he could have done it. They offended him with their weak arguments, for they were like a smoking flax to him; but he would not quench them. He left them for another day when he shall bring forth judgment unto victory. I suppose, if we had seen the Saviour, we should not have thought him "altogether lovely"; for his heavenly beauty was not of the kind that strikes the natural eye. Hence the impossibility of any painter ever being able to paint him, for though he must have been superlatively lovely, it must have been a beauty with which nobody would be charmed unless their eyes were opened to perceive the beauty of holiness. His was the loveliness of virtue, the charm of purity, and not that sensuous beauty which excites desire and kindles the passions of mankind. He was loveliness itself; but only to those who know what loveliness is. About his dress there was nothing remarkable. He wore the ordinary smock-frock of the country, a garment without seam, woven from the top throughout: a very serviceable, useful piece of work-day apparel, but possessing nothing in it of official dignity, or princely richness, to distinguish him from an ordinary person. As for the place where he lived, it was no bishop's palace, nor even an ordinary manse; for he had not where to lay his head.

He sought no dignity and no honour. As for his companionships, they were of the lowest, for it is said of him, "This man receiveth sinners and eateth with them"; "Then drew near unto him all the publicans and sinners for to hear him." The offcasts of society delighted in his discourses, and they gathered round him to receive blessings at his hand. He lifted them up from the dunghill, renewed them, and set them among princes. He was the last person in the world to be hampered by pride. There was nothing of the kind about him. He was the personification of love. He condescended, but he did not seem to condescend; for graciousness was natural to him. He did it so really that one almost forgot the condescension in the altogether naturalness of the way in which he sympathized with all grief, and helped all who came for succour. Hence the proud despised him. Those who looked for dress and garb, as so many do in our day; those who looked for a show of learning, quotations from great writers, continual perplexities to human minds, could not see much in him. Those who wanted a display of power, a leader bold and brave to drive out the Romans, and play Judas Maccabeus for the people, turned away and said, " He is nothing but an ordinary Nazarene."

His followers, too, were another cause of the contempt poured upon him; for his chosen friends were to those who knew them nothing but common fishermen. Indeed, that is all they were. Unlearned and ignorant men they are said to have been, though they baffled the pretended wisdom of the age in which they lived. How could he have selected such followers? There were scribes, and there were Pharisees; there were Rabbis and Rabbonis; he might surely have called some of those to follow him; but, you see, the Saviour was not a preacher that at all attracted the *élite* of society. Those highly cultured minds, as a rule, went to hear Rabbi Simeon, the Pharisee, who expounded points of no earthly importance; but Jesus was one of whom it is written, "The common people heard him gladly." And so the wise ones ran him down as "a Nazarene." "Look," said they, "look and see who they are that he has chosen to be his chief helpers. See how the lower orders flock around him. They are no judges; what notion have they of profound learning and research? They like a man who is ignorant, for he is like themselves. They have no taste, they have no education, and so they gather to one of themselves." "Ah!" said one of these wiseacres, "I am ashamed of him—quite ashamed. Indeed, I shall speak to him, for he ought not to be so lost to all sense of propriety." And so he goes to the Master and says, "Do you hear the boys crying, 'Hosannah!' in the temple? Hearest thou what these say?" He thought that the Lord would be ashamed of having such admirers as mere street boys; but the Saviour answered, "Have you never read"—as if he was going to question this great man's reading—"have you never read, Out of the mouth of babes and sucklings he hath perfected praise"? He was not ashamed even of chits of children that strewed the pathway for him, nor ashamed of the sick and sinful people that gathered around him, nor ashamed of the poor fishermen that were the lieutenants of his salvation army; but rather did he rejoice therein, and say, " Father, I thank thee that thou hast hid these things from the wise and prudent, and hast revealed them unto babes. Even so, Father, for so it seemed good in thy sight." But the higher classes, the refined and the cultivated, said, "Tush! he is nothing but a Nazarene."

Well, then, when they came to listen to *his doctrine* they were not a bit more pleased, nor did they hold him any higher in esteem. What do you think he taught them? Among other things it is reported that he said, "Except a man be born again he cannot see the kingdom of God": and, would you believe it, he said this not to one of the lower order at all, but to a learned gentleman who was a ruler in Israel? Why, it has come to a pretty pass, this, to tell educated people, refined, æsthetic people, that they must be born again, or else they cannot see the kingdom of God—to insist upon regeneration as a thing as necessary to a philosopher as to a prostitute, as necessary to a senator as to a jail-bird;

as needful to the purest as to the most defiled. Oh no, we cannot bear such levelling doctrine! It is shocking. So they turned their backs to him and called him a Nazarene. When a man tells you unpalatable truth it is very easy and natural to call him bad names. If you cannot answer him anyhow else you can always answer him by reviling him.

And, then, what do you think he said beside that? On one occasion he had the audacity to say—and I am sure the Pharisees thought it was audacity indeed—" Except ye eat my flesh, and drink my blood, there is no life in you." What could the man mean—that they, even they the sons of Abraham who were born free; the priests who had partaken of the sacrifices, must actually eat *him?* Did they think that they would accept *his* teaching as food for their souls? I wonder if they went as far as that in understanding him; but if they did they liked it no better. They were indignant that he should say that the only food for their souls must be himself; that unless he became their life, and the nourishment of that life; unless he became part and parcel of their very being, they could not be saved! Even those who did think a little of him said that after this they must give him up. They could not stand *that,* and so they walked no more with him.

He went even further. Why, he actually dared to tell the scribes and Pharisees who had fasted so many times in the week, and never ate bread without washing their hands, and tithed the mint and the cummin, that there was nothing in all this, and he said—" Ye blind guides, ye hypocrites, ye strain at a gnat, and ye swallow a camel." He went on to tell them that all their outside religion was a lie and a falsehood unless the inner part of the soul were cleansed. He said that it was not that which a man ate or drank, but that which came out of the man that really defiled him. People said, " Did you ever hear such talk as that? Why, he is putting us all down, we that are the best people out. If we are not good, who can be?—we that are the leaders of society, the pink of perfection. We do swallow a widow's house sometimes, but we always do that behind the door. It is true that we are not as clean inside as we should be; but then we always make clean the outside of the cup and platter. Nobody can say but what we do, and he has been talking against us; and at the same time he is inviting the fallen to himself, and saying, 'Come unto me, all ye that labour and are heavy laden, and I will give you rest.'" " Well, well," they said, " we cannot bear it: he is nothing but a Nazarene"; and so they turned their backs upon him.

Dear friends, to-day Jesus Christ is as much despised as ever by those ungodly and vain-glorious men who understand what his gospel is. How frequently you will find in the public newspapers, and in the magazines of those who think themselves the cultivated class, remarks against the doctrine of justification by faith. You and I are simpletons enough to believe that we are justified by faith in Christ Jesus, because God has told us so, and we sing—

"Nothing in my hands I bring,
Simply to the cross I cling";

and they tell us that this is inconsistent with public morality; that the masses ought to be told that unless they behave themselves they cannot possibly go to heaven, and so on :—which thing they have been told times without number, and they have grown worse the more they have been told it. When we tell about free grace, which pardons the vilest through faith in Christ, men are changed, and made moral and holy, but our unbelieving critics choose to ignore all that, and go and talk against what is the very essence of the gospel of Christ, as though it were a poor, miserable thing, only fit for a set of fanatics to preach. "Only believe, and you shall be saved," say they, "that is their absurd doctrine." Thus, in other words, they repeat the old abuse, and call us Nazarenes.

But if you want to see the ungodly world foam at its mouth,—oh if you want to see rage get to its worst, and wish to see pretended learned men upon their mettle, preach the doctrine of atonement by blood! Tell them that remission of sin is by substitution—that Christ stood in the sinner's stead, and took the sinner's sin, and that without shedding of blood there is no remission of sin. See how they writhe and rage! They cannot bear this horrible doctrine of atonement by sacrifice; and yet, most learned sirs, it is upon that horrible atonement that our hope depends; it is upon that horrible doctrine that we hinge our destiny for time and for eternity; and we are not ashamed to bring it out with all plainness of speech, for the precious blood of Christ, God's dear Son, and that alone, cleanseth us from all sin. "Ah, well," they say, "that is just the old story which your Puritan fathers used to tell; that is the old Methodist doctrine: that is your Presbyterianism, and as James the First said, Presbyterianism is no religion for a gentleman." These learned men admire the broad-church school, where everything is taken to be true except the truth. Still Jesus is to the mass of mankind the despised Nazarene.

I will not dwell longer upon it, however, because you that know the Lord need not be told that he is to this day despised and rejected of men. Call yourself a Christian, and forget what Christianity is, and you will have easy times of it. Instead of preaching the simple gospel of Christ get fine music, and fix up fine shows, turn the place of worship into a conservatory, or a theatre, and there will be no persecution for you. Of course not, that is not Jesus Christ; but preach Jesus Christ, and see if all the dogs will not howl at you directly. You shall have ill names, and wicked stories, and all sorts of jests poured upon you. Go through the world as a respectable professor of religion, and never let fall a single distinctive truth from your lips, never perform one single distinctive action of Christianity, but just do as others do, and live as others do, and I will warrant you you shall be in a whole skin from the first of January to the end of December; but be a Christian, and live your Christianity and speak it out, and see how long you will be before they of your own house are at war with you. If we are true to the Master we shall find that we have not enlisted in a service which is all fine feathers and music, but stern fighting is to be done. There is war to be borne and hardness to be endured by every good soldier of the cross, for still Jesus is called the Nazarene.

II. But now, secondly, our other text informs us that CHRIST'S FOLLOWERS HAVE BEEN KNOWN AS THE SECT OF THE NAZARENES—that is to say, they must expect to bear a measure of the indignities poured upon their leader.

Dear young friends, I want to press some matters home upon you who have lately joined the church, and also upon you who love the Lord, but have never yet confessed it.

If you follow Christ fully you will be sure to be called by some ill name or other. For, first, they will say how *singular* you are. "Mine inheritance," says God, "is unto me as a speckled bird. The birds round about her are against her." If you become a true Christian you will soon be a marked man. They will say, "How odd he is!" "How singular she is!" They will think that we try to make ourselves remarkable, when, in fact, we are only conscientious, and are endeavouring to obey what we think to be the word of God. Oftentimes that is the form of contempt: practical Christians are set down as intentionally eccentric and wilfully odd. Mothers have brought that charge against daughters who have been faithful to Christ because they would not go into gaiety, or indulge in vain apparel; and many a working man has said it to his fellow man by way of accusation, "You must be different from anybody else." This difference, which God has made a necessity, men treat as a mere whim of our own. If we do not come out from among them, and be separate, we cannot expect to be housed beneath the wings of the Eternal; but if we do, we may reckon upon being regarded by those around us as strange, unfriendly creatures.

Then, again, they will say to the genuine Christian, "Why, you are so *old-fashioned!* Look at you now! You believe the same old things that they used to believe in Oliver Cromwell's day—those old Puritanical doctrines. Do you not know that the world has made a great progress since those times, and we have entered upon the nineteenth century; a wonderful century, never was century like it. There was only one Solomon centuries ago, but we are all Solomons now, the very least of us, while the greater ones far excel a thousand Solomons rolled into one. The nineteenth century! And here are you, you still stick to an old book that was written, half of it ages ago, and the other half is at least eighteen hundred years old! Will you never move with the times? Will you get as far as Moses, and Jesus, and John, and stick there?" Yes, exactly there. We go not an inch beyond Jesus Christ, the same yesterday, to-day, and for ever. We try to hold fast the faith that was once delivered to the saints. In ordinances we hold to the olden baptism, and the ancient supper; in doctrine we abide by the truths which Paul taught among the Gentiles, for we feel that we cannot improve upon them. We would wish to exhibit the same spirit as Jesus Christ our Lord, for we know we shall never improve upon his perfections. Therefore they say, "You are so old-fashioned;" and we answer that for this we tender no apology.

When that form of criticism does not take effect they laugh at *our faith*. They say, "You simple-minded people have great capacity for believing! Look at us, we are far too sensible to believe anything. We do not feel sure about anything. What we think we know to-day we are not certain of; we are so receptive that we may learn the reverse to-morrow. We get our faith out of our own moral consciousness, and compel even the Scriptures to plead at the bar of our inward conceptions. We do not want to have things revealed to us and to have a book, and bind ourselves down to a book revelation; we are our own teachers, judges, and infallible guides, and the very idea of absolutely certain truth is abhorred by us. As to this Spirit of God that you trust in, it is sheer enthusiasm. There is nothing in it, and we wonder that you should be so credulous, when instead of that you ought to be rational, and believe in Huxley and Tyndall. Do not be credulous and believe in God, but be rational and believe in Bradlaugh, and Voltaire, and Tom Paine." This is another sting for the Nazarenes, but happily it has small power to vex us, since our reverence for the authorities of modern wisdom is not sufficient to make us fear their scoffs. Time was when Christianity was opposed by men of real ability, masters in learning, but in the present age its antagonists are men of much smaller calibre, whose lack of argument is scantily concealed by the outrageous absurdities which they invent. Instead of attempting to overwhelm us by the weight of their learning, they endeavour to surprise us with unexpected hypotheses, which we are more inclined to ridicule than to refute; and then, with mock sobriety, they assert that our bewilderment is defeat. The spears of the phalanx of reason are seen no more, but the shafts of folly stand thick upon our shields. In this, also, we shall conquer through the blood of the Lamb. Meanwhile we leave sneers of contempt to those who are such masters of them. It is for Nazarenes to receive, but not to return, contumely.

Another arrow of contempt is the assertion that Christian people *have not their liberty.* " Look at you, you dare not go to the theatre; you dare not drink." " Why," says one man, " I like a jolly drink sometimes; and if I were a Christian, I could not enjoy that great privilege." No, friend, you certainly would lose that booze of yours. As far as we are concerned we have no ambition in that direction. Some of us know a little of what the amusements of the ungodly are, and we are astonished that you should be able to find content in them, for they do not suit our taste at all. We never envy hogs their wash. Let them have their trough well-filled as often as they please. We have no taste in that direction. But you need not say that we have no liberty because we do not feed out of the swine trough, for such liberty we never desired. We have liberty to serve God and do good, and this is the freedom which we covet. We have liberty to do as we like, for we like to do what God would have us do, and we pray that our likes may every day be more and more conformed to the liking of God. There is not much after all in the taunt, " You God-fearing people are cowardly; you dare not enjoy yourselves." We live daily so as to give this taunt the lie, for we are a happy people, a free people, even we who are of the sect of the Nazarenes.

Again, some turn round upon true Christians for their *not being very choice in their company.* If we associated only with the rich and great, whose society, as far as I know of it, is about the poorest thing out, we should then be acting properly. Keep to "society," and society will smile upon you; but if you attend meetings where you call a costermonger your brother, where the washerwoman is your sister, where so long as people love Christ you count them the best of company, then you are low and vulgar, a Philistine, or a Nazarene. If you are willing to be a true brother to a black man, or to one who is an outcast in condition, who was actually seen with a broom sweeping a crossing, then, of course, you cannot expect to be recognised by anybody who is anybody. Listen to the world's ridicule of true Christian churches where there is real brotherly love and true fraternity. They cannot endure it. Well, they may do without it then, but this shall be my glory, that God has made of one blood all nations of men that dwell upon the face of the earth, and that where there is a touch of grace in any man, his dress and his rank are nothing to me. Real believers in Jesus are truly our brothers and sisters in Christ, however poor or however illiterate they may be. This is the very genius of Christianity. To the poor the gospel is preached: as soon as men enter into the church of Christ, all outward distinctions are forgotten, and they are one in the gracious family of God their Father. This, however, is the subject of contempt even among those who profess and call themselves Christians. Many of your fine ladies and gentlemen would not own Jesus himself if he were now upon earth, and as for his disciples, I am sure they would get the cold shoulder on all sides. I, for one, never expect to see saints fashionable, nor holiness popular: let us be content to be low and vulgar in men's esteem for the Lord's sake.

And then, if God's servants will preach the truth outright, or if not being preachers they will hold it, and dare to avow it, I warrant you they will soon meet with some contemptuous title or other. Pare down the gospel, cut away its angles, draw the lion's teeth, and then at once you shall be friends with the world; but hold the doctrines of grace, bring forth the atonement, speak out plainly, have your convictions and state them, and soon the hounds will be after you full cry. Say that the Bible and the Bible alone is the religion of true Christians, and that we are not bound by prayer-books, synods, conferences, or anything of the kind, but only by the word of God, and you shall see what you shall see, for here and there and everywhere all sorts of people will be against you. Live a godly, gracious life, and you will not escape persecution. You may be happily circumstanced so as to live among earnest Christians, and so escape persecution—but take the average Christian man in this city, and he will have a hard time of it if he is faithful, and he will be pointed at by some opprobrious name or other, something like Paul was when they said he was a ringleader of the sect of the Nazarenes.

III. Now, listen to me as I close. THERE IS, AFTER ALL, NOTHING DESPICABLE IN EITHER CHRIST OR HIS PEOPLE. I feel half ashamed to say such a thing, or that it should ever be necessary to be said that there is nothing to despise in Jesus What is there to be ashamed of in him? He is the Son of the Highest. He is "God over all, blessed for ever," and if he stooped—and stoop he did—and became lower than the lowest by the sufferings of death, even the death of the cross, he did it out of such glorious disinterestedness of kindness to fallen men, that he is thereby revealed as the grandest of all characters. His is the sublimest of all lives. Angels have never ceased to wonder and adore, and even the enemies of Christ have often been struck dumb as they have seen the splendour of the love that moved him to stoop so low. And what if he has revealed a plain gospel? Would you have the illiterate left out in the cold? What if he did preach the gospel to sinners? Who wanted the gospel but sinners? What if he did not flatter the pride of those who thought themselves good? Is it not true that "the whole have no need of a physician, but they that are sick"? For my part, I bless my Master that he has given us a common-place gospel. Sublime it is beyond sublimity, but plain it is so that a little child may understand it. A man with slender wit may find his way to heaven guided by the light of the Holy Spirit, and this is one of the grandest proofs of the profound wisdom of God. Glory be to Jesus Christ that he did not come here to tantalize the multitude by a gospel only suitable to the *élite*, that he did not come here to proclaim doctrines that could only be learned in the universities, and could never be understood except by such men as Isaac Newton or Robert Boyle. I bless the name of Jesus that he came to give a gospel to the poor and needy, to the simple and the childlike; and while I do it, I feel that I hear him saying again, "I thank thee, O Father, Lord of heaven and of earth, that thou hast hid these things from the wise and prudent, and hast revealed them unto babes."

The practical point is this: *there is nothing to be ashamed of in being a Christian.* I am afraid that there are some Christians that we have need to be ashamed of, and that we ourselves do many unworthy things. Christians ought to be reflections *of* Christ, but I fear they often cast reflections *upon* Christ. Oh ye that despise Christ, when you find out our faults, and speak against us for them, you treat us justly, and we cannot complain; but why lay our crimes at our Saviour's door? If you find us false to our profession, if we are not like our Master, if we are not true to him, you may well ridicule us, and we cannot answer you. We must be beaten as with whips of scorpions when we are untrue to our Leader; but why blame *him?*

The fact is that the ungodly revile those who are true to the Lord Jesus. Well, when they do, there is nothing in that to be ashamed of. What if I believe the truth! shall I be ashamed of it? What if I fear God! shall I be ashamed of it? Let those be ashamed who do not fear him. What if I believe in prayer! What if I receive answers to prayer! Shall I blush about that? Let those blush to scarlet who never pray, or have no God to hear their prayers.

Shall I be ashamed because I try to do what is right, and have a conscience before God, and cannot enjoy loose pleasures, or listen to lascivious song? Shall I be ashamed of chastity and truth? Why then let angels be ashamed of purity; let the stars be ashamed of light; let the sun be ashamed of day. There is nothing to be ashamed of in things honourable and of good repute. What are some of you at—you who are, I trust, Christians, that you never come out and own your religion? What will your Master say to you in the day of his appearing? What honour can you expect to share with him if you will not share his shame? If any man wants to spit on Christ, let him do me the honour to spit on me. If any man will rail on Christ, let him do me the pleasure to rail on me, for if I may stand between him and my Master, I shall be promoted by the deed. Napoleon's Mamaluke flung himself in the way of the bullet to save the emperor's life. Shall not Christ be served after that fashion? Shall we not be willing to be Nazarenes for the Nazarene? Shall we not glory to be despised and rejected of men for his sake, if by any means we may bring honour to him? I trust it shall be so; and yet some of you have not even been baptized into his name, though you know that it is his command. You have never joined with his people in church fellowship, and yet wish to share their joys. You let them fight the battle alone. You think, I suppose, to slink into heaven by the back door, and not to be found among the soldiers of Christ till the crowns are distributed? Ah, sirs, you miss a great honour in not standing shoulder to shoulder with the rank and file of Christ's chosen. Angels would leave heaven if they could, to come and fight for Christ. They would be glad to leave their rest to bear the hardness which a follower of Christ must endure for his dear Captain's sake. Jesus is coming! He is on his way! He may come to-night. He may come before another Sabbath's bells shall ring; and oh if I have never confessed him, if I have been ashamed of him, how shall I face him? Hear this, ye cowards! What will you say when he appeareth? Be wise and confess him betimes. Come ye out from among the ungodly. Be ye separate. Confess your Lord and Master. "He that with his heart believeth, and with his mouth maketh confession of him, shall be saved." "He that believeth and is baptized shall be saved. He that believeth not shall be damned." God save us from being ashamed of the Nazarene. Amen.

The Great Itinerant

"Who went about doing good"—Acts x. 38.

You will observe, if you read the chapter before us, that Peter's sermon was short and much to the point. He preached Jesus Christ to Cornelius immediately and unmistakably. He gave a very admirable sketch of the life of Jesus, of which he affirmed himself to have been an eye-witness, and he brought forward in his closing sentence just that simple gospel which it is our joy to preach. "To him give all the prophets witness, that through his name whosoever believeth in him shall receive remission of sins." This should be an instructive example to all professed ministers of the gospel. We might say less about other matters without loss, if we would say more about the Lord Jesus. If we should omit some other teaching, if there were more of a savour of the name and of the person of Jesus Christ in our ministry, the omissions might be tolerated. It is a strange thing that men should profess to be sent of God, and yet talk about everything except the great message which they are sent to deliver. My errand as a minister is to preach Christ, and it will avail me little to have been clear and earnest upon other points, if I have neglected to set forth Christ crucified. To put my own views of doctrine or moral practice in the place of Jesus, is to put out the sun, and supply its place with a farthing rushlight; to take away the children's bread, and offer them a stone. We commend Peter as an example to all who preach or teach, either in the street, the sick-chamber, or the house of prayer; do as Peter did; come at once to the soul of your ministry, and set forth Christ crucified in plain and simple language. If any should plead that the subject should be adapted to the audience, we see from the narrative that there is sure to be something in the history of Christ applicable to the case before us. Peter purposely gave prominence to certain points in the history of the Master which would be most likely to enlist the sympathy of Cornelius. He says of him, "He is Lord of all;" as much as to say, "He is not Lord of the Jews only, but also of the Gentiles, and therefore, O Cornelius, his dominion reaches to you. He is to be worshipped and adored, and he is to become a blessing, and a propitiatory sacrifice, not only to Israel's hosts, but even to the Italian band; and therefore thou, O Centurion, mayst take heart." Perhaps the words of our text were uttered by Peter concerning Christ because they also would be sure to attract the notice of a man who was "A devout man, and one that feared God with all his house, which gave much alms to the people, and prayed to God alway." He did as much as say, "Thou goest about doing good, Cornelius. It is the very soul of thy life to help the needy, to feed the hungry, and to clothe the naked: Jesus also went about doing good in a higher sense, and I hold him up to thee as one to be beloved by every devout and generous heart."

Other points are to be noticed in Peter's address, which were evidently adapted to the case before him, but we have said enough to prove that there is something in the story of Jesus suitable to win the attention, and to gain the heart of any congregation, large or small. Only let the Holy Spirit help us to dilate upon the gospel of the Lord Jesus, and we have no need to wander abroad for foreign themes; we can sit at the foot of the cross, and find a perpetually profitable subject there. No need to gather the sheaves of science, or the sweet flowers of poesy; Christ Jesus is both our science and our poetry, and as ministers we are complete in him. When we come forth to preach him, and to lift him up, we are armed from head to foot, and rich with weapons for our spiritual warfare; though learning and art have had no hand in fashioning our panoply, we need not fear that we shall meet a single foe who can withstand the terror of those celestial arms. God grant us grace in all our teachings to keep close to Jesus Christ, for his love is a theme most fit for all cases, and most sweet at all times.

The few words which we have taken for our text, are an exquisite miniature of the Lord Jesus Christ. "He went about doing good." There are not many touches, but they are the strokes of a master's pencil. The portrait cannot be mistaken for anyone else. The mightiest conquerors may gaze upon its beauties, but they cannot claim that it is intended to portray their lives. Alexander, Cæsar, Napoleon—these went about conquering, burning, destroying, murdering; they went not about doing good. Prophets too, who professed to have been sent of God, have compassed sea and land to make proselytes, but the good which they accomplished none could see. Mahomet's career was fraught with incalculable evil. The few good men and true who, like Howard, have perambulated the world, seeking to minister to the necessities of mankind, have wept over the heavenly portrait, and sighed that they are not more like it. This is what they sought to be, and so far as they copied this portrait, this is what they were; but they fall short of the original, and are not slow to confess their shortcomings. What Peter here draws in words, God's divine grace drew, in some measure, in lines of real life in the case of Howard and some other followers of Jesus of Nazareth; still, in the highest and fullest sense, these words are applicable to none but the Master, for his followers could not do such good as he achieved. His is the model, and theirs the humble copy; his the classic type, and theirs the modest imitation. He did good, and good only: but the best of men, being men at the best, sow mingled seed; and if they scatter handsful of wheat, there is here and there a grain of darnel; however carefully they may select the grains, yet the cockle and the hemlock will fall from their hands as well as the good seed-corn of the kingdom. Of the Master, and only of the Master, it is true in the fullest, and the broadest, and most unguarded sense, "He went about doing good."

Two things this morning: first I shall want you, dear brethren, to *consider him;* and then, in the second place, to *consider yourselves.*

I. The first occupation will be pleasing, as well as profitable. Let us CONSIDER HIM.

1. Consider first, *his object.* He went about, but his travel was no listless motion, no purposeless wandering hither and thither—"He went about *doing good.*" O man of God, have a purpose, and devote thy whole life to it! Be not an arrow shot at random, as in child's play, but choose thy target, and swift as the bullet whizzies to the mark, so fly thou onwards towards the great aim and object of thy life. Christ's object is described in these words, "doing good." Of this we may say, that this was his *eternal purpose.* Long before he took upon himself the nature of man, or even before man was formed of the dust of the earth, the heart of Jesus Christ was set upon doing good. In the eternal council in which the sacred Three entered into stipulations of gracious covenant, Christ Jesus became the Surety of that covenant in order that he might do good—good in the highest sense—good in snatching his people from the misery which sin would bring upon them, and good in manifesting the glorious attributes of God in a splendour which could not otherwise have surrounded them. His delights of old were with the sons of men, because they afforded him an opportunity, such as he could find nowhere else, of doing good. He did good, it is true, among the angels, for the heavenly harps owe all their music to his presence. Among the devils there was no room for positive good; they were given over to evil; but even there restraining goodness found work for itself in binding them down in iron bands, lest their mischief should grow too rampant. On earth, however, was the widest scope and amplest room for goodness in its largest sense; not merely the goodness which restrains evil, and the goodness which rewards virtue, but that greater goodness which descends to ruined sin-stricken mortals, and lifts them up from the dunghill of their miserable degradation, to set them upon the throne of glory. It was the eternal purpose of the Lord Jesus Christ, before the lamps of heaven were kindled, or stars began to glitter in the vault of night, that he would do good.

This was his *practical object,* when he made his ever-memorable descent from the throne of his splendour to the manger of his poverty. Angels might well sing at Bethlehem, "Glory to God in the highest, and on earth peace, good will toward men," for Jesus Christ came not condemning the world, but doing good. His presence in the manger did good, as it cheered both rich magi and poor shepherd, both learned and illiterate, both Simeon and Anna, with the knowledge that God had come down to men. His childhood afterwards did good, for though it was so unobtrusive and obscure that a few words suffice to set it forth, yet he has become the very mirror of childhood's dutiful obedience to this day. Ye know how his after life was one practical carrying out of the solitary object which brought him from the throne of glory to the abodes of sinful men. He "went about doing good." Nor was this his purpose merely and the object of his errand, but his *official prerogative.* He received the name of Jesus at his birth, "For he shall save his people from their sins." He was named "Christ," because the Spirit of the Lord was upon him, and he was anointed to preach good tidings to the meek, and to open the prisons to them that were bound. Jesus Christ is the title which bespeaks one whose office it is to do good. Mention any name you please which belongs to the Saviour, and you will see that it is incumbent upon him, *ex officio*, to go about doing good. Is he a Shepherd? he must do good to his sheep. Is he a Husband? he must love his Church and give himself for her, that he may cleanse and perfect her. Is he a Friend? he "sticketh closer than a brother" and doeth good. Is he "the Lion of the tribe of Judah?" it is not to do damage or mischief to innocence and weakness, but that, strong as a lion when he tears his prey, he may rend in pieces the foe of truth and goodness. Is he a Lamb? herein his goodness shows itself most completely, for he lays down his life that his Israel may go free when the destroying angel smites Egypt. Everywhere it was his peculiar prerogative and his special business to go about doing good. But more, it was not only his intention and the object of his errand, and his prerogative, but *his actual performance*. He did good in all senses. Jesus Christ wrought physical benefit among the sons of men. How many blind eyes first saw the light through the touch of his finger! How many silent ears heard the charming voice of affection after he had said "Be open"! Even the gates of death were no barrier to the errands of his goodness; the widow at the gate of Nain felt her heart leap within her for joy when her son was restored; and Mary and Martha were glad when Lazarus came forth from his grave. He did good physically. We have thought that our Lord did this not merely to show his power and universality of his benevolence, and to teach spiritual truth by acted parables, but also to say to us in these days, "Followers of Jesus, do good in all sorts of ways. You may think it to be your special calling to feed souls, but remember that your Master broke loaves and fishes to hungry bodies. You may deem it your chief object to instruct the ignorant, but remember that he healed the sick. You may make it your chief joy to pray for the healing of sick spirits, but remember that he rescued many bodies from incurable disease." As much as lieth in us let us do good unto all men, and good of all sorts too; though it be specially to the household of faith, and specially in a spiritual sense. Let no act of mercy seem beneath him who is a follower of the man that went about doing good. There is a spirit springing up among us which is very dangerous, though it wears the garb of excessive spirituality. It is unpractical and unchristlike— a spirit which talks in this fashion—"The sons of men tried to improve the world and make it better; but as for Enoch, the man of God, he knew that the world was so bad that it was of no avail to attempt to better it, and therefore he left it alone, and walked with God." It may be well, they say, for such carnal-minded Christians as some of us, to try and improve society and to give a better tone to morals; but these dear spiritual brethren are so taken up with divine things, and so assured that the mission is of a supercelestial character, that they will have nothing to do with blessing mankind, being quite sufficiently occupied with blessing themselves and one another. I pray God that we may never fall into the unpractical speculations and separations of certain brethren whose superior sanctity they must allow us to suspect. The large-heartedness of the Lord Jesus Christ is one of the most glorious traits in his character. He scattered good of all sorts on all sides. Let us, if we profess to be his followers, never be straitened even by pretended spirituality. Do good "as *much* as lieth in you," to the utmost extent of your power, and let that be of every sort. It strikes me that the Lord Jesus also did much *moral good*. Where he did not save spiritually, yet he elevated. I am not sure that that poor adultress was ever truly converted, and yet I know that he said, "Neither do I condemn thee: go, and sin no more;" and I can well believe that in this respect, at least, she would sin no more. I do not know that the Pharisees ever became followers of the man of Nazareth; and yet I cannot conceive that they could have listened to his stern rebukes against their hypocrisy without being in some measure humbled if not enlightened. Or if *they* were not better, at any rate, their professions would not be so readily allowed; society would receive, as it were, a tonic from those sharp and bitter words of the Master, and become too strong and masculine to receive any longer the lofty boastings of those mere pretenders. Jesus Christ, when he sat down on the mount, did not deliver a spiritual sermon of the style commonly classed under that head. That sermon on the mount is for the most part morality—good high, heavenly morality, higher than any teacher ever reached before; but there is very little in it about justification by faith, or concerning atonement, very little about the doctrine of election, or the work of the Holy Spirit, or final perseverance. The fact is the Master was doing moral as well as spiritual good; and coming among a degraded people who had set darkness for light and light for darkness, bitter for sweet and sweet for bitter, he thought it a part of his vocation to preach to them truth on that subject as well as upon the higher themes concerning his advent, and his salvation. Dear friends, this admonishes us to seek the moral good of the people among whom we dwell. The Christian minister must not lay aside his ministry to become the mere moralist lecturer, but he may and should lecture upon morals, and he can say some things in lectures which he could not say in sermons. Let him by all means occasionally leave the pulpit for the platform, if he can do service to society; let him do good in every possible shape and way. I trow that it is the Christian minister's place not simply to preach the high and glorious doctrine of the cross, but also to deal with the current sins of mankind as did the prophets of old, and to inculcate those virtues most needed in the state, as did men God sent in the ages which are past. Jesus Christ went about doing good, we say, of a moral kind as well as of a spiritual order, but still the Saviour's great good was *spiritual*. This was the great end that he was driving at—the bringing out of a people prepared to receive himself and his salvation. He came preaching grace and peace. His great object was the spiritual emancipation of the bondaged souls of men. Beloved, how he sought after this! What tears and cries went up to God from the mountain's bleak summit! With what earnest intercession did he plead with men when he addressed them concerning repentance and faith! "Woe unto thee Bethsaida! woe unto thee Chorazin!" were not words spoken by one who had a tearless eye. "Woe unto thee Capernaum!" was not the desolating curse of one who had a hard unsympathetic heart. The Saviour, when he wept over Jerusalem, was only doing once before men what he did all his life before God. He wept over sinners; he longed for their salvation. "Never man spake like that man," for having the highest truth he spake it after the highest fashion. Never the ostentation of eloquence, never the affectation of oratory, but ever the earnest, still, small pleading voice which "doth not break the bruised reed, nor quench the smoking flax." He went about in his daily preaching instructing the people because he found them as sheep without a shepherd, and therefore "he taught them many things." Physical, moral, spiritual good, good of all sorts the Saviour did—and while I close this point as to his object of life, let me say that he did something more than all this: he wrought *enduring good* which abides with us now. The good that holy men do is imperishable. The Scripture saith, "Their works do follow them," but not to the grave—upward their works ascend. If our works followed our bodies, they would rot in the tomb; but they follow our souls, and therefore mount up to immortality. Look ye upon the world now and see whether Jesus Christ is not still in spirit going about doing good. He has gone up to glory, but the spirit of his life and of his teaching is still among us. And what is his religion doing? Ask ye of our sires and they will tell you how this land was translated from a region of savages into the abode of peace and joy. Look ye yourselves in your own day to the far off islands of the south, and see how they have been transformed from dens of the wild blood-loving cannibals, into abodes of civilized men. Jesus Christ's gospel flies like an angel through the midst of heaven, proclaiming good news to men; and wherever its foot rests but for an hour, it transforms the desert into an Eden, and makes the wilderness blossom as the rose. May the Saviour help us so to live, that when we die we may have sown some seeds which shall blossom over our tomb.

Thus we have given an outline of the Saviour's doing good. May we add this sentence as a comfort to any here who are seeking Jesus. If it were his eternal purpose and his life's mission to do good, and he went about to find out the objects of it, why should he not do good to you? If he healed the blind, if he gave spiritual sight, why should he not give it *to you?* O may the desire be breathed by thee, poor seeking soul, breathed solemnly but hopefully to him—"O thou who in the days of thy flesh didst take pity upon misery and wretchedness in every shape, take pity upon me! Save me with thy great salvation!" Rest assured, beloved hearer, that prayer should not go up to heaven in vain. His ear is open still to hear the plaint of woe, and his hand is ready still to giving the healing touch, and the voice to say, "I will, be thou clean." May he do good in *you* this morning.

2. A short time may be profitably spent in considering *the mode* in which this object was compassed. We are told that he "*went about* doing good," which seems to suggest several points. First of all he did the good *personally*. He "went about doing good." He might, if he had chosen, have selected his place, and having seated himself, he might have sent out his apostles as ambassadors to do good in his stead; but you will recollect that when he sent them out, it was not that they might be proxies, but that they might be heralds; he sent them two and two unto every place whither he himself would come. They were to be to him what John the Baptist had been at his first

coming. Jesus Christ entered the field of labour in person. It is remarkable how the evangelists constantly tell us that he touched the leper with his own finger, that he visited the bedside of those sick with fever, and in cases where he was asked to speak the word only at a distance, he did not usually comply with such a request, but went himself to the sick bed, and there personally wrought the cure. A lesson to us if we would do good well, to do it ourselves. There are some things which we cannot do ourselves. We cannot remain among our families in England for instance, and preach the gospel in Hindostan. We cannot be engaged this morning in listening to the Word, and at the same time visiting the lodging-house or den of iniquity in some back street. There are some works of mercy which are best performed by others, but we can make these more personal by looking after the worker and taking a deeper interest in him, and by attending him with our prayers. I would that much more of benevolence were performed by men themselves. I do not care to speak against societies, but it is such an odd thing that if I have twenty-one shillings to give away, I cannot give them to a deserving family myself, but I must make it into about fifteen shillings before it goes at all, by paying it into a royal something or other society, and then it proceeds by a roundabout method, and at last is delivered to the poor by a mere hand without a soul, and is received by the poor, not as a gift of charity, but rather as a contribution from an unknown something with a secretary, which needs a place in which to drop its funds. Why should you not go and give away the twenty-one shillings yourself, lovingly and tenderly? It will be better than letting somebody else pare it down to fifteen, and give it away coldly and officially. So much depends upon the way of doing good. The look, the word, the prayer, the tear, will often be more valuable to the widow than that half-crown which you have given her. I heard a poor person once say, "Sir, I went to So-and-so for help, and he refused me; but I would sooner be refused by him than I would have money given to me by So-and-so," mentioning another who gave it with a sort of, "Well, you know I do not approve of giving anything to such as you are, but there it is—you must have it I suppose, so be off with you." Give your alms away yourselves, and you will learn by so doing, it will enable you to exercise Christian virtues. You will win a joy which it were not worth while to lose, and you will confer, in addition to the benevolence that you bestow, a blessing which cannot be conferred by the person who is your substitute. He went about doing good. He did it himself Oh! some of you, preach yourselves, I pray you! Talk to the Sunday-school children yourselves! Give away tracts—that is well enough if you cannot speak—but do try and talk yourselves. The influence of that hand laid upon your friend's shoulder, that eye of yours looking into his eye as you say, "Friend, I wish you were converted, my soul longs for your salvation;" there is more in that influence than in a whole library of tracts. Seek souls yourselves. Fish with your own hooks; you cannot help being successful if you imitate your Master, and *yourselves* do good in the power of the Holy Spirit.

The Saviour not only "went about doing good" personally, but *his very presence did good.* The presence of the Saviour is in itself a good, apart from the blessings which he bestowed. At the sight of him courage revived, drooping faith grew strong, hope brushed a tear from her eye and smiled. The sight of Jesus Christ as once it calmed the waves and hushed the winds, did so a thousand times in men souls. Even devils, when they saw him, cried out and trembled. Sinners wept at the sight of his pitying goodness. The woman who brake the alabaster box of precious ointment, felt that the only fit place to break it was near to him. His presence made her sacred action yet more sweet. What cannot men do when Christ is there? And, O beloved, if we be anything like our Master, our presence will be of some value. There are some of my brethren, when I see them I feel strong. You go into a little prayer-meeting, and numbers are not there; but such a saint is there, and you feel, "Well, if he be there, there is a prayer-meeting at once." You have work to do; it is very hard and toilsome, and you cannot prosper in it; but a brother drops into your little Sunday-school, or into your class, and looks at it, and you feel, "Well, if I have that man's sympathy, I can go on again." Therefore be careful to give your presence as much as you can to every good work, and do not isolate yourself from those actually engaged in labours of love.

Does not our Lord's going about doing good set forth his *incessant activity?* He did not only the good which was round about him, which came close to hand—he did not only the good which was brought to him, as when men were brought on their beds, and laid at his feet, but he "went about." He could not be satisfied to be still. Throughout the whole land of Judea, from Dan to Beersheba, he trod its weary acres. Scarcely a village or a hamlet which had not been gladdened by the sight of him. Even Jericho, accursed of old, had been blessed by his presence, and a great sinner had been made a great saint. Everywhere he went casting salt into the bitter waters, and sowing with sunshine the abodes of sadness. He was ever active in God's service. Oh! the creeping, crawling manner in which some people serve the Lord. The very way in which some people mumble through religious exercises, is enough to make one sick at heart, to think that the solemn offices of religion should be entrusted to such inanimate beings. If God of old said of Laodicea, that he would spew that Church out of his mouth, what will he do with those professors in modern times, who are the very pink of propriety, but who were never touched with fire from heaven, and know not what *the* word "zeal" means? Our Master was here, and there, and everywhere. Let us gird up the loins of our mind, and be not weary in well doing; but be "stedfast, unmovable, always abounding in the work of the Lord."

Does not the text also imply that Jesus Christ *went out of his way to do good?* "He went *about* doing good." There were short cuts which he would not take, because there were persons dwelling in the roundabout way who must be met with. "He must needs go through Samaria." It is is said that that city lay in the straightest way to Jerusalem. So it was, but it was not the right way, because the Samaritans so hated those whose faces were towards Jerusalem, that they maltreated them whenever they could. Yet the Master did not care for perils of waylaying enemies. He did not select the smoothest or the safest road, but he selected that in which there was a woman to whom he could do good. He sits down on the well. I wot it was not merely weariness that made him sit there; and when he said, "I thirst: give me to drink," it was not merely that he was thirsty; he had another weariness—he was patient over that woman's sin, and longed to reveal himself to her: he had another thirst—he did not mean merely "Give me water out of that well;" when he said, "Give me to drink," he meant "Give me your heart's love, my soul pants for it; I want to see you—a poor adulterous sinner—saved from sin." How else do we understand the words which he said to his disciples, when they wondered that he spoke with the woman? He said, "I have meat to eat that ye know not of, for it is my meat and my drink to do the will of him that sent me." He had received meat and drink in seeing that woman leave her water-pot, and go away to tell her fellow-sinners, "Come, see a man which told me all things that ever I did. Is not this the Christ?" He went round about after the objects of his gracious desires. So must the Christian. You must not be content to do good in the regular circle of your movements: that is so far so well, but go beyond your old line. Break through the bounds of propriety every now and then, and do an odd thing. I do believe that sometimes these odd expedients achieve more than regular methods. That was a quaint expedient of those who brake up the roof to let down a palsied man that Jesus might heal him. There has been a good deal said about that roof. According to some people it was not a roof at all but a sort of awning, but this morning we will stick to our old version that which tells us "they brake up the tiling," this must have made it a very bad look-out of those down below; but I dare say those up top argued—" Well, the Saviour is there, and if anybody shall be hurt by a tile or two he can easily heal them. Anyhow we will get this man before him, for this is the case in which we feel most concerned." Ah! dear friends, many people are so particular about making a little dust or breaking up a few tiles, but our mind is, never care about that, there will be time to clean the repair after souls are saved, and for so great an end as salvation we may neglect some few niceties and punctilios, and be most of all vehemently desirous that we may do good.

We have not quite done with the text yet. It means too that Jesus *Christ went far in doing good.* The district of Palestine was not very large, but you will observe that he went to the limit of it. He was as it were the bishop of the Holy Land and he never went out of the diocese, for he said he was not sent except to the lost sheep of the house of Israel. But he went to the verge of it. He went to the coasts of Tyre and Sidon. If he might not go over the mark yet he will go up to the edge; so if there should happen to be any limit to your doing good in any particular place at least go to the end of the limit. However, I rather like Rowland Hill's thought: when he was blamed for preaching out of his parish he claimed that he never did so, for the whole world was his parish. Make the world the sphere of your occupations, according to the parable "the field is the world." I admire the Lord's going about not simply for the miles he travelled, but for the space of character over which he passed. He "went about." It is nothing wonderful that he went as far as Tyre and Sidon, but it is much that he went as far as publicans and sinners. I do not wonder that he went from Dan to Beersheba, but I have wondered often that he went so far as to save harlots by his grace. We may in this sense go about doing good without travelling across the sea. A minister once announced to his congregation one Sunday morning, "I am going on a mission to the heathen." Now he had not told his deacons about it, and they looked at one another. The good people in the congregation some of them began to take out their pocket handkerchiefs; they thought their minister was going to leave them—he was so useful and necessary to them that they felt sad at the bare idea of loosing him. "But" he added, "I shall not be out of town:" So you may go on a mission to the heathen without going out of this huge town of ours. You might almost preach to every sort of literal heathen within the bounds of London; to Parthians, Medes, and Elamites and the dwellers of Mesopotamia. There are men of every colour, speaking every language under heaven, now living in London; and if you want to convert Mahometans, Turks, Chinese, men from Bengal, Java, or Borneo, you may find them all here. There are always representatives of every nation close at our door. If you want men who have gone far in sin, great foreigners in that respect, you need not certainly leave London for that; you shall find men and women rotten with sin, and reeking in the nostrils of God with their abominations. You may go about doing good, and your railway ticket need not cost you one farthing. No doubt Christ's *perseverance* is intended in our text, for when rejected in one place, he goes to another. If one will not hear, another will. The *unity* of his purpose is also hinted at. He does not go about with two aims, but this one absorbs all his heart—"doing good." And the *success*, too, of his purpose is here intended. He went about, and not only tried to do good, but he did it; he left the world better than he found, it when he ascended to his Father God.

3. One moment concerning *the motive* of Christ's doing good. It is not far to seek. *He did good partly because he could not help it.* It was his nature to do good. He was all goodness, and as the clouds which are full of rain empty themselves upon the earth, even so must he. You will have observed that all the good things which God has made are diffusive. There is light; you cannot confine light within narrow limits. Suppose we were to grow so bigoted and conceited as to conceive that we had all the light in the world inside this Tabernacle. We might have iron shutters made to keep the light in, yet it is very probable that the light would not agree with our bigotry, but would not come in at all, but leave us in the dark for wanting to confine it. With splendid mirrors, Turkey carpets, jewellery, fine pictures, rare statuary, you may court the light to come into palatial halls, it comes, it is true, but as it enters it whispers, "And I passed through the iron grating of a prison, just now. I shone upon the poor cottager beneath the rude thatched roof, I streamed through the window out of which half the glass was gone, and gleamed as cheerily and willingly upon the rags of poverty as in these marble halls." You cannot clip the wings of the morning, or monopolize the golden rays of the sun. What a space the light has traversed doing good. Millions of miles it has come streaming from the sun, and yet further from yonder fixed star. O light! why couldst thou not be contented with thine own sphere, why journey so far from home? Missionary rays come to us from so vast a distance that they must have been hundreds of years in reaching us, and yet their mission is not over, for they flash on to yet remoter worlds. So with the

air; as far as the world is concerned, the air will throw itself down the shaft of the deepest coal pit, climb the loftiest Alp, and although men madly strive to shut it out, it will thrust itself into the fever lair and cool the brow of cholera. So with water. Here it comes dropping from every inch of the cloudy sky, flooding the streets, flushing the foul sewers, and soaking into the dry soil. Everywhere it will come, for water claims to have its influence everywhere felt. Fire, too, who can bind its giant hands? The king cannot claim it as a royal perquisite. Among those few sticks which the widow woman with the red cloak has been gathering in the wood, it burns as readily as in Her Majesty's palace. It is the nature of Jesus to diffuse himself; it is his life to do good. His grand motive no doubt is *the display of the glorious attributes of God.* He went about doing good in order that Jehovah might be revealed in his splendour to the eyes of adoring men. He is the manifestation of Godhead; he is the express image of his Father's person, "In him dwelleth all the fullness of the Godhead bodily," and through heaven, and earth, and sky, and sun, and stars, all show forth something of the goodness of God, yet the life of Jesus is the fullest and clearest manifestation of the beneficence of deity that ever will be accorded to the sons of men. This is an object worthy of God, to manifest himself, and such an object Christ set before him when he came to do good among the sons of men.

I have not said enough about the Saviour, but still as much as time allows us, and I will close that point with this one thing: if Jesus Christ went about doing good, and if his motive was simply God's glory, poor troubled sinner, cannot he glorify God *in you?* You need pardon: you will be an illustrious instance of God's grace if he should ever save you. Have hope. If Jesus Christ goes about, you are not too far off. If he looks upon the most forlorn, you are not in too desperate a plight. Cry to him when your spirit is overwhelmed, yet look to the rock that is higher than you. "From the ends of the earth have I cried unto thee, O God, and thou heardest me." May it be your joy to-day to find him your friend, who "went about doing good."

II. We were in the second place to CONSIDER OURSELVES. This is the application of the subject.

Consider ourselves then as to the past, with sorrow and shamefacedness. Have we gone about doing good? I fear me there are some here who never did any spiritual good. The tree is corrupt, and it cannot bring forth good fruit. The fountain is bitter, and it cannot yield sweet water. Ye must be born again before you can go about doing good. While your nature is as father Adam left it, good cannot come from you. "There is none that doeth good, no not one." How clearly this is true in some persons, as proved by their very profession. The profession of some men is one in which they cannot hope to do good. There are some in all callings who either do positive harm, or at any rate cannot imagine that they are doing any good. Let them repent themselves. "Every tree that bringeth not forth good fruit is hewn down and cast into the fire." God grant that neither our character nor our vocation may stand in the way of our doing good. But you who have new hearts and rights spirits, and are saved by faith in the precious blood of Jesus, have you done all the good you could? *I* dare not say yes—I wish I dare. No, Master, there must have been many times when I might have served thee when I have not done it. I have been an unprofitable servant. I have not done what was my duty to have done. Ah! some of you have missed a world of joy in having done so little good. Ye have not given, therefore you are not increased. You never gave to others much, and so they have not given back to you full measure, pressed down and running over. You have not borne the burdens of others, and so your own burden has become heavy and intolerable. Christians, in looking back upon the past, must you not drop tears of regret, and do you not bless that preserving love which still follows you—yea, which will never let you go, but despite your barrenness and unfruitfulness, will not cease to work upon you till it has made you meet to be partakers of the inheritance of the saints in light, who day without night serve God in his temple?

As to the *future*. The old question comes up, if any man says to-day, "I am resolved to go about doing good"—is he able to do it? And again, the reply comes, we must first be good, or else we cannot do good. The only way to be good is to seek to the good One, the good Master. If thou hast a new heart and a right spirit, then go thy way and serve him; but if not, pause awhile. Unto the wicked God saith, "What hast thou to do to declare my statutes?" He will have clean-handed men to do his work. Wash first in the brazen laver if thou wouldst be a priest. God will not have men for his servants who would defile the sacred place. "Be ye clean that bear the vessels of the Lord." God give us to rest implicitly upon the Lord Jesus Christ by a living faith, and so to be cleansed in his precious blood, and then we may resolve to go forth and live for Him. Have we any work to do now that we can set about at once? If we have, whatsoever our hand findeth to do, let us do it. Let us not be asking for greater abilities than we have. If we can get them, let us do so; but meanwhile let us use what we have. Go, thou housewife, to thy house, and from the lowest chamber to the top go thou about doing good: here is range enough for thee. Go, thou teacher, to thy little school, and among those boys or girls, let thine example tell, and there is range enough for thee. Go, thou worker, to thy shop, and amongst thy fellow-workmen, let fall here and there a word for Christ; above all, let thine example shine, and there is work for thee. You domestic servants, the kitchen is sphere enough for you. You shall go about doing good from the dresser to the fireplace, and you shall have width enough and verge enough to make it a kingdom consecrated to God. Without leaving your position any one of you, without giving up the plough, or the cobbler's lapstone, or the needle, or the plane, or the saw, without leaving business—without any of you good sisters wanting to be nuns, or any of us putting on the serge and becoming monks—in our own calling let us go about doing good. The best preparation for it will be, renew your dedication to Christ, be much in earnest prayer, seek the sanctifying influences of the Holy Spirit, and then go forth in your Master's strength with this as your resolve—that as portraits of Jesus Christ it shall be said of you, "He went about doing good." May God add his blessing for the Saviour's sake. Amen.

Our Compassionate High Priest

"Who can have compassion on the ignorant, and on them that are out of the way; for that he himself also is compassed with infirmity"—Hebrews v. 2.

THE high priest looked Godward, and therefore he had need to be holy; for he had to deal with things pertaining to God. But at the same time he looked manward; it was for men that he was ordained, that, through him, they might deal with God; and therefore he had need to be tender. It was necessary that he should be one who could have sympathy with men; else, even if he could succeed Godward, he would fail to be a link between God and man, from want of tenderness and sympathy with those whom he sought to bring nigh to Jehovah.

Hence, the high priest was taken from among men that he might be their fellow, and have a fellow-feeling with them. No angel entered into the holy place; no angel wore the white garments; no angel put on the ephod and the breastplate with the precious stones. It was a man ordained of God, who for his brothers pleaded in the presence of the Shekinah. Many of us, I trust, have a desire within our hearts to come to God; but we need a high priest, in order that we may draw nigh, one who shall be a man as well as God. We may reflect with joy upon the Godhead of our great High Priest. Inasmuch as it is his right, he counts it not robbery to be equal with God; but he communes with the Father as one that was by him, as one brought up with him, who was daily his delight, rejoicing always before him. But we ought also to be very grateful that we can come into touch with our High Priest on his human side, and rejoice that he is truly man. For thus saith the Lord, " I have laid help upon One that is mighty : I have exalted One chosen out of the people ; " he is anointed, it is true, with the oil of gladness above his fellows, but still he and they are one, "for which cause he is not ashamed to call them brethren."

Those who came to the high priest of old, were not often of the rough sort. Those who wished to have fellowship with God through the high priest in the tabernacle or the temple, were generally the timid ones of the people. Remember how she who came when Eli was high priest was " a woman of a sorrowful spirit"; and the high priests had to deal with many such. The sons and daughters of affliction were those who mostly sought the divine oracle, and desired to have communion with God; hence the high priest needed not only to be a man, but a man of tender and gentle spirit. It was necessary that he should be one with whom those with broken hearts, and those who were groaning under a sense of sin, would like to speak. They would dread an austere man, and would, probably, in many cases, have kept away from him altogether. Now, the mercy for us is, that our great High Priest is willing to receive the sinful and the suffering, the tried and the tempted; he delights in those that are as bruised reeds and smoking flax; for thus he is able to display his sacred qualifications. He " can have compassion." It is his nature to sympathize with the aching heart; but he cannot be compassionate to those who have no suffering, and no need. The heart of compassion seeks misery, looks for sorrow, and is drawn towards despondency; for there it can exercise its gracious mission to the full.

Often, when we are trying to do good to others, we get more good ourselves. When I was here one day this week, seeing friends who came to join the church, there came among the rest a very diffident, tender-hearted woman, who said many sweet things to me about her Lord, though she did not think that they were any good, I know. She was afraid that I should not have patience with her and her poor talk; but she said one thing which I specially remember : " I have to-day put four things together, from which I have derived a great deal of comfort," she told me. " And what are they, my sister ? " I asked. " Well," she said, " they are those four classes—' the unthankful and the evil, the ignorant and those that are out of the way.' Jesus ' is kind unto the unthankful and to the evil', and he ' can have compassion on the ignorant, and on them that are out of the way,' and I think that I can get in through those four descriptions. Though I am a great sinner, I believe that he will be kind to me, and have compassion upon me." I stored that up; for I thought that one of these days I might want it myself; I tell it to you, for if you do not want it now, you may need it one of these days; you may yet have to think that you have been unthankful and evil, ignorant and out of the way, and it will give you comfort to remember that our Lord Jesus is kind to the unthankful and to the evil, and that he " can have compassion on the ignorant, and on them that are out of the way."

On this latter subject, I would speak at this time, wishing to comfort some who are of a sorrowful spirit, and others who may yet have need of such consolation as this topic gives.

Notice in our text, first, *the sort of sinners with whom our High Priest is concerned*, namely, "the ignorant and them that are out of the way"; secondly, *the sort of High Priest with whom sinners have to deal*— One "who can have compassion on the ignorant, and on them that are out of the way"; and, thirdly, *the sort of infirmities in men that may be sanctified to great uses.* " For that he himself also is compassed with infirmity," is said of an earthly high priest; this it was that made him fit to be a high priest; and there are certain infirmities that we might almost glory in, for they enable us to be like priests unto God, and make us helpful to his sorrowing and suffering children.

I. First, then, let us carefully observe THE SORT OF SINNERS FOR WHOM OUR HIGH PRIEST IS CONCERNED. While it is true that he is willing to receive all sorts of sinners, there are many who never come to him, nor submit to his authority. With those who proudly and rashly stand before God on their own merit, he has nothing to do; but with others of a different character he is greatly concerned.

The people who claim Christ's aid are generally *those who have a very low opinion of themselves*. Out of all the tribes of Israel, those that came to the high priest, to ask him to present their sacrifice to God for them, and to speak a word from God to them, were God-fearing people. No doubt hypocrites, occasionally, did come, and some of a proud spirit who trusted in their own offerings; but I should think that, all the year round, the high priest saw some of the humblest and best people in all Israel. Men and women, in sore trouble, would come to him; and these chastened spirits would be choice spirits. Men and women who were conscious of sin, and longing for pardon, would come to the high priest; men and women who had not sinned after the similitude of a public transgression, who nevertheless felt evil darkening their conscience within, would draw near to him; men and women who had lost the light of God's countenance, and who came longing to have it back again, because they could not live without it, would approach the courts of God's house. All these would be welcome visitors at the high priest's door, and would receive his sympathy and compassion. Such are the people whom Christ our great High Priest now delights to bless. The proud and self-satisfied cannot know his love; but the poor and distressed may ever find in him comfort and joy, because of his nature, and by means of his intercession.

As with the high priest of Israel in the olden time, amongst those who come to our High Priest, are *many whose fear and distress arise from ignorance*. Oh, dear friends, if all the ignorant were to come, we should all come; for we are all ignorant; but there are some who fancy it is otherwise with them. They imagine they know all things, and, professing themselves to be wise, they become fools. These know not their need of the great High Priest. Their folly is proved by their light esteem of him. But among those who come to our great High Priest in heaven, there are none but those who are ignorant.

In the first place, there is a *universal ignorance*. Notwithstanding all that great men may say about what they evolve from their own consciousness, I think that the only thing that a man can evolve from his own consciousness is folly and sin; for there is nothing else there. If he goes on evolving, he will evolve greater folly and greater sin, that is all. But when the Lord deals with men, he makes them feel that they know very little. What do we know of sin? The larger proportion of our sins are probably unknown to us. We do them, and scarcely observe that we have committed them. And who knows the evil that lies in any one sin? Who is he that can weigh his iniquities in scales, or his errors in balances? Upon that one dread subject of sin, we are all like babes; we have not begun to learn more than the alphabet of that awful knowledge. Sinful we are, but it is a part of the effect of sin that we do not know the extent of our sinfulness, and we should not know it at all, if it were not for the teachings of the Holy Spirit.

Again, what do we know of ourselves? Does any man truly know himself? "The proper study of mankind is man," says Pope. I am not sure of that; but I am certain that the proper study of mankind is Christ; for in him we not only can learn about man, but much more besides. But how little we know of ourselves, of our natural weakness, of our evil tendencies, of our proneness in this direction, or in that! "Who can understand his errors? Cleanse thou me from secret faults."

What do we know of God the unsearchable? Is not he past finding out? Who can sufficiently tell of his nature, or of his wondrous attributes? Who can speak adequately of his greatness, or of his glory? Who can number up his years, or declare the whole of his lovingkindness? "O the depth of the riches both of the wisdom and knowledge of God! How unsearchable are his judgments, and his ways past finding out!" On this great subject, as well as on the other topics I have mentioned, there is a universal ignorance. As compared with the light of God, we are in the dim twilight. He that seeth best only seeth men as trees walking.

But, in addition to the ignorance that is universal, there is also a *comparative ignorance* on the part of some; and because of this, the compassion of Christ flows forth to them. Those who are ignorant in this way, are the kind of sinners whom he has come to help as a High Priest. He puts them in a class by themselves.

There are, first, the recent converts—young people whose years are few, and who probably think that they know more than they do; but who, if they are wise, will recognize that, even by reason of the fewness of their years, their senses have not been fully exercised to discern between good and evil. You must not ask them questions about the deep things of God. They have to be satisfied with those blessed parts of Scripture where a lamb may wade; they must not meddle with those parts where leviathan has to swim. Many truths are either above them or below them, much experience is too deep for them. In the presence of many of God's ways, they are compelled to say, "Such knowledge is too wonderful for me; it is high, I cannot attain unto it." The Lord Jesus Christ can take little boys and girls to his bosom; and he does so, while they are as yet ignorant of many things. He loves them; he teaches them; he has compassion on them; and he says of them, "Suffer the little children to come unto me, and forbid them not: for of such is the kingdom of God." Christ receives them in spite of their lack of knowledge, and therefore we must treat such very tenderly. "Take heed that ye despise not one of these little ones;" for our great High Priest has compassion upon their ignorance, and he instructs them. "All thy children shall be taught of the Lord, and great shall be the peace of thy children," when they trust in him who sympathizes with them, and who cares for them.

Others there are who are ignorant because of their little opportunity of getting instruction. Are there not many who are so placed that they nave little chance even of learning to read? We are thankful that there will be few left of that sort by-and-by. But there are others who, if they could read, have scarcely sufficient time allowed them to read their Bibles, and who, when they have read them, are very like the Ethiopian eunuch, in that they do not comprehend what they have read. If the question were addressed to them, "Understandest thou what thou readest?" they could truly say, "How can I, except some man should guide me?" There are many, all over our land, who are situated in places where they cannot often hear the gospel, and when they do hear it, it is so mixed up and confused, that it is small wonder they cannot make head or tail of it. Constantly do we meet with persons of that kind, whose ignorance is excusable; for they have had no teaching. They have not had opportunities of reading and searching, as most of us have had; upon these our great High Priest has compassion, and often with their slight knowledge they show more of the fruits of the Spirit than some of us produce even with our more abundant light.

Further than that, there are many that are of a very feeble mind. You can only with difficulty get a thought into their brain, and if you try to get in another idea on the top of it, the second one seems to knock the first one out. They never learn much, and they are so constructed that they never will. In our pilgrim band we have a number who are like Mr. Feebleinind; we may try all that we can with him, but we shall never make a hero of him. Others are like Mr. Ready-to-halt, with his crutches; he did dance once, you will remember, when Giant Despair's head was cut off; but still he had to go on his crutches even then, and he never gave them up till he crossed the river; then he left them to anybody that wanted such things, and, I fear me, there are many who want them to-day. We have those in our company who never will be able to give a systematic statement of the doctrines of grace, though they are full of grace. They could never explain how they were saved; but they *are* saved. I daresay the snail could never explain how he got into the ark, but he did get in; and these feeble ones are in Christ, though they cannot fully explain how they came to that blessed position. Some of these good people are not very apt to receive knowledge: they are not "learnable", if I may coin a word to express my meaning. We cannot make them learn. They are willing to be taught, they are teachable; but they are not "learnable." Ah, well, our blessed High Priest can have compassion on the ignorant, and the feeble-minded!

Beside the universal ignorance of which we have spoken, and this comparative ignorance, there is a *sinful ignorance*. We have some who are ignorant, and no excuse is to be made for them; their ignorance is to be condemned; and if these words reach any who are thus guilty, I would beseech them to pray God to pardon their guilt, and cease to sin in this way any longer. I mean those who are ignorant for want of attention. They are so full of business, and have such a great many other things to think of, that they do not value the means of grace. They say that they cannot attend, but we know that where there is a will there is a way. Perhaps they go once on a Sunday, and never more all the week. Now, if I had to eat one meal a week, and only one, I should want it to be a very good one; but I think that I should hardly be in a good condition for the next one the week following. It is a grand thing to get a little bit by the way, by coming on a Thursday night, or a morsel or two on a Monday, at the prayer-meeting. This stays the heart, and keeps the soul in good order.

Some will never be much above the ignorant, because they have not the ambition to learn. They do not set themselves to study the things of God. They do not sufficiently prize the revelation of God. I pray that they may be stirred up to do so. Though they have been guilty of neglectfulness and forgetfulness, they are not to be deprived of the sweetness of this text. Our Lord can have compassion on the ignorant, and on such as are out of the way. Here stands the great company to which his compassion goes out, and its name is written, "*The ignorant.*" I think that we had better all get into this class; indeed, I am sure that we had better join it, and thus obtain our Lord's compassion. I have seen, at a railway-station, gentlemen with first-class tickets walking up and down the platform unable to find a first-class carriage, and if the train was going on they have jumped in the third-class, so as to get to their journey's end. If there is any man here who does not think that he ought to be put down quite among the ignorant, jump in, brother, because you will get to your journey's end in this compartment, and there is no carriage, just now, for any wise person. There is nothing provided in the train that starts from this text, except that which is provided for the ignorant. The Lord help us personally to rejoice that he can have compassion on the ignorant!

Now comes another description of the sort of sinners for whom our High Priest is concerned. There are *many whose fears arise from being out of the way.* The Lord "can have compassion on the ignorant, and on them that are out of the way." I remember that, when I felt myself to be a very great sinner, and verily thought I was more of a sinner than anybody else, these words were very, very much blessed to me. I read them, "and on them that are out of the way"; and I knew that I was an out-of-the-way sinner. I was then, and I am afraid that I am now, somewhat like a lot out of the catalogue, an odd person who must go by himself. Very well; our High Priest can have compassion on those that are odd, on those that are out-of-the-way, on those who do not seem to be in the common run of people, and do not go with the multitude, but who must be dealt with individually, and by themselves. He can have compassion upon such.

But now let us look at the more exact meaning of the text.

To be out of the way is, in the case of all men, *their natural state.* "All we like sheep have gone astray; we have turned every one to his own way." That is where we are all by nature, and our own way is out of *the* way. Therefore, Christ can have compassion upon all of us who come to him; for he has learnt to deal with those who are out of the way, and such, literally, are we all.

In addition to that, men have gone out of the way by *their own personal folly.* We had enough original sin; but we have added to that another kind of originality in evil.

> "Like sheep we went astray,
> And broke the fold of God;
> Each wandering in a different way;
> But all the downward road."

But there are some who wander most foolishly. You wonder why they sin in the particular way that they do. There seems to be no reason for it, no motive for it, no special temptation in that direction, and yet they will do it. They wander out of the way by themselves. Have you done so, dear friend? The Lord can have compassion on those that are out of the way.

Some are out of the way because of *their seduction from the way by others*. False teachers have taught them, and they have taken up with the error brought before them by a stronger mind than their own. In some cases persons of evil life have had a fascination over them. It is wonderful how, in the cases of young men and young women, they frequently seem to be not themselves, but the evil embodiment of another. They are ruled and governed by the will of somebody else, and not by their own. Thus they are led out of the way. They are like sheep that "have been scattered in the cloudy and dark day." Ah, poor friend, it is ill that you should have been the victim of another's temptation! Do not blame your tempter; blame yourself; but, at the same time, remember that Christ has compassion upon those who have been led out of the way. As by the will of another you were beguiled from the true path, so by the love of Another shall you be won back again, even as it has been with many of us.

Many are out of the way because of *their backslidings after grace has come to them*. Our text comprehends backsliders who were once in the way. To such we may say, "Ye did run well, who did hinder you, that ye should not obey the truth?" Something has been an occasion of stumbling to such; and now, though sitting in the house of God, they know that they are not what they once were, nor what they ought now to be, nor what they must be, nor what I hope they will be, even before I shall finish my discourse. "Turn, O backsliding children, saith the Lord; for I am married unto you." Why will ye wander from the only source of good? "Take with you words, and turn to the Lord." "Come now, and let us reason together, saith the Lord: though your sins be as scarlet, they shall be as white as snow; though they be red like crimson, they shall be as wool." The Lord calls you in infinite tenderness; for he can have compassion upon backsliders, and stop them from becoming apostates, bringing them back unto himself, according to his divine purpose.

Others are out of the way because of *their consciousness of special sin*. Is there here anyone conscious of some great sin in years gone by? Is there a crimson spot upon your hand, which you have tried to wash out, but cannot; some act of your life which you would fain undo, and remove? There it is, still there, always there. Does it fret you by night, and weary you by day, to think of that gross iniquity of yours? Ah, it has put you out of the way! Perhaps you did not grasp all the consequences of what you were doing when you did it. Be comforted by this gracious text. Hear your High Priest pray, "Father, forgive them; for they know not what they do." He pleads your ignorance. You "did it ignorantly in unbelief"; and while this does not excuse you, it puts you in the list of those who are both ignorant and out of the way. Come to this compassionate High Priest, and trust your case in his dear hands; they were pierced because of your sin. Trust your iniquity with him; his heart was opened and set abroach because of your transgression. Come, trust in him. He died because of your sin. "He is able also to save them to the uttermost that come unto God by him, seeing he ever liveth to make intercession for them."

Thus I have, very feebly, set forth the sort of sinners for whom Christ is High Priest; those who are ignorant, and those who are out of the way. This message is for almost everybody here, except my friend over there, who knows everything, and never did anything wrong. He does not want any Christ, and I will not bother him with one. "They that are whole have no need of a physician, but they that are sick," saith the Lord Jesus; and he further adds this word, which shuts out you who never did any harm, "I came not to call the righteous, but sinners to repentance." To be so very learned and so very good in your own estimation is no recommendation to Christ, but the reverse. He comes to men who need compassion, and those he teaches to profit, and leads in the way everlasting.

II. Having seen the sort of sinners with whom our High Priest is concerned, let us, in the second place, look at THE SORT OF HIGH PRIEST WITH WHOM SINNERS HAVE TO DEAL.

Now, if I go back to the high priest under the law, the type would be a fine fatherly man, whose very face invited confidence. I should think that all the people were glad when the high priest was very tender and compassionate. Possibly they had occasionally a high priest who was very high and very mighty; one who was very glad when his day's service was over. If sinners wanted to see him, he was not visible; and when he did talk with them, he was not very gentle. Sometimes he may have said to them, "Now you are stupid, you talk nonsense;" and when any of them were very sad, he said, "You ought to know better than to indulge this foolish nervousness of yours." I think that they were not sorry when that high priest was taken from them. But the pattern high priest was a fatherly-looking man, with love in his eyes, a smile on his face, one who had often sorrowed himself, one to whom all the people could go naturally. There are such men still alive. They are like a harbour for ships. Sometimes it brings a very heavy burden upon them, but yet they are happy men to have such a burden to carry. I think that some of those high priests must have seen a great deal of sin, and a great deal of mercy and divine love. When the poor people went up to the temple, one would say, "I must go in and see the high priest. I have such a burden, and he will be able to help me." Another would say, "No, I shall not go in; I do not need now to take up his time myself. Did not you hear him speak? Why, what he said was just the very thing that I wanted. God gave him the very word that my distress required, and so I can go away in peace." But here and there one would say, "Ah! but I must tell him. It does me good to unburden my heart." Now that is the kind of high priest that we should all have wished for had we been living in those days; but our Lord Jesus is something incomparably better than that.

He is One who can bear with ignorance, forgetfulness, and provocation. How do I know it? Because he bore so wonderfully with the ignorance of people when he was here. It was with a very tender accent that he said to one of his disciples, "Have I been so long time with you, and yet hast thou not known me, Philip?" He had told them many, many times the same thing over again, and yet he was not above repeating it, he had such compassion on them. Sometimes he could not say what he would have liked to say, and yet he bore with the poor men who did not know the burden he had on his heart: he only said, "I have yet many things to say unto you, but ye cannot bear them now." And when, after he had taught them, they still forgot, he did not chide them. I never find that he turned one of them away because of their stupidity; he did not even cast off Thomas for his unbelief. He let them still linger about his person, despite their false notions and their forgetfulness. They must often have grieved him through their ignorance, and through getting out of the way, especially when they got into the way of each desiring to be the greatest. But notwithstanding all, our Lord was never like Moses. Of him it is written that the people of Israel "provoked his spirit, so that he spake unadvisedly with his lips"; but never an impatient word came from those lips into which grace was so abundantly poured. There was never such a meek, and gentle, and quiet spirit as our divine Lord and Master possessed. I need not dwell on that, for you all know what compassion he had upon the ignorant sons of men.

Again, *he is One who can feel for grief, because he has felt the same.* When I have explained compassion as implying meekness of disposition, I have not given you the full meaning of the expression. Not only has our Lord compassion on the ignorant by being gentle towards them, but he sympathizes with them by having a fellow-feeling with them. They got out of the way, and into the thorns; they wandered, and fell into a maze; they were lost on the dark mountains, but he was "a man of sorrows, and acquainted with grief." "In all their affliction he was afflicted." Because of that fellow-feeling he is always very tender and pitiful; and if he finds any of his children sorrowing, he has abundant compassion upon them.

Moreover, *he is One who lays himself out tenderly to help such as come to him.* He did so when he was here in body, and he is the same now; all his life was given in tenderness. You never find Christ throwing bread and meat to the hungry crowd as we throw bones to dogs. He made them sit down on the green grass, and then he blessed the food, and gave it to his disciples, and they distributed it in a quiet, orderly way. And the Lord Jesus Christ has a very loving way now of helping his people. So tenderly does he do it, that the doing of it is almost as great a wonder as the thing that is done. He abounds towards us in all wisdom and prudence, and we may each one say, "Thy gentleness hath made me great." Oh, he is a wonderful Saviour! There is none like him for sympathizing with us, and dealing tenderly with us.

Another thing I have to say of him that never can be said of anybody else, is, that *he is One who never repelled a single person.* Not even the most ignorant, the most out of the way, was ever turned back from him. It was always true: "This man receiveth sinners." And for ever this other word is settled in heaven, "Him that cometh to me I will in no wise cast out."

I have not time to go into this matter fully, but all who have read the life of Christ know what a gentle and tender High Priest he was towards men.

> "Now, though he reigns exalted high,
> His love is still as great.
> Well he remembers Calvary,
> Nor let his saints forget."

His heart is on earth, though he has ascended into the heavens. If anyone here groans after him to-night, he will hear that groan; and if the wish does not come to a vocal sound at all, but if your heart only aches after him, he will feel that ache of your heart, and know what it means; and if you do not know how to pray, the very desire to pray he will interpret. He can have compassion on the ignorant. And if you do not know what you want, but only know that it is something that you must have or die, he will give it to you; for he will interpret your wordless desires, and what you cannot read yourself, he will read for you. But, oh, you must have him; you must have him; you cannot get to God without him! I pray that you may feel such confidence in his tenderness that you may come and take him as your own High Priest: if you do, he will be yours at the moment of acceptance. He will never refuse the seeker. He will not hide himself from his own flesh. He will never be distant and strange to any penitent sinner. If thou desirest him, it is because he desires thee; and if thou hast a spark of wish for him, he has a furnace of desire for thee. Come, and welcome. He can have compassion on the ignorant, and on them that are out of the way. God bless these words! I pray that he may do so, to very many.

III. Now, I want to speak to those of you who are the people of God. I can imagine that some of you here are troubled, perhaps ill, and that you cannot get on as you would like in the world. You seem compassed with infirmities. I want to remind you that there may be a blessing even in your weakness; and that this may be the more clearly seen we will look, in the third place, at the SORT OF INFIRMITY WHICH MAY BE SANCTIFIED AND MADE USEFUL.

The high priest of old was compassed with infirmities, and this was part of his qualification. "Yes," says one, "but he was compassed with sinful infirmities; but our Lord Jesus had no sin." That is quite true, but please remember that this does not make Christ less tender, but more so. Anything that is sinful hardens; and inasmuch as he was without sin, he was without the hardening influence that sin would bring to bear upon a man. He was all the more tender when compassed with infirmities, because sin was excluded from the list. We will not, then, reckon sin in any form as an infirmity likely to be turned to a great use, even though the grace of God abounds over the sin; but, beloved friends, let me try and speak to some of you who wish to do good, and set forth some of the things which were sore to bear at the time, and yet have been rich in blessing since.

First think of *our struggles in finding mercy*. Years ago you had a hard time of it when you were seeking the Saviour. I had, and I have always been very glad of it ever since. It was a long while before I could perceive the eternal light, and cast myself on Christ. I thank God that it was so, because I have had to deal with hundreds—I might say, thousands—in a similar case; and if I had found Christ, as many dear friends do, very readily and very easily, I could not have guided them; but now I can sit down by the side of them, and say, "What! have you got into the dark? I have been in the dark, too. You are down in the low dungeon, are you? Well, I was in the lowest dungeon of all. I can show you the way to where the jug of water stands, and the bit of brown bread. I know the way, for I have been there." If you have not had a certain experience, you cannot so well help others who have; but if you were compassed with infirmity in your first coming to Christ, you may use that in helping others to come to him.

Again, *our grievous temptations* may be infirmities which shall be largely used in our service. "What a blessing it would be to live without temptations!" says one. I do not believe it would be a blessing at all. I think that, being without temptation is more of a temptation than having a temptation. There is no devil that is equal to no devil, for when there seems to be none, we get so very quiet and so very easy, and think that everything is going on well, when it is not. Be glad if you have been tempted. Remember that temptation is one of the best books in a minister's library. To be tried, to be afflicted, to be downcast, to be tested—all this helps you to deal with others. You cannot be unto others a helper unless you have been compassed with infirmities. Therefore accept the temptations which trouble you so much, as a part of your education to make you useful to others.

Our sickness may turn out to be in the same category. Of course we would like to be always well. I think that health is the greatest blessing that God ever sends us, except sickness, which is far better. I would give anything to be perfectly healthy; but if I had to go over my time again, I could not get on without those sick beds and those bitter pains, and those weary, sleepless nights. Oh, the blessedness that comes to us through smarting, if we are ministers and helpers of others, and teachers of the people! I do not say that too much of it is to be desired, but the Lord knows how much is too much, and he will never afflict us beyond that he will enable us to bear. But just a touch of sickness now and then may help you mightily. I have heard some brethren preach the gospel in a terribly heartless way. It has been the gospel, but it has been as hard as a Brazil nut; little children could never get at the kernel. These brethren had never had any trouble or affliction; and if you have never had any, you may try to be very tender, but it will be like an elephant picking up a pin; you may try to be patient and sympathetic, but you will not be able to manage it. Glory in your infirmities, then, and in your sicknesses, for they shall be made useful in you for the comfort of God's sick people.

Our trials, too, may thus be sanctified. He that has had no troubles, and no trials, what mistakes he makes! He is like the French lady in the time of famine, who said that she had no patience with the poor people starving because of the price of bread. You could always buy a penny bun for a penny, she said; and therefore she thought there need not be any poverty at all. She was one of the rich ones of the earth. I do not suppose that she had ever had a penny bun in her life, or a penny either. Ah, dear friends! you must, if you are ready to help others, be yourself compassed with infirmity.

Our depressions may also tend to our fruitfulness. A heart bowed down with despair is a dreadful thing. "A wounded spirit who can bear?" But if you have never had such an experience, my dear brother, you will not be worth a pin as a preacher. You cannot help others who are depressed unless you have been down in the depths yourself. You cannot lift others out of despondency and depression, unless you yourself have sometimes need to be lifted out of such experiences. You must be compassed with this infirmity, too, at times, in order to have compassion on those in a similar case.

Herein I think that every one of us should try to make use of all his weaknesses. *Our whole nature as feeble men* may be turned to the noblest use if it calls forth our compassion towards others. Thank God that you are not a man of iron. We had the Iron Duke once, who did famous things, but in a different fight from ours. An iron preacher would need to have iron hearers; and then, I am afraid, that there would come a crash before long. No, no; we must have our weakness and infirmity consecrated to God, and laid at his feet. Let us go, in all our weakness and infirmity, and try to help others who are as ignorant and as out of the way as we once were; and, God blessing us, when we are weak, we shall be strong. When we are less than nothing, the all-sufficiency of God will be all the more manifested. Here I must stop, for our time has gone. May the Lord bless the word, both to the sinner and to the saint, for his name's sake! Amen.

The Ever-living Priest

"And they truly were many priests, because they were not suffered to continue by reason of death: but this man, because he continueth ever, hath an unchangeable priesthood. Wherefore he is able also to save them to the uttermost that come unto God by him, seeing he ever liveth to make intercession for them"—Hebrews vii. 23—25.

THE apostle Paul is very much at home with his theme whenever he is extolling his Master. When handling the Jewish types and figures, with which he was so familiar, he was charmed to point out how far superior the Lord Jesus Christ is to any and all the priests of the Old Testament dispensation. In this case he is dwelling upon the special honour of our Lord, because his priesthood is without end, seeing he himself is not put forth from the priesthood by reason of death. A common priest served from thirty to fifty years of age, and then his work was done: priests of the house of Aaron, who became high priests, held their office through life. Sometimes a high priest would continue in his office, therefore, for a considerable length of time, but in many cases he was cut off as other men are by premature death; hence there was priest after priest of the order of Aaron to go within the veil for the people. Our Lord is of another race, being a priest according to the order of Melchisedec, "having neither beginning of days nor end of life." He was made a priest not after the law of a carnal commandment, but after the power of an endless life. He continueth to make intercession for the people of God by virtue of his eternal life and perpetual priesthood. In this respect the true Messiah, the Lord Jesus Christ, rises above all former priests: they were indeed but types and shadows of himself.

This superiority of our Lord Jesus Christ is a topic which will not interest everybody. To many persons it will seem a piece of devotional rapture, if not an idle tale. Yet there will ever be a remnant according to the election of grace to whom this meditation will be inexpressibly sweet. Who are the people that will be interested by this theme? They are indicated in the text: they that come unto God by Jesus Christ. The people who are in the habit of using Christ as their way of access to God are those who will value him beyond all price, and such persons will delight to hear him extolled in the highest terms.

We will begin our discourse, then, by the enquiry : Do we come unto God by Jesus Christ ? Hearken, and answer for yourselves. Do we come unto God at all ? Do we recognize the Lord our God as a person who should be approached ? Are we now approaching to him ? Are we among those who are always coming to God, to whom at the last the great Judge shall say, "You have been coming, continue to come. Come, ye blessed of my Father, inherit the kingdom prepared for you" ? Or are we departing from God by forgetting him, or rebelling against him, so that we shall be among that number to whom the Judge shall say, "You have long been departing, continue to do so. Depart, ye cursed, into everlasting fire in hell, prepared for the devil and his angels" ?

Are we coming to God ?—that is the question. Is the direction of our lives towards God ? We are either going to God or from God, and by this we may forecast our everlasting destiny. The direction in which the arrow is flying prophesies the target in which it will be fixed : the way the tree is inclining, that way foretells the place of its fall, and where the tree falleth, there it will lie. So let us judge ourselves this day : which way are we drifting ? Have we ever come to God by sincere repentance of our wanderings ? Have we come to him by faith, and are we reconciled to him ? Do we come to him in prayer ? Do we come to him day by day, speaking with him and desiring to walk with him ? Do we come to God by communion with him, having fellowship with the Father and with his son Jesus Christ ? Do we, in fact, know the meaning of what it is to draw nigh unto God ? It is ill with us if we either have no God, or if he seems to be very far off, an almost unrecognizable phantom, an idea never fully realized, much less approached ! Blessed are they that know the name of the Lord and that walk with him, rejoicing in the light of his countenance. It is to such that Jesus is precious as their way of access to the Father.

In the description there is a little word of distinction ; for the people who are said to be saved by the great Intercessor are those who come unto God *by him*. Certain persons talk of coming to God as Creator, and Ruler, and even as Father, but they do not think of his dear Son as their way of approach. They forget or else deny the declaration of our Lord Jesus—" No man cometh unto the Father, but by me." Yet this saying is true. There is no true way of approach to God except through Jesus Christ, the one Mediator between God and man. A deep abyss divides us from God, and only that ladder which Jacob saw can bridge the gulf. Our Lord Jesus, being God and man in one person, reaches from side to side of the chasm. Coming near to us, this ladder stands at our foot in the human nature of our Lord, and it reaches right up to the infinite Majesty by reason of the divine nature of our Redeemer. God and man, in one person, unites God and man in one league of love. We come unto God by Jesus Christ. Prayers in which Christ is forgotten are insults to the God of revelation : faith in which Jesus is not the foundation of our hope is mere delusion. God cannot accept us if we will not accept his Son. O sinner, one door hath God opened in heaven : if thou wilt not go in by that door thou shalt never enter within the walls of the new Jerusalem. God bids thee come to him by one in whom he is well pleased ; and if thou wilt not be pleased with Jesus thou canst not come to the Father.

O ye who are daily users of this royal way to God, you will forgive me if I hide myself behind my Lord this day, and seek to do nothing more than, in all simplicity, to set forth his unchangeable priesthood and endless life. Pray the Lord to help me to extol the great high priest of our profession, and also to help you all to join in the praise of Jesus in the power of his Holy Spirit.

In the text there are four subjects for your consideration : they are joined together as links of a golden chain, and they are all full of encouragement for you. Here is a great Saviour with *an endless life*, secondly, with *an endless priesthood;* thirdly, with *an endless intercession;* and fourthly, with *an endless salvation:* "He is able to save them to the uttermost that come unto God by him, seeing he ever liveth to make intercession for them."

I. First, we have in our Lord Jesus Christ a priest with AN ENDLESS LIFE. I want you to think earnestly upon this very simple theme : it is in the simplicities that we find our greatest consolations. Our Lord Jesus is not as Aaron, who had to be stripped of his garments on the top of Mount Hor, and to die in the mount ; neither is he like to any of the sons of Aaron who in due time suffered the infirmities of age, and at last bowed their heads to inevitable death. He died once, but death hath no more dominion over him ; it is witnessed of him that he liveth.

We clearly perceive that our Lord Jesus possesses endless life *as God*, for how shall Godhead expire? It is not possible for the Godhead to cease or to suspend its existence. Our Lord is "God over all, blessed for ever"; and in this respect he is necessarily everlasting as to his life.

But our Lord ever lives also in respect to *his manhood*. Though he died unto sin once, he soon rose again from the dead, his body never having seen corruption. He died *in* his priesthood and *for* his priesthood, but never *from* his priesthood. By his resurrection his manhood was fully restored to a life which dieth no more. We speak of him, as "he that liveth, and was dead, and is alive for evermore." This is a very sweet truth to those who are in Christ Jesus. The Lord Jesus Christ had lived one life as a man : why did he not end that life as a man when he died on the cross ? It shows his deep attachment to our manhood, that he retained the human nature after his great sacrifice had been presented and accepted. The fact that he again appeared as a man among men, and carried human nature into his glorified estate is clear evidence of his deep attachment to our humanity. If some glorious spirit from on high, angel or archangel, had loved a race of emmets, and had condescended for the salvation of these tiny creatures to assume their nature, and if in that nature he had died for them, you would naturally expect that at the conclusion of his labours and sufferings he would lay aside the form of his humiliation and return to the greatness of his former estate. But our Lord Jesus Christ, whose stoop of condescension when he assumed our nature was greater than any archangel could have achieved, having taken our human nature, and having bled and died in it, continued to wear it after he had said, "It is finished," after he had risen from the dead, and after he had taken his seat at the divine right hand ! He hath become so wedded to us, so truly one flesh with us, that he will not be divided from us in nature. He sits upon the throne of God, not in his pure Godhead, but as one that has been slain, clothed in a body like our own. What manner of love is this! What bliss to know that my kinsman liveth! Truly many waters could not quench his love to manhood, nor could death itself destroy it. The Son of God is still the Son of man. He whom angels worship is not ashamed to call us brethren, for as partaker of our nature he lives, and will live for ever.

He ever lives, then, as God and as man; and I prolong the blended thoughts by saying that he ever lives *in his relationship to us.* This you have already seen to be the case, because he lives in our nature: but now I beg you to note that he lives as God and man *for us.* I love to read these words—"He ever liveth to make intercession for them." This is one great object for which he lives. To make intercession for those that come unto God by him is the business of his life. Is not this wonderful? If some influential and powerful person should say to you, "I live to promote your interest; wherever I go and whatever I do, whatever I seek and whatever I obtain, I live for you"—it would show great friendship, and excite in us great expectations. Would it not? Yet here is the Lord Jesus declaring that he lives for us: for us he appears in the presence of God, for us he has gone to the many mansions of the Father's house, for us he constantly intercedes with God. Oh, the deep debt of gratitude we owe to this glorious One, who having died for us, now lives for us!

It is more than if a brother should say, "I live my whole life for you"; for, remember, this might be said to be the second life which our Lord gives to us. He lived for us here below a whole lifetime! He laid down that life for us; and now he lives again for us. I know not how to speak what I feel concerning the surpassing greatness of his love. He could not be content to give his life once for us, but he must needs take it again and then give it over again for us. See how he loves us: he died for us! See how he loves us: he lives again for us! He lives for sinners, for he lives to intercede, and for whom is intercession but for those who need an advocate? "If any man sin we have an advocate." May I say that Jesus lives two lives for us?

Yet more, it is said, "He ever liveth to make intercession for us": so that the whole life of Christ throughout eternity,—his boundless, endless, glorified existence is still for his people. He glorifies the Father, and makes glad the hosts of heaven; but still this is the set purpose of his heart, to live for us. "He loved me, and gave himself for me" is true; but we may read it in the present tense if we like, and it is still true: "He loves me, and he gives himself for me." Christ loved his church, and gave himself *for* it, and now he loves his church and gives himself *to* it. What inspiration lies in the endless life of Christ for us! Let our lives be lived wholly for him since he lives wholly for us.

This truth of the living Christ should be remembered in our greatest need. Dear friends, there is an almighty and divine One in heaven who ever lives for our highest benefit. Let us adore him most lovingly. This should show us how great our need is, that we always want a living Saviour to interpose for us. A dying Saviour was not enough; we still require every moment of our lives a living Saviour engrossed with the care of our spirits, interposing on our behalf in all manner of ways, and delivering us from all evil. Our hour of necessity is ever present, for Jesus is ever guarding us, and his work is never a superfluity. Herein should lie our great comfort : we should fall back upon this truth whenever our burden presses too sorely upon our shoulders. Jesus lives : my great Redeemer lives for me : lives in all fulness of power and glory, and devotes that life, with all that pertains to it, to the preservation of my soul from every ill. Can I not rest in this? With such a keeper why should I be afraid? Must I not be safe when One so vigilant and so vigorous devotes his life to my protection? What innumerable blessings must come to those for whom Jesus spends the strength of his endless life!

II. Secondly, I must carry you on to another and kindred subject: ENDLESS PRIESTHOOD. Our Lord is ordained unto an unchangeable priesthood; or rather, as the margin hath it, to a priesthood "which passeth not from one to another." His office cannot be taken up by a successor: it is not transferable, but belongs to himself alone, seeing he ever liveth to carry it out in his own person. We have only one priest, and that one priest we have for ever.

In this we are *not like Israel of old;* for, as we have already seen, a high priest would die. I can conceive that to many Jewish believers the death of a priest was a great affliction. I could imagine an Israelite saying, "And so he is dead: that good man, that tender-spirited minister, that gentle and affectionate shepherd. I have told him all my heart, and now he is taken from me. I went to him in my youth in deep distress of conscience: he offered a sacrifice for me when I was unclean, and brought me near to the holy place. Since then I have gone to him when I have needed guidance; he has consulted the oracle on my behalf, and my way has been made plain. He knows the secrets of my family; he knows those delicate griefs which I have never dared to tell to anybody else. Alas! he is dead, and half my heart has perished. What a gap is made in my life by his decease!" The mourner would be told that his son had become his successor; but I think I hear him say, "Yes, I am aware of it: but the young man does not know what his father knew about me; and I could never again lay bare my heart. The son can never be in entire sympathy with all my sorrows as his good old father was. No doubt he is a good man, but he is not the same person : I reverenced every hair in the grey beard of the old high priest. I have grown up with him, and he has helped me so many, many times; it is so sad that I shall see his face no more." There would always be the feeling in some minds that the next high priest might not be quite so acceptable with God, or so tender towards the congregation, as he who had passed away. He might be a man superior in education, but inferior in affection : he might be more austere and less tender, he might have greater gifts and less fatherliness. At any rate, it would seem like having to begin again when one went for the first time to the new priest : it would be a break in the continuity of one's comfort. The quiet flow of life would be marred, as when a river comes to its rapids, and an impassable fall causes a break in the navigation, and a necessary unloading of the vessel and a laborious *portage* instead of an easy passage down a gently flowing stream. "Oh," says one good Israelite, "the venerable high priest who has just fallen asleep was my friend; we took sweet counsel together, and walked to the house of God in company. He was in my house when my beloved child died; he was with me when the partner of my bosom, the light of my eyes, was taken away from me at a stroke. His long experience he used for my instruction and comfort: but, alas! it is all gone, for the saint of God is dead." Beloved, here is our comfort: We have only *one* priest, and he ever liveth. He had no predecessor and he will have no successor, because he ever liveth personally to exercise the office of high priest on our behalf. My soul reposes in the faith of his one sacrifice, offered once and no more. There is but one presenter of that one sacrifice, and never can there be another, since the One is all-sufficient, and he never dies. Jesus reads my heart, and has always read it since it began to beat: he knows my griefs and has carried my sorrows from of old, and he will bear both them and me when old age shall shrivel up my strength. When I myself shall fall asleep in death he will not die, but will be ready to receive me into his own undying blessedness. Brethren, our Lord in glory

" Looks like a lamb that has been slain,
And wears his priesthood still."

Do we not rejoice in the unbroken continuity and everlasting perpetuity of the priesthood of Christ?

Again, we are *not as Israel is at this moment*. Alas, poor Israel! after all her privileges of the past, where is she now? She is without a high priest; she does not dare even to think of anointing one of her Cohens to that office. She is without an altar or a sacrifice. Once a year on the day of atonement she has something which bears the shadow of sacrifice; but it is a worship of her own devising and not after the law of Moses or the ordinances of God. She is left without priest, altar, temple, or sacrifice; and the outlook of her sons and daughters as to the future life is for the most part exceeding dark and dismal. I am assured that nothing is more unwelcome to a Jew than the thought of death; and it may well be so. Beloved, we are not without a priest. Our faith beholds Jesus passed into the heavens and abiding there in the glory of his once-offered sacrifice, ever living to intercede for us. Jesus is to my soul at this moment as living a person as I am myself, and even more so. I have come to look on friends and dear ones as passing shadows; I see written across their brows the word "mortal"; but Jesus is the one friend who only hath immortality, and therefore can never be lost to me. His sacrifice is for ever effectual, and his priesthood is for ever in exercise. Christ's priesthood remaineth without end. What bliss it is to be a believer in Jesus, and thus to have one priest, and never to desire another!

We are *not as the votaries of Rome*. That Babylon hath many priests within her borders. Some say that these priests are substitutes for Christ; if so, the assertion is a flat blasphemy against him who is a priest for ever, and needs no substitute. Others say they are the vicars of Christ, carrying on his work now that he is gone, by presenting the unbloody sacrifice of the mass. This also is clean contrary to the teaching of the apostle in this passage, wherein he proves that this man, because he continueth for ever, hath a priesthood which cannot be passed from one to another. In this he shows that our Lord is different from the Aaronic priests who had their office taken up by those who followed them, whereas Jesus, like Melchisedec, hath no successor, but exercises his office in his own proper person according to the power of an endless life. We know no priests on earth now, save that in a secondary sense the Lord Jesus hath made all believers to be kings and priests unto God. We have now no special order of persons set apart to represent their fellows before God. Under the Mosaic dispensation there were many priests not suffered to continue by reason of death ; but under the Christian dispensation we have only one priest, who continueth ever in an untransferable priesthood ; this is the apostle's argument. But this is not true if bishops and presbyters are priests in the sense in which they now claim to be so. I count the very thought of our having other sacrificing priests than the Lord Jesus to be derogatory to the one unique, completely-accomplished sacrifice of our Great High Priest who abides alone in his personal office for ever and ever. Wherefore, brethren, despise in your very souls the pretensions of a human priesthood either in the Church of England or in the Church of Rome. If any man call himself a priest otherwise than as all the people of God are priests, we rate him at no higher value than Korah, Dathan and Abiram, to whom Moses said, " Ye take too much upon you, ye sons of Levi." They claimed a priesthood which did not belong to them, as all men do who intrude into the priesthood in these days. Our Lord Jesus walks in that supreme, solitary majesty which was foreshadowed in Melchisedec—and in that spirit he fulfils a priesthood which renders all other priests a superfluity and a mockery. What have we to do with more sacrifices when the one sacrifice is offered once for all ? Brethren, hold fast this precious truth and rejoice in it.

III. Now I conduct you, thirdly, to the fact of ENDLESS INTERCESSION.—" Seeing he ever liveth to make intercession for them."

If I were to read this passage, " Seeing he ever liveth to interpose for them," it would not be an incorrect reading. The Lord Jesus Christ in his perpetual priesthood lives on purpose to be the advocate, defender, patron, mediator, and interposer for his people. You that come to God by him will highly esteem this constant service rendered to you by your Lord. Whereas Christ by his death provided all that was necessary for your salvation, he, by his life, applies that provision which he made in his death. He lives on purpose to see brought home to you, and enjoyed by you, all those blessed boons and privileges which he purchased upon the tree, when he died in your room and stead. Had he not lived for you, his death for you would have miscarried. He would then have begun the work, and provided all the materials for its completion, but there would have been none to render those materials available, and to complete the building whose foundation had been laid in so costly a manner. We are pardoned by the death of Christ, but we are justified by his resurrection. We are saved because he died ; but that salvation is brought home and secured to us because he sitteth at the right hand of God, and continually maketh intercession for us. I want you to-day to think as much of a living Christ as you have ever thought of a dead Christ. You have sat down at the foot of Calvary, your eyes suffused with tears, and you have said, How delightful it is to behold his love written out in crimson characters in yonder streams of blood, which his very heart pours out for our redemption! I want you now to sit at the foot of his throne, and, as far as your dim eyes will permit, behold his splendour, and see how he spends his glory-life in perpetual intercession for you. He is as much ours on the throne as on the tree. He is ever living to apply to us with his own hands what he purchased by the nailing of those hands and the piercing of his heart upon the cross of our redemption.

Why is it so needful that Jesus ever-living should always be interceding for us? I answer, first, it is most becoming *God-ward*. The great principle which God would teach to men is this—that sin is so hateful to him that the sinner can only approach his justice through a Mediator. This truth is most clearly set forth in the fact that even now that we are washed in the blood of the Lamb, there is no approach unto God except through the intercession of Christ. Does not this teach the grand principle of the evil of sin, and teach it in the plainest manner? The distance which sin puts between the sinner and God, and the necessity of mediation in order that a just God may commune with the imperfect—are not these fully taught by the institution of the perpetual intercession of the Son of God? This is as much a declaration of the righteousness of God as was the substitutionary death on Calvary.

Moreover, the intercession of Christ is needful God-ward to illustrate the union, co-operation, and inter-communion of the divine Trinity in the work of our salvation. The Son of God intercedes in heaven, and the Holy Spirit intercedes on earth. If Jesus intercedes, it is of necessity that the Father be there with whom he may intercede. The Son pleads and the Father hears and answers, and in consequence conveys to us by the Holy Ghost the blessings purchased by his Son. Thus, Father, Son, and Holy Spirit are brought before our minds as all concurring in the believer's salvation. A mediator who is not only man, but also one person of the blessed Trinity, continues to intercede for us, and thus we see how God remembers us.

Once again, our own communion with God is openly declared, while there sits on the throne of God a man who is also God, pleading with the Godhead. Man is always standing in glory in connection with God. The perpetual intercession of Christ is a perpetual recognition of the communion which now exists between God and once fallen, but now restored, manhood. We ought to look upon Christ pleading in glory as the sign, token, and evidence, that man is reconciled to God, that man speaks with God, that God speaks with man, and that once again the old dominion is restored to man ; for we see Jesus, who was made a little lower than the angels, for the suffering of death crowned with glory and honour.

The perpetual intercession is necessary God-ward. But it is even more necessary *man-ward*. Think, brethren and sisters, though we have been forgiven through the precious blood, yet we in many things offend, and therefore we need every day a fresh application of the blood of sprinkling. Conscience accuses us for daily flaws and faults, and it is therefore well for us that it is written, "He maketh intercession for the transgressors." Where would our hope be of continual preservation from the weaknesses and sins of our nature did not Jesus constantly plead for us? The way is rough, the world is sinful, our wanderings are many, our wants are incessant, and therefore we need the eternal intercession. We are never out of danger, and therefore always need the guardian prayer; we are never above weakness and folly, and therefore require the perpetual patronage of our protector. What man is there among you that is not full of wants? What woman is there among you that does not need to come to the mercy-seat many times a day? Jesus is always there, waiting to present our petitions; ever making our persons, our petitions, and our praise acceptable with God. Brethren, we are daily pressed, either with conflict with inbred sin or suffering in the body, with service of our Lord or sympathy for our brethren; and for all these we need help out of the holy place, help which can only come by way of the throne of the heavenly grace. We need an interposer, at whose feet we may lay down our burdens, into whose ears we may tell our sorrows: therefore Jesus ever liveth to make intercession for us.

Our great Intercessor also obtains for us those precious gifts and graces which are needful for our growth and usefulness. His is the hand which leads us onward to those attainments of the spiritual life which are needful for our serviceableness in this world, and for our meetness for the life to come. The higher virtues would be beyond our reach if his prayers did not bring us more and more of the Spirit of God to make us perfect in every good work to do his will.

Have you forgotten also that there is an enemy who is always alive and always full of malice? He acts as the accuser of the brethren, who accuseth them day and night before God; and were it not for our glorious Advocate, who for Zion's sake doth never hold his peace, what would become of us? This accuser is also a tempter, who subtly contrives plots for our overthrow. It is at times true of us as it was of Peter—"Simon, Simon, Satan hath desired to have you, that he may sift you as wheat: but I have prayed for thee." How often are we hidden from evil by the prayers of Jesus! We do not know, my brethren, how many poisoned arrows are caught upon the shield of our Lord's intercession. The intercession of Christ as with ten thousand hands is always scattering benedictions. Job asks, "Hast thou entered into the springs of the sea?" Surely our Lord's intercession is the source of an ocean of blessedness. If we had but eyes enlightened of the Holy Ghost we should see the mountain full of horses of fire, and chariots of fire round about the people of God. Who guides those horses? who directs those chariots? who is the captain of the hosts of spirits that encompass the camp of God? Who, but the Prince Immanuel, who by his all-powerful intercession ruleth all things for us.

The Lord Jesus by his unceasing pleas keeps all the powers of darkness in check, and moves all the powers of light for our rescue. His prayers form an atmosphere of blessing in which we live and move. We do not know, we cannot begin to calculate, the depths of our obligation to the ceaseless care of our unwearied Intercessor. Even when time shall be no more, and all the saints shall be saved, their continuance in bliss will be due to his endless intercession.

Think of it—Jesus always praying, never ceasing! His very appearance in heaven is a plea. The memory of his finished work is a plea.

His constant thought of us is a pleading with God. Not with tears and cries will he pray, as he did in the days of his flesh; nor perhaps even with words will he plead; for his spirit speaks to the spirit of God without such vocal instrumentality as creatures require. This much we know, he is always praying, always prevailing, and consequently always showering down upon us blessings beyond all count, the most of which we scarcely recognize; and yet if they were withheld we should perish miserably. Lord Jesus, thy dying blood is well matched by thy living plea, and our hearts rejoice in this because of these two sure proofs of thy love and grace.

IV. That brings me to my fourth point, which is—For this cause, therefore, there is ENDLESS SALVATION in the power of Jesus. "He is able to save without end, or to the uttermost, them that come unto God by him." That word "uttermost" includes within it *a reference to time.* Because our Lord Jesus never dies, he is endlessly able to save. At all times his power to save remains. He was able to save some of you forty years ago, but you would not come to him that you might have life: he is able to save you now though you have passed your fourscore years in impenitence. If you come unto God by him, he will save you however multiplied your sins. Beloved, many years ago, as boys and girls, some of us put our trust in the Redeemer, and he forgave us our trespasses. Happy day! Happy day! We are much further advanced in life at this time, and our strength grows less as the shadows lengthen; but Jesus is evermore the same, and is still able to save to the full. No diminution has taken place as to his ability to save. He that helped us in the seven struggles of our youth, and the seventy burdens of our manhood, will help us to seventy times seven, if need be. We need not fear old age or death, seeing he always has the dew of his youth, and is always our friend, laying out his life for us, even as once he laid it down for us.

He is abundantly able to save: *from the uttermost of evil to the uttermost of good he can save us.* As he ever lives in the fulness of life, so he can save to the fulness of salvation. His name is Jesus—the Saviour, and as Jesus, the Saviour, he lives. He has not renounced his office, nor allowed any part of his life to run to another purpose: he lives to save.

The Lord Jesus Christ is now, "seeing he ever liveth," able to save to the uttermost *in point of our sin.* Whatever the sin of any one here may be, if he come to God by Jesus Christ, it shall be forgiven him. God forbid I should try to make a list of human crimes; what purpose would it serve? The reading of the details of vice is very defiling: I will not therefore attempt a catalogue of crimes into which mortals sink. Sorry scoundrels come here at times; there may be dreadful characters at this moment mingled with this vast congregation, and truly I am not sorry that they are hearing the gospel: but whoever you may be, the text draws a circle of hope around you, as it says—" He is able to save them to the uttermost that come unto God by him." Whatever your offence, if you will now come to God, and confess it, and ask mercy through the name of Jesus, he is able to save you to the extreme limit of your need. If you have gone as far in sin as is possible, and are forced to own that if you could have gone further you would have done so, yet there is forgiveness. O my hearer, though your hand were even red with murder, yet the blood of Christ could wash it clean. "All manner of sin and of blasphemy shall be forgiven unto men." Yes, let the silver trumpet sound it out! Ye chief of sinners, hear the news! The Saviour lives that to the uttermost he may save such as you. Come, then, to your living Lord, ye that groan under the load of deadly guilt, for he can take it all away.

So, too, he saves to *the uttermost of our need and misery.* One old divine says if we were to climb a great hill from which we could see wide fields of spiritual distress and poverty, and if all this represented our experience, yet the Lord is able to spread salvation all round the far-off horizon, and encompass all our wants. Come, poor trembler, climb the mountain, and look far over this terrible wilderness. As far as ever thou canst see, or foresee, of dreaded need in years to come, so far and much further can the salvation of Jesus reach. As far as with the telescope of apprehension thou canst spy out trials in life and woes in death, so far is Jesus able to save thee. The uttermost will never be reached by thee, but it has long ago been provided for by him. All thy capacious emptiness can ever need to fill it, he has provided. Though thy heart should like a horse-leech cry, "Give, give," Jesus can satisfy its hunger. Though like the sea that swallows up a navy and is not full, thy soul should never cease its cravings, yet Jesus can content thee. All that thou canst require he can surely give thee, since he ever liveth by the power of an endless life to be the fulness of every emptied soul.

Jesus can save you *to the uttermost of your desires.* I want you to think of all you would like to be in righteousness and true holiness; for all that will Jesus do unto you ere he has done with you. I asked a young convert the other day "Are you perfect yet?" "Oh dear, sir," she said, "No." I asked, "Would you not like to be?" Her eyes twinkled, as well they might, and she said, "That is what I long for." It will be heaven to be perfect. Jesus is able to make us perfect, and he has resolved to do it; as it is written, "I shall be satisfied, when I awake, with thy likeness." In that likeness he will cause us to awake if we come unto God through him. Jesus will save us to the highest degree.

The Lord Jesus Christ will also save us *entirely:* he will work out the salvation of the whole man, body, soul, and spirit. He ever lives to save his people to the utmost, that is to say, all his people, and all of every one of his people. Nothing essential to manhood shall be left to perish in the case of those whom he redeems. All that which the first Adam ruined the second Adam shall restore. The Canaan of manhood from Dan to Beersheba shall be conquered by our Joshua. As yet the body is dead because of sin, though the spirit is life because of righteousness; but the day comes when the body also shall be delivered from the bondage which sin has brought upon it. Not a bone, nor a piece of a bone, of a redeemed one shall be left in the hands of the enemy. God's deliverances are always complete. When the Lord sent his angel to bring Peter out of prison, he said to the slumbering apostle, "Cast thy garment about thee, and follow me." That garment might be only a fisherman's cloak, but it must not be left in Herod's hands. He said also, "Bind on thy sandals"; for when the angel of the Lord sets a man free, he will not leave even a pair of old shoes behind him. The redemption of Christ is perfect: it reaches to the uttermost. He seems to say to sin, and Satan, and death, as the Lord said to Pharaoh: "Not a hoof shall be left behind." All that he hath redeemed by price he will also redeem by power, and to that end he makes ceaseless intercession before God.

"To the uttermost," from all our doubts and fears, and follies, and failures, Jesus will bring us by his endless intercession. "To the uttermost," from every consequence of the fall, and personal sin, and actual death, Jesus by his intercession will save us. "To the uttermost." Oh, think of it! To the resurrection life, to clearance at the judgment seat, and to the highest glories of heaven, and to boundless bliss throughout the ages he will save us. Right on while thou endurest, O eternity, the pleading of the High Priest shall save the chosen company, who for ever rising into something higher and yet higher, shall prove more and more the heights and depths of everlasting bliss! Because he lives we shall live also, and because he ever intercedes we shall for ever be glorified.

There I leave my subject, only coming back to the one enquiry, *Do you come unto God by Jesus Christ?* If so, the text speaks comfortably to you. It speaks not only of the church as a whole, but also of each individual believer: Jesus intercedes for each one of those who "come unto God by him." You, dear friend, though unknown to fame are known to Jesus. You, dear sister, hidden away in obscurity, are not hidden from the all-seeing eye of the divine Mediator. His breastplate bears your name, yea, he has graven it upon the palms of his hands, and he will never forget those whose memorials are thus perpetually with him. May the living blessing of the ever-living Saviour be with you to-day and for ever! Amen.

The Sinner's Advocate

"My little children, these things write I unto you, that ye sin not. And if any man sin, we have an advocate with the Father, Jesus Christ the righteous "—1 John ii. 1.

THE Apostle John presents us with a very clear and emphatic testimony to the doctrine of full and free forgiveness of sin. He declares that the blood of Jesus Christ, God's dear Son, cleanseth us from all sin, and that if any man sin, we have an Advocate. It is most evident that he is not afraid of doing mischief by stating this truth too broadly; on the contrary, he makes this statement with the view of promoting the sanctity of his "little children." The object of this bold declaration of the love of the Father to his sinning children is "that ye sin not." This is a triumphant answer to that grossly untruthful objection which is so often urged by the adversaries of the gospel against the doctrines of free grace—that they lead men to licentiousness. It does not appear that the Apostle John so thought, for in order that these "little children" should not sin, he actually declares unto them the very doctrine which our opponents call licentious. Those men who think that God's grace, when fully, fairly, and plainly preached, will lead men into sin, know not what they say, nor whereof they affirm. It is neither according to nature nor to grace for men to find an argument for sin in the goodness of God. Human nature is bad enough—and far be it from me to flatter that leprous criminal, that reeking mass of corruption—but even a natural conscience revolts at the baseness of sinning because grace abounds. Shall I hate God because he is kind to me? Shall I curse him because he blesses me? I venture to affirm that very few men reason thus. Man has found out many inventions, but such arguments are so transparently abominable that few consciences are so dead as to tolerate them. Bad as human *nature* is, it seldom turns the goodness of God into an argument for rebelling against him; as for souls renewed by grace, they never can be guilty of such infamy. The believer in Jesus reasons in quite another fashion. Is God so good?—then I will not grieve him. Is he so ready to forgive my transgressions?—then I will love him and offend no more. Gratitude hath bands which are stronger than iron, although softer than silk. Think not, sirs, that the Christian needs to be flogged to virtue by the whip of the law! Dream not that we hate sin merely because of the hell which follows it! If there were no heaven for the righteous, the sons of God would follow after goodness, because their regenerated spirit pants for it; and if there were no hell for the wicked, from the necessity of his new-born nature the true Christian would strive to escape from all iniquity. Loved of God, we feel we must love him in return. Richly, yea, divinely forgiven, we feel that we cannot live any longer in sin. Since Jesus died to rid us from all uncleanness, we feel that we cannot crucify our Lord afresh, and put him to an open shame. We need no nobler or more cogent arguments to lead a man to thorough consecration to God's cause and detestation of all evil than those fetched from the free grace of God. And what if some men do pervert the doctrine? Do not wicked minds corrupt everything? What truth is there in Scripture with which a man may not ruin himself if he will? Did not the prophetic eye of our Lord anticipate this when it was written that to some the Word of God is "a savour of death unto death?" Have there not been in all ages men who hold the truth of God in licentiousness? When were there not evil men to wrest Scripture to their own destruction? Shall we keep back the children's bread least the dogs should steal the crumbs? Shall we destroy health-restoring drugs because fools may poison themselves therewith? Shall all the trees be cut down for fear the owls should build their nest in them? Shall the sea be dried up because sharks swim in it? Shall the pure virgin truth be condemned because gross villains have forged her name and abused her character? God forbid. Let us never blush to preach the whole Gospel, and to preach its full forgiveness of sin in the boldest and baldest manner, believing that the naked breasts of truth are her best armour, and that she is least protected when she is encumbered with a coat of mail of human reasoning and prudence.

As God shall help me, then, believing that the doctrine of free grace and of God's infinite love to his people is a doctrine which will lead the "little children of God" to avoid all sin, I intend this morning to preach that doctrine, and God grant that the result may be according to his mind and will.

I. We commence our exposition of the text with the remark that THE SAINT IS STILL A SINNER.

Our apostle says—"If any man sin." The "if" may be written in as small letters as you will, for the supposition is a matter of certainty. "If any man sin?" Although the gentle hand of the beloved disciple uses such mild and tender terms, putting it as a supposition, as though it were an astonishing thing after so much love, and mercy, and kindness, that we should sin, yet John very well knew that all the saints do sin, for he has himself declared that if any man says that he does not sin he is a liar, and the truth is not in him. Saints are, without exception, sinners still. Far be it from us to deny that divine grace has wrought a wondrous change, it were no grace at all if it had not. It will be well to note this change. *The Christian no longer loves sin;* it is the object of his sternest horror; he no longer regards it as a mere trifle, plays with it, or talks of it with unconcern. He looks upon it as a deadly serpent, whose very shadow is to be avoided. He would no more venture voluntarily to put its cup to his lip than a man would drink poison who had once almost lost his life through it. Sin is dejected in the Christian's heart, though it is not ejected. Sin may enter the heart, and fight for dominion, but it cannot sit upon the throne. It haunts the town of Mansoul, and lurks in dens and corners to do mischief, but it is no longer honoured in the streets, nor pampered in the palace. The head and the hands of Dagon are broken, although the stump remains.

The Christian *never sins with that enormity of boasting of which the unregenerate are guilty.* Others wallow in transgressions, and make their shame their glory, but if the believer falleth he is very quiet, mournful, and vexed. Sinners go to their sins as children to their own father's orchard, but believers slink away like thieves when they have been stealing forbidden fruit. Shame and sin are always in close company in a Christian. If he be drunken with evil he will be ashamed of himself, and go to his bed like a whipped cur. He cannot proclaim his transgressions as some do in the midst of a ribald crowd, boasting of their exploits of evil. His heart is broken within him, and when he has sinned he goes with sore bones for many and many a day.

Nor does he sin *with the fulness of deliberation* that belongs to other men. The sinner can sit down by the month together, and think over the iniquity that he means to perpetrate, till he gets his plans well organised and has matured his project; but the Christian cannot do this. He may put the sin into his mouth and swallow it in a moment, but he cannot continue to roll it under his tongue. He who can carefully arrange and plot a transgression is still a true child of the old serpent.

And again, *he never chews the cud of his sin;* for after he has sinned, however sweet it may have been in his mouth, it becomes bitterness in his bowels, and glad enough would he be to be rid of it altogether. The retrospect of sin to a converted man is nothing but blackness and darkness in his heart.

The Christian, unlike other men, *never finds enjoyment in his sin;* he is out of his element in it. Conscience pricks him; he cannot, even if he would, sin like others. There is a refined taste within him, which all the while revolts at the apparently dainty morsel of sin. The finger of grace, with its secret and mysterious touch, turns all the honey into gall, and all the sweetness into wormwood. If the Christian shall sin, and sin I grant he will, yet it shall always be with half-heartedness; still he clings to the right, the evil that he would not he does, while the good that he would do he fails to perform.

You will notice too, how different the Christian is *as to the habit of sin.* The ungodly man is frequent in overt deeds of rebellion, but the Christian, at least in open acts of crime and folly, rather falleth into than abideth in them. The swallow dippeth with his wing the brook, and then he is up again into the skies, soaring toward the sun; but the duck can swim in the pool or dive under the water—it is in its element. So the Christian just touches sometimes with his wing—alas! for him— the streams of earth, but then he is up again where he should be; it is only the sinner that can swim in sin and delight therein. You may drive the swine and the sheep together side by side; they come to some mire, and they both fall into it, and both stain themselves; but you soon detect the difference in nature between them, for while the swine lies and wallows with intense gusto, the sheep is up again, escaping as soon as possible from the filth. So with the Christian; he falls, God knoweth how many times, but he riseth up again—it is not his nature to lie in sin; he abhors himself that ever he should fall to the ground at all: while the ungodly goeth on in his wicked way till sin becomes a habit, and habit like an iron net has entangled him in its meshes.

There are all these degrees of difference between the Christian and the ungodly man, and far more, for the believer is a new creature, he belongs to a holy generation and a peculiar people; the Spirit of God is in him, and in all respects he is far removed from the natural man, but for all that we must come back to that with which we started—that the Christian is a sinner still. He is so *from the imperfection of his nature.* His nature is such that he cannot but sin until the old Adam shall die in him, and that will not be till the funeral knell is tolled for himself. Sin, by reason of his imperfection, pollutes the best thing the believer does. Sin mars his repentance. There is filth in our tears, and unbelief in our faith. The best thing we ever did apart from the merit of Jesus only swelled the number of our sins, for when we have been most pure in our own sight, yet, like the heavens, we are not pure in God's sight, and as he charged his angels with folly, much more must he charge us with it, even in our most angelic frame of mind. The song that thrills to heaven, and seeks to emulate seraphic strains, has still mortal infirmity in it. The prayer which moves the arm of God is still a sinful prayer, and only moves that arm because the Sinless One, the great Mediator, has stepped in to take away the sin of our supplication. I dare to say it, the best faith or the highest degree of sanctification to which a Christian ever attained on earth, has still so much of the creature's infirmity in it as to be worthy of God's eternal wrath in itself considered. There is so much sin about the highest and loftiest thing to which the creature can attain, that we mournfully confess—"We are altogether as an unclean thing, and all our righteousnesses are but as filthy rags."

As the Christian thus sins in his devout performances, *so he constantly errs in the every-day tenour of his life.* Sins of omission to wit, how many of these may be compressed into a single hour! Oh! what multitudes of things we have left undone! Remember that these make up a very great part of the sin which brings the curse. " I was thirsty and ye gave me no drink; sick and in prison and ye visited me not." Have we no sins of commission? Our thoughts, our imaginations, our words, and must I not say our deeds, have these been what they should be? If any man dare to tell me that he lives for a single day without a sinful deed, I will dare to tell him that he never knew himself. Do but see your own chamber. If you disturb it I see but little dust floating about in it, but if a stray sunbeam shall enter through the window I see millions upon millions of little motes dancing up and down, and I discover that the whole of what I supposed to be clear, pure air, is filled with innumerable atoms of all sorts of things, and that I am breathing these even in the purest atmosphere. So is it with our heart and life. When the Spirit shines into us we see that the atmosphere of life is as full of sin as it can hold, and a man may sooner count the hairs of his head, or the sands upon the sea-shore, or the drops of the dew of the morning upon the grass, than count the sins of a single day. O Lord, thou knowest us, but we know not ourselves; yet this much we know, that we are a people full of sin and laden with iniquity. You will tell me these are little sins, but I remind you that a multitude of grains of sand may overload a vessel quite as surely as bars of iron, and therefore these daily iniquities should be confessed with care, and repented of with sincerity. The Christian, then, from the imperfection of his nature, sins. The old unchanged fountain of Marah must send forth bitter water. The old Adam can do nothing else but sin. Fire can do nothing but burn; water can do nothing but quench fire; everything acts according to its nature. The new nature that is in us cannot sin, because it is born of God; it is so heavenly and divine that it never stoops to anything like sin. There is a spark of the celestial and of the perfect within every believer which never can be quenched; but the old Adam, that which made Paul cry out—" O wretched man that I am, who shall deliver me from the body of this death"—must sin, and as certainly as sparks fly upward, so certainly the old nature will commit iniquity.

Moreover, *many Christian people sin from certain peculiar infirmities.* You know, each of you, what your own infirmity may be; at least I hope you have been watchful enough to discover it. Some sin *through shortness of temper;* they are not long-winded in patience with their fellow-creatures; they are vexed; they grow hot; perhaps they imagine some cause for anger where there is none, and they wax warm, and speak unadvisedly with their tongue. This gives much trouble to many of the most gracious of men. A hasty temper is a perpetual temptation. There are others *who have a high and proud spirit,* and if they fancy they are a little snubbed or put into the back-ground, at once they feel inclined to resent it. There—listen to him—" I am not to be thus trodden upon! Who dares to treat me thus?" Many who have done good service for Christ have had to carry that thorn in their flesh even down to their graves. Sensitiveness, a high spirit, a suspicious temperament, these are like blisters to the feet of a pilgrim, he will always walk painfully, if not slowly. Some of us have to contend with *sloth.* Perhaps we are afflicted with a torpid liver, and the physician has never been able to touch the complaint. God help the man thus afflicted, for he will need to whip himself every day to his duty, and often he will feel so dull and sleepy, that he will wish for Cowper's "lodge in a vast wilderness, some boundless contiguity of shade " that he might hide himself in quiet from the toil of the spiritual harvest. How many we know, dear friends, who have to contend with *constant unbelief brought on through depression of spirits.* Their nerves, perhaps, have experienced a great shock at some period in life, and, constitutionally they look always at the black side of affairs. If they see a grassy knoll they suspect it to be an extinct volcano; and if they happen to be in a green valley where the mountains frown like the battlements of heaven, they are dreadfully afraid that an avalanche must certainly come down and destroy them. They cannot help it; it is a peculiarity of their constitution, but it leads them into much sin, and should cause them much repentance before the face of the living God. So I might go on to mention the peculiarity of some *who are suffering from bashfulness;* they will often be tempted to hold back where they ought to go forward, and if not to disavow their Master yet not to procaim their love for him so boldly as they should do. The Christian, when he reads this verse, "If any man sin," may well say—"Ah! indeed I do; through these infirmities I constantly commit iniquity." And then, dear friends, we all sin *from the assaults of evil.* There are times when we are not watchful, and as Satan is always on his watch-tower he is sure to attack us just then. We wear our vizor up and then in flies the stone from the infernal sling. We have forgotten a piece of our armour, and the foeman spies our nakedness and cuts us deep, leaving a scar for years. The *temptations of the world,* when we are thrust into ungodly company, and *the trials of business and even of the household,* all these in unguarded moments may take the Christian off his feet Ah, my brethren, he who was not a whit behind the very chief of the apostles yet called himself the chief of sinners; and we with far inferior graces must take the lowest place, acknowledging that in us, that is in our flesh, there dwelleth no good thing. Sinner is *my* name, sinner my nature, but thanks be to him who came to save sinners, I am a sinner saved.

II. I now leave that point for a second one full of comfort. OUR SINS DO NOT DEPRIVE US OF OUR INTEREST IN CHRIST.

Note the text. "If any man sin we *have* an advocate." Yes, we have him though we do sin; we have him still. It does not say—" If any man sin he has forfeited his advocate," but " we have an advocate," sinners though we are. All the sin that a believer ever did or can be allowed to commit, cannot destroy his interest in the Lord Jesus Christ. Into whatsoever he may be suffered to fall, yet none of these things can by any possibility touch his title deeds. Indeed in some characters Jesus is only mine when I can claim the name of sinner. I cannot have an advocate unless I do sin, I do not want one. Who wants an advocate to plead his cause in a court of law if there is no suit against him? Sin is a charge against me; I am a sinner; I have an advocate. I have today a brother in Christ? "Go, tell my brethren," said he; and yet they had all forsaken him, and therefore were all sinners, but he was their brother still. I have a husband in Christ too, though I sin. "Israel hath forsaken me," saith God, "and played the harlot; she hath gone a-whoring from me, but return, return, for I am married unto thee." She is his wife still, you see, though she had gone into adultery. The Christian, even when he has stained and fouled himself, is the spouse of Christ still for all that. We are members of his body, and if so the members cannot be removed or taken off and on—limbs are not so easily removed. Did not Christ wash Peter? Peter was a member of Christ's own body, and yet Peter wanted washing. O blessed picture, the Head washing the feet. So at this day, stained though we be, we are claimants of Christ as Head of our body. And, beloved, we know that notwithstanding all our sin we are perfectly justified in Christ, for he justifieth the ungodly. We know, too, that we are perfectly accepted, for we are accepted in the Beloved, and not in ourselves. Notwithstanding all our iniquities we are pardoned, for the fountain is opened for sin and for all uncleanness, not for righteousness and purity, but for sin and for uncleanness; therefore we conclude that all our sins do not deprive us of that which Christ is to us, namely, the fountain of life, and light, and purity, and safety. Oh! my brethren, if our first title to Christ had depended on our good works, then it would fall when our works grew bad, but he loved us when we were as bad as we could be.

> "He saw us ruined in the fall,
> Yet loved us notwithstanding all."

He chose us when we were sinners; he bought us when we were sinners; he loved us when we were dead in trespasses and sins; and if we are as bad as that to-day, he loves us still. If our right to heaven rested on the covenant of works, that unstable tenure, it would soon fail us; but seeing it rests on the covenant of grace, which has no conditions in it, but which is of pure immutable grace from first to last, therefore be it known unto you, O sons of God, that notwithstanding all your faults and failings, wanderings and backslidings, he is your God and you are his children; he will be your God to all eternity, and you shall be his children world without end. "What a bold thing to say?" says one. Yes, and did I not tell you that I meant to say it to the little children that they sin not; believing that the bold open statement of the fact that all the sin that a believer can commit cannot mar his interest in Christ, though it may mar his enjoyment of that interest for the present, believing, I say, that this doctrine instead of driving men to sin, will draw them to love that gracious and immutable God, who notwithstanding all our sin, and care, and woe, will never suffer us to perish.

III. Now let us change the note a little. Our third point is, THAT THE ADVOCATE IS PROVIDED ON PURPOSE TO MEET THE FACT THAT WE ARE STILL SINNERS.

If I be a sinner then there is a court, and there is one who sits as Judge—the Father. There is a charge against me, otherwise I should not want an advocate to meet it, and this implies that I have sinned. There is an adversary to press his suit against me, and he would hardly venture to do this if there were no sin. There must be a right of reply on my part; I must have the right to put in a disclaimer in court, and to stand up and plead before the bar of justice. He who has a right to plead in court is the man who is accused, and the man who has some offence. If I were neither accused nor had been a sinner, then I should have no right to occupy the time of the court; but being a sinner, and being brought up upon that charge, and having one who presses the charge against me, I have a right to reply, and that reply, through God's good grace, I have a right to make through my advocate.

Let us say concerning our advocate, that he is ordained with a special view to sinners; all his names and attributes prove him to be a suitable advocate for such. You and I, who though saved are still sinners, may safely put our case into his hands, for see who he is—"*Jesus Christ the righteous.*"

"*Jesus.*" Ah! then he is an advocate such as I want, for he loves me and takes an interest in me. Jesus is the name of one who became man for my sake. He knows what sore temptations mean; he understands what trials mean, what afflictions mean. I am glad I have one who will be interested in my welfare, and will plead for me as a friend for a friend, and as a brother for a brother. I thank God that though I sin I still have Jesus who is my "brother born for adversity," the friend of sinners, and will therefore plead the sinner's part. Is his name Jesus? Then he is sure to succeed, because "they shall call his name Jesus, for *he shall save* his people from their sins;" his very name implies his success. Is his name Jesus? Then if he do not succeed in my case his honour is compromised. He is called Jesus because he does save sinners, if he does not save me he is no Jesus. If I, a sinner, trusting in him, give him my cause to plead as my advocate, and I be tried, and the verdict be against me, he is no Jesus; he may lay down his claim to be Jesus, for he does not and cannot save his people from their sins. Beloved friends, do you not see how the saint is regarded as a sinner because he who is his advocate is the appointed Saviour of sinners. He is put down as their advocate, I say, because he is the sinner's friend. I never heard of his pleading for the righteous; I never dreamed of his being the friend of the sinless. I find him always on the side of publicans and sinners, offenders, and those who have gone out of the way; and therefore I conclude, that sinner though I be, continually sinning as I am, I may leave my case with Jesus, for he is just the advocate the sinner wants.

Notice, next, it is "Jesus *Christ*"—Christos—the anointed. This shows *his authority* to plead. There are only certain gentlemen who can plead in the Court of Chancery, and only certain others that can enter the Common Pleas, or the King's Bench. Jesus Christ has a right to plead, for he is the Father's own appointed, the Father's own anointed. My soul, thou hast a good pleader, one whom God himself has chosen to plead the sinner's cause. If he were of thy choosing he might fail, but if God hath laid help upon one that is mighty, do thou put thy trouble where God has laid his help. He is Christ, and therefore authorised; but I add, he is Christ, and therefore *qualified*, for the anointing has also qualified him for his work. He can plead better than Judah pleaded when he spake for Benjamin. He can plead so as to move the heart of God and prevail. What words of tenderness, what sentences of persuasion will he use when he stands up to plead for me! But more, he is Christ, that is, he is God's Messiah; therefore God would not send him unless he *guaranteed him.* If God should send into this world a Saviour who could not save, then God would have no mercy. God's appointing and sending Christ is a guarantee of Christ's success. Oh! my soul, thou hast one well-fitted to be thine advocate, and one that cannot but succeed; leave thyself entirely in his hands.

Notice next, it is "Jesus Christ *the righteous.*" This is not only his character, but it is his plea. It is his character, and if my advocate be righteous then I am sure he would not take up a bad cause. I do not know, it may be right for a lawyer to plead for a villain when he knows him to be a villain, but this I think, the greater villain the lawyer is the better qualified would he be to do it. But my Lord and Master, the great advocate, would not plead a bad cause, for he is Jesus Christ *the righteous;* therefore if I sin, if I be put down among the any men that sin, yet if he pleads for me my case must be good, for he would not take up a bad one. But how can he do this? Why, because he meets the charge of unrighteousness against me by this plea on his part, that *he* is righteous. He seems to say to the great Father in the day when the sinner stands arraigned—"Yes, my Father, that sinner was unrighteous, but remember that I was accepted as his substitute; I stood to keep the law for him, and gave my active obedience; I went up to the cross and bled, and so gave my passive obedience; I have covered him from head to foot with my doing and my dying; I have so arrayed him that not even the angels are adorned as he is, for though they may be clothed with the perfect righteousness of a creature, I have given him the righteousness of God himself; I am become unto my people the Lord their righteousness; see, I have taken the jewels out of my crown to bedeck them; the garments from my own back to cover them, and the blood from my own veins to make the dye in which I have dipped their garments, till they are purpled with imperial glory." What can there be asked more for the sinner than this? Jesus Christ the righteous stands up to plead for me, and pleads his righteousness; and mark, he does this not if I do not sin, but if I do sin. There is the beauty of my text. It does not say—"If any man do not sin we have an advocate;" but "if any man sin we have an advocate," so that when I have sinned, and come creeping up to my closet with a guilty conscience and an aching heart, and feel that I am not worthy to be called God's son, I have still an advocate, because I am one of the any men that sin. I sin, and I have an advocate. Oh! I know not how to express the joy I feel in my soul to be able to put it so! It is not—"If any man be righteous we have an advocate;" it is not—"If any man be prayerful, and careful, and godly, and walk scripturally, and in the light," and so on, but "If any man *sin* we have an advocate." Oh! my soul, there is the music of God's heart in those words; music such as the prodigal heard at the festival which welcomed his return. "If any man sin we have an advocate with the Father, Jesus Christ the righteous."

IV. And now we turn to our fourth point which is, that THIS TRUTH, SO EVANGELICAL AND SO DIVINE, SHOULD BE PRACTICALLY REMEMBERED. It should be practically remembered, dear friends, *at all times.* Every day I find it most healthy to my own soul to try and walk as a saint, but in order to do so I must continually come to Christ as a sinner. I would seek to be perfect; I would strain after every virtue, and forsake every false way; but still, as to my standing before God, I find it happiest to sit where I sat when first I looked to Jesus, on the rock of his works, having nothing to do with my own righteousness, but only with his. Depend on it, dear friends, the happiest way of living is to live as a poor sinner and as nothing at all, having Jesus Christ as all in all. You may have all your growths in sanctification, all your progress in graces, all the development of your virtues that you will; but still I do earnestly pray you never to put any of these where Christ should be. If you have begun in Christ then finish in Christ. If you have begun in the flesh and then go on in the flesh, we know what the sure result will be. But if you have begun with Jesus Christ as your Alpha, let him be your Omega. I pray you never think you are rising when you get above this, for it is not rising, but slipping downwards to your ruin. Stand still to this—

> " Nothing in my hands I bring,
> Simply to thy cross I cling."

Still a sinner, but still having an advocate with the Father, Jesus Christ, the righteous—let this be the spirit of your every-day life.

Make this essentially the rule of your life *on particular occasions*. Here let me say a word that may at once comfort and enlighten some here who are in darkness. When the Spirit of God gives you a clearer view of your own depravity, mind that you hold to this : " If any man sin we have an advocate with the Father." Perhaps when you were first converted you did not suspect the depth of wickedness that lay under, in your heart; perhaps you did not even believe that you could be so unutterably bad as you really were. But lately the fountains of the great deep have been broken up and you have been horrified; you are almost driven mad, or else into despondency and despair, by this discovery of your innate corruption, until you fly to this,—" Sinner as I am, and never more consciously so than I am now that God's Spirit has enlightened me, I yet know that if any man sin we have an advocate with the Father, and I, black, foul, and filthy, more foul and filthy than I ever thought myself to be, put my case into the hand of my advocate, and leave it there for ever." When after this you have fallen into sin, and oh! I may address some member of this Church who has done this though the pastor knows it not—you have fallen into some sin that pricks your conscience; you carry about with you a something that will not let you sleep at night; there is a sin that disturbs you, and you wish you could forget that you had committed it; you have gone before God as David did; you have used the language of the fifty-first Psalm, but you cannot get rid of that sin; you believe you are a child of God sometimes, but that sin has got into your conscience, and, like a cancer, is eating into your comfort. My brother, now is your time; " If any man sin, we have an advocate with the Father." Jesus Christ is of no use to you if he will only save you when you have no sin. Let me repeat it: now you are a sinner; now you are condemned by the verdict of your own conscience; now you have sinned, sinned wilfully and foully, and God forbid that I should extenuate your sin; yet let your sin be as gross, and black, and hellish, as it may be, if you believe in Jesus Christ you have an advocate with the Father, and through that advocate your cause shall speed, and your sin shall be put away. Perhaps you will tell me that your sin has had some gross aggravation about it. If you are a Christian it has, for a Christian always sins worse than other men; if the sin be not in itself so bad as other men's, it is worse in you. For a king's favourite to play the traitor is villainy indeed. For one that has been highly favoured, as you have been, with love-visits from Jesus, to be false to him; oh! this is shame, double shame to him. For you who have been washed in his blood to crucify him afresh, what shall I say to that? You deserve the hottest wrath of God and the deepest hell. But thus saith the Lord unto thee—"I have blotted out thy sins like a cloud, and like a thick cloud thine iniquities; return unto me." "If any man sin, we have an advocate with the Father." It does not say, "If some men sin we have no advocate;" or, "if some men sin in an aggravated way." No, it is not put so. It says, "If *any* man sin, we have an advocate with the Father;" so that though you have heaped aggravations one upon another, and your crime has been as foul as any that could have been committed, still you can say, "we have an advocate." Fly with a humble, contrite heart, and throw thyself at the feet of that advocate, and by his blood and by his wounds he will plead for thee, and thou shalt prevail.

What if I add to all this, that you have so sinned as to bring a scandal upon the name of God, upon his Church, and upon his cause? Oh! my brother, you may well weep in secret; you may weep tears of blood for having done this; but still, for all that, I cannot shut the gate where God sets it wide open. I have not a thunderbolt for you; if you be a child of God, still mercy is free, and still it is preached to you—"If any man sin," publicly, like David, so as to make God's enemies to blaspheme, yet still "we have an advocate with the Father, Jesus Christ the righteous." Oh! what splendid mercy is this! Archangel never dreamed of such mercy as this to sinners, to real sinners, to hugely vile sinners, to black, hellish sinners, to devilish sinners, to such as no adjective can be found to describe them. Yet, if they believe in Jesus, sin as they may, they have still "an advocate with the Father, Jesus Christ the righteous."

I wish I could meet the case of that brother yonder, who has long given up all hope of ever being restored. He has been excommunicated; he has been driven away from the society of the godly; he thinks though he is in this house this morning he has no business here; and sometimes the devil has tempted him to make away with himself, and he has said, if I must be lost I may as well be lost at once. Ah! but, my brother, you dare not do it with such a text of Scripture as this before your eyes. The Lord loves you still, and if he ever loved you, all your sin cannot wean his heart from you. You may have gone to the utmost length of your tether, but he has so tied you that you can never go beyond it. You may have got to the very extremity and edge of the precipice, but over that edge you must not and you shall not go. This day he sends me to stop you. Return! return! return! a Father bids you return. You are feeding swine to-day, and all foul and filthy as you are, you would fain fill your belly with their husks; but you cannot; you have a hunger that husks can never satisfy. Your Father waits to receive you. Come, he will meet you; he will fall upon your neck and kiss you; he will set you at his own table, and there shall be music and dancing for you. The best robe awaits thee, prodigal! The fatted calf is killed for thee! Come. O believe it; believe that God is able to do this great thing for thee. "As high as the heavens are above the earth, so high are his thoughts above thy thoughts, and his ways above thy ways."

> "What though your numerous sins exceed
> The stars that fill the skies,
> And, aiming at the eternal throne,
> Like pointed mountains rise,"

yet still the red sea of Jesus' blood shall cover the tops of the mountains of your sins, till, like Noah's ark, that floated twenty cubits upwards, the tops of the mountains shall be covered. "If any man sin"—here you see, there is nothing said about goodness, nothing about virtue, or tenderness of heart—it is only put, "If any man sin, we have an advocate."

O thou that believest in Jesus, pray for those who believe not, that they too may have an advocate. If you and I have come and put our trust in him, and found a shelter in his wounds, let us never be satisfied till we see our children, our brothers, our sisters, our friends, our kinsfolk brought to this advocate. Go ye, and tell it wherever your voices can be heard, that Jesus Christ receiveth sinners, and that he eateth with them. Go and say that he is the sinner's friend, and that he is willing to take them as they are, and wash them, and make them whiter than snow. Since you have proved it yourself, and need to prove it every day, try and bring others to the conviction of it, that they with you may sing to the praise of that divine love which has given the advocate to every believer, whatever his guilt and condemnation may have been.

The Lord bless you now, for Jesus' sake. Amen.

The Way

"Jesus saith unto him, I am the way"—John xiv. 6.

THE most precious things lie in the smallest compass. Diamonds have much value in little space. Those scriptural sayings which are fullest of meaning are many of them couched in the fewest words. Who shall measure the depth of that sentence, "God is love"? or that other, "God is light"? Who shall know the lengths and breadths of this declaration, "Christ is all"? How clearly is the whole gospel condensed into that line, "By grace are ye saved"! There are many more divine words of a like character, all short, and as sweet as they are short, precious beyond comparison, and as brief as precious. Our text, with its four words, and those all monosyllables, and none of more than three letters, is among the chief of these Bibles in miniature. "I am the way." It were difficult, and it were as wicked as difficult, to be otherwise than simple in preaching when such a text as this is the theme. May God grant that some of you may be reached by my simple testimony, and led in the way to heaven; may those who are in the way already be strengthened, and comforted, and quickened in it; may God be glorified and sinners converted, and then our hearts shall be exceeding glad.

I. We shall go at once to the text, and consider, in the first place, HOW JESUS CHRIST IS THE WAY, AND HOW HE COMES TO BE SO.

How he is the way. A way supposes two points—from which and to which. Christ is the way from man's ruin to the Father. Our Lord was speaking of man's coming to the Father, so we know whither the way leads, and we know very well that the way were of no service unless it came to where we are by nature, and that is in the place of ruin and of wrath. Christ is the way that leadeth from the City of Destruction to the Celestial City—from the ruin of our father Adam right up to the glory of our Father who is in heaven.

Christ is the way, then, first, *from the guilt of sin* to the Father. The great difficulty was—How is sin to be put away? Many attempts have been made to remove it, but there is no way of our escaping from the guilt of sin except by Jesus Christ. Some have hoped for pardon from future good conduct, but as we all know that the payment of a future debt can by no means discharge a past debt, so that even the perfect future obedience of man, could he achieve it, could not touch his past sins. Self-righteousness, therefore, even if it could reach perfection, would not be "the way." Some hope much from the mercy of God, but the law knows nothing of clearing the sinner of guilt by a sovereign act of mercy—that cannot be done; for then God's justice would be impugned, his law would be virtually annulled. He will by no means clear the guilty. Every transgression must have its just recompense of reward, so that the absolute mercy of God as such is not the way out of the guilt of sin, for that mercy is blocked up by avenging justice, and over the face of that star of hope called absolute mercy there passes an eclipsing shadow, because God is righteous as well as gracious. There is no way by which a sinner can escape from the guilt of sin but that which is revealed in Jesus Christ. God has sent forth his Son, his only Son. The Word was made flesh and came under the law : upon that mysterious being who combined both Godhead and manhood in one person, the Lord has laid the iniquity of us all. By imputation the transgressions of his elect have been laid upon their Covenant Head, so that he was numbered with the transgressors, and he bare the sin of many. He voluntarily undertook to be the substitute and covenant surety of his chosen; and in this way, by the transferring of sin from the sinner to Christ, the sinner ceases to be regarded as a sinner, and his guilt is removed. Here is the way for that sinner to approach the Father. His sin is laid upon Christ, who became the substitute for all sinners that ever have believed or ever shall believe on him, and he himself is clear. The whole mountain mass of the sins of believers lies not on them any longer, but on Christ. He hath taken their transgressions, he hath borne their iniquities, their sins are moved from them and laid on him. Now hark! The only way in which sin can be taken from any one of us is by this method; it is not imputed unto us, it is imputed unto him; but think not that the sin which was laid upon Christ of old lies upon Christ now. It does not, for the day came when the punishment for all that sin was demanded; the sword of vengeance awoke against human sin, and it would have smitten all the flock, and the sheep would have been destroyed, but the Shepherd came into the place of the flock, and he bore the strokes of the sword; and there upon yonder once accursed, but now for ever blessed, tree, the Saviour endured the fulness of divine wrath on account of sin. Now, where is the sin of his people? He hath cast it into the depths of the sea. By bearing its punishment he has caused it no more to exist ; it is as though it had never been; it is annihilated, it is gone, if it be searched for, it cannot be found. Jesus Christ by his taking the sin and then discharging all the liability that was due to God from that sin, has for ever finished transgression—mark the word, made an end of sin, and brought in everlasting righteousness for his people. Now, sinner, if thou wouldst get away from thy sin, Christ is the way ; this is the way by which thou canst escape from it. I have already told thee that thy future reformation cannot remove thy past sin, neither can the mercy of God, considered as an attribute by itself, clear thee from thy sin; but this wonderful deed of love and wisdom, this marvellous transaction that makes heaven and earth ring with grateful songs, when glorified spirits see further into it, and when angelic intellects are able to grasp it, this wondrous transaction can clear thee from sin as it has cleared many of us; for we are this day before God justified, so that none can lay anything to our charge. Sinners we are in ourselves, but not sinners before God's judgment-seat, for Jesus has made us clean; we are whiter than snow, our sins being removed from us far as is the east is from the west by our great atoning Substitute. Here is a way consistent with divine justice, a way exactly meeting what you need. Oh, I pray God that while the words are used, "I am the way," your spirit may say, " Blessed be his name, Jesus shall be my way, I will this day believe on him and thus escape from my guilt."

The text refers to the guilt of sin, but then "I am the way" is as true concerning *the wrath of God* on account of sin. You will see at once, and, therefore, I need not use many words about it, that the way to escape from wrath is to escape from the sin which causes the wrath. Remove the cause, you remove the effect. Now, when the sin of God's people was moved from them to Christ, the wrath of God went where the sin went, and it fell upon Christ, until he said, " My God, my God, why hast thou forsaken me?" and when that bitter cup of wrath had been drained to its dregs, it was emptied for ever, and not one drop was left for a believing soul to taste. The wrath of God towards the believer has ceased to be, and at this moment there is no angry thought in God's heart towards a justified person. Whosoever has believed in Christ, his sins were laid on Christ, and punished in Christ, and God is not and cannot be angry with the man for whom Jesus was a substitute, for he has no sins for God to be angry with. " Oh," say you, "but does he not sin?" He does, but it is not imputed to him, according to the saying of the psalmist in the thirty-second Psalm: " Blessed is he whose transgression is forgiven, whose sin is covered. Blessed is the man unto whom the Lord imputeth not iniquity." He commits sin, but it is not imputed to him, and so the wrath never comes on him; he is free from guilt and wrath; God has love to him, unbounded love, and though he may chasten him, yet this is not in anger, but with purposes of love to him for his spiritual and everlasting good. So you see Christ is the way out of divine wrath as well as out of our sin.

And, listen. There comes upon us in consequence of sin, when the Lord deals with us and makes us see sin, *a deep and terrible depression of spirit*, in some more and in some less, but in every case " when the commandment came, sin revived, and I died." Sin as soon as it is really felt in the soul to be sin, kills us, blasts our former hopes, crushes our pride, lays us like bruised and mangled things before the burning throne of justice. Oftentimes souls have been heard to cry, " There is no soundness in my flesh because of thine anger; neither is there any rest in my bones because of my sin. For mine iniquities are gone over mine head: as an heavy burden they are too heavy for me. My wounds stink and are corrupt because of my foolishness." Many such expressions, it may be, you, my awakened hearer, have been made to utter, but, oh! if thou comest to see that all this sin of thine is not thine, that in Christ Jesus God hath put away thy sin by thy Saviour's bearing it and enduring its punishment, I say, if thou seest this, thou wilt speedily rejoice. In a moment those waves of wrath will pass away from thee, and thy spirit will sing, "Hope thou in God: for I shall yet praise him, who is the health of my countenance, and my God." I know a truly awakened conscience never will believe in the pardon of sin without atonement first made; but when you hear that atonement has been made, that Christ suffered instead of you, that his death has glorified the justice of God more than your lying in hell could have glorified him, that his atonement is to God's injured law a better vindication than even your eternal destruction, do you not see it, do you not lay hold on it, and doth not your heart leap at the sound of this glorious gospel of the blessed God? Christ is the way, then, out of the guilt of thy sin, out of the wrath of God for thy sin, and out of thy sense of that wrath.

But more, Christ is the way to escape from the *power of sin*. The great object of a penitent soul is to get away from the tyrrany and slavery of evil habits and of corrupt desires. A man may break off some of his sins by his own unaided efforts. For instance, no man need be a drunkard, common determination may have done with those intoxicating cups. No man need be a swearer; let him understand what a wantonness of iniquity there is in that sin, and he may surely give it up. Still, sin dwells in fallen creatures, and the imagination of the thoughts of their hearts is evil, and that continually. Who can bring a clean thing out of an unclean? Man, thy sinfulness is such that thou canst not cease from sin. But man, there is a power above and beyond thee which can deliver thee from the power of sin and make thee holy; it is found in Christ Jesus, in Christ Jesus as I have preached him to thee this day. Let me tell thee my own experience. Whenever I feel that I have sinned, and desire to overcome that sin for the future, the devil at the same time comes to me and whispers, "How can you be a pardoned person and accepted with God while you sin in this way?" If I listen to this I drop into despondency, and if I continued in that state I should fall into despair, and should commit sin more frequently than before; but God's grace comes in and says to my soul, "Thou hast sinned; but did not Jesus come to save sinners? Thou art not saved because thou art righteous; for Christ died for the ungodly." And my faith says, "Though I have sinned, I have an advocate with the Father, Jesus Christ the righteous, and though I am guilty, yet by grace I am saved, and I am a child of God still." And what then? Why, then the tears begin to flow, and I say, "How could I ever sin against my God who is so good to me? Now I will overcome that sin," and I get strong to fight with sin through the conviction that I am God's child. Doubts and fears, and the thought that God is angry only drive you further into sin, but the faith which in the teeth of sin yet believes in God's love, and still believes in the perfect pardon Christ has given, which God himself can never take back again; that holy faith which still clings to the cross with, "If I perish I perish, but to this atoning sacrifice I cling;" that faith, I say, makes you strong against sin. The saints in glory overcame through the blood of the Lamb, and there is no other way of overcoming. The precious blood of atonement wherever sprinkled kills sin, and he that lives in the full belief of it will be purified from sinful habits, as saith that precious text: "If we walk in the light, as he is in the light, we have fellowship one with another, and the blood of Jesus Christ his Son cleanseth us from all sin." It is walking under a sense of divine love as manifest in Christ, it is walking with the full conviction of pardon through the blood that brings to us freedom from the reigning power of sin. So, soul, Jesus Christ is "*the way*" to escape from sin, its guilt, its wrath, its fear, its power.

Now we must have a word or two upon the other end of the way. I said it was *from* sin, *to* what? *To the Father.* Now the way to the Father is alone by Jesus Christ. We have for this the express saying of Christ: "No man cometh unto the Father, but by me." We hear talk of getting to God the Father by nature, but it is a ladder too short to reach the Infinite. God is somewhat seen in his works, but I believe those who have seen the grandest works of God, and have also seen God in Christ, will tell you that God is no more mirrored in his works than is the whole universe in a dewdrop. Earth is not broad enough to reflect the image of God. He doth not mirror himself in the sea, it is a glass too small to show the Deity; he cannot reveal his whole glory in the materialism of this poor world of ours, its axles would groan and crack beneath the weight of Deity. It is in Christ that Jehovah reveals himself more fully than in all nature, though you summon sun, moon, and stars, and read all their hieroglyphs, God is revealed in Christ in a way in which he cannot be in anything of time or of space.

Learn, then, that we get our best apprehensions of the Father through the Son. "He that hath seen me hath seen the Father." It is only by Christ that we realise the Fatherhood of God. I do not believe any man has any idea of what the Fatherhood of God is till he knows Jesus Christ, as the first-born among many brethren, and knows the power of his atonement to bring us near to God. The common Fatherhood doctrine that God is the Father of us all, because he made us all, is not true in the most real and tender sense of Fatherhood. A potter makes ten thousand vessels, but he is not the father of one of them. It is not everything that a man makes that he is the father of, or if he be so called, it is only in a modified sense. We are God's children when we are created anew in Christ Jesus; when regeneration has made us partakers of the divine nature. Sonship is no ordinary privilege common to all mankind, it is the high prerogative of the chosen; for what saith the Scripture: "Behold, what manner of love the Father hath bestowed upon us, that we should be called the sons of God: therefore the world knoweth us not, because it knew him not." When we are adopted into the divine family, then and not till then do we know God as the Father. As for unbelievers, they have not known the Father, for our Lord saith, "O righteous Father, the world hath not known thee." He that hath seen Christ hath seen the Father, and only he; but the very essence of Christ is seen in his expiatory death, and therefore we can never grasp the Fatherhood of God till we have believed in the atonement of his Son. "Whosoever denieth the Son, the same hath not the Father, but he that acknowledgeth the Son hath the Father also." May we then realise the Father through knowing in very deed the Lord, for to a knowledge of the Father he is the only way.

Again, Jesus is the way to *conscious acceptance with the Father*. I know, my dear troubled friend, you feel this morning that you would give anything and everything if you could know that God had accepted you, and loved you, and that you were his dear child. Now, you can never know this until first you come to the cross, and see Jesus Christ dying there, as a substitute for you and for all who trust him. You trust him— your sins are on him, you are clear—the very next feeling of your soul will be, "I am not only pardoned in Christ, but I am accepted before God in Christ Jesus, for Christ's sake, and as one with Christ I am now dear to God ; and what is very marvellous, I am as dear to God as Jesus Christ himself is, I am brought as near as Christ is, I am what Christ is, for he who was once my representative in my sin, and bore the wrath for me, is now my representative in his glory, and has obtained favour and innumerable blessings for me." This is a blessed thing. "The Father himself loveth you." "Made nigh by the blood of Christ." "Beloved, now are we the sons of God, and it doth not yet appear what we shall be : but we know that, when he shall appear, we shall be like him ; for we shall see him as he is." The gift of Christ to us is a full proof of divine love, and wherever it is received it is the proof of God's love to the receiver.

So, too, the way to have *communion with the Father* is the same. "Oh, how I long to talk with God," saith one; " he seems to be a long way off, and the thick darkness shuts him out from me. O that I could speak with him, even though the only word I said were that of the returning prodigal: " Father, I have sinned against heaven and before thee." Beloved, when you see Jesus Christ who bore your sins in his own body on the tree, when you see him ascending up to heaven, you have access with boldness unto God, because Christ has entered within the veil and stands in the presence of God for you. You do talk with God when you draw near in Jesus Christ. Your conviction that all your sin is put away through him, that you are accepted through him, that you live in him as the member lives in the body, that he is your Covenant Head, and that his honours and glories are all reflected upon you, this assured belief brings you so near to God that as a man speaketh with his friend, even so do you commune with him. "Truly, our fellowship is with the Father, and with his Son Jesus Christ."

Again, we by Jesus *come to resemble the Father*. There is no way to get the likeness of the Father, except by learning God's love in the person of his dear Son. Here, too, Christ is the way. You imitate Christ, and so become like the Father; you commune with Jesus Christ, and as you talk with him, his character sacredly operates upon yourself, and you are changed from glory to glory, as by the image of the Lord. I do believe, dear brethren, that the moment we forget Christ, and then seek after personal sanctification, we are trying to get to our journey's end by declining to tread the road to it. It is, at least I find it so, impossible to grow in grace except by abiding evermore at the foot of the cross. When I know by faith, not by any other evidence than by faith, that Jesus loved me, and gave himself for me; when I see grace, magnified in sin, laid on him rather than on me, and see justice magnified, in that sin being put away by him; and when I see grace and justice together, clasping hands in solemn covenant to secure my soul against all fear of risk, then I feel that I am master over sin, then I feel my soul loves God, yearns after God, mounts up to

God—and then it is she becomes more like God than she was before. So Christ is the way from sin, with all we can say of it, to the Father, with all the blessed things that flow from his throne.

II. WHAT SORT OF WAY IS CHRIST, AND FOR WHAT SORT OF PEOPLE?

First, let me say he is *the king's highway*, which means that he is the divinely-appointed way from sin to the Father. If we came to you, dear friends, who are seeking salvation, and told you of a way of mercy, you would naturally enquire, "Who said it was the way? Who appointed it?" And if we replied that it was appointed by the last Council at Rome, I should not wonder if you felt serious doubts about the matter, and questioned whether a council of men could infallibly determine the way of grace; but I have to tell you this day that Jesus Christ is " the way " of God's appointment. Thus saith the word: "Being justified freely by his grace through the redemption that is in Christ Jesus: whom God hath set forth to be a propitiation through faith in his blood, to declare his righteousness for the remission of sins that are past, through the forbearance of God; to declare, I say, at this time his righteousness: that he might be just, and the justifier of him which believeth in Jesus." God the Father devised this plan of salvation by the transference of sin to Christ, and by the punishment of Christ the substitute, instead of us. It is clear to me that if God is satisfied with the way, I ought to be; if he, the aggrieved party, feels that Christ has finished the work, and that he can now justly forgive us, why need we raise questions? O God, if thou canst look at Jesus and be well pleased in him, surely I can; if thou art perfectly content with the sufferings and death of thy dear Son, surely I may be. Now, then, because it is the king's highway, (I recommend you, my hearers, to be very clear here), if thou art trusting in Christ who is the way of divine appointment, if he were to fail thee, which he cannot do, the blame would not lie with thee, but with him who appointed it. I speak reverently. But he has appointed a way which cannot fail, for he is infinite wisdom and infinite power.

Then, as the king's highway it is an open way, I can come to it and need ask no man's leave. If I am treading the king's highway I cannot be a trespasser there. Poor sinner, Christ is the way from your sin to God, and you need ask nobody's leave to come to God through Jesus Christ. "He is able to save them to the uttermost that come unto God by him." "Him that cometh to me," said he, "I will in no wise cast out." Come thou and welcome, God appoints the way, and when he appoints the way, he puts it thus in 1 John ii. 21, "And he is the propitiation for our sins: and not for ours only, but also for the sins of the whole world." In order that any sinner in the whole world who wills to come to the Father by Christ, may pluck up courage and perceive that his sins have been laid on Jesus.

Again, it is *a perfect* way. "I am the way." The way from sin to the Father by Christ is complete. It would not be complete unless it came down where you are, but it does. Where are you? Up to your throat in drunkenness? Where are you? Defiled by evil living? Soul, there is a road from where you are right up to the immaculate perfection of the blessed at God's right hand, and that road is Christ. You have not to make a road to get to Christ, Christ comes to you where you are. The good Samaritan did not ask the wounded man to come to him, and promise that then he would pour in the oil and wine, but he came where he was and poured it in. Christ will come where you are. Saul of Tarsus did not go far to meet Christ. He was riding to the devil as fast as he could, but he was suddenly struck down, there and then where he was, and as he was, and Jesus spake life to him. He can do just the same with you. You think you have some preparations to make, some feelings to pass through, something or other to perform before you may believe that Christ has taken your sins; but all you can do to make yourself fit for Christ is to make yourself unfit; all your preparations are but foul lumber—put them all away. Thou must come as thou art, as a sinner, for Jesus came not to call the righteous, but sinners to repentance: "the whole have no need of a physician, but they that are sick;" and if as thou art thou wilt come and take God's way, and trust Jesus with all thy heart to save thee, thou wilt find he will prove to be the very Saviour thou needest, for he is so perfect a road that there is nothing needed at the beginning. And nothing will be needed at the end. Some have supposed that faith in the atoning sacrifice may carry us a certain way, and after that we must stand on another footing. God forbid I should say a single word against good works. Did I not the other Sabbath morning address you from these words, "Without holiness no man shall see the Lord"? But good works are not the way to heaven, in whole or in part; they are fruits of salvation; they are the sure products of those who are saved, but they do not save a man. A faith that produces no works will never save anybody; but that which saves men is not the work which comes from the faith, but the faith itself, the faith in Jesus Christ. The top and bottom, the beginning and end of salvation, lies in the Redeemer, and not in us. "I am Alpha and Omega, the beginning and the ending," saith the Lord. If you think that you are to patch up Christ's robe of righteousness, or that Jesus is to begin and you are to complete, you know nothing of Christ, and need to be taught something of yourself. It must be all Christ or no Christ, all mercy or no mercy. Grace must lay the foundation, and grace must put on the topstone, or else there can be no salvation. "I am the way," then, means that Christ is the way from where the sinner now is right up to where God is, and he that gets Christ shall come to the Father.

Christ is a *free* way. There is not a toll-bar at the entrance, nor all along the road. Many are afraid to come into this road to heaven, because they cannot pay the charges—but there are no charges whatever. Whosoever wills to have Christ may have him for the taking. He that will pay for Christ cannot have him at all. You may have him for the asking; he is freely given. The way in which to have Christ is the way in which you have water, that is, by drinking; receive Christ, for "unto as many as received him, to them gave he power to become the sons of God, even to as many as believed on his name." There are no legal conditions of salvation laid down anywhere. I know it is sometimes said that repentance and faith are conditions: from one point of view, and in one aspect, I might tolerate the term, but truly and really there is no bargain made between God and a sinner; it is never you do this and I will do that; it is always, "I will do this for you, and then you shall believe and repent as the result." If faith be in one respect a condition, it is in another respect a gift of God, and though we are commanded to repent, yet Jesus is exalted on high to give repentance. So you, poor sinners, who have no repentance, or anything of your own, I bid you come to Jesus Christ for everything. He is the way, and the whole way. This is a free way—nothing to pay, nothing to do, nothing to be, nothing to bring, no merits, no deservings, no preparations; it is all of grace; all the gift of God to the very vilest of the vile. Oh, it does sometimes seem too big to be true, that all for nothing I a great sinner shall be saved; but when I think of what the Saviour is, that he is God, that he came from heaven, and became a man for my sake, that he, the God-man, Immanuel, was born and died, and bore the wrath of God, I can believe it; and, O my Lord, I dare no more add any of my drivelling merits to the worth of thy dear Son than of stitching some foul, infected rags from a dunghill to a garment made of wrought gold. How could I put any nothingness of mine, that only my folly calls anything, side by side with the ever-precious merits of thy dear Son?

Again, let me add, it is a *permanent* way. Jesus says, "I am the way—not a way for Abraham, Isaac, and Jacob, only, but for you; not for the apostles, and martyrs, and early saints, only, but for you.

"His precious blood
Shall never lose its power,
Till all the ransom'd church of God
Be saved to sin no more."

It is a way that never has been broken up, and never will be. All the floods of all his people's sins have never made a swamp or bog-hole in this blessed way; all the earthquakes and upheavals of our rebellious natures have never made a gap or chasm in this glorious way. Straight from the very gates of hell, where the sinner is by nature, right up to the hill-tops of heaven, this glorious causeway runs in one unbroken line, and will for ever and for ever, till every elect one shall be gathered safe into the eternal home.

Let me add, it is a *joyful* way. You noted in the chapter we read that the redeemed are to return with songs, and everlasting joy is to be upon their heads. All believers in Christ as such are a happy and rejoicing people. "But," saith one, "I have seen believers mourn!" That is because they wander from the way. If they continued simply trusting in the substitution of Christ, if they kept their eye on him, and on him only, they would know no sorrow. Where there is no sin there is no sorrow; and when the believer knows that he has no sin, for it is put away in Christ, then also he has no sorrow, but his peace is like a river, because his righteousness is as the waves of the sea. Dear heart, if thou wouldst be happy, come unto Christ, and abide with him.

Lastly, on this point, he is *the only* way. So is he the only way that you cannot be saved if you trust anywhere else. This way which God has planned of laying sin upon the Substitute, is such that it is the only possible way, and therefore God will not have you insult his wisdom and his grace by trying to patch up another. Do not try to find a way by thine own feelings or thine own works; there is no such a way. All these supposed ways will end in disappointment and in ruin. Jesus

Christ is the one foundation, build on him. God help thee to say, "I will now cast myself flat upon Christ, having no confidence in myself; I will make him my confidence, he shall be my all in all." If you have done that, you are a saved soul; go your way, and rejoice with joy unspeakable.

Thus we see what kind of way it is, but *for what sort of people is it made?* Hurriedly in these two or three words, I reply, for all sorts of people. Christ is the way to heaven for anybody and everybody who is led to walk therein. Christ is the way to heaven for thee, poor wanderer, though thou hast sought the theatre and music hall, and worse places, to drive away thy melancholy. Come to Jesus, for he is the way to peace, the very way for a wanderer like you. Christ is the way for exiles, for banished ones, for those who have not seen the face of God for many a day, though once they rejoiced in him. Backslider, if you would get back to your God, Christ is the way.

Christ is the way for captives. You, who hear your chains clanking about you to-day, who feel as if you never would be free, take heart, take heart, there is a way of escape yet, and Christ is that way. Make a desperate push for it, and say, " I will throw myself into his arms, if he reject me I shall be the first one, but I will even go and rest on the bloody sacrifice of that dear Son of God, who sweat great drops of blood because of my heavy sins, my heavy, heavy sins.

Christ is the way, let me add, for the poorest of the poor. Our Master, when he makes a feast, sends us out to bring in men from the highways and hedges, highwaymen and hedgebirds, those who have not a house or a friend of their own. Ye who are lowest of the low and vilest of the vile, ye who are all but in hell, and are condemned already, ye who lie at hell's dark door, bound in affliction and iron, shut out from mercy, as ye think, Christ is the way for you; for all who long to escape from sin; for all who would come to God; for all who have a desire after mercy or eternal life. The great trumpet is blown, and may they come that are ready to perish, may the most needy and abject, and lost, and self-condemned, say, " I will come now and trust in Jesus who died the just for the unjust to bring us to God."

III. The last point is, HOW WE MAKE CHRIST OUR WAY, AND WHETHER HE IS OUR WAY NOW.

How do we make Christ our way? Why, as we make any other way our way? We hear a man say, "This is my way." How does he make that his way? Has he got the title-deeds of it? Has he a charter from his Majesty? No, nothing of the sort. The way in which I shall make the Clapham-road my way after I have done preaching is by getting into it; and the way in which Christ becomes a sinner's way is simply by going to Christ. That is all. You have no legal rights, no forms or ceremonies to go through, you have but to come to the king's highway by trusting Christ, and Christ is yours. " But may I," says one, " without any warrant come and trust Christ? " What warrant do you want? The only warrant is God's permission, and you have a great deal more than that, you have God's command, which is more than a permission, for he hath said, " Go ye into all the world, and preach the gospel to every creature ; he that believeth and is baptised shall be saved, but he that believeth not shall be damned."

In believing you do what that gospel warrants by its command. "Believe in the Lord Jesus Christ, and thou shalt be saved," is God's word; you certainly have a right to do what God commands you to do, so that your right to trust Christ lies in God's command. He says he will save you through what Christ has done. Will you believe him? Will you believe him so as to trust to-day in what Christ has done? If you do not, you make God a liar; if you do, you glorify God by believing his testimony, and you glorify his Son by trusting in his work, and you are saved.

Now, in order to keep the way your own, all you do is to continue in it. How do you keep any other way as your own? By any charter, by any fresh right that you had not at first? No, not at all. "This is my way," say I, as long as I still keep to that way; if I turn the other way I cannot say that it is my way, at least nobody would believe a way to be my way if I went in a contrary direction. If I leap over the hedge and go off in another direction and say, "This is my way," I lie. Man alive, that is your way which you go, your possession of the way lies in your keeping the way. So now, Christian, Christ continues yours by the same way in which he became yours; that is, by your still trusting him, not by anything you do, or are by yourself, or in yourself. Because Jesus lives you live also, not because of anything you do. "The just shall live by faith," not by any other means. You are not to begin in the Spirit and then be made perfect in the flesh; you are not to begin to walk by confidence in Christ and afterwards go on to walk by confidence in your own evidences and graces. Your evidences and graces will always shine best when you think the least of them, and always will be brightest with God when you look most at his dear Son, and not at them. If you ever take your best virtues and sanctifications and make them a ground of hope, you are building on that which will crumble beneath you in the time of trial; but as long as you keep to this, " Still a sinner, but still washed in the blood; still in myself guilty, but no guilt of mine imputed to me, all laid on my Substitute; still my best prayers, my best hymns, my almsgivings, my preachings, my all, all defiled—but yet I am clean through him that washes my feet and makes me clean in his most precious blood." This is the way to live, the way to live evermore, not only as a beginner, but when you are advanced in grace—the way to live when you are becoming a mature matron or veteran soldier, and the way when you come to die. It is especially, then, in those last moments that we fling everything away but just what Christ has done. We might have been troubling ourselves a great deal before about marks, evidences, and so on; but when it comes to the last, we are like the good man who, on his dying bed, tried to pick out what was good and what was bad of his own doings, but he said he was a long while judging them, but they were so much of a muchness that he at last tied them all up in one bundle and flung them over, and rested on Christ alone. That is the very best thing for us all to do even now:—

"None but Jesus, none but Jesus,
Can do helpless sinners good."

This will not make you unholy but holy. If you believe this, you will seek to honour and glorify God with all your might, and when you have done all, you will feel that you are unprofitable servants, and into his dear arms you will cast yourselves, and pray that the hands that were pierced may still embrace you and keep you safe in death and in eternity.

Now, the question to finish with is this, "*Is Christ my way to-day?*" Oh, I know many of you could rise up and say, "Yes, he is, he is all my salvation and all my desire:—

"Nothing in my hands I bring,
Simply to the cross I cling."

"My God, thou knowest all things; thou knowest my soul's only reliance is on thy dying, thy risen, thy ever-living Son, who is my hope, my all.

But, perhaps, there are some here who are not in this way, because they do not even know it. I believe there is no doctrine so little known in England as the gospel; while a great many doctrines are preached, and very properly so, and the precepts are preached, yet there are hearers who have heard for years, and yet do not know this fundamental, essential doctrine of the gospel—that God laid sin on Christ that he might take sin off from us, and punished him that he might be just and yet the justifier of the ungodly. If you have never heard it before you have heard it now; you will not perish, therefore, with that excuse. If you put aside that way of salvation, it will not be because you have never heard it. If you perish, there will be no excuse for you.

But there are some who do not believe this plan to be divine, when they hear it and understand it, they scout it; some will say it is inconsistent with the pursuit of morality; others will say it is fantastic or unjust; one will say this and another that; but though the cross of Christ be to them that perish foolishness, to us who are saved, it is the wisdom of God and the power of God, and God forbid we should preach any other gospel to you. Some there are who even hate it, they will gnash their teeth at the idea of being pardoned through the merit of another, their righteous self feels indignant at being insulted by being put right out of the market. Ah, cast not thy soul away out of mere hate to God, but kiss him whom God has made King this day, and trust in him who is priest for ever after the order of Melchisedec, to put away the sin of man by his own great sacrifice. Come now to him and take the atonement and the peace which he brings. Some are not saved because they are too fearful to come this way, but to such I would speak very gently. The bruised reed he will not break, the smoking flax he will not quench. Let not your sense of sin make you think little of my Master. You are a great sinner, but he is a greater Saviour. Do not say that you have matched Christ, or overmatched him. Come, Goliath sinner, the Son of David can conquer thee or save thee yet: "Though your sins be as scarlet, they shall be as white as snow; though they be red like crimson, they shall be as wool." Think of David, how foully he had transgressed, yet with all the lust-stains, and the murder-spots upon him, he had faith enough to say, "Purge me with hyssop, and I shall be clean: wash me, and I shall be whiter than snow." And so shall you be whiter than snow, when once the bloody sacrifice of Christ in all its merit has become yours, as it may this very morning if you simply trust in him. May my God the Eternal Spirit, may my God the blessed Father, may my God, even Jesus the Son, draw many reluctant hearts now, and his shall be the praise. Amen.

"Eyes Right"

"Let thine eyes look right on, and let thine eyelids look straight before thee"—Proverbs iv. 25.

THESE words occur in a passage wherein the wise man exhorts us to take care of all parts of our nature, which he indicates by members of the body. "Keep thy *heart*," says he, "with all diligence; for out of it are the issues of life. Put away from thee a froward *mouth*, and perverse *lips* put far from thee. Let thine *eyes* look right on, and let thine *eyelids* look straight before thee. Ponder the path of thy *feet*, and let all thy ways be established. Turn not to the right hand nor to the left: remove thy *foot* from evil." It is clear that every part of our nature needs to be carefully watched, lest in any way it should become the cause of sin. Any one member or faculty is readily able to defile all the rest, and therefore every part must be guarded with care. We have selected for our meditation the verse which deals with the eye. These windows of light need to be watched in their incomings, lest that which we take into our soul should be darkness rather than light; and they need to be watched in their outgoings, lest the glances of the eye should be full of iniquity, or should suggest foolish thoughts. Hence the wise man advises, " Let thine eyes look right on, and let thine eyelids look straight before thee." Have eyes and use them. Using them, take care to use them honestly.

Some persons are always as if they were asleep. They go through the world mooning about, seeing nothing, or seeing men as if they were trees, with a sight which is not sight, but blindness hidden. The shadows of this transient life impress them, and that is all: they have never awakened yet to the true life and its solemn realities. They have never seen anything in very truth; for it is faith that sees, and of faith they have none. That which is apart from faith is not visible to the soul, however clear it may be to the eye. We have thousands around us who need to be startled out of that slumber in which they see the fabrics of their dreams, and the unsubstantial fancies of the hour. They say, "We see," but scales are on their eyes. I fear we have such in all our congregations, lulled to sleep even by the preacher's tones, to whom the fact of coming to their accustomed seat, and listening to the usual hymns, tends rather to confirm them in a sluggard's slumber than to stir their souls to action. O ye sluggards, may God awaken you by grace, lest he arouse you by the thunderbolts of his vengeance! It is time that your eyes began to look right on, and your eyelids straight before you.

Many others are somewhat awake mentally, but they are not looking right on, neither do their eyelids look straight before them. They are staring about them, star-gazing, wondering what will be seen next: always ready, like the Athenians, to hear and see some new thing. They move, it is true, but it is in a labyrinth which leads to nothing, in a circle which ends where it began; they toil and slave, but it is all in the shadow land: of substantial work they do nothing. An active idleness, a diligent laziness, is all that their life is made up of; for, as yet, they have no purpose—no purpose worth being the aim of an immortal soul. An arrow will never strike the mark if it travels in a zigzag direction; and the man whose life has no aim whatever, who pursues this, and then that, and then the other, what will he achieve? Are not many like "dumb driven cattle," going they know not where? They have never yet discovered that this life is a preface to a life of diviner mould. They do not regard the present as the lowly porch of the glorious edifice of the future. They have not thought that time is but the doorstep of eternity, a thing of small account, save that it is linked with the endless ages; and so they seek after this, and then after that, and then after the other; and always after that which is too poor, too trifling to be the object of a mind capable of fellowship with God. How many there are whose spirit is agitated by a mere nothing, resembling

"Ocean into tempest tost
To waft a feather or to drown a fly"!

To beings who lead such purposeless lives we would address the words of the wise man, "Let thine eyes look right on, and let thine eyelids look straight before thee." Have something to do, and do it. Have something to live for, and live for it. Get to know the right way, and, knowing the right way, keep to it with full purpose of heart and concentration of faculty. O man, see whither thou art going, and go that way, with thine eyes open, resolutely marking every step as thou takest it. Look where thou oughtest to look, and then follow thine eyes, which shall thus be useful outriders to thy life, and help to make thy way safe and wise. When thou hast sent thine eyes before thee to make sure of the way, it will be safe to follow. Look before you leap, and only leap when looking bids you do so.

If a man is to let his eyes look right on, and his eyelids straight before him, then *he is to have a way, and that way is to be a straight way*, and in that straight way he is to persevere. You cannot see to the end of a crooked way. You can only see a small part of a way that twists and winds. Choose, then, a direct path which has an end which you dare think of and look upon. Some men's lives are such that they dare not think of what the end of them must be. They would not long pursue their present track if they were forced to gaze into that dread abyss, which is the only possible close of an evil course. The way of transgressors is hard in itself, but it is hardest of all when we behold their dreadful end. "Surely thou hast set them in slippery places. Thou castest them down into destruction." You need to have a way, and a straight way, and a way whose end you dare contemplate, or else you cannot carry out the advice of Solomon, "Let thine eyes look right on, and let thine eyelids look straight before thee."

Every wise man will conclude that *the best way for a man is the way which God has made for him.* He that made us knows what he made us for, and he knows by what means we may best arrive at that end. According to divine teaching, as gracious as it is certain, we learn that the way of eternal life is Jesus Christ. Christ himself says, "I am the way, the truth, and the life"; and he that would pursue life after a right fashion must look to Jesus, and must continue looking unto Jesus, not only as the author, but as the finisher of his faith. It shall be to him a golden rule of life, when he has chosen Christ to be his way, to let his eyes look right on, and his eyelids straight before him. He need not be afraid to contemplate the end of that way, for the end of the way of Christ is life and glory with Christ for ever. "It doth not yet appear what we shall be: but we know that, when he shall appear, we shall be like him; for we shall see him as he is." A friend said to me the other day, "How happy are we to know that whatever happens to us in this life it is well!" "Yes," I added, "and to know that if this life ends it is equally well, or better." Then we joined hands in common joy to think that we were equally ready for life or death, and did not need five minutes' anxiety as to whether it should be the one or the other. Brethren, when you are on the King's highway, and that way is a perfectly straight one, you may go ahead without fear, and sing on the road.

With all my heart I invite any who have never yet begun to live after a right fashion, to take Christ to be the way of life to them; and then I entreat them to let their eyes look straight on, and their eyelids straight before them, and to follow Jesus without giving a glance either to the right hand or to the left till it shall be said of them, even in glory, "These are they which follow the Lamb whithersoever he goeth."

I. I shall make my earnest appeals to the heart and conscience by beginning with this first exhortation : LET CHRIST BE YOUR WAY. You that are young, let him be your way from your youth. You that have hitherto gone the wrong road until your hairs have grown grey in the service of iniquity, turn, I beseech you, and take to the way of salvation. May his Spirit turn you, and you will be turned, then will Jesus become your way from henceforth.

If Christ be your way, you will begin first to seek *to have Christ.* "How shall I have him?" says one. Dost thou desire him? Wilt thou accept him? He is thine. The act of accepting Christ secures Christ to us; for the Father freely gives him to all who freely accept him. Some are troubled through ignorant and unbelieving fears, and are saying, "I wish I could lay hold on Jesus! I wish I knew that Christ was mine!" Art thou willing to have him? Who made thee willing? Dost thou desire him? Who made thee desire him? Who but the Spirit of the Lord? Wilt thou now take Jesus to be thy Saviour, to save thee from thy sin? Then depend on it he is thine. There was never any difficulty with him to give himself to thee; the difficulty was to bring thee to receive him; and now that thou dost receive him, remember this—"As many as received him, to them gave he power to become the sons of God, even to them that believe on his name." Jesus himself has said it, "Him that cometh to me I will in no wise cast out"; and therefore, since thou comest, thou shalt never be cast out. Jesus has accepted thee, for thou hast accepted him. But I pray you, none of you rest until you have Christ. Let your eyes look right on, and your eyelids straight before you, till you find him. Look nowhere else but to him and after him. Shut yourself up in your room: determine not to come out again until you have him, and it shall not be long before you find him. Concentrating all your gaze upon the Crucified, light shall come from him, causing the scales to fall from your eyes, and you shall see him, even you that could not see; and you shall cry in delight, "He is mine, he is mine." Remember how David said to his son, "If thou seek him, he will be found of thee." Think of the words of the prophet, "Seek ye the Lord while he may be found, call ye upon him while he is near."

When you have Christ, the next business of your life must be *to know Christ*. Seek to know more of him, to know him better, to know him more practically, to know him more assuredly. "That I may know him," said the apostle, after he had been a believer in him for fifteen years. That same man of God speaks of "the love of Christ, which passeth knowledge," even his knowledge, which was of the fullest sort; so that he meant to go on learning more and more of Christ, and he did not count himself to have attained. Christian men and women, you do not know your great Master yet. Here have some of us been nearly forty years in his service, and yet we could not describe him to our own satisfaction. Why, we hardly know the power of the hem of his garment yet. We have not descended far down into the mines of his perfections. How little know we of our hidden wealth in Christ Jesus! Oh, that we studied Scripture more, that we were more teachable, and waited more humbly upon the Lord for the light of his Spirit from day to day! Well says our singer—

> "Hoard up his sacred word,
> And feed thereon and grow;
> Go on to seek to know the Lord,
> And practise what you know."

In this matter let your eyes look right on, and your eyelids straight before you. Other men may have their pursuits, this is yours; stick to it earnestly. The science of a crucified Saviour shines like the moon in the midst of the stars as compared with all the other sciences which men may know; study it with your whole power of mind and heart. The angels on the mercy-seat of the ark stood always looking downward, and bending over. Hence the apostle says, "Which things the angels desire to look into"; and if *they* desire to look into the ark of the covenant and its sacred mysteries, how much more should we!

When you come to know somewhat of what he is, then go on *to obey Christ*. Is there anything that he has bidden you do? Do it. Some Christians have never yet been baptized: how will they answer for wilful neglect of a known duty? Others have been Christians for years, and yet have never communed at the Lord's table. Jesus said, "If ye love me, keep my commandments." Do they keep his commandments? It was his dying request, "This do in remembrance of me," and yet they will not fulfil it. Even such a tender request they slight, as though it were of no importance whatever, as if their Lord was a mere nobody whose wishes might well be overlooked. What shall I say of many of the biddings of our holy gospel, many of those sweet precepts which are to be used in the family, and in the business, and in the field? What forgetfulness there is of them! What refusings to follow Christ! He might come to us and say, "If I be a Master, where is mine honour?" Truly, it ought to be one of the first thoughts of a Christian to find out the Lord's will; and when he knows it, obedience should follow immediately. His eyes should look right on, and his eyelids straight before him. What said the blessed virgin to those who were at the feast? Note the words, "Whatsoever he saith unto you, do it." It was well spoken of the favoured mother, and it remains as a golden precept for us all—"Whatsoever he saith unto you, do it." Make no reserve, exercise no choice, but obey his command. When you know what he commands, do not hesitate, question, or try to avoid it, but "do it": do it at once, do it heartily, do it cheerfully, do it to the full. It is but a little thing that, as our Lord has bought us with the price of his own blood, we should be his servants. The apostles frequently call themselves the bond-slaves of Christ. Where our Authorized Version softly puts it "servant" it really is "bond-slave." The early saints delighted to count themselves Christ's absolute property, bought by him, owned by him, and wholly at his disposal. Paul even went so far as to rejoice that he had the marks of his Master's brand on him, and he cries, "Let no man trouble me: for I bear in my body the marks of the Lord Jesus." There was the end of all debate: he was the Lord's, and the marks of the scourges, the rods, and the stones were the broad-arrow of the King which marked Paul's body as the property of Jesus, the Lord. Now, if the saints of old time gloried in obeying Christ, I pray that you and I, forgetting the sect to which we may belong, or even the nation of which we form a part, may feel that our first object in life is to obey our Lord, and not to follow a human leader, or to promote a religious or political party. This one thing we mean to do, and so follow the advice of Solomon, as he says, "Let thine eyes look right on, and let thine eyelids look straight before thee." Beloved, let us endeavour to be obedient in the minute as well as in the greater matters, for it is in details that true obedience is best seen. Let us copy the faintest touches in the life of our great Exemplar.

That being attended to, remember, if Christ be your way, you have further to seek *to be like him*, not only to do as he did, but to be as he was; for "as he was, so are we in this world." What a man *does* is important, but what a man *is* is all-important. The ring of the metal is something, but if its ring could be imitated by a base coin, it would be nothing. It is, after all, the substance of the metal that decides its value. O man, what art thou? If thou be a twice-born man, thou art a partaker of the nature of Christ; but if not, thou art under the curse which cleaves to the old nature as leprosy cleaves to the leper. "As we have borne the image of the earthy, we shall also bear the image of the heavenly"; and we must begin to bear that heavenly image even now. As born again into the headship of the Second Adam, we should seek to be as much like the Second Adam as we are already by nature like the first Adam, through our first birth. The second birth should be as operative to produce the image of the second Adam, as the first was to produce the image of the first Adam. Alas! "the earthy" is impressed upon us very distinctly; we cannot spend an hour without discovering the clear stamp of nature's die. Oh, that "the heavenly" could be quite as clearly discerned! This, therefore, we must aim at, though as yet we have not attained it. Here is something to be thought of very carefully, and I charge you, by the Holy Ghost, let your eyes look right on, and your eyelids straight before you, that you may be transformed from glory to glory into the image of the Lord. God grant that it may be so with every one of us!

Now, supposing that we have attended to all this, if Christ is our way, and our model, there is something more, namely, that we seek *to glorify Christ*, and labour to win others to him. Here is a grand field for all our energies. O Christian people, what are we left in this world for, except to bring others to Jesus? Are we not left in this wilderness that we may find out more of the good Shepherd's stray sheep, and work for him and with him to bring them in. I fear we forget this. Are not some of you indifferent as to whether your fellow-men are lost or saved? Have not some of you, in your families, come to this pass—that you see your brother an infidel, your sister frivolous, your parents godless, and yet it does not fret you? I think that if I had a godless relative, it would break my night's rest, not now and then, but always. A brother, a father, a child unsaved! What mean ye by taking your ease? If the spirit of Christ be in us, the tears that fell from the eyes of Jesus will find their like upon our cheeks. We shall weep day and night because men are not gathered unto eternal life. Nor will this be a loss to us, for blessed are the mourners in Zion. Blessed are they that mourn because others abide in sin and reject the Lord!

Now, concerning the salvation of our fellow-men; we shall never compass it unless our eyes look right on, and our eyelids straight before us. Before we win souls, we must live for souls. We need men and women who live to convert others to Christ. The minister had better quit his pulpit if it be not his one burning desire to bring hearts to Jesus' feet. If a divine impulse be not upon him, driving him to seek the souls of men, let him go elsewhere with his windy periods. Professors have little right to be in Christ's church, unless they are passionately in earnest to increase his kingdom by the salvation of their fellow-men. O my brothers and sisters, on whom is the blood-mark of redemption, I charge you concerning this matter to "let your eyes look right on, and let your eyelids look straight before you"! Seek souls as dogs hunt their game; eye, nostril, ear all open, and every muscle strained. Converts are not gained by dreamers. We cannot imitate Jesus as a Saviour of men by being dull and heartless. In any point in which we follow our Lord let us do it with all our soul.

Thus much upon the first point: let Christ be your way in all things, and keep to that way.

II. Following the text again, only working it a little differently, the second exhortation is, SET YOUR EYES ON HIM AS YOUR WAY. If Christ be your way, and you follow him to have him, to know him, to obey him, to be like him, and to glorify him, then set your eyes on him as the way. Think of him, consider him, study him, and in all things regard him as first and last to you.

First, *that you may know the way of life*, let your eyes be fixed on him. Soul, art thou in the dark? Kneel down and pray, and look Christward. Saint, art thou bewildered? Go by the way of the cross, the way of the Crucified, for that is the true and sure path. Sinner, art thou burdened? Wouldst thou be rid of thy burden? Run Christward. Any direction given thee to go anywhere else will misdirect thee. I say not to any one I meet to-night, "Go to the wicket-gate." Neither will I bid you look to any light within, and run that way. My only direction is, "Go to Jesus." You see that cross, and him who bled thereon! Stand still, and look that way, and your burden shall fall from your shoulders. Where Jesus died, you shall live. Where Christ was wounded, you shall be healed. "Let your eyes look right on, and let your eyelids look straight before you." Know the road; you will never know it too well: the more you know it the happier you will be in it. "To Christ!" "To Christ!" "To Christ!" That is the sole inscription upon every finger-post of the road to heaven. Keep you to the King's highway.

Since Christ is the way, let your eyes be fixed on him as the way *that you may follow him well,* may follow him wholly. Gather up all your faculties to go after your Lord. Be not like Lot's wife, who longed, and looked, and lingered, and was lost. Away, away, away from Sodom, altogether away: let no eye steal in that direction. Away, away, away to Christ, to Christ alone. All eyes must be for Jesus, who cries, "Look unto me, and be ye saved." As the ploughman looks to the end of the furrow, and keeps right on, even so must you look only to Jesus. What hast thou to do with anything but Christ, sinner? I tell thee that thou hast nothing even to do with thine own sins, but to lay them down at his feet. He is all; the beginning and the end. "Let thine eyes look right on, and let thine eyelids look straight before thee."

Look alone to Jesus, and do this *to keep your spirits up.* Some men's eyes do not look right on, and their eyelids do not look straight before them, for they look back upon that part of the road which they have traversed, and grow content with that which they have already attained. They live in *retrospection.* When you begin to look back at what you have done, and rub your hands, and say with self-satisfaction, "I remember when I did right well," wisdom warns you that this is not the right kind of look. What have you to look back upon? Poor, weak creature! Forget that which is behind, and press forward to something better and higher. When you sinful souls get looking back upon your past bad lives I am glad of that, but still I do not want even you to keep your eyes always in that direction. You will get no comfort in looking into the foul ditch of your own transgressions. Look, look, look before you! Look where the cross stands. Run that way. Let thine eyelids look straight before thee to the atoning sacrifice; away from the past, which he will graciously blot out, to Jesus only.

Some spend much of their time in what is called *introspection*. Now introspection, like retrospection, is a useful thing in a measure; but it can readily be overdone, and then it breeds morbid emotions, and creates despair. Some are always looking into their own feelings. A healthy man hardly knows whether he has a stomach, or a liver; it is your sickly man who grows more sickly by the study of his inward complaints. Too many wound themselves by studying themselves. Every morning they think of what they should feel: all day long they dwell upon what they are not feeling; and at night they make diligent search for what they have been feeling. It looks to me like shutting up your shop, and then living in the counting-house, taking account of what is not sold. Small profits will be made in this way. You may look a long while into an empty pocket before you find a sovereign, and you may look a long time into fallen nature before you find comfort. A man might as well try to find burning coals under the ice, as to find anything good in our poor human nature. When you look within, it should be to see with grief what the filthiness is; but to get rid of that filthiness you must look beyond yourself. I remember Mr. Moody saying that a looking-glass was a capital thing to show you the spots on your face; but you could not wash in a looking-glass. You want something very different when you would make your face clean. So let your eyes look right on—

> " To the full atonement made,
> To the utmost ransom paid."

Forget yourself, and think only of Christ.

Some not only unduly practise retrospection and introspection, but they carry much too far a sort of *circumspection*. They look all around them: they look upon their past, and their present, and their fears and their doubts, and from all these things they judge their condition, and decide their state of mind. You recollect Peter. He cried to his Lord, "Bid me come unto thee on the water." He receives permission. Down the side over the boat goes Peter. To his intense surprise he is standing on a wave. Peter had never done such a thing before in his life as walk on the water. He might have kept on standing on the wave, and he might have walked all the way to Jesus, if he had kept his eyes on his Master until he reached him. The waters would have borne him up as well as a granite pavement; but Peter began to look at the billows, and he listened to the howling of the wind, and then to the beating of his own heart; and down he went; and then he had to cry to his Master. "Let thine eyes look right on, and let thine eyelids look straight before thee": thou canst walk the waters all the way to the golden shore, if thou canst but stop thine eyes to all things else.

Surely I may use the text as an illustration of that closing of the eyes. "Let thine eyes look right on." "I understand that," says one, "for I trust. But you cannot look with your eyelids." What can that mean? Remember that you can shut your eyes with your eyelids to a great many things, and so cease to see them; and in the matter of faith-sight a great many things are best not seen. So, when you would otherwise see the danger, and all the difficulties and the doubts, do not look with your eyes, but look with your eyelids. Not to look at the difficulties at all is all the look they deserve. Let your eyelids shut out the view which would create distrust. Do not see, do not feel, "only believe." Believe Christ, and believe nothing else. "Let God be true, but every man a liar." If all the sins thou hast ever done should come rolling up like Atlantic billows, and if all the devils in hell should come riding on the crests of those waves, howling as they come, take no notice of them. Christ has said, he that believeth in him hath everlasting life; believe thou in him, and thou hast the everlasting life as surely as Christ is the Christ of God. Draw down the blinds, and see nothing, know nothing, believe nothing but the living word of the living Saviour. "Let thine eyes look right on, and let thine eyelids look straight before thee." When thou closest thine eyes to consider, thou canst see a good deal with closed eyes, but still look thou right on to the one and only trust.

You must also let your eyes look right on, dear friends; for *if you begin to look two ways at a time, you will miss the Lord Jesus, who is your way.* Under the Jewish law no man who had a squint was allowed to be a priest. He is described as one who had "a blemish in his eye." I wish they would make a similar law with regard to spiritual sight in preachers nowadays, for certain of them are sadly cross-eyed. When they preach free grace they squint fearfully towards free-will; and if they look to the atonement, they must needs see in it more of man than of Christ. See how they look to Moses and to Darwin; to revelation and to speculation! A great many people would fain be saved, but they squint: they look a little towards sin, and the flesh, and the world, and they make provision for personal gain, and personal ease. In this case they fail to see Christ's strait and narrow way of the denial of self, and the crucifixion of the flesh. If thou wouldst have salvation, "Let thine eyes look right on, and let thine eyelids look straight before thee." Look not a little this way, and a little that way, or thou wilt never run aright. "I could believe that I was a Christian," says one, "if I felt more happy. I could trust Christ if I felt my nature changed." That is a squint which ruins the faith-look. That is trying to look two ways at once. You cannot do it: it will ruin you. It would spoil the beauty of the sweetest countenance if we could use our eyes to look otherwise than straight on. We have some friends who, if they wish to see us, look over there, and yet we are not there. Avoid this spiritual blemish; it has no advantages—"Let thine eyes look right on." Look to Christ alone, to him as thy whole salvation. Have nothing to do with thy good works as a ground of trust, or thou art a lost man. I charge thee, have nothing to do even with thy faith and thy repentance as a ground of trust. Trust not thy trust, but trust alone in what Christ has done. If thou shalt trust thy best feelings or thy worst feelings, thy prayers or thy praises, thy almsgivings or thy consecration in any degree, thou hast made an antichrist of them. Strip thyself of thy last rag, and let Christ clothe thee from top to toe. Be thou hungry unto famishing, and clean out the last crumb thou hast in the pantry, for then only wilt thou feed on Christ, the bread of life. Let him be both bread and wine, and make up the whole of a feast for thee. Thou shalt have salvation surely enough if this be what thou dost. But let not Jesus bring the bread, and carnal confidence the wine: take a whole Christ to be all thy salvation and all thy desire, and thy peace shall be unbroken. Let the Holy Spirit bring thee to that oneness of trust which makes both eyes meet at their proper focus, and let that focus be the Lord Jesus. "Let thine eyes look right on, and let thine eyelids look straight before thee."

III. But my time has almost expired, and I have only to lay emphasis on one more matter. LET YOUR EYES DISTINCTLY AND DIRECTLY LOOK TO CHRIST ALONE. I have gone over this before, but I need to hammer at it again, in order to clench the nail. *Look not to any human guide*, but look to Christ Jesus alone. We have no faith in priests; but it is a very easy thing to fix your faith upon a minister, and hear what he says, and believe it because he says it. I charge you, believe nothing that I tell you if it cannot be supported by the Word of God. I am content to stand or to fall by this: "To the law and to the testimony: if they speak not according to this word, there is no light in them." I will quote the authority of no other book, whoever may have composed it; no ancient book, let it belong even to the earliest days of the church. This one inspired volume is the text-book of our religion. Follow Holy Scripture, and you have an infallible chart. Our Lord Jesus Christ is the one apostle and high priest of our profession; follow him. Not even mother or father, or the brightest saint that ever lived, must divide you from your perfect Guide. "Let your eyes look right on, and let your eyelids look straight before you," and hear the gracious words of him who bought you with his blood as he cries, "Follow me."

Then, again, *look to Christ directly and distinctly for yourself.* I warn you against putting any trust in national religion, or in family and birthright godliness. A personal Christ must be laid hold of by a personal faith. You must yourself repent, yourself believe, yourself get a grip of him, and of none but him. You must use your own eyes: "Let your eyes look right on, and let your eyelids look straight before you."

Again, *look not to any secondary aims.* Seek first the kingdom of God and his righteousness. In seeking Christ, make no bargain with gain or reputation; be content to lose all gold and all honour if you may but win Christ. To follow religion for pelf would be a mean act of hypocrisy, and to leave it for the same reason is equally vile. Let your eyes be fixed on following your Lord, and as to any worldly consequences, bring your eyelids into use, keep them fast closed, and go right on in implicit obedience to your Lord.

Forget all things else when seeking Christ, and when you have found Christ. It is no ill thing for a man, when he is under concern of soul, to let his business and everything go till he finds his Saviour. I urge no one to such a course, but I have noticed many converts who have done this who have soon found rest. If a captain were busy about the comfort of his passengers in their cabins, but all the while knew that there was a great leak in the ship, and it would soon go down, and to this he paid no heed whatever, you would say to him, "How foolish you are to mind the little, and neglect the great!" But if he told the passengers, "Breakfast cannot be prepared with our usual care, for all hands are pumping or repairing the vessel," you could not blame him when you knew that every man's help was needed to save the ship from going down. In times of extreme danger, secondary things must give place to the main thing. If this house were to take fire you would not stay to sing the last hymn, even if I gave it out. May the Holy Spirit lead some of you to feel that you must be saved! You must be saved, and therefore you must put other things into a second place. Remember how Bunyan pictures the man running for his life, and when his neighbours called to him to stop, he put his fingers in his ears, and as he ran he shouted, "Eternal life! Eternal life! Eternal life!" That man was a wise man. Imitate him; if you have not found eternal life, run for it, with your "eyes right on, and your eyelids straight before you."

And, lastly, *take care that you continue gazing upon Christ until you have faith in him.* "Faith cometh by hearing, and hearing by the word of God." Go on hearing the Word of God till faith come thereby. Do you ask me how faith comes? It is the gift of God, but it usually comes in a certain way. Thinking of Jesus, and meditating upon Jesus, will breed faith in Jesus. I was struck with what one said the other day of a certain preacher. The hearer was in deep concern of soul, and the minister preached a very pretty sermon indeed, decorated abundantly with word-painting. I scarcely know any brother who can paint so daintily as this good minister can; but this poor soul, under a sense of sin, said, "There was too much landscape, sir. I did not want landscape; I wanted salvation." Dear friend, never crave word-painting when you attend a sermon; but crave Christ. You must have Christ to be your own by faith, or you are a lost man. When I was seeking the Saviour I remember hearing a very good doctrinal sermon; but when it was over I longed to tell the minister that there was a poor lad there who wanted to know how he could be saved. How I wished he had given half a minute to that subject! Dr. Manton, who was usually a clear and full preacher of the gospel, when he preached before the Lord Mayor, gave his lordship something a cut above the common citizens, and so the poorer folk missed their portion. After he had done preaching his sermon, an aged woman cried, "Dr. Manton, I came here this morning under concern of soul, wanting a blessing, and I have not got it, for I could not understand you." The preacher meekly replied, "The Lord forgive me! I will not so offend again." He had overlooked the poor, and had thought mainly of my Lord Mayor. Special sermons before Mayors, and Queens, and assemblies are seldom worth a penny a thousand. The gospel does not lend itself to show performances. I am not here to give you intellectual treats: my eyes look right on to your salvation. Oh that yours may look that way! Go after Christ, dear friend. Seek after Christ with your whole heart and soul. Feel that the one thing you must have is to be reconciled to God by the death of his Son. Keep on with that cry, "None but Christ: none but Christ." Make this your continual litany—

> ' Give me Christ, or else I die;
> Give me Christ, or else I die."

Then you will soon find him. "Let your eyes look right on, and let your eyelids look straight before you," and you shall see the Lord of grace appearing to you through the mist and through the cloud, that self-same Saviour who stands in the midst of us even now, and cries, "Look unto me, and be ye saved, all the ends of the earth: for I am God, and there is none else."

The One Foundation

"For other foundation can no man lay than that is laid, which is Jesus Christ "—
I Corinthians iii. 11.

UPBUILDING is very important, but the first question must always concern the foundation. However quickly, however cleverly a man may build, if the foundation be unsound he is a foolish builder; and however slowly, however laboriously a man may proceed, his building will not put him to shame if he has set his walls erect upon a firm basis. This is emphatically true in spiritual things, for there the foundation is of the utmost importance. The hearer of the word, who is not a doer also, comes to a fatal end, because, as the Saviour says, he has built upon the sand, and therefore his fabric in the day of storm and flood is swept away, while he who hears the word and does it is secure because he digs deep and lays his foundation upon a rock, and therefore his building survives the rains of trial from above, the floods of persecution from without, and the mysterious winds of Satanic temptation which howl from every quarter. The best masonry must crack and fall if the groundwork is unstable: the higher the pinnacle the speedier its fall if the base is insecure.

As to what the foundation is in the religion of Jesus Christ there is no question. This verse declares it to be decided beyond controversy. A man may build the superstructure in some measure according to his own taste and judgment, but it must be based upon the one foundation; there may be room for varieties of style in the upper building, but there can be no variety in the groundwork. That is fixed for ever by the unchanging God, who says, " Behold, *I lay* in Zion a foundation stone." It must be acknowledged that all Christian minds and lives do not take exactly the same form and fashion : there are among the best of Christian builders certain grades of excellences,—one man builds with gold, another with silver, and a third with precious stones; but as to the foundation, all are on a level, Christ is all and in all. Whether the gracious life be rich as a golden palace, or pure as a temple of silver, or substantial as a tower of marble, whether it be public or obscure, wide or narrow, it must in every case be built upon the same basement of eternal rock : " for other foundation can no man lay than that is laid." You may say "we will agree to differ" about matters which concern the superstructure, but we must agree to agree as to the foundation; for if we are not at one with the plain statement of the text we are in the wrong.

The apostle is dogmatic to the very last degree : "Other foundation can no man lay." "But," saith one, "various teachers did lay other foundations." The apostle will not admit that they were foundations: they were not worthy of the name, the imposture was too shallow to succeed. No builder if he looked upon a heap of sand poured into an excavation would admit that it was a foundation. If he saw a mass of decayed vegetation and garden rubbish heaped together no architect would for one moment allow it to be spoken of as a "foundation." Paul declareth that there is but one foundation, and that there is none beside it, or beyond it; and that the one only, unalterable, immovable, everlasting foundation is Jesus Christ. It is not to be imagined that there are other foundations somewhat differing and only a little inferior to the Lord Jesus: there is no other, and no other can be laid. It is not a question of comparison, but of monopoly. All other groundworks and principles, whatever may be said in their praise, are mere falsehoods if they are set forth as foundations, for the Lord Jesus has exclusive possession of that title, and in him alone all that is fundamental is summed up; "Neither is there salvation in any other : for there is none other name under heaven given among men, whereby we must be saved."

And truly, when you think that God from all eternity has made his only-begotten Son to be the foundation and corner stone, it will be seen that this rock goes deep into the very nature of things, ay, deep as infinity itself; and, therefore, there cannot be two of the kind, for of whom else is it written that verily he was fore-ordained before the foundation of the world? Of whom else is it said, "I was set up from everlasting, from the beginning, or ever the earth was"? When you think that this foundation is nothing less than divine, for Christ is very God of very God, it is as impossible that there should be two foundations as that there should be two Gods. You must imagine two redemptions before you can conceive of two groundworks for our confidence. Who will dream of two atonements, two Saviours, two Christs? Yet must such a thing be ere there can be two foundations. None but Jesus, the divine Saviour, could sustain the weight of a single soul with all its sins, much less of all the souls which are built up into the temple of God. Jesus alone can sustain our eternal interests, deliver us from eternal wrath, or lift us into eternal bliss. "There is one God, and one mediator between God and men, the man Christ Jesus." His own words in prophecy are very positive—"I, even I, am the Lord, and beside me there is no Saviour"; and equally express is his personal declaration—"I am the way, the truth, and the life: no man cometh into the Father, but by me."

I will sketch out my discourse with these four lines, which I may not always be able to keep from intersecting each other, but they shall each be marked deeply and broadly, so that none can help seeing them. First, *no church but what is built on Christ;* secondly, *no gospel but what is built on Christ;* thirdly, *no hope of salvation but what is built on Christ;* and fourthly, *no Christian but what is built on Christ.*

I. First, there is NO CHURCH BUT WHAT IS BUILT ON CHRIST. I mean, of course, no true, no real church. There are many churches in the world, so called, but this may be laid down as a first principle that there is but one church, and that this one church is built upon Christ alone. Whatever community, congregation, hierarchy, sect, or corporation may call itself a church, or even *the* church, if it is not built upon Christ it is not a church at all. No matter how great in numbers, nor how ancient, nor how wealthy, nor how learned, nor how pretentious, bigoted, dominant, or exclusive it may be, it is not Christ's church if it is not built upon Christ.

To begin with, *a foundation is the first portion* of a building; and so is the Lord Jesus first and foremost with his church, for his people were chosen in him. God has always had in his purpose and decree a chosen people, but he has had no such people apart from Christ. The apostle saith: "Blessed be the God and Father of our Lord Jesus Christ, who hath blessed us with all spiritual blessings in heavenly places in Christ: according as he hath chosen us in him before the foundation of the world." We were chosen in Christ Jesus; he is "the first born among many brethren," and the Lord has "predestinated us to be conformed to the image of his Son." The first setting apart of the church and making it to be the peculiar inheritance of God was in connection with Christ.

> "'Christ, be my first elect,' he said,
> Then chose our souls in Christ our head."

We were never otherwise chosen, nor otherwise beloved, nor otherwise appointed to eternal life than as regarded in Christ Jesus, and one with him. No single soul can be said to be elect otherwise than as it is considered in connection with Christ; much less then is there a church of God apart from the eternal purpose concerning Christ Jesus, the covenant head, and federal representative of his people. The foundation must be laid first, and so was our Lord Jesus Christ first appointed. "Therefore thus saith the Lord God, Behold, I lay in Zion for a foundation a stone, a tried stone, a precious corner stone, a sure foundation." Jesus is called by the Father "Mine elect in whom my soul delighteth," and there are none elect except such as are in him in the eternal purpose of grace.

But next, *a foundation is the support of all,* and there is no church but that which derives all its support from Christ Jesus. If there be any company of people calling themselves a church who depend for salvation and eternal life upon anything beside, or beyond the merit of Christ's atoning blood, they are not a church. That all things are of God, and that he hath reconciled us unto himself by Christ Jesus, is a truth never to be doubted. The atoning Saviour is the corner-stone of the church. He is the one rock of our salvation, the one pillar of our strength. As living stones we are built up into a spiritual house, but we one and all rest and depend upon him, and upon no other. To us the word of the Lord has come with power,—"Therefore let all the house of Israel know assuredly, that God hath made that same Jesus, whom ye have crucified, both Lord and Christ." The great atoning sacrifice of Christ must be the sole reliance of the whole church as well as of each individual, and this must be set forth with great clearness and distinctness as its first and greatest doctrine—salvation by Christ Jesus: "In whom we have redemption through his blood, the forgiveness of sins, according to the riches of his grace." The atonement taken away, no church remains. Call the community a religious club if you like, but it is no church when once the atonement made by the Lord Jesus, through his death in the room and stead of his people, is denied or ignored.

Nor do we judge a community to be worthy of the name of a church which places its dependence for its present power and future progress anywhere but in the almighty Saviour. Jesus saith, "Because I live ye shall live also," and the church must draw its daily life from the immortality of her glorious Head. He that loved us and died for us and rose again is pledged to keep his own, and on that pledge let them repose their faith. Because all power is given unto him in heaven and in earth, therefore go we forth to teach the nations. He has said, "Lo, I am with you alway, even unto the end of the world," therefore have we strength to go forth for the conquest of the world. But if we depend upon an arm of flesh, upon the secular power, upon carnal wisdom, upon education, or eloquence, or prestige, or upon our own zeal and ardour, and not upon Christ, we are leaving the rock for the sand. We cannot thus build up Christ's church, nor ought we to attempt it. The strength of a living church is the living Christ. We must be very careful on this point, that when we are zealous in building we build only upon Christ and by Christ, for edifices otherwise erected will fall in heaps. We must as a church not only rely upon the Christ that died, but upon the Christ who is gone into the glory and sits at the right hand of God, ruling and reigning on our behalf, who also shall shortly come to gather together the scattered, and to reign amongst his own. The true church, like a vine, derives the life-sap of its branches from Jesus the stem, and from no other source. She can say of her glorious Redeemer, "My soul, wait thou only upon the Lord, for my expectation is from him." Other communities may lean on princes, but she comes up from the wilderness leaning on her Beloved; other congregations may look to human greatness for support, but her eyes are towards the hills whence cometh her help; her help cometh from the Lord which made heaven and earth.

Furthermore, *a foundation has the shaping of the building,* and the true church shapes and forms itself upon the Lord Jesus as its groundplan and outline. The shape of a building must, to a very large extent, be determined by its foundation. If you have ever traced the foundations of an ancient abbey or castle, as they have appeared on a level with the soil, you have proceeded to infer the form of the building from the run of the ground line. Here was a sharp angle, there was a circular tower; there was a buttress, and there was a recess. The building must have followed the ground line, and so must every true church be built upon Christ, in the sense of following his word and ordinances to the best of its knowledge and understanding. The law of Christ is the law of the church. All the decrees of popes and councils, all the resolutions of assemblies, synods, presbyteries, and associations, and all the ordinances of men as individuals, however great they be, when they are all put together, if they at all differ from the law of Christ, are mere wind and waste paper, nay, worse, they are treasonable insults to the majesty of

King Jesus. Those who build apart from the authority of Christ build off of the foundation, and their fabric will fall. There is no law and no authority in a true church but that of Christ himself; we who are his ministers are his servants and the servants of the church, and not lords or law-makers. To his law a faithful church brings all things as to the sure test. As churches we are not legislators, but subjects; it is not for us to frame constitutions, invent offices, and decree rites and ceremonies, but we are to take everything out of the mouth of Christ, and to do what he bids us, as he bids us, and when he bids us. Parliaments and kings have no authority whatever in the church, but Christ alone rules therein. If any portion of a church be not based upon Christ it is a mere deforming addition to the plan of the great Architect, and mars the temple which God has built, and not man. What a blessed thing it is to feel that you belong to a church which has a rock under it, because it is constituted by Christ's authority. We feel safe in following an ordinance which is of his commanding, but we should tremble if we had only custom and human authority for it. How secure we feel in believing a doctrine which is of our Lord's teaching, for we can say, "this is not mere opinion, this is not the judgment of a wise man, this is not the decree of councils, but this is the Master's own declaration." Not one of his words shall ever fall to the ground. There is in his authority no change, for ever is his word settled in heaven, and he is in himself the same yesterday, to-day, and for ever. Steadfast is that church which carefully follows his guiding line, but that which departeth from his fixed rule and authority hath left the foundation, and therein ceased to be a church.

A foundation is indispensable to a building, and so Christ is indispensable to a true church. In a house you could do without certain of the windows, you might close a door, and you might remove parts of the roof, and still it might be a house, but you cannot have a house at all if you take away the foundation; and so you cannot have a church of Christ if Jesus Christ be not there as the foundation and corner stone. When sermons are preached without so much as the mention of Christ's name, it takes more than charity, it requires you to tell a lie to say "That was a Christian sermon"; and if any people find their joy in a teaching which casts the Lord Jesus into the background, they are not his church, or else such teaching would be an abomination to them. Yet have I heard it said that from some ministries you may go away like Mary Magdalene from the sepulchre, exclaiming, "They have taken away my Lord, and I know not where they have laid him." One told me the other day that he had heard a discourse from a Christian pulpit which would have been applauded by Jews and Mahometans, for there was not a trace of Christ in it. Another declared that in another place he heard priests, and clergy, and sacraments so much puffed up that as for faith in the Lord Jesus it seemed to be a very small matter. Brethren, this is not so in the church of Christ. There the Lord Jesus is Alpha and Omega—first and last, beginning and end. True Christians make much of Christ; indeed, they make all of him: and as for priests and preachers they say, "Who then is Paul, and who is Apollos, but ministers by whom ye believed, even as the Lord gave to every man"? O brethren, let us see to this. If anything be put into Christ's place we make it an antichrist, and we are not Christians, but anti-Christians. The true church saith, "Give us what learning and eloquence you will, but we cannot be content except **Christ** be glorified; preach us what you may, we will never be satisfied unless he who is the express image of the Father shall be set forth in our midst." Then, I say, she speaketh like the true bride of Christ, but if she can be content to see her Lord dishonoured she is no chaste spouse of Christ.

Let us put this, our first point, in a few sentences. It is not the union of men with men that makes a church if Jesus Christ be not the centre and the bond of the union. The best of men may come into bonds of amity, and they may form a league, or a federation, for good and useful purposes, but they are not a church unless Jesus Christ be the basis upon which they rest. He must be the ground and foundation of the hope of each and of all.

Neither can a church be created by a mere union to a minister. It is most good and pleasant to see brethren dwelling together in unity; it is most advantageous that between the pastor and his flock there should be perfect love, but the relationship must not be exaggerated beyond due bounds. Brethren, there must be no glorying in men, nor blind following of them. A body formed of individuals whose religion lies in drinking in the theories and opinions of a religious teacher falls short of being a church of God. The church is not built on Paul, nor upon Apollos, nor upon Cephas, but upon the sole authority of Jesus Christ. We are not to be believers in Luther, Calvin, Wesley, or Whitefield, but in Christ. Of such believers a true church must be composed. Neither is a church made by the following of any particular form or rite. We have one Lord, one faith, one baptism; and we are bound to be loyal to Christ in his ordinances as in all else, but it is not the practice of an ordinance which constitutes a church. It is well to be united and bound together in loyalty to the faith once delivered to the saints, but, unless there is vital, personal union with the person of Christ on the part of the members of the church, their association may constitute a league for the defence of orthodoxy, or a confederation for the maintenance of a form of religious thought, but it is not a church. No, most blessed Lord, thou must be there, or nothing is there! Pastors, elders, deacons, teachers, evangelists, these are courses of precious stones in the heavenly temple, but without thee they are no church, for the foundation is wanting. All thy saints come to thee and rest on thee, O Christ; and in thee all the building, fitly framed together, groweth unto an holy temple in the Lord. Thou, O Christ, art the seed-corn out of which the church grows, the stem from which it branches, the head in which it lives, the shepherd by whom it is fed, the captain by whom it is marshalled, the husband to whom it is married: thou art, indeed, the all in all of the church which thou hast redeemed with thine own blood.

> "God hath a sure foundation given,
> Fixed as the firm decrees of heaven
> The changeless everlasting rock,
> That braves the storm, and bides the shock.
> *There build:* the gates of hell in vain
> Against that rock their war maintain.
> Christ is the rock, the corner stone,
> God rears his beauteous house thereon."

Thus far, then, we have declared that there is no church except that which is built on Jesus Christ. This truth we assert in the face of all men, let them make what they will of it.

II. Secondly, we assert that there is NO GOSPEL BUT WHAT IS BUILT ON JESUS CHRIST. There are many pretended gospels in the world. Paul said once "another gospel," and then he corrected himself, and said, "which is not another," for strictly speaking there is only one gospel, and there cannot be two. The good news, God's good news to men, is one. There never were two gospels, for there never were two Saviours or two redemptions, and there never will be; but a Saviour and a redemption are necessary to a gospel, and therefore there can be only one. The foundation of the gospel is one, namely Jesus Christ, and there is no other possible foundation. For, first, *there is but one Mediator, by whom God speaks words of grace.* "There is one God, and one mediator between God and men, the man Christ Jesus." If then, beloved, any man shall come to you and say, "God hath spoken to me, and bidden me say to you somewhat other and above what Jesus hath said," receive him not. If any man say unto you, "I have a revelation from heaven, and God bids me speak," if he speak not according to the words of Christ Jesus he is a false prophet, and cometh not from God at all. Yea, moreover, if bishop, or council, or church speak otherwise than Christ has spoken, the truth is not in any of them. All that ever spake from God, both before Christ and after Christ, have spoken after their manner and measure in the same fashion as Christ Jesus the Lord, for the voice of God is not two, but one, and the word of God is not two or three, but one; and now at this day ye may rest quite certain that, if God hath anything to say unto us, he hath in these last days spoken to us by his Son, and his own hand has closed and sealed the revelation of God. Woe unto us if we hear him not, and woe unto us if we listen to other voices. Indeed, if we be the sheep of Christ we shall not regard new voices, for our Lord hath said it, "A stranger will they not follow, for they know not the voice of strangers." The true gospel comes through Christ as the Mediator, and through him alone, and that which comes otherwise is not the gospel.

The true gospel has Christ's divine person as its glory, and there can be no gospel without this. Christ is God, and in him dwelleth all the fulness of the Godhead bodily. In the person of Christ the divinity has come down to us to heal our diseases and remove our griefs. Now, if you hear of a gospel which begins by saying that Christ is not the Only-begotten of the Father, or that he is not the Son of God, close your ears to it, for it is not the gospel of God. Unless Jesus be extolled as certainly God over all, blessed for ever, the preaching is not the gospel.

Jesus Christ is the essence of the gospel: he himself is the good news, as well as the medium of it. The good news is that God hath sent his only-begotten Son into the world that we might live through him. Eternal redemption has been obtained for us by the life, death, and resurrection of the Lord Jesus, and this is the gospel. There is pardon through his blood, justification through his righteousness, and sanctification through his Spirit. Complete salvation is freely provided for believers in him, and the grace of God through him is abundantly displayed to the very chief of sinners. God hath made him to be unto us wisdom, and righteousness, and sanctification, and redemption; in fact, all the blessings that are needed to lift man up into the favour of God, and keep him there for ever, are stored up in the person of Jesus, in whom God's love hath displayed itself to the fullest degree. Jesus is the sum and substance, crown and glory of the gospel. If, then, you hear a gospel in which the freewill of man is spoken of as the main agent, in which the works of man, or the forms and ceremonies practised by priests, are set up as being fundamental things, reject such teaching, for it is not the good news from heaven. The one good news is this,—" God was in Christ, reconciling the world unto himself, not imputing their trespasses unto them." Let others preach what they please; as for us, " we preach Christ crucified." Jesus himself preached the very gospel of the gospel when he cried, " Come *unto me,* all ye that labour and are heavy laden, and I will give you rest."

Now then, brethren, for I speak to many of you who teach the gospel, I beseech you to recollect my simple text of to-day, and henceforth teach nothing apart from Christ. The teaching of doctrines is not the teaching of the gospel if those doctrines be held in a dry, didactic style apart from Christ. Suppose I preach the doctrine of election—that is one thing; but unless I preach that we are chosen in Christ I have left out the foundation, and my teaching crumbles to the ground: as a bowing wall shall it be, and as a tottering fence. Suppose I preach final perseverance, it is well; but I have not preached the gospel unless I show that it is because Jesus lives we shall live also, and that the preservation of the saints depends on their union with him. Suppose I am teaching justification, it is not the true justification unless it is the righteousness of God in Christ Jesus which I hold forth. Herein I commend to you the example of the earlier preachers of the church. From such of their writings as remain we gather that they dwelt much upon the actual events of the Redeemer's life. They are not always so clear as one could wish upon the great doctrines as Paul gives them to us, but there is one point in which they excel. You may not hear enough from them about justification by faith, but you hear a great deal concerning the precious blood of Christ: they do not always speak so clearly upon regeneration as we could desire, but they speak much of the resurrection of Christ, and of the newness of life which his saints enjoy in virtue thereof. Pardon to them is a washing in the blood of Christ: conversion is being called by Christ: resurrection is a risen Christ. Everything is brought out as a matter of fact arising from the actual life and death of the Saviour, and I am free to confess that I greatly admire this way of preaching the gospel. How does Paul put it? What was the gospel to him? Hear him: " Moreover, brethren, I declare unto you the gospel which I preached unto you, which also ye have received, and wherein ye stand; by which also ye are saved, if ye keep in memory what I preached unto you, unless ye have believed in vain. For I delivered unto you first of all that which I also received, how that Christ died for our sins according to the scriptures; and that he was buried, and that he rose again the third day according to the scriptures; and that he was seen of Cephas, then of the twelve." Thus, you see, Paul's body of divinity was the life and death of that only embodied divinity, the Lord Jesus. My brethren, always set forth the gospel in close connection with your Lord, fetching it, as it were, out of him. The juice of the grape is pleasant, but if you would know what it is in all its purity keep the grapes near you, and press them in the vineyard where they grow. So the gospel is the wine of Christ, but it is sweetest when it flows fresh from the cluster. Preach Jesus Christ himself when you preach his doctrine, or else you may make the doctrine to be like the stone at the door of his sepulchre, whereas it ought to be like a throne of ivory on which, like another Solomon, your Lord sits resplendent.

Some preach experience, and they do well; but they should be exceedingly careful to keep Jesus very prominent. We have a school of brethren who preach little else than experience, and I do not condemn them; but what is the experience of a poor fellow-sinner to me? How does it help me to hear that he groans as I do, or sings as I do? It may be of some small service to me, but there are more excellent things. I want to know how Jesus felt, and what Christ can do for my brother and for me. Experience is admirable when Jesus Christ is set forth in it; but if you take up an experimental vein of things, whether of human corruption, or of human perfection, and Jesus Christ is put in the background, you are marring the gospel. Jesus is the one foundation, and there is no gospel apart from him.

So, too, with practice. By all means let us have practical preaching, and plenty of it, and let it come down sternly and faithfully on the vices of the times; but merely to preach against this and that vice, and extol this and that virtue, is a mission fit enough for Socrates or Plato, but does not well beseem a minister of Jesus Christ. Set Jesus forth, my practical brother. His example shames vice and encourages virtue. Set him up as the mirror of all perfection, and in him men will see what they ought to be, and learn how to come at it. Jesus Christ, then, is the only gospel. We leave that point, being abundantly sure that you are persuaded of it.

III. Thirdly. THERE IS NO HOPE OF SALVATION BUT THAT WHICH IS BUILT UPON CHRIST. This is another point upon which I need not speak much. I will only spend a few minutes in talking upon certain other hopes. No doubt some think it must be well with them because they were brought up from their childhood most respectably, their parents were excellent Christian people, and they believe that they themselves, having never done anything very wrong, are no doubt safe. Ah, my dear hearers, if this is your only hope, you are lost, for you are dead in sin. That which is born of the flesh,—the best of flesh that ever was—is flesh, and flesh and blood cannot inherit the kingdom of God. You must be born again, you must have a far better hope than any which can spring out of your birth and your relations. "Ay, but," saith another, "I had all the ceremonies of the church performed upon me." Yes, and it makes no difference to me what church it was. If you are building even upon rites which God has given, they will not suffice you; they cannot bear the weight of your soul. Baptism, the Lord's Supper, or fifty thousand sacraments, if men were to make so many, would not help you one solitary inch. The only foundation for your soul's hope must be Christ, and none of these outward things. "Ah," saith another, "but I have diligently performed a great many good works." I would to God you had ten times as many good works; but if you have committed one single sin no works can save you. All the good works of the best men that ever lived would make but a rotten foundation for them if they were to place reliance thereon. Abound in good works, but do not trust them. Human merit is a foundation of sand. "But I have had special spiritual feelings," says one; "I have been broken down, I have been lifted up." Yes, you may have been crushed down to hell's door, and lifted up to heaven's gate, but there is nothing in feelings and excitements which can be a ground of hope. "Why," says one, "it has troubled me that I have not had these feelings." Do not let it trouble you, but go to Jesus Christ and rest in him; feelings or no feelings. High frames and low frames are delusions all, if they be trusted in. We can no more be saved by our feelings than by our works. "Oh, but," saith another, "I have confidence that I am saved, for I have had a wonderful dream, and, moreover, I heard a voice, and saw a vision." Rubbish all! Dreams, visions, voices! Throw them all away. There is not the slightest reliance to be placed upon them. "What, not if I saw Christ?" No, certainly not, for vast multitudes saw him in the days of his flesh, and died and perished after all. "But surely a dream will save me." It will give you a dreamy hope, and when you awake in the next world your dream will be gone. The one thing to rest upon is the more sure word of testimony:—Christ Jesus came into the world to save sinners, and whosoever believeth in him is not condemned. I believe in him, and, therefore, I am not condemned. Why do I believe my sin to be forgiven? Because Jesus died to put away the sins of believers, and there is no condemnation to those who are in him. Why do I believe myself to be justified? Because he that believeth is justified; the word of God says so. How do I know that I am saved? Because Jesus Christ has declared that whosoever believeth in him is not condemned. To believe in him is to trust in him, to make him my foundation. I do trust in him, he is my foundation, and I am saved, or else his word is not true. I know that his word is true, and therefore I am at rest. It is written, "He that believeth in him hath everlasting life." I believe in him, therefore I have everlasting life. I have his promise that I shall never perish, neither shall any pluck me out of his hand; therefore I shall never perish, neither shall any separate me from his love.

You see, then, there is no hope of salvation but what is fixed upon Christ alone; and I do invite and entreat you, if any of you have any hope which goes beyond Christ or beside Christ, get rid of it, throw it on a dunghill, and loathe it as an insult to God. Do as the man did with the bad bank note. When he found it was a forgery he buried it, and ran away as fast as he could, for fear anybody should think the note had ever been in his possession. So, if you are trusting in anything that is not of Christ, bury your faith, and run away from it, for it is a false confidence, and will work ill to your soul. Let your faith cry, "None but Christ": all-saving faith delights in that cry. For eternal salvation, "other foundation can no man lay than that is laid."

IV. Our last point is this,—there is NO CHRISTIAN BUT THE MAN BUILT ON JESUS CHRIST. Here is a Christian, and of one thing in him I am sure: I cannot tell whether he holds Arminian views or Calvinistic views, but if he is a Christian he has no foundation but Christ. Here is a person who reverences the Pope, here is another who glories in the name of Protestant, here is a third who is a Baptist: which is the Christian out of these? I answer, he is the Christian that is built on Christ, whoever he may be; but if he can do without Christ he is not worthy the name of Christian. What do we mean? Why this. I mean first, every man to be a Christian must *rest his whole soul upon Christ* as to eternal salvation. There must be no stuttering or stammering over that; there must be no mixing up the merits of Jesus with priests or ceremonies: no, it must be a clear, straight line,—Christ for me, Christ everything for me, my sole and only hope. Any deviation here is fatal. On the cross is written, *Spes unica,* and it remains the one only hope of a burdened soul.

Next, if you are to be a Christian, *Christ must be your model;* by the aid of his Holy Spirit, you must try to do what he would have done in your position and under your circumstances. You are not to say, "I cannot follow Christ in this": you are never to renounce his leadership. If you do you must give up being a Christian, because you are bound to take up his cross and follow him. He claims to be your King when he becomes your Saviour. A true Christian is a man who builds upon Christ as his model as walls are built on a foundation. A true Christian is one whose growing up is in Christ, for, strange to say, the temple of God grows. Nor need we wonder, for it is a living temple. I have seen magnificent pieces of architecture, masterpieces, and it has struck me when I looked at them that they must have grown. An ordinary, clumsy bit of work displays the mason and the carpenter, but perfect architecture looks as if it grew; and Christ's church does grow, for Christ's people grow. But all our up-growing must come out of Christ. When a man says, "Years ago I used to worship with these Christian people, and I felt very happy with them, but I have now more education and have got beyond them," he is guided by his pride and not by grace. No true Christian talks so. The higher he grows the more he grows into Christ; the wiser he is the more he shows the wisdom of Christ. If he has begun aright he may advance as far as he can, but he never can advance beyond Christ; he will get to be less and Christ will be more and more to him, for he is not a Christian who does not still stick to this,—that the foundation goes as far as he means to go, and he builds never beyond that, but builds upward upon that, and upon that alone.

And he, again, is the true Christian who *lives for Christ,* to whom Christ's glory is the great object of his being. He is a Christian who reckons that time wasted which is not used for Jesus, that substance wasted which is not used in obedience to Jesus: who considers that he does not live except as Christ lives in him.

Brothers and sisters, I pray that you may all be Christians of this sort, only do let it be with you evermore Jesus Christ. I do not like to preach a sermon without feeling the presence of my Master. I have done so, but never to my own comfort. I cannot bear to come away from the Monday evening prayer-meeting without feeling that the Lord has been there, and he generally is. The true heart does not like to engage in any kind of enterprise without first consulting him, and doing it in his sight. We are a very busy church, and I want you, as a busy church doing a great deal, always to keep the Master near you. The most holy work gets to be mere routine, to be done mechanically, unless we enjoy his dear love, and sweet presence, and blessed smile in the doing of his will. Sit at Jesus' feet with Mary as well as work for him like Martha. May he be the foundation of everything, not only of the church, but of our hope, of our character, of every little thing we do. When you are laying the first stone of a new enterprise, lay it upon Christ with fair colours. Set it in the vermilion of his precious blood; perfume it with the oil of gratitude, and lay it upon him alone; so shall you build for eternity, and glorify his precious name.

The Head Stone of the Corner

"The stone which the builders refused is become the head stone of the corner. This is the Lord's doing; it is marvellous in our eyes. This is the day which the Lord hath made; we will rejoice and be glad in it. Save now, I beseech thee, O Lord: O Lord, I beseech thee, send now prosperity"—Psalm cxviii. 22—25.

It would be difficult, if not impossible, to fix with certainty the occasion which first suggested this psalm: it has even been thought to be purely prophetic, and rather foretelling history than narrating it. I rather incline to the opinion that some Israelitish hero, chosen of God to high office in the midst of his people, had been rejected by their rulers, had passed through many struggles, some of them of the most violent kind, and at last, notwithstanding the rejection of the people and their leaders, had attained to a prominent position, nay, to a chief place in the midst of the nation. The psalm is applicable to Christ, and to him it is referred in the New Testament several times, but probably from the human point of view it was at first intended to celebrate the victory of some chosen man of God who, despite his divine election, had been rejected by his countrymen. Providence conducted him to a crowning success, and he magnified the Lord for it. In some way or other a stone has come to be connected with several persons whose history was of this character. Remember Jacob. He flees from his father's house because Esau threatens to kill him: he appears to be the rejected member of Isaac's family, by whom the house would never be built up. At the end of a day's journey he lies down with *a stone* for his pillow, and as he sweetly slumbers he sees heaven open, beholds the mystic ladder, and rises assured of the love of the Almighty God. By faith thus infused into his soul he becomes strong for his future life, and so lives that now the house of Abraham and Isaac stands represented in the seed of Jacob alone, and Esau with all his dukes has utterly passed away.

The next occurrence of the stone happens in reference to Joseph, of whom the dying Jacob said, "From thence is the Shepherd *the stone* of Israel." He was separated from his brethren by their envy and grievously wounded by their malice. They said, "Behold, this dreamer cometh"; and they sold him for a slave into the stranger's land. From the dungeons of Egypt he climbed to the throne, and became the cornerstone of Israel's house. On his bosom his aged father could lay his head and dream as he did at Bethel; and by his power and wisdom the shepherd family was happily built up.

Then came David, whom his elder brethren despised, and even his father passed him over, until the prophet of God asked for him, that he might be anointed with oil. Out of his hand went that *stone* of Israel which laid low the pride of Philistia. Goliath must bite the ground when the stone of Israel flies from the hand of Israel's shepherd, who was destined to be her king. He was rejected and hated by Saul, so that he wandered about in the wilderness, hiding in cave and rock until the hour came when he was called to the throne. Then the stone which the builders refused became the headstone of the corner, and he and his people confessed that it was the Lord's doing, and it was marvellous in their eyes. Be not afraid, O ye persecuted ones, for you shall fulfil your destiny. It has happened again and again in history that those who have been destined to do great things for the Lord have first of all been compelled to pass through a trying ordeal of misunderstanding and rejection. Such history repeats itself; it may do so in your instance. The speckled bird of the family, the one least beloved, often rises to take the most prominent place. Jephthah was driven out from his father's family, and yet in their distress his brethren were glad enough to make him their champion and accept him as their head. Bow thy head in patience, young man, and bear whatever God or his enemies may lay upon thee, for assuredly as the Lord is in thee and with thee he will bring thee forth, and of thee, too, it shall be true in thine own little way, "The stone which the builders refused, the same is become the head stone of the corner."

At this time, however, we shall confine our application of these verses to our blessed Lord himself, to whom they most evidently refer. Their meaning is focussed upon him, and in reference to him each word is emphatic. He applied them to himself; for Matthew tells us in the twenty-first chapter of his gospel that our Lord said to the chief priests and Pharisees, "Did ye never read in the scriptures, The stone which the builders rejected, the same is become the head of the corner?" You remember also how Peter said in the face of the crucifiers of Christ, "Be it known unto you all, and to all the people of Israel, that by the name of Jesus Christ of Nazareth, whom ye crucified, whom God raised from the dead, even by him doth this man stand here before you whole. This is the stone which was set at nought of you builders, which is become the head of the corner. Neither is there salvation in any other: for there is none other name under heaven given among men, whereby we must be saved." In his first epistle Peter refers again to this psalm in the well-remembered words, "Wherefore also it is contained in the scripture, Behold, I lay in Sion a chief corner stone, elect, precious: and he that believeth on him shall not be confounded. Unto you therefore which believe he is precious: but unto them which be disobedient, the stone which the builders disallowed, the same is made the head of the corner." Of our own exalted Lord we are going to speak at this time, and may the Spirit bear witness in our hearts to his honour.

I. First, I invite your thoughts to CHRIST REJECTED—"the stone which the builders refused." The Lord Jesus came into this world at the fulness of time when the Messiah was expected by those devout men who waited for salvation in Israel. He came born of parents descended from that royal house from which Messiah was prophesied as coming, and he was born in the very city which had been pointed out by seers of old. All details of his life in his early days corresponded with prophetic intimations and answered to the signs which the Lord had appointed. There was nothing in which he did not exactly fit the symbols of the sanctuary and the personal types of history: everything which could speak, cried with one voice, "Behold the Lamb of God." He was clearly placed before the Jewish people as the stone which God would lay in Zion as the foundation of their hopes, but *they persistently refused him*. It was not from want of evidence, for John came prophesying concerning him, and as I have already said he was but the last of a long list of prophets who had all pointed to him as the Anointed of the Lord: and yet Israel rejected him. His own miracles and teaching were more than sufficient evidence of his mission, but Israel would none of him. He was a stone evidently of God's quarrying and preparing. His extraordinary birth marked him out as differing from all the rest of mankind; his surpassing excellence and moral beauty declared him to be destined to the highest position. His person displayed the marvellous love and wisdom of God, and with half an eye, if they had willed to see it, the Jews might have perceived that he was anointed to be the corner stone of the spiritual temple; but yet they refused him. "He came unto his own and his own received him not." He came to those who had the oracles, but in this thing they set at nought the oracle; he came to those who had the law and the prophets, but they were deaf to all holy testimonies and disowned him. Alas, for the blindness of men's hearts.

His rejection was rendered the more remarkable and the more sorrowful because *he was rejected by the builders or leaders of the nation*. "The stone which *the builders* refused." If the common people who were ignorant of the law had not perceived him to be the chosen stone we might not have wondered; but there were men of learning and research among the people, and these rejected him. They had builders who understood spiritual architecture, or professed to do so—the scribes who studied the law, and the priests who taught the people—these were the master-builders, whose business it was to make the selection of the corner stone; but these rejected our Lord. It was not alone the mob of Jerusalem that rejected Christ, but the rulers led the way. True, the many cried, "Crucify him!" but not till they were bribed by the priests, the clergy of the day, by the Sadducees, or sceptical men of science, and by the Pharisees, or ritualistic professors: these were they who sat in Moses' seat, in whom the people had confidence, and by their machinations the people were led to reject the corner stone which the Lord himself had laid.

Concerning this rejection we must also remark that it was no common one: *it was a violent and indignant rejection*. They were not content to say, "He is not the Messiah," but they turned their hottest malice against him; they were furious at the sight of him. This precious stone was kicked against and rolled about with violence, and all manner of ridicule was poured upon it. Nothing would content them but the blood of the man who had disturbed their consciences and questioned their pretensions. "The stone which the builders *refused*" is to be read with a heavy stress upon the word REFUSED. Peter says, "He was set at nought of you builders." They slandered him in life and mocked him in death; they spat their accusations against him when he was free, and gave him over to be defiled with the spittle of the soldiers' mouths when he was bound. They made him live an outcast's life, and then they hung him up to die a felon's death.

This rejection was most unreasonable : they did violence to truth and justice by their evil deed. For which of his works did they stone him? There was nothing in his character which should have incensed them, there was nothing about him which ought to have excited their doubts, much less their wrath; but yet they wilfully and resolutely rejected him. They said, "We will not have this man to reign over us." The cause in part was blind prejudice. They expected a king surrounded with earthly pomp and girt with physical force to break the Roman yoke and create an Israelitish empire more famous than that of Solomon; and because he came as the son of a lowly virgin, robed in a peasant's dress, and humbly dwelt among the sons of men in meekest fashion, therefore they refused him. There was no real reason why he should have been refused because of his humiliation, for was not their Messiah so to come? Did not Isaiah say, "He shall grow up before him as a tender plant, and as a root out of a dry ground: he hath no form nor comeliness; and when we shall see him, there is no beauty that we should desire him." He agreed with the prophecies, but not with their prejudices, and therefore they cried, "Away with him : away with him." Those prejudices were the result of sheer ignorance, for if they had studied the word they would have seen that the Christ of God was not the Christ of their dream; and had they searched the Scriptures they might have known that Jesus of Nazareth was the Lord of glory. They had eyes, but would not see; the light was around them, but they comprehended it not. The pride of their hearts kept them in ignorance; they did not want to know. The proud philosophic Sudducee felt sure of his ground, for he was a thinker, and despised the vulgar many: he did not wish for evidence as to the existence of angel or spirit, or of the resurrection of the dead, and therefore he scornfully rejected the man who brought life and immortality to light. The Pharisee, supremely righteous in himself, did not want to know a man who taught him that he was lost, and came to be the Saviour of sinners. He felt too safe already to need saving.

Thus the Ever-blessed was chased out of the world by the pride which scorns all excellence except its own. Men flung away God's dearest jewel because it outshone their own counterfeit jewellery. Nor was it pride alone, for that mother sin was surrounded with all other evils. They wanted to devour widows' houses in secret, and he exposed them : they wanted to go on saying their long prayers and yet to persecute the righteous, and he unmasked them. Certain of them wanted to be freethinkers, and yet to be thought orthodox, and he denounced them as hypocrites: they denied the essential principles of revelation, but he came forth from the Father to bear witness of God, and therefore they utterly abhorred him. Their sin, as it could not associate with his holiness, raised a clamour against him, and with cunning and malice they denounced, condemned, and utterly rejected the stone which God had appointed to be the foundation and corner-stone of his New Jerusalem. Ah, my brethren, you know what came of it. They threw that chosen stone away, and when they had removed it away from their Babel-building they thought their troubles at an end, when, indeed, they had just begun. That stone was removed out of the way, and yet they stumbled upon it; they stumbled to their own confusion, yea, they stumbled to their own destruction. How broken were they by that stone at the awful siege of Jerusalem, when they and their city perished. Now, also, that stone has been lifted up into heaven by the mighty power of God, and in the fulness of time it will descend upon these foolish builders with terrible effect; for upon whomsoever it shall fall it will grind him to powder. Even while that stone was here they fell upon it and were broken; but when he comes a second time he will fall upon them, and woe unto them in that day. Let us not be among the company of the rejecters; let us not consort with those who cast doubts upon the gospel of Jesus. Rather let our hearts joyfully bless God for appointing him to be the head of the corner; let us accept him in that character and at once build upon him.

> "Chosen of God, to sinners dear,
> And saints adore the name;
> We trust our whole salvation here,
> Nor shall we suffer shame."

God forbid that we should reject the testimony of God concerning his Son, and so make God a liar and bring down eternal wrath upon our own heads. Our safety lies in reception, not in rejection, for to "as many as received him, to them gave he power to become the sons of God, even to them that believe on his name." As for those who reject him, we hear with trembling these words from the lips of the loving Jesus: but those mine enemies, which would not that I should reign over them, bring hither, and slay them before me."

II. With great delight I now pass to the second topic, which is CHRIST EXALTED—"The stone which the builders refused *is become the head stone of the corner*"—that is to say, at this moment Christ has *the chief place of honour* in the building of God. He is the head stone, for he is higher than the kings of the earth: he is higher than all the opposing powers of wisdom or of superstition; and he is the head over all things to his church. Glory be to his name, in the midst of his people he is above all and over all: we worship him with rapture. He is King of kings and Lord of lords, "for by him were all things created that are in heaven, and that are in earth, visible and invisible, whether they be thrones, or dominions, or principalities, or powers: all things were created by him, and for him." There is none like him among the sons of men; in all things he has the pre-eminence. He that was crucified is now enthroned; he that lay in the grave now reigneth in glory.

Nor is he alone eminent for his position of honour, but for his *surpassing usefulness.* He is the head stone of the corner, that stone which joins two walls together, and is the bond of the building. Jew and Gentile are now one in Christ Jesus. It is true he is a stone in Israel's wall, but he is also a stone in the Gentile's wall : in him is neither Jew nor Gentile distinctively, for they are both there inclusively. He hath made both one. The Pharisees would have it that the wall should finish within the line of Judah's race, but not so thought our Master. His heart went forth to the other sheep which he had that were not yet of the fold. This made them wrathful, but their wrath did not prevent his accomplishing his design, and now he is the bond of the building, holding Jew and Gentile in firm unity. This precious corner stone binds God and man together in wondrous amity, for he is both in one. He joins earth and heaven together, for he participates in each. He joins time and eternity together, for he was a man of few years, and yet he is the Ancient of Days. Wondrous corner stone ! Thou dost bind all of us together who are in thee, so that by love of thee we are builded together for a temple of the Holy Ghost. Thou art the perfect bond, the eternal holdfast, the divine cement which holds the universe in one. Is it not written, " By him all things consist " ?

Our Lord Jesus Christ then is brought up from all rejection and shame to which his enemies put him to be by usefulness and by honour the grandest personage upon the face of the earth ; and all this *none the less, but all the more, because he was rejected.* He lost nothing by his enemies. They scourged his back, but they did not rob him of that imperial purple which now adorns him ; they crowned him with thorns, but those thorns have increased the brilliance of his diadem of light ; they pierced his hands, and thereby prepared them to sway an irresistible sceptre of love over men's hearts : they nailed his feet, but those feet stand firm for ever upon the throne of sovereignty : they crucified him, but his crucifixion led him to his greater honour, since he therein finished the work which was given him to do, and now also God hath highly exalted him and given him a name which is above every name. As it has been, so is it, and so shall it be : man's opposition to the gospel will not interfere with it one single whit, but the eternal purposes of Jehovah shall be fulfilled. Our adversaries may mine and undermine, they may openly oppose and secretly assail, but upon this rock, even upon Christ, shall the truth and the church for ever rest, and no harm shall come to it. The Lord will lift the stone which the builders refused, and make it to become the headstone of the corner ; therefore let us not fail nor be discouraged.

Already our text has been fulfilled. Our Lord Christ was dead and buried, but his foes were desperately afraid that he would rise again, and so they rolled a stone to the tomb's mouth and sealed it ; but he rose for all that, and became the first-fruits of them that slept, the headstone of the resurrection. His resurrection utterly defeated those who reckoned upon destroying his power. What could they do against one whom death itself could not silence ? When his resurrection attested his mission, what could they say against him ? Nor was this all, for to add to his honour he was received up into heaven. Beyond the eternal hills he rose, the gates of heaven opening at his coming ; and amidst the acclamation of angels and redeemed spirits he ascended to the highest place that heaven affords. What a change from Gabbatha and all the maltreatment of the Pavement to the sea of glass mingled with fire, and to the seat of infinite majesty! Jesus has gone from the bar to the throne, and there he sitteth in majesty. His adversaries may grind their teeth at him, but the King is set upon the holy hill of Zion beyond their wrath. "Why do the heathen rage, and the people imagine a vain thing?" Jehovah Jesus is King and none can challenge his sovereignty.

At Pentecost, too, this was fulfilled, for when his few and humble disciples were inspired by the Holy Ghost, and began to speak with tongues of fire, all Jerusalem rang with the wonder, and then again the despised and rejected stone was made the head stone of the corner. Very speedily throughout the known world the testimony of his name was made to sound forth till his word had gone forth as far as the sun's utmost track, and all nations beheld the light thereof. Then the gods of the heathen tottered, and colossal systems of idolatry were ground to powder. Glory be unto thee, O Christ; thou didst triumph gloriously in those first ages of thy church! That triumph is proceeding still. It will be consummated by-and-by. What confusion will take hold upon the hearts of his adversaries when he shall be revealed! He is hidden now, and his people with him, but the day draweth nigh when he shall come a second time to be admired in all them that believe. What astonishment will then take hold upon those who refused his righteous claims. Then will they know that this is the Lord's doing; though it will be terrible in their eyes. All intelligent beings, even down to the blackest devil of hell, shall at the second advent of our Lord be obliged to confess that the stone which the builders refused hath become the head stone of the corner. The Man of Nazareth shall be Lord of all before the eyes of all mankind. For that we diligently look. I call upon you, dear brothers and sisters, this morning, greatly to rejoice in the fact which we have thus brought before you. It is a grand truth that Christ Jesus is now enthroned beyond the reach of those who rejected and despised him,

> "Honour immortal must be paid,
> Instead of scandal and of scorn:
> While glory shines around his head,
> And a bright crown without a thorn."

III. Thirdly, I ask your attention to the next point, which is introduced to us by the twenty-third verse. THE EXALTATION OF CHRIST IS DUE TO GOD ALONE,—"*This is the Lord's doing*, and it is marvellous in our eyes." Now, this was so as a matter of history. Jesus Christ's name and work were at length had in honour in the world, but this was due to no man's wisdom, eloquence, or power, but entirely to the Lord, who is wonderful in counsel and great in might. Look, my brethren, if the Scribes and Pharisees had endorsed the claims of our Lord it might have been said that Christianity was grafted upon the old stock of Judaism, and therefore grew with vigour; and if Pilate, or Herod, or any of the great ones, especially if the Cæsar of the day had accepted it, then the following ages would have said, "Oh yes, he derived his power, and was lifted to his place through the prestige of empire and the prowess of arms." But it was not so. All the establishments on earth were against him : rank and station despised the carpenter's son : superstition abhorred his simplicity and spirituality ; ceremonialism would have nothing to do with him who said that the temple was to be destroyed: scepticism could not endure him, for he gave not a jot of ground for its doubts, or food for its speculations; and the kings of the earth, and the statesmen thereof, utterly derided him ; for he spake of a kingdom which was not of this world. And yet he triumphed, and now his name is the most famous among the sons of men. This was not because poets sat waiting upon Parnassus to pour forth their loftiest lays, or because ministrels with their fingers on their harp-strings stood prepared to draw forth matchless music to celebrate his advent. No; the hymns which were composed in his honour had a lowly virgin and an equally humble matron as their authors ; and the music which saluted him was the noise of children in the streets, shouting, "Hosanna to the Son of David." The Son of man owes nothing of his glory to man : his elevation to the throne is the Lord's doing, and marvellous in our eyes.

And while this is true as to the past it remains true at this day, for the gospel of Christ, whenever it spreads in the earth, owes its triumphs entirely to divine interposition. When I consider how hostile is human nature to the gospel, *the very existence of a true Church in the world is to me a miracle.* Nor to me alone does it appear so, for it really is a superhuman work and is wrought by the Lord alone. Just think of it. Why, at this very day, we have all the wisdom and power and eloquence and skill of the superstition of the world arrayed against the simple gospel of Jesus. Though they are agreed in nothing else, they all unite against Christ. He of the Seven Hills has nothing but maledictions for the pure gospel of Jesus, and with him stand a hierarchy clothed with terrible power, and a troop of Jesuits who stick at nothing. Completely organized, numerous, subtle, all pervading, the warriors of Rome are a great host, and not to be lightly thought upon. See how superstition multiplies in this land. See how the builders, appointed by the state to build up a Protestant church, are pulling it down with both hands. These, forsooth, are priests, clergy,—God's heritage! And what are they doing ? Uplifting an idolatrous crucifix in the place of the doctrine of the cross; setting sacraments in the room of the precious blood, and preaching salvation by their own priestcraft instead of salvation by the grace of God through Jesus Christ. The builders are rejecting him, and yet his cause lives on. The wise men on the other side of the house, the builders who affect to be scientific scholars, and persons of advanced thought and thorough culture, these also have their fling against the gospel. For aught I can see of their pretended depth of learning, I would recommend them to attend to their science and obtain a little more culture before they set up for teachers, or they may expose their own shallowness. These boastfully wise men, these self-styled *thinking* men, are all against the gospel of Jesus. When I see the power which at the present time is enlisted on the side of doubt and scepticism, I for my part am astonished that anybody believes the gospel at all, and I feel that it is the Lord's doing and marvellous in mine eye. True faith is supernatural ; it standeth not in the wisdom of man, but in divine power. Wherever Christ is exalted, as, blessed be his name, he is in many churches, it is not because of any wit or skill or power on the part of the minister, but because the Holy Ghost is at work among the people bringing them to Christ. Do not, then, dear brethren, despond on behalf of Christ's cause. The real progress of Christianity must be supernatural. Whenever we fight with the wooden sword of reason we may expect to be defeated; not because the gospel is against reason or contrary to it, but because it is so much above reason that we cannot comprehend it, and, therefore, lose power by healing gospel truth, as if it were a human discovery. If there be not working with Christianity a divine agency altogether above its reasonableness, if there be not, in fact, the Spirit of God working with it to convert men, then it will come to naught and vanish like other systems. Our reliance must be, therefore, not upon evidences which we can bring to prove the truth of the gospel, nor upon eloquence by which we may advance its claims, but upon the Eternal Spirit of God, for it is he, and he alone, who can lift the rejected stone and make it to become the head stone of the corner. It is impossible for blinded human nature to believe the truth of God; and hence we must be born again. Gospel teachings are so humbling, so radical, so pure, so spiritual, so much above our thoughts, that nobody will accept them unless taught of God. His chosen people shall be taught of the Spirit, and the rest will choose to remain in blindness. So it has been, and so it ever shall be; but, beloved, let us not tremble because of this, for despite human blindness, and the opposition of the wise, Christ must reign even to the world's end.

Did I hear a whisper that ministers are nowadays very broad, and have given up the old gospel. I know it, and I am not surprised: the builders are the first to reject the chosen stone. Christ owes little to preachers, and some of his worst enemies are found in their ranks. Unconverted men are in too many pulpits, and are seeking out many inventions to set aside the pure gospel which exalts Christ Jesus. Let them alone, the ditch is gaping for these blind guides. Our Lord can do without them. He owes his victories to himself, and to himself alone; and, therefore, let the faith of his people rest in peace, for if they will have patience they shall see greater things than they have yet beheld. Our text saith that it is not only the Lord's doing and marvellous, but it is marvellous "*in our eyes*," which it could not be if we did not see it. We shall see and we shall marvel. Some of us may have passed away, but you who are younger may live to see modern thought obtain supremacy over human minds: German rationalism which has ripened into Socialism may yet pollute the mass of mankind and lead them to overturn the foundations of society. Then "advanced principles" will hold carnival, and free thought will riot with the vice and blood which were years ago the insignia of "the age of reason." I say not that it will be so, but I should not wonder if it came to pass, for deadly principles are abroad and certain ministers are spreading them. If it ever should be so, do not, O believers, for a single moment despair, but rest certain that the Lord is about to do a marvellous thing in the earth, and that he will lift up once again the stone which the builders have again refused, and cause it to become more than ever the headstone of the corner. Never dream of defeat. Be calm amid all the din of controversy, for the hand which holds the gospel must win the victory. This is the Lord's doing and we shall see it.

IV. Let us now notice that THE EXALTATION OF THE REJECTED CHRIST COMMENCES A NEW ERA. For what saith the twenty-fourth verse? "*This is the day which the Lord hath made; we will rejoice and be glad in it.*" We date from our Lord's resurrection even as the Jews of old counted from the night wherein they went out of Egypt. What is this day which the Lord hath made? I reply first, it is *the day of the gospel.* Through our Lord's exaltation pardon for the guilty is freely preached among all nations, and whosoever believeth in him hath everlasting life. Now is Christ exalted on high to give repentance unto Israel and remission of sins: now is he in the throne of power, that he may be able to save to the uttermost them that come unto God by him. Let us rejoice and be glad in him. How can we rejoice and be glad in him except by believing in him? Come, let us believe the gospel, the gospel of the once rejected but now exalted Saviour: let us put our trust in him, and then let us sing for joy of heart because we have a royal Saviour, an exalted Saviour, an almighty Saviour, in whose hands our souls are safe. The era of the gospel ought to be a time of gladness, for its favours are rich, its light is clear, its promises are abundant, and its truth is certain. To be unhappy now that Jesus reigns is to be ungrateful. It is a royal feast, let us eat to the full, and so honour the King and bless ourselves.

What day is this which the Lord hath made? Why, in the next place, it is *a Sabbath day*, the beginning of a long line of Sabbaths. The day in which our Lord Jesus rose from the dead is now sacred to rest and holy joy. Let us keep it with reverent love, and bless God for making it.

"This is the day the Lord hath made,
He calls the hours his own;
Let heaven rejoice, let earth be glad,
And praise surround the throne.

"To-day he rose and left the dead;
And Satan's empire fell:
To-day the saints his triumphs spread,
And all his wonders tell."

The world calls the Sabbath *Sun*day, do not let us turn it into Cloud-day. Certain good Christian people look upon the Lord's day as a season so solemn that it can only be properly kept by being as dreary as possible. Draw down the blinds, darken the room, chide the children, banish every smile : now we are getting sabbatic. Let us go up to the house of prayer like convicts exercising in the prison yard, and there let us be as decorously miserable as possible; let the preacher be as dull and as monotonous as though he had no subject to preach about but death and destruction, and must preserve an air of melancholy, or none would think him gracious. Such is not the teaching of our Master, nor is it according to his mind and spirit. Herbert well saith of the Sabbath,

"Thou art a day of mirth,
And where the week-days trail on ground,
Thy flight is higher, as thy birth."

It should be "a day most calm, most bright," fit to be called "the endorsement of supreme delight." It is a time of the singing of birds, for the winter of our Lord's humiliation is over and he has risen from the dead; to-day we celebrate the glory of Christ in the highest heavens, as the elect of God and the corner stone of his church : surely it ill becomes us to go about with our hands upon our loins as if we mourned his victory and grudged his honour. No, let us clap our hands with exultation. "The Lord reigneth : let the earth rejoice ; let the multitude of the isles be glad thereof."

Again, "This is the day which the Lord hath made." The resurrection of Christ commences *an era of triumph*. We have spoken of the gospel day, and the Sabbatic day, but it is also a day of victories. As Jesus Christ rose from the dead, so will his truth continually rise from the sepulchre into which men may cast it. As he triumphed over the powers of death and darkness, so will his gospel triumph over all opposition. Whenever at any time your hearts are heavy, I would bid you stand at the open tomb of Christ, and recollect that he arose ; and if he could not be holden by the bands of death, certainly neither himself nor his gospel can be holden by any other bands. His adversaries thrust his gospel into the tomb again ; they proclaim that the old doctrines are effete, but as surely as Jesus our Lord liveth they shall see the truth revive again. Walk ye in patience, for the vision will not tarry. The day cometh when in yet greater power the gospel shall renew its youth, and the world shall assuredly know that the Lord hath done it. Let us rejoice and be glad that we live in an era bright with victories of the right and the true; we may have to fight for them, and wait for them, but they will surely come, and Christ shall reign for ever and ever. I would to God that the thought of the exalted Christ would be the beginning of days to some of you. This day began with sunlight, but at this hour it deepens into gloom ; the skies are overcast, and a tempest is hurrying up. I trust that with my dear hearers it may be the absolute reverse, that if you began this morning amid clouds of doubt and showers of tears, you may see Christ exalted in the highest heaven, because he has offered for you his great atoning sacrifice, and may you look to him, and find clear shining after the rain, a great calm after a great storm.

V. I close by saying that THE EXALTATION OF CHRIST SUGGESTS A PRAYER. The 25th verse supplies us with it. "*Save now, I beseech thee, O Lord : O Lord, I beseech thee, send now prosperity.*" First, it is a prayer *for salvation*. It may mean " God save the King : may Jesus live for ever," and in that sense we would make the heavens ring with it : but we will take it this morning to be a prayer for the salvation of men. Since Christ is the exalted and victorious Saviour, let us beseech him to save all those who are around us. Save them, Lord ! Save them all ! Save them now ! Put it in the present tense. Ask for a display of the present saving power of our exalted Head. O Christ Jesus, Prince and Lord, save the sinners in Zion ; we beseech thee save those who occupy these pews Sabbath after Sabbath, and hear about thee, but do not know thee. Save, too, the strangers that are within thy gates and are strangers to thee as well as to us. Save the careless, good Lord ! Save the anxious ! Save the seekers ! By thy glory at the Father's side, we beseech thee, save men ! Do you believe that Christ Jesus is at the right hand of God ? If you do, all things are possible with him, and he has promised to hear prayer. Hear me then ye thousands of Israel, as I entreat you now to breathe one hearty unanimous prayer to this effect—" Save now, O Lord, we beseech thee." Put the name of your child to the prayer if you please, or that of your wife, or father, or sister, or brother, but do put up the prayer to him who is enthroned on purpose to save. Save now, O Lord. Thou art no more despised and rejected, unveil thy glory by saving men. Thou could'st save even in thine agony: on the cross thou didst save a dying thief; but now in glory thou hast mightier power; therefore, O Saviour, save now. Will you not importunately urge that petition, O ye who know his readiness to hear? Sinners, will you not pray thus for yourselves?

Here now, as we sit together in this dense gloom, so unusual in the month of June, let us feel that the shadow of the Eternal is brooding over us, that the Almighty is now covering us with his wings. Do you not feel near to him? Be ye sure of this, he is very near to you: call upon him while he is near. In all probability we shall in a few moments hear his majestic voice rolling in thunder through the sky, and ere long we shall see the flash of his glittering spear. Let all this deepen our reverence, and prompt us to entreat him now to save us. The God that thunders at his pleasure is near: bow before him and trust in his Son Christ Jesus, and let the prayer go up, "Save now." Do not wait for to-morrow, nor even until the storm has passed over, but *now*, even now, seek his salvation.

The other half of the prayer is for *prosperity*. "O Lord, send now prosperity." This is what we continually need in this church. The prayer is in harmony with the whole passage. Since, Lord, thou hast lifted the chief stone into its place, be pleased to upraise other stones of thy temple into their places; fit them one upon another, and send a prosperous upbuilding. Lord, thou hast conquered all the foes of Christ, come and conquer the foes of thy church to-day. Lord, thou didst gather out a people to his praise and build up a church in the first centuries of Christianity, and then thy Son Jesus was gloriously the corner and head stone; come again and build up thine own church throughout all these lands, a church in which the Lord Jesus shall be exalted even to the highest.

"Send now prosperity." I pray you, beloved, join in this prayer. Pray that Jerusalem may have peace and prosperity, for they that love her and her peace have still felicity. Join in the supplication to the once rejected but now exalted covenant Head of the church, and the Lord will bless you for Jesus Christ's sake. Amen.

The Head of the Church

"He is the head of the body, the church"—Colossians i. 18.

As if to show us that this title of "Head of the church" is to be held in highest esteem, it is here placed in connection with the loftiest honours of our Lord Jesus. In the same breath the Son of God is styled "the image of the invisible God," "the first-born of every creature," the Creator of all existence, and then "the head of the body, the church." We dare not, therefore, think slightly of this title, nor do we hesitate to assert that any levity with regard to it would be as disgraceful as the profane use of any other name of our divine Lord. For any mortal to assume it to himself, we conceive would be equal in blasphemy to the assumption of the mediatorial office; and we should be no more shocked to hear a man claim to be "the creator of all things," than we are now when a mortal is designated, "head of the church."

What is the church? The word signifies an assembly. The church of Jesus Christ is an assembly of faithful men, the whole company of God's chosen, and called out ones, the entire community of true followers of the Lord Jesus Christ. Wherever true believers are, there is a part of the church; wherever such men are not, whatever organisation may be in existence, there is no church of Jesus Christ. The church is no corporation of priests, or confederacy of unconverted men, it is the assembly of those whose names are written in heaven. Any assembly of faithful men is *a* church. The aggregate of all these assemblies of faithful men make up *the* one church which Jesus Christ hath redeemed with his most precious blood, and of which he is the sole and only Head. Part of that church is in heaven, triumphant, part on earth, militant, but these differences of place make no division as to real unity; there is but one church above, beneath. Time creates no separation, the church is always one—one church of the apostles, one church of the reformers, one church of the first century, one church of the latter days, and of this one only church Jesus Christ is the one only Head.

I. WHAT IS MEANT BY OUR LORD'S HEADSHIP OF THE CHURCH? That shall be very briefly our first subject of thought.

We understand this headship to be *the representation of the church* as a body. We speak of counting heads, meaning thereby persons; the head represents the whole body. God has been pleased to deal with mankind as a community, and his great covenant transactions have been with men in a body, and not with separate individuals. That is to say, at the first creation God did not so much deal with each particular person of the human race, as with the whole race represented in one man, namely, the first Adam. It was so ordained that the race should be bound up in his loins, to stand if he stood, to fall if he fell. Hence, my brethren, the fall, hence original sin, hence the sorrows of this life. In order to salvation, which, perhaps, was only possible because we did not fall singly (for the devils falling singly and separately are reserved without hope of mercy unto everlasting fire), God instituted a second federation, of which Jesus Christ is the Head. The apostle calls him the second Adam. He is the Head of that company of mankind who are his chosen, his redeemed, who are known in this world by being led to believe in him, and are ultimately gathered into his rest. Now, Jesus Christ stands to his church in the same position as Adam stood to his posterity. They are chosen in him, accepted in him, and preserved in him: "Saved in the Lord with an everlasting salvation." As his own words declare it, "Because I live, ye shall live also." In the following chapters of the epistle before us, the apostle shows that the saints are buried with Jesus, risen with him, and quickened with him. Even more explicit is he in the fifth of the Romans, where the headship of Adam and of Jesus are compared and contrasted.

Our Lord is Head in *a mystical sense,* explained in Colossians ii. 19: " The Head, from which all the body by joints and bands having nourishment ministered, and knit together, increaseth with the increase of God." The head is to the body indispensable to life; it is the seat of mental life, the temple of the soul; even so Jesus Christ is the vitalising Head of all his people. " He is our life." " In him was life, and the life was the light of men." The life of every member of the mystical body depends upon the life of the mystical Head. Through Jesus Christ every living child of God derives his spiritual life. Not one true member of the church lives by a life of his own. "For ye are dead, and your life is hid with Christ in God." Separation from Christ is spiritual death, "If a man abide not in me, he is cast forth as a branch, and is withered." The head mystically is not merely the source of life and the seat of sensation, but it is the throne of supreme government. It is from the brain that the mandate is issued which uplifts the hand or bids it fall by the side. Man walks or speaks, or sleeps, or rises from his couch, according to the dictate of that mysterious royal something which finds a place for itself within the head. Thus in the true church of God, Jesus Christ is the great directing Head; from him the only binding commands go forth; to him all the really spiritual yield a cheerful homage. His members delight to do the will of their Head. The whole fabric of the church actuated by his life, being filled with his Spirit, most readily concedes to him that in all things he shall have the pre-eminence. In proportion as Christians are truly united to Jesus they are perfectly governed by him, and it is only because of the old nature which abideth in separation from Christ that believers offend and transgress. In so far as they are spiritual men, so far doth Jesus rule them as the head governeth all the members of the body. The head is also the glory of the body. There the chief beauty of manhood dwells. The divine image is best seen in the countenance; the face is the distinguishing glory of man. Man holds his head erect; his countenance is not turned towards the earth like the beast, it glows with intelligence, it is the index of an immortal mind. Beauty chooses as her favoured seat the features of the countenance; majesty and tenderness, wisdom and love, courage and compassion, here hang out their ensigns; all the graces choose the head as their favoured dwelling-place. In this sense right well is our Lord saluted as the "Head." He is fairer than the children of men: grace is poured into his lips. In Jesus Christ all the beauty of the church is summed up. What were all his church without him? A carcase, a ghastly corpse, bereft of all its glory, because divided from its head. What were all the good, and great, and excellent men who have ever lived without Christ? So many ciphers upon a writing table—they count for nothing until their Lord, as the great unit, is put before them to give them power and value; then indeed they swell to a mighty sum, but without him they are less than nothing and vanity. An uncomely thing would be the church of God if she were not comely with the comeliness which Jesus imparts to her? His head is as the most fine gold, his countenance is as Lebanon, excellent as the cedars; he is the chief among ten thousand, and the altogether lovely—glorious is that body of which he is the crown and excellence. Well may the church be called the fairest among women, when her Head thus excelleth all the beauties of earth and heaven.

Another figure which is used to describe the headship of Christ to the church is *the conjugal*. As the Lord made Eve out of the flesh of Adam, so hath he taken the church out of the side of Christ Jesus, and she is of him as Eve was of Adam—she is of his flesh and of his bones. A mysterious union has been established between Christ and his church, which is constantly compared to that of marriage: "For the husband is the head of the wife, even as Christ is the head of the church: and he is the saviour of the body." Jesus is the bridegroom; his church is his bride. They are espoused one to another; in bonds of love they are bound for ever to each other; and they are alike with sacred expectation waiting for the marriage-day, when shall be accomplished the eternal purpose of God and the desire of the Redeemer. As the husband exercises a headship in the house, not at all (when the relationship is rightly carried out) tyrannical or magisterial, but a government founded upon the rule of nature and endorsed by the consent of love, even so Jesus Christ ruleth in his church, not as a despotic lord, compelling and constraining his subject bride against her will, but as a husband well beloved, obtaining obedience voluntarily from the heart of the beloved one, being in all things so admired and had in esteem as to win an undisputed pre-eminence. Such conjugal headship is illustrated by the word of God in the old prophecy, "Thou shalt call me Ishi, and shalt call me no more Baali." Baali and Ishi both mean lord, but the sense differs; the one is a mere ruler, the other a beloved husband. Jesus Christ's kingdom is no tyranny; his sceptre is not made of iron; he rules not with blows and curses, and threats, but his sceptre is of silver and his rule is love. The only chains he uses are the chains of his constraining grace; his dominion is spiritual, and extends over willing hearts who delight to bow before him and to give him the honour due unto his name. These, I think, are the senses in which this word "headship" is used, but there remains one other, these former all qualifying this last, upon which I intend to dwell at some length this morning.

Christ is the Head of his church as *King in Zion*. In the midst of the church of God the supreme government is vested in the person of

Christ. "One is your Master, even Christ, and all ye are brethren." The church is the kingdom of God among men. It is purely spiritual, comprehending only spiritual men, and existing only for spiritual objects. And who is its King? None but Jesus. We can truly say, as they did of old, who proclaimed the kingship of the Crucified, "We have another King, one Jesus." To him the assemblies of the saints pay all regal honour, and at his throne the entire church boweth itself, saluting him as Master and Lord. To no other do we render spiritual obeisance. Christ only and solely is King upon Zion's hill, set there by eternal decree, maintained in that position by infinite power, and appointed to remain upon the throne till every enemy shall be made his footstool. I wish I had eloquence this morning, that I might bear worthy witness to the crown-rights of King Jesus in his church, for I know no subject which it is more necessary to insist upon in these eventful times. Let Jesus be owned as the only Head of the church, and the way out of the present political debate which agitates our nation is clear enough. Ignorance of this truth blinds many, and makes them labour with all their heart for a bad cause, under the notion that they are doing God service. To know this truth is to hold a most weighty trust, with which we must not trifle. Martyrs have bled for this truth, Scotland's heather has been stained in ten thousand places, and her waters have been dyed crimson for the defence of this weighty doctrine. Let us not be slow with unshaken courage to declare yet again that kings and princes and parliaments have no lawful jurisdiction over the church of Jesus Christ, that it beseems not the best of monarchs to claim those royal prerogatives which God has given to his only begotten Son. Jesus alone is the Head of his spiritual kingdom, the church; and all others who come within her pale to exercise power are but usurpers and Antichrist, and not for one moment to be respected in their usurped authority by the true church of the living God. Some churches have not learned this lesson, but are held in leash like dogs by their masters; they crouch down at the feet of the state to eat the crumbs which fall from Mammon's table; and if they are cuffed and beaten by the powers that be, well do they deserve it; and I would almost pray that the whip may fall upon them yet more heavily, till they learn to appreciate liberty, and are willing to take off the dog collar of the State, and be free from human domination. If they lose a little wealth, they will win the solid gold of God's own favour, and the abiding power of his Spirit, which they cannot expect to have while they are traitors to King Jesus, and own not the sole and only headship of Immanuel in the church.

II. We shall now, therefore, in the second place, come to look a little into this headship of Jesus Christ in a regal sense, as to WHAT IT IMPLIES.

Since Christ is the Head of his body, the church, he alone can determine doctrines for her. Nothing is to be received as divinely warranted except it cometh with his stamp upon it. It is nothing, my brethren, to the faithful servant of Jesus Christ that a certain dogma comes down to him with the grey antiquity of the ages to make it venerable. Like a sensible man, the Christian respects antiquity, but like a loyal subject of his King, he does not so bow before antiquity as to let it become ruler in Zion instead of the living Christ. A multitude of good men may meet together, and they may, in their judgment, propound a dogma, and assert it to be essential and undoubted, and they may even threaten perils most abundant to those who receive not their verdict; but if the dogma was not authorised long before they decided it—if it was not written in the Book, the decision of the learned council amounts to nothing. All the fathers, and doctors, and divines, and confessors, put together, cannot add a word to the faith once delivered unto the saints: yea, I venture to say, that the unanimous assent of all the saints in heaven and earth would not suffice to make a single doctrine binding upon conscience unless Jesus had so determined. In vain do men say, " So did the early church "—the early church has no supremacy over us. It is to no purpose to quote Origen or Augustine: quote the inspired apostles, and the doctrine is established, but not otherwise. In the church of God it is never sufficient to say, " So thinks Martin Luther." Who was Martin Luther? A servant of Jesus Christ, and nothing more. It is not sufficient to say, " So teacheth John Calvin," for who is John Calvin? Hath he shed his blood for you, or is he your master? His opinion is to be respected as the opinion of your fellow servant, but in no respect as a doctor or authoritative teacher in the church—for Christ alone is Rabbi, and we are to call no man Master upon earth. Suppose I have received a truth from the very man who was the means of my conversion; I am bound, in candour and affection, to give all respect to him because of the relationship which exists between us, but I must take heed lest this decline into idolatry, and I myself become nothing more than a receiver of truth as the word of man, instead of accepting it as the word of God. I am, therefore, in the most candid manner, but none the less solicitously, to bring to the test every truth which I have received, whether from my father or mother, or my minister, or from some great man of olden times, whose name I have learned to respect; seeking all the while light from above to direct me aright. Nothing is doctrine to the church of God—nothing which has not been taught in the Scriptures. To Christians it is nothing to say that certain doctrines are taught in books of common prayer, or of conference discipline, or of systematic theology; to us it is of small account that either Presbytery, or the Episcopacy, or Independency, have put their stamp upon a certain form of teaching. Authority is no more to us than the snap of a man's finger, unless the truth thus commended derives certainty from the testimony of Jesus Christ himself, who is the Head of his body the church.

So next, since he is the Head, he only can legislate as to the church. In a state, if any knot of persons should profess to make laws for the kingdom, they would be laughed at; and if they should for a moment attempt to enforce their own rules and regulations in defiance of the laws of the country, they would be amenable to punishment. Now the church of God hath no power whatever to make laws for herself, since she is not her own head; and no one has any right to make laws for her, for no one is her head but Christ. Christ alone is the law-maker of the chu ch, and no rule or regulation in the Christian church standeth for anything unless in its spirit at least it hath the mind of Christ to support and back it up. Such-and-such a thing has been thought to be right in the church, and therefore it has been laid down, and made prescriptive; the tradition of the fathers has established a certain custom. What then? Why this—that if we can distinctly see that the custom and prescription are not according to the tenor of holy

Scripture, and the spirit of Christ, neither of them are anything to us. But what if the custom be supported by all the good men of every age? I say that matters nought if the Lord hath not taught it. Our conscience is not to be bound. If a law were backed up by fifty thousand times as many as all the saints, it would have no authority upon the conscience even of the weakest Christian if not laid down by our King himself; and the violation of such a commandment of men would be no sin, but might indeed become a Christian duty in order to let men see that we are not the servants of men, but the servants of Jesus Christ the Lord. In spiritual things it is of the utmost importance to keep this fact clear, that nonconformity is only sinful when it refuses to conform to the will of Christ; and conformity itself is a great sin when it obeys a rule which is not of the Lord's ordaining. When we meet together in church-meeting we cannot make laws for the Lord's kingdom; we dare not attempt it. Such necessary regulations as may be made for carrying out our Lord's commands, to meet for worship, and to proclaim the gospel, are commendable, because they are acts needful to obedience to his highest laws; but even these minor details are not tolerable if they clearly violate the spirit and mind of Jesus Christ. He has rather given us spiritual guidances than legal rubrics and fettering liturgies, and he has left us at liberty to follow the directions of his own free Spirit; but if we make a regulation, thinking it to be very wise, if it be contrary to the Spirit of our Lord, the rule is itself evil, and is not to be borne with; in such a case the church has trenched upon the rights of her Head, and has done what she ought not to have done; she has, in effect, snatched from his hand the sceptre, and set up a schism. Law-making in the church was finished in that day when the curse was pronounced on him who should take from or add to the word of God. Christ alone is the legislator of his church—none but he.

But I go further, and venture to say that Christ is not only the legislator of the church, and has left to us his Statute-book, sufficient to guide us in every dilemma, but he is also the living administrator in the church. He is not here, it is true, but as monarchs often administrate through lieutenants, so the Lord Jesus administereth through his ever living Spirit, who dwells in the hearts of his people. You are not to think of Christ as of one who is dead and buried. If he were here on earth I suppose nobody would claim to be the head of the church but himself. His presence would at once overawe every pretender; and now, though he is not here in person, yet he is not dead. He liveth, he sitteth on the throne prepared for him at the right hand of the Father. In spirit he is here. "Lo! I am with you alway, even unto the end of the world." And what must the true Head of the church think when he sees another put up into his throne, and impiously called by his title! What must the living Head moving in the midst of the church feel in regard to such a blasphemous intrusion as that? He, the Holy Ghost, is the Vicegerent of Christ, the representative of the absent Son of Man. But how does this Spirit administrate the laws of God? I answer, through his people, for the Holy Ghost dwells in true believers; and when they meet together as the Lord's servants, and ask his guidance humbly, they may expect to have it—and opening the Statute-book and seeing plain directions as to their course of action, they may be quite sure that what they do has their Master's sanction. If they look first of all for the direction in their Lord's Law-book, and next seek to be instructed as to its meaning by the Holy Spirit, though they be many minds, they shall be led as one man to choose that course of action which shall be after the mind of Christ. Acting humbly and obediently, not on their own authority, but in the authority of Jesus Christ, who by his Spirit still rules in his church, believers practically show Christ still to be the only Head of his church as to actual administration as well as to legislation.

The sole authority of Jesus Christ in all respects must be maintained rigorously, but churches are very apt to be guided by something else. Some would have us guided by results. We have heard a discussion upon the question whether or no we should continue missionary operations, since there are so few converted! How can the question ever be raised while the Master's orders run thus—" Go ye into all the world, and preach the gospel to every creature"? Spoken by the mouth of Jesus our ruler, that command stands good, and the results of missions can have no effect upon loyal minds either one way or the other as to their prosecution. If from this day for the next ten thousand years not a single soul should be converted to God by foreign missions, if there still remained a church of Christ, it would be her duty with increasing vigour to thrust her sons forward into the mission field; because her duty is not measured by the result, but by the imperial authority of Christ. Equally so the church is not to be regulated by the times. We are told by some that this age requires a different kind of preaching from that of a hundred years ago; and that two hundred years ago, in the Puritanic times, doctrines were suitable which are exploded now; the minister must keep abreast of the age; this is a thoughtful and philosophic period, and the preacher must therefore philosophise, and bring forth his own thinking rather than " mere declamation," which is the learned name for a plain declaration of the gospel of Jesus Christ. But, sirs, it is not so; our King is the same, and the doctrines he has given us have not been changed by his authority, nor the rules he has laid down reversed by his proclamation; he is the same yesterday, to-day, and for ever; let the times be polished or uncouth, let them become philosophical or sink into barbarism, our duty will be still the same, in solemn loyalty to Jesus Christ, to know nothing among men save Jesus Christ and him crucified. But the discoveries of science, we are told, have materially affected belief, and therefore we should change our ways according as philosophy changes. No, it must not so be. This is a stumbling stone and a rock of offence against which he who stumbleth shall be broken. We have the same King still, the same laws still, the same teaching of the word still, and we are to deliver this teaching after the same sort and in the same spirit. *Semper idem* must be our motto—always the same, always keeping close to Jesus Christ and glorifying him, for he and not the times, not the philosophy and not the wit of man, must rule and govern the church of God. If we shall do this, if any church shall do this, namely, take its truth from Jesus' lips, live according to Jesus' word, and go forward in his name, such a church cannot by any possibility fail, for the failure of such a church would be the failure of the Master's own authority. Brethren, he has told us if we keep his commandments, we shall abide in his love. He will be with us always, even to the end of the world, and he has given to his church his Holy Spirit according to the fulness of those words which he uttered when he breathed on his apostles, "Whosoever sins ye remit, they are remitted unto them; and whosoever sins ye retain, they are retained;" so that a church acting for Christ, with his authority denouncing the judgments of God upon sin, shall find those judgments follow; and opening the treasure-house of God's mercy to those who seek Jesus Christ by faith, those treasures shall be freely given according to the church's declaration, which she made in her Master's name. Go in her own name, and she faileth; go in her Lord's name, and she succeedeth. Take with her his sign manual, walk in obedience to his Statute-book, and deliver herself from the lordship of men, and the church's history shall be written in some such lines as these, "Fair as the moon, clear as the sun, and terrible as an army with banners."

I have in these words, I am afraid, rather confusedly stated what I believe Scripture teacheth with regard to the headship of Christ, namely, that he is the only teacher of doctrine, the only maker of spiritual laws, that he is the living administrator of the laws of his own spiritual kingdom, and therefore that no authority is to be yielded unto the church, but that of Christ; and when we have that authority, and are obedient to it, we need entertain no fear as to the result.

III. Thirdly, ON WHAT DOES THIS HEADSHIP REST?

Very briefly, it rests on the natural supremacy of Christ's nature. Who could be head but Jesus? For he is perfect man, which we are not. He is the first-born among many brethren, and we are but the younger and weaker. He is God over all, blessed for ever and ever. Surely, none but he should be king in Zion, since there is no part of the church which is divine except its glorious Head. The headship of Christ is the inevitable and necessary result of his work. Hear how his members sing—

> "Thou hast redeemed our souls with blood,
> Hast set the prisoners free;
> Hast made us kings and priests to God,
> And we shall reign with thee."

Who could be head but he to whom such praise can be awarded? He has washed us in his blood—he must be Head. He has loved us from before the foundation of the world, he must be chief. His right hand and his holy arm hath gotten him the victory—let him be crowned King of kings and Lord of lords. That wine-press wherein he trod his enemies alone, till his garments were dyed with blood, was the guarantee to him that he should sit on his Father's throne and reign for ever and ever.

Moreover, the decree of God has decided this beyond dispute. Read the second Psalm, and learn that when the kings of the earth stood up, and the rulers took counsel together against the Lord and against his anointed, the Lord sitting in the heavens laughed at their conspiracy, and scorned the gathering of his foes, "Yet," saith he, "have I set my my king upon my holy hill of Zion. I will declare the decree: the Lord hath saith unto me, Thou art my Son; this day have I begotten thee." How gloriously the promise reads: "Ask of me, and I shall give thee the heathen for thine inheritance, and the uttermost parts of the earth for thy possession. Thou shalt break them with a rod of iron; thou shalt dash them in pieces like a potter's vessel." It is part of the eternal purpose which constituted the church that Christ should be made its Head; and if there be a church of the living God, it is also inevitable that of that church Christ should be the sole Head. Moreover, brethren, and but once more, is not our Lord the Head of the church by universal acclamation and consent of all the members of that church? We have never set up a rival candidate; no heart renewed by his grace can desire any other king.

> "Let him be crowned with majesty
> Who bow'd his head to death;
> And be his honours sounded high
> By all things that have breath."

Rivals in his blood-bought dominion? Rivals against the Son of David! Let them be swept away as the smoke; let them be as driven stubble to his bow! King Jesus! All hail! Long live the King! Bring forth the royal diadem! See you not how the angels crown him? Hark ye not to the songs of cherubim and seraphim, "For thou art worthy, thou art worthy to take the book, and loose the seven seals thereof"? Hear ye not the everlasting chant of those who have overcome through his blood, "Thou art worthy, thou art worthy, for thou wast slain, and hast redeemed us unto God by thy blood"? while the church on earth joins in the selfsame solemn canticle, "Crown him, crown him, crown him Lord of all, for worthy is the Lamb that was slain." By the supremacy of his nature, by the necessity of his accomplished work, by the decree of the Father, by the universal assent of all the blood-washed, he is the only Head of his own church.

IV. What then, brethren, WHAT THEN DOES THIS CONDEMN?

What does it condemn? It condemns the villanous pretence of a Papal headship. Forsooth, a priest at Rome is the head of the church of Jesus Christ! Well, if the Pope be head of the church—*if he be so*—then see what, according to Scripture, he is. This Pio Nono is this—he is the head of the body, the church "*who is the beginning.*" There was nothing, then, before this aforesaid Pius IX.? "*The first-born from the dead!*" does he claim to have risen from the dead? "*That in all things he might have the pre-eminence;*" is this also the old Italian's right? "For it pleased the Father that in him should all fulness dwell;" blasphemy dares not apply this to the tottering prince whose exchequer needs replenishing with Peter's pence. Yet this is the description of the person who is the Head of the church, and, if Pius IX. be not all that, he is no head of the church. But perhaps he is the second head? Then Christ's church is a monstrous being with two heads. They may make it out to be three one day, perhaps, and then we will call the thing Cerberus, and helldog, and we shall not be far off from the true idea of Popery. Nay, but he is the delegated head. What for? Why should Christ delegate authority which he can wield himself? But we need a delegation, for Christ is absent. But the Holy Spirit is that delegation, and is here. Of all the dreams that ever deluded men, and probably of all blasphemies that ever were uttered, there has never been one which is more absurd and which is more fruitful in all manner of mischief than the idea that the Bishop of Rome can be the head of the church of Jesus Christ. No; these popes die, and are not; and how could the church live if its head were dead? The true Head ever liveth, and the church ever liveth in him.

But it is affirmed that there must needs be a visible headship, and just now we are told every day that we must choose in church matters between the headship of the monarch of England and the headship of the pope at Rome. I beg the gentlemen's pardon, we have no such choice, for when we are asked which we will have to rule us in spiritual things, we say, "Neither—neither for a single moment." We make no bones about the matter, kings and queens are no heads of the church to us. We will no more brook spiritual domination from an English premier than from a Romish pope; we are equally opposed to both—all human headship must go down. To our well beloved queen all honour and reverence as to one of the best of rulers in civil affairs, but in spiritual affairs in the church of Christ she has no ruling power; what she may have *in the church of England* is another question. To us it makes no matter whether it be man or woman, whether it be prince or priest, we will have neither czar, emperor, queen, pope, seraph or angel, to reign in the church of Jesus Christ. The church hath no lawful governor or supreme Lord but Jesus Christ himself. Our Lord, as it seems to me, puts this so plainly in the word, that I marvel men who believe in the Bible should think the state could be at the head of the church. The state-church party have placed a Bible with a crown and a sceptre upon their bills! It is suggestive that the Bible is closed, for if Englishmen were once to read it, it would be fatal to the cause which now claims it, since one of the truths they would read would be this, "My kingdom is not of this world;" and they would hear Christ say, " Render unto Cæsar the things which are Cæsar's"—that is, yield all civil obedience to the civil authority, "but unto God the things that are God's." Leave the Lord to rule in the kingdom of mind and spirit, and let Cæsar keep his kingdom of civil government; let the state do its work and never interfere with the church, and let the church do her work and never interfere with, or be interfered with, by the state. The two kingdoms are separate and distinct. Broad lines of demarcation are always drawn, throughout the whole of the New Testament, between the spiritual and the temporal power, and the mischief is when men cannot see this. Christ is the head of the church, not any one who represents the state. Brethren, just think for a minute what mischief this doctrine of the headship of the state has done. Time was when men could hardly be parish beadles, without coming to take the Sacrament at the established church. Oh! the multiplied hypocrisies which were perpetrated every day by graceless men who came to qualify themselves for office by taking the emblems of our holy faith when they knew not Christ! Such things are more or less inevitable to the system. Think, again, what persecutions have risen out of this error. You cannot put any sect into a position of ascendancy but it falls into persecution; all sects have persecuted in turn when so tempted. There is not a pin to choose between one and the other, except, as I sometimes say, the Baptists have never persecuted, because they have never had an opportunity; but I will not insist even upon that. It is in human nature to do ill when the civil arm is ready to crush conscience, and therefore Christ has taken the temptation out of the way, and put it out of the possibility of his people, if they keep close to his rule, so much as to touch the carnal weapon. The weapons of their warfare, he tells them, are not carnal but spiritual, and therefore mighty through God to the pulling down of strongholds.

What a degradation to the church of Christ to think of having any other head but Christ! Ah! brethren, if the monarch were the most holy and godly person that ever lived, I should tremble for him exceedingly that such a person should in any sense be styled the head of the church. How could such a person pray? How could a poor sinner—and such the best man still is—come before Christ and pray to him and say, "Lord, thou knowest I am the head of thy church"? It seems to me to be such an atrocious claim, such a horrible profanity! I would not, for twice ten thousand worlds, touch that title with so much as the tip of my finger, if I hoped to be saved. I dare not expose my friend, or even my enemy, to the awful risk he must run in assuming such a title. I judge no one, God forbid I should; but if I saw in this world a man absolutely perfect, full of divine knowledge and light, and I were asked by him, "Shall I assume that title?" I should go down on my knees and say, "For God's sake, and for your own soul's sake, touch it not, for how can you, with your light, and knowledge, and love to Christ, take from him one of his grandest names?" But what shall I say when the monarch is the opposite? And such cases have occurred. I need not take you far back in history. The name of George IV. has no remarkable odour of sanctity about it; and the same may be said of Charles II.—I never heard historians say that he was eminent in godliness. But yet these men were heads of the church! I shudder at being compelled to remember such an infamous fact. Men, whose character is not to be thought of without a blush on the cheek of modesty, were heads of the church of Jesus Christ! God have mercy on this land for having fallen so low as this, for I know not that heathen countries have ever blasphemed God more than we have done in allowing heartless debauchers to take upon themselves the name of "head of the church of Christ." No, my brethren, this cannot be endured by us in any church with which we commune; we repudiate it; we shake off the abomination as Paul shook off the viper from his hand into the fire.

The same rebuke is due to that which has been tolerated in many churches, namely, the headship of great religious teachers. Sometimes great teachers while yet alive have been practically regarded as the supreme arbiters of the church. Their will was law, apart from the Book; their decree stood fast, apart from the Scripture. All this was evil. There are certain churches at this day which reverence extremely the names of dead men. "The Fathers"—are they not by some thought to be as great as the apostles? and the names of John Wesley, and John Calvin, and others, I fear very often occupy the place which belongs to Jesus Christ. Let every church of Jesus Christ now declare that she follows not men but obeys her Master alone.

Mark you, brethren, the truth which I have brought out somewhat strongly equally applies to the church itself, for the church is not her own head, she has no right to act upon her own judgment, apart from the statutes of her King; she must come to the Book—everything is there for her. She has no right to use her own judgment apart from the Master. She must go to the Master. She is a servant, and the Master is supreme. The church's power is twofold. It is a power to testify to the world what Christ has revealed. She is set as a witness, and she must act as such. She has, next, a ministerial power, by which she carries out the will of Christ, and doeth his bidding as Christ's servant and minister. A certain number of servants meet in the servants' hall; they have an order given to do such work, and they have also orders given them how to do it. They then consult with each other as to the minor details, how they can best observe the master's rule and do his bidding. They are perfectly right in so doing. But suppose they began to consult about whether the objects proposed by the master were good, or whether the rules which he had laid down might not be altered! They would at once become rebellious, and be in danger of discharge. So a church met together to consult how to carry out the Master's will, how to enforce his laws, does rightly; but a church meeting to make new laws, or a church meeting to rule according to its own judgment and opinion, imagining that its decision will have weight, has made a mistake, and placed itself in a false position. The one doctrine which I have sought to bring forward is this, that he alone who bought the church, and saved the church, is to rule the church; and surely our hearts, without exception, bow to this.

V. But if so, WHAT IS THE LESSON WHICH IT TEACHES TO EACH ONE HERE?

Does not it make each of you enquire, "If the entire church is thus to yield obedience to Christ, and to no one else, am I yielding such obedience? I claim to be a Christian, but am I a Christian of that prejudiced sort who follow that which they are brought up to, and so acknowledge the rules of mothers and fathers instead of the rule of Christ? Have I brought what I avow to be truth to the touchstone of Scripture? Did I ever spend a quarter of an hour in weighing my cherished opinions?" I am afraid the great mass of Christians have never done this, but have sucked in their religion with their mother's milk, and nothing further.

Again, if I be a Christian, am I in the habit of judging what I ought to do by my own whims and wishes, or do I judge by the Statute-book of the King? Many say they do not like this and do not like that, as if that had anything to do with it! What are your likes and dislikes? You are a servant, and bound to give up your own will to the Master. If Christ gives a command, which you imagine to be hard because it does not chime in with your love of ease—my brother, will you not, as a servant of the Master, put your whims aside and endeavour to follow him? Oh, it is a blessed life to lead, to be no longer the servant of men and of self, but to go to Christ daily in prayer, and say, "What I know not, teach thou me." Then you may laugh at Satan's rage, and face a frowning world, for the Master will never leave those who cleave to him. If a man loves the testimonies and commandments of the Most High, God shall be his buckler, his shield, and his high tower; but if he turns aside to his own imaginings, his fall shall be certain. The Lord keep the church in this matter, and her day of victory shall soon come. May Christ be her only Head, and her triumph draweth near. I can see the morning breaking; yonder are the first streaks of light upon the sky: the Master is coming because the church begins to own him—and then shall her happy days begin, and the days of her mourning shall be ended for ever and ever.

Victor Emmanuel, Emancipator

"To open the blind eyes, to bring out the prisoners from the prison, and them that sit in darkness out of the prison house"—Isaiah xlii. 7.

ON a former occasion we contemplated the unconverted man as being bound by the cords of his sins. It was a very solemn and sorrowful topic. I trust it humbled us all, and made those of us whom the Son has made free, feel renewed gratitude for the glorious liberty of the children of God. Sad was the spectacle of the dungeon and the fetters, and the felon bound therewith, a man, a brother, the image of ourselves. It is a great relief to turn to another subject akin to that, but full of cheerfulness and joy. We showed you the prisoner: we have now to speak of him who came to set the prisoners free. We decribed the captive's cords and bonds; we have now to tell you of him whose mighty touch liberates the bond-slaves, and signs the Magna Charta of eternal emancipation. The case of manhood bound like Prometheus to the rock, and preyed upon by the vulture of hell, appeared utterly hopeless, and the more so because the prisoner was his own fetter, and disdained to be free. After all that has been done for man, by the tenderness of God, the simplicity of the gospel, and the clear and plain command; yes, and after all the thunders of threatening, followed by the wooing notes of mercy, the captive continues still the willing slave of sin, and his liberation appeares utterly hopeless. But things impossible with men are possible with God, and where human agency fails, divine agency delights to illustrate its own extraordinary energy. We gladly survey at this time the effectual operations of Jesus the Saviour, the true Victor Emmanuel, who comes to set men free from the bondage of their sins, to whose name be honour and glory world without end.

I. Looking at the first verses of this chapter, we shall consider WHO IT IS THAT SENDS JESUS CHRIST TO ACCOMPLISH THE LIBERATION OF THE SONS OF MEN, because much will depend upon the liberator's credentials, the authority by which he is warranted, and the power by which he is backed.

We sing for joy of heart as we see that the Infinite God himself commissioned the Lord Jesus to be the deliverer of men; and he did this, first, *in his capacity as Creator.* Read the fifth verse, and behold the great author of the Redeemer's commission: "Thus saith Jehovah, he that created the heavens, and stretched them out; he that spread forth the earth, and that which cometh out of it." He, then, who spared not his own Son, but sent him forth on the embassage of love, is Jehovah, who has made the heavens a pavilion of azure, gilded with the sun, and bedecked with stars; the self-same all-sustaining One who bears up the pillars of the universe, and impels the earth in its majestic circuit. He who gave its lustre to every precious stone from the mine, its life to every blade of grass, its fruit to every tree, its motion to every beast and winged fowl—for all these may be said to come out of the earth; he it is who sent the Incarnate God to open the two-leaved gates, and cut the bars of iron asunder, that the slaves of Satan might escape from the thraldom of their sins. Jesus, the Son of God, comes armed with the power of the Creator himself. Rejoice, then, ye that are lost, for surely the power which spake all things out of nothing, can new-create you, though there be nought of good within you to aid the godlike work. Rejoice, ye that are marred and broken, like vessels spoiled upon the potter's wheel, your great Creator puts his hand a second time to the work, and resolves to form you for himself that you may show forth his praise. He by whom you were made in secret, and curiously wrought in the lowest parts of the earth, is able by his mysterious working to create in you a new heart, and infuse into you a right spirit. Is there not hope for the dark chaos of your fallen nature, and that heart of yours which is now without-form and void? Is anything too hard for the Lord? Is there any restraint of his power? It is true your fellow-creatures, be they exalted never so highly by office or character, cannot regenerate you, the very idea is blasphemy against the prerogative of him who alone can create or destroy; but where the will of man, and blood, and birth all fail, the Spirit of the Lord achieves the victory. Thus saith the Lord, "Behold, I create new heavens and a new earth: and the former shall not be remembered, nor come into mind. But be ye glad and rejoice for ever in that which I create: for, behold, I create Jerusalem a rejoicing, and her people a joy." What has John written in the book of his vision? Is it not to the same purpose? He that sat upon the throne saith, "Behold, I make all things new." He who made the light can open your eyes. He who bade the rivers flow, can open springs of penitence within your souls. He who clothed the earth with verdure, can make your barren minds fruitful to his praise. If he piled yon Alpine summits, balanced the clouds which float about them, and formed the valleys which laugh at their feet, he can yet create within the little world of man thoughts that aspire to heaven, desires that ascend to the realms of purity, and good works which are the fair products of his Spirit. Has the Creator sent forth a liberator to captive men? Then is there hope indeed!

He who sent forth the Lord Jesus as his Elect One to restore our fallen race, also describes himself as *the life giver;* for returning to the fifth verse of the chapter before us, we read, "He that giveth breath unto the people upon it, and spirit to them that walk therein." The Lord creates animal life: he puts breath into the nostrils of men and beasts; he gives also mental life—the life which thinks, imagines, doubts, fears, understands, desires. All life comes from the central fountain of self-existence in the great I Am, in whom we live, and move, and have our being. This Eternal One, who has life in himself, has sent forth his Son to give life to those who are dead in trespasses and sins, and he has girded him with his own power, "For as the Father hath life in himself; so hath he given to the Son to have life in himself." It is by the word of Jesus that the dead shall rise, "for the hour is coming, in the which all that are in the graves shall hear his voice, and shall come forth." Arrayed in such life-giving power no case of human corruption can be beyond the Redeemer's skill; even those who rot, like Lazarus, shall come forth when he calls them, and the bonds of death and hell shall be loosed. Thus saith the Lord of life: "Verily, verily, I say unto you, He that heareth my word, and believeth on him that sent me, hath everlasting life, and shall not come into condemnation; but is passed from death unto life." The vision of Ezekiel's valley has become a fact since Jesus has appeared; and it is no marvel that it should be so, since the Eternal and Ever-living God has sent him. He can breathe the Holy Spirit into the dead soul, and give the heart that palpitates with penitence, and leaps with desires after God. He can give eyes to the blind and feet to the lame. All that belongs to life he can bestow—the hearing ear, the speaking tongue, the grasping hand. The great obstacle in his way is spiritual death, and as with a word he can remove it, the salvation of man is no longer a difficulty. Rejoice, ye heavens; and be glad, O earth; for among the graves of our sins, and into the very charnel-house of our corruption, the Quickener has descended, and is quickening whomsoever he will.

Nor is this all; for he who sent the Redeemer is represented in the sixth verse as *the faithful God.* "I the Lord have called thee in righteousness;" that is to say, the God who sends Christ the Saviour is not one who plays with words, and having given a promise to-day, retracts it to-morrow. "He is not a man, that he should lie; neither the son of man, that he should repent." Immutable are his promises and purposes, for they are founded in righteousness. He who has commissioned his chosen messenger is not unrighteous to forget his word. Hath he said, and shall he not do it? Hath he spoken, and shall it not come to pass? Hence, my dear brethren, every gospel promise has the stamp of the divine righteousness upon it, that you may know it to be true. Jesus assures us that, if we believe in him, we shall be delivered. God, who cannot lie, sets his seal to the promise. "He that believeth and is baptised shall be saved," is not only the declaration of Christ, but God himself confirms it. Then, "Amen, so let it be!" The vilest sinner that believeth shall find life and pardon, acceptance and blessedness in Christ Jesus. Thou hast not to deal, O trembler, with one who will interpret his promise at a lower point than thou dost understand it at; but thou hast to deal with One who means more than words can express, whose thoughts are as high above your thoughts, even when enlightened by his Word, as the heavens are above the earth. "Come now, and let us reason together, saith the Lord: though your sins be as scarlet, they shall be as white as snow; though they be red like crimson, they shall be as wool." He who utters these words is the Lord, the faithful Promiser, who has sent forth Christ, not to deceive you with specious pretences, but in very deed and truth to bring abundance of grace to those who trust him.

Reading further in the same verse, you will perceive that the ever-blessed sender of the Lord Jesus is *omnipotent*, for is it not added, "And will hold thine hand, and will keep thee"? By which is meant that God will give to the Mediator all his power. Christ is the power of God. Omnipotence dwells in him who once was slain, but now ever liveth, and he is able to save unto the uttermost them that come unto God by him. In the gospel of Christ there is a putting forth of divine power as manifest as in the creation and in the upholding of the world. Here is our comfort under all the assaults with which the Christian faith is threatened, and under all the disappointments which the Christian church has hitherto undergone; Emmanuel, God with us, is still our strength. We are persuaded that the ultimate victory of the cross is absolutely certain, for "the glory of the Lord shall be revealed, and all flesh shall see it together: for the mouth of the Lord hath spoken it." The creation was a work of omnipotence, and yet it was not accomplished all at once. The Lord could, if he had so willed it, have fashioned this habitable globe in one second of time, and have furnished all its chambers by a single word of his mouth. Instead of this, we have reason to believe that he lingered in the first formation of it, in the beginning, when he created the heavens and the earth; and arranged and disarranged it many times before he came to the final constitution of it in the first six days of time, wherein he modelled it to be a fit abode for man. Even then when he came to the final work, not in one day did he build up chaos into the beautiful house of humanity. Not at first did the firmament divide the waters, or the dry land appear above the seas. Not till the third day did the earth bring forth grass and the herb yielding seed, nor did sun and moon divide the empire of day and night till the fourth day had dawned; while the fowl that fly in the open firmament of heaven, and the living creatures that move in the waters, owned a yet later birth. Everything was gradual. Step by step the Maker advanced, yet was there never anything less than omnipotence in every step of his progress. So, my brethren, the Lord might as easily have converted the whole world to Christ on the day of Pentecost as not, but not so had his decrees appointed. A step was taken in apostolic times, and the light shone forth in darkness; further on, the great division between the heavenly and the earthly became marked and clear, and the church rose like the dry land above the seas of sin, while the plants of the Lord's right-hand planting brought forth their seed and their fruit. Even now the appointed lights make glad the sky, and the time hastens on when the Lord shall more evidently bless his living ones, and say, "Be fruitful, and multiply, and fill the earth;" but all is done by degrees as he appoints. Our impatience would fain stand at the Eternal elbow, and say, "Master, complete thy work, and let our eyes behold the Second Adam in a world restored into a second Eden." But he tarries for awhile, and waits while his great appointed evenings and mornings fill up his week of glorious work. He delights in this noblest labour of his hands, and is not as the hireling who earnestly desireth the shadow that his toilsome task may be ended. He lingers lovingly, and his long suffering is salvation. The Lord's decrees tarry not so long but what in the divine reckoning, and according to the Lord's own estimate, the end will come quickly, but to the presumptuous who dare to say, "where is the promise of his coming?" he seems to linger long. How blessed will be the grand finale of redemption work; then shall the morning stars sing together, and all the sons of God shout for joy. The seventh day of redemption shall eclipse the Sabbath of nature, even as the new heavens and the new earth shall outshine the former: a river purer than Hiddekel shall water the new Eden, the tree of life of richer fruit shall grow in the midst of the garden, and then shall be fulfilled the saying which is written, "Sing, O ye heavens; for the Lord hath done it: shout, ye lower parts of the earth: break forth into singing, ye mountains, O forest, and every tree therein: for the Lord hath redeemed Jacob, and glorified himself in Israel." As we read the promise, "I will hold thine hand, and will keep thee," we see the certainty that the Saviour girt with the allsufficiency of divine strength, will accomplish the work of human salvation. Be of good cheer, O children of God, and comfort yourselves with the belief, "that he shall see his seed, he shall prolong his days, and the pleasure of the Lord shall prosper in his hand." His church has no reason for fear, but every ground of confidence as to her future. Rejoice, O daughter of Zion; for great is the Holy One of Israel in the midst of thee.

> "Fear not, though many a mighty foe
> Against thy walls advance;
> Jehovah's arm will lay them low
> For thy deliverance.
>
> Oh, take him at his royal word,
> That word which cannot lie;
> Thy shield and sword is Israel's Lord,
> Almighty sovereignty."

I know you will tell me, "most men say that the world will end in a few years; is it not written that the Bridegroom cometh quickly?" Yes, but remember that eighteen hundred years ago it was written that he would come quickly, and there have been prophets in all ages who have concluded from this that the end was near, while many believers have been like the Thessalonians, to whom Paul wrote: "Now we beseech you, brethren, by the coming of our Lord Jesus Christ, and by our gathering together unto him, that ye be not soon shaken in mind, or be troubled, neither by spirit, nor by word, nor by letter as from us, as that the day of Christ is at hand." We have been instructed by certain pretended expositors to expect the time of the end for the last seven years, and yet it is possible that it may not arrive for the next seventy thousand years. Perhaps human history, as yet written, is but the first stanza of a wondrous poem, which shall be unfolded page by page for many an age to come, and it may be possible far more rapturous strains of divine mercy and grace in the conversion of men are yet to be read by angels and glorified spirits. If it be so it will still be true that he comes quickly, for what will time be compared with eternity? Even if the space taken up by the world's history be not a brief six thousand years, but sixty thousand times six thousand years, yet will it be but as a drop of a bucket compared with the years of the right hand of the Most High, the lifetime of the Ancient of Days. Fight on hopefully, my brethren, and be not distressed with rumours of times and seasons, but believe ye this, that God is, in Christ Jesus, reconciling the world unto himself, and all the ends of the earth shall see the salvation of our God. Watch daily for the Lord's coming, but yet struggle to advance his empire, for "he shall have dominion also from sea to sea, and from the river unto the ends of the earth." The Lord has not withdrawn his hand from his "elect, in whom his soul delighteth." He will subdue nations before him, he will loose the loins of kings, to open before him the two-leaved gates. With such a deliverer so gloriously upheld, there is no room for fear of failure. Our hope and faith joyfully rest in him to whom the Eternal gives his almightiness wherewith to subdue all things unto himself.

II. We will now advance a little further, the Lord helping us. Having contemplated the glorious One who sent Jesus to the work of man's emancipation, let us, in the second place, consider the SENT ONE HIMSELF.

We have him described in the first verse of this chapter, and the first words which we will select from the description inform us that Jesus is *a chosen one*. "Mine elect, in whom my soul delighteth." God has been pleased to set apart his well-beloved Son to be the Saviour of sinners, and in every way he is most suitable. As man he is supremely adapted for the work; no other of woman born was fitted for the enterprise. Born in a peculiar manner, without taint or blemish, he alone of human kind possessed the holy nature needful to make him God's messenger of love. I tried to show just now that God has girded our Lord with his omnipotence, and this ought to lead every sinner to feel that Christ can save him, for what cannot Omnipotence do? We may not talk of impossibilities or even difficulties when we have almightiness before us. No sinner can be difficult to save, no bonds hard to remove, when God, the Almighty One, comes forth to save. Now look at the other side of the picture, and remember that Christ Jesus was the most suitable person in whom the Father could place the fulness of his saving power. In his complex person he is every way adapted to stand as Mediator between God and man. He who laid help upon one that is mighty, and exalted one chosen out of the people, was guided by infallible wisdom in his choice. None other was so fit as he; in fact there was no other. "Other foundation can no man lay than that is laid." Other door of hope can no man open than that which God has opened in the person of Christ. O sinner, I beseech thee accept what God has wisely chosen. Let God's choice be thy willing choice. At this hour, constrained by the grace of God, say, "If God has chosen the Lord Jesus to be a propitiation for sin, my heart accepts him as the atonement for my sin, feeling that he alone can save me." If thus thou dost elect the Lord's elect One, thou shalt find him precious.

But we are also told in the first verse that the Lord Jesus is *anointed to this work*, as well as a choice one for it. "I have put my Spirit upon him." Now, the Holy Spirit is the greatest of all actors in the world of mind. He it is who can illuminate, persuade, and control the spirits of men. He doeth as he wills with mind, even as in the first creation the Lord wrought as he willed with matter. Now, if Jesus Christ has the fulness of the Holy Spirit resting upon him, it is not supposable that any sinner shall be so desperately enslaved that he cannot set him free. We are about to speak of blind eyes to be opened, but in the light of the Holy Spirit what eye need remain blind? We shall speak of captives to be liberated, but with God's free Spirit to loose him what soul need be bound? Bold men have taught doctrines which have emancipated the minds of their fellows from the slavery of superstition, but the Holy Ghost's teachings deliver minds from bondage of every kind, and make men free before the living God. Trembling sinner, accept Christ as your Saviour; God appoints him; God anoints him. Are not these two reasons sufficient to make him acceptable to your soul?

Furthermore, the Redeemer is spoken of as being *gentle and lowly of heart*, which should commend him much to every lowly and contrite spirit. "A bruised reed shall he not break, and the smoking flax shall he not quench." We need a Saviour who can be touched with the feeling of our infirmities, and Jesus is such. Souls conscious of sin are very tender, and agitated with many fears; to cure a wounded conscience is no fool's work, but fit labour for the most experienced physician. See you, then, how fitted Christ is. He never yet said an unkind word to a soul that desired to find mercy at his hands. In the records of his life you may find him try, but you shall never see him repel, an anxious spirit. When feeble faith could only touch the hem of his garment, yet virtue flowed from him. When the leper said, "Lord, if thou wilt, thou canst make me clean," it was but poor faith, but that faith saved him. Though you cannot yet believe as you would, yet say, "Lord, I believe; help thou mine unbelief," and he will not reject you. Look at the smoking candle-wick which yields no light, but makes much offensive smoke; yet, perchance, a living fire lingers in it, and therefore the tender Saviour will not quench it, but will even fan it to a flame. And that bruised reed, how it mars the music of the pipes; draw it out and break it. So would men do, but not so the sinner's Friend. He makes it perfect yet again, and pours the music of his love through it. O thou who art in thine own esteem utterly worthless, only fit to be thrown away, unfit to live and unfit to die; Jesus Christ, the gentle One, will give thee mercy, if thou seek him, and in giving he will not upbraid thee. O wandering child, Jesus will introduce thee to his Father, who will kiss thee with the kisses of his love, and take off thy rags of sin, and clothe thee with glorious robes of righteousness. Only come thou to him, for he is such an one that he cannot reject thee. "How can I come?" saith one. A prayer will bring thee; an anxious desire will be as a chariot to thee. A trust in him hath brought thee, and Christ is thine, if thou dost now accept him. If thy soul is truly willing to have Christ, Christ hath made thee willing, and has already begun to set thee free. May these thoughts concerning the great Emancipator cheer thee on to confidence in him.

One point more in this direction. The Christ who has come to save the sons of men is *persevering to the last degree.* "He shall not fail, nor be discouraged, till he have set judgment in the earth: and the isles shall wait for his law." Men are unwilling to be saved; they do not desire to be brought out of their prison-houses; but Jesus Christ will not cease to teach, nor cease to seek, nor cease to save, till every one of his elect is redeemed from the ruin of the fall, and until a multitude beyond all count shall surround the Father's throne. I tell thee, soul, if Christ wills to save thee, he will save thee. He will track thy footsteps, wander where thou mayst. If thou shouldest escape time after time, from the arrows of conviction, and plunge again and again into sin, yet will he seek thee out and find thee yet. O delay not, but yield to his power! I pray that he may stretch out his sovereign arm at this moment, and rescue thee from thyself. If thy heart were as adamant, or as the nether millstone, he can dissolve it with a touch. O that the rock-breaking hammer would come down upon thee now! He is mighty to save; may he prove his mightiness in thee!

III. It is time that we expound the text itself, and review THE WORK ITSELF.

According to the text, the Messiah's work of grace is divided into three parts, of which the first is, *to open the blind eyes.* Here is a notable work which brings much glory to our Lord. Man's understanding is perverted from the knowledge of God, from a true sense of sin, from a realisation of divine justice, from a right estimate of salvation. The understanding, which is the eye of the soul, is darkened. But when the anointed Saviour comes, he removes the scales of our mental ophthalmia, and in the light of God we see light, and then the sinner is humbled and bowed down, for he perceives his guilt and the justice of God. Moreover, he is filled with alarm, for he sees the bleeding Saviour bearing Jehovah's wrath, and rightly judges that in every case sin must receive a recompense of wrath; for if sin laid on Christ was punished, how much more must personal sin involve banishment from the presence of the Most High? The sinner is then made to see that the only way in which sin can be removed is through the expiatory sufferings of a substitute. He is led to see that the atonement avails for him upon his believing. He is led to understand what believing is. He *does* believe; he trusts, and then in trusting he is made to see the completeness of pardon, and the glory of the justification which comes to us by faith in Jesus Christ. You may think that this is an easy thing for men to see, trained in the doctrine of it from their childhood, and hearing it incessantly from the pulpit; but, believe me, simple as it seems to be, no man receives it unless it has been given him from heaven. We may say to each one who has seen all this, "Blessed art thou, for flesh and blood hath not revealed it unto thee." Many of us heard the gospel from our childhood, but until the Holy Spirit explained to us what it was to be a sinner, and what it was to believe in Jesus, we did not know even the rudiments of the gospel. We were in darkness ourselves, though the light shone round about us; and well might we be, for our eyes were not opened. When Jesus came we saw it all, and we understood the mystery. Our once blind eyes clearly saw ourselves lost, and Christ suffering instead of us ; we believed in him, our sins disappeared, and we were accepted in the Beloved. My dear friend, if thou art seeking rest, I pray the Lord to open thine eyes to see the simplicities of the gospel. One touch of his finger will make thee wise unto salvation. There is no need for thee to study the twenty-one folio volumes of Albertus Magnus, or even the fifty-two volumes of John Calvin, for the whole secret of the gospel lies in these few words, " Believe and live ;" yet thou canst not open the casket unless the Lord give thee the secret key. It needs an opened eye to see even through a glass window; the clear witness of the gospel is dark to blind eyes.

The next work of the Messiah, according to the text, is *to bring out the prisoners from the prison.* This, I think, relates to the bondage under which a man lies to his sins. Habits of sin, like iron nets, surround the sinner, and he cannot escape their meshes. The man sins, and imagines that he cannot help sinning. How often do the ungodly tell us that they cannot renounce the world, cannot break off their sins by righteousness, and cannot believe in Jesus ? Let all men know that the Saviour has come on purpose to remove every bond of sin from the captive, and to set him free from every chain of evil. I have known men strive against the habit of blasphemy, others against unchaste passions, and many more against a haughty spirit, or an angry temper; and when they have striven manfully but unsuccessfully in their own strength, they have been filled with bitter chagrin that they should have been so betrayed by themselves. When a man believes in Jesus his resolve to become a freeman is to a great extent accomplished at once. Some sins die the moment we believe in Jesus, and trouble us no more; others hang on to us, and die by slow degrees, but they are overcome so as never again to get the mastery over us. O struggler after mental, moral, spiritual liberty, if thou wouldst be free, thine only possible freedom is in Christ. If thou wouldst shake off evil habits or any other mental bondage, I shall prescribe no remedy to thee but this, to commit thyself to Christ the Liberator.

"The gates of brass before him burst,
The iron fetters yield."

Love him, and thou shalt hate sin. Trust him, and thou shalt no more trust thyself. Submit thyself to the sway of the incarnate God, and he will break the dragon's head within thee, and hurl Satan beneath thy feet. Nothing else can do it. Christ must have the glory of thy conquest of self. He can set thee free from sin's iron yoke. He never failed yet, and he never shall. I earnestly entreat any man who desires to break off his sins (and we must break them off or perish by them), to try this divine remedy, and see if it does not give him holy liberty. Ask the thousands who have already believed in Jesus, and their testimony will confirm my doctrine. Faith in the Lord Jesus is the end of bondage and the dawn of freedom.

The last part of this divine work is, *bringing them that sit in darkness out of the prison-house.* This we will refer to those who are truly emancipated, and yet by reason of despondency sit down in the dark dungeon. We have in our pastoral duties constantly to console persons who are free from their sins, having by divine grace got the mastery over them, but yet they are in sadness. The door is open, the bars are broken, but with strange obstinacy of despondency they remain in the cell of fear, in which there is no necessity for them to continue for a moment. They cannot believe that these good things are true to them. They forgiven? They could believe everybody else to be pardoned but themselves. *They* made the children of God? Nay, they could hope for their sisters; they have joy in knowing that their father is a child of God, but as to themselves—can such blessings really fall to the tot of such unworthy ones? We have talked with hundreds of such and tried to console them, but we have only learned our own unskilfulness in the art of consolation. They are rich in inventions for self-torture, ingenious in escaping comfort. But, ah! the blessed Master of our souls, whose business it has been since Adam fell to bind up broken hearts, is never foiled. When his eternal Spirit comes to anoint with the oil of joy, he soon gives beauty for ashes. The mournful sentinel of the night-watches must rejoice when the day breaketh and the Sun of righteousness shines forth.

Although I speak to you in very common-place language, yet the theme is rich. This one thought alone ought to make our hearts dance for joy, to think that the Christ of God undertakes to lift up desponding and despairing spirits into hope and joy once more. I know who will rejoice to hear this. It is yonder good woman, who these many years has been in spiritual bondage. It is yonder young man, who has carried a secret burden month after month. It is yonder aged man, who longs to find Christ ere he gathers up his feet in his dying bed, and who thinks that his hour of grace has passed. Man, it is not so. Christ is still mighty to save. Still doth the message run : " He that believeth on him is not condemned." "Whosoever will, let him take the water of life freely." "Ho, every one that thirsteth, come ye to the waters, and he that hath no money; come ye, buy, and eat; yea, come, buy wine and milk without money and without price." Prisoners of hope, your liberator is near at hand. Trust him and be free. Though it seem a venturesome believing, yet venture on him. He cannot, will not reject you; he will proclaim a jubilee, and set each bondslave free.

See, then, how the great Redeemer blessed us: Jesus the Christ does all things well; he clears the understanding; he breaks the power of sinful habits; he removes the load of despondency; he doth it all. Christ Jesus, Mary's son and Jehovah's son; man, bone of our bone and flesh of our flesh, yet God over all, blessed for ever; he who died on Calvary, whose precious blood is the panacea for all human ills, he it is, and he only, who is the Liberator of our fallen race.

IV. WHAT IS THE DESIGN OF GOD IN ALL THIS?

This question is answered in the next verse to the text: "I am the Lord : that is my name : and my glory will I not give to another." The great end of God in Christ was the manifestation of his own glorious attributes—a simple truth, but big with comfort, for should the sinner who has been an atrocious offender against laws human and divine conceive himself to be an improper subject for the grace of God, I would take him by the hand, and, lest despair drive him to further sin, I would put this truth clearly before him. Where is mercy most glorified? Is it not in passing by the greatest offences? Thou hast great offences; there is room in thee for mercy to be greatly displayed. Where is grace glorified? Is it not in conquering the most violent passions? Thou hast such; grace may therefore be glorified in thee. Why, great sinner, instead of not being a fit subject for grace, I will venture to say that thou art in all respects one of the most suitable. There is elbow-room in thee for grace to work. There is room in thine emptiness for God's fulness. There is a clear stage in thy sinfulness for God's superabounding grace. But you have been a ringleader in the devil's army. Yes, and how can God strike a more telling blow against the hosts of darkness than by capturing you? But you tell me that you are an enormous sinner. How will the Lord of love encourage other sinners to come better than by calling you? For it will be rumoured about among your fellow-sinners:—"Have you heard that such an one is saved?" I know they will jeer, but still, in their secret hearts, they will think it over, and they will say, "How is this?" and they will be led to enquire into the ways of God's grace. A brother told the church, a short time since, a little of his history, and it caused us all to rejoice in sovereign grace. He had lived in all manner of sin and iniquity; his profession had been for some years that of a public runner, and in that course of life he was brought into collision with the scum of society. He was practised, also, in the pugilistic art, and that, we all know, is the very reverse of having an elevating tendency. But he came to the Tabernacle, and here Jesus met with him, and he rejoices now to teach to others the gospel which he once rejected. But what, think you, has he been accustomed to do these three years? Some of our brethren preach in the streets, and he goes with them, and after they have told of what the grace of God can do, he humbly and yet boldly rises and says, "I am a living witness to what grace can do; I can declare to you what God's love has done for me." If the sermon which precedes his little speech has not interested the people, they are quite certain to be struck with his personal testimony, for in some localities many of the street folk know him, and as they look at him they say, "Why, that is old So-and-so. I knew him when he was this and that, and here he is converted;" and his witness-bearing works mightily among his old friends and acquaintances. I say, then, if now I speak to any other who has been a great offender, a drunkard, or what not, if my Master does but set you free and enlist you in his army, there will be such a shout go up in the hosts of Israel as shall make heaven ring, while the Philistines shall tremble, for their Goliath shall be slain, and a new champion raised up from his dead body to fight for the Lord of hosts. If the Lord saved men because of their merits, there would be no hope for great sinners, nor indeed for any one; but if he saves us for his own glory, that he may magnify his grace and his mercy among the sons of men, then none need despair. Up to the very gates of hell would I preach the gospel, and between the jaws of death would I proclaim it. God to glorify his grace sets free the captives, then why should not the most hell-deserving sinner, whose heart is like hardened steel, yet become a monument of Christ's power to save? I remember one who used to say that if God would but have mercy on him he should never hear the last of it, and it may well be the resolve of all of us, that earth and heaven shall never hear the last of our praises if grace shall but save us. As one of our hymns puts it—

> "Then loudest of the crowd I'll sing,
> While heaven's resounding mansions ring
> With shouts of sovereign grace."

Yes, we will each sing loudest, each owing most, each desiring, therefore, to bend the lowest and to praise the most heartily, the grace which has set us free.

Time flies with us; days are rushing past; years are hastening away. How long shall it be ere Christ shall gain your hearts? How long shall ye hear of him, and continue to refuse his grace? How long, ye unconverted ones, will ye hug your chains and kiss your fetters? "Turn ye, turn ye from your evil ways; for why will ye die, O house of Israel?" "Seek ye the Lord while he may be found, call ye upon him while he is near: let the wicked forsake his way, and the unrighteous man his thoughts: and let him return unto the Lord, and he will have mercy upon him; and to our God, for he will abundantly pardon."

The Great Physician and His Patients

"They that be whole need not a physician, but they that are sick"—Matthew ix. 12.

THIS was Christ's apology for mingling with publicans and sinners when the Pharisees murmured against him. He triumphantly cleared himself by shewing that according to the fitness of things he was perfectly in order. He was acting according to his official character. A physician should be found where there is work for him to do, and that it is where healing is required. There was evidently none among the Pharisees, if their own opinion of themselves were to hold good, for they were perfectly whole. There was much to do, according to their own admission, among the publicans and sinners, for they were sore sick; therefore our Lord was in his place, and fittingly executing his office when he sought out those who needed him.

I. We shall have no time for a preface this morning, and therefore let us enter at once into the text by observing that MERCY GRACIOUSLY REGARDS SIN AS A DISEASE.

Sin is more than a disease. If it were only a sickness, men were to be pitied for suffering it; but the element of the perverse will, of voluntary rebellion and designed offence enters into sin, otherwise it were far less truly sin; and this makes it more than a sickness, and worse than a malady. Let us not think that the picture of disease really does set forth all the heinous nature of sin; it is only a generous way in which Mercy chooses to look at it and to deal with it. As Justice views it, all the plague, and venom, and virus, and contagion in the world would be sweet and harmless, compared with one single evil thought or imagination; but Mercy leniently and graciously chooses, in order that it may have a sort of apology for its operations, under the great plan of salvation, to view sin as a disease. It is justified in such a view, for almost everything that may be said of deadly maladies may be said of sin. Let us come to particulars.

Sin is an *hereditary* disease: we are born with a tendency towards it, nay we are born in it. The taint is in our blood: the very centre of our being feels the infection. Born in sin and shapen in iniquity, in sin did our mothers conceive us, and our offspring in like measure received from us that original sin which is part of our fallen nature. Every man born into the world bears within him the seeds of sin, in the bias and current of his mind, nor is this to be wondered at, for "Who can bring a clean thing out of an unclean? Not one." "How can he be clean that is born of a woman?"

Sin, like sickness, *is very disabling*. A sick man cannot carry burdens, climb mountains, run in service, walk with perseverance, or leap for joy. The occupations and the pleasures of other men are things from which he is shut out. Even so does sin prevent our serving God. We cannot pray to him: we cannot praise him aright. In every duty we are weak, and for every good we are feeble.—There is not a single moral power of manhood which sin has not stripped of its strength and glory. If we would run in the way of God's commands, then sin has lamed us; if we would grasp God's promises, evil has paralysed us; if we would see into the mysteries of grace, guilt has blinded us; if we would hear the voice of God, transgression has smitten us with deafness; and if our voices would swell the song of cherubim and seraphim, alas, the plague of our heart within has made us dumb. Of all of us in our measure it may be said through sin, "unstable as water, thou shalt not excel." Sin weakens man's nature for all good.

Sin also, like certain diseases, is a *very loathsome* thing. Some diseases are so extremely disgusting that scarcely can their names be mentioned; but, oh, they are sweetness itself when compared with sin. The most putrid poisonous air that ever blew from a fever hospital, never had such foulness in it as dwells in sin. Pest-houses, and lazar-houses are clean and safe compared with the haunts of vice. In God's esteem, and in the esteem of all holy minds, the most detestable, obnoxious, dreadful thing in the whole world is moral evil. If that could be got rid of, all other evil would cease to be. This is the mother and nurse of all evil, the egg of all mischief, the fountain of bitterness, the root of misery. Here you have the distilled essence of hell; the "quintessence," as the old divines would say of everything that is unlovely, disreputable, dishonest, impure, abominable—in a word—damnable.

Like some diseases, sin is *fearfully polluting*. As the leper cannot be tolerated abroad; as the plague-stricken are separated from their fellows, even so sin separates us from communion with God and holy beings. It is not alone *their* unwillingness to associate with us, as *our* horrible unfitness to have fellowship with them. It is dreadful to bear about with us a cancer, which has reached the stage of sickening rottenness; and yet this is not half so terribly disgusting as sin is to the heart of God. God is very gracious, but he cannot endure sin in his presence, and hence to set forth his hatred of it in type and figure he forbade diseased persons to enter his courts, or even to mingle with the camp of his people. For the unclean there was a plain and clear separation until he had been purified. Sin necessarily shuts us out from God's presence. Into his holy fellowship we must not come, we dare not attempt to come; the fire of his anger would consume us, as it did Nadab and Abihu, if we as sinners should venture near him apart from Christ Jesus. We cannot stand at the altar to officiate as priests before God, though this was the proper lot of manhood, by reason of the leprosy that is on our brow. Our praising God, simple as that might seem, cannot be acceptable in his sight, because of the defilement of our uncircumcised lips. Almighty grace must take away our uncleanliness or we cannot worship. Iniquity is a polluting thing. Everything we do and everything we think of grows polluted through our corruption. The unclean person could not touch a vessel, sit on a bed, or come near a garment without defiling it; and our sin has much the same effect. Our prayers have stains in them, our faith is mixed with unbelief, our repentance is not so tender as it should be, our communion is distant and interrupted. We cannot pray without sinning, and there is filth even in our tears. Well was it for Israel that there was an Aaron to bear the sins of their holy things, and blessed is it for us that Jesus takes the sins even of our best works, and casts them into the depths of the sea.

Sin too may be likened to many sicknesses from its being *contagious*. A man cannot be a sinner alone. "One sinner destroyeth much good." The seeds of sin are winged like thistle-down. You may shut up the leper in a lazar house, but there is no such way of shutting up sin, it *will* get out and spread itself. A man, if he be evil, will make others evil. His children will imitate him; his dependants, feeling his influence, will walk in his footsteps. Even his neighbours cannot look upon his sin without being in some measure infected by it, for "the thought of evil is sin." There is a fierce contagiousness in every form of moral evil; like fire among stubble it spreads most rapidly.

Sin moreover, like many diseases, is very *painful;* and yet, on the other hand, at certain stages it brings on *a deadness,* a numbness of soul preventing pain. The most of men are unconscious of the misery of the fall. They think themselves rich and increased in goods, having need of nothing, when they are naked, and poor and miserable. Sin causes a madness which makes sick souls dream that they are in sound health. They talk as though heaven were their heritage, when they are sitting on the brink of hell. But when sin is really discerned, then it becomes painful. I would sooner suffer—I know not what may be the pangs of some disease, but I feel sure I may say this—I would sooner suffer a complication of all the ills that flesh is heir to, than suffer the plague of a guilty, awakened, enlightened, quickened conscience; for when conscience accuseth a man there is no rest for him either day or night; its little finger is heavier than the loins of all other griefs. When sin becomes exceeding sinful before the eye, then there is a gloom and a heaviness of spirit which crushes the soul into despair, making life bitter, as Pharaoh did the lives of the children of Israel. Speak of Egyptian darkness, it was bright as noon-day compared with the darkness of a mind borne down with its own guilt. Oh what wretchedness was mine before I laid hold on Christ. There are some who feel not so acutely the agony of conflict with sin, but it was *my* lot to feel a horror of great darkness, verging upon despair, so that had I not soon found a Saviour, my soul had chosen strangling rather than life. Believe me, there is no pain so bitter as the pain of sin, and no curse so heavy as the curse which comes from the black lips of our own iniquities; and yet I would to God that some of you felt it now that ye might not feel it hereafter. I would that this whip would fall upon your backs, that you might be flogged out of your self-righteousness, and made to fly to Jesus Christ and find a shelter there.

The disease of sin is *deep-seated*, and has its throne in the heart. It does not lie in the hand or foot, it is not to be removed by amputation, much less by outward applications; no lancet can reach it, it is impossible to cauterize it. The skill of physicians can often extract the roots of disease, but no skill can ever reach this. It has entered the marrow, the very core and centre of our being, and only the Divine one is able to purge us from it.

> "No outward forms can make me clean
> The leprosy lies deep within."

It is in its own nature wholly *incurable*. " Can the Ethiopian change his skin, or the leopard his spots?" If so, then can he that is accustomed to do evil learn to do well. Can a brine fountain send forth sweet waters? Shall the thorn suddenly yield olives? Can the cataract which has been for ever dashing down the steep, reverse its course and return towards the river-head? Shall fire suddenly become gentle and lose its consuming power while the fuel is round about it? Shall the lion of himself eat straw like the ox? Shall the leopard bleat like a lamb? Such changes, being changes of nature, are only to be wrought by divine strength; and so it is not possible for the disease of sin ever to be cured by any human remedies. Man cannot cure himself. He may reform, he may drive the disease inward, and prevent its coming out upon the skin; he may so model, and guide, and restrain himself, that the coarser forms of sin which are condemned among men may not appear in him; but the virus, the essential poison of sin, no man can ever extract from his own heart, nor can another man do it for him. Jehovah Rophi, the healing Lord, must manifest his omnipotent power. The utmost religiousness, the most devout prayers, the greatest possible circumspection, will not avail to remove the taint of sin, if they spring from an unrenewed heart. The carnal mind is enmity against God, and is not reconciled to God, neither, indeed, can it be.

And so, let us close the story of this sickness of sin, by observing that it is a *mortal* disease. It kills not just now, but it *will* kill ere long. Not merely shall the body die as the result of sin, but the soul must be killed for ever with eternal wrath. O sinner, thou little knowest what thy sin will bring thee to; but if thou wilt read in God's Word, thou shalt discover that it will bring thee to the worm that never dies, and to the fire that never can be quenched. Perhaps to-morrow thou mayest know what a full-blown sin is; perhaps to-morrow, I said—that word may be prophetic to some of you—but if not to-morrow, it is but a matter of time, a few months, more or less, and you will be in torment. Sin, when it is ripened, bringeth forth death and damnation. Oh! thou dost not know what that word " to be damned" means! Thou canst play with it sometimes, and lightly hurl it at thy fellow creatures; but couldst thou only once hear the shriek of a damned soul, couldst thou only once see a spirit cast out from the presence of God into eternal misery, surely it would compel thee to cry, "What must I do to be saved."

Enough of this: it is clear that there is a very excellent parallel to be drawn between sin and disease. Humbling as it is, yet the fact is nevertheless most certain, that we are all suffering under the disease of sin.

II. But now, secondly, IT PLEASES DIVINE MERCY TO GIVE TO CHRIST THE CHARACTER OF A PHYSICIAN.

Having deigned to consider sin as a disease, which is a great proof of mercy, it now graciously confers upon Christ the character of a physician. Be it for ever understood that Jesus Christ never came into the world merely to explain what sin is. Moses had for his mission the exposition of sin, Christ has for his mission the eradication of it. We know what sin is through the law: that is as much as the law can do for us. Christ comes, not merely to tell us what it is, but to inform us how it can be removed. Jesus did not come to apologize for sin; Christ never died in order that sin might appear less sinful, that God might be less severe towards sin, or hate it less. God forbid! We never see sin to be so black as when we view its evil as revealed in the sufferings of Jesus, nor is God's wrath ever more intolerable than when we behold it consuming his only-begotten Son. "Behold, and see if there be any sorrow like unto my sorrow, which is done unto me, wherewith the Lord hath afflicted me in the day of his fierce anger." Christ did not come to lay a flattering unction to men's souls, to prevent distress of conscience, to say to them " Peace, Peace!" where there is no peace; no, he came to cure sin, not to film it over;

not to make men forget the disease by drugging them with presumptuous draughts of consolation, but by absolutely removing that which is the cause of their dread and of their fear to make them whole. Christ Jesus did not come in order that you might continue in sin and escape the penalty of it; he did not come to prevent the disease being mortal, but to take the disease itself away. Many people think that when we preach salvation, we mean salvation from going to hell. We do not mean *that*, but we mean a great deal more; we preach salvation *from sin;* we say that Christ is able to save a man; and we mean by that that he is able to save him from sin and to make him holy; to make him a new man. No person has any right to say, "I am saved," while he continues in sin as he did before. How can you be saved from sin while you are living in it? A man that is drowning cannot say he is saved from the water while he is sinking in it; a man that is frost-bitten cannot say, with any truth, that he is saved from the cold while he is stiffened in the wintry blast. No, man, Christ did not come to save thee *in* thy sins, but to save thee *from* thy sins; not to make the disease so that it should not kill thee, but to let it remain in itself mortal, and, nevertheless, to remove it from thee, and thee from it. Christ Jesus came then to heal us from the plague of sin, to touch us with his hand and say, " I will, be thou clean."

When a physician presents himself, one of the first enquiries is, " Is he a regular practitioner? Has he a right to practise? Has he a diploma?" Very properly, the law requires that a man shall not be allowed to hack our bodies and poison us with drugs at his own pleasure without having at least a show of knowing what he is at. It has been tartly said that "a doctor is a man who pours drugs, of which he knows little, into a body of which he knows still less." I fear that is often the case. Still a diploma is the best safeguard mortals have devised. Christ has the best authority for practising as a Physician. He has a divine diploma. Would you like to see his diploma? I will read you a few words of it: it comes from the highest authority, not from the College of Physicians, but from the God of Physicians. Here are the words of it in the sixty-first chapter of Isaiah. "The Spirit of the Lord is upon me, because the Lord hath anointed me to preach good tidings unto the meek. He hath sent me to bind up the broken-hearted." He has a diploma for binding up broken hearts. I should not like to trust myself to a physician who was a mere self-dubbed doctor, who could not show any authorization; I must have him know as much as a man can know, little as I believe that will probably be. He must have a diploma; it must be signed and sealed too, and be in a regular manner, for few sensible men will risk their lives with ignorant quacks. Now Jesus Christ has his diploma and there it is—God hath sent him to bind up the broken-hearted. The next thing you want in a physician is *education;* you want to know that he is thoroughly qualified; he must have walked the hospitals. And certainly our Lord Jesus Christ has done so. What form of disease did he not meet with? When he was here among men it pleased God to let the devil loose, in order that there might be more than usual venom in the veins of poor diseased manhood; and Christ met the devil at his darkest hour and fought with the great enemy when he had full liberty to do his worst with him. Jesus did indeed enter into the woes of men. Walked the hospital! Why the whole world was an infirmary, and Christ the one only physician, going from couch to couch, healing the sons of men.

Something more be it observed, may be said of him, he is experimentally as well as by education qualified in the healing art. I have heard of a celebrated physician that he was wont to try the effect of his medicines upon himself. This has been done in our Master's case. There is not a single disease which he does not know experimentally, for he himself took our sicknesses and infirmities. He was tempted in all points like as we are, yet without sin. He knows his patient's case by having passed through the case himself. There is no brokenness of heart, there is no grief of soul which Jesus Christ has not himself participated in; and though you may say he knows not sin in its infection, yet he knows sin in its imputation, and is, by having suffered all its penalties, perfectly well acquainted with it.

One likes a physician, too, who has *a wide practice*. One does not care for a man's merely understanding his tools; we like to know whether he has used them, and whether he has been successful in his art. Blessed be the name of the beloved Physician! he has the widest imaginable practice. These eighteen hundred years he has been healing sin-sick souls —what am I saying?—these six thousand years he has been "mighty to save;" for before he bodily gave himself to the cross, the virtue of the medicine of his own blood had begun to operate upon the sons of men. O souls, ye may see in heaven the multitudes whom he has healed. There, before the eternal throne, you may view the myriads who have been delivered from all sorts of diseases through the power and virtue of his touch. You need not fear to trust yourselves in his hands, for even the hem of his garment healeth our diseases.

To sum up the virtues of this Physician in a very few words: His cures are very *speedy*—there is life in a look at him; his cures are *radical*—he strikes at the very centre of the disease, and hence his cures are very *sure* and certain. He never fails, and *the disease never returns*. There is no relapse where Christ heals; no fear that one of his patients should be but patched up for a season, he makes a new man of him: a new heart also does he give him, and a right spirit does he put within him. He is a physician, one of a thousand, because he is well-skilled in *all* diseases. Physicians generally have some *specialité*. They may know a little about almost all our pains and ills, but there is usually one disease which they have studied the most carefully, one part of the human frame whose anatomy is as well-known to them as the rooms and cupboards of their own house. Jesus Christ has made the whole of human nature his *specialité*. He is as much at home with one sinner as with another sinner, and never yet did he meet with an out-of-the-way case that was out of the way to him. He has had extraordinary complications of strange diseases to deal with, but he has known exactly in one moment, with one glance of his eye, how to treat the patient. He is the only universal doctor 'at home' in every case; the medicine he gives is a catholicon; it heals in every instance, never failing. *His medicine is himself!* If there be a smart caused by it, it is borne upon his own back. "By his stripes we are healed." "His flesh is meat indeed; his blood is drink indeed:" he himself casts out the disease from poor dying men. We do but trust him, and sin dies: we love him, and grace lives; we wait for him, and grace is strengthened; we see him, as we soon shall, and grace is perfected for ever. O blessed physician for this desperate disease!

III. I cannot, however, tarry longer on that point, but come to the third, which is the main one that I am driving at; namely, THAT NEED IS THAT ALONE WHICH MOVES OUR GRACIOUS PHYSICIAN TO COME TO OUR AID.

He says, "They that are whole need not a physician," and you will see the natural conclusion from his line of reasoning is, "I do not go to the whole, because they do not need me; I go to the sick because they do need me; the reason why I go anywhere is because I am needed." I believe, dear friends, though doubtless there are some exceptions, that if you were to take the medical profession through, you would perceive larger-heartedness, and more humanity there than almost anywhere; and you would find that there is scarcely a physician, certainly none known to me, who would, if he had two urgent cases to consider, make any distinction between the two, except that he would give his first attention to the sufferer who needed him most. Of course if the matters are both trivial, common sense allows a man to select that which will best remunerate him for his skill, but in imminently dangerous cases, necessity decides. The true physician is born with a physician's heart, and feels for the woes of his fellow men; and, though a man has obtained a diploma, he is no physician, and ought not to practise if his soul is not in his work, and his heart full of benevolence to the afflicted.

The true physician having a sympathy and an intense desire to be of service, if there be two persons requiring him, would say, "*This* is in the more imminent danger, I shall go there first." Now what is most certainly only fair to acknowledge concerning human physicians, we must admit with a far greater cogency concerning the great physician of souls. If there were two sinners both perishing, and Christ were not able to save at the same moment more than one, he would go to that one first which needed him most. This is his rule. He acts according to sovereignty, but that sovereignty is under the control of his own infinite mercy, and if he hears a cry from two hearts to-day, if he should give any preference, the preference would be given to that which was the cry of the most lost, the most abject, the most needy sinner. Now think this over and you will see that it is true, and most consolatory. What was it made Christ a physician at all? Was is not because men were sick with sin? Suppose they had been perfect, would Christ have ever been a Saviour if men had not been lost? Brethren, it would have been a work of supererogation; it would have been a folly, a monstrous folly, on his part, to undertake an office which was not required of him. It is *sin* which makes room for his work as a Saviour. I say it—you will understand me—he is only a Saviour because there are sinners, and his Saviourship is based upon our sinnership. He takes that position because he is wanted. Again, what was the main thought which was upon him when he was compounding his great medicine? What was it made him shed great drops of blood?

Was it human guilt, or human merit, think you? Why guilt, and guilt alone. What made him give his back to the scourgers, and his cheeks to the smiters? What made him stretch his arms to the cross and give his feet to the nails? What made him bear the unsufferable wrath of Almighty God? Was it man's goodness? Why you cannot think of such a thing; it was human vileness, villany, degradation, iniquity, which made such sufferings as these all needful. As I see then Christ in his great surgery, compounding the Almighty medicine which is to expel the disease from the veins of humanity, I see him every moment thinking of sin! sin! sin! Man's sin makes him die.

And now that he is in heaven, beloved, what is it that Christ is thinking of there? "He maketh intercession"—what for? For the righteous? If they were self-righteous, perfectly righteous, they would not need intercession from him. "He maketh intercession for the transgressors." He is exalted on high—what for? To reward the good? Nay, verily, but to give repentance and remission of sins—evidently to those who have no repentance and whose sins have need to be forgiven. Up in heaven, Christ still has his eye upon sinners—sinners are the jewels whom he seeks. Where, again, was Jesus Christ when he was on earth? Did he not spend the most of his time among sinners? Was he not always dealing out healing to the sick, life to the dead, and so on? You might ask again, on the other hand, to whom is the gospel sent? What is it? "This is a faithful saying and worthy of all acceptation, that Christ Jesus came into the world to save sinners." That is the gospel—"He that believeth and is baptized shall be saved; he that believeth not shall be damned;" so that those who are bidden to believe are evidently those who deserve to be damned. Need, need, need alone quickens the physician's footsteps, bringing Jesus from the throne of glory to the cross, and in his spiritual power, bringing him every day from the throne of his Father down to broken-hearted heavy-laden souls.

Now, this is very plain talking, and you all receive it, but still the most of people do not understand it. A minister, when he had done preaching in a country village, said to a farm-labourer who had been listening to him, "Do you think Jesus Christ died to save *good* people, or *bad* people?" "Well, sir," said the man, "I should say he died to save good people." "But did he die to save bad people?" "No, sir; no, certainly not, sir." "Well, then, what will become of you and me?" "Well, sir, I do not know. I dare say you be pretty good, sir; and I try to be as good as I can." That is just the common doctrine; and after all, though we think it has died out among us, that is the religion of ninety-nine English people out of every hundred who know nothing of divine grace: we are to be as good as we can; we are to go to church or to chapel, and do all that we can, and then Jesus Christ died for us, and we shall be saved. Whereas the gospel is, that he did not do anything at all for people who can rely on themselves, but gave himself for lost and ruined ones. He did not come into the world to save self-righteous people; on their own showing, they do not want to be saved. He comes because we need him, and therefore he comes only to those who need him; and if we do not need him, and are such good respectable people, we must find our own way to heaven. Need, need alone, is that which quickens the physician's footsteps.

IV. We therefore come to another point, upon which we shall not stay many minutes. It follows, therefore, and the text positively asserts it, that THE WHOLE—THAT THOSE WHO HAVE NO GREAT NEED—NO NEED AT ALL—WILL BE UNAIDED BY CHRIST.

Of course they ought to be left alone. No physician in his senses thinks of sending a prescription, no surgeon thinks of sending his bottles and his boxes of pills to people who profess to be perfectly well. The prescription would be put into the fire and the physic thrown in the streets—the man himself would reckon it to be a gross insult. Christ did not come into the world merely to insult humanity. If humanity be the fine thing it thinks it is, then let it exalt itself as it may, and let it go on with the health it thinks it possesses; let it work out its own salvation if it will allow that even this is required. To send a physician to those who are whole is an insult to the physician too. He knocks at the door, "Who is ill here?" is the first question. "Nobody, we are all well, thank you, sir: we are all well, we thank God: we are not as other men are down the street there, we have no fever, the small-pox never comes here, we never catch the scarlatina, we have nothing of the kind, sir; we are glad to see you—glad to see you, but we have nothing the matter with us." The physician would find at once that he had been hoaxed in being asked there. And that truly is the treatment Jesus Christ gets from a great many people. You hear them say, "Lord have mercy upon us, *miserable* sinners"—dressed in satin and all sorts of furbelows, and as good people as you would find in all the parish; and if you come to question them, they are not "*miserable* sinners" at all. I would like to chalk "miserable sinners" on their backs and see whether they could bear it. It is the same with you—you come here, and if I pray about sinners, there are some of you who say, "Yes, yes, we are sinners;" and yet if I came round and said, "Now let us take the ten commandments—have you broken them?" I daresay there are some here who would say, "Really I do not know that I have in particular done anything wrong; I do not feel that I have erred very remarkably." No, the fact is you insult Christ by sending to him when you are not ill, and it is nothing better than impertinence, though you think it to be a compliment. The whole have no need of a physician: there is no need for a physician's skill. "Why," saith the doctor, as he looks round upon all his store of knowledge, "what is the good of this?—a fool is as good as I am to a man who is not ill. If you were sick, I would try to do my best, but as there is nothing the matter with you, there is no room for me." You may fetch any crossing-sweeper, and he will be of as much use to you as the best physician, when you are not ill. So if you do not confess yourselves really to be sinners, Jesus will have no preciousness in your eyes, he will be but an ordinary person. If you are not sick, there is no likelihood of gratitude. Men will not thank a physician for doing nothing. You will never be thankful to Christ for saving you, if you do not feel that you want saving. Then again, there will be no honour to him. Suppose you went to heaven, and entered there in the same self-righteous frame of mind as you are in now, what would you say? "Well done I." There would be no honour to Christ, no glory to Jesus.

A man must have a deep and conscious need of Christ, or else he cannot illuminate the throne of Christ with glory by his praise, when he shall enter heaven.

Now methinks there is some sweet music in what I have been saying to those of you who do need, though it must sound like a mockery to those of you who think you do not need it.

V. To conclude, it follows then, that THOSE WHO ARE SICK SHALL BE HELPED BY JESUS. Let the question go round these galleries and this area this morning, "Am I sick? Am I sinful? Then I have a need of Jesus, and need is the only thing that will bring Jesus to me?" "Oh!" says one, "but I am so very sinful." Then you have a very great need, and there is room for very great power on the Saviour's part, and that display of grace shall give him very great glory. Sinner, believe on him, that he can save thee; trust him to save thee and let not thy great sin keep thee back. "Oh but I have so many sins!" Then again thou hast the greater need, and as it is need that brings the doctor, so thy many needs will be so many knocks at his door, so many rings at his bell; he will come the faster only plead earnestly every one of these thy sins, and ask him to have pity upon thee. "Yes," say you "but I have been so long sick." Then your case is a very bad one, and there is the more need of his care. He healed the woman that had been thirty-six years disabled, and if you have been thirty-six years—ay, if it be eighty years, he is still able to heal, and your need—let us keep to that—your need is your only plea. You have evidently a very strong plea, for you have a very great need. "Ah," says another, "but I have relapsed since I thought I was healed—I have backslidden." Now there is a special promise given to that form of sickness, "I will heal their backsliding." He does not specially say "I will heal their drunkenness and so on," but here is a special promise for a special case. Now you want him. This is a great sin, this backsliding. Go to him—ask him the rather to come to you. "Yes," says another, "but I cannot feel my sin as I would." This only proves how much you need the Lord Jesus, since you have not even that form of fitness which lies in a deep sense of need; you cannot even feel, for you have the stone in the heart. Oh make this a plea with him. Say "Jesus I want thee more than anybody else, for there are some who have a little health; they can feel they are diseased, but I have not even that. I want thee, oh I want thee more than any." Perhaps you will say "But I cannot believe on him as I would." Then add *that* also to your other sins, confess your unbelief, tell him you have great need of him to give you faith; and go to him, and oh may he help you to believe that he is able to forgive this sin also. "Well," says one, "but I grow worse the more I think about these things." I am glad of it, dear friend, this growing worse is a part of the cure. Suppose you should keep on growing worse, if you should get to feel yourself as black as the devil and as damned as a lost soul, yet still while you are in this world the great physician can heal you, and you have still this great plea, that you want him, you want him. "Oh," says one, "I cannot see how I can plead my need as the only thing." My dear friend, what would you plead, suppose you were publicly begging. If I had to turn to the trade of a beggar, believe me, I would not wear this black coat, or, if I did, I would take care to have it pretty well riddled with holes; because the great thing you have to do when you plead in the street, is to convince the passers-by that you are in need. Some lean wretched-looking fellows have faces which are worth a fortune to them—their cheeks white with consumption—their bodies thin and lean as with starvation—with scarce a handful of rags on them, they squat down in some corner and write on a paper "I am starving," and as you pass them you cannot help it, your hand goes into your pocket—" Here is a case of destitution," you say—and you give them relief. Imitate these vagabonds in all but their deception. Use their logic, the rational argument, that need is a beggar's best plea. You *are* destitute, you *are* starving; spread your case before God. The best case you can make out in order to prevail with God, is a *bad* one. Let it be as bad as it can be and I venture to say the worst is the best. Do not be apologising, attempting to make your sins less than they are; tell him you are a wretch undone without his sovereign grace, and there guilty and vile, and self-abhorred, fall flat before him, say, "Lord Jesus, if thou wantest some one to heal; I am just the man. If thou wantest a case that can be blazoned abroad and that will make the public ears ring and ring again with the praise of thy all-healing medicine, I am thy man, Lord. If thou wantest one full of sores and wounds and putrifying disease like Job upon a dunghill; if thou wantest one that is very far gone, that is rotten through and through, Lord, I am thy man." O think you, sinner, he is just your Saviour, for while he loves to meet with such cases as yours, you should rejoice to meet with such a Saviour as he is; and all you are asked to do is to believe that he can save you and to trust him to do it. If you knew him you would believe him. He loves to save. He can save the vilest. Trust him then, and may the Spirit of God so lead you to understand him, that you can rely upon him, and, if you do, he will say, "Sinner, thy sins be forgiven thee, be of good cheer, go on thy way rejoicing." May God bless these words, for Christ's sake. Amen.

"Supposing Him to Be the Gardener"

"Supposing him to be the gardener"—John xx. 15.

I WAS sitting about a fortnight ago in a very lovely garden, in the midst of all kinds of flowers which were blooming in delightful abundance all around. Screening myself from the heat of the sun under the overhanging boughs of an olive, I cast my eyes upon palms and bananas, roses and camellias, oranges and aloes, lavender and heliotrope. The garden was full of colour and beauty, perfume and fruitfulness. Surely the gardener, whoever he might be, who had framed, and fashioned, and kept in order that lovely spot, deserved great commendation. So I thought, and then it came to me to meditate upon the church of God as a garden, and to suppose the Lord Jesus to be the gardener, and then to think of what would most assuredly happen if it were so. "Supposing him to be the gardener," my mind conceived of a paradise where all sweet things flourish and all evil things are rooted up. If an ordinary worker had produced such beauty as I then saw and enjoyed on earth, what beauty and glory must surely be brought forth "supposing *him* to be the gardener"! You know the "him" to whom we refer, the ever-blessed Son of God, whom Mary Magdalene in our text mistook for the gardener. We will for once follow a saint in her mistaken track; and yet we shall find ourselves going in a right way. She was mistaken when she fell into "supposing him to be the gardener"; but if we are under his Spirit's teaching we shall not make a mistake if now we indulge ourselves in a quiet meditation upon our ever-blessed Lord, "supposing him to be the gardener."

It is not an unnatural supposition, surely; for if we may truly sing—

"We are a garden walled around,
Chosen and made peculiar ground,"

that enclosure needs a gardener. Are we not all the plants of his right hand planting? Do we not all need watering and tending by his constant and gracious care? He says, "I am the true vine: my Father is the husbandman," and that is one view of it; but we may also sing, "My well-beloved hath a vineyard in a very fruitful hill: and he fenced it, and gathered out the stones thereof, and planted it with the choicest vine"—that is to say, he acted as gardener to it. Thus has Isaiah taught us to sing a song of the Well-beloved touching his vineyard. We read of our Lord just now under these terms—" Thou that dwellest in the gardens, the companions hearken to thy voice." To what purpose does he dwell in the vineyards but that he may see how the vines flourish and care for all the plants? The image, I say, is so far from being unnatural that it is most pregnant with suggestions and full of useful teaching. We are not going against the harmonies of nature when we are "supposing him to be the gardener."

Neither is the figure unscriptural; for in one of his own parables our Lord makes himself to be the dresser of the vineyard. We read just now that parable so full of warning. When the "certain man" came in and saw the fig tree that it brought forth no fruit, he said unto the dresser of his vineyard, " Cut it down: why cumbereth it the ground? " Who was it that intervened between that profitless tree and the axe but our great Intercessor and Interposer? He it is who continually comes forward with " Let it alone this year also till I shall dig about it and dung it." In this case he himself takes upon himself the character of the vine-dresser, and we are not wrong in "supposing him to be the gardener."

If we would be supported by a type, our Lord takes the name of "the Second Adam," and the first Adam was a gardener. Moses tells us that the Lord God placed the man in the garden of Eden to dress it and to keep it. Man in his best estate was not to live in this world in a paradise of indolent luxury, but in a garden of recompensed toil. Behold, the church is Christ's Eden, watered by the river of life, and so fertilized that all manner of fruits are brought forth unto God; and he, our second Adam, walks in this spiritual Eden to dress it and to keep it; and so by a type we see that we are right in "supposing him to be the gardener." Thus also Solomon thought of him when he described the royal Bridegroom as going down with his spouse to the garden when the flowers appeared on the earth and the fig tree had put forth her green figs; he went out with his beloved for the preservation of the gardens, saying, " Take us the foxes, the little foxes, that spoil the vines: for our vines have tender grapes." Neither nature, nor Scripture, nor type, nor song forbids us to think of our adorable Lord Jesus as one that careth for the flowers and fruits of his church. We err not when we speak of him, " supposing him to be the gardener." And so I sat me still, and indulged the suggested line of thought, which I now repeat in your hearing, hoping that I may open many roads of meditation for your hearts also. I shall not attempt to think out such a subject thoroughly, but only to indicate in which direction you may look for a vein of precious ore.

I. " Supposing him to be the gardener," we have here THE KEY TO MANY WONDERS in the garden of his church.

The first wonder is *that there should be a church at all in the world;* that there should be a garden blooming in the midst of this sterile waste. Upon a hard and flinty rock the Lord has made the Eden of his church to grow. How came it to be here—an oasis of life in a desert of death ? How came faith in the midst of unbelief, and hope where all is servile fear, and love where hate abounds? "Ye are of God, little children, and the whole world lieth in the wicked one." Whence this being "of God" where all beside is fast shut up in the devil? How came there to be a people for God, separated, and sanctified, and consecrated, and ordained to bring forth fruit unto his name? Assuredly it could not have been so at all if the doing of it had been left to man. We understand its existence, "supposing him to be the gardener," but nothing else can account for it. He can cause the fir tree to flourish instead of the thorn, and the myrtle instead of the briar; but no one else can accomplish such a change. The garden in which I sat was made on the bare face of the rock, and almost all the earth of which its terraces were composed had been brought up there, from the shore below, by hard labour, and so upon the rock a soil had been created. It was not by its own nature that the garden was found in such a place; but by skill and labour it had been formed: even so the church of God has had to be constructed by the Lord Jesus, who is the author as well as the perfecter of his garden. Painfully, with wounded hands, has he built each terrace, and fashioned each bed, and planted each plant. All the flowers have had to be watered with his bloody sweat, and watched by his tearful eyes: the nail-prints in his hands, and the wound in his side are the tokens of what it cost him to make a new Paradise. He has given his life for the life of every plant that is in the garden, and not one of them had been there on any other theory than "supposing him to be the gardener."

Besides, there is another wonder. *How comes the church of God to flourish in such a clime?* This present evil world is very uncongenial to the growth of grace, and the church is not able by herself alone to resist the evil influences which surround her. The church contains within itself elements which tend to its own disorder and destruction if left alone; even as the garden has present in its soil all the germs of a tangled thicket of weeds. The best church that ever Christ had on earth would within a few years apostatise from the truth if deserted by the Spirit of God. The world never helps the church; it is all in arms against it; there is nothing in the world's air or soil that can fertilise the church even to the least degree. How is it, then, that notwithstanding all this the church is a fair garden unto God, and there are sweet spices grown in its beds, and lovely flowers are gathered by the Divine hand from its borders? The continuance and prosperity of the church can only be accounted for by "supposing him to be the gardener." Almighty strength is put to the otherwise impossible work of sustaining a holy people among men; almighty wisdom exercises itself upon this otherwise insuperable difficulty. Hear ye the word of the Lord, and learn hence the reason for the growth of his church below. "I, the Lord, do keep it: I will water it every moment; lest any hurt it, I will keep it night and day." That is the reason for the existence of a spiritual people still in the midst of a godless and perverse generation. This is the reason for an election of grace in the midst of surrounding vice, and worldliness, and unbelief. "Supposing him to be the gardener," I can see why there should be fruitfulness, and beauty, and sweetness even in the centre of the wilderness of sin.

Another mystery is also cleared up by this supposition. The wonder is *that ever you and I should have been placed among the plants of the Lord.* Why are *we* allowed to grow in the garden of his grace? Why me, Lord? Why me? How is it that we have been kept there, and borne with in our barrenness, when he might long ago have said, "Cut it down: why cumbereth it the ground?" Who else would have borne with such waywardness as ours? Who could have manifested such infinite patience? Who could have tended us with such care, and when the care was so ill-rewarded who would have renewed it so long from day to day, and persisted in designs of boundless love? Who could have done more for his vineyard? who could or would have done so much? Any mere man would have repented of his good intent, provoked by our ingratitude. None but God could have had patience with some of us! That we have not long ago been slipped off as fruitless branches of the vine; that we are left still upon the stem, in the hope that we may ultimately bring forth fruit, is a great marvel. I know not how it is that we have been spared, except upon this ground—"supposing him to be the gardener"; for Jesus is all gentleness and grace, so slow with his knife, so tardy with his axe, so hopeful if we do but show a bud or two, or, perchance, yield a little sour berry—so hopeful, I say, that these may be hopeful prognostics of something better by-and-by. Infinite patience! Immeasurable longsuffering! where are ye to be found save in the breast of the Well-beloved? Surely the hoe has spared many of us simply and only because he who is meek and lowly in heart is the gardener.

Dear friends, there is one mercy with regard to this church which I have often had to thank God for, namely, *that evils should have been shut out for so long a time.* During the period in which we have been together as pastor and people, and that is now some twenty-nine years, we have enjoyed uninterrupted prosperity, going from strength to strength in the work of the Lord. Alas! we have seen many other churches that were quite as hopeful as our own rent with strife, brought low by declension, or overthrown by heresy. I hope we have not been apt to judge their faults severely; but we must be thankful for our own deliverance from the evils which have afflicted them. I do not know how it is that we have been kept together in love, helped to abound in labour, and enabled to be firm in the faith, unless it be that special grace has watched over us. We are full of faults; we have nothing to boast of; and yet no church has been more divinely favoured: I wonder that the blessing should have lasted so long, and I cannot make it out except when I fall into "supposing *him* to be the gardener." I cannot trace our prosperity to the pastor, certainly; nor even to my beloved friends the elders and deacons, nor even to the best of you with your fervent love and holy zeal. I think it must be that Jesus has been the gardener, and he has shut the gate when I am afraid I have left it open; and he has driven out the wild boar of the wood just when he had entered to root up the weaker plants. He must have been about at nights to keep off the prowling thieves, and he must have been here, too, in the noontide heat to guard those of you who have prospered in worldly goods, from the glare of too bright a sun. Yes, *he* has been with us, blessed be his name! Hence all this peace, and unity, and enthusiasm. May we never grieve him so that he shall turn away **from** us; but rather let us entreat him, saying, "Abide with us. Thou that dwellest in the gardens, let this be one of the gardens in which thou dost deign to dwell until the day break and the shadows flee away." Thus our supposition is a key to many wonders.

II. Let your imaginations run along with mine while I say that "supposing him to be the gardener" should be A SPUR TO MANY DUTIES.

One of the duties of a Christian is *joy*. That is a blessed religion which among its precepts commands men to be happy. When joy becomes a duty, who would wish to neglect it? Surely it must help every little plant to drink in the sunlight when it is whispered among the flowers that Jesus is the gardener. "Oh," you say, "I am such a little plant; I do not grow well; I do not put forth so much leafage, nor are there so many flowers on me as on many round about me!" It is quite right that you should think little of yourself: perhaps to droop your head is a part of your beauty: many flowers had not been half so lovely if they had not practised the art of hanging their heads. But "supposing him to be the gardener," then he is as much a gardener to you as he is to the most lordly palm in the whole domain. In the Mentone garden right before me grew the orange and the aloe, and others of the finer and more noticeable plants; but on a wall to my left grew common wallflowers and saxifrages, and tiny herbs such as we find on our own rocky places. Now, the gardener had cared for all of these, little as well as great; in fact, there were hundreds of specimens of the most insignificant growths all duly labelled and described. The smallest saxifrage could say, "He is my gardener just as surely as he is the gardener of the Gloire de Dijon or Maréchal Neil." Oh feeble child of God, the Lord taketh care of you! Your heavenly Father feedeth ravens, and guides the flight of sparrows: should he not much more care for you, oh ye of little faith? Oh little plants, you will grow rightly enough. Perhaps you are growing downward just now rather than upward. Remember that there are plants of which we value the underground root much more than we do the haulm above ground. Perhaps it is not yours to grow very fast; you may be a slow-growing shrub by nature, and you would not be healthy if you were to run to wood. Anyhow, be this your joy, you are in the garden of the Lord, and, "supposing him to be the gardener," he will make the best of you. You cannot be in better hands.

Another duty is that of *valuing the Lord's presence, and praying for it*. We ought whenever the Sabbath morning dawns to pray our Well-beloved to come into his garden and eat his pleasant fruits. What can we do without him? All day long our cry should go up to him, "O Lord, behold and visit this vine, and the vineyard which thy right hand has planted." We ought to agonize with him that he would come and manifest himself to us as he does not unto the world. For what is a garden if the gardener never comes near it? What is the difference between it and the wilderness if he to whom it belongs never lifts up spade or pruning-hook upon it? So that it is our necessity that we have Christ with us, "supposing him to be the gardener;" and it is our bliss that we have Christ walking between our beds and borders, watching every plant, training, tending, maturing all. "Supposing him to be the gardener," it is well, for from him is our fruit found. Divided from him we are nothing; only as he watches over us can we bring forth fruit. Let us have done with confidence in man, let us forego all attempts to supply facts of his spiritual presence by routine or rant, ritualism or rowdyism; but let us pray our Lord to be ever present with us, and by that presence to make our garden grow.

"Supposing him to be the gardener," there is another duty, and that is, let each one of us *yield himself up entirely to him*. A plant does not know how it ought to be treated; it knows not when it should be watered or when it should be kept dry: a fruit-tree is no judge of when it needs to be pruned, or digged, or dunged. The wit and wisdom of the garden lieth not in the flowers and shrubs, but in the gardener. Now, then, if you and I are here to-day with any self-will and carnal judgment about us, let us seek to lay it all aside that we may be absolutely at our Lord's disposal. You might not be willing to put yourself implicitly into the hand of any mere man (pity that you should); but, surely, thou plant of the Lord's right-hand planting, thou mayest put thyself without a question into his dear hand. "Supposing him to be the gardener," thou mayest well say, "I would neither have will, nor wish, nor wit, nor whim, nor way, but I would be as nothing in the gardener's hands, that he may be to me my wisdom and my all. Here, kind gardener, thy poor plant bows itself to thy hand; train me as thou wilt. Depend upon it, happiness lives next door to the spirit of complete acquiescence in the will of God, and it will be easy to exercise that perfect acquiescence when we suppose the Lord Jesus to be the gardener. If the Lord hath done it; what has a saint to say? Oh thou afflicted one, the Lord hath done it: wouldest thou have it otherwise? Nay, art thou not thankful that it is even so, because so is the will of him in whose hand thy life is, and whose are all thy ways? The duty of submission is very plain, "supposing him to be the gardener."

One more duty I would mention, though others suggest themselves. "Supposing him to be the gardener," then *let us bring forth fruit to him.* I do not address a people this morning who feel no care as to whether they serve God or not. I believe that most of you do desire to glorify God; for being saved by grace, you feel a holy ambition to show forth his praises who has called you out of darkness into his marvellous light. You wish to bring others to Christ, because you yourselves have been brought to life and liberty in him. Now, let this be a stimulus to your fruit-bearing, that Jesus is the gardener. Where you have brought forth a single cluster, bring forth a hundred, "supposing him to be the gardener." If he is to have the honour of it, then labour to do that which will give him great renown. If our spiritual state were to be attributed to ourselves, or to our minister, or to some of our fellow Christians, we might not feel that we were under a great necessity to be fruitful; but if Jesus be the gardener, and is to bear the blame or the honour of what we produce, then let us use up every drop of sap and strain every fibre, that, to the utmost of which our manhood is capable, we may produce a fair reward for our Lord's travail. Under such tutorship and care we ought to become eminent scholars. Doth Christ train us? Oh let us never cause the world to think meanly of our Master. Students feel that their *alma mater* deserves great things of them, so they labour to make their university renowned. And so, since Jesus is tutor and university to us, let us feel that we are bound to reflect credit upon so great a teacher, upon so divine a name. I do not know how to put it, but surely we ought to do something worthy of such a Lord. Each little flower in the garden of the Lord should wear its brightest hues, and pour forth its rarest perfume, because Jesus cares for it. The best of all possible good should be yielded by every plant in our Father's garden, supposing Jesus to be the gardener.

Thus much, then, on those two points—a key to many wonders, and a spur to many duties.

III. Thirdly, I have found in this supposition A RELIEF FROM CRUSHING RESPONSIBILITY. One has a work given him of God to do, and if he does it rightly he cannot do it carelessly. The first thing when he wakes he asks, "How is the work prospering?" and the last thought at night is, "What can I do to fulfil my calling?" Sometimes the anxiety even troubles his dreams, and he sighs, "O Lord, send now prosperity!" How is the garden prospering which we are set to tend? Are we broken-hearted because nothing appears to flourish? Is it a bad season? or is the soil lean and hungry? It is a very blessed relief to an excess of care if we can fall into the habit of "supposing him to be the gardener." If Jesus be the Master and Lord in all things it is not mine to keep all the church in order. I am not responsible for the growth of every Christian, nor for every backslider's errors, nor for every professor's faults of life. This burden must not lie on me so that I shall be crushed thereby. "Supposing him to be the gardener," then, the church enjoys a better oversight than mine; better care is taken of the garden than could be taken by the most vigilant watchers, even though by night the frost devoured them, and by day the heat. "Supposing him to be the gardener," then all must go well in the long run. He that keepeth Israel doth neither slumber nor sleep; we need not fret and despond. I beg you earnest workers, who are becoming depressed, to think this out a little. You see it is yours to work under the Lord Jesus; but it is not yours to take the anxiety of his office into your souls as though you were to bear his burdens. The under-gardener, the workman in the garden, needs not fret about the whole garden as though it were all left to him. No, no; let him not take too much upon himself. I pray you, bound your anxiety by the facts of the case. So you have a number of young people around you, and you are watching for their souls as they that must give account. This is well; but do not be worried and wearied; for, after all, the saving and the keeping of those souls is not in your hands, but it rests with One far-more able than yourself. Just think that the Lord is the gardener. I know it is so in matters of providence. A certain man of God in troublous times became quite unable to do his duty because he laid to heart so much the ills of the age; he became depressed and disturbed, and he went on board a vessel, wanting to leave the country, which was getting into such a state that he could no longer endure it. Then one said to him, "Mr. Whitelock, are you the manager of the world?" No, he was not quite that. "Did not God get on pretty well with it before you were born, and don't you think he will do very well with it when you are dead?" That reflection helped to relieve the good man's mind, and he went back to do his duty. I want you thus to perceive the limit of your responsibility: you are not the gardener himself; you are only one of the gardener's boys, set to run on errands, or to do a bit of digging, or to sweep the paths. The garden is well enough managed even though you are not head manager in it.

While this relieves us of anxiety it makes labour for Christ very sweet, because if the garden does not seem to repay us for our trouble we say to ourselves, "It is not my garden after all. 'Supposing him to be the gardener,' I am quite willing to work on a barren piece of rock, or tie up an old withered bough, or dig a worthless sod; for, if it only pleases Jesus, the work is for that one sole reason profitable to the last degree. It is not mine to question the wisdom of my task, but to set about it in the name of my Master and Lord. 'Supposing him to be the gardener,' lifts the ponderous responsibility of it from me, and my work becomes pleasant and delightful."

In dealing with the souls of men, we meet with cases which are extremely difficult. Some persons are so timid and fearful that you do not know how to comfort them; others are so fast and presumptuous that you hardly know how to help them. A few are so double-faced that you cannot understand them, and others so fickle that you cannot hold them. Some flowers puzzle the ordinary gardener: we meet with plants which are covered with prickles, and when you try to train them they wound the hand that would help them. These strange growths would make a great muddle for you if you were the gardener; but "supposing him to be the gardener," you have the happiness of being able to go to him constantly, saying, "Good Lord, I do not understand this singular creature; it is as odd a plant as I am myself. Oh, that thou wouldest manage it, or tell me how. I have come to tell thee of it."

Constantly our trouble is that we have so many plants to look after that we have not time to cultivate any one in the best manner, because we have fifty more all wanting attention at the time; and then before we have done with the watering-pot we have to fetch the hoe and the rake and the spade, and we are puzzled with these multitudinous cares, even as Paul was when he said, "That which cometh upon me daily, the care of all the churches." Ah, then, it is a blessed thing to do the little we can do and leave the rest to Jesus, "supposing him to be the gardener."

In the church of God there is a discipline which we cannot exercise. I do not think it is half so hard to exercise discipline as it is not to be able to exercise it when yet you feel that it ought to be done. The servants of the householder were perplexed when they might not root up the tares. "Didst thou not sow good seed in thy field? From whence then hath it tares?" "An enemy hath done this." "Wilt thou then that we go and gather them up?" "Not so," said he, "lest ye root up the wheat with them." This afflicts the Christian minister when he must not remove a pestilent, hindering weed. Yes, but "supposing *him* to be the gardener," and it is his will to let that weed remain, what have you and I to do but to hold our peace? He has a discipline more sure and safe than ours, and in due time the tares shall know it. In patience let us possess our souls.

And then, again, there is that succession in the garden which we cannot keep up. Plants will die down, and others must be put into their places or the garden will grow bare; but we know not where to find these fresh flowers. We say, "When yonder good man dies who will succeed him?" That is a question I have heard many a time, till I am rather weary of it. Who is to follow such a man? Let us wait till he is gone and needs following. Why sell the man's coat when he can wear it himself? We are apt to think when this race of good brethren shall die out that none will arise worthy to unloose the latchets of their shoes. Well, friend, I could suppose a great many things, but this morning my text is, "Supposing him to be the gardener," and on that supposition I expect that the Lord has other plants in reserve which you have not yet seen, and these will exactly fit into our places when they become empty, and the Lord will keep up the true apostolical succession till the day of his second advent. In every time of darkness and dismay, when the heart sinks and the spirits decline, and we think it is all over with the church of God, let us fall back on this, "Supposing him to be the gardener," and expect to see greater and better things than these. We are at the end of *our* wits, but he is not at the beginning of his yet: we are nonplussed, but he never will be; therefore let us wait and be tranquil, "supposing him to be the gardener."

IV. Fourthly, I want you to notice that this supposition will give you A DELIVERANCE FROM MANY GLOOMY FEARS. I walked down the garden, and I saw a place where all the path was strewn with leaves and broken branches, and stones, and I saw the earth upon the flower-beds tossed about, and roots lying quite out of the ground: all was in disorder. Had a dog been amusing himself? or had a mischievous child been at work? If so, it was a great pity. But no: in a minute or two I saw the gardener come back, and I perceived that *he* had been making all this disarrangement. He had been cutting, and digging, and hacking, and mess-making; and all for the good of the garden. It may be it has happened to some of you that you have been a good deal clipped lately, and in your domestic affairs things have not been in so fair a state as you could have wished: it may be in the Church we have seen ill weeds plucked up, and barren branches lopped, so that everything is *en deshabille*. Well, if the Lord has done it our gloomy fears are idle. "Supposing him to be the gardener," all is well.

As I was talking this over with my friend, I said to him—"Supposing him to be the gardener," then *the serpent* will have a bad time of it. Supposing Adam to be the gardener, then the serpent gets in and has a chat with his wife, and mischief comes of it; but supposing Jesus to be the gardener, woe to thee, serpent: there is a blow for thy head within half a minute if thou dost but show thyself within the boundary. So, if we are afraid that the devil should get in among us let us always in prayer entreat that there may be no space for the devil, because the Lord Jesus Christ fills all, and keeps out the adversary. Other creatures besides serpents intrude into gardens; caterpillars and palmerworms, and all sorts of destroying creatures are apt to devour our churches. How can we keep them out? The highest wall cannot exclude them: there is no protection except one, and that is, "supposing him to be the gardener." Thus it is written, "I will rebuke the devourer for your sakes, and he shall not destroy the fruits of your ground; neither shall your vine cast her fruit before the time in the field, saith the Lord of hosts."

I am sometimes troubled by the question, What if roots of bitterness should spring up among us to trouble us? We are all such fallible creatures, supposing some brother should permit the seed of discord to grow in his bosom, then there may be a sister in whose heart the seeds will also spring up, and from her they will fly to another sister, and be blown about till brethren and sisters are all bearing rue and wormwood in their hearts. Who is to prevent this? Only the Lord Jesus by his Spirit. He can keep out this evil, " supposing him to be the gardener." The root which beareth wormwood will grow but little where Jesus is. Dwell with us, Lord, as a church and people: by thy Holy Spirit reside with us and in us, and never depart from us, and then no root of bitterness shall spring up to trouble us.

Then comes another fear. Suppose the living waters of God's Spirit should not come to water the garden, what then? We cannot make them flow, for the Spirit is a sovereign, and he flows where he pleases. Ah, but the Spirit of God will be in our garden, " supposing our Lord to be the gardener." There is no fear of our not being watered when Jesus undertakes to do it. " He will pour water on him that is thirsty, and floods upon the dry ground." But what if the sunlight of his love should not shine on the garden? If the fruits should never ripen, if there should be no peace, no joy in the Lord? That cannot happen " supposing him to be the gardener;" for his face is the sun, and his countenance scatters those health-giving beams, and nurturing warmths, and perfecting influences which are needful for maturing the saints in all the sweetness of grace to the glory of God. So, " supposing him to be the gardener " at this the close of the year, I fling away my doubts and fears, and invite you who bear the church upon your heart to do the same. It is all well with Christ's cause because it is in his own hands. He shall not fail nor be discouraged. The pleasure of the Lord shall prosper in his hands.

V. Fifthly, here is A WARNING FOR THE CARELESS, " supposing him to be the gardener." In this great congregation many are to the church what weeds are to a garden. They are not planted by God; they are not growing under his nurture, they are bringing forth no fruit to his glory. My dear friend, I have tried often to get at you, to impress you, but I cannot. Take heed; for one of these days, " supposing him to be the gardener," he will reach you, and you shall know what that word meaneth, " Every plant which my heavenly Father hath not planted shall be rooted up." Take heed to yourselves, I pray.

Others among us are like the branches of the vine which bear no fruit. We have often spoken very sharply to these, speaking honest truth in unmistakable language, and yet we have not touched their consciences. Ah, but " supposing him to be the gardener," he will fulfil that sentence: " Every branch in me that beareth not fruit he taketh away." He will get at you, if *we* cannot. Would God, ere this old year were quite dead, you would turn unto the Lord with full purpose of heart; so that instead of being a weed you might become a choice flower; that instead of a dry stick, you might be a sappy, fruit-bearing branch of the vine. The Lord make it to be so; but if any here need the caution, I pray them to take it to heart at once. "Supposing him to be the gardener," there will be no escaping from his eye; there will be no deliverance from his hand. As "he will throughly purge his floor, and burn up the chaff with unquenchable fire," so he will throughly cleanse his garden and cast out every worthless thing.

VI. Another set of thoughts may well arise as A QUIETUS TO THOSE WHO COMPLAIN, "supposing him to be the gardener." Certain of us have been made to suffer much physical pain, which often bites into the spirits, and makes the heart to stoop: others have suffered heavy temporal losses, having had no success in business, but, on the contrary, having had to endure privation, perhaps even to penury. Are you ready to complain against the Lord for all this? I pray you, do not so. Take the supposition of the text into your mind this morning. The Lord has been pruning you sharply, cutting off your best boughs, and you seem to be like a thing despised, that is constantly tormented with the knife. Yes, but "supposing him to be the gardener," suppose that your loving Lord has wrought it all, that from his own hand, all your grief has come, every cut, and every gash, and every slip: does not this alter the case? Hath not the Lord done it? Well, then, if it be so, put your finger to your lip and be quiet, until you are able from your heart to say, "The Lord gave and the Lord hath taken away, and blessed be the name of the Lord." I am persuaded that the Lord hath done nothing amiss to any one of his people; that no child of his can rightly complain that he has been whipped with too much severity; and that no one branch of the vine can truthfully declare that it has been pruned with too sharp an edge. No; what the Lord has done is the best that could have been done, the very thing that you and I, if we could have possessed infinite wisdom and love, would have wished to have done; therefore let us stop each thought of murmuring, and say, "The Lord hath done it," and be glad.

Especially I speak to those who have suffered bereavement. I can hardly express to you how strange I feel at this moment when my sermon revives a memory so sweet dashed with such exceeding bitterness. I sat with my friend and secretary in that garden some fifteen days ago, and we were then in perfect health, rejoicing in the goodness of the Lord. We returned home, and within five days I was smitten with disabling pain; and worse, far worse than that, he was called upon to lose his wife. We said to one another as we sat there reading the word of God and meditating, "How happy we are! Dare we think of being so happy? Must it not speedily end?" I little thought I should have to say for him, "Alas, my brother, thou art brought very low, for the delight of thine eyes is taken from thee." But here is our comfort: the Lord hath done it. The best rose in the garden is gone. Who has taken it? The gardener came this way and gathered it. He planted it and watched over it, and now he has taken it. Is not this most natural? Does anybody weep because of that? No; everybody knows that it is right, and according to the order of nature, that he should come and gather the best in the garden. If you are sore troubled by the loss of your beloved, yet dry your grief by "supposing him to be the gardener." Kiss the hand that has wrought you such grief? Brethren beloved, remember the next time the Lord comes to your part of the garden, and he may do so within the next week, he will only gather his own flowers, and would you prevent his doing so even if you could?

VII. "Supposing him to be the gardener," then there is AN OUTLOOK FOR THE HOPEFUL. "Supposing him to be the gardener," then I expect to see in the garden where he works the best possible prosperity: I expect to see no flower dried up, no tree without fruit: I expect to see the richest, rarest fruit, with the daintiest bloom upon it, daily presented to the great Owner of the garden. Let us expect that in this church, and pray for it. Oh, if we have but faith we shall see great things. It is our unbelief that straitens God. Let us believe great things from the work of Christ by his Spirit in the midst of his people's hearts, and we shall not be disappointed.

"Supposing him to be the gardener," then, dear friends, we may expect divine intercourse of unspeakable preciousness. Go back to Eden for a minute. When Adam was the gardener, what happened? The Lord God walked in the garden in the cool of the day. But "supposing HIM to be the gardener," then we shall have the Lord God dwelling among us, and revealing himself in all the glory of his power, and the plenitude of his Fatherly heart; making us to know him, that we may be filled with all the fulness of God. What joy is this!

One other thought. "Supposing him to be the gardener," and God to come and walk among the trees of the garden, then I expect he will remove the whole of the garden upward with himself to fairer skies; for he rose, and his people must rise with him. I expect a blessed transplantation of all these flowers below to a clearer atmosphere above, away from all this smoke and fog and damp, up where the sun is never clouded, where flowers never wither, where fruits never decay. Oh, the glory we shall then enjoy up yonder, on the hills of spices in the garden of God. "Supposing him to be the gardener" what a garden will he form above, and how shall you and I grow therein, developing beyond imagination. "It doth not yet appear what we shall be, but we know that when he shall appear we shall be like him, for we shall see him as he is." Since he is the author and finisher of our faith, to what perfection will he conduct us, and to what glory will he bring us! Oh, to be found in him! God grant we may be! To be plants in his garden, "supposing him to be the gardener," is all the heaven we can desire.

"The Sun of Righteousness"

"In them hath he set a tabernacle for the sun, which is as a bridegroom coming out of his chamber, and rejoiceth as a strong man to run a race. His going forth is from the end of the heaven, and his circuit unto the ends of it: and there is nothing hid from the heat thereof"—Psalm xix. 4, 5, 6.
"The Sun of righteousness"—Malachi iv. 2.

WE should feel quite justified in applying the language of the 19th Psalm to our Lord Jesus Christ from the simple fact that he is so frequently compared to the sun; and especially in the passage which we have given you as our second text, wherein he is called "the Sun of Righteousness." But we have a higher justification for such a reading of the passage, for it will be in your memories that, in the 10th chapter of the Epistle to the Romans, the Apostle Paul, slightly altering the words of this psalm, applies them to the gospel and the preachers thereof. "Have they not heard?" said he, "Yea, verily, their sound went into all the earth, and their words unto the ends of the world." So that what was here spoken of the sun by David, is referred by Paul to the gospel, which is the light streaming from Jesus Christ, "the Sun of Righteousness." We can never err if we allow the New Testament to interpret the Old: comparing spiritual things with spiritual is a good mental and spiritual exercise for us; and I feel, therefore, that we shall not be guilty of straining the text at all when we take the language of David in relation to the sun, and use it in reference to our Lord Jesus Christ.

Do not your hearts often say, "What shall we do, or what shall we say to render honor unto our Redeemer?" Have you not often felt confounded as to what offering you shall bring to him? If you had been possessor of all the worlds, you would have laid them at his feet; if the universe had been your heritage, you would cheerfully have resigned it to him, and felt happy in stripping yourself of everything, that he might be rendered the more glorious by your sacrifice. Since you have not all this wealth, have you not again and again asked of your soul,

> "Oh what shall I do,
> My Saviour to praise?"

I would write the best of poems if so I could extol him, but the faculty is not in me; I would sing the sweetest of songs, and compose the most melting music, if I could, and count art, and wit, and music exalted by being handmaidens to him; but, wherewithal shall I adore him, before whom the best music on earth must be but discord; and how shall I set him forth, the very skirts of whose garments are bright with insufferable light? At such times you have looked the whole world through to find metaphors to heap upon him; you have culled all the fair flowers of nature, and made them into garlands to cast at his feet, and you have gathered all earth's gems and precious things wherewith to crown his head, but you have been disappointed with the result, and have cried out with our poet:—

> "The whole creation can afford
> But some faint shadows of my Lord;
> Nature, to make his beauties known,
> Must mingle colours not her own."

At such times, while ransacking land, and sea, and sky for metaphors, you have probably looked upon the sun, and have said: "This great orb, the lord of light and lamp of day, is like my Saviour; it is the faint image of his excellent glory whose countenance shineth as the sun in its strength." You have done well to seize on such a figure. What Milton calls the golden-tressèd sun is the most glorious object in creation, and in Jesus the fulness of glory dwells; the sun is at the same time the most influential of existences, acting upon the whole world, and truly our Lord is, in the deepest sense, "of this great world both eye and soul; he "with benignant ray sheds beauty, life, and joyance from above. The sun is, moreover, the most abiding of creatures; and therein it is also a type of him who remaineth from generation to generation, and is the same yesterday, to-day, and for ever. The king of day is so vast and so bright that the human eye cannot bear to gaze upon him; we delight in his beams, but we should be blinded should we continue to peer into his face; even yet more brilliant is our Lord by nature, for as God he is a consuming fire, but he deigns to smile upon us with milder beams as our brother and Redeemer. Jesus, like the sun, is the centre and soul of all things, the fulness of all good, the lamp that lights us, the fire that warms us, the magnet that guides and controls us; he is the source and fountain of all life, beauty, fruitfulness, and strength; he is the fosterer of tender herbs of penitence, the quickener of the vital sap of grace, the ripener of fruits of holiness, and the life of everything that grows within the garden of the Lord. Whereas to adore the sun would be idolatry; it were treason not to worship ardently the divine Sun of Righteousness.

Jesus Christ is the great, the glorious, the infinitely blessed; even the sun fails to set him forth; but, as it is one of the best figures we can find, be it ours to use it this day. We will think of Jesus as the Sun this morning; first, *as in the text*; secondly, *as he is to us;* and then, thirdly, for a few minutes, *we will bask in his beams.*

I. First, then, we will contemplate JESUS AS THE SUN IN THE TEXT.

Note how the passage begins: "In them hath he set a tabernacle for the sun." Kings were accustomed in their pompous progresses through their dominions to have canopies of splendour borne aloft over them, so that marching in the midst of their glittering soldiery they were themselves the main attraction of the gorgeous pageant. Our Lord Jesus Christ in his church is, as it were, traversing the heavens in a majestic tabernacle, and, like the sun, scattering his beams among men. The Redeemer is canopied by the adoration of his saints, for he "inhabiteth the praises of Israel." He is from day to day advancing in his glorious marchings through the universe, conquering and to conquer, and he will journey onward till the dispensation shall terminate, and the gospel age shall be closed by his second advent. When the text saith that there is a tabernacle set for the sun in the firmament, we are reminded of Christ as dwelling in the highest heavens. He is not alone the Christ of ancient history, but he is the Christ of to-day. Think not always of him as the lowly man despised and rejected, as nailed to the cross, or buried in the tomb; he is not here, for he is risen, but he still exists, not as a dream or phantom, but as the real Christ. Doubt it not, for up yonder, in the seventh heaven, the Lord has set a tabernacle for the Sun of Righteousness. There Jesus abides in splendour inconceivable, the joy and glory of all those blessed spirits who, having believed in him on the earth, have come to behold him in the heavens.

> "Bright, like a sun, the Saviour sits,
> And spreads eternal noon;
> No evenings there, nor gloomy nights,
> To want the feeble moon."

That Jesus lives is a deep well of consolation to the saints, and did we always remember it our hearts would not be troubled. If we always remembered that Jesus both lives and reigns, our joys would never wither. We worship him, it is true, as one who was slain and hath redeemed us unto God by his blood; but we also extol him as one who is "alive for evermore, and hath the keys of death and of hell."

Let your faith to-day behold Jesus sitting at the right hand of God, even the Father. He sits there because his atoning work is done, and he is receiving the infinite reward which his Father promised him. He is exalted as a king upon his throne, expecting until his enemies are made his footstool. He dwells within his tabernacle of praise, adored and admired by angels and glorified spirits. He sits there, not as a weary one, feeble and exhausted, but with the keys of universal monarchy at his girdle, for "the government is upon his shoulder, and his name is called Wonderful, Counsellor, the mighty God." I want you fully to grasp the thought of the living Saviour,—of the Sun in his tabernacle in the highest heavens, for this must be the fulcrum upon which we shall work this morning. We shall get our leverage here: the living Saviour, the mighty Saviour, the reigning Saviour; he is the church's joy and hope in the present and for all years to come.

The text proceeds to speak of Jesus as the sun, and describes him first as *a bridegroom coming out of his chamber*. A beautiful description indeed of the sun when he rises in the early morning. He comes forth from the vast obscure, as from within a secret chamber. He withdraws the veil of night, and floods the earth with fluid gold. From curtains of purple and vermillion, he looks forth, and scatters orient pearl around him. Clad with a blaze of glory, he begins the race of day. Thus our Lord Jesus Christ when he rose from the dead, was as the sun unveiling itself. He came forth from the sepulchre as a bridegroom from his chamber. Observe that dear name of bridegroom. The Lord of heaven and earth, between whom and us there was an infinite distance, has deigned to take our humanity into union with himself of the most intimate kind. Among men, there is no surer mode of making peace between two contending parties, than for a marriage to be established between them. It has often so been done, and thus wars have been ended, and alliances have been established. The Prince of Peace on heaven's side condescends to be married to our nature, that henceforth heaven and earth may be as one. Our Lord came as the bridegroom of his church out of his chamber, when he was born of the virgin and was revealed to the shepherds and the wise men of the east ; yet, in a certain sense, he still continued in his chamber as a bridegroom all his life, for he was hidden and veiled, the Jewish world knew not their king ; though he spake openly in their streets and sought not mystery, yet he was unknown, they did not discern him; and in some respects he did not then desire to be discerned, for he often bade his disciples to tell no man what was done. That was the time when the bridegroom was in his chamber, being made perfect through suffering and perfectly conformed unto his church, bearing her sicknesses and her sorrows, suffering her wants, enduring her shame, and thus completing the marriage union between the two. To this end, he actually descended by dark steps of anguish into the silent inner room of the grave, and there he slept in his chamber, perfectly wedded to his church. Come and look at him, you who admire the lover of your souls ; he stooped to death and the sepulchre, because manhood had fallen under their yoke; his church was subject to death, and he must die. She deserved to suffer the penalty due to God's insulted law, and, therefore, Jesus bowed his head to the stroke.

> " Yea, said the Son, with her I'll go
> Through all the depths of sin and woe;
> And on the cross will even dare
> The bitter pains of death to bear."

And he did bear them, and in the darksome chamber of the tomb, he proved how true a bridegroom he was to his church. Before his great race began, of which we are soon to speak, it behoved our mighty champion to descend into the lowest parts of the earth, and sleep among the dead. Before every day there is a night wherein darkness seems to triumph. It behoved Christ to suffer, and then to rise again. His descent was necessary to his ascent ; his sojourn in the chamber to his race and victory.

Thus I have introduced to you the prelude of the race, the bridegroom in his chamber. Now observe *the coming out of it.* The sun comes forth, at the appointed hour, from the gates of day, and begins to gladden the earth; even so on the third day, early in the morning, Jesus, our Lord, arose from his sleep, and there was a great earthquake, for the angel of the Lord descended from heaven and rolled back the stone from the door of the sepulchre. Then did the Sun of Righteousness arise. Then did the great Bridegroom come forth from his chamber, and begin his joyful race. It must have been a ravishing sight to have beheld the risen Saviour; well might the disciples hold him by the feet and worship him. Methinks, if ever angels sung more sweetly at one time than another, it must have been on that first Easter morning, when they saw the divine champion break his bonds of death asunder, and rise into the glorious resurrection life. Then was he revealed to the sons of men ; and, no longer hidden : he began to tell his disciples the meaning of those enigmas which had been dark to them; things which they had not understood, which seemed inexplicable, were all opened up by him, for now was his time to come out of his chamber. His words, though plain enough, had aforetime hidden him even from those who loved him; but now he speaketh no more in proverbs, but showeth them openly concerning himself and the Father. He hath laid aside the incognito in which he traversed the earth as a stranger, and he is now divinely familiar with his friends, bidding them even touch his hands and his side. In his death the veil was rent, and in his resurrection the High Priest came forth in his robes of glory and beauty. A little while he was gone away, but he returned from the secret chambers of the ivory palaces, and showed himself unto his disciples. Blessed were the eyes that saw him in that day.

Though during the forty days in which our Lord lingered among his followers upon earth we may truly say that he had come out of his chamber, we perceive that he more fully did so when, after the forty days had been accomplished, he took his disciples to the top of Olivet, and there ascended into heaven, out of their sight. Then had the sun indeed ascended above the horizon to make his glories stream along the heavens. See ye not the angelic bands poising themselves upon the wing in mid-air, waiting until he shall return all glowing with the victory won in long and deadly fight. Mark ye well that matchless spectacle as he is "seen of angels."

> "The helmed cherubim
> And sworded seraphim,
> Are seen in glittering ranks, with wings displayed."

They have hastened to meet the Prince of Glory, and attend him to his ancient patrimony. Right glad are all the heavenly band to welcome back the Captain of the Lord's host, and, therefore, they harp in loud and solemn quire to Heaven's triumphant Heir. As for the glorified of mortal race, redeemed of old by his blood which in the fulness of time was shed, they hail him with gladdest hymn, and lift up their sweetest symphonies to extol him who finished transgression, made an end of sin, and brought in everlasting righteousness. Then the bridegroom came out of his chamber with fit marriage music : his beauties hidden awhile in the chamber, where he was regarded as without form or comeliness, blazed forth with renewed splendour, such as confounded both sun and moon.

In another respect, Christ came out of his chamber at his ascension, because, when he ascended on high, leading captivity captive, he received and gave gifts for men. The gifts were intended for the manifestation of himself. His church, which is his body, was by his own command sitting still in the chamber, tarrying till power was given. But, on a sudden, the bridegroom's power was felt, for there was heard the sound as of a rushing mighty wind, which filled all the place, and then descending upon each favoured head came the cloven tongue, and, straightway, you could see that the bridegroom had come out of his chamber, for the multitude in the street began to hear his voice. It was Peter that spake, we say, but far rather was it Christ, the bridegroom, who spake by Peter. It was the sun, from the chambers of the east, bursting through the clouds, and beginning to shine on Parthians, and Medes, and Elamites, and the dwellers in Mesopotamia, and Rome, and Egypt, and making the multitudes in far off lands to see the day which prophets and kings had waited for, but which had never visited their eyes. Do you hear the joyful motion among the people, the joy mingled with the sorrows of repentance? This is the singing of birds, and these the dewdrops which hail the rising sun. The people cry, "What must we do to be saved?"—the shadows are fleeing. They believe in Jesus, and are baptised into his name,—the true light is shining. Three thousand souls are added in one day to the church, for truly the bridegroom is awaked as one out of sleep, and like a mighty man that shouteth by reason of wine (Psalm lxxviii. 65). Then was the gospel race commenced with a glorious burst of strength, such as only our champion could have displayed. Meditate at your leisure upon this first general manifestation of our Lord to the general multitude. He had not gone out of Israel before. "I am not sent," said he, "save to the lost sheep of the House of Israel." Palestine was his chamber: he went to the windows of it, and looked forth on Tyre and Sidon wistfully; but he had not come forth of his chamber till that day, when the gospel began to be preached to the Gentiles also, and in fulfilment of the gift of Pentecost, when the Spirit was poured out upon all flesh, the apostles went everywhere preaching the word. When even we, the dwellers in the far off northern isles, received the gospel, then, indeed, had the bridegroom come forth out of his chamber.

But enough of this, or time will fail me. After the coming forth, we have to consider in the text *his course*. The course of Jesus has been as that of the sun, or like that of a mighty champion girded for running.

Notice, under this head, *his continuance*. Our Lord's gospel has been no meteor that flashed for a while and then passed away, but it has remained as the sun in the heavens. What systems of philosophy have come and gone since on Calvary the Christ of God was lifted up! What speculations, what lo-heres and lo-theres have shone forth, have dazzled fools, and have been quenched in night, since he left the chamber of his marriage! Yet he continues still the same; nor, brethren, are there any marks of decrepitude either in him or in his gospel. They tell us that the idolatry of Hindostan is evidently crumbling: it falls not yet, but it is worm-eaten through and through. Equally sure is it that the false prophet holds but a feeble sway among his followers, and we can all see that though popery makes desperate efforts, and its extremities are vigorous, yet it is paralysed at its heart, and the Vatican is made to feel that its time of power is short.

As for the gospel, it wears the dew of its youth after eighteen centuries of struggles; and it predominates most in those young nations which have evidently a history before them. The old systems are now most favoured by those nations which are left behind in the race of civilisation, but the peoples whom God has made quick by nature are those to whom he has given to be receptive of his grace. There are grand days coming for the church of God. Voltaire said that he lived in the twilight of Christianity; and so he did, but it was the twilight of the morning, not the twilight of the evening. Glory be unto God, the little cloud the size of a man's hand is spreading; it begins to cover the heavens, and the day is not far distant when the sound of abundance of rain shall be heard. Christ was not a strong man, who bounded forth at a leap, and then put forth no more strength, but he rejoiced to continue his work, and to run his race. He was not a shooting star that sparkles for a moment, but a sun that shall shine throughout the livelong day.

Note next in this metaphor *the unity of our Lord's course,* for it is clear in the text: "Rejoicing as a strong man to run the race." A race is one thing; there is the one goal, and the man gathers up his strength to reach it. He has nothing else to think of. They may throw the golden apples in his road, but he does not observe them; they may sound harp and sackbut to the right, and breathe the lute or sweeter instruments of music to the left, but he is deaf to all; he has a a race to run, and he throws his whole strength into it. This is a fit image of our Lord; he has never turned aside, he has never been compelled to retrace his steps, to revise his doctrine, to amend his system, or change his tactics. On, on, on has the course of Jesus been, shining more and more unto the perfect day.

A certain people now-a-days who yet dare to call themselves Christians, are always hankering after something new, pining for novelties, and boasting of their fresh discoveries, though, forsooth, their fresh things are only fragments of broken images of heresies, which our fathers dashed to shivers centuries ago. The great thinkers of the present day are nothing more than mere translators—you know the London meaning of that word—buyers of old shoes who patch them up, and send them forth again as if they were something new. Old shoes and clouted are common enough among those Gibeonites who would deceive Israel, and whose boast is that they have come from far, and bring us treasures of wisdom from remote regions. Sirs, we want not your new things, for our Lord's race is the same as of old, and as he continues in one course so also will we. To spread righteousness and, in so doing, to save sinners and to glorify God, this is the one purpose of Christ; from it he will never cease, and nothing shall ever tempt him from the pursuit of it. Look, I pray you, with pleasure and see how our Lord, from his first coming out of his chamber until now, has continued still in the gospel to shine forth with rays of glory, without variableness or shadow of a turning. Though we believe not, he abideth faithful, he cannot deny himself; he changes not in work or way. For Zion's sake he worketh hitherto, and the pleasure of the Lord prospers in his hand.

But now, observe next, the notable idea of *strength* which the text conveys to us. "Rejoicing as a strong man to run his race." It is no drudgery to the ascended Lord to carry on his cause :

> " The baffled prince of hell
> In vain new efforts tries,
> Truth's empire to repel
> By cruelty and lies;
> Th' infernal gates shall rage in vain.
> Conquest awaits the Lamb once slain."

There is a race to be run but Jesus is strong enough for it; he does not come panting up to the starting place, and thence go creeping on, but like a strong man he surveys the course. He knows that he is equal to it, and, therefore, he delights in it. When he began his race he was opposed, but the opposition only made him triumph the more readily, for " they that were scattered abroad went everywhere preaching the word." When our Lord arose like the sun, the clouds were thick and heavy, but he painted their fleecy skirts with gold; persecution hung over the eastern horizon, but he turned it into the imperial purple of his sovereignty. As he pursued his course the ice of centuries melted, the dense gloom of ages disappeared. No chains could bind him, and no bonds could hold him. He dashed on with undiminished energy, and the gates of hell could not prevail.

As no cloud has ever stayed the sun as he has "whirled his car along the ethereal plain," so no difficulties impeded the onward course of the gospel in the days of its dawning. To the first days of the church Thomson's lines to the sun are fully applicable—

> "Now, flaming up the heavens, the potent sun
> Melts into limpid air the high-raised clouds,
> And morning fogs, that hover'd round the hills,
> In party-coloured bands; till wide, unveil'd,
> The face of nature shines, from where earth seems
> Far stretch'd around, to meet the bending sphere."

The gospel soon shed its light in every land, and all nations felt its benign power. Men ceased to persecute, and bowed before the cross.

Anon fresh clouds arose, and the church passed through them. Errors and heresies multiplied, filthy dreamers led away a huge apostacy, Rome became the mother of harlots and abominations, but the true church, and the true Christ within her, went right on. The church was not less triumphant in her second trial than in her first. Rome Papal was overcome as surely as Rome Pagan. Popes were no more her conquerors than bloody emperors had been of yore. To the thoughtful eye the sun of Christ is not less bright over the valleys of Piedmont than over the waves of the sea which bore Paul and his fellow apostles. The champion's race was as eager and as triumphant as before.

Since then, dense banks of spiritual deadness and false teaching have barred the visible heavens, and have appeared to mortal sight an ebon wall impenetrable as steel, but the Lord reigneth. He that sitteth in the heavens doth laugh, the Lord doth have them in derision. Strong is his right hand, and his enemies shall be broken. On goes the Sun of Righteousness, nothing impedes him, his tabernacle is above them all, he rideth on the heavens, yea, he rideth on the wings of the wind. Trust ye in the Lord for ever, for in the Lord Jehovah there is everlasting strength. Christ has failed in nothing, the decrees have been executed, the eternal purposes have been fulfilled, the elect have been saved, his kingdom is established, and shall continue as long as the sun. Who shall stay his hand? Who shall resist his will?

Observe, therefore, how the force is coupled with *joy*. Weakness brings sorrow, but strength begets joy. Christ is always glad, and he would have his people rejoice, for his cause goeth right on and he shall not fail nor be discouraged. He rejoices as he divides the spoil with the strong. When a man has a task to do which is easy to him, and which he can readily perform, he sings at his work; and so this day doth Christ rejoice over his church with joy, and triumph over her with singing. His cause goes on in spite of foes, and his strength is so great, that even the battle fills him with delight. I remember to have heard a Welsh preacher make use of the following simile. He was speaking of the joy of Christ in heaven, and he said, " You tell me that the church is sorrowful on earth and I tell you that Christ is joyous in heaven; and then you ask me how this can be ? You see yonder mother with her babe, and she is washing the child; its face is foul and she desires to see it shine with brightness, she would see it white as the marble mingled with the redness of the rose. Therefore she washes it; but the child cries, it is fretful and knows not what is good for it, so it whines and struggles; the mother does not cry, or share its sorrow, she keeps on singing because she knows that all is right, and that her darling will smile like a cherub when all is over; she sees the good results coming, while the babe only feels the present discomfort, so she sings her song and never stops, let the child cry as it may." And so the Lord Jesus has pleasure in his work; he is purifying his church, and making her fit to be presented to himself, and though she winces and laments, it is the flesh that makes her so to do. The Lord sings still joyously, because he sees the end from the beginning! Earth may be swathed in mist, but the sun is never so, he shines gloriously evermore.

The text mentions one other fact connected with Jesus as the sun,— " *There is nothing hid from the heat thereof;* " by which is meant, nothing is able to escape the powerful influence of Christ Jesus. His own chosen people must, in due season, feel his power to save. They may wander as they do, and sin as they may, but when the time appointed comes, they shall be redeemed out of the land of the enemy. The sun's power is felt in the darkest and deepest mines; that there is a sun still shining might be discoverable even in the bowels of the earth! and so, in the darkest haunts of sin, God's elect shall be made to feel the sovereign power and omnipotent grace of our Lord Jesus Christ. When you and I shall die, and when we shall be buried in the grave, we shall not there be hid from the heat of this Sun of Righteousness, for by-and-by he shall kindle life within our bones again; he shall create a soul within the ribs of death, and we shall spring upward as the grass, and as the willows by the watercourses, when the sun renews the year. Our dry bones shall live, and in our flesh shall we see God. Meanwhile, while the gracious operations of Christ thus fall on all his elect, and there is nothing hid from the heat thereof, other operations are at work on all the sons of men. He rules in providence over all people, whether they believe in him or not, and if men do not accept the gospel, yet they are affected by it, in some way or other. Even the darkest parts of the world feel something of the presence of the Christ of God. Responsibility is heaped on those that hear of him and reject him; he becomes a savour of death unto death where he is not a savour of life unto life. There is nothing hid from the heat thereof. Oh, how this ought to encourage you Christian people to work! The Lord has gone before you; there is nothing hid from the heat of his presence. Jesus is King of the darkest settlements of the heathen, and he reigns in the lowest haunts of London's vice. Go there, for you are not intruders; you have a right to go anywhere in your Master's dominions; and the earth is the Lord's, and the fulness thereof. Be not afraid to face the vilest blasphemer, or the most foul-mouthed infidel, for Christ is Master, and if you bring the gospel before his enemy, he will be made to feel its power, either so as to yield to it a willing submission, or else to be condemned by it, In either case, you shall have done your part, and uttered your testimony, and freed your head of his blood.

In these thoughts combined, we see Christ Jesus, the risen Saviour, pursuing his ever glorious course till he shall descend again the second time to take his people to himself to reign with him.

II. Very briefly indeed in the second place. Let us think for a moment of JESUS AS A SUN TO US. Worship and bless our Saviour, it is ever meet and right to do so. Let him be extolled and be very high. Some would give him a secondary place, let it never be so with us. As the sun is the centre, so is Christ; as the sun is the great motor, the first source of motive power, so is Christ to his people; as the sun is the fountain from which light, life, and heat perpetually flow, so is the Saviour; as the sun is the fructifier by which fruits multiply and ripen, so is Christ : and as the sun is the regulator and rules the day, and marks the seasons, even so is Jesus owned as Lord to the glory of God the Father.

Think these thoughts over in the following respects. When you take the *Bible* remember that Christ is the centre of the Scriptures. Do not put election in the centre ; some do, and they make a one-sided system. Do not put man in the centre,—some do, and they fall into grievous errors. Christ is the centre of the entire system of the gospel, and all will be seen to move with regularity when you perceive that he is the chief fixed point ; you cannot be right in the rest unless you think rightly of him. He is the centre and King of all truth.

He is the centre of the *Church* too. Not the pastor, not the church itself, not any rule or government, no bishop, no priest, and no Pope can be our centre, Christ alone is our central sun. We follow as planets where he leads the way: around him we revolve, but we own no other Lord.

Let it be so in *the world*. Believe that even there Christ governs and is the centre of all history. You will understand history better when you know this, for this is the key of the world's story, the reason for the rise and fall of empires. You shall understand all things when you know Immanuel, God with us.

And let him have this place in *your hearts*. There enthrone him! Establish him as the central sun, and let him rule your entire being, enlightening your understanding, warming your hearts, filling all your powers, passions, and faculties with the fulness of his presence. To have Christ in us, the hope of glory—oh, what blessedness! But let us take care that it is so, for we know not Christ aright unless we give him such a place in our hearts as the sun occupies in God's world.

III. But time fails me, and we must now pass on to the last point, and let us for a minute or two BASK IN HIS BEAMS. How shall we do it?

First, we must *realise that he is*. Sinner, saint, Christ lives: he who trod the wave of Galilee lives on. He who was marked with the nails rules on. Oh, sinner, does not that comfort you? The Saviour lives, the redeemer lives; he who forgives sins still lives. Saint, does not this comfort you? The man of the tender heart still lives, with a bosom still to be leaned upon, and with lips still ready to speak endearing words. There is a tabernacle for the sun; he is not extinct; he shineth still, he blesses still. Bask in his beams, then, by realising that he is.

Then come and *lay your souls beneath his divine influence*. O my soul, if thou art guilty come and rest in his atonement, if thou art unrighteous come and take his righteousness. If thou art feeble lay hold upon his strength. If thou canst not pray accept him as thine intercessor. If thou art in thyself nothing, take him to be thy all in all. Some creatures delight to warm themselves in the sun, but oh, what a pleasure it is to sun ones self in the presence of Christ. Never mind how little I am, how nothing I am, how vile I am, how foul I am; all I am he has taken to himself, and all he has belongs to me. I sin, but he has taken all my sin: he is righteous and all his righteousness is mine. I am feeble, he is mighty; his mightiness is mine, I wrap myself in his omnipotence. Christ is all and Christ is mine. Why, I utterly fail when trying to talk about such things as these; talking is but stuttering on such a theme. Faith must enjoy rather than express her delight. Come, plunge ye all into this sea of sweetness, dive deep into this abyss of happiness—Christ Jesus is yours for ever and for ever. The sun is very great but it is all for me, and Christ is very bright and glorious, but he is all my own.

Then next, if you would sun yourself in his beams, *imbibe the joy of his strength*. He is like a bridegroom rejoicing to run his race. Now, brethren and sisters, I am often afraid lest in serving God, we should grow dispirited and downcast, and think that things are not going on as they should. The joy of the Lord is your strength. If you begin to say, "Our cause is very feeble, the gospel will not prevail among us, you will slacken your efforts." Do not so, but remember that Jesus Christ does not fret or sadden himself about his kingdom. He runs on full of strength and rejoices as he runs; and I bid you, in the power of the Holy Spirit, do the same. Cast away your doubts and fears, the kingdom is the Lord's, and he will deliver his adversaries into your hands. I fret and worry myself sometimes about these inventors of new doctrines, and those ritualists who bring up the old rags and stale tallow of the past ages. Let us fret no more, but think that these are only like the clouds to the great sun; the gospel will still proceed in its career. Let us laugh the enemies of God to scorn and defy them to their faces. They defy the Lord God of Israel as did the Philistine of old, but God himself is mightier than they, and the victory is sure to the true church and to the gospel of his Son. Be ye very courageous! Be not alarmed with sudden fear! Trust in Jehovah, for the Lord will surely give unto his own servants the victory in the day of battle.

And brethren, if you would sun yourselves in Christ's beams, let me bid you *reflect his light* whenever you receive it. He is the sun, and you are the planet, but every planet shines, shines with borrowed light. It conceals no light, but sends back to other worlds what the sun has given to it. Cast back on men the light which Jesus gives you. Triumph in Christ's circuit, that it is so broad as to comprehend the world, and compass all time. Enlarge your own hearts, and let your light shine far and wide, believing that the power of God which gives you light will go with the light which you reflect. Comfort your hearts! "Be ye stedfast, unmoveable, always abounding in the work of the Lord, forasmuch as ye know that your labour is not in vain in the Lord." Who shall stop the Christ of God in his race? Let him first go pluck the sun from his sphere. Who shall stay the champion of God who has girt himself for his race? Whosoever cometh in his way woe unto him, for if Samson smote a thousand men hip and thigh, what shall our immortal Samson do? Let all the armies of pope and devil come against him, he will utterly defy them, and drive them like chaff before the wind.

Sing ye unto his name, for he hath triumphed gloriously! Begin the everlasting song, for he is the Lord and God, and to the uttermost ages shall he reign; yea, for ever and ever is he priest and king.

God bless you, for Christ's sake. Amen.

The Way to Honour

"Whoso keepeth the fig tree shall eat the fruit thereof: so he that waiteth on his master shall be honoured"—Proverbs xxvii. 18.

IF a man in Palestine carefully watched his fig tree, and kept it in proper condition, he was sure to be abundantly rewarded in due season, for it would yield him a large quantity of fruit of which he would enjoy the luscious taste. So, according to Solomon, good servants obtained honour as the fruit of diligent service. In those early days, when there were far better relations between servants and masters than unhappily there are nowadays, if a servant carefully waited upon his master he was sure to be honoured for his faithfulness. The Bible is full of such cases. Eleazar, the servant and steward of Abraham, met with much honour at his master's hands. Deborah was a faithful nurse, and what sorrow there was for her at Allon-bachuth, or the oak of weeping. Elisha poured water upon the hands of his master Elijah, and became himself a prophet, endowed with a double portion of his master's spirit. In the New Testament we read of the centurion who so honoured his servant that in his sickness he sent to the Lord Jesus, earnestly entreating him to come and heal him. There were exceptions, of course. There were faithful servants who met with ungenerous treatment; but what rule is there without an exception? The rule was that he who was faithful to his master received honour. I could wish it to be more general for there to be intimate friendly relationships between men and their servants; I would fain see a restoration of family loyalty between heads of households and their dependants, In these times servants, and persons in the employ of others, are looked upon as *hands* to be worked, rather than as *souls* to be cared for. It may be that servants have degenerated, but it may also be the truth that masters have degenerated too. I believe that every Abraham will be likely to find an Eleazar, and every Rebekah a Deborah. Good masters make good servants. Good servants make good masters. Happy is the family where, without forgetting the proper distinctions of position, all are knit together in firm friendship. Alas! the bonds of society have been too much loosened. Oppression on the one hand, and discontent on the other, have rent the commonwealth. Yet there still survive among us instances of personal attachment where servants have served the same masters from their youth up, have continued with them in sickness, and in misfortune, have remained faithful to the family when the master has been scarcely able to remunerate them for their services, and have continued faithful even unto death. I am sure when we have read such stories, or seen such servants ourselves, we have felt that they deserved to be had in honour; and there is a general respect still which is manifested by mankind to the servant that waiteth upon his master. However, I am not going to speak about the duties of masters and servants this evening. At other times we have not hesitated to speak our mind upon that matter, and we shall not fail to do so as occasion requires.

But now we shall speak of a higher Master, who was never unfaithful to a servant yet, and never will be; and we shall speak of a superior service, which brings to those who are engaged in it the highest possible degree of honour. Blessed are they who are servants of the King of kings. Happy is he who takes even the lowest place, and fulfils the meanest office for the Lord Jesus, if any service can be mean that is rendered to our all-glorious Immanuel.

We will begin by considering the *relation of the Lord Jesus Christ to us, and ours to him;* then we shall consider the *conduct which is consistent with that relation;* and then the *reward which is promised to such conduct.*

I. And, first, the RELATION WHICH SUBSISTS BETWEEN OURSELVES AND OUR LORD. He is our Master—*our Master.*

I speak now, of course, only to you who are converted, to you who are true believers and are saved by faith in Jesus Christ. The Lord Jesus is to you your *Master,* in the sense of contrast to all other governing powers. You are men, and naturally moved by all that which moves other men, but still the master motive power with every one of you who is a Christian is the supremacy of Christ. There are some among your fellow servants to whom you render respect, just as in a large firm there are foremen set over different parts of the work, to whom a measure of deference is fitly rendered. Still, as the overseer is not the chief authority, so your earthly superiors are not in the highest sense masters over you. The highest of your fellow workmen in your Lord's service is far, far, far below the Master; ministers and fathers in Christ are not the ultimate authorities to whom you bow, and whatever esteem you may pay even to such glorious names as those of Peter, and James, and John, you still regard them but as your fellow servants. "One is your Master, even Christ, and all ye are brethren." In this sense we are not servants of men, yea, we know no man after the flesh. We are in subjection to the Father of Spirits, but neither to Pope in Rome, nor bishop at home; we are the Lord's free men, and cheerfully obey those whom he sets over us in his church: but we yield to none who claim lordship over us, and would divert us from obeying the Lord Jesus only.

The Christian man has, of course, to attend to the concerns of this life, and while he is attending to them he must throw a measure of his heart into them, or he cannot do them properly; still, the master of our heart is not our business, but our Saviour. A Christian man is thoughtful, and he studies, and reads, and investigates; still, for all that, philosophy does not rule him, nor the news of the day, nor the science of the times. Christ is our Master—master of our thoughts and meditations, the great leader and teacher of our understandings. We are his disciples, and disciples of none else besides. We are affected by the love of family, the love of friendship, the love of country; but there is a love that is higher than all these—a master-love, and this is love to Jesus our Well-beloved, the Bridegroom of our souls. That text is frequently misread,—"No man can serve two masters." The stress is not to be laid upon the word "*two.*" For the matter of that, a man might serve three, or half-a-dozen, or twenty; but the stress is to be laid upon the word "*masters*"—"No man can serve two *masters.*" Only one thing can be the master-passion, only one power can completely master us, so as to be supremely dominant, and exercise imperial lordship over us. No man can have two imperial master-faculties, master-motives, and master-ambitions. *One* is our Master, and that one is Christ. Brethren, as I have said before, we are compelled while we are in this body to yield to this impulse and to that, we are urged forward by this motive and by that, we pursue this end and that, and subordinately none of these things may be sinful, but the master-impulse must be the love of Christ, the master-aim must be Christ's glory, and the master-power that doth possess us, as the Spirit took possession of the prophets of old and carried them right away, must be loyalty to Jesus Christ our Lord. He is our Master, and we stand before him as servants who desire to obey his bidding.

What is, then, the reason why the Lord Jesus Christ has become to us a Master? If we were contending with the ungodly, who challenge us for calling Christ "Master," we could give them a ready enough answer by telling them that he is the Master-man of all men. We would ask them to turn over the pages of history and find a man it was worth while to serve in comparison with the man Christ Jesus. We would appeal to his character, and ask, was there ever a character which could compel homage as his character does? Why, he is a right royal man in all respects: there is nothing about him of meanness or weakness. To know him is to become enthusiastic in his cause. We would then point to his kingdom and the nature and character of it, and ask whether there was a kingdom for which men ought to fight, for which men ought to strive and be willing to die, compared with his kingdom? We would point to the benefits which he confers upon mankind, the blessings which the faith of Jesus Christ has scattered amongst the nations, and ask if there ever was a cause so worthy of zeal as the cause of Christ, which is the cause of humanity, the cause of truth, the cause of right, the cause of God. His are the principles which alone can redeem men from their degradation and misery. We count it easy enough to answer the ungodly in this matter. Whoever *their* leader may be, he is not fit to loosen the shoe latchet of our Master's sandal; whoever he may be, and however they may lift him up, he is only fit to lie in the dust beneath the feet of our Immanuel. He is so excellent, and in his nature so pre-eminent, that we defy anyone to count us foolish for choosing him to be our Master.

But behind all this, deep down in our souls, we have other reasons for calling him our Master, namely, that we belong to him by the purchase of his blood, by the rescue of his grace, and again, by the surrender, the willing surrender, which we have made to him. Christ is our Master because he bought us. When we were sold under sin, when by the justice of God we were condemned to die, when we were utter slaves, he purchased us and redeemed us from all iniquity with a cost which sometimes has seemed to us, for his sake, to be too great. What were ten thousand times ten thousand sinful worms compared with the Son of God? Yet that glorious Son of God laid down his life for us. He loved his church and gave himself for it—a matchless price, indeed, to pay!—and now we are not our own, but are bought with a price. We feel that we should be unjust to Jesus, base to our best Benefactor, if we were to ignore the solemn obligations under which his redemption has placed us. We had been on the road to hell if it had not been for his blood; shall we not walk in the way of his commands? After what he has done for us, nothing is too great for us to do for him. Our body, our soul, our spirit we cheerfully render up to his dominion, neither count we ought of our nature to be our own. As he has redeemed us entirely, so in the entirety of our manhood we belong altogether to him; and if there be a part of our nature which has not been subdued to him, we desire him to conquer it by force of arms, for its rebellion against him is sorrow to ourselves. Jesus is our rightful Lord, his wounds attest it, and if any other lord hath dominion over any other portion of our nature, that lordship is usurped and ought to be cast down.

I said, moreover, that Christ has won us by his power as well as by his blood. There are two redemptions, redemption by price and redemption by power; redemption by price was typified in the paschal lamb and the passover, redemption by power in the passage of the Red Sea, when the children of Israel went through it dry shod, and the Egyptians were drowned. Remember how Jacob spake to his son Joseph and said, "I have given to thee one portion above thy brethren, which I took out of the hand of the Amorite with my sword and with my bow." Now, the Lord Jesus Christ claims us in the same way as Jacob claimed that particular portion, for we are his spoil, taken in battle. Almighty grace bowed us down when we were stiff-necked; almighty grace delivered us from our habits of sin when we were fast bound by them; almighty grace broke the iron bars of our despair and led us into liberty; let all the glory be ascribed unto the Almighty Redeemer. With a high hand and an outstretched arm he brought us forth from the Egypt of our lusts and taught our willing feet the way to the heavenly Canaan. And now we grace his chariot wheels as servants, not in manacles of iron, but in silken fetters of love.

"As willing captives of our Lord
We sing the triumphs of his word,"

and confess him to be our Master and none beside.

Remember that I also said we are his servants and he our Master, because we have willingly surrendered ourselves to him. Recall to your memories that blessed time when you gave yourselves up to Jesus under the sweet constraint of his love. Was it not a good day in which you said—

> "Now, Lord, I would be Thine alone,
> Come, take possession of Thine own,
> For Thou hast set me free;
> Released from Satan's hard command,
> See all my members waiting stand,
> To be employ'd by Thee."

And now at this day, remembering the love of your espousals when you went after your Lord into the wilderness, would you have it otherwise? You were married to him; do you now wish to sue for a divorce against your glorious Bridegroom? Nay, but you can sing with Doddridge,

> " High heaven, that heard the solemn vow,
> That vow renew'd shall daily hear:
> Till in life's latest hour I bow,
> And bless in death a bond so dear."

Now, beloved, as I have shown that Christ had a right to be our Master from the very dignity of his character, and that we yield him service because of his love to us; it only remains for me to add that our position of servants to Christ is an irreversible one. The servant of old when he might go out from bondage, sometimes said, " I love my master, and I love his children, and I love his house. I desire to be his bondsman for ever," and after the same manner would I speak this day. And then, you remember, they took an awl and they bored the man's ear and fastened it to the doorpost, that he might be a servant as long as he lived. Even after that fashion would I say, "Mine ears hast thou opened, and I was not rebellious." Who among us would not wish to bear in our body the marks of the Lord Jesus, to receive the brand which would betoken the irretrievable confiscation of all sinful liberty? Do we not wish to be for ever bound to Christ and crucified with him? This was the teaching of our baptism. When we were baptised we were buried in the water. The teaching was, that we were henceforth to be dead and buried to the world and alive alone for Jesus. It was the crossing of the Rubicon—the drawing of the sword and the flinging away of the scabbard. If the world should call us, we now reply, " We are dead to thee, O world!" One of the early saints, I think it was Augustine, had indulged in great sins, in his younger days. After his conversion he met with a woman who had been the sharer of his wicked follies; she approached him winningly, and said to him, " Augustine," but he ran away from her with all speed. She called after him, and said, " Augustine, it is I," mentioning her name; but he then turned round and said, " But it is not *I;* the old Augustine is dead, and I am a new creature in Christ Jesus." That to Madam Bubble and to Madam Wanton, to the world, the flesh, and the devil, should be the answer of every true servant of Christ: " I live, yet not I, but Christ liveth in me. Thou art the same, O fair false world —thou art the same, but not I. I have passed from death unto life, from darkness into light. Thy siren charms can fascinate me no more. A nobler music is in my ear, and I am drawn forward by a more sovereign spell towards other shores than yours. My bark shall cut her way through all seas and waves till it reaches the fair haven and I see my Saviour face to face." 'Tis irretrievable, then, this step which we have taken, the absolute surrender of our whole nature to the sway of the Prince of peace. We are the Lord's. We are his for ever and for ever. We cannot draw back, and blessed be his name, his grace will not suffer us to do so. "The path of the just is as the shining light, that shineth more and more unto the perfect day."

> "Leave thee! no, my dearest Saviour,
> Thee whose blood my pardon bought;
> Slight Thy mercy, scorn thy favour!
> Perish such an impious thought:
> Leave Thee—never!
> Where for peace could I resort?"

II. The second point of our reflection is to be this. Seeing that we are servants to Jesus, there is A CONDUCT WHICH IS CONSISTENT THEREWITH.

What conduct is consistent in a servant? Is it not, first, that he should own himself to be his master's? Such a servant as is mentioned in the text does not call himself his own, or his time his own. No person who is a servant can say during his work hours—"This time is my time, I can do what I like with it." No, he is a false servant if having sold his time for a reward, he takes it to himself. Servants of Jesus have no time at their own disposal. We have no wealth of our own, we are only stewards; we have no talents, they are our Lord's. When we have traded with our stock, and have multiplied it diligently, we shall say to our Lord, "*Thy* pound hath gained ten pounds." We dare not call the talent ours. If we are true servants, we are always about our Master's business. If we eat or drink, or rest or sleep, we desire to do all to the glory of God. We are never off duty. A policeman may be, but we never are. A soldier may have a furlough, but a Christian never, he must wear both night and day the whole armour of God. We are always to bear the shield, and the sword is always to be in our hands. Even in our recreation we are to remember that our Master may come at any hour, and therefore we are still to be looking for his coming.

As servants it is our duty to learn our Master's will. I am grieved to observe that some of my fellow servants do not want to know their Lord's will. There would not be so many divisions in the church if we all came to Holy Scripture and searched the law and the testimony to know the Lord's will. The Lord's will is fully set forth there, and no other book is of the slightest authority among saints. The Lord's will is not in the prayer-book, it is in the Bible. The Lord's will is not in the canons; the Lord's will is not in the creed of the Baptist church, or the Wesleyan church, or the Congregational church, or the Episcopalian church; his will is in the Scriptures: and if we searched them more and more, and were determined, irrespective of anything that may have been done by the church, or the world, or by government, or by anybody else, that we would all follow our Lord's will, we should come to closer union. We are divided because we do not study the Lord's will as we should. Brethren, we ought to be prepared to give up any doctrine however venerable, any institution however comely, if we do not see it to be the divine will. Obedience is the path of the servant, obedience is his safety and happiness. What have I as a servant to do with anybody but my Master? I am set to do a certain thing, and if passers-by make a remark that I am not doing it according to the usual rules of the trade, what is that to me? Rules and customs are of small consequence. My Master's will must be everything to me if I am a true servant. Somebody will sneeringly remark, "You are acting very singularly." Well, the Master must be accountable for the singularity of conduct which he prescribes. If we are true servants we obey even in the jots and tittles, at all hazards. But we must search the word, for unread Bibles are evidences against rebels, and are unbecoming in believers.

When his master's will is known, every true servant is bound immediately to do it. A servant is not to say, "Sir, I will attend to that to-morrow." If the command be ascertained, it will be as surely disobedience to postpone obedience as to reject the duty altogether. If delay be a part of the command, the delay is justifiable, but, if not, the servant must not tarry. "But surely you forget that the consequences of obedience may be costly and involve great sacrifices?" Servants have nothing to do with consequences; those belong to their masters. "But, perhaps, if I were to follow out the Master's command, I might place myself in a position where I should not be as useful as I now am." You have nothing whatever to do with that except as it may prove a test of your faith: it is a lame obedience which only follows the Master where carnal judgment approves. A servant of God is not to use his judgment as to the rightness of his Master's command; he is to do as he is bidden, for his Lord is infallible. What if the heavens fell through our doing right? God does not want us to sin in order to prop them up. His throne is not rotten so as to need buttresses of iniquity. Consequences of true principles ought never to be considered. There is nothing more vicious in the world than policy; it may be admired in the House of Commons, but it should be detested in the church of God. Far from our minds be every question of policy. If an act be right, let it be done: if Christ bids it, let it be done; and let there be no hesitation in the matter.

It is ours, also, if we are servants, to obey the Master *willingly* and for love of his person. The text says, "He that waiteth *upon his master* shall be honoured." Suppose I, as a minister, know something to be God's will, yet, nevertheless, attend to it with the view of serving you and doing you good as God's church; I shall possibly receive honour from you whom I serve, but that is not the honour which a Christian minister ought to seek. The church is not his master; his Master is in heaven, and if he desires real honour, he must earn it by waiting upon his Master for his Master's sake. Suppose any of you are children, and are doing right in order to please your parents— I will not censure the motive; you will get honour from your parents;

but the right honour is gained by seeking to please God. You must
labour as believers to wait upon your Master ; to come to the house of
God, for instance, not because it is the custom, but because you would
honour the Lord in prayer and praise ; you must give to the poor, not
because others have given so much, but because Jesus loves his people
to be mindful of poor saints ; you must do good, not that others may
say, " See what a zealous man he is ! " but for your Master's sake. I
am afraid we sometimes serve ourselves even in our holiest things; and,
in carrying out our judgment of the Lord's will, we are often the
victims of prejudice or whim, and are not so much determined to do the
Lord's will as to have our own, or to carry out what we call our " principles " in order to show that we are not to be cowed by human
opposition. Ah, brethren, there must be no motive with us but our
Master's honour. " He that waiteth on his master shall be honoured."
Wait on your Master. Take care that you have an eye always to him.
Do your duty because he bids you. Then you shall win the honour
of which the text speaks.

Then observe that this waiting upon the Master is to be performed
personally by the servant. It is not, " The servant who employs
another to wait upon his master shall be honoured," I do not so read
the text, but " He that waiteth upon his master " *himself,* doing *personal*
service to a *personal* master—*he* shall have honour. Jesus Christ did
not redeem us by proxy. He, himself—his own self—bare our sins
in his *own* body on the tree. Let us not attempt to serve God by
merely contributing to the foreign mission, or City Mission, or helping
to support the minister, or something of that sort. We should do that,
but we should not put it in the place of the other. Let us constantly
give our personal service, speaking for Christ with *these* lips, pleading
for his kingdom with *this* heart, running on his errands with *these*
feet, and serving him with *these* hands.

" He that waiteth on his master shall be honoured," even though the
waiting be almost passive. Sometimes our master may not require us
to do anything more than stand still. But you know John, the
footman, behind his master's chair, if his master bids him stand there,
is as true a servant as the other attendant who is sent upon an errand
of the utmost importance. The Lord for wise reasons may make us
wait awhile. Having done all, we may yet have to stand still and see
the salvation of God, and find it to be the hardest work of all. In
suffering especially is that the case ; for it is painful to be laid aside
from the Master's service; yet the position may be very honourable.
There is a time for soldiers to lie in the trenches as well as to fight
in the battle. David made a law that those who tarried with the
baggage were to share the spoil with those who went down to the
fight. This is the rule of the church militant to this day. Some
cannot march to the battle, yet are they to share in the spoil ; they
are waiting on their Master, and they shall be honoured.

On the whole, summing all up in a word, it is ours to abide near to
Christ. Servants wait best when they can see their master's eye
and hear his wish. We are to wait upon our Master humbly,
reverently, feeling it an honour to do anything for him. We are
to be self-surrendered, given up henceforth to the Lord, free men,

and yet most truly serfs of this Great Emperor. We are never so truly free as when we own our sacred serfdom. We are henceforth the body servants of the Lord Jesus Christ. Often Paul calls himself the servant of the Lord and even the slave of Christ; and he glories in the branding iron's marks upon his flesh. "I bear," says he, "in my body the marks of the Lord Jesus; henceforth let no man trouble me." We count it liberty to bear the bonds of Christ. We reckon this to be supremest freedom, for we sing with the psalmist, "I am thy servant; I am thy servant. Thou hast loosed my bonds." "Bind the sacrifice with cords, even with cords to the horns of the altar." Such is the conduct which our servitude to our Lord requires.

III. The third point is, THE REWARD WHICH SURELY COMES TO FAITHFUL SERVANTS. "He that waiteth on his master shall be honoured."

You will observe that he finds his honour in waiting on his master. Now, the Christian may have other honours besides the one of waiting on his Master. He may have poor, wretched, miserable, faded honours. I am always sorry when I see a Christian making himself some great one in the world's esteem. I knew one, and I esteemed him much. He was an earnest, Christian man, but his great ambition was to be the chief magistrate in a certain city, which I shall not name. He lived to reach that post, and his heart exulted greatly; but I noticed that the very night he attained the honour the hand of the Lord went forth against one whom he greatly loved, and in a short time he himself sickened, and went home to his Father and his God. No joy came with the honour, for he had looked at it too long, and with too keen an eye. Not I alone, but those who knew him, judged so too, and we almost thanked God that he did not suffer the child of God, whose crown was in heaven, to be satisfied with being a magistrate here. I have seen men grow very eager after gold, they have had a good business, but have clutched at more and got it, and then sought after more still; and when I have seen chastening come, and sorrow in the household, I have not marvelled at it, for I have understood that Christ meant his servant to take honour from *him*, and if he *would* look after other honour he would find it but a bitter-sweet. There is a law, I believe, that no subject of Her Majesty may take princely rank from any foreign potentate, and it is a law in the kingdom of Christ. What honour can this world confer upon a servant of Christ? I count that to be a scullion in Christ's kitchen would be a greater honour than to be the Czar of all the Russias, or to exercise imperial sway over all the kingdoms of the earth at once. Honour! *Ye* confer honour upon the servant of Christ—ye worldlings! As well might emmets upon their anthills hope to confer dignity upon an angel! Already infinitely superior, it is but degradation to a saint to be honoured by the sons of men. The servant of Christ finds his honour in the service itself. The cultivator of the fig tree looks for figs from the fig tree; the servant of the Master looks for honour from the Master, and he covets no honour besides.

Every faithful servant of Christ is honoured in his Master's honour. If you serve Christ aright you will have to bear his reproach. You must take your share of the cross; for you have already your share of the crown. Thanks be to God, who always causes us to triumph in every place. Paul and the other apostles, when they were suffering for Christ, were always triumphing in Christ at the same time. If there be any honour in the cause of truth and righteousness, and the salvation of men, Christ has it all, but he reflects some of it upon those of his servants who vindicate his righteous cause and propagate his truth. "He that waiteth on his master is honoured" by being permitted to wait upon such a Master. The honour of the Master falls upon the servant, who is honourably distinguished by wearing the livery of the great Prince.

He is honoured too with his Master's approval. Did you ever feel that Christ approved of you? You did some little act of love which nobody knew of but your Lord; he smiled on you, you knew he did, and you felt superabundantly rewarded. You served him, and you were reviled for it, but you took it very joyfully, for you felt that he knew all about it, and as long as your Master was satisfied it did not signify what man could do unto you. For the true Christian his Lord's approval is honour enough.

Sometimes the Lord honours faithful servants by giving them more to do. If they have been faithful in that which is least, he tries them in that which is great. If they have looked after a few little children, and fed the lambs, he says, "Come hither and feed my sheep." If they have trimmed a vine, or a fig tree in a corner, he calls them out and sets them among the chief vines of the vineyard, and says to them, "See after these clusters." Many a man would have been called to wider fields of labour if he had not been discontented or slothful in his narrow sphere. The Lord watches how we do little things, and if great care be taken in them he will give us greater things to do. Elisha poured water upon the hands Elijah, and then the Lord says, "Elijah's mantle shall fall upon his faithful servant, and he shall do even greater miracles."

God also honours the faithful in the eyes of their fellow servants. When I take down from my library-shelf the biography of a holy man I honour him in my soul; I do not mind whether he was a a bishop or a Primitive Methodist preacher, a blacksmith or a peer, I do him honour in my heart. If he served his Master, he will be sure to be elevated into a position of honour in the memory of succeeding ages. There are some men whose doctrines you and I could not endorse, who yet were faithful to the light they had, and therefore we number them amongst the honoured dead, and we are glad to recollect how bold they were against the foe, how meek they were with the little ones, how faithful they were in believing their God, and how courageous in rebuking sin. If you would have honour from your fellow servants, you will never get it by seeking honour from them; you must go to your Master and honour him by waiting upon him, and then there will come to you honour in the eyes of your fellow men.

But, beloved, the chief honour of a faithful servant comes from the blessed Trinity. "If any man will serve me, him will my Father honour." Does it not appear too good to be true that a poor man should be honoured of God the Father, the Creator, the great I Am! I will not speak about it, but leave you to think it over.

And then Jesus Christ will honour us; for he says, that when the master comes and finds the servant waiting for him, he will gird himself and serve him. Can you understand that? There was a certain saturnalia amongst the Romans, which was observed once a year, in which the masters changed places with the servants entirely, and the servants sat at the table and commanded their masters as they liked, while the masters served them. It has been thought by some that our Saviour has drawn the figure from that singular celebration. I hardly think that it can be so, for he would scarcely have cared to use such an illustration. To think of the great Master serving us is strange indeed; yet he has done it. He did so when he took a towel and washed his disciples' feet, and he will do it again; he will gird himself and serve us.

The Holy Spirit will honour us too, for the Holy Spirit often puts great honour upon a faithful man in a way that I cannot explain to you except by a figure. Moses had been a faithful servant, and the skin of his face shone when he came down from the mount. Stephen was a faithful servant, and when he stood up to confront his adversaries, he was full of the Holy Ghost, and a glory gleamed from his face. When the Spirit of God is richly in a man, and that man is faithful to his Master, some gleamings of a supernal splendour will come from him, not visible to human eyes but potent over human hearts. Believers will feel its power, for as one of our poets says, when a good man is in company 'tis even as though an angel shook his wings. You feel the influence of the man, and almost without a word from him, he has honour in the eyes of them that sit at meat with him, for the Holy Ghost is upon him.

Now, dear brethren and sisters, I close by saying we ought faithfully to serve, for we have before us the greatest conceivable reward, a reward which grace enables us to gain. That precious blood which cleanses us, cleanses our service also, it makes us white as snow, and it makes our service white too. We and our work are both accepted in the Beloved. A Christian's works are good works : let no one say they are not, for they are the work of the Spirit of God, and who shall say they are not good? It is an encouragement to go forward when we know that "he that keepeth the fig tree shall eat the fruit thereof;" and that "the servant who waiteth on his master shall be honoured."

There is a black side to this, upon which suffer ye one word. He who doth *not* serve Jesus Christ, will *not* be honoured. In the day when the Lord cometh many that sleep in the dust shall awake, some to glory, but some to shame and everlasting contempt. Oh, the contempt that will be poured upon ungodly men at the last judgment! When God holds up the mirror and they see themselves, they will despise their own image; and when God holds up their characters to men and angels, revealing to all created beings their secret deeds, their evil motives, their base designs, their filthy imaginations, there will go up against such men, dying without faith in Christ, a universal hiss of general execration, to think that they would not believe God, but made God a liar; would not accept the sacrifice of Christ, but trod the blood of the covenant under foot as an unholy thing. Redeemed men will cry, "Shame!" Unfallen angels will cry "Shame!" Holy spirits from a thousand worlds will cry "Shame!" And it will be everlasting contempt. Nothing stings a man like contempt. The poorest among us does not like to be despised, however poor he may be. You do not like to be pointed at and be made the object of derision, yet, sinner, this will be your portion. If you die without believing in Jesus, you will wake up to shame and to everlasting contempt. "Shame shall be the portion of fools"—such shame! Oh, be ashamed to-day, that you may not be ashamed then! Penitent, shame will lead you to fly to Christ, and put your trust in him, and then your transgressions shall be blotted out for ever. May the Spirit lead each one of you to repentance for Jesus' sake. Amen.

The Unrivalled Friend

"A friend loveth at all times, and a brother is born for adversity"—Proverbs xvii. 17.

THERE is one thing about the usefulness of which all men are agreed, namely, friendship; but most men are soon aware that counterfeits of friendship are common as autumn leaves. Few men enjoy from others the highest and truest form of friendship. The friendships of this world are hollow, they are as unsubstantial as a dream, as soon dissipated as a bubble, as light as thistledown. Those airy compliments, those empty sentences of praise, how glibly they fall from the lip, but how little have they to do with the heart! He must be a fool indeed, who believes that there is aught in the complimentary affection but mere flattery or matter of form. The loving cup means not love, and the loud cheering of the toast means not sincere fellowship. With very many, friendship sits very loosely: they could almost write as Horace Walpole does in one of his letters. He says, he takes every thing very easily, "and if," saith he, "a friend should die, I drive down to the St. James's coffee-house, and bring home another," doubtless as cordial and enraptured with the new friend as with the old. Friends in this world are too often like the bees which swarm around the plants while they are covered with flowers, and those flowers contain nectar for their honey; but let November send its biting frosts, the flowers are nipped, and their friends the bees forsake them. Swallow friendship lives out with us our summer, but finds other loves in winter. It has always been so from of old, even until now; Ahithophel has deserted David, and Judas has sold his Lord. The greatest of kings who have been fawned upon by their courtiers while in power, have been treated as if they were but dogs in the time of their extremity; we may, as the poet of the passions—

"Sing Darius, great and good.
* * * *
Deserted in his utmost need,
By those his former bounty fed;
On the cold ground exposed he lies,
With not a friend to close his eyes."

Of all friendship which is not based on principle, we may say with the prophet, "Thou art weighed in the balances, and found wanting." But there is a higher friendship than this by far, and it subsists among Christian men, among men of principle, among men of virtue, where profession is not all, but where there is real meaning in the words they use. Damon and Pythias still have their followers among us, Jonathan and David are not without their imitators. All hearts are not traitorous; fidelity still lingers among men : where godliness builds her house, true friendship finds a rest. Solomon speaking not of the world's sham friends, but of friends indeed, saith, "A friend loveth at all times." Having once given his heart to his chosen companion, he clings to him in all weathers, fair or foul; he loves him none the less because he becometh poor, or because his fame suffers an eclipse, but his friendship like a lamp shines the brighter, or is made more manifest because of the darkness that surrounds it. True friendship is not fed from the barn-floor, or the winefat; it is not like the rainbow, dependent upon the sunshine, it is fixed as a rock, and firm as granite, and smiles superior to wind and tempest. If we have friendship at all, brethren and sisters, let this be the form it takes: let us be willing to be brought to the test of the wise man, and being tried, may we not be found wanting. "A friend loveth at all times."

But I am not about to talk of friendship at all as it exists between man and man; I prefer to uplift the text into a still higher sphere. There is a Friend, blessed for ever be his name, who loveth at all times; there is a Brother, who, in an emphatic sense, was born for adversity. That friend is Jesus, the friend of sinners, the friend of man, the brother of our souls, born into this world that he might succour us in our adversities. I shall take the text, then, and refer it to the Lord Jesus Christ; and unless time should fail us, I shall then refer it to ourselves as in connection with the Lord Jesus Christ, showing that we also ought to love him even as he has loved us, always and under all adversities.

I. First, then, IN REFERENCE TO THE LORD JESUS CHRIST. The first sentence is, "*a friend loveth at all times*," and this leads us to consider, first, *the endurance of the love of Jesus Christ.*

My dear brethren, when we read "a friend loveth at all times," and refer that to Christ, the sentence full as it is, falls short of what we mean, for our Lord Jesus is a friend who loved us before there was any time. Before time began, the Lord Jesus Christ had entered into covenant that he would redeem a people unto himself, who should show forth his Father's praise. Before time began, his prescient eye had foreseen the creatures whom he determined to redeem by blood. These he took to himself by election, these the Father also gave to him by divine donation, and upon these as he saw them in the glass of futurity he set his heart. Long before days began to be counted, or moons to wax and wane, or suns to rise and set, Jehovah Jesus had set apart a people to himself, whom he espoused unto himself, whose names he engraved upon his heart and upon his hands, that they might be taken into union with himself for ever and ever. Meditate on that love which preceded the first rays of the morning, and went forth to you before the mountains were brought forth, or ever he had formed the earth and the world. My brethren, you believe the doctrine of eternal love, meditate thereon, and let it be very sweet unto your hearts:—

> "Before thy hands had made
> The sun to rule the day,
> Or earth's foundation laid,
> Or fashioned Adam's clay,
> What thoughts of peace and mercy flow'd
> In thy dear bosom, O my God!"

He loved you when time began, in the elder days before the flood, and in the far-off periods; for those promises which were spoken in love had reference to you as well as to all the believing seed. All the deeds of love which were wrought as a preface to his coming, all had some bearing towards you as one of his people. There never was a point in the antiquity of our world in which this friend did not love you, every era of time has been a time of love. Love, like a silver thread, runs adown the ages. Chiefly did he lay bare his love eighteen hundred years ago, when down with joyful haste he sped to lie in the manger; and hang as a babe at the virgin's breast. He proved his love to you to a degree surpassing thought when, as a carpenter's son he condescended for thirty years to live in obscurity, working out a perfect righteousness for you, and then spent three years of arduous toil, to be ended by a death of bitterness unutterable. You had no being then, but he loved you, and gave himself for you. For you the bloody sweat that fell amidst the olives of Gethsemane; for you the scourging and the crowning with thorns; for you the nails and spear, the vinegar and lance; for you the cry of agony; the exceeding sorrow "even unto death." He is a friend that loved you in that darkest and most doleful hour, when your sins were laid upon him and with their crushing weight pressed him down, as it were, in spirit, to the lowest hell.

Beloved, having thus redeemed you, he loved you when time began with you. As soon as you were born the eye of his tenderness was fixed upon you. "When Ephraim was a child, then I loved him." It was lovingkindness which arranged your parents' native place and time of birth. You came not into this world, as it were, by chance, or as the young ostrich bereft of a parent's care—the Lord was your guardian; the Lord Jesus Christ looked upon you in your cradle, and bade his angels keep ward around you. He would not let you die unconverted, though fierce diseases waited around you to hurry you to hell. And when you grew up to manhood, and ripened the follies of youth into the crimes of mature years, yet still he loved you. O let your heart be humbled as you remember that if you ever fell into blasphemy, he loved you as you cursed him; that if you indulged in Sabbath-breaking, he loved you when you despised his day; that your neglected Bible could not wean his heart from you, that your neglected prayer closet could not make him cease his affection. Alas! to what an excess of riot did some of his people run! but he loved them notwithstanding all. He was a friend that loved under the most provoking circumstances.

> "Loved when a wretch defiled with sin,
> At war with heaven, in league with hell,
> A slave to every lust obscene,
> Who, living, lived but to rebel."

When justice would have said, "Let the rebel go, O Jesus, be not bound any longer by cords of love to such a wretch," our ever faithful Redeemer would not cast us away, but threw another band of grace around us and loved us still. Consider well, "his great love wherewith he loved us, even when we were dead in trespasses and sins."

I feel as if this were rather matter for you to think over in private, than for me thus hastily to introduce to you in public. May the Holy Spirit however now bedew your hearts with grateful drops of celestial love, as I remind you of the love at all times of this best of friends. You recollect when you were constrained to seek him, when your heart began to be weary of its sin, and to be alarmed at the doom that would surely follow unpardoned transgression; it was his love that sowed the first seeds of desire and anxiety in your heart. You had never desired him if he had not first desired you. There was never a good thought towards Christ in any human breast, unless Christ first put it there. He drew you, and then you began to run after him; but had he left you alone, your running would have been from him, and never towards him. It was a bitter time when we were seeking the Saviour, a time of anguish and sore travail. We recollect the tears and prayers that we poured out day and night, asking for mercy; but Jesus, our friend, was loving to us then, taking delight in those penitential tears, putting them into his bottle, telling the angels that we were praying, and making them string their harps afresh to sweet notes of praise over sinners that repented. He knew us, knew us in the gloom, in the thick darkness in which we sought after God, if haply we might find him. He was near the prodigal's side when in all his rags and filth he was saying, "I will arise, and go to my Father," and it was Jesus through whom we were introduced to the Father's bosom, and received the parental kiss, and were made to sit down where there are music and dancing, because the dead are alive, and the lost is found.

My brethren, since that happy day, this friend has loved us at all times. 1 wish I could say that since that sacred hour when we first came to his feet, and saw ourselves saved through him, we had always walked worthily of the privileges we have received; but it has been very much the reverse. There have been times in which we have honoured him, his grace has abounded, and our holiness has been manifest; but alas! there have been other seasons in which we have backslidden, our hearts have grown cold, and we were on the road to become like Nabal when his heart was turned to a stone within him. We have been half persuaded, like Orpah, to go back to the land of idols, and not like Ruth, to cleave unto the Lord our God. Our heart has played the harlot from the love of Christ, desiring the leeks, and garlick, and onions of Egypt rather than the treasures of the land of promise. But at such times when our piety has been at a low ebb, he has loved us still; there has not been the slightest diminution in the affection of Christ even when our piety has been diminished; he does not set his clock by our watch, or stint his love to the narrow measure of ours. I fear we have often gone further than merely getting poor in grace within; there have been times when God's people have even actually fallen into overt sin; ay, and have descended to sin grievously too, and to dishonour the name of Christ; but herein is mercy, even those actual and accursed sins of ours have not rent away the promise from us, nor turned away the heart of Christ for his beloved. Sinned though we have to our abounding sorrow, I was about to say, for if there could be sorrow in heaven we might eternally regret that we have sinned against such love and mercy, yet for all that our Lord and Saviour would not cast us off, nor will he abjure us come what may.

Reflect, my dear friends, upon all the trying and changeful scenes through which you have passed since the time of your conversion. You have been rich perhaps and increased in goods: you were tempted to forget your Lord, but he was a friend who loved you at all times, and he would not suffer your prosperity to ruin you, but still made his love to dart with healing beams into your soul. But you have been also very poor. The cupboard has been bare, and you have said, "Whence shall I find sufficient to supply my need?" But Christ has not gone away because your suit was threadbare, or your house ill furnished; nay, he has been nearer than ever, and if he revealed himself to you in your prosperity, much more in your adversity. You have found him a faithful friend when all others were unfaithful, true when every one else was a liar. You have been sore sick sometimes, but he it was that made the pillow, and that softened the bed of your affliction. It may be you have been slandered, and those who loved you have passed you by. Some ill word has been spoken in which there was no truth, but it has sufficed to turn away the esteem of many; but your Lord has gone with you through shame and abuse, and never for a single moment has he even hinted that he only loved you because you were had in respect by men. Ever faithful, ever true, has been this friend, who loveth at all times. Ah, there have been times, it may be with you, when you could fain have thrown your very self away, for you felt so empty, so good-for-nothing, so undeserving, ill deserving, hell deserving; you felt fitter to die than to live; you could hardly entertain a hope that any good thing could ever spring from you: but when you have least esteemed yourself, his esteem of you has been just the same; when you were ready to die in a ditch, he has been ready to lift you to a throne; when you felt yourself a castaway, you have still been pressed to his dear bosom, an object of his peculiar regard.

Soon, very soon, your time will come to die: you shall pass through the valley of deathshade, but you need not fear, for the friend that loveth at all times will be with you then. That eminent servant of God, Jonathan Edwards, when he was at his last, said, "Where is Jesus of Nazareth, my old and faithful friend? I know he will be with me now that I need his help," and so he was, for that faithful servant died triumphant. You shall enquire in that last day for Jesus of Nazareth, and you shall hear him say, "Here I am;" you shall find the deathshade vale lit up with supernal splendour, it shall be no death to you, but a passing into life eternal, because he who is the resurrection and the life shall be your helper.

Thus I have hastily run through the life of Christ's love from the beginning that had no beginning, down to the end that knoweth no end, and in every case we see that he is a friend that loveth at all times.

Now, brethren, I shall vary the strain, though still keeping to the same subject. Let us consider *the reality of Christ's love* at all times.

The text says, "A friend loveth at all times," not professes to love, not talks of love, but really does so. Now in Christ's case, the love has become intensely practical. His love has never been a thing of mere words or pretensions; his love has acted out itself in mighty deeds, and signs, and wonders, worthy of a God, such as heaven itself shall not sufficiently extol with all its golden harps.

See then, brethren, Christ has practically loved us at all times. It is not long ago that you and I were slaves to sin, we wore the fetters, nor could we break them from our wrists. We were held fast by evil passions and worldly habits, and there seemed no hope of liberty for us. Jesus loved us at all times, but the love did not let us lie prisoners any longer. He came and paid the ransom price for us. In drops of blood from his own heart he counted down the price of our redemption, and by his eternal Spirit he broke every fetter from us, and to-day his believing people rejoice in the liberty wherewith Christ makes them free. See how practical his love was! He did not leave the slave in his chains and let him remain a captive, but he loved us right out of our prison-house into a sacred freedom. Our Lord found us not long ago standing upon our trial. There we were prisoners at the bar, we had nothing to plead in our defence. The accuser stood up to plead against us, and as he laid many charges and heavy, we were not able to answer so much as one of them. Our great High Priest stood there, and saw us thus arraigned as prisoners at the bar; he loved us, but oh! how efficient was his love—he became an advocate for us; he did more, he stood in our place and stead, stood where the felon ought to stand. He suffered what was due to us, and then covering us with his perfect righteousness, he said before the blaze of the ineffable throne of justice, " Who shall lay anything to the charge of God's elect ? It is Christ that died, yea, rather that hath risen again." He did not love the prisoner at the bar and leave him there to be condemned; he loved him until this day we stand acquitted, and there is therefore now no condemnation to them that are in Christ Jesus. Believer, lift up your heart now, and bless his name who hath done all this for thee.

Our Lord when he came in mercy to us, found us in the rags of our self-righteousness, and in the abject poverty of our natural condition. We were houseless, fatherless; we were without spiritual bread, we were sick and sore, we were as low and degraded as sin could make us. He loved us, but he did not leave us where love found us. Ah! do you not remember how he washed us in the fountain which flowed from his veins; how he wrapped us about with the fair white linen, which is the righteousness of his saints; how he gave us bread to eat that the world knoweth not of; how he supplied all our wants, and gave us a promise, that whatsoever we should ask in prayer, if we did but believe his name, we should receive it! We were aliens, but his love has made us citizens; we were far off, but his love has brought us nigh; we were perishing, but his love hath enriched us; we were serfs, but his love has made us sons; we were condemned criminals, but his love has made us " heirs of God, and joint-heirs with Jesus Christ."

I shall not enlarge here, but I shall appeal to the experience of every believer. In your needs, has not Christ always helped you? you have been in doubt which way to take, and you have gone to him for guidance: did you ever go wrong when you left it to him? Your heart has been very heavy, and you had no friend that you could communicate with, but you have talked with him, and have not you always found solace in pouring out your hearts before him? When did he ever fail you? when did you find his arm shortened, or his ear heavy? Up to this moment has it been mere talk with Christ? no, you know it has been most true and real love—and now in the recollection of it, I beseech you give him true and real praise, not that of the head only, or of the lip, but of your whole spirit, soul, and body, as you consecrate yourself afresh to him. See then the endurance of Christ's love, and see then also the reality of it.

By your patience, I shall notice in the next place *the nature of the love of Christ*, accounting for its endurance and reality. The love of our good friend to us, sprang from the purest possible motives. He has nought to gain by loving us. Some friendship may be supposed to be tinged with a desire of self advantage, to that extent it is degraded and valueless. But Jesus Christ had nought to gain, but everything to lose. "Though he was rich, yet for our sakes he became poor." The love he bears to his people, was not a love which sprang from anything in them. I have no doubt it had a reason, for Christ never acts unreasonably, but that reason did not lie in us. Love between us and our fellows sometimes springs from personal beauty, sometimes for traits of character which we admire, and at other times from obligations which we have incurred, but with Christ none of these things could avail. There was no personal beauty in any one of his elect: there were no traits of character in them that could enchant him, very much on the other hand that might have disgusted him; he certainly was under no obligations to us, for we had not a being then when his heart was set upon us. The love of man to man is sustained by something drawn from the object of love, but the love of Christ to us has its deep springs within himself. As his own courts maintain the grandeur of his throne without drawing a revenue from the creatures, so his own love maintains itself, without drawing any motives and reasons from us, and hence, my brethren, you see why this love is the same at all times. If it had to subsist upon us and what we do, and what we merit, ah! it would always be at the lowest conceivable ebb, but since it leaps up from the great deep of the divine heart, it never changes, it never shall.

Be it also remembered that Christ's love was a wise love, not blind as ours often is. He loved us knowing exactly what we were whom he loved. There is nothing in the constitution of man that Jesus Christ had not perceived; there is nothing in your individuality but what Christ had foreknown. Remember Christ loved his people before they began to sin, but not in the dark. He knew exactly everything they would think, or do, or be; and if he resolved to love them at all, you may rest assured he never will change in that love, since nothing fresh can ever occur to his divine mind. Had he begun to love us, and we had deceived and disappointed him, he might have turned us out of doors, but he knew right well that we should revolt, that we should backslide and should provoke him to jealousy; he loved us knowing all this, and therefore it is that his love abides and endures, and shall even remain faithful to the end.

Brethren, the love of Christ is associated continually with an infinite degree of patience and pity. Our Lord knows that we are but dust, and like as a father pitieth his children, so he pities us. We are but short-tempered, but our Lord is longsuffering. When he sees us sin, he saith within himself, "Alas! poor souls, what folly in them thus to injure themselves." He takes not our cold words in umbrage, so as to put himself in wrathful fume therewith; but he saith, "Poor child, how he hurteth himself by this, and how much he loseth thereby." He even hath a kind look for us when we sin, for he knows it is blotted out through his own blood, and he sees rather the mischief which it is quite sure to bring to the poor soul, than the evil of the sin itself. Jesus hath infinite condescension and patience, and we cannot so provoke him as to turn him from his purpose of grace. He is at all times ready to pardon, and never slow to be moved to forgiveness. Oh, the provocations of men! but the patience of Christ reacheth over the mountains of our provocation, and drowns them all.

Methinks one reason why Christ is so constant in his love, and so patient with us, is that he sees us as what we are to be. He does not look at us merely as what we are to-day in Adam's fall—ruined and lost, nor as we are to-day, but partly delivered from indwelling sin; but he remembers that we are to lie in his bosom for ever, that we are to be exactly like himself, and to be partakers of his glory; and as he sees us in the glass of futurity, as by-and-by to be his companions in the world of the perfect, he passes by transgression, iniquity and sin, and like a true friend he loveth us at all times.

I shall not weary those who know this love. They need no gaudy sentences or eloquent periods to set it forth. Its sweetness lies in itself. You may drink such wine as this out of any cup. He that knoweth the flavour of this divine dainty, asketh not that it be carved this way or that, he rejoiceth but to have it, for the meditation upon it must be sweet. "A friend loveth at all times."

The next sentence of the text is, "*and a brother is born for adversity*." That is to say, a true brother comes out and shows his brotherhood in the time of the trouble of the family. Now let every believer in Jesus here catch the meaning of this with regard to Christ. Jesus Christ was born for you. "Unto us a child is born, unto us a Son is given;" but if at any one time more than another, Christ is peculiarly yours by birth, it is in the time of adversity. A brother born for adversity.

Observe, that Christ was born in the first place, for our adversity, to deliver us from the great adversity of the fall. When our parents' sin had blasted Eden, and destroyed our hopes, when the summer of our joy had turned into the winter of our discontent, then Christ was born in Bethlehem's manger, that the race might be lifted up to hope, and his elect be elevated to salvation. He restored that which he took not away, he rebuilt that which he cast not down. He had never come to be a Saviour if we had not been lost; because our adversity was so great, therefore so great a Saviour was required, and so great a Saviour came.

Our Lord is born for adversity because he has the peculiar art of sympathising with all in adversity. No other but he can claim that he has ranged high and low through all the territories of grief, but this Jesus Christ can justly claim. Every pang that ever rends a human heart has first tried its keen edge on him. It is not possible even in the extremities of anguish to which some are exposed, that any man can go beyond Christ in the endurance of pain. Christ is crowned king of misery, he is the emperor of the domains of woe. He is able therefore to succour all such as are tempted and tried, seeing he is compassed about himself also with a feeling of our infirmities. Look to him suffering on the tree, look to him throughout all his life of shame and pain, and you will see that he was born into adversity, and through being born into it, was born to sympathise with our trials, having learned, as the Captain of our salvation, to be made perfect in sympathy with those many sons whom he brings to glory.

Brethren, the text means more than this however. Jesus Christ is a brother born for adversity, because he always gives his choicest presence to his saints when they are in tribulation. I know many men will think that the presence of Christ with the sick and with the depressed is mere fancy. Ah, blessed fancy! such a fancy as makes them laugh at pain, and rejoice in deep distress, and take joyfully the spoiling of their goods. A blessed fancy truly! Let me declare my heart's witness, and assert that if there be anything real anywhere to the spiritual mind, the presence of Christ is intensely so. Though we do not see his form bending over us, nor mark the lovely light of those eyes that once were red with weeping, though we touch not that hand which felt the nails, and hear no soft footfalls of the feet that were fastened to the cross, yet are we inwardly as certainly conscious of the shadow of Christ falling upon us as ever were his disciples, when he stood in the tempest-tossed vessel, and said to winds and waves, "Peace, be still." Believe me, it is not imagination, nor is it barely faith. It is faith that brings him, but there is a kind of spiritual sense that discovers his presence, and that rejoices in the bliss flowing therefrom. We speak what we do know, and testify what we have seen, when we say that he is a brother born for adversity in very deed, most tenderly revealing himself to his people, as he doth not unto the world.

He is born for adversity, I think, in this sense, that you can hardly know him except through adversity. You may know Christ so as to be saved by him by a single act of faith, but for a full discovery of his beauty it needs that you go through the furnace. Those children of

God whose grassy paths are always newly mown, and freshly smoothed, learn comparatively but little fellowship with Christ, and have but slender knowledge of him, but they that do business on great waters, these see the works of the Lord and his wonders in the deep, and these know the love of Christ which passeth knowledge. "It is good for me that I have been afflicted," many can say, not only because of the restoring effect of sorrow, but because their afflictions have acted like windows, to let them gaze into the very heart of Christ, and read his pity and understand his nature, as they never could have done by other means. Furnace light is memorably clear. Jesus is a brother born for adversity, because in the glimmer of the world's eventide, when all the lamps are going out, a glory shines around him, transforming midnight into day.

He is a brother born for adversity, in the last place, because in adversity it is that through his people's patience he is glorified. I warrant you the sweetest songs that ever come up from these lowlands to the eternal throne, are from sick beds. "They shall sing his high praises in the fires." God's children are too often dumb when they have much of this world's earth in their mouths, but when the Lord is pleased to take away their comforts and possessions, then, like birds in cages, they begin to sing with all their hearts. Praise him, ye suffering ones, your praise will be grateful to him. Extol him, ye mourners, exchange by faith your sorrows for hopes, and bless his name who deserveth to be praised.

II. Now, I shall leave this, and only for a moment turn the text round to a practical purpose, by REFERRING IT TO THE CHRISTIAN.

I hope that what has been spoken has been only the echo of the experience of the most of you. You have found Jesus Christ to be a true brother and a blessed friend, now let the same be true of you. He that would have friends must show himself friendly. If Christ be such a friend to us, what manner of people ought we to be towards him? So, beloved, let us pray and labour to be friends that love Christ at all times. Alas! some professors seem to love him at no time at all. They give him lip homage, but they refuse to give him the exercise of their talents, or the contribution of their substance. They love him only with words that are but air, but they offer him no sweet cane with money, neither do they fill him with the fat of their sacrifices. Such people are windbag lovers, and do nothing substantial to prove their affection. Let it not be so with *us*. Let our love to Christ be so true as to constrain us to make sacrifices for him. Let us deny ourselves that we may spread abroad the knowledge of his truth, and never be content unless in very deed and act we are giving proofs of our love.

We ought to love him at all times. Alas! there are some that prosper in business, who grow too great to love their Saviour. They hold their heads too high to associate with his saints. Aforetime they were with his people, content to worship with them when they were in humble circumstances, but they have prospered in trade, they have laid by a good store of wealth, and now they feel half ashamed to attend the conventicle that was once the very joy of their hearts. They must seek out the world's religion, and they must worship after the world's fashion, for they must not be left behind in society. The people of God are not good enough for them; though they be kings and princes in Christ's esteem, yet are they too poor company for those that have risen so high in the world. Alas, alas! that professed lovers of Jesus should rise too high to walk truthfully and faithfully with Christ : it is no rise at all, but a lamentable fall. Let us cling to him in days of joy, as well as nights of grief, and prove to all mankind that there are no enchantments in this world that can win our hearts away from our best beloved.

We should love Jesus Christ at all times, that is to say, in times when the church seems dull and dead. Perhaps some of you are living in a district just now where the ministry is painfully devoid of power. The lamp burns very low in your sanctuary, the members worshipping are few, and zeal is altogether dead. Do not desert the church, do not flee away from her in the time of her necessity. Keep to your post, come what may. Be the last man to leave the sinking vessel, if sink she must. Resolve as a friend of Christ to love him at all times, and as a brother born into that church, feel that now, beyond all other times, in the season of adversity, you must adhere to her.

It may happen that some here present may to-morrow be found in a workshop, or in some other place, where their business brings them, where some dear child of God will be laughed at and ridiculed. That same man you would have cheerfully owned on the Sabbath as your brother, you delighted to unite your voice with him in prayer, but now, while he stands in the midst of a ribald throng, will you own him, or rather, own Christ in him ? They are making cruel jokes, they are vexing his gracious spirit; now it is possible that a cowardly fear may make you slink away to the other end of the shop, but, oh, if you remember that a friend loveth at all times, you will take up this man's quarrel as being Christ's quarrel, and you, as being a part of the body of Christ, will be willing to share whatever contumely may come upon your fellow Christian, and you will say, "If you mock at him, you may mock also at me, for I also have been with Jesus of Nazareth, and him whom you scoff at I adore." O let us never, by the love that Christ has borne to us, keep back a truth because it may expose us to shame. Let us never be such cowards as to palter with the word of God, because we may then live in silken ease and delicacy. These are not times in which one single particle of truth ought to be repressed. Whatever the spirit of God and the word of God may have taught you, my brethren, out with it for Christ's sake, and let it bring what it will to you, bear that with joy. Since your Saviour bore far more for you, count it joy to bear anything for him. Be a brother born on purpose for adversity. Do you expect to be carried to heaven on beds of ease? do you reckon to win the everlasting laurels without a conflict? What, sirs, would ye stand beneath the waving banners of victory, without having first endured the smoke and the dust of battle? Nay, rather with consecrated courage, follow in the steps of your Master. Love him at all times, give up all for him, and then shall you soon be with him in his glory world without end. God grant a blessing for Jesus' sake. Amen.

The Meat and Drink of the New Nature

"For my flesh is meat indeed, and my blood is drink indeed"—John vi. 55.

WE know that the Saviour spoke of spiritual, not of carnal things, and he spoke of himself not as being in any sense meat for our bodies—that could not be—but as being food for our souls. This statement is very plain to us, but those who heard it at the first found it very hard to understand. Nor need we wonder, for men of the schools who play with letters, words, and phrases, frequently meet with difficulties where none exist. The Jews of our Lord's day had fallen into the foolish habit of taking words to pieces and dwelling upon the syllables and letters, until they seemed to have lost all power of getting at the plain meaning which ordinary language was intended to convey. They blinded their own eyes with the pretence of superior wisdom, made puzzles and riddles out of plain words, raised a huge dust, and sat down in it blinded to the end. Our God has taught us more, and given us to understand more clearly, for his Holy Spirit has given us back the childlike spirit, so that we are willing to see the natural sense which words were meant to reveal. Now we see great force and clear expressiveness in that very language which seemed before to conceal the Saviour's meaning. It was a veil to the Jews, and they saw not: it is an instructive parable to us, which, instead of hiding the truth, shadows it out to us, and softens the light for our weak eyes. We see, I fear, even now but dimly, for our spiritual sight is scarcely clear as yet; but yet we see, blessed be God for that, and we see Jesus, and we see something of his loving meaning. We do more than see: we enjoy, and therefore know to the life what it is to feed upon his flesh, which is meat indeed, and to drink his blood, which is drink indeed.

We cannot attempt to explain the deep mysteries of our text, but rather —as the swallow touches the brook with his wing and is away again— we will glance at these crystal waters of this sacred truth, and then up and away. The text teaches us, first, *what Christ must be to us.* We shall consider, secondly, *what is bound up in this;* and, thirdly, *what reflections naturally arise out of it.*

I. WHAT CHRIST MUST BE TO US. The answer from the text is,

He must be our meat and drink. He must be everything to us—the one thing needful, the indispensable, necessary, all-sufficient supply. He must be the source of strength, the support of life, and we must feel him to be so. He must, to come back to the figure, be meat and drink to us. Our Lord in speaking to the Jews was doubtless thinking of the paschal lamb, and of the time when Israel came out of Egypt; when they not only had the blood of the lamb sprinkled upon their houses for their security, but the lamb itself within them as their sustenance. They sat down to feed upon it before they enjoyed the fulness of redemption by passing out of Egypt from under the bondage of Pharaoh. They did not understand that symbol, and they little knew what our great Lord and Master meant when he employed it to set forth himself, and said, "My flesh is meat indeed, and my blood is drink indeed."

Our Lord Jesus Christ must be to us, then, our spiritual meat and drink. What mean we by that?

First, that *the doctrine of God incarnate must be the food of our souls.* Brethren, we have no doubt as to the true and proper Deity of our Lord Jesus. We have long since passed out of the region of controversy about that, for he has been God to us in the work of salvation and in the new creation which we have experienced through his power. We have, moreover, no doubt about his humanity, but we do not usually dwell enough upon it. We are bound to adore his Deity, but we must not forget that he is as truly man as if he were not God, and as much a brother to us as if he were not the Son of the Highest. Jesus is assuredly man. Now feed on this. The man Christ Jesus heads up a new race: as the first Adam headed up the race of old, and was our federal head to stand or fall for us, and we were to stand or fall in him, so is there now a new head, who brings us up from the ruin of the first Adam's fall and puts us into a new position before the living God. There is a man who has redeemed us. There is a man who has made all the men in him well pleasing to God. There is a man who represents manhood in perfection in the glory above. There is a man in whom all believers are, even as we read that Levi was in the loins of Abraham when Melchisidec met him. We are in Christ, and we stand now before the eternal throne in that blessed representative man. Feed on this doctrine now. Jesus is a real man, though clothed with all power; he is God, and yet he is the mirror of tenderness; he ruleth all things, and yet is touched with the feeling of our infirmities. You must believe this, and you must receive it, and you must rest upon it, otherwise you have no life in you. Some try to turn this fact into a myth, but indeed it is no parable or figure of speech, for the Christ who spoke these words was there before them—one whom they had often seen eat and drink: he spake of himself with his own lips, and was not a phantom or apparition, but a solid existence of flesh and blood. So then it is upon the historical Christ, whose existence is a matter of fact, that my soul must feed, as I believe him to be both human and divine.

But this is not all: *the food to be fed upon is not merely God incarnate, but Christ suffering.* Notice that he puts it "My *flesh* is meat indeed, and my *blood* is drink indeed": when the flesh and the blood are mentioned separately, death is implied. The two being divided and being named together in one connection are the token and emblem of our Saviour's vicarious sacrifice. We also (I am speaking of the brethren worshipping here) have long ago past beyond the region of controversy as to the substitutionary sacrifice of Jesus Christ our Lord; for if it be not so, then is our preaching vain and our hope is also vain, and we are yet in our sins. We have no hope of eternal life save that which begins, centres, and ends in the sacrifice of Jesus Christ. "This man, when he had offered one sacrifice for sins for ever, sat down at the right hand of God"—that is our sole hope. *He* has made expiation for sin.

"He bore, that we might never bear,
His Father's righteous ire."

We are now to build up our souls by feeding upon the suffering, the crucified, the dead, the buried Christ, as having stood as our representative, and as having endured death in our stead. You cannot obtain comfort apart from this if you have felt the weight of sin; and you cannot continue happy apart from this great historical fact if you are conscious of sin. Fly, my hearers, into the wounds of Jesus, and like doves ye shall find shelter in that rock; but with eager wing ye may glide over the waste of human thought without finding a rest for the sole of your weary foot till you light upon the truth of the great substitution. "The Word was made flesh and dwelt among us," is the first bell of heaven's marriage peal, and the second has an equally sweet note of its own—"Christ died for our sins." Ring them both full often. Listen to them as they sound forth—"God *with* us, Christ *for* us." Incarnation, substitution—was there ever better meat and drink for a hungry soul? This surely satisfies the desire of the most hungry spirit—"The blood of Jesus Christ his Son cleanseth us from all sin."

I have, as it were, in those few words set out the viands of the feast. But now I would have you note that our Lord must be to us meat and drink; and *meat is not intended to look at, but to feed on.* I heard the other day that in a certain Socinian place of worship they have gone the length of setting the bread and wine on the table for the people to look at, but they suppose that it is quite unnecessary that they should actually eat and drink. It is fittingly done of them: that is consistent with their creed. They have no Christ to feed upon. There is nothing in their belief which could feed the soul of a mouse, if a mouse had a soul. Why should they attempt to feed the people in figure when really they have no incarnate God or atoning Saviour. If it be indeed true that in one of their places of worship they have exhibited the bread and wine instead of handing it out to be eaten, it is remarkably typical of their bloodless, lifeless gospel, their Christ who is no Deity, their Jesus who is no sacrifice for sin. How can the soul find food there? But we must beware lest we ourselves should ever rest content with merely glancing at Christ and not partaking of him. What is to be done with food, with meat and drink? It is to be received. Food on the table does not nourish; it must be taken into the hand. The cup on the board will never cheer; it must be lifted; it must be appropriated. I know that many of you have by a humble but brave faith appropriated Christ as he is set before you in the gospel. He has bidden you come and eat, and you have come pressed by a sore famine that was in your soul. You have come, and you have said, "He is mine," and you have taken him to yourselves by simple childlike confidence in him. You have well done, continue to do the same. "As ye have received Christ Jesus the Lord, so walk ye in him." Go on receiving him. "To whom coming," says the apostle, "as unto a living stone"; regard him not as one to whom you have come by one act and have done with him, but as one to whom you come continually. "Of his fulness have all we received, and grace for grace," but we are going on receiving, by continuing to believe in him. Hold on to this. Having begun in the spirit, do not hope to be perfected by the flesh. Do not think that you are to be fed afterwards on something other than Christ, but go on receiving, appropriating, and taking home the great truths concerning your Lord. Here, my brethren, is the life of your faith. But even appropriating is not enough to constitute feeding. After taking the morsel, it is put into the mouth, and received inwardly; the draught of wine is poured into the throat and it disappears. Receive truth not only as a matter of creed, but drink it in as the ox sucks in the water when he stands up to his knees in the pool. Take Christ into your very soul—into your *heart's* belief as well as into your mind's belief. Mental beliefs shift and change: the inward soul's belief never alters. I reckon that we know nothing rightly till we have absorbed it, and made it part and parcel of ourselves. The vital truths with regard to our Lord Jesus must go down into the inward parts of the soul, as the food descends into the secret parts of the belly to feed the entire man.

And you know what becomes of the food. It is taken up by the nature itself, and becomes transmuted into it. After its digestion it passes through various processes, and ultimately becomes the life-blood, out of which is built up nerve, muscle, sinew, bone, flesh, heart. Everything comes of it. Now, you must so believe in Jesus that no longer is it a matter of question with you whether you will retain him or not, for if you have inwardly received him you cannot lose him for ever. Oh that blessed "*Quis separabit?*"—"Who shall separate us from the love of God, which is in Christ Jesus our Lord?" It is difficult to deprive a person of that which he has received mentally, for facts learned in childhood are remembered even to old age. No one could compel another to forget, but yet without such compulsion the memory might relax its hold through lapse of years: the mind might part with that which it has received, but no known power could take away from a man that which he has eaten and assimilated. A person may very readily pick my pocket of my purse, but what I ate yesterday he cannot steal. That is mine; it is joined to myself, and has built me up. I do not know what portion of my flesh comes of my morning meal, or of my mid-day repast, but there it is, and there it must be. It has entered into me, and never can be got away from me again. So when the soul takes in Christ's truth with that simple childlike faith which is the mouth, the truth goes into the soul and is thought over, trusted in, delighted in, and becomes so part and parcel of the inner consciousness and of the new nature of the man that it would be henceforth utterly impossible to tear away that truth from him. Pound a true Christian in a mortar and every single atom would say, "I belong to Christ." Grind him finer than the smallest dust of the threshing floor and every minute particle would still say, "Christ is in me." For so it is that the Christ has entered the man, permeated his nature, become his very life, and now it is "I live, yet not I, but Christ liveth in me." Now is the text fulfilled in us, "For ye are dead, and your life is hid with Christ in God. When Christ, who is our life, shall appear, then shall ye also appear with him in glory." "Abide in me," said our Lord, and he gave his own promise to be with us for ever. That is just the result of eating Christ, and to this we must come. Beloved, I have thus explained the matter as well as I can, but as old Rollock says, "The only way to understand feeding upon Christ is to feed upon Christ." This is a practical, personal, experimental business. In learning certain acts you must yourself become a practical scholar, the master cannot teach by merely setting the copy, the scholar must imitate it line by line with his own hand: and so here, I can teach little by words only, you must practise what is spoken. Now feed ye on the Lord Jesus; let each one of you do it. I know what some do: they will not feed on Christ, but they pick over the heavenly bread like dainty folks who have no stomach for their meat. This bit of Christ they would have, but the other does not suit their tooth: justification by faith they would have, but not sanctification,—they do not like that. It is a whole Christ you and I must have—a whole Christ, as to every part of his teaching, character, work, and offices. We must receive him into ourselves without division, rejoicing to take him just as he is. Especially must we receive the spirit of Christ, for "if any man have not the spirit of Christ he is none of his." We must partake in the loving spirit, the self-denying spirit, the generous spirit which lives not within itself, but goes forth in forgiveness of injuries, and in seeking to benefit all mankind. We must have Jesus in us, delighting to take in the whole of him, for he says farther on in this very chapter, "He that eateth *me*"—that is even more comprehensive than his "flesh and his blood"—" He that eateth *me*, even he shall live by me": the entire Christ must be taken into the soul to build up the inner man.

II. Now, secondly, WHAT IS BOUND UP IN THIS EATING OF HIS FLESH AND DRINKING OF HIS BLOOD? Here we will take you back to the context.

And notice, first, that there is for this eating the flesh and drinking the blood of Christ such an essential necessity that *he who has not so eaten and drank has no spiritual life at all.* It is a strong word, "Except ye eat the flesh of the Son of man, and drink his blood, *ye have no life in you.*" He does not mean that they have no natural life; he is speaking about spiritual things. Some that are as foolish as Judaizers in the matter of sticking to the letter, tell us that this means existence, and that no man's eternal existence is certain except that of a believer in Christ. That dogma is not taught here, certainly. Our Lord is not speaking of existence; he is speaking of a far higher thing than existence, namely, *life.* Have you never learned the difference between death and non-existence, and between life and existence? If you have not, you are babes in understanding, and you will often be blundering and losing your way in the midst of texts of Scripture. A man may exist in everlasting death, as, alas, all who die unbelievers must do; but blessed is he who lives! Blessed is he who shall live for ever! Let me repeat the word, "lives"; I did not say exists. What a glorious thing is life. Yet, if I had to explain to you what life is, I might find it far easier by some action of my own to show that I lived than to tell you exactly what life is. He however, who eats Christ has life. He who has not done so has not life. Do you understand this; that unless you have received Christ by faith into your souls you have no life. You can work, you can walk, you can speak; you have all sorts of natural life, but you have not the life everlasting of which Jesus speaks. The life of God is not in you. You are dead, and what a frightful condition that is, and to what horror yet greater does it lead! For wherever there is death the dead thing will go a stage farther on. And what is that stage? Corruption. Only leave a corpse alone long enough, and it must corrupt. Flesh corrupts necessarily. Already there are some signs of corruption about every ungodly man: outward sin, and especially the inward sin of rejecting Christ, are a grievous corruption. Your worm has begun to devour, even the worm that never dies. Then will be reached another stage, for corruption must be cast into the fire. For utter rottenness the end must be burning. O sinner, your fire has begun to burn—the fire that will never be quenched, for sin is the kindling of hell. It is an awful thing to abide in death, and yet he that believeth not on Christ is condemned already, because he hath not believed on the Son of God. It is enough to make you spring from your seats, O ye that are unbelievers, to think that you are not waiting to be tried: you are condemned already. This is not a state of probation, as I often hear it said. Your probation is past. You are condemned already, because you have not believed on the Son of God; and death is upon you now. The sentence has already begun to take effect, and it will go on to the consummation of corruption, till at last the Lord shall say, "Bury my dead out of my sight," and you must be driven from the presence of the Lord and from the glory of his power. There is no life in you unless you have received Christ. Will you think of this, you thinkers? Only think of your being dead. Will you think of this, you ceremonialists, to whom the outward baptism, and the outward Lord's supper, and the church-going and the chapel-going are everything? Unless you have fed on Christ there is no life in you.

Then comes, in the next place, the further truth, namely, that *all who have received Jesus Christ to be to them their meat and drink have eternal life.* "Whoso eateth my flesh, and drinketh my blood, hath eternal life." I do not know how our brethren who doubt the final perseverance of the saints manage to escape from the plain teaching of the text. There are always ways of getting over everything; you can drive a coach and six, they say, through any form of human language. But it does seem to me that if I have eternal life I must eternally live, and cannot possibly die. If I have got eternal life, if words mean anything, I am an eternally saved man. If I have received Jesus Christ into my soul, I have the life in me which will no more die than the life of God, for God's own life is eternal life, and if I have received such life as his, how can I perish? I shall not be slain by sin: the life in me cannot sin, because it is born of God. The life in me will throw off the darts of temptation if it be eternal life. There remains nothing for it but to shake off the death which often surrounds it by reason of the old man, and to mount up like a bird set free from its cage, singing because of its escape, singing in the joy of life, and winging its happy way upward to the throne of God.

Rejoice then, dear friend, that if you have received Christ, you have eternal life in actual possession at this moment. "I do not feel it sometimes," say you. Do not try to live by feeling. It is the most uncertain thing in the world; you might as well try to live by the barometer. Feeling goes up and down, up and down, and changes oftener than the moon. It is hard, uncomfortable living. Live by faith, for it is written, "the just shall live by faith." Your life is a life of trust. Keep to it.

"Ah, but I see so much about me that grieves me." Thank God it grieves you. If you see sin and it does not grieve you, it is a token of death; but if it grieves you, there is life still in you, notwithstanding all the death that surrounds it. You may sometimes have seen a spark in the midst of a heap of autumn leaves which are all damp and will not burn, but only smoulder and smoke, and yet that spark continues to live, and the very smother from the heap proves it is so. There is one who will not quench the smoking flax, but will fan it till it rises to a flame, and then it will devour the leaves which covered it, and dry up the damps which sought to destroy it.

Furthermore, if you believe in Jesus and have received him, you have gathered a life in which Christ giveth us the *victory*, even through his name—a life which will rise, and rise, and rise, and conquer all sin. The believer's inner life must come to absolute perfection, and tread every sin beneath its foot. Very different is this from the doctrine that a man who is a child of God may sin as he pleases and yet be saved. That doctrine is of the devil; but this is quite another doctrine, and ministers to holiness. The quickened man will not willingly and habitually sin, for his seed remaineth in him, and he cannot sin, because he is born of God. The tone and tenor and bearing of his life will be towards holiness and not towards sin, and the Lord who is able to keep him from falling will preserve him to his eternal kingdom and glory, and he that has begun a good work in them will perfect it unto the day of Christ.

Our Lord having thus given us the negative and the positive in our text, tells us that his flesh and blood, or himself, received into the soul, are most efficient nourishment: in it is *satisfaction*. "My flesh is meat *indeed*." The Greek word is "truly," or, some say, "true meat." Now that which we eat for the body is not true meat. As George Herbert says, "When thou art at thy meat eat a bit, and then say, 'Earth to earth I commit.'" It is a deadly business. It is burying earth in earth, and that living grave of earth will be itself buried in earth by-and-by. The eating of material meat is the poor building up of a fabric that must ultimately crumble into nothingness. The meat we eat has all the elements of dissolution about it before we receive it, and it only feeds for a short time,—hence it is not meat indeed.

In the matter of mental food how much there is which is not bread, and can never satisfy the mind. There is nothing in the world that can fill a soul to the full save Jesus. Perhaps I address some thinker who has been trying to satisfy his soul by sniffing up the east wind of speculative philosophy. Ah, well, if you swallow a dose of Kant, or Hegel, Schleiermacher, or any one of those gentlemen, if you do not feel as if you had been eating bubbles and bladders, your mental constitution and mine differ greatly. There is nothing in them all but gas, or vapour less substantial. Why, a man may take down their books—a whole dozen of them—and devour their contents, and then say, "What is it? Is it not much ado about nothing? These thinkings are dreamings, vacuums, airy nothings." All the philosophies that ever were invented could not satisfy a soul. The worst of it is that many do not want to be satisfied. "*We*," say they, "would sooner be seekers after truth than finders of it." They somewhat differ from men of practical common sense who, ordinarily, would rather have money than earn it, and would rather eat their dinners than hunt for them. Still that is their way, and, if they like it, I suppose they must have it. Every creature after its own order. But if you want to be fed, dear friends, depend upon it nothing will feed you but Christ. There was a man of great appetite who lived many years ago, and he began to feast ravenously. He was such a drinker that I may say of him that he drank up Jordan at a draught, and he was such an eater, that, if you heard the story of what was brought to his table, you would be like the Queen of Sheba, utterly astonished, and say that the half was not told you. His name was Solomon, and he fed his soul with all the arts and sciences, and with all the poetries and luxuries of the age, nor did he refrain from laughter and wantonness. There was not a cup he did not drain, nor a dainty from any land, nor a fruit from any tree, of which he did not eat. Yet when he rose up from that abundant banquet, all he had to say was, "Vanity of vanities; all is vanity." I have seen a poor soul feed on Christ in a very humble cottage, upon a bed in a little room, where she has lain alone almost all day and all night long, year after year, with many aches and pains, and scarcely able to lift her hand to her head, with little but dry bread and a cup of water; and yet I have seen in that bedridden woman's pain-worn face a fulness of satisfaction. I have known her speak like one that had not a wish ungratified, nor a grief worth mentioning. I have beheld her when in her sufferings she could scarcely speak, and yet her every word was essential poetry when she spoke of *him*, her best beloved, who had filled her soul even to overflowing. There is no food *indeed*, no drink *indeed*, for soul and spirit, but that which you find in the incarnate God and in the sacrifice of Christ. O ye hungry, come ye hither and eat ye that which is good and let your soul delight itself in fatness. O ye thirsty, come ye hither, for behold the waters are flowing freely, and the wines on the lees are ready for you in Christ Jesus. That is what is bound up in feeding upon Jesus, there is satisfaction in him.

And then there is bound up with it one other matter, namely, *indwelling*. I go over the same ground again. The Lord Jesus says, "He that eateth my flesh, and drinketh my blood, dwelleth in me, and I in him." When you have eaten the bread, it dwells in you and you in it: it goes into you and it is in you; it becomes part of yourself, and you live by it and in its strength. It is a part of the fabric in which you dwell. Even so he that believes in Christ lives in Christ. He does not merely go to Christ; but he enters into Christ. I delight to remember that I am not merely under the shadow of my Lord, but, as David in the caverns of Engeddi, so does my soul hide herself right away in Jesus. We dwell in him, and are at home. Moreover he enters into us by our feeding upon him, so that he becomes our life, the spring of our being, the object of our desire, the motive force of our service. We are woven together—Christ warp and ourselves woof—woven together in a living loom, and so conjoined that it were hard to tell where *he* ends who has no end, and where we begin who are lost in him. We are less than the least of all saints, and yet members of *his* body who is Lord of all.

We must leave the mystery; remarking that if we have fed on Christ for ourselves, we have proof of what good meat it is we have fed on, and we shall always pray, " Lord, evermore give us this bread."

III. I want your attention for a few minutes while, in the third place, we consider WHAT REFLECTIONS ARISE OUT OF THIS TRUTH. I will simply throw them out for you to turn over for yourselves. They occurred to me when I was hearing a brother preach upon a kindred subject. They took hold of my soul; may they prove useful to you.

And the first was this. If I have a life that feeds on Christ *what a wonderful life it must be.* My bodily life is wonderful, yet it only feeds on the fruits of the earth. My mental life is a marvel, but I know that I can build it up with literature and thought. Above all these I have a life which cannot feed on anything but the flesh and blood of the Son of God. What a life that must be! What a wonderful being a man is when God is in him. I almost reverence the meanest saint when I think of this, for he bears about with him not a Koh-i-noor, but a gem of life, compared with which the queenly diamond pales into a glittering vanity. O love divine, dost thou tabernacle in the sons of men! I have been speaking of mysteries, but I ask you to explain which is the greater mystery, the incarnation of God in Christ or the indwelling of the Holy Ghost in believers? They are two wondrous stoops of Deity, which can only be likened to each other, being each one without other parallel. The spiritual life given to the regenerate must be a life of inconceivable excellence and heavenliness since it can only feed on Christ himself.

The next thought is, if we have the life that feeds on such meat as this, *how strong it must be.* They say of such-and-such men that they may well be strong, seeing what good food they have. Ay, but see what food *we* have; how strong we must be. Do we know our own strength? I do not mean our natural strength, for that is weakness, but I mean the strength which lies in the new nature when it has fed on Christ. O brethren, we are strong to do; we are strong to be; we are strong to suffer. And to take an easy illustration of this—the one that occurs to me first—look at how the saints have suffered. Take down " Foxe's Book of Martyrs": read of Marcus Arethusa, stung to death by wasps without a sigh. Think of Blandina tossed on the horns of bulls, exposed in a red-hot iron chair, and yet never flinching. Give up Christ?

They never dreamed of such a thing. Think of Lawrence on the gridiron, and other heroes innumerable, who were made strong because Christ was in them. Ay, and turn to humble men and women, over yonder there in Smithfield, who could clap their hands while every finger burned like a candle, and could shout "None but Christ, none but Christ." Why, they fed on the flesh and blood of Christ, and that made them mighty. They were tortured on the rack like Anne Askew, and yet they scorned to yield. Brave woman! the priests and the friars could not vanquish her. Neither could all the Bishop Bonners in the world burn Christ out of poor Tomkins. When Bonner held the poor man's finger over the candle and said, "How will you like that in every single limb of your body?" Tomkins smiled on the bishop and said that he forgave him the cruelty that he was doing him. Christ in a man makes him a partaker of divine strength. Do you not think, my brethren, that as you are not called to suffer you ought to lay out your strength in the line of doing and giving, and self-denial, and serving Christ by holy living? Certainly you should try to do so, and your strength will be found equal to it. You do not know how strong you are, but Paul shall tell you—"I can do all things through Christ that strengtheneth me." Well may you do all things if you have fed on him who is all, and in all.

Then a third reflection crossed my mind. If we have a life that feeds on this, *how immortal it must be.* We have a text to prove that, and we have given it to you already—"He that believeth on him hath everlasting life." When a man has nothing but bad food, you do not wonder that he dies. It is little marvel that they died by millions in India and China, considering how little nourishment they had during the famine. But if you and I eat Christ, eat the incarnate God and drink his blood, how can we die? What, kill a man that has even a particle of Christ in him! The devil cannot do it: he knows his master. And what does Christ say? "I give unto my sheep eternal life; and they shall never perish, neither shall any man pluck them out of my hand." Oh, blessed truth! We live, not only because our life is itself eternal, but because it feeds on eternal meat. We keep on receiving Christ day by day, for we live upon him: eating is not a work that we finished five-and-twenty years ago, but we continue to feed upon Jesus, and therefore we live. Feeding upon Christ does not mean being converted and then saying, "I am safe, and have no more need to care." Ah, no. It means beginning to receive him in conversion, and continuing to feed upon him evermore; and they who do this may be sure that their life is immortal.

The next thought that struck me was this: if we feed on such meat as this, *how that life must develop.* I do not quite see in myself, and I may say that I do not see in some believers, the full result I should like to see from such food. Has this man been eating such divine food? Let us hear him. He cries, "My leanness, my leanness, woe unto me." He is doing Christ's work spasmodically, feebly, sleepily. He does it without joy, and is soon weary. Is this all he is going to do? Is this all he is going to be? Oh no, brethren, "it doth not yet appear what we shall be." We shall grow; we shall grow. When I hear a man talk about being perfect in the flesh, I hope for the best, and trust that he is not wilfully lying. At any rate, I do not believe him. I would like to *see* his perfection rather than to hear him talk about it. I have generally found that when a cart needs a bell it is a dust cart. I never knew the people of the Bank of England ring a bell when they were going through the streets with bullion, and I do not think it is likely that a man who has much grace will boast of it. Yet I do believe that we can be developed into something very wonderful. A man may grow in grace, and in the knowledge of the Lord till his conversation is in heaven, and he becomes wholly consecrated to the Lord, hating sin, and living like Enoch, who walked with God. There have been such men, and there are such men and women among us still, whose lives glitter with the light of God; why should not we be like them? They are stars in God's firmament, and they shine in the glory of the Most High. The Lord grant us that, feeding on the divine meat, we may develop till the image of Jesus is perfected in us.

And, lastly, he who is thus fed, dear friends, *what company he must keep!* "He that eateth my flesh, and drinketh my blood, dwelleth in me," saith Christ, "and I in him." What heavenly company is this! He goes home at night to his poor family, perhaps, and there is nothing great about his house that you can see; but if your eyes are opened you will see that it is a king's palace, and if you are one of the Lord's, and can step inside, you will see that he has "come to the general assembly and church of the firstborn whose names are written in heaven, and unto God the Judge of all, and unto the spirits of just men made perfect," because he that has Christ in him has heaven around him. All good things are attracted by Christ in man. Put down a little honey, and see how wasps and flies and bees come all around it. What is the sweetest honey in the universe? It is Christ; and if you have Christ in you, his name is as ointment poured forth, therefore do the virgins love him, and they will come where he is. I will tell you yet more,—Christ is never without God, and he that has Christ has the company of the Father. And Christ is never without the Spirit of God, for the Spirit of God is upon him; and he that has Christ is never without the Spirit. What divine society is this! Our Lord Jesus is never unattended by a retinue of sublime intelligences, and so if Christ be in you, he will give his angels charge over you to keep you in all your ways; they shall bear you up in their hands, lest you dash your foot against a stone. O Prince of the blood royal of heaven, O Peer of God's own kingdom, thou art more nearly related to the King of kings than the peers of the realm can be to the Queen, for are you not married to the Prince Imperial? Is he not coming to receive you to himself, that where he is you may be also? If you are feeding on him your union with him is complete. If he is your food, if he is your raiment, if he is your dwelling-place, if he is your all in all, methinks I may compare you to that angel of whom Milton sang, even Uriel, who dwelt in the centre of the sun. It is there we live—in the very substance and essence of all things, and all things move around us like satellites around a central globe, for we are a chosen generation, a royal priesthood, a peculiar people, inasmuch as we have fed on Christ, and Christ dwelleth in us and we in him.

I have not said anything to the unconverted, and yet I have meant it all for them. When you spread a dainty feast, you practically invite the family to come and dine. It is the very best way of enticing them. If they are hungry the meats on the table will make their mouths water, and they will long to partake. Oh, my hearers, whoever you may be, if your mouths water after Christ, come and have him, for he is free to every soul that hungers and thirsts after him.

The Lord give him to you at once, for Jesus's sake. Amen.

The Best Bread

"I am that bread of life"—John vi. 48.

You will observe that our Lord here speaks concerning himself. He speaks not of his words merely, nor of his offices, nor of his work, but of himself. "I am that bread of life." And herein he teaches us all to fix our eye mainly upon his blessed person, and to think of himself first and foremost. He is the centre and soul of all. There is a tendency about us all to get away from Jesus, and to look rather to the streams than to the Fountain-head. Why are we more taken up with bits of glass that sparkle in the light than with the sun himself? That tree of life, in the midst of the Paradise of God—we forget to eat of that; and we wander to the borders of the garden, to pluck the fruit of the forbidden tree of the knowledge of good and evil. I wish that our ministry —that mine especially—might be tied and tethered to the cross. I would have no other subject to set before you but Jesus only. Moses and Elias are well enough in their places; but when they disappear, and Jesus is the better seen, we are gainers by their loss. If I might dig for copper, silver, and gold, I should think it no deprivation to be obliged to find gold only. It is no loss to lose all but Jesus. You may wander from Dan to Beersheba, and you may not sin, for it is all holy ground between the two places; but he is wisest who does not ramble even there, but keeps to Calvary, and is content to speak only of Jesus crucified.

"God forbid," said one who was a great and a wise man—"God forbid that I should glory, save in the cross of our Lord Jesus Christ." Paul would have considered it a terrible calamity if he had become fascinated, or even influenced, by the speculations of the cultured men of his period: he felt that the atoning sacrifice deserved all his admiration, and he had none to spare for anything else.

You know how he fell among certain wise people who were fond of philosophical disquisitions; and to them he said, "I determined not to know anything *among you* save Jesus Christ, and him crucified." He did not endeavour to please his audience by agreeing with them, but the further they went in one direction, the further he went in the other, the more surely to counteract their error. Because they were so broad he would narrow himself to the one theme of the cross. In these times, when the world has run mad upon its idols of human thought, it may be wise to be more strict than ever, and to stand steadfast in Paul's determination—"I determined not to know anything among you save Jesus Christ, and him crucified."

It was *himself*, my brethren, that our Lord set before his hearers as the bread of life; he did not mention anything of doctrine, or of precept, or of ordinance, but himself. He says "I am that bread of life." Of him, therefore, let us think.

It is of the utmost importance to those of you who have spiritual life that you should feed upon the Lord Jesus. It is well to know everything that is revealed, for every word of God is good, and has its uses, and all Scripture is profitable; but the daily household bread, the substantial meat on which we must be nourished if we would grow strong for God and holiness, is Christ himself. "I am that bread of life." We do not get bread anywhere else save in Jesus our Lord. We may find certain minor things apart from him: flavourings, ornaments, and furniture of the table we may get from some other hand; but the bread, the real solid meat, the essence of the festival, is Christ himself. So let us begin with him in our discourse, and continue with him till we close our meditation.

But now, when I have to preach upon a subject like this, I find it necessary to begin a little way from the text. "I am that bread of life." Bread, brethren—bread is for living men and women, but bread is of no use in the tomb. Bread—shall we bring it to a sepulchre? Shall we roll away the stone? Shall we draw out the bodies swathed in linen? Shall we set them upright in ghastly posture, and shall we put bread upon the table before them? To what purpose would it be? It would be a ghastly mockery. If you leave the bread there, and visit again that loathsome banqueting chamber in twelve months' time, the bread will remain untouched; for until there is life, there is no use for bread. And so, at the opening of my discourse, some of you might say, "Bread is intended for living persons; it is for men and women who are quickened. How can we feed upon Christ, for we are dead in trespasses and sins?" You speak most truly; but yet I have a marvel to relate which meets the case. Hearken! That would be a strange kind of bread, would it not, which being put into a dead man's mouth, would make him live? Yet such is the bread that came down from heaven, whereof if a man eat he shall live for ever.

The Lord Jesus Christ is living bread. Bread such as we get from the baker is in itself dead; and if you put it to dead lips, there are two dead things together, and nothing can come of the contact. But our Lord Jesus Christ is living bread; and, when he touches the dead lip of an unregenerate sinner, life comes into it. He brings life even to those who are dead in sin. He says, "Young man, arise," and he sits up upon the bier. He takes a little girl by her hand, and says, "Talitha cumi—Maid, arise," and she sits up in her bed. He calls to Lazarus, who by this time stinketh, and he says, "Lazarus, come forth," and he comes forth, wearing his grave-clothes. He has shuffled down from the niche in the cave, and he has made his way out of the damps of the cold sepulchre. Oh, what a wonderful Christ this is, who is not only bread for the living, but life for the dead! Pray, you who can pray, that he would come here just now, and be life to those who are in the darkness of the Valley of the Shadow of Death, that they may live. When they live, then how gladsome will my text be to them, for life needs bread whereby it may be sustained! The first thing that we want, if we have life, is something for that life to feed upon; and here comes in the text—"I am that bread of life." Your newly-discovered necessities Jesus can meet. Your newly-begotten wants Jesus can supply. Your hunger and your thirst can all be met, not by fifty things, but by one thing, by Jesus Christ himself, in whom there dwells in fulness all that the spiritual life can possibly require.

I. With that to start with, I now make the first observation upon the text itself, which is this—JESUS CHRIST EXACTLY MEETS ALL THE WANTS OF THE NEW LIFE. When a man is born again to God, and gets a new life, he has new wants, new desires, new pains, new longings. He enters upon a novel condition, full of new needs and cravings; the Lord Jesus Christ exactly meets the new case. As the key fits the wards of the lock, so does Christ fit the new heart and the right spirit. He knows how to touch the secrets of our soul, and supply our most mysterious necessities.

According to the text, *the Lord Jesus Christ is the ideal bread*—the ideal supply of man's soul-hunger. Grateful Israelites truthfully judged that there never was such bread in all the world as that which fell in the wilderness in the form of manna. It was very wonderful bread, was it not? Men did eat angels' food, and found it good for them. They went out in the morning, and they gathered manna, and they found it most marvellous meat to sustain them. It was the ideal meat for persons travelling through the great and terrible wilderness. There are different theories of what we ought to eat. One person tells us that, if anybody suffers from rheumatism, he must eat so many pounds of meat in a day. Other doctors have vehemently said, "You must not touch meat. It will heat you if you do. You must keep to a strictly vegetable diet." I believe that these learned persons know one as much as the other about it; and probably the whole of them put together know so little that a very small round nought might encompass all their certain knowledge as to health and disease. But there is one thing we do know, that the bread which the Israelites ate in the wilderness, the manna, was the best sort of food. It was God's own invention; and he who created man best knew what nutriment his life would require. It was not aërated bread, but it was celestial bread which had never been soured with earthly leaven, but had dropped immediately from the sky: the best food that men could eat if they would be healthy, active, and able to endure a hard and toilsome life.

Well now, what that manna was to their bodies—the ideal food of man, which had nothing in it injurious—that our Lord Jesus is to the soul. In him is life for men, and no disease or death. In the manna there was no adulteration, *it was a perfectly pure food:* such food is the Lord Jesus Christ to the spiritual life. He is the bread that came down from heaven, he is the true meat. If our souls live upon Christ, and nothing else but Christ, he will breed no disease within the heart; he will not distort the judgment; he will not inflame the imagination; he will not excite the passions. He would be a perfect man who lived on nothing but this perfect bread. Brethren, if you aspire after holiness of the highest type and order, remember that a man is made by that which he feeds upon, and for the best manhood you need the best food. As certain silk-worms have their silk coloured by the leaves on which they feed, so if we were to feed on Christ, and nothing else but Christ, we should become pure, holy, lowly, meek, gentle, humble; in a word, we should be perfect even as he is. What wonderful meat this must be! O my brethren, if you have ever tried the flesh and blood of Jesus as your souls' diet, you will know that I am not speaking vain words! There is no such sustenance for faith, love, patience, joy, as living daily upon Jesus, our Saviour. You who have never tasted of this heavenly bread, had better listen to the word, " O taste and see that the Lord is good! "

The Lord Jesus Christ is not only the ideal bread, but *he is in himself a sufficient bread*. That manna which the Israelites ate in the wilderness was all that they really wanted. They began a-lusting, and they cried after flesh, and they sighed for the leeks, and the garlic, and the onions, which had charmed their degenerate palates when they dwelt among the Egyptians. Wretched was their taste. They must have been of a coarse mould to grow weary of the food of angels, and sigh for something more rank, more tasty, more heavy. Something injurious they wanted; yet had they but been wise and right they would have known that within the manna there was everything that was sufficient and suitable for them; for the God that made man made manna, and he knew exactly what man wanted. Out of the ovens of heaven he sent man down bread, fresh and hot, each morning, that he might eat to the full, and yet never be surfeited, nor filled with evil humours. They called the manna " light bread"; but what should the food be for those who were always on the march but light, and easy of digestion? Our Lord Jesus is simple in doctrine; but what else do we wish for, even we who are wayfaring men, and all too apt to err?

My brethren, if we do but get a hold of Jesus Christ, and feed on him, he is sufficient for us—sufficient for gigantic labours, sufficient for anguish, and grief, and sorrow; sufficient for the weakest of the babes, for he is the unadulterated milk; sufficient for the full-grown men among us, for he is the strong meat of the kingdom. His flesh is meat indeed. For your spiritual manhood there is bone, gristle, muscle, brain, everything that you want, in Christ. If you feed on him, he will build you up, not in one direction only, but in all ways; for ye are complete in him—thoroughly furnished unto all necessities. Christ Jesus meets all the wants of all his people with a divine sufficiency.

And then there is in Christ what there is in manna—*a sweetness all its own*. I cannot tell you exactly how the manna tasted. Some of them said that it tasted like wafers made with honey. The Jewish notion is that it tasted according to every man's own taste; so that, if he preferred this flavour or that, the manna had that flavour to him, and thus it was to each one a personal and peculiar delicacy. This I know—that there is a sweetness about my Lord which is precisely that which delights *me*. I cannot communicate it to you, for you must each one taste for himself. I believe that our Lord has a flavour to me different from that which he could have to you, because our circumstances and desires somewhat differ. Though there is in the great church of God a sweet community of delight in the Lord, yet each believer has his own special delight. All Israel could claim all Canaan, and yet every Israelite had a little plot of land that was his own; and so all believers can claim all Christ, and yet each believer has a special portion which is altogether his own. Oh, the sweetness that there is in the bread that came down from heaven! Do you not know it? I trust you do, and if so, you do not need me to say more. If you love Jesus, you wish for nothing new. Modern gospels are forthcoming on all sides. You have heard about them, I dare say; but the preachers of them cannot have the delight in preaching their new gospels that I have in preaching the old one. "Oh," I say to myself, "they may preach better than I can; they may be a world more clever; but they have not such a subject to preach of as I have." When I get preaching up Christ, and his precious blood, and eternal love, and covenant securities, there I beat them all. With such a theme I can compete with the most renowned of the world's orators. When I speak on these themes, my lips drop pearls and diamonds. Brethren, when we declare unto you the Lord Jesus we sail upon a sea of sweetness. The novelties of "modern thought" are a Dead Sea, but our gospel is an ocean of living water. He that has Christ to preach has such a subject that angels might envy him, and cry one to another, "Let us go down below, and tell mankind of Jesus and his love." Brethren, to me the pulpit is a throne, and when I am in full swing, with the Lord Jesus Christ as my subject, I would not change places with the seraphim. It is a celestial joy to tell our fellow-men of such a Saviour as Jesus; for all sorts of joys are wrapped up in his thrice-blessed name. When Jesus said, "I am that bread of life," he meant, "I am that choice bread, that satisfying bread, that delicious bread, the like of which was never found elsewhere."

Furthermore, it was bread *suitable for the wilderness*. When they were in the wilderness, it was much better for the tribes to eat what they called "light bread" than for them to be filled with the meat that they had in Egypt, or even the old corn which they enjoyed when they came into Canaan. Manna was suitable food for the climate, and for their condition; and the Lord knew it. So the most suitable meat for us in this vale of tears is Christ Jesus. I believe that there is no meat like it in heaven; but for this world, with its work and its weeping, with its toils and its troubles, its cares and its changes, its wars and its woes, its fears and its frets, there is nothing so suitable as the Lord Jesus.

"Jesus, thou joy of loving hearts!
Thou Fount of life! Thou Light of men!
From the best bliss that earth imparts
We turn unfill'd to thee again.

We taste thee, O thou living Bread,
And long to feast upon thee still!
We drink of thee, the Fountain-head,
And thirst our souls from thee to fill."

Jesus is all the bread that you need while you are on your way to heaven and God.

What I have to say on this point further is—Try it, dear friends. I would be very practical on this point, and say earnestly, *taste and test.* If you wish to know this bread that came down from heaven, and how satisfying, how suitable, how sweet it is—try it.

Let me hand you out a portion of it. The Lord Jesus, the everlasting Son of God, is also man—man, like ourselves. "In all our affliction he was afflicted." He his own self bare our infirmities, and he is at this moment " a Brother born for adversity." Is not this a loaf of nourishing bread for a soul to feed on? I am a man, tried, troubled, burdened, and so is my Redeemer; so is he who sits upon the throne of God. I have to bow in prayer, and agonize in supplication: so did he. I have to endure slander and rebuke: so did he—" He endured such contradiction of sinners against himself." Brothers, sisters, you cannot be in any plight wherein he has never been; you cannot suffer any want so severe, but he also suffered the like. Even if you have not a home, or a lodging, or a bed for the night—" The Son of man had not where to lay his head." He is a partaker with us of the bitter cup of affliction. Now, is not this choice nourishment?

> "Why should I complain of want or distress,
> Temptation or pain? He told me no less;
> The heirs of salvation, I know from his Word!
> Through much tribulation must follow their Lord.
>
> "How bitter that cup no heart can conceive,
> Which he drank quite up, that sinners might live!
> His way was much rougher and darker than mine;
> Did Christ, my Lord, suffer, and shall I repine?"

The sympathy of Jesus, our Brother, is living bread for sorrowing men.

Now for another slice from the same loaf. He died: he bowed his head, and gave up the ghost. It was for sin and sinners that he died. "He his own self bare our sins in his own body on the tree." "The chastisement of our peace was upon him." He has put away our sin by making full atonement to divine justice. Sin has ceased to be so far as those are concerned who believe in him, for he was punished in our stead, and so ended our debt. God will not punish those for whom Christ was punished. He cannot exact the same debt twice, first of the Surety, and then of the sinner. That cannot be. Substitutionary sacrifice is the finest of the wheat. A real atonement is the most satisfactory food for the soul. I know it is so of a truth.

Poor sinner, if you can eat this bread you will not be hungry any more! Feeding upon the glorious doctrine of the vicarious sacrifice of Christ you will find that his flesh is meat indeed, and his blood is drink indeed.

I might continue thus to set forth my Lord as bread for you in his resurrection, in his glorious ascension, in his session at the right hand of God even the Father, where he maketh intercession for transgressors, and in the glory of his Second Advent; but time would fail me. I might cut a slice from this loaf, and speak to you upon our communion with him, upon our acceptance in the Beloved, upon the glory which he wears as our Representative, and wears for us ; but I will not : it is enough for me to introduce the text, and let Jesus say for himself, "I am that bread of life." Certainly there never was such a fruitful and satisfying subject as this of Jesus, our Lord. Oh, that all ministers were shut up to this ! Why leave this bread of heaven for the unsatisfying husks afforded by other topics ?

Very well : that is the first truth we are to remember, namely, that Jesus Christ fully meets all the wants of the new life.

II. But, secondly, IN ORDER THAT JESUS MAY MEET ALL OUR SOUL'S WANTS WE MUST RECEIVE HIM. Bread cannot possibly sustain the body unless it be eaten. You know, dear friends, you might be hungry to-night, and hear about bread, and then be doomed to wait till to-morrow evening without having any of it to eat : that would be a tantalizing business, would it not ? I might then preach again, and tell you about bread, and you might go without all through Saturday, and come here on Sunday, and hear two more sermons about bread, and yet all the while have none of it to eat. It would be trying work. None would like it, unless it were those people who are attempting to fast for forty days, and are likely to die in the process. What good would it do you to keep on hearing of the bread, and never eat of it ? I cannot see any result. Unless it tended to increase your hunger, I do not know what would come of the wisest discourse on bread if you did not eat. Suppose that you should go to a baker's window, and stand there for an hour, and stare at the bread, I do not think that the sight would fill you much. No, you must eat, or else there might be tons of bread within reach, and yet you would die of famine. You might be buried in a grave of bread, and it would be of no use to you. Even manna would not nourish you unless you ate it. You must receive food into yourself, or it is not food to you. The Saviour himself, if you do not receive him by faith, will be no Saviour to you. Mark that.

Here is a brother who never eats bread, but instead of eating he studies the theory of nutrition, and he is ready to discuss with any one the whole system of digestion and assimilation. He has a theory that bread should always be baked in a certain way, and he feels bound to discuss, and discuss, and discuss, till all is mouldy. My dear friend, you may discuss if you like, but I want to eat ; and I think that, if you intend to live, and not to drop down dead in your discussion, you had better eat a bit yourself, and not put discussion into the place of eating. Some of you have been hearing the gospel for years, and you have never fed upon Christ yet ; but you have a great liking for religious controversy. Why, perhaps, this very afternoon you have been discussing this "ism" and that "ism." Wherefore all this chopping of logic ? Why do you not eat, friend ? Why do you not eat ? What is the use of talking about bread when your fainting body pines for a substantial meal ? You are at this time ready to fight anybody about the shape that the portions of bread ought to take when they are cut up for a feast. No, no, I am not going to accept your challenge ! I am hungry, and want food, and to me the form of it does not matter much. Bread is nothing to anybody till he eats it ; and even our Lord Jesus is nothing to any man until he believes in him, until he receives him, until he takes him into himself. That is the one thing that is wanted; and the Lord Jesus Christ silently hints as much when he says, "I am that bread of life." When he calls himself bread, he does in effect say, "Partake of me; eat me; feed upon me."

Here comes in the enquiry—How do we receive Christ into us as we take bread into our bodies?

First, by *believing everything that is revealed about him.* The Father's witness, and the Holy Ghost's witness, and his own witness concerning himself—we have all these in God's most holy Word. Take the Book, and read it. Augustine, after years of tossing to and fro, found peace with God by hearing a little child say, "Take, and read." I suppose that the child was singing to itself, and hardly knew what it was saying as it repeated to itself the two words—"Tolle, lege; tolle, lege; tolle, lege." "Take up, and read." That voice struck the ear of the perplexed thinker as though it were the voice of God, and he took the Scripture, and read the Scripture, and no sooner had he read it than he found Christ. I would entreat each one of you to do this, in order that you may find rest for your soul. Believe what is revealed in Holy Scripture. Ye search the Scriptures, for in them ye think ye have eternal life, and they are they which testify of Christ; but ye will do well if ye go to Christ himself, and find life. To believe in him, think of him. As the look of faith which saves is *to* Jesus, so is it *from* Jesus. By looking we learn to look. As we know of him we believe in him. Believe what is spoken about Christ, and so feed on him.

Then, next, *trust him for yourself.* That is *the* point—the hinge of the whole business. He is a Saviour. I believe *that:* but I go further, and resolve—he shall be *my* Saviour. May I say that? Yes, for I am permitted to do so, inasmuch as he says, "Him that cometh to me I will in no wise cast out." Scripture saith that he is exalted on high to give repentance unto Israel, and remission of sins. Therefore, I look to him to give me repentance and remission of sins. I trust to him in that respect, and he is mine. He has said, "It is finished." The atonement is finished, and I believe that it is finished for me. A prominent point about the offering under the old law was that the person who came with the sacrifice laid his hands on it, and said, "This is mine." You must do the same with Jesus. Lay your hands on him, and say, "This is mine. This sacrificial death is for me." "Oh, but," says one, "suppose he is not mine. What if I were to take him to myself without warrant?" Suppose such a thing for one moment; yet he would be yours. If I was hungry, and I ate a bit of bread, and after I had eaten it somebody said, "It is not yours," I should reply, "Perhaps not, but how will you take it from me? It has nourished me, and refreshed me; it is mine, and none can deprive me of it." There is the point, you see: if you take Christ Jesus into yourself, the devil himself may say you had no right to him, but he cannot take away that which you have eaten. Jesus himself will not quarrel with you, nor blame you for taking him, for he has said, "Him that cometh to me I will in no wise cast out." You may summon a poor man before the magistrate, and say, "He is a thief, for he stole bread from my counter." You may put him in prison for the theft, though I hope you would not if hunger drove him to the act; but you cannot get your

THE BEST BREAD

bread away from him if he has eaten it. So, if you come to Christ, and take him into yourself, he is yours, and you shall live by him. Jesus says, "He that eateth me, even he shall live by me." Nor death, nor hell, nor time, nor eternity, can take Jesus away when once you have him within you. "Who shall separate us from the love of Christ?" Swallow, then, the divine truth. Let it go down quickly, for fear anybody should come before it has fully entered into your soul. Once there, it is yours! They say that possession is nine points of the law; and I should think in the case of eating that it is the whole ten points, or any other number of points, for there is no getting re-possession of that which a man has actually eaten. Get Christ, and Christ is yours —yours by a kind of possession, which will never be disputed before the courts of heaven.

This, then, is to feed upon Christ—to believe that which is revealed about him, and then to appropriate him to yourself by personal faith.

Furthermore, to feed upon Christ means to meditate much upon him —to think much of him. Brothers, there are many sweet doctrines in the Bible which I delight to make my own by reading, marking, learning, and inwardly digesting them; for they are parts of the great circle of truth which is revealed of God. But I find that I am never so comforted, strengthened, and sustained, as by deliberately considering Jesus Christ's precious death and atoning sacrifice. His sacrifice is the centre of the circle, the focus of the light. There is a charm, a divine fascination, about his wounds.

O sacred head, once wounded! O dear eyes, so red with weeping! O cheeks, with spittle all bestained! I could for ever gaze, admire, and adore! There is no beauty in all the world like that which is seen in the countenance "more marred than that of any man." This one vision is enough for all eyes for all time. There is no sustenance to the heart like the sustenance that comes of his flesh and his blood, given up in anguish and in death to work out our redemption. Beloved, this is the bread of heaven. "Take, eat," says he, "this is my body, which is broken for you." What food is this! What life ought that to be which is nourished by such bread!

But time flies so quickly that I cannot dwell upon these points as they deserve to be dwelt upon. Oh, live near the cross! Build your house on Calvary! Frequent Gethsemane! Listen to the groans of your pleading Lord! Be much with a dying Christ. Be much with a risen Christ. Be much with a reigning Christ. Be much in anticipation of a coming Christ. For the more you are with him, the more will your soul be filled with satisfaction, and influenced to sanctification. He shall satiate your soul as with marrow and with fatness, and your mouth shall praise him with joyful lips, for he can say, and none other, "I am that bread of life." Receive him, then, and you shall find it so.

III. Now thirdly—and this shall be but a word or two—notice this solemn fact: NOT TO FEED UPON CHRIST IS THE SURE MARK OF DEATH. Terrible fact. The Lord Jesus Christ has said it—"Except ye eat the flesh of the Son of man, and drink his blood, ye have no life in you." A great preacher, but he does not feed on Christ! You have no life in you. A forward professor, but he does not feed on Christ!

You have no life in you. A very knowing theologian, and a clever controversialist; but he does not feed upon the incarnate God! There is no life in you. A daring speculator in modern thought, but he does not care, he says, for the blood of Christ: he even sneers at the mention of it! You have no life in you. Hard words! Hard words! Hard words, if they be true, are better than soft words if they be false. But this is the sure test : "What think ye of Christ?" If he is not bread to your souls, you have no life in you. If anybody were to say to me, " I have a man at home who stands in my hall, and has stood there for years, but he has never eaten a mouthful of bread all the time, nor cost me a penny for food," I should say to myself, " Oh, yes, that is a bronze man, I know, or a plaster cast of a man. He has no life in him, I am sure; for if he had life in him, he would have needed bread." If we could live without eating, it would be a cheap method of existence, but I have never found out the secret, and I do not mean to make experiments. If you are trying it, and have succeeded in it so far that you can live without Christ, the bread of life, I fear your life is not that of God's people, for they all hunger and thirst after Jesus, the bread of heaven. O my dear hearer, once a professor, once a church-member, if you have given up Christ, and you get on well without him, you have no life in you! The dead can do without bread, but the living cannot. Jesus tells us, "I am that bread of life," and if you are doing without him you are doing without the bread of life, and the reason is that you are without life itself.

IV. Next, and the fourth head, shall be with equal brevity—THOSE WHO FEED UPON CHRIST ARE SUPREMELY BLESSED. They shall never hunger. They shall hunger after more of Jesus, but not after anything else besides Jesus. I was greatly pleased some time ago to hear a gentleman say, who had tried to preach another doctrine, that a certain neighbourhood which he spoke of was so impregnated with what was called " the gospel" that he could not succeed with his speculations. He said that if men once drank this gospel doctrine it made them so bigoted in their love for it that the most clever person could not get them out of it. I thought to myself, " This witness is true." An enemy declared it, and it was therefore all the more striking. The subtlest deceivers may try as long as they please, but when we have once fed upon Christ they cannot get us off from him. They call us away from him ; they proffer us all manner of novelties ; but in vain : " Try our thought! Try our science! Try our purgatory ! Try our larger hope!" But we hear the pails rattle, and we hear the swine clamouring, and we are not anxious to taste the mixture, or unite in the festival. We are not so selfish as to steal this new wash from those whom it delights. Let those have it who can feed on it; but as for ourselves, we mean to feed on the bread of heaven. The gospel is to us such satisfying bread that all the rest is draff.

> Should all the forms that men devise
> Assault my soul with treacherous art;
> I'd call them vanity and lies,
> And bind the gospel to my heart.

Every true child of God is so far a bigot that he prefers the bread of his Father's house to the husks of the far country. He cannot give up the gospel, and he will not, for it satisfies his whole being. What more does he want? Why should he make a change?

Moreover, he has in Christ food that he can never exhaust. He may feed, and feed, and yet he shall never find that he lacks for meat. I have many an old book in my library in which there have been bookworms, and I have sometimes amused myself with tracing a worm. I do not know how he gets to the volume originally, but being there he eats his way into it. He bores a hole in a direct line, and sometimes I find that he dies before he gets half-way through the tome. Now and then a worm has eaten his way right through from one wooden cover to another; yes, and through the cover also. This was a most successful book-worm. Few of us can eat our way quite so far. I am one of the book-worms that have not got half-way into my Bible yet; but I am eating my way as fast as I can. This one thing I have proved to myself beyond all question: I shall never, never exhaust this precious Book; much less shall I exhaust the wondrous person of my divinely-blessed Lord. He is that bread which came down from heaven. He is utterly inexhaustible.

Brethren, feeding upon Jesus we have an immortal blessedness: we shall never die. If we have fed on Christ, we shall fall asleep, but it will be in Jesus. Some whom we love have lately fallen asleep: they will awake with him in the morning. But we shall never die. We shall only pass into a higher stage of life: for that food on which we feed shall be in us the pledge of an immortality equal to the immortality of the Christ who has become our bread.

V. I had much more to say to you, but the time has gone. All that I will say further is this. If any of you desire to have Christ, you may depend upon it that you may have him, because bread is meant to be eaten: JESUS IS PROVIDED TO BE RECEIVED. What is the use of bread if it is never eaten? If you go to the Orphanage, you will see a large batch of bread there kept upon the shelves. It must not be eaten the first day, you know, it would go too fast, and would not be very wholesome for the youngsters. It must get rather staler by being kept a little while. Now suppose that I were to go down there, and say to the baker, "Lock that door: I want to keep that bread. I am going away to Mentone, and I shall take the key with me, that I may save that bread." Suppose I were to do so, and come back in a couple of months' time. Should I say to myself, "I have saved that batch of bread"? I am afraid that it would turn out to be very bad economy. Let us go and look at the loaves which we have kept from use! Come away at once! The sight is not pleasant. Decay and corruption have fallen upon what we have hoarded. It would be a poor matter for the bread. Why, it is the very end of bread, the object of bread, the portion of bread, to be eaten. It is honoured in being eaten: it would be degraded by being left to grow stale and mouldy. Now the Lord Jesus Christ is never so famous a Christ as when sinners come and feed upon him. This precious bread must be eaten, or it has not answered its design. What say you to a doctor who has no patients? What say you to a Saviour who never saves anybody? The honour of a physician lies in the persons that he heals; and the honour of a Saviour lies in the persons that he saves. Christ has become the bread of heaven on purpose for you to have him, and for me to have him. He came into the world to save sinners, and if he does not save sinners he has come for nothing. It is his business to save sinners. Now, if a man sets up in business, and never does any business, his undertaking is a failure. " Poor man ! " you say, " he has made a great mistake."

I know a brother here who wanted to take a certain shop in a wide street, but his wiser friends said, " Do not take that shop for a baker's. It is not in a good eating locality. You must open a shop in one of the streets where there are plenty of poor people, who will buy the bread every morning. Make it good and cheap, and it will not stop long on the shelves." I noticed in the newspaper that a certain drink-shop was " in a good drinking locality." I am sorry that there are such localities. But, assuredly, a good eating locality must be the very place for vending bread. I think that this Tabernacle stands in a good eating locality. Many are here now who are hungry after Christ, and it is a blessed fact that they may have him, and feed upon him without stint. And what is the price ? The price ? The difficulty with all other traders is to get you up to their price; but my difficulty is to get you down to mine—for the bread of heaven is *without price*. Even if you offer a farthing, I cannot take your bid. You may have all for nothing, and have it at once; but not a penny can be accepted from you. The gospel provides a full Christ for empty sinners, pardon on earth and bliss in heaven, and all for nothing. Take it as a free gift, and it is yours. What would you pay ? What could you pay ? Did Israel pay for the manna ? It would have been an insult to God to imagine it. Go your way, and bless the name of the Lord, for this is the gospel—" He that believeth and is baptized shall be saved."

Spiritual Appetite

"The full soul loatheth an honeycomb; but to the hungry soul every bitter thing is sweet"—Proverbs xxvii. 7.

It is a great blessing when food and appetite meet together. Some have appetite and no meat, they need our pity; others have meat but no appetite, they may not perhaps win our pity but they certainly require it. We have heard of a gentleman who was accustomed to take an early morning walk and frequently met a poor man hastening to his labour. One morning he said to him, " I have to walk thus early of a morning to get a stomach for my meat." "Ah," said the other, " and I have to trudge to work thus early to get meat for my stomach." Neither of them was quite satisfied with his position: the happy conjunction of the appetite and the food could alone secure content. Are we thankful enough when we have both?

It has often happened that men have been so luxuriously fed that appetite has departed from them altogether. The Israelites when they were in the wilderness became at last so squeamish that though they were fed with the bread of heaven, and for once men did eat angels' food, yet they said, " Our soul loatheth this light bread;" and thousands in the world are in great danger of falling into the same condition, for the rarest luxuries are unenjoyed by them. They pick and choose as if nothing were good enough for them, and like the old Roman gluttons they require sea and land, earth and air to be ransacked for their gratification, and then crave pungent sauces and strange flavourings ere they can eat. The fact is, the old proverb is true, that the best sauce for meat is hunger, and while the confectioner and the cook may labour with a thousand arts to produce a dainty dish, nature teaches us the way to enjoy our meat, namely, not to eat it till we want it, and then to partake of only so much as our bodies require. That hunger gives a relish even to objectionable diet is certain. Our forefathers found it possible to live upon food which we could not touch. Even so late as the reign of Queen Elizabeth the mass of the poor seldom tasted wheaten bread, but fed on rye or barley cakes, and often had to be content with bread made of beans, peas, tares, oats, or lentils, and even these had to be frequently mixed with acorns. They had a saying that "hunger setteth his foot in the horse's manger," meaning that food which was only fit for horses was devoured by men in the time of famine. Those delicate people, who are for ever complaining of this and that, and regretting the " good old times," would change their tune if they had a trial of such fare, and would earnestly pray to be projected again into the times in which we live.

The rules which apply to the bodily appetite equally hold true of the mind. We easily lose our taste for anything of which we have our fill. Many men of the world have gone the round of amusement, and now nothing can please them; they have worn out all their playthings, and are tired of every game. Poor things, more wearied of their follies than the slave by his servitude ! For them laughter and mirth have become ghastly mockeries, men singers and women singers are no delight, and instruments of music are discordant, gardens and palaces are dreary, and treasures of art a vexation of spirit. By the road of folly they have reached the very point to which Solomon came with all his wisdom, and like him they cry, " Vanity of vanities, all is vanity."

In a higher order of things the same process can be observed. In the pursuit of knowledge men may come to loathe honeycombs through sheer repletion. Many a literary man has reached such a condition of fastidiousness, that the books which he can enjoy are as few as the fingers of his hand. With a toss of the head he passes by volumes with which ordinary readers are charmed. His delicate poetical taste is shocked by the hymns which delight his countrymen, and his ear is tortured by the tunes to which they are sung. For my part, I would sooner retain the power of enjoying a simple hymn, sung to a tune which delights the multitude, than find myself proclaimed king of critics; and I would sooner be able to sit down and read a child's story book with interest, than rise into the sublime condition of those literary gentlemen who glance over every book with a sharp critical eye, and see nothing meriting their attention ; in fact, never will see anything worth reading, unless the book is written by themselves or one of their party. "The full soul loatheth an honeycomb ; but to the hungry soul every bitter thing is sweet."

I should not have said so much upon this principle of our nature if it had not happened to enter into religion. It is upon religious fastidiousness that I have to speak this morning. Men in the things of God have not always an appetite for the sweetest and most precious truth. The gospel of Jesus revealed from heaven is full of marrow and fatness, but the condition of men's minds is such that they cannot perceive its excellence, but regard it as a tasteless thing at best, while some even treat it as though it were wormwood and gall to them. They feed upon the husks of the world with greedy relish, but turn from the provisions of mercy with disdain. They are full of the meat from the flesh pots of Egypt, and for the bread of heaven they have no desire; nor will they till the Holy Spirit quickens them into spiritual life, and makes them feel the keen pangs of spiritual hunger.

The three points of my discourse will be as follows:—first, that *Jesus Christ is in himself sweeter than the honeycomb;* secondly, *there are those that loathe even him;* and then thirdly, blessed be his name, *there are others who appreciate him.*—"To the hungry soul every bitter thing is sweet."

I. Let us begin, then, with the assured truth that JESUS CHRIST IS HIMSELF SWEETER THAN THE HONEYCOMB. Whether you believe it or not, the fact remains, the incarnate word is sweeter than honey or the honeycomb: whether it be your privilege to revel in the delightful knowledge of his love or not, that love will still be equally precious. That Jesus Christ is sweeter than the honeycomb is clear, if we consider who he is and what he gives and does. If you think of it you will see that *it must be so.* Our Lord is the incarnation of divine love. The love of God is sweet, and Jesus is that love made manifest. "God so loved the world,"—I pause to ask how much? Where shall we see at a glance the fulness of that love? Turn your eyes to Jesus, he alone answers the question. "God so loved the world that he gave his only-begotten Son." There bleeding upon Calvary we see the heart of the Father revealed in the pierced heart of his only-begotten Son. Jesus is the focus of the love of God. The boundless goodness of the ever-loving God finds its best expression in the person of the Redeemer :—surely then he must be sweet beyond compare. When God takes his love, and culls the choicest flower from it, and hands it down to earth for men to gaze upon it as the token of his favour, we may be sure that its fragrance surpasses conception. God is love, and when that love is concentrated in one individual that it may be afterwards diffused through multitudes, there mus, be an infinite sweetness in that blessed person. Judge ye what I say ;—must it not be so?

Moreover, Jesus Christ is in himself the embodiment of boundless mercy to sinners as well as love to creatures. God loved men, for he had made them, but he could not bless them, for he must judge them for their offences. Lo, Jesus Christ has vindicated the divine honour, satisfied the law, and now the mercy of God can descend freely to men, even to the rebellious and the undeserving. Who would find mercy let him look where Jesus died upon the tree, and he shall find it blooming freely from the crimsoned ground. Who would behold mercy in all its plenitude, let him go where Jesus stands with open hands welcoming the vilest of the vile to the feast of love, cleansing their every stain, and robing them in garments of salvation. He must be sweet from whom such sweetness flows that he makes the foulest and most offensive of mankind acceptable to God. If his merits turn our hell to heaven, our gall of bitterness into joy and peace, it is not possible that even the honeycomb dripping with virgin honey should fitly set him forth. Ye bees that wander over fairest flowers, your choicest gatherings can never rival the quintessences of delight which must dwell in one in whom the mercy of God is concentrated.

Ye poverty-stricken sons of men, Christ must be sweet, for he meets all your wants. Sweet is liberty to the captive, and when the Son makes you free, you are free indeed ; sweet is pardon to the condemned, and Jesus proclaims full forgiveness and salvation ; sweet is health to the sick, and Jesus is the great physician of souls ; sweet is light to those who are in darkness and to eyes that are dim, and Jesus is both sun to our darkness and eyes to our blindness : all that men can want, all that the most famished souls can pine after is to be found in the person and work of the Lord Jesus, and therefore sweet he must be.

He is sweet because, whenever he comes into a man's heart, he breathes into it the sweetness of abounding peace. Oh the rest our souls have known when we have leaned upon his bosom ! "The peace of God which passeth all understanding" has kept our heart and mind by Jesus Christ. Our soul has drank nectar from his wounds. Nor has it been bare peace alone, the glassy pools of rest have bubbled up into fountains of joy. In Jesus we have rejoiced and do rejoice and will rejoice all the day. No happiness can be more divine than the bliss of knowing him and feeding upon him, and being one with him. All the true peace and joy that are known on earth, I might have said that are known in heaven among the ransomed throng, all come through Jesus Christ our Lord, whose name is the sum of delights. Those spices must be sweet indeed from which the sacred oil of joy distils ; that honey must be infinitely sweet of which one single drop fills a whole life with rejoicing.

It is clear that sweet our Lord must be, because his very name is redolent of celestial hope to believers. No sooner do we taste of Jesus, than, like Jonathan in the wood, our eyes are enlightened and we see the invisible ; the veil is taken away and we behold a way of access to our Father God, and to the joys of his right hand. Once understand that Jesus has borne our sins and carried our sorrows, and we see that the felicities of eternity are prepared for us. His name is the *open sesame* of the gates of Paradise ; learn but to pronounce the name of Jesus from your heart as all your confidence, and you have learned a magic word which will scatter troops of opposing foes and will open the two-leaved gates, and cut the bars of iron in sunder if they stand betwixt your soul and heaven. Since Jesus is all this, and vastly more than any human tongue can tell, it is clear upon the very face of it that he must be sweet.

But we are not left to the supposition and inference that it must be so, we know *it is so*. Our Lord is as the honeycomb, for he is sweet to God himself. The taste of the High and Holy One who shall venture to judge ? What the Lord himself calls sweet must be sweet indeed. Now, the very smell of Christ's sacrifice, nay, I will go further, the very smell of that which was the type of Christ in the days of Noah was so pleasing to God that it is written, "The Lord smelled a sweet savour of rest, and he said, I will no more destroy the earth with a flood." If the very smell of that which was but the emblem of the bleeding Lamb was grateful to Jehovah, how sweet to the divine Father must the Lord Jesus himself be in his actual sacrifice. Why, the very sight of the blood—and, mark you, not the blood of Christ, but only the blood of a lamb slain in type of Christ—the very sight of that blood sprinkled on the lintel turned away the destroying angel from Israel of old, for the Lord said, "When I see the blood I will pass over you." Now, if a mere glimpse of the type of Jesus' atoning blood be so satisfactory to the heart of God, what must the sight of Jesus be, for he has been obedient to death, even the death of the cross? If I had time I might mention the many ways in which our Lord is set forth in Scripture as being sweet to the Father; all the senses are represented as being gratified; the Lord hears his voice crying from the ground and answers it with blessing; he tastes his sacrifice as wine which makes glad the heart of God, and he feels his touch as the Daysman laying his hand both upon judge and offender. In every possible way Jesus is most sweet and pleasant to the divine mind. Hear how from the highest heaven the Lord declares, "This is my beloved Son in whom I am well pleased." The Lord is well pleased for his righteousness' sake. Now, if the heart of Deity itself is satisfied and filled to the full with content, there must be an infinite sweetness in the person of the Lord Jesus. That honeycomb must be sweet with which the Triune God is satisfied.

Moreover, our Lord Jesus is sweet to the angels in heaven. Did they not watch him when he was here below with careful eyes? When first they missed him from the courts above they flew with eager haste to discover where he was, and when they found that he was come to this poor planet they made the night bright with their radiance, and sweet with their chorales. While he tarried here they watched his devious footsteps, they ministered to him in the wilderness, and in the garden, and at other times they waited in their legions, eager to deliver him if he would but have beckoned them to use their celestial weapons. When they saw him at last, ready to ascend, I can well believe that the poet's words are no fiction, but describe a fact—

> "They brought his chariot from on high
> To bear him to his throne;
> Clapp'd their triumphant wings and cried,
> 'The glorious work is done.'"

He was "seen of angels," and was very dear and precious to them. Surely he who attracts all those bright intelligences, and causes them to gaze upon him unceasingly, and pay him divine honours, must be sweet indeed.

Sweet is Christ, beloved, for it is his presence that makes heaven what it is. You are in a garden, and smelling a dainty perfume, you say to yourself, "Whence cometh this?" You traverse the walks and borders to discover the source of the pleasant odour, and at last you come upon a rose: even thus, if you were to walk amongst those fruitful trees which skirt the river of the water of life you would perceive a peerless perfume of superlative delight, but you would not have to ask yourself, "Whence comes this fragrance?" There is but one rose even in the Paradise of God which is capable of scattering such perfume of joy, and that is the "Rose of Sharon," that famous "plant of renown," which has diffused fragrance over both earth and heaven. Well may he be sweet to us, since when he was broken like the alabaster box of precious ointment, he filled all the chambers of the house of God both above and below with an unrivalled sweetness.

If you want proof from nearer home, let me remind you how sweet the Well-beloved is to his own people. What was it that first attracted us to God? Was it not the sweetness of Christ? What was it that banished all the bitterness of our fears? Was it not the sweetness of his pardoning love? What is it that holds us so that we cannot go, which enchains us, seals us, nails us to the cross, so that we can never leave it? Is it not that he is so sweet that we shall never find any to compare with him, and therefore must abide with him because there is nowhere else to go? Brethren and sisters, I appeal to you who know Jesus, are ye not satisfied? I mean not only satisfied with him, but satisfied altogether? Does he not fill and over-fill your souls? When you enjoy his presence what other joy could you imagine? When he embraces you have you any heart left for other delights? Do you not say, "He is all my salvation, and all my desire." My cup runneth over, my Lord Jesus, when I have communion with thee.

> "Jesus, to whom I fly,
> Doth all my wishes fill;
> What though the creature streams are dry,
> I have a fountain still."

All the saints will tell you that Christ is most sweet and altogether lovely, and some of them will confess that sometimes his sweetness overcomes them, carries them right away, and bears them out of themselves. The eagle wings of Jesus' love uplift us to the gates of heaven, and this will happen to us even when there is nothing on earth to make us happy, and all without and within is dark. When the poor body is full of pain, and every nerve is unstrung by disease, even then Jesus comes and lays his fingers amid the strings of our poor nature, until charmed by his touch, they pour forth a music which might teach the harps of heaven his praise. In his presence our heart is glad beyond all gladness; we are beatified if not glorified. Would God it might be always so. My dear Lord and Master is very sweet, but my lips fail me, and I blush at my poor attempts to speak his praises.

One thing that proves how sweet he is, is this,—he removes all bitterness from the heart which truly receives him. The quassia cup of sickness is no longer bitter when a drop of his love falls into it. In his society sick beds grow into thrones, wherein the invalid does not so much pine as reign; the lonely chamber becomes a royal reception room, the hard bed a couch of down, and the curtains are transformed into banners of love. So, too, his love digs out of the garden of life the roots of the rue of care and the wormwood of anxiety. A man may be vexed with a thousand anxieties, but in communion with Christ he will find rest unto his soul. The delectable hydromel of fellowship with Jesus effectually drowns the taste of the world's bitterness. Saints in persecution have found the love of Christ cleanse their mouths from every taste of hatred's gall; they have been able to bear imprisonment and think it liberty, to regard chains as ornaments, to find the rack a bed of roses, and the blazing stake a chariot of fire to bear them to their reward. If a child of God were called in the pursuit of duty to swim through a sea of hell's most bitter pains, yet with the honied sweetness of Christ's love in his mouth he would not so much as taste the sea of gall. As to death, we have learned to swallow it up in victory; surely its bitterness is past. Where else find you such delicious dainties? Where else such all-subduing sweetness? Jesus is bliss itself.

Thus have I shown sufficiently that facts have proved that Jesus is sweet as the honeycomb, but I detain you just a moment to notice that *he is incomparably so.* Honey, I might almost say, is not only sweet, but sweetness itself. Whether I am right or not in speaking thus of honey, I shall be right enough in saying it of Jesus Christ: he is not only sweet, but sweetness itself. We need not say of him that he is good, for he is essential goodness. He is not only loving, but love. Whatever good thing you may seek in the world you shall find it thinly spread here and there upon good men, as God deals out these precious things by measure; but the fulness of all good you shall find in Jesus Christ. He is not the sweet odour, but the ointment which gives it forth; he is not the rill, but the fountain from which it springs; he is not the beam of light, but the sun from which it proceeds. Honey is the conglomeration and compounding of a thousand sweets. The bees visit all sorts of flowers, knowing by a cunning wisdom denied to us where all dulcitudes are hidden: they take not only the nectar of the ruddy rose but also of the snow-white lily, and gathering ambrosia from all the beauties of the garden they thus concoct a luscious sweetness altogether unsurpassable. Even thus my Lord is all excellences compounded and commingled in divine harmony, a rare confection of all perfections to make one perfection, the meeting of all sweetnesses to make one perfect sweet. They said of Harry the Eighth that if all the lineaments of a tyrant had been lost, they might have been painted afresh from his life; and surely we may say of Christ that if all the sweetness and light of manhood had been forgotten, if all the love of mothers, the constancy of martyrs, the honesty of confessors, and the self-sacrifice of heroes, had departed, you would find it all treasured up in the person of the Lord Jesus Christ.

Each bee as he performs his many journeys selects what he thinks best, and brings it to the common store, and I doubt not they have each a dainty tooth, so that each one chooses the best he finds. Oh, ye preachers of the gospel, ye may each seek out the richest thoughts and words ye can to set out my Lord. Oh, ye who are the mighty orators of the church, ye may utter the choicest language of poetry or prose, and so you may bring all sweets together, but you shall never match the altogether peerless sweetness which dwells in the person and work of Jesus the well-beloved.

Honey is a healthy sweet, though many sweets are not so. Children have been made sick and even poisoned by berries whose sickly sweetness has decoyed them to their hurt, but as for our Lord the more you feed on him the more you may. Christ is health to the soul, yea, strength and life. Eat, yea, drink abundantly, O beloved. Hast thou found honey? eat not too much, but hast thou found Jesus? eat to the full, and eat on still, if so thou canst, for never shalt thou have too much of him.

II. Secondly—THERE ARE THOSE WHO LOATHE THE SWEETNESS

OF OUR LORD. This loathing shows itself variously. Some loathe him so as to trample on him, and this I find to be the translation given in the margin, "The full soul tramples on a honeycomb." God have mercy upon these boastful ones who persecute his saints, revile his name, and despise his gospel. If there be any such here, may sovereign mercy change their hearts, or a fearful judgment awaits them.

Others show that they loathe Christ because they are always murmuring at him; if they do not find fault with the gospel itself, they rail at its ministers. Nobody can please them. John comes neither eating nor drinking, and they say he hath a devil; the Master comes eating and drinking and they say—behold a man gluttonous and a wine bibber. One man preaches very solemnly and they call him heavy, another mingles humour with his discourse and they accuse him of frivolity; one minister uses a lofty rhetoric, he is too flowery; another speaks in simpler style, he is vulgar. This generation, like the generations which have gone before, cannot be satisfied, but it is Jesus they are discontented with. O ye carping critics of the gospel, you find fault with the dish, but it is a mere excuse; you do not like the meat. If you hungered after the meat you would not object to the platter on which it is served; but because you love it not you complain of the dish and the carver.

Often this loathing is shown by an utter indifference to the gospel. The great mass of our fellow-citizens will not attend a place of worship at all, or if they do attend it is but seldom; and when they come they leave their hearts behind them, so that the word goes in at one ear and out at the other. The suffering Saviour is nothing to them; heaven and hell are nothing to them; whether they shall be lost or saved is nothing to them. Thus they show their loathing.

Perhaps some here present loathe our Lord at bottom, and yet think not so. They attend to his word, but what is the attention? They care for Jesus, but they care so little that it leads to no practical result. Some of you that after ten years of hearing the gospel are still unconverted, and after twenty years of the enjoyment of gospel privileges you still have never tasted the honey of the word. If you thought it sweet you would have tasted of it before now: you loathe it or else you would not let it stand right under your nose untasted for years. You must be surfeited or you would not allow this honeycomb to lie untouched so long. You have meant to eat of it, you say. Yes, but I never knew a hungry man sit without eating for six hours at a table meaning to eat all the while. No, he lays to as soon as grace has been said; and in your case the grace has been said a great many times, and yet you sit with the sweets of mercy before you, and refuse to eat thereof. I cannot account for it on any other theory but that there is a secret loathing in your soul.

This loathing is manifest by many signs. There is the Bible, a book of infinite sweetness, God's letter of love to the sons of men. Is it not dreadfully dry reading! A three-volume novel suits a great many far better. That is loathing the honeycomb. There is the gospel ministry. Sermons are dull affairs, are they not? Now, I will admit that some sermons are dreary and empty as a desert, but when Christ be honestly and earnestly preached how is it you are so weary? Others are fed, why do you complain? The meat is right enough, but you have no appetite for it, for the reason given in the text. When a man loathes Christ he finds prayer to be bondage, and, if he carries it on at all, it is a very dull exercise, yielding no enjoyment. As to meditation, that is a thing neglected altogether by the godless many. The Sabbath with some persons is a very weary day, they are glad when it is over. I heard one say the other day he thought the Sunday ought to be spent in recreation; upon which a friend replied that he wished he might find true re-creation, for he needed to be created anew in Christ Jesus, and then he would judge the Sabbath to be the best day of the week. Alas, these dull Sabbaths, and these dreary preachers, and this dull praying and singing, and all this weariness, are sure signs that you are full souls, and therefore loathe the honeycomb.

This loathing comes of a soul's being full, and souls may be full in a great many ways. Some are full because they have never yet discovered their natural depravity and nothingness; have never known that they are condemned by the law of God. These full souls who are what they always were, good people as they have always been from their birth, do not want a Saviour, and therefore they despise him. Why should the whole value a physician? Is he not intended for the sick? Alas for you full ones, for your time of hunger will come when there will be no more feasts of love, and then, as Dives could not obtain a drop of water, you also will be denied a crumb of consolation.

Some people are full with enjoying the world. They have wealth and they are perfectly content with it; or they have no wealth, but still they are pleased with the grovelling pursuits of their class. Their thoughts never rise; they are like the cock on the dunghill that scratched up a diamond and said, " I would sooner have found a grain of barley." They are satisfied if they have enough to eat and drink and wear, but they think not of divine things. They are full of the world, and therefore loathe the honeycomb.

Some are full of confidence in outward religiousness. They were christened when they were babes, and they were confirmed, and if that does not save people what will? A bishop's hands laid on you! Think of that!! Since that they have taken the sacrament, and they have always been told that if you go regularly to your place of worship, and especially if you pay twenty shillings in the pound you will do very well—at least if you do not what will become of your neighbours? These full souls do not appreciate free grace and dying love, and salvation by the blood of Christ seems to them to be but idle babble.

Some are full of self-conceit—they know everything,—they are great readers and profound philosophers. Their thoughts have dived to the bottom of infinity; they are so nice in their criticisms that they

" Can a hair divide
Betwixt the west and north-west side."

It is not possible to satisfy them. The knowledge of Christ crucified is foolishness and a stumbling-block to them.

Others are full of the pride of rank. Yes, they are very glad to hear that the poor people hear the gospel, and they have no doubt that the plain preaching of the gospel is very useful to the lower orders, but respectable people who live in the West End and ride in carriages do not require such preaching; they are too respectable to need saving, and so their full souls loathe the honeycomb.

But we need not stop any longer talking about them, for we shall do them no good as long as they are full. If the angel Gabriel were to preach Christ to them it would be as a sounding brass and as a tinkling cymbal. Serve up the meat as well as you may, but never will it be appreciated till the guest has an appetite. The Lord send them an appetite by the work of His Holy Spirit!

III. And so I close with the third point, which is this—THERE ARE SOME WHO DO APPRECIATE THE SWEETNESS OF CHRIST. I would to God I could find such out this morning. Hungry souls, we are brethren. If you are hungry after pardon, mercy, and grace, I remember when I was in your condition. What would you give to have Christ? "I would give my eyes," says one. Give him your eyes, then, by looking to him, and you shall have him. "What would I give," saith one, " to be delivered from my besetting sin! I hunger after holiness." Soul, you may have deliverance from besetting sins, and have it for nothing. Jesus Christ has come into the world to save his people from their sins, and looking to him he will deliver you from that disease which now makes you love sin, and he will give you a taste for holiness, and a principle of holiness by the Holy Ghost, and you shall henceforth become a saint unto God. He turns lions into lambs, and ravens into doves; nothing is impossible with him. You have but to trust your soul with him and you shall have pardon, peace, holiness, heaven, God, everything.

Those who hunger are those, then, who know the sweetness of Christ, but they must do more than that: being hungry, *they must feed*, for though the text does not say so, it is very clear that merely being hungry does not make meat sweet, it is only sweet when you eat it. If meat were placed where we could not reach it, and we were hungry, we should be inclined to think it bitter, after the model of the fox and the grapes in the fable. If there were a Saviour, but we could not reach him, it would make our life still more miserable. Poor soul, if you want Christ, receive him, it is all you have to do. The bread is before you, eat it. The fitness which is needed for eating is an appetite—you have it: lay to, then, by holy faith; receive Christ into yourself, and he will be sweet indeed to you.

The text says that the hungry man's appetite makes even bitter things sweet. Is there anything bitter in Christ? Yes, there was much in him that was bitter to himself, and that is the very sweetest part to us. Those pangs and griefs of his, and woes unutterable, and bloody death, how bitter! The wormwood and the gall were his; but to our believing soul these bitter things are honeycombs. Christ is best loved when we view him as crucified for us.

There are other bitters with Christ. We must repent of sin, and to carnal minds it is a bitter thing to hate sin and leave it; but to those who hunger after Christ, repentance is one of the daintiest of graces. Christ requires of his people self-denial and self-sacrifice, and unrenewed nature nauseates these things, but souls eager after Jesus are glad to deny themselves, glad to give of their substance, glad even to suffer hardships for his dear sake; even bitter things for him are sweet.

There are doctrines also which are very distasteful to carnal minds; they cannot away with them, they are angry when they are preached even as those who left our Lord when he said "Except ye eat my flesh and drink my blood, there is no life in you." Those who hunger after Christ prize the doctrines of grace; only let them know what Jesus teaches and every syllable is at once acceptable to their minds.

It may be there are ordinances which you shrink from; you have felt baptism especially to be a cross, but when your soul fully knows the sweetness of Christ, and your mind perceives that it is his ordinance, you feel at once that the bitter thing is sweet to you for his dear sake. Possibly you may have to suffer some measure of persecution, and be despised and nick-named for Jesus' sake. Thank God they cannot imprison you and put you to death, but even if they could, if you have an appetite for Christ, you will eat the bitter herbs as well as the Paschal Lamb, and think that they do well together. Christ and his cross—you will give your love to both and shoulder the cross right bravely and find it a sweet thing to be despised for the love of Jesus Christ your Lord.

Have but an appetite for Christ and the little prayer meeting, though there be but few poor people at it, will be sweet to you. That poor broken-down preaching, which is the best that the minister is able to give, will become sweet to you because there is a savour of Christ in it. If you can only get a leaf torn out of the Bible, or half a leaf, it will be precious to you. Even to hear a child sing a hymn about Christ will be pleasant. You remember Dr. Guthrie, when dying, asking his friend to sing him "a bairn's hymn." He wanted a child's hymn then; a little simple ditty about Christ was what the grand old man desired in his departing moments; and when your soul hungers after Jesus Christ you will love simple things if they speak of him. You will not be so dainty as some of you are. You must have a comfortable cushion to sit upon; when you are hungry you are glad to stand in the aisles. Full souls must needs have a very superior preacher; they say of the most successful evangelist, there is nothing in him, he only tells a lot of anecdotes: but when you are hungry you will rejoice that the man preaches Christ, and the faults will vanish. I remember my father telling me when I was a boy, and did not like my breakfast, that he thought it would do me good to be sent to the Union-house for a month, and see if I did not get an appetite. Many Christians need to be sent under the law a little while, and Moses would cure them of squeamishness, so that when they came back to Jesus and his love they would have a zest for the gospel.

The lesson from all this is—*pray for a good appetite for Christ*, and when you have it *keep it*. Do not spoil it with the unsatisfying dainties of the world, or by sucking down modern notions and sceptical philosophies—those gingerbreads and unhealthy sweetmeats so much cried up now-a-days. Do not waste a good appetite upon anything less sweet than the true honeycomb. When you have got that appetite for Christ *indulge it.* Do not be afraid at any time of having too much of Christ. Some of our brethren seem alarmed lest they should grow perfect against their wills. Dear brother, go into that river as far as you please, there is no likelihood of your being drowned. You will never have too much grace, or peace, or faith, or consecration. Go in for the whole thing; indulge your appetite to the very full. We cannot say it to our children with honey before them, but we may say it to God's children with Christ before them—" Eat, yea, eat abundantly."

Pray the Lord to give other people appetites. It is a grand thing to hear of ten and twenty thousand rushing to hear the gospel; I hope it is because they are hungering for it. When the Lord gives the people the appetite I am certain he will find them the meat, for it is always true in God's family that whenever he sends a mouth he always sends meat for it, and if any one of you has a mouth for Christ this morning, come to him and be filled to the full.

While you pray to God to give others an appetite, *try and create it.* How can you create it? Many an appetite has been created in the streets amongst poor starving wretches by their passing the place where provision is prepared—the very smell of it has made their mouths water. Tell sinners how happy you are; tell sinners what Christ has done for you; tell them how he has pardoned you, how he has renewed your nature; tell them about your glorious hope; tell them how saints can live and die triumphant in Christ, and you will set their mouth a-watering. That is half the battle; when once they have an appetite they are sure to have the meat. May the Lord the Holy Spirit send that appetite to sinners throughout the whole of London, and to Jesus Christ, who satisfies all comers, shall be glory for ever. Amen.

The Fourfold Treasure

"But of him are ye in Christ Jesus, who of God is made unto us wisdom, and righteousness, and sanctification, and redemption: that, according as it is written, he that glorieth, let him glory in the Lord"—1 Cor. i. 30, 31.

WE meet somewhere in the Old Testament with the expression "salt without prescribing how much." Beyond all question the name, person, and work of Jesus are the salt and savour of every true gospel ministry, and we cannot have too much of them. Alas! that in so many ministries there is such a lack of this first dainty of the feast, this essence of all soul-satisfying doctrine. We may preach Christ without prescribing how much, only the more we extol him the better. It would be impossible to sin by excess in preaching Christ crucified. It was an ancient precept, "With all thine offerings thou shalt offer salt;" let it stand as an ordinance of the sanctuary now: "With all thy sermonisings and discoursings thou shalt ever mingle the name of Jesus Christ; thou shalt ever seek to magnify the alpha and omega of the plan of redemption." The apostle in the first chapter of this epistle was anxious to speak to the Corinthians about their divisions and other serious faults; but he could not confine himself to that unpleasant theme; as naturally as possible his heart bounded over the mountains of division to his Lord and Master. Divisions did but remind him of the great uniting one who has made all his people one, and human follies did but drive him nearer to the infallible Christ who is the wisdom of God. Though Paul had to write many sharp things to those ancient Plymouth Brethren at Corinth, yet how sweetly did he prevent all bitterness by dipping his pen in the honeyed ink of love to the Lord Jesus, and admiration of his person and work! Let us, dear friends, if we have to preach, preach Christ crucified; and if we are private persons, let us in our household life, and in all our conversation, make his name to be as ointment poured forth. Let your life be Christ living in you. May you be like Asher, of whom it is said, he dipped his foot in oil; may you be so anointed with the Spirit of your Lord that wherever you put down your foot, you may leave an impression of grace. The balmy south wind bears token of having passed over sunny lands ; may the ordinary bent and current of your life bear evidence in it that you have communed with Jesus.

To-night we have before us a text which is extraordinarily comprehensive, and contains infinitely more of meaning than mind shall grasp, or tongue shall utter at this hour. Considering it carefully, let us observe, first, that the apostle here attributes the fact that we are in Christ Jesus to the Lord alone. He shows that there is a connection between our very being as Christians, and the love and grace of God in Christ. "Of him" (that is of God) "are ye in Christ Jesus." So we will first speak about *our spiritual existence*. Then Paul goes on to write of *our spiritual wealth*, which he sums up under four heads: wisdom, righteousness, sanctification, and redemption; but which indeed, I might say, he sums up under one head, for he declares that Christ is made of God unto us all these four things: and then he closes the chapter by telling us where *our glorying* ought to go—it should return to the source of our spiritual existence and heavenly wealth. "He that glorieth, let him glory in the Lord."

I. To begin, then, where God began with us—OUR SPIRITUAL EXISTENCE.

"Of him are ye in Christ Jesus." Different translators have read this passage in divers ways. "Of him," they think properly should be "Through him:" that is, "Through God we are in Christ Jesus." Are you this day united to Christ—a stone in that building, of which he is both foundation and topstone—a limb of that mystical body, of which he is the head? Then you did not get there of yourself. No stone in that wall leaped into its place; no member of that body was its own creator. You come to be in union with Christ through God the Father. You were ordained unto this grace by his own purpose, the purpose of the Infinite Jehovah, who chose you, or ever the earth was. "Ye have not chosen me, but I have chosen you." The first cause of your union with Christ lies in the purpose of God who gave you grace in Christ Jesus from before the foundation of the world. And as to the purpose, so to the power of God is your union with Christ to be attributed. He brought you into Christ; you were a stranger, he brought you near; you were an enemy, he reconciled you. You had never come to Christ to seek for mercy if first of all the Spirit of God had not appeared to you to show you your need, and to lead you to cry for the mercy that you needed. Through God's operation as well as through God's decree you are this day in Christ Jesus. It will do your souls good, my brethren, to think of this very common-place truth. Many days have passed since your conversion, it may be, but do not forget what a high day the day of your new birth was; and do not cease to give glory to that mighty power which brought you out of darkness into marvellous light. You did not convert yourself; if you did, you still have need to be converted again. Your regeneration was not of the will of man, nor of blood, nor of birth; if it were so, let me tell you the sooner you are rid of it the better. The only true regeneration is of the will of God and by the operation of the Holy Ghost. "By the grace of God I am what I am." He "hath begotten us again unto a lively hope." "He that hath wrought us to the selfsame thing is God." "Of him are ye in Christ

Jesus." Through the operation and will and purpose of God are you this day a member of Christ's body and one with Jesus. Give all the glory, then, to the Lord alone.

But suppose we read it as we have it in the text, and then we shall not have an allusion to the source of our spiritual life, but to the dignity of it. "Of God are ye in Christ Jesus." Being in Christ you are of God. Not of the earth earthy now, not of Satan, not of the bondage of the law, not of the powers of evil, but of God are you ; God's husbandry, God's people, God's children, God's beloved ones. " Ye are of God," little children, " and the whole world lieth in wickedness." On you hath God's light shone, to you hath God's life come, in you God's love is made manifest, and in you shall God's glory be fully revealed. What a dignity is this to be "of God !" Some have thought it a great thing to have it said, " These are they which are of the prince's household," and others have been yet more boastful when they have been pointed at as parts of an imperial court; but you are of the divine family, descended from him who only hath immortality. " They shall be mine, saith the Lord, in the day when I make up my jewels." " For the Lord's portion is his people, Jacob is the lot of his inheritance." Of God, are you, every one of you who are in Christ Jesus: ye are Christ's, and Christ is God's. The Creator, the Upholder, the Sublime, the Invisible, the Infinite, the Eternal claims you. You have a part and lot with him, and you are herein uplifted to the highest degree of exaltation because you are in Christ.

Here, then, you have the dignity of the Christian life—it is *of* God, as its source is through God.

But note the essence of the Christian life. " Of God are ye *in Christ Jesus.*" You have no life before the Lord, except as you are in Christ Jesus. Apart from him, you are as the branch that is severed from the vine—dead, withered, useless, obnoxious, rotten. Men gather these branches, and cast them into the fire, and they are burned. A ghastly sight it must be on the battle-field, to see on all sides arms, legs, and various portions of limbs torn away from the bodies to which they belonged, and scattered in hideous disorder ! Once of the utmost service, these severed limbs are useless now. Every one knows that they are dead, for they cannot live divided from the vital regions : even thus if you and I could be separated from Christ, our vital head, death—spiritual death—must be the inevitable result. Our life hinges upon union to our Lord. " Because I live, ye shall live also." Out of Christ we abide in death, but in Christ we live, and we are of God. Our spiritual being, and the fact that our spiritual being is an exalted one, both hang upon this—that we are in Christ. Beloved Christian friends, I can congratulate you upon your being able to know that you are in Christ, and that so you are of God; but I must not speak so broadly to all this congregation. I must rather put a grave enquiry, and ask each of my hearers: Are you all in Christ Jesus ? Could the apostle write to you, and say : " Of God are you in Christ Jesus." Have you ever been the subject of a work of God, putting you into Christ Jesus ? Are you now of God in Christ Jesus, so as to be depending for everything upon him, dwelling in him, and he in you; feeling his life within you, and that your life is hid with him in God ? Beloved hearer, there is no joy in this world like union with Christ. The more we can feel it, the happier we are, whatever our circumstances may be. But if you are without Christ, you are without hope. Joy comes not where Jesus comes not. No Saviour, then no peace in life or death. Oh remember, beloved hearer, that you will soon die. Where, where will you look for consolation in your last moments? Your soul will soon have to fly through tracks unknown, and face the burning throne of judgment. What will you do then, without the hand of love to guide you and the righteousness of Christ to cover you? He who wraps himself about with Christ's matchless robe can say—

> "Bold shall I stand in that great day,
> For who aught to my charge shall lay?
> While through thy blood absolved I am
> From sin's tremendous curse and shame."

But he that hath no Saviour, it were better for him that he had never been born. That day is cursed, and hath no blessing, on which he first saw the light. Jesus Christ is willing to receive you if you desire to come to him. Noah's ark was shut, but not until the flood came, it was open till then; Christ is the ark of the covenant, and the door is not shut yet. Let not this, however, cause you to delay, for the flood will rise, and the rains will fall, and then to those who shall knock at the door, it will be said, "Too late! too late! Ye cannot enter now."

Of him, beloved believers in Christ, are ye in Christ Jesus. All you are, even to your bare existence as Christians, you have to trace to "the God and Father of our Lord Jesus Christ, which according to his abundant mercy hath begotten us again unto a lively hope by the resurrection of Jesus Christ from the dead, to an inheritance incorruptible and undefiled, and that fadeth not away."

II. Now let us turn to the second part of our subject, and contemplate OUR SPIRITUAL WEALTH. Christ Jesus is of God made unto us wisdom, righteousness, sanctification, and redemption. Here are four things—only it is to be noticed that in the original Greek the second and third have a peculiar connecting link, which the others have not. The wisdom stands alone, and the redemption, but the righteousness and sanctification have a special link, as though we should be taught that they always go together, that they should always be considered as united—a warning to modern theology, which so often divideth what God hath joined together.

Let us take the first blessing first, asking to be partakers of it at this very moment. Jesus Christ is made unto us *wisdom*. You noticed when we read the chapter that the apostle had been speaking of some other wisdom which he treated somewhat roughly. It had set itself up in opposition to the cross of Christ, and the apostle handled it with no gentle handling. There have always been those in the world who have conceived that wisdom would come to them as the result of the exercise of their own thoughts assisted by culture; that is to say, they hoped to know divine truth by their own thoughts and the additional light arising from the thoughts of other men. They fancied that wisdom would rise out of the human mind, and would not need to be taught us from above. There were those in

Paul's days who were always ruminating, considering, contemplating with themselves, and then disputing, dialoguing, and conversing with others. These were the philosophers of the time. They looked for wisdom through man, and expected to find it in the shallow brain of a poor son of Adam. They so believed that they themselves were wise; that though they affected modesty and did not call themselves "the Sophoi, or wise," but "the Philosophoi," or lovers of wisdom, yet for all that, in their innermost hearts they esteemed themselves to be an inner circle of instructed persons, and they looked upon the rest of mankind as the unilluminated and the ignorant. They had found a treasure which they kept to themselves, and virtually said to their fellow-men, "You are almost without exception hopelessly ignorant." Now, the apostle, instead of pointing to his own brain, or pointing to the statue of Socrates or Solon, says Jesus Christ is made of God unto us wisdom. We look no more for wisdom from the thoughts that spring of human mind, but to Christ himself; we do not expect wisdom to come to us through the culture that is of man, but we expect to be made wise through sitting at our Master's feet and accepting him as wisdom from God himself. Now, as it was in the apostle's day, so is it very much at this present. There are those who will have it that the gospel—the simple gospel—such as might have been preached by John Bunyan or Whitfield, or Wesley, and others, was very well for the many, and for the dark times in which they lived—the great mass of mankind would be helped and improved by it; but there is wanted, according to the wiseacres of this intensely luminous century, a more progressive theology, far in advance of the Evangelism now so generally ridiculed. Men of mind, gentlemen of profound thought, are to teach us doctrines that were unknown to our fathers; we are to go on improving in our knowledge of divine truth till we leave Peter and Paul, and those other old dogmatists far behind. Nobody knows how wise we are to become. Brethren, our thoughts loathe this; we hate this cant about progress and deep thought; we only wish we could know as much of Christ as the olden preachers did. We are afraid that instead of getting into greater light through the thinkings of men, the speculations and contemplations of the scribes, ancient and modern, and the discoveries of the intellectual and eclectic, have made darkness worse, and have quenched some of the light that was in the world. Again has it been fulfilled: "I will destroy the wisdom of the wise, and will bring to nothing the understanding of the prudent. Where is the wise? where is the scribe? where is the disputer of this world? hath not God made foolish the wisdom of this world?" It seemeth to me to be greater wisdom to believe what Christ hath said than to believe what my deepest thoughts have discovered; and though I have thought long upon a subject, and turned it over and over, and think I know more of it than another man, yet, in one simple word of Christ there is more wisdom than in all my thoughts and ruminatings. I am never to look to myself for wisdom, and to fancy that I am the creator of truth or the revealer of it; but ever to go to him, my Lord, my teacher, my all, and to believe that the highest culture, the best results of the highest education are to be found by sitting at his feet, and the best results of the deepest meditation, too, are to be gained in lying down in the green pastures, beside the still waters, where he, as the good Shepherd, leads me. Brethren, when we read that Christ is made of God unto us wisdom, let us recollect what wisdom is. Wisdom is, I suppose, the right use of knowledge. To know is not to be wise. Many men know a great deal, and are all the more fools for what they know. There is no fool so great a fool as a knowing fool. But to know how to use knowledge is to have wisdom. Now, that man is wise in three respects who has Christ for his wisdom. Christ's *teaching* will make him wise of thought, and wise of heart. All you want to know of God, of sin, of life, of death, of eternity, of predestination, of man's responsibility, Christ has either personally, or by his Spirit in the word of God, taught you. Anything that you find out for yourself, anything over and above revelation, is folly, but whatever he has taught is wisdom; and he has so taught it that if you learn it in the spirit in which he would have you learn it, it will not be dry, dead doctrine to you, but spirit and life; and his teaching will endow you with wisdom as well as knowledge. Scholars at the cross-foot let us always be. Never let us go to any other school than Schola crucis, for the learners of the cross are the favourites of wisdom. Let Corpus Christi be the college in which we study. To know Jesus, and the power of his resurrection, this is wisdom.

But, in addition to profiting by our Lord's instruction, the Christian learns wisdom through his Master's *example*. "Wherewithal shall a young man cleanse his way?" How shall I be made wise in action? Policy says, "Adopt this expedient and the other;" and the mass of mankind at this age are guided by the policy of the hour; but policy is seeming wisdom and real folly. Remember it is always wisest to act in any condition as Jesus would have acted, supposing him to have been in that condition. Never did he temporise. Principle guided him, not fashion nor personal advantage. You shall never be a fool if you follow Christ, except in the estimation of fools; and who wishes to be wise in a fool's esteem? But sometimes it may be said: "To do as Christ would have done would involve me in present difficulty or loss." It is true; but there is no man that loseth aught in this life for Christ's sake who shall remain a loser, for he shall receive tenfold in this life, and in the world to come life everlasting. The wisest action is not always the most pecuniarily profitable. It is wise sometimes for men to be poor, ay, even to lose their lives. Truest wisdom—not sham wisdom, not temporary wisdom—you shall manifest by following the example of Christ, though it lead you to prison or to death. His teachings and his example, together, will give you the wisdom which cometh from above.

Above all, if you have the Redeemer's *presence*, he will be made of God unto you wisdom in a very remarkable sense. Never forget or doubt that Jesus is still with his people. They who know how to enter into the secret place of the tabernacles of the Most High, find him still at the mercy-seat. He feedeth among the lilies, and they who know the lilies know where to find him; and those who live with him, and catch his spirit, have their garments perfumed as his are with myrrh, and aloes, and cassia. These may be thought to be mad by some, and others may call them fanatical enthusiasts; but these are the wisest of mankind. O happy men that live at the gates of heaven while yet on earth, that sit at the feet of the blessed in the heavenly places in Christ Jesus while they are toiling along through the pilgrimage of this life! This is to be wise, to have Christ's teaching, Christ's example, and above all, Christ's presence; so may the poorest find the Lord Jesus made of God unto them wisdom.

Pause just a minute. Let none of us ever be so foolish as to suppose that when we have received Jesus and his gospel, we have occasion to blush when we are in the company of the very wisest of the present day. Carry a bold face when you confront the brazen faced philosophy which insults your Lord. The man who does not believe the Bible does not know so much as thou dost. Blush not, though with mimic wisdom the unbeliever tries to laugh or argue thee down. He who knows not Christ, though he propounds wonderful theories as to the creation of mankind and the formation of the world, and though he has a glib tongue, is only an educated fool, a learned idiot, who thinks his own rushlight brighter than God's own sun. "Ah! but he has been to college, and he has a degree, and he is esteemed by men; for he has written books that nobody can comprehend." "The fool hath said in his heart, There is no God;" and I do not care even if he be a Solon, if he has said that there is no God, he is a fool. Do not blush, then, if you find yourself in his company; do not make yourself the blushing one because the fool is there. Self-conceit were to be avoided and loathed; but this is not self-conceit, but a holy courage in a case which demands of you to be courageous. To know Christ is the best of all philosophy, the highest of all sciences. Angels desire to look into this; but I do not know that they care a fig for half the sciences so valued among men. If you know Christ you never need be afraid of being ashamed and confounded whatever company you may be in. If you stood in a senate of emperors, or amidst a parliament of philosophers, and only told them of the God that came in human flesh, and loved, and lived, and died to redeem mankind, you would have told them a greater mystery and a profounder secret than reason could discover. Be not ashamed, then, amid the intellectual pride of this boastful age.

At the same time let me remind you of another evil: do not seek to complete your wisdom at any other source: be satisfied that in keeping close to Christ you have the highest and truest wisdom. As I would not have you cowed before the pretender, neither would I have you envy him, or seek to supplement the wisdom that is in Christ Jesus by the wisdom that is of man. Are you so foolish, having begun with Jesus, will you end with a German neologian, or a French wit, or a Puseyite dreamer? Have you taken Christ's word to be your guide, and will you go and tack on to that some decree of Convocation, some rubric of a church, some minute of Conference, or other invention of human brain and fallen fancy? God forbid! Array yourself solely in this armour of gold, and go forth and gleam in the sun, and angels themselves shall marvel at you as they see your brightness. "Jesus Christ is made of God unto you wisdom."

It is high time for us to proceed to review the next blessing. He is made of God unto us *righteousness*. This was a great want of ours, for naturally we were unrighteous, and to this hour in ourselves we are the same. Righteous we must be to be acceptable with God, but righteous we certainly are not personally, and by merit. All our righteousnesses are as filthy rags, and we are unable to stand before the great King; but there is one who says: "Take away his filthy garments from him," and that same Deliverer, even the Lord Jesus Christ, is made of God unto us righteousness. You know how we usually speak of this as a double work. His blood cleanseth us from all guilt; by it pardon is bestowed upon the believer. He that looks to Christ is absolved from all sin—completely so. Then, in addition to that cleansing, which we call pardon, there is the clothing, the arraying in the righteousness of Christ—in a word, there is justification by faith. The doctrine of imputed righteousness seems to me to be firmly established in the word of God. Yet I have sometimes fancied I have heard a little too much stress put upon the word "imputed," and scarcely enough upon the word "righteousness;" for though I know that righteousness is imputed to us, yet I believe it is not all the truth that we are righteous by imputation. It is true, most true, but there is something true beyond it. Not only is Christ's righteousness imputed to me, but it is mine actually, for Christ is mine. He who believes in Jesus, has Jesus Christ to be his own Christ, and the righteousness of Christ belongs to that believer, and is his. We are not merely imputedly righteous, but the righteousness of our substitute is legally, actually, truly our righteousness. I am not now speaking of nature—that would have to do with sanctification—but I am speaking of repute before God. He reckons us to be righteous in Christ, and he does not reckon wrongly; the imputation is not a legal fiction or a charitable error. We are righteous. Depend upon it, God's imputation is not like human imputation, which makes a thing to be what it is not : we are in Christ made actually righteous, because we are one with him. Do you think that there is an unrighteous member of Christ's body? God forbid! Do you think Christ mystical to be a building with an unholy stone in it? Is Christ a vine with branches, which bear deadly fruit? As he is, so are we also in this respect. His salt has seasoned the whole lump. In the mystical body, every member is made righteous before God, because joined to the living head. Here is an actual righteousness given to us through the righteousness of Jesus Christ our Lord. He is made of God unto us righteousness. Consider this, O believer—you are to-night righteous before God. You are a sinner in yourself worthy to be condemned, but God does not condemn you, nor ever will he do so, for before the eye of his justice you are arrayed in perfect righteousness. Your sin is not upon you: it was laid upon the Scapegoat's head of old. All your iniquities were made to meet upon the head of the Crucified Saviour : he bore your transgressions in his own body on the tree. Where are your sins now? You may ask the question without fear, for they have ceased to be. "As far as the east is from the west, so far hath he removed our transgressions from us." "He hath cast our iniquities into the depths of the sea." Glory be to his name, there is no sin in existence against a believer. Is it not written : "He hath finished transgression, made an end of sin [what stronger expression can there be?], and brought in everlasting righteousness"? And that is true of you to-night, Christian, as true of you to-night as it will be when you are in heaven. You are not so sanctified to-night as you will be in the glory land, but you are as righteous as you can be even there. In God's sight you are as much "accepted in the Beloved," as you will be when you stand on the sea of glass mingled with fire. You are beloved of God, and dear to him and justified, so that even to-night you can say: "Who shall lay anything to the charge of God's elect? It is God that justifieth. Who is he that condemneth?" You cannot lift up a louder boast than that, even when you shall see your Saviour, and shall be like him because you see him as he is. By faith this righteousness is yours at this present moment, and will always be yours without a change; yours when your spirit is cast down, as much as when your joys abound. You are accepted not because of anything in yourself, but because you stand in the Lord your righteousness.

I remarked some time ago that the next blessing in our text is pinned on to this one. I need not not say much about that fact, but just note it. Righteousness and sanctification must always go together, and though they are two different things, or else there would not have been two different words, yet they blend into each other most remarkably, hence the Greek joins the two words by a close link. Our *sanctification* is all in Christ; that is to say, it is because we are in Christ that we have the basis of sanctification, which consists in being set apart. A thing was sanctified of old, under the law, when it was set apart for God's service. We were sanctified in Christ Jesus when we were set apart by the divine Spirit to be the Lord's own peculiar people for ever. Election is the basis of sanctification. Moreover, the power by which we are sanctified comes to us entirely by virtue of our union with Christ. The Holy Spirit who sanctifies us through the truth, works in us by virtue of our union with Jesus. That which becomes holy in us is the new life. The old nature never changes into a holy thing; the carnal mind is not reconciled to God, neither, indeed, can be. The old man is not sent to the hospital to be healed, but to the cross to be crucified. It is not transformed and improved, but doomed to die and to be buried. The ordinance of baptism, which is placed at the outset of Christian life, is meant to show, by our immersion in the liquid tomb, that it is by death and burial that we pass into life by the power of resurrection. If any man be in Christ, he is not an old creature mended up: he is a new creature. "Old things are passed away; behold all things are become new." Now, it is because this new life is the great, the true matter of sanctification, and because it comes to us by virtue of our oneness with Christ, that Jesus Christ is made to us the power and the life by which we are sanctified. Beloved, let your hearts add another meaning: let Jesus always be the motive for your sanctification. Is it not a strange thing that some professors should look to Christ alone for pardon and justification, and run away to Moses when they desire sanctification? For instance, you will hear persons preach this doctrine: "The Christian is to be holy, because if he be not holy he will fall from grace and perish." Do you not hear the crack of the old legal whip in all that? What is that but the yoke of that covenant which none of our fathers were able to bear? It is the bondage of Egypt, not the freedom of the children of God. Christ talks not so, nor his gospel. Think not to make thyself holy by motives of that kind. They are not right motives for a child of God. How then should we urge the child of God to holiness? Should it not be in this way: "Thou art God's child: walk worthy of him who is thy Father"? His love to thee will never cease. He cannot cast thee away: he is faithful and never changes, therefore love him in return. This is a motive fit for the child of the free woman, and it moves his heart. The child of the bond woman is driven by the whip, but the child of the free woman is drawn by cords of love. "The love of Christ constraineth us;" not fear of hell, but love of Christ; not fear that God will cast us away, for that he cannot do, but the joy that we are saved in the Lord with an everlasting salvation constrains us to cling to him with all our heart and soul, for ever and ever. Rest assured, if motives fetched from the gospel will not kill sin, motives fetched from the law never will. If you cannot be purged at Calvary, you certainly cannot be cleansed at Sinai. If " the water and the blood, from the riven side which flowed," are not sufficient to purify thee, no blood of bulls or of goats—I mean, no argument from the Jewish law, or hope of salvation by your own efforts—will ever furnish motives sufficiently strong to cast out sin. Let your reasons for being holy be found in Christ, for he is made of God unto you sanctification! I have ever found, and I bear my witness to it, that the more entirely for the future as well as for the present, I lean upon my Lord, the more conscious I am of my own emptiness and unworthiness; and the more completely I rest my whole salvation upon the grace of God in Christ Jesus, the more carefully do I walk in my daily life. I have always found that self-righteous thoughts very soon lead to sinful actions; but that, on the other hand, the very faith which leads to assurance, and makes the heart rest in the faithfulness of God in Christ, purifies the soul. "He that hath this hope in him purifieth himself, even as he is pure." Jesus, the Saviour, saves us from our sins, and is made of God to us "sanctification."

Now, the last item of our boundless wealth catalogued in the text is "*redemption.*" Somebody says: "That ought to have come first; because redemption, surely, is the first blessing that we enjoy." Ay, but it is the last as well. It is the *alpha* blessing, I grant you that—but it is the *omega* blessing too. You are not yet redeemed altogether. By price you are—for he that redeemed you on the tree did not leave unpaid a penny of your ransom; but you are not yet altogether redeemed by power. In a measure, you are set free by divine power, for you have been brought up out of the Egypt of your sin, you have been delivered from the galling bondage of your corruption, and led through the Red Sea, to be fed upon the heavenly manna; but you are not altogether redeemed by power as yet. There are links of the old chains yet to be snapped from off you, and there is a bondage still about you from which you are ere long to be delivered. You are "waiting for the adoption, to wit, the redemption of the body." You will fall asleep, rejoicing that you were redeemed; but you will not, even when you die, have received the full redemption. When will that come—the full redemption? Only at the second advent of the Lord Jesus; for when the Lord shall descend from heaven with a shout, then the bodies of his saints, which have long been lying in the prison-house of the sepulchre, shall be redeemed by a glorious redemption from the power of death. "I know that my redeemer liveth." The bodies of the saints shall come again from the land of the enemy. Then their body, soul, and spirit—their entire manhood, which Christ hath bought, shall be altogether free from the reign of the enemy. Then will redemption be completed. Remember the saints in heaven without us cannot be made perfect, that is to say, they wait till we arrive among them ; and when all the rest of the chosen ones shall be gathered in, and the fulness of time has come, then shall the bodies of the dead arise ; and then, in body and soul made perfect, the year of the redeemed shall have fully come. "Lift up your heads; for your redemption draweth nigh." Here, then, is my joy, that Christ is my redemption. My soul is free from slavery, but my poor trembling and much suffering body feels the chains of death. Weakened by pain, my body shall in all probability bow before the stroke of death's sword. Unless the Lord soon come, it must be the portion of this frame to feed the worm and mingle with the dust; but, O my body, thou art redeemed, and thou shalt rise in power and incorruption; thou shalt yet adore the Lord without weariness, and without pain shalt thou serve him day and night in his temple. Even thou, O my weary body ; even thou shalt be made glorious like unto the Lord himself. Thou shalt rise and live in the brightness of his presence.

All, then, that you can possibly want, O Christian, is in Christ. You cannot conceive a need which Jesus does not supply. "Wisdom, righteousness, sanctification, redemption," you have all in him. Some gather a flower here ; some gather another there ; some will go farther, and pluck another there ; and some will go yet beyond to grasp a fourth ; but when we win Christ we have a posey ; we have all sweet flowers in one.

> "All human beauties, all divine,
> In my Beloved meet and shine ;
> Thou brightest, sweetest, fairest one,
> That eyes have seen or angels known."

But we cannot stay on this tempting subject, though even amid my present pain I would fain talk on by the hour together ; and therefore I must finish with the last point ; and on that only a word.

You see then, brethren, our very existence as Christians, and all that we possess as Christians, we get from God by Jesus Christ; *let all our glory then be unto him.* What insanity it is to boast in any but in our Lord Jesus ! How foolish are they that are proud of the beauty of their flesh—worms' meat at the best ! How foolish are they who are proud of their wisdom ! The wisdom of which a man is proud, is but folly in a thin disguise. How foolish are they that are vain of their wealth ! He must be a poor man who can think much of gold. He must be a beggar indeed who counts a piece of dirt a treasure. They that know Christ, always value these things at their right estimate, and that is low indeed. If any glory—and I suppose it is natural to us to glory, there is a boasting bump on all our heads—let us glory in the Lord; and here is a wide field and ample sea-room. Now, put out every stitch of canvas, run up the topgallants, seek as stiff a breeze as you will, there is no fear of running on a lee shore here, or striking a rock, or drifting on a quicksand! O men, O angels, O cherubim, O seraphim, boast in Jesus Christ! Wisdom, righteousness, sanctification, and redemption is he, therefore ye may boast and boast, and boast again! You will never exaggerate. You cannot exceed his worth, or reach the tithe of it. You can never go beyond the truth, you do not even reach beyond the skirts of his garments. So glorious is God that all the angels' harps cannot sound forth half his glory. So blessed is Christ that the orchestra of the countless multitudes of the redeemed, though it continue for ever and for ever its pealing music, can never reach to the majesty of his name or the glory of his work. "Give unto the Lord, O ye mighty, give unto the Lord glory and strength. Give unto the Lord the glory due unto his name." Let time and space become great mouths for song; let the infinite roll up its waves; let all creatures lift up their voices in praise of him that liveth and was dead; but chiefly, O my soul, since to him thou owest in a double sense thine existence, give thy praise to him from whom all blessing comes. Give thou the homage of thine intellect to him who is thy wisdom. Let thy conscience and love of rectitude adore him who has made thee righteous. Give the tribute of thy soul to him who sanctifies thee; let thy sanctified nature consecrate itself continually; and to him that hath redeemed thee give thou never-ceasing praise. I wish it were possible for me to rise to the height of my text, but my wings flag; I cannot ascend as the eagle, and face the full blaze of the sun; I can but mount a little as the lark, and sing my song, and then return to my nest. God grant you to know the Lord Jesus in his fulness in your personal experience.

O you to whom Christ is no wisdom, how foolish are you! O you to whom he is no righteousness, you are condemned sinners! O you to whom he is no sanctification, the fire of God's wrath will consume you! O you to whom he is no redemption, you are slaves in hopeless bondage! God deliver you! May you be led to put your trust in Jesus even now.

The Lord's Famous Titles

"The LORD looseth the prisoners: the LORD openeth the eyes of the blind: the LORD raiseth them that are bowed down: the LORD loveth the righteous: the LORD preserveth the strangers; he relieveth the fatherless and widow: but the way of the wicked he turneth upside down"—Psalm cxlvi. 7—9.

THIS morning, as well as I could, looking to God for help, I tried, in Christ's stead, to persuade men to be reconciled to God. I showed that there was a great spiritual drought, and neither dew nor rain to be had except as God should send it; and I tried to press my hearers to go to God, to wait upon him, to look to him, and through the mediation of the Lord Jesus Christ, to seek and find in God all that would be needful for their eternal blessedness. I pressed hard, and some yielded, not to my pressure, but to a divine impulse that went with my pleading. There were some who did not yield this morning, so I am going to make another attempt to win them now, calling in our August Ally, even the Divine Spirit, without whom we can do nothing. May he bring many to God in penitence to-night!

You know that it helps men to come to a person when they know who he is, and how good he is, and how likely it is that they will find benefit by coming to him. My text tells us something about God, the Lord Jehovah. Five times the word occurs at the head of a sentence, Jehovah, Jehovah, Jehovah, Jehovah, Jehovah. Sometimes, when a great king or prince has a high day, a herald proclaims the titles of his majesty. He is prince of this, and lord of that, and emperor of the other;—too often, a lot of empty sounds. But when we come to speak of God, every title of his falls short of what is his real glory and honour. To-night we have five of his titles put together, five wonderful achievements of God, five things for which the

Lord would have himself noted. I want each one of you here to hear about them, and to say, "That encourages me," or "That cheers me," or "That helps me." At any rate, out of the five great magnets that I will try to use to-night, may one or other draw all our reluctant hearts to God, that we may find rest and peace in him!

I. There are five famous titles of God here. The first one is, THE EMANCIPATOR. Read the latter part of the seventh verse: "The Lord looseth the prisoners."

It is God's glory that he is an Emancipator. How often, in the Old Testament, and in the New, too, you find the Lord loosing the prisoners! It was so notably in the case of Joseph, when God brought him out of the prison, and set him up as Lord over all Egypt; and still more notably in the case of Israel in Egypt when, with a high hand, and a stretched-out arm, the Lord brought forth his people from all the tyranny of Pharaoh, whom he destroyed in the Red Sea. You may keep on reading Scripture, and you will continually find that it is true, "The Lord looseth the prisoners."

I want some of you who are here to catch at that thought. Are you *mentally a prisoner*, under gloom, to-night? Did a cloud come over you a little while ago? Does it rest upon your mind still? Can no physician remove it? Listen to this word: "The Lord looseth the prisoners." Are you in the bondage of error? Have you been misled by false teachers? Have you fallen into mistakes about the Word of God? Are you denying the great truths which would comfort you? Are you believing the great errors which becloud your spirit? Come to God for teaching. He can emancipate you from any form of error, even though you have been brought up in it from a child. "The Lord looseth the prisoners." Or have you come under some gross delusion? Are you the victim of some false impression which you cannot shake off? I pray you, if you are harried and worried by temptations of Satan, and he seems to have a firm foothold in your spirit, and cannot be driven out, let this text, like a silver bell, ring out comforting music to you, "The Lord looseth the prisoners." Oh, that you who are in mental bonds might be set free to-night!

There are, however, worse bonds than those, the chains of *moral slavery*. This man is a drunkard; and though he has taken the pledge, he cannot escape from the terrible craving which intemperate habits have brought upon him. Ah! friend, come you to Christ; he can take away the love of strong drink, and set you free. "The Lord looseth the prisoners," and he can do that for men and women who have given themselves up as lost. God have mercy upon wretched women when they become the prey of strong drink! To my certain knowledge, this evil is becoming much more common than it was a few years ago. More frequently do we have to mourn over fallen sisters than we did some years back. It is sad that it should be so; but the glorious fact remains that "the Lord looseth the prisoners." Do not despair, poor woman! Have hope of deliverance; God can loose thee yet from the bonds of strong drink. Has anyone here fallen into bondage to a lust? Has some evil passion got a tight hold on you, and you cannot break the bonds? There is one who can set you free; ay! though you have been indulging in the evil for many years, and seem to be wedded to an evil habit from which you cannot escape, still is it true, "The Lord looseth the prisoners." Do not trust in yourself to get quit of the evil; but look to him who died for sin upon the cross, and trust in him, for it is written, "He shall save his people from their sins." I cannot stay to-night to mention all the kinds of moral bondage into which men and women fall; but let this sweet message be like a stray note from the harps of angels to all who are in the prison-house, "The Lord looseth the prisoners."

Perhaps you are held fast in *spiritual bondage*. This is where we are all by nature; we are born slaves. Are you, to-night, my friend, conscious that you are a slave to sin? Are you fast bound by your trespasses? O spiritual bondsman, there is an Emancipator who can take your chains from you! "If the Son shall make you free, ye shall be free indeed;" and he is able to do it with a single word. Only trust him, only yield yourselves up to him as willing captives, and you shall be free from that moment. God make you free to-night! Ay, and he can loose you from every iniquity in which you may be enslaved!

There is another kind of emancipation which the Lord is constantly giving to the prisoners of hope, even deliverance from this present evil world. You are sick to-night, you are sad, you are cast down and troubled, because of the burden of the flesh. "The Lord looseth the prisoners." There is many a prisoner who has been loosed during the last week or two; dear members of this church who had been confined to sick beds. The Lord has opened the cage door, and the bird, set at liberty, has gone carolling up to the skies. The body has been put into the grave, and lies imprisoned there in durance vile; but he shall come, who himself rose from the dead, and when his feet shall touch the earth again, and the angelic trumpet shall sound the summons, their bodies shall come forth—

"From beds of dust and silent clay
To realms of everlasting day;"

for "the Lord looseth the prisoners."

Here is a theme for a whole evening's discourse; but I do not want to take up any more time over this point. I wish rather to drive home this wedge; if you are prisoners, if you are under any form of bondage, come to God in Christ Jesus, and put your trust in him, for "the Lord looseth the prisoners."

II. We must hasten on, to notice a second famous title for the Lord, that is, THE ILLUMINATOR: "The Lord openeth the eyes of the blind."

If you will kindly look at your copies of the Bible, you will find that the words "the eyes of" are inserted in italics by the translators, so that the text really is, "The Lord openeth the blind." Ah, he opens the very soul of the blind, and lets light in where there are no eyes! Have you not noticed that it is so? If anybody were to say to me, "Mr. Spurgeon, pick out a dozen of the happiest people that you know," ten of them would be blind people. We have some dear friends, members of this church, who are among the happiest souls that God has ever made. It is long since they saw the light; but

God has opened their hearts in such a way that they enjoy a wonderful quietness of spirit, great placidity of mind, and an inward light and splendour which persons with eyes might well envy. I have noticed that blind people are often among the happiest people; and blind Christians certainly might take the chief place among us for their quiet and rest of mind. The Lord Jesus Christ opens the blind, he comes and sheds a light when the windows of the body are closed, and gives light within, so that they are full of brightness.

But if you like to take the text as it is in our translation, it will do very well. *When the Lord Jesus Christ was here, he opened the eyes of the blind.* He touched many a sightless eyeball, and the light streamed in. Read the Evangels through, and you will find this miracle constantly recurring. Blindness is a very common ailment in the East; and the miracle of recovering the sight of the blind was therefore frequent with our Lord.

Next, *the Lord enables blind souls to see.* Here is a great mercy. The Lord has opened the eyes of many a man, who could not see himself, and so proved how blind he was, and could not see the Lord, and so showed still more how blind he was. The Lord has given the inner sight to many a man who was without spiritual understanding, to whom the gospel seemed a great mystery, of which he could make neither head nor tail. The Lord has made the scales to fall from many blind mental eyes, and enabled those who were blind first to see themselves, and then to see their Saviour. Blessed be his name!

And whenever the blind of earth fall asleep in Jesus, and enter into heaven, *they shall have no blindness in glory.* There, their eyes shall see the King in his beauty; they shall behold his face, and rejoice in his love. Jehovah is a great Eye-opener: cannot some of you blind people catch at this truth, and say, "Then we will come to him, for we want to have our eyes opened"?

Perhaps someone says, "Sir, I do not quite comprehend all that you say. I have been a hearer for some time, and I want to understand the gospel. I try to grasp it; but, somehow, I cannot get at the truth." Come, in prayerful faith, to God himself to-night, and he will explain it to you. I can hold the light to your eyeballs; yet, if they are blind, I cannot make you see; but the Lord can give the sight as well as the light, and I beseech you to ask it at his hands to-night. There is nothing really difficult in the gospel; and if you will come to Jesus like a teachable child, and ask to be instructed of him, you will find that it is all plain to him that believeth. Of the way of holiness it is written, "The wayfaring men, though fools, shall not err therein."

If you come to God for grace, dear friend, he will never stint you. You need not be poor Christians; you may be "rich to all the intents of bliss." You need not have shallow grace; you may, if you wish, get into "waters to swim in." Giving will not impoverish him, withholding will not enrich him; but, rather, giving enriches him, it enriches his very heart with great joy, for he delights to give. Come and take freely, and learn the liberality of God. I remember one who called himself "a gentleman-commoner upon the bounty of

God." Some of us can take the same title; we have had a hand-basket portion for many years; not a sackful at a time, but a hand-basketful. That is a good way of living. If a girl gets a portion from her father, and the old gentleman never gives her anything else, she does not receive so much as her sister who has a hand-basket portion many days in the week. A present often comes to her from the old house at home. Father sends it every time with his love, and she receives more love and more thought, and he, too, receives more gratitude in return, perhaps, than if he had given his daughter one lump sum, and then his generosity was all over. It is a blessed way of learning the liberality of God, to be receiving freely and receiving continually from him: "he giveth more grace."

Come, then, to God by Jesus Christ, because he is, first, the Emancipator, and, secondly, the Illuminator.

III. Now for the third bright title of the Lord, that is, THE COMFORTER. Read the middle sentence of verse 8: "The Lord raiseth them that are bowed down."

Some are bowed down with *bereavement.* Well may she be bowed down who has just committed to the earth the beloved of her heart; and well may he go mourning whose firstborn son has been taken from him by a sudden stroke. Well may some lament, who have lost the choicest friend that man ever had, and find that half their life is gone in the death of that beloved one; yet, "The Lord raiseth them that are bowed down." Come, tell your grief to him who pitied the widow at the gate of Nain. Come, pour out your sorrow before him who wept with the beloved sisters at Bethany when Lazarus was dead. He can help you, for he "raiseth them that are bowed down."

Some are bowed down sadly by *the burdens of life.* They have more to carry than most men have. They stagger along from day to day beneath a load that threatens to crush them into the dust. Oh, come to my Lord, who gives new strength to bear burdens, for he raiseth up those that are bowed down! It is wonderful what a man can do when God has laid his hand on him, and said to him, "Be strong." You are faint, and you will faint without your God; but you will be strong if you come and trust him, for "Jehovah raiseth them that are bowed down."

Maybe, you are bowed down *with inward distress.* Ah, there is no cure for some forms of distress but to go straight away to God! The scandal of our ministry is the despondency that we cannot disperse. How often I have come down from talking with some dear friends here, whose minds have been distracted, and I have had to confess myself "dead beat." God has helped me to comfort many: it is my lot, almost wherever I may be, to be followed up by persons suffering in mind. I sometimes laugh and tell them that "birds of a feather flock together," and that they must think me half-cracked, and so they come to me to sympathize with them. Well, so be it; there is a kind of sympathy between me and them. But I have learnt this lesson, that to bring comfort to a mind diseased is not within the preacher's power except his Master shall specially qualify him for the task; and, in any case, I say to you, dear troubled friends, go straight away to him of whom you read these sweet words, "The Lord raiseth them that are bowed down."

Have I the extreme felicity, to-night, of addressing in this congregation one who is bowed down by *a sense of sin?* Where art thou, Magdalen, hiding thy face in tears? Where art thou, poor erring prodigal, longing to come back to thy Father; but too bowed down to start upon the journey? List: "The Lord raiseth them that are bowed down." He loves to find the poor sinner crouching on the dunghill, putting his head into the dust in very despair of heart, and he delights to come, and put his hand upon him, and say, "Stand upon thy feet; fear not." There is a great God of mercies, who glories in doing wonders of grace, forgiving even the blackest sin. I say again, I would like to ring this text, like a silver bell, in the ears of every penitent sinner here, and say, "The Lord raiseth them that are bowed down."

IV. We are getting on with our text, for we have come to the fourth great title. God is THE REWARDER: "The Lord loveth the righteous." Come, dear friends, here is a wafer made with honey; here is a feast of fat things, full of marrow, for you who are the people of God, you whom he has accounted righteous because the perfect righteousness of Christ has been imputed to you.

First, "the Lord loveth the righteous" with a love of *complacency.* He takes delight in them; he loves them, not merely with a love of benevolence that desires their good; but he looks with pleasure and delight at righteous men, those whom he has made righteous, those who love him because they are righteous, and who are like him in being righteous. The Lord looks at them, and rejoices over them. How that ought to cheer any of you who have been made holy by God's grace! The Lord's delight is in you; he calls you his Hephzibahs, saying, "My delight is in them." Wherever there is anything of Christ, anything of righteousness, anything of holiness, there is evidence of the Lord's love. So, in the first place, "the Lord loveth the righteous" with a love of complacency.

He does more than that; he loves the righteous with a love of *communion.* Remember how the Lord puts it, by the mouth of Isaiah, "For thus saith the high and lofty One that inhabiteth eternity, whose name is Holy; I dwell in the high and holy place, with him also that is of a contrite and humble spirit, to revive the spirit of the humble, and to revive the heart of the contrite ones." I doubt not that God often talks with righteous men. "The secret of the Lord is with them that fear him." He lets them speak to him, and he speaks to them in return. Do you know anything about this communion with God? If you do not, never say that others do not, for we are as honest and truthful as you are, and we bear our testimony that there is such a thing as walking with God; we declare, from happy, heartfelt experience, that there is such a thing as talking with God, and knowing that he loves us, and that his love is shed abroad in our hearts by the Holy Ghost which is given unto us.

God also loves his people with a love of *favour.* He loves them so that he will give them anything that they need. Yes, he has said, through the psalmist, "No good thing will he withhold from them that walk uprightly." He loves the righteous so that, when they go into their chamber to pray to him, he may let them plead a little while because it is for their good to do so, but he will always yield to their desires. He has said, "Delight thyself also in the Lord; and he shall give thee the desires of thine heart." He does do that with his people. The Lord loveth the righteous so as to favour them with extraordinary blessings, things of which I cannot talk here; for there is many a love-passage between Christ and the righteous soul that must never be told. We do not talk of our love-passages in the streets, that would be half profane; nor can we even tell of them here. There are favours which the Lord shows to his righteous people, which they know, and he knows, but which no one else can know till that day when all things shall be revealed.

And once more, the Lord loves the righteous so that he will *honour* them. If men are righteous, the world will hate them; and as a proof of its hatred, it will begin to bespatter them. There are always some in the world who say, "Throw plenty of mud, some of it will stick;" and oh, how they delight to throw it! Their hands seem to take to the dirt naturally. But, beloved, if you follow God fully, your character will never be long tarnished. Do not try to answer those who slander you. If an ass kicked you, would you kick the ass? If a fool brings a charge against you, do not reply to him. Let him rail on; God will vindicate you. Remember that Psalm from which I quoted just now, the thirty-seventh: "Commit thy way unto the Lord; trust also in him; and he shall bring it to pass. And he shall bring forth thy righteousness as the light, and thy judgment as the noonday." It may even happen to a man that he may perform an action that will never be understood while he lives; but the true man of God lives for eternity, not for time. He says, "I do not care if it takes five hundred years for the righteousness of my action to be seen by my fellow-men; it will not make it any more righteous when they do see it, nor will it be any less righteous while they do not see it. What have I to do with men? I serve the living God." If you get into that condition of heart, you can trust your reputation, your life, your usefulness, entirely with God, for "the Lord loveth the righteous." A day shall come when all the world shall know it, when they who are righteous shall shine forth as the sun in the kingdom of their Father, and God shall say of them, "Well done, good and faithful servants, enter into the joy of your Lord."

Now, then, will you not come to him, since his favourites are the best people in all the world? Kings and princes have often been known to choose their associates among the worst of their subjects, men who ministered to their baser passions. The favourites of kings have often been the offscouring of the earth; but our King loves the righteous. He will have none to be his courtiers, to come near to him, to dwell before his face, but those that walk uprightly, through his mighty grace. I think that there is something very inviting there to you who are of a true heart, something which ought to induce you to come to such a God as this, the Lord who loveth the righteous.

V. But now, last of all, and, perhaps, sweetest of all, the fifth name of God is THE PRESERVER: "The Lord preserveth the strangers·

he relieveth the fatherless and widow: but the way of the wicked he turneth upside down." My time is so nearly gone that I can only just ask you to apply, by God's help, the few words that I shall say.

Notice, first, that *God preserveth strangers.* In all nations, in the olden time, strangers were driven out; they did not want any foreigners settling among them. In this country, in almost every village, it used to be the practice for a stranger to be regarded as a kind of mad dog; and if he happened to wear a different garb from that of the villagers, all the boys hooted him. It seems that our depraved humanity is naturally unkind to strangers. I often hear people say even now, " Oh, he is a foreigner!" O you proud Englishman! is he not as good as you? You are a foreigner when you get to the other side of the English Channel. It was God's order to his ancient people that they were to be kind to strangers. Wherever they came, they were to be allowed to dwell, and were to be taken care of. God put it thus to Israel : " Thou shalt neither vex a stranger, nor oppress him: for ye were strangers in the land of Egypt;" and because God loved them when they were strangers in Egypt, they were to take especial care of strangers and foreigners who came into their midst.

What a grand trait this is in God's character, " The Lord preserveth the strangers " ! If any of you feel quite strangers here to-night, if you are strangers to religion, strangers to religious observances, strangers to everything that is good, if you feel, when you hear the gospel, that you are altogether strange to it, it sounds so oddly in your ears, come along, dear stranger, " The Lord preserveth the strangers"! Come under the shadow of his wings, and you shall find shelter there. Father is dead, mother is dead, friends are all gone, and even in the very village where you were born you are a stranger; come along, your God is not dead, your Saviour liveth: " The Lord preserveth the strangers."

Then notice the next sentence in our text: "*He relieveth the fatherless and widow.*" If you turn to the first Books of the Bible, you will see there God's great care of the fatherless and the widow. Who had the tithes? Well, the Levites; but also the poor, and the stranger, and the fatherless, and the widow. If you look at Deuteronomy xiv. 28, or xxvi. 12, you will find that the tithes were not for the priests exclusively, but they were also for the widow, and the fatherless, and the strangers. Besides this, the Israelites were never to glean their fields twice, for the gleanings were for the widow and the fatherless; and they were never to shake the olive tree or any fruit tree twice, but to leave what remained upon it for the widow and the fatherless. There was also this law made, that they should never take as a pledge the raiment of a widow. That is pretty often done in London; but it might not be done then, the garment of the widow might never be taken in pledge. Wherever the legislation of God for his people touched upon the widow and the fatherless, it was immeasurably kind. Now, then, you who feel like widows, you who have lost your joy and earthly comfort, you who feel like the fatherless, and cry, " No man careth for my soul," oh, may the sweet Spirit of the Lord entice you to come to him, for, as I reminded you in the reading, "A father of the fatherless, and a judge of the widows, is God in his holy habitation."

But the view of God's character would not be complete if it was not added, "*The way of the wicked he turneth upside down.*" You see, the godly, and they who trust God, are always in danger from the wicked; but he turns the way of the wicked upside down. Take a specimen. Joseph's brethren sell him into Egypt, and make a slave of him. God turns this arrangement upside down, and makes a prince of him. Think of Mordecai. Haman will have him hanged; he has the gallows ready, but Haman gets hanged on his own gallows. God knows how to make the malice of men promote the benefit of those against whom they turn their cruelty. "The way of the wicked he turneth upside down."

Be thou just, and fear not. Rest in Christ's atoning sacrifice; trust him only. Come thou to thy God, and be his servant henceforth, and for ever, and thou shalt see how he will break thy bonds, and open thine eyes, and cheer thy spirit, and indulge thee with his love, and preserve thee even to the end. "There shall no evil befall thee, neither shall any plague come nigh thy dwelling." God bless you, dear friends, and may you all come to God to-night, through Jesus Christ our Lord! Amen.

Christ Our Life—Soon to Appear

"When Christ, who is our life, shall appear, then shall ye also appear with him in glory"—Colossians iii. 4.

My discourse on Sabbath mornings is very frequently the gathering up of the thoughts and experiences of the week—a handful of barley which I have gleaned among the sheaves; but I could not thrust upon you this morning the poverty-stricken productions of my own insufferable dulness of brain, weariness of heart, and sickness of spirit during this week, for this were a sure method of making you partakers of my misery. I have wandered through a wilderness, but I will not scatter handfuls of the hot sand among you. I have traversed the valley of the shadow of death, but I will not repeat the howlings of Apollyon. This day of rest is appointed for a far better purpose.

Scarcely knowing how to fulfil the appointed service of this morning, I sit me down and remember the ancient minstrel, who, when the genius of song had for a time departed from him, was nevertheless called upon to discourse sweet music. What could he do but lay his fingers among the strings of his harp, and begin some old accustomed strain. His fingers, and his lips moved at first mechanically; the first few stanzas dropped from him from mere force of habit, and fell like stones without life or power, but by and by, he struck a string which woke the echoes of his soul, a note fell on his heart like a blazing torch, and the smouldering fire within his soul suddenly flamed up; the heaven-born muse was with him, and he sang as in his better times. So may it be my happy lot this morning: placing my fingers on the strings which know so well the name of Jesus, and beginning to discourse upon a theme which so constantly has made these walls to ring, although at first insipid periods try your patient ears, yet shall they nevertheless lead to something that may kindle in you hope, and joy, and love, if not rapture and delight. O for the wings of eagles to bear our souls upward towards the throne of our God. Already my heart warms with the expectation of a blessing! Does the earth feel the rising of the sun before the first bright beams gild the east? Are there not sharp-witted birds, which know within themselves that the sunbeams are on the road, and therefore begin right joyously to wake up their fellows to tell them that the morning cometh leaping over the hills? Certain hopeful, joyful thoughts have entered within our heart, prophetic of the Comforter's divine appearing, to make glad our souls. Does not the whole earth prophecy the coming of the happy days of spring? There are certain little bulbs that swell, and flowers that peep from under the black mould, and say, "We know what others do not know, that the summer's coming, coming very soon;" and surely there are rising hopes within us this morning, which show their golden flowers above our heaviness, and assure us with joyful accents, that Christ is coming to cheer our heart yet again. Believer, you shall once again behold his comfortable presence; you shall no longer cry unto him out of the depths, but your soul shall lean upon his arm, and drink deep of his love. Beloved, I proceed in the hope that the gracious Lord will favour his most unworthy servant, and in his own mercy fulfil our best expectations.

Our text is a very simple one, and bears upon its surface four thoughts; namely, that *Christ is our life;* that, secondly, *Christ is hidden, and so is our life;* that, thirdly, *Christ will one day appear;* and, fourthly, that *when he appeareth we also shall appear with him in glory.*

I. The first most precious and experimental doctrine lies in these words, "CHRIST WHO IS OUR LIFE."

We hardly realize that we are reading in Colossians when we meet with this marvellously rich expression. It is so like John's way of talking. See his opening words in his gospel, "In him was life, and the life was the light of men." Remember how he reports the words at Lazarus' tomb, "I am the resurrection and the life." How familiarly he speaks of the Lord Jesus under the same character in his first epistle: "That which was from the beginning, which we have heard, which we have seen with our eyes, which we have looked upon, and our hands have handled, of the Word of life; for *the life* was manifested, and we have seen it, and bear witness, and shew unto you that eternal life which was with the Father, and was manifested unto us." How close John cleaves to Jesus! He does not say, as the preacher of this morning will—Christ is the food of our life, and the joy of our life, and the object of our life, and so on, no, but "Christ *is* our life." I think that Peter or James would have said, "He is the *strength* or guide of our life," but John must needs put his head right into the Saviour's bosom, he cannot talk at a distance, or whisper from a second seat, but his head must go sweetly down upon the Saviour's heaving bosom; he must feel himself in the closest, nearest possible contact with his Lord; and so he puts it, "The life was manifested," getting to the very pith and marrow of it at once. Paul has somewhat of the same loving spirit; and if not entitled to be called "that disciple whom Jesus loved," the angel might well have addressed him as he did Daniel, "O man, greatly beloved." Hence, you see, he leaps at once into the depths of the truth, and delights to dive in it. Whereas others, like the Israelites, stand outside the bound which surrounds the mount, he, like Moses, enters into the place where God is, and beholds the excellent glory. We, I fear, must compass this holy truth round about, before we can fully enter into it. Blessed is it to wait at the doors of such a truth, though better far to enter in. Let it be understood that it is not natural but spiritual life of which the text treats, and then we shall not mislead the ignorant.

1. *Christ is the source of our life.* "For as the Father raiseth up the dead, and quickeneth them; even so the Son quickeneth whom he will." Our Lord's own words are—"Verily, verily, I say unto you, he that heareth my word, and believeth on him that sent me, hath everlasting life, and shall not come into condemnation; but is passed from death unto life. Verily, verily, I say unto you, the hour is coming, and now is, when the dead shall hear the voice of the Son of God; and they that hear shall live." Four verilies, as if to show the importance of the truth here taught to us. We are dead in sin. That same voice which brought Lazarus out of the tomb, brings us out of our grave of sin. We hear the Word of God, and we live according to the promise— "Awake thou that sleepest, and arise from the dead, and Christ shall give thee light." (Eph. v. 14.) Jesus is our Alpha, as well as our Omega: he is the Author of our faith, as well as its finisher. We should have been to this day dead in trespasses and sins, if it had not been said, "And you hath he quickened." It is by *his* life that we live; he gives us the living water, which is in us a well of water springing up unto everlasting life.

2. *Christ is the substance of our spiritual life.*

What is life? The physician cannot discover it; the anatomist hunts in vain for it, through flesh, and nerve, and brain. Be quick, sir! with that scapel of yours; "life's just departed," men say; cut quick to the heart, and see if you cannot find, at least, some lingering footprint of the departed thing called life. Subtle anatomist, what hast thou found? Look at that brain—what canst thou see there but a certain quantity of matter strangely fashioned? Canst thou discover what is life? It is true that somewhere in that brain and in that spinal cord it dwells, and that heart with its perpetual pumpings and heavings has something or other to do with it, but where is the substance, the real substance of the thing called life? Ariel's wings cannot pursue it— it is too subtle. Thought knows it but cannot grasp it; knows it from its being like itself, but cannot give a picture of it, nor represent what it is. In the new nature of the Christian there is much mystery, but there is none as to what is its life; if you could cut into the centre of the renewed heart you would find sure footprints of divine life, for you would find love to Jesus, nay, you would find Christ himself there. If you walk in search of the springs of the sea of the new nature, you will find the Lord Jesus at the fount of all. "All my springs are in thee," said David. Christ creates the life-throbs of the believer's soul, he sends the life-floods through the man according to his own will. If you could penetrate the brain of the believer you would find Christ to be the central thought moving every other thought, and causing every other thought to take root and grow out of itself; you would find Christ to be the true substance of the inner life of the spiritual nature of every soul quickened by the breath of heaven's life.

3. *Christ is the sustenance of our life.* What can the Christian feed upon but Jesus' flesh and blood? As to his natural life he needs bread, but as to his spiritual life, of which alone we are now speaking, he has

learned that "man shall not live by bread alone, but by every word which proceedeth out of the mouth of God shall man live." "This is the bread which cometh down from heaven, that a man may eat thereof, and not die. I am the living bread which came down from heaven; if any man eat of this bread, he shall live for ever: and the bread that I will give is my flesh, which I will give for the life of the world." We cannot live on the sand of the wilderness, we want the manna which drops from on high; our skin bottles of creature confidence cannot yield us a drop of moisture, but we drink of the rock which follows us, and that rock is Christ. O wayworn pilgrims in this wilderness of sin, you never do get a morsel, much less a meal, to satisfy the craving hunger of your spirits, except ye find it in Christ Jesus. When you feed on him your soul can sing, "He hath satisfied my mouth with good things, so that my youth is renewed like the eagle's," but if you have him not, your bursting wine vat and your well filled barn can give you no sort of satisfaction; rather you lament over them in the words of wisdom, "Vanity of vanities, all is vanity!" O how true are Jesus' own words, "For my flesh is meat indeed, and my blood is drink indeed. He that eateth my flesh, and drinketh my blood, dwelleth in me, and I in him. As the living Father hath sent me, and I live by the Father: so he that eateth me, even he shall live by me."

Christ is the solace of our life. Noah's ark had but one window, and we must not expect more. Jesus is the only window which lets light into the Christian's spirit when he is under sharp affliction. Kirke White's picture of his midnight voyage, when one star alone of all the train could guide the mariner's foundering bark to the port of peace, is a faint but truthful representation of the Christian's life in its hour of peril. Paul says that during his disastrous voyage "neither sun nor stars for many days appeared, and no small tempest lay on them, and all hope that they should be saved was taken away, but then, just then, the angel of God stood at his side;" and even so will the Lord Jesus appear to his saints in their extremities, and be their joy and safety. And, brethren, if Christ appear, what mattereth it where we are?

> "Midst darkest shades if he appear
> My dawning is begun;
> He is my soul's bright morning star,
> And he my rising sun."

Do not talk of poverty! Our tents are the curtains of Solomon, and not the smoke-dried skins of Kedar, when Christ is present. Speak not of want! There are all manner of precious fruits laid up for my beloved when he cometh into my cot. Speak not of sickness! my soul is no longer sick except it be of love, but full of holy health when once the sun of righteousness hath risen with healing beneath his wings. Christ is the very soul of my soul's life. His loving kindness is better than life! There is nothing in life worth living for but Christ. "Whom have I in heaven but thee, and there is none upon earth that I desire beside thee!" The rest is mere skim milk and curds fit to be given to the swine, but Christ is the cream; all else is but the husk and bran, and coarse gritty meal, the Lord Jesus is the pure flour. All that remaineth is the chaff; fan it, and the wind shall carry it away, or the fire shall burn it, and little shall be the loss; Christ is the golden grain, the only thing worth having. Life's true life, the true heart's blood, the innermost fount of life is in Jesus.

To the true Christian, *Christ is the object of his life.* As speeds the ship towards the port, so hastes the believer towards the haven of his Saviour's bosom. As flies the arrow to its goal, so flies the Christian towards the perfecting of his fellowship with Christ Jesus. As the soldier fights for his captain, and is crowned in his captain's victory, so the believer contends for Christ, and gets his triumph out of the triumphs of his Master. "For him to live is Christ;"—at least, it is this he seeks after, and counts that all life apart from this is merely death in another form. That wicked flesh of his, that cumbrous clay, those many temptations, that Satanic trinity of the world, the flesh, and the devil, all these mar his outward actions; but if he could be what he would be, he would stand like the bullock at Christ's altar to be slaughtered, or march forward like a bullock in Christ's furrow to plough the blood-bought field. He desires that he may not have a hair of his head unconsecrated, nor heave one breath which is not for his Saviour, nor speak one word which is not for the glory of his Lord. His heart's ambition is to live so long as he can glorify Christ better on earth than in heaven, and to be taken up when it shall be better for him and more honourable for his Master that he should be with Jesus where he is. As the river seeks the sea, so, Jesus, seek I thee! O let me find thee and melt my life into thine for ever!

It follows from all this, that *Christ is the exemplar of our life.* A Christian lays the life of Christ before him as the schoolboy puts his copy at the top of the page, and he tries to draw each line, down-stroke and up-stroke, according to the handwriting of Christ Jesus. He has the portrait of Christ before him as the artist has in his studio his Greek sculptures, busts and torsos; he knows that there is all the true anatomy of virtue in Christ. If he wants to study life, he studies from Christ; or, if he would closely learn the beauties of the antique, he studies from the Saviour, for Christ is ancient and modern, antique and living too, and therefore God's artists in their life-sculpture keep to the Saviour, and count that if they imitate every vein, and fetch out every muscle of their great copy, they shall then have produced the perfection of manhood. I would give nothing for your religion if you do not seek to be like Christ; where there is the same life within, there will, there must be, to a great extent, the same developments without. I have heard it said, and I think I have sometimes noticed it, that husbands and wives who are truly knit together in near and dear conjugal affection, grow somewhat like each other in expression, if not in feature. This I well know, that if the heart is truly wedded to the Lord Jesus, and lives in near fellowship with him, it must grow like him. Grace is the light, our loving heart is the sensitive plate, Jesus is the person who fills the lens of our soul, and soon a heavenly photograph of his character is produced. There will be a similarity of spirit, temper, motive, and action; it will not be manifest merely in great things but in little matters too, for even our speech will bewray us.

Thus you see after all, I have only been wading along the banks, or at best conducting you up to the knees in the gently flowing stream of my text. Experience must lead you further, for there is a great deep here; Paul could perceive it, for *he* does not say as I have been saying, "Jesus is the source of our life, the substance of our life, the solace of our life, the object of our life, the exemplar of our life;" but he says, "Christ *is* our life," and so he is indeed. Just as we have a natural life of which we know so little, so we have a spiritual life which is more mysterious far, and of that we know beyond its effects and operations little more than this, that Christ *is* that life, that when we get Christ we have eternal life, that if we have life it is only because we have Christ in us, the hope of glory.

I must pause a minute here, just to say that what is true concerning our spiritual life *now*, is *equally true of our spiritual life in heaven*. Different as are the circumstances of the life in heaven and the life on earth, yet as to real essence there is only one life in both places. Saints in heaven live by precisely the same life which makes them live here. Spiritual life in the kingdom of grace and in the kingdom of glory is the same, only here it is uneducated spiritual life, there it is educated and trained; here it is undeveloped, it is the babe, the child, there it is developed, manifested, perfected; but in very deed the life is precisely the same. Saints need not to be born again after once being regenerate. You who have been born again, have now within you the life which will last on throughout eternity; you have the very same vital spark of heavenly flame which will burn in glory, world without end.

It will be no digression if we here remark, that as we have eternal life in having Christ, this *marks our dignity*. "Christ our life !" Why, this cannot be said of princes or kings! What is their life? Talk of blue blood and pedigree, and so on, here is something more, here is *God's own Son, our life!* You cannot say this of angels. Bright spirits! your songs are sweet and your lives are happy, but Christ is not your life! Nay this cannot be asserted of archangels. Gabriel! thou mayest bend thyself before God's throne, and worship him in praise too high for me, but thou canst not boast what I can surely claim, that Christ is my life! Even those mysterious presence-angels of whom we read in Ezekiel and Revelation, called the four living creatures, though they seem to bear up the moving throne of deity, creatures who appear to be an embodiment of divine power and glory, yet even of these it is not written that Christ is their life. Herein men, redeemed, elect, favoured men rise to a supernatural height, for they can say what no spirits but those redeemed by blood may venture to assert, "Christ is our life." Does not this account for *Christian holiness?* How can a man live in sin if Christ is his life ? Jesus dwell in him and he continue in sin ? Impossible! Can he sin without his life ? He *must* do so if he sins, because Christ cannot sin, and Christ is his life. Why, if I see the saint never so self-denying, never so zealous, never so earnest, never so like his Lord, it is no wonder now, when I understand that Christ is his life.

See *how secure* the Christian is. No dagger can reach his life, for it is hidden beyond the skies. No temptation, no hellish blast, no exhalation from the Stygian pits of temptation can ever with burning fever or chill consumption waste the life of the Christian spiritually. No, it is hid with Christ, it *is* Christ, and unless Christ dies, the Christian's life dies not. Oh how safe, how honoured, how happy is the Christian!

But we may not linger longer, time warns us to proceed. There is much more than ever we shall be able to bring out. Let down your buckets, here is a deep well; I hope you have something to draw with. You that have life within have. You that have not, may look down the well and see the darkness, or the reflection of the water, but you cannot reach the cooling flood. It is only you who can draw, who can know the excellence of this living water. I pray the Lord help you to drink to the full and draw again, for there is no fear of ever draining the inexhaustible fulness of this deep truth of God.

II. Now, as our Lord Jesus has not yet appeared in his glory, OUR LIFE IS THEREFORE HIDDEN.

"The earnest expectation of the creature waiteth for the manifestation of the sons of God," but as yet they are unknown and unmanifested. The major part of the believer's life is not seen at all, and never can be by the unspiritual eye. Where is Christ? To the worldling at the present moment there is no such person as Christ, he says, "I cannot see him, touch him, hear him. He is beyond all cognizance of my senses, I do not believe in him." Just such is spiritual life to the unbeliever. You must not expect because you are a Christian that unbelievers will begin to admire you, and say, "What a mystery! This man has a new life in him, what an admirable thing, what a desirable possession, we wish we partook of the same." Nothing of the kind. They do not know that you have such a life at all. They can see your outward actions, but your inward life is quite out of reach of their observation. Christ is in heaven to-day, he is full of joy; but the world does not know his joy; no worldly heart is boasting and rejoicing because Christ is glad in heaven. Christ to-day is pleading before the Father's throne, but the world does not see Christ's engagements; Christ's occupations are all hidden from carnal eyes. Christ at this present moment reigns, and has power in heaven, and earth, and hell; but what does the worldly man see of it? Jesus has fellowship with all his saints everywhere, but what does the ungodly discern? I might stand and preach until midnight concerning my Lord, but all that men who are unconverted would gain would be to hear what I have to tell, and then to say, "Perhaps it is true," but they could not possibly discern it, the thing is beyond the cognizance of sense. So is our spiritual life. Beloved, you may reign over sin, but the sinner does not comprehend your being a king. You may officiate as a priest before God, but the ungodly man does not perceive your priesthood and your worship. Do not expect him to do so; your labour is lost if you try by any way to introduce him to these mysteries, except by the same door through which you came yourself. I never try to teach a horse astronomy; and to teach an unconverted man spiritual experience would be a folly of the same sort. The man who knows nothing of our inner life takes up "Pilgrim's Progress," and he says, "Yes, it is a very wonderful allegory." It is, sir, but unrenewed minds know nothing about it. When we have sometimes read explanations of the Pilgrim's Progress, we could not but detect that the writer of the explanation had need to have had it explained to himself; he could describe the shell, but the kernel of the nut was far beyond his reach; he had not learned to crack the shell, and to feed upon the meat. Now it must be so, it must be so, if Christ is our life; Christ has gone away and cannot be seen; it must be so that the greater proportion of the spiritual life must be for ever a secret to all but spiritual men. But then there is a part which men do see, and that I may liken to Christ when he was on earth: Christ seen of men and angels. What did the world do with Christ as soon as they saw him? Set him in the chair of state and fall down and worship his absolute perfection? No, not they: "He was despised and rejected of men, a man; of sorrows and acquainted with grief." Outside of the camp was his place; cross-bearing was for him the occupation, not of one day, but of every day. Did the world yield him solace and rest? Foxes, ye have your holes, ye birds of the air, ye have your nests, but the Son of man had not where to lay his head. Earth could afford him no bed, no house, no shelter; at last it cast him out for death, and crucified him, and then would have denied him a tomb, if one of his disciples had not begged his body. Such you must expect to be the lot of the part of your spiritual life which men can see; as soon as they see it to be spiritual life, they will treat it as they treated the Saviour. They will despise it, "Sure!" say they, "pretty fancies, fine airs, nice ideas." You expect them to give you comfort, do you—worldlings to give you comfort! Do you think that Christ will have anywhere to lay his head in this world to-day any more than he had one thousand eight hundred years ago? You go about to find what God gives the foxes and the birds, but what he never meant to give to you in this world, a place whereon to lay your head. Your place to lay your head is up yonder on your Saviour's bosom, but not here. You dream that men will admire you, that the more holy you are and the more Christ-like you are, the more peaceable people will be towards you. My dear friends, you do not know what you are driving at. "It is enough for the disciple that he be as his master, and the servant as his lord. If they have called the master of the house Beelzebub, how much more shall they call them of his household?" I believe if we were more like Christ we should be much more loved by his friends, and much more hated by his enemies. I do not believe the world would be half so lenient to the Church, now-a-days, if it were not that the Church has grown complacent to the world. When any of us speak up boldly, mercenary motives are imputed to us, our language is turned upside down, and we are abhorred of men. We get smooth things, brethren, because I am afraid we are too much like the prophets who prophecied peace, peace, where there was no peace. Let us be true to our Master, stand out and come out and be like him, and we must expect the same treatment which he had; and if we receive it we can only say, This is what I expected;—

> "Tis no surprising thing
> That we should be unknown;
> The Jewish world knew not their king,
> God's everlasting Son."

III. CHRIST WILL APPEAR. The text speaks of it as a fact to be taken for granted. "When Christ, who is our life, shall appear." It is not a matter of question in the Christian church whether Christ will appear or not. Has not Christ appeared once? Yes, after a

CHRIST OUR LIFE—SOON TO APPEAR

certain sort. I remember reading a quaint expression of some old divine, that the book of Revelation might quite as well be called an Obvelation, for it was rather a hiding than a revealing of things to come. So, when Jesus came it was hardly a revealing, it was a hiding of our Lord. It is true that he was "manifest in the flesh," but it is equally true that the flesh shrouded and concealed his glory. The first manifestation was very partial; it was Christ seen through a glass, Christ in the mist of grief, and the cloud of humiliation. Christ is yet to appear in the strong sense of the word "appearing;" he is to come out and shine forth. He is to leave the robes of scorn and shame behind, and to come in the glory of the Father and all his holy angels with him. This is the constant teaching of the word of God, and the constant hope of the Church, that *Christ will appear*. A thousand questions at once suggest themselves: How will Christ appear? When will Christ appear? Where will Christ appear? and so on. What God answers we may enquire, but some of our questions are mere impertinence. How will Christ appear? I believe Christ will appear in person. Whenever I think of the second coming, I never can tolerate the idea of a spiritual coming. That always seems to me to be the most transparent folly that can possibly be put together, because Christ cannot come spiritually, he always is here: "Lo! I am with you alway, even unto the end of the world." Christ's spiritual coming never can be that which is spoken of in Scripture, as the day of our release. I sometimes say to brethren, "Do you think if Christ were to come spiritually now, we should observe the ordinances better?" "Yes, certainly." "Do you think, for instance, the ordinance of the Lord's Supper would be better attended to?" "Yes, no doubt it would." Yes, but then this proves that this is not the coming which the Bible speaks of, because it is expressly said of the Lord's Supper, that we are to do it in remembrance of him, *till he come*. A spiritual coming would make us do it more zealously; there must be another form of coming which would justify our giving up the supper altogether, and that must be of a personal character, for then, and then only, might the Supper properly cease. We shall not need to have a supper to remind us of the person, when the person himself shall be present in our midst reigning and triumphant in his Church. We believe in a personal reign and coming of our Lord Jesus Christ. But how will he come? He will doubtless come with great splendour; the angels of God shall be his attendants. We gather from Scripture, that he will come to reign in the midst of his people, that the house of Israel will acknowledge him as King, yea, that all nations shall bow down before him, and kings shall pay him homage. None shall be able to stand against him. "Those that pierced him shall wail because of him." He will come to discern between the righteous and the wicked, to separate the goats from the sheep. He will come graciously to adjudge his people their reward according to their works. He will give to those who have been faithful over a few things to be rulers over many things; and those who have been faithful over many things shall be rulers over many cities. He will come to discern between the works of his people; such as are only wood, hay, and stubble, will be consumed; such as are gold and silver, and precious stones, will stand the fire. He will come to condemn the wicked to eternal punishment, and to take his people up to their everlasting mansions in the skies. We look for such a coming, and without entering into minute details, drawing charts, and painting pictures, we are content to believe that he is coming in his glory, to show himself to be what he ever was—King of kings, and Lord of lords, God over all, blessed for ever; to be adored and worshipped, and no more to be despised and rejected of men. When will he come? That is a question which unbelief asks with a start. Faith replies, "It is not for you to know the times and seasons, of that day and of that hour knoweth no man." Some simpleton says, "But we may know the week, month, or year." Do not trifle with God's Word and make a fool of yourself, because you must know that the expression means that you do not know anything about the time at all, and never will know. Christ will come in a time when we look not for him, just perhaps when the world and the Church are most asleep, when the wise and the foolish virgins have alike fallen into a deep slumber; when the stewards shall begin to beat their fellow-servants, and to drink, and to be drunken; at midnight, or perhaps not till cock-crowing, he will come like a thief, and the house shall be suddenly broken up; but come he will, and that is enough for you and for me to know; and when he cometh we shall appear, for as *he* shall appear, *we* shall also appear with him in glory.

IV. The fourth thought is, THAT WHEN CHRIST SHALL APPEAR, WE ALSO SHALL APPEAR.

Do you ever feel like those lions in the Zoological Gardens, restlessly walking up and down before the bars of their cage, and seeming to feel that they were never meant to be confined within those narrow limits? Sometimes they are for thrusting their heads through the bars, and then for dashing back and tearing the back of their dungeon, or for rending up the pavement beneath them, as if they yearned for liberty. Do you ever feel like that? Does your soul ever want to get free from her cage? Here is an iron bar of sin, of doubt, and there is another iron bar of mistrust and infirmity. Oh! if you could tear them away, could get rid of them all, you would do something for Christ—you would be like Christ. Oh! if you could but by some means or other burst the bands of this captivity! but you cannot, and therefore you feel uneasy. You may have seen an eagle with a chain upon its foot, standing on a rock—poor unhappy thing! it flaps its wings—looks up to the sun—wants to fly right straight ahead at it and stare the sun out of countenance—looks to the blue sky, and seems as if it could sniff the blue beyond the dusky clouds, and wants to be away; and so it tries its wings and dreams of mounting—but that *chain*, that *cruel chain*, remorselessly holds it down. Has not it often been so with you? You feel, "I am not meant to be what I am, I am sure I am not; I have a something in me which is adapted for something better and higher, and I want to mount and soar, but that chain—that dragging chain of the body of sin and death will keep me down." Now it is to such as you that this text comes, and says to you, "Yes, your present state is not your soul's true condition, you have a hidden life in you; that life of yours pants to get out of the bonds and fetters which control it, and it shall be delivered soon, for Christ is coming, and when Christ shall appear you shall appear,—the same appearance that belongs to him belongs to you. He shall come, and then your day of true happiness, and joy, and peace, and everything that you are panting for, and longing for, shall certainly come too." I wonder whether the little oak inside the acorn—for there is a whole oak there, and there are all the roots, and all the boughs, and everything inside that acorn—I wonder whether that little oak inside the acorn ever has any premonition of the summer weather that will float over it a hundred years hence, and of the mists that will hang in autumn on its sere leaves, and of the hundreds of acorns which itself will cast, every autumn, upon the earth, when it shall become in the forest a great tree. You and I are like that acorn; inside of each of us are the germs of great things. There is the tree that we are to be,—I mean there is the spiritual thing we are to be, both in body and soul even now within us, and sometimes here below, in happy moments, we get some inklings of what we are to be; and then how we want to burst the shell, to get out of the acorn and to be the oak! Ay, but stop. Christ has not come, Christian, and you cannot get out of that till the time shall come for Jesus to appear, and then shall you appear with him in glory. You will very soon perceive in your rainwater, certain ugly little things which swim and twist about in it, always trying if they can to reach the surface and breathe through one end of their bodies. What makes these little things so lively, these innumerable little things like very small tadpoles, why are they so lively? Possibly they have an idea of what they are going to be. The day will come when all of a sudden there will come out of the case of the creature that you have had swimming about in your water, a long-legged thing with two bright gauze-like wings, which will mount into the air, and on a summer's evening will dance in the sunlight. It is nothing more nor less than a gnat; you have swimming there a gnat in one of its earliest stages. You are just like that; you are an undeveloped being; you have not your wings yet, and yet sometimes in your activity for Christ, when the strong desires for something better are upon you, you leap in foretaste of the bliss to come. I do not know what I am to be, but I feel that there is a heart within me too big for these ribs to hold, I have an immortal spark which cannot have been intended to burn on this poor earth, and then to go out; it must have been meant to burn on heaven's altar. Wait a bit, and when Christ comes you will know what you are. We are in the chrysalis state now, and those who are the liveliest worms among us grow more and more uneasy in that chrysalis state. Some are so frozen up in it that they forget the hereafter, and appear content to remain a chrysalis for ever. But others of us feel we would sooner not be than be what we now are for ever, we feel as if we must burst our bonds, and when that time of bursting shall come, when the chrysalis shall get its painted wings and mount to the land of flowers, then shall we be satisfied. The text tells us—" When Christ, who is our life, shall *appear*"—when he comes out in all his glory—"we also shall appear with him in glory." If you would like these gracious promises drawn out into detail with regard to the body, you may listen to just such words as these. "It is sown a soulish body, it is raised a spiritual body. The first man is of the earth earthy, the second man is the Lord from heaven. As is the earthy such are they also that are earthy; as is the heavenly such are they also that are heavenly." Whatever Christ's body is in heaven, our body is to be like it; whatever its glory and strength and power, our vile body is to be fashioned like unto his glorious body. As for our soul, whatever of absolute perfection,—whatever of immortal joy Christ possesses we are to possess that; and as for honour,—whatever of esteem and love Christ may have from intelligent beings, we are to share in the same; and as for position before God—whatever Christ has—we are to stand where he stands. Are his enemies put to confusion? So are ours. Do all worlds discern his glory? they shall discern ours too. Is all dishonour wiped away from him? so shall it be from us. Do they forget for ever the shame and spitting, the cross and the nails? so shall they in our case. Is it for ever "Glory! and honour! and power! and dominion! and bliss without end?" so shall it be in our case. Let us comfort one another therefore, with these words, and look up out of our wormhood, and our chrysalis state, to that happier and better day when we shall be like him, for we shall see him as he is.

All this has nothing to do with a great many of you. You will die but you will never rise like Christ. You will die, *and you will die;*— why did I say "and you will die?" Why because you will have to feel the second death, and that second death, mark you, is as much more tremendous than the first as the trumpet of the angel is more terrible than the voice of the preacher can be this morning. Oh I would that Christ were your life, but you are dead, and God will say of you one of these days as Abraham said of Sarah, "Bury the dead out of my sight," and you must be put out of his sight as an obnoxious putrid thing. Oh that he would quicken you this day! "There is life," says the hymn, "in a look at the crucified One." God help you to exercise one look at that Christ of whom I spoke, and then you shall join with the rest of his people in saying, "Christ is our life."

May God bless these feeble words of mine, and own them because of their weakness, the more to illustrate his own grace and power, for Jesus' sake. Amen.

A Portrait No Artist Can Paint

"He had in his right hand seven stars: and out of his mouth went a sharp two-edged sword: and his countenance was as the sun shineth in his strength"—Revelation i. 16.

WHILE reading this description given by John of what he saw in the isle called Patmos, I think you must have noticed that it would be quite impossible for any painter to depict it upon canvas, and equally impossible for any sculptor to embody it in stone or marble. Those who have attempted to copy the lines here given have signally failed; they may paint a picture of the garment down to the feet, and the golden girdle; but the rest, if it be viewed from an artist's aspect, would be found to be incongruous: "His head and his hairs were white like wool, as white as snow; and his eyes were as a flame of fire." No great painter would ever venture to give us a portrait of our Lord with his head and his hair "white like wool, as white as snow." If he did, it would be quite impossible to depict eyes that were "as a flame of fire." How would it be possible to make us realize, with the aid of any pen or pencil, that his feet were "like unto fine brass, as if they burned in a furnace"? The task would have to be given over as quite hopeless when it reached this point: "He had in his right hand seven stars: and out of his mouth went a sharp two-edged sword: and his countenance was as the sun shineth in his strength."

I believe that this difficulty of giving a truthful representation of the Lord Jesus Christ is according to the divine purpose. Nothing, it seems to me, can be more detestable to the Lord's heart and mind than the worship of his image in any shape. If any are determined to break the law about making graven images, and bowing down before them, then let the idol be the image of something that is on the earth beneath, or in the water under the earth; but, O ye idolaters, pray do not, as it were, make the Lord Jesus Christ accessory to your idolatry. *That*, he never really can be, for he abhors it. "Get thee behind me, Satan," would be his answer to every proposal that his image should be worshipped, for he could not endure it. It is a dreadful thing that men should ever dare attempt to make any likeness of the Son of God himself to be the occasion of sin. If ye must make an image, make it if ye will of a serpent, or of an ox, but not of the Son of God, who came on purpose to redeem us from this among other sins. Let us not degrade his sacred personage by making even it to be an image before which we prostrate ourselves.

I know it is said that idolaters do not worship the image, and that they worship God through the image; but that is expressly forbidden. The first commandment is, "Thou shalt have no other gods before me." Then the second commandment forbids the worshipping of God by or through any symbol or image whatsoever: "Thou shalt not make unto thee any graven image, or any likeness of any thing that is in heaven above, or that is in the earth beneath, or that is in the water under the earth : thou shalt not bow down thyself to them, nor serve them." The worship of the image of Christ appears to me to be not the more excusable form of idolatry, if there be any that is less evil than others, but it seems to me to be the more intensely wicked form of it, since it is making even the glorious personage of the Lord Jesus subsidiary to an act of transgression against the commandments of his Father. If we cannot say concerning the divine and human personage of our Lord, "Ye saw no similitude," yet we can say, "Ye saw no similitude such as can be engraven in any way whatever."

The fact is, that we have, in this apocalyptic vision, very extraordinary hieroglyphics put together. Hieroglyphic language does not aim at the artistic and the poetic; a hieroglyph has a higher object than the mere gratification of taste. It is intended to give us mental ideas,—not ideas for the eye, but ideas for the heart; not what we shall see, but that which we shall feel and understand. Hence, these figurative representations of different parts of our Lord's person, though they cannot be put together so as to form a picture, are, nevertheless, deeply instructive to every loving and reverent heart.

So I want you, dear friends, without wishing to make a complete portrait of your Lord, to try to follow the teaching in this verse. There are three things here; first, *the stars in Christ's hand:* "He had in his right hand seven stars." Then, secondly, there is *the sword in his mouth:* "Out of his mouth went a sharp two-edged sword." And then, thirdly, there is *the glory of his face:* "His countenance was as the sun shineth in his strength."

I. First, then, when John saw our Lord Jesus Christ, he naturally looked to his hand, and therefore he saw THE STARS IN HIS HAND.

Note, dear friends, that our Lord Jesus has a hand. He is not, as some fancy, an abstract idea of a personage without life. He has a hand, and that hand is a working hand. The hand that was pierced by the nail is not paralysed; it has strength to hold in itself seven stars. The hand that wrought out our redemption has not ceased to work for us. Christ holds in his hand that which he bought with the blood of his heart. John saw that his Lord held in his right hand seven stars. Let us always think of our Lord Jesus Christ as full of power, and actively using it; let us think of him at this moment as having a deft, and skilled, and mighty right hand, which he will lift up on the behalf of all those who put their trust in him. On the right hand of the Majesty on high there sits a right-handed Christ, still carrying on according to his own good pleasure the work of the Lord, which ever prospereth in his hand.

When John looked at Christ's right hand, he tells us that in it he saw seven stars. These are generally understood to be the ministers of the seven churches of Asia; we are told, in the twentieth verse, that "the seven stars are the angels of the seven churches," and I do not know who the angels of the churches can be unless they are the messengers of the churches, those ministers of whom Paul wrote, "they are the messengers of the churches, and the glory of Christ." At any rate, we shall take it for granted that these stars represent the pastors of the churches, the ministers of Christ.

These stars are said to be in the Lord's right hand, first, because *he made them stars.* They are in the hand of him who made them what they are. Under the old covenant, there were to be, in the tabernacle, seven lights always burning upon the seven-branched candlestick, or lampstand; but John saw in Christ's hand seven stars; not ordinary lamps, but stars shining with a greater brilliance and a more heavenly light than could ever be seen in the oil-fed lamps in the ancient tabernacle. If any man in the Church of God shines like a star to guide others to the port of peace, he owes his light entirely to Christ. It must be so, because it is Christ's right hand that has made him what he is; he is a light because Christ has given him light, he owes his spiritual radiance entirely to him who is the Lord and Giver of light in the midst of his Church. My dear brethren in the ministry, if you want to shine for Jesus, you must be made into stars to be held in his right hand. There is no possibility of your being of spiritual use to your fellow-men, or exercising a ministry that shall tend to their eternal salvation, except as you are made into a light to be held in the right hand of the Lord Jesus Christ. All the education in the world, all the natural talent that any possess, all the acquired practice of oratory, all the powers which are the result of long experience, can never make a good minister of Jesus Christ. The stars are in the right hand of Christ; ministers are not made by men, but by the Lord himself, if they are worthy to be called ministers at all. So, the stars are in his right hand, first, because he made them.

They are there, next, dear friends, because *he holds them up.* Every Christian has to face great perils, and every Christian has need to pray to the Lord, "Hold thou me up, and I shall be safe." But ministers of Christ, ministers whom he makes to be stars, are exposed to sevenfold peril. Against the leaders of the spiritual Israel the sharpest arrows of the enemy are sure to be shot; the word seems to be still passed round to our adversaries as in the ancient day of battle, when the king of Syria said to his captains, "Fight neither with small nor great, save only with the king of Israel." If there be anywhere a captain who leads the way, and comes to the very front of the host, the temptations that gather about him will be most fierce and terrible. Slander, misrepresentation, and every kind of evil shall dog his heels; and he above all men who are on the face of the earth must cry to his Lord, "Hold thou me up, and I shall be safe." The mercy is, that the true minister of Christ is held up in Christ's right hand. He shall be kept faithful even unto death, he shall not fall; and, God helping him, he shall be caused to shine on right to the end of his ministry. Every now and then, we hear a rumour that some of God's own children have fallen from grace; I do not believe it. It is said that they have fallen away and perished; I do not believe it. Those of you who live till next November, and go out late at night, may see a great many shooting stars; and some of your little children will cry, "Look, father, the stars are falling;" and possibly some children will believe that stars have fallen from their places. Take the telescope, and look at the heavens; sweep the sky as far as the range of the instrument will permit. Jupiter is all right, and Saturn, and Mars, and Venus, and Mercury, and all the planets, they are all in their places; and the fixed stars are shining on as they have done ever since the Lord first kindled them to charm away the gloom of night. I do not know what these shooting stars may be, there have been many guesses with regard to them; neither do I know what these apostates may be, there have been a great many guesses about those that did flame out so brightly once. But I do know this, that Jesus still holds the seven stars in his right hand, and he will not drop even one of them; they shall not be reduced to six, or five, or four, or three, or two, or one, or vanish altogether; neither shall it ever be so with any of the true sons of God. Our Lord himself has said, "They shall never perish, neither shall any man pluck them out of my hand. My Father, which gave them me, is greater than all; and no man is able to pluck them out of my Father's hands." If you, my brother, are kept in the right hand of Christ, then you *are* kept. If you wish and hope to shine for Jesus through all the years that you shall live, then you must be held in his right hand, for he alone, who made you, can hold you up.

Next, are not the stars represented as being in Christ's right hand, because *he holds them out*, as well as holds them up? As a man holds a lamp in his hand, and holds it up and out as far as he can, that its light may shine the farther, so does Christ hold his servants up. Sometimes he holds some of them up high aloft above the multitude, so that, on the Sabbath, they rise quite out of themselves. They say what they could never have thought of saying by themselves; and they are enabled to plunge into mysteries which aforetime had not been opened up to them; and there are given unto them burning words that shine as well as burn, for their Lord lifts them up, and holds them out. Dear friends, pray much for us, who are called to preach the gospel, that we may always be lifted up in the right hand of Christ. If we try to shine simply with our own natural brightness, it will be a very poor, miserable exhibition of darkness; and if we try to work ourselves up, as some do, into a state of excitement, we may goad ourselves into a condition of semi-madness, and lead others into the same folly, but no good will come out of it. That elevation of spirit which comes from the right hand which once was pierced for us, that lifting up of holy speech which is given through contact with the right hand of him who spake as never man spake, that is the kind of uplifting that we want. Pray, beloved, that every star in the right hand of the Lord Jesus Christ may be held up and held out, and so shine yet farther and farther across the wild waste of the waters of sin and sorrow.

Do you not also think that, by the stars being in the right hand of Christ, is meant that *he claims them as his own?* Every faithful minister is Christ's property; he belongs to his Lord, and he recognizes that blessed fact. "Ye are not your own, for ye are bought with a price," is true of all who believe in the Lord Jesus Christ; but it is specially true of as many as are called out from among their fellows that they may be the mouth of God, and that God may speak by them to the feeding of his flock, and to the bringing home of his lost sheep. They are peculiarly and especially in the hand of Christ, for they belong entirely to Christ.

Is not this *the highest honour any man can have*, that he should be in Christ's right hand because he belongs to Christ? You see, it is specially mentioned that these stars are not in the left hand of Christ, but in his right hand, as if the Lord intended to put peculiar and special honour upon his servants who are faithful to him. Brethren, it does not become any of us who preach the gospel to seek honour of men. What is it, after all? What is the value of commendation from the lips of men? Suppose they should praise us, and flatter us, and say that we are "thoughtful men," "abreast of the times," and I know not what,—all such stuff as this is but carrion, fit for the scavengers of the earth, but not worthy to be set before the angels of the churches. The true servants of Christ may well be satisfied to eat of the crumbs that fall from his table, rather than to feast upon the dainties that load the tables of the ungodly. If our hearts be wholly set on shining for Christ, and shining for nothing but Christ, and shining with nothing but Christ's own light, and the light of Christ's own truth, then are we as the stars in his right hand, beloved of him, and precious in his sight. Verily I say unto you, there shall be a glorious reward at the last for those who are made by Christ into stars, and who are held up, and held out in the right hand of their Lord, and so claimed by him as peculiarly and specially his own.

So much, then, concerning the ministers of Christ. Brethren, pray for us; and pray for all the preachers of the Word, that they may be stars in the right hand of Christ.

II. But now, secondly,—and upon this I would dwell with great emphasis,—notice THE SWORD WHICH COMES OUT OF CHRIST'S MOUTH. "Out of his mouth went a sharp two-edged sword."

The conquering power of the gospel is in Christ himself; it does not lie with his ministers. The power with which Christ contends for the mastery against all the powers of darkness resides not with his servants, but dwells within himself. The two-edged sword of the Lord is in the mouth of the Lord. We shine, dear friends,—such little twinkling stars as any of us are,—we shine, and God blesses the shining; but if ever there is a soul saved, we have not saved it; and if ever there is an enemy of Christ who is wounded and slain, the deed is not done by our sword. By ourselves, we have no power; the really effectual work is done by Christ himself, and by him alone. The sword that goes out of our mouth is a poor blunt instrument, which can accomplish nothing; it is the sword that goes out of Christ's mouth that does everything in the great battle for the right. Notice how the right hand of Christ has to be used even to hold up these stars; ministers are not his right hand, they are only as stars that he holds up with his right hand. They derive all their power from him; but even when they are held up by his right hand, they are not the real warriors, it is not their strength with which the battle is fought and won; the power is in Christ himself, it is out of his mouth that there goeth the sharp two-edged sword that wins the victory.

Notice, dear friends, that the power of the Lord Jesus Christ to conquer men is *a power which is like a sword.* "The sword of the Spirit, which is the Word of God," comes out of the mouth of Christ himself; and coming out of his mouth, it does several things, which I will briefly mention to you.

First, it is a discerner of the thoughts and intents of the heart. This sword pierces "even to the dividing asunder of soul and spirit, and of the joints and marrow." When I am preaching most earnestly, some of you may find it possible to go to sleep; while I am talking to you even about the most sacred things, they may glide over you as oil might run down a slab of marble; but if my Lord speaks to you, you will be compelled to feel the power of this sword that goeth out of his mouth. Every Word that comes by his Spirit out of his mouth will seem to rip you open, and lay you bare, for, "all things are naked and opened unto the eyes of him with whom we have to do;" and he can make you feel that he is discerning the thoughts and intents of your hearts. The Lord Jesus Christ, when he comes into our midst, brings his fan in his hand, and with it he will throughly purge his floor; with every movement of that fan, and every breath of his Spirit, he is separating the chaff from the wheat. There is no escaping his observation when he is at work amongst us; private thoughts are detected, the secrets of the heart are laid bare, and the precious and the vile are severed the one from the other when he is working in the midst of his Church, for out of his mouth goeth the Word which is sharper than a two-edged sword.

When this sword comes out of the mouth of Christ, it wounds as well as discerns. As a sword cuts, pierces, pricks, and wounds, so does the Word of God. I do not wonder that people are sometimes angry with the Word of the Lord; who would not be angry when he is cut as with a sharp sword? I am not surprised that others retire to weep as if their hearts would break; who would not weep when the knife cuts into his flesh and touches his very marrow? When the Lord Jesus Christ blesses the Word by his Spirit, the wounded are all round him. The ungodly begin to tremble, and the godly ones, finding that Christ is fighting against the sin that is within them, are wounded and bleeding in a hundred places because of that two-edged sword of his which cuts through coats of mail, and wounds even to the dividing asunder of soul and spirit.

Out of Christ's mouth comes, not only a wounding but a killing sword. When he speaks with power,—and, oh! how I wish that he would do so just now!—sinners feel that their self-righteousness is killed, and that all their carnal hopes are killed. They can say—and I trust that some of you can say, with John,—"'When I saw him, I fell at his feet as dead.' I was alive till I saw Christ, I seemed to be all that I wanted to be till I saw Christ; but when I saw him on the cross, when I read the mystery of his passion, and understood what it cost him to redeem a soul from death, then I saw what a sinner I must be, and I also saw what would be the result of my sin if I had to bear the penalty of it, and then, 'I fell at his feet as dead.'"

Brethren and sisters, let us pray the Lord Jesus Christ to use that sword which is in his mouth, constantly to use it among us; for what is the use of the seven stars in his right hand, what is the use of anything, unless Christ's own voice is heard, and Christ's own truth is driven home to the hearts of men? We have a good deal of preaching, nowadays, do we not? But one Word out of Christ's mouth would be worth fifty thousand out of the mouths of the greatest preachers who have ever lived. Oh! if HE will but speak, the preacher may be very illiterate, and he may not have much to say; but if God speaks through him, there will be a power about his message which cannot be resisted. On the other hand, the preacher may be one who has been well trained and taught, and he may speak eloquently, so as to please his hearers, but if God does not speak through him, what mere froth it is! It is gone like a vapour, and no result comes of it all. Do let us keep on crying that the Master himself may be at work in our midst, with the sword of the Spirit, which is the Word of God, proceeding out of his mouth.

Did you notice that the text said that *out of Christ's mouth there went a sharp sword?* There is nothing so sharp as God's Word. When we are speaking, it is very seldom that God blesses merely our words; it is usually what we quote from the Scripture that is the means of the salvation of our hearers. I think it was McCheyne who said, "It is not our word, but God's Word, which saves souls." I notice that, in most conversions, the point of decision has been reached when a text has been quoted. The word which God has blessed has been mainly Scriptural; even if the truth has not been spoken in the exact words of inspiration, yet it has been most clearly and manifestly a quotation from the Scripture put into other words. There is nothing so sharp as the Word of God. People will get round what we say, but they cannot get round what God says. They can ignore your opinion, and my view of the case, and another person's dictum upon it; but they cannot forget that which comes to them with this message, "Thus saith the Lord," "It is written;" and when the Spirit of God applies the truth to their hearts, it is indeed a sharp sword.

It is also *two-edged*, for the text calls it "a sharp two-edged sword." There is no handling this weapon without cutting yourself, for it has no back to it, it is all edge. The Word of Christ, somehow or other, is all edge. I remember preaching a sermon upon the resurrection, on purpose to see whether God would bless it to the conversion of sinners; there were many brought to Christ by that discourse. With the same intention, I have preached divine sovereignty, and the election of grace, and I have seen many won to Christ by those stern truths. I have often noticed that, when I have been preaching for the comfort of God's people, there have always been sinners wounded even then, for the Word is all edge; and even the consolations of the gospel, while they cheer the believer, will cut the sinner in twain. There is something even about that which is the sweetest truth to the believer which is sour to the unbeliever, and cuts into his conscience. Only let us preach the gospel, and we shall never find any other weapon like it. As David said of Goliath's sword, so may we say of the sword of the Spirit, "There is none like that, give it me." When I am invited to preach the novel doctrines of the present age, or to try the modern methods of fighting the devil, I look these new weapons up and down, and I advise those who offer them to me to send them to the Exhibition of Inventions up in the West of London. You may see them there, but you will never see them here. The old sword suits my hand, and God blesses it to the cutting and the wounding and the killing of sinners; God the Holy Spirit, who made it, uses it most effectually; so, by the grace of God, we will keep to it, and use no other, as long as we live.

I beg all of you, who try to bring sinners to Christ, to stick to that old sword, the two-edged sword that goeth out of Christ's mouth. If souls are not saved by the preaching of the truth, they will not be saved by the telling of lies. I have sometimes heard really awful doctrine preached at revival services, and an easy-going brother has said, "Well, you see, it was an evangelistic meeting." Yes, but you should not tell lies at evangelistic meetings. "Oh, but then, if we were to preach the same truth to these sinners that you would proclaim to a company of believers, it would not do them any good!" Well, then, nothing else will, depend upon it. If the truth will not have any effect upon them, your toning of that truth down, or your screwing it up will not improve it, but will spoil it. I believe that the very gospel that comforts saints is the gospel that saves sinners, that there is but one gospel for all purposes and all people, and that, therefore, two gospels will never be required. You have only to strike this way with one edge of the sword, and then that way with the other edge of it, or to swing it to and fro, like that ancient warrior did with his great two-handed sword, and you will strike sinners down right and left, smiting the self-righteous this way, and the licentious the other way. Only keep you to that grand old sword which the apostles used, which was in the martyrs' hands, and by which Christ himself triumphed, is triumphing, and will triumph even to the end.

III. The third part of my subject will have but few words from me, and perhaps the fewer I shall say, the better it will be. The point to which it refers is, THE GLORY OF CHRIST'S FACE: "His countenance was as the sun shineth in his strength." I will not attempt to explain these words, but will only call your attention to one or two thoughts concerning them.

First, what do you see in Christ's right hand? Seven stars; yet how insignificant they appear when you get a sight of *his face!* They are stars, and there are seven of them; but who can see seven stars, or, for the matter of that, seventy thousand stars, when the sun shineth in his strength? How sweet it is, when the Lord himself is so present in a congregation that the preacher, whoever he may be, is altogether forgotten! I pray you, dear friends, when you go to a place of worship, always try to see the Lord's face rather than the stars in his hand; look at the sun, and you will forget the stars. If you look for the stars, it may be that you will see neither star nor sun, for the Lord may withdraw his light from his servants because you are looking to them rather than looking to him. In Christ's hand are the stars, but his countenance is "as the sun shineth in his strength."

What does this mean but that there is about our Divine Lord *an inexpressible, indescribable, infinite splendour?* No man can look at the sun,—it would blind him,—the sun when it shineth in its strength; not when it is rising in the morning, nor yet when it is setting in the evening, nor yet when a cloud passes over it; but the sun in its strength, no man can look at that, he would soon lose his eyes if he did. So, who shall ever know, much less tell, the glories of the Lord Jesus Christ? To know him, is our great ambition; but his love surpasseth knowledge. That is our confession after years of endeavouring to search into the height and depth and length and breadth of his love. Think of your Lord, then, as covered with inconceivable glory.

But this expression is to be regarded also as setting forth Christ's *overpowering pre-eminence.* The best of his servants are only stars, but he is the Sun. In Christ there is more light than there is in all the prophets, saints, and apostles who have ever lived. All their light came from him, but all their light was still remaining in him; and all the light that ever shall be, throughout all the ages, will be as nothing compared with the light that there is in him. One said of Harry the Eighth that, if all the tyrants who ever lived had been dead, they might all have been considered as reproduced in that one man. I may say of our Lord Jesus Christ something very different, that is, if all the good things and all the virtuous things and all the loving things that have ever been since the world began were gone, they are all to be found in him. As the sun is the great source of light and heat, so there is an overpowering pre-eminence about the Lord Jesus Christ.

Yet, further, this is *a communicable excellence.* The sun, when he shineth in his strength, is pouring out his light; the sun has not light merely for himself, but his light is for all the worlds that are round about him, as the face, the glory, the excellence, the merit of Christ, is for all his people. He is for ever pouring it forth, and this is his splendour, that he shines upon the sons of men to fill them with joy.

Yet this figure of the sun has in it something *justly terrible.* Who could fight against the sun that shineth in his strength? If all the powers that be contended against the sun, and attempted to invade his territory, the sun would consume them all. And who shall fight against thee, O Sun of righteousness? Thou shalt utterly consume them in the day of thy wrath. There will be something terrible about the face of Christ when he comes to judgment; then shall men cry, "Hide us from the face of him that sitteth upon the throne." But to his people there is something in his face that is *intensely joyful.* We shall never be in the dark, for our Lord's face is like the sun. Put out all the lamps, and let all temporal comfort and all spiritual comfort vanish, yet spare us Christ, give us but to see his face, and to be favoured with his smile, and we shall need no candle, neither light of any other sun, for the face of Christ "is as the sun that shineth in his strength."

Dear friends, are you on the Lord's side? Are you on Jesus Christ's side? If so, be happy that you have such a Saviour. Are you an opponent of his? Then tremble, and bow before him. "Kiss the Son, lest he be angry, and ye perish from the way, when his wrath is kindled but a little. Blessed are all they that put their trust in him." May he send this choice blessing to you all, for his dear name's sake! Amen.

Christ with the Keys of Death and Hell

" I have the keys of hell and of death "—Revelation i. 18.

THEN hell and death, terrible powers as they are, are not left to riot without government. Death is a land of darkness, as darkness itself, without any order, yet a sovereign eye surveyeth it, and a master hand holdeth its key. Hell also is a horrible region, where powers of evil and of terror hold their high court and dread assembly; but hell trembles at the presence of the Lord, and there is a throne higher than the throne of evil. Let us rejoice that nothing in heaven, or earth, or in places under the earth, is left to itself to engender anarchy. Everywhere, serene above the floods, the Lord sitteth King for ever and ever. No province of the universe is free from the divine rule. Things do not come by chance. Nowhere doth chance and chaos reign, nowhere is evil really and permanently enthroned. Rest assured that the Lord hath prepared his throne in the heavens, and his kingdom ruleth over all; for if the lowest hell and death own his government, much more all things that are on this lower world.

It is delightful for us to observe, as we read this chapter, that government of hell and of death is vested in the person of the Man Christ Jesus; he who holdeth the keys of these dreadful regions, is described by John as " One like unto the Son of man," and we know that he was our Lord Jesus Christ himself. John saw a strange and glorious change in him, but still recognised the old likeness, perhaps impressed by the nail-prints and other marks of manhood which he had seen in him while yet he was in the days of his flesh. What an honour is thus conferred upon mankind! Unto which of the angels said he at any time, " Thou shalt bear the keys of hell and of death"? Yet these keys are committed to the Son of man, and Jesus Christ, bone of our bone and flesh of our flesh, made in all points like unto his brethren, ruleth over all. Yet manhood is not so exalted as of itself and apart from Godhead, for while the description given of our Lord by John, as he saw him at Patmos, is evidently human, yet is it also convincingly divine. There is a glow of glory about that mysterious manhood, which stood between the golden candlesticks, that comes not of the Virgin Mary nor of Nazareth, but is a light apart, belonging only to the everlasting God, whose Son the Redeemer is, and whose equal he counts it not robbery to be. Jesus, in essence, is "God over all, blessed for ever." Let us rejoice, then, in the condescension of God, in taking man into such union with Godhead, that now in the person of Christ man hath dominion over all the works of God's hands; and he ruleth not only over all sheep and oxen, and all fowl of the air, and fish of the sea, and whatsoever passeth through the paths of the sea, but death and Hades also are committed to the dominion of the glorified man. "At the name of Jesus every knee should bow, of things in heaven, and things in earth, and things under the earth; and that every tongue should confess that Jesus Christ is Lord, to the glory of God the Father."

The metaphor of keys is intended, no doubt, to set forth the double thought of our Lord's possessing both the rightful and the actual dominion over death and hell. The rightful dominion, I say, for often it has been the custom when kings have come to the gates of loyal cities, for the mayor, or high bailiff, or governor of the city, to present the keys in formal state, in recognition that his majesty was the lawful owner and rightful sovereign of the borough. So Christ hath the keys of hell and death—that is to say, he is rightfully the Lord over those dark regions, and rules them by indefeasible title of sovereignty. But in commonest life the key is associated with actual possession and power. When the tenant gives up the key to the landlord, then the owner has the house again under his power, and in his possession, by that act and deed. So Christ is not only *de jure* (according to right), but *de facto* (according to fact), Lord over hell and death. He actually rules and manages in all the issues of the grave, and overrules all the councils of hell, restraining the mischievous devices of Satan, or turning them to subserve his own designs of good. Our Lord Jesus Christ still is supreme; his kingdom, willingly or unwillingly, extends over all existences in whatever regions they may be.

It may be well here to remark, that the word translated "hell," though it may be rightfully referred to the region of lost and damned spirits, yet need not be restricted thereto. The word is "Hades," which signifies the dwelling place of spirits, and so it may include both heaven and hell; no doubt it does include them both in many places, and I think in this. Our Lord then hath the keys of heaven, and hell, and death. Wherever separate spirits are now existing, Christ is King, and over the iron gate through which men pass into the disembodied state, the authority of Christ is paramount. All hail! thou brightness of the Father's glory, be thou evermore adored!

Come we now to consider this text in the following lights; first, as we may be enabled and strengthened, we shall consider *the power of the keys*; secondly, we shall consider *the key of this power*; and then, thirdly, *the choice reflections locked up in this doctrine of the keys*.

I. What is intended by THE POWER OF THESE KEYS here mentioned?

A key is first of all used *for opening*, and hence our Lord can open the gates of death and hell. It is his to open the gate of the separated spirits, to admit his saints one by one to their eternal felicity. When the time shall come for us to depart out of this world unto the Father, no hand but that of the Wellbeloved shall put that golden key into the lock and open the pearly gate which admits the righteous to the spirit-land. When we have tarried awhile as disembodied spirits in Paradise, it will be Christ's work to open the gates of the grave wherein our bodies shall have been confined, in order that at the trump of the archangel we may rise to immortality. He is the resurrection and the life ; because he lives, we shall live also. At his bidding every bolt of death's prison house shall be drawn, and the huge iron gates of the sepulchre shall be rolled back. Then shall the body sown in weakness be raised in power, sown in dishonour be raised in glory. We need not ask the question, " Can these dry bones live ? " when we see in the hands of our omnipotent Saviour the golden key. Death in vain shall have gathered up the carcases of millions as his treasure, he shall lose all these treasures in a moment, when the Lord shall let go his captives, not for price nor for reward. In the Egypt of the grave no Israelite shall remain a prisoner; there shall not a hoof be left behind; of all that the Father gave to Christ he wil llose nothing, but will surely raise it up at the last day. Christ has purchased the bodies as well as the souls of his people; he hath redeemed them by blood, and their mortal frames are the temples of the Holy Ghost; rest assured he will not lose a part of his purchase. It is not the will of our Father in heaven that the Redeemer should be defrauded of any part of his purchased possession. " Thy dead men shall live, together with my dead body shall they arise."

But a key is also used *to shut* the door, and even so Jesus will both shut in and shut out. His golden key will shut his people in in heaven, as Noah was shut in the ark—

" Far from a world of grief and sin
With God eternally shut in."

There is no fear that glorified saints shall fall from their high estate, or that they shall perish after all the salvations which they have experienced. Heaven is the place of eternal safety. There the gates shall be fast shut by which their foes could enter, or by which their joys could leave them. But, alas! there is the dark side to this shutting of the gate. It is Christ, who, with his key shall shut the gates of heaven against unbelievers. When once the Master of the house hath risen up and hath shut to the door, it will be useless for mere professors to come with anxious knock and bitter cry, " Lord, Lord, open unto us;" for I wot that the Son of David, when he shutteth, shutteth so that no man openeth, and he himself repenteth not of what he has done. Once let him close mercy's gate upon the soul of a man, and the iron bar shall never be uplifted. O may none of you know what it is to see Christ shut the door of heaven in your face. It will be terrible when you are expecting to enter into the marriage supper to find yourselves thrust forth into "outer darkness, where shall be weeping, and wailing, and gnashing of teeth." Jesus, with his sovereign key, has locked out of heaven all sinners who die impenitent, and shut out of heaven all sin; shut out of heaven all temptation, all trouble, and all pain and death; shut out of heaven all the temptations of the devil, and not even the howlings of that dog of hell shall be heard across the jasper walls of that New Jerusalem.

A key is used to shut and to open, and so it is used to shut in, in reference to hell, those spirits who are immured there. "Between us and you," said Abraham to Dives, "there is a great gulf fixed: so that they that which would pass hence to you cannot; neither can they pass to us, that would come from thence." It is Christ's key that hath shut in the lost spirits, so that they cannot roam by way of respite, nor escape by way of pardon. May you never be so shut in. Christ hath the key by which he shutteth in Satan. He is to be bound for a thousand years, but Jesus shall hold the chain, for only our Immanuel could bind this old dragon. When temptation is kept away from a Christian it is the Saviour's restraining power which holdeth back the arch enemy; and if the enemy cometh in like a flood it is by permission of Jesus that the trial comes. Every roaming of the lion of the pit is permitted by our Master, or he could never go forth on his devouring errands. The key that shall bind the old dragon in those blessed days of the millennial rest, is in our Lord's power, and the final triumph, when no sin shall any further be known on earth, and evil shall be pent up in the grim caverns of hell, will be achieved by Christ Jesus, the Man, the Mediator, our Lord and God. To open, then, and to shut out, to shut in and to shut out, these are the work of the keys.

By the keys we must further understand here that our Lord *rules*, for the key is the Oriental metaphor for government. He shall have the key of David: "the government shall be upon his shoulder." We understand by Christ's having the keys of hell that he rules over all that are in hell; hence *he rules over the damned spirits*. They would not in this life have this Man to rule over them, but in the life to come they must submit whether they will or not. In that seething caldron every wave of fire is guided by the will of the Man Christ, and the mark of his sovereignty is on every iron chain. This the ungodly will be compelled to feel with terror, for although the ferocity of their natures will remain, yet the boastfulness of their pride shall be taken from them. Though they would still revolt, they shall find themselves hopelessly fettered, and powerless to accomplish their designs. Though they would fain continue stouthearted as Pharaoh, and cry, "Who is the Lord, that we should obey his voice?" they shall find their loins loosed like Belshazzar's on that dreadful night when his city was destroyed; they shall wring their hands in anguish and bite their tongues in despair. One of the great terrors of the lost in hell will be this, that he who came to save was rejected by them, and now only reveals himself to them as mighty to destroy. He who held out the silver sceptre when they would not touch it, shall for ever break them with a rod of iron for their wilful impenitence. Ye despisers, behold and wonder! If ye will not honour the Lord willingly, ye shall submit by force of arms. What must be the consternation of those that were loudest against Christ on earth, the men who denied his deity, the infidels who vented curses upon his blessed name—your Voltaires and Tom Paines, who were never satisfied except when they uttered bitter words against the Man of Nazareth? What will be their amazement! What confusion to the wretch who said he would crush the wretch, to find himself crushed by him whom he despised! What consternation and confusion shall overwhelm that man who said he lived in the twilight of Christianity, to find himself where the blaze of Christ's glory shall for ever be as a furnace to his guilty soul! O that none of us may know what it is to be ruled in justice by Christ because we would not be ruled by mercy. "Kiss the Son, lest he be angry, and ye perish from the way, when his wrath is kindled but a little. Blessed are all they that put their trust in him." But beware, ye that forget him, lest he tear you in pieces and there be none to deliver.

As in hell Christ has power over all the damned spirits, so our text implies that he has power over all *the devils*. It was wilfulness, doubtless, that made Satan revolt against God. Peradventure, Milton's poetic surmise is not far from the truth, and Satan did think it "better to rule in hell than serve in heaven;" but, fool that he was, he has to serve in hell with a service ten thousand times more irksome than that which would have been his lot in heaven. There, firstborn Son of the Morning, brightest of the angels of God, how happy might have been his perpetual service of the Most High; but now blighted by the scathing thunderbolts of Jehovah, he crawls forth from his den degraded, going like the serpent on his belly, with dust to be his meat, debased beneath the very beasts of the field, and cursed above all cattle, going forth for meanest ends, seeking to tempt others that they may come into the same loathsome condition with himself. Yet, mark how even in those temptations of his, Satan is ruled by Christ! He permits the foul fiend to tempt, but there is always a "Hitherto shalt thou go, and no further," just as Satan was permitted to try Job up to a certain point, but beyond that point he must not heap up the patriarch's agony; thus in all cases Christ rules Satan by restraining him. Yea, and even in that which he is permitted to do, God strengtheneth his servants so that Satan gets no honour in the contest, but retires continually more and more disgraced by being defeated by the poor sons of Adam. Cunning spirit as he is, he is worsted in the conflict with poor creatures who dwell in flesh. Ay, and better still, out of all the temptations of Satan, God's people are made to derive profit and strength. In our exercises and conflicts, we are taught our weakness and led to fly to Christ for strength; and so, as Samson's slain lion yielded him honey, out of the eater cometh forth meat, and out of the strong cometh forth sweetness. An abject slave of Christ art thou, O Satan; a very scullion in the kitchen of providence. When thou thinkest most to effect thine own purposes, and to overthrow the Kingdom of Christ on earth, even then what art thou but a mere hack, accomplishing still the purposes of thy Master, whom in vain thou dost blaspheme! Lo, at Christ's girdle are the keys of hell. Let the whole legion of accursed spirits tremble.

Brethren, I have said that the word "Hades" here may include both hell and heaven, or the whole state of separated spirits. Hence we are bound to remark, that our Saviour rules over all *the glorified spirits in heaven*, and all the angels that are their associates and ministering spirits. Is not this a delightful reflection, that the Redeemer is the King of angels, for in times of danger he can send an angel to strengthen us, or, if needs be, twenty legions of angels would soon find their way to stand side by side with the weak but faithful warrior of the cross. O believer, thou canst never be cast where divine succours cannot reach thee. Angels see their way by night, and journey over mount and sea with unwearied flight, unimpeded by wind or tempest. They can meet thine enemy, the prince of the power of the air, and overcome him for thee; as doubtless oftentimes they do unknown to us, in mysterious battles of the spirits. Thou shalt never be left to perish, while the chariots of God which are twenty thousand, even thousands of angels, are all at the beck and command of him who has redeemed thee with his precious blood.

Joyous is the thought that Jesus rules over all redeemed spirits in heaven, for we hope to be there soon, and this shall be among our dearest joys that, without temptation, without infirmity, without weariness, we shall serve our Lord day and night in his temple. My brethren, of all the joys of heaven, next to that of being with Christ, one delights to think of serving Christ. Ah! how rapturous will be our song! How zealously we will praise him! How earnest shall be our service! If he should give us commissions to distant worlds, as perhaps he will; if he shall prepare us to become preachers of his truth to creatures in unknown orbs; if he shall call us through revolving ages to publish to new created myriads the wondrous grace of God in Christ, with what ardent pleasure will we accept the service! How constantly, how heartily will we tell out the story of our salvation by the precious blood of Jesus! O that we could serve him here as we wish; but we shall serve him there without fault or flaw. Oh, happy heaven, because Jesus hath the key of it, and reigns supreme, when shall we stand upon thy sea of glass before his throne?

One more remark is wanted to complete the explanation of the power of the keys. Our Lord is said to have the keys of death, from which we gather that *all the issues of death* are at his alone disposal. No man can die unless as Jesus opens the mystic door of death. Even the ungodly man owes his spared life to Christ. It is the intercession and the interposition of Jesus that keeps breath even in the swearer's nostrils. Long since hadst thou been consumed in the fire of God's wrath, O sinner, had not Jesus used his authority to keep thee out of the jaws of death. As for his saints, it is their consolation that their death is entirely in his hands. In the midst of fever and pestilence, we shall never die until he wills it; in the times of the greatest healthiness, when all the air is balm, we shall not live a second longer than Jesus has purposed; the place, the circumstance, the exact second of our departure, have all been appointed by him, and settled long ago in love and wisdom. A thousand angels would not hurl us to the grave, nor could a host of cherubim confine us there one moment after Jesus said, "Arise." This is our comfort. We are "immortal till our work is done;" mortal still, but immortal also. Let us never fear death, then, but rather rejoice at the approach of it, since it comes at our dear Bridegroom's bidding. There be some who count it a most notable expectation, that perhaps they may be among the number of those who shall not sleep, but be alive and remain at the Lord's coming. I am sure I would not disturb any joy which they can derive from such a contemplation. For my own part, if I had the choice, I would prefer to die, for it seems to me that such as do not die, while they cannot have any preference over them that fall asleep (for we are told they shall not prevent them that are asleep) will lose much of desirable experience. They will never be able to say in heaven, "I was made like unto my dying Saviour;" they can never say that they have slept in the grave as he did; they can never say, "My body came forth in the resurrection as his did." I would fain be in all points made like unto my Lord, to have fellowship with him in all respects. "To die," saith the apostle, "is gain." I will add, a gain I would not lose, and "Death is yours," saith the apostle, nor would we have it rent away from us; though the prospect of our Lord's coming is sweet, immeasurably sweet, yet the prospect of going to him meanwhile if so he wills it, is not without its sweetness too. Christ hath the key of death, and therefore death to us is no longer a gate of terror.

Thus have I, as best I could, while suffering much bodily pain, laboured to open up to you what is the power of the keys in the Redeemer's hands.

II. What is THE KEY OF THIS POWER? Whence did Christ obtain this right to have the keys of hell and death? Doth he not derive it first of all from *his Godhead?*

In the eighteenth verse, he saith, "I am he that liveth," language which only God can use, for while we live, yet it is only with a borrowed life, like the moon that shineth with a borrowed light, and as the moon cannot say, "I am the orb that shineth," neither can man say, "I am he that liveth." God saith, "I am, and there is none beside me," and Jesus being God, claimeth the same self-existence. "I am he that liveth." Now, since Christ is God, he certainly hath power over heaven, and earth, and hell. There can be no dispute concerning the divine prerogative. He is the creator of all things; he is the preserver of all things; all power belongeth unto him. As for all things that are apart from him, they would vanish as a puff of air is gone, if so he willed it: he alone existeth; he alone is; therefore let him wear the crown, let him have undivided rule. That doctrine of the deity of Christ, how I tremble for those who will not receive it! Brethren, if there be anything in the word of God that is clear and plain, it is surely this; if there be any doctrine that is necessary for our salvation, it is this. How could we trust to a mere man? If there be anything that can give us comfort when we come to rest upon Christ, it is just this, that we are not looking to an angel nor depending upon a creature, but are resting upon him who is Alpha and Omega, the beginning and the end, the Almighty God. O you who dare trust in a man, I pity you for your credulity; but you who cannot trust in Jesus, the living God, I may well blame you for your unbelief. Having such a rock of our salvation as the ever-living and ever-blessed God, let the thought kindle in our souls the purest joy.

But the key to this power lies also in our Saviour's *conquests.* He hath the keys of death and hell because he hath actually conquered both these powers. You know how he met hell in the dreadful onset in the garden; how all the powers of darkness there combined against him. Such was the agony of that struggle, that he sweat great drops of blood falling to the ground; yet he sustained the brunt of that onset without wavering, and kept the field unbeaten. He continued still to wrestle with those evil powers upon the cross, and in that thick midday

midnight into which no curious eyes could pry, in the midst of that
darkness he continued still to fight, his heel bruised, but breaking
meanwhile the dragon's head. Grim was the contest, but glorious was
the victory, worthy to be sung by angels in eternal chorus. Take down
your sweetest harps ye seraphs, lift up your loudest notes ye cherubim,
unto him that fought the dragon and overcame him, to Michael the great
archangel of the covenant, unto him be glory for ever and ever. Well
doth Jesus deserve to rule the provinces which he hath subdued in
fight. He has conquered the king of hell and destroyed the works of
the devil, and good right hath he to be King over the domain of the
vanquished.

As to death, ye know how our Lord vanquished him! By death he
conquered death. When the hands were nailed, they became potent to
fight with the grave; when the feet were fastened to the wood, then
began they to trample on the sepulchre; when the death pangs began
to thrill through every nerve of the Redeemer's body, then his arrows
shot through the loins of death, and when his anguished soul was ready
to take its speedy flight, and leave his blessed corpse, then did the
tyrant sustain a mortal wound. Our Lord's entrance into the tomb was
the taking possession of his enemies' stronghold; his sleep within the
sepulchre's stony walls was the transformation of the prison into a couch
of rest. But especially in the resurrection; when, because he could
not be held by the bonds of death, neither could his soul be kept in
Hades, he rose again in glory, then did he become the "death of death
and hell's destruction," and rightfully was he acknowledged the plague
of death and the destruction of the grave. As if to prove that he had
the keys of the grave, Jesus passed in and passed out again, and he
hath made free passage now for his people, free entrance, and free exit.
Whether, when our Lord died, his soul actually descended into hell
itself we will not assert or deny; the elder theologians all asserted that
he did, and hence they inserted in the Creed, the sentence, "He
descended into hell," meaning, many of them, at any rate, hell itself.
It was not till Puritanic times that that doctrine began to be generally
questioned, when it was, as I think rightly asserted, that Jesus Christ
went into the world of separated spirits, but not into the region of the
damned. Well, it is not for us to speak where Scripture is silent, but
why may it not be true that the Great Conqueror cast the shadow of
his presence over the dens of his enemies as he passed in triumph by the
gates of hell? May not the keepers of that infernal gate have seen his
star, and trembled as they also beheld their Master like lightning fall
from heaven? Would it not add to his glory if those who were his
implacable foes were made to know of his complete triumph? At any
rate, it was but a passing presence, for we know that swiftly he sped to
the gates of heaven, taking with him the repentant thief to be with him

that day in Paradise. Jesus had opened thus the grave by going into it, hell by passing by it, heaven by passing into it, heaven again by passing out of it, death again by rising from it into this world, and heaven by his ascension. Thus passing, and repassing, he has proved that the keys are at his girdle. At any rate, by his achievements, by his doings, he hath won for himself the power of the keys.

We have one more truth to remember, that Jesus Christ is installed in this high place of power and dignity by the Father himself, as *a reward for what he has done.* He was himself to "divide the spoil with the strong," but the Father had promised to give him a "portion with the great." See the reward for the shame which he endured among the sons of men! He stooped lower than the lowest, he has risen higher than the highest; he wore the crown of thorns, but now he wears the triple crown of heaven, and earth, and hell: he was the servant of servants, but now he is King of kings, and Lord of lords. Earth would not find him shelter, a stable must be the place of his birth, and a borrowed tomb the sepulchre of his dead body; but now, all space is his, time and eternity tremble at his bidding, and there is no creature, however minute or vast, that is not subject to him. How greatly hath the Father glorified him whom men rejected and despised! Let us adore him; let our hearts, while we think over these plain but precious truths, come and spread their riches at his feet, and crown him Lord of all.

III. THE PRACTICAL BEARING of the whole subject appears to be this—according to the seventeenth verse—"*Fear not.*"

This manifestation of Christ, as having the keys of death and hell, was given to the trembling John, who had fallen down with astonishment and dread as one dead, to comfort him, and as if to make this clear the words were spoken, "Fear not." Beloved, those words I would address to you this morning, "Fear not." Why need you fear? There is no possible cause for fear for believers, since Jesus lives. "But I may be very poor," saith one.

> "Since Christ is rich, can you be poor?
> What can you want beside?"

"But I may be very sick," saith another. "I will make all their bed in their sickness," saith the Lord; and since Christ is with you, sickness shall work your soul's health. "Ah," saith another, "I may be grievously tempted." But while he liveth, he will pray for you that your faith fail not, though Satan hath desired to have you. Yes, but you yourselves are very frail, you say, and you fear that in some dark hour that frailty may overcome your faith. Yes, but he ever liveth, and you are one with him, and who shall destroy you while the vital energy pours from your covenant Head into you as a member of his body?

I say again, there is no possible cause for fear to any soul that believeth in Christ. You shall ransack the corruptions of your heart within; you shall count your trials without; you shall imagine all the tribulations that shall come to-morrow; you shall reflect on all the sins that were with you yesterday and in the past; you shall peer into the shades of death and horrors of hell, but I declare solemnly to you that there is nothing in any of these which you, believing in Christ, have any cause to fear. Nay, if they all should unite, if the whole together, the world, the flesh, the devil, in trinity of malice should all come against you, while you have a living faith in a living Saviour, "Fear not" is but the logical inference from that precious fact. Carry this fearlessness in your life, and be happy as a king. Oh, with nothing else but a living Saviour, how rich ought a saint to be! and with everything else, but missing that living Saviour, how miserable the richest and the greatest of men always would be, if they did but know their true state as before the Lord!

Now, observe, that this "Fear not" may be specially applied to the matter of the grave. We need not fear to die, because Jesus has the key of the grave; we shall never pass through that iron gate with an angel to be our conductor, or some grim executioner to lead us, as it were, through the Traitor's Gate, or into a dreary place of hideous imprisonment. No, Jesus shall come to our dying bed, in all the glory of his supernal splendour, and shall say, "Come with me, from Lebanon, my spouse, with me from Lebanon : look from the top of Amana; for the day breaketh, and the shadows flee away." The sight of Jesus, as he thrusts in the key and opens that gate of death, shall make you forget the supposed terrors of the grave, for they are but suppositions, and you shall find it sweet to die. Since Jesus hath the sepulchre's key, never fear it again, never fear it again. Depend upon it, your dying hour will be the best hour you have ever known; your last will be your richest moment, better than the day of your birth will be the day of your death. It shall be the beginning of heaven, the rising of a sun that shall go no more down for ever. Let the fear of death be banished from you by faith in a living Saviour.

Some saints have a fear of the world of spirits. "Oh," say they, "it must be a dreadful thing to enter that unknown land. We have stood and peered as best we could through the mist that gathers over the black river, and have wondered what it must be like to have left the body, and to be flitting, a naked soul, through that land from which no traveller hath e'er returned." Ah! but, perhaps, you imagined that you were sailing into an enemy's country, but Jesus is King in Hades, as well as Lord of earth. It is not as though you crossed the channel from England into France, and were among a people speaking nother language, and owning another sovereignty. It is but as passing the Tweed from England to Scotland, you do but pass from one province of your Lord's empire into another, and indeed from a darker into a brighter territory of the same one sovereign. In that spiritland they speak the same tongue, the tongue of the New Jerusalem, which you have already begun to lisp; they own the King whom you here obey; and when you shall enter into the assemblies of those disembodied spirits you shall find them all singing to the praise of the same glorious One whom you have adored to-day, rejoicing in the light which was your light on earth, and triumphing in his love which was your Saviour here below. Be of good courage, Jesus is King of Hades. Fear not.

Neither, brethren, ought we to fear the devil. We ought to be watchful against him, but we must not fear him so that he may get an advantage from our fear. "Resist the devil, and he will flee from you;" stand trembling and he will attack you worse than ever. The boldness of courageous faith is that which makes the devil tremble. Well may you be brave, for when he comes howling at you like a lion, you may taunt him thus, and say, "Ah, show thy teeth and howl, and yell, but thou art chained; thou canst do no more than threaten me. Thou thinkest to worry me, but thou canst not devour me, and therefore I defy thee. Avaunt, in the name of Jesus Christ who bruised thee, dragon of hell, avaunt!" The courage that shall enable thee thus to deal with the enemy while it gives glory to thy Lord and Master, shall give rapid victory unto thee. He is a chained enemy; this leviathan hath a bit between his jaws and a hook in his nose. He may vex thee for awhile, but thou shalt be "more than conqueror through him that loved thee;" therefore fear not. That is the lesson from the text to the child of God.

One other word to the believer of God. Should not this contemplation make us say, "Let us worship him who hath the keys of hell and death: let us come into his presence with thanksgiving, and show ourselves glad in him with songs"? Preaching is not the great end of the Sabbath-day; listening to sermons is not the great aim of Sundays. It is a means; what is the end? Why, the end, so far as we can attain it on earth, is for us to glorify God in service, and especially in the singing of his praises. Worship rendered to God in prayer and praise is the true fruit of the Sabbath, and I am afraid we are behind in this. I wish that when believers come together they would oftener render unto Christ the coronals of their hymns, to crown him Lord of all. His enemies miss no opportunity to spite him; those that hate his gospel are zealous to bring shame upon it. Oh, miss no opportunities to extol him with your praises, and to honour him with the holiness of your lives and the zeal of your service. Is he King over heaven, and death, and hell? Then shall he be King over the triple territory of my spirit, soul, and body; and I will make all my powers and passions yield him praise.

To conclude. If to the righteous the lesson from all this is, "Fear not," methinks the lesson to the ungodly is, "Fear and tremble." Christ hath the keys of death. Then you may die this moment: you may die ere you reach your homes. You have not the key of death, you cannot therefore prolong your life; but Christ hath it, and he can end the times of his longsuffering just when he so wills it. And what would it be to some of you if the gate of death were opened for you, and you were driven through it like dumb driven cattle this very day? O man, what would become of thee, O woman what would become of thee, if now those eyes should glaze, and that pulse should stop? I beseech thee consider thy ways, and turn thee unto God, lest thou die and perish on a sudden. Remember, soul, that if thou wouldst fight it out with Christ, and be his enemy, yet thou canst not, for he is Lord, and will be Lord. Even shouldst thou fly to hell to escape him, he ruleth there. "If I make my bed in hell thou art there." "Oh," said one who had gone into the backwoods of America far away, and there met a preacher, "I thought I had escaped these Methodists, and here comes a parson worrying me even here." "Yes," said the other, "if you went to heaven you would find religion there, and if you go to hell you will, I am afraid, find preachers even there."

If religion thus follows a man, how much more does the power of God surround him! You cannot escape from the Lord of all true preachers, if you can escape from them. Wherever you may go, there shall the remembrances of his rejected love pierce you like barbed arrows. Even in hell shall the glory of his power, which you could not thrust down though you tried to do it, strike you with a deeper despair. I implore you to listen to his gospel. He that believeth and is baptised, shall be saved. This is the message he gave us when he was taken up, almost the last word he spake ere he rose into his glory. "Go ye, therefore, and teach all nations, baptising them in the name of the Father, and of the Son, and of the Holy Ghost." O then, yield to his gospel: believe, that is, trust implicitly in him who died on the cross of Calvary to make atonement, and now liveth to make intercession. Trust in him, and then come forth and confess your trust: be baptised in his name, confessing your sins, and acknowledging yourself to be his disciple. This is the gospel: reject it at your peril. Submit to it, I beseech you, for Christ's sake.

Jesus Christ Himself

"Jesus Christ himself"—Ephesians ii. 20.

"JESUS CHRIST himself" is to occupy all our thoughts this morning. What an ocean opens up before me! Here is sea-room for the largest barque! In which direction shall I turn your thoughts? I am embarrassed with riches. I know not where to begin: and when I once begin where shall I end? Assuredly we need not go abroad for joys this morning, for we have a feast at home. The words are few, but the meaning vast—"Jesus Christ himself."

Beloved, the religion of our Lord Jesus Christ contains in it nothing so wonderful as himself. It is a mass of *marvels*, but he is THE miracle of it; the wonder of wonders is "The Wonderful" himself. If *proof* be asked of the truth which he proclaimed, we point men to Jesus Christ himself. His character is unique. We defy unbelievers to imagine another like him. He is God and yet man, and we challenge them to compose a narrative in which the two apparently incongruous characters shall be so harmoniously blended,—in which the human and divine shall be so marvellously apparent, without the one overshading the other. They question the authenticity of the four Gospels; will they try and write a fifth? Will they even attempt to add a few incidents to the life which shall be worthy of the sacred biography, and congruous with those facts which are already described? If it be all a forgery, will they be so good as to show us how it is done? Will they find a novelist who will write another biography of a man of any century they choose, of any nationality, or of any degree of experience, or any rank or station, and let us see if they can describe in that imaginary life a devotion, a self-sacrifice, a truthfulness, a completeness of character at all comparable to that of Jesus Christ himself? Can they invent another perfect character even if the divine element be left out? They must of necessity fail, for there is none like unto Jesus himself.

The character of Jesus has commanded respect even from those who have abhorred his teaching. It has been a stumbling-stone to all objectors who have preserved a shade of candour. Jesus' doctrine they could refute, they say; his precepts they could improve, so they boast; his system is narrow and outworn, so they assert : but himself—what can they do with him ? They must admire him even if they will not adore him; and having done so they have admired a personage who must be divine, or else he wilfully left his disciples to believe a lie. How will they surmount this difficulty? They cannot do so by railing at him, for they have no material for accusation. Jesus Christ himself silences their cavillings. This is a file at which these asps do bite, but break their teeth. Beyond all argument or miracle, Jesus Christ himself is the proof of his own gospel.

And as he is the proof of it, so, beloved, he is the *marrow* and essence of it. When the apostle Paul meant that the gospel was preached he said, " Christ is preached," for the gospel is Christ himself. If you want to know what Jesus taught, know himself. He is the incarnation of that truth which by him and in him is revealed to the sons of men. Did he not himself say, " I am the way, the truth, and the life"? You have not to take down innumerable tomes, nor to pore over mysterious sentences of double meaning in order to know what our great teacher has revealed, you have but to turn and gaze upon his countenance, behold his actions, and note his spirit, and you know his teaching. He lived what he taught. If we wish to know him, we may hear his gentle voice saying " Come and see." Study his wounds, and you understand his innermost philosophy. " To know him and the power of his resurrection " is the highest degree of spiritual learning. He is the end of the law and the soul of the gospel, and when we have preached his word to the full, we may close by saying, " Now, of the things which we have spoken this is the sum,—we have an high priest who is set on the right hand of the throne of the majesty in the heavens."

Nor is he alone the proof of his gospel and the substance of it, but he is the *power* and force by which it spreads. When a heart is truly broken for sin, it is by him that it is bound up. If a man is converted, it is by Christ, the power of God. If we enter into peace and salvation it is by the gracious manifestation of Jesus himself. If men have enthusiastically loved Christianity, it is because first of all they loved Christ : for him apostles laboured, and for him confessors were brave ; for him saints have suffered the loss of all things, and for him martyrs have died. The power which creates heroic consecration is " Jesus Christ himself." The memories stirred by his name have more influence over men's hearts than all things else in earth or heaven. The enthusiasm which is the very life of our holy cause comes from himself. They who know not Jesus know not the life of truth, but those who dwell in him are filled with power, and overflow so that out of the midst of them streams forth living water. Nor is it only so, beloved; for the power which propagates the gospel is Jesus himself. In heaven he pleads, and therefore does his kingdom come. " The pleasure of the Lord shall prosper in his hand." It is from heaven that he rules all things so as to promote the advance of the truth. All power is given unto him in heaven and in earth, and therefore are we to proclaim his life-giving word with full assurance of success. He causes the wheel of providence to revolve in such a manner as to help his cause; he abridges the power of tyrants, overrules the scourge of war, establishes liberty in nations, opens the mysteries of continents long unknown, breaks down systems of error, and guides the current of human thought. He works by a thousand means, preparing the way of the Lord. It is from heaven that he shall shortly come, and when he cometh, when Christ himself shall put forth all his might, then shall the wilderness rejoice and the solitary place be glad. The reserve force of the gospel is Christ Jesus himself. The latent power which shall at last break every bond, and win universal dominion, is the energy, the life, the omnipotence of Jesus himself. He sleeps in the vessel now, but when he arises and chides the storm there will be a deep calm. He now for awhile concealeth himself in the ivory palaces of glory, but when he is manifested in *that day* his chariot wheels shall bring victory to his church militant.

If these things be so, I have a theme before me which I cannot compass. I forbear the impossible task, and I shall but briefly note some few apparent matters which lie upon the surface of the subject.

Brethren, "Jesus Christ himself" should always be the prominent thought of our minds as Christians. Our theology should be framed upon the fact that he is the Centre and Head of all. We must remember that "in him are hid all the treasures of wisdom and knowledge." Some of our brethren are mainly taken up with the doctrines of the gospel, and are somewhat bitter in their narrow orthodoxy. We are to love every word of our Lord Jesus and his apostles, and are to contend earnestly for the faith once delivered unto the saints, but yet it is well always to hold truth in connection with Jesus and not as in itself alone the sum of all things. Truth isolated from the person of Jesus grows hard and cold. We know some in whom the slightest variation from their system arouses their indignation, even though they admit that the brother is full of the Spirit of Christ. It is with them doctrine, doctrine, doctrine: with us, I trust, it is Christ himself. True doctrine is to us priceless as a throne for our living Lord, but our chief delight is not in the vacant throne, but in the King's presence thereon. Give me not his garments, though I prize every thread, but the blessed wearer whose sacred energy made even the hem thereof to heal with a touch.

There are others of our brethren who delight above measure in what they call experimental preaching, which sets forth the inner life of the believer, both the rage of depravity and the triumph of grace: this is well in due proportion, according to the analogy of faith: but still Jesus himself should be more conspicuous than our frames and feelings, doubts and fears, struggles and victories. We may get to study the action of our own hearts so much that we fall into despondency and despair. "Looking unto Jesus" is better than looking unto our own progress: self-examination has its necessary uses, but to have done with self and live by faith in Jesus Christ himself is the best course for a Christian.

Then, there are others who rightly admire the precepts of the gospel, and are never so happy as when they are hearing them enforced, as, indeed, they ought to be; but after all the commands of our Lord are not our Lord himself, and they derive their value to us and their power over our obedience from the fact that they are *his* words, and that he said, "If ye love me, keep my commandments." We know the truth of his declaration, "If a man love me he will keep my sayings," but there must be the personal love to begin with. Brethren, all the benefits of these three schools will be ours if we live upon Jesus himself. They gather each a flower, but our divine "plant of renown" has all the beauty, and all the fragrance, of all that they can gather; and without the thorns which are so apt to grow on their peculiar roses. Jesus Christ himself is to us precept, for he is the way: he is to us doctrine, for he is the truth: he is to us experience, for he is the life. Let us make him the pole star of our religious life in all things. Let him be first, last, and midst; yea, let us say, "He is all my salvation and all my desire." And yet do not, I beseech you, disdain the doctrine, lest in marring the doctrine you should be guilty of insult to Jesus himself. To trifle with truth is to despise Jesus as our Prophet. Do not for a moment underrate experience, lest in neglecting the inner self you also despise your Lord himself as your cleansing Priest; and never for a moment forget his commandments lest if ye break them ye transgress against Jesus himself as your King. All things which touch upon his kingdom are to be treated reverently by us for the sake of himself: his book, his day, his church, his ordinances, must all be precious to us, because they have to do with him; but in the front of all must ever stand " Jesus Christ himself," the personal, living, loving Jesus; Christ in us the hope of glory, Christ for us our full redemption, Christ with us our guide and our solace, and Christ above us pleading and preparing our place in heaven. Jesus Christ himself is our captain, our armour, our strength, and our victory. We inscribe his name upon our banner, for it is hell's terror, heaven's delight, and earth's hope. We bear this upon our hearts in the heat of the conflict, for this is our breastplate and coat of mail.

I shall not endeavour to say anything this morning which will strike you as beautiful in language, for to endeavour to decorate the altogether Lovely One would be blasphemy. To hang flowers upon the cross is ridiculous, and to endeavour to adorn him whose head is as the most fine gold, and whose person is as bright ivory overlaid with sapphires, would be profane. I shall but tell you simple things in simple language: yet are these the most precious and soul-satisfying of the truths of revelation.

I. With Jesus Christ himself we begin by saying, first, that Jesus himself is THE ESSENCE OF HIS OWN WORK, and therefore *how readily we ought to trust him.* Jesus himself is the soul of his own salvation. How does the apostle describe it? "He loved me, and gave *himself* for me." He gave his crown, his throne, and his joys in heaven for us, but that was not all—he gave himself. He gave his life on earth, and renounced all the comforts of existence, and bore all its woes; he gave his body, he gave his agony, he gave his heart's blood: but the summary of it is, he gave himself for me. "Christ loved the church and gave himself for it." "Who his own self bare our sins in his own body on the tree." No proxy service here! No sacrifice which runs as far as his own person and there stops! There was no limit to the grief of Jesus like that set upon the suffering of Job,—"Only on himself lay not thine hand," or "Only spare his life." No, every reserve was taken down, for he gave himself. "He saved others; himself he could not save," because he himself was the very essence of his own sacrifice on our behalf. It is because he is what he is that he was able to redeem us: the dignity of his person imparted efficacy to his atonement. He is divine, God over all, blessed for ever, and therefore infinite virtue is found in him; he is human, and perfect in that humanity, and therefore capable of obedience and suffering in man's place and stead. He is able to save us because he is Immanuel—"God with us." If it were conceivable that an angel could have suffered the same agonies, and have performed the same labours, as our Lord, yet it is not conceivable that the same result would have followed. The pre-eminence of his person imparted weight to his work. Always think then when you view the atonement, that it is Jesus himself who is the soul of it. Indeed the efficacy of his sacrifice lies there; hence the apostle in the Hebrews speaks of him as having "by himself purged our sins." This purging was wrought by his sacrifice, but the sacrifice was himself. Paul says, "he offered up himself." He stood as a priest at the altar offering a bloody sacrifice, but the offering was neither bullock, nor ram, nor turtle dove; it was himself. "Once in the end of the world hath he appeared to put away sin by the sacrifice of himself." The sole reason why we are well-pleasing with God is because of him, for he is our sweet savour-offering; and the only cause for the putting away of our sin is found in him because he is our sin-offering. The cleansing by the blood, and the washing by the water, are the result, not of the blood and the water in and of themselves and separate from him, but because they were the essentials of himself. You see this, I am persuaded, without my enlarging upon it.

Now, because of this, *the Lord Jesus Christ himself is the object of our faith.* Is he not always so described in Scripture? "Look unto *me*, and be ye saved, all ye ends of the earth,"—not "look to my cross," nor "look to my life," nor "to my death," much less "to my sacraments or to my servants," but "look unto *me*." From his own lips the words sound forth, "Come *unto me* all ye that labour and are heavy laden, and I will give you rest." In fact, it is the Christian's life motto, "Looking unto Jesus, the author and finisher of our faith." May I not go further and say, *how very simple and how very easy and natural ought faith to be henceforth?* I might be puzzled with various theories of the atonement, but I can believe in Jesus himself: I might be staggered by the divers mysteries which concern theology, and overpower even masterminds, but I can confide in Jesus himself. He is one whom it is difficult to distrust: his goodness, gentleness, and truth command our confidence. We can and do trust in Jesus himself. If he be proposed to me as my Saviour, and if faith in him be that which saves me, then at his dear feet I cast myself unreservedly, and feel myself secure while he looks down on me. He who bled that sinners might be saved cannot be doubted any more: "Lord, I believe; help thou mine unbelief." Now you who have been looking to your faith, I want you to look to Jesus himself rather than at your poor feeble faith. Now you who have been studying the results of faith in yourselves and are dissatisfied, I beseech you turn your eyes away from yourselves and look to Jesus himself. Now you who cannot understand this and cannot understand that, give up wanting to understand for the while, and come and look at Jesus Christ himself, "that the God of our Lord Jesus Christ, the Father of glory, may give unto you the spirit of wisdom and revelation in the knowledge of him." The Lord grant us grace to view Jesus Christ himself in the matter of our salvation as all in all, so that we may have personal dealings with him, and no more think of him as a mere idea, or as an historical personage, but as a personal Saviour standing in the midst of us, and bidding us enter into peace through him.

II. "Jesus Christ himself" is as we have said THE SUBSTANCE OF THE GOSPEL, *and therefore how closely should we study him.* While he was here he taught his disciples, and *the object of his teaching was that they might know himself,* and through him might know the Father. They did not learn very fast, but you see what he meant them to learn by the observation he made to Philip, "Have I been so long time with you, and yet hast thou not known *me,* Philip ?" He meant them to know himself; and when he had risen from the dead the same object was still before him. As he walked with the two disciples to Emmaus they had wide choice of subjects for conversation, but he chose the old theme, and "beginning at Moses and all the prophets, he expounded unto them in all the Scriptures the things concerning himself." No topic was one half so important or profitable. No mere man may come to teach himself, but this divine One can have nothing better to reveal, for he himself, the incarnate God, is the chief of all truth. Hence our Lord was concerned to be known to his people, and therefore again and again we read that "Jesus showed himself unto his disciples." Whatever else they may be ignorant of, it is essential to disciples that they know their Lord. His nature, his character, his mind, his spirit, his object, his power, we must know—in a word, we must know Jesus himself.

This also, beloved, is the work of the Holy Spirit. "He shall glorify me : for he shall receive of mine, and shall shew it unto you." The Holy Ghost reveals Christ to us and in us. Whatsoever things Christ hath spoken while he was here, the Holy Ghost opens to the mind and to the understanding, and thus by speaking of Christ within us he carries on the work which our Lord began when here below. The Comforter is the instructor and Jesus is the lesson. I dare say you long to know a thousand things, but the main point of knowledge to be desired is Jesus himself. This was his teaching, and this is the Holy Spirit's teaching, and *this is the end and object of the Bible.* Moses, Esaias, and all the prophets spake of him, and the things which are recorded in this book were written that ye might believe that Jesus is the Christ, and that believing ye might have life through his name. Precious is this book, but its main preciousness lies in its revealing Jesus himself, it is the field which contains the pearl of great price, the casket which encloses heaven's brightest jewel. We have missed our way in the Bible if its silken clue has not led us to the central chamber where we see Jesus himself. We have never been truly taught of the Holy Ghost, and we have missed the teaching of the life of Christ, unless we have come to abide in Jesus himself. To know him is our beginning of wisdom and our crown of wisdom. To know him is our first lesson on the stool of penitence and our last attainment as we enter heaven. Our ambition is that we may know the love of Christ which passeth knowledge. Here is our life study, and we have good associates in it, for these things the angels desire to look into. May the Lord grant that the eyes of your understanding may be enlightened, that we may know what is the hope of his calling, and what the riches of the glory of his inheritance in the saints.

Beloved, because Jesus is the sum of the gospel *he must be our constant theme.* "God forbid that I should glory save in the cross of our Lord Jesus Christ." "I determined not to know anything among you save Jesus Christ and him crucified." So spake men of old, and so say we. When we have done preaching Christ we had better have done preaching; when you have done teaching in your classes Jesus Christ himself, give up Sunday school work, for nothing else is worthy of your pains. Put out the sun, and light is gone, life is gone, all is gone. When Jesus is pushed into the background or left out of a minister's teaching, the darkness is darkness that might be felt, and the people escape from it into gospel light as soon as they can. A sermon without Jesus in it is savourless, and worthless to God's tried saints, and they soon seek other food. The more of Christ in our testimony the more of light and life and power to save. Some preachers are guilty of the most wearisome tautology, but this is not laid to their charge when their theme is Jesus. I have heard hearers declare that their minister appeared to have bought a barrel organ on which he could grind five or six tunes and no more, and these he ground out for ever and ever, amen. They have been weary, very weary, of such vain repetitions; but to this day I never heard of anybody against whom the complaint was urged that he preached Christ too much, too often, too earnestly, or too joyfully. I never recollect seeing a single Christian man coming out of a congregation with a sorrowful face saying, "He extolled the Redeemer too highly: he grossly exaggerated the praises of our Saviour." I do not remember ever meeting with a case in which the sick upon the bed of languishing have complained that thoughts of Jesus were burdensome to them. I never recollect that a single book has been denounced by earnest Christian men because it spoke too highly of the Lord, and made him too prominent. No, my brethren, he who is the study of the saints must be the daily theme of ministers if they would feed the flock of God. No theme so moves the heart, so arouses the conscience, so satisfies the desires, and so calms the fears. God forbid we should ever fail to preach Jesus himself. There is no fear of exhausting the subject, nor of our driving away our hearers, for his words are still true, "I, if I be lifted up, will draw all men unto me."

III. Jesus Christ himself is THE OBJECT OF OUR LOVE, and *how dear he should be.* We can all of us who are really saved declare that "We love him because he first loved us." We have an intense affection for his blessed person as well gratitude for his salvation. The personality of Christ is a fact always to be kept prominently in our thoughts. The love of a truth is all very well, but the love of a person has far more power in it. We have heard of men dying for an idea, but it is infinitely more easy to awaken enthusiasm for a person. When an idea becomes embodied in a man it has a force which in its abstract form it never wielded. Jesus Christ is loved by us as the embodiment of everything that is lovely, and true, and pure, and of good report. He himself is incarnate perfection, inspired by love. We love his offices, we love the types which describe him, we love the ordinances by which he is set forth, but we love himself best of all. He himself is our beloved; our heart rests only in him.

Because we love him we love his people, and through him we enter into union with them. Our text is taken from a verse which says, "Jesus Christ himself being the chief corner stone." He is the binder at the corner, joining Jew and Gentile in one temple. In Jesus those ancient differences cease, for he "hath made both one, and hath broken down the middle wall of partition between us; to make in himself of twain one new man, so making peace." We are at one with every man who is at one with Christ. Only let our Lord say, "I love that man," and we love him at once; let us only hope that our friend can say, "I love Jesus," and we hasten to respond, "And I love you for Jesus' sake." So warm is the fire of our love to Jesus that all his friends may sit at it, and welcome. Our circle of affection comprehends all who in any shape or way have truly to do with Jesus himself.

Because we love himself we delight to render service to him. Whatever service we do for his church, and for his truth, we do for his sake, even if we can only render it to the least of his brethren we do it unto him. The woman with the alabaster box of precious ointment is a type which we greatly prize, for she would only break the precious box *for him,* and every drop of its delicious contents must be poured only upon his head. The bystanders complained of waste, but there can be no waste in anything that is done for Jesus. If the whole world, and the heavens, and the heaven of heavens were all one great alabaster box, and if all the sweets which can be conceived were hived within it, we would wish to see the whole broken, that every drop of the sweetness might be poured out for Jesus Christ himself.

> "Jesus is worthy to receive
> Honour and power divine;
> And blessings more than we can give,
> Be Lord, for ever thine."

Oh our Beloved, if we can do anything for thee, we are charmed at possessing such a privilege. If we are allowed to wash thy disciples' feet, or to care for the poorest of thy poor, or the least lamb of thy flock, we accept the office as a high honour, for we love thee with all our hearts. Our love to Jesus should be as much a matter of fact as our affection for our husband, wife, or child, and it should be far more influential upon our lives. Love to our Lord is, I trust, moving all of you to personal service. You might have paid a subscription and allowed others to work, but you cannot do it when you see that Jesus gave himself for you. Jesus himself demands that I myself should be consecrated to his praise. Personal service is due to a personal Christ, who personally loved and personally died for us. When nothing moves us to zeal, when the jaded spirit cannot follow up its industries, let but Jesus himself appear, and straightway our passions are all in a blaze, and the fiery spirit compels the flesh to warm to its work again. We even glory in infirmity when Jesus is near, and venture upon works which else had seemed impossible. We can do anything and everything for "Jesus Christ himself."

IV. Fourthly, our Lord Jesus Christ himself is THE SOURCE OF ALL

OUR JOY. *How ought we to rejoice when we have such a springing well of blessedness.* In times of sorrow our solace is Jesus himself. It is no small ground of comfort to a mourner that Jesus himself is a man. How cheering to read, " Forasmuch as the children are partakers of flesh and blood, he also himself took part of the same." The humanity of Christ has a charm about it which the quietly sorrowful alone discover. I have known what it is to gaze upon the incarnation with calm repose of heart when my brain has seemed to be on fire with anguish. If Jesus be indeed my brother man, there is hope at all times. This is better balm than that of Gilead, " Himself took our infirmities, and bare our sicknesses"; "For in that he himself hath suffered, being tempted, he is able also to succour them that are tempted." Pain, hunger, thirst, desertion, scorn, and agony Jesus himself has borne. Tempted in all points like as we are, though without sin, he has become the chief Comforter of the sorrowful. Many and many a sufferer in the lone watches of the night has thought of him and felt his strength renewed. Our patience revives when we see the Man of Sorrows silent before his accusers. Who can refuse to drink of his cup and to be baptized with his baptism?

"His way was much rougher and darker than mine :
Did Christ, my Lord, suffer, and shall I repine?"

The darkness of Gethsemane has been light to many an agonized soul, and the passion even unto death has made the dying sing for joy of heart. Jesus himself is the solace of our soul in sorrow, and when we emerge from the storm of distress into the deep calm of peace, as we often do, blessed be his name, he is our peace. Peace he left us by legacy, and peace he creates in person. We never know deep peace of heart until we know the Lord Jesus himself. You remember that sweet word when the disciples were met together, the doors being shut for fear of the Jews, " Jesus himself stood in the midst of them, and said, Peace be unto you." Jesus himself you see brought the message ; for nothing but his presence could make it effectual. When we see him our spirit smells a sweet savour of rest. Where can an aching head find such another pillow as his bosom?

On high days and holidays our spirits soar beyond rest : we ascend into the heaven of joy and exultation; but then it is our Lord's joy which is in us making our joy full. " Then were the disciples glad when they saw the Lord," and then are we glad also. By faith we see Jesus himself enthroned, and this has filled us with delight, for his glorification is our satisfaction. " Him also hath God highly exalted, and given him a name which is above every name." I care not what becomes of me so long as he is glorified. The soldier dies happy when the shout of victory salutes his ear, and his failing sight beholds his prince triumphant. What a joy to think that Jesus is risen—risen to die no more : the joy of resurrection is superlative. What bliss to know that he has ascended, leading captivity captive, that he sitteth now enthroned in happy state, and that he will come in all the glory of the Father to break his enemies in pieces as with a rod of iron. Here lies the grandest joy of his expectant church. She has in reserve a mighty thunder of hosannahs for that auspicious day.

If there is any joy to be had, O Christian, that is both safe and sweet, a joy of which none can know too much, it is to be found in him whom as yet you see not, but in whom believing you rejoice with joy unspeakable and full of glory.

We must tear ourselves away from that thought to turn to another, but assuredly it is rich in happy memories and in blessed expectations.

V. Fifthly, JESUS CHRIST HIMSELF IS THE MODEL OF OUR LIFE, and therefore *how blessed it is to be like him.* As to our rule for life, we are like the disciples on the mount of transfiguration when Moses and Elias had vanished, for we see " no man save Jesus only." Every virtue found in other men we find in him in greater perfection; we admire the grace of God in them, but Jesus himself is our pattern. It was once said of Henry VIII., by a severe critic, that if the characteristics of all the tyrants that had ever lived had been forgotten, they might all have been seen to the life in that one king: we may more truly say of Jesus, if all graces, and virtues, and sweetnesses which have ever been seen in good men could all be forgotten, you might find them all in him: for in him dwells all that is good and great. We, therefore, desire to copy his character and put our feet into his footprints. Be it ours to follow the Lamb whithersoever he goeth. What saith our Lord himself? " Follow me," and again, " Take my yoke upon you and learn of me, for I am meek and lowly in heart, and ye shall find rest unto your souls." Not Christ's apostle, but Christ himself, is our guide; we may not take a secondary model, but must imitate Jesus himself. By the indwelling of the Holy Spirit and his gracious operations we are developing into the image of Christ till Christ be formed in us; and we thus develop because the heavenly life in us is his own life. " I in them," said he, and again, " I am the life." For " we are dead, and our life is hid with Christ in God." " He that hath the Son hath life, and he that hath not the Son hath not life." It is not passing through baptism, nor bearing the name of Christ, it is having Jesus himself in our hearts that makes us Christians, and in proportion as he is formed in us and the new life grows we become more and more like him. And this is our prospect for eternity, that we are to be with him and like him, for " when he shall appear, we shall be like him, for we shall see him as he is." Think of him, you that mourn your imperfectness to-day—think of Jesus Christ himself, and then be assured that you are to be like him. What a picture! Come, artist, bring your best skill here. What can you do? All pencils fail to depict *him*. It needs a poet's eye as well as an artist's hand to picture the Lovely One. But what can the poet do? Ah, you also fail; you cannot sing him any more than your friend can paint him. Fruitful conception and soaring imagination may come to your aid, but they cannot prevent your failure. He is too beautiful to be described—he must be seen. Yet here comes the marvel—" We shall be like him "—like Jesus Christ himself. O saint, when thou art risen from the dead how lovely thou wilt be! Wilt thou know thyself? To-day thou art wrinkled with old age, scarred with the marks of disease and pain, and perhaps deformed by accident, or blanched with consumption, but none of these shall blemish thee then. Thou wilt be without spot or wrinkle, faultless before the throne.

> " O glorious hour! O blest abode!
> I shall be near and like my God.'

And not in bodily form alone shall we be like unto him whose eyes are as the eyes of doves, and whose cheeks are as beds of spices; but in spirit and in soul shall we be perfectly conformed to the Well-beloved. We shall be holy even as he is holy, and happy as he is happy. We shall enter into the joy of our Lord—the joy of Jesus himself. I say not that we can be divine—that cannot be; but still, brothers to him that is the Son of God, we shall be very near the throne. O what rapture to know that my next of kin liveth, and when he shall stand in the latter day upon the earth I shall not only see God in this my flesh, but I shall be like him, for I shall see him as he is. Christ himself then becomes to us unspeakably precious, as the model of our present life and the image of the perfection towards which the Holy Ghost is working us.

VI. Lastly, HE IS THE LORD OF OUR SOUL. *How sweet it will be to be with him.* We find to-day that his beloved company makes everything move pleasantly whether we run in the way of his commands, or traverse the valley of the shadow of death. Saints have lain in dungeons, and yet they have walked at liberty when he has been there; they have been stretched on the rack, and even called it a bed of roses when he has stood by. One lay on a gridiron, with the hot fires beneath him; but amidst the flames he challenged his tormentors to do their worst, and laughed them to scorn, for his Lord was there. Martyrs have been seen to clap their hands when every finger burned like a lighted candle, and they have been heard to cry, " Christ is all," " Christ is all." When the Fourth, like unto the Son of God, walks in the furnace, all the fire can do is but to snap their bonds and set the sufferers free. Oh, brethren, I am sure your only happiness that has been worth the having has been found in knowing that he loved you and was near you. If you have ever rejoiced in the abundance of your corn and wine and oil, it has been a sorry joy; it has soon palled upon your taste, it never touched the great deeps of your spirit; and anon it has gone and left you sore wearied in heart. If you have rejoiced in your children, and your kinsfolk, and your bodily health, how readily has God sent a blight upon them all. But when you have rejoiced in Jesus you have heard a voice bidding you proceed to further delights. That voice has cried, " Drink, O friends, yea, drink abundantly, O beloved;" for to be inebriated with such joy as this is to come to the best condition of mind, and to fix the soul where it should be. We are never right till we come out of ourselves and into Jesus; but when the ecstatic state comes, and we stand right out of self, and stand in him, so that whether in the body or out of the body we can scarcely tell, God knoweth; then are we getting back to where God meant man to have been when he walked with him in Eden, getting near to where God means we shall be when we shall see him face to face. Brethren, what must the unveiled vision be! If the sight of him here be so sweet, what must it be to see him hereafter! It may be we shall not live till he cometh, for the Master may tarry; but if he doth not come, and we therefore are called to pass through the gate of death, we need not fear. I should not wonder if when we pass under the veil and come out in the disembodied state, one of our astonishments will be to find Jesus himself there waiting to receive us. The soul hoped that a convoy of ministering angels would be near the bed and would escort it across the stream and up the mountains to the Celestial

City; but no: instead thereof the spirit will be saluted by the Lord himself. Will it be amazed and cry: "It is he, e'en he, my best Beloved, Jesus himself; he has come to meet me. Heaven might have been too great a surprise; even my disembodied spirit might have swooned away, but it is he, the man Christ Jesus whom I trusted down below, and who was the dear companion of my dying hours. I have changed my place and state, but I have not changed my Friend nor changed my joy, for here he is!" What a glance of love will that be which he will give to us and which we shall return to him. Shall we ever take our eyes away from him? Shall we ever wish to do so? Will not the poet's words be true,

> "Millions of years my wondering eyes,
> Shall o'er thy beauties rove;
> And endless ages I'll adore
> The glories of thy love."

Within a week it may be our meeting with Jesus himself may take place; perhaps within an hour. A poor girl lying in the hospital was told by the doctor or the nurse that she could only live another hour; she waited patiently, and when there remained only one quarter of an hour more, she exclaimed: "One more quarter of an hour, and then——" she could not say what, neither can I; only Jesus himself hath said, "Father, I will that they also, whom thou hast given me, be with me where I am; that they may behold my glory." And as he has prayed, so shall it be, and so let it be. Amen and Amen.

Jesus Only

"And when they had lifted up their eyes, they saw no man, save Jesus only "—
Matthew xvii. 8.

THE last words will suffice us for a text, "Jesus only." When Peter saw our Lord with Moses and Elias, he exclaimed, "Master, it is good to be here," as if he implied that it was better to be with Jesus, and Moses, and Elias, than to be with Jesus only. Now it was certainly good that for once in his life he should see Christ transfigured with the representatives of the law and the prophets; it might be for that particular occasion the best sight that he could see, but as an ordinary thing an ecstacy so sublime would not have been good for the disciples; and Peter himself very soon found this out, for when the luminous cloud overshadowed him, and the voice was heard out of heaven, we find that he with the rest became sore afraid. The best thing after all for Peter was not the excessive strain of the transfiguration, nor the delectable company of the two great spirits who appeared with Jesus, but the equally glorious, but less exciting, society of "Jesus only." Depend on it, brethren, that ravishing and exciting experiences and transporting enjoyments, though they may be useful as occasional refreshments, would not be so good for every day as that quiet but delightful ordinary fellowship with "Jesus only," which ought to be the distinguishing mark of all Christian life. As the disciples ascended the mountain side with Jesus only, and as they went back again to the multitude with Jesus only, they were in as good company as when they were on the mountain summit, Moses and Elias being there also; and although Jesus Christ in his common habiliments and in his ordinary attire might not so dazzle their eyes as when they saw his raiment bright as the light, and his face shining as the sun, yet he really was quite as glorious, and his company quite as beneficial. When they saw him in his everyday attire, his presence was quite as useful to them as when he robed himself in splendour. "Jesus only," is after all upon the whole a better thing than Jesus, Moses, and Elias. "Jesus only," as the common Jesus, the Christ of every day, the man walking among men, communing in secret with his disciples, is a better thing for a continuance while we are in this body than the sight even of Jesus himself in the excellence of his majesty.

This morning, in trying to dwell upon the simple sight of "Jesus only," we shall hold it up as beyond measure important and delightful, and shall bear our witness that as it was said of Goliath's sword, "there is none like it," so may it be said of fellowship with "Jesus only." We shall first notice *what might have happened to the disciples after the transfiguration;* we shall then dwell on *what did happen;* and then, thirdly, we shall speak on *what we anxiously desire may happen to those who hear us this day.*

I. First, then, WHAT MIGHT HAVE HAPPENED to the three disciples after they had seen the transfiguration.

There were four things either of which might have occurred. As a first supposition, *they might have seen nobody* with them on the holy mount; they might have found all gone but themselves. When the cloud had overshadowed them, and they were sore afraid, they might have lifted up their eyes and found the entire vision melted into thin air; no Moses, no Elias, and no Jesus. In such a case they would have been in a sorry plight, like those who having begun to taste of a banquet, suddenly find all the viands swept away; like thirsty men who have tasted the cooling crystal drops, and then seen the fountain dried up before their eyes. They would not have gone down the mountain side that day asking questions and receiving instruction, for they would have had no teacher left them. They would have descended to face a multitude and to contend with a demon; not to conquer Satan, but to stand defeated by him before the crowd; for they would have had no champion to espouse their cause and drive out the evil spirit. They would have gone down among Scribes and Pharisees to be baffled with their knotty questions, and to be defeated by their sophistries, for they would have had no wise man, who spake as never man spake, to untie the knots and disentangle the snarls of controversy. They would have been like sheep without a shepherd, like orphan children left alone in the world. They would henceforth have reckoned it an unhappy day on which they saw the transfiguration; because having seen it, having been led to high thoughts by it, and excited to great expectations, all had disappeared like the foam upon the waters, and left no solid residuum behind. Alas! for those who have seen the image of the spirits of just men made perfect, and beheld the great Lord of all such spirits, and then have found themselves alone and all the high companionship for ever gone.

My dear brethren and sisters, there are some in this world, and we ourselves have been among them, to whom something like this has actually occurred. You have been under a sermon, or at a gospel ordinance, or in reading the word of God for awhile delighted, exhilarated, lifted up to the sublimer regions, and then afterwards when it has all been over, there has been nothing left of joy or benefit, nothing left of all that was preached and for the moment enjoyed, nothing, at any rate, that you could take with you into the conflicts of every-day life. The whole has been a splendid vision and nothing more. There has been neither Moses, nor Elias, nor Jesus left. You did remember what you saw, but only with regret, because nothing remained with you. And, indeed, this which happens sometimes to us, is a general habit of that portion of this ungodly world which hears the gospel and perceives not its reality; it listens with respect to gospel histories as to legends of ancient times; it hears with reverence the stories of the days of miracles; it venerates the far-off ages and their heroic deeds, but it does not believe that anything is left of all the vision, anything for to-day, for common life, and for common men. Moses it knows, and Elias it knows, and Christ it knows, as shadows that have passed across the scene and have disappeared, but it knows nothing of any one of these as abiding in permanent influence over the mind and spirit of the present. All come and all gone, all to be reverenced, all to be respected, but nothing more; there is nothing left so far as they are concerned to influence or bless the present hour. Jesus and his gospel have come and gone, and we may very properly recollect the fact, but according to certain sages there is nothing in the New Testament to affect this advanced age, this enlightened nineteenth century; we have got beyond all that. Ah! brethren, let those who can be content to do so, put up with this worship of moral relics and spiritual phantoms; to us it would be wretchedness itself. We, on the other hand say, blessing the name of the Lord that we can say it, that there abides with us our Lord Jesus. At this day he is with us, and will be with us even to the end of the world. Christ's existence is not a fact confined to antiquity or to remote distance. By his Spirit he is actually in his church; we have seen him, though not with eyes; we have heard him, though not with ears; we have grasped him, though not with hands; and we feed upon his flesh, which is meat indeed, and his blood, which is drink indeed. We have with us at this very day Jesus our friend, to whom we make known our secrets, and who beareth all our sorrows. We have Jesus our interpreting instructor, who still reveals his secrets to us, and leads us into the mind and name of God. We have Jesus still with us to supply us with strength, and in his power we still are mighty. We confess his reigning sovereignty in the church, and we receive his all-sufficient succours. The church is not decapitated, her Head abides in vital union with her; Jesus is no myth to us, whatever he may be to others; he is no departed shade, he is no heroic personification: in very deed there is a Christ, and though others see him not, and even we with these eyes see him not, yet in him believing we rejoice with joy unspeakable and full of glory. Oh, I trust it will never be so with us, that as we go about our life work our religion shall melt into fiction and become nothing but mere sentiment, nothing but thought, and dream, and vision; but may our religion be a matter of fact, a walking with the living and abiding Saviour. Though Moses may be gone, and Elias may be gone, yet Jesus Christ abideth with us and in us, and we in him, and so shall it be evermore.

Now, there was a second thing that might have happened to the disciples. When they lifted up their eyes *they might have seen Moses only.* It would certainly have been a very sad exchange for what they did see, to have seen Moses only. The face of Moses would have shone, his person would have awed them, and it would have been no mean thing for men of humble origin like themselves to walk down the mountain with that mighty king in Jeshurun, who had spoken with God face to face, and rested with him in solemn conclave by the space of forty days at a time. But yet who would exchange the sun for the moon? Who would exchange the cold moonbeams of Moses and the law for the sunny rays of the Saviour's divine affection? It would have been an unhappy exchange for them to have lost their Master whose name is love, and to have found a leader in the man whose name is synonymous with law. Moses, the man of God cannot be compared with Jesus, the Son of God. Yet, dear brethren, there are some who see Moses only. After all the gospel preaching that there has been in the world, and the declaration of the precious doctrines of grace every Sabbath day, after the clear revelations of Scripture, and the work of the Holy Spirit in men's hearts, yet we have among us some who persist in seeing nothing but Moses only. I mean this, there are some who will see nothing but shadows still, mere shadows still. As I read my Bible I see there that the age of the symbolical, the typical, the pictorial, has passed away. I am glad of the symbols, and types, and pictures, for they remain instructive to me; but the age in which they were in the foreground has given way to a clearer light, and they are gone for ever. There are, however, certain persons who profess to read the Bible and to see very differently, and they set up a new system of types and shadows—a system, let me say, ridiculous to men of sense, and obnoxious to men of spiritual taste. There are some who delight in outward ordinances; they must have rubric and ritual, vestments and ceremonial, and this superabundantly, morning, noon and night. They regard days, and seasons, and forms of words and postures. They consider one place holy above another. They regard a certain caste of men as being priestly above other believers, and their love of symbols is seen in season and out of season. One would think, from their teachings, that the one thing needful was not ".Jesus only," but custom, antiquity, outward performance, and correct observance! Alas! for those who talk of Jesus, but virtually see Moses, and Moses only. Ah! unhappy change for the heart if it could exchange spiritual fellowship with Jesus for outward acts and symbolical representations. It would be an unhappy thing for the Christian church if she could ever be duped out of the priceless boons which faith wins from her living Lord in his fulness of grace and truth, to return to the beggarly elements of carnal ordinances. Unhappy day, indeed, if Popish counterfeits of legal shadows should supplant gospel fact and substance. Blessed be God, we have not so learned Christ. We see something better than Moses only.

There are too many who see Moses only, inasmuch as they see nothing but law, nothing but duty and precept in the Bible. I know that some here, though we have tried to preach Christ crucified as their only hope, yet whenever they read the Bible, or hear the gospel, feel nothing except a sense of their own sinfulness, and, arising out of that sense of sinfulness, a desire to work out a righteousness of their own. They are continually measuring themselves by the law of God, they feel their shortcomings, they mourn over their transgressions, but they go no further. I am glad that they see Moses, may the stern voice of the lawgiver drive them to the law-fulfiller; but I grieve that they tarry so long in legal servitude, which can only bring them sorrow and dismay. The sight of Sinai, what is it but despair? God revealed in flaming fire, and proclaiming with thunder his fiery law, what is there here to save the soul ? To see the Lord who will by no means spare the guilty, but will surely visit transgression with eternal vengeance, is a sight which never should eclipse Calvary, where love makes recompense to justice. O that you may get beyond the mount that might be touched, and come to Calvary where God in vengeance is clearly seen, but where God in mercy fills the throne. Oh, how blessed is it to escape from the voice of command and threatening and come to the blood of sprinkling, where " Jesus only" speaketh better things!

Moses only, however, has become a sight very common with some of you who write bitter things against yourselves. You never read the Scriptures or hear the gospel without feeling condemned. You know your duty, and confess how short you have fallen of it, and therefore you abide under conscious condemnation, and will not come to him who is the propitiation for your sins. Alas, that there should be so many who with strange perversity of unbelief twist every promise into a threatening, and out of every gracious word that drips with honey manage to extract gall and wormwood. They see the dark shadow of Moses only; the broken tablets of the law, the smoking mount, and the terrible trumpet are ever with them, and over all an angry God. They had a better vision once, they have it sometimes now; for now and then under the preaching of the gospel they have glimpses of hope and mercy, but they relapse into darkness, they fall again into despair, because they have chosen to see Moses only. I pray that a change may come over the spirit of their dream, and that yet like the apostles they may see "Jesus only."

But, my brethren, there was a third alternative that might have happened to the disciples, *they might have seen Elijah only.* Instead of the gentle Saviour, they might have been standing at the side of the rough-clad and the stern-spirited Elias. Instead of the Lamb of God, there might have remained to them only the lion who roared like the voice of God's own majesty in the midst of sinful Israel. In such a case, with such a leader, they would have gone down from the mount, and I wot that if John had said, "Command fire from heaven," Elias would have consumed his foes, the Pharisees like the priests of Baal would have found a speedy end, Herod's blood, like Ahab's, would have been licked up by dogs, and Herodias, like another Jezebel, would have been devoured of the same. But all this power for vengeance would have been a poor exchange for the gracious omnipotence of the Friend of sinners. Who would prefer the slayer of the priests to the Saviour of men ? The top of Carmel was glorious when its intercession brought the rain for Israel, but how poor it is compared with Gethsemane, whose pleadings bring eternal life to millions! In company with Jesus we are at Elim beneath the palm tree, but with Elias we are in the wilderness beneath the stunted juniper. Who would exchange the excellency of Olivet for the terrors of Horeb ? Yet I fear there are many who see Elias only. Prophecies of future woe fascinate them rather than thoughts of present salvation. Elias may be taken representatively as the preparer of Christ, for our Lord interpreted the prophecy of the coming of Elias as referring to John the Baptist. There are not a few who abide in the seeking, repenting, and preparing state, and come not to "Jesus only." I am not myself fond of even using the term "preparing for Christ," for it seems to me that those are best prepared for Christ who most feel themselves unprepared; but there is no doubt a state of heart which prepares for faith—a sense of need, a consciousness of sin, a hatred of sin, all these are preparations for actual peace and comfort in Christ Jesus, and oh! how many there are who continue year after year merely in that preliminary condition, choosing the candle and refusing the sun. They do not become believers, but are always complaining that they do not feel as yet fit to come to Christ. They want Christ, they desire Christ, they would fain have Christ, but they stay in desire and longings, and go no further. They never get so far as to behold "the Lamb of God that taketh away the sin of the world." The voice from heaven to them they always interpret as crying, "The axe is laid unto the root of the trees; bring forth therefore fruits meet for repentance." Their conscience is thrilled, and thrilled again, by the voice that crieth in the wilderness, "Prepare ye the way of the Lord." Their souls are rent and torn by Elijah's challenge, "If the Lord be God, follow him: but if Baal, then follow him;" but they remain still halting between two opinions, trembling before Elias and not rejoicing before the Saviour. Unhappy men and women, so near the kingdom, and yet out of it; so near the feast, and yet perishing for want of the living bread. The word is near you (ah, how near!), and yet you receive it not. Remember, I pray you, that merely to prepare for a Saviour is not to be saved; that to have a sense of sin is not the same thing as being pardoned. Your repentance, unless you also believe in Jesus, is a repentance that needs to be repented of. At the girdle of John the Baptist the keys of heaven did never hang; Elias is not the door of salvation; preparation for Christ is not Christ, despair is not regeneration, doubt is not repentance. Only by faith in Jesus can you be saved, but complaining of yourselves is not faith. "Jesus only" is the way, the truth, and the life. "Jesus only" is the sinner's Saviour. O that your eyes may be opened, not to see Elias, not to see Moses, but to see "Jesus only."

You see, then, these three alternatives, but there was also another: a fourth thing might have happened when the disciples opened their eyes—*they might have seen Moses and Elias with Jesus*, even as in the transfiguration. At first sight it seems as if this would have been superior to that which they did enjoy. To walk down the mountain with that blessed trio, how great a privilege! How strong might they have been for the accomplishment of the divine purposes! Moses could preach the law and make men tremble, and then Jesus could follow with his gospel of grace and truth. Elias could flash the thunderbolt in their faces, and then Christ could have uplifted the humbled spirits. Would not the contrast have been delightful, and the connection inspiriting? Would not the assemblage of such divers kinds of forces have contributed to the greatest success? I think not. It is a vastly better thing to see "Jesus only," as a matter of perpetuity, than to see Moses and Elias with Jesus. It is night, I know it, for I see the moon and stars. The morning cometh, I know it cometh, for I see no longer many stars, only one remains, and that the morning star. But the full day has arrived, I know it has, for I cannot even see the morning star; all those guardians and comforters of the night have disappeared; I see the sun only. Now, inasmuch as every man prefers the noon to midnight and to the twilight of dawn, the disappearance of Moses and Elias, indicating the full noontide of light, was the best thing that could happen. Why should we wish to see Moses? The ceremonials are all fulfilled in Jesus; the law is honoured and fulfilled in him. Let Moses go, his light is already in "Jesus only." And why should I wish to retain Elias? The prophecies are all fulfilled in Jesus, and the preparation of which Elias preached Jesus brings with himself. Let, then, Elias go, his light also is in "Jesus only." It is better to see Moses and Elias *in* Christ, than to see Moses and Elias *with* Christ. The absence of some things betokens a higher state of things than their presence. In all my library I do not know that I have a Lennie's English Grammar, or a Mavor's Spelling Book, or a Henry's First Latin Exercises, nor do I regret the absence of those valuable works, because I have got beyond the need of them. So the Christian wants not the symbols of Moses, or the preparations of Elias, for Christ is all, and we are complete in him. He who is conversant with the higher walks of sacred literature and reads in the golden book of Christ's heart, may safely lay the legal school-book by; this was good enough for the church's infancy, but we have now put away childish things. "We, when we were children, were in bondage under the elements of the world: but when the fulness of the time was come, God sent forth his Son, made of a woman, made under the law, to redeem them that were under the law, that we might receive the adoption of sons. And because ye are sons, God hath sent forth the Spirit of his Son into your hearts, crying, Abba, Father. Wherefore thou art no more a servant, but a son; and if a son, then an heir of God through Christ." My brethren, the principle may be carried still further, for even the most precious things we treasure here below will disappear when fully realised in heaven. Beautiful for situation was the temple on Mount Zion, and though we believe not in the sanctity of buildings under the gospel, we love the place of solemn meeting where we are accustomed to offer prayer and praise; but when we enter into perfection we shall find no temple in heaven. We delight in our Sabbaths, and we would not give them up. O may England never lose her Sabbaths! but when we reach the Jerusalem above, we shall not observe the first day of the week above the rest, for we shall enjoy one everlasting Sabbath. No temple, because all temple; and no Sabbath-day, because all Sabbath in heaven. Thus you see the losing of some things is gain: it proves that we have got beyond their help. Just as we get beyond the nursery and all its appurtenances, and never regret it, because we have become men, so do Moses and Elias pass away, but we do not miss them, for "Jesus only" indicates our manhood. It is a sign of a higher growth when we can see Jesus only. My brethren, much of this sort of thing takes place with all Christians in their spiritual life. Do you remember when you were first of all convinced and awakened, what a great deal you thought of the preacher, and how much of the very style in which he spoke the gospel! But now, though you delight to listen to his voice, and find that God blesses you through him, yet you have sunk the thought of the preacher in the glory of the Master, you see no man save "Jesus only." And as you grow in grace you will find that many doctrines and points of church government which once appeared to you to be all important, though you will still value them, will seem but of small consequence compared with Christ himself. Like the traveller ascending the Alps to reach the summit of Mont Blanc; at first he observes that lord of the hills as one horn among many, and often in the twistings of his upward path he sees other peaks which appear more elevated than that monarch of mountains; but when at last he is near the summit, he sees all the rest of the hills beneath his feet, and like a mighty wedge of alabaster Mont Blanc pierces the very clouds. So, as we grow in grace, other things sink and Jesus rises. They must decrease, but Christ must increase; until he alone fills the full horizon of your soul, and rises clear and bright and glorious. up into the very heaven of God. O that we may thus see "Jesus only!"

II. Time hastens so rapidly, this morning, that I know not how I shall be able to compress the rest of my discourse into the allotted space. We must in the most rapid manner speak upon WHAT REALLY HAPPENED.

"They saw no man, save Jesus only." This was all they wanted to see for *their comfort*. They were sore afraid: Moses was gone, and he could give them no comfort; Elias was gone, he could speak no consolatory word; yet when Jesus said, "Be not afraid," their fears vanished. All the comfort, then, that any troubled heart wants, it can find in Christ. Go not to Moses, nor Elias, neither to the old covenant, nor to prophecy: go straight away to Jesus only. He was all the *Saviour* they wanted. Those three men all needed washing from sin; all needed to be kept and held on their way, but neither Moses nor Elias could have washed them from sin, nor have kept them from returning to it. But Jesus only could cleanse them, and did; Christ could lead them on, and did. Ah! brethren, all the Saviour we want, we find in Jesus only. The priests of Rome and their Anglican mimics officiously offer us their services. How glad they would be if we would bend our necks once again to their yoke! But we thank God we have seen "Jesus only," and if Moses has gone, and if Elias has gone, we are not likely to let the shavelings of Rome come in and fill up the vacancy. "Jesus only," is enough for our comfort, without either Anglican, Mosaic, or Roman priestcraft.

He, again, was to them, as they went afterwards into the world enough for *a Master*. "No man can serve two masters," and albeit, Moses and Elias might sink into the second rank, yet might there have been some difficulty in the follower's mind if the leadership were divided. But when they had no leader but Jesus, his guidance, his direction and command were quite sufficient. He, in the day of battle, was enough for their captain; in the day of difficulty, enough for their direction. They wanted none but Jesus. At this day, my brethren, we have no Master but Christ; we submit ourselves to no vicar of God; we bow down ourselves before no great leader of a sect, neither to Calvin, nor to Arminius, to Wesley, or Whitfield. "One is our Master," and that one is enough, for we have learned to see the wisdom of God and the power of God in Jesus only.

He was enough as *their power* for future life, as well as their Master. They needed not ask Moses to lend them official dignity, nor to ask Elias to bring them fire from heaven, Jesus would give them of his Holy Spirit, and they should be strong enough for every enterprise. And, brethren, all the power you and I want to preach the gospel, and to conquer souls to the truth, we can find in Jesus only. You want no sacred state-prestige, no pretended apostolical succession, no prelatical unction; Jesus will anoint you with his Holy Spirit, and you shall be plenteously endowed with power from on high, so that you shall do great things and prevail. "Jesus only." Why, they wanted no other motive to constrain them to use their power aright. It is enough incentive to a man to be allowed to live for such a one as Christ. Only let the thought of Christ fill the enlightened intellect, and it must conquer the sanctified affections. Let but Jesus be well understood as the everlasting God who bowed the heavens, and came down and suffered shame, and ignominy, that he might redeem us from the wrath to come; let us get but a sight of the thorn-crowned head, and those dear eyes all red with weeping, and those sweet cheeks bruised and battered by the scoffers' fists; let us but look into the tender heart that was broken with griefs unutterable for our sakes, and the love of Christ must constrain us, and we shall thus "judge, that if one died for all, then were all dead: and that he died for all, that they which live should not henceforth live unto themselves, but unto him which died for them, and rose again." In the point of motive believers do not need the aid of Moses. That you ought to do such a thing because otherwise you will be punished will but little strengthen you, nor will you be much aided by the spirit of prophecy which leads you to hope that in the millennial period you will be made a ruler over many cities. It will be enough to you that you serve the Lord Christ; it suffices you if you may be enabled to honour him, to deck his crown, to magnify his name. Here is stimulus sufficient for martyrs and confessors, "Jesus only." Brethren, it is all the *gospel* we have to preach, it is all the gospel we want to preach—it is the only ground of confidence which we have for ourselves; it is all the hope we have to set before others. I know that in this age there is an overweening desire for that which has the aspect of being intellectual, deep, and novel; and we are often informed that there are to be developments in religion even as in science ; and we are despised as being hardly men, certainly not thinking men, if we preach to-day what was preached two hundred years ago. Brethren, we preach to-day what was preached eighteen hundred years ago, and wherein others make alterations they create deformities, and not improvements. We are not ashamed to avow that the old truth of Christ alone is everlasting; all else has gone or shall go, but the gospel towers above the wrecks of time: to us "Jesus only" remains as the sole topic of our ministry, and we want nothing else.

For "Jesus only" shall be *our reward*, to be with him where he is, to behold his glory, to be like him when we shall see him as he is, we ask no other heaven. No other bliss can our soul conceive of. The Lord grant we may have a fulness of this, and "Jesus only" shall be throughout eternity our delight.

There was here space to have dilated at great length, but we have rather given you the heads of thought than the thoughts themselves. Though the apostles saw "Jesus only," they saw quite sufficient, for Jesus is enough for time and eternity, enough to live by and enough to die by.

III. I must close, though I would fain linger. Brethren, let us think of WHAT WE DESIRE MAY HAPPEN to all now present.

I do desire for my fellow Christians and for myself, that more and more the great object of our thoughts, motives, and acts may be "Jesus only." I believe that whenever our religion is most vital it is most full of Christ. Moreover, when it is most practical, downright, and common sense, it always gets nearest to Jesus. I can bear witness that whenever I am in deeps of sorrow, nothing will do for me but "Jesus only." I can rest in some degree in the externals of religion, its outward escarpments and bulwarks, when I am in health; but I retreat to the innermost citadel of our holy faith, namely, to the very heart of Christ, when my spirit is assailed by temptation, or besieged with sorrow and anguish. What is more, my witness is that whenever I have high spiritual enjoyments, enjoyments rich, rare, celestial, they are always connected with Jesus only, other religious things may give some kind of joy, and joy that is healthy too, but the sublimest, the most inebriating, the most divine of all joys, must be found in Jesus only. In fine, I find if I want to labour much, I must live on Jesus only; if I desire to suffer patiently, I must feed on Jesus only; if I wish to wrestle with God successfully, I must plead Jesus only; if I aspire to conquer sin, I must use the blood of Jesus only; if I pant to learn the mysteries of heaven, I must seek the teachings of Jesus only. I believe that anything which we add to Christ lowers our position, and that the more elevated our soul becomes, the more nearly like what it is to be when it shall enter into the region of the perfect, the more completely everything else will sink, die out, and Jesus, Jesus, Jesus only, will be first and last, and midst and without end, the Alpha and Omega of every thought of head and pulse of heart. May it be so with every Christian!

There are others here who are not yet believers in Jesus, and our desire is that this may happen to them, that they may see "Jesus only." "Oh," saith one, "Sir, I want to see my sins. My heart is very hard, and very proud; I want to see my sins." Friend, I also desire that you should, but I desire that you may see them not on yourself, but on Jesus only. No sight of sin ever brings such true humiliation of spirit as when the soul sees its sins laid on the Saviour. Sinner, I know you have thought of sins as lying on yourself, and you have been trying to feel their weight, but there is a happier and better view still. Sin was laid on Jesus, and it made him to be covered with a bloody sweat; it nailed him to the cross; it made him cry, "Lama Sabachthani;" it bowed him into the dust of death. Why, friend, if you see sin on Jesus you will hate it, you will bemoan it, you will abhor it. You need not look evermore to sin as burdening yourself, see Jesus only, and the best kind of repentance will follow. "Ah, but," saith another, "I want to feel my need of Christ more." You will see your need all the better if you look at Jesus only. Many a time an appetite for a thing is created by the sight of it. Why, there are some of us who can hardly be trusted in a bookseller's shop, because though we might have done very well at home without a certain volume, we no sooner see it than we are in urgent need of it. So often is it with some of you about other matters, so that it becomes most dangerous to let you see, because you want as soon as you see. A sight of Jesus, of what he is to sinners, of what he makes sinners, of what he is in himself, will more tend to make you feel your need of him than all your poring over your poor miserable self. You will get no further there, look to "Jesus only." "Ay," saith another, "but I want to read my title clear, I want to know that I have an interest in Jesus." You will best read your interest in Christ, by looking at him. If I want to know whether a certain estate is mine, do I look into my own heart to see if I have a right to it? but I look into the archives of the estate, I search testaments and covenants. Now, Christ Jesus is God's covenant with the people, a leader and commander to the people. To-day, I personally can read my title clear to heaven, and shall I tell you how I read it? Not because I feel all I wish to feel, nor because I am what I hope I yet shall be, but I read in the word that "Jesus Christ came into the world to save sinners," I am a sinner, even the devil cannot tell me I am not. O precious Saviour, then thou hast come to save such as I am. Then I see it written again, "He that believeth and is baptised, shall be saved." I have believed, and have been baptised; I know I trust alone in Jesus, and that is believing.

As surely then as there is a God in heaven I shall be in heaven one day. It must be so, because unless God be a liar, he that believeth must be saved. You see it is not by looking within, it is by looking to Jesus only that you perceive at last your name graven on his hands. I wish to have Christ's name written on my heart, but if I want assurance, I have to look at his heart till I see my name written there. O turn your eye away from your sin and your emptiness to his righteousness and his fulness. See the sweat drops bloody as they fall in Gethsemane, see his heart pierced and pouring out blood and water for the sins of men upon Calvary! There is life in a look at him! O look to him, and though it be Jesus only, though Moses should condemn you, and Elias should alarm you, yet "Jesus only" shall be enough to comfort and enough to save you. May God grant us grace every one of us to take for our motto in life, for our hope in death, and for our joy in eternity, "Jesus only." May God bless you for the sake of "Jesus only." Amen.

The Rule of the Race

"Let us run with patience the race that is set before us, looking unto Jesus the author and finisher of our faith; who for the joy that was set before him endured the cross, despising the shame, and is set down at the right hand of the throne of God "—Hebrews xii. 1, 2.

THE apostle saith, "Let us run." He has in his mind's eye the Olympic games, where all the different tribes of Greece were gathered together in general assembly to display the prowess of the race. Among the athletic exercises were foot-races. The apostle makes this foot-race an illustration of the Christian life. We must run with patience along the appointed course if we would win the prize of our high calling.

He stands with us at the starting-point, and earnestly says to us, not "Run," but, "Let us run." The apostle himself is at our side as a runner. The presence of such a comrade is most inspiring. It is good doing good things in good company. "Let us run," saith he, "with patience the race that is set before us." Who will back out of a race wherein so great a saint takes his place at our side? Ho, ye who aspire to be associated with the excellent of the earth, press forward side by side with an apostle! "Let us run," from Paul's lip, puts wings upon our heels.

Before we start, with a wave of the hand the apostle directs us to the spectators who throng the sides of the course. There were always such at those races: each city and state yielded its contingent, and the assembled throng watched with eager eye the efforts of those who strove for the mastery. Those who look down upon us from yonder heavens are described as "so great a cloud of witnesses." These compass us about. Thousands upon thousands, who have run this race before us, and have attained their crowns, behold us from their heavenly seats, and mark how we behave ourselves. This race is worth running, for the eyes of "the nations of them which are saved" are fixed upon us. This is no hole-and-corner business, this running for the great prize. Angels, and principalities, and powers, and hosts redeemed by blood, have mustered to behold the glorious spectacle of men agonizing for holiness, and putting forth their utmost strength to copy the Lord Jesus. Ye that are men, now run for it! If there be any spiritual life and gracious strength in you, put it forth to-day; for patriarchs and prophets, saints, martyrs, and apostles look down from heaven upon you.

Our apostle, anxious that we should so run that we may obtain, points to certain burdens and impediments which he foresees will hinder us, and he says, "Let us lay aside every weight." Note how he includes himself, so that his warning may not sound like upbraiding. We cannot win if we are weighted: the pace will have to be very swift, and we cannot get to it, or keep it up, if we have weights to carry. Unloaded, we shall find the race taxing all our powers; but weighted, we shall be doomed to failure. Oh, to lay aside all carking care, fretfulness, ambition, anger, greed, and selfish desire! These were never worth the labour they have cost us; but now that we have become running men, we *must* have done with them. Down they must go, till the last ounce is on the ground. Like the Greek footman, we would strip; and instead of adding weight, we would diminish even our own bulk, that we may fly along the course. O ye that would win, heed the caution, and "lay aside every weight," whether it be great or small; and press towards the mark! Run for it, man! Thou hadst need do nothing else but run.

Still attentively considering us, the apostle notes that even when the weights are laid aside, there is a garment about us which will assuredly twist about our feet, and throw us down. Sin, as well as care, must be laid aside. It doth easily beset us, and therefore we must be the more careful to be rid of it. Our original sin, our natural tendencies, our constitutional infirmities—these must be laid aside as garments unsuitable for men who are running the heavenly race. We cannot win heaven and wear sin. Heaven is for the holy: "there shall in no wise enter into it anything that defileth." Darling sins must go first: these, as they are most loved, will have the most power to hinder. Every kind of sin must be watched against, struggled against, and mastered. "Sin shall not have dominion over you." We hope to see all our tendencies to sin killed and buried—buried so deep that not even a bone of a sin shall be left above ground. This will be heaven to us.

Do I not hear you say, "May God help us"? This must be a tough race which requires such stripping as this. If every weight of care must be laid aside, and every rag of sin, who is sufficient for these things? How can we poor limping mortals run in such a race as this? Even the starting is beyond us: how much more must perseverance in it outreach our strength! See, my brethren, how we are driven to free grace, how we are driven to the power of the Holy Spirit! The race which is set before us most clearly reveals our helplessness, and our hopelessness, apart from divine grace. The race of holiness and patience, while it demands our vigour, displays our weakness. We are compelled, even before we take a step in the running, to bow the knee, and cry unto the strong for strength. We dare not retreat from the contest; but how can we begin a struggle for which we are so unfitted? Who will help us? To whom shall we look? Does not all this very admirably introduce the verse which is specially my text—"Looking unto Jesus, the author and finisher of our faith"?

But the apostle has not quite done with us, for he warns us to remember the rules of the course in these words, "Let us run with patience the race that is set before us." You are not to run anyhow, or anywhere: you must keep the appointed course, or you might as well stand still. The way of God's command, the way of obedience, the way of humble trustfulness, the spiritual way, the way of the life given from above—this, and no other way will do, for this is the race set before you! Do you shrink? Does the way seem too mysterious, too contrary to the flesh, too trying? All this adds to the force of the precept—"Looking unto Jesus." Because the way itself and the rules of the running are such as your nature will fight against, therefore look the more earnestly to the great Captain of your salvation.

In a race a great point is the way in which a man keeps his eyes. He cannot run straight who hath a squint eye to this or to that. Straightforward is the best running; but he who has his eye on this and on that will run crookedly, and waste his strength. Look to the end, and then run in a direct line. I have read of a competition between certain young ploughmen who were set to plough for a prize. The most of them made very crooked work of it. After they had ended, one of the judges said, "Young man, where did you look while you were ploughing?" "I kept my eyes well on the plough handles, sir, and saw what I had to hold." "Yes," the judge said, "and your plough went in and out, and the furrow is all crooks." He asked the next ploughman, "and where did you look?" "Well, sir," he answered, "I looked at my furrow, I kept my eye always on the furrow that I was making. I thought I should make it straight that way." "But you did not," answered the judge, "you were all over the place." To the next he said, "What did you look at?" "Well, sir," he said, "I looked between the two horses to a tree that stood in the hedge at the other end of the field, right in front of me." Now that man went straight because he had a fixed mark to guide him. This helps us to appreciate the wisdom of the text, "Looking unto Jesus." Run: run straight: you cannot run straight except you keep your eye on one who is always the same. "Looking unto Jesus, the author and finisher of your faith," you will have a sure preservative from wandering. Spiritual ploughmen, take heed that ye look not back, but plough a straight furrow towards Jesus on the throne! Spiritual runners, make a covenant with your eyes that you will look only to him who is the great end of all your running! Looking unto Jesus means life, light, guidance, encouragement, joy: never cease to look on him who ever looks on you.

To help us, the apostle describes the mark to which we are to look in four ways. "Look unto *Jesus*," the Saviour, is the sum and substance of it all; but he is set forth before us in four lights: first, *the author of faith;* secondly, *the finisher of faith;* thirdly, *the pattern of faith;* and lastly, *the goal* or *the end of faith*. We must look to Jesus Christ in each of these four respects. Oh, for the Holy Spirit's help while I speak thereon!

I. First, then, we are to look to Jesus as THE AUTHOR OF FAITH. The apostle would have us view the Lord Jesus as the starter of the race. When a foot-race began, the men were drawn up in a line, and they had to wait for a signal. Those who were in the race had to look to the starter; for the runner who should get first by a false start would not win, because he did not run according to the rules of the race. No man is crowned unless he strives lawfully. The starter was in his place, and the men stood all waiting and looking. At last he dropped his glove, or a handkerchief, and away they went. Our word at starting in the Christian life is, "Look unto Jesus." We must fix our eye on "the beginner of our faith"; for if we do not begin by looking to him, however quickly we may hurry along, we shall run in vain, and labour in vain. To what purpose will your running be, if the umpire determines that you started improperly?

The beginning of faith is "looking unto Jesus." Let us consider this. We have to look to Jesus, first, by *trusting in that which he has wrought for us.* It is described in these words—" Who for the joy that was set before him endured the cross, despising the shame." Jesus has endured the suffering and shame which were due to us. O soul, thou canst never start on the road to heaven unless thou dost look to him who "endured the cross" on thy behalf! Thy sin will make thee to endure the wrath of God for ever, unless thou dost look to him who bore our sins in his own body on the tree. Thou must get a faith's view of the Lamb of God, which taketh away the sin of the world, or else thou hast not even begun the heavenward race. Dost thou look upon thine own righteousness with pleasure? This is an ill start for thee, thy back is on the prize. "As many as are of the works of the law are under the curse." Dost thou look to thy frames and feelings? Thou wilt make a bad start with these, for they will guide thee into a fog, in which thou wilt lose the track. Look thou to Jesus, the suffering Saviour. He by his bearing the cross has removed thy heaviest weights, and by his death has destroyed thine entangling sin. He can renew thy nature by his resurrection power, and save thee from the dominion of sin by his glorious reign. If thou lookest alone to him, thou startest well; but not else.

The Greek word for "looking" is a much fuller word than we can find in the English language. It has a preposition in it which turns the look away from everything else. You are to look from all beside to Jesus. Fix not thy gaze upon the cloud of witnesses; they will hinder thee if they take away thine eye from Jesus. Look not on the weights and the besetting sin—these thou hast laid aside; look away from them. Do not even look upon the race-course, or the competitors, but look to Jesus and so start in the race. What hast thou to trust to but his blood and righteousness? Beware that thou set up nothing as a rival confidence. Look off from everything thou hast ever relied upon in days gone by, and say to thy soul, "None but Jesus." Thou must have a single eye and a single hope. "Christ is all," and he must be all to thee, or thou art out of the race altogether.

The instructive original has in it the word "*eis*," which is translated "unto," but in addition has the force of "into." We shall do well if we look unto Jesus, but better still if we are found "looking *into*

Jesus." I want you, when you begin your divine life, to take care that you look to Jesus with so penetrating a gaze that your "unto" grows to an "into." Read not only the outside of the volume of his life, but loose the seals thereof and read his heart. Dive into the meaning of what he has done for you. Look at his enduring the cross, know what it means, and enter into the fellowship of his sufferings. Study well the sin-bearing, the curse-bearing, the forsaking, and the sorrow unto death. Think how the Lord Jesus came under shame for your sakes, and see how he rose above it all. Look to him till you are familiar with the different views of the one great Sacrifice. Under the law, a poor man brought his two young pigeons, and the birds were divided in the middle, and so offered. A richer man brought a lamb or a bullock; this was divided carefully, and all its anatomy laid bare: this was to be done with the leg, and that with the shoulder, and there was an ordinance concerning the fat and the inwards. Thus some believers know the details of the sacrifice, and we want you, dear friends, to be among this better-instructed class. May you discern the Lord's body, and penetrate into the secrets of his soul, and so begin your Christian life with an intelligent and instructed faith. This will secure better running throughout the rest of the road. Still you must look to Jesus only, whether you know little or much. It is not your knowledge, but himself that must be your one ground of trust. You must take Jesus to be Alpha as well as Omega. To you his name stands at the head of the book, and it is also the Amen which closes it. To your experience the Scripture is true—"In the beginning was the Word." You begin to run when you look to Jesus.

But then, dear friends, we also begin looking unto Jesus, because of *what he has wrought in us.* I would remind you who are a good way on in the course of those first eager paces with which you started heavenward. Did you not begin with looking unto Jesus? As you have received Christ Jesus the Lord, so continue in him. The Lord Jesus first called us out of darkness into his marvellous light. He sweetly inclined us to think upon himself as the way, and made us wishful to become heavenly footmen. It was he that quickened us, even as of old he raised the dead. The Father quickeneth whomsoever he will, and even so does Jesus. Even now I seem to hear his voice crying, "Lazarus, come forth!" Well do we recollect when serious thought, anxious desire, deep repentance, lingering hope, and trembling faith entered our souls through "looking unto Jesus." Did he not give us pardon at our setting out? It was by looking to him that the great load of sin fell from off our conscience. With pardon of sin came a great loathing of sin: washed in the precious blood we could not wantonly repeat the stains. Our earliest repentance and its fruits came from "looking unto Jesus." Our heart of stone had been hardened by looking elsewhere, but the vision of the sacred head encrowned with thorns did the softening work. We looked and were enlightened, enlivened, enraged against sin, and enamoured of Jesus.

Our first acceptance with God came from looking to Jesus by faith. We found ourselves accepted in the Beloved. O my friend, do you remember that rapturous moment when you perceived that the robe of righteousness had covered you from head to foot, and that your filthy raiment had been taken away? You cannot forget that time of love. At that moment you felt the love of God within your spirit like a consuming fire, burning up your sin. You also were filled with love to the Lord your God. You wondered how it came there till you perceived that you loved him because he first loved you. Then was every evil abhorred of your soul; then were you ready for any holy service; then self-denial became a pleasure to you; then you forsook the company of the wicked, and sought the society of the saints. The love of Jesus had started you upon a race which otherwise you would not have chosen: you were converted, turned, turned quite round. You owned that henceforth you were not your own, and could not run towards self: you were bought with a price, and therefore must run towards your Redeemer. A sight of the Crucified did it all.

Thus, dear friends, Jesus is the beginner of our race of faith by what he has wrought for us, and by what he has wrought in us.

Have I any here this morning who are about to start for heaven? Mind that you start aright. I pray you, do not fall into any delusion. Do not imagine that your life will avail you anything, however good and moral it may have been, unless you begin by looking unto Jesus. Mr. Bunyan, in his "Pilgrim's Progress," frequently speaks of those who tumbled over the wall, or came in by other irregular ways; but they all missed the end. As they came in without Christ, so they went out without hope. One who came near to the celestial city, who had not come in at the gate, was made to know that there is a backway to hell, even from the gate of heaven. You must begin with looking unto Jesus, or you will end with a fearful looking for of judgment. Doth not Jesus say, "I am the beginning"? Would you set up another beginning? He must be the first letter of your hope, or else you do not even know the alphabet of salvation.

II. But now, secondly, we must look to Jesus as THE FINISHER OF FAITH. As Jesus is at the commencement of the course, starting the runners, so he is at the end of the course, the rewarder of those who endure to the end. Those who would win in the great race must keep their eyes upon him all along the course, even till they reach the winning-post.

You will be helped to look to him when you remember that he is the finisher of your faith *by what he has wrought for you;* for the text saith, "He endured the cross, despising the shame, and is set down at the right hand of the throne of God." You also shall have heaven, for he has it; you shall sit upon the throne, for he sits there. Look to his passion on the cross, to begin with; look to his session on the throne, that you may hold on to the end. Look to Jesus as dying for the pardon of your sin, but as living for the justification of your souls. Incarnation and death have led on to intercession and endless life.

Jesus has sat down: he takes his rest because he has completed his work. Here on earth he was filled with shame, but yonder in glory he is full of honour, for he is set down "at the right hand of God." Here he was bound and led captive; there he is King of kings and Lord of lords, for he sits at the right hand of the throne of God. Here on earth we see his manhood, born in a manger, living in poverty, dying the ignominious death of the cross; there we adore his divine glory, for he is "at the right hand of the throne of God." Think of your Saviour as your God, clothed with all power and authority. Surely this should urge you to quicken your pace, and never to become weary or faint. You began by looking to him as a sufferer, persevere by looking to him as a victor. "Be of good cheer," said he, "I have overcome the world." In that fact he gives you an assurance of your own victory. The seed of the woman has bruised the serpent's head, and therefore the Lord will tread Satan under your feet shortly. The death of Christ is our death for sin; but the life of Christ is our life unto holiness. The shame of Christ was our shame, and the triumph of Christ is our triumph. Wherefore, looking unto Jesus let us run.

We are helped to run to the end, not only by what Jesus has done for us, but *by what Jesus is doing in us*. Beloved, you that are in the middle of the race, remember that Jesus *sustains* you. Every atom of your strength for running comes from your Lord. Look to him for it. Do not take a step in creature strength; nor seek after any virtue, or growth, or progress apart from his life and grace. He saith, "From me is thy fruit found." He works all our works in us, and because he worketh in us to will and to do of his own good pleasure, therefore we work out our own salvation with fear and trembling.

We are not only sustained by looking unto Jesus, but we are *inspirited* thereby. If we win a glance from his eye, our feeble knees are confirmed. We take breath as we behold him on the throne, and dash forward again. Those dear eyes of his are to us as stars are to the mariner. Jesus says to us, "Come on, I am victorious, and so shall you be." A sight of the exalted Leader fires the zeal of each believer, and makes him run like a roe, or a young hart.

Looking unto Jesus, you will get many a *direction;* for, as he sits at the winning-post, his very presence indicates the way. If our eyes are up to him, as the eyes of a servant to her mistress, we shall run well. "Be ye not as the horse, or as the mule, which have no understanding, whose mouth must be held in with bit and bridle"; but say with David, "Thou shalt guide me with thine eye." A look from the eye of Jesus is enough for a saint; and if you, my hearer, are indeed "looking unto Jesus," you will avoid crooks and turns, and will take the shortest road to holiness and eternal glory. Consider him who endured such contradiction of sinners against himself, and you will not grow weary, neither will you miss your way.

Look to Jesus, for by that look he *draws* you. The great magnet up yonder is drawing us towards itself. Christ's cords of love give us speed. The more in the power of the Holy Spirit you meditate upon our Lord's passion on the cross and his session on the throne, the more will you be drawn towards him, and the faster will you move. "Draw me, we will run after thee" is the cry of the Old Testament Church, and it is ours also. Lord, we would look that thou mayest draw.

While we are running we look to our Lord as the finisher of faith, and we see him leaning forward and *holding out the crown*.

> " 'Tis his all animating voice
> That calls us from on high;
> 'Tis his own hand presents the prize
> To our aspiring eye."

The sight of the crown removes all weight from our crosses. The race ceases to be severe when we see Jesus enthroned. I see him to-day at the end of the course holding out the wreath to me, and saying, "He that shall endure unto the end, the same shall be saved." Oh that you may each one see him, and feel that "the crown of glory that fadeth not away" is worthy of a life's running. Thus will Jesus, by holding out the reward, become the finisher of faith.

When the race is over, Jesus will appear as the finisher of faith by coming forward to *crown you* with his own right hand. Yes, his hand shall award the prize, and his lips shall say, "Well done, good and faithful servant." Jesus himself will admit the faithful to the place which he has gone to prepare for them. Wherefore be of good courage and run! Jesus at the end of the race will enthrone us with himself: "Let us run."

I invite you, taking the sense of the word "looking" which I have already hinted at, to turn over in your mind these things. *Look away from* all self-denials, difficulties, labours, sufferings, temptations, and persecutions; and equally look away from all pleasures, profits, and preferments, and look to Jesus, who has won the race himself, and now helps you in the race, and holds out the crown at the end of it. Look till you begin to *look into him* and see somewhat of his inward glory, and of its outflowings to his redeemed. Say to yourself, "All things are in him for me. All spiritual blessings God doth bestow upon me according to his riches in glory by Christ Jesus. Doth the Father bless me in my enthroned Lord? Then my feet shall not weary in the heavenward way. Does Jesus lean forward as if he would crown me even now? Then I will quicken my pace to come to him. Does the Holy Spirit help my infirmities? Then will I run swiftly in his strength.

Thus I have tried in my own feeble way to set before you Jesus as the Author and the Finisher of faith: look to him and run.

III. Let us next consider our Lord Jesus as THE PATTERN OF OUR FAITH. Run, as Jesus ran, and look to him as you run, that you may run like him. How did our Lord pursue his course?

You will see this if you first note *his motive:* "Who for the joy that was set before him." Jesus had a motive in all that he did. Men do not do much if they act from mere feeling, and have no underlying design. Indeed, a life without an object must be a frivolous, useless life. Jesus had before him the great joy of glorifying the Father in the salvation of his chosen. For this he lived, for this he died: it was a joy to him to think of accomplishing this object. Beloved, if you want to run your race aright, it must be for the glory of God, and in the hope of the salvation of your fellow-men. These two things, blended into one, must be your joy. Oh that this motive took possession of our entire being! The chief end of man is to glorify God: let it be my chief end, even as it was my Lord's. Oh that I might glorify thee, my Creator, my Preserver, my Redeemer! To this end was I born, and for this end would I live in every action of my life. Brethren, we cannot run the race set before us unless we feel thus. We must, like the Saviour, seek the glory of God by saving our fellow-men. Live for this. Live to seek out the wandering sons of men, and thus to be a shepherd under the Great Shepherd. Learn from him to carry the lambs in your bosom. There is no running heavenward unless the service of God is a joy to us. We run in an approved fashion when we spend and are spent in glorifying God. May you throughout eternity have to rejoice that you were not fruitless! Oh, may none of you be written down as "creation's blot, creation's blank"; but may you all have the joy of glorifying God on earth, and finishing the work he has given you to do!

Wherein are we to imitate Jesus? First, we are to copy *his endurance*. He "endured the cross." Ours is a trifling cross compared with that which pressed him down; but he endured it. He took it up willingly, and carried it patiently. He never rebelled against it, and never relinquished it. He bore the cross till the cross bore him, and then he bore death upon it. He could say, "It is finished." Brethren, let us do the same. Are you persecuted, are you poor, are you sick?—take up the appointed cross. Christ ran with a cross on his shoulder, and so must we run. Do not try to escape trouble: the followers of the Crucified must be familiar with the cross. Endure it patiently, joyfully, in the strength of God. "Looking unto Jesus," behold *his* cross whenever you begin to faint under your own. Think of the bloody sweat, the scourging, the wounds, the blasphemies of men, the forsaking by God! Behold and see if there was ever sorrow like unto his sorrow, or endurance like to his endurance. Shoulder your cross, and run towards the Crucified.

Imitate your Lord in *his magnanimity*. He endured the cross, "despising the shame." Shame is a cruel thing to many hearts. Our Lord shows us how to treat it. See, he puts his shoulder under the cross, but he sets his foot upon the shame. He endures the one, but he despises the other. What! Shall his disciples make much of that which he despised? Are you such gentlemen, that none may come between the wind and your nobility? I wonder when I hear some people say, "I cannot stand being laughed at." Does laughter break bones? "But ridicule is very sharp!" Is it? Do the wounds bleed? "Well," cries one, "a keen sarcasm from a wit stings you!" Does it? Have you no cure for such bites? Some of us have in our minds been like Marcus Arethusa, who was stung to death by wasps; and yet we are none the worse, but rather are we all the better, for there remains no place whereon a new sting can operate. Oh, that some of you, who are so tender, could have thicker skins in this respect! I heard of a prayer the other day which I did not quite like at first, but there is something in it after all. The good man said, "Lord, if our hearts are hard, make them soft; but if our hearts are too soft, make them hard." I know what he meant, and I think I can pray that last prayer for some of my friends who are so delicate that a sneer would kill them. May the Lord harden them till they can despise the shame! Answer shame by making it see that you are ashamed of the scorner. Laugh at the laughter of fools, despise their despising. With glorious greatness of spirit Jesus remained unprovoked amid the cruel taunts of godless men. Run through the ribald throng. Shut your ears and run, despising the shame.

Our Saviour is to be imitated in *his perseverance*. For the joy that was set before him he endured the cross, despising the shame, and "is set down." He never stopped running till he could sit down at the right hand of the throne of God; and that is the only place where you may sit down. My brother, Satan puts before you a comfortable arm-chair, and he says, "Take thine ease." No, no; run till you can sit down at the right hand of the throne of God. There are many dainty little arbours all along the Hill Difficulty, with settles and tables; and men, if they get into them, are very apt to fall asleep, and lose their roll of comfortable assurance: therefore, pass these arbours by. Runners must not sit down: that were to throw the race away. The only running that will save is persevering running. From starting-point to winning-post there must be no pausing. We must practise daily obedience, daily holiness, daily service. An off-and-on religion is a false religion. We must keep to the running till God gives us rest. Our Lord has won the victory. His enthronement "at the right hand of God" has well rewarded the man Christ Jesus for the depth of his shame and misery. We must not cease our following of him till we triumph too. When we have finished our course, then we shall receive our crowns; but as yet we must copy the Captain of salvation by running steadily on.

Our Lord's body bore five wounds, and these shall help your memory to think of the five virtues in which you are to imitate your Lord. The piercing of the right hand is the memorial of his *faith*. He believed in God in the depth of his agony, and trusted that he would deliver him. Oh, for more faith! The left hand wound is his *patience*. He "endured, as seeing him who is invisible," he reviled not again; he said "Thy will be done." The foot-wound reminds me of his *humility*, and how he was obedient to death, even the death of the cross; and that other foot-wound suggests to me his *perseverance*. His feet were nailed to the wood: his soul was joined to his work. Best of all, in yon great wound in his side I see his love. The spear opened a passage to his heart. Love as Jesus loved, loving God and loving men; then shall you triumph as he triumphed, and he will crown you as he himself is crowned. God help you so to run.

IV. Lastly, our text sets before us Jesus as THE GOAL OF FAITH. We are to run "looking unto Jesus" as the end that we should aim at. We go towards our Lord every step that we take. True faith neither goes away from Christ Jesus, nor takes a roundabout road to Jesus, nor so much as dreams of going beyond Jesus. We have wise men about us nowadays who are going a long way beyond the gospel. The old faith which inspired apostles, enabled the glorious army of martyrs to lay down their lives, and produced the noblest of human characters in past ages, is not good enough for the superfine sophists of these days. This boastful nineteenth century demands a new God, a new Christ, a new heaven, a new hell, a new gospel, and everything else new except a new heart. But we, brethren, are not going to run in that direction. We run towards Christ, and that is the good old way, "the way the holy prophets went." We never expect to get beyond the teaching of our Lord Jesus either in this life or in the life to come. The end of our conversation is, "Jesus Christ the same yesterday, to day, and for ever."

Now, we are to run towards him, looking unto him. Looking to Jesus and running to Jesus will look well and run well together. The eyes outstrip the feet, but this also is well; for the feet will thus be made to move the faster. Look you that you may *see more of Jesus*. I have already told you what differences there are in men's perceptions of Christ: now I want you to keep on looking and running, that you may be among the best instructed, seeing most of him and in him. Those who have seen most of Jesus have only taken a cupful out of the great ocean of his fulness. We who live in this land of murk and cloud may imagine that we have seen the sun, for now and then he peeps out through a veil of mist; but ask an Italian who lives beneath the clear blue sky, where the sun is at home, and walks the heavens without a veil, and he will tell you that an Englishman does not see the sun. For myself, the sun seems in those regions to brighten my nature, and lighten my mind: the lord of day talks to my heart and makes it dance for joy. Many a believer lives in a foggy atmosphere of doubts and fears; he sees his Lord now and then, but it is not half a sight. Oh that we could all dwell under the unclouded skies of full assurance, and see Jesus more nearly! I urge you in your running to come nearer and nearer to Jesus, that you may see him more and more clearly.

Let us run towards Jesus that we may *grow more like him*. It is one of the virtues of Jesus that he transforms into his own image those who look at him. He photographs himself upon all sensitive hearts. There are no looking-glasses that I know of which improve the looker's eye; but this mirror of God, as you look into it, enlightens your eyes and beautifies your character. As you see Christ you become Christians. O beloved, our lives would not be so faulty, so wrinkled, so uncomely, if our eye were more completely taken up with beholding the transcendent charms of the altogether Lovely One! It would make us glorious if we saw more of the glory of Jesus.

Run that you may *come nearer* to Jesus. Seek after more near and dear fellowship with him. He is not far away from us. He is absent as to his corporeal frame, but he is with us in spirit. He comes very close to us at times, when he finds us fit for the joy. We remember him from the Hermons and the hill Mizar. We can never forget the golden moments and the hallowed places wherein he has manifested himself unto us as he doth not unto the world. There are hours when our head is on the bosom of Christ. There are times when we sit at his feet and hear his words, and looking up behold his beauty, and are ravished therewith. Run towards him till you are nearer to him in communion than up till now you have been. This is worth running for; but you will not have it without running. Remember how the spouse in the Song could not find her Lord till she had gone through the streets of the city mourning till she embraced him.

Keep on looking and running till you are with him. Oh, I talk to you now about being with him, but how soon this may be realized in the most literal sense! During my ministry in this place it has occurred two or three times, that when the service has ended, dear friends have essayed to go to their homes, but they have died in this House of Prayer. What must it be to go from this congregation to the assembly above? What a change from the poor talk of the preacher to the voice of the Well-Beloved! We do not know how near to Jesus on the throne we may now be. The sea fog is around our vessel. Could we see before us, the white cliffs of our native shore are almost within touch. Think not that we are far out at sea. Within the next week, perhaps, some of us will see the King in his beauty. We may spend next Sunday in heaven! Does anybody shrink from such a prospect? No: each heir of heaven says "Amen; so let it be." Then the sweat of the race will be wiped away, and the sweet of the triumph will begin. Then the fatigue and distress will have ended, and the rest and the glory will have commenced. I would cheer you with the thought that you are much nearer the winning-post than you think. How soon you may sit among the blood-washed throng! You older brethren and sisters in the course of nature must be there soon: be glad of it. Do not talk about being on the wrong side of seventy: you are on the right side, for you are so much nearer heaven. Formerly when great ships went to the Indies, the passengers would for a while toast the friends they left behind. But when they were in the Indian Ocean, they began to drink the health of friends ahead. Though comparatively young, I have many, many friends who are in the land beyond, to which I am making my way. I salute the glorified. Some of the dearest and best people that ever lived were members of this church, but they are now safely landed on the celestial shore. They are waiting and watching for us. We are coming, brethren! We will be with you soon. Best of all, our Lord is there. Once crowned with thorns, his head is now radiant with the diadem of universal dominion. He will come to welcome us on that blessed shore. Hasten, O time! Be like a seraph with six wings and bear us swiftly to that golden strand where we shall see the face of him we love, and shall be

> "Far from this world of grief and sin,
> With God eternally shut in."

Amen.

Alpha and Omega

"I am Alpha and Omega, the beginning and the end, the first and the last "—
Revelation xxii. 13.

EVERY Sunday-school child knows that there is no great mystery hidden in the words "Alpha and Omega." We have here the names of the first and last letters of the Greek alphabet, so that the sense would be, "I am A and great O," in the Greek, or in plain English, "I am A and Z." "Jesus is the Alpha and Omega—A and Z—the beginning and the end, the first and the last."

Our text demands no preface; indeed, I do not know how I could venture to put a single letter before Alpha. Let us therefore come to our subject at once.

In three ways I shall talk of the text. First, I shall *bring certain doctrines to it;* secondly, we will *look at the doctrines which are really in it;* and then thirdly, at *the lessons which naturally flow from it.*

I. At the outset, WE SHALL BRING CERTAIN TRUTHS TO THE TEXT. This is a much too common method of preaching, and one which I am very far from admiring as a custom. When some preachers get a text, the enquiry is not what truth is in the passage, but what sense shall they thrust upon it? Full often the poor text is served as a cook treats a bird; it is first killed, and then stuffed with any kind of fancies that the preacher may have chopped up ready to hand. By frankly stating that my first observations are not in the verse before us, I shall avoid sanctioning such methods of abusing God's Word. The thoughts to which I now give utterance, have been suggested by divers commentators, and certainly, if they be not the legitimate offspring of the text are closely connected with it.

1. Of things which we may fairly bring to the text, let us notice first, that *our Lord may well be described as the Alpha and Omega in the sense of rank.* He is *Alpha, the first,* the chief, the foremost, the first-born of every creature, the Eternal God. Man by nature is not the first even among creatures, for angels excel him far; nor are angels the chief, for our glorious Lord infinitely transcends them. He who made is greater than they who are made; and he who sends is greater than those

who are sent. Jesus Christ stands Alpha in honourable degree; no angel can vie with him. "Being made so much better than the angels, as he hath by inheritance obtained a more excellent name than they." "For unto which of the angels said he at any time, thou art my Son, this day have I begotten thee? . . . And again, when he bringeth in the firstbegotten into the world, he saith, And let all the angels of God worship him." As for the Son, he hath appointed him heir of all things, by whom also he made the worlds, but of the angels it is asked—"Are they not all ministering spirits, sent forth to minister for them who shall be heirs of salvation?"

Alpha was frequently used by the Hebrews to signify the best, just as we are accustomed to use the letter A. We say of a ship, for instance, that it is "A 1." So Jesus Christ may truly be said to be the Alpha, the first in this sense. Call him by whatever title Scripture has affixed to him, and he is the first in it. Is he a prophet? Then all the prophets follow at a humble distance, bearing witness of him. Is he a priest? Then he is the Great High Priest of our profession; he is the fulfilment of all that which the priest did but typically set forth. Let him mount his throne as king, then he is King of kings, and Lord of lords; "his dominion is an everlasting dominion, and his kingdom is from generation to generation." If he be the builder of his Church, he is the wise Master-builder; if a shepherd, he is the Great Shepherd who shall appear; if the corner-stone, he is the chief corner-stone—in fact, it mattereth not what title, or which character he beareth, he is in all these respects the Alpha, as much surpassing all things that may be compared to him, as the sun excelleth the stars, or as the sea exceedeth the drops of the dew.

But, beloved, though our blessed Lord is thus Alpha—the first—he was once in his condescension made *Omega, the last*. How shall I describe the mighty descent of the Great Saviour. Down from the loftiness of his Father's glory, and from the grandeur of his own divine estate, he stooped to become man. There is a vast distance from the Alpha of Deity, down to that letter which stands for manhood; but to this he came, he was made a little lower than the angels, for the suffering of death. But this is not enough; he stoops lower than man, yea, there is a verse in which he seems to put himself on a level with the least of all creatures that have life—he says, "I am a worm, and no man; a reproach of men, and despised of the people." His Father forsook him; the wrath of heaven rolled over him. He was so utterly crushed and broken, that he was poured out like water, and brought into the dust of death. Marshal the creatures of God in their order, in the dread day when Jesus hangs upon the cross, and you must put him for misery, for weakness, for shame as the last, the Omega. How marvellous is this tremendous sweep of his humiliation, that from the highest throne in glory he should descend into the lowest depths of the tomb. Death bringeth the creature to its very lowest degradation, and maketh it as though it were nought. Jesus died, and as I see the incorruptible body lying in Joseph's sepulchre, I can but marvel that ever the great Alpha should come so low as to yield up the ghost, being subjugated beneath the power of the last adversary.

Now, this is not in the text, but it may be fairly brought to it I think, and, without any compulsion, it may shake hands with the passage as being near of kin to it.

2. We will make another observation which is not in the text, but which is still a very precious truth, namely, that Jesus Christ is Alpha and Omega *in the book of holy Scripture.* Open the first page, and a discerning eye will see Jesus Christ in Genesis. We know that the worlds were made by him, and as we hear that majestic sentence, "Let *us* make man in our own image after *our* likeness," we at once discern him as one of the sacred Trinity. We go onward to the fall, and at the gates of Eden the promise of the woman's seed consoles us; we advance to the days of Noah, and lo, we see the Saviour typified in the ark, which bears a chosen company out of the old world of death into the new world of life; we walk with Abraham, as he sees Messiah's day; we dwell in the tents of Isaac and Jacob, feeding upon the gracious promise; we leave the venerable Israel talking of Shiloh on his deathbed; we see his seed brought out of Egypt, and eating the Lamb of God's passover; we reach the age of the law, and here the types crowd in upon us; but time permits not even a glance—suffice it to say, in brief, that we view the face of Jesus in almost every page, and behold his character painted to the life in nearly every book. Prophets and kings, priests and preachers, all look one way—they all stand as the cherubs did, over the ark, desiring to look within, and to read the mystery of God's great propitiation. In the New Testament we find our Lord the one constant theme of every page. It is not an ingot here and there, or dust of gold thinly scattered, but here you stand upon a solid floor of gold, for the whole substance of the New Testament is Jesus crucified. What would be left of the evangelists if you could remove Christ from them? What are Paul's Epistles if Jesus be taken away? The whole of the Pauline literature sinks in a moment if Jesus be withdrawn. And what have Peter, James, Jude, or John to write upon but the same subject? Is it not Jesus still? Do not shut the book too hastily, for see its closing sentence is bejewelled with the Redeemer's name. "Surely I come quickly. Amen. Even so, come, Lord Jesus. The grace of our Lord Jesus Christ be with you all. Amen." Brethren, we should always read Scripture in this light; we should consider the Word to be as a mirror into which Christ looks down from heaven; and, then, we looking into it see his face reflected as in a glass—darkly, it is true, but still in such a way as to be a blessed preparation for seeing him as we shall see him face to face. This volume contains Jesus Christ's letters to us, perfumed by his love. These pages are the garments of our King, and they all smell of myrrh, and aloes, and cassia. Scripture is the golden chariot in which Jesus rides, and it is paved with love for the daughters of Jerusalem. The Scriptures are the swaddling bands of the holy child, Jesus; unrol them and you find your Saviour. Talk not to us of bodies of divinity—the only body of divinity is the person of Christ. As for theology, Christ is the true theology—the incarnate Word of God; and if you can comprehend him you have grasped all truth. He is made unto us wisdom; getting him you have the wisdom of the Scriptures. The quintessence of the Word of God is Christ. Distil the book—and reach its essential

quality, and you have discovered Jesus of Nazareth, the Son of God, and the King of the Jews. He is the Alpha and Omega of holy Scripture.

3. Another fact is also sweetly true, although not perhaps in our text. Jesus Christ is *the Alpha and Omega of the great law of God.* Brethren, the law of God finds not a single letter in human nature to meet its demands. You and I are neither Alpha nor Omega to the law, for we have broken it altogether. We have not even learned its first letter—"Thou shalt love the Lord thy God with all thy heart," and certain I am we know but very little of the next—"thy neighbour as thyself." Even though renewed by grace, we are very slow to learn the holiness and spirituality of the law; we are so staggered by the letter that we often miss its spirit altogether. But, beloved, if you would see the law fulfilled, look to the person of our blessed Lord and Master. What love to God is there! O brethren, where shall we find anything to be compared to it? "The zeal of thine house hath eaten me up." "Wist ye not that I must be about my Father's business?" "My meat and my drink is to do the will of him that sent me." What love to man you find in him. Talk not of the good Samaritan; here is one who is better than he; the Samaritan did but give his wine and his oil, and his twopence, but Jesus gives himself—gives his heart's blood instead of wine, and the anointing of the Holy Spirit instead of oil, while for food he gives his own flesh and blood for poor humanity to feed upon. Jesus loved in such a way that, as we said on Thursday night, all the love that ever gleamed in human bosom, if it could be gathered together, would be but as a spark, while his great love to man would be as a flaming furnace heated seven times hotter than human imagination can conceive. Do not, beloved friends, if you are in Christ Jesus, permit legal fears to distress you at the remembrance of your failures in obedience, as though they would destroy your soul. Seek after holiness, but never make holiness your trust. Seek after virtue, pant for it; but when you see your own imperfections, do not therefore despair. Your saving righteousness is the righteousness of Christ; that in which God accepts you is Christ's perfect obedience; and we say of that again, in the words of the text, Jesus Christ is "Alpha and Omega, the beginning and the end." There is not a precept which he has not fulfilled in its widest sense. As for the spirit of the law, it breathes through his whole life of holiness and service; and as for the letter of the law, he hath carried it out to its extremity. The commandment may be exceeding broad, but not broader than the life of Christ; the law may ask perfection, but it could not ask and could not have a greater perfection than is found in the person of him whose name is, "The Lord our Righteousness."

Brethren, these three matters I cannot affirm to be in the text, but can you blame me for bringing them forward? They stand in such a near connection with the exact sense of the passage, that they cannot well be omitted. May the Lord bless them to you.

II. Now we will take the text itself, and show what are THE TRUTHS WHICH WE ASSUREDLY BELIEVE TO BE IN IT.

1. Our Lord Jesus is Alpha and Omega in the *great alphabet of being.* Reckon existences in their order, and you begin—"In the

beginning was the Word." Proceed to the conclusion, suppose that all the universe has melted like the hoar-frost of the morning—imagine that all worlds are extinguished as the sparks from the forge—conceive that, as a painted bubble passes away for ever, so the whole creation has departed—What then? What is the Omega? Why assuredly Jesus Christ would still be "God over all, blessed for ever. Amen." This we are quite sure is in the text, because the expression "Alpha and Omega" is only used four times, and on the second occasion we find it in the eleventh verse of the first chapter of the Book of the Revelation, in a connection which leads us to conclude that it must relate to the eternity and self-existence of our Lord; for the seventeenth verse explains the eleventh thus, "Fear not; I am the first and the last: I am he that liveth, and was dead; and, behold, I am alive for evermore, Amen; and have the keys of hell and of death." Those expressions manifestly refer to the eternity of Christ; to his self-existence, his having life in himself; to the fact that death did by no means destroy his self-existence, and that now since his resurrection he liveth for evermore, death hath no more dominion over him. Beloved, this is a great theme. When we begin to talk of the eternity of the person of our Lord Jesus Christ, we are overwhelmed by the glory of our subject. We need the eagle eye and the eagle wing of John to see and soar into heavenly things. I read the other day a work by an ancient author, and in the chapter upon the eternity of God I could not help noticing that there was hardly a word of more than one or two syllables, sure sign of the sublimity of the theme, and of the inability of man to see more than its most simple outline. Will you go back six thousand years, when the world has newly emerged from darkness, will you fly on, if you can, through all the ages of the geological periods, if such there were. Can you journey back millions of years? Can you, can you, can you reach in spirit the time when as yet cherubim were not born, when the solemnity of silence had never been disturbed by song of seraph, when the unnavigated ether had never been stirred by the wing of angel? There is no world, no sun, no stars; space alone exists. Can you go further back till space is gone? You cannot. It is impossible; you are lost; for you can only think of space and time. But if you could by any stretch of imagination multiply the millions of years of which we dreamed just now, by another million times, and that a million million million times more, and those on still as far as ever human arithmetic can go, ay, and beyond the possibilities of angelic computation, yet even then you have not begun to fathom the eternity in which God hath dwelt alone. Certainly there was an age in which God was dwelling alone, not in solitude, for, as the fathers very rightly say, you must not use the term "solitude" in reference to God, since the three Divine Persons everlastingly delighted in each other, and so knew no solitude—yet there was and is an aloneness in our God, since he is before all things. Can your thoughts attain to that age of God in lonely glory: in that eternity we know that Jesus was. He, whom though we have not seen his face, unceasingly we do adore, was then the eternal Son. The Word was God. Jesus was Alpha. To fly as far in the other direction, when the little river of time shall have been absorbed into the deep ocean of eternity, when all the world shall have departed even as the motes which dance in the sunbeam are seen no more when the sunbeam is gone; yet still Jesus shall be the Omega. It has been well observed by Dr. Gill, that no doubt the words "Alpha and Omega" are comprehensive—they take in all the letters between. Certainly God comprehends all creatures. God is that without whom there is nothing, and in whom are all things. Philo, the Jew, compares the great God to a tree, and all creatures to the leaves and fruits, which are all in the tree; but the metaphor is not complete, because you may remove fruit from the tree, but there can be no creature out of the power and will of God by which alone it can exist at all. If you remove the fruits from the tree, the tree has at least lost something; but if all creatures were destroyed, yet still the Lord would be as infinitely God as he is now; if the creatures were multiplied, God were no more—and if diminished, he were no less. The creatures may be likened to the waves, and God to the great sea; the waves cannot exist apart from the sea, nor the creatures apart from God: but no earthly figure of the Divine can be complete; for the waves are a portion of the sea, but the creatures are not God, nor do they contribute to his essence or attributes. The sea would be diminished if the waves were gone; but if you could take all creatures away, God would be no less God, nor less infinite than he is now. In fact, the moment we begin to talk of infiniteness, we know nothing of diminishing or of increasing. O brethren, we must leave this subject in the silence of reverent humility, for my little boat is out of sight of shore already, and I must not venture further on this great and wide sea.

> "Great God, how infinite art thou!
> What worthless worms are we!
> Let the whole race of creatures bow,
> And pay their praise to thee."

A deaf and dumb man in one of the institutions in Paris, was asked to write upon the slate his idea of God's eternity, and he wrote the following forcible lines. "It is *duration* without beginning or end; *existence* without bounds or dimensions; *present* without past or future. His eternity is youth without infancy or old age, life without birth or death, to-day without yesterday or to-morrow." "I am Alpha and Omega, the beginning and the end, the first and the last."

2. Another truth is most certainly in the text, namely, that *Jesus Christ is Alpha and Omega in the alphabet of creating operations*. Who was it that began to make? Not an angel, for the angel must first be made. Did matter create itself? Was there an effect without a cause? It is contrary to our experience and our reason to believe any such thing. The first cause stands first, and the first cause is God in the divine Trinity, the Son being one Person of that Trinity. He is Alpha because his hand first of all winged angelic spirit, and made his ministers a flame of fire. He first made all things out of nothing. He moulded the clay from which man was made; all things were made by him, and without him was not anything made that is made. As he alone began, so his power maintains the fabric of creation; all things consist by him. Christ is the great iron pillar of the universe, and the creatures

twine about him as the vine doth about its prop. These things are not, they vanish like a dream if Jesus withdraw his power. He upholdeth all things by the word of his power. Brethren, there may be creations going on at the present moment; fresh globes may even now be fashioned between the hands of Omnipotence, if so; in every one of these Immanuel hath a share. At this very moment new comets may be launched like thunderbolts upon their fiery way, but not without the Son of God. Human souls issue from the womb of creation every hour, but in their sustenance and sending forth the mighty God is ever present. On, on, on, as the works of God shall be enlarged and extended, as the universe shall grow on every side, Christ shall be there still; his Father's delight, with whom he taketh counsel—his equal, bearing with him the name of Alpha and Omega. If this world shall be rolled up like a worn-out vesture, *he* shall roll it up; if the stars shall wither, it shall be at Jesu's bidding; if the sun shall be quenched, his breath shall blow out its coal; and if the moon shall be black as sackcloth of hair, Christ's hand shall extinguish the lamp. He shall do it all, even until the end shall come, for he is Omega as well as Alpha.

3. So again, beyond a doubt, our text intends that Christ is Alpha and Omega *in all covenant transactions.* Beloved, here is a theme worthy of many discourses from the most eminent divines. The thoughts of God, the eternal decrees, the inscrutable purposes of Jehovah, these are deep things; but we know this concerning them, that from first to last they all have a relation to Christ. Concerning our race and the elect out of it, the whole matter is encompassed in the person of the Redeemer. Speak ye of election? "Mine elect in whom my soul delighteth," is Christ's name. We are chosen in him from before the foundation of the world. Speak of our being predestinated to be sons —we are only made so in him who stands as the elder brother. Every separate individual of the chosen tribe stands only by virtue of an union which was established from of old between his person and the person of the Redeemer. Search for the celestial fountain from which divine streams of grace have flowed to us, and you find Jesus Christ as the well-spring of covenant love. If your eyes shall ever see the covenant roll, if you shall ever be permitted in a future state to see the whole plan of redemption as it was mapped out in the chambers of eternity, you shall see the blood-red line of atoning sacrifice running along the margin of every page, and you shall see that from beginning to end one object was always aimed at—the glory of the Son of God. The Father begins with exalting Jesus, and concludes with glorifying him with the glory which he had with him before the world was. How I do love the doctrines of grace when they are taken in connection with Christ. Some people preach the Calvinistic points without Jesus; but what hard, dry, marrowless preaching it is. Oh, dear friends, the letter killeth; it breedeth in men a controversial, quarrelsome spirit; but when you preach the doctrines of grace as they are in Christ, as Dr. Hawker would have preached them, when you talk of them as Rutherford would have talked of them, oh, then, a holy unction rests upon them, and they become inestimably precious; and let every believer remember he does not get these doctrines as he should get them, unless

he receives them in Christ. Everywhere the Lord Jesus is to be considered not as the friend of a day, or our Saviour only in his life on earth, but as the Lamb slain from before the foundation of the world, the anointed Mediator set up from everlasting days. By faith I see him as the eternal Son of God; I see him standing in the purpose of the Father as the covenant head of the elect. I see him in due time born of a woman, but I do not forget that his goings forth are of old from everlasting, and that before the day-star knew its place his delights were with the sons of men. I see him; he cries "It is finished!" he bows his head, I do not, however, forget that he is not dead, but that when the world shall die and time shall conclude its reign, then he who is the Ancient of days shall live, and shall flourish in immortal youth. Alpha and Omega is Jesus Christ, then, in the eternal purposes and in the covenant transactions of God.

4. Jesus Christ is certainly Alpha and Omega *in all salvation-work as it becomes apparent in act and deed.* That this is the meaning of the text I am clear, because in the first passage where the Alpha and Omega occurs—namely, in the first chapter of the Revelation, eighth verse—you will see that all the works of salvation are ascribed to our Lord. Read the fifth verse, "Jesus Christ, who is the faithful witness, and the first-begotten of the dead, and the prince of the kings of the earth. Unto him that loved us, and washed us from our sins in his own blood, and hath made us kings and priests unto God and his Father; to him be glory and dominion for ever and ever. Amen. Behold, he cometh with clouds; and every eye shall see him . . . I am Alpha and Omega." Now, we have here a summary of the great transactions of saving grace. You have here that *he loved us*—loved us before the world was, with an everlasting love; you have next, that *he washed us* from our sins in his own blood, in which you have his redemption, and our consequent pardon, justification, and sanctification, all of which come to us through him. As for our glory, it is the result of his second advent, therefore, "Behold, he cometh," makes him the Omega, as the "Unto him that loved us," made him the Alpha. I need not repeat to you who know so well that "There is none other name given under heaven whereby we must be saved," and that in no part or portion of that salvation can any other name be admitted into partnership with his. Jesus must begin. Jesus must conclude. It is very striking to observe the commencement and the perfection of the spiritual life both laid at Jesus' door in the sixth verse of the twenty-first chapter—"I am Alpha and Omega, the beginning and the end. I will give unto him that is athirst of the fountain of the water of life freely." So then, if you have any thirst, you must come to Jesus Christ at the beginning, to get the water of life. If you have been led to know your own emptiness—if you have received from his Spirit a hungering and a thirsting after righteousness, go not to the law; look not within; but come to the Alpha, drink and be satisfied. If, on the other hand, life is near its close; if you have been preserved in holiness; if you have been kept in righteousness, remember still to trust in the Omega; for these words follow, "He that overcometh shall inherit all things; and I will be his God, and he shall be my son." So that the

inheriting of all things, the final overcoming of all spiritual foes, comes through Jesus, just as did the first drink of living water. The first breath which heaves the spiritual lungs, the first light which greets the newly-opened eye, comes from Jesus who is the beginning; and the last shout of faith, the last shout of holy joy which shall admit the saints into the paradise of God, shall proceed from him who is the end. Beloved, lay thou back upon Christ with all thy strength; lean on him with all thy weight. He who began will finish: he never was Alpha yet without being Omega too. Nothing shall change his purpose: neither heaven, nor earth, nor hell, can afford a motive to turn him from his way of love. "He is of one mind, and who can turn him? What his soul desireth, even that he doeth."

5. There is one more truth which I conceive to be in the text. Jesus is Alpha and Omega not only in the individual salvation of every saint, but *in the whole chain of the Church's history*. Where shall I say that the Church began? Why, very speedily after there was a seed of the serpent, there was also a seed of the woman. Surely the line of demarcation began hard by the gates of Eden; there we see Abel worshipping God in faith, and Cain who was of the wicked one and slew his brother. Do we not thus early see in Abel's sacrifice the Lamb of God which taketh away the sin of the world. Follow the Church through all her varied fortunes, and you will find her always bearing the banner of the Lion of the Tribe of Judah at her fore-front. No matter if she wanders about in sheep-skins and goat-skins, destitute, afflicted, tormented, Christ is still the day-star of her comfort. In her victories, his name is the loudest note; others may have slain their thousands, but the Son of David his ten thousands. No name wakes up the minstrelsy of Israel like the name of Messias, the coming one. Nothing can move the feet of Zion's maidens so joyously in the sacred dance; nothing can make the daughters of Jerusalem smite their timbrels to a more joyful strain than this—"He cometh; he cometh who shall judge the world in righteousness, and his people with truth." Since the first advent of our Lord, has not the Church ever carried Jesus as her standard. Where will you find the Church without Christ? Jesus is yonder, among the snowy mountains of Switzerland, and his Church is with him though her sons bear the approbrious names of heretics, schismatics, traitors, and worse. The Church of Rome had forgotten her first husband, and played the harlot, committing fornication with the kings of the earth; but there was a faithful bride found for the Son among the Albigenses and the Waldenses, in whose homes Jesus dwelt. What was their battle cry?—what the note they chanted round the family hearth?—what the name they pressed to their bosom when they dare not sing for fear the foe should fall upon them? Was it not the name of Jesus? And when the dark ages passed away, what light do I see gleaming yonder? What doth Luther proclaim? What doth Calvin teach? It is the great name of Jesus which is their common theme. What say you, brothers and sisters? do you not join hands in solemn covenant, and say to-day, "His name shall endure for ever; his name shall be remembered as long as the sun." Do you not long for the time when "all nations shall be blessed in him, all people shall call him blessed?" Surely you yourselves

will help to fulfil the promise, "one generation shall praise his name to another, and shall declare his mighty acts." But the end cometh; Jehovah's banner will soon be furled; his sword shall be sheathed for ever; the unsuffering kingdom shall be proclaimed; swords shall be broken, and spears shall be snapped; the sun shall look upon no battlefield, but shall greet the reign of universal peace. What then? Jesus' name shall then be known everywhere, men shall talk of him and think of him by day and by night. Prayer, also, shall be made for him continually, and daily shall he be praised. They who dwell in the wilderness shall bow before him, and his enemies shall lick the dust. Then cometh the end. The judgment throne is set. The wicked are summoned. The righteous on the right hand have received their rewards—from whose hand? From the hand of the Omega who closes the chapter with his benediction, "Come, ye blessed of my Father." Here are the wicked; hell is gaping for them; the tongues of flames lick up the multitudes as the lion devoureth his prey. Who is this that pronounces the thundering sentence, "Depart, ye cursed?" It is the Omega. That same face which once was bedewed with tears, is now brighter than the sun with flashes of lightning; the voice which said, "Come to me, ye weary," now saith, "Depart, ye cursed." He began—he ends—the Alpha is the Omega. But it is an end without end. Long, long through the ages of eternity, amid heaven's perfect inhabitants, his name shall be the perpetual theme of song. Down there, amidst the howlings of the damned, they shall, against their will, declare his awful justice; they shall proclaim, in the eternal moanings, the power of the pierced feet which shall tread them as clusters in the winepress, until their blood floweth forth to the horses' bridles. In eternity, heaven and earth and hell shall adore Jesus as Alpha and Omega. Hallelujah, hallelujah, Jesus Christ reigneth still as the Lord God omnipotent—Alpha and Omega!

III. By your patience we will notice A FEW THINGS WHICH FLOW OUT OF THE TEXT.

1. The first is this—Sinner, saint, *let Jesus be Alpha and Omega to thee to-day in thy trust.* Poor soul, art thou willing to be saved? But dost thou say, "I have not this qualification, or that recommendation?" Ah, do not begin with thyself as the Alpha. Come to Jesus as you are, and let him be Alpha to you. Are you black? Let him wash you. Is your heart hard? Let him soften it. Are you a dead good-for-nothing soul? Are you ragged and wretched? Are you lost, ruined, and undone; do not stop to write Alpha first; do not stop to begin your own salvation. Sinner, remember there is no preparation wanted for Christ. Just lean upon him wholly. Take him to begin with—nay let him take thee to begin with. Drop into his arms now, repose upon him *now*, you will never get the true salvation unless the first letter in it be Christ, for he is the Alpha. It will all have to be begun over again if you begin with humblings, with repentings, with convictions, or with anything but Christ; it must all be done over again, I say, unless you begin with Jesus. There he is. His wounds are flowing, his heart is breaking, his soul is in anguish—there is the Alpha of your salvation. Look and live. "Look unto me and be ye saved all ye ends of the earth." Child of God, let him be the Omega of

your salvation. If you have begun with him, do not now confide in yourself. Shall I say to you as Paul did to the Galatians, "Having begun in the Spirit, are ye now made perfect in the flesh?" "As ye have received Christ Jesus the Lord, so walk ye in him." Your first hope was through looking to Jesus, will you now look to your sanctifications, to your prayings, to your evidences, to your humblings, to your communings. Away with all these, if they pretend to be the ground of your soul's comfort. Remember, child of God, that to the end of the chapter it must be as it was in the beginning—

"None but Jesus, none but Jesus,
Can do helpless sinners good."

Up in that chamber of yours, with strong cryings and tears you turned to God and you never had any comfort till you looked to Jesus only, and in that other chamber where you shall lie a-dying with the death-damp heavy on your brow—you shall have no comfort but Jesus only. You passed through the river of conviction, and Jesus forbade your drowning; you shall go through the stream of death, and he shall still keep your head above the waves. Alpha and Omega should Christ be to every one of us as our trust this morning.

2. Beloved, if we have trusted him, *let him be Alpha and Omega in our love.* Oh, give him the first place in your love, young woman; may the Holy Ghost win thy young heart for my Lord and Saviour. Let the flower of thy heart be offered to him in the bud. O you, young children, who are your mother's delight, and your father's care, I pray that your first dawning days may be consecrated to the Saviour; let him be Alpha with you. I trust he is Alpha to some of us, and has been so for years. We can use the words of the Psalmist, "I was cast upon thee from the womb. Thou hast been my God from my youth up. Truly I am thy servant, and the son of thine handmaid." You who are growing old and grey-headed, let him have the Omega of your love. As you lean upon your staff, bending downward as if to salute your graves, bear loving recollection of all the years of his patience, and the days of his faithfulness to you. Breathe the prayer "Now, also, when I am old and grey-headed, O God, forsake me not." See to it that you forsake him not, but clasp him with an expiring grasp as the Omega of your soul's delight.

3. But, surely, brethren, our Lord should be the Alpha and Omega *of our life's end and aim.* What is there worth living for but Christ? Oh, what is there in the whole earth that is worth a thought but Jesus? Well did an old writer say, "If God be the only Eternal, then all the rest is but a puff of smoke, and shall I live to heap up puffs of smoke, and shall I toil and moil merely to aggrandize myself with smoky treasures that the wind of death shall dissipate for ever?" No, beloved, let us live for eternal things, and what is there of eternal things that can be chosen but our Lord? O let us give him next year the Alpha of our labour. Let us begin the year by working in his vineyard, toiling in his harvest field. This year is almost over. There is another day or two left—let us serve him till the year is ended, going forward with double haste because the days are now so few. "Lord teach us

to number our days, that we may apply our hearts unto wisdom." Let your time and your talents, your substance and your energies, all be given to my Master, who is worthy to be your soul's Alpha and Omega.

4. Lastly, Jesus crucified should be the Alpha and Omega of *all our preaching and teaching*. Woe to the man who makes anything else the main subject of his ministry. "God forbid that I should glory save in the cross of our Lord Jesus Christ, by whom the world is crucified unto me, and I unto the world." Do not tell me you preach sound doctrine, you preach rotten doctrine, if you do not preach Christ—preach nothing up but Christ, and nothing down but sin. Preach Christ; lift him up high on the pole of the gospel, as Moses lifted up the serpent in the wilderness, and you will accomplish your life's end, but preach orthodoxy, or any form of doxy; if you have left out Christ, there is no manna from heaven, no water from the rock, no refuge from the storm, no healing for the sick, no life for the dead. If you leave out Christ, you have left the sun out of the day, and the moon out of the night, you have left the waters out of the sea, and the floods out of the river, you have left the harvest out of the year, the soul out of the body, you have left joy out of heaven, yea, you have robbed *all* of its all. There is no gospel worth thinking of, much less worth proclaiming in Jehovah's name, if Jesus be forgotten. We must have Jesus, then, as Alpha and Omega in all our ministrations among the sons of men.

And now I am very conscious this morning that I have only ploughed the surface; I wish I could drive into the subsoil of such a glorious text as this, but I suppose that the ploughman who can do this, had need to have been caught up to the third heaven, and even then would fail. Who shall know anything of God but those who have seen him, and have beheld his glory in heaven? As for us, our eyes are holden. We have Jesus among us, but we perceive not his excellent glory; but like Peter, and James, and John, we sleep while Jesus is transfigured. The theme is far too high for me. Who can know God but God? Who can reveal him but the only-begotten? And who can comprehend the fulness of him who is the beginning and the end, the first and the last? It is enough if we have a saving acquaintance with the Redeemer, enough for our peace and joy, but gracious Lord, teach us more. Amen.

The Amen

"The Amen"—Revelation iii. 14.

THE word "Amen" is much more full of meaning than may be supposed, and as a title of our Lord Jesus Christ it is eminently suggestive. As you know the word is a Hebrew one, which has been very properly conveyed not only into our language, but into most, if not all the languages of Christendom. It is a happy circumstance that some of these words should have had vitality enough in them to be transplanted into other tongues, and still to flourish; it gives some faint foreshadowing of the united worship of celestial spirits; and it indicates the Lord's will that the Hebrew race shall not be forgotten by his Church, and that the language of his well-beloved Israel stills sounds sweetly in his ear. AMEN signifies, *true, faithful, certain*, but its sense will be better seen by carefully noting its uses. It had at least three forms of practical meaning. First, it was used in the sense of *asserting;* when a person would give peculiar authority to his words, he either commenced or concluded with the word Amen; and thus declared as with the solemn "yea, yea," of an honest truth-loving man, *certainly, assuredly, so it is.* Our Saviour uses the term frequently. The word which we translate "Verily, verily," is this word "Amen." You must have observed that John who has a quick eye for the divine moods of the Lord Jesus notes with unerring fidelity the repetition of the asserting word. Whenever our blessed Lord was about to say something peculiarly solemn, into which he would throw the full weight of his authority, he asserted it by the doubling of the word "Amen, amen," or "Verily, verily," at the commencement of it. The second sense of the word Amen slightly varies from *asserting*, and may be more properly described as *consenting*. There is a memorable instance of this in the case of the woman who drank the water of jealousy. (Numbers v. 22.) When she drank the water of jealousy, it was enacted that if she had been guilty of the crime laid to her door, certain terrible results should follow as the effect of this water; she, at the time she drank it, said "Amen, amen;" that is, she gave her consent that such-and-such pangs should fall upon her if she had been really guilty of adultery. And a more memorable instance still is that of the people assembled upon Mount Ebal and Gerizim; when the threatenings and the blessings were both read in their hearing, the people said "Amen, amen." So let it be. Of the like character is the case in the book of Nehemiah; when Ezra blessed Jehovah, the great God, all the people answered, Amen, with lifting up of their hands. A third meaning of the word Amen is what we may call *petitionary.* In this sense we use it at the close of our prayers. "Our Father who art in heaven" is not a complete model of public prayer till it concludes with "Amen." In the ancient Church it was customary for the entire congregation to say Amen. Paul alludes to this custom in that expression in the Corinthians, where he speaks of persons praying in an unknown tongue; he says, "How should he that occupieth the room of the unlearned say Amen at thy giving of thanks, seeing he understandeth not what thou sayest?" We have it put on record by Jerome, that at Rome the people were accustomed to say Amen in the gatherings of the early Christians so heartily, I might add so lustily, that it was like the dash of a cataract, or a clap of thunder. I could wish that we more uniformly and universally said Amen at the close of public prayer; I am sure it would be scriptural and apostolic, and I believe it would be useful to you all. Perhaps the custom was dropped on account of the irregular way in which the brethren said Amen. I have heard the same irregularity in certain rustic Methodist congregations, when I have thought that the Amen was put in the wrong place; and could have wished the custom to be discontinued altogether, because certain illiterate, rash, but zealous brethren said Amen when there was nothing to say Amen to, and so rather created ridicule than reverence, and showed as much folly as fervour. However, a judicious revival of the custom would, I doubt not, be useful in the Church of God. It then signifies, "So be it, so let it be," and is virtually the consent of the entire congregation to the prayer which has been put up. Observe the devout Amen of Benaiah, at the close of David's dying prayer, with the remarkable addition, "The Lord God of my lord the king say so too." (1 Kings i. 36.) Notice also how the psalmist closes several of the psalms, such as the forty-first and the seventy-second with the emphatic conclusion, "Amen and Amen."

> "Let every creature rise and bring
> Peculiar honours to our King;
> Angels, descend with songs again,
> And earth, repeat the long AMEN."

Should you desire still further to enquire into the use and meaning of this remarkable word, there is a valuable sermon upon it in the works of Abraham Booth which you may read, as I have done, to great advantage. If anything should lead to the revival of its use more generally in public worship, it will be matter of great congratulation.

It strikes me that I might have divided my discourse this morning very fairly under these three heads—*asserting, consenting, petitioning.* For in each of these our adorable Lord Jesus Christ is certainly "the Amen." He asserts the will of God—he asserts God himself. God the Son is constantly called the *Logos,* the Word; he who asserts, declares and testifies God. In the second place, we know that Jesus Christ consents to the will, design, and purpose of Jehovah. He gives an Amen to the will of God—is, in fact, the echo, in his life and in his death, of the eternal purposes of the Most High. And, thirdly, he is "the Amen" in the petitionary sense; for to all our prayers he gives whatever force and power they have. It is his Amen to our supplication which makes it prevalent at the throne of the Most High. In these three senses Christ may well be called "THE AMEN."

But we have preferred to divide the discourse another way. Our blessed and ever-to-be-adored Lord Jesus is, first, "*the Amen*" *in reference to God;* secondly, "*the Amen*" *as viewed in himself;* and, thirdly, I trust some of us have distinctly trusted him to be "*the Amen*" *in regard to ourselves.*

I. Refresh your memories upon the great truth, OUR LORD IS SUPERLATIVELY GOD'S AMEN.

Let us review the various points in which he is "the Amen" of God. We must speak, of course, of God after the manner of men; let that grain of salt be understood to savour all that we say. Jesus is "the Amen" of the divine *purposes.* There was a day before all days, when there was no day but the Ancient of days;—a time before all times, when He who made all time dwelt alone. Then in his august mind he conceived the plan of redemption. He foresaw the world ruined by sin. He determined that a number whom no man could number should be redeemed unto himself to be for ever his children, the beloved of his soul. These purposes he made, and fixed them fast:— there should be a people who should show forth his praise for ever and ever. These purposes were but purposes until God said Amen to them, and made them valid and sure decrees by determining to give his own dear Son. If God had not resolved to give the Lord Jesus Christ to be a redeemer, the purpose of redemption would have had no Amen. If he had not appointed Christ to be the head of the body, his purpose concerning the body would have lacked the Amen. The giving of our souls to Christ according to the Scriptures was a most ancient covenant transaction; and the gift of the Son to us was of equally ancient date, for he is regarded by God as the Lamb slain from before the foundation of the world. That gift of Christ to us in the eternal covenant was the mighty Father's virtually stamping his decree and making it valid and good. Long ere you and I had a being, before this great world started out of nothingness, God had made every purpose of his eternal counsel to stand fast and firm by the gift of his dear Son to us. He was then God's Amen to his eternal purpose.

When our Lord actually came upon the earth, he was then God's Amen to the long line of *prophecies.* One by one the servants of God had testified concerning the coming Messiah. Some had spoken evangelically with Isaiah; others with a more legal savour as Moses; but their testimony was to the same effect, that in due time a prophet should be raised up, and that there should be born of a virgin a man who should at the same time be "the Wonderful, the Counsellor, the Mighty God, the Everlasting Father." These promises followed thick and fast, all of them cohering, each one manifesting the self-same coming One; but there was no Amen to them, they were things hoped for, but not the substance thereof; till at last, in the silence of midnight, angels sweetly sang his advent, "Glory to God in the highest, on earth peace, goodwill toward men! For unto you is born this day in Bethlehem a Saviour, which is Christ the Lord." That babe among the horned oxen, that carpenter's son, was God's declaration that prophecy was the voice of heaven. Now, ye prophets, sleeping in your tombs, it is witnessed that ye lied not. Now hath God himself come forth and set to his seal that ye are true. In the blessed form of Mary's child, God's Amen appears both to shepherds and to wise men.

In the same sense also Christ was God's Amen to all the Levitical *types*. The morning and the evening lamb, the red heifer, the turtle doves, and the two young pigeons whose blood stained the altar, the sacrificial bullock, the scapegoat, the plentiful sprinklings of blood—all these were man's avowal that he believed in God, and at the same time God declaring to man that he had provided a sacrifice. Yonder smoking bullock offered by Aaron and his sons is nothing yet, it is but a figure, it lacks the Amen to give it body, force, substance. That uplifted knife, that priest clad in fair white linen, that blood spilt upon the altar—all these are nothing, they want a soul put into them. When Jesus Christ came, and especially when up to the cross as to the altar he went as a victim and was laid thereon, then it was that God solemnly put an Amen into what otherwise was but typical and shadowy. "It is finished," said the Saviour, and then was, as our poet puts it,—

> "Finish'd all the types and shadows
> Of the ceremonial law!
> Finish'd all that God had promised;
> Death and hell no more shall awe:
> It is finish'd!
> Saints, from hence your comfort draw."

"The Amen" is set to the purposes, to the prophecies, and to the types.

It is exceedingly worthy of your regard, that Christ is God's Amen to *the Majesty of his law*. That was a very solemn Amen which God gave on the top of Sinai, when he came with ten thousand of his holy ones, and the mountain smoked beneath his feet. As I hear those words, "Thou shalt love the Lord thy God with all thy heart, with all thy soul, and with all thy strength;" that blast of the trumpet waxing exceeding loud and long, that crack of thunder, and yon mighty flashes of great lightnings were God's Amen. AMEN rolled in peals along the wilderness of Kadesh, made the tents of Kedar tremble, and made the hinds to calve, and broke even the lofty cedars of Lebanon. It was such a terrible Amen that the people begged that they might hear it no more; their hearts were subdued with the terror of the dread appearances of God's law, though he revealed it in the hands of a mediator by angels. But, dear friends, I can point you to a more solemn Amen than that, more terrible than Sinai, although ye can better bear the sight. God has said, "The soul that sinneth it shall die;" "Cursed is every one that continueth not in all things that are written in the book of the law to do them." There stands the Son of God. He has not sinned himself, but he has the sins of all his people imputed to him. He has never broken the law, but all our breaches thereof were laid on him. Now what will God say to him? God meets him as he once met Adam in the garden, but Jesus did not hide himself as Adam did, he met stern Justice face to face. There he is, the sinner's substitute;

what will the infinitely just Jehovah say now? The law says he is accursed, for he has sin upon him; will the Father consent that his own Beloved shall be made a curse for us? Hearken and hear the Lord's Amen. "Awake, O sword, against the man that is my fellow, saith the Lord." What, does God the Father say Amen? Can it be? It is even so. He says, Amen. And what an awful Amen too, when the streaming sweat of blood started from every pore of his most blessed and immaculate body, and fell in terrible clots upon the frosty ground. O God, thou didst say Amen indeed to all the terror of thy law when Christ had to cry, "I am exceeding sorrowful, even unto death." Yet louder still is that Amen at Golgotha where stands the Saviour, mocked, despised, rejected; at the Roman column, torn with scourges, and in the seat of mockery crowned with thorns. There the law seemed to say, "The sinner is to be despised and rejected, the sinner is a shameful thing, worthy to be spit upon, the sinner deserves to be crowned with thorns;" and God says, Amen, and his own dear Son who stood in the sinner's place was made to set forth God's awful assent to the demands of justice. Yonder along the streets of Jerusalem, over stones as hard as the hearts of Jerusalem's sons and daughters, harder they could not be, he goes, leaving a blood-track up to Calvary's mound; and there, when hands and feet are pierced, and his soul pierced with something worse than nails, and his heart made to drink of draughts more bitter than wormwood mixed with gall, and his soul the subject of worse temptations than the mere thrusting out of the tongue or the jeer and the jibe of the multitude; there where his soul died within him because God forsook him, and he shrieked "Eloi! Eloi! lama sabachthani?" there it was that God said sternly and dreadfully *Amen* to that sentence, "Cursed is every one that hangeth on a tree." Beloved, if you want to see to the fullest degree how God hates sin, and with what vengeance he pursues iniquity, you must see him hunt that sin right into the shelter which it sought to find in his own dear Son. Though it never was his sin, but our sin laid upon him, yet God spared not his own Son. You have only to see how he was smitten of God and afflicted, because the chastisement of our peace was upon him, and with his stripes we are healed, and you will see at once that Jehovah does not reckon sin to be a trifle.

It must have been a very grand sight to stand in the valley between Ebal and Gerizim and to hear the law read, and then to have heard the six tribes upon Gerizim all say to the blessings solemnly, Amen; like a peal of thunder it must have started from the ten thousand lips of the children of Israel. And then how dreadful, in what subdued awe-stricken tones, like the low murmur of a threatening tempest, must have sounded the dreadful Amen from Ebal, when all the threatenings were read. "Cursed be he that confirmeth not all the words of this law to do them. And all the people shall say Amen." But mark this word, it was a far more solemn thing when God spake than when the tribes spake, and he did speak upon Calvary in tones the thunder of which reverberate throughout all ages, and are heard in dreadful mutterings in the abyss of hell. Jehovah, whom cherubs sing as "Holy, Holy, Holy, Lord God of Hosts," then said "Amen, so let it be! Vengeance, take thy fill! Justice, slay the victim! Let the innocent substitute bleed for men."

Our Lord Jesus, so far from destroying the law, came to be God's Amen to its penalty, and to sanction and to establish it as the law of God for ever.

We have not, however, exhausted this topic. Jesus Christ is, as you know, very blessedly God's Amen to all his *covenant promises,* for is it not written that " all the promises of God in him are yea and in him Amen." The apostle Paul seems to have hit upon the very spirit of Christ's name, Amen, when he says, " He that spared not his own Son, but delivered him up for us all, how shall he not with him also freely give us all things?" When God gave his Son he did virtually give all covenant blessings to his people. The gift of Jesus Christ was God's making every promise which had ever gone before the coming of Christ sure and certain. Christ was the wax melted in the fire, upon which God set the stamp of his own honour that he would be true to the covenant engagements which he had made. Brethren, if the saying of Amen upon Mount Gerizim to the blessing of the law had something delightfully cheering and comfortable about it, how much more divinely sweet was Jehovah's Amen when Jesus Christ rose from the dead triumphant, how much more when up the everlasting hills he rode in glorious triumph, leading captivity captive. Devout spirits, come ye hither and mark God's Amen to the blessings of the covenant; see yonder the mighty throng of angels, and hear their song as they sing, " Lift up your heads, O ye gates; and be ye lift up, ye everlasting doors, that the King of Glory may come in." Do you desire to hear God's Amen? Hear it as he bids his Son, amidst universal acclamations, sit upon his throne and reign with him, expecting till his enemies be made his footstool. Oh, greatly blessed are you, ye saints who are one with Jesus, for God has blessed him, and therefore you! On high enthroned are ye, O saints, for Christ enthroned stands! Him hath God exalted, and he has exalted all his saints in him. He joys not for himself alone; the meanest Christian has a part in all the glories of the Saviour. The enthronization of Christ is God's solemn declaration and Amen that he will bless all his people, and make them kings and priests to reign for ever and ever.

Once more, Jesus Christ will be God's Amen at *the conclusion of this dispensation* in the fulness of time. I am not going into curious questions about how this dispensation will end. I have my own notions about it, other people have theirs. I believe, if some people were as reticent about theirs as I am about mine, they would not sell so many twopenny books, nor make so many foolish guesses at futurity. I know just this about that, that Jesus Christ will come in due time, and that when he cometh, whether immediately, or after a millennial reign, two things will surely happen : namely, that the righteous will be rewarded, and that the wicked will be condemned. These two things I can make quite sure of. Now, when God shall put into his dear Son's mouth those words, "Come, ye blessed of my Father, inherit the kingdom prepared for you from before the foundation of the world," that will be a most solemn Amen to God's purpose made concerning those saints; indeed, it will be the Amen to the covenant in the whole of its range, and to the entire work of grace from the first to the last: then, as they come streaming up the sky in glorious pomp, to reign with Jesus Christ for ever, death and hell, and the assembled world shall mark with shame and dismay God's Amen to his own eternal purposes, and to the work of his glorified Son. When, turning to the left, the Judge shall say, "Depart, ye cursed, into everlasting fire in hell," before the word is spoken, the ungodly will recognize Christ as being "the Amen" to all that God had threatened; in their cries to the rocks to hide them, in their shrieks to the mountains to fall upon them, they will at once discover to assembled multitudes that they perceive Jesus to be "the Amen," making God's threatenings true: and when his voice shall have cursed them for ever, it will be the weighty Amen throughout eternity, the emphatic re-asserting at once of their guilt and of their punishment, that their sentence came from Jesus, that same Jesus who died for sinners, and whom sinners crucified and rejected. Had it come from any other lips the sentence had not been so dreadful; but coming from the man as well as from the God, it shall be humanity assenting to God's verdict, as well as God declaring and enforcing the sanctions of his law. Oh sinner! may Christ never be God's Amen to you in that sense; but, on the contrary, may you hide in the wounds of Jesus, and find all the blessings in him yea and in him Amen to you!

I have thus said sufficient upon that point if God bless it to you; and so let us turn to our second head.

II. Our Redeemer took this as a personal title to himself. He called himself "the Amen;" and so he is. Our second point, then, is, THAT HE IS OUR AMEN IN HIMSELF. He proved himself to be Amen; the God of truth, sincerity, and faithfulness *in his fulfilment of covenant engagements.* The Lord Jesus Christ undertook to bring many saints to glory. His Father gave him a people to be his for ever; and he undertook, in suretyship engagements, that every one of these should be delivered perfect and complete when they should be required at his hands. He undertook, in order to this, that he would suffer, bleed, and die for his Church; that all her debts should be discharged from his own veins; that a perfect righteousness should be wrought out for her, in which she should stand all beauteous in the sight of God. Brethren, I leave it to your own judgment, you who know the Lord Jesus, whether he has not faithfully kept his engagements. He has been "the Amen" to the full, in this respect. "Lo I come! In the volume of the book it is written of me: I delight to do thy will, O God." From old eternity he declared himself to be ready to go through the work, and when the time came, he was straitened till the work was done. When he was a servant in the house of his Father, he might have gone out free if he had pleased, he might have left the service had he willed, but he said, "I love my Master, and I love my Master's children;" and so, like a man who would not accept of freedom under the old Jewish law, his ear was fastened to the doorpost of God's house, and he became the servant of his people for ever. "Mine ear hast thou opened." Beloved, he has fulfilled his service. Seven years of toil for Rachel were achieved by Jacob, and seven years afterwards, and our Master has achieved the same. He has paid the price of his Beloved to the uttermost farthing, and up till now it can be said of him, "Having loved his own which were in the world, he loved them unto the end." "Of all whom thou hast given me I have lost none." Let us praise and bless his name as we see him in covenant engagements faithful and true, "the Amen."

He was also "the Amen" in all *his teachings*. We have already remarked that he constantly commenced with "Verily, verily." The Pharisees in their teachings began with insinuating doubts, beclouding the mind with mystifications, and raising needless difficulties. It was considered to be the right thing for a philosopher never to teach dogmatically; but Christ never spoke in any other way. You find him beginning, "Verily, verily, I say unto you." Christ as teacher does not appeal to tradition, or even to reasoning, but gives himself as his authority. He quotes indeed the authority; of "It is written;" and speaks of the things which he had seen and heard of his Father, but this he states upon the authority of his own oneness with the Father. He comes clad with divine authority, and he does not deign to dispute or to argue, but he claims for his words that they are *Amen*. We have accepted his teachings I hope in that same spirit. I do not open the evangelists to find Christ's words to cavil over them. I do not turn to the epistles to criticise the teachings of my Lord, nor to raise difficult questions wherewith to wrangle with the great Teacher. The position of a Christian is at his Master's feet, not disputing but receiving; not questioning, but believing; and in this sense Christ claims as a prophet and teacher to be "the Amen."

He is also "the Amen" in all *his promises*. Sinner, I would comfort thee with this reflection. Jesus Christ said, "Come unto me all ye that labour and are heavy laden, and I will give you rest." If you come to him, you will not find that he has revoked that promise, but he will say "Amen" in your soul; that promise shall be true *to you*. He said in the days of his flesh, "The bruised reed I will not break, and the smoking flax I will not quench." Oh thou poor, broken, bruised heart, if thou comest to him he will say Amen to thee, and that shall be true in *thy* soul as in hundreds of cases in bygone years. These are his own words, which he spake to his servant John: "The Spirit and the Bride say come; and let him that heareth say come; and whosoever will, let him take the water of life freely." He says Amen to all those Comes, and when thou comest and art anxious to drink, he will say Amen to *thy* coming and to *thy* drinking, for he declares to thee, "Him that cometh to me I will in no wise cast out." From the throne of God whereon he is highly exalted, he utters the very selfsame sentence now, and says Amen to that which he declared before. Christian, is not this very comforting to thee also, that there is not a word which has gone out of the Saviour's lips which he has ever retracted? "I have not spoken in secret, in the dark places of the earth: I said not to the seed of Jacob, Seek ye my face in vain." No stopping of Christ's bills; they shall be duly honoured when the time comes. If thou gettest a hold of but half a promise, thou shalt find it true. Beware of him who is called "Clip-promise," who will run away with much of the comfort of God's Word; but if thou shouldst even get a clipped promise God will honour it, he will still keep to his Word. "Let God be true, and every man a liar." Thou hast to deal with Jesus Christ, "the same yesterday, to-day, and for ever." Therefore be not afraid.

> His very word of grace is strong
> As that which built the skies;
> The voice that rolls the stars along
> Speaks all the promises."

I must not, however, tarry here. Jesus Christ is yea and Amen in all *his offices*. He was a priest to pardon and cleanse once; he is Amen as priest still. He was a King to rule and reign for his people, and to defend them with his mighty arm; he is an Amen King, the same still. He was a prophet of old to foretell good things to come; his lips are most sweet, and drop with honey still—he is an Amen Prophet. He is Amen as to the merit of his blood:—

> "Dear dying Lamb, thy precious blood
> Shall *never* lose its power."

He is Amen as to his righteousness. That sacred robe shall remain most fair and glorious when nature shall decay. He is Amen in every single title which he bears; your Husband, never seeking a divorce; your Head, the neck never being dislocated; your Friend, sticking closer than a brother; your Shepherd, with you in death's dark vale; your Help and your Deliverer; your Castle and your High Tower; the horn of your strength, your confidence, your joy, your all in all, and Amen in all.

I must close all this by reminding you that he is Amen with regard to *his person*. He is still faithful and true, immutably the same. Not less than God! No furrows on that eternal brow—no palsy in that mighty arm—no faintness in that Almighty heart—no lack of fulness in his all-sufficiency—no diminution in the keenness of his eye—no defalcation in the purpose of his heart. Omnipotent, immutable, eternal, omnipresent still! God over all, blessed for ever. O Jesus, we adore thee, thou great Amen. He is the same, too, as to his manhood. Bone of our bone still; in all our afflictions still afflicted. Our brother in ties of blood as much to-day as when he wore a peasant's garb, and said, "Foxes have holes, and the birds of the air have nests; but the Son of Man hath not where to lay his head." The same heart of sympathy, the same bowels of compassion still; remembering us, and bidding us remember him. Not for a moment changed because of the change of his condition. Not for an instant unmindful of us because of the harps of angels and the songs of the redeemed. As quick to hear a sigh or catch a tear to-day as when in the days of his flesh he comforted his people and carried the lambs in his bosom. The Amen Saviour! Oh! blessed be his name. Let us worship him as the great Mediator between God and our souls, feeling joy to think that in all this he suffers no shadow of a change.

> "Blessings for ever on the Lamb
> Who bore the curse for wretched men;
> Let angels sound his sacred name,
> And every creature say, AMEN."

III. But I must roll all this up, and leave you to digest and to enjoy the sweetness of the truths which are contained in that short title, "the Amen;" because I have to close now by saying that THE LORD JESUS IS EXPERIMENTALLY GOD'S AMEN TO EVERY BELIEVING SOUL.

We may say in the first place that *he is God's Amen in us.* Beloved, it is not impossible to prove the existence of God by argument; it is not altogether difficult to demonstrate the reasonableness of the gospel by syllogism and by logic. None but the man who is deficient of brains, I think, need be long without being assured of the authenticity of Scripture; but let me say to you that all that argument, reasoning, and logic can do for you is less than nothing and vanity. You will doubt in the teeth of argument, and be sceptical in the face of demonstration as long as your heart does not love the truth; your head may be convinced, but your heart will always supply enough atheism to keep your head at work; and your head will always be willing to receive an abundant supply from that nethermost cavern of your depravity. But let me say to you if you want to know God you must know Christ; if you want to be sure of the truth of the Bible you must believe Jesus; and I warrant you that when you have once looked up and seen incarnate God bearing your sins; when you have thrown yourself flat upon the Rock of Ages, and have felt the inward joy and peace which flow from believing in God, you will have heard an Amen to that old Book, and an Amen to the existence of God, and an Amen to the gospel, which Satan himself can never remove from your remembrance. You will be confident where once you were diffident, you will believe with a Lutheran vigour when once you have laid hold of Jesus Christ. I believe that this is the keynote of all true believing, to lay hold on Jesus Christ.

> "Till God in human flesh I see
> My thoughts no comfort find."

But when I get Christ, my thoughts not only have comfort but they get a solid conviction that the things must be true. Perhaps there are few among you here that are troubled with sceptical doubts, but they will afflict some of us; and I can say with regard to them whenever they come across my soul in any shape or form, I find the short and quick answer is this, I know one thing, namely, that I am not what I used to be. I know that I have entered into a new world. I feel spiritual heavings in my soul, spiritual longings, emotions, desires, to which I was an utter stranger once. I know there has been as great a metamorphosis passed upon me as though a swine should suddenly become a seraph. I know that the very thought of Jesus keeps me back from sin, and impels me in the path of duty. I know that his name exercises such a charm over me that no magician's wand ever wrought such wonders. My rocky heart melts, my frozen soul dissolves at the touch of his love; and I, a clod of dead earth, suddenly get wings, and fly and commune with the eternal God. Why, that must be true which has done all this for me; it cannot be a lie, it must be true. I feel within myself that my own consciousness must be true, and the Lord Jesus has so interwoven and intertwisted himself with my being, nay, overlaid and covered my being, that, though I should doubt all beside, I could not doubt the existence and divine power of my Lord Jesus Christ. Depend on it, dear friend, if you want to know the gospel, you must receive Jesus Christ, and when you know him you know the gospel. Mahomet, you know, is not Mahommedanism; but Jesus is Christianity. Jesus himself is the Bible; Jesus is God's Word. Trust him, and you shall doubt no more.

Next, Jesus Christ is "the Amen," not only in us, but "*the Amen*" *for us.* When you pray, dear friend, you say Amen. Did you think of Christ? Did you look to his wounds? Did you offer your prayer through him? Did you ask him to present it before God? Did you expect to be heard by virtue of his intercession? If not, there is no Amen to your prayer. But if you have prayed, though it were but a sigh or a tear, if you were looking to the Cross, Jesus Christ's blood said Amen, and your prayer is as certain to be heard in heaven as it was heard on earth; as sure as it came from your inmost soul and Christ was pleaded in it, the answer must certainly come.

And now I want, dear friends, that Jesus Christ should be God's Amen in all our hearts, as to all the good things of the covenant of grace this morning; I am sure he will be if you receive him. We who have believed have entered into rest. If you have Christ you have entered into rest. "Being justified by faith we have peace with God." You that have Christ, have peace with God this morning. "Being justified by faith we have peace with God." "He that believeth and is baptized shall be saved;" if you have Christ, you are saved. Christ is God's Amen. Get Christ, and you have the promises; get Jesus, and you are like the man who has an estate and is secure of his property because he holds the title deeds. He says, "I have got the estate." "Where is it?"—he shows you the title deeds. "Oh," says another man, "that is not the estate; that is far away in the north of England." "I have it however," says the owner, and he folds up his deeds, ties them round, and puts them away in his chest. "I have possession of the estate." Well, dear friends, we have heaven, we have God himself, because we have Christ, and Christ is the title deeds of all things. May you

"Read your title clear,
To mansions in the skies,"

and the Lord make Jesus to be to your hearts, to-day, joyfully and blessedly his own Amen.

All and All in All

"Christ is all, and in all"—Colossians iii. 11.
"That God may be all in all"—1 Corinthians xv. 28.

IN our two texts there are three "alls" rising one out of the other, the first leading to the second, and the second conducting to the third. You will notice at once that the first two are in the present tense: "Christ *is* all," and "Christ *is* in all." The third one refers to the future, it is yet to be fulfilled; when the great consummation shall come, then shall God be "all in all."

I shall not detain you with any sort of preface, for my sole endeavour at this time will be to impress these texts upon your memory, in the hope that the Spirit of God may make them a living and abiding influence upon your hearts and lives; that to you Christ may be all, that Christ may be in you all, and that so, in all that you do, and say, and are, God may be all in all.

I. We begin at THE FOUNDATION WHERE ALL BLESSING BEGINS: "Christ is all."

These are but few words, yet what divine shall ever fully expound them? "Christ is all." Here is sea-room enough for all godly mariners; yet with the best wind that ever blew to speed the ship along, and with every sail set, and filled with the breeze from heaven, who shall ever be able to go from one shore of this great truth to the other,—"Christ is all"? I shall not venture upon such a voyage; I can but look across this sea, and ask you kindly to notice the connection in which the text stands, that we may learn exactly what the apostle meant. Writing "to the saints and faithful brethren in Christ which are at Colosse," Paul says, "There is neither Greek nor Jew, circumcision nor uncircumcision, Barbarian, Scythian, bond nor free: but Christ is all."

That is to say, *in the matter of salvation,* "*Christ is all.*" That which had often seemed the most important thing in the world, is here thrown into the background by the apostolic declaration, "There is neither Greek nor Jew." For a long time, it seemed as if the eternal light was only revealed to the eyes of the seed of the house of Israel. They sat in the brightness, and all the rest of the world lay in dense darkness. But, behold, the Christ has come, "a light to lighten the Gentiles," and henceforth salvation is "not of blood, nor of the will of the flesh, nor of the will of man," but, "Christ is all."

It is a great privilege to be born of godly parents, to have come of a race that for generations has feared the Lord; but let no man trust merely in his natural descent. If you had sprung from a lineage of saints, if every one of your progenitors had feared God, yet still, nothing of all this could avail for your own salvation. "Christ is all." Now may the Gentile dog eat of the crumbs that fall from the Master's table where he feeds his Israel; nay, the dog is transformed into a child, he who was far off is made nigh. In the person of the Lord Jesus Christ, both Jew and Gentile are made one, and all the sheep of the Good Shepherd are sheltered in the same fold. We who believe in Jesus are children of him who was called the father of the faithful; and though, according to the flesh, "Abraham be ignorant of us, and Israel acknowledge us not," yet by faith we become the spiritual seed of the great father of all believers. As he believed in a son being born according to God's promise, and in a seed to which the covenant promises were given, even so do we; and entering into union with Christ Jesus, that blessed Son of the promise, we become joint-heirs with him, "heirs of God, and joint-heirs with Christ." You see, then, dear friends, that it is not race, or pedigree, or descent that saves the soul, but that "Christ is all."

Then Paul goes on to say, "There is neither circumcision nor uncircumcision;" from which I gather that *there is nothing in outward ceremonies which can save.* Everything is still of Christ: "Christ is all." That circumcision in the flesh was ordained of God, and it was the mark of the seed that he had chosen. It was not, therefore, lightly to be spoken of; but now, "we are the circumcision, which worship God in the Spirit, and rejoice in Christ Jesus, and have no confidence in the flesh." At this day, even the ancient divine ordinance is put in the background, for "Christ is all." So is it with every other ordinance, whether ordained of God or of man. It must never be placed in the front, as if it were the means of salvation. I say to you who may have been sprinkled, or to you who may have been immersed; to you who may bow at your altars, or to you who may come to the communion table;—I do not place all these rites on a level, certainly, for some are of God and some are not; but I do place them all on a par in this respect, that they enter not into the essence of our salvation;—and I say to all of you, "These things cannot save you, for 'Christ is all.'" Be you who you may, and do you what you may, you shall not be saved because of your natural birth, nor because of any supposed holy acts that you may perform, neither shall you be saved by any transactions that may be the work of a human priest. You must have Christ as your Saviour, and you must rest in him alone, or you cannot be saved. He is the one foundation; and "other foundation can no man lay than that is laid, which is Jesus Christ," for "Christ is all." The Lord Jesus Christ sums up everything that ordinances can possibly mean, and all that pedigree and descent can possibly bring, and he is infinitely more than all of them.

Read on in this Epistle, and you will find that, as race and ceremonialism are both put into the background, so also is *culture:* "There is neither Barbarian nor Scythian, but Christ is all." Of course, it was for many reasons much better to be a Roman citizen than to be a rude barbarian, and it is much better now to be a civilized man than an untutored Indian of the Wild West; but so far as vital godliness and the soul's salvation are concerned, there is no difference. The simplest and most illiterate, upon believing in Jesus Christ, shall find that "Christ is all." And the most learned and most fully instructed, if they bring any of their learning and their culture, and put it side by side with Christ as a ground of trust, shall sorrowfully discover that none of those things can be placed on an equality with him, but that "Christ is all."

I rejoice, brethren, in this truth. If the gospel of Christ were something eclectic, which could only be received by a superior few, what a poor prospect there would be for the great mass of people among whom we dwell! If the gospel of Christ were a matter so deep and profound that it could not be understood except by years of educated thought, where would they be who are this day lying upon the bed of sickness, expecting soon to stand before God, who have never had any culture, and perhaps can scarcely read the letters of a boy's schoolbook? Blessed be God, we have a remedy for sin's sickness which the Great Physician understands; and if he is well acquainted with it, it matters not whether the patient fully comprehends it or not! Blessed be God, the effect of Christ's medicine does not depend upon the degree in which we can realize how it acts; but if we receive it by faith, if it penetrates into the heart, if it takes possession of the affections, it will work in us that wondrous change by which we shall be delivered from the love of sin, and saved both from its condemnation and its power. Thank God for a simple gospel! Blessed be his name that "Christ is all"! If, by the teaching of the Holy Spirit, you have learnt that Christ died for the ungodly, if you know that he is the Son of God, and the one great propitiation for sin, and if you accept him as such, you have that which has delivered you from going down into the pit, for God has found a ransom even for you.

Once more. By this expression, Paul means us to understand that *all conditions and positions of men in this life are put on a level before Christ,* for he adds, "There is neither bond nor free; but Christ is all." When the gospel of Jesus Christ came into the world, it contemplated the saving of bondmen as well as of freemen. Of course, there was a great distinction between being bond or free, and the apostle wrote, "If thou mayest be made free, use it rather;" but as to the real power of God's grace, there was no distinction between the noblest citizen of Rome and the poor slave who wore an iron collar, and was fastened, like a dog, at his master's gate. Christ's grace could enter into the heart of the servile, as well as into the heart of the noble, and could work alike in each. Now, hear ye, sirs. It is well that you should be industrious, that you should be thrifty, and that you should make your way in the world; but this is not the way to eternal life. What though you should work till your finger ends were raw? What though you labour during the livelong day and night, and stint yourselves of needed sustenance, that you may hoard up gold and silver? With all this, you cannot buy salvation, or be an inch nearer to it. "Christ is all." And if you lie penniless upon a workhouse bed, there is that in Christ which can save you. If you beg your meat from door to door, yet shall you not stand at a disadvantage with this great and blessed gospel, for it comes freely to you with this message, and, as it asks of you no learning, so it asks of you no wealth, no rank, and no position; for, from first to last, "Christ is all."

Thus have I taken the words in their connection, and they are full of important teaching. Remember that they mean just this,—that, *to the man who is saved, Christ is all his trust.* Our healing lies in his stripes. Our life lies in his death. Our pardon lies in his having suffered the punishment due to us. Our eternal life is in the fact that he once died for us, and that he now liveth to make intercession for us. "Christ is all." You must not add anything to Christ as your ground of confidence; but just lean the weight of your sin, and your sorrow, and your necessity, and your desires, wholly and entirely upon him who liveth to stand for you before God. Christ, then, is all our trust.

And, as for our belief, *Christ is all our creed.* What he has taught us personally, and of his Holy Spirit through the Epistles,—what he gives us in his Word,—this is what we believe, and nothing else. The Bible and the Bible alone is the religion of a Christian. "Christ is all;" and all the truth that there is in this Book is in him. This revelation of the Word of God is the self-same revelation as that which is made in the Christ himself, who is the true Logos, the Word of God. "Christ is all" as our creed.

And, further, *Christ is all as our example.* You may safely do what he did, and you may not do what he would not have done. You may judge of the right or wrong of everything by this question,—What would Jesus Christ do in these circumstances? You may know thus what you should do; and what you cannot suppose he would have thought of doing, you must not venture to do, for "Christ is all." He draws a ring around us, and we must not go outside that circumference. He is the atmosphere in which we are to live. He is about us; he is above us; he is beneath us; he is within us; he is everywhere; and to us, if we be Christians, "Christ is all."

There is the foundation of all our faith and hope, and I want you who preach, and you who teach the children, always to keep to this one truth, that "Christ is all." Many other things have a measure of instruction in them; but Christ is all that is necessary. If you want to save men, if you wish truly to elevate men, if you desire still further to exalt them to the very highest degree of which human nature is capable, remember that "Christ is all" as your lever, and in him is your fulcrum, and in him is the power to use the lever. "Christ is all." You need not go abroad for anything, for " ye are complete in him." The ship is furnished from stem to stern in him. The house, from its foundation to its roof-tree, is all complete in him. " Christ is all." Oh, to know him! Oh, to have him as our own! Oh, to live wholly upon him! Oh, to grow like him, and ever to keep before our mind's eye this great truth that " Christ is all "!

II. Now we are going a step farther, to consider the second part of our first text: " Christ is all, *and in all.*" This is a matter of experience, and it reveals to us HOW THE WORK OF GRACE PROCEEDS. Christ is in all his people, this gracious possession is the work of the Spirit of God, by whose means Christ is formed in us, the hope of glory.

To my mind, it is a very beautiful thing that the Lord Jesus Christ, when he comes into the soul, *does not annihilate any part of the personality,* but shines in each separate being, for he is not only all, but he is in all his people. There is, for instance, the Greek,—the " Gentile "— shall be the word. Very well, the grace of God does not turn the Gentile into a Jew; he remains a Gentile, but Christ is in him, and therefore he is made into a new creature. There have been some beautiful specimens of holiness and grace found in many of the Gentile nations dwelling in the islands of the sea, or among all sorts and conditions of men scattered up and down the world, and Christ has shone gloriously in them. Then comes the Jew. When he is saved, Christ is in him. The apostles of Jesus were mostly, at least, of that race, and many later believers have been of the seed of Abraham; but Christ has been in them, and gloriously has he displayed himself in them. The Lord Jesus Christ, dwelling in the Jew, leaves him still a member of the house of Abraham; but, through the presence of the Lord Jesus within him, how wondrously his whole character is exalted! Then you have the man who is circumcised and the man who is uncircumcised, and in each of these, if he be saved, Christ dwells, and each one therefore lives according to his light, and his knowledge, and his standing. Christ enters into the barbarian, and though in certain natural respects he remains to a large extent what he was before, yet, as soon as ever Christ enters into him, all of his barbarism that is sinful disappears. He still retains the free spirit of the child of the wilderness or the son of the woods, but how grandly has Christ displayed himself in such men as he is! The personal piety of a Red Indian, or of an African freshly taken from the wilds of the Dark Continent, has been as brilliant and as beautiful,—certainly as fresh, and bright, and clear, and striking, as the piety of the most educated of the Caucasian race. Whether he be barbarian or Scythian, if Christ is formed in him, the hope of glory, it is only another form of the same exquisite beauty.

It is always a pity when our missionaries try to make other nations into English people. If we have pride enough to think so, we may regard ourselves as the model for others to imitate, but it would be a great pity if we should be such a model that every native of Hindostan must copy the Englishman. I like the worship of our black friends in Jamaica, and in the Southern States of America, with its delightful simplicity, its vivacity,—ay, and I venture to say, even its grotesqueness; and I would not have a black man begin slavishly to imitate the white man. Let him continue to be a black man, and let Christ shine in the black man's face right gloriously. Ay, let a man be a brown man, or a yellow man, or a red man, or whatever colour God made him, the more he keeps to his own nationality, and reflects the glory of Christ from that angle, the more will Christ's gospel triumph, and the more will Christ himself be honoured.

The apostle adds, as we have already noticed, "Neither bond nor free: but Christ is all and in all." May the day speedily come when there shall not be a bondsman under heaven; but in those days of the worst of all slavery, the Christian slaves were among the most brilliant gems in the Redeemer's diadem. Oh, what brave deeds they did for the Crucified One! I should think that it was harder to be a Christian freeman, in those days, than to be a Christian slave; but whether bond or free, whether the man took his place in the Forum among the senators, or his lot was cast yonder amongst the slaves, in either case, if Christ was in him, the light shone gloriously from him, and God was magnified thereby. Christ is all, and Christ is in all his people, each one remaining the same in his individuality, but Christ shining in each one.

I must again refer you to the connection of our text, and ask you to read in the 9th and 10th verses, where Paul says, " Ye have put off the old man with his deeds; and have put on the new man, which is renewed in knowledge after the image of him that created him." You recollect that Adam was made in the image of God, and that he lost that image by his sin; but when Christ enters into a man, and he is created anew in Christ Jesus, then *he receives afresh the image of God.* The image of God is Christ Jesus, for he is the express image of his Father's glory. He that hath seen Christ hath seen the Father; and, inasmuch as Christ enters into all believers, and makes them like himself, the image of God is thereby restored in all believers.

So, note again, that because Christ dwells in him, *every believer becomes a copy of Christ.* Read the 13th verse: "Forbearing one another, and forgiving one another, if any man have a quarrel against any: even as Christ forgave you, so also do ye." Is not that beautiful,— Christ in every believer, that Christ the image of God, and that Christian the image of Christ, so that, just as Jesus freely forgave, so does every Christian freely forgive? Do you find it difficult to forgive one who has wronged you? Then you will find it difficult to get to heaven. If you cannot enter heaven unless you are like Christ, how can you be like Christ unless you can freely forgive? This seems a grand opportunity for you to stand on the same platform with Christ, and in some respect to do the works of Christ when, having been slighted, ungratefully treated, misrepresented, slandered, and injured, you can say, "I as freely forgive you as the Lord Jesus Christ forgave me." This is the token and evidence that Christ is in you, when you become imitators of Christ, as dear children. It is a remarkable fact, as I have often said to you, that, although our Lord Jesus Christ is more perfect than any other example,—indeed, the only perfect example,—yet it is more easy to imitate Christ than it is to imitate some of the best of his people. That is curious, but it is a fact. I know a brother whom I greatly admire, an eminent Christian, —I would not mention my own name in the same day with his, he lives so near to God, and is such a truly gracious man,—yet I could not imitate him. It is quite impossible that my nature should ever become exactly like his. Another brother, whom I used to know,— he is now with God,—was equally good, but he was as different from the other good man as anyone could be, they were as opposite as the poles, in their temperament and behaviour. The first brother I mentioned is solid, calm, quiet, unexcitable, and I should think that he very seldom laughs, and that even then he does not know that he has done it. My other friend used sometimes literally to roar with laughter; he was full of earnest love for the souls of men, and God blessed him greatly in his service; but he had a merry vein and a humorous spirit, and I was more at home with him than I was with the first one. Yet the Lord Jesus Christ is far more easy to imitate than either of my two friends, for sometimes I am so depressed that I cannot show all the cheerfulness of the one; and at other times, having such a humorous vein in my nature, I should be hypocritical and unnatural if I suppressed it, and always acted as if I were as solemn as death itself. But in the case of our Lord Jesus Christ, albeit that there is never any mention of laughter, yet there were ripples of holy pleasantry in his life and in his character, though he was "a man of sorrows, and acquainted with grief." He is more of a man than the best of other men, and more imitable, though altogether inimitable, than those who can be imitated, and perhaps can even be excelled.

What is more, Christ in each one of these believers *creates them all into one body.* Read the 14th and 15th verses: "And above all these things put on love, which is the bond of perfectness. And let the peace of God rule in your hearts, to the which also ye are called in one body; and be ye thankful." The same life is in all believers,— in you and in me;—well, then, we are one. The same life is in ten thousand Christians; then they also are all one. If the same life quickens them, and they live under the same influences, and they act according to the same rule, then are they one, and Christ becomes the glorious Head of a body which he renders glorious by quickening it with his own indwelling.

I like to think of this blessed truth,—Christ in all believers creating them into one body: this is the beginning of true unity. Here, for instance, is a man who says that he is baptized as I am; but if he has not the life of God within him, I cannot get on with him; whatever he may call himself, I am not in union with him. There, perhaps, comes a Methodist, and we begin to talk about the Lord Jesus Christ, and I find that he loves him with all his heart, and I know that I do, though I wish that I loved him more, and we two get on together directly; we feel that we are one in Christ because of the one life which quickens us. Do you not feel it to be so? Have you not been reading a book, sometimes, and said to yourself, "Oh, what a blessed book this is! How full of the divine life"? Yes; and after you have read it, you have been surprised to find that the person who wrote it was a Romanist,—for there are many books of that kind,— or the writer was a member of some church that, in many respects, lies in very dangerous error. You say to yourself, "I do not care where this man lived, or what he did, I am one with him as far as he is one with Christ." The one common feeling of union to Christ, and Christ being in us, makes us feel that we are one with each other. Wherever there is, as Augustine used to say, "*aliquid Christi*,"— "anything of Christ,"—there our love must go forth, we cannot help it. Christ in you all makes you into one body, and unites you together in a mysterious and unique manner. There is not a parallel to it anywhere else; it gives such a living, loving, abiding, undeniable unity that, even if you wish to forget it, you cannot. If the man is in Christ, you must love him, do what you may, for you are one body with him.

Such is this manifestation of Christ in his people, that it leads, further, to *the offering of one oblation*. Read the 16th verse: "Let the Word of Christ dwell in you richly in all wisdom; teaching and admonishing one another in psalms and hymns and spiritual songs, singing with grace in your hearts to the Lord." Yes; all God's people love God's Word; they all find a great sweetness in "psalms, and hymns, and spiritual songs," they all delight to sing praises unto the Most High. Montgomery truly wrote,—

"The saints in prayer appear as one,"

but it is equally true that the saints in praise appear as one, and the saints in love to the Word of God appear as one, because Christ being in them, and Christ being one, they are knit to one another. Oh, how blessed it is for us to have Christ in us!

And lastly upon this point, all that I have said leads up to *each one acting to the glory of one name*, for if Christ be in you, the 17th verse is true of you: "Whatsoever ye do in word or deed, do all in the name of the Lord Jesus, giving thanks to God and the Father by him." What a life to lead,—Christ taking such entire possession of a man that everything he does, he does as if Christ himself were doing it, because he does it in Christ's name and by Christ's power! As Paul wrote to the Corinthians, "Whether therefore ye eat, or drink, or whatsoever ye do, do all to the glory of God," so that it shall no longer be yourselves that do it, but Christ that dwelleth in you. This shall sanctify the commonest actions of everyday life, and make the whole of the Christian's career to be sublime, so that, while he treads the earth beneath his feet literally, he is also doing it spiritually, and all the while his conversation is in heaven.

I must just linger one minute here. You all agreed with me when I spoke about Christ being all, you understood clearly that he is the only ground of our hope; can you also go with me in this part of my subject, Christ is in all his people? Is Christ formed in *you*, the hope of glory? Do you know anything about an indwelling Christ? Verily I say unto you, the Christ on the cross will never save you unless there be also Christ within you; it is the Christ on the cross in whom we trust, but the outcome of that trust is that he is born in our hearts. His power comes from his love, his grace, his truth, himself; and we live because he lives in us. Do you understand this? If you do not, I pray God that you may, for, unless Christ be in you, you know what the apostle says: "Examine yourselves, whether ye be in the faith; prove your own selves. Know ye not your own selves, how that Jesus

Christ is in you, except ye be reprobate." If you are disapproved of God, Christ is not in you; if Christ is not in you, you are disapproved of God. But if he lives in you, you are "accepted in the Beloved," and that life of yours shall never die out, but you shall by-and-by behold your Saviour's face in the kingdom of his glory.

Brethren, we are not what we ought to be, we are not what we want to be, we are not what we shall be; but we are something very different from what we used to be. The change in us is as great as in that blind man who said, "One thing I know, that, whereas I was blind, now I see." The change is not merely external, but it is vital. The Lord has taken away the heart of stone out of our flesh, and given us back the heart of flesh which belonged to man in his unfallen nature, and then upon this heart of flesh he has also wrought wondrously, making it sentient to spiritual influences which once did not affect it, and writing upon the fleshy tablets of that renewed heart his perfect law. Glory be to the name of Jehovah, a notable miracle has been performed upon us, a miracle so marvellous that it is comparable to the resurrection from the dead, and in some respects it even surpasses the wonders of creation itself. We shall tell this story in the streets of the New Jerusalem, and we shall draw around us attentive crowds as we narrate our experience, and tell the tale of the sin which ruined us, and of the mercy which reclaimed us.

Thus have we gone up the second stave of this golden ladder. First, "Christ is all;" next, "Christ is in all."

III. Now kindly turn back in your Bibles to our other text,—the 1st Epistle to the Corinthians, 15th chapter, and 28th verse,—"That God may be all in all." First, Christ is all; next, Christ is in all his people; but THE CONSUMMATION, the top-stone of all is, "that God may be all in all."

The passage in which this text stands seems to be a very difficult one to understand; and the common meaning that is given to it, by nearly every interpreter I have ever met with, I do not believe or accept. It seems to a great many to be taught here that there is to come a time, called "the end", when the Lord Jesus Christ, having conquered all his enemies, is to resign his position, abdicate his throne, and cease to be King, "that God may be all in all." Let us read the connection of the passage: "For as in Adam all die, even so in Christ shall all be made alive. But every man in his own order: Christ the firstfruits; afterward they that are Christ's at his coming. Then cometh the end, when he shall have delivered up the kingdom to God, even the Father; when he shall have put down all rule and all authority and power. For he must reign, till he hath put all enemies under his feet. The last enemy that shall be destroyed is death. For he hath put all things under his feet. But when he saith all things are put under him, it is manifest that he is excepted, which did put all things under him. And when all things shall be subdued unto him, then shall the Son also himself be subject unto him that put all things under him, that God may be all in all." The general meaning given to these words is, that there is to be a time when the mediatorial kingdom of Christ will come to an end of itself, and he will deliver up the kingdom to God, ceasing himself to be

King. I can only say that, if this is the teaching of this text, it is not taught anywhere else in the whole Bible; nobody can find any parallel passage to it, or anything like it; neither do I believe that it is taught in the Bible at all, neither here nor anywhere else. And I can say that for this reason, that I cannot see that there is to be any end whatever to the mediatorial kingdom of Christ.

You perceive that *it is the Son who is to be subject to the Father;* but it is of the Son that we read in the first chapter of the Epistle to the Hebrews, "Unto the Son he saith, Thy throne, O God, is for ever and ever," where the Father, manifestly speaking to the Son, in his complex person, declares that his throne is to be for ever and ever. Brethren, in the day when the Christ shall have overcome all his enemies, and death itself shall be destroyed, there will be no abolition of his mediatorial kingdom. There still stands in the Scriptures this promise of our Lord Jesus Christ: "To him that overcometh will I grant to sit with me in my throne, even as I also overcame, and am set down with my Father in his throne." Does that mean that we are to have a temporary reign with a temporary Christ,—a brief rule with a short-lived Monarch? I do not believe it.

Moreover, *the priesthood enters into the mediatorial office most eminently;* yet "the Lord sware and will not repent, Thou art a priest for ever after the order of Melchisedec." If the priesthood is to continue for ever,—and Melchisedec was king as well as priest,—then the kingdom of Christ is to continue, world without end. Moreover, in the Book of the Revelation,—not to mention the almost innumerable passages to the same effect,—we find that, when the kingdoms of this world become the kingdoms of our Lord, it is added, "*and of his Christ; and he shall reign for ever and ever.*" When the kingdoms are brought back, they will be the kingdoms of our God and of his Christ. Then we read of "the throne of God and of the Lamb;" and when all kingdoms are subdued, and the Lord God Omnipotent reigneth, then we are told to expect the announcement, "The marriage of the Lamb is come, and his wife hath made herself ready." What does all this mean but a continuance of that dispensation in which the Christ, the Son of man, as the Son of God, shall be still at the head of his people, still their Priest, and still their King, and still reigning? And that is exactly what this passage says, if you will kindly look at it again, and dismiss all previous prejudices from your minds.

The fact is, our Lord Jesus Christ has performed, and is still performing, *a work which will end in putting everything into its proper order.* Now, the proper order, according to the first Epistle to the Corinthians, the eleventh chapter, and the third verse, is this: "I would have you know, that the head of every man is Christ; and the head of the woman is the man; and the head of Christ is God." This is how it stands: the woman with the man for her head, the man with Christ for his Head, and Christ with God for his Head. Such is the Scriptural order,—an order which has been disturbed all through except with regard to the Father and the Son, for God has ever been the Head of Christ. Now, Christ has come into the world to restore that right order from the bottom right up to the top; and it is to be so restored, first, by Christ becoming the Head of men, when he shall have put down all his enemies under his feet, and when he shall have put down all rule and all authority and power, "for he must reign, till he hath put all enemies under his feet. The last enemy that shall be destroyed is death." Christ is come into the world that all the evil that is in the world should be subdued, and he will drive it out of the world yet. There shall remain no power that shall dare revolt against the majesty of heaven. Over the whole surface of this globe, beneath the new heavens, and on the new earth, there shall yet be the kingdom established of which Jesus Christ shall be the supreme Head, and over which he shall reign for ever, King of kings and Lord of lords. The Lord hasten it in his own time!

Well, and what then?" asks one; "does it not say that he is to deliver up the kingdom to God, even the Father, and to be subject to the Father?" Exactly so. Supposing that India had been in revolt against our Queen, and that a Viceroy had been sent there, and that he had warred against all the rebellious tribes and kingdoms, and they had all been conquered. He telegraphs to the Queen, "Your Majesty's empire is at your feet." Does he therefore cease to be Viceroy? Not necessarily in the least degree. He may still remain as ruler there, and yet have delivered up the kingdom. I believe that to be the meaning of this passage, that Christ has so conquered the kingdom that it is all God's.

But what does it mean when it says that *then* shall the Son also be subject unto the Father? It means that he is subject now, and that even then he will continue to be subject to the Father; that is all. It cannot mean that, at a certain time, Christ will *become* subject to God, because he has been so ever since that day of his glorious humiliation when, for his people's redemption, he took upon himself the form of a servant ; and that condition is not to cease. He is still to be the Representative of God even when he shall have put down all power and all authority under his feet, and when God has put all things under his feet. It is manifest that he that did put all things under him is not himself under him; and it is clear, from the text, that even then God shall be the Head of Christ. I do not know whether you catch my thought yet, but it is just this,—all evil subdued, all the saints having Christ dwelling in them, Christ the Head of all these saints, and then God as God still, all the more surely and securely supreme over all things, for the Head of Christ is God, and God is all in all.

The conclusion of the whole matter is this, that every day this should be the great consummation to be kept in view, "that God may be all in all." For this the heroic labours of the Son of man here on earth ; for this, his cruel death ; for this, his rising again ; for this, his grasping of the mediatorial sceptre ; for this, his ruling in providence ; for this, his management of the world's affairs ; for this, his second coming and the glory of his saints. All this, while it continues to bring glory to him, has been done in subjection to his great Father's will; he has accomplished it all as the Father's Representative and Messenger, sent by him here to do it ; and then, when it is all done, and he shall reign for ever and ever, even then the Son himself shall continue in that position in which he put himself long, long ago,